MW00778254

DISIONARIO DE LINGUA FRANCA NOVA

ELEFEN–ENGLES ENGLES–ELEFEN

Compiled by
Simon Davies
and
George Boeree

evertype
2018

Published by Evertype, 19A Corso Street, Dundee, DD2 1DR, Scotland.
www.evertype.com.

A catalogue record for this book is available from the British Library.

ISBN-10 1-78021-217-6
ISBN-13 978-1-78021-217-7

Typeset in Baskerville by Michael Everson.

Cover design by Michael Everson.

Printed and bound by LightningSource.

CONTENTS

Preface

Lingua Franca Nova (also known as Elefen) is the product of almost 20 years of work on the part of the original author and many dozens of others. It was developed with a number of specific goals that were met with considerable online interest, such as a grammar that is simple and easily learned, and an attention to aesthetics rarely seen in international auxiliary languages. Other than the absence of grammatical gender and conjugation, it looks, sounds and feels like a natural Romance language.

Its vocabulary was constructed on the basis of the Romance languages (specifically Portuguese, Spanish, Catalan, French and Italian), which together have about 800 million speakers spread all around the world. In addition, they are languages well known to many others, including English speakers, and already contain much of the scientific and other academic vocabulary that derives from Latin and Greek. By choosing a collection of related languages, Elefen avoids a dependence on any single language and the cultural animosities that might arise, while at the same time preserving a sense of coherence.

Simon Davies has used his considerable knowledge of language and programming to construct a dictionary that is both comprehensive and easy to use, and accords with our online searchable dictionary at *elefen.org*. Many other speakers have commented on its development and suggested concepts and words that have since been included. I myself have also done so, and tried to keep a close eye on the aesthetic aspect of the language.

We believe this dictionary will make a nice addition to your libraries.

George Boeree
creator of Lingua Franca Nova

Prefasa

Lingua franca nova (ance conoseda como elefen) es la produida de cuasi 20 anios de labora par la autor orijinal e multe deses de otras. Lo ia es developada con alga goles spesifada cual ia encontra un cuantia notable de interesa enlinia, per esemplo un gramatica simple e fasil aprendable, e un atende a estetica cual on vide rara en linguas aidante internasional. Estra la asentia de jenero gramatical e conjuga, lo aspeta, sona e pare como un lingua romanica natural.

Sua vocabulo ia es construida sur la funda de la linguas romanica (spesifada portuges, espaniol, catalan, franses e italian), cual ave en junta sirca 800 milion parlores sperdeda tra la mundo. Plu, los es linguas bon conoseda par multe otras, incluinte la parlores de engles, e conteni ja la plu de la vocabulo de siensa e otra campos de academia cual deriva de latina e elinica. Par eleje un colie de linguas relatada, elefen evita un depende de cualce lingua individua e la odias cultural cual ta pote mostra se, ma conserva a la mesma tempo un senti de coere.

Simon Davies ia usa sua sabes estendosa de linguistica e programi per construi un disionario cual es e completa e fasil usable, e cual acorda con nosa disionario xercable enlinia a *elefen.org*. Multe otra parlores ia comenta sur sua developa e ia sujesta consetas e parolas cual ia deveni incluida a pos. Me mesma ia fa tal ance, e ia atenta manteni un vijila sur la aspeta estetical de la lingua.

Nos opina ce esta disionario va es un bon ajunta a vosa bibliotecas.

George Boeree
creor de lingua franca nova

Introduction

We have tried to make this book as easy as possible to use. It consists of a list of Elefen words with their English equivalents, and a similar list in the opposite direction.

Both sections have been created by automated means from the database that underlies our online dictionary at *elefen.org*. This material started life as a simple word list on a web page, but over the course of ten years, we have developed it into a comprehensive lexicon, gradually adding words and phrases to meet the demands of practical use of the language. The second half of this book was initially generated by an automated reversal of the database, but the result has undergone extensive manual editing to improve its presentation, clarify meanings and remove straightforwardly deducible items, such as most English derivations in *-ed*, *-ing*, and *-ly*.

We use Oxford spelling throughout, i.e. British English and preferring *-iz-* to *-is-* in the many words like *characterize* and *civilization*. American spellings are included in parentheses and duly labelled; an example from the first half of the book is **traveller** (US **traveler**). We also include American turns of phrase, such as *bar hop*, *slowpoke*, and *trunk* for the boot of a vehicle, but we only label these if confusion could arise.

Of course no dictionary can ever be complete; time passes, languages evolve, older dictionaries seem quaint. The Elefen database will doubtless continue to grow as speakers discover new things to talk about or punchier ways of expressing themselves. We have taken every care to eliminate typing mistakes and ensure consistency, but apologize for any errors that remain.

Elefen–English

Technically, Elefen's vocabulary consists of *roots*, such as **sifra** "cipher", from which other words are derived by adding prefixes and suffixes, e.g. **nondesifrable** "indecipherable". However, this dictionary is a list of *words*, not roots, and so **nondesifrable** appears under *n*, rather than as part of the entry for **sifra**. Our approach keeps each entry short and practical, and bypasses the problem posed by words like **representa** "represent" that occupy a grey area between roots and derivatives.

The entries are in alphabetical order, ignoring hyphens, spaces and the difference between capitals and lowercase letters. Geographical names like **Lago Albert**, **Mar Artica** and **Montes Ural** are ordered by their second

Introdui

Nos ia atenta fa ce esta libro es tan fasil usable como posible. Lo conteni un lista de parolas elefen con sua corespondentes engles, e un lista simil en la otra dirije.

Ambos partes ia es creada par metodos automata, usante la banco de datos cual es la funda de nosa disionario enlinia a *elefen.org*. Esta materia ia comensa vive como un lista simple de parolas en un paje ueb, ma tra la curso de des anios, nos ia developa lo a un vocabulo completa, gradal ajuntante parolas e espresas per sasia la esijes de la usa pratical de la lingua. La dui du de esta libro ia es inisial jenerada par un reversa automatida de la datos, ma la resulta ia es estendosa editada par mano per boni sua presenta, clari sinifias e sutrae cosas fasil deduable, como la plu de derivadas engles usante la codas *-ed*, *-ing*, e *-ly*.

Nos usa la spele de Oxford tra la libro, pd engles brites e preferente *-iz-* e no *-is-* en la multe parolas como *characterize* e *civilization*. Speles american es incluida en brasetas ronda con eticeta conveninte; un esemplo en la dui prima de la libro es **traveller** (US **traveler**). Nos inclui ance espresas american, como *bar hop*, *slowpoke*, e *trunk* per un portabagaje, ma nos eticeti estas sola si confusa ta pote aveni.

Natural, sempre, no disionario pote es completa; tempo pasa, linguas evolui, disionarios plu vea pare anticin. Sin duta, la banco de datos elefen va continua crese en cuando parlores descovre temas nova per discute o modos plu astuta de espresa se. Nos ia atende forte per elimina maltapes e garantia la coere, ma nos solisita un pardona si alga eras resta.

Elefen–engles

Tecnical, la vocabulo elefen es composada de *radises*, como **sifra**, de cual on deriva otra parolas par ajunta prefisas e sufisas, pe **nondesifrable**. An tal, esta disionario es un lista de *parolas*, no radises, e donce **nondesifrable** apare su *n*, e no parteni a la entrada per **sifra**. Nosa metodo fa ce cada entrada resta corta e pratical, e evita la problem levada par parolas como **representa** cual ocupa un area neblosa entre radises e derivadas.

La entradas es en ordina alfabetal, iniorante ifenes, spasios e la difere entre leteras major e minor. Nomes jeografial como **Lago Albert**, **Mar Artica** e **Montes Ural** es ordinada par sua elemento du; si esta elemento no ave

element; if this element does not have an entry of its own (as **artica** does), they are listed as **Albert, Lago** and **Ural, Montes**.

Each entry starts with an Elefen form in bold. Multiple entries with the same form but different origins are marked with a superscript digit, e.g. **cometa**[1] "comet" and **cometa**[2] "snack" (derived from **come** "eat"). In such cases, roots are listed before derivatives. Superscript digits are also occasionally used to present two forms that have the same origin but very different semantics, such as **media**[1] "middle" and **media**[2] "means", or **auto**[1] "car" and **auto-**[2] "auto-, self-". Prefixes are listed after any other homonymous forms, and suffixes follow prefixes.

We supply pronunciations using the International Phonetic Alphabet in square brackets for a few Elefen words, including those whose stress falls on an irregular syllable: this syllable is preceded by a vertical mark ˈ; e.g. **ura** [uˈra] "hooray" has final stress and **ferovia** [feroˈvia] "railway" is stressed on the **vi**, not the **ro**. For the glide of a diphthong, the pronunciation shows [w] or [j]; where two consecutive vowels do not form a diphthong, we show [i] or [u]; e.g. **canoiste** [kanoˈiste] "canoeist" has four syllables altogether. An IPA note is also given for any proper name whose spelling does not match its pronunciation, e.g. **Idaho** [ˈajdaho], and the entry for each letter of the alphabet includes the sound of that letter's name in square brackets: [a], [be], [ke], etc.

An abbreviation then follows, indicating the form's part of speech:

abbr. abbreviation
adj. adjective
adv. adverb
conj. coordinating conjunction
det. determiner
interj. interjection
n. noun
pl. plural (used with *n.* and *pron.*)
pref. prefix
prep. preposition
pron. pronoun
suff. suffix
subord. subordinating conjunction
v. verb
vi. intransitive verb
vt. transitive verb

A determiner is a word like **la** "the", **esta** "this", **mea** "my" or **oto** "eight" that introduces a noun phrase and clarifies the scope of reference.

Some suffixes are further categorized as *adj.suff.* (forming adjectives), *n.suff.* (forming nouns) or *v.suff.* (forming verbs). More specifically still, the abbreviations *vi.suff.* and *vt.suff.* are used to clarify the three verbal suffixes **-i**[3], **-i**[4], and **-i**[5].

A handful of adjectives bear the additional label (*prenominal*), indicating that they precede the noun except when qualified by adverbs (**un bon idea** "a good idea", **un idea multe bon** "a very good idea"). Similarly, the special adverbs **ia**, **ta**, **va**, and **no** are labelled (*preverbal*) to denote that they always precede the verb.

sua propre entrada (como **artica** ave), los es listada como **Albert, Lago** e **Ural, Montes**.

Cada entrada comensa con un forma elefen en leteras spesa. Un serie de entradas con la mesma forma ma orijinas diferente es marcada con un supraindise, pe **cometa**[1] (un ojeto sielal) e **cometa**[2] (derivada de **come**). En tal casos, radises es listada ante derivadas. A veses rara, nos usa supraindises ance per presenta du formas cual ave la mesma orijina ma sinifias multe diferente, como **media**[1] (entre du cosas) e **media**[2] (un metodo), o **auto**[1] (un veculo) e **auto-**[2] (un prefisa). Prefisas es listada pos cualce otra formas omonim, e sufisas segue prefisas.

Nos furni pronunsias usante la Alfabeta Fonetical Internasiona en brasetas reta per un pico de parolas elefen, incluinte los cual es asentuada a un silaba noncoerente: esta silaba es presededa par un linia vertical ˈ; pe **ura** [uˈra] ave un asentua final e **ferovia** [feroˈvia] es asentuada a **vi**, no **ro**. Per la semivocal de un diftongo, la pronunsia indica [w] o [j]; do du vocales en serie no formi un diftongo, nos mostra [i] o [u]; pe **canoiste** [kanoˈiste] ave cuatro silabas en junta. Un nota en AFI es ance donada per cualce nom propre de cual sua spele no acorda con sua pronunsia, pe **Idaho** [ˈajdaho], e la entrada per cada letera de la alfabeta inclui la nom de acel letera en brasetas reta: [a], [be], [ke], etc.

Un corti segue alora, indicante la categoria sintatical de la forma:

abbr. corti
adj. ajetivo
adv. averbo
conj. conjunta
det. determinante
interj. esclama
n. nom
pl. plural (usada con *n.* e *pron.*)
pref. prefisa
prep. preposada
pron. pronom
suff. sufisa
subord. sujunta
v. verbo
vi. verbo nontransitiva
vt. verbo transitiva

Un determinante es un parola como **la**, **esta**, **mea** o **oto** cual introdui un formula nomin e clari la estende de refere.

Alga sufisas es plu categorida como *adj.suff.* (forminte ajetivos), *n.suff.* (forminte nomes) o *v.suff.* (forminte verbos). An plu spesifante, nos usa la cortis *vi.suff.* e *vt.suff.* per clari la tre sufisas verbal **-i**[3], **-i**[4] e **-i**[5].

Un pico de ajetivos porta la eticeta ajuntada (*prenominal*), indicante ce los presede la nom cuando los no es cualida par averbos (**un bon idea**, **un idea multe bon**). Simil, la averbos spesial **ia**, **ta**, **va** e **no** es eticetida como (*preverbal*) per nota ce los presede sempre la verbo.

The indicator *abbr.* is always followed by the abbreviation's expansion, e.g. **ovn** *abbr.* (*ojeto volante nonidentifiada*) "UFO". This dictionary presents all Elefen abbreviations in lowercase letters and without dots—a simple and internally consistent convention—but writers may choose **OVN** or **o.v.n.** or even **O.V.N.** if they prefer. Abbreviations are pronounced letter by letter: [o ve ˈen].

Quite often, two or three parts of speech are given in one fell swoop, reflecting the fact that any adjective or verb in Elefen can be reused without change as a noun, as in **comeda mexican** "Mexican food", **un mexican** "a Mexican"; or **la ximine ia colasa** "the chimney collapsed", **la colasa de la ximine** "the collapse of the chimney". The form **mexican** is labelled *adj.* & *n.*, and **colasa** is *vi.* & *n.*, implying that the English equivalents ("Mexican" and "collapse, slump, flop") correspond to both parts of speech.

Another frequent combination is *vi.* & *vt.*, as seen in **crese** "grow", or in verbs such as **rapidi** "accelerate" that contain the intransitive suffix **-i**[3] "become". The fact that **rapidi** is marked *vi.* shows that its suffix is not the transitive **-i**[4] "use, apply" found in words like **telefoni** *vt.*

The first part of speech shown in an entry is the fundamental one. For example, **abri** is fundamentally an intransitive verb, but can be reused without change as a transitive verb or a noun. In a few cases, e.g. **divini** or **fotomanica**, the fundamental part of speech has no convenient English equivalent, but we include it anyway in order to make the derivation pattern explicit.

The part of speech is followed by one or more English equivalents to the Elefen form. Where several translations are given, commas separate those that are more or less interchangeable; semicolons mark wider boundaries.

English words are annotated with italic glosses in parentheses to clarify the applicable meaning. As an example, the label (*eye*) at **pupil** indicates that "pupil" here has its anatomical sense, as opposed to denoting a student. The Latin taxonomical names of living things are regularly included in the same way. Rarer English words are also labelled: "babka (*cake*)", "cation (*chemistry*)". In a case like (*including chess*) at **bispo**, the translation "bishop" is appropriate in both its basic religious sense and the specialized meaning of a chesspiece. The label (*colloquial*) indicates a word or sense whose use is normally restricted to informal situations.

Selected entries then offer examples of usage, introduced by "e.g." and demonstrating how a word behaves in context, particularly in cases where native English speakers risk being led astray. Alternatively, or in addition, some entries contain a sentence or two of discussion, written in English and introduced by a dash. A good example is the preposition **a**, which also illustrates the use of bullets (•) to break a lengthy entry into smaller sections.

La indica de un corti (*abbr.*) es sempre segueda par la forma completa de la corti, pe **ovn** *abbr.* (*ojeto volante nonidentifiada*). Esta disionario presenta tota cortis elefen en leteras minor e sin puntos—un pratica simple e interna coerente ma scrivores pote eleje **OVN** o **o.v.n.** o an **O.V.N.** si los prefere. On pronunsia cortis par spele la leteras: [o ve 'en].

No noncomun, du o tre categorias sintatical apare en junta, refletante ce en elefen on pote reusa cualce ajetivo o verbo sin cambia como un nom, como en **comeda mexican**, **un mexican**; o **la ximine ia colasa**, **la colasa de la ximine**. La forma **mexican** ave la eticetas *adj.* & *n.*, e **colasa** ave *vi.* & *n.*, implicante ce la traduis engles ("Mexican" e "collapse, slump, flop") coresponde a ambos categorias.

Un plu combina frecuente es *vi.* & *vt.*, videda en **crese**, o en verbos como **rapidi** cual conteni la sufisa nontransitiva **-i**[3] (deveni). Ce **rapidi** ave la marca *vi.* mostra ce sua sufisa no es la **-i**[4] transitiva (usa, aplica) cual on trova en parolas como **telefoni** *vt.*

La categoria prima mostrada en un entrada es la fundal. Per esemplo, **abri** es fundal un verbo nontransitiva, ma on pote reusa lo sin cambia como un verbo transitiva o un nom. En un pico de casos, pe **divini** o **fotomanica**, la categoria fundal no coresponde a un parola conveninte en engles, ma nos inclui lo an tal per clari la via de deriva.

La categoria es segueda par un o plu corespondentes engles de la forma elefen. Do plu ca un tradui es donada, un virgula separa los cual es relativa intercambiable; un punto-virgula marca un distingui plu larga.

Parolas engles es anotada con glosas apoiada en brasetas ronda per clari la sinifia pertinente. Como esemplo, la eticeta (*eye*) a **pupil** indica ce "pupil" ave asi sua sinifia anatomial, e no es un parola per un studiante. Nos inclui la nomes tasonomial latina de viventes en la mesma modo. Nos eticeti ance parolas engles plu rara: "babka (*cake*)", "cation (*chemistry*)". En un caso como (*including chess*) a **bispo**, la tradui "bishop" conveni en e sua sinifia relijial fundal e la sinifia spesialida de un peso de xace. La eticeta (*colloquial*) indica un parola o sinifia de cual sua usa es normal restrinjeda a situas nonformal.

Entradas diversa ofre alora esemplos de usa, introduida par "e.g." e mostrante como un parola condui en contesto, spesial en casos cual risca malgida persones de ci sua propre lingua es engles. Alternativa, o en ajunta, alga entradas conteni un o du frases de discute, scriveda en engles e introduida par un linia orizonal. Un bon esemplo es la preposada **a**, cual esempli ance la usa de puntones (•) per divide un entrada longa a partes plu corta.

More frequently, such bullets draw the eye to each additional part of speech for the Elefen form, as at **automati**, which is both the verb "to automate" and the noun "automation".

The entry for an Elefen form often ends with one or more phrases containing that form. For instance, **ordina** "order" offers **en ordina** "in order", **ordina de viaja** "itinerary" and **ordina sua plumas** "preen", among others. Plural forms are seldom explicitly listed, but when they do appear, they appear here—the plural being Elefen's only inflection—e.g. **aparatos** in the entry for **aparato**. Phrases are listed in alphabetical order. Their parts of speech are not shown, except in rare cases where more than one is involved, as with **colpa con pede** and **mori de famia**, each of which is both a verb ("kick", "starve") and a noun ("kick", "starvation")—or, strictly speaking, a verb phrase and a noun phrase.

Finally, an entry may end with a cross-reference to one or more other relevant words, as when **odori** "smell" says: See *ole*. A special case of this is that for certain countries, such as China, the dictionary contains both a native name (**Jonguo**) and an international form (**Xina**): these are always cross-referenced from each other.

English–Elefen

Dictionaries of English vary greatly in how they arrange compound words such as **aircraft**, **air force** and **air-to-air**. Some list these as subentries of **air**; others treat them as standalone words. We prefer the latter option—presenting compound words as entries in their own right—as we believe it makes this half of the book considerably easier to navigate. Moreover, it is analogous to the way we list words, not roots, in the first half. Our alphabetical ordering therefore simply ignores hyphens and spaces: **blood** precedes **blood cell** and **bloodless**, which precede **blood-pressure gauge**, **bloodshed** and **bloody**.

As in the Elefen–English section, phrases appear at the end of a suitable entry. For example, **with abandon** and **take into account** can be found in the entries for **abandon** and **account**. **Catch cold** can be found under both **catch** and **cold**. Forms like **account for** and **act of kindness**, involving a preposition, are treated as phrases, as are plurals. For convenience, various compounds also appear as phrases; e.g. **ammo belt** has an entry of its own, but shows up at **belt** as well.

Homonymous entries are numbered with superscript digits, and glosses and part-of-speech indicators are deployed in much the same way as in the Elefen section. Note, however, that we do not mark the transitivity of English verbs, as this is rather less clear-cut than in Elefen and would complicate the entries to an unnecessary degree. Dictionary users who are unsure whether

Plu comun, tal puntones atrae la oio a cada categoria ajuntada de la forma elefen, como a **automati**, cual es e un verbo e un nom.

La entrada per un forma elefen fini frecuente con un o plu espresas cual conteni acel forma. Per esemplo, **ordina** ofre **en ordina**, **ordina de viaja** e **ordina sua plumas**, entre otras. Lo es rara ce formas plural es direta listada, ma cuando los apare, los apare asi—car la plural es la sola infleta de elefen—pe **aparatos** en la entrada per **aparato**. Espresas es listada en ordina alfabetal. Sua categorias sintatical no es mostrada, estra en casos noncomun cuando plu ca un pertine, como a **colpa con pede** e **mori de famia**, de cual cada es e un verbo e un nom—o, per dise esata, un formula verbin e un formula nomin.

Final, un entrada pote fini con un refere a un o plu otra parolas pertinente, como cuando **odori** dise: See *ole*. Un caso spesial de esta es ce, per alga paises, la disionario conteni e un nom local (pe **Jonguo**) e un forma internasional (**Xina**): cada de estas refere sempre a la otra.

Engles–elefen

Disionarios de engles varia multe en sua modo de ordina parolas composada como **aircraft**, **air force** e **air-to-air**. Algas lista estas como suentradas de **air**; otras trata los como parolas nondependente. Nos prefere la metodo du—la presenta de composadas como sua propre entradas—car nos crede ce lo fasili notable la naviga tra esta dui de la libro. Plu, lo es analoja a nosa modo de lista parolas, no radises, en la dui prima. Donce nosa ordina alfabetal iniora simple ifenes e spasios: **blood** presede **blood cell** e **bloodless**, cual presede **blood-pressure gauge**, **bloodshed** e **bloody**.

Como en la parte elefen–engles, espresas apare a la fini de un entrada conveninte. Per esemplo, on pote trova **with abandon** e **take into account** en la entradas per **abandon** e **account**. **Catch cold** es trovable su e **catch** e **cold**. Formas como **account for** e **act of kindness**, incluinte un preposada, es tratada como espresas, como ance plurales. Per oportunia, alga composadas apare ance como espresas; pe **ammo belt** ave sua propre entrada, ma es egal presente a **belt**.

Entradas omonim es numerida con supraindises, e glosas e indicadores de categoria sintatical es mostrada en esensal la mesma modo como en la parte elefen. Nota, an tal, ce nos no marca la transitivia de verbos engles, car esta es alga min clar definida ca en elefen e ta complica la entradas a grado nonesesada. A usores de la disionario ci no es serta esce un verbo

a given Elefen verb can behave intransitively are advised to consult the Elefen–English section.

American spellings appear alongside their British counterparts, e.g. **behaviour** (US **behavior**). Each is also given its own cross-reference entry, e.g. **cozy** pointing to **cosy**, except where this would be adjacent to the main entry. Multiple consecutive cross-references are occasionally combined into one, as when **esth-...** points to **aesth-...**

elefen spesifada pote condui nontransitiva, nos recomenda consulta la parte elefen–engles.

Speles american apare a lado de sua corespondentes brites, pe **behaviour** (US **behavior**). Cada reseta ance sua propre entrada referente, pe **cozy** enviante a **cosy**, estra do esta ta es visina a la entrada xef. De ves a ves, nos redui un serie de multe referes a un sola combinada, como cuando **esth-...** envia a **aesth-...**

Grammatical overview

This is a brief summary of the main points of Elefen grammar. For a much more comprehensive explanation, please consult the online grammar at *elefen.org*. We hope to publish a detailed grammar as a companion volume to this dictionary.

Pronunciation

The vowels have their Spanish or Italian sounds. A sequence of two vowels is pronounced as two syllables: **aora** [ˈaora], **trae** [ˈtrae]; but as a diphthong if its second vowel is **i** or **u**: **pais** [pajs], **auto** [ˈawto], **euro** [ˈewro], **moia** [moja]. At the start of a word, **i** and **u** are pronounced like *y* and *w* in *yet* and *wet* when they are followed by another vowel: **ioga** [ˈjoga], **ueste** [ˈweste]. **Cu** and **gu** have the sounds *kw* and *gw* before a vowel: **acua** [ˈakwa], **segue** [ˈsegwe]. The addition of a prefix or suffix never creates a diphthong: **reuni** [reˈuni] (not *[rewni]), **cloi** [ˈkloi] (not *[kloj]).

The consonants have their English sounds, except that **c** and **g** are always hard (as in *cat* and *get*); **s** is always as in *hiss* (never as in *his*); **j** sounds like the *s* in *pleasure*; **n** is like *ng* in *think* when before **c** and **g**; **x** is like the *sh* in *shop*; and *r* is preferably trilled or flapped as in Spanish and Italian. The letter **h** is rare. **K**, **q**, **w**, and **y** only occur in proper names, where they are typically pronounced like **c**, **c**, **u**, and **i** respectively.

The stressed vowel (marked with a vertical line ˈ preceding the stressed sylable in these examples) is the one that precedes the last consonant of a word: **matemaˈtica**, **matematiˈcal**, **aˈsentua**; failing that, the stress falls on the first vowel: **ˈtrae**, **ˈsua**, **ˈfria**. The plural ending **-s** does not affect the stress: **ˈpoma**, **ˈpomas**. A final diphthong is stressed: **caˈcau**. Final **-ui** is a special case, pronounced as two syllables with the **u** taking the stress: **proˈdui**.

Here are the letter values in the International Phonetic Aphabet with the names of the letters spelled out in Elefen:

a	[a]~[ɑ]	*a*	/a/	**j**	[ʒ]	*je*	/ʒe/	**s**	[s]	*es*	/es/
b	[b]	*be*	/be/	**k**	[k]	*ka*	/ka/	**t**	[t]	*te*	/te/
c	[k]	*ce*	/ke/	**l**	[l]	*el*	/el/	**u**	[u], [w]	*u*	/u/
d	[d]	*de*	/de/	**m**	[m]	*em*	/em/	**v**	[v]	*ve*	/ve/
e	[e]~[ɛ]	*e*	/e/	**n**	[n], [ŋ]	*en*	/en/	**w**	[w], [v]	*wa*	/wa/
f	[f]	*ef*	/ef/	**o**	[o]~[ɔ]	*o*	/o/	**x**	[ʃ]	*ex*	/eʃ/
g	[g]	*ge*	/ge/	**p**	[p]	*pe*	/pe/	**y**	[i], [j]	*ya*	/ja/
h	[h]	*hax*	/haʃ/	**q**	[k]	*qua*	/kwa/	**z**	[z]	*ze*	/ze/
i	[i], [j]	*i*	/i/	**r**	[r]~[ɾ]	*er*	/er/				

Nouns, adjectives and adverbs

The plural of a noun is formed by adding **-s** if it ends in a vowel, or **-es** if it ends in a consonant: **gato** "cat", **gatos** "cats"; **can** "dog", **canes** "dogs".

Most adjectives follow the noun: **tre canes grande** "three large dogs". Any adjective can be used as a noun meaning a person or thing that has the stated characteristic. There are many examples in this dictionary: **un solve posible** "a possible solution"; **un posible** "a possibility" (something that is possible); **me va esplica la posibles** "I will explain the possibilities"; **me gusta la prima** "I like the first one".

Adjectives are also reused without change as adverbs, with the order of words making the difference clear. Adverbs follow verbs and precede other adjectives: **tu ia core rapida** "you ran very fast"; **esta bus es estrema vea** "this bus is extremely old". Adverbs can also be placed at the start of a sentence: **vera me no comprende** "I really don't understand".

Comparison of adjectives uses **plu** "more", **min** "less", **la plu** "most" and **la min** "least": **tu es plu alta ca me** "you are taller than me", **la taxe la min interesante de la dia** "the least interesting task of the day".

Verbs

With the sole exception of **es** "be", all verbs end in either **-a**, **-e**, or **-i**.

The past and future tenses are indicated by preceding a verb with **ia** and **va** respectively: **me ia dansa** "I danced, I have danced", **me va salta** "I will jump". When a verb refers to a hypothetical situation, it is preceded by **ta**: **si me ta es min fatigada, me ta corti la erba** "if I were less tired, I would mow the lawn". The combination **ia ta** corresponds to "would have" in English: **me ia ta aida tu** "I would have helped you".

To negate a verb, precede it (and **ia**, **va**, or **ta**) with **no**: **tu no ia telefoni** "you didn't phone".

Commands either omit the verb's subject altogether (**vade a via** "go away") or are introduced by **ta ce** (**ta ce me pensa** "let me think").

Infinitives are unmarked: **me espera revide tu** "I hope to see you again"; **me viaja per vide la mundo** "I travel in order to see the world"; **regarda acel filma ia es un mal esperia** "watching that film was a bad experience".

Any verb can be used as a noun meaning an occurrence of the verb's action or state, or its immediate result: **tua condui es xocante** "your behaviour is shocking"; **un tradui de un canta** "a translation of a song".

Participles are formed with **-nte** "-ing" (**-ente** in the case of **es**) and **-da** "-ed": **la polisior riente** "the laughing policeman"; **suscrivente la**

documento, me ia stornui "(while) signing the document, I sneezed"; **la fenetras es rompeda** "the windows are broken".

The subject of a sentence always precedes the verb, and the direct object (if there is one) always follows: **la gato xasa la scural** "the cat chases the squirrel". Any intransitive verb can be turned into a transitive verb by simply adding a direct object; the intransitive subject is then equivalent to the direct object of the transitive verb: **la patatas boli** "the potatoes are boiling"; **me boli la patatas** "I am boiling the potatoes".

Questions and clauses

Yes/no questions are introduced by the word **esce**: **esce la patatas boli?** "are the potatoes boiling?" Colloquially, one can simply add **no?** "no?" if one is expecting confirmation or **si?** "yes?" if one is less sure what the answer will be: **la patatas boli, no?** "the potatoes are boiling, aren't they?"; **la patatas boli, si?** "the potatoes are boiling, are they?"

Another type of question uses words like **ci** "who", **cual** "which, what", **cuando** "when", **do** "where", **como** "how", **cuanto** "how many, how much" and **perce** "why". These words usually appear at the start of the question, but they can also occupy the place where the answer would otherwise go: **cual es tua filma favoreda?** or **tua filma favoreda es cual?** "what's your favourite film?"; **cuanto tu ia come?** or **tu ia come cuanto?** "how much did you eat?"

Indirect or reported questions use the same techniques, and the question word always comes first: **me no sabe esce la patatas boli** "I don't know if/whether the potatoes are boiling"; **los ia demanda cual es mea filma favoreda** "they asked what my favourite film was". In the last example, English says "was" but Elefen retains the present tense of the direct question: **los ia demanda cual ia es mea filma favoreda** would mean "they asked what my favourite film had been".

Relative clauses use **ci** "who" or **cual** "which, that": **la om ci abita asi** "the man who lives here"; **un libro cual me ia leje resente** "a book (that) I recently read". Unlike in English, these words cannot be omitted. The same is true of **ce**, which forms clauses that report statements, thoughts and so on: **la idea ce la Tera orbita la Sol** "the idea that the Earth orbits the Sun"; **tu ia dise ce tu va aida** "you said you would help" (retaining the tense of the direct statement "I will help").

Function words

Learners may find it instructive to explore the following words in the Elefen–English section of the dictionary.

Determiners

tota "all", **ambos** "both"; **la** "the", **un** "a"; **esta** "this", **acel** "that"; **cual** "which, what", **cuanto** "how many, how much"; **cada** "each", **cualce** "any", **alga** "some", **no** "no"; **mea** "my", **tua** "your (*singular*)", **sua** "his, her, its, their", **nosa** "our", **vosa** "your (*plural*)"; **multe** "many, much", **poca** "few", **plu** "more", **min** "less".

Numbers

zero "0", **un** "1", **du** "2", **tre** "3", **cuatro** "4", **sinco** "5", **ses** "6", **sete** "7", **oto** "8", **nove** "9", **des** "10", **des-un** "11", **des-du** "12", … **dudes** "20", **dudes-un** "21", … **novedes-nove** "99", **sento** "100", **sento-un** "101", … **sento-dudes-tre** "123", … **mil** "1000", … **du mil des-sete** "2017", … **milion** "million". These are cardinal numbers ("two", "three", etc.) when they precede a noun, and ordinals ("second", "third", etc.) when they follow: **oto menses** "eight months", **la mense oto** "the eighth month".

Pronouns

me "I", **tu** "you (*singular*)", **el** "he, she", **lo** "it", **nos** "we", **vos** "you (*plural*)", **los** "they", **on** "one", **se** "-self (*reflexive*)"; **ci** "who", **algun** "someone", **cualcun** "anyone", **cadun** "everyone", **nun** "no one", **lunlotra** "each other".

Adverbs

cisa "maybe", **cuasi** "almost", **tan** "so", **tro** "too"; **asi** "here", **ala** "there"; **an** "even", **ance** "also"; **ancora** "still", **aora** "now", **alora** "then"; **ja** "already", **nunca** "never", **sempre** "always"; **cuando** "when", **do** "where", **como** "how", **perce** "why"; **donce** "therefore".

Prepositions

a "at, to", **ante** "before, in front of", **asta** "until", **ca** "than", **como** "like", **con** "with", **contra** "against", **de** "of, from", **en** "in", **entre** "between", **estra** "outside, except", **longo** "along, according to", **par** "by", **per** "for", **pos** "after, behind", **sin** "without", **sirca** "around", **su** "under", **supra** "over", **sur** "on", **tra** "through", **ultra** "beyond".

Coordinating conjunctions

e "and", **o** "or", **ma** "but".

Subordinating conjunctions

ce "that", **esce** "whether", **afin** "in order that", **car** "because", **si** "if".

Word formation

Elefen derives words by adding prefixes and suffixes. Each has an entry in the dictionary.

The following are the most commonly encountered prefixes:

anti- anti-
auto- auto-, self-
bon- well-
des- dis-, un- (*undoing*)—simplifies to **de-** before *s*, *z*, *x* or *j*
estra- step- (*relation*)
inter- inter-
mal- mis-, ill-
media- mid-
non- non-, un-—simplifies to **no-** before *n*
pos- post-
pre- pre-
re- re- (*repetition or backward direction*)
su- sub-, under-
supra- super-, over-
vis- vice-

Numbers and fractions are also occasionally used as prefixes. With family members, numbers denote increasingly distant generations, like sequences of *great-* in English: **treneta** "great-great-granddaughter".

Most suffixes start with a vowel. When one of these is added to a word that already ends in a vowel, the existing vowel is dropped (**jua** "game", **jueta** "toy"), unless it was the only vowel in the original word (**bu** "owl", **buin** "owl-like"). There are two exceptions: **tre** "three" forms **tri** "third" and **truple** "triple". If a suffix would bring two instances of the same vowel together, one is dropped: **comedia** "comedy", **comediste** "comedian".

Here are the most common suffixes. The letter *x* represents the rest of the suffixed word:

-a *n.* (alternating with **-o**) female; fruit
-able *adj.* -able, -ible, able to be *x*-ed
-ador *n.* -er, tool or machine that does *x* or processes *x*
-al *adj.* pertaining to *x*
-an *adj.* pertaining to region or era *x*
-da *adj.* -ed (*passive participle*)
-eria *n.* place or shop associated with *x*
-es *adj.* pertaining to country *x*
-esa *n.* female equivalent of historical male title *x*
-eta *n.* (occasionally also *v.* or *adj.*) smaller or reduced variant of *x*
-i[3] *vi.* become *x*, e.g. *corti*
vt. cause the direct object to become *x*, e.g. *corti capeles*
n. fractional number, one of *x* parts into which something is divided
-i[4] *vt.* use tool *x* on, apply substance *x* to, e.g. *axi lenio*, *buri pan*
-i[5] *vt.* emit (the optional direct object as) fluid *x*; e.g. *vomiti sangue*
-i[6] *adj.* pertaining to country *x*
-ia *n.* -ness, -ity, the characteristic of being *x*, e.g. *cortia*
-ica[2] *adj.* pertaining to environment, era or country *x*

-ica[3] *adj.* suffering from medical or psychological problem *x*

-in *adj.* -like, -ish, -y, similar to *x*

-isme *n.* -ism, belief in *x*, prejudice against *x*, etc.

-iste *adj.* -istic, pertaining to belief *x* *n.* -ist, believer of *x*, practitioner of field of study *x*, player of instrument *x*

-nte *adj.* -ing (*present active participle*)

-o *n.* (alternating with **-a**) male; tree

-on *n.* larger or augmented variant of *x*

-or *n.* -er, person who does *x* or works with *x*

-osa *adj.* -ful, -y, full of *x*

-sce *adj.* pertaining to country *x*

-uple *adj.* involving *x* instances, e.g. *triple* "triple"
n. group of *x* members, e.g. *triple* "trio"

The suffixes **-an**, **-es**, **-i**, **-ica** and **-sce** all form words for inhabitants and languages of countries, but are not interchangeable: each country has a specific suffix, based on similarity to the native form.

Elefen has far fewer compound words than English. Those that do exist are like "pickpocket": they consist of a verb plus a noun, and mean "a person or thing that does the specified action to the specified item", sometimes metaphorically. Typical examples include **abrivia** "pioneer", **covreoio** "eyepatch", **gardacosta** "coastguard", **parapluve** "umbrella", **plenimano** "handful" and **portaculpa** "scapegoat".

A

A[1] [a]~[ɑ], **a** *letter* A, a.

a[2] *prep.* • at, in, on (*a point in space or time*); e.g. *nos senta a la table*; *la barco es a mar*; *me va parti a la fini de la semana*; *a 26 julio 1887*; *a la ora des-sinco.* • (*in relation*) to; e.g. *tu sta tro prosima a la borda*; *la pen parteni a me*; *la forma de Italia es simil a un gama*; *a la min.* • in the direction of, to, toward, towards, unto; e.g. *el desira viaja a la Luna*; *de ves a ves*; *me va dona un oso a tua can*; *la idea pare bon a me*; *la sorsor ia cambia se a un capra*; *on va eleje tu a presidente*; *el ia pinti sua mures a jala*; *tradui un poesia a elefen.* • (*influencing another*) to (*do something*); e.g. *el comanda la soldatos a ataca la fortres.*—*Me instrui tu a comprende* means that I want *you* to understand, whereas *me instrui tu per comprende* means that the aim is for *me* to understand. • (*clarifying, if necessary, that the following preposition indicates motion towards a location*); e.g. *la gato ia salta a sur la table*; *me pone la libros (a) en la saco.* • (*converting the following preposition into an adverb indicating location or motion*); e.g. *la saco es a supra*; *me va pone la saco a supra*; *la gato ia salta a su*; *el ia resenia la teatral a pos.* See *ante, contra, cuando, do, en, entre, pos, sirca, su, supra, sur.*

a[3] *interj.* ah, aha.

-a[4] *n.suff.* female; fruit; e.g. *tio/tia*; *pero/pera*; *oranio/orania.* See *-o*.

a-[5] *pref.* a-.

a-uu *interj.* awhoo (*howling*).

aa *abbr.* (*ante aora*) before now, before the present, ago.

abaco *n.* abacus.

abadal *adj.* abbatial.

abade *n.* abbot. **abade xef** head abbot, archimandrite.

abaderia *n.* abbey.

abadesa *n.* abbess.

abadia *n.* abbacy (*post, period*).

abaia *vt.* & *n.* bark; squawk, crow, caw; e.g. *abaia un comanda.*

abaieta *vt.* & *n.* yap, yip.

abalon *n.* abalone (*Haliotis*).

abandona *vt.* abandon, strand, maroon, desert, orphan; jilt, forsake, relinquish, give up on, leave behind, chuck; time out (*software*). • *n.* abandonment; timeout (*software*). **abandona la scola** drop out of school. **abandona militar** desertion. **abandona sua posto** abandon one's post, desert.

abandonada *adj.* abandoned, deserted, forlorn, forsaken.

abandonor *n.* deserter; dropout.

abcaz *adj.* & *n.* Abkhaz, Abkhazian (*person, language*).

Abcazia *n.* Abkhazia.

abea *n.* bee, honeybee (*Apis*). **abea laborante** worker bee. **abea mas** drone. **rea de abeas** queen bee.

abeon *n.* bumblebee (*Bombus*).

abeor *n.* beekeeper.

aberia *n.* beehive, hive, apiary.

abeto *n.* fir (*Abies*).

Abisinia *n.* Abyssinia, Ethiopian Empire.

abisinian *adj.* & *n.* Abyssinian.

abita *vt.* live in, inhabit, reside in, dwell in, settle in; e.g. *el abita un aparte*; *el abita en Moscva*; *el abita en la campania*; *el abita un caseta en la campania.* • *n.* habitation, residency, dwelling (*state*).

abitable *adj.* habitable, inhabitable, liveable (US livable).

abitablia *n.* habitability, inhabitability, liveability (US livability).

abitada *adj.* inhabited, lived-in; manned. • *n.* habitat. **abitada de studiantes** hall of residence, student residence, dormitory.

abital *adj.* residential.

abitante *adj.* residential, resident.

abiteria *n.* residence, abode, dwelling, accommodation, quarters, billet, domicile.

abitor *n.* inhabitant, resident, denizen. **abitor de cava** cave dweller, caveman, cavewoman. **abitor luante** lodger. **abitores** inhabitants, residents, population.

abitua *vi.* get used (*to*), become habituated, become accustomed, become inured; grow addicted; acclimatize, acclimate; e.g. *el abitua a labora en la note*; *el ia abitua a eroina.* • *vt.* accustom, habituate, inure; addict. • *n.* habit, habituation, convention; addiction. **abitua sosial** social habit, social convention. **mal abitua** bad habit, vice.

abituada *adj.* accustomed, used.

abitual *adj.* habitual.

abituante *adj.* habit-forming, moreish, addictive.

abjad *n.* abjad (*writing system*).

ablativa *adj.* & *n.* ablative (*grammar*).

-able *adj.suff.* -able, -ible; e.g. *comable*; *lejable*; *lodable*; *notable*; *vidable.*

aboli *vt.* abolish, do away with, get rid of, scrap, axe. • *interj.* down with …, no more …; e.g. *aboli la gera!* • *n.* abolition, abolishment.

abolisme *n.* abolitionism.

aboliste *adj.* & *n.* abolitionist.

aborta *vi.* abort, terminate, be cancelled (US canceled), come to nothing; miscarry. • *vt.* abort, terminate, cancel, foil. • *n.* abortion, termination. **aborta natural** *vi.* miscarry. • *n.* miscarriage.
abortada *adj.* abortive.
abortiste *adj.* & *n.* abortionist.
abrable *adj.* openable, foldout.
abracadabra *interj.* abracadabra, hocus pocus.
abrasa *vt.* & *n.* embrace, hug, cuddle, clinch. **abrasa ursin** bear hug.
abrasable *adj.* embraceable, huggable.
abrasador *n.* clamp. **abrasador de diton** thumbscrew. **abrasador fisada** vice (US vise).
abrasadorin *adj.* vicelike (US viselike).
abrasante *adj.* embracing, hugging; tight, tight-fitting, skintight, close-fitting, form-fitting, figure-hugging.
abri *vi.* open, open up; undo, unfasten, come undone, come unbuttoned, come untied, fall open; turn on, switch on (*tap, power*). • *vt.* open, open up; undo, unfasten, unbutton, untie, open; turn on, switch on. • *n.* opening, aperture, orifice (*action, result*). **abri la via de** pioneer.
abribote *n.* can opener, tin opener.
abribotela *n.* bottle opener.
abricoca *n.* apricot (*fruit*).
abricoco *n.* apricot (*tree*: *Prunus armeniaca*).
abrida *adj.* open, opened; unabashed. **de fonte abrida** open-source. **pico abrida** slightly open, ajar.
abridia *n.* openness.
abrinte *adj.* opening. **abrinte vias** pioneering, groundbreaking.
abrioio *n.* eye-opener, revelation.
abrisita *n.* opening quotation mark.
abrivia [abriˈvia] *n.* pioneer, pathfinder, trailblazer.
abrotano *n.* southernwood (*plant*: *Artemisia abrotanum*).
abugida *n.* abugida, alphasyllabary (*writing system*).
abunda *vi.* abound. • *n.* abundance, plenty, plenitude.
abundante *adj.* abounding, abundant, bountiful, plentiful, copious.
Acaba *n.* Aqaba. **Golfo Acaba** Gulf of Aqaba, Gulf of Eilat.
acad *adj.* & *n.* Akkadian (*person, language*).
academia *n.* academy. **academias** academia, academe.
academial *adj.* academic.
academin *adj.* academic, irrelevant in practice.
academiste *n.* academician, academy member.
Acadia *n.* Acadia (*French colony*).
acadian *adj.* & *n.* Acadian.
acantisita *n.* New Zealand wren (*Acanthisittidae*).
acanto *n.* acanthus (*plant*: *Acanthus*).
acantosefalo *n.* acanthocephalan (*worm*: *Acanthocephala*).
acariase *n.* mange.
acariasica *adj.* mangy, mangey.
acaro *n.* mite (*arachnid*: *Acariformes, Parasitiformes*).
acasi *vi.* & *vt.* randomize, jumble, shuffle, mix.
acasia[1] *n.* acacia, thorntree, wattle (*Acacia*).
acasia[2] *n.* randomness, arbitrariness, jumble.
acasisme *n.* opportunism.
acasiste *adj.* opportunistic, taking the opportunity. • *n.* opportunist.
acaso *adj.* random, arbitrary, erratic, haywire, accidental, incidental, adventitious, fortuitous. • *adv.* randomly, arbitrarily, by chance, by accident, accidentally, incidentally. • *n.* chance, luck, accident (*event*). **acaso locada** adventitious, placed accidentally. **bon acaso** happy chance, piece of good luck, serendipity.
acc *abbr.* (*ance conoseda como*) a.k.a.
Acea *n.* Achaea (*Greek region*).
acean *adj.* & *n.* Achaean.
acel *det.* that, those, yonder, yon. • *pron.* that, that one; the former. **aceles** those, those ones. **par acel** thereby.
acemenan *adj.* & *n.* Achaemenid (*dynasty*).
acenio *n.* achene (*botany*).
Aciten *n.* Aquitaine, Aquitania (*French region*).
aclama *vt.* acclaim, cheer, cheer for. • *n.* acclamation, cheer, cheering. **aclama final** curtain call.
acne *n.* acne.
acompania *vt.* accompany, escort. • *n.* accompaniment, companionship, company, concomitance.
acompaniable *adj.* companionable.
acompaniada *adj.* accompanied. **acompaniada par** accompanied by, in the company of.
acompaniante *adj.* accompanying, concomitant, incidental.
acompanior *n.* companion, partner, escort.
acompaniste *n.* accompanist.
Aconcagua, Monte *n.* Aconcagua.
aconito *n.* aconite, monkshood, wolfsbane (*plant*: *Aconitum*).
acorda *vt.* agree to, consent, assent, accede, be in agreement (*about*), concur, accord; agree (*grammar*); match up, correspond, tally (*with*); be compatible; e.g. *el ia acorda canta.* • *n.* agreement, accordance, consent, consen-

sus, concord, congruence, congruity, compatibility; entente; chord (*music*). **acorda con testa** nod one's head. **acorda de coesiste** modus vivendi, agreement to coexist. **acorda de nonrevela** non-disclosure agreement. **acorda formal** formal agreement, contract, deal, covenant, terms. **acorda unida** unanimity. **en acorda unida** unanimous.
acordable *adj.* compatible.
acordada *adj.* agreed, consensual. **formal acordada** formally agreed, contractual.
acordante *adj.* agreeing; compatible, congruent, congruous; in tune.
acordion *n.* accordion. **acordion diatonica** melodeon, melodion.
acre *n.* acre.
acrete *vi.* accrete. • *n.* accretion.
acrilica *adj.* & *n.* acrylic.
acrofobia *n.* acrophobia.
acromata *adj.* achromatic, black and white.
acromion *n.* acromion.
acronim *adj.* acronymic, acronymous. • *n.* acronym.
acropoli *n.* acropolis.
acrostica *adj.* & *n.* acrostic.
acrotera *n.* acroterion, acroterium.
acrupi *vi.* & *vt.* crouch, squat, hunker, duck. **acrupi se** crouch down, squat down. **acrupi temosa** cower, cringe, shrink.
actinica *adj.* actinic.
actinicia *n.* actinism (*chemistry*).
actinido *n.* actinide (*chemistry*).
actinio *n.* actinium (*element*).
acua *n.* water. • *pref.* aqua-. **acua de banio** bathwater. **acua de cala** bilge, bilgewater. **acua de calce** whitewash. **acua de cloaca** waste water, slop, sewage. **acua de mar** seawater. **acua de pluve** rainwater. **acua de rosa** rosewater. **acua dulse** fresh water. **acua mineral** mineral water. **acua salosa** saltwater. **acua suteran** underground water, groundwater. **de acua dulse** freshwater. **de acua salosa** saltwater. **pinti con acua de calce** whitewash.
acuacultur *n.* aquaculture.
acuaduto *n.* aqueduct.
acual *adj.* aquatic.
acuamarin *adj.* & *n.* aquamarine.
acuarela *n.* watercolour (US watercolor). **depinta con acuarela** paint in watercolours (US watercolors). **depinta de acuarela** watercolour (US watercolor) painting.
acuatinje *n.* aquatint.
acuavit *n.* aquavit, akvavit (*drink*).
acueria *n.* aquarium.
acui *vt.* water.
acuifer *n.* aquifer.
acuin *adj.* watery, runny, thin, non-viscous.
acuor *n.* water carrier, water bearer. **Acuor** *n.* Aquarius (*constellation*).
acuosa *adj.* watery, aqueous; waterlogged, sodden, soggy.
acupunturiste *n.* acupuncturist.
acusa *vt.* accuse, charge, impeach, indict, arraign, prosecute. • *n.* accusation, legal charge, impeachment, arraignment. **acusa de malcondui** accuse of wrongdoing, impeach. **acusa formal** charge.
acusada *adj.* accused. • *n.* accused, defendant.
acusante *adj.* accusing, accusatory.
acusativa *adj.* & *n.* accusative (*grammar*).
acusor *n.* accuser, plaintiff, prosecutor.
acustica *n.* acoustics.
acustical *adj.* acoustic.
acusticiste *n.* acoustician.
acuta *adj.* acute (*medical*).
adajio *adj.* adagio.
Adam *n.* Adam.
Aden *n.* Aden. **Golfo Aden** Gulf of Aden.
adenoidal *adj.* adenoidal.
adenoide *n.* adenoid, pharyngeal tonsil.
adere *vi.* & *vt.* stick, adhere, cling. • *n.* stickiness, adhesion, adhesiveness, adherence.
aderente *adj.* adhesive, sticky, tacky. • *n.* adhesive; sticker, sticky label.
aderor *n.* adherent, adept, aficionado.
aderosa *adj.* clingy, sticky.
adiabatica *adj.* adiabatic (*physics*).
adial *adj.* valedictory.
adio *interj.* goodbye, farewell, adieu. • *n.* farewell, send-off, valediction.
adipos *adj.* adipose.
adirije *vt.* address. • *n.* address; path (*of a computer file*). **adirije de eposta** email address. **adirije ueb** web address, URL.
adn *abbr.* (*asida desosiribonucleal*) DNA.
adobe *n.* adobe.
adolese *vi.* be a teenager, pass through adolescence. • *n.* adolescence.
adolesente *adj.* adolescent, teenage, teen. • *n.* adolescent, teenager.
adomen *n.* abdomen, midriff.
adomenal *adj.* abdominal.
adonis *n.* adonis.
-ador *n.suff.* -er (*tool, machine*); e.g. *computador; cloador; silentador.*
adora *vt.* adore, worship, revere. • *n.* adoration, worship, reverence, worshipfulness.
adorable *adj.* adorable, cute.
adorablia *n.* adorability.
adorante *adj.* adoring, worshipful, reverent.
adormi *vi.* fall asleep, go to sleep. • *vt.* send to sleep, put to sleep.
adorminte *n.* sleeping pill, hypnotic.

adoror *n.* adorer, worshipper (US worshiper), devotee.
adota *vt.* adopt, espouse; take up. • *n.* adoption.
adotada *adj.* adopted. • *n.* adoptee. **enfante adotada** adoptive child, child by adoption. **enfante tempora adotada** foster child.
adotante *adj.* adopting. **jenitores tempora adotante** foster parents. **madre tempora adotante** foster mother.
adotor *n.* adopter.
adriatica *adj.* Adriatic. **Mar Adriatica** Adriatic Sea.
adron *n.* hadron (*particle*).
adsorbe *vt.* adsorb. • *n.* adsorption.
aduador *n.* adductor (*muscle*).
adui *vt.* adduct (*muscle*). • *n.* adduction.
adula *vt.* adulate, flatter, fawn over, grovel to, toady to, suck up to, coax, wheedle, cajole, ingratiate, kowtow. • *n.* flattery, fawning, adulation, sycophancy.
adulante *adj.* adulatory, flattering, fawning, sycophantic, obsequious, deferential, fawning, ingratiating, unctuous, grovelling (US groveling), toadyish, smarmy.
adulor *n.* flatterer, adulator, sycophant, toady.
adulte *adj.* & *n.* adult, grown-up.
adultera *vt.* adulterate, tamper with; commit adultery, fornicate, adulter, philander. • *n.* adultery, affair, fornication.
adulterante *adj.* adulterous.
adulteror *n.* adulterer, fornicator.
adulti *vi.* become adult, grow up, mature.
adultia *n.* adulthood.
adventisme *n.* Adventism (*Christianity*).
adventiste *adj.* & *n.* Adventist.
aec *abbr.* (*ante la eda comun*) BCE (*before the common era*), BC (*before Christ*).
afasia *n.* aphasia (*medical*).
afasica *adj.* & *n.* aphasic.
afelio *n.* aphelion (*astronomy*).
-aferese *n.suff.* -aphaeresis (US -apheresis).
afeta *vt.* affect, have an effect on, influence, impinge on. • *n.* influence.
afetable *adj.* susceptible.
afgani *adj.* & *n.* Afghanistani, Afghani, Afghan.
Afganistan *n.* Afghanistan.
afidavit *n.* affidavit.
afido *n.* aphid (*Aphidoidea*).
afin *subord.* so that, in order that; e.g. *me va leva tu afin tu vide*. See *car*.
afirma *vt.* affirm, state, aver. • *n.* affirmation.
afirmante *adj.* affirming, affirmative.
afisa *vt.* affix, attach; mount (*a picture*). • *n.* affixing, affixation; affix; attachment (*email*).
afluente *n.* tributary.
afoca *vi.* & *vt.* drown. • *n.* drowning.
afonda *vi.* & *vt.* sink, scuttle.
afondada *adj.* sunken.
afonia *n.* aphonia (*medical*).
afonica *adj.* aphonic.
Africa *n.* Africa. **Africa norde** Northern Africa. **Africa sude** Southern Africa. **Africa susaharan** Subsaharan Africa. See *Sudafrica*, *Republica de Africa Sude*.
african *adj.* & *n.* African.
africans *adj.* Afrikaner. • *n.* Afrikaner; Afrikaans.
africante *adj.* & *n.* affricate.
afro *adj.* & *n.* afro.
afroamerican *adj.* & *n.* Afro-American, African American, Negro, black.
afroasian *adj.* Afro-Asiatic, Afrasian, Hamito-Semitic.
afrodisica *adj.* aphrodisiac, aphrodisiacal. • *n.* aphrodisiac.
afroeurasian *adj.* Afro-Eurasian.
agape *n.* agape (*Christianity*).
agar *n.* agar, agar-agar (*substance*).
agarico *n.* agaric (*fungus*: *Agaricales*).
agata *n.* agate.
agave *n.* agave (*plant*: *Agave*).
ageta *n.* splinter, sliver, chip, chipping.
ageti *vi.* & *vt.* splinter, sliver, chip.
agi *vi.* & *vt.* sharpen, hone, whet.
agia *n.* sharpness, acuteness, acuity, keenness.
agila *n.* eagle (*Aquilinae*). **Agila** *n.* Aquila (*constellation*). **agila de mar** sea eagle (*Haliaeetinae*).
agileta *n.* eaglet.
agilin *adj.* aquiline; eagle-eyed.
agin *adj.* needlelike.
aglutina *vt.* agglutinate.
aglutinante *adj.* agglutinative.
agnostica *adj.* & *n.* agnostic.
agnosticisme *n.* agnosticism.
ago *n.* needle, hand (*clock*, *compass*). **ago de croxe** crochet needle, crochet hook. **ago de pino** pine needle. **ago de tricota** knitting needle.
agopuntur *n.* acupuncture.
agora *n.* agora.
agorafobia *n.* agoraphobia.
agorafobica *adj.* agoraphobic. • *n.* agoraphobe.
agosto *n.* August.
-agra *n.suff.* -agra (*pain*).
agrega *vi.* aggregate, combine, conglomerate, agglomerate. • *n.* aggregation, aggregate, combination, conglomeration, conglomerate, agglomeration (*action*, *result*).
agrimonia *n.* agrimony (*Agrimonia*).
agronomia *n.* agronomy.
agronomial *adj.* agronomic, agronomical.

agronomiste *n.* agronomist.
agu [a'gu] *adj.* sharp, pointed, pointy; acute, keen (*sense*); acute (*angle*).
aguti *n.* common agouti (*rodent*: *Dasyprocta*).
aha [a'ha] *interj.* aha.
ahimsa *n.* ahimsa (*Buddhism*, *Hinduism*).
ai *interj.* oh dear, sigh, alas, alack.
aiai *n.* aye-aye (*primate*: *Daubentonia madagascariensis*).
aiatola *n.* ayatollah.
aicido *n.* aikido.
aida *vt.* help, assist, aid, abet, help out; serve (*customer*); improve. • *interj.* help, mayday. • *n.* help, assistance, aid, succour (US succor). **aida medical** medical assistance, healthcare. **aida sosial** welfare, dole. **sin aida** without help, by oneself, on one's own.
aidador *n.* assistant, wizard. **aidador personal** personal digital assistant, PDA, handheld computer, palmtop.
aidamemoria *n.* reminder, memory aid, aide-mémoire, mnemonic. **aidamemoria secreta** cheatsheet.
aidante *adj.* helping, auxiliary, ancillary; complicit.
aidaoia *n.* hearing aid.
aidapasea *n.* walker, walking frame.
aidaservor *n.* busboy, busgirl, busser.
aidor *n.* helper, helpmate, assistant, aide, acolyte, accomplice, sidekick. **aidor de xasa** hunting guide, gillie, ghillie, gilly. **aidor militar** adjutant. **aidor sosial** social worker, caseworker.
aidosa *adj.* helpful, constructive. • *n.* samaritan.
aidosia *n.* helpfulness.
ailanto *n.* ailanthus (*tree*: *Ailanthus*).
ainstainio *n.* einsteinium (*element*).
aira *n.* air; (*colloquial*) weather. **con aira fluetante** draughty (US drafty). **de aira a aira** air-to-air. **de aira a tera** air-to-surface, air-to-ground. **en la aira** in the air, aloft, in mid air, mid-air. **sin aira** airless; out of breath, breathless.
airador *n.* snorkel, breathing mask, aerator.
airal *adj.* aerial, in the air, of the air; overhead (*cable*).
airi *vt.* air, aerate. • *n.* aeration.
airo- *pref.* aero-.
airobial *adj.* aerobic. **eserse airobial** aerobic exercise, aerobics.
airobio *n.* aerobe.
airocompania *n.* airline.
airodinamica *n.* aerodynamics.
airodinamical *adj.* aerodynamic, streamlined.
airofolia *n.* aerofoil (US airfoil).
airograf *n.* airbrush.
airografi *vt.* airbrush.
airojel *n.* aerogel, frozen smoke.
airolito *n.* aerolite (*meteorite*).
airolojia *n.* aerology.
airolojial *adj.* aerological.
aironautica *n.* aeronautics.
aironautical *adj.* aeronautical.
airoporto *n.* airport. **airoporto de jetos** jetport.
airoposta *vt.* & *n.* airmail.
airosa *adj.* airy.
airosol *n.* aerosol.
airospasio *n.* airspace; aerospace.
airostato *n.* aerostat (*including balloon*). **airostato dirijable** airship, dirigible. **airostato nonrijida** blimp, non-rigid airship. **airostato rijida** zeppelin, rigid airship. **airostato semirijida** semirigid airship.
Aiti *n.* Haiti.
aitian *adj.* & *n.* Haitian.
ajena *vi.* & *vt.* kneel, kowtow. **ajena se** kneel down, genuflect.
ajenda *n.* agenda, day planner, appointment book, diary; docket, to-do list.
ajendi *vt.* schedule, put in one's diary.
ajendida *adj.* scheduled.
ajenero *adj.* agender, gender-neutral, unisex. • *n.* agender person.
ajente *n.* agent, broker, intermediary, attaché. **ajente asecurinte** underwriter. **ajente de aposta** bookmaker, bookie. **ajente de cambia** stockbroker. **ajente de imobila** estate agent, real estate agent, realtor. **ajente de intercambia** broker, intermediary. **ajente de potia** powerbroker. **ajente de sposi** matchmaker. **ajente media** middleman. **ajente secreta** secret agent.
ajenteria *n.* agency. **ajenteria de aida** relief agency. **ajenteria de compensa** clearing house. **ajenteria de intercambia** brokerage. **ajenteria secreta** secret service.
ajetival *adj.* adjectival.
ajetivin *adj.* adjectival, adjective-like.
ajetivo *n.* adjective.
ajil *adj.* agile, nimble, sprightly, lithe, limber.
ajilia *n.* agility, nimbleness.
ajiografia *n.* hagiography.
ajiografiste *n.* hagiographer.
ajita *vt.* agitate, excite, upset, fluster, worry, trouble, perturb. • *n.* agitation, excitement, ado, tizzy, trouble.
ajitada *adj.* agitated, excited, upset, distraught, restless, restive, fitful, fidgety.
ajitor *n.* agitator.
ajitprop *n.* agitprop.
ajunta *vt.* add, append, annex; impart (*quality*); e.g. *ajunta sal a la sopa*; *ajunta tre nomes nova a un lista*; *ajunta du e du e fini con sinco*. • *n.*

addition, annexation. **en ajunta** in addition, besides, furthermore, moreover. **en ajunta a** in addition to, besides.
ajuntable *adj.* addable, subsidiary, supplementary, extra. • *n.* accessory, accoutrement, appurtenance; add-on, add-in, plug-in, extension module.
ajuntada *adj.* additional, in addition, extra, ancillary, supplementary. • *n.* annexe (US annex), extension, appendix, addendum, adjunct.
ajusta *vi.* adjust, adapt, acclimatize. • *vt.* adjust, adapt, fit, tune, configure, calibrate; tune up (*music*). • *n.* adaptation, adaption, adjustment, calibration; tune-up; (*software*) setting, configuration (*action, result*). **ajusta a** adjust to, adapt to, accommodate (*change*).
ajustable *adj.* adaptable, adjustable, tunable, configurable, flexible.
ajustablia *n.* adaptability, adjustability.
ajustada *adj.* adapted, adjusted, fitted, tuned, configured.
ajustador *n.* adjuster, adapter, tuner (*device*).
ajustal *adj.* adaptive.
ajusteta *vi.* & *vt.* fine-tune, tweak.
ajustisme *n.* adaptationism.
ajustiste *n.* adaptationist.
ajustor *n.* adapter, adjuster, fitter, tuner (*person*).
-al[1] *adj.suff.* -al, -y (*pertaining to*); e.g. *siensal*.
-al[2] *n.suff.* -al (*aldehyde*).
ala[1] [a'la] *adv.* there, yonder; to there, thither. **a ala** to there, thither. **de ala** from there, thence.
ala[2] *n.* wing; fly, flap. **con alas** winged, alate.
Alabama *n.* Alabama (*US state*).
alabastrin *adj.* alabaster (*in smoothness and whiteness*).
alabastro *n.* alabaster.
alantoide *n.* allantois (*membrane*).
alarma *vt.* alarm. • *n.* alarm, siren. **alarma de nebla** foghorn.
alaroja *n.* redwing (*bird: Turdus iliacus*). **alaroja american** red-winged blackbird (*Agelaius phoeniceus*).
Alaska *n.* Alaska (*US state*). **Golfo Alaska** Alaskan Sea.
alaskan *adj.* Alaskan.
alaui *adj.* & *n.* Alawite, Alawi (*Islam*).
Albania *n.* Albania. See *Xciperia*.
albanian *adj.* & *n.* Albanian. See *xcip*.
albatros *n.* albatross (*Diomedeidae*).
albedo *n.* albedo (*astronomy*).
Albert, Lago *n.* Lake Albert.
Alberta *n.* Alberta (*Canadian province*).
albinisme *n.* albinism.
albino *adj.* & *n.* albino.
Alboran, Mar *n.* Alboran Sea.
album *n.* album, scrapbook.
albumen *n.* albumen, egg white.
albumina *n.* albumin (*protein*).
alburno *n.* bleak (*fish: Alburnus, Chalcalburnus*).
alcalifilia *n.* alkaliphilia.
alcalifilica *adj.* alkaliphilic. • *n.* alkaliphile.
alcalin *adj.* alkaline. • *n.* alkali, base. **alcalin corodente** caustic soda, lye.
alcalini *vi.* & *vt.* alkalize. • *n.* alkalization.
alcalinia *n.* alkalinity.
alcaloide *n.* alkaloid.
alcalose *n.* alkalosis (*medical*).
alcano *n.* alkane, paraffin.
alce *n.* elk (*UK*), moose (*Alces alces*).
alcen *n.* alkene (*chemistry*).
alceta *n.* auklet (*bird: Aethia, Ptychoramphus*).
alcil *n.* alkyl (*chemistry*).
alcimica *n.* alchemy.
alcimical *adj.* alchemical.
alcimiciste *n.* alchemist.
alcin *n.* alkyne (*chemistry*).
alco *n.* auk, razorbill, little auk, dovekie (*bird: Pinguinus impennis, Alca torda, Alle alle*).
alcol *n.* alcohol, booze. **alcol nonlegal** bootleg, moonshine. **de alcol** alcoholic (*drink*). **sin alcol** non-alcoholic.
alcolomania *n.* alcoholism.
alcolomanica *adj.* & *n.* alcoholic (*person*).
alcolometre *n.* breathalyser (US breathalyzer).
alcolosa *adj.* alcoholic (*drink, content*).
alcova *n.* alcove, recess, nook, bay. **alcova de arbores** bower. **alcova de jardin** arbour (US arbor).
aldehido *n.* aldehyde.
aldosterona *n.* aldosterone (*hormone*).
ale *n.* ale (*beer*).
alef *n.* aleph (*Hebrew letter* א).
alega *vt.* allege, claim, adduce. • *n.* allegation, claim.
alegada *adj.* alleged.
alegoria *n.* allegory.
alegorial *adj.* allegorical.
alelo *n.* allele (*genetics*).
aleluia *interj.* hallelujah, alleluia.
alemande *n.* allemande (*dance, music*).
alena *n.* awl, bradawl.
alerjen *adj.* allergenic. • *n.* allergen.
alerjia *n.* allergy.
alerjica *adj.* allergic.
alerjiste *n.* allergist.
aleta *n.* winglet, flipper; aileron. **aleta de coda** fluke (*whale*).
aletera *vi.* alliterate. • *n.* alliteration.
aleterosa *adj.* alliterative.
aletin *adj.* flipperlike.
aleuron *n.* aleurone (*botany*).
aleut *adj.* & *n.* Aleut (*person, language*).

aleutian *adj.* Aleutian. **Isolas Aleutian** Aleutian Islands. **Montes Aleutian** Aleutian Range.
Alexandria *n.* Alexandria (*Egyptian city*).
alexandrian *adj.* Alexandrian.
alexandrin *adj.* alexandrine (*poetry*).
alexia *n.* alexia (*medical*).
alfa *n.* alpha (*Greek letter* A, α).
alfabeta *n.* alphabet. **alfabeta roman** Roman alphabet, Latin alphabet.
alfabetal *adj.* alphabetic, alphabetical.
alfabeti *vt.* alphabetize, sort, put into alphabetical order.
alfabetisme *n.* literacy.
alfabetiste *adj.* literate.
alfalfa *n.* alfalfa (*Medicago sativa*).
alfanumeral *adj.* alphanumeric.
alga *det.* some, certain, a certain (*unspecified identity*); some, several, a few, a little, a small amount of (*unspecified quantity*); any (*in a question or negative statement*). • *adv.* somewhat, rather, fairly, quite. • *pron.* some (*singular or plural*); several; e.g. *alga de la pan*; *alga de la botecas*; *alga dise.* **a alga dia** one day, someday. **a alga grado** somewhat, rather, fairly, quite, to some degree, to some extent. **alga cosa** something; anything (*in a question or negative statement*). **alga de mundo** some people. **alga min** *adj.* a little less, a few less. • *adv.* a little less. **alga o otra** such and such, some ... or other. **alga plu** *adj.* a little more, a few more. • *adv.* a little more. **algas** some, several, a few (*people or things, optional plural pronoun*); e.g. *algas dise.* **en alga loca** somewhere, in some place. **en alga modo** somehow. **en alga parte** somewhere, in some area. **per alga tempo** for some time (*intention*), for a while, awhile. **tra alga tempo** for some time.
algal *adj.* algal.
alge *n.* alga. **alges** algae, seaweed.
algoncian *adj.* Algonquian (*language family*).
algoncin *adj.* & *n.* Algonquin (*language*).
algoritmal *adj.* algorithmic.
algoritmo *n.* algorithm.
algun *pron.* someone, somebody; anyone, anybody (*in a question or negative statement*).—*Algun* does not pluralize. The forms *alga* or *algas* are used instead.
alia *vi.* & *vt.* ally; alloy. • *n.* alliance, league, coalition, fellowship. **alia se con** ally oneself with, become allies with, join with.
aliada *n.* ally; alloy.
alias *n.* alias.
aliasi *vt.* alias.
alibi *n.* alibi.
alidada *n.* alidade (*device*).
aliena *vt.* alienate. • *n.* alienation.
aligator *n.* alligator (*Alligator*).
alinia *vi.* & *vt.* align, line up. • *n.* alignment. **alinia a destra** *v.* right-align, flush right. • *n.* right alignment, ragged left. **alinia a sinistra** *v.* left-align, flush left. • *n.* left alignment, ragged right. **alinia plen** *v.* justify (*margins*). • *n.* (*full*) justification. **alinia se** align oneself, get into alignment.
aliniada *adj.* aligned, lined up, in alignment; flush (*text*).
alio *n.* garlic (*Allium sativum*).
alise *n.* trade wind.
alitose *n.* halitosis, bad breath.
aljebra *n.* algebra.
aljebral *adj.* algebraic.
aljebriste *n.* algebraist.
-aljia *n.suff.* -algia (*pain*).
-aljica *adj.suff.* -algic.
almanaco *n.* almanac.
alno *n.* alder (*Alnus*).
alo[1] [a'lo] *interj.* hello, hi, yo (*greeting*); hey, yoo-hoo (*calling*). **alo ala** hello there, hi there, ahoy there.
alo-[2] *pref.* allo- (*other*).
aloata *n.* howler monkey (*Alouatta*).
aloda *n.* lark, skylark (*Alaudidae*).
aloe *n.* aloe (*plant: Aloe*).
alojen *adj.* & *n.* halogen.
alopatia *n.* allopathy.
alopatica *adj.* allopathic.
alor *n.* winger; wingman.
alora *adv.* then (*at that time*); therefore, consequently, in that case; e.g. *la vive alora ia es plu simple*; *si tu come tua vejetales, alora tu pote come un torteta.* • *conj.* then, so. • *interj.* well, now, now then, right, right then, so. **asta alora** until then, yet; see you next time, bye for now. **de alora** from then on, since then, any longer. **la re alora** the then king. See *a pos*.
alosa *n.* shad (*fish: Alosa, Caspialosa*). **alosa arengin** alewife (*Alosa pseudoharengus*).
alosauro *n.* allosaur, allosaurus (*Allosaurus*).
alotropia *n.* allotropy.
alotropo *adj.* allotropic. • *n.* allotrope.
alpaca *n.* alpaca (*animal: Vicugna pacos*).
alpan *adj.* alpine, Alpine.
alpe *n.* alp. **Alpes** Alps.
alsea *n.* hollyhock (*plant: Alcea rosea*).
alselafo *n.* hartebeest (*antelope: Alcelaphus buselaphus*).
alta *adj.* high, lofty; upper, higher; tall; majestic, great. • *adv.* highly, greatly. • *n.* top, top half, upper part. **a alta** up; upward, upwards, aloft. **a alta de** near the top of; up, towards the top of. **alta de bicini** bikini top. **alta de roba** bodice. **alta e diniosa** statuesque. **la altas e la basas** the highs and lows, the ups and downs, vicissitudes. **la plu alta** highest, tallest, top-

most, uppermost. **plu alta** higher, taller, upper.
altai *adj.* & *n.* Altai, Altay (*person*, *language*). **Montes Altai** Altai Mountains.
altaica [alta'ika] *adj.* Altaic.
altar *n.* altar. **Altar** *n.* Ara (*constellation*).
altea *n.* althaea, marshmallow (*Althea*).
altera *vi.* & *vt.* alter, modify, customize. • *n.* alteration, modification, customization.
alterable *adj.* alterable, modifiable, customizable.
alterada *adj.* altered, modified.
alterante *n.* accidental (*music*); modifier.
alterna *vi.* alternate, take turns. • *vt.* alternate; flip, toggle (*setting*). • *n.* alternation.
alternador *n.* alternator.
alternante *adj.* alternating. • *n.* alternant.
alternativa *adj.* alternative. • *n.* alternative, recourse, fallback; answer (*to a rival concept*).
alti *vi.* rise, soar. • *vt.* lift, raise, elevate; exalt; promote. • *n.* rise; exaltation; promotion.
altia *n.* height, altitude, elevation; highness, majesty. • *interj.* your highness, your majesty. **altia de ex** x-height (*typography*). **altia de tono** pitch. **sua altia** his highness, her highness.
altimetre *n.* altimeter.
alto *adj.* & *n.* alto, countertenor (*music*).
altruisme *n.* altruism.
altruiste *adj.* altruistic. • *n.* altruist.
alum *n.* alum (*substance*).
aluminio *n.* aluminium (US aluminum).
alusina *vt.* hallucinate. • *n.* hallucination, apparition, illusion, vision. **alusina oiada** auditory hallucination. **alusina videda** visual hallucination.
alusinal *adj.* hallucinatory, psychedelic.
alusinalia *n.* psychedelia.
alusinojen *adj.* hallucinogenic. • *n.* hallucinogen.
aluvia *n.* alluvium (*geology*).
aluvial *adj.* alluvial.
alveolal *adj.* alveolar. • *n.* alveolar consonant.
alveolite *n.* alveolitis.
alveolo *n.* alveolus, air sac; tooth socket.
am *abbr.* (*ante mediadia*) a.m.
ama *vt.* love, cherish. • *n.* love, affection. **ama uniladal** unrequited love. **cade en ama** fall in love. **comensa ama** fall in love. **fa de ama** lovemaking, sex. **fa la ama** make love, have sex.
amable *adj.* loveable (US lovable), likeable (US likable), kind, nice, endearing, pleasant, affable.
amablia *n.* loveableness (US lovableness), kindness, niceness, affability.
amaca *n.* hammock.
amaceta *n.* deckchair.
amada *adj.* loved, beloved, cherished. • *n.* beloved, lover, loved one, heartthrob. **amada vera** true love. **bon amada** well-loved.
amamelia *n.* witch hazel (*Hamamelis*).
amanda *n.* almond (*nut*). **con amandas** amandine, almondine.
amando *n.* almond (*tree*: *Prunus dulcis*).
amanita *n.* fly agaric, fly amanita (*Amanita muscaria*).
amante *adj.* loving, friendly, kind.
amaperil *n.* daredevil.
amar *n.* splashdown (*of spacecraft*).
amaranto *n.* amaranth (*Amaranthus*).
amarga *adj.* bitter (*taste*, *emotion*), acerbic, acrid; embittered, acrimonious, rancorous. **amarga-dulse** *adj.* bittersweet.
amargi *vi.* grow bitter. • *vt.* embitter.
amargia *n.* bitterness, acerbity, rancour (US rancor).
amarilis *n.* amaryllis (*plant*: *Amaryllidaceae*).
amarina *adj.* & *n.* Amhara, Amharic (*person*, *language*).
amasa *vt.* knead, work.
amasador *n.* kneading machine.
amato *n.* hobby, pastime, avocation.
amator *n.* hobbyist, amateur, dilettante.
amazona *n.* Amazon (*mythology*).
Amazonas *n.* Amazon (*region*). **Foresta Amazonas** Amazon Rainforest. **Rio Amazonas** Amazon River.
ambar *adj.* amber (*colour*). • *n.* amber (*resin*).
ambargris *n.* ambergris (*substance*).
ambasada *n.* embassy, consulate.
ambasador *n.* ambassador, envoy, emissary, high commissioner.
ambi- *pref.* ambi-.
ambidestrosa *adj.* ambidextrous.
ambie *vt.* surround.
ambiental *adj.* environmental.
ambiente *adj.* ambient, surrounding. • *n.* surroundings, environment, context; atmosphere (*place*, *event*), ambience, milieu, locale.
ambientisme *n.* environmentalism.
ambientiste *n.* environmentalist.
ambifilia *n.* ambiphilia.
ambifilica *adj.* ambiphilic. • *n.* ambiphile.
ambigua *adj.* ambiguous, equivocal. • *n.* ambiguity (*something ambiguous*).
ambigui *vi.* become ambiguous. • *vt.* make ambiguous.
ambiguia *n.* ambiguity (*quality*).
ambivale *vi.* be ambivalent, have mixed feelings. • *n.* ambivalence.
ambivalente *adj.* ambivalent.
ambliopia *n.* amblyopia, lazy eye (*medical*).
ambliopica *adj.* amblyopic. • *n.* amblyope.

ambos *det.* & *pron.* both; e.g. *ambos formas es coreta.* **ambos de ... e** both ... and; e.g. *ambos de la maior e sua sposa es asi.* **ambos de nos** both of us, us both.
ambrosia *n.* ambrosia (*Ambrosia*).
ambulansia *n.* ambulance.
amburger *n.* hamburger, burger. **amburger con ceso** cheeseburger.
ameba *n.* amoeba (US ameba).
amebin *adj.* amoeboid (US ameboid).
amebiside *n.* amoebiside (US amebicide).
amen *interj.* amen, so be it, let it be.
amento *n.* catkin.
America *n.* America. **America Norde** North America. **America Sentral** Central America. **America Sude** South America.
american *adj.* American; US. • *n.* American. See *SUA, esuan.*
americani *vi.* & *vt.* Americanize. • *n.* Americanization.
amerisio *n.* americium (*element*).
ameta *n.* (*my*) dear, darling.
ametista *n.* amethyst.
amfetamina *n.* amphetamine.
amfi- *pref.* amphi-.
amfibin *adj.* amphibious.
amfibio *n.* amphibian (*Amphibia*).
amfibraco *n.* amphibrach.
amfiteatro *n.* amphitheatre (US amphitheater).
amfora *n.* amphora.
ami [a'mi] *n.* friend, mate, pal, chum, buddy, crony. **ami de cor** girlfriend, boyfriend. **ami de jua** playmate. **ami fema** female friend, girl friend. **ami mas** male friend, boy friend.
amia *n.* friendship, amity, fellowship.
amida *n.* amide (*substance*).
amidon *n.* starch. **amidon de mais** cornstarch, cornflour.
amidoni *vt.* starch.
amidonida *adj.* starched.
amidonosa *adj.* starchy.
amigdala *n.* amygdala.
amil- *pref.* amyl-.
amilase *n.* amylase.
amiloide *n.* amyloid.
amiloidose *n.* amyloidosis.
amin *adj.* friendly, nice, amiable, amicable, genial, congenial, neighbourly, personable, chummy, pally.
amina *adj.* & *n.* amine (*chemistry*).
amini *vi.* become friends. • *vt.* befriend, make friends with.
aminia *n.* friendliness.
aminoasida *n.* amino acid.
aminobutirica *adj.* aminobutyric.
amir *n.* emir, amir.
amira *vt.* admire. • *n.* admiration.
amirable *adj.* admirable, fine.
amiral *n.* admiral.
amiralia *n.* admiralty, admiralship.
amirante *adj.* admiring.
amirati *adj.* & *n.* Emirati.
amiria *n.* emirate. **Amirias Arabi Unida** United Arab Emirates.
amiror *n.* admirer.
amix *adj.* & *n.* Amish.
amnesia *n.* amnesia.
amnesica *adj.* & *n.* amnesiac, amnesic.
amnestia *vt.* amnesty, grant amnesty to. • *n.* amnesty.
amnial *adj.* amniotic.
amnio[1] *n.* amnion (*membrane*).
amnio-[2] *pref.* amnio-.
amniosentese *n.* amniocentesis.
amoc *adj.* amok, amuck. **sindrom amoc** amok syndrome.
amonia *n.* ammonia.
amonio *n.* ammonium.
amor *n.* lover, girlfriend, boyfriend, paramour. **amor de belia** aesthete (US esthete). **amor de comeda** gourmand. **amor de plaser** hedonist.
amortador *n.* shock absorber.
amorti *vt.* muffle, deaden, dampen; amortize, absorb (*cost*). • *n.* amortization.
amosa *adj.* affectionate, fond; amorous.
amosia *n.* affection, fondness; amorousness.
amper *n.* ampere, amp. **cuantia de amperes** ampage, amperage.
amperimetre *n.* ammeter.
ampola *n.* ampoule; lightbulb.
amputa *vt.* amputate; e.g. *amputa la gama de algun.* • *n.* amputation.
amputada *adj.* amputated. • *n.* amputated limb; amputee.
an[1] *adv.* even. **an con** despite, in spite of, regardless of, notwithstanding, even with, even in the face of. **an con tota** after all, despite everything, at least, if nothing else. **an cuando** even when, even while, even as. **an no** not even. **an nunca** never at all, not even once. **an pos** even after, despite, in spite of, notwithstanding (*something that has already happened*). **an pos tota** after all, despite everything. **an si** even if, though, although, even though, albeit, despite the fact that, in spite of the fact that, notwithstanding that, while, whilst. **an sin** even without, despite the lack of. **an tal** even thus, even so, nevertheless, nonetheless, however, anyway, anyhow, yet, still, be that as it may, despite that, having said that, all the same, at least, if nothing else.
-an[2] *adj.suff.* & *n.suff.* -an, -ian (*pertaining to a region or period*); e.g. *italian*; *suburban*; *victorian.* See *-es, -i, -ica, -sce.*

-an[3] *n.suff.* -an (*saturated hydrocarbon*).
ana- *pref.* ana-.
anabatisme *n.* Anabaptism (*Christianity*).
anabatiste *adj.* & *n.* Anabaptist.
anabolal *adj.* anabolic.
anaboli *vi.* anabolize (*biology*). • *n.* anabolism.
anacardia *n.* cashew (*nut*).
anacardio *n.* cashew (*tree: Anacardium*).
anaconda *n.* anaconda (*Eunectes*).
anacron *adj.* anachronistic. • *n.* anachronism.
anafor *adj.* anaphoric. • *n.* anaphor (*word that refers back*).
anaforia *n.* anaphora.
anagram *n.* anagram.
anagramal *adj.* anagrammatic.
anagrami *vi.* & *vt.* anagrammatize.
anal *adj.* anal.
analesica *adj.* analeptic.
analisable *adj.* analysable (US analyzable).
analisador *n.* analyser (US analyzer). **analisador sintatical** syntax analyser (US analyzer), parser.
analisal *adj.* analytic, analytical.
analise *vt.* analyse (US analyze), dissect; parse. • *n.* analysis, dissection, breakdown. **analise numeral** numerical analysis. **analise tro detaliosa** overanalyse (US overanalyze).
analiseda *adj.* analysed (US analyzed). • *n.* analysand, analytic patient.
analisor *n.* analyst.
analoja *adj.* analogous, analogue (US analog). • *n.* analogue (US analog), analogy (*something analogous*).
analojia *n.* analogy (*comparison*); analogousness.
anamnese *n.* anamnesis (*medical*).
anamorfosal *adj.* anamorphic.
anamorfose *n.* anamorphosis (*optics, biology*).
ananas *n.* pineapple (*plant, fruit: Ananas*).
anapestal *adj.* anapaestic (US anapestic).
anapesto *n.* anapaest (US anapest).
anarcia *n.* anarchy, lawlessness.
anarciosa *adj.* anarchic.
anarcisme *n.* anarchism.
anarciste *n.* anarchist.
anastomose *n.* anastomosis (*anatomy*).
Anatolia *n.* Anatolia, Asia Minor.
anatolian *adj.* & *n.* Anatolian.
anatomia *n.* anatomy.
anatomial *adj.* anatomical.
anatomiste *n.* anatomist.
anc *n.* ankh (*cross*).
anca *n.* hip, rump. **anca e coxa** haunch.
ancaran *adj.* angora (*cat, goat, rabbit*).
ance *adv.* also, as well, too, likewise. **como ance** as well as, plus. **con ance** with the addition of, plus.
ancilosauro *n.* ankylosaurus (*Ankylosauria*).
ancilose *n.* ankylosis (*medical*).
ancilostoma *n.* hookworm (*Ancylostoma*).
ancilostomiase *n.* hookworm, ancylostomiasis.
ancor *n.* anchor. **cade la ancor** drop anchor. **leva la ancor** weigh anchor.
ancora *adv.* still (*ongoing*); even (*more, less*). **ancora no** still not, not yet. **ma ancora** but still, and yet, nevertheless, nonetheless, however.
ancoreria *n.* anchorage.
ancori *vt.* anchor.
Andalusia *n.* Andalusia (*Spanish region*).
Andaman *n.* Andaman. **Isolas Andaman** Andaman Islands. **Mar Andaman** Andaman Sea.
Andes *n.pl.* Andes.
Andora *n.* Andorra.
andoran *adj.* & *n.* Andorran.
-andria *n.suff.* -andry.
andro- *pref.* andro- (*male*).
androfilia *n.* androphilia.
androfilica *adj.* androphilic. • *n.* androphile.
androfobia *n.* androphobia.
androfobica *adj.* androphobic. • *n.* androphobe.
androide *adj.* & *n.* android.
androjen *n.* androgen.
androjine *adj.* androgynous, hermaphroditic, epicene. • *n.* androgyne, hermaphrodite.
androjinia *n.* androgyny, hermaphroditism.
andromeda[1] *n.* andromeda, pieris (*plant: Andromeda, Pieris*).
Andromeda[2] *n.* Andromeda (*mythology, constellation*).
androseo *n.* androecium (*botany*).
anela *vt.* long for, yearn for, pine for, hanker for, crave, deeply desire, covet. **anela de casa** homesickness, longing for home. **anela de pais** homesickness (*abroad*).
anelante *adj.* yearning. **anelante sua casa** homesick. **anelante sua pais** homesick (*abroad*).
aneleta *n.* washer; picot.
aneli *vi.* & *vt.* loop, ring.
anelido *n.* annelid (*worm: Annelida*).
anelo *adj.* ring-shaped, annular. • *n.* ring, loop (*material*); link (*chain*); hoop, quoit; circuit, lap (*racetrack*); torus, closed curve; ring, kroužek (*diacritic*). **anelo de ago** eye of a needle. **anelo de onca** eye (*fastener*). **anelo de spageti** spaghetti hoop, spaghetti ring, spaghettio. **anelo fortinte** grommet, reinforcement ring.
anelosa *adj.* ringed.
anemia *n.* anaemia (US anemia).

anemica *adj.* anaemic (US anemic).
anemometre *n.* anemometer.
anemone *n.* anemone (*Anemone*). **anemone-de mar** *n.* sea anemone (*Actiniaria*).
anestese *vt.* anaesthetise (US anesthetize). • *n.* anaesthetisation (US anesthetization).
anestesente *n.* anaesthetic (US anesthetic).
anestesia *n.* anaesthesia (US anesthesia).
anestesiste *n.* anaesthetist (US anesthetist).
aneto *n.* dill (*plant: Anethum graveolens*).
aneurisme *n.* aneurysm.
angila *n.* eel (*Anguilliformes*).
angilin *adj.* eel-like.
anglican *adj.* & *n.* Anglican.
anglicanisme *n.* Anglicanism (*Christianity*).
anglosason *adj.* & *n.* Anglo-Saxon, Old English.
Angola *n.* Angola.
angolan *adj.* & *n.* Angolan.
angostura *n.* angostura (*Angostura, Galipea*).
Anguila *n.* Anguilla.
anguilan *adj.* & *n.* Anguillian.
anguli *vi.* & *vt.* angle.
angulida *adj.* angled.
angulo *adj.* angular. • *n.* angle, corner. **angulo reta** right angle.
angulometre *n.* protractor.
angusa *vt.* distress, appall (US appal), harrow. • *n.* agony, anguish, anxiety, dismay, consternation, distress, stress (*mental*).
angusada *adj.* distressed, anxious, agonized, anguished, in anguish.
angusante *adj.* distressing, appalling, harrowing, hurtful.
ani *n.* ani (*bird: Crotophaga*).
anial *adj.* annual, yearly.
anilina *n.* aniline (*substance*).
anima *vi.* animate, come to life. • *vt.* animate, bring to life, vivify. • *n.* animation (*action, film*); cartoon. **anima suspendeda** suspended animation.
animada *adj.* animated, animate; brought to life. • *n.* animated character, cartoon character.
animal *adj.* & *n.* animal. **animal amada** pet. **animal de casa** pet. **animal de pelux** stuffed toy, plush toy, soft toy, cuddly toy. **animal xasada** game, big game. **animales** animals, fauna. **animales nosiva** vermin.
animali *vi.* & *vt.* zoomorphize. • *n.* zoomorphism.
anime *n.* anime (*animation*).
animisme *n.* animism.
animiste *adj.* & *n.* animist.
animor *n.* animator, cartoonist; cheerleader.
aninga *n.* darter, snakebird (*Anhinga*).
anio *n.* year. **anio de lus** light year. **anio de recolie** vintage. **anio estendeda** leap year. **anios pasada** years gone by, yesteryear.
anion *n.* anion (*chemistry*).
anis *n.* anise, aniseed (*plant: Pimpinella anisum*). **seme de anis** aniseed (*seed*).
aniso- *pref.* aniso- (*unequal*).
aniversario *n.* anniversary, birthday, jubilee. **aniversario dusento** 200th anniversary, bicentenary, bicentennial. **aniversario sento** 100th anniversary, centenary, centennial. **aniversario sento sincodes** 150th anniversary, sesquicentennial.
anjel *n.* angel. **anjel gardante** guardian angel.
anjelica *n.* angelica (*plant: Angelica*).
anjelin *adj.* angelic.
anjina *n.* angina. **anjina de peto** angina pectoris.
anjio- *pref.* angio- (*blood vessels*).
anjioma *n.* angioma.
anjiopatia *n.* angiopathy.
anjioplastia *n.* angioplasty.
anjiosperma *n.* angiosperm.
anjiotensina *n.* angiotensin.
ano *n.* anus.
anodo *n.* anode.
anomal *adj.* anomalous. • *n.* anomaly (*something anomalous*).
anomalia *n.* anomalousness, anomaly (*quality*).
anomalur *n.* flying squirrel, anomalure (*Pteromyinae, Anomaluridae*).
anomia *n.* anomia (*medical*).
anona *n.* annona (*plant: Annona*).
anonim *adj.* anonymous, faceless, incognito.
anonimia *n.* anonymity.
anorac *n.* anorak (*garment*).
anorexia *n.* anorexia.
anorexica *adj.* & *n.* anorexic.
anosia *n.* anoxia (*medical*).
anosica *adj.* anoxic.
anota *vt.* annotate. • *n.* annotation.
anotor *n.* annotator.
ansi *vi.* dread, fret, become anxious. • *vt.* worry, rattle.
ansia *n.* anxiety, worry, unease, nervousness, apprehension, dread, angst, trepidation.
ansiosa *adj.* anxious, worried, nervous, apprehensive, rattled, fretful, jittery, fraught.
anstrom *n.* angstrom (*unit of length*).
antartica *adj.* Antarctic. **Antartica** *n.* Antarctica, Antarctic. **Mar Antartica** Antarctic Ocean, Southern Ocean.
ante *prep.* • in front of, before (*in space*); e.g. *mea peto es ante mea dorso*; *un can dormi ante la boteca*; *la casa sta ante un colina.* • (*moving*) to the front of, in front of; e.g. *me veni ante tu per*

demanda per tua pardona. • before (*in time*), earlier than, prior to, ahead of; e.g. *janero veni ante febrero*; *me espera fini la labora ante la reposa de sol.*—*Ante* by itself is a preposition. When *before* means *beforehand*, the translation is *a ante*. If *before* introduces a subordinate clause, i.e. if it means *before the time when*, use *ante cuando* instead. • *pref.* ante-. **a ante** *prep.* (*moving*) to the front of, in front of; e.g. *el ia lansa la bal a ante la arbores*; *par macina de tempo, el ia viaja a ante sua nase.* • *adv.* (*located*) in front, ahead; (*moving*) forward, forwards, forth; (*occurring*) before, beforehand, formerly, previously, earlier, ago. • *interj.* onward, onwards, on we go. **a du dias a ante** two days before, two days earlier. **a du dias ante aora** two days ago. **a multe tempo a ante** a long time before, a long time previously, long ago. **a multe tempo ante aora** long ago, a long time ago. **ante fini de** by (*at the latest*), no later than; e.g. *el va fini la labora ante fini de lundi.* **ante tota** above all. **de ante** *prep.* moving from ahead of, from in front of. • *adv.* from ahead, from in front. See *cuando.*

antecarga *vt.* muzzle-load (*gun*).

antena *n.* antenna; aerial.

anteporto *n.* outer harbour (US harbor).

antera *n.* anther.

anterior *adj.* anterior, rostral. • *n.* forepart; forequarters (*animal*).

antesala *n.* anteroom.

antestadio *n.* proscenium.

anteultima *adj.* penultimate, second from last, last but one.

anteurbe *n.* outskirts, approaches.

anti- *pref.* anti- (*opposition*); e.g. *antisosial*; *antiavional*; *antifungal*; *antieroe*; *antiproton.*

antiabortiste *adj.* & *n.* antiabortionist.

antiasida *n.* antacid.

antiavional *adj.* antiaircraft.

antibaterial *adj.* & *n.* antibacterial, antibiotic.

antica *adj.* ancient, antique. **eda antica** antiquity, ancient times.

anticalia *n.* antique (*object*), vintage item.

anticalior *n.* antique seller, antiquarian.

anticia *n.* antiquity (*quality*), seniority.

anticin *adj.* quaint, old-fashioned, dated, archaic, antiquated, frumpy; legacy (*software, hardware*). • *n.* archaism, dated expression; old fogey, old geezer (*person*).

anticoagulante *n.* anticoagulant.

anticolinerjica *n.* anticholinergic.

anticonvulsante *n.* anticonvulsant.

anticorodente *adj.* anticorrosive.

anticorpo *n.* antibody.

Anticristo *n.* Antichrist.

antidepresante *adj.* & *n.* antidepressant.

antidiabetica *n.* antidiabetic.

antielmintal *n.* anthelmintic, antihelminthic, vermifuge, vermicide, wormer, dewormer, drench (*medicine*).

antiepilesica *n.* antiepileptic.

antieroe *n.* antihero, antiheroine.

antifebral *n.* antipyretic.

antifona *n.* antiphon (*music*).

antifonia *n.* antiphony.

antifungal *adj.* & *n.* antifungal.

antige [antiˈge] *adj.* anti-gay.

antigovernal *adj.* antigovernment.

antigravita *n.* antigravity.

Antigua *n.* Antigua. **Antigua e Barbuda** Antigua and Barbuda.

antiguan *adj.* & *n.* Antiguan.

antiinflamante *adj.* & *n.* anti-inflammatory. **antiinflamante nonsteroidal** NSAID, non-steroidal anti-inflammatory drug.

antiistaminal *n.* antihistamine.

antiiudisme *n.* antisemitism.

antiiudiste *adj.* anti-Jewish, antisemitic. • *n.* antisemite.

antijen *adj.* antigenic. • *n.* antigen.

antilean *adj.* Antillean.

antileprosa *n.* antileprotic.

Antiles *n.pl.* Antilles. **Antiles Major** Greater Antilles. **Antiles Minor** Lesser Antilles. **Antiles Nederlandes** Netherlands Antilles.

antilocapra *n.* pronghorn antelope (*Antilocapra*).

antilope *n.* antelope (*Alcelaphinae, Antilopinae, Hippotraginae, Reduncinae, Cephalophinae*).

antimalarial *n.* antimalarial.

antimateria *n.* antimatter.

antimicrobial *adj.* & *n.* antimicrobial, antibiotic, antiseptic, germicide.

antimonio *n.* antimony.

antimonopolial *adj.* antitrust.

antineutron *n.* antineutron.

antinomia *n.* antinomy.

antiosidinte *adj.* & *n.* antioxidant.

antipape *n.* antipope.

antiparticula *n.* antiparticle.

antipatia *n.* antipathy, aversion, deep dislike.

antipatiosa *adj.* antipathetic, averse.

antipoda *adj.* antipodean, antipodal. • *n.* antipode.

antiproton *n.* antiproton.

antiprotozonal *n.* antiprotozoal.

antipsicosica *n.* antipsychotic.

antirascal *adj.* anti-scratch, scratch-resistant.

antisemita *adj.* antisemitic. • *n.* antisemite.

antisemitisme *n.* antisemitism.

antisenesente *adj.* antiageing (US antiaging).

antisepsica *adj.* & *n.* antiseptic.
antisiclon *n.* anticyclone, high-pressure area.
antisistemal *adj.* antiestablishment.
antisosial *adj.* antisocial, sociopathic.
antispasmal *n.* antispasmodic.
antitesal *adj.* antithetical.
antitese *n.* antithesis.
antitosal *n.* antitussive, cough medicine.
antitoxina *n.* antitoxin.
antituberculosica *n.* antituberculous drug.
antivenenal *n.* antivenom.
antivirusal *adj.* antiviral; antivirus (*software*).
antixocal *adj.* antishock, shockproof.
antoloji *vt.* anthologize. • *n.* anthologization.
antolojia *n.* anthology.
antolojiste *n.* anthologist.
antonim *adj.* antonymous, opposite. • *n.* antonym, opposite.
antonimia *n.* antonymy.
antoserotal *n.* hornwort (*plant*: *Anthoceros*).
antrasita *n.* anthracite (*substance*).
antrax *n.* anthrax.
antro *n.* antrum (*anatomy*).
antropo- *pref.* anthropo-.
antropolojia *n.* anthropology.
antropolojial *adj.* anthropological.
antropolojiste *n.* anthropologist.
antropometria *n.* anthropometry.
antropometrial *adj.* anthropometric.
antropomorfe *adj.* anthropomorphic.
antropomorfia *n.* anthropomorphism.
antroposentral *adj.* anthropocentric, anthropic. **prinsipe antroposentral** anthropic principle.
antrostomo *n.* whippoorwill (*bird*: *Antrostomus*).
anunsia *vt.* announce, advertise, publicize. • *n.* announcement, advertisement, advertising, advert, ad, publicity, prospectus, blurb, hype. **anunsia de mori** obituary, necrology. **bon anunsia** good press, good publicity.
anunsieta *n.* classified advertisement, small ad, want ad.
anunsior *n.* announcer, crier; adman.
anura *n.* anura (*amphibian*: *Anura*).
anxa *n.* reed.
anxo *n.* ancho (*chili*).
anxoa *n.* anchovy (*Engraulis*).
aora *adv.* now, currently, at present, at this time; right now, immediately, at once. **ante aora** before now, ago. **aora e alora** now and then, now and again, from time to time, on occasion, occasionally. **asta aora** until now, so far, to date, yet, up to this point. **de aora** from now on, henceforth. **no aora** not now. **per aora** for now, for the moment, for the time being.
aoristo *n.* aorist (*grammar*).
aorta *n.* aorta (*anatomy*).
aortal *adj.* aortic.
aortite *n.* aortitis.
aoto *n.* night monkey, owl monkey, douroucouli (*Aotus*).
ap *n.* application, app (*software*).
Apalatxia *n.* Appalachia.
apalatxian *adj.* Appalachian. **Montes Apalatxian** Appalachian Mountains.
aparateta *n.* thingy, thingummy, thingamajig, thingamabob, whatsit, wossname, whatchamacallit, doodad, doobry, doohickey, hickey; widget, gizmo, control (*user interface*).
aparato *n.* device, gadget, piece of apparatus. **aparato de puleas** block and tackle. **aparato dental** brace (*teeth*). **aparato fisada** fixture. **aparatos** apparatus, equipment, hardware, tackle, rigging, paraphernalia. **aparatos de pexa** fishing tackle. **aparatos de vela** tackle (*ship*).
apare *vi.* appear, become visible, show up, turn up, surface. • *vt.* cause to appear, manifest, conjure. • *n.* appearance. **apare corta** appear briefly, put in an appearance, show one's face. **apare lenta** fade in. **apare prima** first appearance, debut.
apartait *n.* apartheid.
aparte *n.* apartment, flat, tenement; unit (*commercial*, *residential*). **aparte apical** penthouse. **aparte misera** tenement. **aparte sin asendador** walk-up.
apatia *n.* apathy.
apatica *adj.* apathetic.
apatosauro *n.* apatosaurus, brontosaurus (*Apatosaurus*).
apatxe *adj.* & *n.* Apache (*person*, *language*).
apela *vt.* appeal, say in appeal. **apela a** appeal to, petition.
apelor *n.* appellant.
apena *adv.* hardly, scarcely, barely, just, by a small amount, with difficulty.
apendis *n.* appendix (*anatomy*, *publishing*), appendage.
apendisectomia *n.* appendectomy (*surgery*).
apendisite *n.* appendicitis.
apesta *vi.* stink, reek, pong, niff. • *n.* stink, stench.
apestante *adj.* stinking, fetid.
apestosa *adj.* stinky.
apetito *n.* appetite.
apical *adj.* apical.
apico *n.* apex, tip, peak, vertex; heyday, prime, zenith.
apicomplexa *n.* sporozoon (pl. sporozoa) (*organism*: *Apicomplexa*).
aplanata *adj.* aplanatic. • *n.* aplanat, aplanatic lens.

aplasia *n.* aplasia (*medical*).
aplasica *adj.* aplasic.
aplaudi *vt.* applaud, clap. • *n.* applause, clapping, ovation.
aplaudor *n.* applauder. **aplaudores** claque.
aplica *vt.* apply (*substance, physical force*), spread; exact, inflict (*revenge*). • *n.* application (*applying, using*); appliqué (*sewing*). **aplica se a** apply oneself to (*task*). **aplica sua mente a** apply one's mind to.
aplicable *adj.* applicable, relevant, appropriate.
aplicador *n.* applicator.
aplo- *pref.* haplo- (*single*).
aploide *adj.* & *n.* haploid.
apnea *n.* apnoea (US apnea) (*medical*).
apnica *adj.* apneic.
apo- *pref.* apo-.
apocalisal *adj.* apocalyptic.
apocalise *n.* apocalypse, armageddon, doomsday, catastrophe; revelation (*religious*).
apocrifa *adj.* apocryphal. **apocrifas** apocrypha.
apoia *vi.* lean, tilt, slant, tip, skew, prop (*position, movement*); bank (*aircraft*); italicize. • *vt.* lean, tilt, slant, skew, prop (*position, movement*); bank (*aircraft*); italicize.
apoiada *adj.* tilted, leaning, slanting, skew, askew, lopsided, crooked, wonky; oblique, italic.
apojeo *n.* apogee (*astronomy*).
aponable *adj.* wearable.
apone *vt.* put on (*garment*), don.
aponeurose *n.* aponeurosis (*anatomy*).
apoptose *n.* apoptosis, programmed cell death.
aposa *vt.* appose, juxtapose, collocate. • *n.* apposition, juxtaposition, collocation.
aposada *n.* adposition (*grammar*).
aposta *vt.* & *n.* bet, wager, gamble; e.g. *aposta sento euros ce esta va aveni*. **aposta coletiva** sweepstake. **aposta contra** bet against, wager against. **aposta per** bet on, wager on.
apostada *n.* stake, stakes.
aposteria *n.* betting shop, betting parlour (US parlor).
aposteriori *adj.* a posteriori.
apostol *n.* apostle.
apostolal *adj.* apostolic.
apostor *n.* bettor, better; backer (*of horse*).
aprende *vt.* learn.
aprendor *n.* learner, pupil, apprentice, trainee.
april *n.* April.
apriori *adj.* a priori.
aproba *vt.* approve, approve of, assent to, endorse; confirm (*action on computer*). • *n.* approval, confirmation.
aprosima *adj.* approximate, rough. • *adv.* approximately, roughly, some.
aprosimi *vi.* & *vt.* approximate. • *n.* approximation.
aprosiminte *adj.* & *n.* approximant (*consonant*). **aprosiminte ladal** lateral approximant (*consonant*).
apside *n.* apse; apsis.
apto- *pref.* hapto- (*attachment*).
ara *n.* macaw (*Ara* and related genera).
arabesca *adj.* & *n.* arabesque.
arabi *adj.* & *n.* Arab, Arabic, Arabian. **Mar Arabi** Arabian Sea. **Penisola Arabi** Arabian Peninsula.
Arabia *n.* Arabia. **Arabia Saudi** Saudi Arabia.
arac *n.* arrack, arak (*drink*).
aracide *n.* peanut (*Arachis hypogaea*).
aracnido *n.* arachnid (*Arachnida*).
aracno- *pref.* arachno- (*spider*).
aracnofobia *n.* arachnophobia.
aracnofobica *adj.* arachnophobic. • *n.* arachnophobe.
aracnoide *n.* arachnoid.
aradi *vt.* plough (US plow), till.
arado *n.* plough (US plow).
Arafura, Mar *n.* Arafura Sea.
Aragon *n.* Aragon (*Spanish region*).
aragones *adj.* & *n.* Aragonese.
Aral, Mar *n.* Aral Sea.
Aram *n.* Aram (*biblical region*).
arami *adj.* & *n.* Aramaic, Aramean, Aramaean.
aramo *n.* limpkin (*bird*: *Aramus guarauna*).
aranca *vt.* wrench, jerk, yank, snatch, wrest, tug, heave. • *n.* jerk, yank, tug, twist.
arania *n.* spider (*Araneae*). **arania de rede embutin** funnelweb spider.
aranieta *n.* baby spider.
aranin *adj.* spidery, arachnoid.
aranja *vt.* arrange (*music*). • *n.* arrangement.
aranjor *n.* arranger.
arbitra *vt.* arbitrate on, mediate on. • *n.* arbitration, mediation.
arbitraje *n.* arbitrage.
arbitror *n.* referee, umpire, official, arbiter, arbitrator.
arbor *n.* tree. **arbor de pan** breadfruit (*Artocarpus altilis*). **arbor joven** young tree, sapling.
arboral *adj.* arboreal.
arboran *n.* treepie (*bird*: *Crypsirina, Dendrocitta, Platysmurus, Temnurus*).
arboreria *n.* arboretum.
arboreta *n.* bush, shrub. **arboreta de rosa** rosebush. **arboretas** bushes, shrubbery.

arboretin *adj.* shrublike, shrubby.
arborin *adj.* treelike.
arbuto *n.* arbutus (*plant*: *Arbutus*, *Epigaea*).
arca *n.* ark. **arca de la acorda** ark of the covenant.
arcabus *n.* arquebus, hackbut.
arcada *n.* arcade.
arcanjel *n.* archangel.
arcea *n.* archaeon, archaea, archaebacterium (*organism*).
arcenemi [arkene'mi] *n.* archenemy, nemesis.
arceo- *pref.* archaeo- (US archeo-).
arceolojia *n.* archaeology (US archeology).
arceolojial *adj.* archaeological (US archeological).
arceolojiste *n.* archaeologist (US archeologist).
arceopterix *n.* archaeopteryx (*Archaeopteryx*).
arcetipal *adj.* archetypal.
arcetipo *n.* archetype.
arci[1] *vi.* arch (*back*, *roof*). **arci a retro** backbend.
arci-[2] *pref.* archi-, arch- (*chief*).
arcibispia *n.* archbishopric, archdiocese.
arcibispo *n.* archbishop.
arciduxe *n.* archduke.
arcin *adj.* bow-shaped.
arcipelago *n.* archipelago.
arciteta *n.* architecture.
arcitetal *adj.* architectural.
arcitetor *n.* architect.
arcitrava *n.* architrave.
arcivador *n.* file cabinet, filing cabinet. **arcivador de revisas** version control system, revision control system.
arcival *adj.* archival.
arciveria *n.* archive, depository, record office, repository, registry.
arcivi *vt.* archive, log, chronicle, file.
arciviste *n.* archivist.
arcivo *n.* record (*information*), register, log; file, folder, document wallet; folder, directory. **arcivos anial** annals.
arcivolta *n.* archivolt, voussure (*architecture*).
arco *n.* arc (*geometry*, *electrical*, *narrative*); arch, archway (*architecture*); bow (*weapon*, *music*). **arco apoiante** flying buttress. **arco de pede** arch (*foot*), instep. **arco de porte** doorway. **arco de sielo** rainbow. **arco longa** longbow. **arco sigmoide** ogee (*architecture*, *mathematics*, *etc.*). **xuta con arco** archery.
arconte *n.* archon (*Athenian judge*).
arcor *n.* archer. **Arcor** *n.* Sagittarius (*constellation*).
ardador *n.* burner, incinerator.
arde *vi.* burn, blaze. • *vt.* burn, sear, incinerate. **arde de ereses** auto-da-fé. **arde par sol** sunburn. **arde sacrifial** immolate. **arde un fondable** blow a fuse.
ardeda *adj.* burned, charred. • *n.* burn (*injury*). **ardeda par sol** sunburned.
ardente *adj.* burning; ardent, passionate.
ardeta *vi.* smoulder (US smolder).
ardin *adj.* glowing, aglow.
ardosia *n.* slate.
are *n.* are (*unit of area*).
area *n.* area. **area abital** residential area, uptown. **area neblosa** grey (US gray) area (*of unclear definition*).
areal *adj.* areal.
areca *n.* areca palm (*Areca*).
arem *n.* harem, seraglio.
aremon *n.* brush finch (*Arremon*, *Atlapetes*, etc.).
arena *n.* sand, grit. **arena movente** quicksand.
arenga *vt.* harangue, rant at. • *n.* rant, tirade, diatribe.
arenge *n.* herring (*Clupea*). **arenge fumida** smoked herring, kipper.
areni *vt.* sandblast.
arenin *adj.* sandy, gritty.
arenito *n.* sandstone.
arenor *n.* sandman.
arenosa *adj.* sandy, sand-covered.
areola *n.* halo, nimbus; areola.
aresta *vt.* arrest, seize, apprehend. • *n.* arrest; custody. **aresta acaso** arbitrary arrest. **aresta nonlegal** illegal arrest.
arestada *adj.* arrested, under arrest, in custody.
argon *n.* argon.
arhat *n.* arhat (*saint*).
aria *n.* aria.
arianisme *n.* Arianism (*Christianity*).
ariete *n.* battering ram.
aril *n.* aril, arillus (*botany*).
aristocrata *adj.* aristocratic, highborn. • *n.* aristocrat. **aristocratas** aristocrats, aristocracy, peerage.
aristocratia *n.* aristocracy.
aristolocia *n.* aristolochia, birthwort, pipevine (*plant*: *Aristolochia*).
aritmetica *n.* arithmetic.
aritmetical *adj.* arithmetic, arithmetical.
aritmeticiste *n.* arithmetician.
aritmia *n.* arrhythmia.
aritmica *adj.* arrhythmic.
ariva *vi.* arrive; (*colloquial*) come (*orgasm*). • *n.* arrival; advent (*including religious*).
ariveria *n.* arrivals hall.
arivor *n.* arrival (*person*), newcomer.
Arizona *n.* Arizona (*US state*).
arjenti *vi.* become silver. • *vt.* silver, silverplate.
arjentida *adj.* silver-plated.

arjentifer *adj.* argentiferous.
arjentin *adj.* silvery.
Arjentina *n.* Argentina. **arjentina** *adj.* Argentinian, Argentine. • *n.* Argentinian. **Mar Arjentina** Argentine Sea.
arjento *adj.* silver (*colour*). • *n.* silver (*element*). **arjento dorada** gilded silver, vermeil. **de arjento** (*made of*) silver.
arjentor *n.* silversmith.
arjila *n.* clay.
arjilosa *adj.* clayey.
Arkansas [ˈarkansa] *n.* Arkansas (*US state*).
arlecin *n.* harlequin.
arma[1] *n.* weapon. **arma de xoca eletrical** electroshock weapon. **armas** weapons, arms, armaments, munition, ordnance, weaponry. **armas lejera** light weapons, small arms. **ave plu armas ca** outgun. **con armas** armed. **furni armas a** arm. **porta armas** bear arms. **sin armas** unarmed.
arma[2] *vt.* arm. • *n.* armament (*action*).
armada *n.* army, legion, armada, host.
armadilo *n.* armadillo (*Cingulata, Dasypodidae*).
armario *n.* cupboard, cabinet, armoire. **armario de libros** bookcase. **armario de mur** wall cabinet. **armario de vestes** wardrobe. **construi de armarios** cabinetmaking.
armarior *n.* cabinetmaker.
armatur *n.* armature (*literature, sculpture*); key signature; framework (*software*).
Armenia *n.* Armenia. See *Haiastan.*
armenian *adj.* & *n.* Armenian (*person, language*). See *haiaren.*
armeria *n.* armoury (US armory), arsenal.
arminian *adj.* & *n.* Arminian.
arminianisme *n.* Arminianism (*Christianity*).
armoni *vi.* & *vt.* harmonize.
armonia *n.* harmony.
armonial *adj.* harmonic. • *n.* harmonic (*frequency*).
armonica *n.* harmonica, mouth organ, mouth harp.
armonio *n.* harmonium (*musical instrument*).
armoniosa *adj.* harmonious, compatible, congruous, eurhythmic.
armor *n.* armourer (US armorer).
armur *n.* (*suit of*) armour (US armor); carapace, shell (*animal, plant*). **armur de gama** greave. **armur de peto** breastplate.
arn *abbr.* (*asida ribonucleal*) RNA.
arnes *n.* harness, sling.
arnesi *vt.* harness.
arnica *n.* arnica (*plant: Arnica*).
arpa *n.* harp.
arpejio *n.* arpeggio.
arpia *n.* harpy; harridan, hag, gorgon, crone. • *n.* harpy eagle (*Harpiinae*).
arpiste *n.* harpist.
arpon *n.* harpoon.
arponi *vt.* harpoon.
arsenico *n.* arsenic.
artal *adj.* artistic.
arte *n.* art. **arte de altar** altarpiece. **arte de governa** statesmanship, statecraft. **arte deco** art deco. **arte inferior** kitsch. **artes bela** fine arts, beaux arts. **artes de presenta** performing arts. **artes vidable** visual arts.
artemisia *n.* mugwort, sagebrush (*plant: Artemisia*).
arteria *n.* artery. **arteria carotide** carotid artery.
arterial *adj.* arterial.
arterieta *n.* arteriole.
arteriografia *n.* arteriography.
arteriosclerose *n.* arteriosclerosis.
arterite *n.* arteritis.
artesian *adj.* artesian (*well*).
artica *adj.* Arctic. **Artica** *n.* Arctic. **Mar Artica** Arctic Ocean.
article *n.* article (*document*); record, row (*data*). **article de crede** article of faith. **article de cuantia** partitive article. **article de defini** definite article. **article de lavabo** toiletry. **article de nondefini** indefinite article. **article de novas** news item.
artifis *adj.* artificial, synthetic, manmade.
artifisia *n.* artifice, artificiality.
artileria *n.* artillery, ordnance.
artileriste *n.* artillerist, artilleryman.
artin *adj.* arty, artsy.
artisan *n.* artisan, craftsman, craftswoman, tradesman, tradeswoman.
artisania *n.* craft, trade, craftsmanship, handicraft.
artiste *adj.* artistic. • *n.* artist.
artosa *adj.* artful, artistic.
artrite *n.* arthritis (*medical*).
artritica *adj.* arthritic.
artro- *pref.* arthro-.
artropodo *n.* arthropod (*Arthropoda*).
artrose *n.* arthrosis, osteoarthritis.
Aruba *n.* Aruba (*island*).
aruban *adj.* & *n.* Aruban.
arum *n.* arum (*plant: Arum*).
as *n.* ace (*card*).
asafetida *n.* asafoetida (US asafetida) (*plant: Apiaceae*).
asal *adj.* axial.
Asam *n.* Assam (*Indian state*).
asames *adj.* & *n.* Assamese.
asana *n.* asana (*yoga*).
asaro *n.* wild ginger (*Asarum*).

asasina *vt.* assassinate, murder. • *n.* assassination, murder.
asasinor *n.* assassin, murderer.
asbesto *n.* asbestos.
asbestose *n.* asbestosis.
ascarido *n.* ascarid (*worm*: *Ascarididae*).
asclepia *n.* milkweed (*plant*: *Asclepias*).
asconde *vi.* hide, be in hiding, lurk, skulk. • *vt.* hide, conceal, efface, tuck away, cover up, screen, stash, shield from view. • *n.* hiding, cover-up. **sin asconde** above board, openly.
ascondeda *adj.* hidden, concealed, latent, tucked away; lurking, stealthy. • *adv.* stealthily, by stealth.
asconderia *n.* hideout, hiding place.
ase[1] *n.* axle, shaft; axis. **ase x** x-axis. **ase y** y-axis.
-ase[2] *n.suff.* -ase (*enzyme*).
-ase[3] *n.suff.* -asis (*medical*).
asecura *vt.* insure. • *n.* insurance, indemnity. **asecura mutua** mutual insurance.
asecurada *adj.* insured. • *n.* policyholder.
asedable *adj.* accessible, approachable.
asede *vt.* access; accede to. • *n.* access.
aseja *vt.* besiege. • *n.* siege.
asejor *n.* besieger.
aselera *vi.* accelerate, speed up; expedite, hasten. • *n.* acceleration.
aselerador *n.* accelerator; gas pedal, throttle. **aselerador de particulas** particle accelerator.
aselomorfo *n.* acoelomorph (US acelomorph) (*organism*: *Acoelomorpha*).
asembla *vi.* assemble, gather, meet, come together, muster. • *vt.* assemble, amass, bring together, put together. • *n.* gathering, get-together, meeting, rally, jamboree; (*political*) assembly. **asembla de grevores** picket.
asemblable *adj.* self-assembly, flat-pack. • *n.* kit, flat pack.
asemblador *n.* assembler (*software*).
asembleria *n.* assembly rooms, assembly hall, meeting hall, meetinghouse.
asemblor *n.* assembly member, assemblyman, assemblywoman.
asendador *n.* elevator, lift.
asende *vt.* ascend, rise, climb, go up, mount. • *n.* ascent, ascension, rise, upswing, upturn.
asendente *adj.* ascending, ascendant, rising, upward, upswept. • *n.* ancestor, forebear, forefather; ascender, upstroke. • *prep.* up, towards the top of.
asendeplato *n.* dumb waiter.
asente *adj.* absent, missing. • *n.* absentee; truant. **asente sin permete** absent without leave, awol.
asenti *vi.* become absent, depart. • *vt.* make absent. **asenti se** excuse oneself.
asentia *n.* absence. **asentia permeteda** leave, furlough.
asentor *n.* accentor (*bird*: *Prunella*).
asentua *vt.* emphasize, accentuate, stress, prioritize. • *n.* emphasis, accent, stress.
asentuada *adj.* emphatic, stressed.
asentuante *adj.* emphatic.
aser *n.* steel; frizzen (*gun*). **aser nonosidinte** stainless steel, inox steel.
asera *n.* maple fruit, maple key, samara.
asero *n.* maple (*Acer*).
asesal *adj.* asexual, non-sexual. • *n.* asexual person, non-sexual person.
asesalia *n.* asexuality.
aseseta *n.* boil, furuncle (*abscess*).
aseso *n.* abscess.
aseta *vt.* accept, condone, abide by; admit, acknowledge, grant, concede (*point in an argument*); pass (*a law*). • *n.* acceptance. **pos aseta ce** granted that.
asetable *adj.* acceptable, passable, reasonable, valid, admissible, allowable.
asetablia *n.* acceptability.
asetador *n.* outlet, socket (*electric*).
asetante *adj.* accepting. **asetante ce** granted that.
asetato *n.* acetate.
asetica *adj.* acetic. • *n.* acetic acid.
asetilcolina *n.* acetylcholine.
asetilen *n.* acetylene.
asetona *n.* acetone.
asfalto *n.* asphalt, tarmac, macadam, blacktop, asphalt concrete.
asfixia *vi.* asphyxiate. • *n.* asphyxia, asphyxiation.
asfodelo *n.* asphodel (*plant*: *Asphodelus*, *Asphodeline*).
asi [a'si] *adv.* here; to here, hither. **a asi** to here, hither. **asi e ala** here and there, in various places, dotted about. **de asi** from here, away, away from here, hence. **de asi a ala** back and forth, to and fro.
Asia *n.* Asia. **Asia este** East Asia, Far East. **Asia sude-ueste** Southwest Asia, Near East, Middle East.
asiamania *n.* orientalism.
asiamanica *adj.* & *n.* orientalist.
asian *adj.* & *n.* Asian, Asiatic.
asida *adj.* acid, acidic, sour, tart, acerbic. • *n.* acid. **asida acrilica** acrylic acid. **asida desosiribonucleal** deoxyribonucleic acid, DNA. **asida-dulse** *adj.* sweet-and-sour. **asida fosforica** phosphoric acid. **asida latica** lactic acid. **asida nitrica** nitric acid. **asida nucleal** nucleic acid. **asida ribonucleal** ribonucleic acid,

RNA. **asida sulfurica** sulphuric (US sulfuric) acid. See *adn*, *arn*.
asidental *adj.* accidental.
asidente *n.* accident (*mishap*). See *acaso*.
asidi *vi.* sour, turn sour. • *vt.* acidify, make sour. • *n.* acidification.
asidia *n.* acidity, sourness, tartness.
asidofilia *n.* acidophilia.
asidofilica *adj.* acidophilic. • *n.* acidophile.
asidua *adj.* assiduous, diligent, hardworking, industrious. • *n.* wonk.
asiduia *n.* assiduousness, diligence, hard work.
asilido *n.* robber fly (*Asilidae*).
asimina *n.* pawpaw (*tree, fruit: Asimina*).
asinia *vt.* assign, allocate, allot, appoint (*tasks, resources*), deploy; earmark; ascribe; e.g. *asinia roles a la juores*. • *n.* assignment, allocation, allotment, appointment, deployment. **asinia roles** assign roles, cast.
asiniada *adj.* assigned. **loca asiniada** allotted place, allotment; berth.
asino *n.* donkey, ass, jackass (*Asinus*).
asinor *n.* donkey driver, donkey rider.
asinto *n.* wormwood, absinthe (*plant, drink*).
asintota *n.* asymptote (*mathematics*).
asintotal *adj.* asymptotic.
asion *n.* stock, share.
asioneria *n.* stock market, stock exchange.
asionor *n.* stockholder, shareholder.
Asiria *n.* Assyria (*ancient region*).
asirian *adj.* & *n.* Assyrian.
asma *n.* asthma.
asmica *adj.* & *n.* asthmatic.
asoluta *adj.* absolute, utter. • *adv.* absolutely, utterly.
asolutisme *n.* absolutism.
asolutiste *n.* absolutist.
ason *n.* axon (*anatomy*).
asona *vi.* assonate. • *n.* assonance.
asonante *adj.* assonant.
asoran *adj.* Azorean.
asorbe *vt.* absorb, assimilate, ingest, soak up, incorporate, entrain. • *n.* absorption, assimilation, incorporation, uptake.
asorbente *adj.* absorbent.
Asores *n.pl.* Azores.
asosia *vi.* associate, hobnob; be involved; map (*to*). • *vt.* associate, partner; associate (*mentally*). • *n.* association, partnership, consortium, society; association (*mental*); mapping. **asosia carital** charitable organization, registered charity. **asosia de comersia** chamber of commerce. **asosia secreta** secret society.
asosior *n.* associate, partner, colleague.
asparago *n.* asparagus (*plant, vegetable: Asparagus officinalis*).
asparajina *n.* asparagine (*amino acid*).
aspartame *n.* aspartame (*sweetener*).
aspartato *n.* aspartate (*amino acid*).
asperula *n.* asperula (*plant: Asperula*).
aspeta *vi.* look (*have a certain appearance*), appear; e.g. *el aspeta como un capra*; *tua capeles aspeta bela*. • *n.* aspect, appearance, guise, look. **aspeta continuante** continuous aspect. **aspeta de fas** facial appearance, physiognomy. **aspeta nonperfeta** imperfective aspect. **aspeta perfeta** perfective aspect.
aspica *n.* aspic.
aspira *vt.* aspire to, dream of. • *n.* aspiration, dream, ambition.
aspirante *adj.* aspiring, ambitious.
aspirina *n.* aspirin.
aspiror *n.* candidate, applicant, nominee, postulant.
asta *prep.* • as far as, up to, down to, until (*reaching a point but going no further*); e.g. *me va acompania tu asta la porte*; *moiada asta sua pel*; *la preso ia cade asta sento euros*; *studia pajes 25 asta 42*. • until, till, up to (*in time*); e.g. *el ia dormi asta mediadia*.—*Asta* by itself is a preposition. If *until* introduces a subordinate clause, i.e. if it means *until the time when*, it is translated as *asta cuando*. **asta doman** see you tomorrow. **asta plu tarda** see you later. **asta reuni** bye, goodbye, see you, ta-ta. **asta revide** bye, goodbye, see you. See *cuando*.
astatica *adj.* astatic.
astato *n.* astatine (*element*).
asteca *adj.* & *n.* Aztec.
asteni *vi.* abstain, refrain, desist, eschew, forbear, deny oneself, forgo, recuse. • *n.* abstinence, abstention, forbearance, abnegation, self-denial. **asteni de seso** celibacy. **asteni de vota** abstention from voting.
astenia *n.* asthenia (*medical*). • *n.suff.* -asthenia.
astenica *adj.* asthenic.
asteninte *adj.* abstinent, abstemious, ascetic; chaste, celibate; teetotal.
astenisme *n.* asceticism.
astenor *n.* abstainer, ascetic. **astenor de alcol** teetotaller (US teetotaler).
aster *n.* aster (*plant*).
asterida *n.* asterid (*plant*).
asteroide *n.* asteroid.
astigmata *adj.* astigmatic.
astigmatia *n.* astigmatism.
astragalo *n.* astragalus, milkvetch (*plant: Astragalus*).
astral *adj.* astral.
astrata *adj.* abstract. • *n.* abstraction (*something abstract*).
astrati *vi.* become abstract. • *vt.* abstract, abstract out.
astratia *n.* abstractness, abstraction (*quality*).

astratisme *n.* abstractionism.
astrinje *vt.* cause to contract, be astringent (*anatomy*).
astrinjente *adj.* astringent. • *n.* astringent, toner.
astro- *pref.* astro-.
astrobiolojia *n.* astrobiology.
astrobiolojial *adj.* astrobiological.
astrobiolojiste *n.* astrobiologist.
astrofisica *n.* astrophysics.
astrofisiciste *n.* astrophysicist.
astrolabio *n.* astrolabe (*device*).
astrolojia *n.* astrology.
astrolojial *adj.* astrological.
astrolojiste *n.* astrologer, astrologist.
astronauta *n.* astronaut, cosmonaut, spaceman, spacewoman.
astronomia *n.* astronomy.
astronomial *adj.* astronomical.
astronomiste *n.* astronomer.
astruzo *n.* ostrich (*Struthio camelus*).
asturian *adj.* & *n.* Asturian.
Asturias *n.pl.* Asturias (*Spanish region*).
astuta *adj.* astute, clever, smart, cunning, savvy, shrewd, witty, incisive, punchy. **astuta de rede** internet-savvy. **astuta de ueb** web-savvy. **es plu astuta ca** outwit, outsmart, outthink, outfox. **tecnical astuta** tech-savvy.
astutia *n.* astuteness, cleverness, wittiness, wit, esprit, cunning, savvy, shrewdness, acumen. **astutia comersial** business acumen.
asurda *adj.* absurd, nonsensical, ludicrous, preposterous, ridiculous, risible, far-fetched. • *n.* absurdity (*something absurd*), nonsense, drivel, flimflam, hogwash, poppycock. • *interj.* absurd, nonsense, rubbish.
asurdia *n.* absurdity (*quality*), ludicrousness, preposterousness, ridiculousness.
asusta *vt.* frighten, scare, terrify, horrify. • *n.* fright, scare.
asustada *adj.* frightened.
asustante *adj.* frightening, terrifying, terrible, horrible, horrid, horrific, horrendous, fearsome, awful, dreadful, frightful, grotesque, atrocious, creepy, scary, spooky. • *adv.* terribly, horribly, awfully.
asustavia *n.* scarecrow.
asustor *n.* bogeyman, boogeyman.
ata *vi.* act. • *n.* action, act, deed (*thing done, legal document, section of drama*); (*an*) activity. **ata esajerada** overact, ham. **atas de gera** acts of warfare, hostilities. **bon ata** good deed, act of kindness.
ataca *vt.* attack, assault, charge, storm, besiege, raid, aggress, assail, tackle, belabour (US belabor). • *n.* attack, assault, aggression, foray, onslaught, offence (US offense), offensive, raid; paroxysm, seizure, fit, bout. **ataca de aira** air raid. **ataca de cor** heart attack, coronary. **ataca de rie** fit of laughter. **ataca par suiside** suicide attack. **ataca serebral** stroke, transient ischemic attack. **ataca sortinte** sally, sortie.
atacable *adj.* vulnerable, assailable, open to attack.
atacada *adj.* attacked, besieged, under attack.
Atacama, Deserto *n.* Atacama Desert.
atacante *adj.* attacking, aggressive, belligerent.
atacor *n.* attacker, aggressor, assailant, besieger; forward, striker.
atacosa *adj.* aggressive.
atalanta *n.* red admiral (*butterfly*: *Vanessa atalanta*).
atavisme *n.* atavism.
ataviste *adj.* atavistic.
ataxia *n.* ataxia (*medical*).
ataxica *adj.* ataxic.
ateisme [ate'isme] *n.* atheism.
ateiste [ate'iste] *adj.* atheistic, godless. • *n.* atheist.
atenable *adj.* reachable, attainable, achievable.
atende *vt.* pay attention to, attend to, heed, take into account; keep an eye on, mind, look after, take care of (*temporarily*); attend, serve (*master*). • *interj.* look out, watch out, be careful, fore. • *n.* attention, heedfulness. **atrae atende** draw attention. **atraente atende** attention-getting, conspicuous, obtrusive. **nontraente atende** inconspicuous, unobtrusive. **sin atende** careless. **sin atrae atende** inconspicuously, unobtrusively, without drawing attention. See *cura*.
atendente *adj.* attentive, alert, attendant, heedful; careful, rigorous, clear-headed, wakeful.
atendor *n.* attendant, caretaker, sitter; squire. **atendor de bebe** babysitter. **atendores** attendants, entourage, retinue.
atendosa *adj.* fastidious, meticulous.
ateni *vt.* reach, attain, achieve, accomplish, score; catch up with. • *n.* attainment, achievement, accomplishment, feat. **ateni fasil** easy achievement, cakewalk, piece of cake. **ateni min ca espetada** underachieve. **ateni plu ca espetada** overachieve.
atenta *vt.* attempt, try, endeavour (US endeavor), essay. • *n.* attempt, try. **atenta colpa** try to hit, take a swing at. **atenta criminal** criminal attempt. **atenta e era** trial and error. See *proba*.

atera *vi.* land, make landfall, arrive at port. • *vt.* land. • *n.* landing, landfall.
aterador *n.* lander (*space travel*).
atereria *n.* runway, landing strip.
ateroma *n.* atheroma (*medical*).
aterosclerose *n.* atherosclerosis.
atesta *vt.* attest, testify, give as evidence; vouch, acknowledge. • *n.* testimony, evidence, testament, testimonial. **atesta falsa** *v.* commit perjury, perjure. • *n.* perjury. **atesta final** will, last will and testament. **Atesta Nova** New Testament. **Atesta Vea** Old Testament. **atesta vival** living will. **sin atesta** intestate.
atestante *adj.* attesting, evidential, evidentiary.
atestor *n.* testator; witness, eyewitness.
Atica *n.* Attica (*Greek region*). **atica** *adj.* & *n.* Attic (*person, language*).
Atina *n.* Athens.
ativa *adj.* active, busy. • *n.* asset; active (*verb*).
ativi *vi.* activate. • *vt.* activate, trigger, precipitate, deploy. • *n.* activation, deployment.
ativia *n.* activity, activeness, bustle, dealings. **ativia volcanal** volcanic activity, volcanism.
ativisme *n.* activism.
ativiste *n.* activist, militant.
atlantica *adj.* Atlantic. **Mar Atlantica** Atlantic Ocean.
Atlantida *n.* Atlantis.
Atlas *n.* Atlas. **Montes Atlas** Atlas Mountains.
atleta *n.* athlete.
atletal *adj.* athletic.
atletisme *n.* athletic activity, sports, athletics. **atletisme lejera** track-and-field athletics. **atletisme pesosa** weightlifting and wrestling.
atmosfera *n.* atmosphere.
atmosferal *adj.* atmospheric.
-ato *n.suff.* -ate (*chemistry*).
atol *n.* atoll.
atom *n.* atom.
atomal *adj.* atomic.
atomi *vi.* & *vt.* atomize.
atonia *n.* atony (*medical*).
atonica *adj.* atonic.
ator *n.* actor, performer, player, thespian. **ator esajerada** ham. **ator fema** female actor, actress. **ator mas** male actor. **atores** actors, cast.
atrae *vt.* attract, allure, entice. • *n.* attraction, allure, enticement. **atrae minor** minor attraction, sideshow. **atrae per turistes** tourist attraction, sight.
atraente *adj.* attracting.
atraosa *adj.* attractive, pretty, cute, winsome. • *n.* attractive person, bombshell.
-atresia *n.suff.* -atresia (*medical*).
atribui *vt.* attribute, credit (*with*); e.g. *atribui un cualia a algun*; *atribui esta obra a acel autor*. • *n.* attribution.
atribuida *adj.* attributed, credited. • *n.* attribute, quality.
atricorno *n.* scrub-bird (*Atrichornis*).
atrio *n.* atrium, hall, lobby, foyer, vestibule. **atrio de presentores** green room.
atrofia *vi.* atrophy, wither. • *n.* atrophy, atrophying, withering.
atrofica *adj.* atrophic.
atropina *n.* atropine (*substance*).
atuarial *adj.* actuarial.
atuario *n.* actuary.
aturdi *vt.* stun, daze, bewilder, bedazzle, befuddle, stupefy, knock out. • *n.* knockout; bewilderment.
aturdida *adj.* stunned, dazed, stupefied, dopey.
aturdinte *adj.* stunning, bewildering, stupefying; breathtaking.
au *interj.* ow, ouch.
Auad *n.* Awadh, Audh, Oudh (*Indian region*).
auadi *adj.* & *n.* Awadhi.
audio *adj.* & *n.* audio.
audiolojia *n.* audiology.
audiolojiste *n.* audiologist.
audiomanica *n.* audiophile.
audiometre *n.* audiometer.
audiovideo *adj.* audiovisual.
augur *n.* augur.
auguria *n.* augury, auspices.
aulacode *n.* cane rat (*Thryonomys*).
aulo *n.* aulos (*musical instrument*).
aumenta *vi.* augment, increase, increment, supplement, boost, surge, redouble; appreciate (*in value*); tighten (*rules*). • *n.* augmentation, increase, surge, supplement, boost, upsurge, increment. **aumenta con** increase by (*an addition*). **aumenta de salario** wage rise, wage raise, pay rise, pay raise.
aumental *adj.* supplementary, supplemental, incremental.
aura *n.* aura.
aurora *n.* aurora. **aurora norde** Aurora Borealis, northern lights. **aurora sude** Aurora Australis, southern lights.
Australasia *n.* Australasia.
australasian *adj.* Australasian.
Australia *n.* Australia.
australian *adj.* & *n.* Australian. **Baia Australian Grande** Great Australian Bight. **Desertos Australian** Australian Deserts.

australopiteco *n.* australopithecus (*primate: Australopithecus*).
austronesian *adj.* Austronesian.
autentica *adj.* authentic, genuine.
autentici *vi.* & *vt.* authenticate, certify, authenticate, vet; log in (*software*). • *n.* authentication, verification, certification; certificate.
autenticia *n.* authenticity, genuineness.
autenticida *adj.* authenticated; logged in (*software*).
autisme *n.* autism.
autiste *adj.* autistic.
auto[1] *n.* car, automobile, auto. **auto de fuji** getaway car. **auto de serie** stock car. **auto de xoca** bumper car, dodgem. **auto esplorante** scout car. See *automobil.*
auto-[2] *pref.* auto-, self- (*reflexive or automatic action*); e.g. *autopilote*; *autodestrui.*
autoaderente *adj.* self-adhesive, self-sticking.
autoaida *n.* self-help.
autoarpa *n.* autoharp.
autobiografia *n.* autobiography, memoirs.
autobiografial *adj.* autobiographical, autobiographic.
autoboni *n.* self-improvement.
autocaravan *n.* motor home, recreational vehicle, RV, campervan.
autoclave *n.* autoclave.
autocompatia *n.* self-pity.
autoconsensa *adj.* self-conscious.
autocontradise *vt.* contradict oneself.
autocontradisente *adj.* self-contradictory.
autocopia *vt.* self-replicate, autoreplicate. • *n.* self-replication.
autocopiante *adj.* self-replicating, autoreplicating.
autocoreti *vi.* self-correct.
autocoretinte *adj.* self-correcting.
autocrata *adj.* autocratic, dictatorial, sovereign, totalitarian. • *n.* autocrat, dictator.
autocratia *n.* autocracy, autarchy, dictatorship, sovereignty, totalitarianism.
autocreada *adj.* self-made.
autodefende *n.* self-defence (US self-defense).
autodepinta *n.* self-portrait.
autodestrui *vt.* self-destruct.
autodestruinte *adj.* self-destructive.
autodetermina *vt.* self-determine, self-direct. • *n.* self-determination.
autodisiplina *n.* self-discipline.
autoduta *n.* self-doubt.
autoempleada *adj.* self-employed.
autoerotica *adj.* autoerotic.
autoesplicante *adj.* self-explanatory.
autoesposa *n.* autoexposure.
autoevidente *adj.* self-evident.
autofida *n.* self-confidence, morale, assertiveness, aplomb.
autofidante *adj.* self-confident, assertive, self-assured; smug.
autoflue *vi.* & *vt.* word-wrap. • *n.* word wrap.
autoidentia *n.* self-identity.
autoimune [awtoiˈmune] *adj.* autoimmune.
autoimunia *n.* autoimmunity.
autoinstruida [awtoinstruˈida] *adj.* self-taught, autodidact.
autojiro *n.* autogyro, autogiro, gyroplane, gyrocopter.
automanica *n.* car enthusiast, automobilist.
automata *adj.* automated, automatic. • *n.* automat, automaton, automata. **automata de banco** ATM, cash machine, cashpoint. **automata de discos** jukebox, nickelodeon.
automati *vt.* automate. • *n.* automation.
automobil *n.* automobile, car.
automobilal *adj.* automotive.
automobili *vt.* transport by car.
automorfe *adj.* automorphic.
automotiva *vi.* motivate oneself. • *n.* self-motivation.
automotivada *adj.* self-motivated, showing initiative.
autonal *adj.* autumnal.
autono *n.* autumn, fall.
autonom *adj.* autonomous, independent, self-governing, sovereign.
autonomi *vi.* gain independence, become autonomous.
autonomia *n.* autonomy, independence, sovereignty, self-rule.
autonomida *adj.* self-proclaimed, self-styled.
autoodia *n.* self-hatred, self-loathing.
autopilote *n.* autopilot.
autopoleni *vi.* self-pollinate. • *n.* self-pollination, autogamy.
autopropulsa *vt.* self-propel. • *n.* self-propulsion.
autopsia *n.* autopsy, postmortem.
autor *n.* author, writer, creator. **autor de anunsias** copywriter. **autor teatral** playwright.
autoreali *vi.* self-realize, self-actualize. • *n.* self-realization, self-actualization.
autoregula *vi.* self-regulate.
autoremedia *vt.* self-limit.
autoremediada *adj.* self-limited (*disease*).
autoreproxa *n.* self-reproach.
autorespeta *n.* self-respect, self-esteem.
autorespirador *n.* scuba, aqualung.
autorestrinje *n.* self-restraint, self-control.
autorestrinjeda *adj.* self-restrained, self-controlled.

autori *vt.* authorize, empower. • *n.* authorization.
autoria[1] *n.* authority, mandate, jurisdiction.
autoria[2] *n.* authorship.
autorida *adj.* authorized, certified, qualified.
autoriosa *adj.* authoritative, canonical; plenipotentiary. • *n.* authority; leader.
autoritar *adj.* authoritarian, high-handed, bossy, officious. • *n.* authoritarian.
autoritarisme *n.* authoritarianism.
autoritariste *adj.* & *n.* authoritarian.
autosacrifia *n.* self-sacrifice.
autosasiada *adj.* self-satisfied, smug, complacent.
autoservi *n.* self-service.
autostopa *vi.* hitchhike. • *n.* hitchhiking.
autostopor *n.* hitchhiker.
autosufisinte *adj.* self-sufficient.
autotrof *adj.* autotrophic. • *n.* autotroph.
autotrofia *n.* autotrophia.
autovia [awto'via] *n.* motorway, highway, carriageway, superhighway, turnpike. **autovia verde** parkway.
ava *n.* grandmother.
avalanxa *vi.* & *n.* avalanche.
avansa *vi.* advance, go forward, surge. • *vt.* advance; forward (*document*). • *interj.* advance, forward, forwards, onward, onwards, on we go. • *n.* advance, incursion, surge, inroad. **avansa grande** breakthrough. **avansa min** lag behind, dawdle, straggle. **avansa parlante a** accost. **avansa rapida** fast-forward. **avansa subita** breakaway (*sport*). **fa avansas a** make advances to, make a pass at, come on to, hit on.
avansada *adj.* advanced; late. • *n.* vanguard, spearhead (*attack*).
avar *adj.* avaricious, greedy, acquisitive, grasping, rapacious; miserly, stingy, mean, grubby, close-fisted, tight-fisted. • *n.* miser, scrooge.
avaria *n.* greed, meanness, miserliness, avarice.
avatar *n.* avatar.
ave *vt.* have, own.—*Ave* does not mean *have* as in *you have done well* (*tu ia fa bon*) or *having eaten, she slept* (*pos come, el ia dormi*). **ave un metre de longia** be a metre (US meter) long. **no ave** do not have, lack, be without. **on ave** there is, there are, there exists. **on ave asi alga ideas** here are some ideas. **on ave un problem** there is a problem. **on no ave** there is not, there are not.
avena *n.* oat, oats (*Avena*).
aveneria *n.* venue.
aveni *vi.* happen, occur, take place, transpire. • *vt.* cause to happen, stage, hold (*event*). • *n.* happening, occurrence, event, incident; (*special*) occasion; outbreak. **avenis corente** current events. **avenis de la ora** current events, latest news. **avenis nova** news, current events.
avenosa *adj.* eventful.
aventura *vi.* adventure. • *n.* adventure, escapade.
aventurante *adj.* adventurous (*person*).
aventuror *n.* adventurer.
aventurosa *adj.* adventurous (*activity*).
averbal *adj.* adverbial.
averbin *adj.* adverbial.
averbo *n.* adverb. **averbo de demanda** interrogative adverb. **averbo-sujunta** *n.* subordinating adverb, relative adverb.
avertador *n.* alarm, buzzer, siren.
averti *vt.* warn (*of danger*), caution. • *n.* warning, caution.
avesta *n.* avesta (*scripture*).
avi *n.* grandparent.
avia *n.* bird. **avia cantante** warbler, songbird. **avia de acua** waterbird, waterfowl. **avia de cultiveria** fowl, farm bird. **avia de mar** seabird. **avia de paradiso** bird of paradise (*Paradisaeidae*). **avia de tona** thunderbird. **avia tentante** decoy. **avia xasada** gamebird. **avia xasante** bird of prey. **avias de cultiveria** poultry, farm birds.
avial *adj.* avian.
avicultur *n.* aviculture.
avieria *n.* aviary.
avieta *n.* chick, fledgling, birdie.
avion *n.* aeroplane (US airplane), aircraft. **avion comersial** commercial aircraft, airliner. **avion de mar** seaplane, hydroplane. **avion liscante** glider. **avion sin pilote** drone, unmanned aerial vehicle. **avion xasante** fighter aircraft. **sur avion** on board.
avioneria *n.* aircraft hangar.
avioneta *n.* (*small*) drone.
avioni *vt.* airfreight. • *n.* aviation; airfreight.
avionica *n.* avionics.
avionor *n.* aviator.
avisa *vt.* advise, notify, give notice, alert. • *n.* advice, warning, notice, notification, alert, bulletin, prompt; caveat, proviso. **avisa de via** road sign, street sign. **avisa vidable** visual alert.
aviseta *vt.* & *n.* hint, tip.
avo *n.* grandfather.
avocado *n.* avocado (*tree, fruit: Persea americana*).
avocato *n.* lawyer, barrister, solicitor, attorney, counsel. **avocato acusante** prosecuting attorney, prosecutor. **avocato de corte** barrister. **avocato defendente** defence (US defense) attorney, defence (US

defense) lawyer. **avocato frodante** shyster. **avocato jeneral** attorney general. **avocato personal** solicitor.
avoseta *n.* avocet (*bird: Recurvirostra*)
ax *n.* ash, æsc (*Latin letter* Æ, æ).
axa *n.* ax (US axe). **axa de gera** battleax (US battleaxe), poleax (US poleaxe).
axcenazi *adj.* Ashkenazi (*Judaism*). • *n.* Ashkenazi Jew.
axeta *n.* hatchet, tomahawk. **axeta de carnor** cleaver, butcher's knife.
axi[1] [aˈʃi] *interj.* atishoo.
axi[2] *vt.* chop, hack, hew. **axi a picos** mince.
axia *n.* adze (*tool*).
axida *adj.* chopped. **axida a picos** minced, finely chopped.
axila *n.* armpit, underarm.
axilal *adj.* axillary, underarm.
axiom *n.* axiom, convention, postulate.
axiomal *adj.* axiomatic.
axiomi *vt.* axiomatize. • *n.* axiomation.
axisa *n.* abscissa (*coordinate*).
Axoca *n.* Ashoka (*Indian emperor*).
axocan *adj.* Ashokan.
axolote *n.* axolotl (*amphibian: Ambystoma mexicanum*).
axon *n.* broadaxe (US broadax).
axor *n.* axeman (US axman).
axram *n.* ashram (*hermitage*).
axu [aˈʃu] *interj.* achoo.
Axum *n.* Aksum (*Ethiopian city*).
azalea *n.* azalea (*plant: Rhododendron, Pentanthera, Tsutsuji*).
Azerbaidjan *n.* Azerbaijan.
azerbaidjani *adj.* & *n.* Azerbaijani.
azimuta *n.* azimuth (*astronomy*).
azor *n.* goshawk, hawk (larger members of *Accipitrinae*).
azospermia *n.* azoospermia (*medical*).
azotemia *n.* azotemia (*medical*).
Azov, Mar *n.* Sea of Azov.
azul *adj.* light blue, sky blue, baby blue, powder blue, azure. • *n.* azure, light blue, baby blue, powder blue. **azul de sielo** sky blue. **azul verdin** greenish blue, greeny blue. **verdin azul** greenish-blue, greeny-blue.
azuli *vi.* & *vt.* turn light blue.

B

B [be], **be** *letter* B, b.
ba *interj.* bah, nonsense, rubbish, who cares?
babau *n.* bogeyman, boogeyman, bogey, bogles, bugaboo, bugbear.
babca *n.* babka (*cake*).
babela *vt.* babble, gab, gabble, mutter, gibber, witter, prattle, prate, waffle, bumble, talk nonsense. • *n.* gibberish, gobbledygook, gobbledegook, bafflegab, jargon, patter, balderdash, piffle, baloney, drivel, bunkum, twaddle. **babela bela** blah blah blah.
babelosa *adj.* gibberish, jargon-filled.
Babilonia *n.* Babylonia.
babilonian *adj.* babylonian.
babirusa *n.* babirusa, deer pig, pig deer (*Babyrousa*).
babuin *n.* baboon (*Papio*, *Mandrillus*).
baca *n.* berry. **baca de peper** peppercorn.
bacara *n.* baccarat (*card game*).
bacelita *n.* bakelite.
bacin *adj.* berrylike.
baclava *n.* baklava (*dessert*).
Bactria *n.* Bactria (*ancient region*).
badaui *adj.* & *n.* Bedouin.
badminton *n.* badminton.
badmintonor *n.* badminton player.
Baffin *n.* Baffin. **Baia Baffin** Baffin Bay. **Isola Baffin** Baffin Island.
bagaje *n.* baggage, luggage.
bagel *n.* bagel.
bagete *n.* baguette (*bread*). **bagete plenida** Italian sandwich, submarine sandwich, sub, hoagie, hoagy, grinder, hero.
bahai [ba'hai] *adj.* & *n.* Baha'i.
bahaisme [baha'isme] *n.* Baha'i, Baha'ism (*religion*).
bahaman *adj.* & *n.* Bahamian.
Bahamas *n.pl.* Bahamas.
baia *n.* bay, bight.
Baical, Lago *n.* Lake Baikal, Lake Baykal.
baieres *adj.* & *n.* Bavarian.
Baiern *n.* Bavaria.
baieta[1] *n.* baize (*fabric*).
baieta[2] *n.* cove, inlet.
baioneta *n.* bayonet.
bait *n.* byte.
bal *n.* ball. **bal bonodorosa** pomander. **bal de bolo** bowl, bowling ball. **bal de canon** cannonball. **bal de carne** meatball. **bal de foco** fireball. **bal de futbal** football. **bal de naftalina** mothball. **bal de neva** snowball. **bal de pasta** dumpling, gnocco. **bal de tenis** tennis ball. **bal oto** eightball. **bales de pasta** gnocchi.
bala *vt.* baa, bleat. See *maa*.
Balabak, Streta *n.* Balabac Strait.
balaclava *n.* balaclava.
balada *n.* ballad.
baladador *n.* personal stereo, walkman. **baladador dijital** MP3 player, digital audio player.
balador *n.* balladeer.
balalaica *n.* balalaika (*musical instrument*).
balansa *n.* seesaw; scales. **Balansa** *n.* Libra (*constellation*). **balansa fratal** vernier (*fractional scale*).
balansador *n.* outrigger.
balansi *vt.* seesaw, balance, swing (*up and down*).
balasti *vt.* ballast.
balasto *n.* ballast.
balbuta *vt.* & *n.* stutter, stammer; splutter, sputter.
balcan *adj.* Balkan. **Balcanes** Balkans (*mountains*, *region*).
balcon *n.* balcony. **balcon media** mezzanine.
baldacin *n.* canopy, baldaquin, tabernacle, marquee, awning.
balde *n.* bucket, pail.
baldon *n.* bin, dustbin, rubbish bin, litter bin, trash can, garbage can, ashcan. **baldon de resicli** recycling bin, recycle bin.
baldoni *vt.* bin, throw away, chuck out, toss, toss out.
balear *adj.* Balearic. **Isolas Balear** Balearic Islands. **Mar Balear** Balearic Sea.
balena *n.* whale (*Cetacea*). **Balena** *n.* Cetus (*constellation*).
balenor *n.* whaler.
balenotera *n.* rorqual (*whale*: *Balaenopteridae*).
balesta *n.* crossbow.
baleston *n.* arbalest (*weapon*).
baleta *n.* bullet.
baletiste *n.* ballet dancer, ballerina.
baleto *n.* ballet.
Balgaria *n.* Bulgaria.
balgarsce *adj.* & *n.* Bulgarian (*person*, *language*).
Bali *n.* Bali.
balia *vi.* yawn; gape. • *n.* yawn.
baliante *adj.* yawning, gaping, agape, wide open.
balio *n.* bailiff.
balistica *n.* ballistics.
balistical *adj.* ballistic.
balmol *n.* softball (*sport*).
balo *n.* dance (*event*). **balo de debuantes** debutantes' ball, cotillion. **balo formal** ball. **balo vivosa** lively dance (*event*), hop,

bop, hoedown, hootenanny, shindig, corroboree.

balon *n.* balloon; (*speech*) bubble. **balon de aira calda** hot-air balloon. **balon de avisa** warning balloon (*software*).

balonor *n.* balloonist.

balotxi *adj.* Baloch, Baluch, Balochi.

Balotxistan *n.* Balochistan, Baluchistan.

balsa *n.* raft.

balsam *n.* balm, balsam, liniment. **balsam de labio** lip balm, lip salve, chapstick.

balsamal *adj.* balsamic.

balsami *vt.* embalm.

balsi *vt.* raft, send by raft.

baltica *adj.* Baltic. **Baltica** *n.* Baltic (*region*). **Mar Baltica** Baltic Sea.

balustre *n.* baluster, railing.

bambola *vi.* wobble, totter, teeter, be unsteady; stagger, reel, bumble, lurch, toddle, walk unsteadily; flounder, flail.

bambolante *adj.* tottering, staggering; tipsy.

bambu [bam'bu] *n.* bamboo (*plant, stem: Bambusa, Arundinaria, Dendrocalamus*).

banana *n.* banana (*plant, fruit: Musa*).

banca *n.* bench (*seat*), pew.

bancarota *adj.* bankrupt, insolvent.

bancaroti *vi.* go bankrupt, go bust. • *vt.* bankrupt, make bankrupt.

bancarotia *n.* bankruptcy.

banceta *vi.* & *n.* banquet, feast.

banco *n.* bank (*money*). **banco de arena** sandbank. **banco de datos** database, data bank. **banco de oios** eye bank.

bancor *n.* banker.

bancsia *n.* banksia (*plant: Banksia*).

banda *n.* band, tape, strip, strap, streamer; track (*mix*); lane (*traffic*); swathe. **banda audio** audio tape. **banda de calsa** garter (*band around leg*). **banda de capeles** hairband, bandeau. **banda de crise** emergency lane, hard shoulder. **banda de cuoro** leather band, thong. **banda de frecuentia** frequency band, waveband. **banda de lenio** strip of wood, lath. **banda de oios** blindfold. **banda de rota** tread (*tyre*). **banda de sona** soundtrack. **banda de suo** sweatband. **banda de taie** waistband. **banda de testa** headband. **banda de xapo** hatband. **banda elastica** elastic band, rubber band. **banda emostasal** tourniquet. **banda erugin** caterpillar track, continuous track, tank tread. **banda fortinte** strengthening strip, wale. **banda larga** broadband. **banda medical** bandage. **banda medical aderente** band-aid, sticking plaster. **banda ru** rumble strip (*on road*). **banda solosa** sunbelt (*sunny region*). **banda transportante** conveyor belt. **banda video** video tape.

Banda, Mar *n.* Banda Sea.

bandana *n.* bandana, kerchief.

bande *n.* band, ensemble, combo (*people*). **bande marxante** marching band.

bandera *n.* flag, banner, banderole.

bandereta *n.* pennant. **banderetas** bunting.

banderor *n.* flagman.

bandeta *n.* stripe (*pattern*), streak.

bandetosa *adj.* stripy, striped, tabby.

bandi *vt.* tape, tape up; strap. **bandi la oios** blindfold.

bandicute *n.* bandicoot (*Peramelidae*).

bandin *adj.* straplike, strap-shaped.

banditia *n.* banditage, brigandage.

bandito *n.* bandit, outlaw, highwayman, brigand.

bandolera *n.* bandolier (*belt*).

bandura *n.* bandura (*musical instrument*).

bangalo *n.* bungalow, ranch house.

bangla *adj.* Bengali, Bangla. • *n.* Bengali, Bangla (*person, language*).

Bangladex *n.* Bangladesh.

bani *vt.* bathe. • *n.* bath, bathing. **bani de sangue** bloodbath. **bani de spuma** foam bath, bubble bath (*activity*). **bani su sol** sunbathe.

banieria *n.* spa, bath, bath house (*communal*). **banieria mineral** mineral bath, spa. **banieria termal** thermal bath, spa.

banio *n.* bathtub, bath, tub. **banio de vortis** whirlpool bath, hot tub, jacuzzi, spa.

baniomaria *n.* double boiler, water bath, bain-marie.

banior *n.* bather.

banjiste *n.* banjo player.

banjo *n.* banjo.

banlam *adj.* & *n.* Min Nan, Ban-Lam (*person, language*).

bantu *adj.* & *n.* Bantu (*person, language*).

banxi *n.* banshee.

baobab *n.* baobab (*Adansonia*).

bar *n.* bar, pub, bar room, saloon.

bara *n.* bar, rod, rail; slash (*punctuation*). **bara de confeto** candy bar, confectionery bar. **bara de dentes** rack (*for pinion*). **bara de molas** splinter bar. **bara de musli** muesli bar, granola bar, flapjack. **bara de pesas** barbell. **bara de rola** scrollbar. **bara de tira** tow bar, tow hitch. **bara de titulo** title bar (*software*). **bara de utiles** toolbar (*software*). **bara de xocolada** chocolate bar. **bara inclinada** slash, forward slash, oblique stroke, solidus. **bara natural** health bar (*food*). **bara reta** straightedge (*tool*). **bara reversada** backslash. **bara traversante** crossbar. **bara vertical** vertical slash, bar, pipe symbol. **baras de**

arjento silver bullion. **baras de oro** gold bullion.
baracuda *n.* barracuda (*Phyraena barracuda*).
Barain *n.* Bahrain.
baraini *adj.* & *n.* Bahraini.
Barat *n.* India. See *India*.
barata *adj.* cheap, inexpensive. • *n.* bargain (*cheap item*).
baratamanica *n.* cheapskate, pinchpenny, tightwad.
barati *adj.* & *n.* Indian (*person, language*). See *indian*.
baratia *n.* cheapness.
barba *n.* beard. **barba de balena** baleen. **barba de jenas** whiskers, sideburns, sideboards.
barbadian *adj.* & *n.* Barbadian, Bajan (*person, language*).
Barbados *n.* Barbados.
barbar *adj.* barbarian, barbaric, barbarous. • *n.* barbarian.
barbaria *n.* barbarism.
barbecu [barbeˈku] *n.* barbecue, barbeque, BBQ, barbie.
barbeta *n.* goatee.
barbi *vt.* give a beard to.
barbida *adj.* bearded.
barbiturica *adj.* barbituric. • *n.* barbiturate. **asida barbiturica** barbituric acid.
barbo *n.* barbel (*Barbus*).
Barbuda *n.* Barbuda.
barbudan *adj.* & *n.* Barbudan.
barcasa *n.* barge.
barceria *n.* marina.
barceta *n.* dinghy. **barceta de palo** punt.
barco *n.* boat. **barco-bus** *n.* water bus, water taxi, sightseeing boat. **barco de canal** canalboat, narrowboat. **barco de embarca** ship's tender. **barco de faro** lightvessel, lightship. **barco de remos** rowboat, rowing boat. **barco de salva** lifeboat. **barco de vela** sailboat. **barco longa** longboat. **barco teatral** showboat. **barco tirante** tug, tugboat, towboat. **barco vicing** Viking boat, longboat, longship. **estra barco** overboard. **sur barco** on board.
barcon *n.* ship. **barcon abandonada** hulk, wreck. **barcon blindada** battleship, armoured (US armored) ship. **barcon de carga** cargo ship, freighter. **barcon de gera** warship. **barcon de soldatos** troopship. **barcon de turi** cruise ship, cruise liner. **barcon de vapor** steamship, steamboat. **barcon de vela** sailing ship. **barcon prima** flagship. **barcon privata** private ship, privateer. **barcon ruinada** shipwreck. **barcon spasial** spaceship, spacecraft, starship.
barconeria *n.* boatyard, shipyard.
barconi *vt.* ship, send by ship.
bardal *adj.* bardic, skaldic.
bardana *n.* burdock, hordock (*plant: Arctium*).
barde *n.* bard, skald.
Barents, Mar *n.* Barents Sea.
bareta *n.* bolt (*door, gun*); barrette, hairslide.
bari *vt.* bar, block off; cross out, strike through.
baril *n.* barrel, cask, butt, hogshead.
barileria *n.* cooperage, barrel factory.
barileta *n.* keg.
barilor *n.* barrelmaker, cooper.
bario *n.* barium (*element*).
barion *n.* baryon (*particle*).
barisentral *adj.* barycentric.
barisentro *n.* barycentre (US barycenter).
bariste *n.* bartender, barman, barmaid, barkeep, mixologist; barista.
baritono *adj.* & *n.* baritone.
barmitsva *n.* bar mitzvah.
baroca *adj.* baroque.
barometre *n.* barometer.
baron *n.* baron, lord.
baronesa *n.* baroness.
baroneta *n.* baronet.
baronia *n.* barony.
basa *adj.* low (*position*); lower (*part*); short (*height*); shallow (*depth*); deep (*tone*); low, mean, unkind, base. • *n.* bottom, bottom half, lower part. **a basa** down; downward, downwards. **a basa de** near the bottom of; down, towards the bottom of. **basa de bicini** bikini bottom. **basa de catran** low in tar, low-tar (*cigarette*). **plu basa** lower, deeper, shorter.
basalto *n.* basalt.
bascetbal *n.* basketball (*sport*).
bascetbalor *n.* basketball player.
base *n.* base (*headquarters, chemistry, linguistic, numbers, baseball*).
basebal *n.* baseball, hardball.
basebalor *n.* baseball player.
basi *vi.* lower. • *vt.* lower, reduce in height; debase, degrade; demote. • *interj.* down with …, no more …; e.g. *basi la regulas!* • *n.* abasement (*action*); demotion. **basi se** lower oneself, abase oneself, belittle oneself, deign (*to do*). **basi sua regarda** look down.
basia *n.* lowness; meanness; abasement (*state*).
basil *n.* basil (*Ocimum basilicum*).
basilica *n.* basilica.
basilisco *n.* basilisk (*lizard, mythology: Basiliscus*).
basilo *n.* bacillus (*bacterium*).
basin *n.* basin, bowl (*geography*). **Basin Grande** Great Basin. **basin idrografial** watershed.

basiste *n.* bassist, bass player.
basmati *n.* basmati rice.
baso *adj.* & *n.* bass (*music*).
basofilia *n.* basophilia
basofilica *adj.* basophilic. • *n.* basophil.
bason *n.* bassoon.
Bass, Streta *n.* Bass Strait.
basta *vi.* be ample, be more than enough, more than suffice.
bastante *adj.* ample, more than enough, more than sufficient. • *adv.* amply, enough, sufficiently.
bastardia *n.* bastardy, illegitimacy.
bastardo *n.* bastard.
basteta *n.* stick, twig, small branch. **basteta de dentes** toothpick. **de bastetas** wicker.
basti *vt.* cane (*punish*).
bastion *n.* bastion, bulwark.
basto *n.* stick, cane, rod; ramrod. **basto cavalin** hobbyhorse. **basto curva** crook, staff, crosier, crozier. **basto de mesura** measuring stick, measuring rod. **basto de olio** dipstick. **basto de pasea** walking stick. **basto de tambur** drumstick. **basto de zucar** candy cane. **basto eletrical** electric prod, stun baton. **basto majial** wand, magic wand.
baston *n.* bat, club, truncheon; skittle, pin (*bowling*). **baston de golf** golf club.
bastoni *vt.* bludgeon, batter, cudgel, club, beat, thrash, clobber, pummel.
batador *n.* beater, whisk, churn; thresher; clapper (*bell*). **batador eletrical** beater. **batador engranada** crank beater, egg-beater.
batalia *vt.* battle, combat, fight. • *n.* battle, fight, fighting, combat. **batalia per** campaign for.
batalion *n.* battalion.
batalior *n.* fighter, combatant; campaigner.
bate *vt.* beat, thrash, thresh, batter, pound, pummel; beat up, do over; slam (*door*); flap; whip (*into a froth*), churn.
bateovo *n.* eggbeater.
bateporte *n.* door knocker.
bateria *n.* bacterium, eubacterium (*Bacteria, Eubacteria*). **baterias** bacteria.
baterial *adj.* bacterial.
bateriolojia *n.* bacteriology.
bateriolojial *adj.* bacteriological.
bateriolojiste *n.* bacteriologist.
baterioterapia *n.* bacteriotherapy.
bateriside *n.* bactericide.
baterivor *adj.* bacterivorous. • *n.* bacterivore.
bateta *vt.* & *n.* knock, rap, tap (*at door*); beat (*heart*); flutter (*wings*). **bateta de cor** heartbeat. **bateta de ungulas** hoofbeat.
batetador *n.* knocker (*door*).
batic *n.* batik (*dyeing*).
batiscopio *n.* bathyscope, aquascope.
batisfera *n.* bathysphere.
batisme *n.* Baptist religion.
batista *n.* batiste (*fabric*).
batiste *adj.* & *n.* Baptist.
batiza *vt.* baptize, christen. • *n.* baptism, christening.
batizeria *n.* baptistry, baptistery.
batmitsva *n.* bat mitzvah.
bava *vi.*, *vt.* & *n.* dribble, trickle; drool, slobber.
bazar *n.* bazaar; jumble sale, fete.
bazuca *n.* bazooka.
bearnes *adj.* Béarnaise (*French region, sauce*).
beatifia *vt.* beatify. • *n.* beatification.
beatifiante *adj.* beatific.
Beaufort, Mar ['bofort] *n.* Beaufort Sea.
bebe *adj.* & *n.* baby, babe, infant, tot. **bebe de la buma** baby boomer. **bebes** babies, litter.
bebeta *n.* newborn, neonate.
bebia *n.* babyhood, infancy.
bebop *n.* bebop (*music*).
becasia *n.* woodcock (*bird: Scolopax*).
becerel *n.* becquerel (*unit of radioactivity*).
becin *adj.* beaklike.
beco *n.* beak, bill; snout, muzzle; mouthpiece (*music*); nib (*pen*); spout (*jug*). **beco de Bunsen** Bunsen burner.
becobarcin *n.* boat-billed heron, boatbill (*bird: Cochlearius cochlearius*).
becocrusada *n.* crossbill (*bird: Loxia*).
becoibisin [bekoibi'sin] *n.* ibisbill (*bird: Ibidorhyncha struthersii*).
becosapatin *n.* shoebill (*bird: Balaeniceps rex*).
becosisorin *n.* skimmer (*bird: Rynchopidae, Rynchops*).
becospatulin *n.* spoonbill (*bird: Platalea*).
becospesa *n.* grosbeak (*bird: Carduelinae*).
bedel *n.* beadle (*officer*).
begonia *n.* begonia (*Begonia*).
Beijing *n.* Beijing, Peking.
beje *adj.* beige.
bela *adj.* beautiful, lovely, pretty, stunning, gorgeous, elegant, handsome. • *n.* belle, beau. **estrema bela** extremely beautiful, exquisite, gorgeous, ravishing.
beladona *n.* belladonna, deadly nightshade (*Atropa belladonna*).
Belau *n.* Palau. **belau** *adj.* & *n.* Palauan.
beleria *n.* beauty salon, beauty shop, beauty parlour (US parlor).
beleta *adj.* pretty, cute, pert. • *n.* pretty thing, pretty one, cutie.
belga *adj.* Belgic. **belgas** Belgae (*ancient tribe*).
beli *vi.* become beautiful. • *vt.* beautify, make beautiful, embellish, prettify. • *n.* beautification.

belia *n.* beauty, loveliness, prettiness, pulchritude.
Beliz *n.* Belize.
belizan *adj.* & *n.* Belizian.
beljes *adj.* & *n.* Belgian.
Beljia *n.* Belgium.
beltin *n.* beltane (*pagan holiday*).
beluga *n.* beluga, white whale (*Delphinapterus leucas*).
belvedere *n.* belvedere, gazebo.
bemol *adj.* & *n.* flat (*music*).
ben *n.* item for sale; commodity. **benes** goods, ware, wares, merchandise, commodities. **benes de arjento** silverware. **benes de coce** cookware. **benes de cose** haberdashery, notions. **benes de cosina** kitchenware. **benes de fero** ironware. **benes de vitro** glassware. **benes dorada** giltware. **benes furada** stolen goods, booty, loot, swag. **benes nonlegal** illegal goods, contraband.
benedictin *adj.* & *n.* Benedictine (*monk*).
benefica *vi.* benefit, gain advantage. • *vt.* benefit, give advantage to, favour (US favor). • *n.* benefit, behalf, sake; perk.
beneficada *n.* beneficiary.
beneficante *adj.* beneficial, salutary, conducive.
beneficor *n.* benefactor.
beneria *n.* warehouse, storehouse, repository, depot.
Bengala *n.* Bengal. **Golfo Bengala** Bay of Bengal.
Benin *n.* Benin.
benines *adj.* & *n.* Beninese, Beninois.
benzen *n.* benzene. **anelo de benzen** benzene ring.
benzoica *adj.* benzoic. **asida benzoica** benzoic acid.
Beograd *n.* Belgrade.
berber *adj.* & *n.* Berber.
berberis *n.* barberry, berberis (*plant: Berberis*).
bercelio *n.* berkelium (*element*).
bereta *n.* beret; biretta.
bergamota *n.* bergamot, bergamot orange (*Citrus bergamia*).
bergamoto *n.* bergamot tree.
beril *n.* beryl (*gem*).
berilio *n.* beryllium (*element*).
Bering *n.* Bering. **Mar Bering** Bering Sea. **Streta Bering** Bering Strait.
Beringia *n.* Beringia.
Bermuda *n.* Bermuda.
bermudan *adj.* & *n.* Bermudan.
besa *vt.* kiss, smooch. • *n.* kiss.
besaculo *n.* (*colloquial*) kiss-ass, kiss-up (*sycophant*).
besaorea *n.* (*colloquial*) kiss-ass, kiss-up (*sycophant*).
beseta *vt.* peck, lightly kiss. • *n.* peck, light kiss.
bestia *n.* beast. **bestia de carga** pack animal, beast of burden, workhorse. **bestia de servi** service animal, support animal, helper animal. **bestia de tira** draught (US draft) animal. **bestia imajinal** imaginary beast. **bestias** beasts, livestock.
bestin *adj.* bestial.
bestinia *n.* bestiality.
beta[1] *n.* beet, beetroot (*plant, vegetable: Beta vulgaris*).
beta[2] *n.* beta (*Greek letter* Β, β). **a beta** in beta, being beta-tested. **varia de beta** beta version.
betel *n.* betel (*plant, stimulant: Piper betle*).
beton *n.* concrete. **beton fortida** reinforced concrete. **de beton** (*made of*) concrete.
betong *n.* bettong (*marsupial: Bettongia*).
betonica *n.* betony, bishopwort (*plant: Stachys officinalis*).
betul *n.* birch (*Bertula*).
bevable *adj.* drinkable, potable.
beveria *n.* drinking establishment, pub, tavern.
bevi *vt.* drink, imbibe, quaff.
bevida *n.* drink, beverage, libation. **bevida de alcol** alcoholic drink. **bevida ofreda** libation. **bevida sin alcol** non-alcoholic drink.
bexamel *n.* bechamel, white sauce.
bezica *n.* bezique (*card game*).
bezoar *n.* bezoar (*biology*).
bi- *pref.* bi-.
biatlon *n.* biathlon.
biatlonor *n.* biathlete.
Biblia *n.* Bible.
biblial *adj.* biblical.
biblio- *pref.* biblio-.
bibliofilia *n.* bibliophilia.
bibliofilica *n.* bibliophile.
bibliografia *n.* bibliography.
bibliografial *adj.* bibliographical.
bibliografiste *n.* bibliographer.
biblioteca *n.* library.
bibliotecor *n.* librarian.
bicarbonato *n.* bicarbonate. **bicarbonato de sodio** sodium bicarbonate.
bicini *n.* bikini.
bide *n.* bidet.
bidimensional *adj.* two-dimensional.
biela *n.* connecting rod (*machinery*).
Bielarus *n.* Belarus.
bielarusce *adj.* & *n.* Belarusian.
bies *n.* bias (*fabric*).
bifasal *adj.* biphasic.
bifocal *adj.* bifocal. • *n.* bifocals.

bigama *adj.* bigamous.
bigamia *n.* bigamy.
bigamiste *n.* bigamist.
bigel *n.* beagle (*dog*).
bigin *n.* beguine, biguine (*dance*).
bijenero *adj.* bigender. • *n.* bigender person.
bilabial *adj.* & *n.* bilabial (*consonant*).
biladal *adj.* bilateral, two-sided.
bilal *adj.* bilious, biliary.
bilaterio *n.* bilateral (*Bilateria*).
bilbi *n.* bilby, rabbit bandicoot (*Macrotis lagotis*).
bile *n.* bile, gall.
bileta *n.* ticket; coupon, voucher; bill (*paper money*), note, banknote. **bileta de deta** chit, IOU. **bileta de rasca** scratchcard. **bileta de rasca e gania** scratchcard (*instant lottery*). **bileta de un dirije** one-way ticket. **bileta de vade e reveni** round-trip ticket, return ticket.
bileteria *n.* ticket office, box office.
biletor *n.* ticket collector, conductor, guard.
bilia *n.* marble (*ball*).
biliarderia *n.* billiards hall, billiards room, poolhall, poolroom, snooker hall.
biliardo *n.* billiards, pool, snooker. **biliardo american** pool. **biliardo engles** snooker. **biliardo franses** carom billiards.
biliardor *n.* billiards player.
bilingual *adj.* bilingual. • *n.* bilingual, bilingual person.
bilingualisme *n.* bilingualism.
bilion *det.* (*a*) billion, (*a*) thousand million, (*a*) milliard. • *adj.* billionth (*ordinal*).
bilioni *vi.* & *vt.* split into a billion parts. • *n.* billionth (*fraction*).
bilionor *n.* billionaire.
bimetal *adj.* bimetallic.
binaria *adj.* binary.
binoculal *adj.* binocular.
binoculo *n.* binoculars. **binoculo de teatro** opera glasses.
binomial *adj.* binomial.
binomio *n.* binomial.
bio- *pref.* bio-.
biocimica *n.* biochemistry.
biocimical *adj.* biochemical.
biocombustable *n.* biofuel.
biodegrada *vi.* biodegrade. • *n.* biodegradation.
biodegradante *adj.* biodegradable.
biodiversa *adj.* biodiverse.
biodiversia *n.* biodiversity.
biofilia *n.* biophilia.
biofilica *adj.* biophilic. • *n.* biophile.
biofisica *n.* biophysics.
biografia *n.* biography.
biografial *adj.* biographical, biographic.
biografiste *n.* biographer.
biojenese *n.* biogenesis.
biojeografia *n.* biogeography.
biolojia *n.* biology. **biolojia matematical** mathematical biology.
biolojial *adj.* biological.
biolojiste *n.* biologist.
biomasa *n.* biomass.
biomecanica *n.* biomechanics.
biometria *n.* biometrics, biometry, biostatistics.
biometrial *adj.* biometric, biometrical.
bionica *n.* bionics.
bionical *adj.* bionic.
biopsia *n.* biopsy.
bioritmo *n.* biorhythm.
biosfera *n.* biosphere.
biosintese *n.* biosynthesis.
biotecnolojia *n.* biotechnology.
bipartida *adj.* bipartite.
bipartisan *adj.* bipartite.
bipede *adj.* bipedal. • *n.* biped.
biplana *n.* biplane.
bipolal *adj.* bipolar.
bir *n.* beer. **bir blonde** lager. **bir forte** stout.
birazal *adj.* biracial.
bireria *n.* brewery.
biriani *n.* biryani, biriani (*food*).
biror *n.* brewer.
bisc *n.* bisque (*soup*).
Biscaia *n.* Biscay. **Golfo Biscaia** Bay of Biscay.
biscoto *n.* cookie, biscuit, cracker. **biscoto arenin** shortbread, shortcake. **biscoto de jinjer** gingersnap, ginger nut. **biscoto dur** hardtack. **biscoto savoian** ladyfinger, lady's finger, sponge finger. **biscoto seca** rusk, zwieback.
bisel *n.* bevel.
biseli *vt.* bevel, chamfer.
bisepe *n.* biceps (*muscle*).
bisesal *adj.* bisexual.
bisesalia *n.* bisexuality.
bisicle *n.* bicycle, bike. **bisicle motorida** motorized bicycle, moped. **bisicle orizonal** recumbent bicycle. **bisicle per du** tandem.
bisicli *vt.* bicycle, cycle.
bisiclisme *n.* bicycling, cycling (*sport, pastime*).
bisicliste *n.* bicyclist, cyclist.
Bismarck, Mar *n.* Bismarck Sea.
bismuto *n.* bismuth.
bison *n.* bison (*Bison*).
bispal *adj.* episcopal.
bispia *n.* bishopric, diocese.
bispo *n.* bishop (*including chess*).
bistro *n.* bistro.

bisturi *n.* scalpel, lancet.
bitio *n.* bit, binary digit.
bitnic *n.* beatnik.
bitume *n.* bitumen, asphalt (*viscous pitch*).
bitumosa *adj.* bituminous.
bivaca *vi.* bivouac. • *n.* bivouac encampment.
bivalvo *n.* bivalve, clam (*Bivalvia*).
Bixcec *n.* Bishkek.
bizantian *adj.* Byzantine.
bizara *adj.* bizarre, outlandish, kinky, kooky, madcap, zany, wacky. • *n.* weirdo, oddball, dingbat, kook.
blanca *adj.* white; Caucasian, Caucasoid. • *n.* white. **blanca de ovo** egg white. **blanca-negra** *adj.* black and white. **grisin blanca** greyish white, hoary. **Mar Blanca** White Sea.
blanceta *n.* whitefly (*Aleyrodoidea*).
blanci *vi.* & *vt.* whiten, bleach, blanch.
blancida *adj.* whitened, bleached.
blancin *adj.* whitish.
blancinte *adj.* whitening. • *n.* bleach, whitener.
blanco *n.* target (*shooting*); butt (*of joke*). **blanco de eserse** practice target.
blanda *adj.* bland, mild, plain, weak (*food, medicine*); insipid, anodyne, vapid; wimpy. • *n.* pablum, pap; wimp.
blandia *n.* blandness, weakness, plainness.
blasfema *vi.* blaspheme; swear, curse, cuss. • *n.* sacrilege, profanation, blasphemy; swearing, cursing, curse, swearword, expletive.
blasfemal *adj.* sacrilegious, profane, blasphemous.
blasfemante *adj.* swearing, cursing, foul-mouthed.
bleni *n.* blenny (*fish*: *Blennioidei*).
bleta *n.* chard (*plant*: *Beta vulgaris susp. vulgaris*).
blinda *vt.* armour-plate (US armor-plate).
blindada *adj.* armoured (US armored), armour-plated (US armor-plated).
blineta *n.* blintz (*pancake*).
blini *n.* blini (*pancake*).
bloci *vt.* block, clog, obstruct, stonewall. • *n.* blockage, obstruction. **bloci de via** roadblock.
blocinte *adj.* blocking. • *n.* blocker. **blocinte de canales de calsio** calcium-channel blocker. **blocinte de resetadores beta** beta blocker.
bloco *n.* block, chunk, slab, obstacle; block (*group of buildings*); bloc (*alliance*). **bloco de desinias** sketch pad. **bloco de notas** notepad, scratchpad. **bloco de paper** pad of paper.
blog *n.* blog, web log.
blogi *vt.* blog.
blogor *n.* blogger, blog author.
blogosfera *n.* blogosphere.
blonde *adj.* blonde, blond, fair-haired, fair. • *n.* blonde. **blanca blonde** *adj.* & *n.* platinum blonde. **roja blonde** *adj.* & *n.* strawberry blonde.
blondia *n.* blondness.
blu *adj.* & *n.* dark blue, navy. **blus** blues (*music*).
blueta *n.* cornflower, bluet (*Centaurea, Houstonia*).
blugras *n.* bluegrass (*music*).
blui *vi.* & *vt.* turn blue.
bluin *adj.* bluish, blueish.
blusa *n.* blouse.
boa *n.* boa (*snake, scarf*: *Boidae*).
bob *n.* bobsled, bobsleigh.
bobia *n.* silliness, tomfoolery.
bobin *n.* spool, reel, bobbin.
bobini *vt.* spool, wind.
bobo[1] *adj.* silly, goofy, corny, loopy, nutty, bonkers. • *n.* goofball, goon, nincompoop, pillock, prat.
bobo[2] *n.* booby, gannet (*bird*: *Sula, Morus*).
bobolince *n.* bobolink (*bird*: *Dolichonyx oryzivorus*).
bobor *n.* bobsledder.
boca *n.* mouth (*anatomy, river, cave*), gob; muzzle (*gun*). **boca de leon** snapdragon (*plant*: *Antirrhinum*). **boca de venti** vent. **boca plen** mouthful.
bocal *adj.* oral, buccal, of the mouth.
boceta *n.* nozzle, showerhead.
bocon *n.* maw.
boctxoi *n.* bok choy (*cabbage*).
Bod *n.* Tibet. **bod** *adj.* Tibetan. • *n.* Tibetan (*person, language*). See *Tibet, tibetan*.
bodi *n.* bodysuit, body, teddy. **bodi de bebe** onesie, babygro, romper. **bodi de dansa** leotard. **bodi de nada** one-piece swimsuit. **bodi de sporte** leotard. **bodi longa** bodystocking, unitard.
bodisatva *n.* bodhisattva (*Buddhism*).
bodjpuri *adj.* & *n.* Bhojpuri.
bodran *n.* bodhrán (*musical instrument*).
Boemia *n.* Bohemia.
boemian *adj.* & *n.* Bohemian.
bogi *n.* bogie (*wheel system*).
Bohai, Mar *n.* Bohai Sea.
Bohol *n.* Bohol (*island*). **Mar Bohol** Bohol Sea.
boia[1] *n.* buoy.
boia[2] *adj.* Boiian. **boias** Boii (*ancient tribe*).
boicota *vt.* & *n.* boycott.
bol *n.* basin, bowl, tureen. **bol bonodorosa** potpourri. **bol de lava** dishpan, washing-up bowl, washtub. **bol de leto** bedpan. **bol de mole** mortar. **bol de salada** salad bowl. **bol e piston** mortar and pestle.

bola *vi.* bubble, effervesce. • *n.* bubble.
bolante *adj.* bubbling, effervescent.
bolero *n.* bolero.
boleta *n.* small bowl, porringer.
bolevar *n.* boulevard, avenue. **bolevar a plaia** promenade, esplanade, boardwalk. **bolevar de pasea** promenade, mall.
boli *vi.* boil, seethe. • *vt.* boil (*something*). **boli lenta** *vi.* & *vt.* simmer.
bolida *adj.* boiled. **dur bolida** hardboiled.
bolide *n.* bolide; hotrod.
boling *n.* bowling. **boling de des bastones** ten-pin bowling. **boling de nove bastones** nine-pin bowling.
bolinte *adj.* boiling.
Bolivia *n.* Bolivia.
bolivian *adj.* & *n.* Bolivian.
bolo[1] *n.* lawn bowling, bowls, bocce, pétanque.
bolo[2] *n.* bolus (*biology*).
bolosa *adj.* bubbly.
bolsa *n.* handbag, pouch, purse, pocketbook.
bolseta *n.* wallet, purse, billfold.
bolson *n.* rucksack, backpack, knapsack; holdall, carryall, gymbag, sports bag. **bolson de scola** schoolbag. **bolson de spala** satchel.
bolsonor *n.* backpacker.
bolxevic *adj.* & *n.* Bolshevik.
boma *n.* boom.
bomba *n.* bomb, bombshell. **bomba de foco** firebomb. **bomba de idrojen** hydrogen bomb, H-bomb. **bomba ensendente** incendiary bomb. **bomba nucleal** nuclear bomb, nuke. **bomba-orolojo** *n.* time bomb. **bomba umana** human bomb, suicide bomber.
bombador *n.* bomber (*aircraft*).
bombarda[1] *vt.* bombard, barrage, pelt. • *n.* bombardment, bombing, barrage, blitz, salvo, volley. **bombarda con foco** firebomb. **bombarda con petras** stone. **bombarda de lado** broadside.
bombarda[2] *n.* bombarde (*musical instrument*).
bombeta *n.* mine (*bomb*). **planta bombetas** mine, plant mines.
bombetador *n.* minelayer.
bombi *vt.* bomb. • *n.* bombing. **bombi nucleal** nuke.
bombis *n.* silkmoth (*Bombyx*). **bombis de morero** domesticated silkworm (*Bombyx mori*).
bombisila *n.* waxwing (*bird: Bombycilla*).
bombor *n.* bomber (*person*), bombardier.
bon *adj.* (*prenominal*) good, nice; valid. • *adv.* well, nicely. • *interj.* well, right; good, OK, okay. • *pref.* good-, well- (*added to verbs: a better variant of the action, often a specialized sense*); e.g. *bonodori*; *bondise*. **fa la plu bon cual on pote** do one's best. **la plu bon** best, optimal, optimum. **ma bon** oh well (*mild disappointment*). **multe bon** very good, excellent, primo, top-notch. **no bon e no mal** so-so, comme ci comme ça. **plu bon** *adj.* better, preferable. • *adv.* preferably, rather.
Bonaire *n.* Bonaire (*island*).
bonajustada *adj.* well-adjusted; in tune.
bonbon *n.* bonbon (*confectionery*).
bondaje *n.* bondage (*sexual*).
bondi *vi.* bound, bounce, lope. • *n.* bound.
bondise *vt.* bless. • *n.* blessing, benediction, beatitude. **bondises** blessings.
bonfem *n.* nice woman, nice lady, good-natured woman.
bonformida *adj.* well-formed.
bongo[1] *n.* bongo (*drum*).
bongo[2] *n.* bongo (*antelope: Tragelaphus eurycerus*).
boni *vi.* improve, become good, get better. • *vt.* improve, ameliorate, better, enhance, emend, revamp. • *n.* improvement, enhancement.
bonia *n.* goodness.
bonida *adj.* improved.
bonintendente *adj.* well-intentioned, well-meaning.
bonobo *n.* bonobo, pygmy chimpanzee (*Pan paniscus*).
bonodori *vi.* smell good; aromatize. • *vt.* aromatize, give a nice smell to. • *n.* aromatization.
bonodorinte *adj.* aromatic, fragrant.
bonodorosa *adj.* aromatic, fragrant.
bonom *n.* nice guy, decent chap, good-natured fellow, average Joe.
bonparla *n.* eloquence.
bonparlante *adj.* well-spoken, eloquent, articulate.
bonparlor *n.* speaker, orator.
bonpensante *adj.* well-thinking, right-minded.
bonpronunsia *n.* elocution.
bonreputada *adj.* reputable, of good repute.
bonsai *n.* bonsai.
bonsona *n.* euphony, mellifluousness.
bonstate *n.* welfare, well-being, morale, weal.
bonumorosa *adj.* in a good mood, cheerful, jovial, light-hearted, gay (*dated*); sanguine.
bonvendeda *adj.* bestselling. • *n.* bestseller (*book, author*).
bonveni *vt.*, *n.* & *interj.* welcome.
bonvenida *adj.* welcome.
bonveninte *adj.* welcoming, hospitable.
bonvestida *adj.* well-dressed, smart, dapper, debonair, rakish.
bonvole *n.* good will, goodwill, benevolence.

bonvolente *adj.* benevolent, magnanimous, beneficent.
bonvolor *n.* volunteer. **es un bonvolor** volunteer.
boraja *n.* borage (*plant*: *Borago*).
borax *n.* borax (*substance*).
borbon *n.* bourbon (*whisky*).
borda *vt.* border. • *n.* edge, border, brink, verge, rim; outskirts, outlying regions; brim (*hat, cup*); threshold (*metaphor*). **borda de mar** seaside. **borda de troteria** kerb (US curb). **borda fronte** peak (*cap*). **sin borda** borderless, brimless, rimless.
bordel *n.* brothel, bordello, whorehouse.
bordelor *n.* brothelkeeper, madam.
bordo *adj.* maroon, puce. • *n.* bordeaux, claret.
borio *n.* bohrium (*element*).
borla *n.* tassel.
Borneo *n.* Borneo.
boro *n.* boron (*element*).
borxt *n.* borscht, borshch.
bosanova *n.* bossa nova.
bosce *n.* copse, grove, small wood, orchard, woodland. **bosce de arboretas** shrubland, scrubland, brush. **bosce de frutas** orchard.
bosceta *n.* thicket, bushes; rough (*golf*).
boscin *adj.* wooded, sylvan.
boscor *n.* woodsman, woodman.
Bosnia *n.* Bosnia. **Bosnia e Hersegovina** Bosnia and Herzegovina.
bosnian *adj.* & *n.* Bosnian, Bosniak (*person, language*).
boson *n.* boson (*particle*).
Bosporo, Streta *n.* Bosphorus Strait, Bosporus Strait.
bota *n.* boot. **bota de cauxo** rubber boot, wellington, welly, gumboot. **bota militar** jackboot.
botanica *n.* botany.
botanical *adj.* botanical.
botaniciste *n.* botanist.
bote *n.* can, tin.
boteca *n.* shop, store, boutique, commercial unit. **boteca completa** one-stop shop. **boteca de cose** fabric store, haberdasher's. **boteca de departes** department store. **boteca de te** teashop. **boteca de utiles** tool shop, hardware store, ironmonger's. **boteca descontante** discount store. **boteca sin imposta** duty-free shop, duty-free store.
botecor *n.* shopkeeper.
botela *n.* bottle, flask. **botela de acua** water bottle, canteen.
boteleta *n.* phial, vial.
boteli *vt.* bottle.
boteria *n.* cannery.
boti *vt.* can, tin.
botida *adj.* canned, tinned.
Botnia, Golfo *n.* Gulf of Bothnia.
boton *n.* button, knob. **boton de presa** snap fastener, press stud, popper.
botoni *vt.* button.
botonin *adj.* buttonlike, knobby.
botor *n.* bittern (*bird*: *Botaurinae*).
Botsuana *n.* Botswana. See *tsuana*.
botulisme *n.* botulism.
boval *adj.* bovine.
bove *n.* ox, cow, bull, bovine (*Bos*). **Bove** *n.* Taurus (*constellation*). **bove fema** cow. **bove mas** bull. **boves** cattle, oxen.
boveta *n.* calf. **boveta fema** heifer.
bovin *adj.* cowlike, bovine.
bovor *n.* cowherd, cowboy, wrangler.
boxe *vt.* box. • *n.* boxing, pugilism. **boxe de pedi** *v.* kickbox. • *n.* kickboxing. **boxe de pesa media** middleweight boxing. **boxe pesosa** heavyweight boxing. **boxe plumin** featherweight boxing. **boxe profesal** professional boxing, prizefight. **boxe solitar** shadowboxing.
boxor *n.* boxer, pugilist. **boxor de pedi** kickboxer. **boxor profesal** professional boxer, prizefighter.
braci- *pref.* brachy- (*short*).
braciopodo *n.* brachiopod (*Brachiopoda*).
braciosauro *n.* brachiosaur, brachiosaurus (*Brachiosaurus*).
bradi- *pref.* brady- (*slow*).
bradipo *n.* sloth (*Megalonychidae, Bradypodidae*).
Brahmaputra, Rio *n.* Brahmaputra River.
braille [braj]~[brajl] *n.* Braille.
Brama *n.* Brahma.
braman *n.* brahmin, brahman.
brancia *n.* gill.
brandi *vt.* brandish, flourish, wield, wave; swing (*club*). **brandi per colpa** swing at.
brasa *n.* ember. **brasas** embers; afterglow (*emotion*).
brasador *n.* brazier, hibachi.
brasal *adj.* bracchial.
brasaleta *n.* bracelet, bangle, wristband. **brasaleta de talo** anklet.
braseta *n.* bracket, parenthesis. **braseta angulo** angle bracket. **braseta curva** round bracket, parenthesis. **braseta reta** square bracket. **braseta risa** curly bracket, brace. **entre brasetas** *adj.* in brackets, parenthetical. • *adv.* in brackets, parenthetically, by the way.
braseti *vt.* bracket.
brasetida *adj.* bracketed. • *adv.* in brackets. • *n.* parenthesis, parenthetical phrase.
brasi *vt.* apply one's arm to. • *n.* stroke (*swimming*).

Brasil *n.* Brazil.
brasilera *adj.* & *n.* Brazilian.
braso *n.* arm. **braso alta** upper arm. **braso basa** forearm.
bratea *n.* bract (*botany*).
brava *adj.* decent, worthy, gallant. • *interj.* bravo.
bravata *n.* bravado, bluster, bombast, swagger.
bravator *n.* blowhard, braggart.
bravatosa *adj.* bombastic, swaggering, swashbuckling. • *n.* swashbuckler.
brecdansa *vi.* breakdance. • *n.* breakdance, breakdancing, B-boying.
Bres *n.* Brittany; Duchy of Brittany.
bresonica *adj.* & *n.* Breton (*person*, *language*).
bretela *n.* brace (*UK*), suspender (*US*); shoulder strap. **bretela de calsa** suspender (*UK*), garter (*US*). **sin bretelas** strapless.
breteleta *n.* spaghetti strap, noodle strap.
Breton, Capo *n.* Cape Breton.
bretsel *n.* pretzel; ampersand.
breviario *n.* breviary.
bri *n.* brie (*cheese*).
bricabrac *n.* junk, odds and ends, bric-a-brac.
bricabraceria *n.* junk shop, charity shop.
brice *n.* brick; ingot, bar. **brice de beton** concrete block, cement block. **brice de carbon** briquet, briquette. **brice de sene** cinder block, breeze block, besser block.
brici *vt.* brick, brick up.
bricola *vi.* do odd jobs, tinker. • *n.* DIY, do-it-yourself, odd jobs.
bricoleta *vi.* potter (US putter) about.
bricolor *n.* tinker.
bricor *n.* bricklayer, brickie.
brida *n.* bridle (*straps*).
bridi *vt.* bridle.
brigada *n.* brigade. **brigada de pompores** fire department, fire brigade.
brigador *n.* brigadier.
brigantin *n.* brigantine, brig.
brije *n.* bridge (*card game*).
brilia *vi.* shine, gleam. • *vt.* cause to shine, polish, burnish. • *n.* brilliance, splendour (US splendor), lucidity, gleam. **brilia de mente** brainwave, brainstorm. **brilia de sol** sunshine. **cuantia de brilia** brightness; magnitude (*astronomy*).
briliamobila *n.* furniture polish.
briliante *adj.* shining, shiny, bright, brilliant, glossy, gleaming, lustrous, splendid, lucid, lurid, resplendent, vibrant. • *n.* shiner; brightener; sequin.
briliasapato *n.* shoe polish.
brilieta *vi.* glow. • *n.* sheen, glow, lustre (US luster).
brilion *n.* glare, dazzle.
brinca *vt.* hop, skip, gambol, caper, cavort, flit across. • *n.* hop, skip, gambol, caper, flit.
brincacorda *n.* skipping.
brincacuadro *n.* hopscotch.
brincadorso *n.* leapfrog.
brincor *n.* hopper, skipper, leaper.
brinda *vt.* toast, raise one's glass to. • *n.* toast.
briox *n.* brioche (*bread*).
briozon *n.* bryozoon (pl. bryozoa) (*organism*: *Briozoa*).
Britan *n.* Britain, Britannia. **Britan Grande** Great Britain (*island*). **Britan Nova** New Britain (*island*).
Britania *n.* Britannia (*personification of Britain*).
brites *adj.* British (*person*, *language*). • *n.* Briton, Brit.
broca *n.* drill bit.
brocada *n.* brocade (*fabric*).
brocol *n.* broccoli (*plant*, *vegetable*: *Brassica oleracea*).
brode *vt.* embroider. • *n.* embroidery, needlework, needlepoint.
broma *vt.* joke, jest, tease. • *n.* joke, gag, tease, pleasantry, zinger, wisecrack. **broma de parolas** pun, wordplay, play on words.
bromelia *n.* bromeliad (*plant*: *Bromeliaceae*).
bromido *n.* bromide (*chemistry*).
bromo *n.* bromine.
bromor *n.* joker, jester, jokester, comedian.
bromosa *adj.* jocular, facetious.
bromosia *n.* jocularity, facetiousness, levity.
broncal *adj.* bronchial.
bronciol *n.* bronchiole.
broncite *n.* bronchitis.
bronco *n.* bronchus, bronchi.
broncodilatante *n.* bronchodilator.
broncoscopi *n.* bronchoscopy.
broncoscopio *n.* bronchoscope.
bronze *n.* bronze; tan, suntan. **bronze dorada** gilded bronze, vermeil. **de bronze** (*made of*) bronze.
bronzi *vi.* & *vt.* tan.
brosa *n.* brush, paintbrush. **brosa de capeles** hairbrush. **brosa de dentes** toothbrush.
brosi *vt.* brush; groom (*animal*).
brosin *adj.* brushlike, bushy (*tail*).
broti *vi.* bud.
broto *n.* bud. **broto de rosa** rosebud.
brox *n.* brooch.
brun *adj.* brown; brunette; swarthy. • *n.* brown; brunette. **brun oranin** tawny. **brun pal** light brown. **brun rojin** reddish brown, auburn, rugous. **pal brun** light brown, beige, fawn.
Brune *n.* Brunei. **brune** *adj.* & *n.* Bruneian.
bruni *vi.* turn brown. • *vt.* sear, brown (*cookery*); bruise. • *n.* bruise.

brunin *adj.* brownish.
Brunswick Nova *n.* New Brunswick (*Canadian province*).
brusca *adj.* brusque, curt, blunt, terse, short, peremptory.
bruta *adj.* rough (*marble, estimate*), untreated, uncut (*gem*), coarse (*sand*), unrefined (*sugar*), unfinished, crude, gross (*national product, income, profit, tax, tonnage*); uncouth, brutish, loutish, boorish, gruff, surly, crass. • *n.* brute, boor, lout, ruffian, lowlife, vulgarian.
Bruxelles [bruˈʃeles] *n.* Brussels.
bubon *n.* bubo (*swollen lymph node*).
bubonal *adj.* bubonic.
buce *n.* bouquet, bunch of flowers.
buceta *n.* posy, nosegay.
buco *n.* hole, gap, breach, lacuna. **ateni la buco con un colpa** score a hole in one (*golf*). **buco de baril** bunghole. **buco de boton** buttonhole. **buco de clave** keyhole. **buco de cloaca** manhole. **buco de culo** (*colloquial*) arsehole (US asshole) (*anus, insult*). **buco de palo** posthole. **buco de posta** letterbox, mail slot. **buco de refuja** foxhole. **buco de respira** blowhole. **buco de spia** spyhole, peephole. **buco de strada** pothole. **buco de verme** wormhole. **buco negra** black hole.
bucosa *adj.* full of holes, holey.
Bucuresti *n.* Bucharest.
Buda *n.* Buddha.
budisme *n.* Buddhism.
budiste *n.* Buddhist.
budlea *n.* buddleia (*plant: Buddleia*).
bufalo *n.* water buffalo, buffalo (*Bubalus*).
bufe *n.* buffet, potluck (*meal*).
buferia *n.* cafeteria, buffet restaurant.
bufon *n.* clown, buffoon, jester; joker, wildcard; catchall.
bufonal *adj.* clown. **bufonales** antics, buffoonery.
bufonia *n.* clowning, antics, buffoonery, horseplay.
bugainvilea *n.* bougainvillea (*Bougainvillea*).
bugi *n.* boogie, boogie-woogie (*dance, music*).
buin *adj.* owl-like.
bujeta *vt.* & *n.* budget.
bujia *n.* spark plug.
bula *n.* blister.
bulbal *adj.* bulbous (*growing from a bulb*).
bulbin *adj.* bulbous, bulblike.
bulbo *n.* bulb. **bulbo de lus** lightbulb. **bulbo flax** flashbulb.
bulbul *n.* bulbul (*bird: Pycnonotidae*).
buldog *n.* bulldog.
buldozer *n.* bulldozer.
bulgur *n.* bulgur (*food*).
buli *vi.* & *vt.* blister.
buliabes *n.* bouillabaisse.
bulimia *n.* bulimia.
bulimica *adj.* & *n.* bulimic.
bulion *n.* bouillon, broth, stock, consommé.
bulon *n.* bolt (*including nut*). **bulon xef** kingpin (*bolt, person*).
buloni *vt.* bolt.
bulteta *n.* small bump, small lump, weal.
bulti *vi.* & *vt.* bulge.
bulto *n.* bulge, bump, lump, protuberance, burl, slub, gob, nub, nubbin.
bultosa *adj.* bumpy, lumpy.
buma *vi.* boom (*increase explosively*). • *n.* boom. **buma de bebes** baby boom. **buma economial** economic boom. **Buma Grande** Big Bang.
bumerang *n.* boomerang.
buncer *n.* bunker, dugout.
buo *n.* owl (*Strigidae*). **buo de neva** snowy owl (*Bubo scandiaca*). **buo real** Eurasian eagle owl (*Bubo bubo*).
bur *n.* butter. **bur de aracide** peanut butter.
burca *n.* burqa, burka, chadri (*garment*).
Burcina Faso *n.* Burkina Faso.
burcinabe *adj.* & *n.* Burkinabé.
burcini *n.* burkini, burqini (*swimsuit*).
bure *n.* bourrée, bourée, borreia, borry, bore (*dance, music*).
Burgonia *n.* Burgundy. **burgonia** *adj.* burgundy (*colour*). • *n.* burgundy (*wine*).
burgunda *adj.* & *n.* Burgundian.
buri *vt.* butter.
buril *n.* burr, burin, dental tool, engraving tool.
burin *adj.* buttery.
burino *n.* thick-knee, stone-curlew, dikkops (*bird: Burhinidae*).
burito *n.* burrito.
burjes *adj.* bourgeois, middle-class.
burjesi *vi.* become middle-class, become gentrified. • *vt.* gentrify. • *n.* gentrification.
burjesia *n.* bourgeoisie, middle class.
burla *vt.* taunt, tease, mock, jeer, deride, laugh at, heckle, lampoon, scoff. • *n.* taunt, tease, jeer, mockery, ridicule, derision.
burlable *adj.* laughable, risible, ridiculous, ludicrous.
burlada *n.* stooge.
burlante *adj.* taunting, mocking, derisive.
burleta *vt.* rib, josh, banter, tease (*good-naturedly*). • *n.* banter, persiflage.
burlor *n.* teaser, mocker, heckler, scoffer.
Burma *n.* Burma, Myanmar. See *Miama*.
burman *adj.* & *n.* Burmese (*person, language*). See *miama*.
buro *n.* desk, bureau (*furniture*).
burocrata *adj.* bureaucratic. • *n.* bureaucrat.
burocratia *n.* bureaucracy.

burosa *adj.* buttery.
bursa *n.* bursa (*anatomy*).
bursite *n.* bursitis (*medical*).
burundes *adj.* & *n.* Burundian.
Burundi *n.* Burundi.
bus *n.* bus, coach. **bus de dona sangue** bloodmobile.
busino *n.* whelk (*Buccinidae*).
busola *n.* compass (*for finding north*). **Busola** *n.* Pyxis (*constellation*).
busor *n.* bus driver, coach driver.
bustier *n.* bustier. **bustier tubo** tube top, boob tube.
busto *n.* bust (*sculpture*).
bustrofedon *adj.* & *n.* boustrophedon.
but- *pref.* but- (*chemistry*).
Butan *n.* Bhutan. **butan** *adj.* & *n.* Bhutanese, Bhutanse. See *Druciul*, *drucpa*.
butano *n.* butane.
buteo *n.* buzzard, buzzard-hawk, hawk (*Buteoninae*).
butil *n.* butyl (*chemistry*).
butirica *adj.* butyric. **asida butirica** butyric acid.
bux *n.* box tree, boxwood (*Buxus*).
buxido *n.* bushido (*samurai code*).
buzuci *n.* bouzouki (*musical instrument*).
bzz *interj.* buzz.

C

C [ke], **ce** *letter* C, c.
ca *prep.* & *subord.* than; e.g. *mea can es plu intelijente ca me.*
caa *interj.* caw, crow.
cabal *n.* cabal, caucus.
cabala *n.* kabbalah, kabbala (*Judaism*).
cabana *n.* cabin, hut, shed, cabana. **cabana bruta** shack, hovel. **cabana de arbor** tree house, tree fort. **cabana de lenio** woodshed. **cabana de troncos** log cabin. **cabana de utiles** tool shed.
cabare *n.* cabaret, floor show; nightclub, dinner theatre, boîte.
cabe *vi.* fit; e.g. *tua valis no cabe en mea auto*; *acel xapo cabe a tu.*
cabestro *n.* halter.
cabina *n.* cabin (*ship*, *aircraft*).
cable *n.* cable. **cable coasal** coaxial cable. **cable eletrical** power cable.
cabuci *n.* kabuki (*drama*).
caca *n.* (*colloquial*) poo, poop, crap, cack (*dung*, *anything worthless*). **caca de bove** bullshit.
cacara *vi.* & *n.* cackle.
cacareta *vi.* & *n.* chuckle, chortle.
cacatu [kaka'tu] *n.* cockatoo (*Cacatuida*).
cacau *n.* cocoa, cacao (*Theobroma cacao*).
caci[1] *adj.* khaki (*colour*). • *n.* khaki (*fabric*).
caci[2] *n.* persimmon (*tree*, *fruit*: *Diospyros*).
caci[3] *vt.* (*colloquial*) poo, poop, crap, cack.
cacin *adj.* (*colloquial*) crappy.
cacto *n.* cactus (*Cactaceae*).
cada *det.* each, every. • *pron.* each, each one, every one. **a cada matina** every morning. **a cada ora** every hour. **a cada ves** every time, each time, on each occasion, always. **a un ves en cada anio du** once every two years. **a un ves en cada duple de anios** once every two years. **a un ves en cada pico de anios** once every few years. **cada cosa** each thing, everything (*individually*). **en cada loca** everywhere. **en cada parte** everywhere, throughout. **per cada** each, apiece.
cade *vi.* fall, fall down, tumble, tip over, topple, collapse; crash (*aircraft*). • *vt.* fell, knock over, knock down; cut down (*tree*); drop; omit. • *n.* fall, collapse, crash; wipeout (*surfing*). **cade a jenos** fall to one's knees, kneel down. **cade a tera** *vi.* fall to earth; crash (*aircraft*). • *vt.* knock to earth, unhorse. **cade comica** pratfall. **cade e pedi** dropkick, punt (*ball*). **fa ce lo cade** fell, knock over.
cadena *n.* chain (*including shops*, *hotels*); range (*mountains*); string (*characters*); pipeline (*software*); thread (*correspondence*); warp (*textiles*). **cadena de claves** keychain, key fob. **cadena de construi** assembly line. **cadena de orolojeta** watch chain, fob. **cadena de verbos** verb chain. **cadena leteral** string literal (*software*). **cadena nural** food chain. **cadena vacua** empty string, null string (*software*).
cadeni *vt.* chain, enchain.
cadjen *adj.* & *n.* Cajun.
cadmio *n.* cadmium.
caduca *adj.* deciduous.
cadun *pron.* everyone, everybody.
caduseo *n.* caduceus (*herald's wand*, *medical symbol*).
cafador *n.* coffeemaker. **cafador de filtro** percolator.
cafe [ka'fe] *n.* coffee (*plant*, *seed*, *drink*: *Coffea*). **cafe con lete** coffee with milk, white coffee. **cafe con lete calda** coffee with hot milk, café au lait. **cafe pronto** instant coffee.
caferia *n.* café, coffee shop, coffeehouse, canteen.
cafia *n.* keffiyeh, kufiya (*headdress*).
cafina *n.* caffeine.
cafini *vt.* caffeinate. • *n.* caffeination.
caftan *n.* kaftan (*garment*).
caiac *n.* kayak.
caiman *n.* caiman, cayman (*Caiman*). **Isolas Caiman** Cayman Islands.
caje *n.* cage. **caje de avia** birdcage. **caje de coneo** rabbit hutch.
caji *vt.* cage, encage.
cala[1] *n.* (*ship's*) hold.
cala[2] *n.* calla lily, marsh calla, bog arum (*Calla palustris*).
calalit *adj.* Greenlandic (*person*, *language*). • *n.* Greenlander. See *gronlandes.*
Calalitnunat *n.* Greenland. See *Gronland.*
calamar *n.* squid (*Teuthida*).
calamo *n.* calamus, gladdon, sweet flag, sweet myrtle (*plant*: *Acorus calamus*).
calau *n.* hornbill (*bird*: *Bucerotidae*).
calaza *n.* chalaza (*biology*).
calcaneo *n.* calcaneus, heel bone.
calcario *n.* limestone.
calce *n.* lime (*substance*).
calci *vi.* & *vt.* calcify. • *n.* calcification.
calcolitica *adj.* & *n.* Chalcolithic, copper age.
calcula *vt.* calculate, reckon, work out. • *n.* calculation, reckoning.
calculable *adj.* calculable.
calculador *n.* calculator.

calculo[1] *n.* pebble; counter (*game piece*); stone (*medical*). **calculo bilal** gallstone. **calculos** pebbles, gravel, shingle. **calculos nonfisada** loose pebbles, scree.

calculo[2] *n.* calculus. **calculo diferensial** differential calculus. **calculo integral** integral calculus. **calculo vetoral** vector calculus.

calda *adj.* hot. **alga calda** warm. **calda e seca** hot and dry, torrid. **comfortosa calda** comfortably hot, toasty.

caldador *n.* heater.

caldera *n.* kettle, boiler. **caldera de te** tea kettle.

calderon *n.* cauldron.

caldi *vi.* & *vt.* heat, warm. • *n.* heating, warming. **caldi global** global warming.

caldia *n.* heat, warmth.

caldiplato *n.* plate warmer.

Caledonia Nova *n.* New Caledonia.

caledonian *adj.* & *n.* Caledonian.

calendario *n.* calendar; timescale.

calendula *n.* marigold (*Calendula*).

calia *vi.* curdle.

caliada *adj.* curdled. • *n.* curd, junket.

caliante *adj.* curdling. • *n.* curdling agent.

calibre *n.* calibre (US caliber), bore.

calibro *n.* calliper (US caliper).

calico *n.* calico, chintz, dungaree (*fabric*).

calidoscopial *adj.* kaleidoscopic.

calidoscopio *n.* kaleidoscope.

calidris *n.* stint, sandpiper (*Scolopacidae*).

califa *n.* caliph.

califia *n.* caliphate.

California *n.* California (*US state*). **California Basa** Baja California. **Golfo California** Gulf of California, Sea of Cortez.

californio *n.* californium (*element*).

caligrafia *n.* calligraphy, artistic writing.

calimba *n.* kalimba, mbira, sansa, thumb piano (*musical instrument*).

calio *n.* rennet (*substance*).

calipso *adj.* & *n.* calypso.

calix *n.* chalice, calyx. **Calix Santa** Holy Grail.

calma *adj.* calm, still, tranquil, sedate, quiescent, serene, level-headed, unruffled, uneventful.

calmi *vi.* calm, calm down, settle, subside, abate. • *vt.* calm, calm down, becalm, settle, soothe, lull, reassure; sedate, tranquillize (US tranquilize). • *n.* calming, reassurance, sedation.

calmia *n.* calm, calmness, stillness, quiescence, composure, serenity.

calminte *adj.* calming; sedative, sedating, soporific, emollient, tranquillizing (US tranquilizing). **medisin calminte** sedative, soporific, tranquillizer (US tranquilizer).

calmitose *n.* cough syrup.

calo *n.* callus, corn.

caloria *n.* calorie. **caloria grande** large calorie. **caloria peti** small calorie.

calorial *adj.* caloric.

caloriosa *adj.* calorie-laden.

calosa *adj.* callous, insensitive, cruel, hardened.

calosia *n.* callousness, insensitivity, cruelty, hardness.

calsa *n.* stocking. **calsas** hosiery, hose.

calsedonia *n.* chalcedony (*mineral*).

calseta *n.* sock.

calsio *n.* calcium.

calson *n.* tights, pantyhose.

caluna *n.* heather (*Calluna*).

calva *adj.* bald, hairless.

Calvario *n.* Calvary, Gagulta, Golgotha (*hill*).

calvi *vi.* bald, go bald. • *vt.* make bald.

calvia *n.* baldness, alopecia.

calvinisme *n.* Calvinism (*Christianity*).

calviniste *adj.* & *n.* Calvinist.

calvinte *adj.* balding.

camaleon *n.* chameleon (*Chamaeleonidae*). **Camaleon** *n.* Chamaeleon (*constellation*).

camamber *n.* camembert (*cheese*).

cambia *vi.* change, transform. • *vt.* change, transform, amend, convert; replace; cash (*a cheque*), cash in. • *n.* change, transformation, transition, amendment. **cambia calda** hot-swap. **cambia de bus** connection, change of bus. **cambia de clima** climate change. **cambia de engrana** gear change. **cambia de tren** connection, change of train. **cambia esta a acel** change this to that, replace this with that. **cambia la grandia de** resize.

cambiable *adj.* changeable. **calda cambiable** hot-swappable. **fasil cambiable** easily changed, amenable to change, labile.

cambion *n.* upheaval, sea change.

cambra *n.* chamber. **cambra de bola** bubble chamber. **cambra de combusta** combustion chamber. **cambra de fusil** chamber (*gun*). **cambra de gas** gas chamber. **cambra de resona** echo chamber. **cambra de venta** wind tunnel.

cambrian *adj.* & *n.* Cambrian (*geology*).

camel *n.* camel (*Camelus*).

camelia *n.* camellia (*plant*: *Camellia*).

camelor *n.* camel driver, camel rider, cameleer.

cameo *n.* cameo (*jewellery*, *literature*, *minor acting role*).

camera *n.* camera. **camera compata** compact camera. **camera de trafica** traffic enforcement camera, speed camera. **camera pronto** instant camera. **camera**

ueb webcam. **camera vijilante** CCTV camera.

camerada *n.* comrade, companion, compatriot, crony, sidekick. **camerada de aparte** flatmate. **camerada de barco** shipmate. **camerada de clase** classmate. **camerada de leto** bedfellow. **camerada de sala** roommate. **camerada de scola** schoolmate. **camerada de selula** cellmate; cubemate.

cameradia *n.* comradeship, camaraderie.

cameror *n.* camera operator, cameraman, camerawoman.

Camerun *n.* Cameroon.

camerunes *adj.* & *n.* Cameroonian.

camfor *n.* camphor.

camion *n.* truck, lorry; truckload. **camion de pompores** fire engine, fire truck. **camion jigante** juggernaut. **camion sesionida** articulated truck, articulated lorry, tractor trailer, semitrailer truck, semi.

camioneta *n.* small truck, pickup.

camioni *vt.* truck (*send by truck*).

camionor *n.* trucker, truck driver, lorry driver, teamster.

camisa *n.* shirt. **camisa de juta** hairshirt, cilice. **camisa de note** nightshirt. **camisa de polo** polo shirt. **camisa de sera** dress shirt. **camisa T** tee, T-shirt.

camiseta *n.* top, collarless shirt, tee, T-shirt; undershirt. **camiseta corta** crop top, belly shirt, half-shirt. **camiseta de nuca** halterneck, haltertop. **camiseta de sporte** athletic shirt, A-shirt, sleeveless T-shirt, muscle shirt, singlet, vest (*UK*), tanktop (*US*), wifebeater. **camiseta gainin** tube top, boob tube.

camison *n.* smock, smock-frock, tunic. **camison blanca** alb, surplice. **camison de malie** hauberk, coat of mail. **camison de restrinje** straitjacket.

camofla *vt.* & *n.* camouflage.

camomila *n.* camomile (US chamomile) (*Chamaemelum*).

campa *vi.* camp, encamp, bivouac. • *n.* camping; camp, bivouac, temporary shelter. **campa avansada** advanced camp, outpost. **campa de base** base camp. **campa de consentra** concentration camp. **campa de labora** labour (US labor) camp. **campa de mata** death camp. **campa de prisoni** prison camp. **campa isolida** isolated camp, outpost.

campana *n.* bell, chime. **campana de bove** cowbell.

campaneria *n.* bell tower, campanile.

campaneta *n.* handbell; doorbell. **campaneta blu** bluebell (*various plants*).

campania[1] *n.* countryside, rural area, boondocks.

campania[2] *vi.* campaign, canvass. • *n.* campaign.

campanial *adj.* rural, rustic, country, bucolic.

campanian *n.* rural person, country dweller, peasant, hayseed, bumpkin, yokel, hick, rube. **campanianes** peasantry.

campanin *adj.* bell-like, bell-shaped.

campaniol *n.* vole (*Arvicolini, Ellobiusini, Lagurini, Myodini, Pliomyini*).

campanior *n.* campaigner.

campanula *n.* bellflower, harebell, Scottish bluebell (*plant: Campanula*).

Campeche [kam'petʃe] *n.* Campeche (*Mexican state*). **Baia Campeche** Bay of Campeche, Campeche Sound.

campefaje *n.* cuckoo shrike (*Campephagidae*).

camperia *n.* campsite.

campidanes *adj.* & *n.* Campidanese (*language*).

campion *n.* champion (*including of a cause*), champ, winner, prize-winner; paladin (*knight*).

campioni *vi.* become the champion. • *vt.* crown as champion.

campionida *adj.* prize-winning, award-winning.

campo *n.* field (*grass, knowledge, activity*); discipline; pitch, course (*sport*). **campo bancal** banking sector. **campo comun** common (*land*). **campo de avion** airfield, aerodrome, airstrip. **campo de batalia** battlefield, battleground. **campo de bombetas** minefield (*physical or metaphorical*). **campo de criceta** cricket pitch. **campo de futbal** football pitch, soccer pitch. **campo de gera** battlefield. **campo de golf** golf course. **campo de jua** playing field. **campo de ris** paddy, rice field. **campo de scola** playground, schoolyard. **campo de sporte** sports field. **campo de tenis** tennis court. **campo de vide** field of vision. **campo privata** private sector. **campo reposante** fallow field. **en la campo de oia** within earshot. **en la campo de vide** in the field of vision, within eyeshot.

Camputxa *n.* Cambodia. **camputxa** *adj.* & *n.* Cambodian.

camusa *n.* chamois (*animal: Rupicapra rupicapra*); shammy, chamy (*leather*).

camusin *adj.* chamois-like. • *n.* moleskin.

can *n.* dog, pooch, mutt (*Canis familiaris*). **can coleriosa** cur. **can de pastor** sheepdog. **can de pastor deutx** German shepherd dog, Alsatian. **can de pastor scotes** collie. **can-de-prado** *n.* prairie dog (*rodent:*

Cynomys). **Can Grande** Canis Major (*constellation*). **can misera** cur. **Can Peti** Canis Minor (*constellation*). **can regalada** lapdog (*dog, person*). **Canes de Xasa** Canes Venatici (*constellation*).
cana *n.* reed, cane (*Phragmites*, *Arundo* and many other genera); rod (*fishing*). **cana de zucar** sugarcane (*Saccharum*).
canaba *n.* hemp, cannabis, marihuana, marijuana (*plant, material, drug*: *Cannabis sativa*).
canabinoide *n.* cannabinoid (*drug*).
canabor *n.* cannabis user, pothead, stoner.
canada[1] *adj.* & *n.* Kannada (*person, language*).
Canada[2] *n.* Canada.
canadian *adj.* & *n.* Canadian.
canal *n.* canal, channel, ditch, duct, flume. **canal suteran** underground channel, culvert.
canaleta *n.* gutter (*street, roof*); sluiceway.
Canan *n.* Canaan (*biblical region*).
cananes *adj.* & *n.* Canaanite (*person, language*).
canape *n.* canapé.
canario *n.* canary (*Serinus*). **Isolas Canario** Canary Islands.
canasta *n.* canasta (*card game*).
cancan *n.* cancan (*dance*).
candela *n.* candle; candela, candlepower.
candelabro *n.* candelabra, chandelier.
canela *n.* cinnamon (*plant, spice*: *Cinnamomum*).
caneria *n.* kennel, doghouse.
caneta *n.* puppy, pup, doggie, whelp.
cangareta *n.* joey.
cangari *vi.* behave like a kangaroo. **cangari a enfantes** look after children, babysit.
cangaru [kaŋgaˈru] *n.* kangaroo (*Macropus*).
canibal *n.* cannibal, anthropophage.
canibalisme *n.* cannibalism.
canido *n.* canid, canine (*Canidae*).
canin *adj.* canine, doglike.
canion *n.* canyon, gorge, ravine, chasm; gap (*to be bridged metaphorically*).
canix *n.* poodle.
canji *n.* kanji (*writing system*).
cano *n.* barrel (*gun*). **cano lisa** smooth bore. **cano raiosa** rifled bore.
canoa *n.* canoe. **canoa escavada** dugout. **vade par canoa** canoe.
canoisme [kanoˈisme] *n.* canoeing.
canoiste [kanoˈiste] *n.* canoeist.
canolo *n.* cannolo (*dessert*). **canolos** cannoli.
canon[1] *n.* canon (*literature, music*).
canon[2] *n.* cannon (*gun*).
canonal *adj.* canonical.
canonera *n.* gunboat.
canonor *n.* cannoneer, cannonier, artilleryman.
cansela *vt.* cancel, revoke, abrogate, annul, repeal, belay, nix; erase, rub out, delete, expunge. • *n.* cancellation, abrogation, erasure, annulment, revocation, write-off. **cansela sua enscrive** unsubscribe.
canselable *adj.* cancellable (US cancelable), revocable, erasable.
canselador *n.* canceller (US canceler) (*device*).
canselor *n.* chancellor.
canseloreria *n.* chancellery, chancery.
canser *n.* cancer.
canserosa *adj.* cancerous, malignant.
canserosia *n.* malignancy.
canta *vt.* sing, croon. • *n.* song. **canta de avias** birdsong. **canta de cuna** lullaby. **canta de folclor** folk song. **canta de gondolor** barcarole. **canta de loda** song of praise, paean. **canta de marinores** shanty, chanty. **canta de natal** carol. **canta gregorian** Gregorian chant, plainchant, plainsong. **canta grupal** group singing, songfest. **canta lenta** *v.* & *n.* chant. **canta melodiosa** *v.* & *n.* warble. **canta sincrona** mime, lip-sync.
cantada *n.* cantata, song (*score and lyrics*).
cantalupo *n.* cantaloupe.
canteta *n.* ditty.
cantilever *n.* cantilever.
cantileveri *vt.* cantilever.
cantin *adj.* singsong.
canto *n.* street corner (*general area*).
canton *n.* canton.
cantor *n.* singer, vocalist, cantor; songbird, warbler (*Oscines*, *Parulinae*, *Sylviidae*). **cantor-composor** *n.* singer-songwriter. **cantor fondal** backing singer. **cantor sincrona** playback singer, lipsyncher.
caodai *adj.* Cao Dai; Caodaist. • *n.* Cao Dai; Caodaism (*religion*). • *n.* Caodaist.
caos *n.* chaos, tumult, haphazard, mayhem, snafu. **Caos** *n.* Chaos (*mythology*).
caososa *adj.* chaotic, irregular.
capa[1] *n.* cape, cloak, serape.
capa[2] *n.* kappa (*Greek letter* Κ, κ).
capara *n.* caper (*plant, bud*: *Capparis spinosa*).
capas *adj.* able, capable, skilled, skilful (US skillful), proficient, accomplished, adept, adroit, competent, professional, amenable, efficient. **capas de era** capable of error, fallible. **capas de susede** capable of success, viable. **tro capas** overqualified, overskilled.
capasi *vi.* grow capable. • *vt.* enable.
capasia *n.* ability, capability, capacity, power, faculty (*power*); talent, skill, knack, gift; proficiency, competence, prowess, artistry; efficiency, performance. **ave la capasia** be qualified. **capasia eletrical** capacitance.

capel *n.* hair (*of the scalp, one strand*). **capeles** hairs, hair (*collectively*). **capeles brosin** flat-top. **Capeles de Berenise** Coma Berenices (*constellation*). **capeles de pajo** pageboy bob. **capeles erisin** spiked hair. **capeles irocuoi** mohican (US mohawk). **capeles militar** military haircut, buzzcut, crewcut. **capeles rastafari** dreadlocks. **capeles reta** straight hair. **capeles risa** curly hair. **con capeles roja** red-haired, red-headed, ginger. **par un capel** by a hair's breadth, barely.

capeleria *n.* barbershop, hair salon.

capeleta *n.* facial hair, body hair (*one strand*). See *pelo*.

capeli *vt.* add hair to.

capelin *adj.* hairlike.

capelon *n.* bristle, awn, arista. **capelones** stubble.

capelonosa *adj.* stubbly.

capelor *n.* hairdresser, hairstylist, barber.

capelosa *adj.* hairy (*head*).

capeta *n.* hood (*garment*); bonnet (UK), hood (US) (*vehicle*). **capeta de motor** bonnet, hood (*vehicle*). **capeta laxe** cowl.

capetor *n.* hoodie (*person*).

capi *vt.* cape, cloak.

capibara *n.* capybara (*animal: Hydrochoerus hydrochaeris*).

capilar *adj.* & *n.* capillary.

capital *adj.* & *n.* capital (*city, economics, architecture*). **capital riscosa** venture capital.

capitali *vt.* capitalize.

capitalisme *n.* capitalism.

capitaliste *n.* capitalist.

capitan *n.* captain, leader.

capitol *n.* chapter.

capitolio *n.* capitol (*building*).

capo *n.* headland, cape, promontory. **Capo Verde** Cape Verde.

caporal *n.* corporal (*officer*).

capoverdean *adj.* & *n.* Cape Verdean.

capra *n.* goat (*Capra*). **Capra** *n.* Capricornus, Capricorn (*constellation*).

capreta *n.* kid (*young goat*).

capri *vi.* rear up; do a wheelie, pull a wheelie. • *n.* wheelie.

caprifolia *n.* honeysuckle (*Lonicera, Diervilla*).

caprimuljo *n.* goatsucker, nightjar, nighthawk (*Caprimulgidae*).

caprin *adj.* goatlike; capricious.

capriol *n.* roe deer (*Capreolus*). **capriol mas** roebuck.

capris *n.* caprice, whim, whimsy.

caprisal *adj.* arbitrary.

caprisia *n.* capriciousness, whimsy.

caprisosa *adj.* capricious, whimsical.

capsula *n.* capsule. **capsula de percute** percussion cap. **capsula de tempo** time capsule. **capsula spinosa** bur, burr.

capsuli *vt.* encapsulate. • *n.* encapsulation.

caputxin *n.* capuchin (*monkey: Cebus*).

caputxino *n.* cappuccino (*coffee*).

car *subord.* because, cos, as, since, for; e.g. *me surie car me es felis*. See *afin*.

cara *adj.* dear, beloved, cherished, darling, cute; expensive, costly, pricey. • *n.* dear, beloved, darling.

Cara, Mar *n.* Kara Sea.

caracal *n.* caracal (*wild cat: Caracal caracal*).

caracara *n.* caracara (*bird: Polyborinae*).

caracol *n.* snail, escargot (*Gastropoda*); at sign.

caracul *n.* karakul sheep; astrakhan (*fabric*).

caradrio *n.* plover, dotterel, killdeer (*bird: Charadrius*).

carafa *n.* jug, pitcher, carafe, decanter, flagon.

carafin *adj.* juglike, jug-shaped; akimbo.

carafon *n.* large container with spout. **carafon de acua** watering can, jerrycan. **carafon de gasolina** gasoline can, gas can, jerrycan.

carambola *n.* starfruit, carambola (*Averrhoa carambola*).

caramel *n.* caramel. **caramel de bur** butterscotch. **caramel dur** toffee. **caramel mol** fudge. **caramel tirada** taffy.

carameli *vi.* & *vt.* caramelize.

caraoce *n.* karaoke.

carate *n.* karate.

carater *n.* character (*including in fiction*), personality.

carato *n.* carat, karat.

carator *n.* karateka, karate expert.

caravan *n.* caravan (*towed vehicle, travellers*); trailer, camper.

caravela *n.* caravel (*ship*).

carbido *n.* carbide (*chemistry*).

carboidrato [karboi'drato] *n.* carbohydrate.

carbon *n.* coal. **carbon bitumosa** bituminous coal. **carbon de lenio** charcoal.

carbonato *n.* carbonate. **carbonato de calsio** calcium carbonate. **carbonato de sodio** sodium carbonate, washing soda, soda ash.

carboni *vi.* & *vt.* carbonize, char.

carboniferosa *adj.* & *n.* Carboniferous (*geology*).

carbonil *n.* carbonyl (*chemistry*).

carbono *n.* carbon.

carbosil *n.* carboxyl (*chemistry*).

carbura *vt.* carburate. • *n.* carburation.

carburador *n.* carburettor (US carburetor).

carburante *adj.* carburating. • *n.* fuel (*for engine*).

cardamom *n.* cardamom (*plant, spice: Amomum, Elettaria*).
cardan *n.* gimbal, universal joint.
cardeta *n.* goldfinch (*bird: Carduelis*).
-cardia *n.suff.* -cardia (*heart*).
cardial *adj.* cardiac.
cardigan *n.* cardigan.
cardinal *n.* cardinal (*church, bird: Cardinalis*).
cardio[1] *n.* cockle (*Cardiidae*).
cardio-[2] *pref.* cardio- (*heart*).
cardiograf *n.* cardiograph.
cardiografia *n.* cardiography.
cardiogram *n.* cardiogram.
cardiolojia *n.* cardiology.
cardiolojial *adj.* cardiological.
cardiolojiste *n.* cardiologist.
cardiomiopatia *n.* cardiomyopathy.
cardiomiopatica *adj.* cardiomyopathic.
cardionosiva *adj.* cardiotoxic.
cardiopatia *n.* cardiopathy.
cardiopatica *adj.* cardiopathic.
cardiopulmonal *adj.* cardiopulmonary.
cardiotonica *adj.* cardiotonic.
cardiovascular *adj.* cardiovascular.
cardo *n.* thistle (*Cynareae*).
caren *adj.* & *n.* Karen (*person, language*).
carera *n.* career, calling, occupation, job, profession, vocation, métier.
careral *adj.* career-related.
careria *n.* carriage house.
careror *n.* career man, career woman.
caresa *vt.* caress, stroke, fondle, pet.
careta *n.* cart, handcart, pushcart, trolley, barrow. **careta de bebe** stroller, buggy, pushchair. **careta de compra** shopping cart, shopping trolley. **careta de jardin** wheelbarrow, barrow.
carga *vt.* load, stow, ship; upload; charge (*electrically*); burden, afflict, subject, encumber, foist. • *n.* load, burden, cargo, freight, shipment; upload; charge (*electric*). **carga de labora** workload. **carga profitosa** payload. **cargas** cargo items.
cargada *adj.* loaded, charged. **plen cargada** fully loaded, fully charged.
cargador *n.* charger; magazine (*gun*).
cargosa *adj.* burdensome.
cari[1] *n.* curry.
cari[2] *vi.* become endeared. • *vt.* endear.
cariatide *n.* caryatid.
caribe *adj.* Carib; Caribbean. • *n.* Carib (*language, people*). **Caribe** *n.* Caribbean. **Isolas Caribe** Caribbean Islands. **Mar Caribe** Caribbean Sea.
carilion *n.* carillon (*music*).
carioca *n.* carioca (*dance*).
cariofilo *n.* carnation (*Dianthus caryophyllus*).
carisma *n.* charisma, mystique.
carismal *adj.* charismatic (*religion*).
carismosa *adj.* charismatic (*showing charisma*).
carita *n.* alms, almsgiving, charity, handout.
carital *adj.* charitable, charity.
carlino *n.* pug (*dog*).
carma *n.* karma.
carmesi *adj.* & *n.* crimson.
carnaval *n.* carnival, festival, fiesta.
carnavalor *n.* carnival worker, carny.
carne *n.* flesh, meat. **carne axida a picos** minced meat. **carne de avia** fowl, poultry (*meat*). **carne de bove** beef. **carne de boveta** veal. **carne de gal** chicken (*meat*). **carne de ovea** mutton. **carne de oveta** lamb (*meat*). **carne de peto** breast, brisket. **carne de porco** ham, pork. **carne de servo** venison. **carne fumida** smoked meat, cured meat. **carne moleda** ground meat. **carne per canones** cannon fodder (*soldiers*). **carne salosa** salted meat, cured meat. **carne secida** dried meat, cured meat, jerky. **carne xasada** game (*meat*).
carneria *n.* butcher's shop.
carni *vt.* flesh out, put flesh on.
carnivor *adj.* carnivorous. • *n.* carnivore.
carnor *n.* butcher. **carnor de avia** poulterer.
carnosa *adj.* fleshy, meaty, beefy.
caro *n.* coach, carriage, buggy, wagon, trolley, cart; carriage (*typewriter*). **caro de bebe** baby carriage, pram. **caro de bove** oxcart. **caro de canon** gun carriage. **caro de carnaval** carnival float. **caro de feno** haycart, haywagon, haywain. **caro de gera** chariot. **caro de golf** golf cart, golf buggy. **caro de parade** parade float. **caro lejera** cabriolet, cab (*two-wheeled carriage*). **caro per du** surrey.
caroba *n.* carob (*bean, powder*).
carobo *n.* carob (*plant: Ceratonia siliqua*).
Carolina *n.* Carolina. **Carolina Norde** North Carolina (*US state*). **Carolina Sude** South Carolina (*US state*).
caron[1] *n.* caron, haček, wedge (*diacritic*).
caron[2] *n.* carriage, coach (*for royalty, weddings, etc.*).
caronia *n.* carrion.
caror *n.* coachman, carriage driver; charioteer. **Caror** *n.* Auriga (*constellation*).
carota *n.* carrot (*plant, root: Daucus carota*).
carotide *adj.* carotid.
carpa *n.* carp (*Cyprininae*).
carpal *adj.* carpal (*anatomy*).
carpel *n.* carpel (*botany*).
carpenta *vt.* carpenter. • *n.* carpentry, woodwork, woodworking, joinery.
Carpentaria, Golfo *n.* Gulf of Carpentaria.

carpentor *n.* carpenter, woodworker, joiner (*furniture, doors*). **carpentor de teto** joiner (*roofs*).
carpino *n.* hornbeam (*tree*).
carpo *n.* carpus (*anatomy*).
carsinojen *adj.* carcinogenic. • *n.* carcinogen.
carsinojenese *n.* carcinogenesis.
carsinoma *n.* carcinoma.
carta *n.* card. **a la carta** à la carte (*menu*). **carta blanca** carte blanche. **carta de banca** bank card. **carta de credito** credit card. **carta de identia** identity card, ID card. **carta de jua** playing card. **carta de memoria** memory card. **carta de oras** timetable; timecard, timesheet. **carta de puntos** scorecard, scoreboard. **carta de telefon** phone card. **carta de Valentin** valentine. **carta madral** motherboard (*computer*). **carta otometrial** eye chart. **carta postal** postcard.
Cartago *n.* Carthage.
cartamo *n.* safflower (*Carthamus tinctorius*).
cartel *n.* cartel.
cartesian *adj.* Cartesian.
cartesianisme *n.* Cartesianism.
cartilaje *n.* cartilage, gristle.
cartilajosa *adj.* cartilaginous, gristly.
cartin *adj.* cardlike.
cartografia *n.* cartography, mapmaking.
cartografial *adj.* cartographic, cartographical.
cartografiste *n.* cartographer, mapmaker.
carton *n.* cardboard, posterboard; placard. **carton ondin** corrugated cardboard.
cartuli *adj.* & *n.* Georgian (*person, language*). See *Sacartvelo*.
cartun *n.* caricature, cartoon (*still*). **banda de cartunes** comic strip, cartoon strip. **cartunes** comics.
cartuniste *n.* cartoonist; comics artist.
cartusia *n.* charterhouse, Carthusian monastery.
cartusian *adj.* & *n.* Carthusian (*monk*).
cartux *n.* shell (*ammunition*); cartridge, casing; cartouche.
caruncula *n.* caruncle, wattle, dewlap; jowl.
carusel *n.* merry-go-round, roundabout, carousel (*entertainment, conveyor belt*).
carvi *n.* caraway (*plant: Carum carvi*).
casa *n.* house, home, household, menage. **a casa** at home; homeward, homewards, home. **a casa de** in the house of, at the home of. **casa campanian** country house, villa. **casa de avia** nest box, birdhouse. **casa de can** kennel, doghouse. **casa de club** clubhouse. **casa de cultiveria** farmhouse. **casa de eglesor** parsonage. **casa de estate** summerhouse. **casa de gales** henhouse. **casa de garda** guardhouse, gatehouse. **casa de jua** playhouse, Wendy house. **casa de publici** publishing house, press. **casa de site** townhouse. **casa flotante** houseboat. **casa longa** longhouse. **casa misera** hovel, slum. **casa movable** mobile home. **casa sur palos** pile dwelling, house on stilts. **en casa** indoor; indoors. **estra casa** outdoor; outdoors, out of doors. **sin casa** homeless.
casca *n.* skin, hull, peel (*fruit*), rind (*fruit, cheese*), pod (*seed*), shell (*egg, animal*), integument. **casca de noza** nutshell. **casca de onion** onion skin. **casca de ovo** eggshell. **sorti de casca** hatch.
cascade *vi.* cascade. • *n.* cascade, waterfall, cataract. **cascade jelada** frozen waterfall, icefall. **cascades** cascades, waterfalls, falls.
cascin *adj.* podlike, pod-shaped.
casco *n.* hull.
casena *n.* casein (*protein*).
caserna *n.* barracks.
caseta *n.* cottage.
casi *vt.* house, accommodate. **casi bon** accommodate well, fit well around. **casi tempora** lodge, billet, quarter, canton.
casia *n.* cassia (*plant: Cassia*).
casino *n.* casino.
Casiopea *n.* Cassiopeia (*mythology, constellation*).
caso *n.* case, instance, situation, circumstance, scenario; legal case, cause. **caso de ama** love affair. **caso la plu bon** best-case scenario. **caso la plu mal** worst-case scenario. **en acel caso** in that case. **en caso ce** in case, if it should happen that. **en caso de** in case of. **lo es un caso de** it's a case of, it's a matter of, it's a question of, it's to do with. **per caso** in case, just in case. **per caso ce** in case (*to guard against the possibility that*). **per caso de** in case of.
casola *n.* pot, pan. **casola de presa** pressure cooker. **casola per bulion** stock pot. **casola per sopa** soup pot.
casoleta *n.* saucepan, sauce pot.
casolon *n.* casserole. **casolon de fero** Dutch oven. **casolon per caldi** chafing dish. **casolon per rosta** roasting pan.
cason *n.* mansion. **cason de campania** country house, chateau.
caspa *n.* dandruff, dander.
caspian *adj.* Caspian.
Caspio, Mar *n.* Caspian Sea.
casta *n.* caste (*social class*).
castania *n.* chestnut (*tree, nut: Castanea*). **castania de acua** water chestnut (*Eleocharis dulcis, Trapa natans*).
castanieta *n.* castanets.

castel *n.* castle. **castel de salta** bouncy castle.
Castelia *n.* Castile (*Spanish region*).
castelian *adj.* & *n.* Castellano, Castilian (*person, language*).
castor *n.* beaver (*Castor*).
castra *vt.* castrate. • *n.* castration.
castrada *adj.* castrated. • *n.* castrato.
casual *adj.* casual, informal, nonchalant, offhand, easygoing, folksy.
casualia *n.* casualness, nonchalance.
casuari *n.* cassowary (*bird*: *Casuarius*).
casula *n.* chasuble (*garment*).
cat *n.* qat, khat (*plant, leaves*: *Catha edulis*).
cata- *pref.* cata-, kata- (*down*).
cataboli *vi.* catabolize (*biology*). • *n.* catabolism.
catacana *n.* katakana (*writing system*).
catacomba *n.* catacomb.
catal *n.* katal (*unit of catalytic activity*).
catalan *adj.* & *n.* Catalan.
catalesia *n.* catalepsy.
catalesica *adj.* cataleptic.
catalise *vt.* catalyse (US catalyze).
catalisente *adj.* catalytic. • *n.* catalyst.
catalogi *vt.* catalogue (US catalog), index.
catalogo *n.* catalogue (US catalog), index, directory.
catalogor *n.* cataloguer (US cataloger).
Catalunia *n.* Catalonia (*Spanish region*).
catamaran *n.* catamaran.
catana *n.* katana (*sword*).
cataplasma *n.* poultice.
Catar *n.* Qatar.
catarata *n.* cataract.
catari *adj.* & *n.* Qatari.
cataro *n.* common cold, catarrh, nasopharyngitis, rhinopharyngitis. **ave cataro** have a cold.
catatonia *n.* catatonia.
catatonica *adj.* catatonic.
catecisme *n.* catechism (*Christianity*).
catedral *n.* cathedral.
categori *vt.* categorize, classify. • *n.* categorization, classification.
categoria *n.* category, class. **categoria sintatical** lexical category, syntactic category, part of speech.
cateter *n.* catheter.
cateteri *vt.* catheterize. • *n.* catheterization.
cateto *n.* cathetus (*geometry*).
cation *n.* cation (*chemistry*).
Catmandu *n.* Kathmandu.
catodal *adj.* cathodic.
catodo *n.* cathode.
catolica *adj.* & *n.* Catholic, Roman Catholic.
catolicisme *n.* Catholicism, Roman Catholicism.
catran *n.* tar. **catran de tabaco** tar.
catrani *vt.* tar.
catura *vt.* capture, catch, apprehend, nab. **per catura** wanted (*criminal*).
caturada *adj.* captured, captive.
caturamosca *n.* flycatcher, chat (*Muscicapidae*).
caturamus *n.* mousetrap.
caturor *n.* captor, catcher.
cauboi *n.* cowboy (*North American*), buckaroo.
caucasian *adj.* Caucasian (*of the Caucasus*).
Caucaso *n.* Caucasus, Caucasia. **Caucasos** Caucasus Mountains. **Montes Caucaso** Caucasus Mountains.
caucasoide *adj.* Caucasoid.
cauri *n.* cowrie (*shell, mollusc*: *Cypraeidae*).
causa *vt.* cause, entrain, wreak, underlie, result in. • *n.* cause, grounds; causation. **par causa ce** because. **par causa de** because of, due to, owing to, thanks to.
causal *adj.* causal.
causalia *n.* causality.
cauta *adj.* cautious, careful, wary, prudent, heedful, conservative, circumspect.
cauterador *n.* cautery.
cauteri *vt.* cauterize. • *n.* cauterization.
cautia *n.* caution, carefulness, prudence, discretion, heedfulness.
cauxi *vt.* rubberize. • *n.* rubberization.
cauxo *n.* rubber.
cava[1] *n.* cave, grotto. **cava de bir** beer cellar, rathskeller. **cava de vino** wine cellar.
cava[2] *n.* kava (*plant*: *Piper methysticum*).
cavalal *adj.* equine.
cavaleta *n.* foal; easel, trestle, sawhorse, sawbuck; gantry; kickstand (*bicycle*). **Cavaleta** *n.* Equuleus (*constellation*).
cavalin *adj.* horselike.
cavalo *n.* horse, steed (*Equus caballus*); knight (*chess*); horsepower (*measurement*). **cavalo de corsa** racehorse. **cavalo de gera** warhorse. **cavalo-de-mar** *n.* seahorse (*Hippocampus*). **cavalo fema** mare. **cavalo mas** stallion. **cavalo osilante** rocking horse. **cavalo peti** pony.
cavalor *n.* horse rider, horseman, horsewoman, equestrian; knight, cavalryman, cavalier; knight (*tarot*). **cavalores** cavalry. **titulo de cavalor** knighthood.
cavaloral *adj.* horseriding, equestrian.
cavalori *vi.* be knighted. • *vt.* knight.
cavaloria *n.* chivalry; horsemanship.
caveta *n.* cavity, hollow, pit; socket (*joint*). **caveta nasal** nasal cavity.
cavetin *adj.* hollow.
cavia *n.* cavy, guinea pig (*Cavia, Caviinae*).
caviar *n.* caviar.
cavil *n.* peg, dowel. **cavil de rota** linchpin.
cavon *n.* cavern.
cavor *n.* caver, potholer, spelunker.

caxa *n.* box, coffer; case, casing, housing. **caxa de arena** sandbox, sandpit. **caxa de carton** cardboard box, carton. **caxa de come** lunch box. **caxa de ensofable** snuffbox. **caxa de esibi** display case, showcase, vitrine, shadow box. **caxa de fosfores** box of matches, matchbox. **caxa de junta** mitre (US miter) box. **caxa de leto** footlocker. **caxa de olio** oil pan, sump. **caxa de pan** breadbox, bread bin. **caxa de Pandora** Pandora's box. **caxa de posta** mailbox, postbox. **caxa de utiles** toolbox. **caxa rejistrante** cash register, till. **caxa secur** safe, locker, strongbox.
caxalote *n.* sperm whale (*Physeter macrocephalus*).
caxer *adj.* kosher, kasher.
caxeta *n.* drawer; cassette. **caxeta audio** audio cassette. **caxeta video** video cassette.
caxi *vt.* box, encase; embed, imbed, nest. **caxi bon** encase well, fit well around.
caxin *adj.* boxlike, boxy.
caxmir[1] *n.* cashmere.
Caxmir[2] *n.* Kashmir.
caxmiran *adj.* Kashmiri.
caxofa *n.* artichoke (*Cynara cardunculus*).
caxon *n.* chest, crate, soapbox. **caxon funeral** coffin.
caxor *n.* cashier, clerk, purser, bursar, scrivener.
cazac *adj.* & *n.* Kazakh, Kazakhstani (*person, language*).
Cazacstan *n.* Kazakhstan.
cazu [ka'zu] *n.* kazoo, mirliton (*musical instrument*).
cd *abbr.* (*disco compata*) CD.
ce *subord.* that; e.g. *me vide ce tu es triste*; *los insiste ce nos parti*.—*Ce* does not mean *what?*. Nor is it used for *which* in *the chair which broke* or *that* in *the dog that barked*. It introduces a clause that reports the content of something like a statement or thought, and it cannot be omitted.
cea *n.* kea (*bird*: *Nestor notabilis*).
cebab *n.* kebab, kabob, shish kebab.
cela *vi.* chelate (*chemistry*). • *n.* chelation.
celada *adj.* chelate. • *n.* chelate complex.
celante *adj.* chelating. • *n.* chelant, chelating agent.
celaterapia *n.* chelation, chelation therapy.
celi *n.* ceilidh (*social event*).
celpi *n.* kelpie (*mythology, dog*).
celsius *n.* Celsius, centigrade. See *grado*.
celta *adj.* Celtic. • *n.* Celtic, Celt. **Mar Celta** Celtic Sea.
celtiberian *adj.* & *n.* Celtiberian.
celvin *n.* kelvin (*unit of temperature*).
Cenia *n.* Kenya.
cenian *adj.* & *n.* Kenyan.
ceratin *n.* keratin.
ceratinosite *n.* keratocyte.
cerem *n.* chereme (*unit of sign language*).
Cerno *n.* Cornwall.
cernoica [kerno'ika] *adj.* Cornish (*person, language*).
cerosen *n.* kerosene.
cerubin *n.* cherub. **cerubines** cherubs, cherubim.
cesadilia *n.* quesadilla (*tortilla*).
ceso *n.* cheese. **ceso cremosa** cream cheese. **ceso-de-testa** *n.* headcheese, brawn (*jellied meat*). **ceso limburgan** limburger.
cetognato *n.* chaetognath (US chetognath) (*worm*: *Chaetognatha*).
cetona *n.* ketone (*chemistry*).
cetsal *n.* quetzal (*Pharomachrus, Euptilotis*).
cetxap *n.* ketchup.
cetxua *adj.* & *n.* Quechua (*person, language*).
cexa *vt.* complain, whine, kvetch, whinge, gripe, rant, carp. • *n.* complaint, rant, grievance.
cexeta *vt.* grumble.
cexor *n.* complainer, whiner, whinger, grouch.
cexosa *adj.* whiny, whiney, whingey, grouchy, querulous.
Chesapeake, Baia ['tʃesapik] *n.* Chesapeake Bay.
Chihuahua [tʃi'wawa] *n.* Chihuahua (*Mexican state*). **chihuahua** *n.* chihuahua (*dog*). **Deserto Chihuahua** Chihuahuan Desert.
ci[1] *pron.* who, whom (*interrogative, relative*); e.g. *ci es tu?*; *el ia demanda ci me ia vide*; *la om ci senta en la auto es mea avo*; *me conose la fem con ci tu ia parla*.—*Ci* is the equivalent of *cual* for referring to people, animals or personified things. **de ci ... sua** whose; e.g. *la fem de ci tu ia trova sua clave es mea fia*.
ci[2] *n.* chi (*Greek letter* Χ, χ).
cianti *n.* chianti (*wine*).
ciasma *n.* chiasma (*genetics*).
cibuts *n.* kibbutz.
Ciclades *n.pl.* Cyclades (*islands*).
cidonia *n.* quince (*Cydonia oblonga*).
cifose *n.* kyphosis (*medical*).
Ciiv *n.* Kiev.
cile *n.* chyle (*substance*).
cilia *n.* keel; carina. **Cilia** *n.* Carina (*constellation*).
Cilicia, Mar *n.* Cilician Sea.
cilo- *pref.* kilo-.
cilobait *n.* kilobyte.
cilogram *n.* kilogram.
cilolitre *n.* kilolitre (US kiloliter).

cilometre *n.* kilometre (US kilometer). **cilometres** mileage (*distance travelled*).
cilovate *n.* kilowatt.
cilovate-ora *n.* kilowatt-hour.
cilt *n.* kilt.
cimera *n.* chimera (*mythology*).
cimica *n.* chemistry. **cimica matematical** mathematical chemistry.
cimical *adj.* & *n.* chemical.
cimiciste *n.* chemist.
cimo *n.* chyme (*substance*).
cimono *n.* kimono.
cimosina *n.* rennin (*enzyme*).
cimosintesal *adj.* chemosynthetic.
cimosintese *vt.* chemosynthesis.
cimoterapia *n.* chemotherapy.
cimotrof *n.* chemotroph (*organism*).
cimotrofia *adj.* chemotrophic. • *n.* chemotrophia.
Cimri *n.* Wales.
cimrica *adj.* & *n.* Welsh (*person, language*).
cincaju *n.* kinkajou (*animal: Potos flavus*).
cinesiolojia *n.* kinesiology.
cinesiolojiste *n.* kinesiologist.
cinestesia *n.* kinaesthesia (US kinesthesia).
cinestesica *adj.* kinaesthetic (US kinesthetic).
cinetica *adj.* kinetic.
cinina *n.* quinine.
cinorinco *n.* kinorhynch (*organism: Kinorhyncha*).
cinua *n.* quinoa (*Chenopodium quinoa*).
cionis *n.* sheathbill (*bird: Chionis*).
ciosco *n.* kiosk, booth, stand, stall. **ciosco de bande** bandstand. **ciosco de peaje** tollbooth. **ciosco de polisia** police box. **ciosco de telefon** telephone booth, telephone box, phone box. **ciosco de vota** voting booth, polling booth.
cipa *n.* skull cap, kipa, kippah, yarmulke, zucchetto, taqiyah, topi, kufi, beanie.
ciprica *adj.* & *n.* Cypriot.
Cipros *n.* Cyprus.
ciptxac *adj.* & *n.* Kipchak (*person, language*).
cipu *n.* quipu (*Inca device*).
Cirgistan *n.* Kyrgyzstan.
cirgiz *adj.* & *n.* Kyrgyz, Kyrgyzstani (*person, language*).
Ciribas *n.* Kiribati. **ciribas** *adj.* & *n.* Kiribati.
cirilica *adj.* & *n.* Cyrillic.
ciromansia *n.* chiromancy, palmistry, palm reading.
ciroperatica *n.* chiropractic, chiropraxis.
ciropraticor *n.* chiropractor.
cirotero *n.* bat (*animal: Chiroptera*).
cisa *adv.* maybe, perhaps, possibly.
citian *adj.* & *n.* Kittian. See *San Kitts*.
citina *n.* chitin (*substance*).
citinosa *adj.* chitinous.
citon *n.* chiton (*garment*).
ciui[1] *n.* kiwi (*bird: Apteryx*).
ciui[2] *n.* kiwi fruit, Chinese gooseberry (*plant, fruit: Actinidia chinensis*).
cix *n.* quiche.
clac-clac *interj.* tap-tap, knock-knock.
clace *vi.* & *n.* clack, clatter; tap dance.
claceta *n.* clapperboard.
clacor *n.* tap dancer.
clado *n.* clade (*biology*).
clama *vt.* call, summon, summons, invoke, draft.—When *call* means *name*, it can be clearer to use *nomi*. • *n.* call, summons, invocation. **clama a servi militar** *v.* & *n.* draft, call to military service. **clama de avia** birdcall. **clama de nomes** roll call. **clama dulse** whinny.
clamada *adj.* called, summoned, invoked. • *n.* callee, draftee.
clan *n.* clan.
claneta *n.* subclan, sept.
clar *adj.* clear, unblocked, unstained; transparent, see-through, limpid, pellucid; plain (*to see or understand*), explicit, lucid, perspicuous; blatant. • *adv.* clearly, explicitly; by far, far and away, easily. **es clar** be clear, stand out clearly.
clarestorio *n.* clerestory (*architecture*).
clari *vi.* become clear. • *vt.* clarify, elucidate, enunciate. • *n.* clarification.
claria *n.* clarity, transparency, lucidity, perspicuity.
clarida *adj.* clarified.
clarineta *n.* clarinet.
clarinetiste *n.* clarinettist (US clarinetist).
claron *n.* clarion (*trumpet*).
claroscur *n.* chiaroscuro.
clarvide *vt.* be clairvoyant, see the future. • *n.* clairvoyance.
clarvidente *adj.* clairvoyant, prescient. • *n.* clairvoyant, fortuneteller.
clase *n.* class. **clase alta** upper class, gentry. **clase basa** lower class. **clase de turiste** tourist class, economy class. **clase media** middle class. **de clase alta** upper-class, posh. **de clase basa** lower-class, plebeian. **de clase media** middle-class.
clasi *vt.* classify. • *n.* classification.
clasica *adj.* classic, classical. • *n.* classic.
clasicisme *n.* classicism.
clasisme *n.* classism.
clasiste *adj.* snobbish, snobby, snooty, class-conscious. • *n.* snob.
claustrofobia *n.* claustrophobia.
claustrofobica *adj.* claustrophobic. • *n.* claustrophobe.
clave *n.* key (*lock*); wrench, spanner; password. **clave ajustable** adjustable wrench.

clave alta treble clef. **clave basa** bass clef. **clave de arco** keystone. **clave de musica** clef. **clave engles** monkey wrench. **clave exagon** Allen key, Allen wrench. **clave restrinjeda** passkey. **clave xef** master key, passkey.
clavesimbal *n.* harpsichord.
clavesimbaliste *n.* harpsichordist.
clavi *vt.* lock. **clavi de braso** armlock. **clavi de testa** headlock.
clavicordio *n.* clavichord.
clavicula *n.* clavicle, collarbone.
clavor *n.* locksmith, keymaker.
claxon *n.* klaxon, horn, hooter.
claxoni *vt.* honk, hoot, sound one's horn; guffaw.
clematis *n.* clematis (*Clematis*).
cleptocrata *n.* cleptocrat, kleptocrat.
cleptocratia *n.* cleptocracy, kleptocracy.
cleptomania *n.* kleptomania.
cleptomanica *adj.* & *n.* kleptomaniac.
clica *vi.* click; rattle; chatter (*teeth*). • *vt.* click (*mouse, link*). • *n.* click; rattle; chatter. **clica destra** *v.* & *n.* right click (*mouse*). **clica duple** *v.* & *n.* double click. **clica media** *v.* & *n.* middle click. **clica simple** *v.* & *n.* single click. **clica sinistra** *v.* & *n.* left click. **clica truple** *v.* & *n.* triple click.
clicador *n.* rattle (*toy, device*).
cliceta *n.* ratchet.
cliente *n.* client, customer. **clientes** customers, clientele.
clima *n.* climate, weather, clime.
climal *adj.* climatic.
climatolojia *n.* climatology.
clina *n.* cline (*biology*).
clinica *n.* clinic, dispensary.
clinical *adj.* clinical.
clip *n.* clip (*audio, video, fastener*); paper clip. **de clip** clip-on.
clipi *vt.* clip, clip on.
clitico *n.* clitic.
clito *n.* (*colloquial*) clit (*clitoris*).
clitorectomia *n.* clitorectomy, clitoridectomy (*surgery*).
clitoris *n.* clitoris.
clitorisal *adj.* clitoral.
clixe *adj.* clichéd, hackneyed. • *n.* cliché, platitude.
clo *n.* nail.
cloaca *n.* drain, sewer; cloaca (*anatomy*).
cloador *n.* nail gun.
cloeta *n.* tack.
cloi [ˈkloi] *vt.* nail.
clone *vt.* clone. • *n.* cloning (*action*); clone (*product*).
clorantasea *n.* chloranthaceae (*Chloranthaceae*).
clori *vt.* chlorinate. • *n.* chlorination.
clorido *n.* chloride. **clorido de polivinil** polyvinyl chloride, PVC.
cloro[1] *n.* chlorine.
cloro-[2] *pref.* chloro-.
clorofila *n.* chlorophyll.
clorofluorocarbono *n.* chlorofluorocarbon.
clorofonia *n.* chlorophonia (*Chlorophonia*).
cloroformo *n.* chloroform.
cloroplasto *n.* chloroplast.
clorose *n.* chlorosis, blight.
clox *n.* cloche (*hat*).
cluable *adj.* shuttable, fastenable.
cluador *n.* shutter (*camera*).
club *n.* club.
clubor *n.* club member.
clui *vi.* & *vt.* close, shut; turn off, switch off (*tap, power*). • *n.* closure, shutoff. **clui la boca** shut up.
cluida *adj.* closed; shut.
cluisita *n.* closing quotation mark, unquote.
clusa *n.* lock (*waterway*). **clusa de aira** airlock.
cmer *adj.* & *n.* Khmer (*person, language*).
cnidario *n.* coelenterate (*organism: Cnidaria*).
co- *pref.* co- (*with, together*).
coabita *vi.* cohabit. • *n.* cohabitation.
coabitor *n.* cohabiter, cohabitant, housemate, flatmate, roommate.
coagula *vi.* coagulate; clot, clot up (*blood*). • *n.* coagulation, concretion.
coala *n.* koala (*Phascolarctos cinereus*).
coan *n.* koan (*Zen*).
coarde *adj.* cowardly, gutless; wimpy, spineless. • *n.* coward; wimp.
coardia *n.* cowardice.
coasal *adj.* coaxial.
coautor *n.* coauthor.
coaveni *vi.* coincide. • *n.* coincidence. **coaveni partal** overlap. **par coaveni** coincidentally, by coincidence.
coaveninte *adj.* coincidental. • *adv.* coincidentally, by coincidence.
cobalto *n.* cobalt.
cobra *n.* cobra (members of *Elapidae*, esp. the genus *Naja*).
coc *n.* coke (*fuel*).
coca *n.* coca (*plant: Erythroxylaceae*).
cocaina *n.* cocaine.
coc-coc-coc *interj.* cluck.
coce *vi.* cook. • *vt.* cook; fire (*pottery*). **coce lenta** *vi.* & *vt.* stew, braise. **coce su sielo** cookout. **coce tro multe** overcook, overdo. **coce tro poca** undercook.
coceda *adj.* cooked; fired. **lenta coceda** stewed, braised. **tro poca coceda** undercooked, underdone.
coclea *n.* cochlea.
cocleal *adj.* cochlear.

cocni *adj.* & *n.* cockney.
coco *n.* coconut (*plant, fruit*: *Cocos nucifera*).
cocon *n.* cocoon.
coconspiror *n.* co-conspirator, fellow schemer.
coctel *n.* cocktail.
coda *n.* tail; coda; ending (*grammar*). **coda anelida** ringtail. **coda de camisa** shirt-tail. **coda de cavalo** horse's tail; ponytail (*hairstyle*).
codal *adj.* caudal (*towards the tail*); trailing, closing.
codeina *n.* codeine.
codetas *n.pl.* bunches, pigtails (*unplaited*).
codi *vt.* betail, add a tail to.
codida *adj.* caudate, tailed.
codigi *vt.* code, encode, codify. • *n.* encoding (*action*).
codigida *adj.* coded. **codigida par color** colour-coded (US color-coded). **permanente codigida** hard-coded.
codigo *n.* code (*laws*, *software*), encoding. **codigo de baras** bar code. **codigo de Morse** Morse code. **codigo fisical de sinias** character encoding (*e.g.* *UTF-8*). **codigo numeral de sinias** character code (*numeric representation of characters*).
codo *n.* elbow; cubit.
codon *n.* codon (*genetics*).
coecipor *n.* teammate.
coedal *adj.* of the same age, peer. • *n.* peer.
coedita *vt.* coedit.
coeditor *n.* coeditor.
coeduca *vt.* coeducate. • *n.* coeducation.
coemprende *n.* joint venture.
coencargada *adj.* collegial, with shared responsibility.
coere *vi.* cohere, stick together. • *n.* coherence, cohesion, consistency.
coerente *adj.* coherent, cohesive, consistent, regular, rational.
coesiste *vi.* coexist. • *n.* coexistence.
cognisial *adj.* cognitive.
cognisio *n.* cognition.
coicoi *adj.* & *n.* Khoikhoi, Khoi, Hottentot (*person*, *language*).
coion *n.* (*colloquial*) ball, nut, bollock (*testicle*).
coiote *n.* coyote (*Canis latrans*).
coipu *n.* coypu, nutria, river rat (*Myocastor coypus*).
coisan *adj.* & *n.* Khoisan (*person*, *language*).
col[1] *n.* cabbage (*plant*, *leaves*: *Brassica oleracea*). **col de Bruxelles** [bruˈʃeles] Brussels sprout. **col risa** kale. **folia de col** collard greens, borekale.
col[2] *n.* kohl (*cosmetic*).
cola[1] *n.* glue, paste.
cola[2] *n.* cola, kola (*plant*, *nut*, *drink*: *Cola*).
Cola, Penisola *n.* Kola Peninsula.
colabora *vi.* collaborate, cooperate, liaise. • *n.* collaboration, cooperation.
colaborante *adj.* collaborating, collaborative.
colaboror *n.* collaborator, colleague, co-worker, fellow worker.
coladal *adj.* collateral.
colajen *n.* collagen.
colal *adj.* cervical.
colar *n.* collar. **colar aletin** wing collar. **colar enrolada** turtleneck. **colar fronsosa** ruff. **colar ronda** round neck, crewneck. **sin colar** collarless.
colareta *n.* necklace.
colasa *vi.* & *n.* collapse, slump, flop.
colasable *adj.* collapsible.
colbasa *n.* kielbasa, kubasa, kolbassa (*sausage*).
coleo *n.* coleus (*plant*: *Solenostemon*).
coler *adj.* angry, mad, irate, indignant. • *n.* hothead, spitfire.
colera *n.* cholera.
coleri *vi.* turn angry, rage. • *vt.* anger, madden, outrage, enrage.
coleria *n.* anger, wrath, ire, rage, outrage, indignation.
coleriosa *adj.* full of anger, enraged, wrathful, aggressive.
colesterol *n.* cholesterol.
coletiva *adj.* mass, collective, bulk. • *n.* collective (*farm*, *factory*).
coletivisme *n.* collectivism.
coletiviste *adj.* & *n.* collectivist.
coli[1] *n.* collie (*dog*).
coli[2] *vt.* glue, paste.
colibri *n.* hummingbird (*Trochilidae*).
colico *n.* colic (*medical*).
colidador *n.* collider.
colide *vi.* collide, crash. • *n.* collision, crash. **colide multiple** multiple collision, pile-up.
colie *vt.* collect, gather, accumulate; pick, garner. • *n.* collection, set, accumulation, repertoire, repertory; medley, omnibus. **colie caxida** box set. **colie de armas** arsenal. **colie de filos** strand (*threads or wires*). **colie de presentas** repertory, repertoire. **colie de selos** stamp collecting; stamp collection. **colie de sinias** character set, character repertoire (*e.g. Unicode*). **colie de tambures** drum kit. **colie grande** large collection, panoply. **colie la resta** glean (*harvest*). **colie miscada** assortment, miscellany, hotchpotch, hodgepodge.
coliebal *n.* ballboy, ballgirl.
coliflor *n.* cauliflower (*plant*, *vegetable*: *Brassica oleracea*).
colina[1] *n.* hill, butte, mesa.

colina[2] *n.* choline (*substance*).
colinabo *n.* swede, rutabaga (*plant, vegetable*: *Brassica napobrassica*).
colinerjica *n.* cholinergic.
colineta *n.* hillock, mound, bank, hummock, knoll; tumulus, barrow.
colino *n.* bobwhite (*bird*: *Colinus*).
colinosa *adj.* hilly.
colio *n.* mousebird (*Coliidae*).
collor *n.* collector. **collor de selos** stamp collector.
colirabano *n.* kohlrabi (*plant, vegetable*: *Brassica oleracea*).
colite *n.* colitis (*medical*).
colo *n.* neck. **colo de botela** bottleneck. **colo de monte** mountain pass. **colo de utero** cervix.
colobo *n.* colobus (*monkey*: *Colobus, Procolobus*).
colocolo *n.* colocolo (*wild cat*: *Leopardus colocolo*).
colofon *n.* colophon (*publishing*).
coloide *adj.* colloidal. • *n.* colloid.
Colombia *n.* Colombia.
colombian *adj.* & *n.* Colombian.
colombina *n.* aquilegia, columbine (*plant*: *Aquilegia*).
colon *n.* colon. **colon iritable** irritable bowel.
colona *n.* column, pillar; column (*text*); file (*chess*). **colona de leto** bedpost. **colona sinco** fifth column.
colonal *adj.* colonic.
coloni *vt.* colonize, settle. • *n.* colonization, settlement.
colonia *n.* colony, plantation (*colony*), settlement; rookery.
colonial *adj.* colonial.
colonialisme *n.* colonialism.
colonialiste *adj.* colonialistic. • *n.* colonialist.
colonin *adj.* columnlike.
coloniste *n.* colonist, colonial, settler. **coloniste prima** pioneer.
color *n.* colour (US color), complexion. **sin color** colourless (US colorless).
Colorado *n.* Colorado (*US state*). **Rio Colorado** Colorado River.
colori *vt.* colour (US color).
colorida *adj.* colour (US color).
coloroja *adj.* (*derogatory*) redneck.
colorosa *adj.* colourful (US colorful), technicolor, colour (US color).
coloseo *n.* colosseum, coliseum.
colostomia *n.* colostomy.
colostro *n.* colostrum (*biology*).
colpa *vt.* hit, strike, knock, blow, bump, jolt, impact, butt, whack, bonk, thump, pelt, smite, bat, blast. • *n.* hit, strike, stroke, knock, jab, blast, blow, bump, jolt, impact, bonk, thump, thud; coup. **colpa a lado** sideswipe. **colpa a supra** uppercut. **colpa a tera** knock down, knock over, fell. **colpa con dito** *v.* & *n.* flick. **colpa con palma** *v.* & *n.* slap, smack, spank. **colpa con pede** *v.* & *n.* kick. **colpa con testa** *v.* headbutt; head (*football*). • *n.* headbutt; header (*football*). **colpa de cavalo** unhorse, unseat. **colpa de mori** death blow, coup de grâce. **colpa de palacio** palace coup. **colpa de stato** coup d'état, coup. **colpa de tona** thunderclap. **colpa forte** hard blow, wallop, whack, wham, crackdown, haymaker. **colpa metalin** metallic thud, clunk. **colpa sever** severe blow, crackdown. **colpa xef** main blow, brunt. **no colpa** miss (*target*). **par sola un colpa** in one fell swoop.
colpador *n.* blaster (*weapon*).
colpamosca *n.* flyswatter, flyswat.
colpeta *vt.* pat, dab, daub; flick; putt (*golf*). • *n.* pat, light blow; flick.
colpetador *n.* putter (*golf club*).
colposcopi *n.* colposcopy.
colposcopio *n.* colposcope.
colugo *n.* colugo, cobego, flying lemur (*Dermoptera*).
Columbia Brites *n.* British Columbia.
colxa *vt.* quilt.
colza *n.* rape, cole, colza (*plant*: *Brassica napus*); rapeseed; rape oil, rapeseed oil, canola.
com- *pref.* com- (*with, together*).
coma *n.* coma.
comable *adj.* edible. • *n.* food, foodstuff.
comadre *n.* midwife.
comadria *n.* midwifery.
comanda *vt.* command, order, dictate, ordain; order (*food, goods*); e.g. *comanda alga cosa a/de algun*; *comanda ce algun fa alga cosa*. • *n.* command, order, directive, decree, fiat, commission, warrant, writ, behest. **comanda per apare** *v.* & *n.* summons, subpoena. **comanda temprana** *v.* & *n.* preorder. **par comanda** custom, custom-made, bespoke, custom-order, special-order, customized, on demand, tailored, tailor-made.
comandante *adj.* commanding, imperative, peremptory. • *n.* imperative.
comando *n.* commando.
comandor *n.* commander, commandant, commodore. **comandor militar** military commander, warlord.
combate *vt.* fight, combat, brawl. • *n.* fight, combat, brawl, bout. **combate airal** aerial combat, dogfight. **combate de bove** bullfight. **combate de gales** cockfight. **combate prosima** hand-to-hand combat.

combator *n.* fighter, combatant. **combator de bove** bullfighter.
combatosa *adj.* combative, aggressive, militant.
combatosia *n.* aggression.
combina *vi.* combine, amalgamate, aggregate, concoct; consolidate. • *n.* combination, combo, amalgam, amalgamation, aggregate, concoction; consolidation.
combinatoria *n.* combinatorics.
combusta *vi.* combust. • *n.* combustion.
combustable *adj.* combustible. • *n.* combustible, fuel. **combustable de fosil** fossil fuel.
combustablia *n.* combustibility.
come *vt.* eat, dine, ingest, sup. • *n.* meal, dinner, supper, repast. **come con sua oios** ogle, leer at. **come de matina** breakfast. **come de matina tarda** brunch. **come de negosia** business lunch. **come de sera** supper, dinner, evening meal. **come en un restorante** eat out. **come media** lunch, luncheon. **come retirable** takeaway, takeout. **come tro multe** eat too much, overeat. **con du comes** half-board (*hotel*). **con tre comes** full-board (*hotel*). **de come** prandial. **pos come** postprandial.
comeda *n.* food, grub, nosh, victual. **comeda de bestias** fodder. **comeda de mar** seafood. **comeda favoreda** favourite (US favorite) food, delicacy. **comeda fibrosa** roughage. **comeda major** staple (*food*). **comeda rapida** fast food. **comeda sin nuri** junk food. **comedas** groceries.
comederia *n.* grocery, grocery store, supermarket.
comedia *n.* comedy, romp. **comedia de situas** situation comedy, sitcom.
comedial *adj.* comic, comedic, humorous.
comediste *n.* comedian.
comedor *n.* grocer.
comefoco *n.* fire eater.
comensa *vi.* commence, begin, start; set off (*on journey*); kick off; proceed with; e.g. *la corsa comensa.* • *vt.* commence, begin, start, take up; establish, set up; e.g. *on comensa dansa*; *nos comensa la viaja.* • *n.* commencement, beginning, start, inception, onset, novitiate; preliminary (*attempt, round of competition*); kickoff, faceoff (*sport*). **a la comensa de** at the beginning of, early in. **comensa en via** set off. **comensa riscosa** risky start, gambit. **de comensa** preliminary.
comensada *adj.* begun, started, underway.
comensal *adj.* initial.
comensante *adj.* beginning, starting, incipient, setting off, afoot. **comensante de** starting from, leaving from.
comensor *n.* beginner, novice, novitiate, neophyte, rookie, newbie, noob, newcomer, plebe, tenderfoot. **comensor egosa** upstart. **per comensores** for beginners, entry-level.
comenta *vt.* comment, remark, observe, commentate. • *n.* comment, remark. **comenta astuta** witticism. **comentas** comments, commentary; feedback.
comentor *n.* commentator, commentor. **comentor de sporte** sports commentator, sportscaster.
comeria *n.* eatery, fast-food restaurant, canteen, lunchroom.
comersia *vt.* trade, do business. • *n.* trade, commerce, business. **comersia frodante** racket, racketeering.
comersial *adj.* commercial, business, enterprise, mercantile.
comersiali *vi.* commercialize; go to market. • *vt.* commercialize; put on the market. • *n.* commercialization.
comersin *adj.* businesslike.
comersior *n.* businessperson, businessman, businesswoman. **comersior nononesta** wheeler-dealer.
comespada *n.* sword swallower.
cometa[1] *n.* comet (*astronomy*); kite (*toy*).
cometa[2] *vt.* snack. • *n.* snack, refreshment.
comforta *vt.* comfort, make comfortable. • *n.* comfort.
comfortada *adj.* comforted. **es comfortada par** be comforted by, take comfort in.
comfortante *adj.* comforting, pleasant.
comfortosa *adj.* comfortable, comfy.
comica *adj.* comical, funny, humorous, risible, wacky, zany.
comision *n.* commission (*committee, payment*).
comisionor *n.* commissioner.
comite *n.* board, committee; panel (*experts*). **comite de vila** town council. **comite dirijente** board (*trustees*). **comite local** local council.
comiteria *n.* board room, committee room.
comitor *n.* committee member, commissioner.
como *adv.* (*interrogative*) how; e.g. *como on abri esta caxa?* • *interj.* what, huh, eh? (*confusion*). • *subord.* as, like, in the way that; e.g. *acel es como on debe condui*; *salta tan alta como tu pote.* • *prep.* like, similarly to, qua; e.g. *el rie como un iena*; *tan alta como me.* **como si** as if, as though, like. **no como** *prep.* unlike. • *subord.* unlike how.
comoda *n.* chest of drawers, dresser. **comoda de cosina** sideboard (*displaying or storing dishes*).
comodeta *n.* nightstand, bedside table.

comodo *n.* Komodo dragon, Komodo monitor (*lizard*: *Varanus komodoensis*).
comor *n.* eater, diner.
comorbosa *adj.* comorbid (*medical*).
Comori *n.* Comoros. **comori** *adj.* & *n.* Comorian.
comosa *adj.* comatose.
compania *n.* company, firm, business; troupe. **compania asecurinte** underwriter. **compania nova** startup.
compara *vt.* compare, liken; e.g. *compara custas*; *compara la filma con la libro*; *compara vives a naras*. • *n.* comparison; simile. **compara con realia** *v.* compare with reality. • *n.* reality check. **sin compara** incomparable.
comparable *adj.* comparable.
comparada *adj.* comparative. • *adv.* comparatively.
comparativa *adj.* & *n.* comparative.
comparte *n.* compartment; cubbyhole, pigeonhole.
comparti[1] *vt.* share, have in common; share out, distribute. • *n.* share, portion, serving, helping (*food*). **comparti de fixes** file sharing. **comparti un leto** share a bed, be bedfellows.
comparti[2] *vt.* compartmentalize. • *n.* compartmentalization.
compartida *adj.* shared, common. • *adv.* in common.
compartidia *n.* sharedness, commonality.
compas *n.* compass (*for drawing circles*). **Compas** *n.* Circinus (*constellation*).
compata *adj.* compact.
compatador *n.* compactor, steamroller.
compati *vi.* & *vt.* compact, compress.
compatia *vt.* pity, feel sorry for, feel compassion for, sympathize with, commiserate with. • *n.* pity, compassion, kindness, consideration, sympathy, condolence, heartstrings, pathos. **sin compatia** pitiless, merciless, inhumane, cut-throat.
compatiable *adj.* pitiable, worthy of compassion.
compatiosa *adj.* compassionate, humane, kind, kind-hearted, soft-hearted, warm-hearted, considerate, tender, sympathetic, selfless.
compendio *n.* compendium. **compendio de bestias** bestiary.
compensa *vt.* compensate, make amends for. • *n.* compensation, damages, indemnity, reparation, restitution. **compensa tro multe** overcompensate.
compete *vi.* compete, contest, strive, vie. • *n.* competition (*action*), contest, rivalry, fray.
competor *n.* competitor, contestant, contender, rival. **competor favoreda** frontrunner.
competosa *adj.* competitive.
compila *vt.* compile.
compilador *n.* compiler (*software*).
compilor *n.* compiler (*person*).
compleso *n.* complex; compound, plant, facility, campus; complex (*psychological*). **compleso de casas** housing estate. **compleso de datos** data centre (US center).
completa *adj.* complete, comprehensive, exhaustive, thorough, utter, outright, plenary. • *adv.* completely, comprehensively, exhaustively, thoroughly, utterly, altogether. • *n.* whole; suit, outfit (*clothes*). **completa con pantalon** pantsuit, trouser suit. **completa de negosia** business suit. **completa de sera** evening suit, black tie. **completa de sporte** tracksuit.
completi *vi.* (*become*) complete. • *vt.* complete, finalize, fulfil (US fulfill), complement, consummate; fill in, fill out (*form*). • *n.* completion, fulfilment (US fulfillment). **completi la testo** fill in the blank. **completi un negosia** cut a deal.
completia *n.* completeness.
completinte *adj.* completing, fulfilling, complementary, supplementary. • *n.* complement.
complica *vt.* complicate. • *n.* complication, complexity, intricacy.
complicada *adj.* complicated, complex, intricate, involute.
composa *vt.* compose. • *n.* composition, makeup.
composada *adj.* composed, compound, composite. • *n.* compound; montage. **composada de** composed of, consisting of, comprising. **es composada de** be composed of, consist of, comprise.
composante *adj.* & *n.* component, constituent. **composante major** key component.
composor *n.* composer.
compra *vt.* buy, purchase, shop. • *n.* purchase (*action*). **compra manica** shopping spree. **pote compra** afford (*to buy*).
comprada *n.* purchase (*object*).
compramania *n.* spending spree, splurge.
compramanica *n.* spendthrift.
comprendable *adj.* understandable, intelligible, comprehensible.
comprende *vt.* understand, comprehend. • *n.* understanding, interpretation, comprehension, insight.
compresa *vt.* compress; pressurize. • *n.* compression; pressurization.
compromete *vi.* compromise, make concessions, accommodate. • *n.* compromise, concession, trade-off.
compror *n.* buyer, purchaser, shopper.

compulsa *vt.* compel. • *n.* compulsion.

computa *vt.* compute. • *n.* computation, computing. **computa distribuida** grid computing.

computador *n.* computer; central processing unit, CPU. **computador de mano** handheld computer. **computador de table** desktop computer. **computador personal** personal computer. **computador portable** laptop, portable computer. **computador portable peti** netbook. **computador sentral** mainframe computer. **computador tabletin** tablet computer.

comun *adj.* common, general, ordinary, plain, banal, prevalent, mundane, commonplace; frequent, rife; shared, in common. • *adv.* commonly, generally, widely; often, oftentimes, frequently; in common.

comunia *n.* commonness, ordinariness, prevalence, commonality; community, commonwealth; communion. **comunia legal** commune, municipality.

comunial *adj.* communal.

comunica *vt.* communicate; pass on (*illness*). • *n.* communication. **sin comunica** without communication, incommunicado.

comunicable *adj.* communicable, contagious, infectious.

comunicada *adj.* communicated. **sesal comunicada** sexually transmitted.

comunicador *n.* communicator, intercom. **comunicador de porte** doorphone, intercom, talkback.

comunisme *n.* communism.

comuniste *n.* communist.

comuta *vi.* & *vt.* switch on, turn on, come on, connect, go live (*machine*); enable (*software feature*). • *n.* connection, joint, junction. **boton de comuta** power button, power switch, on/off switch.

comutada *adj.* on, switched on, turned on, live; connected, online; enabled.

comutador *n.* switch (*electric*), toggle.

con[1] *prep.* • with, in the company of, going along with; e.g. *me jua tenis con mea sore*; *el nada con la flue.* • with (*having or including*); e.g. *cafe con lete*; *un can con oreas longa*; *tu roji con embarasa.* • with, by means of, using (*a tool*); e.g. *me scrive con un lapis*; *compra bonbones con monetas.* **con ce** at the same time as, accompanied by a situation in which; e.g. *los pasea con ce la pluve cade.*

con-[2] *pref.* con- (*with, together*).

conaseda *adj.* cognate. • *n.* sibling, sib, cognate.

conasedia *n.* siblinghood, cognacy.

conca *n.* shell, seashell. **conca de bivalvo** clamshell. **conca de cardio** cockleshell. **conca de strombo** conch shell, conch.

concava *adj.* concave.

concin *adj.* shell-like.

concista *vt.* conquer, take by force, subjugate. • *n.* conquest.

concistor *n.* conqueror, conquistador.

conclave *n.* conclave.

conclui *vi.* conclude, come to a conclusion. • *vt.* conclude, bring to a conclusion. • *n.* conclusion, coda, denouement.

concluinte *adj.* conclusive.

concombre *n.* cucumber (*Cucumis sativus*). **concombre-de-mar** *n.* sea cucumber (*Holothuroidea*). **concombre vinagrida** pickle, gherkin.

concreta *adj.* concrete, tangible.

concreti *vi.* & *vt.* concretize, reify.

concubina *n.* concubine; mistress, paramour, kept woman.

concurso *n.* contest, competition (*event*). **concurso de belia** beauty contest. **concurso de elimina** knockout, elimination match.

concursor *n.* contestant, competitor.

condena *vt.* condemn (*disapprove, declare punishment*), convict, sentence, doom, censure. • *n.* condemnation, conviction, sentence, indictment, demerit. **condena a enferno** damn.

condenada *adj.* condemned. • *n.* condemned, convict.

condensa *vi.* condense. • *n.* condensation (*action*).

condensada *adj.* condensed. • *n.* condensation (*product*), condensate.

condensador *n.* capacitor, condenser.

condo *n.* condominium, condo.

condom *n.* condom.

condor *n.* condor, New World vulture (*Cathartidae*).

condui *vi.* behave, conduct (*oneself*), comport. • *n.* behaviour (US behavior), demeanour (US demeanor), comportment, conduct. See *gida.*

conduisme *n.* behaviourism (US behaviorism).

conduiste *n.* behaviourist (US behaviorist).

conduta *vt.* conduct (*energy*). • *n.* conduction.

condutador *n.* conductor (*energy*).

condutante *adj.* conducting, conductive.

coneo *n.* rabbit (*Leporidae*).

coneria *n.* warren.

coneta *n.* baby rabbit, bunny.

confere *vi.* confer; parley. • *n.* conference, convention (*meeting*), symposium, powwow; parley. **confere academial** academic conference, colloquium, seminar. **confere**

de xefes summit (*meeting*). **confere jornaliste** press conference. **confere video** video conference.

confesa *vt.* confess, admit, avow. • *n.* confession, admission.

confeseria *n.* confessional.

confeti *vt.* candy.

confeto *n.* sweet, confection. **confeto de jelatin** jelly bean, jelly baby, gum drop. **confeto de menta** mint. **confeto de menta peperin** humbug, bullseye. **confeto dur** hard candy, gobstopper. **confetos** sweets, candy, confectionery.

confetor *n.* confectioner.

confida *vt.* confide, entrust (*valuables, secret*); e.g. *el ia confida a me ce la compania es cuasi bancarota.* • *n.* confiding.

confidada *adj.* confided, confidential (*secret*). • *n.* confidant, confidante.

confirma *vt.* confirm, corroborate, clinch. • *n.* confirmation (*including religious*), corroboration, clincher; evidence. **confirma con testa** nod one's head, give a nod.

confirmable *adj.* confirmable, testable.

confisca *vt.* confiscate, sequester, impound. • *n.* confiscation.

conflue *vi.* converge; merge. • *n.* convergence, confluence; merger.

confluente *adj.* confluent.

confonde *vt.* confound, puzzle, perplex, baffle, bewilder, mystify. • *n.* puzzlement, perplexity, bafflement, bewilderment.

confondeda *adj.* puzzled, quizzical.

conforma *vi.* conform, match, hew. • *n.* conformity. **conforma de sangue** cross-matching (*blood types*).

conformante *adj.* conforming, compliant.

conformiste *n.* conformist.

confusa *vt.* confuse, bewilder, muddle, addle, scramble. • *n.* confusion, bewilderment, muddle, mix-up.

confusable *adj.* confusable, mistakable.

confusada *adj.* confused, muddled.

confusador *n.* scrambler.

confusante *adj.* confusing.

confuzisme *n.* Confucianism. See *Kongzi.*

confuziste *n.* Confucian.

conga *n.* conga (*dance, music*); conga drum.

Congo *n.* Congo (*region*). **Republica de Congo** Republic of the Congo. **Republica Democrata de Congo** Democratic Republic of the Congo. **Rio Congo** Congo River. See *Zair.*

congoles *adj.* & *n.* Congolese.

congrega *n.* congregation (*religious, administrative*), flock. **congrega de sorsores** coven.

congresa *n.* congress.

congresor *n.* member of congress, congressman, congresswoman.

congro *n.* conger (*eel: Conger*).

coniac[1] *n.* cognac, brandy.

coniac[2] *n.* konjac, konjak, konnyaku, voodoo lily, elephant yam, devil's tongue (*plant: Amorphophallus konjac*).

conifer *adj.* coniferous. • *n.* conifer.

conio *n.* hemlock (*plant, poison: Conium maculatum*).

conjela *vi.* congeal.

conjenital *adj.* congenital.

conjesta *vi.* congest, engorge. • *n.* congestion. **conjesta de nas** nasal congestion, stuffy nose. **conjesta de trafica** traffic congestion, traffic jam. **conjesta de troncos** logjam. **conjesta sin sorti** gridlock.

conjestada *adj.* congested, stuffy.

conjestosa *n.* bottleneck.

conjuga *vi.* conjugate. • *n.* conjugation.

conjunta *n.* coordinating conjunction.

conjuntiva *n.* conjunctiva (*anatomy*).

conjuntivite *n.* conjunctivitis, pinkeye.

Connecticut [ka'netikat] *n.* Connecticut (*US state*).

cono *adj.* conic, conical. • *n.* cone. **cono de pino** pinecone.

conom *n.* cognomen.

conopofaje *n.* gnateater (*bird: Conopophagidae*).

conosal *adj.* cognitive.

conose *vt.* know (*person, place, etc.*), be acquainted with, be familiar with (*by experience rather than learning*), cognize; e.g. *me conose tua sore; tu conose Roma?; el conose la problem ma no sabe la detalias.* • *n.* knowledge (*of person, place, etc.*), acquaintance (*with*), familiarity. **comensa conose** get to know, become acquainted with, familiarize oneself with. **dona conose a** familiarize. **recomensa conose** become reacquainted with, refamiliarize oneself with. See *sabe.*

conoseda *adj.* known, familiar. • *n.* acquaintance (*person*). **conoseda como** known as, referred to as. **poca conoseda** little-known, esoteric.

conosor *n.* connoisseur, maven.

conota *vt.* connote. • *n.* connotation.

consela *vt.* counsel, advise. • *n.* counsel, advice.

conselor *n.* counselor, advisor, adviser, consultant. **conselor privata** confidant, confidante, confessor.

consensa *adj.* conscious, aware, mindful, lucid, cognizant.

consensi *vi.* become conscious, become aware. • *vi.* make conscious, make aware.

consensia *n.* consciousness, awareness, mindfulness, lucidity, cognizance.

consenta *vi.* meet, be in session. • *n.* meeting, session, sitting.
consentra *vi.* concentrate (*attention, substance*). • *n.* concentration, focus.
consentrador *n.* hub (*computer*).
consentral *adj.* concentric.
consepi *vt.* conceive (*pregnancy*). • *n.* conception.
conserna *vt.* concern, be important to, be of interest to; relate to, have to do with. • *n.* concern, matter of importance, business, affair. **acel no conserna tu** that does not concern you. **acel no es tua conserna** that is none of your business, that is no concern of yours. **conserna xef** priority, prime concern.
consernada *adj.* concerned, solicitous.
consernante *prep.* concerning, regarding, with regard to.
conserta *n.* concert. **conserta de avias** dawn chorus.
consertina *n.* concertina.
conserto *n.* concerto.
conserva *vt.* conserve, preserve, store, enshrine. • *n.* conservation, preservation. **conserva de fruta** preserve (*marmalade*). **conserva de natur** conservationism.
conservalisme *n.* conservatism (*political*).
conservaliste *adj.* & *n.* conservative (*political*).
conservante *n.* preservative.
conserveria *n.* conservation site, (*wildlife*) reserve.
conservor *n.* curator, conservator, guardian (*museum, collection*). **conservor de natur** conservationist.
conseta *n.* concept, conceit.
consetable *adj.* conceivable.
consetal *adj.* conceptual.
conseti *vi.* form as a concept. • *vt.* conceive (*concept*), conceptualize. • *n.* conception (*of concept*).
considera *vt.* consider, ponder, puzzle, mull, mull over; take into account. • *n.* consideration. **considera tarda** afterthought. **considera xef** priority, most important consideration. **si on considera** if one considers, to judge by, judging by, going by.
considerante *adj.* considering; taking into account. **considerante ce** considering that, given that, as, since.
consiensa *n.* conscience.
consiensosa *adj.* conscientious, dutiful.
consilio *n.* council, cabinet (*political*). **consilio de ministros** government, cabinet (*political*). **consilio governante** government, cabinet (*political*). **consilio ombral** shadow government, shadow cabinet.
consilior *n.* councillor (US councilor).
consinia *vt.* consign. • *n.* consignment.
consinieria *n.* consignment store.
consisa *adj.* concise, succinct, brief, compact, condensed, laconic, terse, pithy, snappy, to the point.
consol *n.* console, control panel, instrument bank.
consola *vt.* console, solace, comfort, cheer, support, soothe. • *n.* consolation, solace, comfort, cheer, support.
consolada *adj.* consoled. **es consolada par** be consoled by, take solace in, find consolation in.
consolador *n.* dildo.
consolida *n.* larkspur (*plant: Consolida*).
consolor *n.* consoler (*person*).
consonante *adj.* consonant (*language, music*). • *n.* consonant. **consonante con vose** voiced consonant. **consonante sin vose** voiceless consonant.
conspira *vi.* conspire, plot, scheme, collude, connive. • *n.* conspiracy, intrigue, connivance, scheme, plot, machination, collusion. **teoria de conspira** conspiracy theory.
conspiror *n.* conspirator, schemer, plotter.
constante *adj.* constant, invariant, stable, steady, permanent. • *n.* constant, invariant; coefficient.
constela *vi.* constellate. • *n.* constellation.
constipa *vt.* constipate. • *n.* constipation.
constipada *adj.* constipated.
constitual *adj.* constitutional.
constitui *vt.* constitute, establish. • *n.* constitution, charter (*organization*).
constrinje *vt.* constrain, constrict, inhibit. • *n.* constraint, condition, damper.
constrinjeda *adj.* constrained, inhibited, uptight, anal-retentive.
constrinjente *adj.* constraining, constricting. • *n.* obstruent (*consonant*). **constrinjente de pompas de protones** proton-pump inhibitor.
construeria *n.* building site, construction site.
construi *vt.* build, construct. • *n.* construction. **construi de petra** stonework, masonry. **en construi** under construction, in the works.
construida *n.* building, edifice.
construinte *adj.* building, constructing, constructive.
construor *n.* builder, constructor.
consul *n.* consul.
consuleria *n.* consulate.
consulta *vt.* consult. • *n.* consultation.
consuma *vt.* consume, deplete, expend, exhaust, use up, spend, ingest. • *n.* consumption, depletion; footprint (*software*).

consumante *adj.* consuming. **consumante de tempo** time-consuming.
consumisme *n.* materialism, consumerism.
consumiste *adj.* materialistic, consumerist. • *n.* materialist, consumerist.
consumor *n.* consumer.
conta *vt.* count, enumerate. • *n.* count (*action, amount*), quantity, tally; account (*bank, online, etc.*). **conta de abitores** census. **conta desendente** *v.* count down. • *n.* countdown. **conta reversada** *v.* count down. • *n.* countdown. **ultra conta** beyond count, countless, innumerable.
contable *adj.* countable.
contablia *n.* accounting, accountancy, bookkeeping.
contador *n.* counter (*device*). **contador de Geiger** Geiger counter.
contagota *n.* eyedropper.
contajira *n.* tachometer.
contamina *vt.* contaminate, pollute. • *n.* contamination, pollution.
contaminada *adj.* contaminated, polluted.
contaminante *n.* contaminant, pollutant.
contata *vt.* contact, touch. • *n.* contact, contiguity, touch.
contatante *adj.* contacting, touching, contiguous.
conte *n.* count, earl.
contempla *vt.* contemplate, gaze. • *n.* contemplation. **contempla la stelas** stargaze.
contemplante *adj.* contemplating, contemplative.
contempora *adj.* & *n.* contemporary.
contenador *n.* container, holder, receptacle, caddy. **contenador secinte** desiccator.
conteni *vt.* contain.
contenida *n.* content. **contenidas** contents.
conteninte *adj.* containing; continent (*medical*).
contente *adj.* glad, content, satisfied.
contentia *n.* contentment.
contesa *n.* countess.
contesto *n.* context.
contia *n.* county, shire, earldom.
continental *adj.* continental.
continente *n.* continent, mainland.
continua *vi.* continue; e.g. *la labora continua.* • *vt.* continue, perpetuate, carry on (*doing*), keep (*doing*), still be (*doing*); e.g. *el continua labora; el continua la labora.* • *n.* continuity, continuum, continuation. **esta va continua** to be continued.
continuante *adj.* continuing, continuous, continual, contiguous.
contor *n.* counter, teller; accountant, bookkeeper.
contorni *vi.* be outlined, appear as an outline. • *vt.* outline.
contorno *n.* contour, outline.
contorse *vi.* contort, squirm, writhe. • *vt.* contort, distort, warp; misrepresent. • *n.* contortion, distortion.
contorsor *n.* contortionist.
contra *prep.* • against, versus, opposing, opposed to (*something undesirable*); e.g. *batalia contra un enemi; tu ata contra mea desiras; secur contra acua.* • against (*a vertical surface*); e.g. *la scala sta contra la mur; la bisicliste ia cade contra la serca.* • *pref.* contra-. **a contra** by contrast. **contra ce** although, while (*contrast*), whilst, despite the fact that. **contra esta** against this, however, nonetheless.
contrabanda *vt.* smuggle. • *n.* smuggling; contraband. **contrabanda umana** human trafficking.
contrabandor *n.* smuggler, rumrunner.
contrabaso *n.* double bass.
contracolpa *n.* countercoup.
contraconsepal *adj.* & *n.* contraceptive. **contraconsepal intrauteral** intrauterine contraceptive device, IUD, coil.
contraconsepi *n.* contraception, birth control. **contraconsepi urjente** emergency contraception.
contracultur *n.* counterculture.
contracultural *adj.* counterculture, countercultural.
contracusa *vt.* recriminate. • *n.* counteraccusation, recrimination.
contrademostra *vt.* disprove. • *n.* disproof.
contradise *vt.* contradict. • *n.* contradiction. **contradise se** contradict oneself.
contradisente *adj.* contradictory.
contrae *vi.* contract (*shrink*). • *n.* contraction, spasm.
contrafatal *adj.* counterfactual.
contraforte *n.* buttress.
contraindente *vt.* apply a hanging indent to. • *n.* hanging indent.
contraindica *vt.* contraindicate. • *n.* contraindication.
contrainteroga *vt.* cross-examine. • *n.* cross-examination.
contralto *adj.* & *n.* contralto (*music*).
contramove *vi.* parry, counteract.
contraprodui *vt.* be counterproductive, backfire.
contraproduinte *adj.* counterproductive.
contrapuntal *adj.* contrapuntal.
contrapunto *n.* counterpoint.
contrarebela *vi.* perform counterinsurgency. • *n.* counterinsurgency.
contrarebelor *n.* counterinsurgent.
contrareclama *n.* counterclaim.

contraspia *vt.* perform counterespionage. • *n.* counterespionage.
contrasta *vi.* & *n.* contrast. **en contrasta con** contrasted with, in contrast to, as opposed to. **par contrasta** by contrast, however, nevertheless, nonetheless.
contrastada *adj.* contrasted. **contrastada con** contrasted with, in contrast to, as opposed to.
contrata *vi.* (*enter into*) contract. • *vt.* contract (*someone to do something*). • *n.* contract, legal document; covenant. **contrata de asecura** insurance policy. **contrata de lua** lease. **contrata de paia** payment schedule.
contrataca *vt.* counterattack, retaliate against. • *n.* counterattack, retaliation.
contratal *adj.* contractual.
contraterorisme *n.* counterterrorism.
contrateroriste *adj.* & *n.* counterterrorist.
contrator *n.* contractor.
contrautopia [kontrau'topia] *n.* dystopia.
contrautopial [kontrautopi'al] *adj.* dystopian, Orwellian.
contravenena *n.* antidote.
contri *adj.* & *n.* country (*music*).
contribui *vt.* contribute. • *n.* contribution; allowance, stipend.
contribuor *n.* contributor; taxpayer.
controla *vt.* control. • *n.* control, thrall. **controla de trafica airal** air traffic control. **su controla de** under the control of, subject to.
controlable *adj.* controllable.
controlada *adj.* controlled.
controlador *n.* controller, driver (*software*). **controlador de aparato** device driver. **controlador de primador** printer driver.
controlamanica *adj.* & *n.* control freak.
controlante *adj.* controlling, in charge.
controleria *n.* control room.
controlor *n.* controller (*person*).
controversa *adj.* controversial, contentious. • *n.* controversy (*something controversial*).
controversia *n.* controversy (*quality*).
contusa *vi.* bruise. • *n.* bruise, contusion. **contusa serebral** concussion.
conveni *vi.* suit, be suitable, be appropriate; be compatible. • *n.* suitability, appropriateness; compatibility.
conveninte *adj.* suitable, suited, proper, fit, appropriate, commensurate, expedient; compatible. • *adv.* suitably, appropriately, duly. **conveninte per primi** suitable for printing, printer-friendly.
converje *vi.* converge. • *n.* converging, convergence.
converjente *adj.* converging, convergent.
conversa *vi.* converse. • *n.* conversation, dialogue (US dialog). **conversa intima** pillow talk. **conversa privata** private conversation, tête-à-tête. **conversa replicosa** witty conversation, repartee, badinage.
conversal *adj.* conversational, colloquial, casual.
conversor *n.* converser, interlocutor.
convertable *adj.* convertible.
converti *vi.* & *vt.* convert. • *n.* conversion.
convertida *n.* convert.
convesa *adj.* convex.
conveta *vi.* convect. • *n.* convection.
convetante *adj.* convective.
convinse *vt.* convince, persuade, cajole, disabuse, sway. • *n.* convincing, persuading, persuasion.
convinsente *adj.* convincing, compelling, persuasive, plausible.
convoia *n.* convoy. **convoia de autos** motorcade. **convoia de furnis** supply convoy.
convulsa *vi.* convulse, spasm. • *n.* convulsion, spasm.
convulsante *adj.* convulsive, jerky.
Cook, Isolas *n.pl.* Cook Islands.
coopera *vi.* cooperate, liaise. • *n.* cooperation, teamwork.
cooperante *adj.* cooperating, cooperative.
coordina *vt.* coordinate. • *n.* coordination.
coordinada *n.* coordinate. **coordinada cartesian** Cartesian coordinate. **coordinada x** x-coordinate. **coordinada y** y-coordinate.
copa *n.* cup (*without handles*), goblet, beaker. **Copa** *n.* Crater (*constellation*). **copa de forno** ramekin, ramequin. **copa de portaseno** bra cup.
copec *n.* kopek (*currency*).
copernisio *n.* copernicium (*element*).
copi *vt.* cup, scoop, bail.
copia *vt.* copy, replicate, transfer. • *n.* copy, replica. **copia de securia** backup copy. **copia e coli** *v.* & *n.* copy and paste, cut and paste. **copia esata** *v.* replicate. • *n.* replication. **copia per securia** back up, make a backup copy of.
copiador *n.* copier.
copilote *n.* copilot.
copin *adj.* cuplike, cupped, cup-shaped.
copior *n.* copier, copyist.
coprolito *n.* coprolith, coprolite.
copta *adj.* Coptic (*Christianity*). • *n.* Copt.
copula *vi.* copulate, mate, have sex. • *n.* copulation, coitus, mating, lovemaking, sex.
cor *n.* heart (*including cards*), core, kernel; crux. **cor de pais** heartland. **sin cor** heartless.

coraje *n.* courage, bravery, valour (US valor), nerve. **sin coraje** cowardly, gutless, spineless.
coraji *vt.* encourage, urge, exhort, embolden, foster, hearten. • *n.* encouragement, exhortation.
corajinte *adj.* hortative, exhortative, exhortatory.
corajosa *adj.* brave, courageous, valorous, valiant, bold, plucky, feisty, gutsy, stout-hearted.
coral[1] *n.* coral. **Mar Coral** Coral Sea.
coral[2] *adj.* choral. • *n.* chorale.
corasa *n.* cuirass.
corasida *n.* battleship, dreadnought (*warship*).
Corcovado *n.* Corcovado. **Golfo Corcovado** Corcovado Gulf.
corda *n.* cord, rope, lanyard; chord (*geometry*). **corda de abri** ripcord. **corda de campana** bell pull, bell rope. **corda de salva** lifeline. **corda de vestes** clothesline. **corda elastica** elastic cord, bungee, bungee rope. **corda ombilical** umbilical cord. **corda tensada** tightrope. **corda vosal** vocal cord. **sin corda** cordless.
cordato *n.* chordate (*organism*: *Chordata*).
cordeta *n.* string, twine; shoelace, shoestring, bootlace; thin strap. **cordeta fronsinte** drawstring.
cordetin *adj.* stringy.
cordi *vt.* & *n.* cordon.
cordita *n.* cordite.
cordon *n.* thick rope, cable, hawser.
core *vi.* run, flow. • *n.* run (*including cricket*), running. **core de distantia longa** *v.* run long-distance. • *n.* long-distance running, endurance running. **core lenta** *v.* jog. • *n.* jog, jogging. **core sin restrinje** careen, career, hurtle. **core tra bates** run the gauntlet. **core tra campania** cross-country running.
corea[1] *n.* leash, strap, thong. **lia con corea** leash, strap.
corea[2] *n.* chorea (*medical*).
Corea[3] *n.* Korea. **Baia Corea** Korea Bay, Korean Bay. **Corea Norde** North Korea. **Corea Sude** South Korea. **Streta Corea** Korea Strait. See *Tehan*, *Txoson*.
corean *adj.* & *n.* Korean (*person*, *language*). See *hangugo*.
coredor *n.* corridor, aisle, passageway, hall, hallway. **coredor de mori** death row. **coredor esterna** breezeway.
coregon *n.* whitefish (*Coregoninae*).
corein *adj.* straplike.
corelata *vi.* correlate. • *n.* correlation.
corente[1] *adj.* current, ongoing, topical, present, up to date. • *adv.* currently, nowadays. **corente dominante** mainstream. **corente traversal** crosscurrent. **corente xef** mainstream.
corente[2] *n.* current (*water*, *electricity*); courante (*dance*, *music*). **con la corente** downstream. **contra la corente** upstream. **corente alternante** alternating current, AC. **corente de aira** airstream. **corente de jeta** jet stream. **corente direta** direct current, DC. **corente eletrical** electric current.
corenti *vt.* update, bring up to date.
coreografia *n.* choreography.
coreografiste *n.* choreographer.
coresponde *vi.* correspond, match (*communicate*, *be equivalent*). • *n.* correspondence, equivalence.
corespondente *adj.* corresponding, equivalent, matching. • *n.* correspondent (*letter writer*, *reporter*); counterpart, equivalent, answer (*to*).
coreta *adj.* correct, right; appropriate, proper, impeccable.
coretable *adj.* correctable, corrigible.
coreti *vi.* become correct. • *vt.* correct; proofread, emend. • *n.* correction, discipline.
coretia *n.* correctness.
coretor *n.* corrector, proofreader, copyreader.
corevisor *n.* coeditor.
corgi *n.* corgi.
coriandro *n.* coriander (*plant*, *spice*), cilantro, Chinese parsley (*Coriandrum sativum*).
corin *adj.* heartlike, heart-shaped, cordate.
corindon *n.* corundum (*crystal*).
corion *n.* chorion (*biology*).
corional *adj.* chorionic.
coriste *n.* chorister.
cormo *n.* corm (*botany*).
cormoran *n.* cormorant, shag (*Phalacrocoracidae*).
cornalina *n.* carnelian (*gem*).
cornamusa *n.* bagpipe, bagpipes. **cornamusa eres** uilleann pipes.
cornamusor *n.* piper.
cornea *n.* cornea.
corneal *adj.* corneal.
corneo *n.* dogwood (*plant*, *wood*: *Cornus*).
corneta *n.* cornet (*musical instrument*). **corneta engles** English horn. **corneta natural** bugle, natural trumpet, natural cornet.
cornetor *n.* bugler.
cornin *adj.* horny, hornlike.
cornisa *n.* ledge, sill, cornice. **cornisa de fenetra** windowsill. **cornisa de foco** hob (*surface beside a fire*).
corno *n.* horn (*animal*, *music*), antler. **corno alpan** Alphorn, Alpenhorn. **corno de**

abunda cornucopia, horn of plenty. **corno de servo** antler.
coro *n.* chorus, choir.
corode *vi.* corrode. • *n.* corrosion.
corodente *adj.* corroding, corrosive, caustic.
corola *n.* corolla (*botany*).
corolario *n.* corollary.
corona *n.* crown. **Corona Norde** Corona Borealis (*constellation*). **Corona Sude** Corona Australis (*constellation*).
coronel *n.* colonel.
coroneta *n.* coronet, tiara, diadem.
coroni *vt.* crown. • *n.* crowning, coronation.
coronin *adj.* crownlike, crown-shaped.
coror *n.* runner, jogger.
corpal *adj.* corporal, corporeal, somatic.
corpeta *n.* corpuscle.
corpi *vi.* become embodied. • *vt.* embody, be the embodiment of. • *n.* embodiment.
corpin *adj.* bodylike, close-fitting, figure-hugging, form-fitting, tight-fitting, skintight.
corpo *n.* body (*person*, *animal*, *vehicle*); corps (*military*); corpus (*texts*). **corpo de comunica** signals corps. **corpo mamelin** mammillary body. **corpo mor** dead body, corpse, cadaver, carcass. **de corpo capas** able-bodied. **sin corpo** bodiless, disembodied, incorporeal.
corpora *vi.* incorporate. • *n.* incorporation; corporation, guild; corporate (*company*).
corsa *vi.* race. • *n.* race; racing. **corsa de autos** motor racing, car racing, auto racing. **corsa de cavalos** horse race; horseracing. **corsa de dragsteres** drag race. **corsa de orienta** orienteering. **corsa de ostaculos** hurdle race. **corsa de rele** relay race. **corsa de salta** steeplechase. **corsa de sci** cross-country skiing.
Corse *n.* Corsica.
corseto *n.* corset, girdle, bodice.
corsetor *n.* corsetiere.
corsor *n.* racer. **corsor de ostaculos** hurdler.
corsu *adj.* & *n.* Corsican (*person*, *language*).
corta *adj.* short, brief, stubby. **corta pos** shortly after. **pos corta** soon, shortly.
cortador *n.* clippers (*electric*).
corte *n.* court (*law*, *royal*); courthouse, courtroom. **corte de apela** court of appeal, appellate court. **corte militar** court martial, military court. **corte suprema** supreme court.
cortea *vt.* court, woo, date. • *n.* courtship, date, dating.
corteal *adj.* courting, dating. **compete corteal** *v.* & *n.* rut. **mostra corteal** courtship display. **periodo corteal** mating season, rut, oestrus (US estrus).
corteor *n.* date, wooer, suitor.
cortes *adj.* courteous, polite, cordial, decorous, urbane.
cortesan *n.* courtesan, hetaera.
cortesia *n.* courtesy, politeness, civility, etiquette, manners, decorum, propriety. **cortesia de rede** netiquette.
cortex *n.* cortex; bark (*tree*). **cortex de tanin** tanbark. **cortex serebral** cerebral cortex.
cortexal *adj.* cortical.
corti *vi.* shorten. • *vt.* shorten, cut short, trim, prune, crop, lop, abbreviate, abridge, curtail. • *n.* trim, abbreviation (*action*, *result*). **corti de barba** shave. **corti de capeles** haircut. **corti de perspetiva** foreshortening. **corti la barba** shave. **corti la erba** cut the grass, mow the lawn.
cortia *n.* brevity.
corticosteroide *adj.* & *n.* corticosteroid.
cortierba *n.* lawnmower, mower. **cortierba puiable** push mower, unmotorized lawnmower.
cortina *n.* curtain, drape. **cortina alta** valance. **cortina enrolante** window blind, window shade. **cortina venezian** venetian blind, jalousie. **cortinas** curtains, drapery. **sin cortina** uncurtained.
cortisona *n.* cortisone (*hormone*).
cortiungia *n.* nail clipper.
cortor *n.* cutter, mower (*person*).
Corvatsca *n.* Croatia.
corvatsce *adj.* & *n.* Croatian (*person*, *language*).
corveta *n.* corvette (*ship*).
corvo *n.* crow, raven (*Corvus*). **Corvo** *n.* Corvus (*constellation*). **corvo american** American crow (*Corvus brachyrhynchos*). **corvo blanca-negra** pied crow (*Corvus albus*). **corvo comun** carrion crow (*Corvus corone*). **corvo de jungla** jungle crow (*Corvus macrorhynchos*). **corvo gris** hooded crow, hoodie (*Corvus cornix*). **corvo pexante** fish crow (*Corvus ossifragus*).
corvon *n.* raven (*Corvus albicollis*, *Corvus corax*, *Corvus crassirostris*, *Corvus ruficollis*, etc.).
cosa[1] *n.* thing, affair, matter, entity. **no cosa** nothing. **no cosa plu ca** nothing more than, merely, simply, just.
cosa[2] *adj.* & *n.* Xhosa (*person*, *language*).
cosador *n.* sewing machine.
coscrive *vt.* co-write, coauthor.
coscrivor *n.* co-writer, coauthor.
cose *vt.* sew, stitch. • *n.* sewing, stitching, needlework. **cose de orlo** hemstitch. **cose laxe** baste.
coseda *adj.* sewn, stitched. **coseda par mano** handsewn, handstitched.
cosina *n.* kitchen.
cosinal *adj.* culinary.
cosineta *n.* kitchenette.

cosineto *n.* bearing (*machinery*).
cosini *vt.* cook. • *n.* cooking, cookery, cuisine, cooking style. **cosini refinada** haute cuisine.
cosinor *n.* cook.
cosinus *n.* cosine.
cosix *n.* coccyx, tailbone.
cosmetica *adj.* & *n.* cosmetic.
cosmetolojia *n.* cosmetology.
cosmetolojiste *n.* cosmetologist.
cosmogonia *n.* cosmogony.
cosmolojia *n.* cosmology.
cosmolojiste *n.* cosmologist.
cosor *n.* sewer, seamster, seamstress.
cosovan *adj.* & *n.* Kosovan.
Cosovo *n.* Kosovo.
cosponsor *n.* cosponsor.
cosponsori *vt.* cosponsor.
costa *n.* coast, shore, seashore, seacoast, waterside. **a lado de costa** off the coast. **Costa de Ivor** Ivory Coast, Côte d'Ivoire. **Costa Rica** Costa Rica. **sin costa** landlocked. See *ivorian*.
costal *adj.* coastal, littoral, offshore. • *adv.* offshore.
costarican *adj.* & *n.* Costa Rican, Costarican.
costela[1] *n.* rib; chop (*meat*). **costela de porco** pork rib, spare rib.
costela[2] *n.* co-star.
costeleta *n.* cutlet.
costelin *adj.* ribbed, corded. • *n.* rib, ridge, wale (*fabric*).
costudiante *n.* fellow student.
costum *n.* custom, routine, usage, social convention.
costumal *adj.* customary, default, pro forma. • *adv.* customarily.
costur *n.* seam. **costur interna** inseam.
costurin *adj.* seamlike.
cosuscrive *vt.* cosign.
cosuscrivor *n.* cosigner, cosignatory.
cotanjente *n.* cotangent.
cotel *n.* knife, shiv. **colpa con cotel** *v.* & *n.* stab, jab. **cotel composada** Swiss army knife. **cotel de pox** pocket knife, folding knife, jackknife, penknife. **cotel de xef** chef's knife. **cotel ejetable** flick knife, switchblade. **cotel osilante** herb chopper, mezzaluna, hachoir.
coteli *vt.* cut, stab (*with knife*).
cotiledon *n.* cotyledon (*botany*).
cotinga *n.* cotinga (*bird: Cotingidae*).
cotino *n.* smoke tree (*Cotinus*).
coto *n.* koto (*musical instrument*).
coton *n.* cotton (*plant, fibre: Gossypium*). **coton asorbente** cotton wool. **coton de zucar** cotton candy, candyfloss. **de coton** (*made of*) cotton.
coturnix *n.* quail (*bird: Coturnix*).
covalente *adj.* covalent.
covre *vt.* cover, coat. • *n.* coverage, coat, coating. **a covre de** covering, coating, all over. **covre completa** full coverage. **covre partal** overlap.
covrebuco *n.* stopgap.
covrecasola *n.* saucepan lid.
covrecolo *n.* neckscarf; gorget (*throat protector*).
covrecuxin *n.* cushion cover, pillowcase.
covreda *adj.* covered, overcast.
covrefenetra *n.* shutter.
covregama *n.* legging (*protective*).
covrejeno *n.* kneepad.
covreleto *n.* blanket, quilt, duvet.
covrelibro *n.* dust jacket.
covrente *adj.* covering, coating. • *prep.* covering, coating, all over. • *n.* cover, covering, lid, top. **covrente desfisable** slipcover.
covreoio *n.* eyepatch.
covreorea *n.* earmuff, earmuffs.
covrepeto *n.* bib (*overalls*).
covreplato *n.* dish cover.
covresentro *n.* hubcap.
covreseso *n.* loincloth, breechcloth, breechclout; cache-sexe.
covreta *n.* placket; fly, flies.
covretable *n.* tablecloth.
covretesta *n.* headgear, headwear.
covreteta *n.* nipple shield; pastie.
covretibia *n.* shinpad, shinguard.
covretota *n.* overalls, coverall, boilersuit, jumpsuit.
covrevaso *n.* tea cosy.
covreveranda *n.* awning.
coxa *n.* thigh.
coxea *vi.* limp, hobble. • *n.* limp.
coxeante *adj.* lame, gimpy; shaky, wobbly, rickety, wonky.
coxeor *n.* limper, gimp.
coxinilia *n.* scale insect (*Coccoidea*).
cozac *adj.* & *n.* Cossack.
cozatxoc *n.* kozachok, kazachok (*dance*).
crabe *n.* crab (*Brachyura*). **Crabe** *n.* Cancer (*constellation*). **crabe de rio** crayfish (*Astacoidea, Parastacoidea*).
crac[1] *n.* & *interj.* crack, crunch, snap.
crac[2] *n.* crack, crack cocaine.
cracen *n.* kraken.
cracer *n.* cracker, saltine.
craci *vi.* & *vt.* crack, crunch, scrunch, snap.
cracinte *adj.* crunchy.
cracosa *adj.* crunchy, crisp, crispy.
crampo *n.* cramp (*muscle*).
crampon *n.* crampon, stud (*boot*).
cranial *adj.* cranial.
cranio *n.* skull, cranium.

crase *vt.* crush, squash, mash, crumple, flatten, smash, run over. • *n.* crushing, squashing. **crase su pede** crush under foot, trample, tread on.
crasenoza *n.* nutcracker (*Nucifraga*).
crasula *n.* jade plant, friendship tree, lucky plant, money tree (*Crassula ovata*).
crater *n.* crater. **crater volcanal** caldera.
craton *n.* craton (*geology*).
cravata *n.* necktie, tie. **cravata papilin** bow tie.
crea *vt.* create, make, craft, cause to exist. • *n.* creation (*action*); genesis. **crea corente** improvisation.
creada *adj.* created. • *n.* creature, creation (*product*).
creante *adj.* creating, creative.
credable *adj.* believable, credible, plausible.
credablia *n.* credibility.
crede *vt.* believe. • *n.* belief, creed, credo, doctrine, conviction. **crede falsa** fallacy. **no crede** disbelieve.
credito *n.* credit (*money*). **par credito** on credit.
creditor *n.* creditor.
credor *n.* believer.
credosa *adj.* credulous, gullible, trusting, superstitious.
credosia *n.* credulity.
crema *adj.* cream (*colour*). • *n.* cream, lotion. **crema ardeda** crème brûlée, burnt cream, Trinity cream. **crema asida** sour cream. **crema baieres** Bavarian cream, bavarois. **crema bateda** whipped cream. **crema catalan** crema catalana. **crema de bur** buttercream. **crema de caramel** crème caramel, caramel custard, caramel pudding, flan. **crema de la crema** crème de la crème. **crema de menta** crème de menthe. **crema de ovos** custard. **crema de rasa** shaving cream, shaving foam. **crema de sosia** cream of society, high society. **crema de zucar** marshmallow cream, marshmallow topping. **crema engles** crème anglaise, custard. **crema italian** panna cotta. **crema jelada** ice cream. **crema rojinte** rouge. **crema solal** suncream, sunblock.
cremeria *n.* creamery.
cremeta *n.* custard.
cremi *vt.* cream (*add cream to*).
cremin *adj.* creamy (*creamlike*).
cremosa *adj.* creamy (*full of cream*).
creol *adj.* & *n.* creole. **creol aitian** *adj.* & *n.* Haitian Creole, Kreyol Ayisyen.
creor *n.* creator.
creosa *adj.* creative.
creosia *n.* creativity.
creosota *n.* creosote.
crepe *n.* crêpe, pancake, flapjack, hotcake.
crepita *vi.* & *n.* crackle, sizzle.
crese *vi.* & *vt.* grow, develop, expand, increase. • *n.* growth, development, expansion; growth (*thing that has naturally grown*), excrescence. **crese dentes** teethe. **crese rapida** grow quickly, burgeon.
cresedas *n.pl.* produce (*fruit and vegetables*).
cresente *adj.* growing, increasing. • *adv.* increasingly, more and more, ever more. • *n.* crescent; croissant; crescendo. **sempre cresente** ever growing, ever increasing.
creson *n.* cress (*Brassicaceae*). **creson de acua** watercress (*Nasturtium*).
crespa *adj.* frizzy.
crespi *vi.* & *vt.* frizz.
cresta *n.* crest (*wave, bird, heraldic*), ridge. **cresta de gal** cockscomb. **cresta de la arte** state of the art. **cresta de la tecnolojia** state of the art. **cresta de neva** snowbank. **cresta sajital** sagittal crest. **cresta spumosa** whitecap.
cresti *vi.* crest (*wave*).
creta *n.* chalk.
cretasica *adj.* & *n.* Cretaceous (*geology*).
creti *vt.* chalk (*up*).
cretin *adj.* cretinous. • *n.* cretin.
creve *vi.* burst, puncture. • *n.* puncture. **creve de cor** heartbreak.
crevecor *n.* heartbreaker; tearjerker.
creveda *adj.* burst, punctured. **con cor creveda** heartbroken.
cri *adj.* & *n.* Cree (*person, language*).
cria *vt.* & *n.* cry, shout, scream, yell, yelp, bawl, outcry. **cria burlante** jeer, catcall.
cribaje *n.* cribbage (*card game*).
criceta *n.* cricket (*sport*).
criceto *n.* hamster (*Cricetinae*).
cricetor *n.* cricketer.
crici *vt.* jack up.
crico *n.* jack (*for lifting*).
crieta *vt.* & *n.* whimper.
cril *n.* krill (*crustacean*).
Crim *n.* Crimea.
crimin *n.* crime, offence (US offense). **crimin de gera** war crime. **crimin de odia** hate crime. **crimin major** felony. **crimin minor** misdemeanour (US misdemeanor). **crimin organizada** organized crime, mob, racket.
criminal *adj.* criminal, delinquent, nefarious.
criminali *vi.* & *vt.* criminalize.
criminalia *n.* criminality; underworld.
criminolojia *n.* criminology.
criminor *n.* & *n.* criminal, delinquent, lawbreaker, malefactor, hoodlum, felon, crook.
crimsce *adj.* & *n.* Crimean.
-crin *adj.suff.* -crine (*secreting*).

crinera *n.* mane, mop (*hair*); horsehair.
crinoide *n.* crinoid (*organism*: *Crinoidea*).
criofilia *n.* cryophilia.
criofilica *adj.* cryophilic. • *n.* cryophile.
criojen *adj.* cryogenic, cryonic.
crior *n.* crier, shouter; screamer (*bird*: *Anhimidae*).
criosirurjia *n.* cryosurgery.
criovolcan *n.* cryovolcano.
criovolcanisme *n.* cryovolcanism.
cripto- *pref.* crypto-.
criptografia *n.* cryptography, cryptology.
criptografiste *n.* cryptographer, cryptologist.
cripton *n.* krypton.
criptonita *n.* kryptonite.
cris *n.* kris (*dagger*).
crisalida *n.* chrysalis, pupa.
crisantemo *n.* chrysanthemum (*Chrysanthemum*).
crise *n.* crisis, emergency. **crise coler** temper tantrum. **crise mental** mental breakdown, nervous breakdown.
crisol *n.* crucible, melting pot.
crisopa *n.* lacewing (*insect*: *Chrysopidae*).
cristal *adj.* crystalline. • *n.* crystal. **cristal licuida** liquid crystal.
cristali *vi.* & *vt.* crystallize, effloresce. • *n.* crystallization.
cristalografia *n.* crystallography.
cristian *adj.* & *n.* Christian. **mundo cristian** Christendom.
cristiani *vi.* & *vt.* Christianize. • *n.* Christianization.
cristianisme *n.* Christianity.
Cristo *n.* Christ.
criterio *n.* criterion (pl. criteria).
Criti *n.* Crete.
critica[1] *vt.* criticize, reproach, lambast, tell off, henpeck; critique. • *n.* criticism, reproach, sideswipe; critique.
critica[2] *adj.* & *n.* Cretan.
criticante *adj.* critical, mordant, trenchant.
criticiste *n.* critic (*art*).
criticor *n.* critic, opponent.
Crixna *n.* Krishna.
crixnaisme [kriʃna'isme] *n.* Krishnaism, Hare Krishna.
crixnaiste [kriʃna'iste] *adj.* & *n.* Krishnaist.
croceta[1] *n.* croquette (*food*).
croceta[2] *n.* croquet (*game*, *shot*).
croco *n.* crocus (*Crocus*).
crocodil *n.* crocodile (*Crocodylidae*).
cromatica *adj.* chromatic.
cromato *n.* chromate (*chemistry*).
cromi *vt.* chrome-plate, chromium-plate.
cromida *adj.* chrome-plated, chromium-plated. • *n.* chrome.
cromo[1] *n.* chromium.
cromo-[2] *pref.* chromo-.
cromorno *n.* krummhorn (*musical instrument*).
cromosoma *n.* chromosome.
cronica *adj.* chronic (*medical*).
crono- *pref.* chrono-.
cronolojia *n.* chronology.
cronolojial *adj.* chronological.
cronolojiste *n.* chronologist.
cronometre *n.* chronometer, stopwatch, timer.
cronometri *vt.* time. • *n.* timing, measurement of time.
cronometriste *n.* timekeeper.
crosta *n.* crust, scab, rind (*cheese*).
crosti *vi.* & *vt.* encrust, cake. • *n.* encrustation.
crostosa *adj.* crusty.
crotal *n.* rattlesnake, rattler (*Crotalus*, *Sistrurus*).
croxe *vt.* crochet.
cru *adj.* raw, uncooked, crude, gross.
cruel *adj.* cruel, ruthless, vicious, cut-throat.
cruelia *n.* cruelty, ruthlessness, viciousness.
cruji *vi.*, *vt.* & *n.* creak (*low-pitched*), groan.
crujinte *adj.* creaking, creaky.
crumpeta *n.* crumpet (*cake*).
crup *n.* croup (*medical*).
crus *n.* cross; crucifix. **Crus** *n.* Crux (*constellation*). **crus de vias** crossroads. **Crus Roja** Red Cross.
crusa *vi.* cross, intersect. • *n.* crossing, intersection. **crusa plana** level crossing, grade crossing. **crusa sua brasos** cross one's arms, fold one's arms. **crusa sua gamas** cross one's legs.
crusada *vi.* & *n.* crusade.
crusador *n.* crusader.
crusante *adj.* crossing, intersecting, crisscross.
crusca *n.* bran.
cruser *adj.* cruising. • *n.* cruiser (*warship*). **cruser de batalia** battlecruiser (*warship*).
crusi *vt.* crucify. • *n.* crucifixion.
crusin *adj.* crosslike, cross-shaped, cruciform.
crustaseo *n.* crustacean, shellfish (*Curstacea*).
crut *n.* crwth (*musical instrument*).
cruton *n.* crouton.
ctenoforo *n.* ctenophore (*organism*: *Ctenophora*).
cuac *interj.* quack (*duck*); ribbit (*frog*).
cuaci *vi.* & *n.* quack; croak.
cuadrador *n.* set square, carpenter's square. **Cuadrador** *n.* Norma (*constellation*).
cuadral *adj.* quadratic, square (*root*).
cuadrante *n.* quadrant.
cuadri *vi.* square, become square. • *vt.* square, make square.
cuadrida *adj.* squared.

cuadrilia *n.* quadrille (*dance, music*).
cuadro *adj.* & *n.* square, check.
cuadrosa *adj.* checked, checkered.
cuaga *n.* quagga (*zebra*: *Quagga quagga*).
cuai *n.* chopstick.
Cuait [ku'ajt] *n.* Kuwait.
cuaiti [ku'ajti] *adj.* & *n.* Kuwaiti.
cual *det.* (*interrogative*) what, which. • *pron.* (*interrogative*) what, which, which one; (*relative*) which, that (*cannot be omitted*); e.g. *un ata cual merita es lodada*; *la vino cual tu bevi es multe vea.* **cual cosa?** what, which thing? **cual de enferno?** what the hell? **cual de mundo?** what on earth? **cual es la data?** what is the date? **cual es la ora?** what is the time? **de cual ... sua** whose, of which; e.g. *me no ave plu la caxa de cual tu ia trova sua covrente.* **sur cual ... lo** (*interrogative*) about what ... it?; (*relative*) which, that ... it; e.g. *sur cual el ia demanda esce me gusta lo?*; *esta es la libro sur cual me ia dise ce me va mostra lo a tu.*— English tends to use a more compressed structure for such sentences than is possible in Elefen, saying *what was he asking if I liked?* and *this is is the book which I said I would show you.*
cualce *det.* any (*at all*), whichever (*you like*); e.g. *prende cualce carta*; *cualce vestes va sufisi.* • *pron.* any (*no matter which*), whichever; so-and-so. **a cualce caso** in any case, anyhow, anyway, nonetheless, nevertheless. **a cualce ora** at any time of the day (*at all*), whenever (*you like*). **a cualce ves** on any occasion (*at all*), at any time, whenever (*you like*), ever. **cualce cosa** anything (*at all*), whatever (*you like*). **cualces** any (*people or things, optional plural pronoun*). **en cualce loca** anywhere (*at all*), wherever (*you like*). **en cualce modo** in any way (*at all*), by any means (*you like*), in whatever way.
cualcun *pron.* anyone, anybody (*doesn't matter who*), whoever (*you like*), whosoever. • *n.* everyman, man in the street. **cualcun ci** anyone who, whoever.
cuale *n.* quale (*philosophy*).
cuali *vi.* qualify (*for something*), be eligible (*for something*). • *vt.* qualify (*someone for something, grammar*). • *n.* qualification.
cualia *n.* quality, feature, trait, attribute, property, characteristic, aura. **cualia de labora** quality of work, workmanship. **cualia de parla** quality of speech, diction. **cualia de vive** quality of life, well-being, welfare. **cualia spesial** feature, special feature. **cualia unica** idiosyncrasy. **cualias nesesada** necessary qualities, right stuff. **de cualia alta** high-quality, vintage. **sin cualias** featureless.
cualial *adj.* qualitative.
cualinte *adj.* qualifying, eligible. • *n.* qualifier (*grammar*).
cuando *adv.* (*interrogative*) when; (*relative*) at which time; e.g. *cuando nos va parti?*; *me no sabe cuando me va reveni*; *febrero, cuando la aira es fria.* • *subord.* when; e.g. *nos va parti cuando la sol reposa*; *me ia come ante cuando vos ia ariva.* **a cuando** as (*at the moment when*). **ante cuando** before (*the time when*). **asta cuando** until, till (*the time when*). **de cuando** since the time when, ever since. **en cuando** while, whilst, as, during the time when. **estra cuando** except when, unless. **pos cuando** after (*the time when*). **sempre cuando** whenever.
cuanti *vt.* quantify. • *n.* quantification.
cuantia *n.* quantity, amount, magnitude; number (*quantity, not position in sequence*). **cuantia de abitores** population (*figure*). **cuantia de mores** death toll. **cuantia de regardores** audience size, ratings, viewing figures. **cuantia persental** percentage.
cuantial *adj.* quantitative.
cuanto[1] *det.* & *adv.* (*interrogative*) how many, how much. • *subord.* as many as, as much as, inasmuch as, as far as, so far as, to the extent that; e.g. *el ia aida cuanto el ia pote.* **per cuanto tempo** how much time, how long (*intended*); e.g. *per cuanto tempo tu va labora?* **tra cuanto tempo** how much time, how long (*elapsed*); e.g. *tra cuanto tempo tu abita ja asi?*
cuanto[2] *n.* quantum. **cuantos** quanta.
cuarc *n.* quark. **cuarc alta** top quark. **cuarc asendente** up quark. **cuarc basa** bottom quark. **cuarc desendente** down quark. **cuarc encantada** charm quark. **cuarc strana** strange quark.
cuaresma *n.* lent (*Christianity*).
cuaresmal *adj.* lenten.
cuarzo *n.* quartz.
cuasar *n.* quasar.
cuasi *adv.* almost, nearly, virtually, practically, not quite, just less than. • *pref.* quasi-. **cuasi cadun** almost everyone.
cuatri *vi.* quarter. • *n.* quarter, fourth (*fraction*). • *pref.* quarter-. **Cuatri Vacua** Empty Quarter, Rub al Khali, Great Sandy Desert.
cuatrida *adj.* quartered; quarto (*book size*).
cuatrigalon *n.* quart.
cuatrim *n.* 25-cent piece, quarter, farthing (*coin*).
cuatrinegra *adj.* & *n.* quadroon.
cuatro *det.* four. • *adj.* fourth (*ordinal*). • *pref.* quadr-, quadri-.
cuatroangulo *adj.* quadrangular. • *n.* quadrangle.
cuatrodes *det.* forty. • *adj.* fortieth (*ordinal*).
cuatrodesi *n.* fortieth (*fraction*).

cuatrojemelo *adj.* & *n.* quadruplet.

cuatroladal *adj.* quadrilateral, quadrangular. • *n.* quadrilateral, quadrangle.

cuatronaria *adj.* quaternary.

cuatropede *adj.* quadrupedal. • *n.* quadruped.

cuatruple *adj.* quadruple. • *n.* quartet, foursome.

cuaxiorcor *n.* kwashiorkor (*medical*).

Cuba *n.* Cuba.

cuban *adj.* & *n.* Cuban.

cubi *vi.* become a cube. • *vt.* cube.

cubida *adj.* cubed, to the third power.

cubisme *n.* cubism.

cubiste *adj.* & *n.* cubist.

cubo *adj.* cubic, cubical. • *n.* cube.

cucabura *n.* kookaburra (*Dacelo*).

cucaraxa *n.* cockroach, roach (*Blattaria*).

cuci *n.* cookie (*web*).

cucu *n.* cuckoo (*Cuculidae*).

cucui *n.* candlenut, candleberry (*tree*: *Aleurites moluccana*).

cucurucu *interj.* cock-a-doodle-doo, crow.

cudzu *n.* kudzu (*plant*: *Pueraria*).

cuecer *adj.* & *n.* Quaker.

cuecerisme *n.* Quakerism (*Christianity*).

cuer *adj.* (*non-conforming*) queer.

cuerca *n.* acorn.

cuerco *n.* oak (*Quercus*). **cuerco de suber** cork oak (*Quercus suber*). **cuerco sempreverde** evergreen oak, live oak (*Quercus virginianus*). **de cuerco** oak, oaken.

cuicstep *n.* quickstep (*dance*).

cuieta *adj.* quiet, calm, soft, faint, stealthy. • *adv.* quietly, calmly, softly, faintly, stealthily; pianissimo.

cuieti *vi.* & *vt.* quieten, calm, calm down.

cuietia *n.* quiet, calm, quietness, calmness.

cuietisme *n.* quietism.

cuietiste *n.* quietist.

cuiscal *n.* grackle (*bird*: *Quiscalus*).

cuiz *n.* quiz.

culeta *n.* (*colloquial*) bun, butt cheek (*buttock*).

culier *n.* spoon, scoop. **culier de table** tablespoon (*spoon, measurement*). **culier de te** teaspoon (*spoon, measurement*).

culieri *vt.* (*transfer by*) spoon.

culierin *adj.* spoonlike, spoon-shaped.

culieron *n.* ladle.

culmina *vi.* culminate, climax, peak, crest. • *n.* culmination, climax, peak, summit, top, crest; paragon; punchline. **culmina con** culminate with, be surmounted with, be topped with. **culmina de arbor** treetop. **culmina de colina** hilltop. **culmina de monte** mountaintop.

culminante *adj.* culminating, peaking, climaxing, climactic.

culo *n.* (*colloquial*) arse, ass, bum, butt, booty, fanny (*US*), rump, tush (*buttocks*); (*insult*) arse, jerk, schmuck, prat.

culom *n.* coulomb (*unit of charge*).

culote *n.* French knickers, tap pants.

culpa *vt.* & *n.* blame.

culpable *adj.* guilty, blameworthy, culpable, responsible, liable.

culpablia *n.* guilt, responsibility, liability.

cultiste *n.* cultist.

cultiva *vt.* cultivate, farm, grow (*something*); till, work (*the soil*). • *n.* crop, cultivation, agriculture, husbandry; culture (*medical*). **alterna de cultiva** crop rotation. **cultiva de uvas** viticulture. **cultiva luante** sharecrop.

cultivable *adj.* cultivatable, cultivable, arable, farmable, growable.

cultivada *adj.* cultivated, farmed. **cultivada a casa** homegrown.

cultivador *n.* cultivator, tiller, rototiller, rotavator.

cultival *adj.* agricultural, agrarian.

cultiveria *n.* farm, farmstead, plantation. **cultiveria grande** plantation, latifundium.

cultivor *n.* farmer, grower, agriculturalist, cultivator (*person*). **cultivor luante** sharecropper.

cultivorisme *n.* agrarianism.

culto *n.* cult. **culto de personalia** personality cult.

cultur *n.* culture, lifestyle, ethos.

cultural *adj.* cultural.

cuman *adj.* & *n.* Cuman.

cumbia *n.* cumbia (*dance, music*).

cumcuat *n.* kumquat (*Fortunella*).

cumin *n.* cumin (*plant, seed*: *Cuminum cyminum*).

cumula *vi.* accumulate, hoard, accrue. • *n.* accumulation, accrual, backlog, build-up, pile-up. **cumula de neva** snowpack.

cumulador *n.* accumulator (*software, cryptography, energy*).

cumulante *adj.* cumulative.

cumulin *adj.* cumulous (*like cumulus clouds*).

cumulo *adj.* cumulus (*cloud*). • *n.* cumulus.

cumulonimbo *adj.* & *n.* cumulonimbus (*cloud*).

cumulor *n.* hoarder.

cumulosa *adj.* cumulous (*containing cumulus clouds*).

cuna *n.* cradle.

cuneforma *adj.* & *n.* cuneiform.

cuneo *n.* wedge, chock, shim; wedge (*golf club*).

cungfu *n.* kung fu.

cunilingo *n.* cunnilingus. **fa cunilingo** perform cunnilingus.

cuno *n.* (*colloquial*) pussy, fanny (*UK*), cunt (*vagina*). **leca la cuno** (*colloquial*) eat out, go down on (*cunnilingus*).
cuol *n.* quoll (*animal*: *Dasyurus*).
cuorin *adj.* leathery.
cuoro *n.* leather. **cuoro suave** suede. **cuoro vernisida** patent leather. **de cuoro** (*made of*) leather.
cuorum *n.* quorum.
cuota *n.* quota, allowance.
cupe *n.* coupé (*car*).
Cupido *n.* Cupid.
cupola *n.* dome, cupola. **cupola jeodesial** geodesic dome. **cupola onionin** onion dome.
cupolin *adj.* domelike, dome-shaped.
cupre *n.* copper. **de cupre** (*made of*) copper.
cupri *vt.* copper.
cuprica *adj.* cupric.
cuprita *n.* cuprite.
cupror *n.* coppersmith.
cuprosa *adj.* cuprous.
cura *vt.* care, care for, take care of, nurse, nurture, minister to. • *n.* care, concern, nurture; care (*means of treatment*); custody. **ci cura?** who cares? (*disinterest*). **cura personal** grooming, personal hygiene. **cura prima** primary care. **me no cura** I don't care (*disinterest*). **sin cura** carefree, mindless, thoughtless. See *atende*.
Curan *n.* Qur'an, Koran.
curante *adj.* careful, deliberate; custodial.
curare *n.* curare (*resin*).
Curasau *n.* Curaçao (*island*).
curcuma *n.* turmeric (*plant, spice*: *Curcuma longa*).
curdi *adj.* & *n.* Kurdish, Kurd (*person, language*).
Curdistan *n.* Kurdistan.
cureta *n.* curette (*tool*).
cureti *vt.* perform curettage. • *n.* curettage.
curgan *n.* kurgan (*mound*).
curio *n.* curium (*element*).
curiosa *adj.* curious, inquisitive, nosy, nosey (*wanting to know more*).
curiosi *vi.* become curious, pry. • *vt.* intrigue, arouse curiosity.
curiosia *n.* curiosity.
curling *n.* curling (*sport*).
curlo *n.* curlew (*bird*: *Numenius*).
curor *n.* carer, nurse.
curso *n.* course, path, track, trail, circuit, trajectory, tract; fairway (*golf*). **curso alta** upper course (*river*). **curso basa** lower course (*river*). **curso de corsa** racetrack, racecourse, raceway. **curso de dijesta** digestive tract, alimentary tract. **curso de mus** mouse trail (*software*). **curso de ostaculos** obstacle course. **curso de respira** respiratory tract. **curso de studia** course of study. **curso de trata** course of treatment. **curso de vose** vocal tract. **curso enlinia** online course, internet course. **curso intensa** crash course. **curso par coresponde** correspondence course. **curso projetada** itinerary, projected course. **cursos** courses, curriculum. **estra cursos** extracurricular.
cursor[1] *n.* cursor (*software*).
cursor[2] *n.* courser (*bird*: *Cursorius*, *Rhinoptilus*).
curva *adj.* curved, bent (*naturally*). • *n.* curve, bend, bight. **curva ornosa** flourish, ornate curve.
curvable *adj.* bendable.
curvi *vi.* & *vt.* curve, bend; bend down, stoop. **curvi se a ante** hunch forward, hunch over.
curvia *n.* curvature.
curvida *adj.* bent.
curvosa *adj.* curvy, curvaceous, voluptuous, rubenesque, zaftig.
cuscus *n.* couscous (*food*).
cusin *n.* cousin.
cusina *n.* female cousin.
cusino *n.* male cousin.
custa *vt.* cost. • *n.* cost, price, expense, fare. **a bon custa** affordable. **a custa de** at the cost of, at the expense of. **cosa sin custa** freebie, giveaway. **custa de instrui** tuition fee, tuition. **custa de lua** rent. **custa de viaja** travel cost, airfare. **custa per la compror** consumer price, street price, price in the shops. **deside la custa de** price. **sin custa** free, for free, gratis, gratuitous, toll-free.
custosa *adj.* costly, expensive, dear, pricey.
cutanea *adj.* cutaneous.
cuticula *n.* cuticle. **cuticula laserada** hangnail.
cuxan *adj.* Kushan (*dynasty*).
cuxin *n.* cushion, pillow; buffer. **cuxin de favas** beanbag. **cuxin de jenos** kneeler, hassock. **cuxin de securia** safety cushion, airbag. **cuxin de testa** pillow.
cuxineta *n.* pad.
cuxini *vt.* cushion, pad.
cuxinida *adj.* cushioned, padded.

D

D [de], **de** *letter* D, d.

-da *adj.suff.* -ed; e.g. *ascondeda*; *tu ia asconde un mesaje e me ia trova tua mesaje ascondeda*; *la mesaje ia es ascondeda.*—*-da* creates a passive form, such as *ovos fritada*. This is not the same thing as the past tense in *el ia frita la ovos*, even though both are *fried* in English. • *n.suff.* -ee (*person or thing that is -ed*); e.g. *empleada*; *comeda*.

Dacia *n.* Dacia (*ancient region*).

dacota *adj.* & *n.* Dakota (*person, language*).

dadaisme [dada'isme] *n.* dadaism.

dadaiste [dada'iste] *adj.* dadaist.

dado *n.* die, dice. **dados** dice.

dafnia *n.* daphnia (*crustacean*).

daga *n.* dagger, dirk. **daga magra** stiletto.

dagara *adj.* & *n.* Dagaaba (*people*), Dagare (*language*).

dagereotipo *n.* daguerreotype.

dageta *n.* bodkin (*needle*).

daiciri *n.* daiquiri (*drink*).

Dakota *n.* Dakota. **Dakota Norde** North Dakota (*US state*). **Dakota Sude** South Dakota (*US state*).

dalia *n.* dahlia (*Dahlia*).

dalit *adj.* & *n.* Dalit (*caste*).

Dalmasia *n.* Dalmatia.

dalmasian *adj.* & *n.* Dalmatian (*including dog*).

daltonisme *n.* colour (US color) blindness.

dama *n.* lady, dame, gentlewoman, matron; bridesmaid; queen (*chess, cards*). **dama de onora** maid of honour (US honor). **damas** draughts (*UK*), checkers (*US*) (*game*).

damasco *n.* damask (*fabric*).

damia *n.* ladyship.

damin *adj.* ladylike.

dana *vt.* & *n.* damage. **dana criminal** vandalism.

danante *adj.* damaging, injurious.

dandi *n.* fop, dandy, poseur, hipster, popinjay.

dandia *n.* foppery.

Danmarc *n.* Denmark. **Streta Danmarc** Denmark Strait.

dansa *vi.* dance, prance; flicker (*flame*). • *n.* dance. **dansa cuadro** square dance. **dansa de folclor** folk dance. **dansa de moria** danse macabre. **dansa de ventre** belly dance. **dansa un valsa** dance a waltz.

dansce *adj.* Danish (*person, language*). • *n.* Dane; Danish.

dansor *n.* dancer.

Danubio, Rio *n.* River Danube.

Dardanelia, Streta *n.* Dardanelles.

dardo *n.* dart.

darma *n.* dharma (*religion*).

darmstatio *n.* darmstadtium (*element*).

darvix *n.* dervish.

Darwin *n.* Darwin.

darwinisme *n.* Darwinism.

data *n.* date (*calendar*).

dati *vt.* date (*determine the date of, write a date on*).

datila *n.* date (*fruit*).

datilal *adj.* dactylic.

datilo[1] *n.* date (*tree*: *Phoenix dactylifera*).

datilo[2] *n.* dactyl (*poetry*).

dativa *adj.* & *n.* dative (*grammar*).

dato *n.* datum. **datos** data.

datura *n.* datura (*plant*: *Datura*).

dau *n.* Tao, Dao.

dauisme *n.* Taoism, Daoism.

dauiste *n.* Taoist, Daoist.

Davis, Streta *n.* Davis Strait.

de[1] *prep.* • from, of, since (*a point of origin in space or time*); e.g. *me es de London*; *el ia parti de Paris*; *Frans es a norde de Espania*; *me ia sta a no plu ca un metre de la asidente*; *me estrae el de la casa*; *el ia es salvada de mori*; *el ia asconde de la polisia*; *un cavalo difere de un bove*; *aprende de tua frate*; *esta libro veni de la sentenio 17*; *la boteca funsiona de lundi asta jovedi*; *el labora de la ora cuando el velia.* • made of, composed of, consisting of; e.g. *un veste de seda*; *un anelo de oro.* • of, belonging to (*an owner or whole*); e.g. *la casa de Juan*; *la rota es un parte de la veculo.* • of (*specifying, adding detail*); e.g. *la idea de progresa*; *un arbor con altia de dudes metres.* • (*a quantity*) of; e.g. *un tas de cafe*; *tre caxas de libros*; *cuatro metres de altia*; *plen de aira.* • (*forming the equivalent of a compound noun*); e.g. *avia de mar*; *oculo de sol*; *tenis de table.* • from (*indicating motion away from the location shown by the following preposition*); e.g. *me move mea mano de su la table.* • (*converting the following preposition into an adverb indicating motion away from a location*); e.g. *la gato ia salta de sur.* **a 24 oras de la dia** 24 hours a day, around the clock, round the clock. **de ci** of whom, whose. **de cual** of which, whose. **de esta** thereof. **de esta loca** from this place, away. See *ante, cuando, do, en, estra, pos, su, sur, supra.*

de-[2] *pref.* de-.

debatable *adj.* debatable.

debate *vt.* & *n.* debate.

debe *vt.* owe (*debt*); be obligated to, have to, need to, must (*duty, obligation, social correctness*); should, ought to; e.g. *un bon sitadan debe vota.* • *n.* duty. **como lo debe es** as it

should be, as things should be. **debe de casa** homework. **ta debe** should, ought to (*simple conditional, or polite, or commenting without expectation*); e.g. *nos ta debe aida ma no pote.* **tu debe deside** you must decide, you decide.

debente *adj.* owing, indebted, overdrawn.

debil *adj.* feeble, weak, infirm, puny, thready. • *n.* weakling, pipsqueak, wimp, pushover, runt; weakness (*weak point*), foible.

debili *vi.* weaken, languish, attenuate. • *vt.* weaken, enfeeble, debilitate, enervate. • *n.* attenuation, debilitation, enervation.

debilia *n.* weakness, frailty, infirmity.

debua *vi.* & *n.* debut, premiere.

debuante *n.* debutant, debutante.

deca- *pref.* deca- (*ten*).

decaedro *adj.* decahedral. • *n.* decahedron.

decagon *adj.* decagonal. • *n.* decagon.

decagram *n.* decagram.

decal *n.* decal; rubdown, dry transfer.

decalitre *n.* decalitre (US decaliter).

decalogo *n.* decalogue (US decalog), Ten Commandments.

decametre *n.* decametre (US decameter).

decano *n.* dean (*religious, university*); elder (*religious*); doyen, doyenne.

decanta *vt.* decant.

decantador *n.* decanter.

declara *vt.* declare, state, assert, claim, maintain, intimate, profess. • *n.* statement, declaration, assertion, claim, intimation, manifesto. **declara falsa** falsehood. **declara nonsabe** plead ignorance.

declina *vi.* decline (*including grammar*). • *n.* declension, declination; downturn.

deco *adj.* art deco.

decora *vt.* decorate (*including with an honour*), adorn, trim, garnish. • *n.* decoration, decor, ornament, garnish, adornment, trim, topping; scenery (*theatrical*).

decoror *n.* decorator.

decupaje *n.* decoupage (*art*).

dedica *vt.* dedicate, devote. • *n.* dedication, devotion, commitment.

dedicada *adj.* dedicated, devoted, committed, staunch.

deduable *adj.* deducible, inferable, derivable.

deduador *n.* abductor (*muscle*).

dedui[1] *vt.* deduce, infer, derive, educe. • *n.* deduction, inference, derivation.

dedui[2] *vt.* abduct (*muscle*). • *n.* abduction.

deduinte *adj.* deductive, inferential.

defende *vt.* defend, advocate. • *n.* defence (US defense). **defende de tese** viva voce, oral defence (US defense). **sin defende** defenceless (US defenseless), helpless, vulnerable.

defendor *n.* defender, advocate, apologist, proponent; guardian (*of child or invalid*). **defendor de la popla** ombudsman.

defeta *n.* defeat, downfall, wipeout. **defeta completa** crushing defeat. **sin defeta** undefeated.

defetisme *n.* defeatism.

defetiste *n.* defeatist.

defeto *n.* defect, glitch, bug.

defetosa *adj.* defective, faulty. • *n.* dud.

defia *vt.* defy, challenge. • *n.* defiance, challenge.

defiante *adj.* defiant, challenging, recalcitrant.

defini *vt.* define, delineate. • *n.* definition; clue (*in word game*).

definida *adj.* defined, definite.

defininte *adj.* definitive.

defior *n.* challenger.

defla *vi.* deflate. • *n.* deflation.

degrada *vi.* degrade. • *vt.* degrade, cheapen, demean. • *n.* degradation.

degradante *adj.* degradable. • *adj.* degrading, derogatory.

dejela *vi.* & *vt.* defrost, unfreeze, thaw. • *n.* thaw.

dejelada *adj.* unfrozen. **acua dejelada** meltwater.

dejenera *vi.* degenerate, deteriorate, run down, decay. • *n.* degeneration, decay, decadence.

dejenerada *adj.* degenerated, degenerate, decadent.

dejeta *vt.* throw away, discard, dump, dispose of, get rid of, jettison. • *n.* disposal.

dejetable *adj.* disposable; rubbish, trashy, of poor quality.

dejetada *n.* garbage, waste, trash, rubbish, litter, refuse, waste material. **dejetadas flotante** jetsam.

dejeteria *n.* garbage dump, rubbish heap, landfill (*site*), dumping ground, transfer station; dustheap, slag heap.

dejetor *n.* sanitation worker, garbage man, dustman.

dejuna *vi.* stop fasting, break one's fast.

dejunta *vi.* unjoin, become unjoined, decouple, disconnect. **dejunta se de** unsubscribe.

Delaware [ˈdelawer] *n.* Delaware (*US state*). **Baia Delaware** Delaware Bay.

delega *vt.* delegate. • *n.* delegation.

delegada *adj.* delegated. • *n.* delegate, commissary.

deleta *vt.* delight, exhilarate. • *n.* delight, glee, exhilaration; delicacy, appetizer, aperitif, starter, hors d'oeuvre, antipasto, amuse-gueule.

deletada *adj.* delighted.

deleteria *n.* delicatessen, deli.

deletosa *adj.* delightful, delicious, delectable, luscious, sensuous, scrumptious, yummy.

delfin *n.* dolphin (*Delphinidae*, *Odontoceti*); dauphin. **Delfin** *n.* Delphinus (*constellation*).

delfinio *n.* delphinium, larkspur (*plant*: *Delphinium*).

delicata *adj.* delicate, fine, dainty, sensitive, tender. **delicatas** delicates, lingerie.

delirio *n.* delirium.

deliriosa *adj.* delirious.

delta *n.* delta (*Greek letter* Δ, δ; *river mouth*).

deltoide *n.* deltoid (*muscle*).

delude *vt.* disappoint, let down; dash (*hopes*). • *n.* disappointment, anticlimax, letdown. **delude de suspende** anticlimax.

deludente *adj.* disappointing, anticlimactic.

deluvia *vt.* flood, deluge; washout. • *n.* major flood, deluge, torrent. **deluvia subita** flash flood.

deluvial *adj.* torrential.

demagogia *n.* demagogy, demagoguery.

demagogo *n.* demagogue.

demanda *vt.* ask, inquire, enquire; e.g. *me demanda a tu do tu abita*; *el va demanda ce nos aida*.—One can *demanda de algun* or *demanda a algun*; the former is more polite or suggests that the question is more difficult. The object of *demanda* is the question itself. To *ask for* something, use *demanda per*. • *n.* question, inquiry, enquiry, query. **demanda a se** ask oneself, wonder. **demanda autorespondente** rhetorical question. **demanda codal** tag question, question tag. **demanda gidante** leading question. **demanda per** ask for, request. **fa un demanda** ask a question, pose a question, put a question.

demente *adj.* demented, insane, crazy, mad. • *n.* lunatic, madman, madwoman.

dementeria *n.* madhouse, nuthouse, bedlam, lunatic asylum, insane asylum.

dementi *vi.* go crazy, go insane, go mad. • *vt.* make crazy, drive mad, madden, unhinge.

dementia *n.* dementia, insanity, lunacy, madness.

demiurgo *n.* demiurge.

demo- *pref.* demo- (*people*).

democrata *adj.* democratic. • *n.* democrat.

democrati *vi.* & *vt.* democratize.

democratia *n.* democracy.

demografia *n.* demography.

demografial *adj.* demographic.

demografiste *n.* demographer.

demon *n.* demon, daemon.

demonal *adj.* demonic.

demoni *vt.* demonize. • *n.* demonization.

demonim *adj.* demonymic. • *n.* demonym.

demonin *adj.* demonic, devilish.

demonolojia *n.* demonology.

demostra *vt.* prove. • *n.* proof. **demostra empirical** empirical proof.

demostrable *adj.* provable.

demostrablia *n.* provability.

demotica *adj.* demotic, vernacular, informal, colloquial, casual (*speech*). • *n.* vernacular, vulgate.

Denali, Monte *n.* Mount Denali, Mount McKinley.

dendrite *n.* dendrite.

dendritosa *adj.* dendritic.

dendrocronolojia *n.* dendrochronology.

dendrolojia *n.* dendrology.

dendrolojial *adj.* dendrological.

dendrolojiste *n.* dendrologist.

denge *n.* dengue, dengue fever.

denim *n.* denim. **de denim** (*made of*) denim.

denova *adv.* again, anew, afresh.

densa *adj.* dense, thick.

densi *vi.* thicken, condense. • *vt.* thicken, condense; compress (*data*). • *n.* thickening; compression (*data*).

densia *n.* density, thickness, consistency; resolution (*image*).

dental *adj.* dental. • *n.* dental (*consonant*).

dente *n.* tooth; tine, prong; sprocket. **dente canin** canine tooth. **dente canin superior** eyetooth. **dente conein** bucktooth. **dente molente** molar. **dente sisorante** incisor. **dentes** teeth, dentition.

dentela *n.* lace, lacework. **dentela de lenio** fretwork.

denteleon *n.* dandelion (*Taraxacum*).

dentin *n.* dentine (US dentin).

dentiste *n.* dentist.

denton *n.* tusk, fang.

dentosa *adj.* toothy, toothed.

denunsia *vt.* denounce, decry. • *n.* denouncement.

denunsior *n.* denouncer, whistleblower.

departe *n.* department, bureau. **departe de investiga** bureau of investigation. **departe de securia esterna** foreign intelligence agency. **departe de securia interna** domestic intelligence agency.

depende *vi.* depend, rely; e.g. *nos depende de tu*; *la responde depende de fatores diversa*. • *n.* dependence, dependency; reliance, addiction.

dependente *adj.* dependent, conditional, provisory; addicted. • *n.* dependant, ward; addict. **dependente de** dependent on. **dependente si** on condition that, provided that.

depinta *vt.* paint, depict. • *n.* painting (*art form*, *artwork*), depiction. **depinta de per-**

sones portraiture. **depinta mural** mural. **depinta personal** portrait.
depintin *adj.* picturesque.
depintor *n.* painter. **Depintor** *n.* Pictor (*constellation*).
deplora *vt.* deplore, bemoan.
deplorable *adj.* deplorable, appalling, abysmal, awful, atrocious.
depone *vt.* deposit (*including financial*). • *n.* sedimentation.
deponeda *adj.* deposited; sedimentary. • *n.* sediment, silt.
deporta *vt.* deport. • *n.* deportation.
deportada *adj.* deported. • *n.* deportee.
depresa *vt.* depress (*push down, sadden*). • *n.* depression; trough (*wave*). **depresa climal** low-pressure area, depression, weather system. **depresa economial** economic depression.
depresada *adj.* depressed, dejected, down, melancholy.
depresante *adj.* depressant.
derbi *n.* derby (*horse race, sporting event*).
deriva *vi.* & *vt.* derive. • *n.* derivation.
derivable *adj.* derivable.
derivada *adj.* derived, derivative. • *n.* derivative; spinoff.
derma *n.* dermis (*anatomy*).
dermatero *n.* earwig (*Dermaptera*).
dermatite *n.* dermatitis.
dermatolojia *n.* dermatology.
des[1] *det.* ten. • *adj.* tenth (*ordinal*). **des-du** *det.* twelve. • *adj.* twelfth (*ordinal*). **deses** tens; (*loosely*) dozens.
des-[2] *pref.* dis-, un- (*added to verbs: undoing or reversal of an action*); e.g. *descarga*; *dejela*.—*Des-* simplifies to *de-* before *s, z, j* or *x*.
desaclama *vt.* boo.
desacorda *vt.* disagree, conflict, clash, contravene. • *n.* disagreement, discord, discordance, discordancy, dissonance, clash, conflict, contention.
desacordante *adj.* disagreeing, discordant, dissonant, out of tune, clashing.
desagi *vi.* become blunt. • *vt.* blunt, dull.
desajusta *vi.* & *vt.* detune.
desali *vt.* desalinate. • *n.* desalination.
desaliasi *vt.* anti-alias.
desambigui *vi.* & *vt.* disambiguate. • *n.* disambiguation.
desamini *vt.* unfriend.
desapare *vi.* disappear, vanish; dispel. **desapare lenta** fade out.
desapone *vt.* take off (*garment*), remove, doff.
desaprende *vt.* unlearn.
desaproba *vt.* disapprove, deprecate, mind. • *n.* disapproval, deprecation.
desaprobante *adj.* disapproving, askance.
desarma *vt.* disarm. • *n.* disarmament.
desarnesi *vt.* unharness.
desasembla *vt.* disassemble, dismantle.
desasentua *vt.* de-emphasize.
desasosia *vi.* disassociate, dissociate. • *n.* disassociation, dissociation.
desasosiante *adj.* dissociative.
desastre *n.* disaster, crash, catastrophe, calamity, cataclysm.
desastrosa *adj.* disastrous, catastrophic.
desativi *vi.* & *vt.* deactivate; defuse. • *n.* deactivation.
desautentici *vi.* & *vt.* log out (*software*).
desbandi *vi.* disband.
desbari *vt.* unbar, unblock.
desbloci *vt.* unblock, unclog.
desbombetor *n.* deminer.
desbotoni *vt.* unbutton.
desbridi *vt.* unbridle; debride. • *n.* unbridling; debridement.
descafini *vt.* decaffeinate. • *n.* decaffeination.
descalci *vi.* & *vt.* decalcify.
descalpi *vt.* scalp.
descami *vt.* descale.
descamida *adj.* descaled.
descapasi *vi.* & *vt.* incapacitate, disable, impair, vitiate, cripple.
descapasia *n.* disability, handicap, impairment.
descapasida *adj.* incapacitated, disabled, handicapped, impaired, crippled. • *n.* disabled person, handicapped person; invalid.
descapeli *vt.* depilate, remove hair from.
descapelinte *adj.* depilatory.
descarga *vt.* discharge, unload, offload, unburden; flush (*toilet*); download. • *n.* download.
descarni *vt.* remove flesh from, flesh, pick clean.
descascador *n.* peeler, potato peeler, vegetable peeler.
descasci *vt.* peel (*fruit, egg*), shell (*nut*).
descasi *vt.* evict.
desclavi *vt.* unlock.
desclipi *vt.* unclip.
desclori *vt.* dechlorinate.
descoli *vt.* unstick, peel off.
descolori *vt.* discolour (US discolor).
descome *vt.* (*colloquial*) puke, barf, spew, chunder, throw up (*vomit*).
descomforta *n.* malaise, discomfort.
descomposa *vt.* decompose, break down.
descomposada *adj.* decomposed, rotten. • *n.* compost.
descompresa *vt.* decompress. • *n.* decompression.
descomuta *vi.* & *vt.* switch off, turn off, shut off, shut down, disconnect (*machine*); disable (*software feature*). • *n.* shutoff, disconnection.

descomutada *adj.* off, switched off, turned off; disconnected, offline; disabled.
descondena *vt.* overturn the conviction of, quash a guilty verdict against.
desconfusa *vt.* unmuddle, unscramble.
desconjesta *vi.* decongest.
desconjestante *n.* decongestant.
desconstrui *vt.* demolish, knock down (*building, wall*).
desconta *vt.* discount. ● *n.* discount, rebate (*business*).
descontamina *vt.* decontaminate. ● *n.* decontamination.
descontinua *vt.* discontinue, phase out.
descontinuada *adj.* discontinued, defunct.
desconvinse *vt.* dissuade.
descorador *n.* decorer, corer.
descoraji *vt.* discourage, demoralize, dishearten, unnerve. ● *n.* discouragement, despondency.
descorajida *adj.* discouraged, dejected, demoralized, disheartened, despondent, heartsick.
descori *vt.* decore, core.
descoroni *vt.* uncrown.
descorpi *vi.* become disembodied.
descorpida *adj.* disembodied.
descovrable *adj.* discoverable.
descovre *vt.* discover, uncover, find out, ascertain. ● *n.* discovery.
descovror *n.* discoverer.
descremi *vt.* skim.
descremida *adj.* skimmed (*milk*).
descriminali *vi.* & *vt.* decriminalize.
descrivable *adj.* describable.
descrive *vt.* describe. ● *n.* description.
descrivor *n.* describer.
descrusa *vt.* uncross (*arms, legs*).
descuali *vt.* disqualify (*someone*). ● *n.* disqualification.
desculpa *vt.* exculpate, exonerate, vindicate, acquit. ● *n.* exoneration, vindication, acquittal.
desculpada *adj.* exonerated. **es desculpada** be exonerated, be acquitted, get off.
descura *vt.* neglect. ● *n.* negligence, apathy.
descurada *adj.* neglected, overgrown, derelict.
descurante *adj.* negligent, neglectful, derelict.
descurvi *vi.* & *vt.* unbend.
desdefetador *n.* debugger.
desdefeti *vt.* debug.
desdui *vi.* & *vt.* split into twelve. ● *n.* twelfth (*fraction*).
desduple *n.* dozen.
desecreti *vi.* & *vt.* declassify.
desecuilibra *vi.* & *vt.* imbalance, unbalance, throw off balance, tip over, topple, knock over, overbalance.
desecuri *vi.* & *vt.* unlock, untether. **desecuri la polsos de** uncuff. **desecuri la talos de** unshackle.
deseleje *vt.* deselect.
deseli *vt.* unseal.
deselminti *vt.* deworm, worm, drench.
desemafori *vt.* unlock (*database*).
desembarca *vt.* disembark, deplane.
desembla *vi.* be in disguise, disguise oneself, dissemble. ● *vt.* disguise. ● *n.* disguise, guise.
desemblante *adj.* disguise, in disguise, undercover, incognito. **polisior desemblante** plainclothesman, plainclothes officer.
desembraji *vt.* declutch.
desembre *n.* December.
desemi *vt.* pit, stone (*fruit*).
desemplea *vt.* dismiss, fire, sack, lay off (*employee*). ● *n.* dismissal, sacking, layoff.
desenama *vt.* disenamour (US disenamor), cause to fall out of love.
desenamada *adj.* disenamoured (US disenamored). **deveni desenamada par** fall out of love with. **es desenamada par** be disenamoured (US disenamored) with.
desencanta *vt.* disenchant. ● *n.* disenchantment.
desende *vt.* descend, decline, go down; alight, get off. ● *n.* descent.
desendente *adj.* descending, descendent. ● *n.* descendant, scion; descender, downstroke. ● *prep.* down, towards the bottom of. **desendentes** descendants, posterity.
desenerji *vt.* de-energize, enervate. ● *n.* enervation.
desengrana *vi.* & *vt.* disengage (*gear, enemy*). ● *n.* disengagement.
desenio *n.* decade. **es en sua desenio oto** be in one's seventies. **la desenio de 1970** the 1970s.
desenrola *vi.* unroll, unwind, uncoil, unfurl.
desenscrive *vt.* unsubscribe.
desensela *vt.* unsaddle.
desensosi *vi.* & *vt.* desensitize.
desentera *vt.* unearth, disinter, exhume, dig up. ● *n.* unearthing, exhumation.
desentri *vi.* & *vt.* decentralize, decentre (US decenter).
desenvolve *vt.* unwrap.
desepara *vi.* desegregate. ● *n.* desegregation.
deser *n.* dessert, pudding.
deserita *vt.* disinherit.
deserti *vi.* & *vt.* turn into a desert. ● *n.* desertification.
deserto *n.* desert, wasteland, waste.
desfa *vt.* undo. ● *n.* undoing.

desfase *vi.* be out of phase. **desfase de ora** jetlag.
desfaseda *adj.* out of phase.
desfibi *vt.* unbuckle.
desfida *vt.* distrust, mistrust.
desfisa *vt.* unfasten, detach, unlatch, undo, dislodge, remove. • *n.* detachment, removal.
desfisable *adj.* detachable, removable.
desfisada *adj.* detached.
desflori *vt.* deflower.
desfoli *vt.* exfoliate, defoliate, shed skin. • *n.* exfoliation, shedding of skin.
desfolinte *n.* exfoliant, defoliant.
desforesti *vt.* deforest. • *n.* deforestation, forest clearance.
desformi *vi.* & *vt.* deform, buckle. • *n.* deformation, deformity.
desfrati *vi.* & *vt.* defragment. • *n.* defragmentation.
desgrupi *vi.* ungroup, disband.
desi *vi.* split into ten. • *n.* tenth (*fraction*); tithe. • *pref.* deci- (*a tenth*).
desibel *n.* decibel.
deside *vt.* decide, resolve. • *n.* decision, verdict, resolution.
desidente *adj.* decisive. • *n.* tiebreak, runoff, play-off.
desidentifia *vt.* deidentify. **desidentifia se** deidentify oneself, log out (*software*).
desidrata *vi.* dehydrate. • *n.* dehydration.
desifrable *adj.* decipherable.
desifri *vt.* decode, decipher, decrypt. • *n.* decryption.
desigram *n.* decigram.
desil *n.* decile (*statistics*).
desilitre *n.* decilitre (US deciliter).
desilude *vt.* disillusion. • *n.* disillusionment.
desim *n.* ten-pence piece, ten-cent piece, dime (*coin*).
desimal *adj.* decimal.
desimetre *n.* decimetre (US decimeter).
desindente *vt.* unindent, outdent.
desinfesta *vt.* weed; exorcise.
desinfestante *adj.* weeding. • *n.* weedkiller.
desinfeta *vt.* disinfect.
desinfetante *adj.* disinfecting, disinfectant. • *n.* disinfectant. **desinfetante de boca** mouthwash.
desinia *vt.* draw, sketch, illustrate; design, plan (*creatively*); landscape (*garden*). • *n.* drawing, sketch, illustration; design, configuration. **desinia aidada par computador** computer-aided design, CAD.
desiniador *n.* graphics program.
desinieta *vt.* & *n.* doodle.
desinior *n.* designer, draughtsman (US draftsman), illustrator. **desinior de jardines** landscape designer.
desinstala *vt.* uninstall, deinstall.
desintegra *vi.* disintegrate, crumble, unravel. • *n.* disintegration.
desintegrable *adj.* disintegratable, crumbly, friable.
desintensi *vi.* & *vt.* reduce, assuage.
desinteresa *vt.* disinterest, fail to interest. • *n.* disinterest.
desinteresada *adj.* disinterested.
desinturi *vt.* unbelt, unstrap.
desira *vt.* desire, wish for, fancy. • *n.* desire, wish. **desira nonpratical** wishful thinking. **desira sesal** *v.* lust. • *n.* sexual desire, lust, libido.
desirable *adj.* desirable. • *n.* desirable feature, amenity.
desirada *adj.* desirable. • *n.* object of desire. **si desirada** optional, if desired.
deslegali *vi.* & *vt.* illegalize, delegitimize, outlaw.
deslia [desˈlia] *vt.* untie, unbind, disconnect, unplug.
desliada *adj.* untied, unbound.
desloca *vt.* dislocate, displace, offset, shift. • *n.* dislocation, displacement, offset, shift. **desloca blu** blue shift. **desloca de vocales** vowel shift. **desloca roja** red shift.
deslocada *adj.* dislocated, displaced, askew, awry.
desmacia *vt.* remove makeup from.
desmaciante *n.* cleanser.
desmaia *vi.* faint, swoon. • *n.* faintness (*feeling faint*), syncope.
desmalerbi *vt.* weed.
desmarania *vt.* disentangle, untangle, unravel, unsnarl.
desmarca *vt.* unmark, deselect.
desmasci *vt.* unmask.
desmasi *vi.* & *vt.* emasculate. • *n.* emasculation.
desmateri *vi.* & *vt.* dematerialize. • *n.* dematerialization.
desmembri *vt.* dismember.
desmili *vi.* & *vt.* split into ten thousand. • *n.* ten-thousandth (*fraction*).
desmilitari *vi.* & *vt.* demilitarize. • *n.* demilitarization.
desmisca *vt.* unmix, unscramble.
desmisteri *vi.* & *vt.* demystify. • *n.* demystification.
desmiti *vi.* & *vt.* demythologize.
desmodula *vt.* demodulate.
desmonta *vt.* dismount.
desmotiva *vt.* demotivate. • *n.* disincentive.
desmovabli *vi.* & *vt.* immobilize; demobilize. • *n.* immobilization; demobilization.
desnazi *vi.* & *vt.* denazify. • *n.* denazification.
desneblador *n.* demister, defogger.
desnebli *vi.* & *vt.* demist, defog; deblur.
desnevi *vt.* clear snow from.

desobedi *vt.* disobey. • *n.* disobedience.
desobedinte *adj.* disobedient, insubordinate.
desocupa *vt.* vacate.
desodori *vi.* & *vt.* deodorize.
desodorinte *n.* deodorant; air freshener, deodorizer.
desonci *vt.* unhook.
desonora *vt.* dishonour (US dishonor), humiliate, disgrace, discredit, compromise. • *n.* dishonour (US dishonor), humiliation, disgrace, ignominy, opprobrium.
desonorada *adj.* dishonoured (US dishonored), ignominious.
desonorosa *adj.* dishonourable (US dishonorable), disgraceful.
desordina *vt.* mess up, make a mess of, muss, rumple, dishevel, clutter. • *n.* disorder, disarray, clutter, mess, muzz.
desordinada *adj.* messy, untidy, disorderly, sloppy, slovenly, scruffy, bedraggled, dishevelled, unkempt.
desorganiza *vt.* disorganize. • *n.* disorganization.
desorganizada *adj.* disorganized, ragtag, scatterbrain, scatty, sloppy.
desorienta *vi.* disorient, disorientate. • *n.* disorientation.
desosiribonucleal *adj.* deoxyribonucleic.
despaci *vt.* unpack. • *n.* unpacking.
despeli *vt.* skin, flay, excoriate, flense.
despelida *adj.* skinless, skinned.
despera *vi.* despair. • *n.* despair, desperation.
desperante *adj.* desperate.
despersonali *vi.* & *vt.* depersonalize.
despeta *vt.* despise, scorn, disdain, revile, look down on. • *n.* contempt, scorn, disdain.
despetable *adj.* despicable, loathsome, execrable, contemptible, pissant.
despetada *adj.* despised, despicable.
despetante *adj.* pejorative.
despeteni *vt.* dishevel, mess up (*hair*).
despetenida *adj.* dishevelled, uncombed, messy, tangled, unkempt.
despetosa *adj.* contemptuous, scornful, disdainful, dismissive, contemptuous, cavalier.
despini *vt.* unpin.
despioli *vt.* delouse.
despiriti *vt.* dispirit.
despiritinte *adj.* dispiriting, soul-destroying.
desplanta *vt.* dig up, uproot.
desplantador *n.* trowel.
desplase *vt.* displease. • *n.* displeasure.
desplasente *adj.* disagreeable, unpleasant, displeasing, nasty, horrid, horrible, distasteful, sordid.
desplia [desˈplia] *vt.* unfold.
desplumi *vt.* pluck (*feathers*).
despolali *vi.* & *vt.* depolarize. • *n.* depolarization.
despolvi *vt.* dust.
despone *vt.* depose, oust, remove from office. • *n.* deposition, ouster.
despopla *vt.* depopulate. • *n.* depopulation.
despota *n.* despot.
despotia *n.* despotate.
despotin *adj.* despotic.
desprendable *adj.* disposable, expendable.
desprende *vt.* get rid of, throw away, discard, dispense with, dispose of, waive. • *n.* disposal.
despreti *vi.* become defrocked. • *vt.* defrock, unfrock, laicize.
desprogrami *vt.* deprogramme (US deprogram), remove brainwashing from.
desradisi *vi.* & *vt.* uproot.
desramador *n.* billhook, pruning hook, lopper.
desrami *vt.* remove branches, prune, cane.
desrefere *vi.* & *vt.* dereference (*software*).
desregula *vt.* deregulate. • *n.* deregulation.
desreli *vt.* derail.
desrespeta *vt.* disrespect. • *n.* disrespect, insolence.
desrespetosa *adj.* disrespectful, flippant, overfamiliar.
desrisi *vi.* & *vt.* uncurl.
desroji *vi.* become less red. • *vt.* remove red from; remove red-eye from (*photo*).
desrompe *vi.* cease to be broken. • *vt.* mend, repair, patch, troubleshoot.
desruidi *vt.* denoise, remove noise from.
destabli *vi.* & *vt.* destabilize. • *n.* destabilization.
destapi *vt.* unplug, unseal, unstop, uncork, uncap.
destartari *vt.* descale; remove tartar.
desteni *vt.* let go of, lose one's grip on, unhand.
destensa *vi.* untense, untighten, relax, take it easy. • *n.* relaxation; detente.
destensante *n.* relaxant. **destensante de musculo** muscle relaxant.
destesti *vt.* behead, decapitate. • *n.* beheading, decapitation.
desteti *vt.* wean.
destexe *vt.* unweave, unpick, unravel.
destexeda *adj.* unravelled (US unraveled), frayed.
destina *vt.* destine. • *n.* destination; destiny, fate, kismet; addressee.
destinada *adj.* destined, bound.
destorse *vi.* untwist.
destra *adj.* right (*not left*); starboard. • *n.* right (*not left*). **a destra** on the right. **a destra de** on the right of.

destricota *vt.* unravel.
destrisme *n.* rightism.
destriste *adj.* right-wing, rightist. • *n.* right-winger, rightist.
destroni *vt.* dethrone.
destrosa[1] *n.* dextrose (*sugar*).
destrosa[2] *adj.* handy, dextrous, skilful (US skillful), deft.
destrosia *n.* dexterity.
destrui *vt.* destroy, demolish, decimate, raze, spoil; blast, zap. • *n.* destruction, demolition.
destruinte *adj.* destructive, ruinous.
destruor *n.* destroyer, demolisher.
desumani *vi.* & *vt.* dehumanize. • *n.* dehumanization.
desumidador *n.* dehumidifier.
desumidi *vi.* & *vt.* dehumidify, desiccate.
desuni *vi.* & *vt.* disunite. • *n.* disunion.
desusa *vt.* disuse, no longer use. • *n.* obsolescence.
desusada *adj.* disused, obsolete, archaic, defunct.
desvalidi *vi.* expire. • *vt.* invalidate, debunk. • *n.* expiration.
desvalidida *adj.* expired, out of date.
desvalua *vt.* devalue, belittle, disparage, denigrate, deprecate, depreciate, trivialize, vilify. • *n.* devaluation, deprecation, depreciation.
desveli *vt.* unveil. • *n.* unveiling.
desveneni *vt.* detox, detoxify.
desventri *vt.* disembowel, gut, eviscerate.
desvermi *vt.* deworm, worm, drench.
desvesti *vt.* undress, disrobe.
desvide *vt.* unsee.
desvisi *vt.* unscrew.
deta *n.* debt, debit, arrears. **deta de jua** gambling debt.
detalia *vt.* detail, itemize; pinpoint. • *n.* detail.
detaliosa *adj.* detailed, elaborate.
deteneria *n.* detention centre (US center).
deteni *vt.* detain. • *n.* detention.
deterjente *n.* detergent, cleanser. **deterjente de platos** dishwashing liquid, washing-up liquid.
determina *vt.* determine, dictate. • *n.* determination.
determinada *adj.* determined; purposeful, resolute. **jenetical determinada** genetically determined, hardwired.
determinante *n.* determiner, determinative (*grammar*). **determinante de demanda** interrogative determiner (*grammar*).
determinisme *n.* determinism.
deterministe *adj.* deterministic. • *n.* determinist.
deteta *vt.* detect, discern. • *n.* detection.
detetador *n.* detector. **detetador de bombas** bomb detector. **detetador de bombetas** mine detector. **detetador de fumas** smoke detector. **detetador de mentis** lie detector. **detetador de metales** metal detector.
detetor *n.* detective, investigator, sleuth, gumshoe, private eye.
detona *vi.* detonate.
detor *n.* debtor.
detrito *n.* detritus; debris, rubble.
detrivor *adj.* detrivorous. • *n.* detrivore.
deuterio *n.* deuterium (*chemistry*).
deuterostomio *n.* deuterostome (*organism: Deuterostomia*).
deutx *adj.* German. • *n.* German (*person, language*).
Deutxland *n.* Germany.
devanagari *n.* Devanagari (*writing system*).
developa *vi.* develop, hone, educe; catch, contract (*illness*). • *n.* development. **developa la gripe** catch cold. **developa tro multe** overdevelop.
developor *n.* developer.
deveni *v.* become, get, grow, turn; e.g. *me deveni vea*; *la eruga ia deveni un papilio.*
devia *vi.* deviate, stray, swerve, go off course. • *n.* deviation, aberration, detour, discrepancy, swerve.
deviante *adj.* deviant, deviating, deviated, stray, astray, awry, aberrant, errant.
devolui *vi.* devolve. • *n.* devolution.
devonian *adj.* & *n.* Devonian (*geology*).
devora *vt.* devour, gobble, scoff.
devorante *adj.* voracious, ravenous, ravening.
dexarnieri *vt.* unhinge.
dezipi *vt.* unzip.
dezuma *vi.* zoom out.
di- *pref.* di- (*two*).
dia[1] *n.* day; daytime. **a cada dia** every day. **a la otra dia** the other day. **de la dia** of the day, du jour. **dia completa** day (*24-hour period*). **Dia D** D-day. **dia de comersia** business day. **dia de labora** working day, workday, weekday, business day. **dia de lava** washday. **Dia de Memoria** Remembrance Day. **dia de paia** payday. **dia de semana** day of the week, weekday. **dia santa** sabbath.
dia-[2] *pref.* dia-.
diabete *n.* diabetes.
diabetica *adj.* diabetic.
diablin *adj.* devilish.
diablo *n.* devil, Satan, Lucifer. **diablo caxida** jack-in-the-box. **diablo tasmanian** Tasmanian devil (*Sarcophilus harrisii*).
diablosa *adj.* diabolic, diabolical.
diacon *n.* deacon, provost.

diacrona *adj.* diachronic.
diafana *adj.* translucent, diaphanous, semi-transparent, sheer, gauzy, filmy, frosted.
diafania *n.* translucency.
diafonia *n.* crosstalk.
diaframa *n.* diaphragm. **diaframa contraconsepal** contraceptive diaphragm.
diagnose *vt.* diagnose; troubleshoot. • *n.* diagnosis, diagnostics. **programes de diagnose** diagnostic tools (*software*).
diagnosiste *n.* diagnostician.
diagonal *adj.* diagonal, slanted.
dial *adj.* daily, diurnal (*once a day*); everyday, quotidian.
dialetica *n.* dialectic.
dialeticiste *n.* dialectician.
dialeto *n.* dialect, patois. **dialeto fonetical** accent.
dialise *n.* dialysis, haemodialysis (US hemodialysis).
dialogo *n.* dialogue (US dialog); dialogue (US dialog) box (*software*).
diamante *n.* diamond (*including cards*). **diamante bruta** uncut diamond; diamond in the rough. **diamante falsa** false diamond, rhinestone.
diamantin *adj.* diamondlike, diamond-shaped.
diametre *n.* diameter.
dianto *n.* pink (*plant*: *Dianthus*).
diapositiva *n.* slide (*photography*).
diarca *n.* diarch (*governor*).
diarcia *n.* diarchy, dyarchy.
diarea *n.* diarrhoea (US diarrhea).
diaspora *n.* diaspora.
diastolal *adj.* diastolic.
diastole *n.* diastole (*biology*).
diatomea *n.* diatom (*organism*: *Bacillariophyceae*).
diatonica *adj.* diatonic.
diazepam *n.* diazepam, valium.
dicdic *n.* dik-dik (*antelope*: *Madoqua*).
dicotiledon *n.* dicotyledon, dicot (*botany*).
dicotomia *n.* dichotomy.
dicotomial *adj.* dichotomous.
dicromata *adj.* dichromatic.
didje *n.* deejay, DJ, disc jockey.
didjeridu [didʒeriˈdu] *n.* didgeridoo, didjeridu.
dierese *n.* diaeresis (US dieresis) (*diacritic*).
dies *adj.* & *n.* sharp (*music*).
dieta *vi.* & *n.* diet. **dieta intensa** crash diet.
dietal *adj.* dietary.
dietiste *n.* dietician.
dietor *n.* dieter.
difere *vi.* differ. • *n.* difference.
diferensia *vt.* differentiate (*mathematics*). • *n.* differentiation.
diferensial *adj.* & *n.* differential.
diferente *adj.* different, disparate, unlike; e.g. *el es multe diferente de sua frate.*
difisil *adj.* difficult, hard, awkward; abstruse. • *adv.* awkwardly, with difficulty. • *n.* difficulty, issue.
difisili *vi.* become difficult, get harder. • *vt.* make difficult, make harder.
difisilia *n.* difficulty (*state*), awkwardness.
difrata *vi.* diffract. • *n.* diffraction.
difteria *n.* diphtheria.
diftongo *n.* diphthong (*vowel sound*).
difusa *vt.* broadcast, diffuse, disseminate, spread. • *n.* broadcast, telecast, broadcasting, diffusion, dissemination. **difusa de novas** newscast, news bulletin. **difusa simultan** simulcast.
digram *n.* digraph.
dijesta *vt.* digest. • *n.* digestion.
dijestable *adj.* digestible.
dijestal *adj.* digestive, alimentary.
dijital *adj.* digital.
dijitale *n.* digitalis, foxglove (*Digitalis*).
dijitali *vi.* & *vt.* digitize, digitalize.
dijito *n.* digit (*numerical*).
dilata *vi.* dilate. • *n.* dilation.
dilatador *n.* dilator.
dildo *n.* dildo.
dilema *n.* dilemma, quandary.
dilijente *n.* stagecoach.
dilui *vt.* dilute, water down. • *n.* dilution.
diluida *adj.* diluted, dilute.
Dimashq *n.* Damascus.
dimension *n.* dimension. **con tre dimensiones** three-dimensional. **en tre dimensiones** in three dimensions, three-dimensionally.
dimensional *adj.* dimensional.
dimetre *n.* dimeter (*poetry*).
diminui *vi.* decrease, decrement, diminish, lessen, shrink, contract, taper, wane, dwindle; depreciate (*in value*). • *vt.* decrease, diminish, lessen, reduce, shrink, mitigate. • *n.* decrease, diminution; depreciation.
diminuida *adj.* shrunken.
diminuinte *adj.* decreasing, shrinking, tapering, tapered.
dimsam *n.* dim sum (*food*).
dinamica *n.* dynamics; dynamic. **dinamica de fluentes** fluid dynamics.
dinamical *adj.* dynamic, dynamical.
dinamicisme *n.* dynamism.
dinamite *n.* dynamite.
dinamitor *n.* dynamiter.
dinamo *n.* dynamo.
dinamometre *n.* dynamometer.
dinar *n.* dinar (*currency*).
dinastia *n.* dynasty.
dinastial *adj.* dynastic.
dine[1] *n.* dyne (*unit of force*).

dine2 *adj.* & *n.* Dine, Navaho, Navajo (*person, language*).
dingo *n.* dingo (*Canis lupus dingo*).
dini *vt.* dignify.
dinia *n.* dignity.
diniosa *adj.* dignified, stately.
dinosauro *n.* dinosaur (*Dinosauria*).
dio *n.* god, deity; God; Allah. **de dio** divine. **dio minor** minor god, demigod. **dio par machina** deus ex machina. **sin dio** godless.
diodo *n.* diode. **diodo de lus** light-emitting diode, LED.
dionia *n.* Venus flytrap (*plant*: *Dionaea muscipula*).
dionisal *adj.* Dionysiac, Dionysian.
Dioniso *n.* Dionysus.
diosa *adj.* numinous.
diosido *n.* dioxide. **diosido de carbono** carbon dioxide. **diosido de silico** silicon dioxide, silica.
diosina *n.* dioxin (*substance*).
diplo- *pref.* diplo- (*double*).
diploide *adj.* & *n.* diploid.
diploma *n.* diploma, degree. **diploma avansada** advanced degree. **(diploma) dotoral** doctorate. **(diploma) laural** bachelor's, baccalaureate. **(diploma) mestral** master's.
diplomata *adj.* diplomatic. • *n.* diplomat, envoy, emissary.
diplomatia *n.* diplomacy. **diplomatia navetal** shuttle diplomacy.
diplopia *n.* diplopia, double vision.
dipno *n.* lungfish (*Dipnoi*).
dipsaco *n.* teasel, teazle, teazel (*plant*: *Dipsacus*).
direta *adj.* direct, straight; immediate, instant, instantaneous; explicit, firsthand, outright. • *adv.* directly, immediately, instantly, straightaway, summarily, at once. **difusa direta** live broadcast, live transmission, live programme (US program). **direta cuando** as soon as.
direto *n.* right, just claim, entitlement; prerogative. **ave la direto** have the right, be entitled, be qualified. **direto de autor** copyright. **direto de vota** right to vote, suffrage, franchise. **direto nativa de tera** native title, native land right. **direto natural** natural right, birthright. **diretos** rights. **diretos de autor** royalties.
dirijador *n.* router (*computer*).
dirijal *adj.* administrative, managerial.
dirije *vt.* direct, steer; manage, administer, administrate, orchestrate, operate, run (*business*). • *n.* direction, heading, bearing; management, administration. **de un dirije** one-way. **dirije se a** direct oneself to, address oneself to (*audience, task*). **en dirije a** in the direction of, toward, towards.
dirijor *n.* director, executive, trustee, manager, administrator, operator, provost. **dirijor de selebra** event planner. **dirijores** administration, management, board (*directors, trustees*).
dirndl *n.* dirndl (*costume*).
dis- *pref.* dys- (*bad, abnormal*).
disacarido *n.* disaccharide.
discador *n.* CD drive, CD player; DVD drive, DVD player, DVD recorder.
discalculia *n.* dyscalculia.
discalculica *adj.* dyscalculic.
disci *vt.* dial (*phone number*).
discin *adj.* disclike, disc-shaped.
disco *n.* disc, discus, roundel; disk, record, CD, DVD; dial (*telephone, radio, etc.*); disco (*music*). **disco compata** compact disc, CD. **disco de hoci** hockey puck. **disco de inisia** startup disk. **disco de vinil** record (*vinyl*). **disco dur** hard disk, hard drive. **disco mol** floppy disk. **disco video** video disc, DVD.
discografia *n.* discography.
discoteca *n.* disco, discotheque.
discreta *adj.* discreet.
discutable *adj.* debatable, up for discussion, moot.
discute *vt.* discuss, talk about, deliberate. • *n.* discussion, deliberation.
dise *vt.* say, state, tell, utter. • *n.* utterance. **dise coreta** be correct, be right (*in what one says*). **dise forte** *v.* assert. • *n.* assertion. **on dise ce** they say that, it is said that, it is rumoured that. **on ta dise** one might say, you could say, as it were. **per dise** namely, that is to say, in other words, to wit, i.e. **per dise esata** strictly speaking.
diseda *adj.* said. • *n.* saying, maxim, adage, proverb. **como diseda par** according to, as said by. **diseda saja** wise saying, word of wisdom, aphorism.
diseno [dise'no] *n.* naysayer.
disenteria *n.* dysentery.
disenti *vi.* dissent. • *n.* dissention.
disentor *n.* dissenter, apostate, non-conformist.
disesi [dise'si] *n.* yesman.
disfajia *n.* dysphagia (*medical*).
disfasia *n.* dysphasia (*medical*).
disforia *n.* dysphoria (*medical*).
disi *n.* flowerpecker (*bird*: *Dicaeidae*).
disionario *n.* dictionary. **disionario de sinonimes** synonym dictionary, thesaurus.
disipa *vi.* dissipate.
disipador *n.* dissipator. **disipador de caldia** heat sink.

disiplina *vt.* discipline, chasten. • *n.* discipline.
disiplinor *n.* disciplinarian, martinet.
disiplo *n.* disciple, protégé.
dislexia *n.* dyslexia.
dislexica *adj.* dyslexic.
disolvable *adj.* dissolvable, soluble.
disolve *vi.* dissolve. • *n.* dissolution; solution (*liquid mixture*).
disolveda *adj.* dissolved. • *n.* solute.
disolvente *adj.* dissolving. • *n.* solvent.
dispepsia *n.* dyspepsia, dyspepsy.
dispepsica *adj.* dyspeptic.
displasia *n.* dysplasia (*medical*).
dispnea *n.* dyspnoea (US dyspnea) (*medical*).
disponable *adj.* available.
disponablia *n.* availability.
dispone *vt.* have available, have at one's disposal; e.g. *nos no dispone un lavabo.*
disposa *vt.* dispose (*someone to*), predispose, incline. • *n.* disposition, predisposition, attitude, approach, stance. **disposa mental** mental attitude, mindset, mentality.
disposada *adj.* inclined, disposed, predisposed.
disprosio *n.* dysprosium (*element*).
disputa *vt.* dispute, quarrel over, argue about, contest, row, impugn. • *n.* dispute, quarrel, argument, debate, conflict, strife, row, feud, dust-up, fracas, wrangle.
disputable *adj.* arguable, controversial.
disputada *adj.* disputed, controversial.
disputeta *n.* spat, minor quarrel.
disputosa *adj.* quarrelsome, argumentative, tetchy, irritable, bad-tempered, ill-tempered, hot-tempered, quick-tempered, irascible, cross, surly, choleric, grouchy, grumpy, peevish, prickly, bolshy, crabby, cantankerous, fractious, pugnacious, scrappy, truculent. • *n.* curmudgeon, hothead.
distante *adj.* distant, remote, distal, far, far away, far out, afar, outlying; aloof. • *adv.* far away, in the distance, distantly. **plu distante ca** farther than, beyond.
distanti *vi.* distance, move away, grow distant. • *vt.* make distant, take far away.
distantia *n.* distance. **a distantia** remote, (*operating*) from a distance. **distantia focal** focal length.
distila *vt.* distil (US distill). • *n.* distillation.
distilada *adj.* distilled. • *n.* distillate, liquor, spirit, booze (*distilled beverage*).
distilador *n.* still, alembic.
distileria *n.* distillery.
distinguable *adj.* distinguishable, distinct.
distingui *vt.* distinguish, differentiate, discriminate, tell apart, characterize. • *n.* distinction, differentiation, discrimination, characterization. **sin distingui** indiscriminate, undifferentiated.
distinguida *adj.* distinct, distinctive.
distinguinte *adj.* selective, discriminating. • *n.* distinguishing feature, idiosyncrasy. **distinguinte leteras major** case-sensitive.
distonia *n.* dystonia (*medical*).
distrae *vt.* distract. • *n.* distraction.
distraeda *adj.* distracted, absent-minded.
distribuador *n.* distributor.
distribui *vt.* distribute, dispense, serve out, hand out, hand round; deal (*cards*). • *n.* distribution. **distribui proportial** distribute proportionally, prorate.
distribuor *n.* distributor.
distrital *adj.* district, regional.
distriti *vt.* district, divide into districts.
distrito *n.* district, precinct, borough, township.
distrofia *n.* dystrophy (*medical*).
distrofica *adj.* dystrophic.
disturba *vt.* disturb, perturb, disrupt, interfere (*with normal functioning*); interrupt, intrude on, impose on, put out, disconcert, unsettle, bother.—*Disturba* suggests a minor interruption; *turba* suggests a more serious upset. • *n.* disturbance, perturbation, disruption, commotion, imposition, ruckus, rumpus; disorder, condition (*medical*). **disturba se (per)** be bothered (*with*), go to the trouble (*of*), make the effort (*of*).
disturbable *adj.* disturbable.
disturbada *adj.* disturbed. **es disturbada par** be bothered by, mind.
disturbante *adj.* disturbing, uncanny.
disulfido *n.* disulphide (US disulfide) (*chemistry*).
disuria *n.* dysuria (*medical*).
dita *vt.* dictate. • *n.* dictation.
ditador *n.* dictaphone.
dital *n.* thimble.
diti *vt.* finger. **diti se** (*colloquial*) touch oneself, wank (*masturbate*).
ditin *adj.* fingerlike.
dito *n.* finger; digit. **dito de anelo** ring finger, fourth finger. **dito de pede** toe. **dito indicante** index finger. **dito martelin** hammertoe. **dito media** middle finger. **dito peti** little finger, pinky, pinkie. **sur ditos de pedes** on tiptoe. See *orteo.*
diton *n.* thumb; inch (*unit of length*). **diton de pede** big toe.
ditransitiva *adj.* ditransitive, divalent (*grammar*).
diurese *n.* diuresis (*medical*).
diuresica *n.* diuretic.
diurna *adj.* daytime, diurnal.
diva *n.* goddess; diva.

divalente *adj.* divalent.
divali *n.* Diwali, Deepavali (*Hindu festival*).
Divehi *n.* Maldives. **divehi** *adj.* & *n.* Maldivian. See *Maldives.*
diverjador *n.* overflow, spillway.
diverje *vi.* divert, diverge, shunt, sidetrack, turn in another direction. • *n.* divergence.
diverjente *adj.* divergent.
diversa *adj.* diverse, motley, various, miscellaneous, several, assorted, numerous, ragtag, sundry, a range of. **cosas diversa** various things, several things.
diversi *vi.* & *vt.* diversify.
diversia *n.* diversity, variety.
diverti *vi.* have fun, enjoy oneself. • *vt.* amuse, entertain, divert, regale. • *n.* amusement, entertainment, diversion, fun, frivolity. **diverti bon** have fun, have a good time.
diverticulite *n.* diverticulitis (*medical*).
diverticulo *n.* diverticulum (*anatomy, medical*).
diverticulose *n.* diverticulosis (*medical*).
divertida *adj.* amused, entertained.
divertinte *adj.* amusing, entertaining, fun, light-hearted.
divertor *n.* entertainer.
dividable *adj.* divisible, capable of being divided.
divide *vi.* divide, part, split, fork, partition, sever. • *vt.* divide, part, split, fork, partition; ration, hand over part of, share out. • *n.* division, parting, splitting, split, partitioning; rationing; septum (*anatomy*). **divide de comeda** food rationing.
divideda *adj.* divided, split, forked, cloven, cleft. • *n.* numerator. **divideda entre** divided by.
dividendo *n.* dividend.
dividente *adj.* dividing, divisive. • *n.* divisor, denominator.
divin *adj.* divine, godlike. • *n.* deity, godhead, deva.
divina *vt.* guess, conjecture, speculate. • *n.* guess, speculation, guesswork. **divina informada** educated guess. **divina ritual** divination.
divinante *adj.* guessing, speculative.
divini *vi.* become divine. • *vt.* deify, apotheosize. • *n.* deification, apotheosis.
divinisme *n.* deism.
diviniste *adj.* deistic, deist. • *n.* deist.
divinor *n.* speculator; soothsayer.
divorsa *vt.* & *n.* divorce.
divorsada *n.* divorcee.
djadjici *n.* tzatziki (*food*).
Djava *n.* Java. **djava** *adj.* & *n.* Javanese (*person, language*). **Mar Djava** Java Sea.
djembe *n.* djembe (*drum*).
Djibuti *n.* Djibouti. **djibuti** *adj.* & *n.* Djibouti, Djiboutian.
djihad *n.* jihad. **djihad grande** greater jihad.
djihadiste *n.* jihadi, jihadist.
djini *n.* genie, jinni, djinn.
djiniu *n.* Jin, Jin-yu (*language*).
djuang *adj.* & *n.* Zhuang (*person, language*).
do[1] *adv.* (*interrogative*) where; (*relative*) where; e.g. *do es la porte?; do nos vade?; me no sabe do la porte es; un parte de la pais do on bisicli multe.* • *subord.* where; e.g. *me es felis do me senta; los escava su do on ia trova la osos.* **a do** to where, where to, whither. **de do** from where, where from, whence. **sempre do** wherever.
do[2] *n.* do (*musical note*).
doberman *n.* Doberman (US Dobermann) (*dog*).
dobro *n.* dobro (*guitar*).
doca *n.* dock, wharf.
doci *vt.* dock.
docor *n.* docker, dock worker, longshoreman, stevedore.
documenti *vt.* document. • *n.* documentation (*action*).
documento *n.* document, certificate. **documento de nase** birth certificate. **documentos** documents, documentation. **documentos de identia** identity documents, credentials. **documentos de rexerca** research material, research documents. **documentos fondal** background material, background documents. **documentos orijinal** source material, source documents. **sin documentos** undocumented.
dodo *n.* dodo (*bird: Raphus cucullatus*).
dogma *n.* dogma.
dogmisme *n.* dogmatism.
dogmosa *adj.* dogmatic.
dolable *adj.* vulnerable.
dolar *n.* dollar.
dole *vi.* feel pain, hurt, ache; e.g. *me dole; mea gama dole.* • *vt.* cause pain to, pain, hurt, afflict; e.g. *mea sapatos dole me.* • *n.* pain, hurt, ache, suffering, affliction, gyp. **dole agu** sharp pain, pang. **dole de cor** heartache (*metaphor*). **dole de dente** toothache. **dole de dorso** backache, back pain. **dole de mundo** world-weariness, Weltschmerz. **dole de orea** earache. **dole de stomaco** stomach ache. **dole de testa** headache. **dole de ventre** bellyache. **doles de mori** death throes. **sin dole** painless.
dolente *adj.* hurtful.
doleta *vi.* & *n.* ache.
doletosa *adj.* achy, aching.
dolico- *pref.* dolicho- (*long*).

dolina *n.* sinkhole, swallowhole, swallet, doline.
dolineta *n.* pothole.
dolmen *n.* dolmen (*tomb*).
dolomita *n.* dolomite (*mineral*).
dolon *n.* agony, extreme pain.
dolosa *adj.* painful, sore.
doma *vt.* domesticate, tame. **doma esibal** dressage.
domada *adj.* domesticated, tame, domestic.
doman *adv.* & *n.* tomorrow. **a la dia pos doman** the day after tomorrow.
domina *vt.* dominate, domineer, subjugate, exert power over; predominate, prevail, obtain. • *n.* domination, dominion, domain, sovereignty, predomination, preponderance. **domina publica** public domain.
dominante *adj.* dominant, domineering, predominant; mainstream.
Dominica *n.* Dominica.
dominican *adj.* & *n.* Dominican (*of Dominica, the Dominican Republic, or the monastic order*). **Republica Dominican** Dominican Republic.
domino *n.* domino. **dominos** dominoes (*game*).
dominor *n.* dominator, dominatrix.
dona *vt.* give, contribute, donate, impart, pass, hand, confer, grant, endow, bestow, award, vouchsafe. • *n.* contribution, donation, grant, endowment. **dona acua a** water (*animals*). **dona lete a** nurse (*give milk to*). **dona un titulo a** entitle.
donada *adj.* given. • *n.* present, gift, donation, contribution; tip, pourboire. **donada a Dio** oblation. **donada de Dio** godsend. **donada per studia** scholarship. **donadas** presents, gifts, largesse (US largess).
donce *adv.* therefore, so, then, consequently, thus, ergo, thereby. • *conj.* therefore, so, and so, ergo; e.g. *me pensa, donce me esiste.* **e donce?** so what? (*disinterest*).
dongle *n.* dongle (*device*).
donor *n.* giver, donor, donator.
donut *n.* doughnut, donut.
dopamina *n.* dopamine.
dora *vt.* gild. **dora de fatos** spin (*political*). **dora la lil** gild the lily.
dorada *adj.* gilded, gilt.
dorado *n.* dorado (*fish: Salminus maxillosus*). **Dorado** *n.* Dorado (*constellation*).
dormeria *n.* dormitory (*sleeping quarters*).
dormeta *vi.* doze, nap, snooze. • *n.* doze, nap, snooze, siesta, catnap.
dormi *vi.* sleep. • *n.* sleep, slumber, shuteye. **dormi paradoxal** REM sleep, paradoxical sleep. **dormi tro longa** oversleep. **sin dormi** sleepless.
dorminte *adj.* sleeping, asleep, dormant.
dormosa *adj.* sleepy, drowsy.
dormosia *n.* sleepiness, drowsiness, somnolence.
doror *n.* gilder. **doror de fatos** spin doctor (*gilder of facts*).
dorsal *adj.* dorsal, of the back.
dorsi *vt.* put one's back to, turn one's back on.
dorso *n.* back, dorsal area; spine (*book*); reverse (*side*); tails (*coin*). **a dorso** on one's back, piggyback. **dorso de mano** back of the hand. **dorso de montania** mountain ridge.
dosa *vt.* dose. • *n.* dose, drench; jigger.
dote *n.* dowry. **dote de bebe** layette.
dotor *n.* doctor. **dotor medical** medical doctor, physician.
dotoral *adj.* doctoral.
dox *n.* dox (*exposure of information*).
doxi *vt.* dox.
Dr *abbr.* (*dotor*) Dr.
dracma *n.* drachma (*currency*).
draga *vt.* dredge, trawl.
dragabombeta *n.* minesweeper.
dragador *n.* dredger, trawler.
dragon *n.* dragon. **Dragon** *n.* Draco (*constellation*).
dragster *n.* dragster (*car*).
draisin *n.* handcar (*railway maintenance vehicle*).
drama *n.* drama.
dramal *adj.* dramatic, theatrical.
dramaturjia *n.* dramaturgy.
drami *vt.* dramatize. • *n.* dramatization.
dramiste *n.* dramatist.
dramosa *adj.* dramatic, dramatical, spectacular, histrionic.
drape *vi.* drape, swag.
dravidian *adj.* Dravidian.
drena *vi.* & *vt.* drain. • *n.* drainage.
drepani *n.* Hawaiian honeycreeper (*bird: Drepanidinae*).
dribla *vt.* dribble (*ball*).
droga *n.* drug.
drogamania *n.* drug addiction, drug habit.
drogamanica *adj.* addicted to drugs. • *n.* drug addict, junkie.
drogi *vt.* drug, dope.
droma *n.* crab plover (*bird: Dromas ardeola*).
dromedario *n.* dromedary.
drongo *n.* drongo (*bird: Dicruridae*).
drosera *n.* sundew (*plant: Drosera*).
Druciul *n.* Bhutan. See *drucpa, Butan.*
drucpa *adj.* & *n.* Bhutanese, Bhutanse. See *butan, Druciul.*
druida *n.* druid.
drupa *n.* drupe (*botany*).
du *det.* two. • *adj.* second (*ordinal*). • *n.* two, deuce (*cards*). • *pref.* great-(*grandparent*). **a du veses** twice. **la monte du de la plu**

altas the second highest mountain. **la monte du la plu alta** the second highest mountain.
duable *adj.* even (*number*).
dual *adj.* dual (*grammar*).
dualia *n.* duality.
duana *n.* customs (*agency*).
duanial *adj.* biennial.
duanor *n.* customs official.
duava *n.* great-grandmother.
duavi *n.* great-grandparent.
duavo *n.* great-grandfather.
dubnio *n.* dubnium (*element*).
ducat *n.* ducat (*coin*).
ducolorida *adj.* two-coloured (US two-colored), piebald, skewbald.
dudes *det.* twenty. • *adj.* twentieth (*ordinal*).
dudesi *vi.* & *vt.* split into twenty. • *n.* twentieth (*fraction*).
dudesim *n.* five-pence piece, five-cent piece, nickel (*coin*).
duel *n.* duel.
dufel *n.* duffel, duffle.
dugong *n.* dugong (*animal: Dugong dugon*).
dui *vi.* halve, split in two, bisect, fork, bifurcate. • *n.* half, moiety. • *pref.* half-, semi-, hemi-. See *emi-*, *semi-*.
duicalson *n.* leggings.
duiconsensa *adj.* semiconscious.
duiconsensia *n.* semiconsciousness.
duida *adj.* halved, half.
duifrate *n.* half-brother.
duigalopa *vi.* & *n.* canter.
duilus *n.* twilight, half light.
duiplen *adj.* half full.
duisentim *n.* halfpenny, ha'penny, halfpence.
duisore *n.* half-sister.
duivive *n.* half-life.
dulse *adj.* sweet; nice, gentle, dulset; cute. **dulse per la oios** *adj.* nice to look at, pleasing on the eye. • *n.* (*colloquial*) eye candy.
dulsi *vi.* & *vt.* sweeten.
dulsia *n.* sweetness, gentleness, cuteness.
dulsimer *n.* dulcimer. **dulsimer martelida** hammered dulcimer.
dulsinte *n.* sweetener.
dumensal *adj.* bimonthly (*once every two months*).
duna *n.* dune. **duna de neva** snowdrift.
duneta *n.* great-granddaughter.
dunete *n.* great-grandchild.
duneto *n.* great-grandson.
duodeno *n.* duodenum (*anatomy*).
duple *adj.* double, twofold, duplex, dual. • *adv.* doubly, twice. • *n.* double, pair, couple, duet, couplet, dyad. **deveni un duple** become a couple. **divide a duples** divide into pairs, pair up. **en duples** two by two, in pairs, in couples. **grupi a duples** group into pairs, pair up.
dupli *vi.* double, duplicate. • *vi.* double, duplicate; dub, overdub (*audio*). • *n.* duplication, redundancy; dubbing (*audio*).
duplia *n.* duality.
duplida *adj.* doubled, duplicated; dubbed, overdubbed.
duplinte *adj.* duplicating, redundant.
duplisme *n.* dualism, duality, dichotomy, bifurcation.
dupliste *n.* dualist; duettist.
dupunto *n.* colon.
dur *adj.* hard, firm, tough, resistant to pressure; harsh, hostile (*environment*); difficult.
dura[1] *vi.* endure, continue to exist, last, hold out, eke out. • *n.* endurance, stamina, staying power, durability. **dura plu longa ca** outlast. **dura tra** last for, endure for (*a specified time*).
dura-[2] *pref.* dura- (*hard*).
duramadre *n.* dura mater (*anatomy*).
durante *adj.* durable, resilient, robust, sturdy, hardy, strong, tough, lasting, long-lasting.—*Durante* does not mean *during*.
duri *vi.* & *vt.* harden, toughen, hard-boil.
durzi *adj.* & *n.* Druze (*Islam*).
dusento *det.* two hundred. • *adj.* two hundredth (*ordinal*).
dusobrin *n.* grandniece or grandnephew (*cousin of one's grandchildren's generation*).
dusobrina *n.* grandniece.
dusobrino *n.* grandnephew.
duta *vt.* doubt. • *n.* doubt, qualm, reservation. **dutas** doubts, scruples, reservations. **sin duta** doubtless, undoubted; undoubtedly. **sin duta tu era** you must be mistaken.
dutable *adj.* doubtable, dubitable, questionable, open to doubt.
dutada *adj.* doubted, dubious, doubtful.
dutante *adj.* sceptical (US skeptical), doubtful.
dutia [du'tia] *n.* female cousin of one's grandparents' generation.
dutie *n.* cousin of one's grandparents' generation.
dutio [du'tio] *n.* male cousin of one's grandparents' generation.
duto *n.* duct, shaft (*tunnel*); tract, vessel. **duto de caldi** heating duct, flue. **duto de fuma** flue. **duto sangual** blood vessel.
dutosa *adj.* doubtful, doubting.
dux *n.* shower, sprinkler; shower stall, shower cubicle. **dux vajinal** vaginal douche.
duxal *adj.* ducal.
Duxanbe *n.* Dushanbe (*city*).
duxe *n.* duke.

duxesa *n.* duchess.
duxi *vt.* shower, sprinkle; water (*flowers*). • *n.* shower (*occurrence*). **duxi se** take a shower.
duxia *n.* duchy.
duxierba *n.* garden sprinkler.
dvd *abbr.* (*disco video dijital*) DVD.

E

E[1] [e]~[ɛ], **e** *letter* E, e.
e[2] *conj.* and. **e … e** both … and; e.g. *e esta e acel.* **e/o** and/or.
e-[3] *pref.* e- (*electronic*).
ebano *n.* ebony (*Ebenaceae*).
ebefrenia *n.* hebephrenia (*medical*).
ebefrenica *adj.* hebephrenic.
ebonita *n.* ebonite (*rubber*).
ec *abbr.* (*de la eda comun*) CE, AD, anno domini.
ecdisozon *n.* ecdysozoon (pl. ecdysozoa) (*organism*: *Ecdysozoa*).
ecg *abbr.* (*eletrocardiograf*) ECG, EKG.
ecidna *n.* echidna, spiny anteater (*Tachyglossidae*).
ecimose *n.* ecchymosis (*medical*).
ecinodermato *n.* echinoderm (*organism*: *Echinodermata*).
ecipo *n.* crew, team, squad, cadre. **ecipo prima** first team, varsity.
ecipor *n.* crew member, team member.
eclampsia *n.* eclampsia (*medical*).
ecler *n.* éclair (*cake*).
ecletica *adj.* eclectic, catholic.
ecleticisme *n.* eclecticism.
eclis *n.* eclipse. **eclis anelo** annular eclipse.
eclisal *adj.* & *n.* ecliptic.
eclisi *vi.* & *vt.* eclipse.
eco[1] *n.* echo. **fa un eco** echo.
eco-[2] *pref.* eco-.
ecograf *n.* echograph, sonograph, ultrasonograph.
ecografi *vt.* echograph, sonograph, ultrasonograph.
ecografia *n.* echography, sonography, ultrasonography.
ecogram *n.* echogram, sonogram, ultrasonogram.
ecolalia *n.* echolalia (*medical*).
ecoloca *vt.* echolocate. • *n.* echolocation.
ecolojia *n.* ecology.
ecolojial *adj.* ecological. **ecolojial sana** environmentally friendly, eco-friendly.
ecolojiste *n.* ecologist.
ecomersia *n.* e-commerce.
economia *n.* economy; economics. **economia de mercato** market economy. **economia libraliste** liberal economy, laissez-faire economy. **economia matematical** mathematical economy.
economial *adj.* economic.
economiste *n.* economist.
ecosa *adj.* echoic.
ecoside *vt.* commit ecocide, destroy the environment. • *n.* ecocide.
ecosistem *n.* ecosystem.
ecotono *n.* ecotone (*biology*).
ecoturisme *n.* ecotourism.
ectare *n.* hectare (*unit of area*).
ecto- *pref.* hecto- (*hundred*).
ectoderma *n.* ectoderm (*anatomy*).
ectogram *n.* hectogram.
ectolitre *n.* hectolitre (US hectoliter).
ectometre *n.* hectometre (US hectometer).
-ectomia *n.suff.* -ectomy (*surgery*).
ectopia *n.* ectopia (*medical*).
ectopica *adj.* ectopic.
ectoplasma *n.* ectoplasm.
Ecuador *n.* Ecuador.
ecuadoran *adj.* & *n.* Ecuadoran.
ecuatoginean *adj.* & *n.* Ecuatorial Guinean, Ecuatoginean. See *Gine Ecuatoral.*
ecuator *n.* equator.
ecuatoral *adj.* equatorial.
ecui- *pref.* equi-.
ecuidistante *adj.* equidistant.
ecuiladal *adj.* equilateral.
ecuilibra *vi.* & *vt.* balance, poise. • *n.* balance, equilibrium, kilter. **ecuilibra idrostatical** hydrostatic balance, hydrostatic equilibrium.
ecuinote *n.* equinox. **ecuinote de autono** autumnal equinox. **ecuinote de primavera** vernal equinox.
ecuisito *n.* horsetail (*plant*: *Equisetum*).
eczema *n.* eczema (*medical*).
ed *n.* eth (*Latin letter* Đ, ð).
eda *n.* age (*measure of years*); age, era. **ante la eda comun** before the common era (*BCE*), before Christ (*BC*). **de la eda comun** common era (*CE*), anno domini (*AD*). **eda comun** common era. **eda de bronze** bronze age. **eda de fero** iron age. **eda de petra** stone age. **eda glasial** ice age. **eda grande** longevity. **eda matur** old age. **eda media** middle age. **eda oro** golden age, heyday, halcyon days. **eda scolal** school age.
edema *n.* oedema (US edema) (*medical*).
Eden *n.* Eden.
eder *n.* eider, eider duck (*Somateria*).
edera *n.* ivy (*Hedera*).
ederdon *n.* eiderdown.
edipal *adj.* Oedipal.
Edipo *n.* Oedipus.
edisme *n.* ageism (US agism).
ediste *adj.* ageist (US agist).
edita *vt.* edit. • *n.* editing; edit, edition.

editador *n.* (*software*) editor, editing program. **editador de fasimil** WYSIWYG editor.
editor *n.* editor.
editorial *n.* editorial.
edonisme *n.* hedonism, sybaritism.
edoniste *adj.* hedonistic. • *n.* hedonist, sybarite.
-edro *n.suff.* -hedron (*geometric solid*).
educa *vt.* educate, school, edify. • *n.* education, edification. **educa ajuntada** further education. **educa coletiva** mass education. **educa de liseo** secondary education. **educa de universia** higher education, tertiary education. **educa prima** primary education.
educable *adj.* educable.
educada *adj.* educated, schooled, learned.
educal *adj.* educational.
educor *n.* educator.
Edward, Lago *n.* Lake Edward.
efedra *n.* ephedra (*plant*: *Ephedra*).
efedrina *n.* ephedrine (*drug*).
efemera *adj.* ephemeral. • *n.* mayfly (*Ephemeroptera*). **efemeras** ephemera.
efeto *n.* effect; consequence, impact, footprint. **efeto de Doppler** Doppler effect. **efeto de moda** bandwagon effect. **efeto invernerial** greenhouse effect. **efeto spesial** special effect. **en efeto** in effect, effectively.
efrata *vt.* burgle (US burglarize). • *n.* burglary.
efrator *n.* burglar.
egal *adj.* equal, equivalent, tantamount; tied, drawn. • *n.* tie, draw (*match result*); toss-up. **sin egal** without equal, unequalled (US unequaled), unrivalled (US unrivaled), unmatched, matchless, peerless, nonpareil.
egalador *n.* equalizer (*filter*).
egali *vi.* equalize, become equal, catch up. • *vt.* equalize, make equal. • *vt.* match, rival, equate to, catch up with. • *n.* equation. **atenta egali** try to catch up, play catch-up. **egali diferensial** differential equation.
egalia *n.* equality, parity, equivalence.
egalinte *adj.* equalizing. • *n.* equalizer.
egalisme *n.* egalitarianism.
egaliste *adj.* egalitarian.
egipsian *adj.* & *n.* Egyptian.
Egipte *n.* Egypt. **Egipte antica** Ancient Egypt. See *Misre*.
egiptolojia *n.* Egyptology.
egiptolojiste *n.* Egyptologist.
eglefin *n.* haddock (*Melanogrammus aeglefinus*).
eglesa *n.* church (*building*, *organization*).
eglesal *adj.* ecclesiastic.
egleseta *n.* chapel.
eglesor *n.* member of the clergy, clergyman, clergywoman, cleric, parson, pastor, minister, chaplain. **eglesor alta** prelate. **eglesor fema** clergywoman. **eglesor mas** clergyman. **eglesores** clergy.
ego *n.* ego, self. **otra ego** alter ego. **sin ego** selfless.
egoisme [ego'isme] *n.* selfishness.
egoiste [ego'iste] *adj.* selfish, egotistical. • *n.* egoist.
egomania *n.* egomania.
egomanica *adj.* egomaniac, egomaniacal.
egosa *adj.* egotistical, arrogant, insolent, haughty, conceited, vainglorious, overweening, puffed-up, overbearing, pretentious, affected, ostentatious, full of oneself, conceited, stuck-up, bold, brash, high-handed, snippy, snotty, supercilious, uppity.
egosentral *adj.* egocentric.
egosia *n.* egotism, arrogance, insolence, conceit.
egoverna *n.* e-government.
egreta *n.* egret (*bird*: *Egretta*).
ejacula *vt.* ejaculate. • *n.* ejaculation.
ejean *adj.* Aegean.
ejemonia *n.* hegemony.
Ejeo *n.* Aegean (*region*). **Mar Ejeo** Aegean Sea.
ejeta *vt.* eject. • *n.* ejection, ouster.
ejetada *adj.* ejective. • *n.* ejective (*consonant*).
ejitalido *n.* bushtit, long-tailed tit (*bird*: *Aegithalidae*).
el *pron.* he, she; him, her; it (*animal or personified thing*). **el ci** he who, she who, the one who; e.g. *el ci osa gania.*
ela *pron.* she, her.—The normal word for either *she* or *he* is *el*. The word *ela* is occasionally used for reasons of clarity and style if, for example, one is narrating a conversation between a woman (*ela*) and a man (*elo*).
Elam *n.* Elam (*ancient civilization*).
elaman *adj.* & *n.* Elamite.
Elas *n.* Greece. See *elinica*.
elastan *n.* elastane, lycra, spandex. **de elastan** (*made of*) elastane, lycra, spandex.
elastica *adj.* elastic, stretchy, stretch. • *n.* elastic.
elasticia *n.* elasticity.
elefante *n.* elephant (*Elephantidae*). **elefante-de-mar** *n.* elephant seal, sea elephant (*Mirounga*).
elefantiase *n.* elephantiasis.
elefantin *adj.* elephantine.
elefen *adj.* & *n.* Elefen, Lingua Franca Nova.
elefeni *vi.* & *vt.* Elefenize, translate into Elefen.
elefeniste *n.* Elefenist, Elefen speaker, Elefen advocate.

elejable *adj.* electable, eligible, alternative, optional, discretionary. • *n.* option, alternative, choice.
elejablia *n.* elegibility, electability.
elejal *adj.* electoral, elective.
eleje *vt.* choose, select, pick, elect, opt. • *n.* choice, election, selection. **eleje natural** natural selection. **eleje no partisipa** opt out. **eleje par comite** co-opt. **eleje partisipa** opt in.
elejedas *n.pl.* chosen ones, elect.
elejente *adj.* discriminating, choosy.
elejor *n.* elector.
elemento *n.* element (*basic part, including chemical*); factor.
eletrica *n.* electricity.
eletrical *adj.* electrical, electric.
eletrici *vt.* electrify. • *n.* electrification.
eletricida *adj.* electrified, electric.
eletricinte *adj.* electrifying.
eletriciste *n.* electrician.
eletrocardiograf *n.* electrocardiograph, ECG scanner, EKG scanner.
eletrocardiografia *n.* electrocardiography.
eletrocardiogram *n.* electrocardiogram, ECG scan, EKG scan.
eletrocuta *vt.* electrocute. • *n.* electrocution.
eletrodinamica *n.* electrodynamics.
eletrodinamical *adj.* electrodynamic.
eletrodo *n.* electrode.
eletroensefalograf *n.* electroencephalograph.
eletroensefalografia *n.* electroencephalography.
eletroensefalogram *n.* electroencephalogram.
eletrofisiolojia *n.* electrophysiology.
eletroforese *n.* electrophoresis.
eletrolisal *adj.* electrolytic.
eletrolise *vt.* electrolyse (US electrolyze). • *n.* electrolysis.
eletrolito *n.* electrolyte.
eletromagnetal *adj.* electromagnetic.
eletromagnete *n.* electromagnet.
eletromagnetia *n.* electromagnetism.
eletromecanica *n.* electromechanics.
eletromecanical *adj.* electromechanical.
eletromotiva *adj.* electromotive.
eletron *n.* electron.
eletronegativa *adj.* electronegative.
eletronica *n.* electronics (*science*).
eletronical *adj.* electronic. **eletronicales** electronics (*components*).
eletroplaca *vt.* electroplate. • *n.* electroplating.
eletropositiva *adj.* electropositive.
eletrosirurjia *n.* electrosurgery.
eletrostatica *n.* electrostatics.
eletrostatical *adj.* electrostatic.
eleva *vt.* bring up, raise, rear, nurture; breed (*raise animals*). • *n.* upbringing, nurture; breeding, husbandry. **eleva de abeas** apiculture, beekeeping. **eleva de animales** raising animals, breeding animals, animal husbandry. **eleva de enfantes** parenting, raising children. **eleva endogama** inbreed.
eleveria *n.* farm, stud (*breeding animals*).
elevor *n.* breeder (*animals*).
elfin *adj.* elfin, elfish, pixieish.
elfo *n.* elf, pixie, pixy, sprite, hobgoblin.
elianto *n.* sunflower (*plant, bloom: Helianthus annuus*).
elica *adj.* helical, helicoid. • *n.* helix; propeller.
elicador *n.* auger. **elicador de Arcimede** Archimedes' screw.
elicotor *n.* helicopter. **elicotor de ataca** helicopter gunship.
elidi *vt.* elide. • *n.* elision.
elimina *vt.* eliminate, annihilate, obliterate, eradicate, exterminate, extirpate, purge, expunge; knock out (*from contest*). • *n.* elimination, annihilation, obliteration, eradication, extermination, extirpation, purge.
elinica *adj.* Greek, Grecian, Hellenic. • *n.* Greek, Hellene. See *Elas*.
elinici *vi.* & *vt.* hellenize. • *n.* hellenization.
elinisme *n.* Hellenism.
eliniste *adj.* Hellenistic. • *n.* Hellenist.
elio *n.* helium.
eliofilia *n.* heliophilia (*biology*).
eliofilica *adj.* heliophilic. • *n.* heliophile.
eliosentral *adj.* heliocentric.
eliotropo *adj.* heliotrope (*colour*). • *n.* heliotrope (*plant*).
eliporto *n.* heliport.
elise *adj.* elliptic, elliptical. • *n.* ellipse.
elisme *n.* illeism (*referring to oneself in the third person*).
elisoide *adj.* ellipsoid, ellipsoidal. • *n.* ellipsoid.
elisurfas *n.* helipad.
elite *adj.* elite.
elitisme *n.* elitism.
elitiste *adj.* elitist.
elizabetan *adj.* Elizabethan.
elmin *adj.* helmetlike, helmet-shaped.
elminto *n.* helminth, parasitic worm (*Platielminto*).
elmintose *n.* helminthiasis, helmintosis, worms.
elmo *n.* helmet, hard hat.
elo *pron.* he, him.—The normal word for either *he* or *she* is *el*. The word *elo* is occasionally used for reasons of clarity and style if, for example, one is narrating a conversation between a man (*elo*) and a woman (*ela*).

em *interj.* um, uh, er, erm (*hesitation*).
ematemese *n.* haematemesis (US hematemesis) (*medical*).
ematita *n.* haematite (US hematite) (*mineral*).
emato- *pref.* haemato- (US hemato-) (*blood*).
ematolojia *n.* haematology (US hematology).
ematoma *n.* haematoma (US hematoma), bruising. **ematoma periorbital** periorbital haematoma (US hematoma), black eye.
ematopoiesal *adj.* haematopoietic (US hematopoietic), haemopoietic (US hemopoietic).
ematopoiese *n.* haematopoiesis (US hematopoiesis), haemopoiesis (US hemopoiesis) (*biology*).
ematozon *n.* haematozoon (US hematozoon) (pl. haematozoa) (*organism*).
ematuria *n.* haematuria (US hematuria) (*medical*).
embarasa *vt.* embarrass, mortify. • *n.* embarrassment, chagrin.
embarasada *adj.* embarrassed, sheepish.
embarasante *adj.* embarrassing.
embarca *vt.* embark, board, go aboard, entrain; undertake, address oneself to (*task*); broach, bring up (*topic*).
embargo *n.* embargo.
emberiza *n.* bunting (*bird*: *Emberiza*, etc.).
embolia *n.* embolism.
embolo *n.* embolus (*medical*).
embosce *vt.* ambush, waylay. • *n.* ambush.
embosceda *adj.* ambushed, waylaid.
embraje *n.* clutch (*mechanism*).
embraji *vt.* apply the clutch (*to*).
embrial *adj.* embryonic, embryonal.
embrio *n.* embryo.
embriolojia *n.* embryology.
embriolojial *adj.* embryological.
embriolojiste *n.* embryologist.
embuti *vt.* funnel.
embutin *adj.* funnel-like.
embuto *n.* funnel (*for pouring*); infundibulum.
Emelia *n.* Emilia (*Italian region*).
emelian *adj.* & *n.* Emilian.
emeri *n.* emery.
emerji *vi.* emerge, emanate, issue; surface; loom up; hatch. • *vi.* cause to emerge; bring to the surface; hatch. • *n.* emergence, emanation.
emerjinte *adj.* emerging, emergent. **nova emerjinte** newly emergent, up-and-coming.
-emese *n.suff.* -emesis (*vomiting*).
emetador *n.* emitter; exhaust (*system*).
emete *vt.* emit, effuse, give off. • *n.* emission, emanation.
emfisema *n.* emphysema (*medical*).
emi- *pref.* hemi-. See *semi-*, *dui-*.
-emia *n.suff.* -aemia (US -emia) (*blood*).
-emica *adj.suff.* -aemic (US -emic).
emiplejia *adj.* hemiplegia.
emiplejica *adj.* hemiplegic.
emisfera *n.* hemisphere.
emo[1] *abbr.* (*en mea opina*) IMO, IMHO.
emo-[2] *pref.* haemo- (US hemo-) (*blood*).
emofilia *n.* haemophilia (US hemophilia).
emofilica *adj.* & *n.* haemophiliac (US hemophiliac).
emoglobina *n.* haemoglobin (US hemoglobin).
emoji *n.* emoji.
emolitica *adj.* haemolytic (US hemolytic).
emopatolojia *n.* haemopathology (US hemopathology).
emopatolojial *adj.* haemopathological (US hemopathological).
emorajal *adj.* haemorrhagic (US hemorrhagic).
emoraje *vt.* & *n.* haemorrhage (US hemorrhage).
emoroide *n.* haemorrhoid (US hemorrhoid).
emosia *vt.* affect, move (*emotionally*). • *n.* emotion, sentiment, emotiveness, emotivity.
emosial *adj.* emotional.
emosiante *adj.* emotive.
emosicon *n.* emoticon.
emosiosa *adj.* sentimental, emotional, labile.
emosiosia *n.* sentimentality.
emosite *n.* haemocyte (US hemocyte), blood cell.
emositoblasto *n.* haemocytoblast (US hemocytoblast).
emostasal *adj.* haemostatic (US hemostatic).
emostase *n.* haemostasis (US hemostasis) (*medical*).
emotoxina *n.* haemotoxin (US hemotoxin).
empapa *vt.* soak, drench, waterlog, macerate; indoctrinate. • *n.* soaking, drenching, maceration; indoctrination.
empapada *adj.* soaked, drenched, sodden, soggy.
empatia *n.* empathy.
empatica *adj.* empathic, empathetic.
empirical *adj.* empirical, objective.
empiricalia *n.* objectivity.
empiricalisme *n.* empiricism.
empiricaliste *n.* empiricist.
emplea *vt.* employ (*person*), hire. • *n.* employment, job. **emplea a stranjer** *v.* outsource. • *n.* outsourcing. **emplea con salario** salaried employment.
empleable *adj.* employable.
empleablia *n.* employability.

empleada *adj.* employed. • *n.* employee, hireling, staffer. **con tro multe empleadas** overstaffed. **con tro poca empleadas** understaffed. **empleada tempora** temporary employee, temp. **empleadas** employees, staff, personnel.
empleor *n.* employer, boss.
emporta *vt.* import. • *n.* importation. **emporta nonlegal** import illegally, bootleg.
emportor *n.* importer.
emprende *vt.* undertake, take on, take over. • *n.* undertaking, venture, enterprise (*project*).
emprendor *n.* entrepreneur.
empresta *vt.* borrow.
emprestor *n.* borrower.
emu *n.* emu (*bird: Dromaius novaehollandiae*).
emulsion *n.* emulsion.
emulsioni *vi.* & *vt.* emulsify.
en[1] *prep.* • in (*a place or condition*), inside, within; e.g. *mea cor es en mea peto; ideas en la mente; nos es en peril; nos es en acorda; vive en felisia; los senta en un sirculo.* • (*moving*) into; e.g. *el ia cade en la rio.* • in, during (*a period of time*); e.g. *en la note; en febrero; en 1770; el ia scrive la libro en sola tre semanas; el ia spende du anios en scrive la prefas.* • in (*a language, medium or manner*); e.g. *un jornal en franses; parla en modo aidosa.* **a en** *prep.* into. • *adv.* within, inside, herein. **de en** *prep.* from within, coming out of. • *adv.* from within. See *cuando.*
en[2] *n.* yen (*currency*).
-en[3] *n.suff.* -ene (*chemistry*).
en-[4] *pref.* en-, in-.
enaira *vi.* take off, lift off, blast off. • *n.* takeoff, lift-off, blast-off.
enama *vt.* enamour (US enamor), cause to fall in love, infatuate. • *n.* infatuation.
enamada *adj.* enamoured (US enamored), infatuated, in love, moonstruck, smitten. **deveni enamada par** fall in love with. **es enamada par** be enamoured (US enamored) with.
encalia *vi.* wash up, run aground, become beached, become stranded, become marooned. • *vt.* beach, strand, maroon.
encanta *vt.* enchant, bewitch, beguile, cast a spell, captivate, charm, enrapture, ravish, jinx, transfix. • *n.* spell, incantation, enchantment, charm, jinx, juju.
encantada *adj.* enchanted, bewitched, spellbound. • *interj.* pleased to meet you.
encantante *adj.* charming, engaging; gorgeous, breathtaking, ravishing.
encantor *n.* charmer, enchanter, enchantress.
encarga *vt.* commission, order, entrust, charge, deputize; e.g. *encarga algun a/con solve la problem.* • *n.* commission, order, responsibility, onus.
encargada *adj.* entrusted, responsible, accountable, answerable, in charge. • *n.* commission (*authorized group*); deputy.
encefalina *n.* enkephalin (*biology*).
enclave *n.* enclave.
enclui *vt.* enclose, shut in, encapsulate, encase.
encontra *vt.* meet, encounter, come across, hook up with. • *n.* meeting, date, appointment, rendezvous, briefing, assignation, session (*therapy, music*). **encontra acaso** *v.* stumble upon. • *n.* chance encounter. **encontra romantica** romantic rendezvous, tryst.
endemica *adj.* & *n.* endemic.
endo- *pref.* endo- (*inside*).
endocrin *adj.* endocrine (*gland*).
endocrinolojia *n.* endocrinology.
endocrinolojial *adj.* endocrinological.
endocrinolojiste *n.* endocrinologist.
endogama *adj.* endogamous, inbred.
endogamia *n.* endogamy, inbreeding.
endojenesal *adj.* endogenous.
endojenese *n.* endogeny.
endometrial *adj.* endometrial.
endometrio *n.* endometrium.
endometriose *n.* endometriosis.
endonim *adj.* endonymous. • *n.* endonym (*local place name*).
endoplasma *n.* endoplasma.
endorfina *n.* endorphin.
endoscopi *n.* endoscopy.
endoscopial *adj.* endoscopic.
endoscopio *n.* endoscope.
endostilo *n.* endostyle (*anatomy*).
endotelio *n.* endothelium (*anatomy*).
enebria *vt.* intoxicate, inebriate. • *n.* intoxication, inebriation, drunkenness.
enebriada *adj.* intoxicated, inebriated, drunk, drunken, tipsy. • *n.* drunk, drunkard.
enebriante *adj.* intoxicating, inebriating. • *n.* intoxicant.
Eneida [ene'ida] *n.* Aeneid (*poem*).
enema *n.* enema.
enemi [ene'mi] *n.* enemy, adversary, foe.
enemia *n.* hostility (*quality*), enmity, malignity, acrimony.
enemin *adj.* hostile, adverse, belligerent, antagonistic, inimical.
enerji *vt.* energize, vitalize.
enerjia *n.* energy, power; verve, vigour (US vigor), pep. **par enerjia de pilas** battery-powered. **par enerjia solal** solar-powered.
enerjiosa *adj.* energetic, vigorous, brisk, lusty, vibrant.

enets *adj.* & *n.* Enets, Samoyed, Samoyedic (*person*, *language*).

enfante *adj.* child. • *n.* child, kid, kiddie, kiddy, bairn, tyke. **enfante con clave** latchkey child. **enfante de sinco anios** five-year-old child, five-year-old. **enfante misera** urchin, guttersnipe. **enfante unica** only child. **enfantes** children, offspring, progeny.

enfantia *n.* childhood, girlhood, boyhood.

enfantin *adj.* childish, childlike, innocent, infantile, puerile.

enfantiside *vt.* commit infanticide. • *n.* infanticide (*action*).

enfantisidor *n.* infanticide (*person*).

enfantor *n.* childminder, nanny, nurse, nursemaid.

enfernal *adj.* infernal.

enfernin *adj.* hellish, damned, damn, blasted, bloody.

enferno *n.* hell, hellfire, inferno, perdition, underworld.

enflue *vi.* flow in. • *vt.* input. • *n.* inflow, influx, input, intake; flow (*tide*).

enforsa *vt.* enforce, apply, implement, bring to bear. • *n.* enforcement, application, implementation.

enforsable *adj.* enforceable.

enforsada *adj.* enforced, in effect.

enforsor *n.* enforcer. **enforsor de corte** bailiff.

engana *vt.* deceive, hoax, bluff, bilk, trick, inveigle. • *n.* deception, subterfuge, hoax, bluff, bunco, deceit, duplicity, con, feint, humbug, setup, skulduggery, wile. **engana sposal** cuckoldry.

enganosa *adj.* deceitful, deceptive, duplicitous, devious, sneaky, underhanded, deceitful, duplicitous, illusive.

England *n.* England.

engles *adj.* English (*person*, *language*). • *n.* English; Englishman, Englishwoman. **engles estuarial** Estuary English.

englesi *vi.* & *vt.* anglicize. • *n.* anglicization.

englesisme *n.* anglicism.

engoli *vt.* swallow, gulp, guzzle, scoff, swig, swill; engulf, envelop.

engrana *vi.* & *vt.* engage (*gear*, *enemy*). • *n.* engagement (*gear*, *combat*); gear (*setting*). **engrana de avansa** drive, forward gear. **engrana de retira** reverse, reverse gear. **engrana mor** neutral (*gear*). **engrana prima** first gear.

engranada *adj.* engaged (*gear*). **engranada a cuatro rotas** four-wheel drive, all-wheel drive, four-by-four.

engranador *n.* gearbox, transmission.

enigma *n.* enigma, conundrum, puzzle.

enigmosa *adj.* enigmatic.

enlinia *adj.* online.

enorme *adj.* enormous, giant, huge, vast, immense, colossal, tremendous, prodigious, terrific. • *adv.* enormously, hugely, vastly.

enormia *n.* vastness, enormity, immensity, bulk.

enotera *n.* evening primrose (*Oenothera*).

enrola *vi.* wind, coil, wind up (*mechanism*); furl; curl up, snuggle. • *n.* roll; coil, skein. **enrola de piano** piano roll.

enrolador *n.* winch, capstan, windlass.

enscrive *vt.* inscribe, subscribe, register (*for activity*), enlist, enrol (US enroll), empanel, impanel, recruit, matriculate. • *n.* inscription, subscription, sub, registration, enlistment, enrolment (US enrollment), conscription. **enscrive de tomba** epitaph. **enscrive su direto de autor** copyright.

enscriveda *adj.* inscribed, subscribed, registered, enrolled, recruited. • *n.* recruit, conscript, draftee.

enscrivor *n.* subscriber.

ensefalite *n.* encephalitis.

ensefalograf *n.* encephalograph.

ensefalografia *n.* encephalography.

ensefalogram *n.* encephalogram.

ensefalomielite *n.* encephalomyelitis.

ensela *vt.* saddle.

ensendador *n.* lighter.

ensende *vi.* catch fire, light, ignite, kindle; fire (*gun*); turn on (*light*, *person*). • *vt.* set fire to, light, ignite, kindle; fire (*gun*); turn on (*light*, *person*). • *n.* ignition. **ensende criminal** arson.

ensendelampa *n.* lamplighter.

ensendente *adj.* igniting, incendiary.

ensendor *n.* firestarter. **ensendor criminal** arsonist.

ensenia *vt.* teach (*a subject*); e.g. *ensenia a enfantes*; *ensenia la regulas a algun*. See *instrui*.

ensenior *n.* teacher, lecturer, pedagogue (US pedagog), schoolteacher, schoolmaster, schoolmistress. **ensenior privata** tutor. **ensenior xef** headteacher, headmaster, headmistress.

ensiclica *adj.* & *n.* encyclical.

ensiclopedia *n.* encyclopaedia (US encyclopedia).

ensinta *adj.* pregnant, gravid.

ensinti *vi.* become pregnant. • *vt.* impregnate.

ensintia *n.* pregnancy.

ensintial *adj.* prenatal.

ensirca *vt.* surround, encircle, enclose, frame, encompass, encapsulate, gird; cup (*as with hands*). • *n.* enclosure, compound, stockade. **ensirca de bebe** playpen. **ensirca de bestias** pen, corral, bullpen, stockyard, run. **ensirca de canes** dog

pound, dog run. **ensirca de cavalos** paddock, corral, stockade. **ensirca de gales** chicken coop, hencoop. **ensirca de oveas** sheep pen, sheepcote, sheepfold, fold. **ensirca de porcos** pigpen, pig sty.
ensircada *adj.* surrounded. **ensircada par tera** landlocked.
ensircante *adj.* encircling, peripheral.
ensofla *vt.* sniff, snort. • *n.* sniff, snort, insufflation.
ensoflable *adj.* sniffable. • *n.* snuff.
enspira *vt.* inhale, breathe in, toke. • *n.* inhalation. **enspira subita** *v.* & *n.* gasp.
enspirable *adj.* inhalable.
enspirador *n.* inhaler.
enspireta *vt.* & *n.* gasp.
entablamento *n.* entablature.
-ente *adj.suff.* & *n.suff.* -ing; e.g. *esente.*—This variant of *-nte* is only used with the verb *es*.
entera *vt.* bury, inter. • *n.* burial.
entereria *n.* landfill (*site*).
enterite *n.* enteritis.
enteror *n.* gravedigger.
entomolojia *n.* entomology.
entomolojiste *n.* entomologist.
entoprocto *n.* entoproct (*organism: Entoprocta*).
entra *vi.* enter, go in, come in; log in (*software*); e.g. *entra a un sala*; *entra a un loca de rede.* • *vt.* admit (*to place*); enter, input. • *n.* admission (*to place*), admittance; entrance, entry, entryway, ingress, check-in, threshold, concourse. **entra par forsa** break in.
entrada *n.* entry (*in list*).
entre *prep.* • between, among, amongst, amid, amidst; within (*a group*); e.g. *viaja entre Paris e Madrid*; *comunica entre comunias*; *tu es entre amis*; *entre la geras mundal.* • divided by, per, out of; e.g. *100 entre 4 es 25.* • *pref.* inter- (*between*). **a entre** in between. **entre cual** between which, within which (*relative*). **entre la du** between the two, in between.
entregama *n.* crotch, crutch.
entreseno *n.* cleavage.
entretempo *adv.* meanwhile, meantime, in the meantime, in the interim.
entretexable *adj.* interlacing, interlocking.
entretexe *vt.* interweave, interlace, interleave, interlock, intertwine, entwine, dovetail.
entretexeda *adj.* interwoven, interlaced.
entropia *n.* entropy.
entxilada *n.* enchilada (*food*).
enurese *n.* enuresis, bedwetting.
envelopa *n.* envelope.
envia *vt.* send, dispatch, transmit, transfer, submit. • *n.* transmission. **envia a mar** launch (*a ship*). **envia a via** send away, send off, dismiss.
enviada *adj.* sent. • *n.* envoy, emissary.
enviador *n.* transmitter.
envior *n.* sender.
envolve *vt.* wrap, wrap up, envelop, swaddle; involve, embroil, enlist, engage, commandeer. • *n.* involvement. **envolve en leto** tuck into bed.
envolveda *adj.* wrapped; involved. **es envolveda en** be involved in, be wrapped up in, be party to, be engaged in.
enzima *n.* enzyme.
enzimolojia *n.* enzymology.
eon *n.* aeon (US eon).
eosene *adj.* & *n.* Eocene (*geology*).
eosin *n.* eosin (*dye*).
eosinofilia *n.* eosinophilia (*medical*).
eosinofilica *adj.* eosinophilic. • *n.* eosinophil.
eparina *n.* heparin (*medical*).
epatal *adj.* hepatic.
epatica *n.* liverwort, liverleaf, hepatic (*plant: Marchantiophyta, Hepaticae*).
epatite *n.* hepatitis.
epe *n.* épée (*sword*).
epi- *pref.* epi-.
epica *adj.* & *n.* epic.
epicanto *n.* epicanthus, epicanthic fold.
epicurisme *n.* epicureanism.
Epicuro *n.* Epicurus (*philosopher*).
epidemica *adj.* & *n.* epidemic.
epidemiolojia *n.* epidemiology.
epidemiolojial *adj.* epidemiological.
epidemiolojiste *n.* epidemiologist.
epiderma *n.* epidermis.
epidermal *adj.* epidermal.
epididimo *n.* epididymis (*anatomy*).
epifania *n.* epiphany. **sera de epifania** Epiphany Eve, Twelfth Night.
epifenomeno *n.* epiphenomenon.
epiglotal *adj.* epiglottal. • *n.* epiglottal (*consonant*).
epiglote *n.* epiglottis.
epigraf *n.* epigraph.
epigram *n.* epigram.
epigramal *adj.* epigrammatic.
epigramor *n.* epigrammatist.
epilesia *n.* epilepsy.
epilesica *adj.* epileptic.
epilogo *n.* epilogue (US epilog), afterword.
epinefrina *n.* epinephrine, adrenaline.
episcopalian *adj.* & *n.* Episcopalian.
episcopalianisme *n.* Episcopalianism (*Christianity*).
episentro *n.* epicentre (US epicenter).
episodial *adj.* episodic.
episodio *n.* episode, instalment (US installment). **episodio de caldi** hot flash, hot flush.
epistemolojia *n.* epistemology.

epitelial *adj.* epithelial.
epitelio *n.* epithelium (*anatomy*).
epiteto *n.* epithet.
epoca *n.* epoch.
eponim *adj.* eponymous. • *n.* eponym.
eposidal *adj.* epoxy.
eposido *n.* epoxide (*chemistry*).
eposta *vt.* & *n.* email.
epsilon *n.* epsilon (*Greek letter* Ε, ε).
Er *n.* Ireland (*island*), Ireland (*country*), Republic of Ireland. **Er Norde** Northern Ireland. **Mar Eres** Irish Sea.
era[1] *vi.* err, make a mistake. • *n.* error, mistake, solecism. **era comica** blooper, outtake. **era grande** big mistake, blunder. **era sosial** gaffe, faux pas, solecism.
era[2] *n.* era (*geology*).
eraldia *n.* heraldry.
eraldial *adj.* heraldic.
eraldo *n.* herald.
erante *adj.* mistaken, wrong, erroneous, fallacious.
erba *n.* grass (*Gramineae*, *Poaceae*); lawn; herb. **erba de cosini** herb. **erba-de-mar** *n.* seagrass (*Posidoniaceae*, *Zosteraceae*, *Hydrocharitaceae*, *Cymodoceaceae*). **erba-de-mate** *n.* yerba maté (*Ilex paraguariensis*).
erbal *adj.* herbal.
erberia *n.* herbarium.
erbin *adj.* grasslike, herbaceous.
erbio *n.* erbium (*element*).
erbisidal *adj.* herbicidal.
erbiside *n.* herbicide, weedkiller.
erbivor *adj.* herbivorous. • *n.* herbivore.
erbolojia *n.* herbology.
erbolojiste *n.* herbologist.
erbosa *adj.* grassy.
eremita *n.* hermit, hermitic, recluse, anchorite, anchoress.
eremiteria *n.* hermitage.
eremitia *n.* hermitry.
eres *adj.* & *n.* Irish, Gaelic (*person*, *language*).
erese *adj.* heretical. • *n.* heretic, infidel.
eresia *n.* heresy.
ereta *vi.* slip, slip up, make a small mistake. • *n.* slip, slip-up, booboo, boob, small mistake, glitch. **ereta de parla** slip of the tongue.
ergativa *adj.* & *n.* ergative (*grammar*).
ergonomia *n.* ergonomics.
ergonomial *adj.* ergonomic.
ergote *n.* ergot (*fungus*).
ergotisme *n.* ergotism (*medical*).
-eria *n.suff.* -ery, -arium (*place*); e.g. *refineria*; *paneria*; *monceria*; *beleria*.
erica *n.* heath (*plant*: *Erica*). **erica arborin** white heather, brier, briar (*Erica arborea*).
Eridano *n.* Eridanus (*constellation*).
Erie, Lago ['iri] *n.* Lake Erie.
erijable *adj.* erectile.
erije *vi.* & *vt.* erect, prick up, put up, stand up straight. • *n.* erection.
erijeda *adj.* erect, pricked up.
eriso *n.* hedgehog (*Erinaceinae*). **eriso-de-mar** *n.* sea urchin (*Echinoidea*).
erita *vt.* inherit. • *n.* inheritance, heritage, heredity, patrimony, birthright, legacy.
eritable *adj.* heritable, inheritable.
eritada *adj.* inherited. **eritada de familia** heirloom.
erital *adj.* hereditary.
eritema *n.* erythema (*medical*). **eritema cutanea** chilblain.
eritor *n.* heir, heiress, heritor, heritrix, scion. **eritor legal** heir apparent.
eritro- *pref.* erythro- (*red*).
eritroblasto *n.* erythroblast (*blood cell*).
eritromisina *n.* erythromycin (*antibiotic*).
eritropoiese *n.* erythropoiesis (*biology*).
eritrosite *n.* erythrocyte, red blood cell.
ermino *n.* ermine, stoat (*Mustela erminea*).
ernia *vi.* herniate. • *n.* hernia, herniation, rupture. **ernia femoral** femoral hernia. **ernia iatal** hiatal hernia. **ernia inguinal** inguinal hernia. **ernia ombilical** umbilical hernia.
erode *vt.* erode, wear away, wear down, weather. • *n.* erosion, attrition.
erodente *adj.* eroding, erosive.
eroe *n.* hero, heroine, protagonist.
eroin [ero'in] *adj.* heroic.
eroina [ero'ina] *n.* heroin (*drug*).
eroisme [ero'isme] *n.* heroism.
erojen *adj.* erogenous.
eron *n.* heron (*Ardeidae*).
Eros *n.* Eros (*mythology*).
erosa *adj.* very wrong, badly mistaken, riddled with errors.
erotica *adj.* erotic, carnal. **eroticas** erotica.
erpes *n.* herpes.
erpetolojia *n.* herpetology.
erpetolojiste *n.* herpetologist.
Ertra *n.* Eritrea.
ertri *adj.* & *n.* Eritrean.
erudita *adj.* erudite, learned, scholarly. • *n.* polymath, savant, scholar.
eruditia *n.* erudition, learnedness, scholarliness, scholarship.
eruga *n.* caterpillar (*Lepidoptera*). **eruga de jeometrido** inchworm, looper. **eruga de seda** silkworm (*Bombyx mori*).
erugin *adj.* caterpillarlike.
eruta *vi.* erupt; break out (*in a rash*). • *n.* eruption; outbreak; rash (*medical*). **eruta de dentes** teething.
es[1] *v.* be, is, are, am; e.g. *tu es bela*; *lo es un jua*.
-es[2] *adj.suff.* & *n.suff.* -ese, -ish (*pertaining to a region*); e.g. *nederlandes*. See *-an*, *-i*, *-ica*, *-sce*.

-es[3] *suff.* -s (*plural of noun that ends in a consonant*); e.g. *canes*. See *-s*.
es-[4] *pref.* ex- (*outside*).
-esa[1] *n.suff.* -ess (*formal female title*); e.g. *prinsesa*.
esa-[2] *pref.* hex- (*six*).
esaedro *adj.* hexahedral. • *n.* hexahedron.
esagram *n.* hexagram.
esajera *vt.* exaggerate, overstate, overdo, caricature. • *n.* exaggeration, hyperbole; spoof.
esajiste *n.* essayist.
esajo *n.* essay.
esamina *vt.* examine, inspect, check, look over, peruse, investigate, scrutinize, probe, audit, vet, test. • *n.* examination, check-up, work-up, inspection; examination, exam, test, scrutiny, probe, audit. **esamina de elejes multiple** multiple-choice examination. **esamina parlada** oral examination. **esamina scriveda** written examination.
esaminada *n.* examinee.
esaminor *n.* inspector, examiner, auditor.
esarca *n.* exarch (*bishop*).
esarcia *n.* exarchate.
esata *adj.* exact, precise, particular, accurate. • *adv.* exactly, precisely, just, verbatim. **esata tal** just so. **o plu esata** or rather, or more precisely.
esatia *n.* accuracy, exactitude, precision, veracity.
esca *n.* tinder.
escava *vt.* dig, scoop, excavate, mine. • *n.* excavation, dig.
escavador *n.* digger, excavator (*machine*).
escaveria *n.* quarry.
escavor *n.* miner, excavator (*person*).
esce *adv.* (*introducing a direct question*). • *subord.* whether, if (*introducing an indirect question*).
esclama *vt.* exclaim, blurt. • *n.* exclamation; interjection (*grammar*).
esclamante *adj.* exclaiming, exclamatory.
esclui *vt.* exclude, keep out; banish, exile, expel, oust, excommunicate, ostracize, disbar. • *n.* exclusion, banishment, excommunication, ostracism.
escluida *adj.* excluded. • *n.* exile, outcast.
escluinte *adj.* exclusive, clannish, cliquey. • *prep.* excluding, other than.
escota *vt.* cut low. • *n.* neckline, cleavage. **con escota V** V-necked. **escota profonda** decolletage. **escota V** V-neck.
escotada *adj.* low-cut, plunging.
escretal *adj.* excretory.
escrete *vt.* excrete. • *n.* excrement; excretion.
escretemania *n.* scatology.
escretemanica *adj.* scatological.
escusa *vt.* excuse. • *n.* excuse, apology, pretext, justification, rationalization. **escusa se** apologize.
escusable *adj.* excusable.
escuta *vt.* listen (*to*), hark, harken, hearken. • *n.* hearing (*legal*). **escuta musica** listen to music. **escuta secreta** eavesdrop.
escutador *n.* headphones, earphone, earphones, earpiece, earbuds, headset. **escutador con microfon** headset. **escutador secreta** wiretap.
escutor *n.* listener. **escutores** audience.
esecuta *vt.* execute (*including kill*), enact (*plan*), perpetrate, carry out, fulfil (US fulfill); run (*software*). • *n.* execution. **esecuta fretada** summary execution.
esecutor *n.* executioner; executor, perpetrator. **esecutor de atesta** executor, executrix.
esede *vt.* exceed, surpass. • *n.* excess, surfeit.
esedente *adj.* exceeding, excessive, supernumerary.
esele *vi.* excel. • *n.* excellence, eminence.
eselente *adj.* excellent, great, wonderful, marvellous (US marvelous), outstanding, eminent, prime, illustrious, fine, grand, terrific, top-notch.
eselentia *n.* excellence, greatness. • *interj.* your excellency, your grace.
esempli *vt.* exemplify, illustrate, epitomize.
esemplo *n.* example, sample, exemplar, model, specimen. **esemplo perfeta** perfect example, paragon, quintessence. **per esemplo** for example, for instance.
esensal *adj.* essential, critical, crucial, inherent, intrinsic, pivotal. • *adv.* essentially.
esense *n.* essence, quintessence, quiddity; crux, gist. **la esense de un arcitetor** the quintessential architect, the architect par excellence.
esenta *vt.* exempt. • *n.* exemption, dispensation, impunity, immunity (*legal*).
esentada *adj.* exempt.
esente *adj.* being. • *n.* being, creature, entity.
eserse *vi.* exercise, work out, drill, train. • *n.* exercise, workout, drill, exertion. **eserse adomenal** abdominal exercise, sit-ups. **eserse con pesas** weight training. **eserse fisical** physical exercise, calisthenics.
esersor *n.* exerciser.
esersosa *adj.* strenuous.
eseta *vt.* except, spare. • *n.* exception; irregularity. **con eseta de** except, except for, excepting, with the exception of. **sin eseta** without exception, whatsoever, at all.
esetante *prep.* except, except for, excepting, with the exception of, other than.
esetosa *adj.* irregular, full of exceptions.

esflue *vi.* flow out. • *vt.* output, emit. • *n.* outflow, output; ebb (*tide*).
esfluente *n.* effluent.
esiberia *n.* exhibition hall.
esibi *vt.* exhibit. • *n.* exhibition; panoply.
esibisme *n.* exhibitionism.
esibiste *n.* exhibitionist, flasher.
esibor *n.* exhibitor.
esije *vt.* demand, require, exact. • *n.* demand, requirement. **con esije ce** on condition that, provided that. **esije judal** injunction. **esije ultima** ultimatum.
esijente *adj.* demanding, bossy, exigent; picky, fussy, choosy, pernickety (US persnickety), finicky, prissy.
esistal *adj.* existential.
esiste *vi.* exist. • *n.* existence.
esistente *adj.* existing, existent, extant.
esistentialisme *n.* existentialism.
esistentialiste *adj.* existential, existentialist. • *n.* existentialist.
esita *vi.* hesitate, falter, balk. • *n.* hesitation. **esita moral** scruples.
esitante *adj.* hesitant, reluctant, halting, faltering.
esitosa *adj.* tentative.
esmalte *n.* enamel.
esmalti *vt.* enamel.
esmeralda *adj.* & *n.* emerald.
eso- *pref.* eso-, exo- (*outside*).
esobiolojia *n.* exobiology.
esobiolojial *adj.* exobiological.
esobiolojiste *n.* exobiologist.
esocrin *adj.* exocrine (*gland*).
esofago *n.* oesophagus (US esophagus), foodpipe.
esogama *adj.* exogamous, outbred.
esogamia *n.* exogamy, outbreeding.
esojenesal *adj.* exogenous.
esojenese *n.* exogeny.
esonim *adj.* exonymous. • *n.* exonym (*international place name*).
esoplaneta *n.* exoplanet.
esorsi *vt.* exorcize. • *n.* exorcism.
esorsiste *n.* exorcist.
esosceleto *n.* exoskeleton.
esosfera *n.* exosphere (*atmosphere*).
esotica *adj.* exotic. **esoticas** exotica.
Espania *n.* Spain.
espaniol *adj.* & *n.* Spanish (*person, language*).
espera *vt.* hope for, wish for; e.g. *espera un dia solosa; on espera ce lo no va pluve.* • *n.* hope, wish. **on espera ce** hopefully, it is hoped that. **sin espera** hopeless, forlorn.
esperable *adv.* hopefully.
esperante *adj.* hoping, hopeful.
esperantiste *adj.* & *n.* Esperantist.
esperanto *adj.* & *n.* Esperanto.
esperia *vt.* experience, undergo, witness. • *n.* experience. **sin esperia** inexperienced.
esperial *adj.* experiential.
esperimenta *vi.* experiment. • *n.* experiment, experimentation.
esperimental *adj.* experimental.
esperimentor *n.* experimenter, experimentalist.
esperiosa *adj.* experienced.
esperta *adj.* expert, consummate. • *n.* expert, specialist, consultant, authority, pundit, maven, whiz. **esperta de cartas** cardsharp, cardshark. **esperta legal** expert witness, legal expert.
espertia *n.* expertise, authority, punditry.
espeta *vt.* expect, anticipate, await, wait for. • *n.* expectation, expectancy, anticipation, waiting. **espeta de vive** life expectancy. **espeta furtiva** lurk, skulk, loiter. **espeta la bon momento** wait for the right moment, bide one's time. **espeta zelosa** eagerly await, look forward to.
espetada *adj.* expected, due, payable.
espetante *adj.* expecting, expectant, waiting.
espetora *vt.* expectorate, cough up.
espetorante *adj.* & *n.* expectorant.
espia[1] *vt.* atone for, expiate, do penance. • *n.* atonement, expiation, penance.
espia[2] *n.* e-spionage (*online stalking*).
espira *vt.* exhale, breathe out; aspirate. • *n.* exhalation; aspiration (*phonetics*).
espirada *adj.* aspirated. • *n.* aspirate (*consonant*).
esplica *vt.* explain, elaborate, elucidate, rationalize, justify. • *n.* explanation, reason, justification, rationale, elaboration, rationalization, exposition; legend (*diagram*). **esije un esplica** demand an explanation, call to account, hold to account. **esplica tro** overexplain, overelaborate, belabour (US belabor).
esplicable *adj.* explainable, explicable.
esplode *vi.* explode, blow up, burst, fulminate. • *vt.* explode, blow up, blast. • *n.* explosion, blast, outburst, outpouring. **esplode con rie** burst out laughing, hoot with laughter.
esplodente *adj.* exploding, explosive; plosive. • *n.* explosive; plosive (*consonant*).
esplora *vt.* explore. • *n.* exploration, excursion, reconnaissance. **esplora de cavas** caving, spelunking.
esplorante *adj.* exploring, exploratory.
esploror *n.* explorer, scout.
esplota *vt.* exploit, take advantage of, avail oneself of, cash in on. • *n.* exploitation. **esplota de forestas** logging (*industry*).
esplotable *adj.* exploitable.
esponental *adj.* exponential (*growth*).

esponente *n.* exponent.

esponenti *vt.* exponentiate (*raise to a power*). • *n.* exponentiation.

esporta *vt.* export. • *n.* exportation.

esportor *n.* exporter.

esposa *vt.* expose; divulge, blab, leak (*information*). • *n.* exposure; leak (*information*). **esposa a radia** irradiate. **esposa lenta** long exposure (*photography*). **esposa par mano** manual exposure.

esposor *n.* exposer, blabbermouth.

espresa *vt.* express, state, convey (*meaning*), assert, articulate. • *n.* expression, assertion; turn of phrase. **espresa clar** express clearly, clarify, enunciate. **espresa cortes** pleasantry. **espresa de fas** facial expression, countenance. **espresa tro usada** cliché. **sin espresa de fas** expressionless, blank, deadpan.

espresada *adj.* expressed. **clar espresada** clearly expressed, perspicuous.

espresisme *n.* expressionism.

espresiste *adj.* & *n.* expressionist.

espreso *n.* espresso.

espresosa *adj.* expressive, demonstrative, soulful.

espulsa *vt.* eject, expel, throw out, cast out, oust, evict, banish, unseat. • *n.* expulsion, ejection, eviction, banishment.

esta *det.* this, these (*demonstrative*). • *pron.* this, this one; the latter. **a esta dias** nowadays, these days. **a esta loca** here, hither, to this place. **a esta ora** at this time. **a esta ves** this time, this once, on this occasion. **en esta** herein. **en esta loca** here, in this place, at this place. **en esta modo** in this way, in this manner, like this, thus, so. **estas** these. **par esta** hereby.

estasia *vi.* be ecstatic, fly high. • *vt.* elate, enrapture. • *n.* ecstasy, bliss, rapture, euphoria, elation.

estasiante *adj.* ecstatic, overjoyed, euphoric, elated, blissful.

estasiosa *adj.* beatific.

estatal *adj.* summer, aestival (US estival).

estate *n.* summer, summertime.

estati *vt.* summer.

estatin *adj.* summery, balmy.

este *adj.* east, eastern, oriental. • *n.* east, orient. **a este** eastward, eastwards. **a este de** to the east of. **este-norde-este** *adj.* east-northeast. **este-sentral** *adj.* central east. **este-sude-este** *adj.* east-southeast.

estendable *adj.* extendable, extensible, tensile.

estendador *n.* extensor (*muscle*).

estende *vi.* extend, stretch, project, span, splay, sprawl; spread, propagate, expand; reach out (*for something*). • *vt.* extend, stretch; spread, propagate, expand; hold out, proffer. • *n.* extent, range, gamut, scope, reach, outreach, extension, spread, expanse, array, propagation, overhang, projection, span. **estende a** extend to, reach. **estende de alas** wingspan. **estende de ase** wheelbase. **estende de teto** eaves. **estende tra** spread through, permeate. **estende tro multe** overextend, overreach.

estendeda *adj.* extended, stretched, outstretched, outspread.

estendisme *n.* expansionism.

estendiste *n.* expansionist.

estendosa *adj.* extensive, expansive, far-reaching, sprawlings.

ester *n.* ester (*chemistry*).

esterna *adj.* outer, exterior, external, extrinsic, extraneous. • *n.* outside, exterior.

esterni *vi.* & *vt.* externalize, exteriorize.

estetica *n.* aesthetics (US esthetics).

estetical *adj.* aesthetic (US esthetic).

esteticiste *n.* aesthete (US esthete); beautician, aesthetician (US esthetician).

Esti *n.* Estonia. **esti** *adj.* Estonian. • *n.* Estonian (*person, language*).

estima *vt.* estimate. • *n.* estimate, estimation; budget. **estima bruta** rough estimate. **estima divinante** guesstimate.

estinguador *n.* fire extinguisher. **estinguador de candela** candle extinguisher, snuffer.

estingui [eˈstiŋgwi] *vt.* extinguish, put out, quench, turn off (*lights*). • *n.* extinguishing; extinction, oblivion.

estinguida *adj.* extinct.

estorsador *n.* wringer.

estorse *vt.* wring, extort. • *n.* extortion, blackmail, shakedown.

estorsin *adj.* extortionate, exorbitant (*cost*).

estorsor *n.* extortionist.

estra *prep.* • outside (*a place or time*); e.g. *abita estra la site*; *estra peril*; *estra la oras de labora*; *estra la familia*. • (*moving*) out of; e.g. *la gato ia core estra la caxa*. • except, except for, excepting, with the exception of, apart from, other than; e.g. *nun estra la golor pote toca la bal*; *me ia vide la serie estra la episodio final*. • *pref.* extra- (*outer, additional*); step- (*relation*). **a estra** *adj.* outward. • *prep.* (*moving*) out of. • *adv.* outside; outwards. **de estra** *prep.* & *adv.* (*moving*) from outside. **estra comprende** beyond comprehension. See *cuando, si*.

estracomun *adj.* extraordinary.

estraconaseda *n.* stepsibling.

estradi *vt.* extradite. • *n.* extradition.

estrador *n.* extractor.

estrae *vt.* extract, remove, bring out, take out, pluck out, excise, excerpt, extricate, glean. • *n.* extraction, excision, removal,

resection. **aida estrae** help out, help (*someone*) to climb out. **estrae de dente** tooth extraction. **estrae fortunas** draw lots.
estraeda *n.* extraction, extract, excerpt, clip (*thing extracted*).
estraenfante *n.* stepchild.
estrafia *n.* stepdaughter.
estrafie *n.* stepchild.
estrafio *n.* stepson.
estrafrate *n.* stepbrother.
estragon *n.* terragon (*plant*: *Artemisia dracunculus*).
estragrande *adj.* extralarge, king-size.
estrajenitor *n.* stepparent.
estralegal *adj.* extralegal.
estralinia *adj.* offline.
estramadre *n.* stepmother.
estramural *adj.* extramural.
estrapadre *n.* stepfather.
estrapola *vt.* extrapolate. • *n.* extrapolation.
estrapoleni *vt.* cross-pollinate. • *n.* cross-pollination, allogamy.
estrasensal *adj.* extrasensory.
estrasore *n.* stepsister.
estrasposal *adj.* extramarital.
estrateran *adj.* & *n.* extraterrestrial, alien.
estrateritorial *adj.* offshore (*finance*).
estravagante *adj.* extravagant, flamboyant, over the top, grandiloquent. • *n.* extravaganza, spectacle, show.
estravagantia *n.* extravagance, panache.
estrema *adj.* extreme; furthest, outermost; radical, drastic, critical, hardcore. • *adv.* extremely, tremendously. • *n.* extreme, extremity (*furthest point*).
estremi *vi.* & *vt.* radicalize. • *n.* radicalization.
estremia *n.* extremity (*quality*).
estremisme *n.* extremism, radicalism, zealotry.
estremiste *adj.* extremist, radical. • *n.* extremist, radical, zealot.
estremofilia *n.* extremophilia.
estremofilica *adj.* extremophilic. • *n.* extremophile.
estrildido *n.* waxbill (*bird*: *Esterldidae*).
estro *n.* oestrus (US estrus). **en estro** in heat, on heat.
estrojen *n.* oestrogen (US estrogen).
estroverti *vi.* be extrovert, be extravert. • *n.* extroversion, extraversion.
estrovertida *adj.* extroverted, extraverted, extrovert, extravert. • *n.* extrovert, extravert.
estruador *n.* extruder; ricer (*utensil*).
estrui *vt.* extrude. • *n.* extrusion.
estuario *n.* estuary, delta, tidal mouth, embouchure, firth.
esuan *adj.* US, American. • *n.* American.
esurban *adj.* exurban. • *n.* exurbanite.
esurbe *n.* exurb (*rich outlying suburb*). **esurbes** exurbia.
esvasa *vi.* flare, open up, open out, spread out; open (*hand*), unclench (*fist*); countersink.
esvasada *adj.* flared.
et- *pref.* eth- (*chemistry*).
eta[1] *n.* eta (*Greek letter* H, η).
-eta[2] *n.suff.* (*smaller or simpler variant*) -ette, -kin, -let, -ling, -ie, -y; e.g. *caseta*; *gradeta*; *boveta*; *camiseta*; *sibileta*. • *v.suff.* (*weaker variant*) -le; e.g. *pluveta*.
eta-[3] *pref.* hepta- (*seven*).
etagon *adj.* heptagonal. • *n.* heptagon.
etametre *n.* heptameter (*poetry*).
etano *n.* ethane.
etanol *n.* ethanol.
etatlon *n.* heptathlon.
etatlonor *n.* heptathlete.
etc *abbr.* (*e tal cosas, e tal continuante*) etc., et cetera, and so on, and so forth, and whatnot.
eter *n.* ether.
etera *n.* hetaera (*moth*: *Hetaera*).
eteri *vt.* etherize.
eterin *adj.* ethereal.
eterna *adj.* eternal, perpetual, ageless, everlasting; lifelong.
eterni *vi.* & *vt.* eternalize, memorialize.
eternia *n.* eternity, perpetuity.
etero- *pref.* hetero- (*different*).
eterodox *adj.* heterodox.
eterojen *adj.* heterogeneous, motley.
eterosesal *adj.* & *n.* heterosexual.
eterosesalia *n.* heterosexuality.
eterotrof *adj.* heterotrophic (*biology*). • *n.* heterotroph.
eterotrofia *n.* heterotrophia.
etica *n.* ethics.
etical *adj.* ethical.
eticeta *n.* label, tag, sticker, docket; tag (*markup*).
eticeti *vt.* label, tag.
eticetida *adj.* labelled (US labeled).
etil *n.* ethyl (*chemistry*).
etilen *n.* ethylene, ethene.
etimolojia *n.* etymology.
etimolojial *adj.* etymological.
etiolojia *n.* aetiology (US etiology).
etnical *adj.* ethnic.
etnicia *n.* ethnicity.
etnico *n.* ethnic group.
etnografia *n.* ethnography.
etnografiste *n.* ethnographer.
etnojenese *n.* ethnogenesis.
etnolojia *n.* ethnology.
etnolojial *adj.* ethnological.
etnolojiste *n.* ethnologist.
eto- *pref.* ecto- (*outside*).

etolojia *n.* ethology.
etolojial *adj.* ethological.
etolojiste *n.* ethologist.
Etruria *n.* Etruria.
etrusca *adj.* & *n.* Etruscan.
eu- *pref.* eu- (*good*).
eucalipto *n.* eucalyptus (*Eucalyptus*).
eucariota *n.* eukaryote, eucaryote (*organism*).
eucariotal *adj.* eukaryotic, eucaryotic.
eucaristia *n.* eucharist.
euclidal *adj.* Euclidean.
Euclide *n.* Euclid.
eucre *n.* euchre (*card game*).
eudicota *n.* eudicot (*botany*).
eufonia *n.* euphonia (*bird*: *Euphonia*).
eufonio *n.* euphonium.
euforbia *n.* euphorbia, spurge (*plant*: *Euphorbia*).
Eufrates, Rio *n.* River Euphrates.
eujenetica *n.* eugenics.
eujenetical *adj.* eugenetical.
eujeneticisme *n.* eugenics.
eumetazon *n.* eumetazoon (pl. eumetazoa) (*organism*).
eunuco *n.* eunuch.
Eurasia *n.* Eurasia.
eurasian *adj.* Eurasian.
eureca *interj.* eureka.
euri- *pref.* eury- (*broad*).
eurilaimo *n.* broadbill (*bird*: *Eurylaimidae*).
euristica *n.* heuristic.
euristical *adj.* heuristic.
euro *n.* euro.
Europa *n.* Europe.
european *adj.* & *n.* European.
europeani *vi.* & *vt.* Europeanize. • *n.* Europeanization.
europio *n.* europium (*element*).
eurosentrisme *n.* Eurocentrism.
eurosentriste *adj.* Eurocentric, Eurocentrist. • *n.* Eurocentrist.
eurosetica *adj.* & *n.* eurosceptic (US euroskeptic).
eurozona *n.* eurozone, euro area.
Euscaleria *n.* Basque Country.
euscara *adj.* & *n.* Basque (*person*, *language*).
eutanasia *vt.* euthanize, euthanase. • *n.* euthanasia.
Eva *n.* Eve.
evacua *vt.* evacuate. • *n.* evacuation.
evacuada *n.* evacuee.
evade *vt.* escape, flee from. • *n.* escape, breakout, getaway. **evade de prison** jailbreak. **evade de realia** escapism.
evador *n.* escapee.
evalua *vt.* evaluate, appraise, assess, measure. • *n.* evaluation, appraisal. **evalua medical** check-up.
evanjelial *adj.* evangelical.
evanjelialisme *n.* evangelicalism.
evanjelio *n.* gospel.
evanjelisme *n.* evangelism.
evanjeliste *adj.* evangelistic. • *n.* evangelist.
Everest, Monte *n.* Mount Everest, Mount Sagarmatha, Mount Chomolungma.
eversa *vt.* evert, turn inside-out. • *n.* eversion.
eversada *adj.* inside-out.
evidente *adj.* evident, in evidence, apparent, obvious, manifest, blatant, flagrant, overt, unmistakable. • *adv.* evidently, obviously, of course.
evidenti *vi.* become evident, turn out (*to be*), prove (*to be*). • *vt.* make evident, expose, reveal.
evidentia *n.* obviousness.
evita *vt.* avoid, evade, elude, dodge, shun, shirk, stay away from, keep away from, bypass, shirk. • *n.* evasion, avoidance. **evita apena** narrowly avoid, have a narrow escape, have a near miss, have a close shave. **evita de scola** truancy. **evita la scola** avoid school, play truant, play hookie.
evitable *adj.* avoidable.
evitante *adj.* evasive, elusive, avoiding. **evitante ce** avoiding, without (*it happening that*). **evitante lus** avoiding light, photonegative.
evitor *n.* avoider, evader. **evitor de imposta** tax dodger.
evoca *vt.* evoke, elicit, remind of, conjure up, call to mind. • *n.* evocation, connotation, resonance.
evocante *adj.* evocative.
evolual *adj.* evolutionary.
evolui *vi.* & *vt.* evolve. • *n.* evolution.
evoluisme *n.* evolutionism.
evoluiste *n.* evolutionist.
exadesimal *adj.* hexadecimal.
exagon *adj.* hexagonal. • *n.* hexagon.
exametre *n.* hexameter.
eziditi *adj.* & *n.* Yazidi.
eziditisme *n.* Yazidism (*religion*).

F

F [ef], **ef** *letter* F, f.
fa[1] *vt.* do, perform; commit (*crime*); have (*shower, dream, etc.*); take (*shower, photo, etc.*); hold (*event*); play (*game, role*).—*Fa* does not mean *make* in the senses of *crea, fabrica* or *prepara*. • *n.* doing, deed. **fa bon** do well; do good. **fa ce** cause (*something to happen or become*), make (*something happen*), render, turn; e.g. *no fa ce me rie; la anunsia ia fa ce el roji.*
fa[2] *n.* fa (*musical note*).
fable *n.* fable, legend, folktale, fairy tale, children's story. **fable moral** moral fable, apologue (US apolog).
fabrica *vt.* make, craft, fabricate, manufacture. • *n.* fabrication, manufacture. **fabrica de vitro** glasswork. **fabrica par mano** handcraft, handicraft.
fabricada *adj.* manufactured, fabricated, manmade. • *n.* artifact. **fabricada a casa** homemade. **ojeto fabricada** artifact.
fabriceria *n.* factory, manufacturing plant, workshop. **fabriceria misera** sweatshop.
fabricor *n.* manufacturer, fabricator, maker, wright. **fabricor de fusiles** gunsmith. **fabricor de rotas** wheelwright. **fabricor de vagones** wainwright.
facir *n.* fakir.
facocero *n.* warthog (*Phacochoerus*).
facula *n.* facula (*astronomy*).
fada *adj.* done. • *n.* deed (*past*). **fada realida** fait accompli.
fago- *pref.* phago- (*eating*).
fagosital *adj.* phagocytic.
fagosite *n.* phagocyte.
fagositose *n.* phagocytosis.
faia *n.* beech (*Fagus*). **noza de faia** beechnut.
faiense *n.* faience.
-faje *n.suff.* -phage (*eater*).
-fajia *n.suff.* -phagia.
fajita *n.* fajita (*food*).
falafel *n.* falafel (*food*).
falanje *n.* phalanx (*crowd*); phalange (*anatomy*).
falaropo *n.* phalarope (*bird: Phalaropus*).
falcon *n.* hawk, falcon, kestrel, falconet (*Falconinae*).
falconor *n.* falconer.
falconoria *n.* falconry.
falda *n.* skirt, kilt. **falda de leto** valance. **falda scotes** kilt.
faldeta *n.* petticoat, half-slip, underskirt.
faldon *n.* apron; tail (*coat*).
falesa *n.* cliff.
fali *vt.* fail (*not succeed*), fail to, flunk; e.g. *el ia fali sua esaminas; tu fali comprende la problem.* • *n.* failure, fault, flaw, failing, lapse; miss; (*surfing*) wipeout. **fali de judi** lapse of judgement. **fali moral** moral failure, moral lapse. **fali paia** fail to pay, default on payment. **fali para** fail to stop, overshoot. **sin fali** faultless, impeccable.
falia *n.* fault (*geology*).
falin *adj.* phallic.
falinte *adj.* failing. **nunca falinte** infallible.
falion *n.* rift. **vale de falion** rift valley.
Falkland, Isolas *n.pl.* Falkland Islands.
falo *n.* phallus.
falsa *adj.* wrong, false, incorrect, untrue, fake, fallacious, counterfeit, bogus, mock, faux, pseudo-. • *n.* fake (*thing*).
falseto *adj.* & *n.* falsetto.
falsi *vi.* become false; be faked. • *vt.* counterfeit, falsify, fake, forge (*money, document*). • *n.* falsification, forgery.
falsia *n.* falseness, falsehood, untruth.
falsor *n.* counterfeiter, forger.
falxe *n.* scythe.
falxeta *n.* sickle.
falxi *vt.* reap, mow, scythe.
falxor *n.* reaper, harvestman.
fama *n.* fame, notoriety, renown, stardom. **mal fama** infamy.
fame *adj.* hungry, ravenous, ravening.
fami *vi.* starve, hunger, famish, go hungry. • *vt.* starve, make hungry.
famia *n.* hunger.
familia *n.* family, household; suit (*cards*). **familia fusada** stepfamily, blended family. **familia real** royal family, royalty. **la familia Braun** the Brown family.—One can also speak of *la Braunes.*
familial *adj.* familial, familiar.
familian *n.* family member.
familin *adj.* familiar.
famion *n.* famine.
famosa *adj.* famous, noted, renowned, historic.
fan *n.* fan, fanatic, aficionado. **fanes** fans, fandom.
fandango *n.* fandango (*dance*).
fanfara *vi.* sound a fanfare. • *n.* fanfare.
fangi *vt.* muddy.
fango *n.* mud, mire. **fango acuin** slurry.
fangosa *adj.* muddy, turbid.
fangosia *n.* muddiness.
fania *n.* fandom (*quality*).
fanin *adj.* fannish.

fantasia *vt.* fantasize, daydream. • *n.* fantasy, daydream, reverie, woolgathering; escapism.
fantasial *adj.* fanciful.
fantasin *adj.* fantastic.
fantasior *n.* dreamer, daydreamer.
fantasma *n.* ghost, phantom, spectre (US specter), phantasm, spook, wraith. **fantasma jemelin** doppelgänger. **fantasma turbosa** poltergeist.
fantasmin *adj.* ghostly, spectral.
fantasmosa *adj.* haunted, spooky.
faor *n.* doer.
farade *n.* farad (*unit of capacitance*).
faraon *n.* pharaoh.
farenhait *n.* Fahrenheit. See *grado*.
farfulia *vt.* & *n.* mutter, mumble, slur.
farina *n.* flour, farina. **farina de mais** cornflour, corn meal.
farinin *adj.* floury, flourlike.
farinjal *adj.* pharyngeal. • *n.* pharyngeal (*consonant*).
farinjali *vi.* & *vt.* pharyngealize.
farinje *n.* pharynx. **farinje bocal** oropharynx. **farinje larinjal** laryngopharynx. **farinje nasal** nasopharynx.
farinjite *n.* pharyngitis.
farinosa *adj.* floury.
fariseo *n.* pharisee.
farmacolojia *n.* pharmacology.
farmacolojial *adj.* pharmacological.
farmacolojiste *n.* pharmacologist.
farmasia *n.* pharmacy, chemist, drugstore, apothecary, dispensary.
farmasial *adj.* pharmaceutical.
farmasiste *n.* pharmacist, chemist, druggist, apothecary.
faro[1] *n.* lighthouse; beacon; headlight, headlamp.
faro[2] *n.* faro (*card game*).
Faro, Isolas *n.pl.* Faroe Islands, Faeroe Islands.
faroisce *adj.* & *n.* Faroese, Faeroese.
farsa *n.* farce, physical comedy, knockabout comedy, slapstick, burlesque, vaudeville, buffoonery.
farsi *adj.* & *n.* Farsi, Persian (*person*, *language*).
farsin *adj.* farcical.
fas *n.* face, physiognomy, visage; dial (*watch*, *clock*, *compass*); heads (*coin*). **a fas de** opposite, facing. **con fas a fas con** face to face with.
fasa *vt.* face.
fasada *n.* façade. **fasada de boteca** storefront.
fasador *n.* phaser.
fasal *adj.* facial.
fasante *adj.* opposite, facing; opposable (*thumb*).
fase *vi.* & *n.* phase.
faseta *n.* facet, aspect.
fasian *n.* pheasant (*Phasianinae*). **fasian galin** grouse (*Tetraoninae*).
fasil *adj.* easy, effortless, straightforward; graceful (*in movement*). • *adv.* easily, gracefully, handily. **fasil aprendable** easily learned, easy to learn.
fasili *vi.* become easy, become easier. • *vt.* facilitate, ease, simplify. • *n.* easing, facilitation.
fasilia *n.* facility, ease, easiness; grace (*in movement*).
fasilinte *adj.* facilitating, labour-saving (US labor-saving).
fasimil *n.* facsimile, exact reproduction.
fasina *vt.* fascinate, intrigue, engross. • *n.* fascination, allure.
fasinada *adj.* fascinated, rapt.
fasinante *adj.* fascinating, engrossing, riveting, compelling.
fasmido *n.* stick insect, stick bug, walking stick (*Phasmatodea*).
fatal *adj.* factual.
fatiga *vt.* tire, exhaust, fatigue. • *n.* tiredness, exhaustion, weariness, lassitude. **fatiga de oios** eyestrain.
fatigada *adj.* tired, weary, exhausted, haggard, gaunt.
fatigante *adj.* tiring, arduous, backbreaking.
fato *n.* fact. **en fato** in fact. **fato suportante** supporting fact, evidence. **la fato ce** the fact that. **par fato** de facto.
fator *n.* factor, coefficient.
fatoral *n.* factorial.
fatori *vi.* & *vt.* factorize.
fatota *n.* factotum, handyman, jack of all trades.
fatua *n.* fatwa.
fatura *vt.* bill, invoice, charge. • *n.* bill, invoice, statement, tab. **fatura tro multe** overcharge.
fauno *n.* faun (*mythology*).
faustian *adj.* Faustian.
fauvisme *n.* fauvism.
fauviste *adj.* & *n.* fauvist.
fava *n.* bean (*plant*, *seed*: *Phaseolus* and others). **fava azuci** azuki bean, aduki, adzuki. **fava blanca** white bean, navy bean, haricot bean. **fava de Lima** lima bean. **fava de oio negra** black-eyed bean. **fava de visia** fava bean, garbanzo bean, broad bean. **fava mung** mung bean. **fava negra** black bean. **fava pintida** pinto bean. **fava roja** kidney bean, frijol. **fava verde** green bean, snap bean.
favin *adj.* beanlike, bean-shaped.
favo *n.* honeycomb.

favorable *adj.* favourable (US favorable), opportune.
favore *vt.* favour (US favor), indulge, privilege; (*garment*) flatter. • *n.* favour (US favor), indulgence, partiality; good turn. **fa un favore a** do (*someone*) a favour (US favor). **favore divin** providence. **per favore** please.
favoreda *adj.* & *n.* favourite (US favorite), privileged.
favorente *adj.* favouring (US favoring), indulgent, partial, preferential; flattering (*garment*).
favorisme *n.* favouritism (US favoritism).
fax *n.* fax.
faxa *n.* fascia, planking, plating, horizontal band.
faxador *n.* fax machine.
faxi *vi.* become bundled. • *vt.* bundle.
faxisme *n.* fascism.
faxiste *adj.* & *n.* fascist.
faxo *n.* bundle, sheaf, fasces, bale, faggot (US fagot).
faxon *n.* beam, rafter, girder, joist. **faxon de cresta** ridgepole. **faxon I** I-beam. **faxon traversal** crossbeam.
fe *n.* fairy, faerie. **fe de aira** sylph. **fe de mar** mermaid, merman.
fea *adj.* ugly, unsightly, grotesque. • *n.* ugly person. **xocante fea** shockingly ugly, hideous.
febre *n.* fever.
febrero *n.* February.
febrosa *adj.* fevered, feverish, febrile.
fecal *adj.* faecal (US fecal).
fece *n.* faeces (US feces), dung, excrement, turd.
feci *vt.* defecate. • *n.* defecation.
federa *vi.* & *vt.* federate, confederate. • *n.* federation, confederacy, confederation (*action*, *result*).
federada *adj.* federated.
federal *adj.* federal.
federalisme *n.* federalism.
federaliste *adj.* federalist, federalistic. • *n.* federalist.
fei ['fei] *vi.* become ugly. • *vt.* make ugly, uglify.
feia ['feja] *n.* ugliness.
fein *adj.* fairylike, fey.
fejoa *n.* feijoa (*tree*, *fruit*: *Acca sellowiana*).
felatio *n.* fellatio. **fa felatio** perform fellatio, fellate.
feldspato *n.* feldspar (*mineral*).
felido *n.* felid, feline (*Felidae*).
felis *adj.* cheerful, cheery, happy, jolly, jocund, glad.
felisi *vi.* & *vt.* cheer up, perk up, hearten, gladden. • *n.* uplift.
felisia *n.* cheerfulness, cheeriness, happiness. **vive en felisia** live in happiness, live happily.
felisinte *adj.* heartening, heartwarming.
feltri *vt.* full (*material*).
feltrin *adj.* feltlike.
feltro *n.* felt.
fem *n.* woman; (*colloquial*) wife. **fem de cabare** showgirl. **fem de carera** career woman. **fem de casa** housewife, homemaker, stay-at-home mom. **fem de corte** female courtier. **fem de mundo** female socialite. **fem de neva** snowwoman. **fem de strada** streetwalker. **fem joven** young woman; maiden, damsel, wench. **fem odiosa** shrew, harridan. **fem servinte** handmaid, handmaiden.
fema *adj.* & *n.* female.
femi *vi.* & *vt.* feminize. • *n.* feminization.
femia *n.* womanhood, femaleness.
femin *adj.* feminine, effeminate, femme, girlish, womanish.
feminia *n.* femininity.
femisme *n.* feminism.
femiste *n.* feminist.
femor *n.* femur, thighbone.
femoral *adj.* femoral.
fendador *n.* splitter (*device*).
fende *vi.* split, cleave. • *n.* split, fission, schism.
fendor *n.* splitter (*person*).
feneria *n.* hayloft.
fenetra *n.* window. **fenetra colorida** stained-glass window. **fenetra de alcovo** bay window, bow window, oriel. **fenetra de bileta** ticket window. **fenetra de esibi** display window, store window, shop window. **fenetra de rede** screen window. **fenetra de teto** skylight. **fenetra xarnierida** casement window.
fenetreta *n.* porthole.
fenilalanina *n.* phenylalanine (*amino acid*).
fenilcetonuria *n.* phenylketonuria (*medical*).
Fenisia *n.* Phoenicia. **fenisia** *adj.* & *n.* Phoenician.
fenix *n.* phoenix. **Fenix** *n.* Phoenix (*constellation*).
feno *n.* hay.
fenobarbital *n.* fenobarbital, fenobarbitone (*drug*).
fenol *n.* phenol (*substance*).
fenolftalein *n.* phenolphthalein (*substance*).
fenomeno *n.* phenomenon.
fenomenolojia *n.* phenomenology.
fenor *n.* haymaker.
fenotipo *n.* phenotype.
ferable *adj.* vulnerable.
feri *vt.* wound, injure, harm, hurt, maim. • *n.* wound, injury.

feria *n.* fairground, fair, fete; trade fair.
ferica *adj.* ferric.
ferida *adj.* wounded, injured, hurt. • *n.* casualty.
ferinte *adj.* wounding, injurious, detrimental.
fermenta *vi.* ferment. • *n.* fermentation.
fermentante *n.* leaven, leavening agent. **fermentante natural** levain. **fermentante nural** nutritional yeast.
fermento *n.* yeast.
fermentosa *adj.* yeasty.
fermio *n.* fermium (*element*).
fero *n.* iron. **fero calda** iron, flat iron (*for pressing*). **fero de cavalo** horseshoe. **fero de golf** golfing iron. **fero de marca** branding iron. **fero forjada** wrought iron. **fero moldida** cast iron. **fero ondin** corrugated iron. **fero per solda** soldering iron. **sin fero** unshod.
feromagnetal *adj.* ferromagnetic.
feromon *n.* pheromone.
ferosa *adj.* ferrous, full of iron.
ferose *adj.* fierce, ferocious.
ferovia [fero'via] *n.* railroad, railway, railroad track. **ferovia streta** narrow-gauge railway. **ferovia xef** mainline.
ferovior *n.* railroad worker, railway worker, railwayman.
fertil *adj.* fertile, fruitful, fecund.
fertilable *adj.* fertilizable.
fertili *vi.* & *vt.* fertilize. **fertili en vitro** in vitro fertilization.
fertilia *n.* fertility.
fertilinte *adj.* fertilizing. • *n.* fertilizer. **fertilinte organica** organic fertilizer, compost.
ferula *n.* splint (*medical*).
festa *n.* holiday, festival. **festa de asende** Ascension Day. **festa de grasia** Thanksgiving Day. **festa de la Tera** Earth Day. **festa de labora** Labour Day. **festa de madres** Mother's Day. **festa de padres** Father's Day. **festa de Res** Epiphany. **festa de Valentin** Valentine's Day. **festa de veteranes** Veterans Day. **festa nasional** national holiday, public holiday, bank holiday.
festi *vt.* celebrate.
festin *adj.* festive.
festuca *n.* fescue (*plant*: *Festuca*, *Vulpia*).
fesur *n.* crack, fissure, cleft, chink, crevice, crevasse, breach, gap; loophole.
fesuri *vi.* & *vt.* crack.
feta *n.* feta (*cheese*).
fetal *adj.* foetal (US fetal).
fetix *n.* fetish; charm, juju.
fetixi *vi.* & *vt.* fetishize. • *n.* fetishization.
fetixisme *n.* fetishism.
fetixiste *n.* fetishist.
feto *n.* foetus (US fetus).
fetutxine *n.* fettuccine (*pasta*).
feudal *adj.* feudal.
feudalisme *n.* feudalism.
feudo *n.* fief, fiefdom, feudal estate, feudal manor.
fez *n.* fez (*hat*).
fi *n.* phi (*Greek letter* Φ, ϕ).
fia *n.* daughter. **fia de batiza** goddaughter. **fia par sposi** daughter-in-law.
fial *adj.* filial.
fiasco *n.* fiasco, flop, debacle. **fa un fiasco** flop, fail humiliatingly.
fibi *vt.* buckle.
fibia *n.* buckle.
fibre *n.* fibre (US fiber), thread, filament; roughage. **fibre de vitro** glass fibre (US fiber), fibreglass (US fiberglass). **fibre otical** optical fibre (US fiber).
fibroblasto *n.* fibroblast (*biology*).
fibrosa *adj.* fibrous, fibroid.
fibrose *n.* fibrosis. **fibrose sistal** cystic fibrosis.
fibrosite *n.* fibrocyte (*biology*).
fibula *n.* fibula (*anatomy*, *brooch*).
fida *vt.* trust, rely on, have faith in, be confident in. • *n.* faith, faithfulness, allegiance, loyalty, fidelity; trust, reliance, confidence. **de fida alta** high-fidelity, hi-fi. **fida algun** trust someone, have faith in someone. **fida jurada** fealty.
fidable *adj.* trustworthy, reliable, responsible, dependable.
fidada *adj.* trusted.
fidalia *n.* reliability.
fidante *adj.* trusting, confident. **tro fidante** overconfident.
fidiste *n.* loyalist.
fidosa *adj.* faithful, loyal, stalwart, true, true-blue.
fidusia *n.* trust (*legal arrangement*).
fidusial *adj.* fiduciary. **reserva fidusial** trust fund.
fidusieria *n.* trust company.
fidusior *n.* fiduciary, depositary, trustee (*money*, *property*).
fie *n.* child, offspring, son or daughter. **fie de batiza** godchild.
fieta *n.* baby son, baby daughter, little one.
fife *n.* fife (*flute*).
figa *n.* fig (*fruit*). **figa bangla** banyan.
figato *n.* liver. **figato grasosa** foie gras.
figo *n.* fig (*tree*: *Ficus*).
figur *n.* figure. **figur de proa** figurehead.
Fiji *n.* Fiji. See *Viti*.
fijian *adj.* & *n.* Fijian.
filantrope *adj.* philanthropic.
filantropia *n.* philanthropy.
filantropiste *n.* philanthropist.

filarmonial *adj.* philharmonic.

Filastin *n.* Palestine.

filastini *adj.* & *n.* Palestinian.

filatelia *n.* philately.

filateliste *n.* philatelist.

filepita *n.* asity (*bird*: *Philepitta*).

fileta *n.* filament (*including of stamen*); thread (*screw*, *bolt*, *nut*).

filetador *n.* threader. **filetador fema** die, spinner, pipe threader. **filetador mas** tap, pipe threader.

filete *vt.* fillet (US filet). • *n.* fillet (US filet), sirloin. **filete de bove** filet mignon, tenderloin.

fili *vi.* become threaded; line up, queue, form a queue, file. • *vt.* thread (*needle*, *beads*, *etc.*); wire (*electronics*); spin (*thread*). • *n.* wiring. **fili sua dentes** floss.

-filia *n.suff.* -philia (*love*).

-filica *adj.suff.* -philic, -philiac. • *n.suff.* -phile.

filigrana *n.* filigree; watermark.

filin *adj.* wiry, threadlike.

filipino *adj.* & *n.* Filipino.

filis *n.* fern (*Pteridophyta*). **filis aletin** bracken (*Pteridium*).

filisin *adj.* fernlike.

filma *vt.* film. • *n.* film, movie. **filma atestante** documentary. **filma composada** montage. **filma de novas** newsreel. **filma de teror** horror movie, slasher. **filma de viaja** travelogue (US travelog).

filmeta *n.* short film, short.

filmografia *n.* filmography.

filo[1] *n.* thread, wire; line (*fishing*); queue, line, line-up, file. **filo de brode** embroidery thread, crewel. **filo de dentes** dental floss. **filo de lana** yarn. **filo de plomo** plumb line. **filo lamosa** razor wire. **filo metal** wire. **filo spinosa** barbed wire, barb wire. **sin filo** wireless, cordless.

filo[2] *n.* phylum.

filo-[3] *pref.* philo- (*love*).

filojenese *n.* phylogenesis, phylogeny.

filojenetica *n.* phylogenetics, phylogeny.

filojenetical *adj.* phylogenetic.

filolojia *n.* philology.

filolojiste *n.* philologist.

filosofi *vt.* philosophize.

filosofia *n.* philosophy, ideology. **filosofia de lege** jurisprudence.

filosofial *adj.* philosophical.

filosofiste *n.* philosopher.

filozon *n.* filozoon (pl. filozoa) (*organism*).

filtri *vt.* filter, seep, percolate. • *n.* filtration.

filtrida *adj.* filtered.

filtro *n.* filter.

final *adj.* last, final, hindmost. • *adv.* finally, at last, in the end. • *n.* final, finale.

finaliste *n.* finalist (*competitor*).

finansia *vt.* finance, fund, defray. • *n.* finance. **finansia matematical** mathematical finance.

finansial *adj.* financial, fiscal.

finansior *n.* financier.

fini *vi.* & *vt.* finish, conclude, end, stop, expire, terminate. • *n.* finish, end, ending, conclusion, expiration; tip, extremity; terminus. **a fini** at last, finally, eventually. **a fini do** at the end of. **es a fini de fa** have just done. **fini de linia** linefeed (*character*). **fini de relata** breakup. **fini de semana** weekend. **fini la scola** finish school, leave school. **fini un negosia** cut a deal. **sin fini** *adj.* endless, unending. • *adv.* endlessly.

finica *adj.* Finnic.

fininte *adj.* finishing, terminating, ending.

finita *adj.* finite, bounded.

finitiva *adj.* finite (*grammar*).

finje *vt.* pretend, act, fake, feign, bluff; pose as, impersonate; affect, assume, purport; e.g. *el ia finje dormi*; *el ia finje ce el dormi*; *el ia finje un maladia*; *el ia finje sua padre*. • *n.* pretence (US pretense), bluff, impersonation, feint, sham, act. **finje superioria** condescend, patronize, talk down to, look down on, look down one's nose at, put on airs. **finje un maladia** malinger, fake an illness.

finjente *adj.* fake, phoney.

finjor *n.* pretender, usurper, fake, faker, phoney, fraud, imposter, impostor, impersonator, poser, ringer. **finjor de maladia** malingerer, skiver.

finjosa *adj.* pretentious, affected, effete.

Finland *n.* Finland. See *Suomi*.

finoio *n.* fennel (*Foeniculum*). **finoio de mar** samphire (*Crithmum maritimum*).

finsce *adj.* Finnish. • *n.* Finn. See *suomi*.

fio *n.* son. **fio de batiza** godson. **fio de puta** (*insult*) bastard, whoreson. **fio par sposi** son-in-law.

fiordo *n.* fjord, fiord.

fiorentin *adj.* Florentine.

firma *adj.* firm, still, steady, steadfast, stationary. **sta firma** stand to attention.

fisa *vt.* attach, fasten, fix, clasp, latch, belay; stick, jam, lodge; save (*data*). **fisa con regarda** stare at, rubberneck.

fisable *adj.* fastenable, fixable.

fisacable *n.* cable tie, zip tie, zap strap.

fisada *adj.* fixed, firm, stuck; sedentary, sessile (*zoology*, *anthropology*). **deveni fisada** get stuck.

fisador *n.* fastener, clasp, hasp, catch, latch.

fisalia *n.* Portuguese man-of-war (*organism*: *Physalia physalis*).

fisante *adj.* fixing, fixative. • *n.* fixative.

fiscorno *n.* fiscorn (*musical instrument*).

-fise *n.suff.* -physis (*growth*).
fisica *n.* physics. **fisica cuantal** quantum physics. **fisica matematical** mathematical physics.
fisical *adj.* physical.
fisiciste *n.* physicist.
fisiolojia *n.* physiology.
fisiolojial *adj.* physiological.
fisiolojiste *n.* physiologist.
fision *n.* fission.
fisionable *adj.* fissionable, fissile.
fisioni *vi.* undergo fission.
fistula *n.* fistula (*medical*).
fitocimica *n.* phytochemistry.
fix *n.* index card, file card, slip, fiche; file (*software*); token (*counter representing money*); chip (*gambling*). **fix PDF** PDF file.
fixador *n.* filer, file manager (*software*).
flajeli *vt.* whip, beat, flagellate, flog. • *n.* flagellation.
flajelo *n.* whip, flagellum.
flama *n.* flame.
flamable *adj.* flammable, inflammable.
flamenco *n.* flamenco (*dance, music*).
flames *adj.* Flemish (*person, language*). • *n.* Fleming.
flami *vi.* flame, flame up. • *vt.* inflame (*feelings*).
flamingo *n.* flamingo (*Phoenicopterus*).
flaminte *adj.* flaming, on fire, aflame, afire; flambé; inflammatory (*provocative*).
flamosa *adj.* flaming.
Flandre *n.* Flanders.
flanela *n.* flannel (*material*).
flanje *n.* flange.
flasida *adj.* flaccid, flabby, limp.
flatule *vt.* break wind, fart. • *n.* flatulence, farting, wind.
flatulente *adj.* flatulent.
flauta *n.* flute, pipe. **flauta de Pan** panpipe, panpipes, pan flute, syrinx. **flauta dulse** recorder.
flautiste *n.* flautist, flutist, piper.
flax *adj.* extremely quick, quick as a flash. • *n.* flash of light.
flaxador *n.* flash (*camera*).
flaxi *vi.* & *vt.* flash.
flebite *n.* phlebitis (*medical*).
flebitica *adj.* phlebitic.
flebotomia *n.* phlebotomy.
flebotomiste *n.* phlebotomist.
flerovio *n.* flerovium (*element*).
flexa *n.* arrow. **Flexa** *n.* Sagitta (*constellation*).
flexable *adj.* flexible, supple, bendy, limber, pliable, pliant; versatile, protean.
flexablia *n.* flexibility.
flexador *n.* flexor (*muscle*).
flexe *vt.* flex (*limb, muscle*). • *n.* flection, flexion.
flexin *adj.* arrowlike, arrow-shaped.
flexor *n.* fletcher.
flirta *vi.* flirt. • *n.* flirtation. **flirta con** flirt with, chat up.
flirtante *adj.* flirtatious, flirty, saucy, fresh, coquettish.
flirtor *n.* flirt, coquette.
floco *n.* flake, floccule. **floco de mais** cornflake. **floco de neva** snowflake.
flocosa *adj.* flaky.
floema *n.* phloem (*botany*).
flor *n.* flower, bloom, blossom. **flor de boton** boutonnière, buttonhole. **flor de pascua** poinsettia.
floreria *n.* florist (*shop*).
Flores *n.* Flores (*island*). **Mar Flores** Flores Sea.
floreta *n.* floret.
flori *vi.* flower, flourish, bloom, blossom; prosper, thrive.
Florida *n.* Florida (*US state*). **Streta Florida** Florida Strait.
florin *adj.* flowerlike. • *n.* florin, guilder.
floriste *n.* florist.
florosa *adj.* flowery, floral (*design*).
flota *vi.* float. • *n.* flotation, floatation; float. **flota en aira** hover, levitate.
flotante *adj.* floating, buoyant, afloat. • *n.* flotsam. **fenetra flotante** popup window.
flotila *n.* fleet (*ships or other vehicles*).
flox *n.* phlox (*plant: Phlox*).
flue *vi.* flow, stream, course. • *vt.* flow, stream; feed (*into a machine*). • *n.* flow; flux; stream (*data*), feed (*news, software*). **con la flue** downstream, downriver. **contra la flue** upstream, upriver. **flue de aira** airflow. **flue de fango** mudslide.
fluente *adj.* flowing, fluent, fluid. • *n.* fluid.
flueta *vi.*, *vt.* & *n.* dribble, trickle. **flueta de aira** draught (US draft).
fluor *n.* fluorine.
fluorese *vi.* fluoresce. • *n.* fluorescence.
fluoresente *adj.* fluorescent.
fluori *vt.* fluorinate.
fluorido *n.* fluoride. **fluorido de sodio** sodium fluoride; fluoride (*in water or toothpaste*).
fluorita *n.* fluorite.
fluorocarbono *n.* fluorocarbon.
fluoroscopio *n.* fluoroscope.
flutua *vi.* fluctuate.
flutuante *adj.* fluctuating, remittent.
fo *n.* pho (*soup*).
fobia *n.* phobia. • *n.suff.* -phobia (*fear*).
fobica *adj.* phobic. • *adj.suff.* -phobic. • *n.suff.* -phobe.
foca[1] *vi.* & *vt.* focus (*light, energy, attention*). • *n.* focus; centrepiece (US centerpiece).
foca[2] *n.* seal (*animal: Phocidae, Otariidae*).

focada *adj.* focused, in focus.
focador *n.* lighter; torch.
focal *adj.* focal.
focatxia *n.* focaccia (*bread*).
foco *n.* fire; passion. **foco de festa** bonfire (*celebratory*). **foco de jardin** bonfire (*of rubbish*). **focos artal** fireworks.
focon *n.* fire, blaze, conflagration. **focon savaje** wildfire, grass fire, forest fire.
focosa *adj.* fiery, passionate, sensual.
fode *vt.* (*colloquial*) fuck, screw, shag, bonk, lay (*have sex with*).
fodeda *adj.* fucking (*colloquial intensifier*).
fol *adj.* foolish, silly, crazy, idiotic, daft, dotty, fatuous, inane, madcap. • *n.* fool, dupe, imbecile, idiot, loony, moron, nincompoop, numpty, airhead, bimbo, chump, twit, goon.
fola *n.* crowd, throng, concourse.
folclor *n.* folklore, lore.
foleta *n.* scrum.
foli *vt.* crowd, pack, clutter, huddle.
folia[1] *n.* leaf, blade (*grass*), frond; leaf, sheet (*paper*). **folia avisante** handbill, flyer. **folia cascadente de stilo** cascading stylesheet. **folia de stilo** stylesheet. **folias** leaves, foliage.
folia[2] *n.* silliness, foolishness, madness, folly.
foliculo *n.* follicle.
folida *adj.* crowded, packed, cluttered.
folieta *n.* leaflet, handout.
folin *adj.* leaflike. • *n.* phyllo, filo (*pastry*).
folio *n.* sketchbook, dossier, binder; folio (*book size*). **folio de calcula** spreadsheet.
foliosa *adj.* leafy.
-fon *n.suff.* -phone (*sound*).
fonda *n.* sling, catapult (*weapon*).
fondable *adj.* meltable, fusible. • *n.* fuse (*electric*).
fondador *n.* smelter.
fondal *adj.* background, backing.
fonde *vi.* melt, smelt. **fonde nucleal** nuclear meltdown.
fondeda *adj.* molten.
fonderia *n.* foundry.
fondeta *n.* slingshot.
fondo *n.* bottom, underside, floor (*of sea*); background, backdrop. **fondo de flores** flowerbed. **fondo de mar** seabed, sea floor, ocean bottom, ocean floor. **fondo de pede** sole. **fondo de rio** river bottom, river bed. **fondo de semes** seedbed.
fondu *n.* fondue.
fonem *n.* phoneme.
fonemal *adj.* phonemic.
fonetica *n.* phonetics. **fonetica oreal** auditory phonetics.
fonetical *adj.* phonetic.
-fonia *n.suff.* -phony (*sound*).
fono- *pref.* phono-.
fonograf *n.* phonograph, gramophone, record player.
fonolojia *n.* phonology.
fonolojial *adj.* phonological.
fonotatica *n.* phonotactics.
fontanel *n.* fontanelle (*anatomy*).
fonte *n.* fountain, fount, fountainhead, spring, well, source. **fonte de inca** inkwell. **fonte de potia** power source, power supply. **fonte de revenu** source of income, moneymaker, earner. **fonte de rio** headwater.
fonti *vi.* spring, well, originate.
fontina *n.* fontina (*cheese*).
fontosa *adj.* original (*work, idea*).
fora *vt.* drill, bore. • *n.* hole.
forador *n.* drill (*tool*). **forador arcin** bow drill. **forador colonin** drill press. **forador de mano** hand drill. **forador engranada** breast drill, eggbeater drill. **forador percusente** hammer drill. **forador puiable** push drill. **punto de forador** drill bit.
foraje *vt.* forage, scavenge, rummage.
forajor *n.* scavenger.
forame *n.* foramen (*anatomy*).
force *n.* fork. **force de ajusta** tuning fork. **force de ferovia** points, switch.
forci *vi.* & *vt.* fork, bifurcate. • *n.* fork, bifurcation, crotch.
forcin *adj.* forklike, fork-shaped, forked.
forcon *n.* pitchfork.
forcor *n.* forker. **forcor de ferovia** pointsman, switchman.
fore *vt.* line. • *n.* (*internal*) lining.
forense *adj.* forensic.
forensia *n.* forensics.
foresta *n.* forest, large wood. **cultiva de foresta** forestry. **foresta orijinal** virgin forest. **foresta pluvosa** rainforest.
foresti *vt.* forest.
forestor *n.* forester.
forestosa *adj.* forested, wooded.
-foria *n.suff.* -phoria (*feeling*).
-forica *adj.suff.* -phoric.
forja *vt.* forge (*metal*).
forjeria *n.* forge, smithy.
forjor *n.* smith, blacksmith.
forma *n.* form, shape, format, formation. • *adj.suff.* -form. **bon forma** well-formedness; fitness (*physical*). **con forma de** with the shape of, shaped like. **de forma duple** dual-format. **en bon forma** in good shape, fit (*physically*). **en forma de** in the form of, taking the form of. **forma completa** full form, expansion (*of abbreviation*). **forma de corpo** body shape, physique. **forma de onda** waveform. **sin forma** without form, formless, amorphous.

formable *adj.* formable, ductile.
formal *adj.* formal, by the book, pro forma; solemn, prim; smart, dressy.
formaldehido *n.* formaldehyde.
formalia *n.* formality.
formalin *n.* formalin (*substance*).
formati *vt.* format.
formato *n.* format.
formi *vi.* & *vt.* form, shape. • *n.* forming, formation.
formica[1] *n.* ant (*Formicidae*).
formica[2] *n.* formica (*plastic*).
formicaleon *n.* antlion (*insect*: *Myrmeleontidae*).
formicor *n.* anteater (*Vermilingua*); antbird (*Thamnophilidae*).
formicosa *adj.* tingling, tingly, prickly, feeling pins and needles.
forminte *adj.* forming, formative.
formosa *adj.* full-figured, buxom, curvaceous, voluptuous, rubenesque, zaftig.
formula *vt.* formulate. • *n.* formula, formulation; phrase (*grammar*). **formula ajetivin** adjective phrase. **formula de loda** doxology. **formula de preposada** preposition phrase. **formula nomin** noun phrase. **formula verbin** verb phrase.
formulario *n.* form (*to fill*), questionnaire.
formulin *adj.* formulaic.
forni *vt.* bake, cook (*in oven*). • *n.* baking.
fornida *adj.* baked. • *n.* bake, baked food.
forno *n.* oven. **Forno** *n.* Fornax (*constellation*). **forno de microonda** microwave oven.
fornon *n.* furnace, kiln.
fornor *n.* baker; ovenbird, woodcreeper (*Furnariidae*).
foro *n.* forum.
foromanica *adj.* forumite. • *n.* forumite, regular commenter.
foronido *n.* phoronid (*organism*: *Phoronida*).
forosa *adj.* porous.
forsa *vt.* force (*strongly or physically*), enforce, coerce, necessitate, compel; impose (*something*), inflict, levy, wreak. • *n.* coercion. **forsa a via** drive away, force back, repel, ward off. **forsa se** exert oneself.
forsada *adj.* forced, compulsory.
forsitia *n.* forsythia (*plant*: *Forsythia*).
fortador *n.* amplifier.
forte *adj.* strong, robust, sturdy, formidable; loud, vehement, forte, stentorian, booming, vociferous, punchy. • *adv.* strongly, robustly; loudly, vehemently. • *n.* force (*including in physics*). **forte de aira** air force (*military*). **forte nonresistable** overwhelming force, juggernaut. **fortes militar** armed forces. **multe forte** very strong; very loud, fortissimo.
forti *vi.* & *vt.* strengthen, fortify, reinforce, potentiate; consolidate. • *n.* strengthening, consolidation.
fortia *n.* strength, force, effort, exertion, fortitude, brawn. **fortia de vive** life force, life energy, vital force, élan vital.
fortiosa *adj.* forceful, forcible.
fortres *n.* fortress, blockhouse, fort, fortification, stronghold, keep. **fortres de site** citadel.
fortuna *n.* fortune, chance, fate, destiny, lot, luck. **bon fortuna** good luck. **bon fortuna nonespetada** windfall. **mal fortuna** bad luck, misfortune, mishap, unfortunate occurrence, accident, adversity, woe.
fortunosa *adj.* lucky, fortunate, auspicious, fortuitous. • *adv.* fortunately.
fosena *n.* porpoise (*Phocoenidae*).
foseta *n.* rut, wheel track.
fosfato *n.* phosphate (*chemistry*).
fosfolipido *adj.* phospholipid (*chemistry*).
fosfor *n.* phosphorus (*element*); match, matchstick.
fosforese *vi.* phosphoresce.
fosforesente *adj.* phosphorescent.
fosil *n.* fossil.
fosili *vi.* & *vt.* fossilize. • *n.* fossilization.
foso *n.* ditch, trench, moat; fossa (*anatomy*).
foson *n.* gully, ravine, arroyo.
fostrot *n.* foxtrot (*dance, music*).
foto[1] *n.* photo, photograph, shot, snapshot, still. **fa un foto** take a photo. **foto airal** aerial photograph. **foto distante** long shot. **foto personal** portrait. **foto prosima** closeup.
foto-[2] *pref.* photo- (*light, photography*).
fotocimical *adj.* photochemical.
fotocopia *vt.* photocopy, xerox. • *n.* photocopy.
fotografi *vt.* photograph.
fotografia *n.* photography. **fotografia a intervales** timelapse photography. **fotografia prosima** closeup photography, macro photography.
fotografial *adj.* photographic.
fotografiste *n.* photographer.
fotograva *n.* photogravure, heliogravure.
fotojen *adj.* photogenic.
fotojornalisme *n.* photojournalism.
fotojornaliste *adj.* photojournalistic. • *n.* photojournalist.
fotomanica *adj.* enthusiastic about photography. • *n.* shutterbug, photography enthusiast.
foton *n.* photon.
fotorealisme *n.* photorealism.
fotorealiste *adj.* photorealistic. • *n.* photorealist.
fotoresetador *n.* photoreceptor.

fotoselula *n.* photocell, photoelectric cell.
fotosensante *adj.* photosensitive.
fotosintese *vt.* photosynthesize. ● *n.* photosynthesis.
fototrof *adj.* phototrophic (*biology*). ● *n.* phototroph.
fototrofia *n.* phototrophia.
fototropia *n.* phototropism.
fototropo *adj.* phototropic (*botany*).
fotovoltaica *adj.* photovoltaic. **efeto fotovoltaica** photovoltaic effect. **enerjia solal fotovoltaica** photovoltaics. **selula fotovoltaica** photovoltaic cell.
fovea *n.* fovea (*anatomy*).
Foxe [foks] *n.* Foxe. **Baia Foxe** Foxe Basin. **Streta Foxe** Foxe Channel.
fractur *n.* fraktur (*lettering*).
frajil *adj.* fragile, frail, brittle, delicate, sensitive, flimsy, frangible, labile, easily damaged.
frajilia *n.* fragility.
Fram, Streta *n.* Fram Strait.
frambosa *n.* raspberry (*Rubus*).
franc *n.* franc (*currency*).
franca *adj.* frank, direct, candid, outspoken, plainspoken, outright, explicit, vocal; straightforward.
francamason *n.* freemason, mason.
francamasonisme *n.* freemasonry, masonry.
francia *n.* frankness, directness.
francisia *n.* franchise (*commercial*).
franco *adj.* Frankish. ● *n.* Frank.
franje *n.* fringe (*border*); bangs, fringe (*hairstyle*).
Frans *n.* France.
franses *adj.* & *n.* French (*person*, *language*).
fransio *n.* francium (*element*).
fransiscan *adj.* & *n.* Franciscan.
frase *n.* sentence; phrase (*music*).
fraseolojia *n.* phraseology.
fratal *adj.* fractional, fractal.
frate *n.* brother; friar. **frate par sposi** brother-in-law. **frates** brothers, brethren.
frateria *n.* brotherhood, fraternity (*organization*).
frateta *n.* younger brother.
frati *vi.* & *vt.* fracture, fragment, shatter, crack. ● *n.* fragmentation, fracture.
fratia *n.* brotherhood, brotherliness, fraternity (*quality*).
fratin *adj.* brotherly, fraternal.
fratiside *vt.* commit fratricide. ● *n.* fratricide (*action*).
fratisidor *n.* fratricide (*person*).
frato *n.* fraction; fragment, shard; snippet, clip, clipping. **frato agu** sharp fragment, shard. **frato seramica** potsherd. **fratos** fragments, shrapnel, smithereens.
fraton *n.* older brother.
frecuente *adj.* frequent, occurring often. ● *adv.* frequently, often, oftentimes.
frecuenti *vi.* become frequent. ● *vt.* make frequent.
frecuentia *n.* frequency. **frecuentia de orolojo** clock speed, clock rate. **frecuentia estrema alta** UHF. **frecuentia multe alta** VHF.
fregate[1] *n.* frigatebird (*Fregatidae*, *Fregata*).
fregate[2] *n.* frigate, full-rigged ship.
freni *vt.* brake, restrain, hold back, immobilize.
freno *n.* brake, restraint (*device*). **freno de mano** handbrake.
frenolojia *n.* phrenology.
frenolojiste *n.* phrenologist.
frenor *n.* brakeman.
freon *n.* freon.
fresa *n.* strawberry (*Fragaria*).
fresca *adj.* fresh, cool; new, up to date.
frescador *n.* air conditioner, air conditioning.
fresci *vi.* & *vt.* freshen.
fresco *n.* fresco (*art*).
fresia *n.* freesia (*plant*: *Freesia*).
fresno *n.* ash (*tree*: *Fraxinus*).
freta *vi.* hurry, hasten, rush, scurry, scamper. ● *vt.* hurry, rush, hustle. ● *n.* haste, rush, hustle. **no freta** take your time, do not rush, do not hurry.
fretada *adj.* rushed, hurried.
fretante *adj.* hurrying, hasty, cursory; impetuous, hot-headed, hare-brained.
fretor *n.* hurrier, hothead.
fretosa *adj.* impulsive, reckless, heedless, slapdash.
fretosia *n.* impulsiveness, recklessness.
freudisme *n.* Freudianism.
freudiste *adj.* Freudian.
fri *vi.* & *vt.* cool, chill, refrigerate. ● *n.* refrigeration. **fri par venta** windchill.
fria *adj.* cold, chilly, frigid, dank, inclement; frappé. ● *n.* cold.
friacua *n.* water cooler.
friador *n.* refrigerator, fridge.
frica *vt.* abrade, scour, cause friction, rub against. ● *n.* friction, abrasion; rubdown.
fricante *adj.* fricative. ● *n.* fricative (*consonant*). **fricante ladal** lateral fricative.
fricase *n.* fricassee (*food*).
fricosa *adj.* abrasive.
frida *adj.* cooled, chilled, refrigerated.
Frigia *n.* Phrygia.
frigian *adj.* Phrygian.
fringilo *n.* chaffinch (*bird*: *Fringilla*).
frinte *n.* coolant, refrigerant.
frisbi *n.* frisbee.

frisce *adj.* Frisian. • *n.* Frisian (*person, language*).
Frisland *n.* Frisia, Friesland.
friso *n.* frieze.
frita *vt.* fry. **frita en uoc** stir-fry.
fritada *adj.* fried. **fritadas** chips (*UK*), fries, French fries.
fritador *n.* fryer.
froda *vt.* defraud, cheat, embezzle, misappropriate, swindle, finagle, grift, gyp, hoodwink. • *n.* fraud, con, trick, rip-off, scam, bunco, bunko, flimflam; corruption, embezzlement, misappropriation.
frodante *adj.* fraudulent, corrupt, sleazy.
frodor *n.* fraud, fraudster, cheater, swindler, phoney, con man, con artist, grifter, huckster, hustler, mountebank.
fronsi *vt.* & *n.* gather (*fabric*). **fronsi sua suprasiles** frown, scowl.
fronsida *adj.* gathered. • *n.* frill, ruche, ruffle, furbelow.
fronsosa *adj.* frilly, ruffled, froufrou.
fronte *adj.* front, forward, fore, advance. • *n.* front; forehead, brow; foreground. **a fronte** forward, ahead. **a fronte de** at the front of, in front of, ahead of. **en fronte de** inside the front of, into the front of. **fronte de acua** waterfront. **fronte de batalia** battlefront. **fronte de lago** lakeside. **fronte de mar** seafront, beachfront. **fronte de rio** riverside. **fronte meteorolojial** weather front. **lobe fronte** frontal lobe. **oso fronte** frontal bone.
frontera *n.* frontier, front line, limit, border, borderline, borderland, boundary, bound.
fronteror *n.* frontiersman.
fronti *vt.* confront, face, tackle (*enemy, problem*). • *n.* confrontation, faceoff, showdown. **fronti corajosa** brave, bravely face.
frontinte *adj.* facing, confronting.
frontispis *n.* frontispiece (*publishing, architecture*).
fronton *n.* gable; pediment; marquee, awning.
frota *vt.* rub, scrub, wipe, smear.
frotador *n.* wiper. **frotador de paraventa** windshield wiper, windscreen wiper.
frugal *adj.* frugal, thrifty, economical, parsimonious, budget-conscious. **es frugal** be frugal, economize, scrimp, skimp.
frugalia *n.* frugality, frugalness, thrift, thriftiness, parsimony.
frustra *vt.* vex, frustrate, exasperate. • *n.* frustration, vexation, exasperation.
frustrante *adj.* frustrating, vexing, exasperating, vexatious.
fruta *n.* fruit. **fruta axida a picos** mincemeat. **fruta confetida** candied fruit. **fruta de pan** breadfruit. **fruta en xirope** compote. **fruta sitrica** citrus fruit. **frutas** fruit, fruits.
fruteria *n.* fruiterer's, greengrocer's (*shop*).
fruti *vi.* fruit, bear fruit.
frutor *n.* fruiterer, greengrocer (*person*).
frutosa[1] *n.* fructose (*sugar*).
frutosa[2] *adj.* fruity, fruitful, prolific.
fu *interj.* phew, whew.
fuca *n.* kelp (*Laminariales, Fucales*).
fucsia *adj.* fuchsia (*colour*). • *n.* fuchsia (*flower: Fuchsia*).
fufu *n.* fufu (*food*).
fuga *n.* fugue (*music, psychology*).
fugal *adj.* fugal.
fugu *n.* pufferfish, blowfish (*Tetraodontidae*).
fuji *vi.* flee, run away, escape, bolt, scram. • *vt.* rout, put to flight. • *n.* flight, escape, getaway. **fuji en manada** stampede. **fuji furtiva** slip away, sneak away, abscond, skedaddle. **fuji per sposi** elope.
fujor *n.* fugitive, runaway.
fulcro *n.* fulcrum, pivot.
fulgoro *n.* planthopper (*insect: Fulgoromorpha*).
fuma *n.* smoke, fume. **sin fuma** smokeless.
fumaria *n.* fumitory, fumiter (*plant: Fumaria*).
fumeria *n.* smokery (US smokehouse).
fumi *vi.* smoke (*emit smoke*), smoulder (US smolder). • *vt.* smoke (*tobacco*); smoke, preserve with smoke (*food*).
fumiga *vt.* fumigate. • *n.* fumigation.
fumor *n.* smoker.
fumosa *adj.* smoky, smokey.
func *adj.* & *n.* funk (*music*).
funcosa *adj.* funky.
funda *n.* base, basis, foundation, substrate, rudiment; foundation, establishment (*organization*). **es la funda de** be the basis of, underlie. **funda de solo** subfloor. **sin funda** baseless, groundless, unfounded.
fundal *adj.* basic, fundamental, elementary, rudimentary, underlying, primal; basal.
fundalisme *n.* fundamentalism.
fundaliste *adj.* & *n.* fundamentalist.
fundi *vt.* found, establish; base (*something on*); entrench, intrench, instil (US instill). • *n.* foundation, establishment (*action*).
fundor *n.* founder.
Fundy, Baia *n.* Bay of Fundy.
funera *n.* funeral.
funeral *adj.* funereal, funeral, funerary.
funereria *n.* funeral parlour (US parlor), undertaker's.
funeror *n.* mortician, undertaker.
fungal *adj.* fungal.
fungiside *n.* fungicide.
fungo *n.* fungus (*Fungi*). **fungo de lenio** dry rot.
funicular *adj.* funicular. • *n.* funicular, cliff railway.

funsiona *vi.* function, operate, work. • *n.* function, functioning, operation; function (*mathematics*, *software*). **funsiona ondal** wave function. See *opera*.
funsional *adj.* functional (*of a function*).
funsionalisme *n.* functionalism.
funsionaliste *adj.* functionalist, functionalistic. • *n.* functionalist.
funsionante *adj.* functioning, functioning.
fura *vt.* steal, purloin, nick, filch, pilfer, swipe; kidnap. • *n.* theft, robbery, larceny, heist. **fura de** steal from, rob, burgle (US burglarize). **fura de enfantes** kidnap, kidnapping (*children*). **fura de identia** identity theft. **fura de persones** kidnap, kidnapping.
furabolsa *n.* pickpocket.
furaboteca *n.* shoplifter.
furacasa *n.* burglar.
furcula *n.* wishbone, furcula.
fureta *vt.* pilfer. • *n.* pilferage.
furgon *n.* van.
furgoneta *n.* people carrier, minivan, MPV.
furia *vi.* be furious, be enraged, go berserk, run amok, rampage. • *vt.* infuriate, enrage. • *n.* fury, rage, apoplexy. **furia publica** furore, outcry.
furiosa *adj.* furious, livid, raging, enraged, apoplectic, berserk.
furlan *adj.* & *n.* Furlan, Friulian (*person*, *language*).
furlong *n.* furlong (*unit of length*).
furnador *n.* dispenser (*machine*).
furni *vt.* supply, provide, furnish, yield, equip, dispense, issue, purvey, render; e.g. *furni acua a la vileta.* • *n.* supply, provision, yield. **furni la come** cater. **furni nonvolente** reluctantly provide, cough up. **furnis** supplies, provisions, material, material resources. **furnis de scrive** writing materials.
furnor *n.* supplier, provider, purveyor. **furnor de come** caterer. **furnor de servi** service provider, public utility. **furnor esterna** third-party supplier.
furon *n.* ferret, polecat (*Mustela putorius*).
furor *n.* thief, robber, burglar, larcenist; kidnapper. **furor acasiste** opportunist thief, looter. **furor de bestias** rustler. **furor de caxas secur** safecracker.
furtiva *adj.* stealthy, shifty, sneaky. • *adv.* stealthily, by stealth. • *n.* lurker, prowler.
furtivia *n.* stealth, stealthiness, shiftiness, sneakiness.
fusa *vi.* fuse, meld, merge, coalesce, blend. • *vt.* fuse, merge, blend; weld. • *n.* fusion, merger.
fusable *adj.* fusible.
fusil *n.* gun, rifle, firearm. **fusil de antecarga** muzzleloader. **fusil de ataca** assault rifle. **fusil de mano** handgun, sidearm, pistol, revolver. **fusil de retrocarga** breechloader. **fusil de sintil** flintlock. **fusil de suber** popgun. **fusil de xasa** shotgun, rifle.
fusili *vt.* shoot (*with a rifle*). • *n.* shooting, shootout.
fusilor *n.* marksman, gunman, rifleman, sharpshooter; fusilier.
fusin *adj.* spindle-shaped, fusiform.
fuso *n.* spindle.
fustan *n.* fustian (*fabric*).
fusuma *n.* fusuma (*screen*).
futbal *n.* football, soccer. **futbal american** American football, gridiron football.
futbalor *n.* footballer, football player, soccer player.
futil *adj.* futile, fruitless, hopeless, pointless, vain, fatuous; fond (*hope*). • *adv.* in vain, to no avail.
futilia *n.* futility, fruitlessness.
futon *n.* futon (*mattress*).
futuna *adj.* & *n.* Futunan. **Uvea e Futuna** Wallis and Futuna.
futur *adj.* future, forthcoming, to come, -to-be, subsequent, eventual, prospective. • *n.* future, posterity. **en la futur** in the future, subsequently. **en la futur distante** in the distant future, eventually.
futuriste *n.* futurist.
futurolojia *n.* futurology.
futurolojiste *n.* futurologist.

G

G [ge], **ge** *letter* G, g.
gaba *n.* GABA (*biology*).
gabardina *n.* gabardine (*fabric*).
Gabon *n.* Gabon.
gabones *adj.* & *n.* Gabonese.
gado *n.* cod (*fish*: *Gadidae*).
gadolinio *n.* gadolinium (*element*).
gadures *adj.* & *n.* Gallurese (*person*, *language*).
gailica *adj.* & *n.* Scottish Gaelic, Scots Gaelic.
gaina *n.* sheath; casing (*of cable*, *sausage*); spathe (*anatomy*). **gaina de cordeta** aglet.
gaini *vt.* sheathe.
gal *n.* chicken (*Gallus gallus*). **gal de venta** weathercock. **gal de xasor** cacciatore (*food*). **gal fema** hen. **gal fema joven** pullet. **gal mas** cock, cockerel, rooster.
gala *n.* show (*entertainment*).
galago *n.* galago, bushbaby, nagapie (*primate*: *Galagidae*).
Galapagos, Isolas *n.pl.* Galápagos Islands.
galasia *n.* galaxy.
galasial *adj.* galactic.
galatosa *n.* galactose (*sugar*).
galea *n.* galley (*ship*).
galego *adj.* & *n.* Galician.
galeon *n.* galleon (*ship*).
galeria *n.* gallery, showroom (*art*); cloister (*architecture*).
galerieta *n.* portfolio (*of work*).
galeta *n.* chick, chicken.
galia[1] *n.* bedstraw, galium (*plant*: *Galium*).
Galia[2] *n.* Gaul (*ancient region*).
galin *adj.* chickenlike.
galinago *n.* snipe (*bird*: *Coenocorypha*, *Gallinago*, *Lymnocryptes*).
galio *n.* gallium (*element*).
Galisia *n.* Galicia (*Spanish region*).
galo *adj.* & *n.* Gaulish; Gaul.
galon *n.* gallon.
galopa *vi.* & *n.* gallop.
galvanica *adj.* galvanic.
gama[1] *n.* leg; stem (*glass*). **con gamas arcida** bowlegged, bandylegged. **gama alta** upper leg. **gama basa** lower leg, shank. **gama de porte** doorpost, jamb.
gama[2] *n.* gamma (*Greek letter* Γ, γ).
-gama[3] *adj.suff.* -gamous.
gamalonga *n.* daddy longlegs, harvester, harvestman (*arachnid*: *Phalangium*).
gamba *n.* shrimp, prawn (*Caridea*).
Gambia *n.* Gambia.
gambian *adj.* & *n.* Gambian.
gamelan *n.* gamelan.
gameta *n.* gamete.
gamotofito *n.* gametophyte.
gami *vt.* & *n.* stride.
-gamia *n.suff.* -gamy (*marriage*, *mating*).
gamon *n.* stilt.
gan *n.* Gan (*language*).
Gana *n.* Ghana.
ganaian *adj.* & *n.* Ghanaian.
ganax *n.* ganache (*food*).
gang *n.* gang.
Ganga, Rio *n.* Ganges River.
ganglio *n.* ganglion (*biology*).
gangrena *n.* gangrene.
gangrenosa *adj.* gangrenous.
gangster *n.* gangster, mobster, racketeer.
gania *vt.* earn, gain; win (*game*); catch (*bus*, *etc.*). **gania la tempo** save time.
ganiada *adj.* earned, gained, won. **difisil ganiada** hard-won, close-fought, closely fought.
ganior *n.* winner. **sin ganior** tied, drawn (*match*).
ganseta *n.* gosling.
ganso *n.* goose (*Anser*, *Branta*, *Chen*); geek, nerd. **ganso mas** gander.
ganteta *n.* mitten.
ganto *n.* glove. **ganto de armur** gauntlet. **ganto de boxe** boxing glove. **ganto de cosini** oven glove.
ganton *n.* muff.
gara *n.* claw, talon.
garaje *n.* garage. **garaje partal** carport.
garantia *vt.* guarantee, ensure. • *n.* guarantee, warranty, guaranty; collateral, security, surety; bail. **garantia de cualia** guarantee of quality, hallmark, imprimatur.
garantior *n.* bondsman, surety.
garda *vt.* guard, stand guard; save (*money*). • *n.* guard; guardianship, tutelage. **garda la casa** housesit. **garda se contra** beware of.
gardacorpo *n.* bodyguard.
gardacosta *n.* coastguard.
gardada *n.* ward (*person*).
gardador *n.* guard (*device*), burglar alarm.
gardafoco *n.* fireguard, fender.
gardaforesta *n.* forest ranger, park ranger.
gardamano *n.* hand guard.
gardaporte *n.* doorkeeper, commissionaire.
gardaporton *n.* gatekeeper.
gardaxasa *n.* gamekeeper.
gardenia *n.* gardenia (*plant*: *Gardenia*).
gardor *n.* guard (*person*), sentry; warder, jailer, gaoler; guardian, custodian, warden; watchdog (*metaphor*). **gardor de pisina** lifeguard. **gardor de plaia** lifeguard.

garga *n.* throat.
gargal *adj.* throaty, guttural.
gargara *vt.* & *n.* gargle.
gargarosa *n.* redpoll (*bird*: *Acanthis flammea*).
gargola *n.* gargoyle.
gari *vt.* claw, scrabble at.
garlanda *n.* garland, wreath, festoon, swag. **garlanda sintilinte** tinsel.
garlandi *vt.* garland, wreathe, festoon.
garnison *n.* garrison.
garota *n.* garotte.
garoti *vt.* garotte.
gas *n.* gas. **gas invernerial** greenhouse gas. **gas nosiva** toxic gas, fumes.
gasal *adj.* gaseous (*of a gas*).
gasi *vi.* become gaseous. • *vt.* make gaseous; gas, expose to gas.
gasin *adj.* gaseous (*like a gas*).
gasolina *n.* gasoline, petrol.
gasolineria *n.* gas station, petrol station.
gasolio *n.* diesel.
gasometre *n.* gasometer.
gasosa *adj.* gaseous (*full of gas*), gassy; carbonated, fizzy.
gaspatxo *n.* gazpacho (*soup*).
gasta *vi.* & *vt.* wear out, age; fray, unravel.
gastada *adj.* worn out, shabby, threadbare, frayed, dilapidated, rundown; (*tyre*) bald. **gastada par clima** weathered, weatherbeaten. **gastada par gera** war-torn.
gastral *adj.* gastric.
gastraljia *n.* gastralgia.
gastrite *n.* gastritis.
gastroenterite *n.* gastroenteritis.
gastroenterolojia *n.* gastroenterology.
gastroenterolojiste *n.* gastroenterologist.
gastrointestinal *adj.* gastrointestinal.
gastropodo *n.* gastropod (*Gastropoda*).
gastrotrico *n.* gastrotrich (*worm*: *Gastrotricha*).
gateta *n.* kitten, kitty, pussy, puss.
gatili *vt.* trigger.
gatilio *n.* trigger.
gatiliomanica *adj.* trigger-happy.
gato *n.* cat (*Felis catus*).
gauda *n.* gouda (*cheese*).
gaulteria *n.* wintergreen (*plant*: *Gaultheria*).
gaus *n.* gauss (*unit of induction*).
gavia *n.* loon, diver (*bird*: *Gavia*).
gavota[1] *n.* gull, seagull (*Laridae*).
gavota[2] *n.* gavotte (*dance, music*).
gaxa *n.* gruel, porridge, mush. **gaxa de avena** porridge, oatmeal. **gaxa de favas** bean porridge; baked beans. **gaxa de orzo** barley porridge. **gaxa de pisos** mashed peas, mushy peas. **gaxa de ris** rice porridge; rice pudding. **gaxa de torta** cake batter, cake mix.
gaxi *vi.* & *vt.* mush.
gaxin *adj.* mushy, sloppy. • *n.* mush, pap, slop.
gaza[1] *n.* gauze. **gaza de ceso** cheesecloth.
Gaza[2] *n.* Gaza, Gaza strip.
gazela *n.* gazelle (*Gazella*).
ge *adj.* & *n.* gay, queer, homosexual.
geco *n.* gecko (*Gekkonidae*).
Genova *n.* Genoa (*Italian city*).
genoves *adj.* & *n.* Genoese.
Georgia ['dʒordʒa] *n.* Georgia (*US state*)
gepardo *n.* cheetah (*Acinonyx jubatus*).
gera *vi.* war, make war. • *n.* war, warfare. **declara un gera contra** wage war on. **gera biolojial** biological warfare. **gera cimical** chemical warfare. **gera fria** cold war. **gera interna** civil war, internecine war. **gera lampin** blitzkrieg. **gera mundal** world war. **gera nucleal** nuclear warfare. **gera psicolojial** psychological warfare.
gerilia *n.* guerrilla. **gera de gerilia** guerrilla warfare.
germanica *adj.* & *n.* Germanic, Teutonic.
germanio *n.* germanium (*element*).
Gernsi *n.* Guernsey.
gernsies *adj.* & *n.* Sarnian (*person*); Guernésiais (*language*).
geror *n.* warrior.
gerosa *adj.* bellicose, warlike.
geser *n.* geyser; gusher, uprush, blowout (*oil*).
gestalt *n.* gestalt.
gestapo *n.* gestapo.
geto *n.* ghetto.
gexa *n.* geisha.
gi *n.* ghee (*butter*).
gibon *n.* gibbon (*Hylobatidae*).
gida *vt.* guide, lead, head; conduct, convey; usher, herd, wrangle; drive (*vehicle*), steer. • *n.* guidance, leadership.
gidador *n.* guide (*device*).
gidor *n.* guide, leader, usher, docent; driver (*vehicle*), chauffeur. **gidor de museo** museum guide. **gidor de turi** tour guide.
giga- *pref.* giga- (*a thousand million*).
gigabait *n.* gigabyte, gig.
gilotin *n.* guillotine.
gilotini *vt.* guillotine.
gimnosperma *n.* gymnosperm (*botany*).
ginco *n.* ginkgo (*tree*: *Ginkgo biloba*).
Gine *n.* Guinea. **Gine-Bisau** *n.* Guinea-Bissau. **Gine Ecuatoral** Equatorial Guinea. **Gine Nova** New Guinea. **Golfo Gine** Gulf of Guinea. See *ecuatoginean*.
ginean *adj.* & *n.* Guinean.
gingam *n.* gingham. **de gingam** (*made of*) gingham.
ginia *vt.* wink, blink, nictate. • *n.* wink, blink (*eyes*).

gitar *n.* guitar. **gitar acustical** acoustic guitar. **gitar baso** bass guitar. **gitar eletrical** electric guitar.
gitariste *n.* guitarist.
gladiator *n.* gladiator.
gladiolo *n.* gladiolus (*Gladiolus*).
glamor *n.* glamour, pizzazz.
glamori *vt.* glamorize.
glamorosa *adj.* glamorous.
glande *n.* gland; glans. **glande salival** salivary gland. **glande suprarenal** adrenal gland.
glareola *n.* pratincole (*bird*: *Glareola*, *Stiltia*).
glasa *vt.* glaze, ice, frost. • *n.* glaze, icing, frosting. **glasa fondente** fondant.
glasada *adj.* glazed, glossy.
glasi *vi.* & *vt.* glaciate. • *n.* glaciation.
glasia *n.* glacier, icecap. **glasia polal** polar icecap.
glasial *adj.* glacial.
glasida *adj.* glaciated.
glasiolojia *n.* glaciology.
glasiolojiste *n.* glaciologist.
glasnost *n.* glasnost.
glaucoma *n.* glaucoma.
gleditsia *n.* honey locust (*tree*: *Gleditsia*).
gli *n.* glee (*music*).
glicojen *n.* glycogen (*biology*).
glifo *n.* glyph, pictogram, pictograph.
glisemia *n.* glycaemia (US glycemia).
glisemial *adj.* glycaemic (US glycemic). **indise glisemial** glycaemic (US glycemic) index.
gliserol *n.* glycerol, glycerin, glycerine.
glisina *n.* wisteria (*plant*: *Wisteria*).
global *adj.* global, worldwide.
globali *vi.* & *vt.* globalize. • *n.* globalization.
globalisme *n.* globalism.
globaliste *n.* globalist.
globin *adj.* globular.
globo *n.* globe. **globo de oio** eyeball.
globulina *n.* globulin (*protein*).
glocenspil *n.* glockenspiel.
glomerulo *n.* glomerulus (*anatomy*).
glori *v.* glorify.
gloria *n.* glory, magnificence, majesty.
gloriosa *adj.* glorious, magnificent, majestic.
glosa *n.* gloss, annotation.
gloseria *n.* glossary.
glotal *adj.* glottal. • *n.* glottal (*consonant*).
glote *n.* glottis.
gloton *adj.* gluttonous. • *n.* glutton.
glotonia *n.* gluttony.
glucagon *n.* glucagon.
glucosa *n.* glucose, blood sugar.
glu-glu *interj.* gobble (*turkey*, *peacock*).
gluma *n.* husk, chaff.
gluon *n.* gluon (*particle*).
glutamato *n.* glutamate (*chemistry*).
glutamina *n.* glutamine (*amino acid*).
glutaminal *adj.* glutamic.
gluten *n.* gluten.
gluteo *n.* buttock, gluteus. **gluteos** buttocks, backside, behind, bottom, rear.
gnais *n.* gneiss (*geology*).
gnatostomulido *n.* gnathostomulid (*organism*: *Gnathostomulida*).
gneto *n.* gnetum (*plant*: *Gnetum*).
gnomon *n.* gnomon.
gnostica *adj.* & *n.* gnostic.
gnosticisme *n.* gnosticism.
gnu *n.* gnu, wildebeest (*Connochaetes*).
go *n.* go (*game*).
Gobi *n.* Gobi. **Deserto Gobi** Gobi Desert.
gobio *n.* goby (*fish*: *Gobiidae*).
gofer *n.* gopher (*rodent*: *Geomyidae*).
gol *n.* goal, target. **fa un gol** score a goal.
golem *n.* golem (*mythology*).
goleta *n.* schooner (*ship*).
golf *n.* golf (*sport*).
golferia *n.* golf course.
golfo *n.* gulf.
golfor *n.* golfer.
golor *n.* goalkeeper, goaltender, goalie.
goma *n.* gum. **goma de cansela** eraser. **goma de mastica** chewing gum.
gombo *n.* okra, gumbo (*plant*: *Abelmoschus esculentus*).
gomin *adj.* gummy, chewy.
gonada *n.* gonad.
gondola *n.* gondola.
gondolor *n.* gondolier.
gongo *n.* gong.
gonorea *n.* gonorrhoea (US gonorrhea), clap.
gorgonzola *n.* gorgonzola.
gorila *n.* gorilla (*Gorilla*).
gospel *adj.* & *n.* gospel (*music*).
gota[1] *vi.* & *vt.* drip. • *n.* drip, drop (*liquid*). **gota de pluve** raindrop.
gota[2] *n.* gout (*medical*).
gotea *vi.* & *vt.* leak; e.g. *la teto gotea*; *acua es goteada par la teto*. • *n.* leak, leakage.
goteante *adj.* leaking, leaky.
goteta *n.* droplet; tiny amount, smidgen, tad.
gotica *adj.* Gothic (*architecture*, *lettering*).
goto *adj.* Gothic (*person*, *language*). • *n.* Goth.
goton *n.* blob, dollop, glob, globule.
governa *vt.* govern, rule. • *n.* government, rule, regime; cabinet. **governa pupetin** puppet government, puppet regime.
governal *adj.* government.
governor *n.* governor.
governoria *n.* governorate.
gradal *adj.* gradual. • *adv.* gradually.
gradalisme *n.* gradualism.
gradeta *n.* rung.

gradi *vt.* grade, rank, rate; stagger (*events, payments*). • *n.* ranking, rating (*measurement*).
gradiente *n.* gradient. **gradiente de consentra** concentration gradient. **gradiente de presa** pressure gradient. **gradiente sosial** social gradient. **gradiente termal** thermal gradient, temperature gradient.
grado *n.* degree, extent; rank, echelon; stair, tread, step; stage, step (*process*). **a no grado** to no extent, not at all. **grado de celsius** degree Celsius, degree centigrade. **grado de farenhait** degree Fahrenheit. **grado de porte** doorstep. **par grado** *adj.* gradual. • *adv.* gradually. **redui de grado** downgrade. **redui la grado de** downgrade.
gradua *vi.* graduate. • *n.* graduation. **gradua de scola** leave school, graduate from school.
graduada *adj.* graduated. • *n.* graduate. **graduada prima** valedictorian.
graduante *adj.* graduating. **graduante de scola** school leaver.
graf[1] *n.* graph (*diagram*).
-graf[2] *n.suff.* -graph (*device*).
grafem *n.* grapheme.
grafemal *adj.* graphemic.
grafi *vi.* & *vt.* graph.
-grafia *n.suff.* -graphy.
grafica *adj.* graphic, graphical. • *n.* graphic; graphic design.
graficiste *n.* graphic artist, graphic designer.
grafiti *n.* graffiti.
grafito *n.* graphite; (*pencil*) lead.
grafitosa *adj.* graffitied, covered in graffiti.
grafolojia *n.* graphology.
grafolojiste *n.* graphologist.
grai *n.* gray (*unit of radiation*).
gralia *n.* rook (*Corvus frugilegus*).
gram[1] *n.* gram, gramme.
-gram[2] *n.suff.* -gram (*output of device*).
gramatica *n.* grammar.
gramatical *adj.* grammatical.
gramaticiste *n.* grammarian.
gran *n.* grain, kernel, grist, cereal seed; cereal crop, corn; particle, pellet (*salt, sand, etc.*). **gran de plomo** lead shot.
granada[1] *n.* grenade.
granada[2] *n.* pomegranate (*Punica granatum*).
granador *n.* grenadier (*soldier*).
granato *n.* garnet (*gem*).
grande *adj.* large, big, great, hefty, sizeable; great, eminent; e.g. *Alexandro la Grande*. **Rio Grande** Rio Grande.
grandi *vi.* & *vt.* enlarge, grow, increase, amplify, magnify, augment, scale up, escalate. • *n.* enlargement, growth, increase, amplification, magnification; augmentation, escalation.
grandia *n.* size, amplitude; stature. **de grandia cambiable** resizable. **de grandia natural** full-size, full-scale, life-size. **de grandia vera** life-size.
grandida *adj.* enlarged, magnified.
grandiosa *adj.* grandiose, grand.
graneria *n.* barn, granary; breadbasket (*region*).
graneta *n.* granule; bagatelle, trinket, trifle, triviality.
granetin *adj.* granular, grainy, crumbly.
grani *vi.* & *vt.* granulate.
granin *adj.* granulated.
granito *n.* granite.
graniza *vi.* hail. • *n.* hail, hailstone.
granuloma *n.* granuloma (*medical*).
granulopoiese *n.* granulopoiesis (*medical*).
granulosite *n.* granulocyte (*medical*).
granulositopenia *n.* granulocytopenia (*medical*).
grapa *n.* staple (*fastener*).
grapador *n.* stapler, staple gun.
grapi *vt.* staple.
gras *n.* fat (*oily animal material*), grease, flab, shortening, lard. **gras de balena** blubber. **gras de bur** butterfat. **gras de porco** lard. **gras de ren** suet.
grasi *vt.* grease, baste.
grasia *vt.* thank. • *n.* gratitude, thanks; grace (*Christianity*). **con grasias a** thanks to. **grasias** thanks, thank you. **grasias a Dio** thank God, thank goodness. **grasias a la sielo** thank heavens.
grasieta *vt.* tip, give a tip (*for service*). • *n.* tip, gratuity.
grasiosa *adj.* grateful, thankful, appreciative. **es grasiosa per** be grateful for, appreciate.
grasosa *adj.* fat, fatty, greasy.
Grau, Mar *n.* Mar de Grau.
grava *vt.* engrave, etch. • *n.* engraving, etching.
gravada *adj.* engraved, graven.
gravador *n.* engraving machine.
grave *adj.* grave, serious, dire, grim, grievous, virulent.
gravia *n.* seriousness, gravity.
gravita *vi.* gravitate. • *n.* gravity.
graviton *n.* graviton.
gravor *n.* engraver.
grebe *n.* grebe (*bird: Podicipedidae*).
gregorian *adj.* Gregorian.
Grenada *n.* Grenada.
grenadian *adj.* & *n.* Grenadian.
Grenadine, Isolas *n.pl.* Grenadine Islands.
greve *vi.* strike (*protest*). • *n.* strike. **greve nonlegal** wildcat strike.
grevor *n.* striker, picketer.
grifon *n.* griffin, griffon, gryphon.

grili *vt.* grill, barbecue, broil, charboil; add a hash sign to, hashtag.
grilia *n.* grill, grillwork, grid, gridiron, grate, lattice, latticework, trellis; broiler; hash sign, hashtag; number sign; pound sign (*US: weight*). **grilia de ximineria** grate (*fireplace*).
grilin *adj.* gridlike, crisscross.
grilo *n.* cricket (*insect: Ensifera*). **grilo verde** katydid, bush cricket (*Tettigoniidae*).
grima *vi.* & *n.* grimace, frown, scowl, glower, glare, sneer; grin (*skull*).
grinse *vi.*, *vt.* & *n.* creak (*high-pitched*), squeak, chirp, grate.
grinsente *adj.* creaking, creaky, squeaky.
grio *n.* griot (*storyteller*).
gripe *n.* influenza, flu. **gripe avial** avian flu, bird flu. **gripe porcal** swine flu.
gris *adj.* grey (US gray), grizzled. • *n.* grey (US gray).
grisi *vi.* & *vt.* grey (US gray), turn grey (US gray), grizzle.
grisin *adj.* greyish (US grayish).
grog *n.* grog (*drink*).
Gronland *n.* Greenland. **Mar Gronland** Greenland Sea. See *Calalitnunat.*
gronlandes *adj.* Greenlandic (*person, language*). • *n.* Greenlander. See *calalit.*
grosela *n.* edible currant (*Ribes*). **grosela negra** blackcurrant (*Ribes nigrum*). **grosela roja** redcurrant (*Ribes rubrum*). **grosela spinosa** gooseberry (*Ribes uva-crispa*).
grr *interj.* grrr (*growling*).
gru *n.* crane (*bird, machine: Gruidae*). **Gru** *n.* Grus (*constellation*). **gru cavaletin** gantry.
grunje *adj.* & *n.* grunge (*music*).
grupal *adj.* group, as a group.
grupi[1] *n.* groupie.
grupi[2] *vi.* & *vt.* group, form a group.
grupo *n.* group, bunch, batch, troop, cohort, posse, cluster, clump. **grupo de odia** hate group. **grupo escluinte** clique, coterie. **grupo laborante** working group, working party. **grupo propre** ingroup.
grupor *n.* grouper (*fish*).
guacamole *n.* guacamole (*food*).
Guadelupe *n.* Guadeloupe.
guadelupean *adj.* Guadeloupean.
guaiava *n.* guava (*tree, fruit: Psidium*).
Guam *n.* Guam (*island*).
guamanian *adj.* & *n.* Guamanian.
Guangdong *n.* Guangdong. **guangdong** *n.* Guang Dong Wa (*language*).
guano *n.* guano.
guarani *adj.* & *n.* Guarani (*person, language*).
Guatemala *n.* Guatemala.
guatemalteca *adj.* & *n.* Guatemalan.
Guayaquil *n.* Guayaquil. **Golfo Guayaquil** Gulf of Guayaquil.
Gudjarat *n.* Gujarat (*Indian state*).
gudjarati *adj.* & *n.* Gujarati (*person, language*).
gugli[1] *vt.* google (*search for*).
gugli[2] *n.* googly (*cricket*).
gugol *n.* googol (*number*).
gugolplex *n.* googolplex (*number*).
Guian Franses *n.* French Guiana.
Guiana *n.* Guyana.
guianan *adj.* & *n.* Guyanese.
guianes *adj.* & *n.* (French) Guianan.
gul *n.* ghoul (*mythology*).
gulag *n.* gulag.
gulax *n.* goulash, gulyás (*soup*).
gulo *n.* wolverine (*animal: Gulo gulo*).
gundi *n.* gundi (*rodent: Ctenodactylidae*).
gupi *n.* guppy (*fish: Poecilia reticulata*).
guptan *adj.* Guptan (*dynasty*).
gurami *n.* gourami (*fish: Osphronemidae*).
gurgula *vi.*, *vt.* & *n.* gurgle, glug, squelch.
gurme *n.* gourmet, gastronome, epicure, epicurean.
guru *n.* guru.
gusta *vt.* like, enjoy, be fond of; e.g. *me gusta leje*; *me gusta esta canta.* • *n.* enjoyment. **no gusta** dislike.
gustable *adj.* likeable (US likable), enjoyable, pleasant, agreeable, welcome, groovy.

H

H [haʃ], **hax** *letter* H, h.
ha *interj.* ha. **ha ha** ha ha (*laughing*).
haca[1] *adj.* & *n.* Hakka (*person*, *language*).
haca[2] *n.* haka (*dance*).
hadj *n.* hajj (*pilgrimage*).
hadji *n.* hajji (*pilgrim*).
hadrosauro *n.* hadrosaur, hadrosaurus (*Hadrosauridae*).
hafnio *n.* hafnium (*element*).
hagis *n.* haggis (*food*).
haiaren *adj.* & *n.* Armenian (*person*, *language*). See *armenian*.
Haiastan *n.* Armenia. See *Armenia*.
haicu *n.* haiku (*poetry*).
haida *adj.* & *n.* Haida (*person*, *language*).
Hainan *n.* Hainan (*island*).
halal *adj.* halal. • *n.* halal meat.
halter *n.* dumbbell.
halux *n.* hallux, big toe (*technical*). **halux valga** bunion.
Hampshire Nova ['hampʃer] *n.* New Hampshire (*US state*).
han[1] *n.* khan, khagan (*governor*).
han[2] *adj.* Han (*dynasty*).
handbal *n.* handball (*sport*).
hangugo *adj.* & *n.* Korean (*person*, *language*). See *corean*.
hangul *n.* hangul, hangeul (*writing system*).
hania *n.* khanate, khaganate.
hantavirus *n.* hantavirus (*medical*).
hanuca *n.* Hanukkah (*Jewish festival*).
haraciri *n.* harakiri (*disembowelment*).
hascala *n.* Haskalah, Jewish Enlightenment.
hasidisme *n.* Hasidism (*Judaism*).
hasidiste *adj.* Hasidic. • *n.* Hasid.
hasio *n.* hassium (*element*).
hausa *adj.* & *n.* Hausa (*person*, *language*).
hawaian *adj.* & *n.* Hawaiian. **Isolas Hawaian** Hawaiian Islands.
Hawaii *n.* Hawaii (*US state*).
haxix *n.* hashish.
he *interj.* hey, ahoy.
Hebrides *n.pl.* Hebrides. **Hebrides Esterna** Outer Hebrides. **Hebrides Interna** Inner Hebrides.
Hecate, Streta *n.* Hecate Strait.
hemicordato *n.* hemichordate (*organism*: *Hemichordata*).
hena *n.* henna (*plant*, *dye*: *Lawsonia inermis*).
henri *n.* henry (*unit of inductance*).
hentai *n.* hentai (*manga*).
Hercule *n.* Hercules (*mythology*, *constellation*).
herculin *adj.* Herculean.
hersegovasce *adj.* & *n.* Herzegovinian.
Hersegovina *n.* Herzegovina.
herze *n.* hertz.
hibatxi *n.* hibachi (*heater*).
hidjab *n.* hijab (*garment*).
hidjra *n.* hejira (*Islam*).
hi hi *interj.* hee-hee, tee-hee (*giggling*).
Himalaia *n.* Himalayas (*region*). **Montes Himalaia** Himalaya Mountains, Himalayas.
himalaian *adj.* Himalayan.
hindi *adj.* & *n.* Hindi (*language*).
hiolito *n.* hyolith (*fossil*: *hyolitha*).
hiphop *adj.* hip-hop (*dance*, *music*).
hipi *n.* hippy, hippie.
Hipocrate *n.* Hippocrates. **jura de Hipocrate** Hippocratic oath.
hiragana *n.* hiragana (*writing system*).
hitita *adj.* & *n.* Hittite (*person*, *language*).
hm *interj.* hmm (*thinking*); ahem (*clearing throat*).
hobit *n.* hobbit.
hoci *n.* hockey, field hockey. **hoci de campo** field hockey. **hoci de jelo** ice hockey. **hoci eres** hurling.
ho ho ho *interj.* ho ho ho.
Hokkaido *n.* Hokkaido (*island*).
holding *n.* holding company.
holmio *n.* holmium (*element*).
holo *adj.* & *n.* Hoklo, Taiwanese Hokkien (*person*, *language*).
holozon *n.* holozoon (pl. holozoa) (*organism*).
holstain *n.* holstein (*cow*).
homeral *adj.* Homeric.
Homero *n.* Homer.
Hongkong *n.* Hong Kong.
Honshu *n.* Honshu (*island*).
hopi *adj.* & *n.* Hopi (*person*, *language*).
Hormuz *n.* Hormuz. **Streta Hormuz** Strait of Hormuz.
hornpip *n.* hornpipe (*dance*, *music*).
Huanghai, Mar *n.* Huang Hai, Yellow Sea. See *Jala*.
Huanghe, Rio *n.* Huang He, Yellow River.
Hudson *n.* Hudson. **Baia Hudson** Hudson Bay. **Rio Hudson** Hudson River. **Streta Hudson** Hudson Strait.
hula *n.* hula (*dance*).
hun *adj.* Hunnic. • *n.* Hun.
huri *n.* houri (*Islam*).
Huron, Lago *n.* Lake Huron.
husar *n.* hussar (*soldier*).
husci *n.* husky (*dog*).
husisme *n.* Hussitism (*Christianity*).
husiste *adj.* & *n.* Hussite.
huterita *adj.* & *n.* Hutterite (*Christianity*).
huti *adj.* & *n.* Houthi (*Islam*).
hutu *adj.* & *n.* Hutu (*person*, *language*).

I

I[1] [i], **i** *letter* I, i.
i[2] *interj.* eek.
-i[3] *vi.suff.* become, -en, -esce, -ify, -ize; e.g. *la acua profondi*; *la visitores grupi.* • *vt.suff.* cause (*someone or something*) to become; e.g. *me pleni la caxa*; *on grupi la visitores.* • *n.suff.* (*fractional number*); e.g. *dui, tri, cuatri.*
-i[4] *vt.suff.* make use of (*tool*), apply (*substance*) to; e.g. *el botoni sua jacon*; *me va telefoni la detalias a tu*; *on ia pinti la mur*; *me va buri la pan.*
-i[5] *vt.suff.* emit (*bodily fluid*); e.g. *urini*; *vomiti sangue.*
-i[6] *adj.suff.* & *n.suff.* -i (*pertaining to a region*); e.g. *arabi.* See *-an, -es, -ica, -sce.*
ia[1] *adv.* (*preverbal*) (*indicating that a finite verb is in the past tense*) -ed, did (*happen*), have (*happened*); e.g. *me ia espera ce tu es asi.* **ia ta** would have (*past hypothetical*); e.g. *si me ta sabe acel, me no ia ta parla.*
-ia[2] *n.suff.* -ness, -ity, -hood, -ship (*abstract quality*); e.g. *felisia*; *en mea enfantia*; *la jornal de la bispia.*
-ia[3] *n.suff.* -y, -ia (*disease*).
i-aa *interj.* eeyore, hee haw, bray.
iac *n.* yak (*Bos grunniens*, *Bos mutus*).
Iaman *n.* Yemen.
iamani *adj.* & *n.* Yemeni.
iambal *adj.* iambic.
iambo *n.* iamb, iambus (*poetry*).
ianci *adj.* & *n.* (*colloquial*) Yankee (*American*).
iang *n.* yang (*philosophy*).
iard *n.* yard (*unit of length*).
-iase *n.suff.* -iase (*disease*).
iate *n.* yacht; cruiser (*pleasure boat*).
iator *n.* yachtsman, yachtswoman.
-iatria *n.suff.* -iatry.
-iatrica *adj.suff.* -iatric.
iatrojen *adj.* iatrogenic (*caused by doctors*).
Iaue *n.* Yahweh.
Iberia *n.* Iberia.
iberian *adj.* & *n.* Iberian.
ibex *n.* ibex (*goat*: *Capra ibex*).
ibis *n.* ibis (*bird*: *Threskiornithinae*).
ibisco *n.* hibiscus (*plant*: *Hibiscus*).
ibride *adj.* hybrid, crossbred, mongrel. • *n.* hybrid, crossbreed, mongrel.
ibridi *vi.* & *vt.* hybridize, crossbreed. • *n.* hybridization.
ica[1] *vi.* hiccup, hiccough. • *n.* hiccup.
-ica[2] *adj.suff.* & *n.suff.* -ic, -ish (*pertaining to a region*); e.g. *cimrica.* See *-an, -es, -i, -sce.*
-ica[3] *adj.suff.* & *n.suff.* -ic, -iac (*suffering from a medical condition*); e.g. *alerjica.*
-ica[4] *n.suff.* -ic (*chemical valency*).
icebana *n.* ikebana (*flower arrangement*).
icon *n.* icon.
iconin *adj.* iconic.
iconoclasia *n.* iconoclasm.
iconoclasiste *adj.* iconoclastic. • *n.* iconoclast.
icor *n.* ichor (*mythology*, *medical*).
icosaedro *adj.* icosahedral. • *n.* icosahedron.
ictiolojia *n.* ichthyology.
ictiolojiste *n.* ichthyologist.
ictiosauro *n.* ichthyosaur, ichthyosaurus (*Ichthyosauria*).
id *n.* id (*psychology*).
Idaho ['ajdaho] *n.* Idaho (*US state*).
idea *n.* idea, concept, issue, notion. **ideas** ideas. **ideas asetada** received wisdom.
ideal *adj.* & *n.* ideal.
ideali *vi.* & *vt.* idealize. • *n.* idealization.
idealia *n.* ideality.
idealisme *n.* idealism.
idealiste *adj.* idealistic, quixotic. • *n.* idealist.
identia *n.* identity, ID. **identia de jenero** gender identity. **identia sesal** sexual identity.
identica *adj.* identical.
identifia *vt.* identify, designate. • *n.* identification, designation. **identifia se** identify oneself, log in (*software*).
identifiable *adj.* identifiable.
identifiada *adj.* identified, designated; logged in (*software*).
identifiante *n.* identifier.
ideogram *n.* ideogram, ideograph.
ideolojia *n.* ideology.
ideolojial *adj.* ideological.
ideolojiste *n.* ideologist.
ides *adj.* & *n.* Yiddish.
idilin *adj.* idyllic.
idilio *n.* idyll.
idiografia *n.* idiography.
idiografial *adj.* idiographic.
idiom *n.* idiom.
idiomal *adj.* idiomatic.
idiopatia *n.* idiopathy.
idiopatica *adj.* idiopathic.
-ido *n.suff.* -ide (*salt*).
idol *n.* idol; heartthrob.
idoli *vi.* be idolized. • *vt.* idolize. • *n.* idolatry.
idolinte *adj.* idolatrous.
idolor *n.* idolater, idol worshipper (US worshiper).
idra *n.* hydra (*organism*: *Hydra*). **Idra** *n.* Hydra (*mythology*). • *n.* Hydra (*constellation*). **Idra Mas** Hydrus (*constellation*).
idrante *n.* hydrant, fire hydrant, fire plug.

idrata *vi.* & *vt.* hydrate, moisturize. • *n.* hydration.
idratador *n.* hydrator.
idratante *adj.* moisturizing. • *n.* moisturizer.
idraulica *n.* hydraulics.
idraulical *adj.* hydraulic.
idro- *pref.* hydro- (*water*).
idrocarbonal *adj.* hydrocarbon.
idrocarbono *n.* hydrocarbon.
idroclorica *adj.* hydrochloric. **asida idroclorica** hydrochloric acid.
idrocloriđo *n.* hydrochloride.
idrodinamica *n.* hydrodynamics.
idrodinamical *adj.* hydrodynamic; streamlined.
idroeletrica *n.* hydroelectricity.
idroeletrical *adj.* hydroelectric.
idrofilia *n.* hydrophilia.
idrofilica *adj.* hydrophilic. • *n.* hydrophile.
idrofobia *n.* hydrophobia.
idrofobica *adj.* hydrophobic. • *n.* hydrophobe.
idrografia *n.* hydrography.
idrografial *adj.* hydrographical.
idrografiste *n.* hydrographer.
idrojen *n.* hydrogen.
idrolise *vt.* hydrolyse (US hydrolyze). • *n.* hydrolysis.
idrolojia *n.* hydrology.
idrolojiste *n.* hydrologist.
idromel *n.* mead (*drink*).
idroplana *n.* hydrofoil.
idroponia *n.* hydroponics.
idroponial *adj.* hydroponic.
idrosa *adj.* hydrous.
idrosefalia *n.* hydrocephalus, water on the brain.
idrosefalica *adj.* hydrocephalic.
idrosfera *n.* hydrosphere.
idrosido *n.* hydroxide. **idrosido de potasio** potassium hydroxide, caustic potash, lye. **idrosido de sodio** sodium hydroxide, caustic soda, lye.
idrosil *adj.* hydroxyl (*chemistry*).
idrostatica *n.* hydrostatics.
idrostatical *adj.* hydrostatic.
idroterapia *n.* hydrotherapy.
idrotermal *adj.* hydrothermal.
idrozon *n.* hydrozoon (pl. hydrozoa) (*organism*).
ie *interj.* yeah, yay.
iena *n.* hyena (*Hyaenidae*).
ienin *adj.* hyena-like.
ier *adv.* & *n.* yesterday. **a la dia ante ier** the day before yesterday.
ierarcia *n.* hierarchy.
ierarcial *adj.* hierarchic, hierarchical.
ieratica *adj.* hieratic (*writing*, *art*).
Ierevan *n.* Yerevan.
ieroglifal *adj.* hieroglyphic.
ieroglifo *n.* hieroglyph.
Ieruxalim *n.* Jerusalem.
ieti *n.* yeti.
ifen *n.* hyphen. See *sinia de junta*.
ifenable *adj.* hyphenatable.
ifeni *vt.* hyphenate. • *n.* hyphenation.
-ifer *n.suff.* -ifer (*producing*, *carrying*).
iftar *n.* iftar (*meal*).
iglu *n.* igloo.
iguana *n.* iguana (*Iguana*).
iguanodon *n.* iguanodon (*Iguanodon*).
iii[1] *interj.* neigh, whinny (*horse*).
i-i-i[2] *interj.* ee-ee-ee, ook (*monkey*).
iin *n.* yin (*philosophy*).
iin-iang *n.* yin-yang.
ijeni *vt.* sanitize.
ijenia *n.* hygiene, sanitation.
ijenial *adj.* hygienic, sanitary.
ijeninte *n.* sanitizer.
ijeniste *n.* hygienist.
-il *n.suff.* -yl (*chemistry*).
ilaria *n.* hilarity, mirth.
ilario *adj.* hilarious, uproarious.
ileo *n.* ileum (*anatomy*).
ilex *n.* holly (*Ilex*).
Iliada *n.* Iliad (*poem*).
ilio[1] *n.* ilium (*anatomy*).
Ilio[2] *n.* Ilium, Ilion (*ancient Troy*). See *Troia*.
Iliria *n.* Illyria.
ilirian *adj.* Illyrian.
Illinois [iliˈnoj] *n.* Illinois (*US state*).
ilote *n.* helot (*social class*).
ilude *vt.* delude. • *n.* delusion, illusion, figment. **ilude de grandiosia** delusion of grandeur. **ilude de paranoia** delusion of paranoia. **ilude de vide** optical illusion, visual illusion.
iludente *adj.* illusive, illusory.
iludiste *n.* illusionist.
im-[1] *pref.* im- (*in*, *into*).
im-[2] *pref.* im- (*not*).
imago *n.* imago (*biology*, *psychology*).
imaje *n.* image, picture, depiction, graphic, illustration, painting, drawing, photo; frame (*movie*). **imaje esajerada** caricature. **imaje matrisin** bitmap image, raster image. **imaje vetoral** vector image, vector graphic. **imajes** images, imagery.
imajeta *n.* thumbnail image.
imaji *vi.* appear as an image. • *vt.* image, picture, depict, illustrate. • *n.* imaging.
imajin *adj.* pictorial.
imajina *vt.* imagine, fancy, ideate, visualize; dream up, think up, think of, come up with, hit on. • *n.* imagination, ideation.
imajinable *adj.* imaginable, conceivable.
imajinal *adj.* imaginary, fictional, fictitious, fanciful, chimeric, chimerical.

imajinosa *adj.* imaginative.
imajor *n.* illustrator.
imam *n.* imam (*Islam*).
imantico *n.* stilt (*bird*: *Himantopus*).
imen *n.* hymen, maidenhead (*anatomy*).
imita *vt.* imitate, mimic, emulate, impersonate. • *n.* imitation, mimicry, emulation, impersonation.
imitador *n.* emulator (*software*).
imitor *n.* impressionist, mimic, impersonator.
imno *n.* hymn, anthem, paean.
imobila *n.* property, premises, piece of real estate, homestead, realty. **con imobila** propertied, landed.
impala *n.* impala (*antelope*: *Aepyceros melampus*).
impasto *n.* impasto (*painting technique*).
impedi *vt.* impede, hinder, prevent, hamper, deter, preclude, thwart; obstruct, block, congest, be in the way. • *n.* blockade, obstacle, congestion, obstruction, impediment, hindrance.
impedida *adj.* congested.
impedinte *adj.* impeding, hindering, inimical.
impenia *vt.* pawn, hock.
impenieria *n.* pawnshop.
impenior *n.* pawnbroker.
imperal *adj.* imperial.
imperalisme *n.* imperialism.
imperaliste *adj.* imperialist.
impero *n.* empire.
imperor *n.* emperor.
imperoresa *n.* empress.
impetigo *n.* impetigo (*medical*).
implanta *vt.* implant. • *n.* implantation.
implantada *adj.* implanted. • *n.* implant.
implica *vt.* imply, entail; implicate, incriminate. • *n.* implication, incrimination. **par implica** by default.
implicada *adj.* implied, implicit, default, tacit. • *n.* default value.
implode *vi.* & *vt.* implode. • *n.* implosion.
implodente *adj.* implosive.
importa *vi.* be important, matter, have import, have significance. • *n.* importance, significance; salience, prominence. **lo no importa** it's not important, never mind, whatever.
importante *adj.* important, significant, momentous; salient, prominent, consequential. **suprema importante** paramount.
imposta *vt.* tax. • *n.* tax, taxation. **imposta de ben** duty, goods tax. **imposta de corpora** corporate tax. **imposta de duana** imports tax, border tax, customs duty. **imposta de emporta** imports tax, border tax, customs duty. **imposta de erita** inheritance tax. **imposta de imobila** property tax. **imposta de revenu** income tax. **imposta de valua ajuntada** value-added tax, VAT. **imposta de vende** sales tax. **imposta interna** inland tax, excise. **imposta regresante** regressive tax. **imposta tro multe** overtax. **sin imposta** taxfree.
impostable *adj.* taxable.
impostor *n.* taxman, publican.
impresa *vt.* impress, imprint, emboss, stamp; make an impression, come across (*as*); instil, inculcate. • *n.* impression, imprint. **impresa de dito** fingerprint. **impresa de diton** thumbprint. **impresa de pede** footprint. **impresa de ungula** hoofprint, hoofmark.
impresable *adj.* impressionable.
impresablia *n.* impressionability.
impresador *n.* stamp.
impresante *adj.* impressive, sonorous.
impresisme *n.* Impressionism (*art*).
impresiste *n.* Impressionist.
improvisa *vt.* improvise, extemporize; jam; cobble together. • *n.* improvisation, extemporization.
improvisada *adj.* improvised, impromptu, extemporary, extemporaneous, freeform.
impulsa *vt.* impel. • *n.* impulse, impulsion, impetus.
imune *adj.* immune, unsusceptible.
imuni *vi.* become immune, develop immunity. • *vt.* immunize. • *n.* immunization.
imunia *n.* immunity.
imunial *adj.* immune (*of the immune system*). **sistem imunial** immune system.
imunodebil *adj.* immunodeficient.
imunodebilia *n.* immunodeficiency, immune deficiency.
imunoglobulina *n.* immunoglobulin.
imunojen *adj.* immunogenic. • *n.* immunogen.
imunolojia *n.* immunology.
imunolojiste *n.* immunologist.
imunosupresante *adj.* immunosuppressive. • *n.* immunosuppressant.
imunoterapia *n.* immunotherapy.
-in[1] *adj.suff.* -ish, -like, -y (*similar to*); e.g. *amin*; *serpentin*.
-in[2] *n.suff.* -yne (*chemistry*).
in-[3] *pref.* in- (*in, into*).
in-[4] *pref.* in- (*not*).
inata *adj.* innate.
inatisme *n.* innatism.
inatiste *n.* innatist.
inca[1] *n.* ink.
inca[2] *adj.* Incan. • *n.* Inca.

incandese *vi.* incandesce, glow, be white-hot. • *vt.* make incandescent. • *n.* incandescence.
incandesente *adj.* incandescent, white-hot.
incarne *vi.* incarnate. • *n.* incarnation.
inci *vt.* ink (*apply ink to*).
inclina *vi.* & *vt.* incline, slope, tip; bow (*bend respectfully*). • *n.* bow. **inclina sua testa** nod one's head.
inclinada *adj.* inclined, sloped, sloping. • *n.* incline, slope, bank.
inclui *vt.* include, subsume, encompass. • *n.* inclusion. **inclui partal** overlap, partially include.
incluinte *adj.* including, inclusive. • *prep.* including, inclusive of.
inco *n.* anvil; incus (*anatomy*).
incore *vt.* incur (*punishment*).
incuba *vt.* incubate, cause to hatch. • *n.* incubation.
incubador *n.* incubator.
incuberia *n.* hatchery.
incubo *n.* incubus.
incuisisio *n.* inquisition.
indente *vt.* dent, nick, nock; indent. • *n.* dent, nick, nock, notch; indent, indentation. **indente de jena** dimple. **indente de surie** dimple.
India *n.* India. **Indias Este** East Indies. **Indias Ueste** West Indies. See *Barat.*
indian *adj.* & *n.* Indian. **Indian** *n.* Indus (*constellation*). **Mar Indian** Indian Ocean. See *barati.*
Indiana *n.* Indiana (*US state*).
indica *vt.* indicate, point to, denote, read, register; bookmark, earmark. • *n.* indication; clue, evidence; sign, trace; harbinger, portent, omen; reading. **indica de ora** timestamp. **indica e clica** point and click. **indica la ora de** timestamp. **indicas de vive** signs of life, life signs, indications of life. **mal indica** bad omen, evil omen.
indicador *n.* indicator, dial, readout; hand (*clock, compass*); marker; bookmark. **indicador de venta** weathervane, weathercock.
indicante *adj.* indicating, pointing, ostensive.
indiceta *vt.* hint. • *n.* hint, clue, slight indication.
indigo *adj.* indigo.
indio *n.* indium (*element*).
indise *vt.* & *n.* index.
individua *adj.* individual, particular. • *adv.* individually, one by one. • *n.* individual.
individual *n.* (*pertaining to an*) individual.
individualia *n.* individuality.
individualisme *n.* individualism.
individualiste *adj.* & *n.* individualist.
Indo, Rio *n.* Indus River.
indoarian *adj.* Indo-Aryan, Indic.
indoeuropean *adj.* & *n.* Indo-European, Aryan.
indoiranian *adj.* & *n.* Indo-Iranian.
Indonesia *n.* Indonesia.
indonesian *adj.* & *n.* Indonesian.
Indoxina *n.* Indochina.
indri *n.* indri, woolly lemur (*Indriidae*).
indu *adj.* & *n.* Hindu.
indui *vt.* induce, induct, inaugurate, swear in. • *n.* induction, inductance; inauguration. **indui magnetal** magnetic induction, magnetic flux density.
induinte *adj.* inductive, inaugural.
induisme *n.* Hinduism.
induiste *adj.* & *n.* Hindu.
industani *adj.* Hindustani.
industri *vt.* industrialize. • *n.* industrialization.
industria *n.* industry.
industrial *adj.* industrial.
industrialiste *n.* industrialist.
inere *vi.* inhere (*be an essential or permanent feature*). **ave la inere de** inherently have, consist in.
inerente *adj.* inherent, immanent.
inerte *adj.* inert, inactive, quiescent.
inertia *n.* inertia, quiescence.
inertial *adj.* inertial.
inerva *vt.* innervate. • *n.* innervation.
infarta *vi.* infarct (*die through lack of blood*). • *n.* infarction. **infarta miocardial** myocardial infarction, heart attack.
inferior *adj.* inferior, second-rate, substandard, tacky. • *n.* inferior, minion, stooge.
inferiori *vi.* & *vt.* subordinate. • *n.* subordination.
inferioria *n.* inferiority.
infesta *vt.* infest; haunt. • *n.* infestation; haunting.
infestada *adj.* infested, haunted.
infeta *vt.* infect. • *n.* infection. **infeta ajuntada** secondary infection. **infeta de palpebra** stye.
infetante *adj.* infectious, contagious, virulent.
infiltra *vt.* infiltrate. • *n.* infiltration.
infinita *adj.* infinite, boundless, unbounded. **infinita peti** infinitesimal.
infinitia *n.* infinity.
infinitiva *adj.* & *n.* infinitive.
infisa *vt.* infix; ingrain. • *n.* infix.
infisada *adj.* infixed; ingrained.
infla *vi.* & *vt.* inflate, distend, swell, bloat, billow, puff up. • *n.* inflation (*including economic*), swelling, bloat, distension.
inflable *adj.* & *n.* inflatable.

inflada *adj.* inflated, swollen, bloated, puffy, puffed-up, tumescent, turgid; pudgy; bouffant; exorbitant.
inflama *vi.* & *vt.* inflame. • *n.* inflammation.
inflamante *adj.* inflammatory.
infleta *vt.* inflect. • *n.* inflection.
influable *adj.* amenable, suggestible.
influablia *n.* suggestibility.
influe *vt.* influence, have influence over, affect, sway. • *n.* influence.
influente *adj.* influential, seminal.
infografia *n.* computer graphics, CGI.
informa *vt.* inform, tell, apprise, acquaint. • *n.* information, info, lowdown, tattle; intelligence (*gathered*), intel. **informa contra** inform on, rat on, sneak on, snitch on. **informa fondal** background information. **informa secreta** classified information.
informada *adj.* informed, apprised, privy.
informatica *n.* information science, computer science.
informor *n.* informer, informant, stool pigeon, stoolie.
informosa *adj.* informative.
infotecnolojia *n.* information technology, IT, ICT.
infra- *pref.* infra- (*below*).
infraordina *n.* infraorder.
infraroja *adj.* & *n.* infrared.
infrastrutur *n.* infrastructure.
infusa *vt.* infuse, brew (*tea*, *coffee*). • *n.* infusion, brew.
ingrediente *n.* ingredient.
inguin *n.* groin, crotch, crutch.
inguinal *adj.* inguinal.
ingux *adj.* & *n.* Ingush (*person*, *language*).
Inguxetia *n.* Ingushetia.
iniora *vt.* ignore, flout, disregard, snub.
iniorable *adj.* negligible.
iniorada *adj.* ignored, unheeded, unregarded, disregarded.
inioror *n.* ignorer. **inioror de lege** lawbreaker, scofflaw.
inisia *vt.* initiate, start, ignite; take the initiative; boot (*software*), initialize. • *n.* initiation, ignition; booting, bootstrapping. **inisia duple** dual-boot (*software*). **inisia multiple** multiboot (*software*). **inisia pronto** instant-on.
inisiador *n.* starter, ignition (*for engine*).
inisial *adj.* initial, leading, opening, preliminary, precursory; default, startup; inchoate. • *adv.* initially; by default. • *n.* initial (*letter*); default; preliminary, prelim. **inisiales ornal** monogram.
inisior *n.* initiator, starter (*person*).
injenia *vt.* engineer. • *n.* ingenuity, engineering.
injenior *n.* engineer. **injenior de sona** sound engineer.
injeniosa *adj.* ingenious.
injeta *vt.* inject; mainline. • *n.* injection.
inonda *vt.* inundate, flood, drown; overwhelm, overpower. • *n.* inundation, flood. **inonda de informa** information overload. **inonda de mercato** dumping (*economic*). **mori par inonda** *v.* drown, be drowned. • *n.* drowning.
inondada *adj.* inundated, flooded, awash. **inondada con lus** floodlit.
inondante *adj.* inundating, overwhelming.
inosente *adj.* innocent (*not intending harm*).
inova *vt.* innovate. • *n.* innovation.
inovor *n.* innovator.
inovosa *adj.* innovative, promethean.
insenso *n.* incense.
inserta *vt.* & *n.* graft; insert, inset. **inserta de oso** bone graft. **inserta de pel** skin graft.
insestal *adj.* incestuous.
insesto *n.* incest.
insetiside *n.* insecticide.
insetivor *adj.* insectivorous. • *n.* insectivore.
inseto *n.* insect (*Insecta*).
insinia *n.* insignia, badge. **insinia de libro** bookplate, exlibris.
insinua *vt.* insinuate, intimate. • *n.* insinuation, intimation, innuendo.
insiste *vt.* insist. • *n.* insistence.
insistente *adj.* insistent, pushy.
insonia *n.* insomnia.
insonica *adj.* & *n.* insomniac.
inspira *vt.* inspire, arouse (*interest*, *action*). • *n.* inspiration.
inspirante *adj.* inspiring, inspirational.
inspiror *n.* luminary.
instala *vt.* install; ensconce. • *n.* installation.
instinto *n.* instinct.
instintosa *adj.* instinctive, instinctual. **senti instintosa** gut feeling.
institual *adj.* institutional.
institui *vt.* institute, establish, set up. • *n.* institution (*action*).
instituida *n.* institute, institution, establishment (*organization*).
instrual *adj.* instructional.
instrui *vt.* instruct, teach, brief, train (*including animals*); e.g. *instrui algun sur la regulas*. • *n.* instruction, teaching, training, tuition, howto, brief, briefing. See *ensenia*.
instruida *adj.* instructed, trained.
instruinte *adj.* instructive, instructional, educational, didactic.
instruor *n.* instructor, trainer, coach, docent.
insulin *n.* insulin.

insulta *vt.* insult, vituperate. • *n.* insult, invective, putdown.
intalio *n.* intaglio (*art technique*).
intarsia *vt.* inlay. • *n.* intarsia, inlay, marquetry.
intata *adj.* intact.
integra *vi.* & *vt.* integrate. • *n.* integration.
integrada *adj.* integrated, inbuilt, built-in.
integral *adj.* & *n.* integral.
inteletal *adj.* intellectual, noetic.
inteletalisme *n.* intellectualism.
inteleto *n.* intellect; noesis. **inteleto artifis** artificial intelligence.
inteletosa *n.* intellectual (*person*). **inteletosas** intellectuals, intelligentsia.
intelijente *adj.* intelligent, intellectual, smart, clever.
intelijentia *n.* intelligence, astuteness, intellect. **esamina de intelijentia** intelligence test, IQ test. **grado de intelijentia** intelligence quotient, IQ.
intende *vt.* intend, plan, mean (*to do*). • *n.* intent, intention, purpose, aim, motive, plan. **con intende ce** so that, in order that (*indicating intended result*). **con intende de** for, with the intention of.
intendeda *adj.* intended, intentional, deliberate, premeditated, meant, wilful (US willful); earmarked.
intendente *adj.* intentional, deliberate, on purpose.
intensa *adj.* intense, intensive; formidable.
intensi *vi.* & *vt.* intensify. • *n.* intensification.
intensia *n.* intensity.
inter- *pref.* inter- (*between, mutually*); e.g. *interata, internasional.*
intera *adj.* entire, whole, total. • *adv.* entirely, wholly, totally, quite. • *n.* whole, entirety, totality.
interajenterial *adj.* interagency.
interata *vi.* interact. • *n.* interaction.
interatante *adj.* interactive.
interatomal *adj.* interatomic.
intercambia *vt.* exchange, interchange, swap, trade, transact, share. • *n.* exchange, interchange, swap, trade, transaction; swinging (*sex*). **par intercambia** in return. **par intercambia per** in exchange for, in return for.
intercambiable *adj.* exchangeable, interchangeable, swappable, fungible.
intercambieria *n.* exchange (*place*).
intercambior *n.* exchanger, moneychanger; swinger.
intercampal *adj.* interdisciplinary.
intercomunica *vt.* intercommunicate.
intercontinental *adj.* intercontinental.
intercredal *adj.* interfaith, cross-faith.
intercultural *adj.* intercultural, cross-cultural, cross-culture.
interdental *adj.* & *n.* interdental (*consonant*).
interdepartal *adj.* interdepartmental, interoffice.
interdepende *vi.* interdepend.
interdependente *adj.* interdependent.
interede *n.* internet. **interede de banda larga** broadband internet.
interelata *vi.* & *vt.* interrelate. • *n.* interrelation, interrelationship.
interesa *vt.* interest, be of interest to. • *n.* interest (*including money*), attention; return (*on investment*), yield, payoff; sake. **interesa composada** compound interest. **per sua propre interesa** for its own interest, for its own sake.
interesada *adj.* interested.
interesante *adj.* interesting, fascinating.
interfas *n.* interface. **interfas de usor** user interface. **interfas grafica de usor** graphical user interface, GUI.
interfase *n.* interphase.
interfere *vi.* interfere, interlope, meddle, hinder, tamper, jigger. • *n.* interference.
interferente *adj.* interfering, meddling, meddlesome.
interferon *n.* interferon (*protein*).
interferor *n.* meddler, busybody, interloper.
intergalasial *adj.* intergalactic.
intergovernal *adj.* intergovernmental.
interjeta *vt.* interject. • *n.* interjection.
interlia *vt.* interconnect, interlink.
interliada *adj.* interconnected, interlinked.
interlingua *n.* international language; Interlingua.
interlinguistica *n.* interlinguistics.
intermisca *vi.* & *vt.* intermingle.
interna *adj.* inner, interior, internal; inland. • *n.* inside, interior, hinterland. **a interna** inside, within. **a interna de** inside, within, in the interior of. **la plu interna** innermost.
internasional *adj.* international.
internasionalisme *n.* internationalism.
internasionaliste *adj.* internationalist.
interni *vi.* & *vt.* internalize, interiorize, take in.
interniste *n.* internist (*medical*).
intero *adj.* integer, integral. • *n.* integer.
interoga *vt.* interrogate, examine, question. • *n.* interrogation, examination, questioning.
interompe *vt.* interrupt, heckle; suspend, cut off; supervene. • *n.* interruption, suspension, breakpoint, cut-off.
interpersonal *adj.* interpersonal.
interplanetal *adj.* interplanetary.
interpol *n.* interpol.

interpola *vt.* interpolate. • *n.* interpolation.
interpone *vt.* interpose.
interpretable *adj.* interpretable, open to interpretation, ambiguous, equivocal.
interpretador *n.* interpreter (*software*).
interpretal *adj.* interpretational, hermeneutic.
interprete *vt.* interpret, construe. • *n.* interpretation, rendition.
interpreteda *adj.* interpreted, interpretive.
interpretor *n.* interpreter (*person*).
intersepi *vt.* intercept. • *n.* interception.
intersesal *adj.* intersex, intersexual. • *n.* intersex person.
intersesalia *n.* intersexuality.
intersposi *vi.* & *vt.* intermarry. • *n.* intermarriage.
interstatal *adj.* interstate.
interstelal *adj.* interstellar.
interstisial *adj.* interstitial.
interstisio *n.* interstice.
intertestal *adj.* intertextual.
intertestalia *n.* intertextuality.
interval *n.* interval (*including musical*), interlude, intermission.
interveni *vi.* intervene, intercede. • *n.* intervention, intercession.
intervisa *vt.* & *n.* interview; debrief. **intervisa pratical** audition.
intervisor *n.* interviewer.
intestin *n.* intestine, bowel. **intestin magra** small intestine. **intestin spesa** large intestine. **intestines** intestines, guts, viscera, entrails; offal, chitterlings.
intestinal *adj.* intestinal.
intima *adj.* intimate, close. • *n.* insider.
intimia *n.* intimacy.
intra- *pref.* intra- (*inner*).
intramural *adj.* intramural.
intrarede *n.* intranet.
intrauteral *adj.* intrauterine.
intravenal *adj.* intravenous.
intro- *pref.* intro- (*inner*).
introdui *vt.* introduce (*substance, topic, law*), insert, institute; broach, bring up (*topic*).—When introducing one person to another, the usual verb is *presenta*. • *n.* insertion, introduction; prelude, overture, prolegomenon. **introdui gradal** phase in.
introduinte *adj.* introductory.
introjeta *vt.* introject (*psychology*). • *n.* introjection.
introspeta *vi.* introspect. • *n.* introspection.
introspetante *adj.* introspective.
introverti *vi.* be introverted. • *n.* introversion, reserve.
introvertida *adj.* introverted, introvert, reserved. • *n.* introvert.
intrui *vi.* intrude, encroach, impinge. • *vt.* intrude, impose. • *n.* intrusion, encroachment.
intruor *n.* intruder.
intruosa *adj.* intrusive.
intuable *adj.* intuitable, intuitive (*design*).
intuba *vt.* intubate. • *n.* intubation.
intui *vt.* intuit. • *n.* intuition, insight. **contra intui** counterintuitive.
intuosa *adj.* intuitive, insightful (*person*).
inuit *adj.* & *n.* Inuit, Eskimo.
invade *vt.* invade, trespass, raid; overrun (*with*). • *n.* invasion, incursion, raid, foray.
invadente *adj.* invading, invasive.
invador *n.* invader, trespasser, raider.
inventa *vt.* invent, devise, contrive, concoct, come up with. • *n.* invention (*action*).
inventada *adj.* invented, devised, contrived, concocted. • *n.* invention (*product*), brainchild.
inventor *n.* inventor.
inventosa *adj.* inventive, creative, original.
inventosia *n.* inventiveness, creativity, originality.
invernal *adj.* winter, hibernal.
inverneria *n.* greenhouse, glasshouse, hothouse.
inverni *vt.* hibernate, winter. • *n.* hibernation.
invernin *adj.* wintry.
inverno *n.* winter.
invernosa *adj.* wintry.
inversa *vt.* invert, upend, turn upside-down, overturn; capsize. • *n.* inverse; inversion.
inversada *adj.* inverted, upside-down, overturned; capsized.
investi *vt.* invest. • *n.* investment.
investiga *vt.* investigate. • *n.* investigation, inquiry, enquiry. **investiga judal** judicial inquiry, inquest.
investigor *n.* investigator; inspector (*police*).
investor *n.* investor, stakeholder. **investor otimiste** bull. **investor pesimiste** bear.
invia *vt.* & *n.* envy.
inviable *adj.* enviable.
inviosa *adj.* envious.
invita *vt.* invite; co-opt. • *n.* invitation; overture (*to communication, negotiation*).
invitada *adj.* invited. • *n.* guest.
invitante *adj.* inviting, appetizing.
iodle *vt.* yodel. • *n.* yodelling (US yodeling).
iodlor *n.* yodeller (US yodeler).
iodo ['jodo] *n.* iodine.
iog *n.* yogh (*Latin letter* Ȝ, ȝ).
ioga *n.* yoga.
iogi *n.* yogi (*yoga expert*).
iogurte *n.* yogurt, yoghurt.
ioio *n.* yo-yo.
ioman *n.* yeoman, beefeater.

ion [jon] *n.* ion (*chemistry*).

ional [jo'nal] *adj.* ionic.

ioni[1] *n.* yoni (*Hinduism*).

ioni[2] ['joni] *vi.* & *vt.* ionize. • *n.* ionization.

Ionia [i'onja] *n.* Ionia (*ancient region of Turkey*).

ionian [ion'jan] *adj.* Ionic, Ionian.

ionica [io'nika] *adj.* Ionian (*of the Ionian Sea*). **Isolas Ionica** Ionian Islands. **Mar Ionica** Ionian Sea.

ionosfera [jono'sfera] *n.* ionosphere.

iora *n.* iora (*bird*: *Aegithina*).

ioruba *adj.* & *n.* Yoruba (*person*, *language*).

iota ['jota] *n.* iota (*Greek letter* I, ι).

Iowa ['ajowa] *n.* Iowa (*US state*).

iper- *pref.* hyper-.

iperasidia *n.* hyperacidity. **iperasidia gastral** heartburn.

iperativa *adj.* hyperactive.

iperativia *n.* hyperactivity.

iperbara *adj.* hyperbaric.

iperbola *n.* hyperbola.

ipercinesia *n.* hyperkinesia.

ipercubo *n.* hypercube, tesseract.

ipereflexia *n.* hyperreflexia (*medical*).

iperestende *vt.* hyperextend. • *n.* hyperextension.

iperfajia *n.* hyperphagia (*medical*).

iperglisemia *n.* hyperglycaemia (US hyperglycemia).

iperglisemica *adj.* hyperglycaemic (US hyperglycemic).

iperico *n.* hypericum, St John's-wort (*plant*: *Hypericum*).

iperidrose *n.* hyperhidrosis (*medical*).

iperinfla *vi.* & *vt.* hyperinflate. • *n.* hyperinflation.

iperlia *n.* hyperlink.

iperlipidemia *n.* hyperlipidaemia (US hyperlipidemia) (*medical*).

iperope *adj.* far-sighted, long-sighted.

iperopia *n.* far-sightedness, long-sightedness.

iperostose *n.* hyperostosis (*medical*).

iperpirexia *n.* hyperpyrexia (*medical*).

iperplasia *n.* hyperplasia (*medical*).

ipersecrete *vt.* hypersecrete (*medical*). • *n.* hypersecretion.

ipersensosa *adj.* hypersensitive.

iperstimula *vt.* hyperstimulate, overstimulate. • *n.* hyperstimulation, overstimulation.

ipertensa *n.* hypertension (*medical*).

ipertensal *adj.* & *n.* hypertensive.

ipertermia *n.* hyperthermia, heatstroke, sunstroke.

ipertesto *n.* hypertext.

ipertiroidia *n.* hyperthyroidism (*medical*).

ipertonia *n.* hypertonia (*medical*).

ipertricose *n.* hypertrichosis (*medical*).

ipertrofia *n.* hypertrophy (*medical*).

iperurisemia *n.* hyperuricaemia (US hyperuricemia) (*medical*).

ipnagojia *n.* hypnagogia.

ipnagojial *adj.* hypnagogic.

ipno- *pref.* hypno- (*sleep*).

ipnosal *adj.* hypnotic, mesmeric.

ipnose *vt.* hypnotize, mesmerize. • *n.* hypnosis, hypnotism, mesmerism.

ipnosiste *n.* hypnotist, hypnotizer.

ipnoterapia *n.* hypnotherapy.

ipnoterapiste *n.* hypnotherapist.

ipo- *pref.* hypo-.

ipocalemia *n.* hypokalaemia (US hypokalemia) (*medical*).

ipocampo *n.* hippocampus.

ipocastania *n.* horse chestnut (*tree*, *nut*: *Aesculus hippocastanum*).

ipocolio *n.* hypocolius (*bird*: *Hypocolius ampelinus*).

ipocondria *n.* hypochondria, hypochondriasis.

ipocondrica *adj.* & *n.* hypochondriac.

ipocrita *adj.* hypocritical. • *n.* hypocrite.

ipocritia *n.* hypocrisy; sellout.

ipoderma *n.* hypodermis, subcutis.

ipodermal *adj.* hypodermic, subcutaneous.

ipofisal *adj.* pituitary, hypophysial.

ipofise *n.* pituitary gland, hypophysis.

ipoglisemia *n.* hypoglycaemia (US hypoglycemia).

ipoglisemica *adj.* hypoglycaemic (US hypoglycemic).

ipogloso *n.* halibut (*Hippoglossus*).

ipogonadia *n.* hypogonadism (*medical*).

ipomania *n.* hypomania (*medical*).

ipomea *n.* morning glory (*plant*: *Ipomoea*).

ipopotamo *n.* hippopotamus, hippo (*Hippopotamus amphibius*).

iposemia *n.* hypoxaemia (US hypoxemia).

iposia *n.* hypoxia (*medical*).

ipotalamo *n.* hypothalamus.

ipoteca *vt.* mortgage, lien. **ipoteca suprima** subprime mortgage.

ipotensa *n.* hypotension (*medical*).

ipotensal *adj.* & *n.* hypotensive.

ipotenusa *n.* hypotenuse.

ipotermia *n.* hypothermia.

ipotesal *adj.* hypothetical.

ipotese *vt.* hypothesize. • *n.* hypothesis.

ipotiroidia *n.* hypothyroidism (*medical*).

Irac *n.* Iraq.

iraci *adj.* & *n.* Iraqi.

iraco *n.* hyrax (*animal*: *Procaviidae*).

Iran *n.* Iran.

irani *adj.* & *n.* Iranian.

irena *n.* fairy-bluebird (*Irena*).

iridio *n.* iridium (*element*).

iriga *vt.* irrigate. • *n.* irrigation.

iris *n.* iris (*eye*, *plant*: *Iris*).

irita *vt.* irritate, annoy, bother, hassle, pester, peeve, irk, rankle. • *n.* irritation, annoyance, nuisance, indignation, pique. **irita par venta** windburn.
iritable *adj.* irritable, touchy, tetchy, peevish, prickly, crabby, edgy, snappy.
iritablia *n.* irritability.
iritada *adj.* irritated, annoyed, bothered, cross, huffy, indignant, aggrieved.
iritante *adj.* irritating, irritant, disagreeable, annoying, bothersome, irksome, obnoxious, pesky.
irocuoi *adj.* & *n.* Iroquois (*person, language*).
ironia *n.* irony.
ironiosa *adj.* ironic, wry.
isberg *n.* iceberg.
iscio *n.* ischium (*anatomy*).
-iside *v.suff.* -icide (*kill*).
Isis *n.* Isis (*Egyptian goddess*).
islam *n.* Islam. See *muslim.*
islamisme *n.* Islamism, Islamic fundamentalism, political Islam.
islamiste *adj.* & *n.* Islamist, Islamic fundamentalist.
Island *n.* Iceland.
islansce *adj.* & *n.* Icelandic, Icelander.
-isme *n.suff.* -ism; e.g. *femisme*; *otimisme*; *simbolisme*; *turisme.*
iso- *pref.* iso- (*equal*).
isobar *n.* isobar.
isoglosa *n.* isogloss.
isola *n.* island, isle.
isolador *n.* insulator (*device*).
isolal *adj.* insular.
isoleta *n.* islet, skerry, river island.
isoli *vi.* & *vt.* isolate, insulate, sequester, quarantine. • *n.* isolation, insulation, quarantine, insularity. **isoli acustical** soundproof.
isolida *adj.* isolated, insulated; out of the way. **acustical isolida** soundproof, soundproofed. **isolida par neva** snowed in.
isolinte *adj.* isolating. • *n.* isolator (*substance*).
isolisme *n.* isolationism.
isoliste *adj.* isolationist.
isomeral *adj.* isomeric.
isomero *n.* isomer (*chemistry*).
isometral *adj.* isometric.
isomorfe *adj.* isomorphic. • *n.* isomorph.
isosele *adj.* isosceles.
isostasia *n.* isostasy (*geology*).
isotopia *n.* isotopy.
isotopo *adj.* isotopic. • *n.* isotope.
Ispaniola *n.* Hispaniola (*island*).
Israel *n.* Israel.
israeli *adj.* & *n.* Israeli.
istamina *n.* histamine.
-iste *adj.suff.* -ist; e.g. *femiste*; *otimiste*; *jeolojiste*; *gitariste*; *jornaliste*, *turiste.*
ister- *pref.* hyster- (*womb*).
isterectomia *n.* hysterectomy (*surgery*).
isteria *n.* hysteria. **isteria coletiva** mass hysteria.
isterica *adj.* hysteric, hysterical.
istmo *n.* isthmus.
istogram *n.* histogram.
istolojia *n.* histology.
istolojiste *n.* histologist.
istoria *n.* history; track record. **istoria fondal** backstory.
istorial *adj.* historical.
istoriografia *n.* historiography.
istoriografiste *n.* historiographer.
istoriste *n.* historian.
Italia *n.* Italy.
italian *adj.* & *n.* Italian.
italica *adj.* italic (*typography*).
italici *vi.* & *vt.* italicize.
-ite *n.suff.* -itis (*inflammation*).
itera *vi.* & *vt.* iterate. • *n.* iteration.
iteral *adj.* iterative.
iterbio *n.* ytterbium (*element*).
itero *n.* jaundice.
-itica *adj.suff.* -itic (*inflamed*).
Itiopia *n.* Ethiopia.
itiopian *adj.* & *n.* Ethiopian.
-ito *n.suff.* -ite.
itrio *n.* yttrium (*element*).
iu *interj.* ew, ugh, yuck, pooh (*disgust*).
iuan[1] [ju'an] *n.* yuan (*currency*).
iuan[2] [ju'an] *adj.* Yuan (*dynasty*).
iuca *n.* yucca (*plant: Yucca*).
iudi *adj.* Jewish. • *n.* Jew. **cosas iudi** Judaica. **iudis** Jews, Jewry.
iudia *n.* Jewishness.
iudisme *n.* Judaism.
iudiste *adj.* Judaic, Jewish.
iugo *n.* yoke.
Iugoslavia *n.* Yugoslavia.
iugoslavian *adj.* Yugoslav.
iupi *n.* yuppie.
iurt *n.* yurt (*tent*).
ivor[1] *n.* ivory.
-ivor[2] *adj.suff.* -ivorous (*eating*).
ivorian *adj.* & *n.* Ivorian. See *Costa de Ivor.*
ivri *adj.* Hebrew. • *n.* Hebrew, Israelite.
ivrisme *n.* Hebraism, Hebraica.

J

J [ʒe], **je** *letter* J, j.

ja *adv.* already.—In addition to its use as a simple equivalent of *already*, *ja* can indicate which of two actions is the earlier: *si tu reveni doman, me va fini ja la labora* (*I will have finished the work*). It is also used to clarify that a present situation extends into the past: *me es ja asi tra tre oras* (*I have been here for three hours*).

jaca *n.* coat, jacket (*suit, sports*), windbreaker, windcheater. **jaca de club** blazer. **jaca de scola** school jacket, blazer. **jaca de sera** tuxedo, dinner jacket.

jacana *n.* jacana (*bird: Jacanidae*).

jacaranda *n.* jacaranda (*tree*).

jaceta *n.* waistcoat, vest (*US*), jerkin. **jaceta de muni** ammunition vest, ammo vest. **jaceta inflable** life jacket, life preserver.

jacon *n.* overcoat, raincoat, greatcoat, topcoat. **jacon de cavalor** surcoat. **jacon de dufel** duffel coat, duffle coat. **jacon de foso** trenchcoat. **jacon de pluve** raincoat, macintosh, mac. **jacon robin** frock coat.

jada *adj.* jade (*colour*). • *n.* jade (*gem*).

jaguar *n.* jaguar (*Panthera onca*).

jaguarundi *n.* jaguarundi (*wild cat: Puma yagouaroundi*).

jai *n.* jay (*bird: Corvidae*). **jai african** piapiac (*Ptilostomus afer*). **jai american** American jay (*Aphelocoma, Calocitta, Cyanocitta, Cyanocorax, Cyanolyca, Gymnorhinus*). **jai blu** bluejay (*Cyanocitta cristata*). **jai eurasian** Eurasian jay, ground jay (*Garrulus, Podocess*). **jai gris** grey (US gray) jay (*Perisoreus*).

jaieta *adj.* jet-black. • *n.* jet (*stone*).

jain *adj.* & *n.* Jain.

jainisme *n.* Jainism, Jain Dharma (*religion*).

jala *adj.* & *n.* yellow. **jala de ovo** egg yolk. **Mar Jala** Yellow Sea. See *Huanghai*.

jalapenio *n.* jalapeño (*pepper: Capsicum annuum*).

jalea *n.* jam (*UK*), jelly (*US*) (*fruit preserve*).

jali *vi.* & *vt.* yellow, turn yellow.

jalin *adj.* yellowish, yellowy, sallow.

Jamaica *n.* Jamaica.

jamaican *adj.* & *n.* Jamaican.

James, Baia [dʒeimz] *n.* James Bay.

jamon *n.* ham (*meat*).

janero *n.* January.

Japan *n.* Japan. **Mar Japan** Sea of Japan. See *Nion*.

japanes *adj.* & *n.* Japanese.

jar *n.* jar (*container*).

jardin *n.* garden, lawn, yard. **jardin de enfantes** kindergarten, nursery. **jardin de inverno** winter garden; sunroom.

jardinor *n.* gardener, landscaper; bowerbird (*Ptilonorhynchidae*).

jari *vt.* jar, can (*preserve in a jar*).

jasinto *n.* hyacinth (*Hyacinthus*). **jasinto de bosce** wild hyacinth, common bluebell, English bluebell, bell bottle (*plant: Hyacinthoides*).

jasmin *n.* jasmine (*Jasminum*).

jat *adj.* & *n.* Jat, Jaat (*person*).

jaz *adj.* & *n.* jazz. **jaz tradisional** traditional jazz, dixieland.

Jazair *n.* Algeria; Algiers.

jazairi *adj.* & *n.* Algerian.

jejuno *n.* jejunum (*anatomy*).

jel *n.* gel, jell.

jela *vi.*, *vt.* & *n.* freeze.

jelada *adj.* frozen. • *n.* frost, hoarfrost.

jelador *n.* freezer, icebox.

jelatin *adj.* gelatinous. • *n.* gel, gelatin, jelly. **jelatin de alcol** jellied alcohol, Sterno.

jelatini *vi.* & *vt.* gelatinize.

jelato *n.* gelato (*ice cream*).

jeleria *n.* icehouse (*storing ice*).

jeli *vi.* & *vt.* gel, jell.

jelin *adj.* icy, icelike, ice-cold. **jelin fria** ice-cold.

jelo *n.* ice. **jelo flotante** floe.

jelosa[1] *adj.* jealous.

jelosa[2] *adj.* icy, frosty.

jelosia *n.* jealousy, envy.

jem *n.* gem, jewel.

jemeli *vi.* & *vt.* geminate. • *n.* gemination.

jemelin *adj.* lookalike. • *n.* lookalike, double, ringer.

jemelo *adj.* & *n.* twin. **jemelo identica** identical twin. **jemelo nonidentica** fraternal twin. **jemelos** twins. **Jemelos** Gemini (*constellation*).

jemi *vt.* & *n.* groan, moan.

jen[1] *n.* gene.

-jen[2] *adj.suff.* -genic (*producing*). • *n.suff.* -gen.

jena *n.* cheek.

jenealojia *n.* genealogy.

jenealojial *adj.* genealogical.

jenealojiste *n.* genealogist.

jenera *vt.* generate. • *n.* generation.

jenerador *n.* generator.

jeneral[1] *adj.* general, generic. • *adv.* generally, in general, as a rule, on the whole, widely, overall, mostly, for the most part. • *n.* general (*officer*).

jeneral[2] *adj.* generic (*of a genus*).

jenerali *vi.* & *vt.* generalize. • *n.* generalization.

jenero *n.* genus, kind, type, genre; gender (*male or female, grammatical*). **de jenero fluente** gender-fluid.
jenerosa *adj.* generous, charitable, magnanimous, big-hearted, bountiful, munificent, liberal.
jenerosia *n.* generosity, largesse (US largess), magnanimity, munificence.
jenese *n.* genesis. • *n.suff.* -genesis (*origin*).
jenetica *n.* genetics.
jenetical *adj.* genetic, inborn. **jenetical alterada** genetically modified, GM.
jeneticiste *n.* geneticist.
jenio *n.* genius, mastermind.
jeniseri *n.* janissary (*soldier*).
jenita *vt.* beget.
jenital *adj.* genital. **jenitales** genitals, genitalia, pudenda.
jenitiva *adj.* & *n.* genitive (*grammar*).
jenitor *n.* parent. **jenitor de batiza** godparent. **jenitor futur** parent-to-be.
jenitoria *n.* parenthood.
jenitoriside *vt.* commit parenticide, commit parricide. • *n.* parenticide, parricide (*action*).
jenitorisidor *n.* parenticide, parricide (*person*).
jenjiva *n.* gum, gums (*anatomy*).
jenjival *adj.* gingival.
jenjivite *n.* gingivitis.
jeno *n.* knee. **con jenos valga** knock-kneed. **con jenos vara** bowlegged. **jenos** knees, lap.
jenom *n.* genome.
jenoside *n.* genocide.
jenotipo *n.* genotype.
jentil *adj.* gentle, kind, genteel, graceful (*socially*).
jentilia *n.* gentleness, kindness, grace (*social*).
jeo- *pref.* geo- (*Earth*).
jeocimica *n.* geochemistry.
jeocucu *n.* roadrunner (*bird: Geococcyx*).
jeodesia *n.* geodesy.
jeodesial *adj.* geodesic, geodetic.
jeodo *n.* geode (*geology*).
jeofisica *n.* geophysics.
jeofisical *adj.* geophysical.
jeografia *n.* geography.
jeografial *adj.* geographical.
jeografiste *n.* geographer.
jeolocali *vt.* geolocate. • *n.* geolocation.
jeolojia *n.* geology.
jeolojial *adj.* geological.
jeolojiste *n.* geologist.
jeomansia *n.* geomancy (*divination*).
jeometre *vt.* survey (*land*).
jeometria *n.* geometry. **jeometria euclidal** Euclidean geometry. **jeometria noneuclidal** non-Euclidean geometry.
jeometrial *adj.* geometrical.
jeometrido *n.* geometrid moth.
jeometriste *n.* geometrician.
jeometror *n.* surveyor (*land*).
jeomorfolojia *n.* geomorphology.
jeopolitica *n.* geopolitics.
jeopolitical *adj.* geopolitic, geopolitical.
jeosentral *adj.* geocentric.
jeosincrona *adj.* geosynchronous.
jeostable *adj.* geostationary.
jeotermal *adj.* geothermal.
jeranio *n.* geranium (*Geranium*).
jerbil *n.* gerbil.
jerboa *n.* jerboa (*rodent: Dipodidae*).
jergo *n.* slang, jargon, argot, cant, parlance.
jergosa *adj.* slangy, jargon-filled.
jerme *vi.* sprout, germinate. • *n.* sprout (*young shoot*); germ (*cereal*); stub (*entry*). **jerme de radis** sucker, shoot (*from the roots*).
jerontolojia *n.* gerontology.
jerontolojiste *n.* gerontologist.
Jersey Nova ['dʒerzi] *n.* New Jersey (*US state*).
Jersi *n.* Jersey.
jersies *adj.* Jèrriais (*language*). • *n.* Jèrriais; Jerseyman (*person*).
jerundio *n.* gerund.
jesi *vt.* plaster.
jeso *n.* plaster (*material*), gesso; gypsum. **molda de jeso** plaster cast.
jesta *vi.* gestate. • *n.* gestation.
jesti *vt.* gesture, gesticulate; beckon. • *n.* gesture.
jesuita *adj.* & *n.* Jesuit.
Jesus *n.* Jesus.
jeta *vi.* & *vt.* jet, squirt, spurt, spout, gush, spray. • *n.* jet, squirt, spurt, spout, gush, spray, outpouring.
jeto *n.* jet, jet plane. **motor de jeto** jet engine.
jiba *n.* hump, hunch (*back*). **jiba lentinte** speed hump, speed bump.
jibosa *adj.* humped, hunched; gibbous (*moon*).
Jibraltar *n.* Gibraltar. **Streta Jibraltar** Strait of Gibraltar.
jibraltarian *adj.* & *n.* Gibraltarian.
jiga *n.* jig, gigue (*dance, music*).
jigante *adj.* giant, gigantic, gargantuan, humongous, jumbo, whopping. • *n.* giant; whopper. **jigante de gas** gas giant (*planet*).
jigantia *n.* giantism, gigantism.
jigolo *n.* gigolo.
jigor *n.* jigger (*dancer*).
jin *n.* gin.
jina *n.* jeans. **jina corta** jean shorts, denim shorts, jorts.
jinarca *n.* gynarch (*governor*).
jinarcia *n.* gynarchy.
jinasio *n.* gymnasium, gym.

jinasta *n.* gymnast, acrobat.
jinastia *n.* gymnastics, acrobatics. **jinastia de aira** aerobatics.
jinastial *adj.* gymnastic, acrobatic (*of acrobatics*).
jinastin *adj.* gymnastic, acrobatic (*like an acrobat*).
jineco- *pref.* gynaeco- (US gyneco-) (*female*).
jinecolojia *n.* gynaecology (US gynecology).
jinecolojial *adj.* gynaecological (US gynecological).
jinecolojiste *n.* gynaecologist (US gynecologist).
jinefilia *n.* gynephilia.
jinefilica *adj.* gynephilic. • *n.* gynephile.
jinefobia *n.* gynephobia.
jinefobica *adj.* gynephobic. • *n.* gynephobe.
jineseo *n.* gynoecium (*botany*).
jinesta *n.* broom (*plant*: *Chamaecytisus*, *Cytisus*, *Genista*, etc.).
jinjer *n.* ginger (*plant*, *spice*: *Zingiber*).
jino- *pref.* gyno- (*female*).
jinsen *n.* ginseng (*plant*, *root*: *Panax*).
jip *n.* jeep.
jira *vi.* turn (*in repeated circles*), rotate, revolve, spin, whirl, twirl, swirl, gyrate, gyre, stir, pivot, swivel, swill; e.g. *rotas jira*; *la Tera jira dial*. • *vt.* rotate, spin, stir; (*colloquial*) joyride, take (*a stolen car*) for a spin. • *n.* spin, gyration. **jira minima** idle (*engine*). See *turna*.
jirabroca *n.* brace (*of brace and bit*).
jirafa *n.* giraffe (*Giraffa camelopardalis*). **Jirafa** *n.* Camelopardalis (*constellation*).
jirante *adj.* rotating, rotary. • *n.* whirligig.
jireta *n.* spinning top. **jireta ivri** dreidel.
jiro *n.* gyrus (*anatomy*).
jiroscopio *n.* gyroscope.
joala *n.* piece of jewellery (US jewelry), jewel. **joala majiosa** amulet, talisman. **joala perforante** piercing. **joalas** jewellery (US jewelry). See *jem*.
joaleria *n.* jewellery (US jewelry) store, jeweller's (US jeweler's) shop.
joalor *n.* jeweller (US jeweler).
joce *n.* jockey.
jogla *vt.* juggle.
joglor *n.* juggler.
joia *vt.* enjoy, rejoice, be joyous, have fun. • *n.* joy, fun, enjoyment, frivolity, gaiety. • *interj.* cheers, enjoy. **sin joia** joyless.
joiosa *adj.* joyous, joyful, merry, fun, exuberant, ebullient, exultant, gleeful, mirthful.
joistic *n.* joystick.
joncila *n.* jonquil (*plant*: *Narcissus jonquilla*).
Jonguo *n.* China. **jonguo** *adj.* & *n.* Chinese. See *Xina*.
Jorjia *n.* Georgia (*Caucasus*). See *Sacartvelo*.
jorjian *adj.* & *n.* Georgian (*person*, *language*).
jornal *n.* journal, magazine, gazette. **jornal de ativia** log (*software*). **jornal de contas** daybook, journal (*accounting*). **jornal de prosegues** proceedings (*society*). **jornal de scandal** tabloid newspaper. **jornal de viaja** log, logbook. **jornal dial** newspaper. **jornal personal** diary.
jornaleria *n.* newsstand, newsagent (*shop*).
jornalisme *n.* journalism. **jornalisme fotografial** photojournalism.
jornaliste *adj.* journalistic. • *n.* journalist, correspondent, newspaperman, newspaperwoman. **jornalistes** journalists, media, press.
jovedi *n.* Thursday.
joven *adj.* young, youthful; boyish, girlish. • *n.* youth, young person, youngster, juvenile; guy, gal; cub (*animal*). **la plu joven** youngest. **plu joven** younger.
jovenal *adj.* juvenile, young people's.
jovenia *n.* youth, youthfulness, girlhood, boyhood.
jovenin *adj.* youthlike, juvenile (*behaviour*); youthful (*appearance*).
jua *vi.* play, gambol, frolic; fool, trifle, dabble. • *vt.* play (*game*, *sport*, *music*, *instrument*). • *n.* game, recreation. **jua de acaso** game of chance. **jua de anelo** quoits, hoopla, ringtoss. **jua de aposta** betting game, gambling game. **jua de asconde** hide and seek. **jua de cartas** card game. **jua de cucu** peek-a-boo. **jua de fortuna** game of chance, gambling. **jua de ieroglifos** rebus. **jua de mima** charades. **jua de parolas** word game. **jua de pulgas** tiddlywinks. **jua de roles** roleplay. **jua de sieca** blind man's bluff, blind man's buff. **jua de table** table game, board game. **jua enerjiosa** romp. **jua piano** play piano. **jua solitar** one-player game, solitaire. **jua un rol** play a role, roleplay. **jua video** video game. **jua xace** play chess.
jubila *vi.* retire (*from work*). • *vt.* retire, superannuate. • *n.* retirement.
jubilada *adj.* retired, emeritus, emerita.
jubilor *n.* pensioner, retired person, retiree.
judal *adj.* judicial.
juderia *n.* judiciary.
judi *vt.* judge, estimate; adjudicate. • *n.* judgement, judging, estimation, ruling. **judi de tempo** timing.
judo *n.* judo.
judor *n.* judge, adjudicator, justice (*person*). **judor local** local judge, magistrate. **judor sivil** magistrate (*civil law*). **judores** judges, tribunal.
jueria *n.* playground, play area.
jueta *n.* toy, plaything. **jueta con** fiddle with, fidget with, toy with, twiddle.

juetor *n.* toymaker.
jugulal *adj.* jugular.
jujutsu *n.* ju-jitsu, jiu-jitsu, ju-jutsu (*martial art*).
jul *n.* joule (*unit of energy*).
julepo *n.* julep (*drink*).
juliana *n.* julienne (*food*).
julio *n.* July.
jumper *n.* pinafore dress, jumper dress, gymslip.
juna *vi.* fast. • *n.* fasting, abstinence from food. **juna political** hunger strike.
junca *n.* junk (*boat*).
junco[1] *n.* rush (*plant*: *Juncus*).
junco[2] *n.* junco (*bird*: *Junco*).
jungla *n.* jungle.
junio *n.* June.
juniper *n.* juniper (*plant*: *Juniperus*).
junta *vi.* join, become joined, connect, hook up (*with*). • *vt.* join together, put together, clasp, conjoin, connect, splice. • *n.* joint, junction, juncture, articulation, connection; conjunction (*grammar*); junta (*government*). **a junta** (*coming*) together. **en junta** together, altogether. **junta angulo** angled joint, mitre (US miter) joint, mitre (US miter). **junta se a** join, subscribe to, participate in (*a group*). **junta selinte** gasket. **junta T** T-junction.
juntada *adj.* joined; adjacent (*to each other*), adjoining, abutting. • *adv.* together.
juntador *n.* coupler.
juntante *adj.* joining, connecting, connective.
juor *n.* gambler, gamer, player.
juosa *adj.* playful, frisky.
Jupiter *n.* Jupiter (*mythology*, *planet*); Jove.
jura *vt.* swear, vow, take oath. • *n.* oath, vow.
jurasica *adj.* & *n.* Jurassic (*geology*).
juria *n.* jury, panel. **juria grande** grand jury.
jurior *n.* juror.
jus *n.* juice. **jus de orania** orange juice. **jus de poma** apple juice, cider (*non-alcoholic*).
jusador *n.* juicer, reamer, orange squeezer, lemon squeezer.
jusciam *n.* henbane (*plant*: *Hyoscyamus*).
jusosa *adj.* juicy, succulent.
justa *adj.* just, fair, equitable, reasonable, judicious, even-handed. • *adv.* justly, fairly.
justable *adj.* justifiable.
justi *vi.* become fair. • *vi.* justify, make fair, account for, vindicate. **justi de gera** casus belli.
justia *n.* justice, fairness, equity. **justia estralegal** vigilantism.
juta *n.* jute (*plant*, *fibre*: *Corchorus*); hessian, burlap, sackcloth, haircloth.

K

K [ka], **ka** *letter* K, k.
Kalahari, Deserto *n.* Kalahari Desert.
Kansas *n.* Kansas (*US state*).
Karakum, Deserto *n.* Karakum Desert, Gara-Gum Desert.
Karimata, Streta *n.* Karimata Strait.
Kattegat *n.* Kattegat.
Kentucky [ken'taki] *n.* Kentucky (*US state*).
Kerguelen, Isolas *n.pl.* Kerguelen Islands.
Kilimanjaro, Monte *n.* Mount Kilimanjaro.
Kivu, Lago *n.* Lake Kivu.
Kizilkum, Deserto *n.* Kyzylkum, Qyzylqum.
Kobenhavn *n.* Copenhagen.
Kongzi ['koŋtsi] *n.* Confucius (*philosopher*). See *confuzisme*.
Kyushu *n.* Kyushu.

L

L [el], **el** *letter* L, l. **con forma de L** L-shaped.
la[1] *det.* the.
la[2] *n.* la (*musical note*).
labia *n.* labium (pl. labia). **labias major** labia majora. **labias minor** labia minora.
labial *adj.* labial.
labiali *vi.* & *vt.* labialize.
labio *n.* lip. **con labios selida** with sealed lips, tight-lipped. **labio fendeda** harelip, cleft lip.
labiodental *adj.* & *n.* labiodental (*consonant*).
labirintin *adj.* labyrinthine.
labirinto *n.* maze, labyrinth.
labora *vi.* work, toil. • *vt.* work, put (*someone*) to work. • *n.* work, labour (US labor), toil, effort. **labora de jardin** gardening. **labora de via** roadworks. **labora en curso** work in progress. **labora fundal** groundwork. **labora nonusosa** makework. **labora par mano** manual labour, manual work, handwork. **labora sin sesa** *v.* work incessantly, toil. • *n.* toil, drudgery, slog. **labora tro multe** work too much, overwork, overexert oneself, overdo it. **oras de labora** working hours. **sin labora** effortless.
laboramania *n.* workaholism.
laboramanica *adj.* workaholic.
laboreria *n.* workplace, laboratory, workshop, facility; workhouse. **laboreria siensal** laboratory, lab. **laboreria sindicatida** closed shop.
laboror *n.* worker, workman, workingman, labourer (US laborer), peasant, journeyman. **laboror migrante** migrant worker, seasonal worker. **laboror noninstruida** unskilled worker, roustabout. **laboror nonsesante** drudge. **laboror par mano** manual labourer (US laborer), blue-collar worker.
laborosa *adj.* laborious, laboured (US labored).
Labrador *n.* Labrador. **Mar Labrador** Labrador Sea.
laca *n.* lacquer. **laca de capeles** hairspray. **laca de goma** shellac.
lace *n.* footman, lackey, flunkey, stooge.
lacrimal *adj.* lacrimal, lachrymal. **oso lacrimal** lacrimal bone, lachrymal bone.
lacrimojen *adj.* lachrymogenic, lachrymatory. **gas lacrimojen** tear gas.
lacros *n.* lacrosse (*sport*).
ladal *adj.* lateral, side; sideways. • *n.* lateral (*consonant*). **ladal fasante** sideways, sideways on.
ladin *adj.* & *n.* Ladin (*language*).
lado *n.* side, flank. **a la otra lado** on the other hand. **a lado** at the side, to the side; to one side, aside, sideways. **a lado de** beside, next to, alongside, by. **a lado de lunlotra** next to each other, side by side. **a lado de via** roadside, by the roadside. **a un lado** on the one hand. **con lado a lado** side by side, abreast; neck and neck. **lado de monte** mountainside. **lado de via** roadside, wayside, hard shoulder.
lageta *n.* pond, tarn, small lake.
lago *n.* lake. **lago de reserva** reservoir.
lagon *n.* lagoon.
Lakshadib, Mar *n.* Lakshadweeb Sea, Laccadive Sea.
lama[1] *n.* blade, razor blade, razor. **lama de arado** ploughshare (US plowshare).
lama[2] *n.* lama (*Buddhism*).
lambada *n.* lambada (*dance*).
lamda *n.* lambda (*Greek letter* Λ, λ).
lame *n.* lamé (*fabric*).
lamenta *vt.* lament, mourn, grieve. • *n.* lamentation, mourning, grief; elegy, dirge, jeremiad.
lamentada *adj.* lamented, mourned, late.
lamentin *adj.* mournful, plaintive, plangent.
lamentor *n.* mourner.
lamentosa *adj.* mournful.
lamina *n.* lamina, laminate, plate; louvre (US louver), slat; lamella, gill (*mushroom*).
lamini *vt.* laminate. • *n.* lamination.
lampa *n.* lamp, light, lantern. **lampa alojen** halogen lamp. **lampa de calce** limelight (*literal*). **lampa de gas** gaslight. **lampa de note** nightlight. **lampa de olio** oil lamp. **lampa de pox** torch (*electric*), flashlight. **lampa de punto** spotlight. **lampa inondante** floodlight. **lampa retro** taillight. **lampa solin** sunlamp. **lampa ultravioleta** ultraviolet lamp, sunlamp.
lampeta *n.* firefly, glow-worm, lightning bug (*Lampyridaeo*).
lampi *vi.* & *vt.* flash.
lampin *adj.* like lightning, breakneck.
lampo *n.* lightning, thunderbolt.
lamposa *adj.* full of lightning.
lamprea *n.* lamprey (*animal: Petromyzonidae*).
lana *n.* wool, fleece. **de lana** wool, woollen, woolly. **lana petenida** worsted (*yarn, fabric*).
landsat *n.* landsat (*satellite network*).
langobarda *adj.* Langobardic, Lombardic (*person, language*). • *n.* Langobard, Lombard.

langosta *n.* spiny lobster, rock lobster, crawfish (*Palinuridae*).
langur *n.* langur, leaf monkey (*Colobinae*).
lanio *n.* shrike (*bird*: *Laniidae*).
lanolin *n.* lanolin (*substance*).
lanosa *adj.* wool-covered, woolly.
lansa *vt.* throw, toss, fling, sling, hurl, chuck, launch, cast, bowl, blast off; project (*image, voice*). • *n.* throw, throwing, toss, launch, cast, blast-off, lift-off; projection. **lansa a mercato** launch onto the market, release, ship. **lansa alta** lob. **lansa con dito** *v.* & *n.* flick. **lansa de borda** throw-in (*football*). **lansa de fenetra** *v.* defenestrate, throw from a window. • *n.* defenestration. **lansa un colpa a** swing at.
lansada *adj.* thrown, launched. **lansada par roceto** rocket-propelled.
lansadardo *n.* spear thrower, atlatl, woomera.
lansador *n.* launcher.
lansaflama *n.* flamethrower.
lansamisil *n.* missile launcher.
lansapetra *n.* catapult.
lansapetri *vt.* catapult.
lansaroceto *n.* rocket launcher.
lanseria *n.* launchpad.
lansi *vt.* spear, lance, skewer, impale, gore.
lansia *n.* spear, lance, javelin.
lansieta *n.* skewer.
lansor *n.* thrower, bowler, hurler, pitcher.
lantanido *n.* lanthanide (*chemistry*).
lantano *n.* lanthanum (*element*).
Laozi [ˈlawtsi] *n.* Laozi, Lao-Tze (*philosopher*).
lapa *n.* limpet (*Patellidae*).
laparoscopi *n.* laparoscopy.
laparoscopial *adj.* laparoscopic.
laparoscopio *n.* laparoscope (*medical*).
laparotomio *n.* laparotomy (*medical*).
lapidario *adj.* lapidary. • *n.* lapidary (*gem worker*).
lapis *n.* pencil. **lapis colorida** coloured (US colored) pencil, colouring (US coloring) pencil.
Laptev, Mar *n.* Laptev Sea.
lardo *n.* bacon.
larga *adj.* wide, broad.
largi *vi.* widen, broaden. • *vt.* widen, broaden, ream.
largia *n.* width. **largia de banda** bandwidth.
larinjal *adj.* & *n.* laryngeal, guttural.
larinje *n.* larynx.
larinjite *n.* laryngitis.
larix *n.* larch (*tree*: *Larix*).
larma *vt.* weep, shed tears, tear. • *n.* tear, teardrop.
larmosa *adj.* tearful, teary, weepy, maudlin.
larva *n.* larva, grub (*insect*). **larva de mosca** maggot. **larva xilofaje** woodworm.
larval *adj.* larval.
lasa *vt.* leave (*in a specified state*); allow, let (*happen*). **lasa ce on entra** admit, allow entry. **lasa ce un cosa cade** let something fall, drop something (*deliberately*); omit something.
lasanie *n.* lasagne.
laser *n.* laser.
lasera *vt.* tear, rend, rip, lacerate, maul. • *n.* tear, laceration.
laserada *adj.* torn, ripped, ragged, tattered.
laseri *vt.* laser.
lasi *vt.* lasso.
lasiva *adj.* lascivious, lecherous, lewd, lustful, licentious, lubricious, salacious, prurient, dissolute; obscene, crude, coarse, dirty, filthy, mucky, naughty, smutty, raunchy.
lasiveria *n.* red-light district, fleshpot.
lasivia *n.* lewdness, lechery.
laso *n.* lasso, noose, lariat.
lata *n.* tinplate, sheet steel.
latce *n.* latke (*pancake*).
latex *n.* latex.
latica *adj.* lactic.
latina *adj.* & *n.* Latin; Latin American, Hispanic, Latina, Latino. **latina poplal** Vulgar Latin.
latitude *n.* latitude. **latitude de sielo** declination.
latolosa *n.* lactulose (*sugar*).
laton *n.* brass.
lator *n.* tinsmith.
latosa *n.* lactose (*sugar*).
latrina *n.* latrine, outhouse, privy.
Latvia *n.* Latvia.
latvisce *adj.* & *n.* Latvian, Lettish.
Lau *n.* Laos. **lau** *adj.* & *n.* Lao, Laotian (*person, language*).
laudano *n.* laudanum (*painkiller*).
laurensio *n.* lawrencium (*element*).
lauri *vt.* laureate (*crown with laurel*).
laurida *adj.* & *n.* laureate.
lauro *n.* laurel (*Lauraceae*). **folia de lauro** bay leaf. **lauro nobil** bay laurel (*Laurus nobilis*).
lava[1] *vt.* wash, launder. • *n.* washing (*action*), ablution. **lava de serebro** brainwashing. **lava interna** lavage, washing out. **lava la serebro** brainwash.
lava[2] *n.* lava (*geology*).
lavabo *n.* sink, washbasin, washstand, washbasin, washbowl.
lavador *n.* washing machine (*clothes, dishes*). **lavador de autos** carwash (*machine*).
lavanda *adj.* & *n.* lavender.
lavaoio *n.* eyewash.
lavaplato *n.* dishwasher.

lavaveste *n.* washing machine; washerman, washerwoman.
laveria *n.* laundry, laundromat. **laveria de autos** carwash (*place*).
lavor *n.* washer, launderer, washwoman, washerwoman.
laxe *adj.* loose, slack, baggy, lax, sloppy.
laxi *vi.* & *vt.* loosen.
laxia *n.* looseness, slackness, bagginess.
laxinte *n.* laxative.
le *n.* lei (*garland*).
leca *vt.* lick, lap. • *n.* lick.
lecabota *n.* (*colloquial*) bootlicker (*sycophant*).
lecaculo *n.* (*colloquial*) arselicker (US asskisser), kiss-ass (*sycophant*).
lederhose *n.* lederhosen.
lega[1] *vt.* bequeath. • *n.* legacy, bequest.
lega[2] *n.* league (*unit of length*).
legal *adj.* legal, valid, lawful, legitimate; forensic.
legali *vi.* & *vt.* legalize, legitimize. • *n.* legalization, legitimization.
legalia *n.* legality, legitimacy.
legalisme *n.* legalism.
legaliste *adj.* legalistic. • *n.* legalist.
lege *n.* law, statute. **par lege** by law; de jure, by right. **sin lege** lawless.
legeria *n.* legislature, legislative branch (*of government*). **legeria con du salones** bicameral legislature. **legeria con un salon** unicameral legislature. **legeria provinsal** statehouse. **legeria statal** statehouse.
legi *vt.* legislate. • *n.* legislation.
leginte *adj.* legislative.
legiste *n.* legist, jurist.
legor *n.* legislator, lawmaker.
legum *n.* legume (*Fabaceae*).
lejable *adj.* readable, legible.
lejablia *n.* readability, legibility.
lejador *n.* reader, reading device.
leje *vt.* read, peruse. • *n.* reading (*action, interpretation, measurement*). **leje de labios** lipreading. **leje rapida** skim.
lejecarta *n.* card reader.
lejedisco *n.* disk drive.
lejemente *n.* mind reader, mentalist.
lejenda *n.* legend.
lejendal *adj.* legendary.
lejera *adj.* light, lightweight, weightless. **tro lejera** underweight.
lejeri *vi.* lighten, become lighter. • *vt.* alleviate, relieve, soothe, mitigate. • *n.* relief.
lejeria *n.* lightness. **lejeria completa** weightlessness, zero gravity.
lejion *n.* legion.
lejionor *n.* legionnaire.
lejor *n.* reader.
lema *n.* lemma (*mathematics, philosophy*); headword (*dictionary*).
leming *n.* lemming (*rodent: Lemmini*).
lemur *n.* lemur (*primate: Lemur*).
lenial *adj.* wooden, wood.
leniería *n.* woodyard, timberyard.
lenio *n.* wood, timber, lumber. **de lenio** wooden, wood. **lenio de foco** firewood. **lenio dur** hardwood. **lenio esterna** sapwood, alburnum. **lenio flotante** drift wood. **lenio interna** heartwood, duramen. **lenio mol** softwood. **lenio presada** particleboard, chipboard. **lenio stratida** plywood.
lenior *n.* woodcutter, lumberjack.
leniosa *adj.* woody.
lenta *adj.* slow; lingering. • *n.* slowcoach, slowpoke, laggard, sluggard.
lente *n.* lens. **lente de angulo larga** wide-angle lens. **lente de grandi** magnifier, magnifying glass. **lente de ojeto** object lens, objective lens. **lente de regarda** eyepiece, ocular lens. **lente de zuma** zoom lens. **lente macro** closeup lens, macro lens. **lente macro de zuma** macro zoom lens.
lenteta *n.* contact lens.
lenti *vi.* & *vt.* slow, slow down, decelerate. • *n.* deceleration, slowdown.
lentil *n.* lentil (*Lens culinaris*). **lentil brun** brown lentil. **lentil roja** red lentil.
lentin *adj.* lenslike, lens-shaped, lenticular.
leon *n.* lion (*Panthera leo*). **Leon** *n.* Leo (*constellation*). **leon-de-mar** *n.* sea lion (*Otariidae*). **leon fema** lioness. **Leon Peti** Leo Minor (*constellation*).
leoneta *n.* lion cub.
leoni *vi.* & *vt.* lionize.
leopardeta *n.* leopard cub.
leopardo *n.* leopard (*Panthera pardus*).
lepilemur *n.* sportive lemur (*Lepilemuridae*).
lepre *n.* hare (*Lepus*). **Lepre** *n.* Lepus (*constellation*).
leprecan *n.* leprechaun.
lepror *n.* sighthound. **lepror afgani** Afghan hound. **lepror engles** greyhound. **lepror eres** Irish wolfhound.
leprosa *adj.* leprous. • *n.* leper.
leprosia *n.* leprosy.
lepton *n.* lepton (*particle*).
lesbian *adj.* lesbian, sapphic. • *n.* lesbian.
lesbianisme *n.* lesbianism.
-lesia *n.suff.* -lepsy (*medical*).
-lesica *adj.suff.* -leptic.
lesion *n.* lesion. **lesion de arde** burn (*injury*).
lesitina *n.* lecithin (*substance*).
leson *n.* lesson, lecture. **dona un leson** give a lesson, give a lecture. **leson moral** moral

lesson, moral (*of story*). **leson privata** tutorial, private lesson.

lesonor *n.* lecturer.

Lesoto *n.* Lesotho. **lesoto** *adj.* & *n.* Lesothan.

letarjia *n.* lethargy, sluggishness, torpor, torpidity, listlessness, languor.

letarjiosa *adj.* lethargic, sluggish, listless, languorous.

lete *n.* milk. **dona lete** nurse, breastfeed. **lete bateda** milkshake. **lete de gal** eggnog. **lete de ris** rice milk. **lete densida** condensed milk. **prende lete** nurse. **prende lete de** milk (*animal*).

letera *n.* letter (*alphabet, postal*), epistle, missive. **letera major** uppercase letter, capital letter, majuscule. **letera minor** lowercase letter, small letter, minuscule. **leteras major o minor** case.

leteral *adj.* literal.

leteratur *n.* literature. **leteratur parlada** oral literature.

leteratural *adj.* literary.

leteri *vt.* letter, do lettering. **leteri con mano** hand lettering.

leteria *n.* dairy.

leteta *n.* cot, crib, cradle; small bed, berth, bunk.

leti *vt.* lactate. • *n.* lactation.

letin *adj.* milky.

leto *n.* bed. **leto ascondeda** wall bed, murphy bed, trundle bed. **leto castelin** bunk bed. **leto de acua** waterbed. **leto de maladia** sickbed. **leto de mori** deathbed. **leto de plumas** featherbed. **leto de sol** sunbed. **leto estragrande** king-size bed. **leto grande** queen-size bed. **leto per du** double bed. **leto per un** single bed. **leto pliable** folding bed, cot. **leto rolante** wheeled bed, hospital bed. **letos jemelo** twin beds (*two single beds*). **ordina la leto** make the bed.

letor *n.* milkman.

letseburges *adj.* & *n.* Luxemburgish, Luxembourgeois.

letuga *n.* lettuce (*Lactuca*). **letuga roman** romaine lettuce, cos lettuce.

leucemia *n.* leukaemia (US leukemia).

leuco- *pref.* leuco-.

leucoplasto *n.* leucoplast (*biology*).

leucosite *n.* leukocyte (*blood cell*).

lev *n.* lev (*currency*).

leva *vi.* rise, lift, levitate, get up, arise. • *vt.* raise, lift, heft, hoist, levitate; hold up; raise, pose (*problem, question*); promote (*in rank*), exalt. • *n.* rise, levitation; promotion, exaltation, uplift. **ante leva de sol** predawn. **leva de luna** moonrise. **leva de pesas** weightlifting. **leva de sol** sunrise, dawn, daybreak. **leva de spalas** shrug. **leva final** proofing (*bread*). **leva sua regarda** look up. **leva sua spalas** shrug.

levacarga *n.* lift truck, forklift truck, sideloader, stacker truck.

levada *adj.* leavened. **levada natural** sourdough.

Levante *n.* Levant (*Mediterranean region*). **Mar Levante** Levantine Sea.

lever *n.* lever. **lever de engrana** gearstick, gearshift.

leveri *vt.* lever, pry, prise. • *n.* leverage.

leviatan *n.* leviathan (*Biblical sea monster*).

levor *n.* lifter. **levor de pesas** weightlifter.

lexem *n.* lexeme.

lexicografia *n.* lexicography.

lexicografial *adj.* lexicographical.

lexicografiste *n.* lexicographer.

lexicolojia *n.* lexicology.

lexicolojial *adj.* lexicological.

lexicolojiste *n.* lexicologist.

lezardo *n.* lizard (*Lacertilia*, but not snakes). **Lezardo** *n.* Lacerta (*constellation*).

lfn *abbr.* (*Lingua Franca Nova*) Elefen, LFN.—To avoid confusion with other possible meanings of the abbreviation *LFN*, the spelling *Elefen* is preferred, including in English.

lia *vt.* tie, bind, strap, tether, moor; connect, link, plug in; liaise; associate (*mentally*). • *n.* link, bond, connection, ligation, linkage; liaison; covenant; suspender (*UK*), garter (*US*); association (*mental*). **lia a tera** ground, earth (*an electrical device*). **lia con filo** wired connection. **lia la gamas de** bind the legs of, hobble, hogtie. **lia la manos e pedes de** hogtie. **lia sin filo** wireless connection. **lia tubal** tubal ligation (*medical*).

liada *adj.* bound, tied.

liador *n.* plug (*electric*).

liama *n.* llama (*animal*: *Lama glama*).

liana *n.* liana (*plant*).

liante *adj.* connecting, connective. • *n.* ligature. **verbo liante** linking verb, copula.

libela *n.* dragonfly, damselfly (*Odonata*).

Liberia *n.* Liberia.

liberian *adj.* & *n.* Liberian.

libi *adj.* & *n.* Libyan.

Libia *n.* Libya.

libidal *adj.* libidinal.

libido *n.* libido, sex drive, lust. **sin libido** frigid.

libidosa *adj.* libidinous, lustful, randy, horny. • *n.* sexpot, voluptuary. **tro libidosa** oversexed.

libra *n.* pound (*weight*).

libralisme *n.* liberalism.

libraliste *adj.* liberal, laissez-faire. • *n.* liberal.

libre *adj.* free, at liberty; freelance. **libre con garantia** free on bail, out on bail.
libreria *n.* bookshop.
libreta *n.* booklet, pamphlet, brochure; libretto. **libreta de fosfores** book of matches, matchbook.
libri *vi.* & *vt.* free, liberate, release, emancipate, unleash, rid. • *n.* liberation, emancipation, release; quittance. **libri con garantia** release on bail. **libri de sclavia** freedom from slavery, manumission.
libria *n.* freedom, liberty, leeway. **libria de jornalisme** freedom of the press. **libria limitada** parole. **libria oservada** probation.
libro *n.* book. **libro anial** yearbook, annual. **libro de aprende** textbook. **libro de cantas** songbook. **libro de consulta** reference book. **libro de contas** ledger. **libro de cuoro** leather-bound book. **libro de eserse** exercise book, practice book. **libro de fables** storybook. **libro de fato** non-fiction book. **libro de imajina** fiction book. **libro de imnos** hymnbook, hymnal. **libro de mapas** atlas. **libro de modeles** copybook. **libro de notas** notebook. **libro de pox** pocketbook, small notebook. **libro de preas** prayerbook, missal. **libro de resetas** recipe book, cookbook. **libro de scola** schoolbook. **libro de stratejia** playbook. **libro de viaja** travel guide; travelogue (US travelog). **libro de xeces** chequebook (US checkbook). **libro dur** hardback, hardcover. **libro enrolada** scroll. **libro mol** paperback, softback. **libro nonvendeda** remaindered book, unsold book.
libromanica *adj.* & *n.* book fanatic, bookworm.
libron *n.* tome.
libror *n.* liberator.
licen *n.* lichen (*plant*: *Ascomycota*, *Basidiomycota*).
liciris *n.* liquorice (US licorice) (*Glycyrrhiza glabra*).
licopodio *n.* clubmoss (*plant*: *Lycopodiaceae*).
licor *n.* liqueur.
Lictenstain *n.* Liechtenstein.
lictenstaines *adj.* Liechtenstein. • *n.* Liechtensteiner.
licuida *adj.* liquid (*including assets*), fluid. • *n.* liquid, fluid. **licuida de coreti** correction fluid, whiteout.
licuidador *n.* liquidizer, blender.
licuidi *vi.* & *vt.* liquefy, liquify, liquidize; liquidate. • *n.* liquidation.
licuidia *n.* liquidity.
licuidor *n.* liquidator.
Lidia *n.* Lydia.
Lietuva *n.* Lithuania.
lietuvisce *adj.* & *n.* Lithuanian.
ligamento *n.* ligament, sinew.
lignito *n.* lignite, brown coal.
Liguria *n.* Liguria. **Mar Liguria** Ligurian Sea.
ligurian *adj.* & *n.* Ligurian.
ligustro *n.* privet (*plant*: *Ligustrum*).
lil *n.* lily (*Lilium*). **lil-de-mar** *n.* sea lily (*Bourgueticrinida*). **lil de neva** snowdrop (*Galanthus*). **lil tigrin** tiger lily (*Lilium lancifolium*).
lila *adj.* lilac (*colour*). • *n.* lilac (*plant*: *Syringa*).
lim *n.* lime (*tree*, *fruit*: *Citrus* × *aurantifolia*, *Citrus* × *latifollia*).
lima *n.* file. **lima de emeri** emery board. **lima de ungia** nail file.
limasa *n.* slug (*Gastropoda*).
limbica *adj.* limbic.
limbo[1] *n.* limbo (*religion*).
limbo[2] *n.* limbo (*dance*).
Limburg *n.* Limburg (*Dutch or Belgian province*).
limburgan *adj.* Limburgish, Limburgian.
limeric *n.* limerick.
limeta *n.* sweet lime, sweet lemon, sweet limetta (*Citrus* × *limetta*).
limfa *n.* lymph.
limfal *adj.* lymphatic.
limfo- *pref.* lympho- (*lymph*).
limfoblasto *n.* lymphoblast (*biology*).
limfoide *adj.* lymphoid.
limfoma *n.* lymphoma. **limfoma de Hodgkin** ['hodʒkin] Hodgkin's lymphoma.
limfopoiese *n.* lymphopoiesis (*biology*).
limfosital *adj.* lymphocytic.
limfosite *n.* lymphocyte, white blood cell. **limfosite B** B-cell. **limfosite NK** natural killer cell. **limfosite T** T-cell.
limi *vt.* file (*smoothe*).
limita *vt.* limit, delimit; cap (*price*). • *n.* limit, boundary, bound, frontier, delimitation, threshold, cut-off, limitation. **limita de tempo** deadline, time limit. **limita masima** upper limit, cap, ceiling. **limitas** limits, bounds, extent, ambit, scope. **pone un limita** impose a limit, draw the line. **sin limita** unlimited, limitless, infinite, boundless, unbounded, countless, innumerable.
limitada *adj.* limited, finite, bounded.
limital *adj.* borderline (*just on the edge*, *personality disorder*).
limon *n.* lemon (*Citrus* × *limon*).
limonada *n.* lemonade.
limonin *adj.* lemony, lemonlike.
limonosa *adj.* lemony.
limpa *adj.* clean.
limpi *vi.* become clean, clean up. • *vt.* clean, clean up, wipe; mop; sweep (*chimney*). **limpi etnical** ethnic cleansing.

limpia *n.* cleanliness.
limpibota *n.* bootblack.
limpida *adj.* cleaned.
limpor *n.* cleaner (*person*), scrubwoman, charwoman, charlady. **limpor de sala** chambermaid.
limusin *n.* limousine, limo.
lince *n.* lynx (*Lynx*). **Lince** *n.* Lynx (*constellation*). **lince rojin** bobcat (*Lynx rufus*).
lineta *n.* linnet, twite (*bird*: *Linaria*).
linga *n.* linga, lingam (*Hinduism*).
lingua *n.* tongue; language; speech (*ability*). **lingua aidante** auxiliary language. **lingua construida** constructed language, conlang, artificial language. **lingua de asembla** assembly language. **lingua de programi** programming language. **lingua de sinia** sign language. **lingua desiniada** planned language, artificial language. **lingua franca nova** Lingua Franca Nova. **propre lingua** native language, native tongue, mother tongue.
linguaje *n.* language (*style*), wording.
lingual *adj.* lingual (*of the tongue*); linguistic (*of language*).
linguine *n.* linguine (*food*).
linguiste *n.* linguist.
linguistica *n.* linguistics. **linguistica computal** computational linguistics.
lini *vt.* line (*mark lines on*).
linia *n.* line, row; rank (*chess*). **en linia reta** in a straight line, in a beeline, as the crow flies. **linia de arbores** treeline. **linia de comandas** command line (*software*). **linia de familia** lineage, family line, line of descent, bloodline, pedigree. **linia de neva** snowline. **linia de sangue** bloodline, pedigree. **linia direta** direct line, hotline. **linia media** midline. **linia orizonal** horizontal line, dash. **vade en linia reta a** make a beeline for.
linial *adj.* linear, lineal.
linida *adj.* lined (*marked with lines*).
linioio *n.* eyeliner.
lino *n.* flax, linseed (*plant*: *Linum usitatissimum*). **olio de lino** linseed oil. **pasta de lino** putty. **seme de lino** linseed. **stofa de lino** linen.
linolio *n.* linoleum, lino.
linosa *adj.* treated with linseed.
lintel *n.* lintel, transom.
linxa *vt.* lynch. • *n.* lynching.
Lion *n.* León (*Spanish region*).
liones *adj.* & *n.* Leonese.
lipido *adj.* lipid (*chemistry*). • *n.* lipid.
lipo- *pref.* lipo- (*fat*).
lipoprotena *n.* lipoprotein.
liposuca *n.* liposuction.
lira[1] *n.* lyre. **Lira** *n.* Lyra (*constellation*).
lira[2] *n.* lira (*currency*).
lirica *adj.* lyrical, lyric.
liriodendro *n.* tulip tree (*Liriodendron*).
liron *n.* dormouse (*Gliridae*).
lisa *adj.* smooth, sleek; crisp (*cloth, paper*).
lisador *n.* smoother, sander. **lisador de banda** belt sander.
Lisboa *n.* Lisbon.
lisca *vi.* slide, slip, glide, coast, swipe. • *vt.* slide, slip, push. • *n.* slip, glide. **lisca de tera** landslide, landslip. **lisca e pone** drag and drop (*software*). **lisca sur acua** aquaplane.
liscable *adj.* slidable, sliding.
liscador *n.* slider; hovercraft.
liscante *n.* glissando.
liscasapato *n.* shoehorn.
lisceta *vi.* glitch, goof, slip, slip up. • *n.* glitch, goof, booboo, boob, slip, slip-up.
liscor *n.* flying possum, flying phalanger, glider (*marsupial*: *Petaurus*).
liscosa *adj.* slippery, slick.
liscosia *n.* slipperiness.
-lise *n.suff.* -lysis (*decomposition*).
lisensa *vt.* license. • *n.* licence (US license), permit. **lisensa de primi** imprimatur.
lisensada *adj.* licensed.
liseo *n.* high school, secondary school, lycee, lyceum.
lisi *vi.* & *vt.* smoothe, streamline; sand (*wood*).
lisia *n.* smoothness.
-lisica *adj.suff.* -lytic.
lisosoma *n.* lysosome (*biology*).
lista *vt.* list, itemize. • *n.* list. **lista cadente** drop-down list. **lista de benes** inventory. **lista de contenidas** packing slip, (*ship's*) manifest. **lista de desiradas** wish list. **lista de eras** errata. **lista de medisines** formulary. **lista de salarios** payroll. **lista de sertis** checklist. **lista negra** blacklist. **pone en lista negra** blacklist.
litania *n.* litany.
litiga *vt.* litigate, prosecute, sue, take to court, arraign, try, proceed against. • *n.* litigation, suit, lawsuit, trial, prosecution, case (*law*). **litiga falsa** mock trial. **litiga nonconcluinte** mistrial.
litigable *adj.* accountable, responsible, actionable.
litigor *n.* litigator, litigant. **litigor de stato** state attorney (*civil law*).
litigosa *adj.* litigious.
litio *n.* lithium.
-lito[1] *n.suff.* -lith (*stone*).
lito-[2] *pref.* litho- (*stone*).
litografi *vt.* & *n.* lithograph.
litografia *n.* lithography.
litolojia *n.* lithology.

litorina *n.* winkle, periwinkle (*mollusc*: *Littorina*).
litosfera *n.* lithosphere, mantle (*geology*).
litote *n.* litotes (*rhetoric*).
litotrof *adj.* lithotrophic (*biology*). • *n.* lithotroph.
litotrofia *n.* lithotrophia.
litre *n.* litre (US liter) (*unit of capacity*).
liturjia *n.* liturgy.
liturjial *adj.* liturgical.
litvac *adj.* Litvak. • *n.* Litvak, Lithuanian Jew.
litxi *n.* lychee (*tree*, *fruit*: *Litchi chinensis*).
livermorio *n.* livermorium (*element*).
lixivia *vi.* & *vt.* leach (*drain*). • *n.* leaching.
lixiviada *n.* leachate.
lo *pron.* it. **lo cual** that which, what; e.g. *lo cual resta parteni a tu*; *me va esplica lo cual me crede*.
lobe *n.* lobe. **lobe de orea** earlobe.
lobosa *adj.* lobed.
lobotomia *n.* lobotomy.
loca *vt.* locate, place, site, position. • *n.* place, location, position, spot, site, locale. **en loca** instead. **en loca de** instead of, in place of, rather than. **en no loca** nowhere. **en no otra loca** nowhere else. **en un otra loca** somewhere else. **loca de nase** birthplace. **loca de note** nightclub, night spot. **loca de orienta** landmark (*navigation*). **loca misera** wretched place, hellhole, dump. **loca ueb** website.
local *adj.* local. **popla local** local people, local population, locals.
locali *vi.* localize. • *vt.* trace, track, pinpoint. • *n.* localization.
localisme *n.* localism, parochialism.
locativa *adj.* & *n.* locative (*grammar*).
locomotiva *n.* locomotive, engine. **locomotiva de vapor** steam locomotive.
locomotivor *n.* engine driver, train engineer.
locusta *n.* locust, grasshopper (*Caelifera*). **locusta solitar** grasshopper (*when not swarming*). **locusta xamante** locust (*Acridoidea*).
loda *vt.* praise, laud, glorify, exalt, commend, extol, eulogize; compliment, congratulate, flatter. • *n.* praise, kudos, compliment, congratulation, glory, exaltation, eulogy, panegyric, encomium, citation, commendation. **con loda masima** with the highest praise, summa cum laude. **loda duple** praise twice, give two thumbs up to. **loda falsa** false praise, hype, puffery. **loda zelosa** praise enthusiastically, rave about.
lodable *adj.* laudable, praiseworthy, commendable.
lodante *adj.* praising, flattering.
lodas *interj.* congratulations, my compliments.
loden *n.* loden (*fabric*).
loes *n.* loess (*soil*).
lofofora *n.* lophophore (*biology*).
lofotrocozoon *n.* lophotrochozoon (*pl.* lophotrochozoa) (*organism*).
logaritmal *adj.* logarithmic.
logaritmo *n.* logarithm.
logo[1] *n.* logo, emblem.
logo-[2] *pref.* logo- (*words*).
logofilia *n.* logophilia, love of words.
logofilica *adj.* logophilic, word-loving. • *n.* logophile, lover of words.
logudores *adj.* & *n.* Logudorese (*person*, *language*).
Logudoro *n.* Logudoro (*Sardinian region*).
lojia[1] *n.* loggia, veranda; box (*theatre*). **lojia de acusada** dock (*in court*). **lojia de atestor** witness stand, witness box. **lojia de juria** jury box.
-lojia[2] *n.suff.* -logy (*study*).
lojica *n.* logic.
lojical *adj.* logical; Boolean. **es lojical** make sense.
lojicalia *n.* logicality.
lojistica *n.* logistics.
lojistical *adj.* logistical.
lolio *n.* ryegrass, darnel (*Lolium*).
lom *n.* loam (*soil*).
lombal *adj.* lumbar.
lombard *adj.* & *n.* Lombard.
Lombardia *n.* Lombardy (*Italian region*).
lombo *n.* loin, loins, lower back.
lomen *n.* lo mein (*food*).
lomosa *adj.* loamy.
lona *n.* canvas, sailcloth. **de lona** canvas. **lona catranida** tarpaulin, tarp. **lona de polietilen** polythene tarpaulin, polytarp.
longa *adj.* long. • *adv.* long, for a long time, for a long way. **como longa** how long. **Isola Longa** Long Island.
longi *vi.* & *vt.* lengthen, elongate, prolong, protract. • *n.* elongation, prolongation.
longia *n.* length, duration. **longia de onda** wavelength. **par longia** lengthwise, lengthways.
longo *prep.* • along, up, down (*following or in parallel with*); e.g. *la folias flota longo la rio*; *un arania rampe longo mea gama*. • according to; e.g. *longo la predise, doman va es an plu calda*.
lonjitude *n.* longitude. **lonjitude de sielo** right ascension.
lonxura *n.* mannikin (*bird*: *Lonchura*).
lori *n.* lory, lorikeet (*bird*: *Loriinae*).
loris *n.* loris (*primate*: *Lorisinae*).
lorisifero *n.* loricifer (*organism*: *Loricifera*).
los *pron.* they; them. **los ci** they who; e.g. *los ci osa gania*.

losa *n.* earthenware. **de losa** earthenware.
losion *n.* lotion. **losion de rasa** aftershave.
loto *n.* lotto, lottery; bingo, keno.
Louisiana [luizi'ana] *n.* Louisiana (*US state*).
lsd *n.* LSD (*drug*).
lua *vt.* rent, hire, lease, let. • *n.* rental, hiring, leasing. **ofre per lua** rent out, hire out.
luable *adj.* rentable, rental, to let.
luau *n.* luau (*Hawaiian feast*).
Lubnan *n.* Lebanon.
lubnani *adj.* & *n.* Lebanese.
lubrica *vt.* lubricate, lube. • *n.* lubrication.
lubricante *adj.* lubricating. • *n.* lubricant, lube.
lucarna *n.* dormer (*window*).
lufa *n.* luffa, loofah (*plant, sponge*: *Luffa*).
luganda *adj.* & *n.* Luganda. See *Uganda*.
luje *n.* luge (*toboggan*).
luji *vt.* luge.
lumbago *n.* lumbago (*medical*).
lumen *n.* lumen (*unit of light*).
lumina *vt.* illuminate, light, enlighten, brighten, highlight. • *n.* illumination (*action, result*), highlight; enlightenment. **Lumina** *n.* Enlightenment. **lumina fondal** backlight, backlighting. **lumina ultravioleta** black light, blacklight.
luminada *adj.* illuminated, lit. **luminada par luna** moonlit. **luminada par sol** sunlit.
luminosa *adj.* luminous, lucid.
luna *n.* moon. **luna de miel** honeymoon. **luna oscur** new moon. **luna plen** full moon.
lunal *adj.* lunar.
lundi *n.* Monday.
luneta *n.* small moon, natural satellite.
lunlotra *pron.* each other, one another; e.g. *la gatos regarda lunlotra*; *la tre frates xuxa a lunlotra*; *la calculos en la caxa clica contra lunlotra*. **con lunlotra** with each other, together. **pos lunlotra** one after another, one by one.
luor *n.* renter, tenant, lodger.
lupa *n.* magnifying glass, magnifier, loupe.
lupin *n.* lupin (*plant*: *Lupinus*).
lupo *n.* wolf (*Canis lupus*). **Lupo** *n.* Lupus (*constellation*).
lupulo *n.* hop (*plant*: *Humulus lupulus*).
lupus *n.* lupus (*medical*).
lus *n.* light (*illumination*). **lus clar de dia** clear light of day, broad daylight. **lus de dia** daylight; daytime, day. **lus de lampa** lamplight. **lus de luna** moonlight. **lus de sol** sunlight. **lus de stela** starlight. **lus final** dusk, twilight. **lus prima** dawn, twilight. **lus refletada** reflected light, glare.
lusio *n.* pike (*fish*: *Esox*).
luso *n.* luxury (*item*).
lusosa *adj.* luxurious, luxuriant, opulent, lavish, sumptuous, sensuous, rich, deluxe, lush, posh, ritzy, swanky. **estrema lusosa** high-end.
lusosia *n.* luxury (*state*).
luta *vi.* wrestle, rassle, grapple, struggle, contend; falter. • *vt.* cause to struggle. • *n.* wrestling, struggle, altercation, contention.
lutefisc *n.* lutefisk (*food*).
luteran *adj.* & *n.* Lutheran.
luteranisme *n.* Lutheranism (*Christianity*).
lutesio *n.* lutetium (*element*).
lutiste *n.* lutist, lute player.
luto *n.* lute.
lutor *n.* wrestler, fighter.
lutra *n.* otter (*Lutrinae*).
lux *n.* lux (*unit of light*).
Luxemburg *n.* Luxembourg.
luxemburges *adj.* Luxembourgish. • *n.* Luxembourger.
Luzon *n.* Luzon (*island*). **Streta Luzon** Luzon Strait.

M

M [em], **em** *letter* M, m.
ma *conj.* but, whereas.
maa *interj.* baa. See *bala*.
Maca *n.* Mecca.
macabre *adj.* macabre, grim, ghoulish, ghastly, grisly, gruesome.
macaca *n.* macaque (*Macaca*). **macaca resus** rhesus monkey, rhesus macaque (*Macaca mulatta*).
macadamia *n.* macadamia (*tree*: *Macadamia*).
macaron *n.* macaroon.
macaroni *n.* macaroni.
Macau *n.* Macau, Macao. **macau** *adj.* & *n.* Macanese.
Macedonia *n.* Macedonia.
macedonsce *adj.* Macedonian.
macero *n.* mackerel (*Scombridae*, *Carangidae*).
macia *vt.* make up, apply cosmetics to. • *n.* makeup, cosmetics. **macia de teatro** greasepaint.
macina *n.* machine, mechanism. **macina de fili** spinning wheel. **macina de soma** adding machine. **macina de tempo** time machine. **macina de vapor** steam engine. **macinas** machines, machinery.
macinal *adj.* mechanical, clockwork.
macineta *n.* device, gadget, contraption.
macini *vt.* mechanize.
maciniste *n.* mechanic, machinist; artificer.
maciste *n.* makeup artist.
macrame *n.* macrame (*art*).
macro *adj.* closeup (*image*). • *n.* closeup; macro (*software*). • *pref.* macro- (*large*).
macrocosmo *n.* macrocosm.
macrofago *n.* macrophage (*biology*).
macrosefalia *n.* macrocephaly (*medical*).
macrosefalica *adj.* macrocephalic, macrocephalous.
macula *n.* macula, macula lutea (*anatomy*).
macular *adj.* macular.
Madagasicara *n.* Madagascar. See *malagasi*.
madalena *n.* madeleine (*cake*).
Madera *n.* Madeira (*island*). **Isolas Madera** Madeira Islands.
madjong *n.* mahjong (*game*).
madona *n.* madonna.
madral *adj.* maternal; maternity (*leave*, *dress*).
madras *n.* madras (*fabric*).
madre *n.* mother. **madre de batiza** godmother. **madre e padre** mother and father, parents. **madre futur** mother-to-be. **madre par sposi** mother-in-law. **madre sin sposo** single mother. **sin madre** motherless.
madria *n.* motherhood, maternity.
madrigal *n.* madrigal (*music*).
madrin *adj.* motherly. • *n.* mother figure, godmother.
madriside *vt.* commit matricide. • *n.* matricide (*action*).
madrisidor *n.* matricide (*person*).
madron *n.* matriarch.
mafia *n.* mafia.
mafior *n.* mafioso, member of a mafia.
Magallanes, Streta *n.* Strait of Magellan.
Magiar *n.* Hungary. **magiar** *adj.* & *n.* Hungarian. See *Ungaria*.
magma *n.* magma (*geology*).
magmal *adj.* magmatic, igneous.
magnesio *n.* magnesium.
magnetal *adj.* magnetic.
magnete *n.* magnet.
magneti *vi.* & *vt.* magnetize. • *n.* magnetization.
magnetia *n.* magnetism.
magnetometre *n.* magnetometer.
magnetometria *n.* magnetometry.
magnolia *n.* magnolia (*Magnolia*).
magra *adj.* thin, slim, slender, svelte, lean, willowy, skinny, narrow, fine, gracile; gaunt, paltry, meagre (US meager).
magri *vi.* thin, slim, emaciate. • *vt.* thin, slim, constrict. • *n.* thinning, emaciation, constriction.
magria *n.* thinness, slimness, slenderness.
Magrib *n.* Morocco. See *Maroco*.
magribi *adj.* & *n.* Moroccan.
mahaiana *adj.* Mahayana (*Buddhism*).
maharaja *n.* maharajah (*Indian prince*).
maharani *n.* maharani (*Indian princess*).
maharixi *n.* maharishi (*Hinduism*).
mahatma *n.* mahatma (*holy person*).
mahimahi *n.* mahi-mahi, dolphinfish (*Coryphaena hippurus*).
Mahore *n.* Mahore (*island*).
mahores *adj.* & *n.* Mahoran.
maia *adj.* & *n.* Mayan.
maiasauro *n.* maiasaurus (*dinosaur*).
Maine [mejn] *n.* Maine (*US state*). **Golfo Maine** Gulf of Maine.
mainel *n.* mullion (*architecture*).
maio *n.* May.
maiones *n.* mayonnaise, mayo.
maior *n.* mayor.
maioral *adj.* mayoral.
mais *n.* corn, maize (*Zea mays*). **mais moleda** hominy.
maitili *adj.* & *n.* Maithil, Maithili (*person*, *language*).

maitnerio *n.* meitnerium (*element*).
majel *adj.* Marshallese. • *n.* Marshallese, Marshall Islander. **Isolas Majel** Marshall Islands.
majenta *adj.* & *n.* magenta.
majenti *vi.* & *vt.* turn magenta.
majia *n.* magic, sorcery. **majia de mano** sleight of hand, prestidigitation.
majial *adj.* magic.
majiosa *adj.* magic, magical.
majiste *n.* magician, conjuror.
majo *n.* mage, magus (pl. magi).
major *adj.* major, key; great; senior, the elder. • *n.* major (*officer*).
majoran *n.* marjoram (*plant*: *Origanum majorana*).
majori *vi.* & *vt.* capitalize, convert to uppercase.
majoria *n.* majority, preponderance.
Makasar, Streta *n.* Makassar Strait.
mal *adj.* (*prenominal*) bad, invalid, wrong. • *adv.* badly, wrongly. • *pref.* mis-, bad-, ill- (*added to verbs: a worse variant of the action, often a specialized sense*); e.g. *malodori*; *maldise*. **fa mal** do wrong. **mal fa** wrongdoing, bad deed. **plu mal** worse.
malacita *n.* malachite (*mineral*).
malacusa *vt.* libel, slander, defame, calumniate, vilify, badmouth. • *n.* libel, slander, defamation, calumny, calumniation, vilification, backbiting.
malacusante *adj.* libellous (US libelous), slanderous, calumnious.
malacusor *n.* libeller (US libeler), slanderer, calumniator.
malada *adj.* sick, ill, unwell, indisposed. • *n.* invalid. **malada de ama** lovelorn, lovesick. **malada de cor** heartsick. **malada de mar** seasick. **malada de posenebria** hung over.
maladeria *n.* infirmary, sick bay.
maladerior *n.* infirmary nurse.
maladi *vi.* sicken, become sick, fall ill. • *vt.* make ill.
maladia *n.* disease, illness, sickness, ailment, malady. **maladia de altia** altitude sickness. **maladia de ama** lovesickness. **maladia de bestias** murrain. **maladia de descompresa** decompression sickness, the bends. **maladia de dormi** sleeping sickness, trypanosomiasis. **maladia de mar** seasickness. **maladia de Parkinson** Parkinson's disease, parkinsonism. **maladia de vola** airsickness.
maladiosa *adj.* sickly.
malagasi *adj.* & *n.* Malagasy. See *Madagasicara*.
malagatani *n.* mulligatawny (*soup*).
malaialam *adj.* & *n.* Malayalam (*person, language*).
Malaisia *n.* Malaysia.
malaisian *adj.* & *n.* Malaysian.
malajusta *n.* maladaptation, maladjustment.
malajustada *adj.* badly adjusted, maladapted, maladaptive, maladjusted, misconfigured; out of tune. • *n.* misfit.
Malaka, Streta *n.* Strait of Malacca.
malalinia *vi.* & *vt.* misalign. • *n.* misalignment.
malaplica *vt.* misapply.
malarcivi *vt.* misfile.
malaria *n.* malaria.
malasinia *vt.* misassign, miscast.
Malaui *n.* Malawi. **malaui** *adj.* & *n.* Malawian. **Lago Malaui** Lake Malawi, Lake Nyasa.
malaventura *n.* misadventure.
malcalcula *vt.* miscalculate. • *n.* miscalculation.
malclasi *vt.* misclassify.
malcolori *vt.* discolour (US discolor).
malcombusta *vi.* backfire (*engine*).
malcomprende *vt.* misunderstand, misapprehend. • *n.* misunderstanding.
malcondui *vi.* misbehave. • *n.* misbehaviour (US misbehavior), misconduct, impropriety, wrongdoing.
malconsela *vt.* misadvise.
malconselada *adj.* ill-advised, inadvisable.
malconseti *vi.* & *vt.* misconceive. • *n.* misconception.
malconstrui *vt.* misconstruct, build badly.
malconta *vt.* miscount.
malcreada *adj.* ill-made. • *n.* miscreant.
malcrede *n.* misbelief.
maldeclara *vt.* misstate.
maldestinada *adj.* ill-fated.
maldiagnose *vt.* misdiagnose. • *n.* misdiagnosis.
maldijesta *n.* indigestion.
maldirije *vt.* misdirect. • *n.* misdirection.
maldisable *adj.* abominable.
maldise *vt.* curse, damn, anathematize, badmouth, jinx; blaspheme. • *n.* curse, jinx, malediction; blasphemy, profanity.
maldiseda *adj.* accursed, abominable.
maldistribui *vt.* misdistribute, misdeal.
Maldives *n.pl.* Maldives. See *Divehi*.
maleje *vt.* misread. • *n.* misreading.
malensende *vi.* & *vt.* misfire (*gun*).
malerba *n.* weed. **estrae malerbas de** weed.
malesperia *n.* ordeal.
malespresa *vt.* misexpress, misspeak.

malfa *vt.* do badly, bodge, botch, bungle, bumble, screw up, make a bad job of. • *n.* misfeed, bodge, botch.
malfamosa *adj.* infamous, notorious.
malfaor *adj.* bodger, botcher, bungler.
malformi *vi.* & *vt.* deform, disfigure. • *n.* deformation, malformation.
malformida *adj.* deformed, malformed, misshapen, grotesque.
malfunsiona *vi.* malfunction, go wrong. • *n.* malfunction.
malfunsionante *adj.* malfunctioning, dysfunctional.
malgida *vt.* misguide, mislead.
malgidada *adj.* misguided, misled, wrongheaded.
malgidante *adj.* misleading, specious.
malgoverna *vt.* misgovern, misrule; misgovernment, misrule.
Mali[1] *n.* Mali.
mali[2] *vi.* turn bad, become corrupt; worsen, degenerate, deteriorate, spoil. • *vt.* make bad, corrupt; worsen, exacerbate, aggravate. • *n.* worsening, degeneration, deterioration, corruption, exacerbation.
malia *n.* evil.
malian *adj.* & *n.* Malian.
malida *adj.* deteriorated, corrupt, degenerate, spoiled (*food*).
malidentifia *vt.* misidentify.
malie *n.* chain mail.
malinforma *vt.* misinform.
malintendente *adj.* ill-willed, cruel.
malinterprete *vt.* misinterpret, misapprehend, misconstrue.
maljudi *vt.* misjudge.
malmaneja *vt.* mismanage, mishandle.
malnara *vt.* garble (*story*).
malnomida *adj.* misnamed; so-called (*disparaging*). • *n.* misnomer. **la X malnomida** the so-called X (*disparaging*).
malnuri *n.* malnutrition.
malnurida *adj.* malnourished, undernourished.
malodori *vi.* smell bad, stink, reek.
malodorinte *adj.* smelly, stinking.
malodorosa *adj.* smelly, malodorous, foul-smelling, stinking, rank. • *n.* stinker.
maloia *vt.* mishear.
malopera *vi.* malfunction, go wrong. • *n.* malfunction.
malparlante *adj.* inarticulate.
malpersepi *vt.* misperceive, mistake for. • *n.* misperception, (*optical*) illusion.
malpersepida *adj.* illusional.
malpone *vt.* misplace, mislay.
malposada *adj.* badly positioned; offside, offsides (*sport*).
malpratica *n.* malpractice.
malprimi *vt.* misprint.
malprimida *adj.* misprinted. • *n.* misprint.
malpronunsia *vt.* mispronounce. • *n.* mispronunciation.
malpunta *vi.* & *vt.* misaim.
malreconose *vt.* misrecognize, mistake for.
malreporta *vt.* misreport.
malrepresenta *vt.* misrepresent. • *n.* misrepresentation, travesty.
malreputa *n.* disrepute.
malreputada *adj.* disreputable, of ill repute.
malsaborosa *adj.* foul-tasting, unpalatable.
malscrive *vt.* & *n.* scribble, scrawl.
malsiniali *vt.* & *n.* miscue.
malsita *vt.* misquote. • *n.* misquotation.
malsonia *vt.* have a nightmare, experience as a nightmare. • *n.* nightmare.
malsonin *adj.* nightmarish.
malspele *vt.* misspell. • *n.* misspelling.
malspende *vt.* squander, waste.
malstate *n.* disrepair, dilapidation.
malta[1] *n.* malt.
Malta[2] *n.* Malta.
maltape *vt.* mistype. • *n.* typing mistake, typo.
maltase *n.* maltase (*enzyme*).
malti[1] *vt.* malt.
malti[2] *adj.* & *n.* Maltese.
maltosa *n.* maltose (*sugar*).
maltradui *vt.* mistranslate. • *n.* mistranslation.
maltrata *vt.* mistreat, revile, abuse, wrong. • *n.* mistreatment, abuse, abusiveness, wrong.
maltratante *adj.* abusive.
maltrator *n.* abuser.
Maluku *n.* Maluku, Molucca. **Isolas Maluku** Maluku Islands, Moluccas. **Mar Maluku** Molucca Sea.
malumorosa *adj.* in a bad mood, sulking, sulky, sullen, brooding, moping, morose; cranky, curmudgeonly, surly, petulant. • *n.* curmudgeon, grump, sourpuss. **es malumorosa** be in a bad mood, sulk, brood, mope.
maluro *n.* Australian wren (*Maluridae*).
malusa *vt.* misuse, abuse. **malusa de drogas** drug abuse.
malva *adj.* mauve (*colour*). • *n.* mallow (*plant*: *Malva*).
malversa *vi.* & *vt.* spill, upset, tip over.
malvestida *adj.* badly dressed, poorly dressed.
malvole *n.* ill will, malice, malevolence, maliciousness, malignance, malignancy, acrimony.
malvolente *adj.* malicious, malevolent, malign, malignant, sinister, evil, wicked, mean-spirited, virulent.

mama *n.* (*colloquial*) mum, mom, mummy, mommy, mama (*mother*).
mamal *n.* mammal (*Mammalia*).
mambo *n.* mambo (*dance*).
mamela *n.* udder, mammary gland, (*colloquial*) boob, tit, knocker (*breast*). **a mamela** suckling.
mamelal *adj.* mammary.
mamograf *n.* mammograph.
mamografi *vt.* mammograph.
mamografia *n.* mammography.
mamogram *n.* mammogram.
mamute *n.* mammoth, mastodon (*Mammuthus*). **mamute lanosa** woolly mammoth (*Mammuthus primigenius*).
Man, Isola *n.* Isle of Man. See *manes*.
mana *n.* manna (*miracle food*).
manacin *n.* manakin (*bird: Pipridae*).
manada *n.* herd, drove, mob (*people, monkeys*), pack (*wolves*), pride (*lions*), flock (*birds*), gaggle (*geese*), school (*fish*), pod (*whales*), swarm (*insects*), horde (*barbarians*); rabble, riffraff, hoi polloi.
manadi *vi.* flock.
manador *n.* drover, herdsman.
manati *n.* manatee, sea cow (*Trichechus*).
manca *vi.* be missing, be wanting, be lacking, fall short; e.g. *me ia trova la rota mancante; un rota manca de la auto.* • *n.* lack, deficiency, insufficiency, dearth, scarcity, deficit, shortage, shortfall, shortcoming.
mancala *n.* mancala (*game*).
mancante *adj.* missing, wanting, lacking, scarce, scant, meagre (US meager), sparse.
mandala *n.* mandala (*Buddhism, Hinduism*).
mandarin *n.* mandarin (*official*); zebra finch (*bird: Taeniopygia guttata*).
mandarina *n.* mandarin, mandarine, clementine.
mandarino *n.* mandarin tree (*Citrus reticulata*).
Mandeb, Streta *n.* Mandeb Strait, Bab-el-Mandeb.
mandibula *n.* jaw, jawbone, mandible.
mandinca *adj.* & *n.* Mandinka (*person, language*).
Mandju *n.* Manchuria (*Chinese region*). **mandju** *adj.* Manchu.
mandola *n.* mandola (*musical instrument*).
mandolin *n.* mandolin (*musical instrument*).
mandragora *n.* mandrake (*plant: Mandragora*).
mandril *n.* mandrill (*monkey*).
maneja *vt.* manage, operate (*machinery*), run (*organization*), administer, administrate, handle (*tool*); cope with. **maneja de casa** housekeeping. **maneja de contas** account management. **maneja de linguas** language planning. **maneja sin** do without, manage without.
manejable *adj.* manageable, tractable.
manejablia *n.* manageability, tractability.
manejal *adj.* administrative.
manejor *n.* manager, administrator, operator, steward, seneschal. **manejor de casa** housekeeper. **manejor de servores** butler.
manera *n.* manner, way of behaving, mannerism. **de bon maneras** well-mannered. **de mal maneras** ill-mannered, uncouth.
manes *adj.* & *n.* Manx. See *Man*.
manga[1] *n.* sleeve; cuff (*blood pressure*). **Isolas de la Manga** Channel Islands. **la Manga** English Channel. **manga de camisa** shirtsleeve. **manga de venta** windsock. **sin manga** sleeveless.
manga[2] *n.* manga (*cartoon*).
manganes *n.* manganese (*element*).
mangera *n.* hose, hosepipe, flexible tube.
mangeri *vt.* hose, hose down.
mango *n.* mango (*Mangifera*).
mangoste *n.* mongoose (*Herpestidae*).
Mani[1] *n.* Mani (*prophet*).
mani[2] *vt.* handle.
mania *n.* mania, addiction, fanaticism; craze, furore. • *n.suff.* -mania (*medical, enthusiasm*).
maniate *n.* magnate, tycoon, mogul.
manica *adj.* manic, maniacal, fanatical; hectic, frantic. • *n.* maniac, fanatic, junkie; addict; (*colloquial*) geek, nerd. • *adj.suff.* -manic.
manicin *n.* mannequin (*dummy, fashion model*).
manico *n.* handle (*for holding*), hilt (*sword, knife*), grip; handlebar; handhold. **manico de porte** door handle, doorknob. **manico de scopa** broomstick. **manicos** handles, handlebars.
manicura *n.* manicure.
manicuror *n.* manicurist.
manioca *n.* manioc, cassava (*tree, root: Manihot esculenta*).
manipula *vt.* manipulate. • *n.* manipulation. **manipula de opina** manipulation of opinion, spin. **manipula distritos elejal** gerrymander. **manipula par autoduta** gaslight.
manipulor *n.* manipulator.
manisme *n.* manichaeanism (US manicheanism).
maniste *adj.* & *n.* manichaean (US manichean).
Manitoba *n.* Manitoba (*Canadian province*).
manitu [mani'tu] *n.* manitou (*life force*).
manivel *n.* crank, crank handle. **arbor de maniveles** crankshaft.
maniveli *vt.* crank.

Mannar, Golfo *n.* Gulf of Mannar.
mano *n.* hand; handful. **con mano destra** right-handed. **con mano en mano** hand in hand. **con mano sinistra** left-handed. **con manos libre** hands free. **de mano destra** (dright-handed (*person*). **de mano sinistra** left-handed (*person*). **fabricada par mano** made by hand, handmade. **mano plen** handful. **par mano** by hand, manual. **sur manos o jenos** on one's hands and knees, on all fours.
manobra *vt.* & *n.* manoeuvre (US maneuver). **manobra plu bon ca** outmanoeuvre (US outmaneuver).
manodestra *n.* right-hander.
manometre *n.* manometer (*pressure-measuring tool*).
manoscrito *n.* manuscript, autograph, codex, typescript.
manosinistra *n.* left-hander, southpaw.
manteni *vt.* maintain, keep (*in the same state*), preserve; monitor. • *n.* maintenance, preservation, upkeep.
mantenida *adj.* maintained, kept.
mantenor *n.* janitor, caretaker, maintenance man, maintenance woman. **mantenor de eglesa** sexton.
manticor *n.* manticore (*mythology*).
mantis *n.* mantis (*insect*: *Mantodea*).
mantra *n.* mantra (*meditation*).
manual *n.* handbook, manual, reference book, guide, guidebook, vade mecum. **manual de instrui** training manual, instruction book. **manual de stilo** style guide, stylebook. **manual prima** primer, basic guide.
manxa *vt.* stain, blemish, blot, mar, tarnish, taint, sully, besmirch, stigmatize, deface, disfigure; smudge, smear. • *n.* stain, blemish, blot, blotch, spot, fleck; smudge, smear; marking (*animals*, *plants*). **manxa de inca** inkblot. **manxa de larmas** tearstain. **manxa frotada** smudge, smear. **manxa solal** sunspot.
manxeta *n.* speckle.
manxosa *adj.* blotchy, smudgy, mottled, dappled.
maoisme [mao'isme] *n.* Maoism (*politics*).
maoiste [mao'iste] *adj.* Maoist.
maori *adj.* & *n.* Maori.
mapa *vt.* map, chart. • *n.* map, mapping, chart. **mapa de releva** relief map. **mapa linial** linear mapping.
mapada *adj.* mapped, charted.
mar *n.* sea, ocean. **a mar** at sea, offshore. **en la mar** in the sea, overboard. **mar alta** high seas, open ocean, open sea, main. **su mar** *adj.* submarine, undersea. • *adv.* under the sea.
marabu [mara'bu] *n.* marabou (*bird*: *Leptoptilos crumeniferus*).
marabut *n.* marabout (*monk*).
maraca *n.* maraca (*musical instrument*).
Maracaibo, Lago *n.* Lake Maracaibo.
Marajo *n.* Marajó (*island*).
maral *adj.* marine, oceanic, maritime, seagoing.
marania *vt.* entangle, tangle, mat, snarl, mess up. • *n.* tangle, mess; thicket.
maraniada *adj.* tangled, matted, messy. **maraniada en jelo** icebound. **maraniada en trafica** stuck in traffic.
maranta *n.* arrowroot (*plant*: *Maranta arundinacea*).
marascino *n.* maraschino (*drink*).
marati *adj.* & *n.* Marathi (*person*, *language*).
maraton *n.* marathon.
marca *vt.* mark, stamp, characterize, typify; select, flag, highlight (*text*). • *n.* mark, stamp, brand (*commercial*), characterization, identifier; marking (*animals*, *plants*). **marca comersial** trademark. **marca como paiada** frank, mark as paid. **marca de colpa** weal, wheal, welt. **marca de cualia** hallmark. **marca de orea** earmark. **marca de paia** mark of payment, frank, franking mark. **marca postal** postmark.
marcada *adj.* marked. **marcada par** characterized by, involving.
marcador *n.* marker, stamp.
marcesa *n.* marchioness, marquise.
Marcesas, Isolas *n.pl.* Marquesas Islands.
marci *n.* marquess, marquis, margrave.
marcia *n.* march (*land*).
marea[1] *vi.* feel dizzy, feel giddy, feel woozy. • *vt.* make dizzy.
marea[2] *n.* tide. **marea alta** high tide. **marea basa** low tide. **marea forte** riptide.
mareada *adj.* dizzy, giddy, groggy, woozy.
mareal *adj.* tidal.
mareante *adj.* dizzying.
mareria *n.* oceanarium.
marexal *n.* marshal (*officer*).
marga *n.* marl (*soil*).
margarina *n.* margarine, marge, oleo.
margarita[1] *n.* daisy (*plant*: *Bellis*).
margarita[2] *n.* margarita (*drink*).
Margarita[3] *n.* Margarita Island.
Mariana *n.* Mariana. **Isolas Mariana** Marianas.
mariatxi *n.* mariachi (*music*).
marieta *n.* ladybird, ladybug, lady beetle (*Coccinellidae*).
marimba *n.* marimba (*musical instrument*).
marin *adj.* sealike, salty, briny, brackish. • *n.* brine, salty water.
marina *n.* navy, fleet, armada.

marinal *adj.* naval.
marinara *n.* marinara (*sauce*).
marineta *n.* flotilla.
marini *vt.* marinate in brine, marinade, pickle, brine.
marinida *adj.* marinated, marinaded, pickled, brined.
marinor *n.* sailor, seaman, mariner; marine.
marioneta *n.* marionette.
marionetor *n.* marionettist.
marjin *n.* margin.
marjinal *adj.* marginal.
marjini *vt.* marginalize. • *n.* marginalization.
marlin *n.* marlin (*fish*: *Istiophoridae*).
Marmara *n.* Marmara (*island*). **Mar Marmara** Marmara Sea.
marmelada *n.* marmalade.
marmo *n.* marble. **de marmo** (*made of*) marble.
marmota *n.* marmot (*rodent*).
marocan *adj.* & *n.* Moroccan.
Maroco *n.* Morocco. See *Magrib*.
marolojia *n.* oceanology, oceanography.
marolojiste *n.* oceanologist, oceanographer.
maror *n.* seafarer, sailor.
marsupial *adj.* & *n.* marsupial.
marsupio *n.* marsupium, pouch.
martan *adj.* & *n.* Martian.
Marte *n.* Mars (*mythology*, *planet*).
martedi *n.* Tuesday.
martel *n.* hammer, mallet; hammer, dog, cock (*gun*); malleus. **martel de aira** pneumatic drill, jackhammer. **martel mol** mallet.
martelable *adj.* malleable.
marteleta *n.* mallet; gavel.
marteli *vt.* hammer.
martelon *n.* sledgehammer.
martes *n.* marten (*animal*: *Martes*).
martin *n.* martin (*bird*: *Hirundinidae*).
martini *n.* martini (*drink*).
Martinic *n.* Martinique (*island*).
martinices *adj.* & *n.* Martiniquan.
martir *n.* martyr.
martiri *vi.* & *vt.* martyr.
martiria *n.* martyrdom.
marto *n.* March.
marxa *vi.* march; stride. • *n.* march. **marxa funeral** funeral march.
marxisme *n.* Marxism.
marxiste *n.* Marxist.
Maryland *n.* Maryland (*US state*).
mas *adj.* & *n.* male.
masa *n.* mass, lump, clot, clod, blob (*shapeless piece*); mass (*physics*).
masacra *vt.* & *n.* massacre, slaughter, bloodbath.
masai *adj.* & *n.* Maasai, Masai (*person*, *language*).
masaje *vt.* & *n.* massage.
masajor *n.* masseur, masseuse.
masapan *n.* marzipan.
masca *n.* mask, face mask. **masca medical** medical mask, face mask.
mascarpone *n.* mascarpone (*cheese*).
masci *vt.* mask.
mascita *n.* mosque.
mascote *n.* mascot.
maseta *n.* small mass, lump, clot.
masi[1] *vi.* form lumps, become lumpy, clot up. • *vt.* make lumpy, clot up.
masi-[2] *pref.* maxi-.
masia *n.* maleness, masculinity, machismo.
masif *n.* massif (*geology*).
masila *n.* maxilla (*bone*).
masima *adj.* maximum, maximal, most. • *adv.* at most. • *n.* maximum, most.
masimi *vi.* & *vt.* maximize, optimize. • *n.* maximization, optimization.
masin *adj.* masculine, boyish, butch.
masiosa *adj.* macho, virile.
masis *n.* mace (*spice*).
masocisme *n.* masochism.
masociste *adj.* masochistic. • *n.* masochist.
masosa *adj.* massive, bulky, unwieldy, cumbersome.
Massachusetts [masaˈtʃusets] *n.* Massachusetts (*US state*).
mastectomia *n.* mastectomy (*surgery*).
mastica[1] *vt.* chew, munch, masticate.
mastica[2] *n.* mastic (*tree*, *resin*: *Pistacia lentiscus*).
mastin *n.* mastiff. **mastin deutx** Great Dane.
masto *n.* mast. **masto florinte** spike, flower cluster. **masto posmedial** mizzenmast. **masto xef** mainmast.
mastoide *adj.* mastoid (*anatomy*). • *n.* mastoid process.
mastosite *n.* mast cell, mastocyte (*biology*).
masturba *vt.* masturbate. • *n.* masturbation, onanism.
mata *vt.* kill, exterminate, execute, slaughter, butcher, slay. • *n.* killing, extermination, execution, slaughter. **mata la debiles** cull. **mata sin intende** *v.* & *n.* manslaughter. **matas per venja** tit-for-tat killings, retaliation killings.
mataderia *n.* abattoir, slaughterhouse.
matador *n.* killing machine.
matajoia *n.* killjoy, spoilsport, wet blanket; (*plot*) spoiler.
matante *adj.* deadly, fatal, lethal, mortal, homicidal.
mate[1] *adj.* matte, matt (*dull*).
mate[2] *n.* maté (*drink*).

matematica *n.* mathematics. **matematica computal** computational mathematics.
matematical *adj.* mathematical.
matematiciste *n.* mathematician.
materas *n.* mattress. **materas de palia** straw mattress, pallet. **materas de plumas** feather mattress, featherbed. **materas inflable** air mattress, air bed, lilo.
materasi *vt.* pad, upholster.
materi *vi.* & *vt.* materialize. • *n.* materialization.
materia *n.* matter, substance, material, stuff. **materia combustable** combustable material. **materia fisionable** fissionable material. **materia flamable** inflammable material. **materia usosa** useful material, grist.
material *adj.* material.
materialisme *n.* materialism.
materialiste *adj.* materialistic, acquisitive. • *n.* materialist.
matina *n.* morning, morn. **a esta matina** this morning. **a matina** in the morning. **a matina doman** tomorrow morning. **a matina ier** yesterday morning. **a matina oji** this morning.
matini *vi.* dawn, become day, become morning. • *n.* dawn, daybreak; threshold (*metaphor*).
mator *n.* killer; matador. **mator en serie** serial killer.
matriarca *n.* matriarch.
matriarcia *n.* matriarchy.
matrilinia *n.* matrilineage.
matrilinial *adj.* matrilineal.
matrioxca *n.* matryoshka (*doll*).
matris *n.* matrix (*mathematical*), two-dimensional array.
matur *adj.* mature, ripe; adult, grown-up; aged. **sesal matur** sexually mature, nubile. **temprana matur** precocious. **tro matur** overripe.
maturi *vi.* & *vt.* mature, ripen; grow up. **maturi sesal** puberty.
maturia *n.* maturity.
maturinte *adj.* maturing, ripening. **sesal maturinte** pubescent.
matxete *n.* machete (*knife*).
maurian *adj.* & *n.* Mauryan (*dynasty*).
Mauris *n.* Mauritius.
maurisian *adj.* & *n.* Mauritian.
mausoleo *n.* mausoleum.
max *n.* match, game. **max desidente** play-off.
maxa *vt.* mash, crush, pulp, squash, squish.
maxador *n.* masher, crusher, pulper. **maxador de patata** potato masher.
maxia *n.* messiah.
maxial *adj.* messianic.
maximin *n.* maximin (*game theory*).
maxo *adj.* macho.
mazaua *adj.* & *n.* Mazahua (*person, language*).
mazurca *n.* mazurka (*dance, music*).
me *pron.* I; me. **la otras de me** my other selves. **la plu joven de me** my younger self.
mea *det.* my. **la mea** mine.
meato *n.* meatus (*anatomy*).
mecanica *n.* mechanics. **mecanica cuantal** quantum mechanics. **mecanica de sielo** celestial mechanics.
mecanical *adj.* mechanical.
mecanicisme *n.* mechanism (*science, philosophy*).
mecaniciste *adj.* mechanistic. • *n.* mechanist.
mecanoresetador *n.* mechanoreceptor (*neuron*).
Mecong, Rio *n.* Mekong River.
mecotero *n.* scorpion fly (*Mecoptera*).
medalia *n.* medal.
medalion *n.* medallion. **medalion ronda** roundel.
medaliste *n.* medallist (US medalist). **medaliste de oro** gold medallist (US medalist).
media[1] *adj.* middle, middling, medium, intermediate. • *n.* middle, centre (US center), median, halfway point, midsection, midst. • *pref.* mid- (*added to nouns: midpoint*); e.g. *mediadia*. **a media** in the middle, midway. **a media de** in the middle of, midway through. **media de anio** midyear. **media de barcon** midship. **media de matina** midmorning. **media de periodo** midperiod, midterm. **media de rio** midstream. **media de semana** midweek.
media[2] *n.* means (*of doing*); measure (*course of action*); medium (*of communication*). **medias** media (*including mass communications*). **medias fluente** streaming media. **medias publica** mass media. **medias sever** austerity measures.
Media[3] *n.* Media (*ancient region*).
mediadia [media'dia] *n.* midday, noon, noontime.
mediaestate *n.* midsummer.
mediainverno *n.* midwinter.
mediajua [media'ʒua] *n.* halftime.
medianote *n.* midnight. **pos medianote** after midnight, in the dead of night, in the middle of the night.
mediapunto *n.* midpoint.
mediasoprano *adj.* & *n.* mezzo-soprano.
mediatinje *n.* midtone, halftone, mezzotint.
mediatrimestre *n.* half-term (*holiday*).
medica *n.* medicine (*profession*).
medical *adj.* medical.

mediciste *n.* medic, doctor, physician. **mediciste abitante** resident (*medical graduate*). **mediciste clinical** clinician. **mediciste comensante** intern (*medical graduate*). **mediciste forense** coroner.

medieval *adj.* medieval. **eda medieval** middle ages.

mediocre *adj.* mediocre, ordinary, average, middling, uninspired, undistinguished, indifferent, unexceptional, unexciting, unremarkable, run-of-the-mill, pedestrian, prosaic, lacklustre (US lackluster), forgettable. **obra mediocre** mediocre work, potboiler.

mediocria *n.* mediocrity.

medisin *n.* medicine (*drugs*), medication. **medisin de fertilia** fertility drug. **medisin enspirable** inhalant. **medisin inferior** nostrum. **medisin lejerinte** palliative.

medisinal *adj.* medicinal.

medisini *vt.* medicate.

medisinida *adj.* medicated, on medication.

medita *vi.* meditate. • *n.* meditation.

mediteranean *adj.* Mediterranean.

Mediteraneo *n.* Mediterranean (*region*). **Basin Mediteraneo** Mediterranean Basin. **Mar Mediteraneo** Mediterranean Sea.

medula *n.* marrow, medulla, pith. **medula de oso** bone marrow. **medula spinal** spinal cord.

medulosa *adj.* pithy.

medusa[1] *n.* jellyfish, medusa (*Medusozoa*).

Medusa[2] *n.* Medusa (*mythology*).

mega- *pref.* mega- (*large, a million*).

megabait *n.* megabyte, meg.

megafon *n.* megaphone, bullhorn, loudhailer.

-megalia *n.suff.* -megaly (*medical*).

megalital *adj.* megalithic.

megalito *n.* megalith.

megalo- *pref.* megalo- (*large*).

megalomania *n.* megalomania.

megalomanica *adj.* megalomaniacal. • *n.* megalomaniac.

megatero *n.* humpback whale (*Megaptera novaeangliae*).

meiose *n.* meiosis (*biology*).

melaiu *adj.* & *n.* Malay (*person, language*).

melamina *n.* melamine (*plastic*).

melancolia *n.* melancholy, melancholia.

melancolica *adj.* melancholy, melancholic, melancholiac. • *n.* melancholiac.

Melanesia *n.* Melanesia.

melanesian *adj.* Melanesian.

melanin *n.* melanin.

melano- *pref.* melano- (*black*).

melanoma *n.* melanoma, melanocarcinoma (*tumour*).

melanose *n.* melanosis (*medical*).

melanosite *n.* melanocyte (*biology*).

melasa *n.* molasses, treacle. **melasa oro** golden syrup.

melasin *adj.* treacly.

melatonina *n.* melatonin (*hormone*).

melma *n.* slime, scum, gunge, gunk, goo, goop, gloop, glop.

melmi *vt.* slime, gunge.

melmosa *adj.* slimy, scummy, gungy, gooey, goopy, gloopy.

melodia *n.* melody, tune.

melodica *n.* melodica (*musical instrument*).

melodiosa *adj.* melodious, melodic, tuneful, singsong.

melodrama *n.* melodrama.

melodramosa *adj.* melodramatic.

melon *n.* melon (*Cucumis*). **melon acuosa** watermelon (*Citrullus lanatus*). **melon de inverno** honeydew melon.

melonjena *n.* aubergine, eggplant (*Solanum melongena*).

mem *n.* meme.

membrana *n.* membrane, web. **membrana mucosa** mucous membrane.

membranin *adj.* membranous, membranelike.

membranosa *adj.* membranous, webbed.

membro *n.* member (*group*), fellow (*society*), affiliate; limb (*arm, leg*).

memorable *adj.* memorable.

memori *vt.* memorize, remember, commit to memory. • *n.* memorization. See *recorda*.

memoria *n.* memory (*as a capacity; including computer*). **de memoria** from memory (*without notes*), by rote. **memoria de dura corta** short-term memory, STM. **memoria de dura longa** long-term memory, LTM. **memoria de state solida** solid-state drive. **memoria flax** flash memory. **memoria sensal** sensory memory, very-short-term memory, VSTM. **memoria vivin** eidetic memory.

menasa *vt.* threaten, menace, intimidate, loom, browbeat; e.g. *el ia menasa me con colpa.* • *n.* threat, menace, intimidation, duress. **su menasa de fusil** at gunpoint.

menasante *adj.* threatening, ominous, forbidding, portentous.

mendelevio *n.* mendelevium (*element*).

mendelisme *n.* mendelianism (*genetics*).

mendeliste *n.* mendelian, mendelianist.

mendica *vt.* beg, scrounge, panhandle. • *n.* begging.

mendicor *n.* beggar.

mendicorin *adj.* beggarly, beggarlike.

menestrel *n.* minstrel, troubadour.

meninjal *adj.* meningeal.

meninje *n.* meninge (*anatomy*).

meninjite *n.* meningitis.
menir *n.* menhir (*standing stone*).
meniscal *adj.* meniscal.
menisco *n.* meniscus.
menonita *adj.* & *n.* Mennonite.
menonitisme *n.* Mennonitism (*Christianity*).
menopausa *n.* menopause.
menora *n.* menorah (*candelabrum*).
menorea *n.* menorrhoea (US menorrhea).
mensal *adj.* monthly.
mense *n.* month; e.g. *la mense agosto*. **per mense** per month, a month.
menstrua *n.* menstruation, period. **menstrua prima** menarche.
menstrual *adj.* menstrual.
menstrui *vt.* menstruate.
mensula *n.* corbel (*architecture*).
menta *n.* mint (*plant*: *Mentha*). **menta fresca** spearmint (*Mentha spicata*). **menta peperin** peppermint.
mental *adj.* mental.
mentalisme *n.* mentalism (*philosophy*, *psychic*).
mentaliste *adj.* mentalistic. • *n.* mentalist.
mente *n.* mind. **con mente clar** clear-headed. **de la mesma mente** like-minded. **de mente debil** weak-minded, feeble-minded. **de mente simple** simple-minded.
menteta *n.* fib, white lie.
menti *vt.* lie, tell a lie. • *n.* lie; mendacity. **menti jigante** whopper.
mentin *adj.* minty.
mentinte *adj.* lying, untruthful, mendacious.
mento *n.* chin.
mentol *n.* menthol.
mentor *n.* liar.
menu [meˈnu] *n.* menu; programme (US program), agenda. **menu cadente** drop-down menu. **menu cascadente** cascading menu.
menur *n.* lyrebird (*Menura*).
mera *adj.* mere; e.g. *nos es mortales mera*; *la pensa mera de comeda ia repulsa el*. • *adv.* merely, only, just, simply, purely, not much more than; e.g. *la sona ia es mera la tona*.
merbromina *n.* merbromin, mercurochrome (*antiseptic*).
mercatiste *adj.* marketing (*company*, *expert*).
mercato *n.* market, emporium, mart. **mercato de pulgas** flea market. **mercato otimiste** bull market. **mercato pesimiste** bear market.
mercator *n.* merchant, market trader.
mercurdi *n.* Wednesday.
Mercurio *n.* Mercury (*mythology*, *planet*). **mercurio** *n.* mercury, quicksilver.
merda *n.* (*colloquial*) shit, crap, turd (*dung*, *anything worthless*); (*insult*) arsehole (US asshole). **merda de bove** (*colloquial*) bullshit, bollocks (*nonsense*).
merdi *vt.* (*colloquial*) shit.
merenge[1] *n.* meringue (*dessert*).
merenge[2] *n.* meringue (*Dominican dance*, *music*). **merenge aitian** méringue (*Haitian dance*, *music*).
meridiano *n.* meridian.
merita *vt.* deserve, merit, be worthy of, warrant, justify, be due, be owed, be entitled to. • *n.* merit, worth; entitlement, desert.
meritada *adj.* deserved, merited, justified.
meritante *adj.* deserving, worthy, entitled. **meritante la labora** worthwhile, worth the effort, worth the trouble.
meritocrata *adj.* meritocratic. • *n.* meritocrat.
meritocratia *n.* meritocracy.
merlan *n.* whiting (*fish*: *Merlangius merlangus*).
merlo *n.* blackbird (*Turdus merula*, *Agelaius phoeniceus*).
merlon *n.* merlon, battlement, embattlement, crenellation, castellation (*architecture*).
merloni *vt.* crenellate, castellate.
merlonida *adj.* crenellated, castellated.
merlonin *adj.* crenellated.
merlusa *n.* hake (*fish*: *Merluccius*).
mero *n.* grouper (*fish*: *Serranidae*).
mersenaria *n.* quahog, hard clam (*mollusc*: *Mercenaria mercenaria*).
mersenario *n.* mercenary (*soldier*).
mertensia *n.* bluebell (*plant*: *Mertensia*).
mervelia *vi.* marvel, wonder, be astonished. • *vt.* astonish, amaze. • *n.* marvel, miracle.
merveliosa *adj.* marvellous (US marvelous), wonderful, awe-inspiring, awesome, majestic, magnificent, glorious, superb, splendid, sublime.
mesaje *n.* message. **mesaje pronto** instant message.
mesajeta *n.* text message, text, SMS.
mesaji *vt.* message, send as a message, text. • *n.* messaging, texting. **mesaji pronto** instant messaging.
mesajor *n.* messenger, courier.
mescal *n.* mescal, mezcal (*drink*).
mescalina *n.* mescaline (*drug*).
mescite *n.* mesquite, mezquite (*plant*: *Prosopis*).
mesensefalo *n.* midbrain, mesencephalon (*anatomy*).
mesenterio *n.* mesentery (*anatomy*).
mesma *adj.* (*prenominal*) same, identical. • *adv.* -self (*emphasising the preceding noun or pronoun*). **el mesma** he himself, she herself (*non-reflexive*). **en la mesma modo** in the same way. **la re mesma** the king himself. **lo es la mesma per cadun** one size fits all. **lo mesma** it itself (*non-reflexive*). **los**

mesma they themselves (*non-reflexive*). **me mesma** I myself (*emphatic*). **nos mesma** we ourselves (*emphatic*). **par sola se mesma** singlehandedly. **se mesma** himself, herself, itself, themselves (*emphatically reflexive*). **tu mesma** you yourself. **vos mesma** you yourselves.
meso- *pref.* meso- (*middle*).
Mesoamerica *n.* Mesoamerica.
mesofilia *n.* mesophilia (*biology*).
mesofilica *adj.* mesophilic. • *n.* mesophile.
mesolitica *adj.* & *n.* Mesolithic (*geology*).
mesomisetozon *n.* mesomycetozoon (pl. mesomycetomozoea) (*organism*: *Mesomycetozoea*).
meson *n.* meson (*particle*).
Mesopotamia *n.* Mesopotamia.
mesotelial *adj.* mesothelial.
mesotelio *n.* mesothelium (*anatomy*).
mesotelioma *n.* mesothelioma.
mesozoica *adj.* & *n.* Mesozoic (*geology*).
mesozon *n.* mesozoan (*worm*).
mestral *adj.* master.
mestre *n.* master; teacher, mentor; maestro, virtuoso. **mestre de selebras** master of ceremonies, MC, emcee, showman.
mestresa *n.* mistress.
mestri *vt.* master.
mestria *n.* mastery.
mestrin *adj.* masterful, masterly.
mesura *vt.* measure. • *n.* measure, measurement, dimension; bar (*music*). **mesuras** measurements, dimensions.
mesurable *adj.* measurable.
mesurador *n.* measuring device, meter.
met- *pref.* meth- (*chemistry*).
meta- *pref.* meta-.
metabolal *adj.* metabolic.
metaboli *vi.* & *vt.* metabolize. • *n.* metabolism.
metabolite *n.* metabolite (*biology*).
metacarpal *adj.* metacarpal.
metacarpo *n.* metacarpus (*bones*).
metacualona *n.* methaqualone, quaalude (*drug*).
metadatos *n.pl.* metadata.
metadon *n.* methadone (*painkiller*).
metafisica *n.* metaphysics.
metafisical *adj.* metaphysical.
metafisiciste *n.* metaphysician.
metafor *adj.* metaphorical, metaphoric, figurative. • *n.* metaphor, trope.
metal *adj.* metal, metallic. • *n.* metal. **arte de metal** metalwork, metalworking. **metal resiclable** scrap, scrap metal.
metalin *adj.* metallic, metal-like.
metalor *n.* metalworker.
metalurjia *n.* metallurgy.
metalurjial *adj.* metallurgical.
metalurjiste *n.* metallurgist.
metamfetamina *n.* methamphetamine, meth.
metano *n.* methane.
metanol *n.* methanol.
metastase *vi.* metastasize (*medical*). • *n.* metastasis.
metatarsal *adj.* metatarsal.
metatarso *n.* metatarsus (*bones*).
metazon *n.* metazoon (pl. metazoa) (*member of the animal kingdom*: *Metazoa*, *Animalia*).
meteor *n.* meteor.
meteorin *adj.* meteoric.
meteorite *n.* meteorite.
meteorolojia *n.* meteorology.
meteorolojial *adj.* meteorological.
meteorolojiste *n.* meteorologist.
metil *n.* methyl (*chemistry*).
metodisme *n.* Methodism (*Christianity*).
metodiste *adj.* & *n.* Methodist.
metodo *n.* method, manner, way, technique, means. **par sua propre metodo** on one's own terms.
metodolojia *n.* methodology.
metodosa *adj.* methodical.
metonim *adj.* metonym (*substitution of name*).
metonimia *n.* metonymy.
metraje *n.* footage (*film*).
metral *adj.* metric.
metre[1] *n.* metre (US meter) (*unit of length, poetry*).
-metre[2] *n.suff.* -meter (*measuring tool*).
-metria *n.suff.* -metry (*measuring*).
metro *n.* subway, underground (*railway*).
metronomo *n.* metronome.
mexa *n.* lock (*hair*), tuft, hank, wisp; wick; fuse (*bomb*). **con mexa** tufted.
mexican *adj.* & *n.* Mexican.
Mexico *n.* Mexico. **Golfo Mexico** Gulf of Mexico. **Mexico Nova** New Mexico (*US state*).
mexin *adj.* tuftlike, tufty.
mezuza *n.* mezuzah (*parchment*).
mi *n.* mi (*musical note*).
Miama *n.* Myanmar, Burma. **miama** *adj.* & *n.* Burmese (*person, language*). See *Burma*, *burman*.
miasma *n.* miasma (*vapour*).
miastenia *n.* myasthenia (*medical*).
miau *interj.* miaow, meow.
miau-iau *adj.* & *n.* Miao-Yao, Hmong-Mien (*person, language*).
miaui *vi.* miaow, meow, mew.
mica *n.* mica (*mineral*).
Michigan ['miʃigan] *n.* Michigan (*US state*). **Lago Michigan** Lake Michigan.
micolojia *n.* mycology.
micolojial *adj.* mycological.
micolojiste *n.* mycologist.

micro- *pref.* micro- (*small, a millionth*).

microarciteta *n.* microarchitecture.

microbio *n.* microbe, bug, germ, virus; glitch, defect (*electronic*). **sin microbios** germfree.

microbiolojia *n.* microbiology.

microbiolojiste *n.* microbiologist.

microcosmo *n.* microcosm.

microcredito *n.* microcredit.

microfarade *n.* microfarad.

microfilma *n.* microfilm.

microfon *n.* microphone, mic, mike.

microlito *n.* microlith (*geology*).

micrometre *n.* micrometre (US micrometer) (*unit of length*); micrometer (*measuring tool*).

micron *n.* micron (*unit of length*).

Micronesia *n.* Micronesia. **Statos Federada de Micronesia** Federated States of Micronesia.

micronesian *adj.* & *n.* Micronesian.

microonda *n.* microwave.

microplastica *n.* microplastic.

microscopial *adj.* microscopic.

microscopio *n.* microscope. **Microscopio** *n.* Microscopium (*constellation*).

microsefalia *n.* microcephaly (*medical*).

microsefalica *adj.* microcephalic, microcephalous.

microsirurjia *n.* microsurgery.

microtelia *n.* microchip, chip.

microtomia *n.* microtomy.

microtomo *n.* microtome (*slicing tool*).

miel *n.* honey.

mielada *n.* honeydew (*substance*).

mielifaje *n.* honeyeater (*bird*: *Meliphagidae*).

mielin[1] *n.* myelin (*biology*).

mielin[2] *n.* honey, sweetheart.

mieloide *adj.* myeloid (*anatomy*).

mieloma *n.* myeloma (*medical*).

mielosite *n.* myelocyte (*biology*).

migra *vi.* & *vt.* migrate. • *n.* migration, immigration, emigration. **migra a** immigrate to. **migra de** emigrate from.

migrania *n.* migraine.

migrante *adj.* migrating. • *n.* migrant.

migror *n.* immigrant, emigrant.

mil *det.* (*a*) thousand. • *adj.* thousandth (*ordinal*). **miles** thousands.

milan *n.* kite (*bird*: *Elaninae*, *Milvinae*).

milenialisme *n.* millennialism.

milenio *n.* millennium.

milflor *n.* millefleurs, millefiori (*art*).

milfolia *n.* yarrow (*plant*: *Achillea millefolium*).

mili *vi.* & *vt.* split into a thousand parts. • *n.* thousandth (*fraction*). • *pref.* milli- (*a thousandth*).

milia *n.* mile. **milia engles** English mile. **milia maral** nautical mile. **milia roman antica** Roman mile.

miligram *n.* milligram.

mililitre *n.* millilitre (US milliliter).

milimetre *n.* millimetre (US millimeter).

milio *n.* millet (*plant*: *Gramineae*, esp. *Panicum miliaceum*, *Eleusine caracana*, *Pennisetum glaucum*).

milion *det.* (*a*) million. • *adj.* millionth (*ordinal*). **miliones** millions.

milioni *vi.* & *vt.* split into a million parts. • *n.* millionth (*fraction*).

milionor *n.* millionaire.

milipede *n.* millipede (*Diplopoda*).

militar *adj.* military, militaristic. • *n.* serviceman, servicewoman; (*the*) military (*organization*). **artes militar** martial arts. **militares** (*the*) military. **servi militar** military service.

militari *vi.* & *vt.* militarize. • *n.* militarization.

militarisme *n.* militarism.

militariste *adj.* militant. • *n.* militarist, militant.

militia *n.* militia.

militior *n.* militiaman, militia member, minuteman.

mima *vt.* mime, pantomime, imitate. • *n.* mime, pantomime, mimesis, mimicry, imitation.

mimeograf *n.* mimeograph.

mimeografia *n.* mimeography.

mimor *n.* mime, mimer (*person*); mockingbird, catbird, thrasher (*Mimidae*).

mimosa *n.* mimosa (*plant*: *Mimosa*, *Acacia dealbata*).

min *det.* less, fewer; e.g. *min enerjia*; *min persones*. • *adv.* less; e.g. *min alta ca*. • *conj.* minus (*arithmetic*). **a la min** at least, as a minimum. **la min** least; e.g. *la lia la min forte*. **la min de** least, fewest, the minority of. **min … min** the less … the less; e.g. *min lo pluve, min la teto gotea*; *min bon es la problem, plu bon es la solve*; *min los ave, plu los vole*. **min ca nun** second to none. **min e min** less and less, ever less.

mina *vt.* mine. • *n.* mining.

minareta *n.* minaret (*mosque tower*).

Mindanao *n.* Mindanao (*island*).

Mindoro *n.* Mindoro. **Streta Mindoro** Mindoro Strait.

mineral *adj.* mineral. • *n.* mineral, ore.

minerali *vi.* & *vt.* mineralize. • *n.* mineralization.

mineralojia *n.* mineralogy.

mineralojial *adj.* mineralogical.

mineralojiste *n.* mineralogist.

mineria *n.* mine.

ming *adj.* Ming (*dynasty*).

mini- *pref.* mini-.

miniatur *adj.* & *n.* miniature.

miniaturi *vt.* miniaturize. • *n.* miniaturization.
miniaturiste *n.* miniaturist.
minibus *n.* minibus.
minitalda *n.* miniskirt.
minima *adj.* minimum, minimal, least; nominal (*cost*). • *adv.* at least. • *n.* minimum, least.
minimax *n.* minimax (*game theory*).
minimi *vi.* & *vt.* minimize, downplay, understate. • *n.* minimization.
minimisme *n.* minimalism.
minimiste *adj.* & *n.* minimalist.
minimoto *n.* minibike (*motorcycle*).
minio *n.* minium, red lead (*pigment*).
minipantala *n.* hotpants, short shorts, booty shorts; (*underwear*) boyshorts, boxer briefs.
miniserie *n.* miniseries.
minislip *n.* minibriefs, bikini briefs, tanga briefs.
ministral *adj.* ministerial.
ministreria *n.* ministry.
ministro *n.* minister (*government*). **ministro de esternas** foreign minister, foreign secretary, secretary of state for foreign affairs. **ministro de internas** home secretary, secretary of state for internal affairs. **ministro xef** prime minister, chancellor.
Minnesota *n.* Minnesota (*US state*).
minor *adj.* minor, slight; junior, the younger (*in names*). • *n.* minor.
minori *vi.* & *vt.* convert to lowercase.
minoria *n.* minority.
minotauro *n.* minotaur.
minueto *n.* minuet (*dance, music*).
minuto *n.* minute.
mio- *pref.* myo- (*muscle*).
miocardial *adj.* myocardial.
miope *adj.* near-sighted, short-sighted, myopic.
miopia *n.* near-sightedness, short-sightedness, myopia.
miosene *adj.* & *n.* Miocene (*geology*).
miosite *n.* myocyte (*biology*).
mira *n.* myrrh (*tree, resin: Commiphora myrrha*).
miracle *n.* miracle.
miraclor *n.* miracleworker.
miraclosa *adj.* miraculous.
miraje *n.* mirage.
mirandes *adj.* & *n.* Mirandes (*person, language*).
miriapodo *n.* myriapod (*arthropod*).
mirica *n.* bayberry (*plant, berry: Myrica gale*).
miror *n.* mirror. **miror de retrovista** rear-view mirror.
mirori *vt.* mirror.
mirto *n.* myrtle (*plant: Myrtus*).
misa *n.* mass (*religious*). **misa de moria** requiem.
misantrope *adj.* misanthropic. • *n.* misanthrope, misanthropist.
misantropia *n.* misanthropy.
misca *vt.* mix, blend, jumble, scramble, intersperse; mingle; shuffle (*reorder*). • *n.* mixture, miscellany, jumble, admixture, hodgepodge, hotchpotch, medley, melange, potpourri. **misca de razas** interbreeding, miscegenation.
miscable *adj.* miscible.
miscada *adj.* mixed, miscellaneous, assorted.
miscador *n.* blender, mixer, mixing machine. **miscador de beton** cement mixer.
miselio *n.* mycelium (*biology*).
misera *adj.* miserable, abject, wretched, piteous, pitiful, downtrodden, pathetic, squalid, crummy, lousy. • *n.* wretch; fleabag.
miseria *n.* misery, abjection, abjectness, squalour (US squalor).
misil *n.* missile, projectile. **misil cruser** cruise missile. **misil de tera a aira** surface-to-air missile. **misil intercontinental** intercontinental missile. **misil luminante** flare.
mision *n.* mission, expedition. **mision fol** fool's mission, fool's errand.
misioneria *n.* mission (*station*).
misioneta *n.* errand.
misionor *n.* missionary.
miso[1] *n.* miso (*soup*).
miso-[2] *pref.* miso- (*hate*).
misojine *adj.* misogynistic. • *n.* misogynist.
misojinia *n.* misogyny.
Misre *n.* Egypt. See *Egipte*.
misri *adj.* & *n.* Egyptian.
Mississippi *n.* Mississippi (*US state*). **Rio Mississippi** Mississippi River.
Missouri *n.* Missouri (*US state*). **Rio Missouri** Missouri River.
misterio *n.* mystery, enigma; whodunnit.
misteriosa *adj.* mysterious, uncanny.
mistica *adj.* mystic, mystical, esoteric. • *n.* mystic.
misticisme *n.* mysticism.
mistral *n.* mistral (*wind*).
mital *adj.* mythical, mythic.
mito *n.* myth, legend.
mitocondrial *adj.* mitochondrial.
mitocondrio *n.* mitochondrion (pl. mitochondria) (*biology*).
mitolojia *n.* mythology.
mitolojial *adj.* mythological.
mitose *n.* mitosis (*biology*).
mitra[1] *n.* mitre (*hat*).

Mitra[2] *n.* Mithras, Mithra.
mitraisme [mitra'isme] *n.* mithraism.
mitraiste [mitra'iste] *adj.* & *n.* mithraist.
mitral *adj.* mitral (*anatomy*).
mitralia *vt.* strafe.
mitraliador *n.* machine gun.
mitralior *n.* machine gunner.
mixino *n.* hagfish.
mixna *n.* Mishnah, Mishna (*Judaism*).
mmm *interj.* hmmm (*thinking*); mmmm, yum (*tasty*).
moa *n.* moa (*bird*: *Dinornithidae*).
mobila *n.* piece of furniture, item of furniture. **mobila de vaso de note** commode. **mobilas** furniture, furnishings.
mobileta *n.* prop.
mobili *vt.* furnish.
moca *n.* mocha (*coffee*).
mocasin *n.* moccasin (*shoe*).
moda *n.* fashion, style, vogue, trend, fad; mood (*grammar*); mode (*software*, *statistics*). **a la moda** in fashion, cool, fashionable, stylish, trendy, chic, hot. **bolsa de moda** designer handbag. **de moda** in fashion, cool, fashionable, stylish, trendy, chic, hot. **de moda pasada** outdated, outmoded, out of fashion, old-fashioned. **moda de capeles** hairstyle. **moda dependente** conditional mood, irrealis mood. **moda indicante** indicative mood. **moda refinada** haute couture. **moda sujuntiva** subjunctive mood.
modal *adj.* modal; sartorial.
model *adj.* model, exemplary, archetypal. • *n.* model, prototype, exemplar, example, archetype, pattern, standard, template, paradigm, mock-up; model (*art*, *fashion*). **model proportial** scale model.
modeli *vt.* model (*make a model of*; *display clothes*). • *n.* modelling (US modeling).
modem *n.* modem.
modera *vt.* moderate, temper, mitigate. • *n.* moderation, mitigation.
moderada *adj.* moderate, sparing, tempered, mitigated.
moderante *adj.* moderating, moderating. • *n.* moderator (*substance*).
moderna *adj.* modern.
moderni *vi.* & *vt.* modernize, update, rework. • *n.* modernization, retrofit.
modernia *n.* modernness, modernity.
modernisme *n.* modernism.
moderniste *n.* modernist.
modernor *n.* modernizer.
moderor *n.* moderator (*person*).
modesta *adj.* modest (*humble*, *avoiding impropriety*), unpretentious. **tro modesta** prudish.
modiste *n.* fashion designer, milliner, modiste, follower of fashion, fashionista.
modo *n.* manner, means, way (*of doing*); e.g. *en modo interesante*. **en multe modos** in many ways, multiply. **en no modo** by no means, in no way. **en no otra modo ca** in no other way than, just, simply, purely. **en otra modo** in another way, otherwise. **modo de parla** way of speaking, parlance. **modo de susta** livelihood, living. **modo de vive** way of life, lifestyle, approach to life.
modosa *adj.* fashionable, stylish, chic, groovy, snazzy.
modula *vt.* modulate. • *n.* modulation.
modulador *n.* modulator.
modulal *adj.* modular.
modulo *n.* module; modulus. • *prep.* modulo (*mathematics*); e.g. *17 modulo 5 es 2*. **modulo estendente** extension module.
mofeta *n.* skunk (*Mephitidae*).
mofo *n.* mould (US mold), mildew.
mofosa *adj.* mouldy (US moldy).
mogano *n.* mahogany (*tree*, *wood*: *Swietenia*). **de mogano** (*made of*) mahogany.
mohair *n.* mohair.
Mohave, Deserto *n.* Mojave Desert, Mohave Desert.
moia *vt.* wet. • *n.* wetting.
moiada *adj.* wet, soaked, drenched.
moisme [mo'isme] *n.* Mohism (*philosophy*).
moiste [mo'iste] *adj.* & *n.* Mohist.
mol[1] *adj.* soft (*not hard or tough*), squishy; tender. See *suave*.
mol[2] *n.* mole (*chemistry*).
mola *n.* spring. **cargada par mola** spring-loaded.
molador *n.* grinder.
molda *n.* mould (US mold), cast (*container*). **molda per pan** bread pan. **molda per tartes** pie pan, pie tin. **molda per tortas** cake pan.
moldi *vt.* mould (US mold), cast.
moldida *n.* moulding (US molding), casting; mould (US mold), cast (*moulded object*).
Moldova *n.* Moldova, Moldavia.
moldovan *adj.* & *n.* Moldovan.
moldur *n.* frame (*picture*), moulding (US molding), cornice. **moldur cablin** cable moulding (US molding). **moldur de solo** baseboard, skirting board. **moldur merlonin** dentil (*architecture*).
moldurador *n.* router (*carpentry tool*).
mole *vt.* grind, pound, pulverize, reduce to powder; gnash (*teeth*).
molecula *n.* molecule.
moleculal *adj.* molecular.
molesta *vt.* molest, harass, harry, hassle. • *n.* molestation, harassment.
moli *vi.* soften; relent. • *vt.* soften; tenderize.
molia *n.* softness.

molibdeno *n.* molybdenum (*element*).
molin *n.* mill. **molin de carne** meat grinder. **molin de peper** pepper mill, pepper grinder. **molin de rio** water mill. **molin de venta** windmill.
molineta *n.* toy windmill, pinwheel; turnstile.
molini *vt.* mill.
molinor *n.* miller.
molo *n.* pier, jetty, quay, quayside, wharf.
molotro *n.* cowbird (*Molothrus*).
molusco *n.* mollusc (US mollusk), shellfish (*Mollusca*).
momental *adj.* momentary.
momento *n.* moment, instant, jiffy, juncture; momentum. **de la momento** of the moment, du jour. **la bon momento** the right moment, the opportunity, the chance. **momento angulo** angular momentum. **momento de torse** torque. **momento linial** linear momentum.
momi *vi.* & *vt.* mummify. • *n.* mummification.
momia *n.* mummy (*preserved*).
monaces *adj.* & *n.* Monacan.
Monaco *n.* Monaco.
monal *adj.* monetary.
monarca *n.* monarch, sovereign; monarch butterfly (*Danaus plexippus*).
monarcal *adj.* monarchic, monarchical, monarchistic.
monarcia *n.* monarchy, sovereignty.
monarcisme *n.* monarchism, royalism.
monarciste *adj.* monarchist, royalist.
monax *n.* woodchuck, groundhog, whistlepig (*rodent*: *Marmota monax*).
moncal *adj.* monastic.
monce *n.* monk, nun. **monce fema** nun. **monce mas** monk. **monce sever** ascetic.
monceria *n.* monastery, convent, abbey, cloister, nunnery, priory.
moncin *adj.* monkish.
moncisme *n.* monasticism.
mone *n.* money, cash, currency. **con mone** in cash. **mone blancida** laundered money. **mone de jua** play money, monopoly money. **mone falsa** counterfeit money. **mone fisical** cash, physical currency. **mone lavada** laundered money. **mone sanguosa** blood money. **mone susia** dirty money, lucre.
monedula *n.* jackdaw (*Coloeus monedula*).
moneria *n.* mint (*money*).
moneta *n.* coin.
Mongol *n.* Mongolia. **mongol** *adj.* & *n.* Mongolian.
mongoloide *adj.* mongoloid.
monisme *n.* monism (*philosophy*).
moniste *n.* monist.
monito *n.* monito del monte, chumaihuén, colocolo opossum (*marsupial*: *Dromiciops gliroides*).
monitor *n.* monitor. **monitor de glucosa** glucose monitor, blood-sugar monitor.
monitori *vt.* monitor, keep an eye on. • *n.* monitoring, surveillance.
mono- *pref.* mono- (*one*).
monoamina *adj.* & *n.* monoamine (*chemistry*).
monoblasto *n.* monoblast (*biology*).
monocini *n.* monokini (*garment*).
monocota *n.* monocot, monocotyledon (*botany*).
monocromata *adj.* monochrome, monochromatic, black and white.
monoculal *adj.* monocular.
monoculo *n.* monocle.
monocultiveria *n.* monoculture, plantation.
monoftongo *n.* monophthong.
monogama *adj.* monogamous.
monogamia *n.* monogamy.
monogamiste *n.* monogamist.
monografi *vt.* monograph.
monografia *n.* monograph.
monografiste *n.* monographer.
monolingual *adj.* monolingual. • *n.* monolingual, monolingual person.
monolitin *adj.* monolithic.
monolito *n.* monolith.
monologo *n.* monologue (US monolog), soliloquy.
monomania *n.* monomania.
monomanica *adj.* monomaniacal. • *n.* monomaniac.
monomer *n.* monomer (*chemistry*).
monomial *adj.* monomial (*mathematics*).
monomio *n.* monomial (*mathematics*).
mononucleose *n.* mononucleosis (*medical*).
monopoli *vt.* monopolize, corner the market.
monopolio *n.* monopoly.
monopolo *n.* monopole (*particle*).
monorel *n.* monorail.
monosacarido *n.* monosaccharide, simple sugar.
monosicle *n.* unicycle, monocycle.
monosido *n.* monoxide. **monosido de carbono** carbon monoxide.
monosilaba *n.* monosyllable.
monosilabal *adj.* monosyllabic.
monosite *n.* monocyte (*biology*).
monositopoiese *n.* monocytopoiesis (*biology*).
monoteisme [monoteˈisme] *n.* monotheism.
monoteiste [monoteˈiste] *adj.* monotheistic. • *n.* monotheist.
monotonia *n.* monotony.
monotono *n.* monotone.

monotonosa *adj.* monotonous, dull, tedious, boring, stodgy.
monson *n.* monsoon.
monstrin *adj.* monstrous.
monstrinia *n.* monstrosity.
monstro *n.* monster. **monstro de Gila** Gila monster (*lizard*: *Heloderma suspectum*). **monstro jigante** behemoth.
monta *vt.* mount, ride, sit on, straddle. **monta la dorso** piggyback.
Montana *n.* Montana (*US state*).
montania *n.* mountains, mountainous area, highlands.
montanial *adj.* mountain, highland.
montanior *n.* mountain dweller, highlander, hillbilly.
montaniosa *adj.* mountainous.
montante *adj.* riding, straddling, astride; horseback, on horseback.
monte *n.* mount, mountain. **a monte** up, uphill, upstream, upward, upwards.
montenegrin *adj.* & *n.* Montenegrin.
Montenegro *n.* Montenegro. See *Tsernagora*.
monton *n.* heap, pile, mound; (*colloquial*) bunch, heap, host, load, shedload, ton (*large quantity*). **monton de dejetadas** garbage heap, rubbish heap, midden. **monton de fece** dunghill, midden. **monton de feno** haystack. **monton de formicas** anthill. **monton de neva** snowdrift. **un monton de** a lot of, a load of, lots of, loads of. **un monton de mone** a fortune. **un monton de ricia** a fortune.
Montserat *n.* Montserrat (*island*).
montseratian *adj.* & *n.* Montserratian.
montur *n.* mount, frame (*lens*), setting, bezel.
monturi *vt.* mount (*one thing on another*).
monumental *adj.* monumental, landmark.
monumento *n.* monument, memorial, landmark, sight; milestone. **monumento de rocas** cairn.
mor *adj.* dead, deceased. • *n.* dead person, deceased, casualty. **Mar Mor** Dead Sea.
mora *n.* blackberry (*plant*, *berry*: *Rubus*).
moral *adj.* moral. **prinsipe moral** moral principle, moral. **regula moral** moral rule, moral.
moralia *n.* morality, morals. **sin moralia** amoral.
moralisme *n.* moralism, moralizing, priggery.
moraliste *adj.* moralistic, sanctimonious, self-righteous, priggish, puritanical. • *n.* moralist, prig, prude.
morbilio *n.* measles.
morbosa *adj.* morbid.
morbosia *n.* morbidity.
morde *vt.* bite. **morde de pulga** fleabite. **morde de serpente** snakebite.
moren *n.* moraine (*geology*).
morena *n.* moray.
morera *n.* mulberry (*berry*).
moreria *n.* morgue, mortuary.
morero *n.* mulberry (*tree*: *Morus*).
-morfe *adj.suff.* -morph.
morfem *n.* morpheme.
morfina *n.* morphine.
morfo- *pref.* morpho-.
morfolojia *n.* morphology.
morfolojial *adj.* morphological.
mori *vi.* die, perish, pass away. • *vt.* deaden. • *n.* death, dying, decease, demise, fatality, casualty, mortality. **mori de famia** *v.* starve. • *n.* starvation. **mori e destrui** death and destruction, carnage. **mori fetal** stillbirth. **pos mori** posthumous.
moria *n.* death (*being dead*).
morida *adj.* deadened.
morinte *adj.* dying, moribund.
mormon *adj.* & *n.* Mormon.
mormonisme *n.* Mormonism, Latter-day Saints.
moro *adj.* Moorish (*medieval*); Moro, Bangsamoro (*Philippine Muslim*). • *n.* Moor; Moro. **Golfo Moro** Moro Gulf.
morsa *n.* walrus.
morso *n.* bit (*bridle*).
mortal *adj.* mortal, perishable.
mortalia *n.* mortality.
mortasa *n.* mortise (*of dovetail joint*).
mortasi *vt.* mortise.
morteri *vt.* mortar, grout.
mortero *n.* mortar, grout (*substance*); mortar (*gun*).
morva *n.* distemper (*disease*).
mos *n.* moss (*Bryophyta*).
mosaica *adj.* & *n.* mosaic.
Mosambic *n.* Mozambique. **Streta Mosambic** Mozambique Channel.
mosambican *adj.* & *n.* Mozambican.
mosarabi *adj.* Mozarabic. • *n.* Mozarab.
mosca *n.* fly (*insect*: *Brachycera*). **Mosca** *n.* Musca (*constellation*). **mosca de carne** blowfly. **mosca de casa** housefly.
mosceta *n.* midge, gnat (*Nematocera*).
moscete *n.* musket (*gun*).
mosceti *vt.* shoot with a musket. • *n.* musketry.
moscetor *n.* musketeer.
moscito *n.* mosquito, gnat (*Culicidae*).
moscovio *n.* moscovium (*element*).
Moscva *n.* Moscow.
mosin *adj.* mosslike.
mososa *adj.* mossy.
mostarda *n.* mustard (*Brassica hirta*, *nigra*, *juncea*).
mostra *vt.* show, exhibit, display, reveal, demonstrate, illustrate. • *n.* exhibition, illus-

tration, audition, demonstration, demo, sample, manifestation. **mostra e dise** *v.* & *n.* show and tell. **mostra emosia** show emotion, emote. **mostra prima** premiere, opening, first showing. **mostra sua autoria** assert one's authority. **mostra un video** show a video, play a video.
mostrable *adj.* demonstrable.
mostrada *adj.* shown, revealed, manifest.
mostral *adj.* demonstrative.
mostrante *adj.* illustrative.
motasila *n.* wagtail (*bird*: *Motacillidae*).
motel *n.* motel.
motif *n.* motif, trope, (*repeating*) pattern. **motif caxmiran** paisley pattern. **motif de puntos** polka dots. **motif spiral** spiral pattern, scrollwork. **sin motif** blank, plain.
motiva *vt.* motivate. • *n.* motive, motivation, incentive. **motiva ascondeda** ulterior motive.
motivante *adj.* motivating, motivational.
moto- *pref.* motor-.
motobarco *n.* motorboat, powerboat, speedboat.
motocareta *n.* sidecar.
motoneuron *n.* motoneuron, motor neuron.
motor *n.* motor, engine. **motor de combusta interna** internal combustion engine. **motor esterna** outboard motor. **motor interna** inboard motor.
motori *vt.* motorize.
motorisme *n.* motoring, driving.
motoriste *n.* motorist, driver.
motosicle *n.* motorcycle, motorbike.
motosiclisme *n.* motorcycling, motorcycle racing, motor racing.
motosicliste *n.* motorcyclist, biker.
motosiera *n.* chainsaw.
mototreno *n.* snowmobile.
movable *adj.* mobile.
movabli *vi.* & *vt.* mobilize. • *n.* mobilization.
movablia *n.* mobility.
move *vi.* move, shift, budge. • *vt.* move, shift, propel, transfer; shovel (*snow, soil, etc.*). • *n.* movement, move, motion, locomotion; movement (*music*). **de move** locomotory. **de move lenta** slow-motion, in slow motion. **move ajitada** fidget. **move caracolin** move at a snail's pace, crawl along. **move furtiva** slink. **move laborosa** move laboriously, manhandle. **move sua casa** move house, move.
moxa *vi.* mosh (*dance*). • *n.* moshing.
Moxe *n.* Moses.
moxeria *n.* mosh pit.
mozabita *adj.* & *n.* Mozabite (*person, language*).
mozarela *n.* mozzarella (*cheese*).
mu *n.* mu (*Greek letter* M, μ).
mua *vi.* pout, sulk. • *n.* pout, moue.
mucilajo *n.* mucilage.
mucin *adj.* gooey, goopy, gloopy.
muco *n.* mucus, phlegm; goo, goop, gloop, glop. **muco acuin** rheum. **muco nasal** nasal mucus, snot, bogey, booger.
mucosa *adj.* mucous, snotty.
muda *adj.* mute, dumb, speech-impaired; speechless. • *n.* mute, speech-impaired person.
mudi *vi.* & *vt.* mute.
mudia *n.* muteness, mutism, dumbness.
muezin *n.* muezzin (*caller to prayer*).
mufin *n.* muffin. **mufin cavetin** popover.
mufinor *n.* muffin seller, muffinman.
mufti *n.* mufti (*Islamic scholar*).
mugre *n.* filth, grime, sludge, muck, mess.
mugrosa *adj.* filthy, squalid, grimy, mucky, messy.
mugul *adj.* & *n.* Mughal, Mogul (*dynasty*).
Muhammad *n.* Muhammad, Mohammed, Muhammed.
mui *vt.* moo, low. • *n.* mooing, lowing.
mujil *n.* mullet (*fish*: *Mugilidae*).
mul *n.* mussel (*mollusc*: *Mytilidae*).
mula *n.* mullah (*Islam*).
muladi *n.* muladi (*Islam*).
mulato *n.* (*derogatory*) mulatto.
muleta *n.* crutch (*support stick*).
mulin *adj.* mulish, stubborn.
mulo *n.* mule.
mulor *n.* muleteer.
multa *vt.* fine, penalize. • *n.* fine, penalty, ticket, forfeit, forfeiture.
multe *det.* many, much, numerous, myriad, a host of, a multitude of. • *adv.* very, really, greatly. • *pron.* much, many (*singular or plural*). **es plu multe ca** outnumber. **multe min** *adj.* many fewer, much less. • *adv.* much less. **multe plu** *adj.* many more, much more. • *adv.* much more. **multes** (*people or things, optional plural pronoun*). **tan multe como posible** as many as possible, as much as possible.
multi- *pref.* multi-.
multia *n.* multitude, host.
multibandal *adj.* multitrack.
multicanalal *adj.* multichannel.
multicolorosa *adj.* multicoloured (US multicolored), multicolour (US multicolor), polychromatic, variegated, motley, mottled, pied, dappled.
multicoral *adj.* multicore.
multicultural *adj.* multicultural.
multidimensional *adj.* multidimensional.
multidirijal *adj.* multidirectional.
multietnical *adj.* multiethnic.
multifasal *adj.* multiphase, multiphasic.

multifasetal *adj.* multifaceted.
multigradal *adj.* multistage.
multiladal *adj.* multilateral, many-sided.
multilingual *adj.* multilingual. • *n.* polyglot.
multilinial *adj.* multilinial.
multimedial *adj.* multimedia.
multimedialia *n.* multimedia.
multinasional *adj.* & *n.* multinational.
multinivelal *adj.* multilevel, multistorey (US multistory).
multipartital *adj.* multiparty, multipartite.
multiple *adj.* multiple. • *adv.* multiply. • *n.* multiple (*number*).
multiplesal *adj.* multiplex.
multipleso *n.* multiplex.
multipli *vi.* become multiple. • *vt.* multiply. • *n.* multiplication; product.
multiplida *n.* multiplicand. **multiplida par** multiplied by, times.
multiplinte *n.* multiplier.
multipolal *adj.* multipolar.
multirazal *adj.* multiracial.
multiselulal *adj.* multicellular.
multistratal *adj.* multilayered.
multitalentosa *adj.* multitalented, protean.
multitaxal *adj.* multitasking.
multitaxia *n.* multitasking.
multiterenal *adj.* off-road, all-terrain. • *n.* off-road vehicle, all-terrain vehicle, sport utility vehicle, SUV, four-wheel drive, four-by-four.
multiusal *adj.* multipurpose, multifunctional, versatile, general-purpose.
multiusoral *adj.* multiuser.
multivalente *adj.* multivalent.
multivariante *adj.* multivariate, multivariant.
multiverso *n.* multiverse.
mundal *adj.* world, worldly (*pertaining to the world*).
mundo *n.* world. **de la mundo** cosmopolitan. **la plu grande de mundo** the world's largest. **mundo consumiste** material world. **mundo de sonia** dream world.
muni *vt.* supply with ammunition. • *n.* ammunition, ammo, munition.
munisipa *n.* municipality.
munisipal *n.* municipal, civic.
munster *n.* munster, muenster (*cheese*).
muon *n.* muon (*particle*).
mur *n.* wall; bulkhead (*ship*). **mur contra esplodes** blast wall.
muraliste *n.* muralist (*artist*).
mureta *n.* partition; board. **mureta blanca** whiteboard. **mureta de avisas** message board, bulletin board, noticeboard. **mureta negra** blackboard, chalkboard.
muritani *adj.* & *n.* Mauritanian.
Muritania *n.* Mauritania.
murmura *vi.*, *vt.* & *n.* murmur, mumble, burble.
muron *n.* rampart, defensive wall, city wall; bulkhead, retaining wall. **muron de mar** seawall. **muron de tera** earthwork.
mus *n.* mouse (*Mus*).
musa *n.* muse.
musaca *n.* moussaka (*food*).
musarania *n.* shrew (*animal: Soricidae*).
muscada *n.* nutmeg (*Myristica*).
muscari *n.* grape hyacinth (*plant: Muscari*).
muscatel *n.* muscat, muscatel (*grape, wine*).
musco *n.* musk deer (*Moschus*); musk.
muscosa *adj.* musky.
musculal *adj.* muscular.
musculo *n.* muscle. **musculos** muscles, musculature.
musculor *n.* muscleman, strongman, he-man.
musculosa *adj.* muscular, muscly, brawny, musclebound.
musculosceletal *adj.* musculoskeletal.
musculosia *n.* muscularity, brawn.
muse *n.* mousse (*food*).
muselina *n.* muslin (*fabric*). **de muselina** (*made of*) muslin.
museo *n.* museum.
musica *n.* music. **musica de asendador** muzak, elevator music, lift music. **musica de folclor** folk music. **musica de salon** chamber music. **musica en conserta** live music. **musica pop** pop music. **musica rap** rap music. **musica roc** rock music.
musical *adj.* musical.
musiciste *n.* musician. **musiciste suportante** supporting musician, sideman.
musicolojia *n.* musicology.
musicolojiste *n.* musicologist.
musin *adj.* mouselike, mousy.
musli *n.* muesli, granola.
muslim *adj.* & *n.* Islamic, Muslim, Moslem, Mohammedan. See *islam*.
mustang *n.* mustang (*horse*).
mustax *n.* moustache (US mustache).
mustela *n.* weasel (*Mustela*).
mustelin *adj.* weaselly, weasel-like.
muta *vi.* mutate, transform, transmute. • *vt.* mutate, transform, transmute, transfigure, transmogrify. • *n.* mutation, transformation, metamorphosis, transmutation, transfiguration. **muta sua pel** shed one's skin. **muta sua pelo** moult (US molt). **muta sua plumas** moult (US molt).
mutable *adj.* mutable, changeable.
mutablia *n.* mutability.
mutada *adj.* mutated. • *n.* mutant.
mutador *n.* transformer.
mutajen *adj.* mutagenic (*genetics*). • *n.* mutagen.

mutila *vt.* mutilate, mangle. • *n.* mutilation.
mutisme *n.* metamorphism (*geology*).
mutua *adj.* mutual, reciprocal. • *adv.* mutually, reciprocally, to each other, to one another.
mutui *vi.* & *vt.* mutualize.
muu *interj.* moo (*cow*).
muxu *n.* mu shu, moo shu (*food*).

N

N[1] [en], **en** *letter* N, n.
n[2] *abbr.* (*numero*) n., no., №.
nabatea *adj.* & *n.* Nabatean (*person, language*).
nabo *n.* turnip (*Brassica rapa*).
nacre *n.* nacre, mother-of-pearl (*substance*).
nacrin *adj.* nacreous.
nada *vi.* & *n.* swim.
nadene *adj.* & *n.* Na-Dene (*person, language*).
naderia *n.* swimming baths, swimming complex, natatorium.
nadir *n.* nadir (*astronomy, misfortune*).
nador *n.* swimmer.
nafta *n.* naphtha (*oil*).
naftalina *n.* naphthalina (*substance*).
naftol *n.* naphthol (*substance*).
naive *adj.* naïve, ingenuous, trusting, innocent, unsophisticated, jejune. • *n.* simpleton.
naivia *n.* naïvety, naïveté, naïveness, innocence, ingenuousness.
Namib, Deserto *n.* Namib Desert.
Namibia *n.* Namibia.
namibian *adj.* & *n.* Namibian.
nana[1] *adj.* dwarf (*including mythology*), midget, gnome. • *n.* dwarf, midget, gnome.
nana[2] *n.* (*colloquial*) nanny (*carer*).
nanisme *n.* dwarfism.
nano- *pref.* nano- (*tiny, a thousand-millionth*).
nanometre *n.* nanometre (US nanometer).
nanosecondo *n.* nanosecond.
napalm *n.* napalm (*liquid*).
nara *vt.* narrate, tell, relate (*story*). • *n.* narration, story, tale, chronicle. **nara de fes** fairy tale. **nara de folclor** folktale. **nara en tre libros** trilogy. **nara fondal** backstory. **naras** stories, fiction. **naras siensal** science fiction.
naral *adj.* fictional, narrative, narrational.
narco- *pref.* narco- (*stupor*).
narcolesia *n.* narcolepsy.
narcolesica *adj.* narcoleptic.
narcose *n.* narcosis.
narcotica *adj.* & *n.* narcotic.
nardo *n.* spikenard (*plant: Nardostachys grandiflora*).
nareta *n.* short story.
narina *n.* nostril, naris (pl. nares).
naror *n.* storyteller, narrator, raconteur.
narsisisme *n.* narcissism.
narsisiste *adj.* narcissistic. • *n.* narcissist.
narsiso *n.* narcissus, daffodil (*plant: Narcissus*).
narval *n.* narwhal (*whale: Monodon monoceros*).
nas *n.* nose.
nasal *adj.* nasal. • *n.* nasal (*consonant*).
nasali *vi.* & *vt.* nasalize.
nase *vi.* be born; come into existence. • *vt.* bear, give birth to. • *n.* birth. **ante nase** prenatal, antenatal. **de nase** natal. **pos nase** postnatal. See *pari*.
naseda *adj.* born. **mor naseda** stillborn. **prima naseda** firstborn.
nasel *n.* nacelle (*vehicle part*).
nasente *adj.* nascent, coming into existence.
nasi *vt.* nuzzle, nose at.
nasion *n.* nation, state. **Nasiones Unida** United Nations. **sin nasion** stateless.
nasional *adj.* national, nationwide. **falsa nasional** pseudo-national.
nasionali *vi.* & *vt.* nationalize. • *n.* nationalization.
nasionalia *n.* nationality.
nasionalisme *n.* nationalism.
nasionaliste *adj.* nationalistic. • *n.* nationalist.
nasturtio *n.* nasturtium (*plant: Tropaeolum*).
natal *n.* Christmas, Noel, Nowell, nativity, yule, yuletide. **arbor de natal** Christmas tree. **de natal** Christmas. **Isola Natal** Christmas Island. **sera de natal** Christmas Eve.
nativa *adj.* native (*to a place*), indigenous. • *n.* native.
nativisme *n.* nativism.
nativiste *n.* nativist.
natron *n.* natron (*substance*).
natur *n.* nature. **natur mor** still life.
natural *adj.* natural, inborn; organic (*food*); artless (*writing*). • *adv.* naturally, of course.
naturali *vi.* & *vt.* naturalize. • *n.* naturalization.
naturin *adj.* naturalistic.
naturiste *n.* naturalist.
nauatl *adj.* & *n.* Nahuatl (*person, language*).
Nauero *n.* Nauru. **nauero** *adj.* & *n.* Nauruan.
nausea *vt.* nauseate. • *n.* nausea, nauseation. **nausea de ensintia** morning sickness.
nauseada *adj.* nauseated, queasy. **nauseada de auto** carsick. **nauseada de mar** seasick. **nauseada de vola** airsick.
nauseosa *adj.* nauseous, queasy.
nautilo *n.* nautilus (*mollusc: Nautilidae*).
Navara *n.* Navarre (*Spanish region*).
nave *n.* nave (*church*).
naveta *n.* shuttle; ferry, ferryboat. **naveta spasial** space shuttle.
naveti *vt.* shuttle, ferry.
navetor *n.* ferryman.
naviga *vt.* navigate. • *n.* navigation. **naviga par vela** *vt.* sail, go sailing. • *n.* sailing.

navigor *n.* navigator.
nazi *adj.* & *n.* Nazi.
nazisme *n.* Nazism.
nb *abbr.* (*nota bon*) NB, nota bene.
ne *n.* nay (*flute*).
neandertalan *adj.* & *n.* Neanderthal.
nebla *n.* fog. **nebla fumosa** smog. **nebla jelada** frozen fog, rime.
neblador *n.* mister, nebulizer.
nebleta *n.* mist, haze.
nebli *vi.* & *vt.* mist up, fog up, steam up; blur.
neblosa *adj.* nebulous, foggy, vague, fuzzy, bleary, hazy; blurry (*image, vision*).
Nebraska *n.* Nebraska (*US state*).
nebulosa *n.* nebula.
necator *n.* hookworm (*Necator*).
necatoriase *n.* hookworm, necatoriasis (*disease*).
necro- *pref.* necro- (*death*).
necrofilia *n.* necrophilia.
necrofilica *adj.* necrophiliac. • *n.* necrophiliac, necrophile.
necrofobia *n.* necrophobia.
necrofobica *adj.* necrophobic. • *n.* necrophobe.
necromansia *n.* necromancy (*divination*).
necromansiste *n.* necromancer.
necropoli *n.* necropolis.
necrose *n.* necrosis (*medical*).
necrosica *adj.* necrotic.
Nederland *n.* Netherlands, Holland.
nederlandes *adj.* & *n.* Dutch, Netherlandish.
nefrite *n.* nephritis (*medical*).
nefritica *adj.* nephritic.
nefro- *pref.* nephro- (*kidney*).
nega *vt.* negate, deny, repudiate, nullify, annul, rescind, overrule, countermand, disavow, disclaim. • *n.* negation, denial, repudiation, annulment, disavowal. **nega con testa** shake one's head.
negable *adj.* deniable.
negativa *adj.* negative. • *n.* negative (*photography*).
negativia *n.* negativity.
negativisme *n.* negativism.
negosia *vt.* negotiate; haggle, bargain. • *n.* negotiation.
negosior *n.* negotiator.
negra *adj.* & *n.* black. **Foresta Negra** Black Forest. **Mar Negra** Black Sea.
negri *vi.* & *vt.* blacken, char, scorch, singe.
negrisil *n.* mascara (*cosmetic*).
negroide *adj.* (*derogatory*) negroid.
nelumbo *n.* lotus (*plant*: *Nelumbo*).
nematodo *n.* roundworm, nematode (*Nematoda*).
nematomorfo *n.* nematomorph (*organism*: *Nematomorpha*).
nemerteo *n.* nemertean (*worm*: *Nemertea*).
neo- *pref.* neo- (*new*).
neoclasica *adj.* neoclassical.
neoclasicisme *n.* neoclassicism.
neoclasiciste *n.* neoclassicist.
neocolonial *adj.* neocolonial.
neocolonialisme *n.* neocolonialism.
neocolonialiste *adj.* & *n.* neocolonialist.
neodimio *n.* neodymium (*element*).
neolitica *adj.* & *n.* Neolithic.
neon *n.* neon.
neopagan *adj.* neopagan.
neoplasma *n.* neoplasm (*medical*).
neotenia *n.* neoteny (*biology*).
neotropical *adj.* neotropica.
neotropico *n.* neotropics.
Nepal *n.* Nepal.
nepali *adj.* & *n.* Nepali, Nepalese.
nepentes *n.* pitcher plant (*Nepenthes*).
nepeta *n.* catnip (*plant*: *Nepeta*).
nerval *adj.* nervous (*of the nerves*).
nervo *n.* nerve. **nervo otical** optic nerve. **nervo serebral** cerebral nerve. **nervo siatica** sciatic nerve.
nervosa *adj.* nervous, jumpy.
nervosia *n.* nervousness.
nesesa *vt.* need, require, lack; need to, have to, must (*physical or essential*); necessitate, entail; e.g. *el va nesesa un seja*; *me nesesa dormi*; *lo nesesa ce nos escuta*. • *n.* need (*state*). **nesesa adota** resort to, have recourse to.
nesesada *adj.* needed, required, necessary, indispensable, must-have, requisite, incumbent. • *adv.* necessarily. • *n.* necessity, need, requirement, must-have, must, prerequisite, wherewithal.
-nesia *n.suff.* -nesia (*islands*).
neta[1] *adj.* & *adv.* nett (US net) (*money*).
neta[2] *n.* granddaughter.
netar *n.* nectar.
netarina *n.* nectarine (*peach*: *Prunus persica*); sunbird (*bird*: *Nectariniidae*).
nete *n.* grandchild.
netisme *n.* nepotism.
neto *n.* grandson.
netsuce *n.* netsuke (*sculpture*).
netunio *n.* neptunium (*element*).
Netuno *n.* Neptune (*mythology, planet*).
neuraljia *n.* neuralgia. **neuraljia siatica** sciatic neuralgia, sciatica.
neuraljica *adj.* neuralgic.
neurastenia *n.* neurasthenia.
neurastenica *adj.* neurasthenic.
neurite *n.* neuritis (*medical*).
neuritica *adj.* neuritic.
neuro- *pref.* neuro- (*nerve*).
neurobiolojia *n.* neurobiology.
neurobiolojiste *n.* neurobiologist.
neurolojia *n.* neurology.

neurolojiste *n.* neurologist.
neuron *n.* neuron. **neuron de sensa** sensory neuron.
neuronal *adj.* neuronal, neural, neurological.
neuropatia *n.* neuropathy.
neuropatica *adj.* neuropathic.
neuropeptido *n.* neuropeptide.
neurose *n.* neurosis, psychoneurosis, hang-up.
neurosica *adj.* & *n.* neurotic.
neurosiensa *n.* neuroscience.
neurosiensiste *n.* neuroscientist.
neurosirurjia *n.* neurosurgery.
neurosirurjial *adj.* neurosurgical.
neurosirurjiste *n.* neurosurgeon.
neurotoxina *n.* neurotoxin.
neurotransmetador *n.* neurotransmitter.
neuton *n.* newton (*unit of force*).
neutra *adj.* neutral; neuter.
neutri *vi.* & *vt.* neutralize, neuter, spay.
neutria *n.* neutrality.
neutrino *n.* neutrino.
neutrofilia *n.* neutrophilia.
neutrofilica *adj.* neutrophilic. • *n.* neutrophile.
neutron *n.* neutron.
neutronal *adj.* neutronic.
neva *vi.* & *n.* snow. **neva dejelada** *v.* sleet. • *n.* sleet; slush. **neva fondeda** snowmelt.
Nevada *n.* Nevada (*US state*).
neveta *vi.* snow lightly, flurry. • *n.* snow shower, flurry, dusting.
Nevis *n.* Nevis.
nevisian *adj.* & *n.* Nevisian. See *San Kitts*.
nevo *n.* mole (*on skin*), birthmark, naevus (US nevus).
nevon *n.* snowstorm, whiteout, heavy snow, deep snow.
nevosa *adj.* snowy.
Newfoundland *n.* Newfoundland. **Newfoundland e Labrador** Newfoundland and Labrador (*Canadian province*).
niama *n.* yam (*plant, tuber: Dioscorea*).
niasina *n.* niacin, nicotinic acid.
nicab *n.* niqab (*veil*).
Nicaragua *n.* Nicaragua.
nicaraguan *adj.* & *n.* Nicaraguan.
nicel *n.* nickel.
niceli *vt.* nickel-plate.
nicelida *adj.* nickel-plated.
nicotina *n.* nicotine.
nictofilia *n.* nyctophilia.
nictofilica *adj.* nyctophilic. • *n.* nyctophile.
nidi *vt.* nest, build a nest (*for*). **nidi se** nestle, snuggle down, ensconce oneself.
nidida *adj.* snug, cosy (US cozy) (*person*).
nidin *adj.* snug, cosy (US cozy) (*place*).
nidinia *n.* snugness, cosiness (US coziness).
nido *n.* nest, roost, eyrie (US aerie); hive; den, lair, burrow; hideaway, hideout, retreat. **nido de abeas** beehive. **nido de formicas** ant nest.
nidor *n.* nestling (*bird*).
Nietzsche *n.* Nietzsche.
nihilisme *n.* nihilism.
nihiliste *adj.* nihilist, nihilistic. • *n.* nihilist.
nihonio *n.* nihonium (*element*).
Nijer *n.* Niger. **Rio Nijer** Niger River.
Nijeria *n.* Nigeria.
nijerian *adj.* & *n.* Nigerian (*of Nigeria*).
nijerien *adj.* & *n.* Nigerien (*of Niger*).
Nilo, Rio *n.* River Nile.
nilon *n.* nylon.
nilotica *adj.* Nilotic (*languages*).
nimbo *adj.* & *n.* nimbus (*cloud*).
nimfa *n.* nymph. **nimfa de acua** naiad. **nimfa de bosce** dryad. **nimfa de mar** nereid.
nimfea *n.* water lily (*Nymphaeaceae*).
nimfomania *n.* nymphomania.
nimfomanica *adj.* nymphomaniac. • *n.* nymphomaniac, nympho.
ninja *n.* ninja, shinobi (*ninjutsu expert*).
ninjutsu *n.* ninjutsu (*martial art*).
niobio *n.* niobium (*element*).
Nion *n.* Japan. **nion** *adj.* & *n.* Japanese. See *Japan*.
nirvana *n.* nirvana (*Buddhism*).
nistagmo *n.* nystagmus (*medical*).
nitrato *n.* nitrate. **nitrato de potasio** potassium nitrate, saltpetre (US saltpeter).
nitrica *adj.* nitric.
nitrito *n.* nitrite.
nitrogliserina *n.* nitroglycerine, nitro.
nitrojen *n.* nitrogen.
nitrojenosa *adj.* nitrogenous.
nitrosa *adj.* nitrous.
Niue [ˈnjue] *n.* Niue. **niue** *adj.* & *n.* Niuean.
nivel *n.* floor, storey (US story), deck (*ship*); level, tier (*scale, hierarchy*). **nivel de mar** sea level. **nivel de oio** eye level. **nivel de tera** ground floor, ground level. **nivel prima** first floor (*above ground level*).
niveleta *n.* landing.
nix *n.* niche (*alcove, ecological*).
no[1] *det.* no; e.g. *no person ia responde*; *el ia trova no problemes*. • *adv.* (*preverbal*) not; e.g. *me no ia comprende*; *la can no es en la jardin*. • *conj.* not, and not; e.g. *me vole esta, no acel*. • *interj.* no; (*question tag*) eh?, isn't it?, don't you?, haven't they? (*etc., typically expecting the answer yes*). **no esta e no acel** neither this nor that. **no plu ca** no more than, merely, simply, just. See *si*.
no[2] *n.* noh (*drama*).
Noa *n.* Noah.
nobelio *n.* nobelium (*element*).

nobil *adj.* noble, well-born, high-born. • *n.* noble, peer. **nobiles** nobles, nobility.
nobili *vi.* & *vt.* ennoble.
nobilia *n.* nobility.
noca *n.* knuckle, fetlock.
noda *vt.* knot, burl. • *n.* knot, node. **noda de capeles** topknot. **noda limfal** lymph node. **noda liscante** slipknot. **noda papilin** bow.
nodosa *adj.* knotty, gnarled, gnarly, nodose.
nodulal *adj.* nodular.
nodulo *n.* nodule.
noia *vt.* bore, tire, stultify. • *n.* boredom, tedium, ennui.
noiada *adj.* bored.
noiante *adj.* tiresome, boring, tedious, dull, humdrum, jejune.
-noide *adj.suff.* -noid (*mind*).
noior *n.* bore.
nom *n.* name, moniker, monicker; noun. **con nom falsa** pseudonymous. **nom ante sposi** maiden name. **nom de arcivo** folder name, directory name. **nom de fix** filename. **nom de gera** nom de guerre. **nom de usor** username. **nom falsa** alias, pseudonym, pen name, nom de plume. **nom familial** family name, surname. **nom individua** first name. **nom madral** matronym. **nom orijinal** original name, maiden name, birth name. **nom padral** patronym. **nom propre** proper noun. **nom teatral** stage name. **nomes** names, nomenclature. **par nom** nominal. **sin nom** nameless, anonymous.
nomada *adj.* nomadic, itinerant. • *n.* nomad, itinerant, traveller (US traveler).
nomadisme *n.* nomadism.
nometa *n.* nickname, sobriquet, soubriquet.
nomi *vt.* name, call, give a name to; appoint; e.g. *on nomi esta forma un exagon*. **nomi per** name for, name after.
nomida *adj.* named, called. **es nomida** be named, be called. **nomida X** named X, called X, known as X.
nomin *adj.* nounal, substantival.
nomina *vt.* nominate. • *n.* nomination.
nominada *n.* nominee.
nominativa *adj.* & *n.* nominative (*grammar*).
non- *pref.* un-, in-, non- (*added to adjectives and nouns: opposite characteristic, or absence of an action or state*); e.g. *nonjusta*; *noncrede*; *nonesesada*.—*Non-* simplifies to *no-* before *n*.
nonabitable *adj.* uninhabitable, unliveable (US unlivable).
nonabitada *adj.* uninhabited; unmanned.
nonabital *adj.* non-residential.
nonabitante *adj.* non-residential.
nonabitor *n.* non-resident.
nonabituada *adj.* unaccustomed, unused.
nonabrida *adj.* unopened.
nonacaso *adj.* non-random, deterministic.
nonacompaniada *adj.* unaccompanied.
nonacorda *n.* incongruity; incompatibility.
nonacordante *adj.* non-consenting; intransigent; incongruent, incongruous, incompatible.
nonaderente *adj.* non-adhesive, non-stick.
nonafetable *adj.* insusceptible.
nonagia *n.* bluntness, dullness.
nonagon *adj.* nonagonal, enneagonal (*nine-sided*). • *n.* nonagon, enneagon.
nonagu [nona'gu] *adj.* blunt, dull; obtuse (*angle*).
nonaidosa *adj.* unhelpful.
nonairobial *adj.* anaerobic.
nonairobio *n.* anaerobe (*organism*).
nonajitable *adj.* phlegmatic, placid, impassive, imperturbable, stolid, unflappable.
nonajustable *adj.* non-adjustable, unadaptable, untunable, unconfigurable, inflexible.
nonajustada *adj.* unadapted, unadjusted, untuned.
nonalcolosa *adj.* non-alcoholic.
nonalfabetisme *n.* illiteracy.
nonalfabetiste *adj.* illiterate, preliterate.
nonalienable *adj.* inalienable.
nonalterable *adj.* inalterable, unmodifiable, uncustomizable, iron-clad.
nonalterada *adj.* unaltered, unmodified.
nonamable *adj.* unloveable (US unlovable), unlikeable (US unlikable).
nonambigua *adj.* unambiguous, unequivocal.
nonamin *adj.* unfriendly, cold, aloof, distant, standoffish, forbidding.
nonanimada *adj.* inanimate.
nonarada *adj.* untold.
nonarmonia *n.* disharmony; incompatibility.
nonarmoniosa *adj.* inharmonious, incompatible, incongruous.
nonasecurada *adj.* uninsured.
nonasedable *adj.* inaccessible, unapproachable.
nonasentuada *adj.* unstressed, atonic.
nonasetable *adj.* unacceptable, invalid, inadmissible. • *n.* no-no.
nonasorbente *adj.* non-absorbent.
nonaspirante *adj.* unambitious.
nonastrata *adj.* figurative (*art*).
nonatacable *adj.* invulnerable, unassailable.
nonatenable *adj.* unreachable, unattainable, unachievable.
nonatendeda *adj.* unattended, untended.
nonatendente *adj.* careless, negligent, imprudent, heedless, absent-minded, inattentive, remiss, slapdash, slipshod.

nonativa[1] *adj.* inactive, languorous, quiescent, dormant.
nonativa[2] *adj.* non-native, adventitious.
nonativia *n.* inactivity, inaction, languor, quiescence.
nonatural *adj.* unnatural, preternatural, otherworldly, unworldly.
nonautentica *adj.* false, fake, faux, ersatz, substitute.
nonavenosa *adj.* uneventful.
nonbevor *n.* non-drinker. **nonbevor de alcol** non-drinker of alcohol, teetotaller (US teetotaler).
nonbinaria *adj.* non-binary; multigender. • *n.* multigender person.
nonblancida *adj.* unbleached.
nonbonvenida *adj.* unwelcome.
nonbonveninte *adj.* unwelcoming, inhospitable.
noncalculable *adj.* incalculable.
noncambiante *adj.* unchanging, changeless, timeless.
noncanselable *adj.* irrevocable, unerasable, indelible.
noncanserosa *adj.* non-cancerous, benign.
noncapas *adj.* unable, incapable, powerless, incompetent, inept, amateurish, unprofessional, hopeless, unqualified, unversed.
noncapasia *n.* inability, incompetence.
noncauta *adj.* impulsive, foolhardy, rash, heedless, hare-brained.
noncautia *n.* impulsiveness, temerity.
noncaxer *adj.* non-kosher.
nonclar *adj.* unclear.
noncoere *n.* incoherence, inconsistency, irregularity.
noncoerente *adj.* incoherent, inconsistent, irregular, erratic, haywire, irrational.
noncolorida *adj.* uncoloured (US uncolored).
noncomable *adj.* inedible.
noncombator *n.* non-combatant.
noncomfortosa *adj.* uncomfortable.
noncompatiosa *adj.* not compassionate, inhumane, unkind, inconsiderate, unsympathetic, hard-hearted, cold-hearted.
noncompleta *adj.* incomplete.
noncompletia *n.* incompleteness.
noncompletida *adj.* uncompleted.
noncomposada *adj.* uncompounded, simplex.
noncomprendable *adj.* unintelligible, incomprehensible, inscrutable, unfathomable.
noncomprendablia *n.* unintelligibility, incomprehensibility.
noncomprende *n.* incomprehension.
noncomun *adj.* uncommon, unusual, infrequent, eccentric, offbeat; original (*idea*). • *adv.* uncommonly, unusually.
noncomunia *n.* unusualness, eccentricity.
nonconcistable *adj.* unconquerable, unbeatable, indomitable.
nonconcluinte *adj.* inconclusive.
nonconfirmada *adj.* unconfirmed, uncorroborated, unsubstantiated.
nonconforma *n.* non-conformity
nonconfusable *adj.* unconfusable, unmistakable.
nonconosable *adj.* unknowable.
nonconoseda *adj.* unknown, unfamiliar. • *n.* stranger.
nonconsensa *adj.* unconscious, unaware, incognizant, insensible.
nonconsensia *n.* unconsciousness, oblivion.
nonconsernada *adj.* unconcerned, blithe, carefree.
nonconsetable *adj.* inconceivable.
nonconsolable *adj.* inconsolable.
nonconstante *adj.* inconstant, fickle, flighty.
nonconstitual *adj.* unconstitutional.
nonconsumable *adj.* inexhaustible.
noncontable *adj.* uncountable, innumerable.
noncontaminada *adj.* uncontaminated, unpolluted.
noncontatante *adj.* discontiguous.
nonconteninte *adj.* incontinent.
noncontenintia *n.* incontinence.
noncontente *adj.* discontented, discontent, malcontent. • *n.* malcontent.
noncontentia *n.* discontent.
noncontrolable *adj.* uncontrollable, intractable; berserk, haywire, runaway, out of control.
noncontrolada *adj.* uncontrolled.
nonconveni *n.* unsuitability; incompatibility.
nonconveninte *adj.* unsuitable, unsuited, incongruous, incompatible; inappropriate, tasteless, unbecoming, unbefitting, unfit, unseemly.
nonconvinsable *adj.* unpersuadable, intransigent.
nonconvinseda *adj.* unconvinced, unswayed.
nonconvinsente *adj.* unconvincing, far-fetched, implausible.
noncorajosa *adj.* faint-hearted, timid.
noncoresponde *vi.* & *n.* mismatch.
noncoreta *adj.* incorrect, wrong; inappropriate, amiss.
noncoretable *adj.* uncorrectable, incorrigible.
noncoretia *n.* incorrectness, wrongness.
noncorodente *adj.* non-corrosive, rustproof.

noncortes *adj.* discourteous, impolite, rude, impudent, cheeky, irreverent, impertinent, sassy, tactless, gruff, surly, mouthy, overfamiliar, presumptuous, unmannerly.
noncortesia *n.* impoliteness, rudeness, impudence, cheek, cheekiness, nerve, irreverence, impertinence, sass.
noncosia *n.* nothingness.
noncostumal *adj.* uncustomary.
noncovreda *adj.* uncovered, not covered. **(retira) noncovreda** overdraft.
noncredable *adj.* unbelievable, incredible; incredibly good, fabulous, fantastic. • *adv.* unbelievably, incredibly.
noncredablia *n.* incredibility.
noncrede *n.* disbelief, incredulity.
noncredente *adj.* disbelieving, incredulous.
noncredor *n.* non-believer, infidel.
noncromatica *adj.* achromatic.
noncualinte *adj.* ineligible.
noncuieta *adj.* uneasy.
nonculpable *adj.* blameless, innocent (*of crime*), not guilty.
nonculpablia *n.* blamelessness, innocence.
noncultivada *adj.* uncultivated, fallow.
noncurante *adj.* uncaring, indifferent, blasé.
noncurantia *n.* indifference.
nondecorada *adj.* undecorated, blank, plain.
nondedicada *adj.* undedicated, non-committal.
nondefendable *adj.* indefensible, untenable.
nondefinida *adj.* undefined, indefinite.
nondemocrata *adj.* undemocratic.
nondemostrada *adj.* unproven, unconfirmed.
nondependente *adj.* not dependent, self-sufficient, standalone; independent, autonomous.
nondescapasida *adj.* unimpaired.
nondescrivable *adj.* indescribable.
nondesideda *adj.* undecided.
nondesifrable *adj.* indecipherable.
nondesirada *adj.* undesired, undesirable, unwanted.
nondestruable *adj.* indestructible.
nondeterminada *adj.* indeterminate.
nondeterministe *adj.* non-deterministic. • *n.* non-determinist.
nondetetada *adj.* undetected.
nondevelopada *adj.* undeveloped.
nondeviante *adj.* undeviating, unswerving.
nondiagnoseda *adj.* undiagnosed.
nondijestable *adj.* indigestible.
nondinia *n.* indignity.
nondiniosa *adj.* undignified.
nondireta *adj.* indirect, roundabout, circuitous, vicarious.
nondirijeda *adj.* undirected, unaimed, aimless.
nondiscreta *adj.* indiscreet. • *n.* indiscreet person, bigmouth.
nondiseda *adj.* unsaid, unspoken, unstated, unvoiced.
nondisolvable *adj.* undissolvable, insoluble.
nondisponable *adj.* unavailable.
nondisponablia *n.* unavailability.
nondisputable *adj.* indisputable, incontrovertible, unimpeachable.
nondisputada *adj.* undisputed.
nondistinguinte *adj.* indiscriminate, undifferentiated.
nondisturbada *adj.* undisturbed, unfazed.
nondividable *adj.* indivisible.
nondivideda *adj.* undivided.
nondocumentida *adj.* undocumented.
nonduable *adj.* odd (*number*).
nondulsida *adj.* unsweetened.
nondutable *adj.* undoubtable, indubitable, unequivocal, unquestionable.
nondutada *adj.* undoubted, unqualified.
nonecuilibra *n.* imbalance.
noneducada *adj.* uneducated, unschooled, uncultured, ignorant, unskilled, menial.
nonegable *adj.* undeniable.
nonegada *adj.* undenied.
nonegal *adj.* unequal, non-equivalent.
nonegalia *n.* inequality, disparity, discrepancy.
nonegosa *adj.* unselfish.
nonelastica *adj.* inelastic.
nonelasticia *n.* inelasticity.
nonelejable *adj.* unelectable, ineligible.
nonemosiada *adj.* unmoved.
nonemosiosa *adj.* unemotional, unfeeling, cold.
nonempatica *adj.* non-empathic, hard-hearted.
nonemplea *n.* unemployment.
nonempleada *adj.* unemployed, jobless.
nonenforsable *adj.* unenforceable.
nonenganante *adj.* guileless, artless.
nonenscrivor *n.* non-subscriber.
nonerante *adj.* inerrant, infallible, unerring.
nonesata *adj.* inexact, imprecise, inaccurate. • *adv.* not exactly, not quite.
nonesatia *n.* inaccuracy.
nonescusable *adj.* inexcusable.
nonesededa *adj.* unsurpassed.
nonesensal *adj.* non-essential, extrinsic.
nonesesada *adj.* unnecessary, undue, dispensable.
nonesiste *n.* non-existence.
nonesistente *adj.* non-existent.
nonesitante *adj.* unhesitating, unfaltering, unflinching.
nonesperia *n.* inexperience.

nonesperta *adj.* inexpert.
nonespetada *adj.* unexpected, unanticipated, unplanned, quirky.
nonespetante *adj.* not expecting, unwitting.
nonesplicable *adj.* unexplainable, inexplicable.
nonesplotada *adj.* unexploited, untapped.
nonespresable *adj.* unspeakable, ineffable.
nonespresosa *adj.* unexpressive, undemonstrative, reticent, taciturn, deadpan.
nonestimable *adj.* inestimable, invaluable, priceless.
nonestrable *adj.* inextricable.
nonestrema *adj.* non-extreme, mild, moderate.
nonetical *adj.* unethical.
noneticetida *adj.* unlabelled (US unlabeled).
noneuclidal *adj.* non-Euclidean.
nonevadable *adj.* inescapable.
nonevitable *adj.* inevitable, unavoidable, inexorable.
nonfatigable *adj.* indefatigable, tireless.
nonfavorable *adj.* unfavourable (US unfavorable).
nonfavoreda *n.* underdog.
nonfavorente *adj.* unflattering (*garment*).
nonfelis *adj.* unhappy, cheerless.
nonfelisia *n.* unhappiness, cheerlessness.
nonferable *adj.* invulnerable.
nonferida *adj.* unhurt, unharmed, uninjured, unscathed.
nonfermentada *adj.* unleavened.
nonfertil *adj.* infertile, sterile, barren.
nonfertilia *n.* infertility.
nonfida *n.* unfaithfulness, disloyalty.
nonfidable *adj.* untrustworthy, unreliable, undependable, irresponsible, erratic, feckless.
nonfidosa *adj.* unfaithful, disloyal.
nonfiltrida *adj.* unfiltered.
nonfininte *adj.* unending, endless, interminable.
nonfinitiva *adj.* non-finite.
nonfinjosa *adj.* unpretentious, naïve.
nonfisada *adj.* unfixed, loose.
nonflamable *adj.* non-flammable.
nonfluente *adj.* non-fluent, faltering, broken, halting (*speech*).
nonflutuante *adj.* unremittent.
nonfocada *adj.* unfocused, out of focus.
nonformal *adj.* informal.
nonformalia *n.* informality.
nonforte *adj.* insubstantial.
nonfortunosa *adj.* unlucky, unfortunate, inauspicious, hapless, lamentable, poor, underprivileged. • *n.* underdog.
nonfrecuente *adj.* infrequent, occasional.
nonfrenida *adj.* unrestrained, rampant.
nonfresca *adj.* stale.
nonfumor *n.* non-smoker.
nonfurtiva *adj.* open, blatant, flagrant, overt.
nongovernable *adj.* ungovernable.
nongradida *adj.* ungraded, unranked, unrated.
nongrandida *adj.* unenlarged, unmagnified.
nongrasiada *adj.* thankless (*task*).
nongrasiosa *adj.* ungrateful, thankless (*person*). • *n.* ingrate.
nongrave *adj.* non-virulent.
nongusta *n.* dislike.
nonidrosa *adj.* anhydrous.
nonijenial *adj.* unsanitary.
nonimajinable *adj.* unimaginable, inconceivable, unfathomable.
nonimitable *adj.* inimitable.
nonimpedida *adj.* unimpeded, unhindered, unobstructed, undeterred.
nonimportante *adj.* unimportant, insignificant, trite, trivial, inconsequential.
nonimpostable *adj.* untaxable.
nonimpresada *adj.* unimpressed, blasé, indifferent.
nonindustrial *adj.* non-industrial.
noninformada *adj.* uninformed.
noninstruable *adj.* untrainable, ineducable.
noninstruida *adj.* untrained, unskilled.
nonintelijente *adj.* unintelligent, obtuse.
nonintendeda *adj.* unintended, inadvertent, unplanned, collateral.
noninteresante *adj.* uninteresting.
nonintuable *adj.* unintuitable, unintuitive (*design*).
nonintuosa *adj.* unintuitive (*person*).
noninvestigada *adj.* uninvestigated, unscreened.
noninvitante *adj.* uninviting, unappetizing.
nonjusta *adj.* unjust, unfair.
nonjustable *adj.* unjustifiable.
nonjustia *n.* injustice, inequity.
nonlegal *adj.* illegal, illicit, unlawful, illegitimate, invalid.
nonlegalia *n.* illegality, illegitimacy.
nonlejable *n.* unreadable, illegible.
nonlejablia *n.* unreadableness, illegibility.
nonleteral *adj.* non-literal, figurative.
nonliada *adj.* unconnected, disjointed.
nonlibre *adj.* unfree, restricted, captive.
nonlibria *n.* captivity.
nonlimitada *adj.* unlimited, infinite, boundless, unbounded, countless, innumerable.
nonlimpa *adj.* unclean.
nonlinial *adj.* non-linear.
nonliscosa *adj.* non-slip.
nonlisensada *adj.* unlicensed.
nonlistada *adj.* unlisted.
nonlodada *adj.* unpraised, unsung.

nonlodante *adj.* unflattering.
nonlojical *adj.* illogical.
nonlojicalia *n.* illogicality.
nonluminada *adj.* unilluminated; unenlightened, benighted.
nonmalida *adj.* unspoiled, uncorrupted, unsullied.
nonmanejable *adj.* unmanageable.
nonmanxada *adj.* unmarked, unblemished, unsullied, untainted, immaculate, pristine.
nonmapada *adj.* unmapped, uncharted.
nonmarinor *n.* non-sailor, landlubber.
nonmatante *adj.* non-fatal.
nonmaterial *adj.* immaterial, insubstantial, intangible.
nonmatur *adj.* immature, unripe, callow.
nonmaturia *n.* immaturity.
nonmedisinida *adj.* unmedicated.
nonmeritada *adj.* undeserved, unmerited, unwarranted, unjustified, undue.
nonmeritante *adj.* unworthy.
nonmesurable *adj.* immeasurable.
nonmesurada *adj.* unmeasured.
nonmetal *adj.* & *n.* non-metal.
nonmetral *adj.* non-metric, imperial.
nonmilitar *adj.* & *n.* civilian.
nonmoderada *adj.* immoderate, intemperate.
nonmodesta *adj.* immodest.
nonmodosa *adj.* unfashionable, unstylish, dowdy, frumpy.
nonmoral *adj.* immoral, unprincipled, unprofessional, unscrupulous.
nonmoralia *n.* immorality, iniquity.
nonmorinte *adj.* undying.
nonmortal *adj.* immortal, imperishable, non-perishable.
nonmortali *vi.* & *vt.* immortalize.
nonmortalia *n.* immortality.
nonmostrada *adj.* unshown, unscreened.
nonmovable *adj.* immovable, immobile.
nonmovente *adj.* motionless, unmoving, stationary, sessile, immobile.
nonmundal *adj.* unworldly.
nonmutable *adj.* immutable.
nonmutablia *n.* immutability.
nonobedinte *adj.* uncompliant.
nonoblidable *adj.* unforgettable.
nonobligada *adj.* unobligated, unbeholden.
nonobligante *adj.* optional, voluntary, not required.
nonocupada *adj.* unoccupied.
nonofendente *adj.* inoffensive; innocent (*joke*).
nonofisial *adj.* unofficial.
nonoiable *adj.* inaudible.
nonoiada *adj.* unheard.
nonolable *adj.* unsmellable, odourless (US odorless).
nonomida *adj.* unnamed, nameless.
nononesta *adj.* dishonest, shady, dodgy.
nononestia *n.* dishonesty.
nonoperable *adj.* inoperable.
nonoportun *adj.* inopportune, inconvenient, untimely.
nonoportunia *n.* inconvenience, hassle.
nonoposada *adj.* unopposed.
nonordinada *adj.* irregular, out of order, disorganized, unsorted, untucked.
nonorganica *adj.* inorganic.
nonorijinal *adj.* unoriginal, banal, trite.
nonormal *adj.* abnormal, aberrant, odd, strange, irregular. • *n.* abnormality, aberration, irregularity.
nonormalia *n.* abnormality (*state*).
nonorminte *adj.* non-normative.
nonortodox *adj.* unorthodox, unconventional. • *n.* maverick.
nonoscurida *adj.* unobscured.
nonosidinte *adj.* rustproof, stainless.
nonosiva *adj.* benign, non-toxic, harmless, innocuous.
nonotada *adj.* unnoted, unnoticed. • *n.* oversight.
nonotenable *adj.* unavailable, unobtainable.
nonpaiada *adj.* unpaid.
nonpalinte *adj.* colourfast (US colorfast).
nonpalpable *adj.* impalpable, intangible.
nonparable *adj.* unstoppable.
nonpardona *n.* grudge, resentment.
nonpardonable *adj.* inexcusable, unforgivable.
nonpardonosa *adj.* unmerciful.
nonparlada *adj.* unspoken; non-verbal.
nonparolal *adj.* non-verbal.
nonpartisan *adj.* non-partisan, impartial.
nonpasable *adj.* implacable.
nonpasiente *adj.* impatient.
nonpasientia *n.* impatience.
nonpasionosa *adj.* passionless, dispassionate.
nonpasteurida *adj.* unpasteurized.
nonpatojen *adj.* non-pathogenic.
nonpausante *adj.* unpausing, non-stop.
nonpaveda *adj.* unpaved.
nonpenetrable *adj.* impenetrable, impregnable.
nonpensable *adj.* unthinkable.
nonperdente *adj.* lossless (*compression*).
nonperfeta *adj.* imperfect, defective. • *n.* imperfection, defect, flaw.
nonperforada *adj.* unperforated, imperforate.
nonperiodal *adj.* irregular, sporadic, intermittent, infrequent.
nonpermanente *adj.* impermanent, short-term.
nonpermanentia *n.* impermanence.

nonpermeable *adj.* impermeable, impervious, hermetic, waterproof, airtight.
nonpermeteda *adj.* disallowed, forbidden, unauthorized. • *n.* no-no.
nonperosa *adj.* efficient, cost-effective. **nonperosa de enerjia** energy-efficient.
nonperosia *n.* efficiency, performance, cost-effectiveness.
nonpersepable *adj.* imperceptible, unnoticeable.
nonpersonal *adj.* impersonal.
nonpertine *n.* irrelevance.
nonpertinente *adj.* irrelevant, invalid, inapplicable, extraneous.
nonpintida *adj.* unpainted.
nonplana *adj.* uneven, wobbly, bobbly.
nonplasente *adj.* unpleasant, disagreeable.
nonplaserosa *adj.* unpleasurable, unenjoyable.
nonpopular *adj.* unpopular.
nonporosa *adj.* non-porous.
nonposible *adj.* impossible. • *n.* impossibility (*something impossible*).
nonposiblia *n.* impossibility (*quality*).
nonpotente *adj.* unable, incapable, impotent.
nonpotentia *n.* impotence.
nonpratical *adj.* impractical, impracticable, inconvenient, unfeasible, infeasible.
nonpredisable *adj.* unpredictable.
nonprejudosa *adj.* unprejudiced, unbiased.
nonpreparada *adj.* unprepared, impromptu, extemporary, extemporaneous, unqualified.
nonprevenable *adj.* unpreventable.
nonprevidable *adj.* unforeseeable.
nonprevideda *adj.* unforeseen, unexpected.
nonprimable *adj.* unprintable.
nonprobable *adj.* improbable, unlikely. • *n.* improbability, long shot (*something unlikely*).
nonprobablia *n.* improbability (*quality*).
nonprobada *adj.* untried, untested; unscreened.
nonproduosa *adj.* unproductive, ineffective, ineffectual, inefficacious.
nonproduosia *n.* unproductiveness, ineffectiveness, ineffectuality, inefficacy.
nonprofesal *adj.* unprofessional. • *n.* nonprofessional, layman, layperson.
nonprofitante *adj.* non-profit.
nonprofitosa *adj.* unprofitable.
nonprofonda *adj.* shallow.
nonprogresa *n.* stalemate, deadlock, standoff, impasse, logjam.
nonpronunsiable *adj.* unpronounceable.
nonproportial *adj.* disproportionate, incommensurate.
nonprotejeda *adj.* unprotected.
nonpublicida *adj.* unpublished.
nonpunida *adj.* unpunished.
nonpur *adj.* impure, unclean.
nonpuria *n.* impurity.
nonputrable *adj.* imperishable, non-perishable.
nonramal *adj.* non-denominational, ecumenical.
nonrasada *adj.* unshaven, unshorn.
nonraspante *adj.* non-abrasive.
nonrazonada *adj.* irrational (*argument*), unjustified.
nonrazonante *adj.* irrational (*person*), unreasonable.
nonreal *adj.* unreal, irreal, illusory.
nonrealable *adj.* unfeasible, infeasible, unworkable, unviable, inviable.
nonrecambiable *adj.* irreplaceable.
nonreconosable *adj.* unrecognizable.
nonreduable *adj.* irreducible.
nonreenviable *adj.* non-returnable, unreturnable.
nonrefinada *adj.* unrefined.
nonrefletante *adj.* non-reflective.
nonreformida *adj.* unreformed.
nonrefutable *adj.* irrefutable.
nonreganiable *adj.* irrecoverable.
nonregardada *adj.* unregarded.
nonregulada *adj.* unregulated, irregular.
nonrelatada *adj.* unrelated.
nonrelijiosa *adj.* non-religious, lay, secular, ungodly. • *n.* layman, layperson. **nonrelijiosas** laymen, laypeople, laity.
nonremediable *adj.* irremediable, uncurable, irrecoverable.
nonremetable *adj.* irredeemable.
nonrenovable *adj.* non-renewable.
nonreparable *adj.* irreparable, unfixable.
nonreparada *adj.* in disrepair, dilapidated.
nonrepentinte *adj.* unrepentant, unapologetic.
nonreportada *adj.* unreported.
nonreprendable *adj.* irretrievable.
nonrepresable *adj.* irrepressible.
nonrepresentante *adj.* unrepresentative.
nonresetante *adj.* unreceptive.
nonresistable *adj.* irresistible, compelling, overwhelming.
nonrespondente *adj.* unresponsive.
nonrestrinjeda *adj.* unrestrained, unrestricted, unconfined, unimpeded, uninhibited, unreserved, wild, frenetic.
nonrevelada *adj.* unrevealed, undisclosed; unturned (*cards*).
nonreversable *adj.* irreversible.
nonritual *adj.* unceremonious.
nonromantica *adj.* non-romantic, aromantic.
nonrompable *adj.* unbreakable, shatterproof.
nonrompeda *adj.* unbroken.

nonsabable *adj.* unknowable.
nonsabe *n.* ignorance, lack of knowledge.
nonsabeda *adj.* & *n.* unknown. **nonsabeda par** unknown by, unbeknown to.
nonsabosa *adj.* ignorant, unknowing, benighted.
nonsaisonal *adj.* unseasonable.
nonsaja *adj.* unwise.
nonsalida *adj.* unsalted.
nonsana *adj.* unhealthy.
nonsanta *adj.* unholy, profane.
nonsasia *vt.* dissatisfy. • *n.* dissatisfaction.
nonsasiable *adj.* insatiable, voracious.
nonsasiada *adj.* unsatisfied, dissatisfied, unsatiated.
nonsasiante *adj.* unsatisfying, unsatisfactory, unrewarding.
nonsaturada *adj.* unsaturated.
nonscrivable *adj.* read-only.
nonscriveda *adj.* unwritten, oral.
nonsecur *adj.* insecure, unsafe, loose.
nonsecuria *n.* insecurity.
nonsecurida *adj.* unsecured, unlocked, untethered.
nonsedente *adj.* unyielding, unrelenting, relentless, unremitting, tenacious, flinty.
nonsegue *n.* non sequitur; non-observance, breach. **nonsegue de acorda** breach of contract. **nonsegue sintatical** anacoluthon.
nonsenesente *adj.* never-ageing (US neveraging), ageless, timeless.
nonsensable *adj.* insensible.
nonsensante *adj.* unsensing, insensate.
nonsensosa *adj.* insensitive, numb, obtuse.
nonsensosia *n.* insensitivity, numbness.
nonsentosa *adj.* unfeeling, unsentimental.
nonsentral *adj.* non-central, off-centre (US off-center).
nonseparable *adj.* inseparable.
nonseparada *adj.* indiscrete.
nonsepsica *adj.* aseptic.
nonseria *adj.* frivolous.
nonserta *adj.* uncertain, insecure, unconfident, unassertive, unsure, iffy, moot, unsure.
nonsertida *adj.* unchecked, unverified, unconfirmed.
nonsesal *adj.* asexual, non-sexual. • *n.* asexual person, non-sexual person.
nonsesante *adj.* unceasing, incessant, continual, non-stop.
nonsiclin *adj.* acyclic.
nonsiensal *adj.* unscientific.
nonsimetre *adj.* asymmetrical, skew.
nonsimetri *vi.* & *vt.* skew.
nonsimetria *n.* asymmetry.
nonsimil *adj.* unlike, unalike, dissimilar.
nonsincrona *adj.* asynchronous, out of sync.
nonsindicatal *adj.* non-union.
nonsinsera *adj.* insincere, disingenuous, glib.
nonsinseria *n.* insincerity.
nonsintomal *adj.* asymptomatic.
nonsirculo *adj.* non-circular, eccentric (*orbit*).
nonsistemal *adj.* unsystemic.
nonsistemosa *adj.* unsystematic, irregular.
nonsivilida *adj.* uncivilized, primitive, savage.
nonsofisticada *adj.* unsophisticated, lowbrow, gauche.
nonsolvable *adj.* unsolvable, insoluble.
nonsosial *adj.* unsocial, unsociable, asocial, detached, distant, remote, cold, aloof, introverted.
nonsperde *n.* non-proliferation.
nonspesialida *adj.* unspecialized.
nonspisida *adj.* unseasoned.
nonsposia *n.* spinsterhood, bachelorhood.
nonsposida *adj.* unmarried, unwed, single. • *n.* bachelor, spinster.
nonstable *adj.* unstable, unfixed, shifting.
nonstablia *n.* instability.
nonsteril *adj.* unsterile.
nonstimulante *adj.* unexciting.
nonstruturida *adj.* unstructured, structureless, freeform.
nonsufisi *n.* insufficiency, inadequacy, deficiency, lack, want, dearth, scarcity.
nonsufisinte *adj.* insufficient, inadequate, deficient, lacking, wanting, scant; meagre (US meager), sparse, paltry; scanty, skimpy.
nonsuportable *adj.* unsupportable.
nonsuportada *adj.* unsupported.
nonsuprapasada *adj.* unsurpassed.
nonsupravideda *adj.* unsupervised.
nonsurprendeda *adj.* unsurprised.
nonsusedosa *adj.* unsuccessful.
nonsusida *adj.* undirtied, unsoiled, unsullied.
nonsuspetada *adj.* unsuspected.
nonsuspetante *adj.* unsuspecting.
nonsustable *adj.* unsustainable.
nonsutrable *adj.* unremovable, irremovable, indelible.
nontatosa *adj.* tactless, indelicate.
nontemal *adj.* off-topic.
nontemosa *adj.* intrepid, fearless.
nontemperada *adj.* intemperate.
nonteni *n.* non-attachment.
nonteral *adj.* unearthly.
nontipal *adj.* untypical, atypical, uncharacteristic.
nontocable *adj.* untouchable, intangible.
nontocada *adj.* untouched.
nontolera *n.* bigotry, intolerance.
nontolerable *adj.* unbearable, intolerable, insufferable.

nontolerante *adj.* intolerant, bigoted.
nontoleror *n.* bigot.
nontonal *adj.* atonal.
nontradisional *adj.* non-traditional, untraditional.
nontraduable *adj.* untranslatable.
nontraduida *adj.* untranslated.
nontransitiva *adj.* intransitive.
nontransparente *adj.* untransparent.
nontrasable *adj.* untraceable.
nontratable *adj.* untreatable, intractable.
nonumana *adj.* inhuman, non-human.
nonumerable *adj.* innumerable, umpteenth.
nonusa *n.* disuse, desuetude.
nonusable *adj.* unusable, useless.
nonusada *adj.* unused, out of use.
nonusosa *adj.* useless, idle, feckless.
nonusual *adj.* unusual, odd, different, unconventional, uncharacteristic, uncustomary. • *adv.* unusually.
nonvalida *adj.* invalid, spurious.
nonvantaje *n.* disadvantage, handicap (*including golf*), demerit, drawback. **con nonvantaje** disadvantaged, handicapped.
nonvariable *adj.* invariable.
nonvariablia *n.* invariability.
nonvasilante *adj.* resolute, decisive.
nonvasinida *adj.* unvaccinated.
nonvenenosa *adj.* non-toxic, non-poisonous, atoxic.
nonvera *n.* untrue thing, untruth.
nonveria *n.* untruth, untrueness.
nonvertebrato *adj.* invertebrate, spineless. • *n.* invertebrate.
nonvidable *adj.* invisible.
nonvidablia *n.* invisibility.
nonvideda *adj.* unseen, unwitnessed.
nonvinsable *adj.* invincible, insurmountable, insuperable.
nonvinseda *adj.* unbeaten, undefeated.
nonviolable *adj.* inviolable, sacrosanct.
nonviolente *adj.* non-violent.
nonvolatil *adj.* non-volatile.
nonvolente *adj.* unwilling, reluctant, indisposed. **volente o nonvolente** willy-nilly, like it or not.
nonxercada *adj.* unsolicited.
nonzelosa *adj.* unenthusiastic, cool.
no-oblida-me *n.* forget-me-not (*plant*: *Myosotis*).
norde *adj.* north, northern, upstate. • *n.* north. **a norde** northward, northwards. **a norde de** to the north of. **Mar Norde** North Sea. **norde-este** *adj.* northeast, northeasterly. • *n.* northeast. **norde-norde-este** *adj.* & *n.* north-northeast. **norde-norde-ueste** *adj.* & *n.* north-northwest. **norde-sentral** *adj.* central north. **norde-ueste** *adj.* northwest, northwesterly. • *n.* northwest.
nordica *adj.* Norse.
norepinefrina *n.* norepinephrine, noradrenaline (*hormone*).
nori *n.* nori, laver, slake (*seaweed*).
Noria *n.* Norway.
norma *n.* norm, standard; par (*golf*). **du su la norma** eagle (*two below par*). **normas** code, ethos. **normas de condui** code of behaviour (US behavior). **normas moral** moral code, ethics. **tre su la norma** albatross (*three below par*). **un su la norma** birdie (*one below par*). **un supra la norma** bogey (*one above par*).
normal *adj.* normal, ordinary, usual, standard, normative, conventional, regular. • *adv.* normally, ordinarily, usually.
normali *vi.* & *vt.* normalize, institutionalize, canonicalize. • *n.* normalization, institutionalization, canonicalization.
normalia *n.* normality, normalcy, regularity.
normande *adj.* & *n.* Norman.
Normandia *n.* Normandy.
normi *vt.* standardize. • *n.* standardization.
norminte *adj.* standardizing, normative.
normoblasto *n.* normoblast (*blood cell*).
norsce *adj.* Norwegian. **Mar Norsce** Norwegian Sea.
nos *pron.* we, us.
nosa *det.* our. **la nosa** ours.
nosebo *adj.* & *n.* nocebo (*medical*).
nosiva *adj.* noxious, toxic, virulent, harmful, pernicious, prejudicial, deleterious, detrimental.
nosolojia *n.* nosology.
nosolojiste *n.* nosologist.
nostaljia *n.* nostalgia.
nostaljial *adj.* nostalgic.
nota *vt.* note, make a note of; minute; mention. • *n.* note, annotation; memorandum, memo, message, short letter; notice (*displayed information*); note (*music*). **nota basa** footnote. **nota bon** by the way, nota bene. **nota codal** endnote. **nota de reseta** receipt. **nota de validi** certificate. **notas** notes; minutes (*of meeting*).
notable *adj.* notable, mentionable, noticeable, remarkable, considerable. • *adv.* notably, noticeably, remarkably, considerably.
notada *adj.* noted. **ja notada** already mentioned, aforementioned.
notario *n.* notary, scrivener, solicitor's clerk.
note *n.* night. **a note** at night, in the night, overnight. **note des-du** Twelfth Night. **note tarda** late night. **per la note** for the

night. **tra la note** throughout the night, overnight.
noti *vi.* become night. • *n.* nightfall, dusk.
notocorda *n.* notochord (*anatomy*).
notor *n.* noter, notetaker, secretary, minute taker.
noturna *adj.* nocturnal. • *n.* nocturne (*art, music*).
nova[1] *adj.* new, novel, recent. • *adv.* newly, freshly. **bon novas** good news, good tidings. **la plu nova** newest, latest. **mal novas** bad news, bad tidings. **novas** news, tidings, current events.
nova[2] *n.* nova (*star*).
nove *det.* nine. • *adj.* ninth (*ordinal*).
novedes *det.* ninety. • *adj.* ninetieth (*ordinal*).
novedesi *n.* ninetieth (*fraction*).
novela *n.* novel. **novela rosa** romantic novel, romance.
noveleta *n.* novella.
novelor *n.* novelist.
novembre *n.* November.
novena *n.* novena (*prayers*).
noveta *n.* novelty, curiosity (*item*).
novi *vi.* & *vt.* split into nine. • *n.* ninth (*fraction*).
novia *n.* newness, novelty.
noza *n.* nut; walnut. **noza de Brazil** Brazil nut.
nozeta *n.* hazelnut, filbert (*nut*).
nozeto *n.* hazel, filbert (*tree: Carylus*).
nozin *adj.* nutlike, nutty.
nozo *n.* walnut tree (*Juglans*). **nozo de Brazil** Brazil nut tree (*Bertholletiar*).
nozosa *adj.* nutty (*full of nuts*).
-nte *adj.suff.* -ing; e.g. *un can dorminte*; *leje es divertinte*. • *n.suff.* -er (*substance, object*); e.g. *pleninte*; *covrente*.
nu *n.* nu (*Greek letter* N, ν).
nube *n.* cloud. **nube de zucar** marshmallow. **nube oscur** dark cloud, pall. **sin nube** cloudless, cloudfree.
nubosa *adj.* cloudy, overcast.
nubosia *n.* cloudiness.
nuca *n.* nape, scruff, back of the neck.
nucleal *adj.* nuclear, nucleic.
nucleo *n.* nucleus, kernel; head (*syntax*).
nucleol *n.* nucleolus (*biology*).
nucleon *n.* nucleon (*particle*).
nucleotido *n.* nucleotide.
nuda *adj.* nude, naked, bare, exposed.
nudi *vi.* & *vt.* strip, bare, denude.
nudia *n.* nudity, nakedness.
nudifilo *n.* wire stripper.
nudisme *n.* nudism, naturism.
nudiste *n.* nudist, naturist.
nuga *n.* nougat (*confectionery*).
numatico *n.* tyre (US tire).
numeno *n.* noumenon (*philosophy*).
numeral *adj.* numeric.
numeri *vt.* number, assign a number to. **numeri de pajes** pagination. **numeri la pajes de** paginate.
numerisme *n.* numeracy.
numeriste *adj.* numerate.
numero *n.* number (*in sequence*); numeral (*grammar*); issue, edition (*periodical*); item, entry (*in list*). **la numero du** the second one. **numero de sinia** character number, code position, code point, code number (*software*). **numero duable** even number. **numero natural** natural number, whole number. **numero nonduable** odd number. **numero primal** prime number. **numero sin custa** freephone number, toll-free number. See *cuantia*.
numerolojia *n.* numerology.
numerolojiste *n.* numerologist.
numismatia *n.* numismatics, coin collecting.
numismatial *adj.* numismatic.
numismatiste *n.* numismatist, coin collector.
nun *pron.* no one, nobody.
Nunavut *n.* Nunavut (*Canadian province*).
nunca *adv.* never, not ever.
nuntxacu *n.* nunchaku, nunchuk (*weapon*).
nuragal *adj.* Nuragic (*civilization*).
nurage *n.* nuraghe (*tower*).
nural *adj.* nutritional.
nuri *vt.* feed, nourish; fuel. • *n.* nourishment, nutrition.
nurinte *adj.* nutritious. • *n.* nutrient.
nuriste *n.* nutritionist.

O

O[1] [o]~[ɔ], **o** *letter* O, o.
o[2] *conj.* or. **o … o** either … or; e.g. *o esta o acel.*
o[3] *interj.* oh; O (*vocative*).
-o[4] *n.suff.* male; tree; e.g. *ava/avo*; *poma/pomo*.
oasis *n.* oasis.
obedi *vt.* obey, follow, observe, abide by, comply with. • *n.* obedience.
obedinte *adj.* obedient, obeying, compliant.
obelisce *n.* obelisk.
obesa *adj.* obese, fat, overweight, plump, corpulent, portly, stout, flabby.
obesia *n.* obesity, fatness.
obi *n.* obi (*sash*).
oblida *vt.* forget. **oblida lo** forget it, forget about it, never mind.
oblidable *adj.* forgettable.
oblidante *adj.* forgetful.
obliga *vt.* oblige, obligate, compel, necessitate, force (*socially*). • *n.* obligation, commitment, duty, responsibility. **obliga finansial** bond.
obligada *adj.* obligated, compelled, beholden.
obligante *adj.* obligatory, compulsory, mandatory.
oboe *n.* oboe.
oboiste *n.* oboist.
obra *n.* opus, work (*of art, literature, music, etc.*). **obra de arte** artwork, work of art, objet d'art. **obra mestral** masterpiece, masterwork, magnum opus.
obus *n.* howitzer (*gun*).
ocapi *n.* okapi (*animal*: *Okapia johnstoni*).
ocarina *n.* ocarina (*musical instrument*).
oce *adj.* OK, okay, all right, alright, good enough, acceptable. • *interj.* OK, okay, all right, alright, yes, yep. **ma oce** oh well (*mild disappointment*).
ocer *adj.* ochre (US ocher) (*colour*). • *n.* ochre (US ocher) (*pigment*).
ocroma *n.* balsa (*tree, wood*: *Ochroma pyramidale*).
oculeria *n.* optician's, glasses store.
oculiste *n.* oculist, optician.
oculo *n.* spectacles, glasses, eyeglasses. **oculo coretinte** corrective glasses. **oculo de sol** sunglasses. **oculo protejente** goggles.
oculon *n.* goggles.
oculta *adj.* & *n.* occult.
oculti *vi.* & *vt.* occult. • *n.* occultation.
ocultisme *n.* occultism.
ocultiste *adj.* occultist, occult. • *n.* occultist.
ocupa *vt.* occupy. • *n.* occupation, occupancy; walk of life.
ocupada *adj.* occupied, busy. **casa nonlegal ocupada** squat.
ocupal *adj.* occupational.
ocupante *adj.* occupying.
ocupor *n.* occupant, occupier; occupying force. **ocupor nonlegal** squatter, illegal occupant.
odalisce *n.* odalisque (*slave*).
ode *n.* ode (*poem*).
odia *vt.* hate, detest, abominate, resent, abhor, loathe, anathematize. • *n.* odium, hatred, animosity, resentment, spite, abomination, acrimony, ill feeling.
odiable *adj.* detestable, abominable, reprehensible, odious, loathsome, execrable, heinous, abhorrent. • *n.* abomination, atrocity.
odiablia *n.* odiousness.
odiada *adj.* hated, detested. • *n.* anathema.
-odinia *n.suff.* -odynia (*pain*).
odiosa *adj.* hateful, spiteful, resentful, bitchy, splenetic, vindictive.
Odisea *n.* Odyssey (*poem*). **odisea** *n.* odyssey.
odjibua *adj.* & *n.* Ojibwa, Chippewa (*person, language*).
odometre *n.* odometer.
odontia *n.* dentistry, odontology.
odontiste *n.* odontologist.
odor *n.* smell, scent, odour (US odor). **bon odor** good smell, aroma, fragrance. **con odor agu** acrid, pungent. **mal odor** bad smell, stink, stench. **sin odor** odourless (US odorless), unscented.
odoreta *n.* whiff, faint smell.
odori *vi.* smell (*give off a smell*); e.g. *la lete odori strana.* • *vt.* cause to smell. **odori bon** smell good. **odori mal** smell bad. See *ole*.
odorosa *adj.* smelly, odorous, strong-smelling, redolent.
ofende *vt.* offend, appall (US appal), shock, trespass against. • *n.* offence (US offense), offensiveness, obscenity, shock, affront, umbrage.
ofendeda *adj.* offended, indignant, resentful. **es ofendeda par** be offended by, resent.
ofendente *adj.* offensive, disgusting, distasteful, obscene.
ofendor *n.* offender.
ofisia *n.* office, agency, bureau, facility; practice (*medical, legal*); position (*authority*). **ofisia a casa** home office. **ofisia de comersia** chamber of commerce. **ofisia de governa** ministry. **ofisia de informa** information office, information bureau. **ofisia de**

intercambia currency exchange, bureau de change. **ofisia de pape** pontificate. **ofisia de polisia** police station. **ofisia de posta** post office. **ofisia de site** town hall, city hall.
ofisial *adj.* official.
ofisior *n.* officer, official (*person*), officeholder, commissar, commissary. **ofisior alta** high-ranking officer, dignitary. **ofisior militar** military officer. **ofisior publica** public official, civil servant, public servant.
ofre *vt.* offer, bid, tender. • *n.* offer, offering, bid. **ofre e compra** supply and demand. **ofre min ca** underbid. **ofre plu ca** outbid. **ofre prometeda** votive offering. **ofre respondente** counteroffer. **ofre se per** volunteer for.
ofror *n.* bidder.
oftalmite *n.* ophthalmia, ophthalmitis.
oftalmo- *pref.* ophthalmo- (*eye*).
oftalmolojia *n.* ophthalmology.
oftalmolojiste *n.* ophthalmologist, oculist.
oftalmoplejia *n.* ophthalmoplegia.
oftalmoscopi *n.* ophthalmoscopy.
oftalmoscopio *n.* ophthalmoscope.
ogam *n.* ogham (*alphabet*).
oganeson *n.* oganesson (*element*).
ogro *n.* ogre (*mythology*).
Ohio [o'hajo] *n.* Ohio (*US state*). **Rio Ohio** Ohio River.
Ohotsc, Mar *n.* Sea of Okhotsk.
oia *vt.* hear. • *n.* (*sense of*) hearing. **no oia** miss, not hear. **oia acaso** overhear. **oia secreta** eavesdrop.
oiable *adj.* audible.
oiada *adj.* heard. **acaso oiada** overheard. **oiadas** hearsay.
-oide *adj.suff.* -oid (*shaped*).
oieta *n.* eyelet, grommet (*hole*).
oio *n.* eye. **con oios protendente** with bulging eyes, bug-eyed. **oio brunida** black eye, shiner. **oio de pex** fisheye; fisheye lens.
ojetal *adj.* objective (*of an object or target*).
ojeto *n.* object (*including grammar*), target, goal, objective, cause. **ojeto sielal** astronomical object, celestial object, heavenly body.
oji ['oʒi] *adv.* & *n.* today.
ojiva *n.* ogive (*architecture, statistics*); warhead. **ojiva nucleal** nuclear warhead.
Oklahoma *n.* Oklahoma (*US state*).
-ol *n.suff.* -ol (*chemistry*).
olable *adj.* smellable, perceptible by smell.
olal *adj.* olfactory.
olandes *adj.* hollandaise. **salsa olandes** hollandaise sauce.
olartica *adj.* holarctic (*ecology*).
ole *vt.* smell (*perceive the smell of*). • *n.* (*sense of*) smell, olfaction. See *odori*.
oleandro *n.* oleander (*plant: Nerium oleander*).
oli *vt.* oil. • *n.* oiling.
olibano *n.* frankincense (*resin*).
oligarca *n.* oligarch.
oligarcia *n.* oligarchy.
oligo- *pref.* oligo- (*few*).
oligosacarido *n.* oligosaccharide (*sugar*).
oligosene *adj.* & *n.* Oligocene (*geology*).
Olimpia *n.* Olympia (*in Greece*).
olimpiada *n.* Olympiad.
olimpial *adj.* Olympic. **Juas Olimpial** Olympic Games, Olympics.
olimpian *adj.* & *n.* Olympian.
Olimpo, Monte *n.* Mount Olympus.
olin *adj.* oily, oil-like.
olio *n.* oil. **olio de balena** whale oil.
oliosa *adj.* oily, full of oil.
olisme *n.* holism.
oliste *adj.* holistic. • *n.* holist.
olito *n.* oolite, ooid (*geology*).
oliva *adj.* olive, olive green. • *n.* olive (*fruit*).
olivo *n.* olive (*tree: Olea europaea*).
olmo *n.* elm (*Ulmus*).
olo- *pref.* holo- (*whole*).
olocausto *n.* holocaust. **Olocausto** *n.* Jewish Holocaust, Shoah.
olografi *vt.* make a hologram of.
olografia *n.* holography.
olografial *adj.* holographic.
ologram *n.* hologram.
olosene *adj.* & *n.* Holocene (*geology*).
om *n.* man; guy, bloke, chap, fellow; (*colloquial*) husband. **om de carera** career man. **om de casa** man of the house, male homemaker, househusband, stay-at-home dad. **om de corte** courtier. **om de mundo** socialite. **om de neva** snowman. **om joven** young man; whelp. **om-lupia** *n.* lycanthropy. **om-lupo** *n.* werewolf, lycanthrope.
-oma *n.suff.* -oma (*tumour*).
omareta *n.* scampi, langoustine, Norway lobster, Dublin Bay prawn (*Nephrops norvegicus*).
omaro *n.* lobster (*Nephropidae*).
Ombai, Streta *n.* Ombai Strait.
ombilical *adj.* umbilical.
ombilico *n.* navel, belly button, tummy button, umbilicus.
ombra[1] *n.* shadow, shade; silhouette.
ombra[2] *adj.* umber (*colour*). • *n.* umber (*pigment*).
ombral *adj.* shadow.
ombri *vt.* overshadow, put into shadow, cast a shadow over; upstage; shade, shade in.
ombrida *adj.* overshadowed, dwarfed; shaded, shady.
ombrin *adj.* shadowy (*like a shadow*).
ombrosa *adj.* shadowy (*full of shadows*).

ome *n.* ohm (*unit of resistance*).
omega *n.* omega (*Greek letter* Ω, ω).
omeleta *n.* omelette (US omelet).
omento *n.* omentum (*anatomy*).
omeo- *pref.* homoeo- (US homeo-) (*same*).
omeopatia *n.* homoeopathy (US homeopathy).
omeopatica *adj.* homoeopathic (US homeopathic).
omeopatiste *n.* homoeopath (US homeopath).
omeostasal *adj.* homoeostatic (US homeostatic).
omeostase *n.* homoeostasis (US homeostasis) (*biology*).
omero *n.* humerus (*anatomy*).
omete *vt.* omit, skip, leave out, cut out. • *n.* omission, cut, skip.
omia *n.* manhood, maleness.
omicron *n.* omicron (*Greek letter* O, o).
omin *adj.* manlike, mannish.
ominido *n.* hominid.
omisidal *adj.* homicidal.
omiside *vt.* murder, commit murder, commit homicide. • *n.* murder, homicide (*action*).
omisideda *n.* murder victim.
omisidente *adj.* murdering, murderous.
omisidor *n.* murderer, homicide (*person*).
omni- *pref.* omni- (*all*).
omnipotente *n.* omnipotent, almighty.
omnipotentia *adj.* omnipotence.
omnipresente *adj.* omnipresent, ubiquitous.
omnipresentia *n.* omnipresence, ubiquity.
omnisiente *adj.* omniscient.
omnisientia *n.* omniscience.
omnivor *adj.* omnivorous. • *n.* omnivore.
omo- *pref.* homo- (*same*).
omoerotica *adj.* homoerotic.
omofobia *n.* homophobia.
omofobica *adj.* homophobic. • *n.* homophobe, homophobic.
omofon *adj.* homophonous. • *n.* homophone.
omojen *adj.* homogeneous, homogene.
omojeni *vi.* & *vt.* homogenize.
omojenia *n.* homogeneity.
omoloja *adj.* homologous. • *n.* homologue (US homolog), homology (*something homologous*).
omolojia *n.* homology (*quality*).
omonim *adj.* homonymous. • *n.* homonym, namesake.
omonimia *n.* homonymy.
omorganal *adj.* homorganic.
omosesal *adj.* & *n.* homosexual.
omosesalia *n.* homosexuality.
on[1] *pron.* one, you, they (*an arbitrary person or people in general*).
-on[2] *n.suff.* (*larger variant*); e.g. *cason*; *denton*; *jacon*.
-on[3] *n.suff.* -on (*particle*); e.g. *neutron*; *foton*; *codon*; *interferon*.
-ona *n.suff.* -one (*chemistry*).
onca *n.* hook. **onca de casola** pothook. **onca de pexa** fishhook.
onci *vt.* hook, hook up; dock, couple.
oncianelo *n.* hook-and-eye closure, hook-and-eye fastener.
oncin *adj.* hooked, hooklike.
oncolojia *n.* oncology.
oncolojial *adj.* oncological.
oncolojiste *n.* oncologist.
onda *vi.* wave, undulate, heave. • *vt.* cause to wave, undulate. • *n.* wave (*including of emotion*), undulation. **onda corta** shortwave. **onda de ataca** assault wave. **onda de caldia** heatwave. **onda de opina** wave of support, groundswell. **onda de xoca** shockwave. **onda sismica** shockwave. **onda spumante** breaker. **ondas** waves; ups and downs, vicissitudes. **ondas de caldia** hot flash, hot flush.
ondante *adj.* undulating, undulant, corrugated.
ondatra *n.* muskrat (*rodent*: *Ondatra zibethicus*).
ondeta *vi.* & *vt.* ripple; flutter (*flag*). • *n.* ripple, wavelet, flutter.
ondin *adj.* wavelike, corrugated.
ondon *n.* surge, torrent, huge wave.
ondosa *adj.* wavy; undulating, heaving.
onduran *adj.* & *n.* Honduran.
Onduras *n.* Honduras.
onesta *adj.* honest, truthful.
onestia *n.* honesty, candour (US candor).
onicoforo *n.* onychophor (*organism*: *Onychophora*).
onion *n.* onion (*plant*, *bulb*: *Allium cepa*).
oniromansia *n.* oneiromancy (*divination*).
onisco *n.* woodlouse, pill bug, roly-poly (*Oniscidea*).
onix *n.* onyx (*mineral*).
onomatopea *n.* onomatopoeia.
onomatopeal *adj.* onomatopoeic.
onora *vt.* honour (US honor), commemorate, credit, glorify. • *n.* honour (US honor), credit (*for achievement*), face; commemoration, homage, honourableness (US honorableness), reverence, glory. **salva la onora** save face. **salvante de onora** face-saving.
onorable *adj.* honourable (US honorable); venerable, reverend (*form of address*).
onorada *n.* honoree, laureate. **vea onorada** time-honoured (US time-honored).
onoral *adj.* honorary, commemorative.

onorosa *adj.* honourable (US honorable), upstanding. • *adv.* honourably (US honorably), with honour (US honor).
onsa *n.* ounce (*unit of weight*).
Ontario *n.* Ontario. **Lago Ontario** Lake Ontario.
onto- *pref.* onto- (*existence*).
ontojenia *n.* ontogeny (*biology*).
ontojenial *adj.* ontogenetic.
ontolojia *n.* ontology.
ontolojial *adj.* ontological, ontologic.
op *interj.* oops, whoops, uh-oh.
opaca *adj.* opaque.
opacia *n.* opacity.
opal *n.* opal (*gem*).
opalin *adj.* opaline, opalescent, iridescent, nacreous.
opalinia *n.* opalescence.
opera[1] *vi.* operate, function, work; operate, perform surgery; e.g. *la macina opera bon*; *la sirurjiste opera sur la pasiente*; *la sirurjiste opera a la tumor*.—*Opera* is similar in meaning to *funsiona*, but suggests that someone is managing the proceedings. • *vt.* operate, work (*machine*, *system*). • *n.* operation, functioning. See *funsiona*.
opera[2] *n.* opera (*music*).
operable *adj.* operable.
operada *n.* operand.
operador *n.* operator (*mathematics*, *logic*).
operante *adj.* functioning, functional, working; operant (*psychology*).
opereta *n.* operetta.
operor *n.* operator (*person*).
-opia *n.suff.* -opia (*eye condition*).
opiato *n.* opiate (*drug*).
-opica *adj.suff.* -opic (*eye condition*).
opina *vt.* opine, think, have an opinion, hold a view. • *n.* opinion, mind.
opinosa *adj.* opinionated.
opio *n.* opium (*drug*).
opioide *n.* opioid (*drug*).
oplita *n.* hoplite (*soldier*).
oportun *adj.* opportune, convenient, handy, expedient. • *n.* opportunity, chance. **acaso oportun** opportunity. **aveni oportun** opportune occasion. **momento oportun** opportune moment.
oportunia *n.* opportunity, convenience.
oportunisme *n.* opportunism.
oportuniste *adj.* opportunistic. • *n.* opportunist.
oposa *vt.* oppose, object, withstand, contrast, counter, demur, counteract, parry, antagonize. • *n.* objection, opposition, antagonism, contrast.
oposada *adj.* opposed, opposite; complementary (*colour*). • *n.* opposite, antithesis; complement (*colour*).
oposante *adj.* opposing, opposite, contrary, adverse, antagonistic, dissident, antithetical, wayward.
oposor *n.* opponent, rival, adversary, antagonist.
oposum *n.* opossum (*marsupial*: *Didelphidae*).
opresa *vt.* oppress. • *n.* oppression.
opresante *adj.* oppressive.
opresor *n.* oppressor.
-opsia *n.suff.* -opsy (*medical*).
optometria *n.* optometry.
optometriste *n.* optometrist, optician, oculist.
-or *n.suff.* -er (*person*); e.g. *joglor*; *xapor*; *modernor*.
ora *n.* hour, time. **ora de adormi** bedtime. **ora de come** mealtime, dinnertime, suppertime. **ora de labora** man-hour. **ora de presa** rush hour, peak hour. **ora de retira** curfew. **ora de te** teatime. **ora favoreda** prime time.
oraculal *adj.* oracular.
oraculo *n.* oracle.
-orafia *n.suff.* -orrhaphy (*medical*).
orangutan *n.* orangutan (*Pongo*).
orani *vi.* & *vt.* turn orange.
orania *adj.* orange (*colour*). • *n.* orange (*fruit*). **orania amarga** bitter orange (*Citrus* × *aurantium*).
oranieria *n.* orangery.
oranin *adj.* orangey. **oranin brun** tawny.
oranio *n.* orange tree (*Citrus sinensis*).
oratorio *n.* oratory.
orbita *vt.* orbit. • *n.* orbit; eye socket.
orbital *adj.* orbital.
orca *n.* orca, killer whale (*Orcinus orca*).
orcectomia *n.* orchectomy (*surgery*).
orcestra *n.* orchestra. **orcestra de jaz** big band, jazz orchestra. **orcestra de salon** chamber orchestra.
orcestral *adj.* orchestral.
orcestri *vt.* orchestrate. • *n.* orchestration.
orceta *n.* goblin, gremlin.
orcidea *n.* orchid (*Orchidaceae*).
orco *n.* orc (*mythology*).
ordina *vt.* order, sort, sequence, arrange, rank, grade, prioritize; tidy, neaten, groom; ordain (*religious*). • *n.* order (*including monks*), arrangement (*including music*), sequence; ordination (*religious*). **en ordina** in order, respectively. **ordina de la dia** order of the day, agenda. **ordina de viaja** itinerary, travel plans. **ordina se** preen, primp. **ordina sua plumas** preen.
ordinada *adj.* ordered, orderly, neat, tidy, trim, shipshape, smart, dressy.
ordinal *adj.* ordinal.
ordovisian *adj.* & *n.* Ordovician (*geology*).

orea *n.* ear. **orea asoluta** perfect pitch. **orea esterna** outer ear, pinna, auricle. **orea interna** inner ear.
oreal *adj.* aural, of the ear; auditory, audial.
orealeta *n.* earring.
oregano *n.* oregano (*plant, spice: Origanum vulgare*).
Oregon *n.* Oregon (*US state*).
oreta *n.* bootstrap (*for pulling boot on*); tab (*of page*). **con oretas** tabbed.
orexina *n.* orexin (*hormone*).
orfan *adj.* orphan, waif. • *n.* orphan, foundling.
orfaneria *n.* orphanage.
orfani *vi.* & *vt.* orphan.
organal *adj.* organic.
organdi *n.* organdy, organza (*fabric*).
organeta *n.* organelle (*biology*).
organica *adj.* organic.
organisme *n.* organism.
organiste *n.* organist.
organiza *vt.* organize, arrange, mount. • *n.* organization, arrangement, setup; institute, society, club, entity. **organiza nongovernal** non-governmental organization, NGO.
organizal *adj.* organizational.
organizor *n.* organizer, producer, impresario.
organo *n.* organ (*anatomy, music*). **organo de enrola** barrel organ, hurdy-gurdy. **organo de vapor** calliope. **organos** organs; offal, giblets. **organos sesal** sexual organs.
organofosforosa *n.* organophosphorus (*substance*).
organotrof *adj.* organotrophic (*biology*). • *n.* organotroph.
organotrofia *n.* organotrophia.
orgasma *vi.* & *n.* orgasm.
orgasmal *adj.* orgasmic (*of orgasm*).
orgasmosa *adj.* orgasmic (*orgasming*).
orgulo *n.* pride, hubris. **orgulo vana** vainglory.
orgulosa *adj.* proud, prideful. **es orgulosa de** be proud of, glory in. **vana orgulosa** vainglorious.
ori *vi.* turn to gold, become golden. • *vt.* make golden, gold-plate. See *dora*.
oria *adj.* & *n.* Oriya (*person, language*).
orida *adj.* gold-plated, gold-filled.
orienta *vt.* orient, orientate. • *n.* orientation.
origami *n.* origami.
orijina *vi.* originate; date (*from*). • *n.* origin, source, provenance, fount, fountainhead.
orijinal *adj.* original, native, aboriginal, autochthonous; original (*work, idea*). • *adv.* originally; né, née. • *n.* original (*not a copy*). **american orijinal** *adj.* & *n.* Native American, American Indian, Amerindian. **australian orijinal** *adj.* & *n.* Australian Aborigine. **es orijinal de** be originally from, originate in.
Orinoco, Rio *n.* Orinoco River.
oriol *n.* oriole (*bird: Oriolus, Icterus*).
Orion *n.* Orion (*mythology, constellation*).
oriteropo *n.* aardvark (*Orycteropus afer*).
orix *n.* oryx (*antelope: Oryx*).
orizon *n.* horizon, skyline. **orizon de avenis** event horizon
orizonal *adj.* horizontal; landscape (*orientation*).
orizonalia *n.* horizontalness, horizontality.
orjia *n.* orgy; spree (*metaphor*). **orjia de mata** killing spree.
orjial *adj.* orgiastic.
orlo *n.* hem; hemline.
ormese *n.* hormesis (*biology*).
ormon *n.* hormone. **ormon tiroidal** thyroid hormone.
ormonal *adj.* hormonal.
ormonin *adj.* hormonelike.
orna *vt.* decorate, adorn. • *n.* decoration, ornament, adornment; dingbat (*typography*). **orna apical** finial. **orna par perfora** openwork. **ornas real** regalia.
ornal *adj.* decorative, ornamental.
orneta *n.* bauble, trinket, trifle, gewgaw, knickknack, curio, souvenir, tchotchke.
ornito- *pref.* ornitho-.
ornitolojia *n.* ornithology.
ornitolojial *adj.* ornithological.
ornitolojiste *n.* ornithologist.
ornitorinco *n.* platypus (*Ornithorhynchus anatinus*).
ornosa *adj.* ornate, baroque, florid, rococo; gaudy, tawdry.
oro *adj.* gold, golden (*color*). • *n.* gold (*element*). **de oro** golden, (*made of*) gold.
orolojeta *n.* watch, wristwatch, pocketwatch.
orolojia *n.* horology.
orolojo *n.* clock. **Orolojo** *n.* Horologium (*constellation*). **con la orolojo** clockwise. **contra la orolojo** counterclockwise, anticlockwise. **orolojo de acua** water clock, clepsydra. **orolojo de arena** hourglass, eggtimer. **orolojo de sol** sundial.
orolojor *n.* clockmaker, watchmaker.
oromo *adj.* & *n.* Oromo (*person, language*).
oror *n.* goldsmith.
orosa *adj.* golden, (*made of*) gold.
oroscopo *n.* horoscope.
ortensia *n.* hydrangea (*plant: Hydrangea*).
orteo *n.* toe. See *dito de pede*.
orteta *n.* kitchen garden, vegetable garden, vegetable patch.
ortica *n.* nettle (*Urtica*).
orticultur *n.* horticulture.

orticultural *adj.* horticultural.
orticulturiste *n.* horticulturist.
orto[1] *n.* market garden, truck farm, orchard.
orto-[2] *pref.* ortho- (*straight*).
ortodontia *n.* orthodontics, orthodontia.
ortodontial *adj.* orthodontic.
ortodontiste *n.* orthodontist.
ortodox *adj.* orthodox, conventional.
ortodoxia *n.* orthodoxy.
ortogonal *adj.* orthogonal.
ortografia *n.* orthography.
ortografial *adj.* orthographic.
ortonectido *n.* orthonectid (*organism: Orthonectida*).
ortonis *n.* logrunner (*bird: Orthonyx*).
ortopedia *n.* orthopaedics (US orthopedics), orthopaedy (US orthopedy).
ortopedial *adj.* orthopaedic (US orthopedic).
ortopediste *n.* orthopaedist (US orthopedist).
orzo *n.* barley (*Hordeum vulgare*).
osa[1] *vt.* dare, venture. • *n.* daring, audacity, boldness.
-osa[2] *adj.suff.* -ful, -ous, -y (*full of, containing much or many*); e.g. *zucarosa*.
-osa[3] *n.suff.* -ose (*chemistry*).
osale *n.* sorrel (*plant: Rumex*).
osante *adj.* daring, audacious, bold.
oscan *adj.* & *n.* Oscan (*person, language*).
oscur *adj.* dark, dim, dusky, gloomy; obscure, little-known. • *n.* dark, darkness, gloom.
oscuri *vi.* & *vt.* darken, dim, obscure, remove light; obfuscate.
oscuria *n.* darkness, obscurity (*quality*).
oscurisme *n.* obscurantism.
oscuriste *n.* obscurantist.
-ose *n.suff.* -osis (*medical*).
Oseania *n.* Oceania.
oseanografia *n.* oceanography.
oseanografial *adj.* oceanographic.
oseanografiste *n.* oceanographer.
oselote *n.* ocelot (*wild cat: Leopardus pardalis*).
oseria *n.* ossuary.
oserva *vt.* observe, watch, sight, reconnoitre. • *n.* observation, reconnaissance, recon, sighting.
oservable *adj.* observable.
oservada *adj.* unobserved.
oservante *adj.* watching, observant.
oserveria *n.* observatory.
oservor *n.* observer, spectator, bystander, onlooker. **oservor de avias** birdwatcher, birder.
osese *vt.* obsess, fixate, infatuate. • *n.* obsession, fixation, infatuation.
oseseda *adj.* obsessed, infatuated, besotted.
osesente *adj.* obsessive.
osesor *n.* obsessive.
Osetia *n.* Ossetia.
osetin *adj.* & *n.* Ossetian (*person, language*).
osi *vi.* & *vt.* ossify. • *n.* ossification.
osida *adj.* ossified.
osidi *vi.* & *vt.* rust, oxidize, tarnish. • *n.* rust, corrosion, oxidation, tarnish.
osidiana *n.* obsidian (*rock*).
osidinte *adj.* rusting, rusty.
osido *n.* oxide. **osido de aluminio** aluminium (US aluminum) oxide, alumina. **osido de calsio** calcium oxide. **osido de fero** iron oxide. **osido de magnesio** magnesium oxide, magnesia.
osijen *n.* oxygen.
osijeni *vt.* oxygenate.
osila *vi.* & *vt.* oscillate, rock, sway, pitch, bob, teeter. • *n.* oscillation, swaying.
osilador *n.* oscillator.
osilante *adj.* oscillating, rocking, swaying, pitching.
osileta *vi.* bob gently; curtsy. • *n.* bob, curtsy.
osiloscopio *n.* oscilloscope.
osimoro *adj.* oxymoronic. • *n.* oxymoron.
osio *n.* leisure.
osiosa *adj.* leisurely, idle. • *adv.* at leisure, idly.
osipital *adj.* occipital. **lobe osipital** occipital lobe. **oso osipital** occipital bone.
osisolda *vt.* weld. • *n.* oxy-fuel welding, oxyacetylene welding, gas welding.
osisoldador *n.* welding torch, oxyacetylene torch.
ositalia *vt.* cut with a torch. • *n.* oxy-fuel cutting, oxyacetylene cutting.
ositaliador *n.* cutting torch.
ositan *adj.* & *n.* Occitan (*language*).
osite *n.* oocyte (*biology*).
ositosina *n.* oxytocin (*hormone*).
osiuro *n.* pinworm (*Enterobius vermicularis*).
osiurose *n.* pinworm infection, enterobiasis.
osmanian *adj.* & *n.* Ottoman, Osmanian, Osmanli (*empire*).
osmio *n.* osmium (*element*).
osmosal *adj.* osmotic.
osmose *n.* osmosis.
oso *n.* bone. **oso de anca** hipbone. **oso de colar** clavicle, collarbone. **oso de jena** cheekbone. **oso de pex** fishbone. **oso de spala** scapula, shoulderblade. **oso de talo** anklebone. **oso medulosa** marrowbone. **osos crusada** crossbones.
ososa *adj.* bony, scraggly, scrawny.
ososia *n.* chutzpah; derring-do.
ospisio *n.* hospice, care home.
ospita *vt.* host, hold (*event*).
ospitador *n.* host (*computer*).

ospitafix *n.* file-hosting service, cloud storage service, cyberlocker.
ospital *n.* hospital. **ospital de madres** maternity hospital.
ospitaleta *n.* sanatorium, sanitorium.
ospitali *vt.* hospitalize. • *n.* hospitalization.
ospitalor *n.* hospital nurse, hospital worker.
ospitia *n.* hospitality.
ospitor *n.* host, hostess. **ospitor de avion** air steward, air stewardess, air hostess. **ospitor de conversa** chat-show host, talk-show host.
ostaculo *n.* obstacle, barrier, hurdle.
ostaje *n.* hostage.
ostenta *vt.* show off, flaunt, emblazon. • *n.* ostentation, affectation, pomp.
ostentosa *adj.* ostentatious, pompous, pretentious, grandiloquent, turgid, bombastic; flamboyant, showy, affected. **testo ostentosa** fustian (*pompous text*).
osteolojia *n.* osteology.
osteolojiste *n.* osteologist.
osteopatia *n.* osteopathy.
osteopatial *adj.* osteopathic.
osteopatiste *n.* osteopath.
osteoporose *n.* osteoporosis.
Osteraic *n.* Austria.
osteraices *adj.* & *n.* Austrian.
ostetrica *n.* obstetrics.
ostetrical *adj.* obstetrical, obstetric, perinatal.
ostetriciste *n.* obstetrician.
ostia *n.* host (*Eucharist*).
ostina *vi.* persist, persevere. • *n.* persistence, perseverance, obstinacy, stubbornness, tenacity.
ostinosa *adj.* obstinate, stubborn, persistent, tenacious, dogged, determined, headstrong, adamant, hard-headed, hell-bent, obdurate, ornery, pig-headed, unshakeable (US unshakable).
ostomia *n.* ostomy (*surgical opening*).
ostra *n.* oyster (*Ostreidae*).
ostrogoto *adj.* Ostrogothic. • *n.* Ostrogoth.
ostror *n.* oystercatcher (*bird: Haematopus*).
otagon *adj.* octagonal. • *n.* octagon.
otal *adj.* octal (*base eight*).
otalmo- *pref.* opthalmo- (*eye*).
otano *n.* octane.
otante *n.* octant. **Otante** *n.* Octans (*constellation*).
otarda *n.* bustard (*bird: Otis*).
otario *n.* eared seal, fur seal (*Otariidae*).
otava *n.* octave.
otel *n.* hotel, inn, hostelry. **otel de jovenes** youth hostel.
oteleta *n.* guest house, boarding house, bed and breakfast, B&B.
otelor *n.* hotelier, hotelkeeper, innkeeper.
otenable *adj.* obtainable, available.
oteni *vt.* obtain, acquire, get, procure; assume (*responsibility*). • *n.* acquisition, procurement.
otenida *n.* acquisition.
otenor *n.* procurer; pimp.
oti *vi.* split into eight. • *vt.* split into eighths. • *n.* eighth (*fraction*). • *pref.* eighth-.
otica *n.* optics. **otica de fibres** fibre (US fiber) optics.
otical *adj.* optical.
oticiste *n.* optical scientist.
otida *adj.* octavo (*book size*).
otigalon *n.* pint (*unit of capacity*).
otimisme *n.* optimism.
otimiste *adj.* optimistic, sanguine, upbeat. • *n.* optimist.
oto *det.* eight. • *adj.* eighth (*ordinal*). • *pref.* octo-.
otobre *n.* October.
otodes *det.* eighty. • *adj.* eightieth (*ordinal*).
otodesi *n.* eightieth (*fraction*).
otodon *n.* octodont (*rodent: octodontidae*).
otojemelo *adj.* & *n.* octuplet.
otolarinjolojia *n.* otolaryngology.
otolarinjolojiste *n.* otolaryngologist.
otolito *n.* otolith (*anatomy*).
otolojia *n.* otology.
otolojiste *n.* otologist.
otomi *adj.* & *n.* Otomi (*person, language*).
otoscopi *n.* otoscopy.
otoscopio *n.* otoscope, auriscope, aural speculum (*medical*).
otra *adj.* (*prenominal*) other; latter (*of two, when the former has already been mentioned*). **a otra parte** elsewhere; apart, separately. **a otra tempos** at other times; formerly. **a otra ves** on another occasion; otherwise. **la un la otra** each other, one another. **la un o la otra** either, either one, either one or the other. **la un pos la otra** one after the other, each in turn; one behind the other, in tandem. **no la un e no la otra** neither, neither one nor the other. **otra ca** other than. **un otra** *det.* & *pron.* another. See *lunlotra.*
otras *pron.* others.
otuple *n.* octet.
oval *adj.* oval, ovate, elliptical. • *n.* oval, ellipse.
ovarial *adj.* ovarian.
ovario *n.* ovary.
ovea *n.* sheep (*Ovis aries*). **Ovea** *n.* Aries (*constellation*). **ovea fema** ewe, female sheep. **ovea gidante** leading sheep, bellwether. **ovea mas** ram, male sheep.
oveal *adj.* ovine.
oveta *n.* lamb.
ovi- *pref.* ovi- (*egg*).

oviduto *n.* oviduct (*anatomy*).
ovin *adj.* egglike, egg-shaped, ovoid.
ovipari *vi.* lay eggs, be oviparous. • *n.* spawn, frogspawn.
oviparia *n.* oviparity.
oviparinte *adj.* oviparous, egg-laying.
oviraptor *n.* oviraptor (*dinosaur: Oviraptor*).
ovn *abbr.* (*ojeto volante nonidentifiada*) UFO.
ovo *n.* egg, ovum. **ovo bolida** boiled egg. **ovo de piolio** nit. **ovo fritada** fried egg. **ovos bateda** scrambled eggs. **ovos de pex** caviar, roe.
ovovivipari *vi.* be ovoviviparous (*lay eggs within oneself*).
ovoviviparia *n.* ovoviviparity.
ovoviviparinte *adj.* ovoviviparous.
ovuli *vt.* ovulate. • *n.* ovulation.
ovulo *n.* ovule (*biology*).
ozon *n.* ozone.

P

P[1] [pe], **pe** *letter* P, p.
p[2] *abbr.* (*paje, pajes*) p., pp.
pacarana *n.* pacarana (*rodent: Dinomys branickii*).
paceta *n.* package, packet, parcel; deck, pack (*cards*). **paceta de proba** test kit. **paceta de survive** survival kit.
paci[1] *vi.* pack, become packed. • *vt.* pack, package, bundle. • *n.* packing.
paci-[2] *pref.* pachy- (*thick*).
pacida *adj.* packed, packaged, bundled.
pacidermo *n.* pachyderm.
Pacistan *n.* Pakistan.
pacistani *adj.* & *n.* Pakistani.
paco *n.* pack, bundle, kit.
padela *n.* pan, fry pan, frying pan, skillet. **padela de crepes** crêpe pan, omelette (US omelet) pan. **padela de grili** griddle. **padela de polvo** dustpan. **padela de sote** sauté pan.
padral *adj.* paternal; paternity (*leave*).
padre *n.* father. **padre de batiza** godfather. **padre futur** father-to-be. **padre par sposi** father-in-law. **padre sin sposa** single father. **sin padre** fatherless.
padria *n.* fatherhood, paternity.
padrin *adj.* fatherly. • *n.* father figure, godfather.
padriside *vt.* commit patricide. • *n.* patricide (*action*).
padrisidor *n.* patricide (*person*).
padron *n.* master, lord, boss; patriarch.
paela *n.* paella.
pagan *adj.* & *n.* pagan, heathen, gentile, infidel.
paganisme *n.* paganism.
pagoda *n.* pagoda.
paia *vt.* pay, compensate, remunerate, finance; e.g. *paia sento euros a algun per sua aida.* • *n.* payment, fee, charge, compensation, remuneration, remittance. **paia ajuntada** surcharge, additional payment, premium. **paia anial** annuity. **paia de asecura** insurance premium. **paia de conjesta** congestion charge. **paia de intercambia** exchange fee, brokerage. **paia en partes** *v.* pay by instalments (US installments), pay on account. • *n.* payment by instalments (US installments), payment on account. **paia mensal** monthly payment. **paia onoral** honorarium. **paia partal** part payment, instalment (US installment). **paia per** pay for. **paia per desemplea** severance pay. **paia per maneja** administration charge, management fee. **paia per servi** service charge. **paia pico** pittance.
paiable *adj.* payable.
paiada *adj.* paid. **paiada par taxe** piecework. **tro multe paiada** overpaid. **tro poca paiada** underpaid.
paior *n.* payer. **paior de imposta** taxpayer.
pais *n.* country, land. **estra la pais** out of the country, abroad. **pais de fes** fairyland, faerie. **pais de mervelias** wonderland. **pais de nase** native land. **propre pais** homeland, motherland, fatherland.
paisan *n.* (*fellow*) countryman, countrywoman.
pajama *n.* pyjamas (US pajamas).
paje *n.* page, sheet of paper. **paje HTML** HTML page. **paje prima** home page. **paje sentral** centrefold (US centerfold). **paje ueb** web page.
pajeria *n.* website.
pajo *n.* page, pageboy; knave, jack (*cards*); valet (*tarot*).
pal *adj.* pale, pallid, ashen, wan, light.
pala *n.* shovel, spade.
paladio *n.* palladium (*element*).
palanca *n.* crowbar.
palasin *adj.* palatial.
palasio *n.* palace; seraglio.
palatal *adj.* & *n.* palatal.
palatali *vi.* & *vt.* palatalize.
palato *n.* palate. **palato dur** hard palate. **palato fendeda** cleft palate. **palato mol** soft palate, velum.
paleo- *pref.* palaeo- (US paleo-) (*ancient*).
paleografia *n.* palaeography (US paleography).
paleografiste *n.* palaeographer (US paleographer).
paleolitica *adj.* & *n.* Palaeolithic (US Paleolithic).
paleontolojia *n.* palaeontology (US paleontology).
paleontolojial *adj.* palaeontological (US paleontological).
paleontolojiste *n.* palaeontologist (US paleontologist).
paleosene *adj.* & *n.* Palaeocene (US Paleocene) (*geology*).
paleotropico *n.* palaeotropics (US paleotropics).
paleozoica *adj.* & *n.* Palaeozoic (US Paleozoic) (*geology*).
paleta *n.* palette; pallet (*for stacking goods*); trowel.
pali[1] *adj.* & *n.* Pali (*language*).

pali[2] *vi.* & *vt.* pale, fade.
palia[1] *n.* straw; thatch. **palias basa** stubble.
palia[2] *n.* paleness, pallor.
paliaso *n.* clown, pierrot, pagliaccio.
palieta *n.* drinking straw.
palindrom *n.* palindrome.
palisandro *n.* rosewood (*tree, wood: Dalbergia*).
Palk, Baia *n.* Palk Bay.
palma *n.* palm (*hand*); palm (*tree: Arecaceae*). **leje de palma** palm reading, palmistry. **palma de mano** palm of the hand.
palmi *vt.* & *n.* slap, smack, spank.
palmin *adj.* palmlike, palmate.
palo *n.* pole, post, rod, stake, spit, picket. **palo de bandera** flagpole. **palo de dirije** signpost, guidepost. **palo de gol** goalpost. **palo de lampa** lamppost, streetlight, streetlamp. **palo de maio** maypole. **palo de oro** goldenrod (*plant: Solidago*). **palo de porte** doorpost. **palo de serca** fencepost.
palon *n.* pylon, caber.
palpa *vt.* touch, feel, handle, palpate, frisk. • *n.* (*sense of*) touch.
palpable *adj.* palpable, tactile, tangible.
palpador *n.* feeler.
palpebra *n.* eyelid.
palpebri *vt.* & *n.* blink.
palpita *vi.* palpitate, throb. • *n.* palpitation.
pampelmus *n.* pomelo, pummelo, pamplemousse, shaddock (*fruit, tree: Citrus maxima, Citrus grandis*).
pan[1] *n.* bread, loaf. **pan de carne** meatloaf. **pan de jinjer** gingerbread. **pan negra** pumpernickel. **pan pascual** paska, Easter bread. **pan plata** flatbread. **pan tostada** toast. **pan tostada con ceso** cheese on toast, Welsh rarebit, Welsh rabbit.
Pan[2] *n.* Pan (*mythology*).
pan-[3] *pref.* pan- (*all*).
Panama *n.* Panama. **Canal Panama** Panama Canal. **Golfo Panama** Gulf of Panama. **Istmo Panama** Isthmus of Panama.
panaman *adj.* & *n.* Panamanian.
panamerican *adj.* pan-American.
panarabi *adj.* pan-Arabian.
pancreas *n.* pancreas (*anatomy*).
panda *n.* panda (*Ailuropoda melanoleuca*).
pandemica *adj.* & *n.* pandemic.
pandion *n.* osprey (*bird: Pandionidae*).
Pandjab *n.* Punjab, Panjab.
pandjabi *adj.* & *n.* Punjabi.
Pandora *n.* Pandora (*mythology*).
panel *n.* panel, pane, panelling (US paneling). **panel a lado** sidebar. **panel basa** wainscot, wainscotting. **panel de caviles** pegboard. **panel de comuta** control panel (*switches, plugs*), plugboard. **panel de poster** billboard, hoarding. **panel de sesto** backboard (*basketball*). **panel de strumentos** instrument panel, control panel, dashboard. **panel de toca** touchpad.
paneria *n.* bakery.
paneta *n.* bread roll, bun. **paneta de salsix** hotdog roll, hotdog bun, frankfurter.
pangermanisme *n.* pan-Germanism.
pangolin *n.* pangolin (*animal: Manis*).
pani *vt.* bread, crumb.
panica *vi.* panic. • *vt.* panic, frighten, scare. • *n.* panic, frenzy, stampede, scare.
panicada *adj.* panicked, frantic, frightened, scared.
panicante *adj.* panicking, panicky.
panjenero *adj.* pangender. • *n.* pangender person.
panor *n.* baker.
panorama *vi.* & *vt.* pan. • *n.* panorama.
panoramador *n.* pan control, pan pot.
pansesal *adj.* pansexual.
pantala *n.* short trousers, short pants, shorts, trunks; breeches, britches, knickerbockers. **pantala de bisicli** cycling shorts, bike shorts. **pantala de jenos** knee-length shorts, Bermuda shorts, boardshorts. **pantala de nada** swim shorts, swimming trunks. **pantala faldin** culottes; skort.
pantaleta *n.* underpants, undershorts, pants (*UK*), shorts (*US*), panties, knickers.
pantalon *n.* trousers, pants (*US*), slacks, bottoms. **pantalon cortida** cut-offs. **pantalon de anca** hipsters, hip-huggers. **pantalon de carga** cargo pants. **pantalon de cavalor** jodhpurs. **pantalon de denim** jeans. **pantalon de sporte** sweatpants, joggers, jogging bottoms, tracksuit bottoms. **pantalon de stribos** ski pants, stirrup pants, salopettes. **pantalon de sura** capri pants. **pantalon esvasante** flared trousers, flares, bellbottoms.
pantan *n.* wetland, swamp, bog, mire, quagmire, marsh, marshland, fen, fenland, bayou, morass. **pantan arborosa** marsh. **pantan erbosa** swamp. **pantan torbosa** peatland, peat bog. **pantan torbosa alta** bog (*ecology*). **pantan torbosa basa** fen (*ecology*).
pantaneria *n.* paludarium (*tank*).
pantani *vi.* become mired, get bogged down.
pantanida *adj.* mired, bogged down.
pantanosa *adj.* swampy, marshy, boggy.
panteisme *n.* pantheism.
panteiste *adj.* pantheistic. • *n.* pantheist.
panteon *n.* pantheon.
pantera *n.* panther (*Panthera pardus*).
pantofla *n.* slipper.
pantofli *vt.* beslipper, put slippers onto; shuffle.
pantoflor *n.* stay-at-home, homebody.

pantomima *n.* pantomime, panto (*musical comedy*).
papa *n.* (*colloquial*) dad, daddy, pop, papa (*father*).
papagaio *n.* parrot, parakeet, budgerigar (*Psittacidae*). **papagaio de mar** puffin (*Fratercula*).
papaia *n.* papaya (*fruit*).
papaio *n.* papaya (*tree*: *Carica papaya*).
papal *adj.* papal, pontifical.
paparazo *n.* paparazzo (pl. paparazzi).
papavera *n.* poppy (*Papaver*).
pape *n.* pope, pontiff.
paper *n.* paper, wrapper. **paper asorbente** blotting paper. **paper de aluminio** aluminium (US aluminum) foil, tin foil. **paper de carbono** carbon paper. **paper de catran** tarpaper. **paper de donadas** wrapping paper, giftwrap. **paper de emeri** emery paper. **paper de letera** notepaper. **paper de mur** wallpaper. **paper de pH** litmus paper. **paper de stanio** tin foil. **paper de vason** toilet paper. **paper diafana** tracing paper, onion skin. **paper maxada** papier mâché. **paper raspante** sandpaper. **paper trinxada** shredded paper, confetti.
papereria *n.* stationery store, stationer's.
papereta *n.* note, scrap of paper. **papereta aderente** sticky note, Post-it note.
paperor *n.* paperhanger, wallpaperer; stationer.
papia *n.* papacy.
papiamentu *n.* Papiamento (*language*).
papila *n.* papilla (*anatomy*). **papila de sabor** taste bud.
papilin *adj.* butterfly-shaped.
papilio *n.* butterfly, moth, lepidopteran (*Papilio*). **papilio de dia** butterfly. **papilio de note** moth. **papilio de vestes** clothes moth.
papiro *n.* papyrus (*plant, paper*: *Cyperus papyrus*).
papiste *n.* papist.
paprica *n.* paprika (*plant, fruit, spice*: *Capsicum annuum*).
Papua *n.* Papua. **Golfo Papua** Gulf of Papua. **Papua Gine Nova** Papua New Guinea.
papuan *adj.* & *n.* Papuan.
papula *n.* papule, pimple (*anatomy*).
par *prep.* • (*made, done, caused*) by, through the agency of, because of; e.g. *surprendeda par la responde*; *ensircada par otra paises*; *un teatral par Shakespeare*; *la ataca de la troianes par la elinicas*. • by means of, using, via (*method, action*); e.g. *viaja par avion*; *codigida par color*; *el ia survive par asconde su la table*. • multiplied by, times; e.g. *2 par 3 es 6*. • differing by (*amount, quality*); e.g. *me es plu alta ca tu par un sentimetre*.
para[1] *vi.* & *vt.* stop, end, halt. • *n.* stop, standstill. • *interj.* stop, wait, whoa.
para-[2] *pref.* para- (*additional*).
parabaleta *n.* bulletproofing; bulletproof vest.
parabola *n.* parable (*story*); parabola (*curve*).
parabomba *n.* bombproof structure.
parabus *n.* bus stop.
paracade *n.* parachute.
paracador *n.* paratrooper.
paracolico *n.* antispasmodic (*drug*).
paracolpa *n.* bumper (*of vehicle*).
paraconstipa *n.* purgative, laxative.
paracua *n.* waterproof container, watertight container; wetsuit.
parada *adj.* stopped. **parada par pluve** stopped by rain, washed out.
parade *vi.* & *vt.* parade. • *n.* parade, cavalcade. **parade de susedosas** charts, hit parade. **parade volante** flypast, flyby.
paradeluvia *n.* levee, flood barrier.
paradiarea *n.* antidiarrhoeal (US antidiarrheal) drug.
paradisal *adj.* paradisiacal (*of paradise*).
paradisin *adj.* paradisiacal, heavenly (*like paradise*).
paradiso *n.* paradise, heaven. **paradiso finansial** tax haven.
paradole *n.* painkiller, analgesic, anodyne, palliative.
parador *n.* barrier, barricade. **parador de arena** sandbar, sandbank, shoal. **Parador Grande de Coral** Great Barrier Reef.
paradox *n.* paradox.
paradoxal *adj.* paradoxical.
parafango *n.* mudguard, fender.
parafebre *n.* febrifuge, antipyretic (*drug*).
parafilia *n.* paraphilia.
parafilica *adj.* & *n.* paraphiliac.
parafina *n.* paraffin.
paraflama *n.* flame-retardant.
parafoco *n.* fire door, fire screen; firewall (*software*).
parafrase *vt.* & *n.* paraphrase.
paragasta *n.* selvage (US selvedge) (*edging*).
paragota *n.* coaster, drinks mat, beermat. **paragota de dentela** doily.
paragraf *n.* paragraph.
paragravita *n.* g-suit, gravity suit.
Paraguai *n.* Paraguay.
paraguaia *adj.* & *n.* Paraguayan.
parajela *n.* antifreeze.
paralampa *n.* lampshade, lightshade.
paralampo *n.* lightning rod, lightning conductor.
paralax *n.* parallax.
paralegal *adj.* paralegal.

paralegaliste *n.* paralegal.
paralel *adj.* parallel, equivalent, concurrent. • *n.* parallel, equivalent.
paralelepipedo *adj.* parallelepipedal. • *n.* parallelepiped.
paralelia *n.* parallelness, equivalence.
paralelisme *n.* parallelism.
paralelogram *adj.* parallelogrammatic. • *n.* parallelogram.
paralimpial *adj.* paralympic. **Juas Paralimpial** Paralympic Games.
paralise *vt.* paralyse (US paralyze); transfix. • *n.* paralysis. **paralise serebral** cerebral palsy.
paraliseda *n.* paralytic.
paramar *n.* dyke, dike, levee, sea embankment.
paramediciste *n.* paramedic.
paramesio *n.* paramecium (*organism*).
parametre *n.* parameter.
parametri *vt.* parameterize. • *n.* parameterization.
paramilitar *adj.* paramilitary.
paramorde *n.* muzzle.
Parana, Rio *n.* Paraná River.
paranoia *n.* paranoia.
paranoica *adj.* paranoid.
paranormal *adj.* paranormal.
paransia *n.* anxiolytic (*drug*).
parapeto *n.* parapet.
paraplejia *n.* paraplegia.
paraplejica *adj.* & *n.* paraplegic.
parapluve *n.* umbrella.
paraporte *n.* doorstop.
parapsicolojia *n.* parapsychology.
parapsicolojiste *n.* parapsychologist.
parario [para'rio] *n.* dam, weir (*river*).
parasangual *adj.* styptic, haemostatic (US hemostatic) (*substance*).
parasangue *n.* styptic, haemostatic (US hemostatic) (*substance*).
parasimpatica *adj.* parasympathetic (*nerves*).
parasital *adj.* parasitic.
parasito *n.* parasite.
parasol *n.* parasol, sun umbrella.
parasuo *n.* antiperspirant.
paratiroide *adj.* & *n.* parathyroid.
paratose *n.* cough medicine, antitussive.
paraventa *n.* windscreen, windshield; windbreak, shelterbelt.
paravide *n.* screen.
paraxoca *n.* shock absorber.
parazon *n.* parazoon (pl. parazoa) (*organism*).
parca *n.* parka (*coat*).
parce *n.* park, parkland. **parce acual** waterpark. **parce de autos** car park (*UK*), parking lot (*US*). **parce de divertis** fairground, amusement park. **parce de venta** wind farm.
parceta *n.* parquet, parquetry (*floor*).
parci *vt.* park (*vehicle*). • *n.* parking.
parcur *n.* parkour.
pardalote *n.* pardalote (*bird*: *Pardalotus*).
pardona *vt.* forgive, pardon. • *n.* forgiveness, clemency, mercy, lenience, leniency. • *interj.* sorry. **demanda per pardona** apologize, beg forgiveness. **pardona de imposta** tax break. **pardona me** pardon me, excuse me, I am sorry. **solisita un pardona** apologize.
pardonable *adj.* pardonable, excusable, forgivable, venial.
pardonosa *adj.* merciful, lenient.
pardonosia *n.* mercifulness, leniency.
pare *vt.* seem (*to do, to be*), appear (*to do, to be*), look (*as if*), give the impression (*of being or doing*); feel (*e.g. happy, cold*); e.g. *la aira pare fria*; *lo pare fria asi*; *esta pare como la solve*; *esta pare es la solve*; *el pare labora*; *el pare laborante*; *lo pare ce el labora*. • *n.* appearance, look, semblance. **pare de realia** verisimilitude. See *aspeta*.
parente *adj.* apparent, ostensible. • *adv.* apparently, ostensibly.
-parese *n.suff.* -paresis (*medical*).
parfe *n.* parfait (*dessert*).
parfum *n.* perfume, cologne.
parfumeria *n.* perfumery.
parfumi *vt.* perfume.
parfumor *n.* perfumer, parfumier.
pari *vt.* give birth to, bear, be in labour (US labor). • *n.* giving birth, childbirth, childbearing, parturition, labour (US labor). **ante pari** prenatal, antenatal. **pos pari** postpartum, postnatal.
paria[1] *n.* pariah, outcast.
Paria[2] *n.* Paria (*Venezuelan region*). **Golfo Paria** Gulf of Paria.
parietal *adj.* parietal (*anatomy*). **lobe parietal** parietal lobe. **oso parietal** parietal bone.
parinte *adj.* giving birth, childbearing, in labour (US labor).
parla *vt.* speak, talk. • *n.* speech, discourse, oratory; oration. **par parla** by speaking, by word of mouth. **parla de** speak of, talk of. **parla deliriosa** rave. **parla evitante** *v.* prevaricate. • *n.* prevarication. **parla merda** (*colloquial*) bullshit, talk bullshit, talk bollocks (*nonsense*). **parla monotonosa** speak monotonously, drone on. **parla papin** pontificate. **parla pigra** drawl. **parla sur** speak about, talk about.
parlada *adj.* spoken, voiced, oral.
parlador *n.* loudspeaker, speaker. **parlador basa** woofer.
parlamania *n.* logorrhoea (US logorrhea), verbal diarrhoea (US diarrhea).
parlamental *adj.* parliamentary.

parlamento *n.* parliament, congress. **membro de parlamento** member of parliament, MP, parliamentarian. **parlamento sin majoria** hung parliament.
parlamentor *n.* member of parliament, MP, parliamentarian.
parlante *adj.* speaking. • *adv.* aloud, out loud.
parleta *vt.* chat, natter, chatter, yak, yack, tattle, socialize. • *n.* chat, natter, chatter, yak, yack, gossip, schmooze. **parleta video** *v.* & *n.* video chat.
parlor *n.* speaker.
parlosa *adj.* talkative, garrulous, loquacious, chatty, voluble. • *n.* chatterbox, gasbag, windbag. **es parlosa** be talkative, effuse.
parmesan *n.* parmesan (*cheese*).
paro *n.* tit, titmouse, chickadee (*bird*: *Paridae*).
parocia *n.* parish.
parocial *adj.* parochial.
parocialisme *n.* parochialism.
parocian *n.* parishioner.
parocior *n.* parish priest, vicar, rector. **casa de parocior** vicarage, rectory.
parodia *vt.* parody. • *n.* parody, travesty, take-off.
parola *n.* word. **parola de moda** fashionable word, buzzword. **parola erante** wrong word, malapropism, dogberryism. **parola evitante** euphemism. **parola grilida** hashtag. **parola nova** neologism. **parola secreta** password, codeword. **parolas crusada** crossword puzzle. **parolas tecnical** terminology, jargon.
parolal *adj.* verbal (*expressed in words*).
paroleta *n.* particle (*grammar*).
parolor *n.* wordsmith; lyricist.
parolosa *adj.* wordy, verbose.
parolosia *n.* wordiness, verbosity, verbiage.
parotida *n.* parotid, parotid gland (*anatomy*).
parotidite *n.* mumps, epidemic parotitis (*medical*).
parsec *n.* parsec (*unit of length*).
partal *adj.* partial, patchy. • *adv.* partially, partly, half-.
parte *n.* part, portion, section, division, segment, partition, instalment (US installment); share, ration. **en no parte** nowhere. **par partes** piecemeal. **parte reservada** spare part.
parteni *vi.* belong, affiliate; be a part of; e.g. *la pen parteni a me.* • *n.* affiliation, membership.
parteninte *adj.* belonging, affiliated. • *n.* appurtenance.
partenojenese *n.* parthenogenesis (*biology*).
parti *vi.* depart, leave, go; e.g. *la tren va parti de la stasion.* • *n.* departure, parting; exodus.
Partia *n.* Parthia (*ancient region*).
partian *adj.* & *n.* Parthian.
particula *n.* particle, speck, grain, mote. **particula beta** beta particle.
particulin *adj.* particulate.
particulosa *adj.* grainy, silty.
partinte *adj.* departing, outbound. **partinte de** starting from, leaving from.
partisan *adj.* partisan, partial, taking sides. • *n.* partisan.
partisipa *vi.* participate, take part, be a part, partake, engage. • *n.* participation; turnout.
partisipante *adj.* participating. • *n.* argument (*mathematics*, *grammar*).
partisipio *n.* participle.
partisipor *n.* participant.
partital *adj.* factional.
partitisme *n.* factionalism.
partito *n.* party (*political*), faction, caucus.
partitur *n.* score, soundtrack (*music*).
partituri *vt.* score.
pas *n.* peace, peacetime.
pasa *vi.* pass (*place*, *time*), elapse. • *vt.* pass, go past, overtake, outpace, lap; pass across, hand over, transfer; pass, spend (*time*). • *n.* passing, transfer, transference, handover, handoff. **en pasa** in passing, by the way, incidentally; en passant (*chess*). **pasa de rena** succession. **pasa la estate** summer, spend the summer. **pasa la inverno** winter, spend the winter. **pasa per oserva** flyby. **pasa su la cilia** keelhaul. **pasa tempo** pass time, idle.
pasada *adj.* past, previous, former, earlier, ex-. • *adv.* previously, formerly, once. • *n.* past (*time*, *tense*), yore; preterite. **en la pasada** in the past; out of the way. **en la pasada distante** in the distant past, long ago. **en la semana pasada** last week. **pasada perfeta** past perfect, pluperfect. **plu bon ca pasada** better than ever.
pasaje *n.* passage (*travel*, *text*, *music*); passageway. **dona pasaje a** give a lift to, give a ride to. **pasaje de frontera** border crossing. **pasaje de traversa** pedestrian crossing, crosswalk.
pasajor *n.* passenger. **pasajor secreta** stowaway.
pasaporto *n.* passport.
pasarin *adj.* sparrowlike. • *n.* passerine, perching bird.
pasaro *n.* sparrow (*Passeridae*). **pasaro americano** New World sparrow (*Emberizidae*). **pasaro de neva** snow finch (*Montifingilla*).
pasatempo *n.* hobby, pastime, recreation.
pascal *n.* pascal (*unit of pressure*).
pascua *n.* Easter. **Isola Pascua** Easter Island, Rapa Nui. See *Rapanui.*
pascual *adj.* Easter.

pasea *vi.* walk, stroll. • *vt.* walk, take for a walk. • *n.* walk. **modo de pasea** gait. **pasea de ganso** goosestep. **pasea en spasio** spacewalk. **pasea grande** stride. **pasea grandiosa** strut. **pasea laborosa** *v.* & *n.* trudge, plod, trek. **pasea lenta** stroll, amble, saunter. **pasea longa** *v.* & *n.* hike, trek. **pasea lunal** *v.* & *n.* moonwalk (*dance*). **pasea ostentosa** sashay.

paseacorda *n.* rope walker, tightrope walker, funambulist.

paseador *n.* treadmill (*wheel, exercise machine*).

paseamania *n.* hiking.

paseamanica *n.* hiker.

paseante *adj.* walking, peripatetic; andante (*music*).

paseor *n.* walker, pedestrian. **paseor nova** toddler.

paseria *n.* walkway, footpath, catwalk. **paseria de plances** boardwalk. **paseria rolante** moving walkway, travelator.

paseta[1] *vi.* tiptoe, walk on one's toes.

paseta[2] *n.* tiny step.

pasi *vt.* pacify, appease, placate, mollify, propitiate. • *n.* pacification, appeasement, placation.

pasiente *adj.* patient, easygoing. • *n.* patient. **pasiente esterna** outpatient. **pasiente ospitalida** inpatient.

pasientia *n.* patience.

pasifica *adj.* Pacific. **Mar Pasifica** Pacific Ocean.

pasiflora *n.* passion flower (*Passiflora*).

pasigrafia *n.* pasigraphy (*writing system*).

pasion *n.* passion.

pasioni *vt.* impassion.

pasionosa *adj.* passionate, impassioned, torrid.

pasisme *n.* pacifism.

pasiste *n.* pacifist.

pasiva *adj.* passive. • *n.* passive (*grammar*).

pasivia *n.* passivity.

pasmacer *n.* pacemaker (*medical*).

paso *n.* step, footstep, pace, tread; stage (*of progress*). **fa un mal paso** stumble, trip, misstep, make a mistake, make a faux pas. **fa un paso** step, take a step, tread, pace. **mal paso** misstep, faux pas. **par pasos** *adj.* step-by-step. • *adv.* step by step.

pason *n.* stride, big step.

pasor *n.* passer-by, passing traveller (US traveler) (*on foot or in vehicle*).

pasosa *adj.* peaceful, tranquil, docile, placid, serene, uneventful, at peace.

paspie *n.* passepied (*dance*).

pasta *n.* paste; dough, pasta. **pasta aplicable** spread, paste, pâté. **pasta arenin** shortcrust pastry. **pasta de dentes** toothpaste. **pasta de frita** batter. **pasta de modeli** plasticine, modelling (US modeling) clay. **pasta de torta** cake mix, cake batter. **pasta dulse** pastry. **pasta folin** filo pastry, thin pastry.

pastel *adj.* & *n.* pastel. **pastel de sira** crayon.

pasteuri *vt.* pasteurize. • *n.* pasteurization.

pasteurida *adj.* pasteurized.

pastinaca *n.* parsnip (*Pastinaca sativa*).

pastix *n.* pastiche, pasticcio; mashup.

pasto *n.* pasture, pasturage. **come a pasto** graze. **usa tro multe la pasto** overgraze.

pastor *n.* herder, herdsman, herdswoman, shepherd, shepherdess; pastor. **Pastor** *n.* Boötes (*constellation*).

pastoral *adj.* pastoral, rural. • *n.* pastoral (*art*).

pastoria *n.* pastoralism, herding.

pastrami *n.* pastrami (*food*).

Patagonia *n.* Patagonia.

patata *n.* potato (*Solanum tuberosum*). **patata dulse** sweet potato (*Ipomoea batatas*). **patata fornida** baked potato, jacket potato. **patatas fritada** French fries, fries, chips (*UK*).

pate *n.* pâté.

patenta *vt.* & *n.* patent.

paternalisme *n.* paternalism (*philosophy*).

pateta *n.* duckling.

pati *vi.* waddle.

-patia *n.suff.* -pathy (*illness*).

-patica *adj.suff.* -pathic, -pathetic.

patin *n.* skate. **patin de rotas** rollerskate.

patina *n.* patina (*sheen*).

patineria *n.* ice rink.

patineta *n.* scooter, kick scooter, push scooter.

patini *vt.* skate; skid.

patinor *n.* skater.

patio *n.* courtyard, (*enclosed*) yard. **patio de cultiveria** barnyard, farmyard. **patio de enfantes** playground, play area.

patlatx *n.* potlatch (*feast*).

pato[1] *n.* duck (*Anatidae*). **pato real** mallard.

pato-[2] *pref.* patho- (*illness*).

patojen *adj.* pathogenic. • *n.* pathogen, germ.

patojenesal *adj.* pathogenetic.

patojenese *n.* pathogenesis.

patolojia *n.* pathology.

patolojial *adj.* pathological.

patolojiste *n.* pathologist.

patriarca *n.* patriarch.

patriarcia *n.* patriarchy.

patrilinia *n.* patrilineage.

patrilinial *adj.* patrilineal.

patriota *adj.* patriotic. • *n.* patriot.

patriotisme *n.* patriotism.

patrulia *vt.* & *n.* patrol.

patrulior *n.* patroller, patrolman. **patrulior estralegal** vigilante.

patxinco *n.* pachinko (*pinball*).

patxisi *n.* pachisi, parcheesi, ludo (*game*).

paund *n.* pound (*currency*), sterling.

pausa *vi.* & *vt.* pause, adjourn; wait; stop (*overnight or before resuming*). • *n.* pause, hiatus, break (*from activity*), adjournment, abeyance, stop-off, stopover, intermission, letup; wait, standby. **loca de pausa** stop, stopping place (*along a journey*). **sin pausa** without pause, continual, incessant, non-stop.

pausada *adj.* paused, adjourned, in abeyance.

pavana *n.* pavane (*dance, music*).

pave *vt.* pave. • *n.* paving (*slabs, asphalt, cobbles*).

paveda *adj.* paved.

pavilion *n.* pavilion.

pavlova *n.* pavlova (*dessert*).

pavo *n.* turkey (*Meleagris gallopavo*).

pavon *n.* peafowl, peacock, peahen (*Pavo, Pavo cristatus*). **Pavon** *n.* Pavo (*constellation*).

paxtu *adj.* & *n.* Pashtun (*person*); Pashto (*language*).

pc *abbr.* (*personal computador*) PC. **pc de table** desktop PC.

pd *abbr.* (*per dise*) i.e., that is to say, namely.

pe *abbr.* (*per esemplo*) e.g., for example.

peaje *n.* toll (*payment*).

peca *vi.* sin. • *n.* sin, infraction.

pecan *n.* pecan, hickory (*tree, nut: Carya*).

pecari *n.* peccary (*animal: Tayassuidae*).

peceta *vi.* commit a misdemeanour (US misdemeanor). • *n.* peccadillo, misdemeanour (US misdemeanor), minor infraction, indiscretion.

peco *n.* pekoe (*tea*).

pecor *n.* sinner.

pecosa *adj.* sinful.

pectina *n.* pectin (*substance*).

pedagojia *n.* pedagogy.

pedagojial *adj.* pedagogic, pedagogical.

pedal *n.* pedal.

pedali *vt.* pedal.

pedante *adj.* pedantic, fussy. • *n.* pedant, nitpicker. **es pedante** be pedantic, quibble, split hairs, nitpick.

pedantia *n.* pedantry, nitpicking, pettifogging.

pede *n.* foot, base. **con pedes nuda** barefoot. **par pede** on foot, by foot. **pede de monte** foothill. **pede de paje** footer. **pede fronte** forefoot. **pede membranosa** webbed foot, webfoot. **ses pedes** fathom (*unit of length*). **su pede** underfoot. **sur cuatro pedes** (*animal*) on all fours.

pedestal *n.* pedestal.

pedeta *n.* paw.

pedi *vt.* & *n.* kick. **pedi cadente** dropkick (*martial arts*). **pedi prima** *v.* kick off. • *n.* kickoff.

pediatria *n.* paediatrics (US pediatrics).

pediatrica *adj.* paediatric (US pediatric).

pediatriste *n.* paediatrician (US pediatrician).

pedicura *n.* pedicure.

pedionom *n.* plains-wanderer (*bird: Pedionomus torquatus*).

pedo- *pref.* paedo- (US pedo-) (*child*).

pedofilia *n.* paedophilia (US pedophilia). **pedofilia omosesal** paederasty (US pederasty).

pedofilica *adj.* paedophilic (US pedophilic). • *n.* paedophile (US pedophile). **pedofilica omosesal** paederast (US pederast).

pedor *n.* kicker.

Pegaso *n.* Pegasus (*mythology, constellation*).

pel *n.* skin, hide, pelt, integument. **pel cru** rawhide. **pel de capra** goatskin. **pel de ovea** sheepskin. **pel de porco** pigskin. **pel de servo** buckskin. **pel de urso** bearskin. **pel de vino** wineskin. **pel mor** dead skin, slough, eschar. **su pel** subcutaneous.

pelagra *n.* pellagra (*medical*).

peleta *n.* film (*thin skin*). **peleta aderente** cling film, cling wrap, Saran wrap.

pelican *n.* pelican (*Pelicanus*).

pelicanin *adj.* pelicanlike.

pelin *adj.* furry, furlike.

pelo *n.* fur, coat (*animal*), body hair (*human*); pile, nap (*of fabric*), grain (*of wood*). **bal de pelo** hairball. **contra la pelo** against the grain. **pelo de jenas** sideburns, sideboards. See *capel*.

pelosa *adj.* furry, hairy, hirsute, shaggy.

peltre *n.* pewter (*metal*).

pelux *n.* plush (*fabric*).

peluxeta *n.* down, fluff, fuzz, lint.

peluxetin *adj.* downy, fluffy, fleecy.

pelvis *n.* pelvis.

pelvisal *adj.* pelvic.

pemfigo *n.* pemphigus (*medical*).

pen *n.* pen. **pen de bal** ballpoint pen, biro. **pen de cartux** cartridge pen. **pen de fonte** fountain pen. **pen de pluma** quill.

penal *adj.* penal (*punishment*).

Penas, Golfo *n.* Gulf of Penas.

pendador *n.* hanger; gallows, gibbet.

pende *vi.* hang, hang down, sag, droop. • *vt.* hang, suspend, dangle.

pendejacon *n.* coathook.

pendente *adj.* pendulous, droopy, saggy. • *n.* pendant. **pendente de recorda** locket.

pendeveste *n.* coathanger.

pendexapo *n.* hat rack, hatstand.

pendor *n.* hangman, executioner.

penduli *vi.* & *vt.* swing (*back and forth*).

pendulo *n.* pendulum; swing.
penetra *vt.* penetrate, breach. • *n.* penetration.
-penia *n.suff.* -penia (*lack*).
penis *n.* penis.
penisal *adj.* penile.
penisilina *n.* penicillin.
penisola *n.* peninsula.
penisolal *adj.* peninsular.
Pennsylvania *n.* Pennsylvania (*US state*).
penombra *n.* penumbra (*shadow*).
pensa *vt.* think; opine, hold an opinion. • *n.* thought, cognition. **pensa a** think of (*have in mind*). **pensa ladal** *v.* think laterally, think outside the box. • *n.* lateral thought, lateral thinking, thinking outside the box. **sin pensa** thoughtless, mindless.
pension *n.* pension. **pension de divorsa** alimony. **pension de jubila** retirement pension.
pensor *n.* thinker. **pensor libre** freethinker.
pensosa *adj.* thoughtful, pensive.
penta- *pref.* penta- (*five*).
pentadatilo *adj.* pentadactyl (*biology*).
pentagon *adj.* pentagonal. • *n.* pentagon.
pentagram *n.* staff, stave (*music*); pentagram, pentacle (*star*).
pentametre *n.* pentameter (*poetry*).
pentatlon *n.* pentathlon.
pentatlonor *n.* pentathlete.
pentecostal *adj.* Pentecostal.
pentecostalisme *n.* Pentecostalism (*Christianity*).
pentecoste *n.* pentecost.
pentobarbital *n.* pentobarbital, pentobarbitone (*drug*).
peon *n.* peon, menial worker, unfree labourer (US laborer); foot soldier, pawn (*chess*). **peon cultival** farmhand.
peonia *n.* peony (*plant*: *Paeonia*).
peote *n.* peyote (*plant, drug*: *Lophophora williamsii*).
peper *n.* (*black, white*) pepper (*vine, spice*: *Piper nigrum*).
peperi *vt.* pepper.
peperin *adj.* peppery (*like pepper*).
peperomia *n.* peperomia (*plant*: *Peperomia*).
peperon *n.* (*hot, sweet, bell*) pepper, capsicum (*plant, fruit*: *Capsicum annuum*). **peperon polvida** cayenne. **peperon roja** red pepper. **peperon verde** green pepper, bell pepper. **salsix de peperon** pepperoni (*sausage*).
peperosa *adj.* peppery (*full of pepper*).
pepita *n.* nugget. **pepita de gal** chicken nugget. **pepita de oro** gold nugget.
-pepsia *n.suff.* -pepsia (*digestion*).
-pepsica *adj.suff.* -peptic.
pepsin *n.* pepsin (*enzyme*).
peptido *n.* peptide (*chemistry*).
per[1] *prep.* • for (*an intended reason or beneficiary*); in order to, to; e.g. *nos labora per mone; viaja per vide la mundo; vestida per un sera de dansa; el ia scrive la libro per sua madre.*—Both *per* and *par* can introduce reasons: *per* indicates an intention; *par* indicates a cause. • for, in exchange for, in return for; e.g. *tu ia paia tro per acel computador; me ia compra lo per mil euros; grasias per tua mesaje.* • for every, per (*in measurements of speed, etc.*); e.g. *viaja a sento cilometres per ora.* • for, on behalf of; pro (*in favour of*); e.g. *vota per la proposa; me parla per mea ami.* • for (*an intended distance or duration*); e.g. *me vade a via per un semana; el va bisicli per tre menses.*—Both *per* and *tra* can introduce distances or durations: *per* suggests an intention; *tra* suggests that the time has actually elapsed or the distance been covered. **paia per ora** pay rate per hour. **per ci** for whom (*relative*). **per cual** for which (*relative*). **per si** in case. See *par, tra.*
per-[2] *pref.* per- (*thoroughly*).
pera *n.* pear (*fruit*).
perca *n.* perch (*Perca*).
percal *n.* percale (*fabric*).
perce [perˈke] *adv.* why, for what, wherefore.—*Perce* is always a question. For *because*, use *car.*
percute *vt.* percuss; tap (*medical*). • *n.* percussion.
percutiste *n.* percussionist.
perde *vt.* lose, misplace; miss (*bus, connection, etc.*). • *n.* loss. **bon perde** good riddance. **perde completa** complete loss, write-off. **perde de consensia** blackout, loss of consciousness. **perde de lus** blackout.
perdeda *adj.* lost, stray (*dog, cat*), astray. **perdeda a mar** *adj.* lost at sea, shipwrecked. • *n.* castaway. **perdeda en batalia** missing in action, MIA.
perdente *adj.* losing; lossy (*compression*).
perdis *n.* partridge (*Phasianidae*). **perdis blanca** ptarmigan (*Lagopus*).
perdor *n.* loser.
peregrina *vi.* peregrinate, make a pilgrimage. • *n.* peregrination, pilgrimage.
peregrinor *n.* pilgrim; peregrine falcon (*Falco peregrinus*).
perene *adj.* & *n.* perennial.
perfeta *adj.* perfect, flawless, immaculate, quintessential. • *adv.* perfectly, by heart.
perfeti *vi.* & *vt.* perfect.
perfetia *n.* perfection.
perfetisme *n.* perfectionism.
perfetiste *adj.* perfectionist, punctilious. • *n.* perfectionist.
perfora *vt.* perforate, pierce, puncture, riddle, run through, punch (*hole*). • *n.* perfora-

tion, puncture. **perfora lombal** lumbar puncture, spinal tap.
perforador *n.* perforator, punch.
pergamin *n.* parchment. **enrola de pergamin** scroll. **pergamin de boveta** vellum.
pergola *n.* pergola, arbour (US arbor).
peri[1] *vt.* waste, misuse, squander. • *n.* waste.
peri-[2] *pref.* peri- (*around*).
pericardio *n.* pericardium (*anatomy*).
pericardite *n.* pericarditis (*medical*).
perielio *n.* perihelion (*astronomy*).
periferia *n.* periphery.
periferial *adj.* peripheral, distal.
perijeo *n.* perigee (*astronomy*).
peril *n.* danger, hazard, peril, jeopardy.
perila *n.* perilla (*plant*: *Perilla*).
perili *vt.* endanger, imperil, jeopardize, compromise.
perilida *adj.* endangered, at risk.
perilosa *adj.* dangerous, hazardous, perilous, precarious.
perimetre *n.* perimeter, circumference, girth.
perin *adj.* pearlike, pear-shaped.
perineo *n.* perineum (*anatomy*).
periodal *adj.* periodic, regular.
periodo *n.* period, spell. **periodo de condena** sentence (*prison*). **periodo de incuba** incubation period. **periodo de ofisia** term of office, tenure.
periodontia *n.* periodontology, periodontics.
periodontiste *n.* periodontist.
periorbita *n.* periorbita (*anatomy*).
periscopial *adj.* periscopic.
periscopio *n.* periscope.
peristalsia *n.* peristalsis (*biology*).
peristalsica *adj.* peristaltic.
peritoneo *n.* peritoneum (*anatomy*).
perjura *vi.* perjure. • *n.* perjury.
perjuror *n.* perjurer.
perla *n.* pearl. **perla de zucar** sugarplum.
perleta *n.* bead.
perlin *adj.* pearly.
perma *vt.* perm. • *n.* perm, permanent wave (*hair*).
permajelada *n.* permafrost.
permane *vi.* be permanent, remain, continue, stay, overstay, linger. • *n.* permanence.
permanente *adj.* permanent, long-term, indelible.
permanentia *n.* permanence.
permea *vt.* permeate, pervade, percolate, suffuse, riddle. • *n.* permeation, perfusion.
permeable *adj.* permeable.
permeada *adj.* permeated; ingrown (*nail*). • *n.* filtrate.
permeante *adj.* permeating, pervading, pervasive.
permete *vt.* permit, allow, let, authorize, grant; condone; e.g. *me permete ce tu reposa*; *me permete tu a reposa*; *me permete un reposa a tu*. • *n.* permission, authorization, right, licence (US license). **permete a se** allow oneself (*to do*), afford (*to do*). **permete ce on vota** enfranchise. **permete entra** admit, allow entry. **permete poesial** poetic licence (US license).
permeteda *adj.* allowed, permitted, allowable, permissible. **es permeteda** be permitted, be allowed.
permetente *adj.* permitting. **permetente ce** although, granted that.
permian *adj.* & *n.* Permian (*geology*).
permuta *vt.* permutate. • *n.* permutation.
pero *n.* pear (*tree*: *Pyrus*).
perosa *adj.* wasteful, inefficient, prodigal, profligate.
perosia *n.* wastefulness, inefficiency.
perosido *n.* peroxide. **idrojen perosido** hydrogen peroxide.
perosisoma *n.* peroxisome (*biology*).
perpendicular *adj.* & *n.* perpendicular.
persegue *vt.* persecute. • *n.* persecution.
perseguor *n.* persecutor.
persentil *n.* percentile.
persento *n.* percent, percentage point. **sincodes persentos** fifty percent.
Perseo *n.* Perseus (*mythology*, *constellation*).
persepable *adj.* perceptible, noticeable, tangible. **apena persepable** barely perceptible, faint. **fasil persepable** salient, conspicuous, standing out.
persepal *adj.* perceptual.
persepi *vt.* perceive, notice, realize, detect, discern. • *n.* perception; interpretation, point of view. **fa ce on persepi** call attention to, draw attention to. **persepi estrasensal** extrasensory perception, ESP.
persepida *n.* percept.
persepinte *adj.* perceptive, discerning, incisive, trenchant.
Persia *n.* Persia (*ancient region*).
persian *adj.* Persian. **Golfo Persian** Persian Gulf.
persil *n.* parsley (*plant*: *Petroselinum crispum*).
persiste *vi.* & *vt.* persist, persevere, linger. • *n.* persistence, perseverance, tenacity.
persistente *adj.* persistent, lingering, tenacious.
person *n.* person. **no person** no one, nobody. **per person** per person, per capita, per head. **person comun** common person, everyman, man in the street. **person de mundo** socialite. **person importante** important person, personage. **per-**

son matur grown-up, adult. **person nondesirada** persona non grata. **persones** people (*individuals*), persons, folk; staff (*of organization*). **persones disponable** available people, manpower.
personal *adj.* personal.
personali *vi.* & *vt.* personalize, customize. • *n.* personalization, customization.
personalia *n.* personality. **personalia alternativa** alternative personality, alter ego.
personi *vi.* & *vt.* personify. • *n.* personification, epitome.
personin *adj.* personlike.
perspetiva *n.* perspective.
pertine *vi.* pertain, relate, apply, be relevant, be associated, have to do with. • *n.* pertinence, relevance. **lo pertine a** it's a case of, it's a matter of, it's a question of, it's to do with.
pertinente *adj.* pertinent, relevant, valid.
pertuse *n.* pertussis, whooping cough.
Peru [pe'ru] *n.* Peru.
peruan *adj.* & *n.* Peruvian.
peruca *n.* wig, toupee.
peruceta *n.* hairpiece, hair attachment.
perucor *n.* perruquier, wigmaker.
perverti *vt.* pervert. • *n.* perversion.
pervertida *adj.* perverse, perverted.
pervertinte *adj.* perverting, perversive.
perxa *n.* perch (*support*).
perxi *vt.* perch.
pesa *vt.* weigh (*have weight, measure weight*). • *n.* weight (*measure, object*).
pesador *n.* scales, weighing machine.
pesah *n.* Pesach, Passover (*Judaism*).
pesca *adj.* peach (*colour*). • *n.* peach (*fruit*).
pesco *n.* peach (*tree: Prunus persica*).
peseta *n.* titbit (US tidbit), morsel, stub (*pencil, cigarette*). **un peseta de** a small quantity of, a little, a few.
pesimisme *n.* pessimism.
pesimiste *adj.* pessimistic, downbeat. • *n.* pessimist.
peso *n.* piece, fragment, slice, scrap; literary work, play (*theatre*), musical piece, track; (*building*) lot, plot (*land*); patch (*repair*); peso (*currency*). **a pesos** in pieces, to pieces, apart. **de du pesos** two-piece. **de pesos** patchwork. **de sola un peso** all-in-one. **de un peso** one-piece. **peso de xace** chesspiece. **peso spesa** thick piece, slab. **repara con pesos** patch.
peson *n.* chunk, hunk, wodge. **un peson de** a large quantity of, a lot of, a load of, lots of, loads of.
pesosa *adj.* heavy, ponderous, hefty. **tro pesosa** overweight; burdensome, onerous.
pesta *vt.* plague, pox. • *n.* pestilence, plague, bane.
peste *n.* pest (*creature*); (*colloquial*) pest, nuisance, hassle, pain in the neck.
pestiside *n.* pesticide.
pesto *n.* pesto (*sauce*).
peta *vt.* & *n.* (*colloquial*) fart. **peta de labios** raspberry, razz, Bronx cheer.
petal[1] *n.* petal.
petal[2] *adj.* pectoral.
petalosa *adj.* petalled (US petaled).
petardo *n.* petard, firecracker, cracker, squib, banger.
petecia *n.* petechia (*medical*).
peten[1] *n.* comb.
peten[2] *n.* scallop (*Pectinidae*).
peteni *vt.* comb.
peti *adj.* small, little, undersized, wee. • *vi.* & *vt.* shrink, reduce in size. • *n.* little thing, little one, runt.
petirosa *n.* European robin (*bird: Erithacus rubecula*).
peto *n.* chest (*anatomy*), breast (*whole chest, including poultry*); bosom, bust. **con peto nuda** bare-chested, bare-breasted, topless.
petra *n.* stone. **petra cubo** sett, paving block. **petra de agi** whetstone. **petra de milia** milestone. **petra de molin** millstone, grindstone. **petra de paso** stepping stone. **petra de pave** paving stone, paving block (*of any kind*). **petra de tomba** tombstone, gravestone, headstone. **petra de zodiaco** birthstone. **petra focosa** flint, firestone. **petra plata** flagstone, paving stone, paver. **petra ronda** round stone, cobblestone. **petra ultima** capstone.
petrel *n.* petrel (*bird: Procellariidae, Hydrobatidae, Pelecanoididae*).
petri *vi.* & *vt.* petrify. • *n.* petrification.
petrida *adj.* petrified.
petrin *adj.* stonelike, stony.
petro- *pref.* petro- (*stone*).
petrocimical *adj.* & *n.* petrochemical.
petrodolar *n.* petrodollar.
petrolio *n.* (*crude*) oil, petroleum.
petrolojia *n.* petrology.
petronia *n.* rock sparrow, petronia (*bird: Petronia*).
petror *n.* mason, stonemason.
petrosa *adj.* stony, full of stones.
petunia *n.* petunia (*plant: Petunia*).
pex *n.* fish. **pex anjelin** angelfish (*Pterophyllum*). **pex arjenta** silverfish (*Lepisma saccharina*). **pex caxin** boxfish (*Ostraciontidae*). **pex de rocas** rockfish (*Sebastes* and other genera). **pex de siera** sawfish (*Pristidae*). **pex de spada** swordfish (*Xiphias gladius*). **pex de vela** sailfish (*Istiophorus*). **pex gatin** catfish (*Siluriformes*). **pex linguin** tonguefish

(*Cynoglossidae*). **pex oro** goldfish (*Carassius auratus*). **pex pipin** pipefish (*Syngnathinae*). **pex plata** flatfish (*Pleuronectiformes*). **pex plenida** gefilte fish. **Pex Sude** Piscis Austrinus (*constellation*). **Pex Volante** Volans (*constellation*). **Pexes** Pisces (*constellation*).

pexa *vt.* fish (*for*). • *n.* fishing, angling. **pexa con serca** seine (*fish with a dragnet*). **pexa per pomas** bob for apples. **pexa ueb** phishing.

pexeria *n.* fishery.

pexeta *n.* minnow (*fish*: *Phoxinus*).

-pexia *n.suff.* -pexy (*fastening*).

pexor *n.* fisherman, angler; kingfisher (*bird*: *Alcedines*). **pexor ueb** phisher.

pf *abbr.* (*per favore*) please.

pH [pe'haʃ] *n.* pH.

pi *n.* pi (*Greek letter* Π, π).

pia *vi.* & *n.* tweet, twitter, beep, bleep, chirp, squeak. **pia longa** *v.* & *n.* squeal.

piador *n.* pager, beeper.

piafa *vi.*, *vt.* & *n.* stamp, stomp (*feet*).

piamadre *n.* pia mater (*anatomy*).

pianiste *n.* pianist.

piano *n.* piano, pianoforte. **piano automata** pianola, player piano. **piano de enrola** pianola, player piano.

piastre *n.* piastre (US piaster) (*currency*).

pibgorn *n.* pibgorn, hornpipe (*musical instrument*).

pica[1] *vt.* & *n.* sting, peck, prick. **pica de spino** pinprick.

pica[2] *n.* pika (*animal*: *Ochotona minor*).

pica[3] *n.* pica (*food craving*).

picador *n.* sting, stinger.

picalili *n.* piccalilli (*sauce*).

picante *adj.* stinging, piquant.

picatarte *n.* rockfowl (*bird*: *Picathartesa*).

picia *n.* tininess, minuteness.

picnica *vi.* & *n.* picnic.

pico[1] *adj.* tiny, teeny, minute, minuscule, miniscule, puny. • *adv.* slightly, a little. • *n.* bit, dash, pinch, smidgen, soupçon, speck, spot, tad, trace, modicum (*tiny amount*); trifle, bagatelle. **pico de pan** crumb, breadcrumb. **pico de sal** pinch of salt. **pico e pico** little by little. **picos** bits, smithereens. **un pico de** a very small quantity of, a little bit of, a few. **un plu pico de** a little more of, a bit more of.

pico-[2] *pref.* pico- (*a million-millionth*).

picolo *n.* piccolo (*flute*).

picon *n.* pick, pickaxe (US pickax).

picor *n.* picador (*bullfighter*); woodpecker (*bird*: *Picinae*).

picosecondo *n.* picosecond.

Piemonte *n.* Piedmont (*Italian region*).

piemontese *adj.* & *n.* Piedmontese (*person*, *language*).

piga *n.* magpie (*bird*: *Cissa*, *Cyanopica*, *Pica*, *Urocissa*). **piga blu** blue magpie (*Urocissa*). **piga comun** Eurasian magpie (*Pica*). **piga itiopian** Stresemann's bushcrow (*Zavattariornis*). **piga sian** azure-winged magpie (*Cyanopica*). **piga verde** green magpie (*Cissa*).

pigmento *n.* pigment, pigmentation.

pigmeo *n.* pygmy.

pigra *adj.* lazy, languid, idle, indolent, lackadaisical, slothful. • *n.* lazy person, lazybones, idler, deadbeat, goldbricker, sluggard, wastrel.

pigri *vi.* laze, lounge, bask, idle; loiter, dawdle, dally, tarry. • *vt.* make lazy.

pigria *n.* laziness, idleness.

pijin *n.* pidgin (*language*).

pijon *n.* pigeon, dove (*Columbidae*). **Pijon** *n.* Columba (*constellation*). **pijon de bosce** wood pigeon (*Columba palumbus*). **pijon de rocas** rock pigeon, rock dove (*Columba livia*).

pijoneria *n.* dovecot, dovecote.

pijoneta *n.* squab (*baby pigeon*).

pil *n.* pill, tablet. **pil de doman** morning-after pill. **pil rombo** lozenge.

pila *vt.* pile, heap, stack. • *n.* pile, heap, stack; battery. **pila de combustable** fuel cell. **pila de lenio** woodpile.

pilaf *n.* pilaf (*food*).

pilastro *n.* pilaster (*column*).

pilipina *adj.* & *n.* Philippine. **Mar Pilipina** Philippine Sea.

Pilipinas *n.pl.* Philippines.—The form is normally *la Pilipinas*.

piloral *adj.* pyloric.

pilori *n.* pillory, stocks. • *vt.* pillory.

piloro *n.* pylorus (*anatomy*).

pilote *n.* pilot.

piloteria *n.* cockpit.

pilsen *n.* pils, pilsner (*beer*).

pimento *n.* allspice, pimento, pimiento, Jamaica pepper (*tree*, *spice*: *Pimenta dioica*).

pimpinela *n.* pimpernel (*Anagallis*, *Lysimachia*). **pimpinela scarlata** scarlet pimpernel (*Anagallis arvensis arvensis*).

pina *n.* fin. **pina dorsal** dorsal fin. **pina ladal** pectoral fin.

pinaculo *n.* pinnacle, spire, steeple.

pinaculor *n.* steeplejack.

pinbal *n.* pinball, flipper.

pineal *adj.* pineal (*anatomy*). **glande pineal** pineal gland.

pinguin *n.* penguin (*Spheniscidae*).

piniacolada *n.* piña colada (*drink*).

piniata *n.* piñata (*container of treats*).

piniin *n.* Pinyin (*transcription*).

pinion *n.* gear, pinion. **pinion cono** bevel gear. **pinion elica** helical gear.

pino *n.* pine (*tree*: *Pinus*).
pinocle *n.* pinochle (*card game*).
pinse *n.* pincers, pliers, tongs. **pinse de cosini** tongs. **pinse de vestes** clothespin, clothespeg. **pinse medical** forceps. **pinse vascular** haemostat (US hemostat).
pinseta *n.* tweezers.
pinsi *vt.* & *n.* pinch, nip, tweeze, tweak.
pinson *n.* finch (*bird*: *Fringillidae*).
pinta *n.* paint. **pinta de acua** water-based paint. **pinta de corpo** body paint. **pinta de emulsion** emulsion paint. **pinta de fas** facepaint. **pinta de olio** oil paint, oil-based paint. **pinta prima** primer.
pinti *vt.* paint. See *depinta*.
pintida *adj.* painted.
pintilabio *n.* lipstick.
pintisil *n.* mascara.
pintiungia *n.* nail polish.
pintor *n.* painter. See *depintor*.
piolio *n.* louse (*insect*: *Phthiraptera*).
piopio *n.* piopio, turnagra (*bird*: *Turnagra*).
pip *interj.* & *n.* squeak, tweet, peep, cheep (*mouse*, *bird*).
pipa *n.* pipe (*smoking*). **pipa de acua** hookah, bong, water pipe.
pipal *n.* pipal, peepul, sacred fig, bo tree, bodhi tree (*Ficus religiosa*).
pipeta *n.* pipette. **pipeta de oio** eyedropper.
pipi *vi.* squeak, tweet, peep, cheep.
pipilo *n.* towhee (*bird*: *Pipilo*).
pipin *adj.* pipelike, pipe-shaped.
pira *n.* pyre (*bonfire*).
piramide *n.* pyramid.
pirania *n.* piranha (*Piranha*).
pirata *n.* pirate, buccaneer. **pirata de rede** hacker, cracker.
pirati *vt.* hack, crack; pirate, bootleg, make a pirate copy of.
piratia *n.* piracy.
pirinean *adj.* Pyrenean.
Pirineo *n.* Pyrenees. **Montes Pirineo** Pyrenees.
pirita *n.* iron pyrite, fool's gold (*mineral*).
piro- *pref.* pyro- (*fire*).
pirogi *n.* pierogi, perogi, varenyky (*dumplings*).
piromania *n.* pyromania.
piromanica *adj.* pyromaniacal. • *n.* pyromaniac.
pirometral *adj.* pyrometric.
pirometre *n.* pyrometer.
pirotecnica *n.* pyrotechnics.
pirotecnical *adj.* pyrotechnical. • *n.* firework display.
pirueta *vi.* & *n.* pirouette.
pirula *n.* bullfinch (*bird*: *Pyrrhula*).
pisa *n.* (*colloquial*) piss, pee, wee (*urine*).
pisea *n.* spruce (*tree*: *Picea*).
pisi *vt.* (*colloquial*) piss, pee, wee (*urinate*).
pisin *adj.* & *n.* Tok Pisin (*language*).
pisina *n.* swimming pool.
piso *n.* pea (*plant*, *seed*: *Pisum sativum*).
pistaxio *n.* pistachio (*tree*, *nut*: *Pistacia vera*).
pistil *n.* pistil (*botany*).
pistol *n.* pistol, handgun. **pistol de cola** glue gun. **pistol eletrical** stun gun, taser. **pistol per solda** soldering gun.
pistoli *vt.* fight with pistols. • *n.* pistol fight, gunfight.
pistolor *n.* gunfighter, gunslinger, gunman.
piston *n.* piston. **piston de mole** pestle. See *bol*.
pita[1] *n.* pitta (*bird*: *Pitta*).
pita[2] *n.* pitta (US pita), Arabic bread, Syrian bread. **pita de falafel** falafel. **pita elinica** gyro, gyros.
Pitagora *n.* Pythagoras.
pitagoran *adj.* Pythagorean.
piton *n.* python (*Pythonidae*).
pitui *n.* pitohui (*bird*: *Pitohui*).
pivote *vi.* & *vt.* pivot, swing round.
pixa *n.* (*colloquial*) cock, dick, prick, knob, willy (*penis*). **suca de pixa** blowjob. **suca la pixa** (*colloquial*) suck off, give a blowjob, blow, go down on (*fellatio*).
pixel *n.* pixel.
pixeli *vi.* & *vt.* pixellate. • *n.* pixellation.
pixeta *n.* (*insult*) jerk, schmuck, prat, dickhead, knobhead, tosser, wanker.
pixon *n.* (*colloquial*) hard-on, stiffy, boner, wood (*erection*).
piza *n.* pizza.
pizeria *n.* pizzeria.
pizicato *n.* pizzicato.
placa *vt.* plate. • *n.* plating; plate (*photographic*, *mechanical*); plaque (*tablet*). **placa de nom** nameplate. **placa de veculo** vehicle registration plate, licence (US license) plate, number plate. **placa dental** dental plaque. **placa tetonical** tectonic plate.
placozon *n.* placozoon (pl. placozoa) (*organism*: *Placazoa*).
plaia *n.* beach, shore, seashore.
plajia *vt.* plagiarize. • *n.* plagiarism.
plajior *n.* plagiarist.
plana *adj.* flat (*not bumpy*), plane, planar, level; smooth, even, flush. • *n.* plane (*surface*); counter, worktop (*surface*). **plana sajital** sagittal plane (*anatomy*). See *plata*.
planador *n.* plane, planing tool, planer.
planaria *n.* planarian (*worm*: *Planaria*).
plance *n.* plank, board, batten. **plance compresada** hardboard. **plance de embarca** gangplank, gangway. **plance de jeso** drywall, plasterboard, sheetrock, wallboard. **plance de lava** washboard.

plance de neva snowboard. **plance de solo** floorboard. **plance de surfa** surfboard. **plance de vela** sailboard.
planceta *n.* board (*small*). **planceta de ceso** cheese board. **planceta de clip** clipboard. **planceta de pan** bread board. **planceta de talia** cutting board.
planci *vt.* board, board up.
plancton *n.* plankton.
planeta *n.* planet.
planetal *adj.* planetary.
planeteria *n.* planetarium.
planeterieta *n.* orrery (*solar system model*).
planetesimo *n.* planetesimal.
planeteta *n.* minor planet, asteroid.
planetolojia *n.* planetology.
planetolojiste *n.* planetologist.
planeton *n.* giant planet. **planeton de gas** gas giant.
plani *vi.* flatten, plane, level, become even. • *vt.* flatten, plane, level, make even.
planida *adj.* flattened. **planida a la polos** oblate.
plano *n.* plain, pampas, flatland. **plano alta** plateau, high plain, mesa, altiplano, paramo, tableland. **plano continental** continental shelf. **plano deluvial** floodplain.
planta[1] *vt.* plant. • *n.* plant; planting. **planta infestante** weed. **plantas** plants, vegetation, flora, greenery.
planta[2] *n.* sole (*foot*). **planta de sapato** sole (*shoe*). **planta interna** innersole, insole.
plantago *n.* plantain, fleawort (*plant*: *Plantago*).
plantal[1] *adj.* plant-related, vegetational.
plantal[2] *adj.* plantar (*of the sole*).
plantano *n.* plantain (*plant, fruit*: *Musa acuminata, Musa balbisiana*).
plantigrada *adj.* plantigrade (*biology*).
plantosa *adj.* verdant.
plantosia *n.* verdure.
plase *vt.* please; humour (US humor). • *n.* pleasingness, pleasantness, agreeableness. **lo plase me** it pleases me, I like it.
plasebo *adj.* & *n.* placebo (*medical*).
plaseda *adj.* pleased.
plasenta *n.* placenta; afterbirth.
plasental *adj.* placental.
plasente *adj.* pleasing, pleasant, agreeable, welcome, complaisant, tasteful.
plaser *n.* pleasure, enjoyment. **plaser odiosa** Schadenfreude. **plaser vergoniosa** guilty pleasure.
plaserosa *adj.* pleasurable, enjoyable.
-plasia *n.suff.* -plasia (*growth*).
plasma[1] *n.* plasma (*medical, gas*).
-plasma[2] *n.suff.* -plasm (*growth*).
plasmasite *n.* plasmacyte (*biology*).
-plasmica *adj.suff.* -plasmic.
plasmodio *n.* plasmodium (*organism*).
-plastia *n.suff.* -plasty (*surgery*).
plastica[1] *adj.* & *n.* plastic. **plastica abrasante** shrink wrap. **plastica de bolas** bubblewrap. **plastica de vitro** glass-reinforced plastic, fibreglass (US fiberglass). **plastica polalida** polaroid.
-plastica[2] *adj.suff.* -plastic (*surgical*).
plasto *n.* plastid (*biology*).
plata *adj.* flat (*level and thin*), flattened, thin; plain (*text file*). • *n.* plate, platen. **plata de cupre** copperplate (*engraving*). **plata de forno** sheet pan. **plata jirante** turntable (*rail*). **plata per biscotos** cookie sheet. See *plana*.
plataforma *n.* platform, podium, rostrum, dais, catwalk. **plataforma de petrolio** oil platform, oil rig. **plataforma de predica** pulpit. **plataforma rolante** rolling platform, dolly.
platan *n.* sycamore (*tree*: *Platanus*).
platdeutx *adj.* & *n.* Plattdeutsch, Low Saxon, Low German (*language*).
plateta *n.* saucer.
plati *vi.* & *vt.* flatten.
platielminto *n.* platyhelminth, flatworm (*Platyhelminthes*).
platin *adj.* flattish.
platino *n.* platinum.
platizon *n.* platyzoon (pl. platyzoa) (*organism*).
plato *n.* plate, dish; course. **lava la platos** wash the dishes, wash up, do the washing-up. **plato de disco** turntable. **plato de la dia** dish of the day. **plato de lenio** trencher. **plato de Petri** Petri dish. **plato miscada** mixed dish, salmagundi. **plato prima** starter, first course. **platos de forno** ovenware.
Platon[1] *n.* Plato (*philosopher*).
platon[2] *n.* platter, tray. **platon de esflue** output tray.
platonica *adj.* platonic.
platonisme *n.* Platonism.
plaza *n.* plaza, (*town*) square.
plectro *n.* plectrum.
-plejia *n.suff.* -plegia (*paralysis*).
-plejica *adj.suff.* -plegic.
plen *adj.* full, filled, gravid, teeming. • *adv.* fully. **es plen de** be full of, abound in, teem with, be rife with, be fraught with, be riddled with. **partal plen** half full.
pleni *vi.* & *vt.* fill, stuff, pad, stock, cram, engorge. • *n.* filling, stuffing (*action*). **pleni la spasio** fill in the blank.
plenia *n.* fullness, satiety.
pleniboca *n.* mouthful; tongue twister.
plenibraso *n.* armful, armload.

plenida *adj.* filled. • *n.* plenum (*filled space*). **plenida de** fed up with.
plenimano *n.* handful.
pleninte *adj.* filling. • *n.* filling, stuffing (*substance*); filler, stopgap, expletive.
plenioio *n.* eyeful.
pleniorea *n.* earful.
plenipunio *n.* fistful.
plenisaco *n.* bagful.
pleo- *pref.* pleo- (*more*).
plesiosauro *n.* plesiosaur (*Plesiosauria*).
pleso *n.* plexus (*anatomy*).
plestosene *adj.* & *n.* Pleistocene (*geology*).
pleura *n.* pleura (*anatomy*).
pleural *adj.* pleural.
pleurite *n.* pleuritis, pleurisy (*medical*).
plia *vt.* fold, bend, crease, tuck. • *n.* fold, bend, crease, tuck; furrow; sulcus. **plia de codo** crook of the arm. **plia de jeno** crook of the leg, back of the knee; genuflection, genuflexion. **plia de jenos** curtsy. **plia de tempo** time warp. **plia sua jenos** curtsy. **plia sua oios** squint, half-close one's eyes. **plia un jeno** genuflect. **plia vosal** vocal fold, vocal cord (*anatomy*).
pliable *adj.* foldable, folding, collapsible, pliable, pliant.
Pliades *n.pl.* Pleiades (*mythology*, *stars*).
plieta *vt.* wrinkle, shrivel, crumple, crimp, wither, pucker, purse, furrow. • *n.* wrinkle, crinkle, crimp, pucker, furrow. **plieta sua fronte** furrow one's brow.
plietosa *adj.* wrinkled, shrivelled (US shriveled), wizened, crumpled, crinkled, crinkly, puckered, puckery, plissé.
pliosene *adj.* & *n.* Pliocene (*anatomy*).
plisa *vt.* pleat (*stitched fold*). • *n.* pleat.
plomin *adj.* leaden.
plomo *n.* lead. **sin plomo** unleaded.
plomor *n.* plumber.
plora *vt.* cry, weep, bawl. • *n.* cry.
ploreta *vt.* & *n.* whimper.
plorosa *n.* crybaby.
ploton *n.* platoon.
plu *det.* more, additional, extra, further, other, another; e.g. *plu tempo*; *plu problemes*; *un plu peso de torta*. • *adv.* more; any more, any further, any longer; in addition, besides, moreover, furthermore; e.g. *plu fria ca*. • *conj.* plus (*arithmetic*). **a la plu** at most. **la plu** the most, the maximum; e.g. *la dia la plu longa*; *mea ami la plu cara*. **la plu de** most, the majority of; e.g. *la plu de persones*. **no plu** no longer, no more, not any more (*time*). **per la plu** mostly, for the most part. **plu … plu** the more … the more; e.g. *plu me deveni vea, min me recorda*; *plu me leje, min me sabe*; *plu me senta, plu me deveni fria*. **plu ca nesesada** more than necessary, excessive, superfluous, redundant, overkill, supernumerary. **plu ca sempre** more than ever. **plu e plu** more and more, ever more. **plu o min** more or less, approximately.
pluf *n.* & *interj.* splash, plop, splat.
plufi *vi.* & *vt.* splash, plop, splat; dabble (*in water*).
pluma *n.* feather, quill. **pluma nonmatur** pinfeather. **plumas** feathers, plumage.
plumasedin *n.* silky-flycatcher (*bird*: *Ptilogonatidae*).
plumbago *n.* plumbago (*plant*: *Plumbago*).
plumeria *n.* plumeria, frangipani (*tree*: *Plumeria*).
plumi *vt.* feather, fletch.
plumin *adj.* feathery, featherlike.
plumon *n.* plume (*feathers*, *smoke*). **plumon de despolvi** feather duster.
plumosa *adj.* feathery (*full of feathers*).
plural *adj.* & *n.* plural.
plurali *vi.* & *vt.* pluralize.
pluralia *n.* plurality.
pluralisme *n.* pluralism.
pluraliste *n.* pluralist.
Pluto *n.* Pluto (*mythology*, *planet*).
plutocrata *n.* plutocrat.
plutocratia *n.* plutocracy.
plutonio *n.* plutonium.
pluve *vi.* rain. • *n.* rain, rainfall. **lo pluve** it's raining.
pluveta *vi.* & *n.* shower, drizzle. **pluveta lamposa** thundershower.
pluvial *n.* plover (*bird*: *Pluvialis*). **pluvial de Egipte** Egyptian plover (*Pluvianus aegyptius*). **pluvial de Magalan** Magellanic plover (*Pluvianellus socialis*).
pluvon *n.* rainstorm, downpour, cloudburst, soaker.
pluvosa *adj.* rainy, wet, inclement.
pm *abbr.* (*pos mediadia*) p.m.
-pnea *n.suff.* -pnea (*breathing*).
pneumato- *pref.* pneumato- (*air*).
pneumo- *pref.* pneumo- (*air*).
pneumonia *n.* pneumonia.
poca *det.* few (*in number*), little (*quantity*).—*Poca* emphasises the smallness of the quantity. A more general way of saying *a few* or *a little* is *alga*. • *adv.* (*only a*) little, not much. • *pron.* little, few (*singular or plural*). **poca min** *adj.* (*only a*) little less, few less. • *adv.* (*only a*) little less. **poca plu** *adj.* (*only a*) little more, few more. • *adv.* (*only a*) little more. **pocas** (*people or things*, *optional plural pronoun*). **tan poca como posible** as few as possible, as little as possible.
pocer *n.* poker (*card game*).
poci *vi.* & *vt.* reduce in quantity.
podcasta *vt.* & *n.* podcast.
podolojia *n.* podiatry, chiropody.

podolojiste *n.* podiatrist, chiropodist.
podometre *n.* pedometer.
poesia *n.* poem, verse; poetry. **mal poesia** bad poetry, doggerel. **poesia de lamenta** elegy.
poesial *adj.* poetic.
poesin *adj.* poetic, picturesque.
poesiste *n.* poet.
pogrom *n.* pogrom (*massacre*).
poi *n.* poi (*food*).
-poiese *n.suff.* -poiesis (*forming*).
poitin *n.* poteen, potheen (*drink*).
polal *adj.* polar.
polali *vi.* & *vt.* polarize. • *n.* polarization.
polalia *n.* polarity (*electric*, *magnetic*).
polca *n.* polka (*dance*).
polder *n.* polder (*reclaimed land*).
polemica *n.* polemic.
polemiciste *n.* polemicist.
polen *n.* pollen.
poleni *vt.* pollinate. • *n.* pollination.
polenta *n.* polenta (*food*).
polex *n.* pollex, thumb (*technical*).
poli- *pref.* poly- (*many*).
poliamia *n.* polyamory.
poliamial *adj.* polyamorous.
poliandria *n.* polyandry (*marriage*).
poliandrial *adj.* polyandrous.
polidatilia *n.* polydactyly (*biology*).
polidatilo *adj.* polydactylic.
poliedro *adj.* polyhedral. • *n.* polyhedron.
poliester *n.* polyester. **de poliester** (*made of*) polyester.
polietilen *n.* polyethylene, polythene.
polifonia *n.* polyphony (*music*).
polifonial *adj.* polyphonic.
poligala *n.* milkwort (*plant*: *Polygala*).
poligama *adj.* polygamous.
poligamia *n.* polygamy (*marriage*, *botany*).
poligamiste *n.* polygamist.
poligon *adj.* polygonal. • *n.* polygon.
polijinia *n.* polygyny (*marriage*).
polijinial *adj.* polygynous.
polimer *n.* polymer.
polimeri *vi.* & *vt.* polymerize. • *n.* polymerization.
polimeria *n.* polymerism.
polimerosa *adj.* polymeric, polymerous.
polimorfe *adj.* polymorphic.
polimorfia *n.* polymorphism.
Polinesia *n.* Polynesia. **Polinesia Franses** French Polynesia.
polinesian *adj.* & *n.* Polynesian.
polinomial *adj.* polynomial.
polinomio *n.* polynomial.
poliomielite *n.* polio, poliomyelitis.
polioptila *n.* gnatcatcher (*bird*: *Polioptilidae*).
polipeptido *n.* polypeptide (*chemistry*).
polipo *n.* polyp.
polisacarido *n.* polysaccharide (*sugar*).
polisia *n.* police.
polisieria *n.* police station.
polisilaba *n.* polysyllable.
polisilabal *adj.* polysyllabic.
polisior *n.* police officer, policeman, policewoman, constable, cop. **polisior barati** sepoy. **polisior canadian** mountie. **polisior engles** bobby. **polisior franses** gendarme. **polisior montante** mounted police officer, trooper.
polistiren *n.* polystyrene. **polistiren estruida** expanded polystyrene, polystyrene foam, styrofoam.
politburo *n.* politburo.
politecnical *n.* polytechnic.
politeisme [polite'isme] *n.* polytheism.
politeiste [polite'iste] *adj.* polytheistic. • *n.* polytheist.
politica *n.* politics; policy. **politica esterna** foreign policy. **politica interna** domestic policy. **politica perilosa** brinkmanship.
political *adj.* political.
politici *vi.* & *vt.* politicize.
politiciste *n.* politician.
poliuretan *n.* polyurethane.
polivalente *adj.* polyvalent.
polivinil *n.* polyvinyl chloride, PVC. **polivinil cuorin** naugahyde.
polo[1] *n.* pole (*magnetic*, *etc.*). **polo de sielo** celestial pole. **Polo Norde** North Pole. **Polo Sude** South Pole.
polo[2] *n.* polo (*sport*). **polo de acua** water polo.
polonesa *n.* polonaise (*dance*).
polonio *n.* polonium (*element*).
polpo *n.* octopus (*Octopoda*).
Polsca *n.* Poland.
polsce *adj.* Polish (*person*, *language*). • *n.* Polish, Pole.
polso *n.* wrist; cuff.
polvi *vi.* turn to dust, effloresce. • *vt.* powder, pulverize, atomize.
polvin *adj.* powdery.
polvo *n.* dust, powder. **covre con polvo** (*cover with*) dust, powder. **polvo cosmetica** cosmetic powder, face powder. **polvo de siera** sawdust. **polvo de talco** talcum powder, baby powder. **polvo negra** black powder, gunpowder. **polvo rojinte** rouge. **polvo xerografial** toner.
polvosa *adj.* dusty.
poma *n.* apple (*fruit*). **poma de Adam** Adam's apple, laryngeal prominence. **poma savaje** crab apple.
pomatostomo *n.* Australian babbler (*bird*: *Pomatostomus*).

pomelo *n.* grapefruit (*fruit, tree: Citrus × paradisi*).
pomis *n.* pumice (*rock*).
pomo *n.* apple (*tree: Malus*).
pomon *n.* pommel (*sword, saddle*).
pomoran *n.* pomeranian (*dog*).
pompa *n.* pump. **Pompa** *n.* Antlia (*constellation*).
pompador *n.* pompadour (*hairstyle*).
pomperia *n.* fire station, fire department.
pompi *vt.* pump. • *n.* pumping; push-up (*exercise*).
pompon *n.* pompom.
pompor *n.* firefighter, fireman.
pone *vt.* put, put down, place, lay, stick; impose. • *n.* placing, placement. **pone se en filo** get in line, queue up, form a queue. **pone sur scafal** shelve.
ponte *n.* bridge. **ponte de pasea** footbridge. **ponte de pontones** pontoon (*bridge*). **ponte levable** drawbridge, lift bridge.
ponteta *n.* scaffolding; scaffold (*gallows*).
ponti *vt.* bridge. **ponti la canion** bridge the gap.
ponton *n.* pontoon (*boat*).
pontxe *n.* punch, toddy, grog (*drink*). **pontxe de ovos** eggnog.
pontxo *n.* poncho (*garment*).
pop *adj.* & *n.* pop (*music*).
popa *n.* stern (*ship*); (*colloquial*) bum, butt, rear, tush (*buttocks*). **Popa** *n.* Puppis (*constellation*).
popal *adj.* aft, astern.
popcorn *n.* popcorn.
popelin *n.* poplin (*fabric*).
popla *vt.* populate. • *n.* population (*action, figure*); people (*a particular community*); populace, (*the*) masses, (*the*) public. **de la popla comun** plebeian. **popla laborante** working people, working masses.
poplada *adj.* populated. **multe poplada** populous.
poplal *adj.* popular (*of or by the populace*).
poplisme *n.* populism.
popliste *n.* populist.
poplo *n.* poplar (*tree: Populus*). **poplo tremante** aspen.
popular *adj.* popular.
populari *vi.* & *vt.* popularize. • *n.* popularization.
popularia *n.* popularity.
por *n.* pore (*opening*).
porceria *n.* pig sty, pigpen.
porceta *n.* piglet; piggy bank.
porcin *adj.* piglike, porcine.
porco *n.* pig, hog, swine (*Sus*); (*insult*) slob. **porco savaje** wild pig, razorback.
porcor *n.* swineherd.
porcospina *n.* porcupine (*Hystricomorpha*).
porfir *n.* porphyry (*rock*).
porifero *n.* porifer (*organism: Porifera*).
porno *adj.* (*colloquial*) porn. • *n.* porn; porno, porn film.
pornografia *n.* pornography, smut.
pornografial *adj.* pornographic.
pornografiste *n.* pornographer.
poro *n.* leek (*plant, vegetable: Allium ampeloprasum*).
porosa *adj.* porous.
-porose *n.suff.* -porosis (*medical*).
porselana *n.* porcelain, china.
porta *vt.* carry, bear, convey, tote; wear. • *n.* carrying, portage. **porta de trapa** trap door.
portabagaje *n.* boot (*UK*), trunk (*US*) (*of vehicle*).
portabal *n.* tee (*golf*).
portabebe *n.* baby sling, babycarrier.
portable *adj.* portable, mobile; wearable. • *n.* portable computer, laptop.
portabroca *n.* chuck (*gripping tool*).
portabulbo *n.* light socket, light fixture.
portacandela *n.* candleholder, candlestick, sconce.
portacaxon *n.* bier.
portaclave *n.* keyring, keychain.
portacoda *n.* hair tie, scrunchie.
portacontenador *n.* container ship.
portacopa *n.* cup holder.
portacua *n.* water trough. **portacua de avias** bird bath.
portaculpa *n.* scapegoat, fall guy, patsy.
portada *adj.* carried; worn. **portada par aira** airborne.
portadetrito *n.* skip, dumpster.
portador *n.* stand, holder, support.
portafeno *n.* trough, manger.
portaferida *n.* stretcher. **portaferida rolante** (*hospital*) trolley, gurney.
portaflexa *n.* quiver.
portaflor *n.* flowerpot.
portafolio *n.* portfolio, briefcase.
portaganto *n.* glovebox, glove compartment.
portagrafito *n.* mechanical pencil, propelling pencil, clutch pencil.
portainca *n.* inkpot, inkstand.
portainserta *n.* stock (*for graft*).
portajoala *n.* jewellery (US jewelry) case, jewellery (US jewelry) box, casket.
portalia [porta'lia] *n.* suspender belt (*UK*), garter belt (*US*).
portalibro *n.* bookstand, lectern.
portamento *n.* portamento, pitch bend (*music*).
portamone *n.* wallet, purse, billfold.
portamortero *n.* mortarboard.

portaovo *n.* eggcup.
portapaper *n.* folder. **portapaper de anelos** ring binder.
portapeca *n.* scapegoat, sacrificial lamb, whipping boy.
portapen *n.* pen holder.
portapil *n.* pillbox.
portapistol *n.* holster.
portaplanta *n.* planter.
portasene *n.* ashtray.
portaseno *n.* bra, brassiere. **portaseno de bicini** bikini top. **portaseno tubo** bandeau top. **sin portaseno** braless.
portaseso *n.* jockstrap; dance belt; codpiece.
portasigareta *n.* cigarette holder.
portaspada *n.* scabbard.
portaspino *n.* pincushion.
portatela *n.* towel rack, towel rail.
portatorxa *n.* torchbearer.
portatronco *n.* andiron (*holding logs in a fire*).
portaveste *n.* clothes rack, clothes rail, clothes rod, clothes pole, clothes horse, clothes airer.
portavion *n.* aircraft carrier.
portavose *n.* spokesperson, spokesman, spokeswoman. **portavose de sindicato** union steward, shop steward.
portaxapo *n.* hatbox.
porte *n.* door. **con porte retro** hatchback (*car*). **porte caruselin** revolving door. **porte contra esplodes** blast door. **porte de asede** hatch. **porte de rede** screen door. **porte-fenetra** *n.* French window, French door. **porte retro** back door, tailgate. **porte xef** front door.
porteta *n.* gate (*field, garden*), gateway; wicket (*gate, cricket*). **porteta de peaje** tollgate.
portico *n.* portico, porch.
porto[1] *n.* port, harbour (US harbor), seaport; port (*computer*). **porto de visita** port of call. **Porto Rica** Puerto Rico. **porto spasial** spaceport (*science fiction*).
porto[2] *n.* port (*wine*).
porton *n.* portal, gate (*castle, town*); sluice, sluice gate, floodgate (*of lock*).
portor *n.* porter, bellboy, bellhop; caddie (*golf*); pallbearer.
portorican *adj.* & *n.* Puerto Rican, Puertorican.
Portugal *n.* Portugal.
portuges *adj.* & *n.* Portuguese.
portulaca *n.* portulaca, purslane (*plant: Portulaca*).
pos *prep.* • behind (*in space or sequence*); e.g. *la gato dormi pos la sofa.* • (*moving*) to behind, to the back of; e.g. *la gato core pos la sofa.* • after, later than, since; in (*e.g. one week's time*); e.g. *desembre veni pos novembre*; *nos esperia la tona pos la lampo*; *me va reveni pos du dias*; *pos come, el ia dormi.*—*Pos* by itself is a preposition. When *after* means *afterwards*, the translation is *a pos*. If *after* introduces a subordinate clause, i.e. if it means *after the time when*, use *pos cuando* instead. • *pref.* post- (*happening later or located behind*); e.g. *posenebria*; *posalveolal*. **a pos** *prep.* behind, to behind; e.g. *la gato ia core a pos la sofa.* • *adv.* behind, at the back, at the rear; (*moving*) to the back; backward, backwards; (*time*) afterward, afterwards, later, then, next, subsequently, since. **de pos** *prep.* from behind; since (*time*); e.g. *mea madre abita asi de pos la mori de sua sposo.* • *adv.* from behind. **e a pos?** and then?, and what happened next? **pos du dias** after two days, two days later. See *cuando*.
posa *vt.* pose, posture, position, arrange, lay out, deploy. • *n.* pose, posture, position, arrangement, layout, deployment. **sin posa** unposed, candid (*photo*).
posalveolal *adj.* postalveolar. • *n.* postalveolar (*consonant*).
posanal *adj.* postanal.
posardador *n.* afterburner.
poscopulal *adj.* postcoital.
posdati *vt.* postdate.
posefeto *n.* aftereffect.
posenebria *n.* hangover.
posesal *adj.* possessive (*grammar*).
posese *vt.* possess, own. • *n.* possession, ownership (*state*).
poseseda *adj.* possessed, owned. • *n.* possession (*item*). **posesedas** possessions, belongings, effects, chattels.
posesente *adj.* possessive (*person*).
posesor *n.* possessor, owner.
posgeral *adj.* post-war.
posgraduada *adj.* & *n.* postgraduate.
posible *adj.* possible, feasible, potential. • *adv.* possibly, maybe, perhaps. • *n.* possibility, opportunity (*something possible*). **otra posible** alternate, alternative, other possibility. **un otra idea posible** an alternative idea, an alternate idea, another possible idea.
posiblia *n.* possibility (*quality*).
posimaje *n.* afterimage.
posimpresa *n.* afterimage, afterimpression.
posirurjial *adj.* postoperative.
positiva *adj.* positive.
positivia *n.* positivity.
positron *n.* positron (*particle*).
posmedia *n.* afternoon.
posmenopausal *adj.* postmenopausal.
posnasal *adj.* postnasal.
posnomal *adj.* & *n.* postnominal (*grammar*).
poso *n.* well (*shaft*). **poso de cloaca** cesspit, cesspool.

pospone *vt.* postpone, procrastinate, delay, defer; suspend (*judgement*). • *n.* postponement, procrastination, delay, deferral, deferment, wait, hold-up, continuance, stay (*of execution*).
posposada *n.* postposition (*grammar*).
posta *vt.* post, mail (*letter, parcel*); post (*accounting, internet, etc.*). • *n.* post, mail; posting. **posta airal** airmail. **posta caracolin** snail mail. **posta de odia** hate mail.
postadio *n.* backstage area.
postal *adj.* postal.
poster *n.* poster; pin-up. **no afisa posteres** stick no bills, post no bills. **poster teatral** playbill.
posteri *vi.* & *vt.* posterize. • *n.* posterization.
posteria *n.* post office.
posterior *adj.* posterior, rear, hind, caudal. • *n.* backside, behind, bottom, rear, derriere, bum, butt, tush; hindquarters; butt, stock (*rifle*).
posto *n.* position, function, office, post, job, capacity. **ave sua posto en** be stationed in, be posted in. **posto fasil** sinecure.
postor *n.* postman, postwoman, mailman.
postraumal *adj.* post-traumatic.
potasio *n.* potassium.
pote *vt.* can, be able to, have the opportunity to, have the chance to. **lo pote es ce** maybe, perhaps, it could be; e.g. *lo pote es ce nos es perdeda.* **ta pote** could, would be able to, might be able to (*simple conditional, or polite, or commenting without expectation*); e.g. *nos ta pote aida.*
potensia *n.* potential.
potensial *adj.* potential.
potente *adj.* able, capable.
potia *n.* power, might, potency, clout; power (*electric, mathematics*). **potia de esecuta** executive power. **potia de judi** judicial power. **potia de legi** legislative power. **potia de spara** firepower. **potia idraulical** waterpower.
potiosa *adj.* powerful, mighty, potent. • *n.* power, (*economic*) leader, mover, powerhouse.
poto *n.* potto (*primate: Perodicticus potto*).
povre *adj.* poor, impoverished, needy, destitute, penurious, indigent; pitiful, pitiable, piteous, pathetic. • *n.* pauper.
povreria *n.* poorhouse, almshouse.
povri *vi.* become poor, fall into poverty. • *vt.* make poor, impoverish.
povria *n.* poverty, penury.
pox *n.* pocket; pouch (*anatomy*); buffer (*software*). **pox de copia** clipboard, copy buffer (*software*).
poxe *vt.* poach, blanch, parboil (*cookery*).
poxi *vt.* pocket.
pradeta *n.* clearing, glade.
prado *n.* meadow, meadowland, prairie.
pragmatica *n.* pragmatics (*linguistics*).
Praha *n.* Prague.
pralin *n.* praline (*food*).
praseodimio *n.* praseodymium (*element*).
pratica *vt.* practise (US practice), rehearse. • *n.* practice, praxis; convention; exercise, rehearsal. **pratica de banco** banking practice. **pratica model** exemplary practice.
pratical *adj.* practical, pragmatic, feasible, down to earth, sensible, level-headed, matter-of-fact, utilitarian, convenient, expedient.
praticalia *n.* practicality, feasibility, sensibility.
praticalisme *n.* pragmatism.
praticaliste *n.* pragmatist.
praticor *n.* practitioner.
-praxia *n.suff.* -praxia (*medical*).
pre- *pref.* pre- (*happening earlier*); e.g. *previde, preistoria.*
prea *vt.* pray, implore, plead, beseech, entreat. • *n.* prayer, entreaty. **prea de grasias** grace. **prea de sera** vesper.
preadolesente *adj.* preadolescent, prepubescent. • *n.* preadolescent, preteen, tween.
preafirma *vt.* preaffirm.
preajusta *vi.* & *vt.* preadjust, preadapt, preset, pretune.
preambul *n.* preamble.
preaverti *vt.* forewarn. • *n.* forewarning.
precaldi *vi.* & *vt.* preheat.
precambrian *adj.* & *n.* Precambrian (*geology*).
precanserosa *adj.* precancerous.
precomanda *vt.* & *n.* preorder.
preconose *vt.* know in advance, have foreknowledge of. • *n.* foreknowledge, precognition.
preconosente *adj.* precognisant.
preconsidera *vt.* premeditate. • *n.* premeditation, forethought, forward planning.
precopula *vi.* & *n.* foreplay.
precopulal *adj.* precoital.
precorsor *n.* pacemaker, pacesetter (*in race*).
preda *n.* prey.
predati *vt.* backdate.
predefini *vt.* predefine.
predeluvial *adj.* antediluvian.
predestina *vt.* predestine. • *n.* predestination.
predetermina *vt.* predetermine, preordain. • *n.* predetermination.
predeterminisme *n.* predeterminism, fatalism.

predeterministe *adj.* predeterministic, fatalistic. • *n.* predeterminist, fatalist.
predica *vt.* preach, moralize; predicate. • *n.* sermon; predicate (*grammar*, *logic*).
predicativa *adj.* & *n.* predicative.
predicosa *adj.* preachy.
predisable *adj.* predictable.
predise *vt.* predict, forecast, prophesy, foretell, prognosticate. • *n.* prediction, forecast, prognosis, prophecy.
predisente *adj.* predicting, prophetic.
predor *n.* predator, raptor.
preeclampsia *n.* pre-eclampsia (*medical*).
preelejal *adj.* pre-election.
preeleje *vt.* preselect.
preenscrive *vt.* pre-register.
preesamina *vt.* precheck, pre-examine, pretest.
preesiste *vi.* pre-exist.
preesistente *adj.* pre-existing.
prefabrica *vt.* prefabricate. • *n.* prefabrication, prefab.
prefabricada *adj.* prefabricated, prefab.
prefasa *vt.* preface. • *n.* preface, foreword, prologue.
preferable *adj.* preferable.
preferal *adj.* preferential.
prefere *vt.* prefer, favour (US favor). • *n.* preference, taste, predilection; setting, option (*software*). **prefere de mano** handedness.
prefereda *adj.* preferred, favourite (US favorite), of choice. • *n.* preference, favourite (US favorite).
prefetia *n.* prefecture.
prefeto *n.* prefect.
prefisa *vt.* prefix; e.g. *on prefisa un silaba a un radis.* • *n.* prefix; area code, dialling (US dialing) code, exchange (*phone*); prefixing, prefixation.
prefortador *n.* preamplifier, preamp.
pregeral *adj.* pre-war.
pregraduada *adj.* & *n.* undergraduate.
pregrasia *vt.* thank in advance.
pregrasias *interj.* thanks in advance.
preistoria [prei'storia] *n.* prehistory.
preistorial [preistori'al] *adj.* prehistoric, prehistorical.
prejual *adj.* pregame, prematch.
prejudi *vt.* prejudge, preconceive. • *n.* prejudice, bigotry, bias, preconception.
prejudosa *adj.* prejudiced, biased, bigoted, tendentious, narrow-minded. **es prejudosa contra** be prejudiced against, discriminate against.
prelavada *adj.* prewashed, preshrunk.
prelitigal *adj.* pretrial.
prematur *adj.* premature. • *n.* premature baby, preemie.
premedical *adj.* premedical, premed.
prememori *vt.* cache.
prememoria *n.* cache, cache memory (*software*).
premenstrual *adj.* premenstrual.
premia *vt.* award. • *n.* awards ceremony.
premiada *adj.* award-winning.
premio *n.* prize, award, accolade; reward. **premio lodante** commendation, honour (US honor), recognition. **premio xef** jackpot, top prize.
premior *n.* prize-winner, award-winner, title holder.
premisa *n.* premise (*principle*).
premisca *vt.* premix.
premoral *adj.* premoral, innocent.
premostra *vt.* presage, augur, portend, foreshadow, forebode, bode.
prende *vt.* take, get, seize, appropriate, confiscate; capture, take (*chess*); pick up; pick (*flower*). • *n.* taking, seizure, appropriation, confiscation; electrical outlet; trick (*card games*). **prende controla** take control, take over. **prende de propria** expropriation. **prende la propria de** expropriate. **prende la rol de** take the role of, be cast as. **prende sua tempo** take one's time.
prendor *n.* taker, catcher.
prenomal *adj.* & *n.* prenominal (*grammar*).
prensil *adj.* prehensile.
preocupa *vt.* preoccupy, concern, engross; worry, cause worry. • *n.* preoccupation, worry; hobbyhorse.
preocupada *adj.* preoccupied. **es preocupada** be preoccupied, worry, brood. **preocupada de custa** cost-conscious.
preordina *vt.* prearrange, preordain.
prepaci *vt.* prepackage.
prepaia *vt.* prepay, pay in advance. • *n.* prepayment.
prepaiada *adj.* prepaid; post-paid (*letter*, *parcel*); pay-as-you-go (*phone*).
prepara *vt.* prepare, set, prime, ready, groom; make (*dinner*, *tea*, *coffee*, *beer*), brew; cure (*meat*). • *n.* preparation, preparations, prep, build-up, warm-up, work-up, readiness; potion, brew, concoction, tonic, elixir. **prepara afrodisica** philtre (US philter). **prepara per inverno** winterize.
preparada *adj.* prepared, ready, set, poised; cured (*meat*). **preparada per batalia** ready for battle, on the warpath.
preposada *n.* preposition (*grammar*).
prepus *n.* prepuce (*anatomy*); clitoral hood; foreskin.
prerejistra *vt.* pre-record.
presa *vt.* press, push, squeeze, hold tight, compress, constrict; pressure, pressurize (*someone to do something*); iron (*clothes*). • *n.*

pressure. **presa de grupo** peer pressure. **presa de manos** handshake, handclasp. **presa manos con** shake hands with. **presa sangual** blood pressure.
presada *adj.* compact, compressed.
presador *n.* press, squeezer; mangle. **presador de vino** winepress.
presalio *n.* garlic press, garlic crusher.
presapantalon *n.* trouser press.
presaveste *n.* (*clothes*) iron.
presbiope *adj.* long-sighted, presbyopic.
presbiopia *n.* long-sightedness, presbyopia.
presbiterian *adj.* & *n.* Presbyterian.
presbiterianisme *n.* Presbyterianism (*Christianity*).
prescolal *adj.* preschool.
prescrive *vt.* prescribe, dictate. • *n.* prescription. **sin prescrive** without prescription, over the counter.
presede *vt.* precede, predate. • *n.* precedence; precession (*astronomy*).
presedente *adj.* preceding, previous, prior, former, precursory. • *n.* precedent, precursor, predecessor, forerunner, antecedent (*thing*); prequel. **sin presedente** unprecedented, history-making, historic, record-breaking.
presedor *n.* predecessor, precursor, forerunner (*person*).
presensa *vt.* foresee, have a premonition. • *n.* premonition, presentiment.
presenta *vt.* present, introduce (*person*); publicize; perform (*feat*, *role*, *script*); award, bestow; submit (*offer*). • *n.* presentation, introduction; publicity (*announcement*); performance, rendition, recital; stunt. **presenta prima** first performance, debut. **presenta teatral** play (*theatrical*), drama. **presenta temprana** matinee. **presentas de promove** promotional material.
presentable *adj.* presentable.
presente *adj.* present (*time*, *not absent*); current, incumbent. • *n.* present (*time*); attendee, person present. **a presente** at present. **es presente a** be present at, attend. **per la presente** for the present, for now, for the moment, for the time being, provisionally.
presentia *n.* presence, attendance.
presentor *n.* presenter, performer, showman; anchor (*news*); lecturer. **presentor de clima** weather presenter, weather forecaster, weatherman, weatherwoman. **presentor de novas** news presenter, news anchor, newsreader, newscaster, anchorman, anchorwoman.
preseta *vt.* squeeze lightly. • *n.* light squeeze.
preside *vt.* preside, chair.
presidental *adj.* presidential.
presidente *adj.* presiding. • *n.* president, chairperson, chairman, chairwoman, speaker (*legislative*). **presidente pasada** ex-president.
presidentia *n.* presidency.
presinapsal *adj.* presynaptic (*biology*).
presipe *adj.* steep, precipitous. • *n.* precipice, crag, cliff, escarpment, chasm, abyss.
presipita *vi.* precipitate (*rain*). • *vt.* precipitate, deposit. • *n.* precipitation.
presipitada *adj.* precipitated. • *n.* precipitate (*substance*).
presirurjial *adj.* presurgical, preoperative.
presivilia *n.* precivilization.
presta *vt.* lend, loan. • *n.* loan. **presta per casa** home loan. **presta per studia** student loan.
prestijia *n.* prestige, status, cachet.
prestijiosa *adj.* prestigious.
prestor *n.* lender, moneylender.
presuposa *vt.* presuppose. • *n.* presupposition.
pretal *adj.* priestly, sacerdotal.
pretaliada *adj.* pre-cut.
prete *n.* priest, priestess, clergyman, clergywoman, pastor. **prete fema** priestess, clergywoman. **prete mas** priest, clergyman, pastor. **prete regulada** canon.
preteme *vt.* fear in advance, have a foreboding, dread. • *n.* foreboding, dread.
preteria *n.* presbytery (*priest's house*).
pretia *n.* priesthood (*state*).
pretitulo *n.* pre-title sequence, pre-credit, cold open (*TV*, *film*).
prevenable *adj.* preventable.
preveni *vt.* prevent, deter, keep (*from doing*), pre-empt, forfend; e.g. *tu preveni ce me escuta*; *tu preveni me de escuta*. • *n.* prevention, deterrence, prophylaxis.
preveninte *adj.* preventing, preventive, preventative, deterring, pre-emptive, prophylactic. • *n.* deterrent, preventive.
preverbal *adj.* & *n.* preverbal (*grammar*).
previdable *adj.* foreseeable.
previde *vt.* foresee, expect, anticipate, preview. • *n.* preview, expectation, anticipation, foresight; advance showing, prevue.
prevideta *n.* trailer, trail (*film*, *TV*).
previdor *n.* seer, visionary.
priapisme *n.* priapism (*medical*).
priapulido *n.* priapulid (*worm*: *Priapulida*).
prima *adj.* first, primary, original; premier; early; former (*of two*). • *adv.* firstly, at first, in the first place, primarily. • *n.* first, original.
primable *adj.* printable.
primador *n.* printer, printing press. **primador-scanador** *n.* printer-scanner.
primajenita *n.* primogeniture (*state or rights of a firstborn*).

primal *adj.* prime (*number*).

primalia *n.* primality.

primate *n.* primate, ape (*Primates*).

primatolojia *n.* primatology.

primatolojiste *n.* primatologist.

primavera *n.* spring, springtime.

primaveral *adj.* spring.

primeria *n.* printing house, printer's.

primeval *adj.* primeval, primordial, primal.

primi *vt.* print. • *n.* printout (*action, result*).

primia *n.* priority. **primia de abri** aperture priority (*photography*). **primia de relasador** shutter priority (*photography*).

primida *adj.* printed. • *n.* print, printed object. **no plu primida** out of print.

primitiva *adj.* primitive, early, inchoate.

primitivisme *n.* primitivism.

primitiviste *n.* primitivist.

primor *n.* printer (*person*).

primula *n.* primrose, primula (*plant: Primula*).

prinse *n.* prince. **Isola Prinse Edward** Prince Edward Island (*Canadian province*). **prinse erital** crown prince.

prinsesa *n.* princess.

prinsia *n.* principality, princedom, princely state.

prinsipe *n.* principle, doctrine, precept, tenet. **de prinsipe** in principle.

prinsiposa *adj.* principled, based on principles.

prisma *n.* prism.

prismal *adj.* prismatic.

prison *n.* prison, jail, jailhouse, gaol, cellblock, clink, lockup, penitentiary. **prison botelin** oubliette. **prison de barcon** brig. **prison suteran** dungeon.

prisoni *vt.* imprison, jail, incarcerate. • *n.* imprisonment, captivity, incarceration, internment.

prisonida *adj.* imprisoned, captive. • *n.* prisoner, convict, inmate, internee, jailbird. **prisonida con libria limitada** parolee. **prisonida de gera** prisoner of war, POW.

prisoninte *adj.* imprisoning, custodial.

priva *vt.* deprive, bereave, dispossess, divest. • *n.* deprivation, bereavement.

privada *adj.* deprived, bereft, dispossessed.

privata *adj.* private, confidential. • *n.* confidence, secret.

privatia *n.* privacy, confidence, confidentiality; seclusion.

pro-[1] *pref.* pro- (*in favour of*).

pro-[2] *pref.* pro- (*forward*).

proa[1] *n.* bow, prow (*of ship*).

proa[2] *n.* proa, perahu (*sailboat*).

proba *vt.* try, try out, try on (*clothes*), trial, test, check; taste. • *n.* try, trial, test, check, screen; taste (*action*). **proba de cualia** quality test, benchmark test. **proba de Pap** Pap test, Pap smear. See *atenta*.

probable *adj.* probable, likely. • *adv.* probably. • *n.* probability, chance (*something likely*).

probablia *n.* probability (*quality, statistic*), likelihood, chances, odds.

probada *adj.* tried, tested; tasted. **longa probada** tried and tested, time-tested.

probiotica *n.* probiotic.

problem *n.* problem; difficulty, issue, setback, drawback, kink, snag. **crea un problem** create a problem, pose a problem. **no plu un problem** no longer a problem, out of the way. **no problem** no problem, you're welcome, don't mention it. **problem medical** medical problem, medical condition.

problemosa *adj.* problematic, worrisome.

proboside *n.* proboscis (*anatomy*).

procaina *n.* procaine, novocaine (*anaesthetic*).

procariota *n.* prokaryote (*organism*).

proclama *vt.* proclaim, declaim, announce, recite, issue. • *n.* proclamation, announcement, edict, ordinance, pronouncement. **proclama papal** papal bull.

proclamor *n.* announcer, crier, barker, bellman.

procomersial *adj.* pro-business.

proconsul *n.* proconsul.

proctolojia *n.* proctology.

proctolojiste *n.* proctologist.

proctoscopi *n.* proctoscopy.

proctoscopio *n.* proctoscope.

produi *vt.* produce. • *n.* production. **produi a stranjer** *v.* outsource. • *n.* outsourcing. **produi en serie** mass production. **produi interna bruta** gross domestic product, GDP.

produida *n.* product, handiwork. **produidas** products, produce.

produor *n.* producer. **produor dirijal** executive producer. **produor-dirijor** *n.* producer-director.

produosa *adj.* productive, prolific, bountiful, effective, effectual, efficacious.

produosia *n.* productiveness, productivity, effectiveness, effectuality, efficacy.

proelejal *adj.* pro-choice.

profesa *n.* profession.

profesal *adj.* professional.

profesalisme *n.* professionalism.

profesor *n.* professor, academic, academician, don, faculty member, prof. **profesores** professors, faculty (*members*).

profeta *n.* prophet.

profil *n.* profile.

profili *vi.* & *vt.* profile.

profilor *n.* profiler.

profita *vi.* profit. • *n.* profit, gain. **crimin no profita** crime does not pay. **profita de** profit from, take advantage of, cash in on. **profita e perde** profit and loss, boom and bust. **profita nonlegal** *v.* profiteer. • *n.* profiteering. **profita subita** bonanza, windfall.

profitosa *adj.* profitable, lucrative.

profonda *adj.* deep, profound, in-depth. • *adv.* deeply, profoundly. • *n.* deep, depths, chasm.

profondi *vi.* & *vt.* deepen.

profondia *n.* deepness, depth, profundity; draft, draught (*of ship*).

profondon *n.* abyss, chasm.

progeral *adj.* pro-war.

prognose *n.* prognosis.

progovernal *adj.* pro-government.

program *n.* programme (US program), schedule; program, application (*software*). **program de calcula** spreadsheet. **program de concurso** quiz show, game show. **program de conversa** chat show, talk show. **program de desinia** graphics program. **program de labora** work schedule, roster, rota. **program de realia** reality show. **program de scrive** word-processing program, word processor. **program ueb** web application. **programes** programs, software. **programes de nube** cloudware. **programes de proba** demo software, demoware, trialware. **programes de rescate** ransomware. **programes libre** free software (*unrestricted*). **programes sin custa** free software (*zero-cost*), freeware. **programes vil** malware.

programal *adj.* programmatic.

programeta *n.* script, batch file, app (*software*).

programi *vt.* program. • *n.* programming. **programi funsional** functional programming. **programi ojetal** object-oriented programming.

programor *n.* programmer.

progresa *vi.* & *vt.* progress, advance. • *n.* progress, advancement, progression, headway, inroad, going.

progresante *adj.* progressing, afoot.

progresisme *n.* progressivism.

progresiste *adj.* & *n.* progressive.

proibi [proˈibi] *vt.* prohibit, forbid, disallow, interdict, ban, proscribe; e.g. *me proibi ce tu parla*; *me proibi tu de parla*; *me proibi la parla a tu*. • *n.* prohibition, interdiction, ban. **proibi de sorti** curfew. **proibi de vota** disenfranchise.

proibida *adj.* prohibited, forbidden, disallowed, banned. **entra proibida** no entry, no admittance. **fumi proibida** no smoking.

proibinte *adj.* prohibiting, prohibitive.

proibiste *n.* prohibitionist.

projenia *n.* progeny, offspring, brood, descendants, litter.

projeta *vt.* project (*light*, *image*, *voice*); plan (*a project*); landscape (*garden*). • *n.* projection; plan, project, undertaking, venture. **projeta legal** bill (*legislative*).

projetador *n.* projector; floodlight, searchlight.

prolaso *n.* prolapse (*medical*).

proletaria *n.* proletariat.

proletarial *adj.* proletarian. • *n.* proletarian, prole.

promedia *adj.* & *n.* average, mean. **per promedia** on average.

promerope *n.* sugarbird (*Promerops*).

promete *vt.* promise, pledge, devote, commit. • *n.* promise, pledge, devotion, commitment, obligation; engagement (*to be married*). **promete de paia** acknowledgement of debt, IOU. **prometes** policy, pledges (*in political campaign*).

prometeda *adj.* promised; engaged (*to be married*), betrothed. • *n.* fiancé, fiancée.

prometente *adj.* promising (*including showing promise*), promissory.

prometio *n.* promethium (*element*).

prometor *n.* devotee.

prometosa *adj.* promising, full of promise.

promiscua *adj.* promiscuous, wanton, libertine. **fem promiscua** libertine, harlot, strumpet, trollop. **om promiscua** playboy, lothario, gigolo.

promiscuia *n.* promiscuity, debauchery.

promontania *n.* promontory, headland.

promove *vt.* promote, support, espouse, advocate, lobby for, promulgate, purvey, proselytize. • *n.* promotion, advocacy, hype; movement (*community with a cause or direction*).

promovor *n.* promoter, lobbyist. **promovor de odia** hatemonger. **promovores** lobby.

prona *adj.* prone, face down, palm down.

pronador *n.* pronator (*muscle*).

proni *vi.* & *vt.* pronate, prostrate. • *n.* pronation.

pronom *n.* pronoun. **pronom de demanda** interrogative pronoun. **pronom-sujunta** *n.* relative pronoun.

pronomal *adj.* pronominal.

pronto *adj.* with little delay; instant (*coffee*), ready. • *adv.* soon, shortly, presently, readily, anon, in a jiffy; immediately, instantly, straight away, post-haste. **la plu pronto** as soon as possible, soonest, immediately,

instantly, instantaneously. **pronto a pos** soon afterwards. **pronto pos** soon after, shortly after.
pronunsia *vt.* pronounce, articulate. • *n.* pronunciation, articulation, accent. **pronunsia clar** pronounce clearly, enunciate. **pronunsia melodiosa** lilt.
pronunsiable *adj.* pronounceable.
prop- *pref.* prop- (*chemistry*).
propaganda *n.* propaganda.
propagandi *vt.* propagandize.
propagandiste *n.* propagandist.
propano *n.* propane.
propanol *n.* propanol (*chemistry*).
propen *n.* propene, propylene (*chemistry*).
propensa *vt.* predispose. • *n.* propensity, predisposition, susceptibility.
propensada *adj.* predisposed (*to*), liable (*to*), tending (*to*), with a tendency (*to*), prone (*to*), subject (*to*), susceptible (*to*).
proportial *adj.* proportional, proportionate, commensurate. • *adv.* proportionally, in proportion, pro rata.
proportio *n.* proportion, ratio, quotient, rate; concentration. **de bon proportio** well-proportioned. **proportio de aspeta** aspect ratio.
proposa *vt.* propose (*including marriage*), suggest, nominate, submit, postulate, propound. • *n.* proposal, proposition, suggestion, motion, nomination; clause (*grammar*); thesis. **proposa autonom** independent clause. **proposa coordinada** coordinate clause. **proposa major** main clause. **proposa suordinada** subordinate clause, subclause, dependent clause.
proposada *adj.* proposed, nominated. • *n.* nominee.
proposor *n.* proposer, proponent.
propre *adj.* (*prenominal*) own, respective, proper (*to*); e.g. *el rasca sua propre dorso*.
propri *vi.* & *vt.* appropriate, adopt, annex, commandeer. • *n.* appropriation, annexation.
propria *n.* property (*possessions*), estate; property, attribute. **propria inteletal** intellectual property.
proprial *adj.* proprietary.
proprior *n.* owner, proprietor, landlord, landlady. **proprior de casa** homeowner. **proprior esplotante** slumlord.
propriosepi *vi.* propriocept. • *n.* proprioception (*sense of one's own movement and orientation*).
propulsa *vt.* propel, power. • *n.* propulsion. **propulsa par jeto** jet propulsion.
propulsada *adj.* propelled, powered.
propulsante *n.* propellant.
prosa *n.* prose.
prosedador *n.* processor.
prosede *vt.* process. • *n.* process, procedure. **prosede complicada** complicated process, rigmarole. **prosede legal** legal process, trial, lawsuit.
prosederia *n.* processing plant.
prosegue *vi.* proceed, process (*move in procession*). • *n.* procession. **prosegue funeral** funeral procession, cortège.
prosima *adj.* near, nearby, proximal, close (*including friend*). • *adv.* nearby, thereabouts, in the vicinity. **de prosima** from close up, point-blank.
prosimi *vi.* near, come near, approach. • *vt.* bring nearer, cause to approach. • *n.* approach (*including to a problem*). **prosimi furtiva** sneak up, sidle up, approach stealthily.
prosimia *n.* proximity, nearness, closeness, contiguity.
prosiminte *adj.* impending, imminent, upcoming.
prosin *adj.* prosaic.
prosion *n.* raccoon (*Procyon lotor*).
prostaglandina *n.* prostaglandin (*biology*).
prostata *n.* prostate.
prostesal *adj.* prosthetic.
prostese *n.* prosthesis, prosthetic. **prostese dental** dentures, false teeth.
prostitui *vt.* prostitute. • *n.* prostitution.
prostituida *n.* prostitute. **fem prostituida** hooker, whore, streetwalker, harlot, strumpet, trollop. **prostituida pasada** reformed prostitute, magdalen.
protactinio *n.* protactinium (*element*).
protea *n.* protea (*plant*: *Protea*).
proteje *vt.* protect, defend, shield, shelter. • *n.* protection, precaution, aegis.
protejeda *adj.* protected, sheltered. • *n.* protectorate.
protejente *adj.* protecting, protective.
protejisme *n.* protectionism.
protejiste *n.* protectionist.
protejor *n.* protector.
protejoria *n.* protectorate.
protele *n.* aardwolf (*animal*: *Proteles cristatus*).
protena *n.* protein.
protende *vi.* & *vt.* protrude, project, extend, jut, stand out, stick out, bulge. • *n.* protrusion, protuberance, prominence, projection, appendage, bulge, nub; tenon (*of dovetail joint*); process (*anatomy*).
protendente *adj.* protruding, prominent.
protesta *vt.* protest, object, demonstrate, picket; rail, fulminate. • *n.* protest, protestation, objection, demonstration, demo (*political*). **protesta par juna** hunger strike. **protesta par senta** sit-in.

protestante *adj.* protesting; protestant. • *n.* protestant.
protestantisme *n.* protestantism.
protestor *n.* protester, picketer.
protista *n.* protist (*organism*: *Protista*).
proto- *pref.* proto- (*first*).
protocol *n.* protocol (*rules*).
proton *n.* proton.
protoplasma *n.* protoplasm (*biology*).
protostomio *n.* protostome (*organism*: *Protostomia*).
prototipal *adj.* prototypical, prototypal.
prototipo *n.* prototype.
protozon *n.* protozoon (pl. protozoa), protozoan (*organism*: *Protozoa*).
protozonal *adj.* protozoic.
Provensa *n.* Provence (*French region*).
provensal *adj.* & *n.* Provençal (*person*, *language*).
proverbal *adj.* proverbial.
proverbo *n.* proverb, adage.
provinsal *adj.* provincial; unsophisticated.
provinsalisme *n.* provincialism.
provinse *n.* province, prefecture, state.
provival *adj.* pro-life.
provoca *vt.* provoke, instigate, foment, incite, stir up, prompt, engender. • *n.* provocation, instigation.
provocante *adj.* provoking, provocative.
provocor *n.* provocateur, instigator, agitator, enabler, mover. **provocor de gera** warmonger.
provolone *n.* provolone (*cheese*).
proxi *n.* proxy server (*computer*).
pruna *adj.* plum (*colour*). • *n.* plum (*fruit*). **pruna seca** prune, dried plum.
pruno *n.* plum (*tree*: *Prunus*).
pruri *vi.* & *n.* itch.
prurinte *adj.* itchy.
Prusen *n.* Prussia. **prusen** *adj.* & *n.* Prussian.
ps *abbr.* (*pos scrive*) PS, postscript.
psefolojia *n.* psephology.
psefolojial *adj.* psephological.
psefolojiste *n.* psephologist.
pseudo- *pref.* pseudo-.
pseudopodo *n.* pseudopod, pseudopodium (pl. pseudopodia) (*anatomy*).
psi *n.* psi (*Greek letter* Ψ, ψ).
psical *adj.* psychic (*of the psyche*).
psice *n.* psyche, mind.
psiciatria *n.* psychiatry.
psiciatrica *adj.* psychiatric, psychiatrical.
psiciatriste *n.* psychiatrist.
psicica *adj.* psychic (*paranormal*).
psico- *pref.* psycho-.
psicoanalesica *adj.* & *n.* psychoanaleptic.
psicoanalisal *adj.* psychoanalytic, psychoanalytical.
psicoanalise *vt.* psychoanalyse (US psychoanalyze). • *n.* psychoanalysis.
psicoanaliste *n.* psychoanalyst.
psicoativa *adj.* psychoactive.
psicobiolojia *n.* psychobiology.
psicojen *adj.* psychogenic (*of psychological origin*).
psicolesica *adj.* psycholeptic (*medical*).
psicolojia *n.* psychology.
psicolojial *adj.* psychological.
psicolojisme *n.* psychologism (*philosophy*).
psicolojiste *n.* psychologist.
psicomotor *adj.* psychomotor.
psicopatia *n.* psychopathy.
psicopatica *adj.* psychopathic. • *n.* psychopath.
psicopatolojia *n.* psychopathology.
psicose *n.* psychosis.
psicosesal *adj.* psychosexual.
psicosica *adj.* psychotic.
psicosomatica *adj.* psychosomatic.
psicososial *adj.* psychosocial.
psicoterapia *n.* psychotherapy.
psicoterapiste *n.* psychotherapist.
psicotropial *adj.* psychotropic.
psilosibina *n.* psilocybin (*drug*).
psoriase *n.* psoriasis (*medical*).
ptero- *pref.* ptero- (*wing*).
pterodatilo *n.* pterodactyl (*Pterodactylus*).
pterosauro *n.* pterosaur (*Pterosuria*).
ptolemean *adj.* Ptolemean, Ptolemaic.
Ptolemeo *n.* Ptolemy (*astronomer*, *dynasty*).
pubica *adj.* pubic. • *n.* pubis. **oso pubica** pubic bone. **pelo pubica** pubic hair.
publica *adj.* public.
publici *vi.* & *vt.* publish, release, issue; air; post (*on web*). • *n.* publication, release, edition, issue; posting.
publiciste *n.* publicist.
publicor *n.* publisher.
pueblo *adj.* pueblo. • *n.* pueblo (*Native American community*).
puia *vt.* push (*trolley*, *button*).
puieta *vt.* & *n.* poke, nudge, jog, prod, prompt.
pulea *n.* pulley.
pulga *n.* flea (*Siphonaptera*); tiddlywink.
pulmon *n.* lung.
pulmonal *adj.* pulmonary.
pulpa *n.* pulp (*including dental*), mush, pap, slop; flesh (*fruit*).
pulpi *vi.* & *vt.* pulp.
pulposa *adj.* pulpy, fleshy (*fruit*).
pulsa *vi.* pulse, pulsate; beat (*music*). • *n.* pulse, pulsation; beat (*music*). **pulsa asentuada** downbeat. **pulsa inversada** backbeat.
pulsante *adj.* pulsing, pulsating, vibrant.
pulsar *n.* pulsar (*astronomy*).

pum *n.* bang, crash, thud, pop (*sound*); slam dunk (*basketball*). ● *interj.* bang, crash, thud, pop, thump, wham, kaboom.
puma *n.* puma, cougar, mountain lion, panther, catamount (*Felis concolor*).
pumi *vi.* & *vt.* bang, slam, clap, pop, thud; slam-dunk.
punable *adj.* punishable.
punc *adj.* & *n.* punk (*music*).
puni *vt.* punish, penalize. ● *n.* punishment, penalty, sanction; penalty (*football*). **puni avertinte** exemplary punishment. **puni de mori** death penalty, capital punishment. **puni eterna** damnation, perdition.
punica *adj.* Punic, Carthaginian.
puninte *adj.* punishing, punitive.
punio *n.* fist. **colpa con punio** *v.* & *n.* punch. **punio ferin** iron fist.
punta *vi.* point, be aimed. ● *vt.* point, aim, bring to bear. ● *n.* aim.
punteta *n.* freckle.
punti *vi.* & *vt.* sharpen, make pointed.
puntida *adj.* pointed, pointy, sharp.
puntilapis *n.* pencil sharpener.
puntisme *n.* pointillism (*art*).
puntiste *n.* pointillist.
punto *n.* point, tip, dot, spot; vertex; item, entry; point (*scoring*); full stop, period; stitch (*sewing*). **a punto de** on the point of, about to, just, just about to. **fa un punto** stitch. **punto cablin** cable stitch. **punto calda** hotspot. **punto crusada** cross-stitch. **punto de cambia** turning point, watershed. **punto de comensa** starting point. **punto de controla** checkpoint. **punto de dito** fingertip. **punto de fini** endpoint. **punto de refere** point of reference, landmark. **punto de vista** viewpoint, point of view, outlook, perspective. **punto G** G-spot (*anatomy*). **punto longa** tack (*stitch*). **punto negra** blackhead, comedo (*acne*). **punto pedante** quibble. **punto-virgula** *n.* semicolon. **puntos** points, score.
punton *n.* bullet, bullet point (*typography*).
puntosa *adj.* dotted, spotty, spotted, speckled, spangled, studded, patterned with dots.
puntua *vt.* punctuate. ● *n.* punctuation.
puntual *adj.* punctual, prompt, on time, in time.
puntualia *n.* punctuality, promptness.
pupa *n.* doll, effigy; pupa (*insect*). **pupa de trapo** rag doll.
pupeta *n.* puppet.
pupetia *n.* puppetry.
pupetin *adj.* puppetlike, dummy.
pupetor *n.* puppeteer.
pupi *vi.* pupate. ● *n.* pupation.
pupil *n.* pupil (*eye*).
pur *adj.* pure, mere; chaste, unadulterated, uncontaminated. ● *adv.* purely, merely.
purador *n.* purifier.
purda *n.* purdah (*female seclusion*).
pure *vt.* & *n.* puree (*cookery*). **pure de fruta** smoothie. **pure de poma** apple sauce, apple puree.
purga *vt.* & *n.* purge. **purga de emosias** catharsis.
purgante *adj.* purging, cathartic.
purgatorio *n.* purgatory.
puri *vi.* & *vt.* purify. ● *n.* purification.
puria *n.* cleanliness, purity.
puriacua *n.* water purifier.
puriaira *n.* air purifier.
purisme *n.* purism.
puriste *adj.* puristic. ● *n.* purist.
puritan *adj.* & *n.* Puritan.
puritanisme *n.* Puritanism (*Christianity*).
purpur *adj.* purple, livid (*colour*).
purpura *n.* purpura (*medical*).
purpuri *vi.* & *vt.* turn purple, turn livid.
purpuria *n.* lividity.
purpurin *adj.* purplish.
pus *n.* pus (*substance*).
pusosa *adj.* purulent.
pustula *n.* pustule, pimple.
puta *n.* (*insult*) whore, slut, bitch, bastard, harlot, strumpet, trollop.
putin *adj.* whorish.
puto *n.* (*insult*) sod, bastard, manwhore.
putong *adj.* & *n.* Putonghua, Mandarin Chinese (*language*).
putrable *adj.* perishable.
putri *vi.* rot, decay, addle, fester, putrefy. ● *n.* rot, decay, putrefaction.
putrida *adj.* putrid, rotten, decayed, rancid. ● *n.* rotten matter.
puxa *vt.* shove, ram, thrust, sweep, jostle, manhandle. ● *n.* shove, thrust.
puxador *n.* thruster.
puzel *n.* jigsaw puzzle.

Q

Q [kwa], **qua** *letter* Q, q.
Qahira *n.* Cairo.
Quebec [ke'bek] *n.* Quebec (*Canadian province*).
quebecan *adj.* & *n.* Quebecois.

R

R [er], **er** *letter* R, r.
rabano *n.* radish (*plant, root: Raphanus sativus*). **rabano blanca** daikon, mooli. **rabano forte** horseradish (*plant, root, sauce: Armoracia rusticana*).
rabi *n.* rabbi.
rabia *n.* rabies.
rabica *adj.* rabid.
raceta[1] *n.* racket, racquet, bat, stick. **raceta de neva** snowshoe.
raceta[2] *n.* rackett (*musical instrument*).
racetabal *n.* racquetball (*sport*).
racite *n.* rickets, rachitis (*medical*).
raconta *vt.* tell, relate. • *n.* anecdote, memoir.
racontal *adj.* anecdotal.
racontor *n.* raconteur.
radar *n.* radar.
radareria *n.* radar post, radar station.
radia *vi.* radiate, broadcast, beam. • *vt.* radiate, broadcast. • *n.* radiation, broadcasting; radiance.
radiador *n.* radiator.
radial *adj.* radial.
radian *n.* radian (*unit of angle*).
radiante *adj.* radiating, radiant, beaming, aglow.
radiato *n.* radiate (*jellyfish: Radiata*).
radical *n.* radical (*chemistry*). **radical libre** free radical (*chemistry*).
radio[1] *n.* radio, wireless. • *pref.* radio-.
radio[2] *n.* radius (*bone*).
radio[3] *n.* radium (*chemistry*).
radioativa *adj.* radioactive.
radioativia *n.* radioactivity, fallout.
radiocomunica *vt.* radio. • *n.* radiocommunication.
radiograf *n.* X-ray machine.
radiografi *vt.* X-ray.
radiografia *n.* radiography.
radiogram *n.* X-ray image.
radiolojia *n.* radiology.
radiolojial *adj.* radiological.
radiolojiste *n.* radiologist.
radiotelefon *n.* radiotelephone, radiophone, walkie-talkie.
radioterapia *n.* radiotherapy.
radis *n.* root. **a radis** at root, basically, fundamentally. **radis cuadral** square root. **radis cuatro** fourth root. **radis cubo** cube root. **radis du** square root. **radis major** taproot. **radis vejetal** root vegetable.
radisal *adj.* radical, fundamental, drastic.
radisi *vi.* take root. • *vt.* cause to take root, entrench, intrench, instil (US instill), inculcate.
radon *n.* radon (*element*).
rafia *n.* raffia (*plant*).
raga *adj.* & *n.* raga (*music*).
raglan *n.* raglan (*sleeve*).
ragnaroc *n.* ragnarok, Götterdämmerung, twilight of the gods.
ragtaim *adj.* & *n.* ragtime (*music*).
ragu [raˈgu] *n.* stew, ragout.
raia *n.* ray, skate (*fish: Batoidea*). **raia de spina** stingray (*Dasyatis pastinaca*).
raial *adj.* radial.
raio *n.* ray, beam (*light*); radius (*circle*); spoke (*wheel*); bolt (*lightning*). **raio de luna** moonbeam. **raio de sol** sunbeam. **raio gama** gamma ray. **raio X** X-ray. **raios diplomata** pinstripes.
raion *n.* rayon (*fibre*).
raiosa *adj.* striped, striate, striated (*including muscle*); rifled (*barrel of gun*).
raja *n.* raja, rajah (*title*).
-raje *n.suff.* -rhage (*medical*).
-rajica *adj.suff.* -rhagic.
ral *n.* rail, crake (*bird: Rallidae*).
ram *n.* RAM (*random-access memory*).
ramadan *n.* Ramadan (*Islam*).
rameta *n.* shoot.
rami[1] *n.* rummy (*card game*).
rami[2] *vi.* & *vt.* branch. • *n.* branching; ramification.
ramin *adj.* branchlike.
raminte *adj.* branching.
ramo *n.* branch; denomination; chapter (*society, religious community*); faction.
ramon *n.* bough.
rampa *n.* ramp, chute.
rampe *vi.* crawl, creep; sneak.
rampor *n.* crawler, creeper (*person, plant*).
rana *n.* frog (*Anura*). **rana grande** bullfrog.
rand *n.* rand (*currency*).
raneta *n.* tadpole, polliwog.
rani *n.* rani, ranee (*title*).
ranin *adj.* froglike, froggy. • *n.* breaststroke.
ranunculo *n.* buttercup (*Ranunculus*).
ranur *n.* slot, groove, aperture, slit, furrow, striation. **en ranur orizonal** letterboxed (*video*). **en ranur vertical** pillarboxed (*video*). **ranur de arado** furrow.
ranuri *vt.* slit.
ranxo *n.* ranch.
ranxor *n.* rancher.
rap *adj.* & *n.* rap (*music*).

Rapanui *n.* Rapa Nui, Easter Island. **rapanui** *adj.* & *n.* rapanui. See *Isola Pascua.*
rapela *vi.* rappel, abseil.
rapi *vt.* rap (*music*).
rapida *adj.* rapid, fast, quick, swift, punctual, prompt, fleet.
rapidi *vi.* & *vt.* speed up, accelerate, quicken; expedite, hasten. ● *n.* acceleration.
rapidia *n.* speed, velocity, rate, pace, tempo.
rapidometre *n.* speedometer, speedo.
rapor *n.* rapper (*music*).
rapsodia *n.* rhapsody.
rara *adj.* rare, uncommon, scarce, infrequent. ● *adv.* rarely, seldom. ● *n.* rarity.
rari *vi.* & *vt.* rarefy, diffuse, dilute.
raria *n.* rareness, rarity.
rarida *adj.* rarefied, tenuous, diffuse, diluted, dilute, sparse, wispy.
rasa *vt.* & *n.* shave.
rasador *n.* razor, shaver.
rasca *vt.* scratch, scrabble. ● *n.* scratch. **rasca glasial** glacial striation.
rascasielo *n.* skyscraper.
rasiona *vt.* ration, allocate. ● *n.* ration, allocation.
raspa *vt.* scrape, abrade, scuff, graze; chafe; grate, grind; rasp (*sound*). ● *n.* abrasion.
raspador *n.* scraper, rasp, grater.
raspante *adj.* scraping, abrasive; raspy.
rastafari *adj.* & *n.* Rastafari, Rastafarian.
rasti *vt.* rake, harrow.
rasto *n.* rake (*tool*).
raston *n.* harrow.
rata *n.* rat (*Rattus*).
ratan *n.* rattan (*fibre, plant: Calameae*).
ratatui *n.* ratatouille (*food*).
rateria *n.* rathole, rat trap.
ratin *adj.* ratlike, ratty.
ravioli *n.* ravioli (*food*).
raza *n.* race, ethnic group, breed. **de raza miscada** of mixed race, mongrel, mestiza, mestizo.
razal *adj.* racial.
razisme *n.* racism.
raziste *n.* racist.
razona *vt.* reason, ratiocinate, argue. ● *n.* reasoning, rational thought, argument, case, reason, motive, purpose. **razona bon** reason well, be right, be correct. **razona coreta** reason correctly, be right, be correct. **razona deduinte** deductive reasoning, syllogism. **razona induinte** inductive reasoning. **sin razona** for no reason, gratuitous; pointless, groundless.
razonada *adj.* rational (*argument*), reasoned.
razonal *adj.* rational (*number*).
razonalisme *n.* rationalism.
razonaliste *adj.* rationalist, rationalistic.
razonante *adj.* rational (*person*), reasoning, reasonable, sapient.
re[1] *n.* king.
re[2] *n.* re (*musical note*).
re-[3] *pref.* re- (*added to verbs: repetition or backward direction*); e.g. *recomensa, reinventa; reveni, redona.*
rea[1] *n.* rhea (*bird: Rhea*).
-rea[2] *n.suff.* -rhea (*outflow*).
rea[3] *n.* queen.
reabri *vi.* & *vt.* reopen.
reafirma *vt.* reaffirm.
reafisa *vt.* reattach.
reajendi *vt.* reschedule.
reajusta *vi.* & *vt.* readapt, readjust.
real[1] *adj.* real, actual, tangible, proper.
real[2] *adj.* royal, regal. ● *n.* royal; real (*currency*).
realable *adj.* feasible, workable, doable, achievable, viable.
reali *vi.* become real, actualize. ● *vt.* realize, make real, actualize, achieve, accomplish, do, effect, enact, implement, bring about; honour (US honor), fulfil (US fulfill), observe (*promise*), answer (*prayer*). ● *n.* realization, achievement, actualization, accomplishment, enactment, implementation, fruition. **reali model** reference implementation.
realia *n.* reality. **en realia** in reality, in fact.
realida *adj.* realized, actualized, accomplished.
realin *adj.* realistic.
realinia *vi.* & *vt.* realign.
realisme *n.* realism.
realiste *n.* realist.
realpolitica *n.* realpolitik.
reanalise *vt.* reanalyse (US reanalyze).
reanima *vt.* reanimate, resuscitate. **reanima cardiopulmonal** cardiopulmonary resuscitation, CPR.
reanimador *n.* resuscitator.
reanimante *adj.* reanimating, resurgent.
reapare *vi.* reappear, resurface. ● *vt.* cause to reappear. ● *n.* reappearance; comeback.
reaplica *vt.* reapply.
reapone *vt.* put (*garment*) back on.
reaprende *vt.* relearn.
rearma *vt.* rearm. ● *n.* rearming, rearmament.
rearmoni *vi.* & *vt.* reharmonize. ● *n.* reharmonization, rapprochement.
reasede *vt.* reaccess.
reasembla *vi.* & *vt.* reassemble, reconvene, regather.
reasinia *vt.* reassign, reallocate, reappoint, recast, redeploy.
reasorbe *vt.* reabsorb. ● *n.* reabsorption.
reata *vi.* react. ● *n.* reaction; reactance; fuss, brouhaha, ado. **reata en cadena** chain

reaction, domino effect. **reata tro forte** overreact.
reatador *n.* reactor (*nuclear*).
reatante *adj.* reactionary. • *n.* reagent.
reateni *vt.* reattain, get back to.
reatenta *vt.* retry.
reativi *vi.* & *vt.* reactivate. • *n.* reactivation.
reativia *n.* reactivity.
reator *n.* reactor, reactionary (*person*).
reatosa *adj.* reactive, sensitive.
reaveni *vi.* reoccur, recur, happen again. • *vt.* cause to happen again, restage. • *n.* recurrence.
rebatiza *vt.* rebaptize.
rebela *vi.* rebel, mutiny, resist authority. • *n.* rebellion, mutiny, resistance, insurrection, insurgency, sedition.
rebelante *adj.* rebelling, rebellious, mutinous, seditious.
rebelor *n.* rebel, mutineer.
rebita *n.* rivet.
rebiti *vt.* rivet.
rebitor *n.* riveter.
rebobini *vt.* rewind, wind back.
rebondi *vi.* rebound, bounce back, ricochet.
recalcula *vt.* recalculate.
recaldi *vi.* & *vt.* reheat, heat up.
recambia *vt.* replace (*an old item with a new one*), supplant. • *n.* replacement (*item*). **recambia la planta de** resole (*shoe*).
recambiable *adj.* replaceable.
recapasi *vi.* & *vt.* re-enable, rehabilitate. • *n.* rehabilitation.
recarga *vt.* reload; recharge.
recargable *adj.* rechargeable.
recasi *vt.* rehouse.
recatura *vt.* recapture.
reclama *vt.* claim, reclaim (*property*, *title*); assert. • *n.* claim, reclaim; assertion, contention.
reclamor *n.* claimant, pretender.
reclasi *vt.* reclassify.
reclina *vi.* lie, recline. • *vt.* lay, lay down. **reclina se** lie down, lie back.
recoce *vi.* & *vt.* recook; anneal.
recoliador *n.* harvester (*machine*).
recolie *vt.* pick up, reap, harvest. • *n.* harvest, crop, bounty, haul, roundup. **recolie de reservas** fundraising, fundraiser (*activity*). **recolie profitosa** cash crop. **recolie reservas** raise funds.
recolior *n.* harvester (*person*). **recolior de reservas** fundraiser (*person*).
recombina *vi.* & *vt.* recombine, reamalgamate.
recombinante *adj.* recombinant.
recomenda *vt.* recommend. • *n.* recommendation. **recomenda forte** *v.* strongly recommend, urge, adjure. • *n.* strong recommendation.
recomensa *vi.* & *vt.* resume, recommence.
recompensa *vt.* recompense, reward. • *n.* recompense, reward, payback, payoff, yield.
recomuta *vt.* reconnect, switch back on.
reconosable *adj.* recognizable.
reconose *vt.* recognize, acknowledge, accredit. • *n.* recognition, acknowledgement, accreditation. **reconose la valua de** recognize the value of, appreciate.
reconsidera *vt.* reconsider.
reconsilia *vi.* reconcile, make up. • *vt.* reconcile. • *n.* reconciliation.
reconsilior *n.* mediator, peacemaker.
reconstitui *vt.* reconstitute. • *n.* reconstitution.
reconstrui *vt.* reconstruct, rebuild, remake, rework, reassemble, refurbish, piece together. • *n.* reconstruction, recon, rebuilding.
reconstruida *adj.* reconstructed, rebuilt.
reconta *vt.* & *n.* recount.
reconverti *vt.* reconvert, convert back.
recorda *vt.* remember, recall, recollect. • *n.* recollection, recall, memory (*particular*). **fa ce on recorda** remind one of, call to mind; prompt (*an actor*); e.g. *el ia fa ce me recorda tua aniversario.* **recorda falsa** *v.* confabulate. • *n.* confabulation, false memory. **recorda felis** reminisce. See *memori.*
recordante *adj.* reminding, redolent. • *n.* reminder, souvenir, keepsake, memento. **recordantes** reminders, memorabilia.
recordo *adj.* record, record-breaking. • *n.* record. **en tempo recordo** in record time.
recore *vi.* recur, reoccur, relapse. • *n.* recurrence, relapse, recidivism.
recorente *adj.* recurrent, relapsing.
recoror *n.* recidivist.
recorsa *vi.* recurse. • *n.* recursion.
recorsante *adj.* recursive.
recovre *vi.* recover, recuperate, get better, convalesce. • *n.* recovery, recuperation.
recrea *vt.* recreate (*create anew*). • *n.* recreation (*repeated creation*, *leisure activity*); playtime; remake (*film*).
recreal *adj.* recreational.
recrese *vi.* & *vt.* regrow, regenerate.
recurso *n.* resource, facility, recourse.
recursosa *adj.* resourceful.
rede *n.* net; network, nexus; mesh, screen, netting. **Rede** *n.* Reticulum (*constellation*). **rede de arania** spider's web, cobweb. **rede de capeles** hairnet, snood. **rede de compania** company network, corporate network. **rede de draga** dragnet. **rede mundal** worldwide web, internet. **rede restrinjente** trammel net.

redeclara *vt.* reassert.
redecora *vt.* redecorate.
rededica *vt.* rededicate.
redefini *vt.* redefine.
redescovre *vt.* rediscover, become reacquainted with.
redesinia *vt.* redesign.
redi *vt.* network.
redifusa *vt.* rebroadcast.
redin *n.* rein (*strap*).
redini *vt.* rein.
redirije *vt.* redirect, reroute, deflect. • *n.* redirection, deflection.
rediscute *vt.* rediscuss, rehash.
redise *vt.* say again, reiterate; rephrase.
redistribui *vt.* redistribute.
redistriti *vt.* redistrict.
redona *vt.* give back, return. • *n.* return. **redona tro poca** shortchange.
redor *n.* networker, network user.
reduable *adj.* reducible.
redui *vi.* reduce, decrease, decrement, lessen. • *vt.* reduce, decrease, scale down, scale back, lessen, curtail; turn down (*volume*). • *n.* reduction, decrease, lessening, cutback. **redui de empleadas** downsizing. **redui de engrana** downshift. **redui de imposta** tax cut, tax reduction. **redui empleadas** downsize. **redui la custa** cheapen. **redui la spende** reduce spending, cut back, retrench.
reduinte *adj.* reducing, reductive.
reduisme *n.* reductionism.
reduvido *n.* assassin bug (*Reduviidae*).
reeduca *vt.* re-educate.
reeleje *vt.* re-elect.
reemerji *vt.* re-emerge.
reenerji *vt.* re-energize, rally.
reenforsa *vt.* re-enforce.
reenscrive *vt.* resubscribe, re-enlist.
reensende *vt.* reignite.
reentra *vi.* re-enter, go back in. • *vt.* readmit. • *n.* re-entry; readmittance.
reenvia *vt.* send back, return, recommit, resubmit.
reenviable *adj.* returnable.
reenvolve *vt.* rewrap; re-engage.
reesamina *vt.* re-examine, reinspect, retest. • *n.* re-examination, reinspection.
reescuta *vt.* relisten, listen again to; listen back to (*a recording*).
reesperia *vt.* re-experience.
reespresa *vt.* re-express, restate.
reevalua *vt.* re-evaluate, reappraise, reassess.
refa *vt.* redo, recommit, do over, do again. • *n.* redoing, do-over, retake.
refabrica *vt.* remake.
refatori *vt.* refactor (*software*).
refere *vi.* refer, allude; e.g. *la autor refere a sua jovenia.* • *n.* reference, cross-reference, referral, allusion, mention; pointer (*software*). **refere a** refer to, reference, cross-reference, mention.
referendo *n.* referendum, plebiscite. **referendo per retira** recall election, recall referendum.
referente *adj.* referring. • *n.* reference. **referente a** referring to, apropos of.
refili *vt.* rewire.
refina *vt.* refine, perfect. • *n.* refinement; grace, poise.
refinada *adj.* refined; graceful, poised, elegant, gracious, sleek.
refinansia *vt.* refinance.
refineria *n.* refinery.
refleta *vt.* reflect. • *n.* reflection.
refletante *adj.* reflecting, reflective, introspective; reflexive (*grammar*).
reflexe *adj.* reflexive, automatic. • *n.* reflex.
reflue *n.* reflux (*chemistry*).
reforesti *vt.* reforest.
reformati *vt.* reformat.
reformeria *n.* reformatory.
reformi *vt.* reform. • *n.* reform, reformation.
reformida *adj.* reformed.
reformisme *n.* reformism.
reformiste *adj.* & *n.* reformist.
reformula *vt.* reformulate.
reforti *vt.* reinforce. • *n.* reinforcement (*action*).
refortinte *adj.* reinforcing, strengthening. • *n.* reinforcement (*person, thing*); strengthener, gusset; booster (*vaccination*).
refrata *vt.* refract. • *n.* refraction.
refratal *adj.* refractive.
refren *n.* refrain, chorus.
refreneta *n.* jingle.
refresci *vi.* & *vt.* refresh, invigorate, reinvigorate, enliven, vivify; update. • *n.* refresh, refresher; update.
refrita *vt.* refry.
refuja *vt.* shelter, give refuge to, give asylum to, harbour (US harbor). • *n.* shelter, refuge, asylum, sanctuary. **refuja se** take refuge.
refujada *n.* refugee.
refujeria *n.* shelter, refuge, asylum, sanctuary. **refujeria contra esplodes** bomb shelter.
refurni *vt.* resupply.
refusa *vt.* refuse, reject, dismiss, deny, decline. • *n.* refusal, rejection, denial.
refuta *vt.* refute, rebut. • *n.* refutation, rebuttal.
refutable *adj.* refutable.
regala *vt.* treat, spoil, pamper, indulge, dote, coddle, mollycoddle, cosset, pander. • *n.* treat, bonus, lagniappe; encore.

regalante *adj.* treating, spoiling, permissive.
regania *vt.* regain, recoup, recover (*money*).
reganiable *adj.* recoverable.
regarda *vt.* look at, behold, regard; watch, view (*film, sport*); overlook (*a view*); take into account; deem, consider to be. • *n.* look, glance, regard. **regarda a su** look down. **regarda a supra** look up. **regarda a via** look away, avert one's gaze, avert one's eyes. **regarda intensa** *v.* stare at, gawk at. • *n.* stare. **regarda la oios de** look in the eye, make eye contact with. **regarda miope** peer at. **regarda un cosa como** see something as, regard something as, consider something to be; e.g. *on regarda el como un autor importante*; *me regarda tu como mea ami la plu prosima*. **turna sua regarda a via** look away, avert one's gaze, avert one's eyes.
regardante *prep.* regarding, as regards, as for, apropos of.
regardeta *vt.* glance at. • *n.* glance.
regardor *n.* viewer (*person*). **regardores** audience.
rege *adj.* & *n.* reggae (*music*).
regex *n.* regular expression, regex (*software*).
regla *n.* ruler, yardstick. **regla de calcula** slide rule. **regla T** T-square.
regresa *vi.* regress, backslide. • *vt.* regress, cause to regress. • *n.* regression.
regresante *adj.* regressive.
regretable *adj.* regrettable, unfortunate. • *n.* regrettably, unfortunately.
regrete *vt.* regret, be sorry for, rue. • *n.* regret, remorse. **sin regrete** unregretful, impenitent.
regretosa *adj.* rueful, wistful.
regula *vt.* regulate, arrange, regularize, modulate. • *n.* rule, regulation, commandment. **regula jeneral** general rule, rule of thumb, guideline. **regula local** by-law.
regulada *adj.* regulated, regular.
regulador *n.* regulator.
reidrata [rei'drata] *vi.* & *vt.* rehydrate.
reincarne [rein'karne] *vi.* reincarnate. • *n.* reincarnation, transmigration.
reinforma [rein'forma] *vt.* reacquaint.
reinisia [rei'nisia] *vt.* & *n.* restart, reset, reboot.
reinstala [rein'stala] *vt.* reinstall.
reinstitui [reinsti'tui] *vt.* re-establish.
reinstrui [rein'strui] *vt.* retrain.
reintegra [rein'tegra] *vt.* reintegrate. • *n.* reintegration.
reinterprete [reinter'prete] *vt.* reinterpret.
reintrodui [reintro'dui] *vt.* reintroduce, reinsert.
reinventa [rein'venta] *vt.* reinvent. • *n.* reinvention.
reinvestiga [reinve'stiga] *vt.* reinvestigate.
reipoteca [reipo'teka] *vt.* remortgage.
reiside [rei'side] *vt.* commit regicide. • *n.* regicide (*action*).
reisidor [reisi'dor] *n.* regicide (*person*).
rejela *vi.* & *vt.* refreeze.
rejenera *vt.* regenerate. • *n.* regeneration.
rejente *adj.* & *n.* regent.
rejentia *n.* regency.
rejeta *vt.* reject, rebuff, veto, blackball; abjure, spurn, deny oneself. • *n.* rejection, rebuff, brushoff; abjuration, abnegation.
rejetiste *adj.* & *n.* rejectionist.
rejimental *adj.* regimental.
rejimento *n.* regiment.
rejion *n.* region, area.
rejional *adj.* regional.
rejionalisme *n.* regionalism.
rejistra *vt.* record, register; tape; log (*software*). • *n.* recording; log (*software*); register (*music, language*).
rejistrador *n.* recorder, recording device; register. **rejistrador de banda** tape recorder.
rejistror *n.* recorder, registrar. **rejistror de puntos** scorekeeper.
rejoveni *vi.* & *vt.* rejuvenate. • *n.* rejuvenation.
rejunta *vt.* rejoin, reassemble, reconnect.
rel *n.* rail, railing, banister, bannister, balustrade. **rel de lampas** lighting rail, lighting track, track lighting. **rel de mano** handrail. **rel gardante** guardrail. **reles** railroad track, rails.
relansa *vt.* throw back, throw again.
relasa *vt.* release, let go, unleash, outgas. • *n.* release. **con relasa gradal** slow-release, time-release.
relasador *n.* shutter release (*camera*).
relata *vi.* relate, be in relation, be associated. • *vt.* relate, associate. • *n.* relationship, relation, association, kinship. **en relata con** in relation to, regarding, as regards, with regard to, regarding, in terms of. **relata de ama** love affair, relationship. **relatas publica** public relations. **sin relata con** irrespective of, regardless of.
relatable *adj.* relatable.
relatada *adj.* related, kindred. **relatadas** relatives, family relations, kin, kinfolk, kith.
relatal *adj.* relational.
relativa *adj.* relative.
relativia *n.* relativity.
relativial *adj.* relativistic.
relava *vt.* rewash.
rele *n.* relay (*electric, race*).
releje *vt.* re-read; proofread.

releva[1] *vt.* throw into relief. • *n.* relief. **releva alta** high relief. **releva basa** low relief, bas-relief.
releva[2] *vi.* rise again. • *vt.* re-raise, raise again.
relia [re'lia] *vt.* bind (*book*). • *n.* bookbinding (*action*); binding (*cover*).
reliada *adj.* bound. **reliada con anelos** ring-bound.
relicia *n.* relic (*object, tradition*)
relicieria *n.* reliquary.
relieria *n.* bindery.
relijial *adj.* religious (*pertaining to religion*).
relijio *n.* religion.
relijiosa *adj.* religious (*displaying religion*), pious, devout, numinous.
relijiosia *n.* piety, devoutness.
relior *n.* bookbinder.
reloca *vt.* move, relocate; translate (*geometry*). • *n.* move, relocation; translation (*geometry*). **reloca se** relocate, move house.
relocali *vt.* relocalize, resettle.
rem *n.* rem (*unit of radiation*).
remastica *vt.* ruminate, chew cud; brood, worry.
remasticante *adj.* ruminant.
remedia *vt.* remedy, cure, heal, redress. • *n.* remedy.
remediable *adj.* remediable, curable.
remediante *adj.* remedial.
remente *vt.* remind, prompt. • *n.* reminder.
remetable *adj.* redeemable.
remete *vt.* remit, absolve, redeem, reprieve, vindicate, acquit. • *n.* remission, absolution, redemption; reprieve, remission.
remetor *n.* redeemer.
remi *vt.* row, paddle.
remisca *vt.* remix.
remize *n.* penduline tit (*bird*: *Remiz pendulinus*).
remo *n.* oar, paddle.
remobili *vt.* refurnish.
remonta *vt.* remount.
remor *n.* rower, oarsman.
remora *n.* remora (*fish*: *Remora*).
remostra *vt.* replay.
ren *n.* kidney.
rena *vt.* reign, rule. • *n.* kingdom, dominion, realm; regime, rule. **rena par la manada** mob rule. **Rena Unida** United Kingdom.
renal *adj.* renal (*of kidneys*).
renante *adj.* reigning, regent.
renara *vt.* retell.
renase *vi.* be reborn. • *n.* rebirth, renaissance, renascence. **Renase** *n.* Renaissance.
renaseda *adj.* reborn.
renasente *adj.* renascent.
renativi *vi.* & *vt.* repatriate. • *n.* repatriation.
rendere *vt.* render (*image, video*).
renegada *adj.* renegade. • *n.* renegade, turncoat.
renegosia *vt.* renegotiate.
reneta *n.* petty kingdom.
renin *n.* renin (*enzyme*).
renio *n.* rhenium (*element*).
reno *n.* reindeer, caribou (*Rangifer tarandus*).
Reno, Rio *n.* River Rhine.
renomi *vt.* rename.
renor *n.* ruler, overlord, potentate
renoreta *n.* kinglet, petty king; kinglet, crest (*bird*: *Regulus*).
renovable *adj.* renewable.
renovascular *adj.* renovascular (*biology*).
renovi *vi.* & *vt.* renew, renovate, upgrade, refurbish, revamp, refinish, remodel. • *n.* renewal, renovation, upgrade, refurbishment.
renovor *n.* renewer, renovator.
renunsia *vt.* resign, abdicate, renounce, deny oneself. • *n.* resignation, abdication, renunciation, apostasy, quitclaim; abnegation, self-denial; disclaimer, waiver. **renunsia formal** abjure, forswear.
renunsior *n.* abdicator; apostate.
renuri *vt.* feed again, feed back; refuel. • *n.* feedback (*audio, video*).
reocupa *vt.* reoccupy. • *n.* reoccupation.
reolojia *n.* rheology.
reolojiste *n.* rheologist.
reordina *vt.* reorder, rearrange, put back in order, tidy up, clear up.
reorganiza *vt.* reorganize. • *n.* reorganization, shakedown, shakeup.
reorienta *vt.* reorient, reorientate.
reostato *n.* rheostat.
repaci *vt.* repack, repackage.
repaia *vt.* repay, pay back, refund, reimburse. • *n.* repayment, refund, reimbursement.
repaiable *adj.* repayable, refundable.
repara *vt.* repair, fix, mend, darn. • *n.* repair, fix, darn. **repara completa** overhaul.
reparable *adj.* reparable, fixable, mendable.
repareria *n.* repair shop.
reparor *n.* repairer, fixer, repairman, repairwoman.
repave *vt.* repave.
repensa *vt.* rethink.
repenti *vt.* repent, feel remorse (*for*), feel contrite, be penitent, regret, be sorry. • *n.* repentance, penitence, penance, contrition, remorse, regret.
repentinte *adj.* repentant, penitent, contrite, remorseful, regretful, sorry, apologetic.
repentor *n.* penitent.
repertorio *n.* repertoire, repertory.

repete *vi.* repeat, echo. ● *vt.* repeat, echo, replay; keep, keep on (*doing*). ● *n.* repetition, replay, reprise, rerun. ● *interj.* ditto.
repetente *adj.* repeating, repetitive.
repetosa *adj.* repetitious.
repinti *vt.* repaint.
repleni *vi.* & *vt.* refill, replenish, restock; backfill. ● *n.* refill, replenishment.
replica *vt.* retort, quip, answer back, snap back. ● *n.* retort, quip, riposte, witty reply, witticism, comeback, bon mot; line (*dialogue*). **replica sismica** aftershock.
repone *vt.* replace (*place again*), put back, restore, reinstate.
repopla *vt.* repopulate.
reporta *vt.* report, brief. ● *n.* report, account, allegation, briefing.
reportor *n.* reporter.
reposa *vi.* rest, relax, repose, lounge, have a rest, take it easy; lie down, settle, pause, ensconce oneself; roost (*birds*); stay (*reside temporarily*), sojourn; set (*sun, moon, planet*). ● *vt.* rest. ● *n.* rest, relaxation, repose, respite, pause; stay, sojourn. **reposa de luna** moonset. **reposa de sol** sunset, sundown. **reposa per la note** *v.* stay for the night. ● *n.* overnight stay.
reposabraso *n.* armrest.
reposadorso *n.* backrest.
reposapede *n.* footstool, ottoman, footrest.
reposatesta *n.* headrest.
reposeria *n.* rest area, rest stop; roost (*for birds*).
reposese *vt.* repossess, foreclose. ● *n.* foreclosure.
reposantosa *adj.* restful.
reprendable *adj.* retrievable.
reprende *vt.* take back, pick up, retrieve, repossess.
represa *vt.* repress. ● *n.* repression.
represable *adj.* repressible.
represante *adj.* repressive.
representa *vt.* represent, stand for, characterize, portray, depict. ● *n.* representation, characterization, portrayal, depiction; notation.
representante *adj.* representative.
representor *n.* representative, spokesperson, proxy, envoy, emissary, deputy.
reprimi *vt.* reprint.
reprodui *vt.* reproduce, propagate, breed, procreate. ● *n.* reproduction, propagation, procreation. **per reprodui** stud, breeding, brood. **reprodui esata** *v.* replicate. ● *n.* replication.
reproposa *vt.* repropose, resubmit.
reprosede *vt.* reprocess. ● *n.* reprocessing.
reproxa *vt.* rebuke, reproach, reprehend, reprimand, admonish, scold, tell off, upbraid, chide, berate, castigate, chastise. ● *n.* reproach, reprimand, admonition.
republica *n.* republic. **Republica de Africa Sentral** Central African Republic. **Republica de Africa Sude** Republic of South Africa, Union of South Africa. See *Sentrafrica*, *Sudafrica*.
republici *vt.* republish.
republicisme *n.* republicanism.
republiciste *adj.* & *n.* republican.
repulsa *vt.* repulse, repel; disgust, horrify, turn off (*person*). ● *n.* revulsion, antipathy, aversion, dislike, disgust, abhorrence.
repulsante *adj.* repulsive, repellent, revolting, disgusting, foul, repugnant, nasty, distasteful, horrible, horrid, grisly, gruesome, horrendous, tasteless, abhorrent, icky, unsightly. ● *n.* repellent (*substance*). **repulsante de insetos** insect repellent.
reputa *vt.* repute, deem. ● *n.* reputation.
reputada *adj.* reputed.
rerasiona *vt.* reallocate.
rereali *vi.* & *vt.* re-enact. ● *n.* re-enactment.
reregarda *vt.* look again, watch again, have another look at; watch back (*a recording*).
rerejistra *vt.* re-record.
rescate *n.* ransom. **rescate finansial** bailout.
rescati *vt.* ransom.
rescrive *vt.* rewrite; write back, write in reply.
resegue *vt.* follow back, retrace. **resegue sua pasos** backtrack, retrace one's steps.
reselable *adj.* resealable.
reseli *vt.* reseal.
resenia *vt.* & *n.* critique, review.
resenial *adj.* critical, analytically reviewed.
resenior *n.* reviewer, critic.
resenta *vt.* reseat. **resenta se** sit back down.
resente *adj.* recent. ● *adv.* recently, lately, the other day. **la plu resente** most recently, last; e.g. *la plu resente, on ia vide el en via a la stasion.* **resente de scola** fresh from school.
reserti *vt.* recheck, reverify.
reserva *vt.* reserve; save (*money*), scrimp, put aside; hoard, stash, stockpile; book (*seat, table*). ● *n.* store, cache, hoard, storehouse, depot, storage, stash, stockpile; savings, kitty, fund (*money*); booking, reservation (*seat, table*); reserve, reservation. **reserva de amorti** sinking fund. **reserva mone per** save money for, budget for. **reservas** reserves, stock (*supplies*).
reservada *adj.* reserved, put aside, on layaway. ● *adv.* in reserve.
reserviste *n.* reservist.

reseta *vt.* receive, get; receive, welcome (*visitors*); catch, contract (*illness*). • *n.* reception; recipe.
resetador *n.* receiver (*device, biology*).
resetante *adj.* receptive.
reseteria *n.* reception, reception area; footprint, reception range (*communications*).
resetiste *n.* receptionist; welcomer.
resetor *n.* recipient.
resiclable *adj.* & *n.* recyclable.
resicleria *n.* recycling plant; junkyard, scrapyard.
resicli *vi.* & *vt.* recycle.
resife *n.* reef.
resina *n.* resin, rosin, gum. **resina de sisto** ladanum, labdanum. **resina eposidal** epoxy resin.
resinia *vt.* resign. • *n.* resignation.
resinosa *adj.* resinous.
resiproca *adj.* reciprocal.
resiproci *vi.* & *vt.* reciprocate.
resiprocia *n.* reciprocity.
resistable *adj.* resistible.
resistador *n.* resistor.
resiste *vt.* resist, withstand, hold out, hold up. • *n.* resistance, unwillingness.
resistente *adj.* resistant, unwilling. • *n.* resistance (*movement*). **resistente a foco** flame-retardant.
resita *vt.* recite. • *n.* recitation.
resitua *vt.* resituate.
resolve *vt.* resolve (*into parts*). • *n.* resolving, resolution.
resoma *vt.* summarize, outline, encapsulate, recapitulate, recap, minute. • *n.* summary, synopsis, outline, résumé, precis, recap; minutes (*of meeting*). **resoma de carera** curriculum vitae, CV, résumé, vita, vitae.
resomal *adj.* synoptic.
resona *vi.* resound, resonate, reverberation, echo; snore. • *n.* resonance, reverberation, echo. **resona densa** *v.* reverberate. • *n.* reverberation (*merged echoes*).
resonador *n.* resonator, sounding board, soundboard.
resonante *adj.* resonating, reverberating, resonant, plangent, sonorous, vibrant.
respele *vt.* respell.
respeta *vt.* respect, esteem, venerate. • *n.* respect, deference.
respetable *adj.* respectable, formidable, staid.
respetada *adj.* respected, esteemed, venerable, august.
respetosa *adj.* respectful.
respira *vt.* breathe, respire. • *n.* breath. **respira debil** *v.* breathe shallowly, breathe weakly. • *n.* shallow breathing, weak breathing. **respira final** *v.* breathe one's last, give up the ghost. • *n.* final breath, last gasp. **respira laborosa** *v.* struggle for breath. • *n.* laboured (US labored) breathing. **respira rapida** *v.* & *n.* pant. **respira ruidosa** *v.* & *n.* wheeze. **sin respira** *adj.* breathless, not breathing. • *adv.* breathlessly. **sistem de respira** respiratory system.
respirador *n.* respirator.
respiral *adj.* respiratory.
respirante *adj.* breathing. **ruidosa respirante** wheezing, wheezy.
respondable *adj.* answerable (*question*).
respondador *n.* answering machine, answerphone.
responde *vt.* respond, answer, reply. • *n.* response, answer, rejoinder.
respondente *adj.* responding, answering, replying, respondent, responsive.
respondor *n.* responder, answerer, replier, respondent.
resposi *vi.* & *vt.* remarry.
resta *vi.* remain, keep; stay (*behind*), be left over; e.g. *alga de la torta resta*; *tu resta mea ami*; *lo resta usosa*. • *n.* remainder, rest, remnant, residual, residue, leftover. **resta a via** stay away, keep away. **restas** leftovers, remains, remnants, dregs.
restante *adj.* remaining, residual. • *n.* remainder, rest, remnant, residual, residue. **restantes** leftovers, remains, remnants, dregs.
restora *vt.* restore, refresh, roll back, make like new. • *n.* restoration, restitution, rollback; refreshment.
restorada *adj.* refreshed, zesty, perky.
restorante *adj.* refreshing. • *n.* restaurant, diner. **restorante de comes retirable** takeaway restaurant, takeout restaurant.
restorantor *n.* restaurateur.
restorisme *n.* restorationism; irredentism (*restoration of territories*).
restoriste *n.* irredentist.
restoror *n.* restorer.
restrinje *vt.* restrict, confine, cramp, curtail; disqualify; restrain, immobilize. • *n.* restriction, confinement, control, interment; condition, precondition, provision, clause, term, stricture, trammel. **restrinje limital** boundary condition. **sin restrinje** *adj.* unrestricted, unconditional; unrestrained. • *adv.* unconditionally; without restraint, with abandon.
restrinjeda *n.* internee (*prisoner*). **restrinjeda a casa** homebound. **restrinjeda a leto** confined to bed, bedridden. **restrinjeda a tera** earthbound.
restrinjente *adj.* restrictive.
restruturi *vt.* restructure, reframe.

resulta *vi.* result, arise. • *vt.* produce, provoke, cause, result in. • *n.* result, consequence, effect, outcome, upshot. **resulta ladal** side effect, offshoot, spinoff, repercussion.
resultante *adj.* resultant, consequent, consequential.
resus *adj.* rhesus (*medical*). See *macaca.*
reta *adj.* straight (*not bent*); right-angled.
retal *adj.* rectal.
retangulo *adj.* rectangular, oblong. • *n.* rectangle, oblong.
retape *n.* retype.
retapeti *vt.* reupholster.
retarda *vt.* retard, slow down, inhibit, postpone, delay, stall, forestall, hold up, stonewall. • *n.* inhibition, delay, stall, lag, lag time, hold-up, wait. **retarda mental** mental retardation. **sin retarda** immediately, straightaway, without delay.
retardada *adj.* retarded, delayed. **mental retardada** mentally retarded.
retenador *n.* retainer (*any retaining device*).
reteni *vt.* keep, retain (*in one's possession*); reserve (*for future use*); keep, store (*in a regular place*); withhold; hold in. • *n.* keeping, retention, storing. **reteni sua respira** hold one's breath.
reti[1] *vi.* straighten. • *vt.* straighten; (*electronics*) rectify (*convert from AC to DC*).
reti-[2] *pref.* recti-.
retia *n.* straightness.
reticulal *adj.* reticular.
reticulo *n.* reticulum (*network, anatomy*); crosshairs, reticule, reticle.
retil *n.* reptile (*Reptilia*).
retilal *adj.* reptilian.
retilinial *n.* rectilinear.
retina *n.* retina (*anatomy*).
retinal *adj.* retinal.
retinopatia *n.* retinopathy.
retinopatica *adj.* retinopathic.
retinoscopi *n.* retinoscopy.
retinoscopio *n.* retinoscope.
retira *vt.* pull back, take back, withdraw, retire, retract, recall, recant, retreat, relent; recoil; log out (*software*). • *n.* withdrawal, retreat, retraction, fallback; recoil, kickback. **retira gradal** phase out. **retira tro multe** overdraw.
retirada *adj.* withdrawn, reserved, reclusive.
retirador *n.* retractor.
reto *n.* rectum (*anatomy*).
retoca *vt.* retouch, touch up.
retorica *n.* rhetoric, oratory.
retorical *adj.* rhetorical.
retoriciste *n.* rhetorician, orator.
retorta *n.* retort (*container*).
retrae *vt.* bring back, fetch, retrieve. • *n.* retrieval.
retraor *n.* retriever (*dog*). **retraor de Labrador** Labrador retriever, Labrador (*dog*). **retraor oro** golden retriever (*dog*).
retro *adj.* rear, back. • *n.* rear, back part; back cover (*book*). • *pref.* retro-; backwards; e.g. *retrosede.* **a retro** back, backwards. **a retro de** at the back of, in back of, behind. **en retro de** inside the back of, into the back of.
retroacronim *n.* backronym.
retroativa *adj.* retroactive.
retrocarga *vt.* breech-load (*gun*).
retroflami *vi.* backfire.
retroflexe *adj.* & *n.* retroflex.
retrogradal *adj.* retrograde, backward, backwards.
retroroceto *n.* retrorocket.
retrosede *vi.* & *vt.* recede; relegate, demote. • *n.* recession; relegation, demotion. **retrosede economial** economic recession.
retrosedente *adj.* receding, recessive.
retrospasi *vt.* backspace.
retrospeta *vt.* look back. • *n.* retrospective, flashback. **en retrospeta** in retrospect, looking back, with hindsight.
retrospetante *adj.* retrospective.
retrova *vt.* find again, find back, recover.
retrovista *n.* rear view.
reumatica *adj.* rheumatic. **febre reumatica** rheumatic fever. **maladia reumatica** rheumatism, rheumatic disorder.
reumato- *pref.* rheumato-.
reumatoide *adj.* rheumatoid.
reumatolojia *n.* rheumatology.
reumatolojiste *n.* rheumatologist.
reuni [re'uni] *vi.* & *vt.* reunite, reunify, regroup, congregate, convoke, convene, meet. • *n.* reunion, reunification, meeting, assembly, convocation, convention, session.
reusa *vt.* reuse.
reusable *adj.* reusable.
rev *n.* rave (*party*).
revade *vi.* go back, return. • *n.* return.
revela *vt.* reveal, disclose, divulge, manifest, evince, vouchsafe. • *n.* disclosure, revelation, mystical vision, manifestation.
revelante *adj.* revealing, giveaway, telltale; scanty, skimpy (*garment*).
revelia *vi.* & *vt.* reawaken.
revende *vt.* resell. • *n.* resale.
revendor *n.* resaler.
reveni *vi.* come back, return, recur. • *n.* comeback, return. **reveni a casa** homecoming. **reveni de caro** carriage return (*character*).
reveninte *adj.* recurring.

revenu *n.* income, revenue, proceeds, earnings.
reversa *vt.* reverse, turn around, roll back; revert. • *n.* reversal, rollback, turnabout; setback; reversion, atavism. **en reversa** in reverse, vice versa.
reversable *adj.* reversible.
reversada *adj.* reversed. • *adv.* in reverse, vice versa, conversely.
revesti *vt.* reclothe; recoat. • *n.* recoat, fresh coat (*of paint*).
revide *vt.* see again. • *n.* seeing again. **asta revide** bye, goodbye, see you.
revisa *vt.* revise, redact. • *n.* revision, version (*including of text, product*).
revisita *vt.* revisit.
revisor *n.* reviser, editor (*of texts for publication*); revisionist.
revista *vt.* review. • *n.* review, periodical, magazine.
revisteta *n.* bulletin. **revisteta de grupo** newsletter, circular.
revive *vi.* live again, come back to life. • *vt.* revive, resuscitate, resurrect, revitalize, relive. • *n.* revival, resuscitation, resurrection, revitalization.
revolta *vi.* revolt, rise up. • *n.* revolution, revolt, uprising (*local rebellion*).
revolui *vt.* revolutionize, overturn. • *n.* revolution (*overthrow of government*), insurgence.
revoluinte *adj.* revolutionary, radical.
revoluisme *n.* revolutionism.
revoluiste *n.* revolutionist, revolutionary, radical, insurgent.
revolver *n.* revolver (*gun*).
-rexe *n.suff.* -rhexis (*rupture*).
rexerca *vt.* & *n.* research.
rexercar *n.* ricercar (*music*).
rexercor *n.* researcher.
Rhode Island [rod 'ajland] *n.* Rhode Island (*US state*).
ri *vi.* flow, stream, course.
riable *adj.* laughable, risible, ridiculous, ludicrous.
Riad *n.* Riad, Riyad.
rial[1] *n.* rial, riyal (*currency*).
rial[2] *adj.* fluvial, riverine (*of rivers*).
ribes *n.* currant (*plant, fruit: Ribes*).
riboflavina *n.* riboflavin (*vitamin*).
ribonucleal *adj.* ribonucleic.
ribonucleotido *n.* ribonucleotide.
ribosa *n.* ribose (*sugar*).
ribosoma *n.* ribosome (*biology*).
ribosomal *adj.* ribosomal.
rica *adj.* rich, wealthy, prosperous, affluent, monied. **nova rica** newly rich, nouveau riche. **rica con fero** rich in iron.
ricetsia *n.* rickettsia (*bacterium*).
rici *vi.* prosper. • *vt.* enrich.
ricia *n.* richness, riches, wealth, means, prosperity, opulence, affluence, mammon.
ricota *n.* ricotta (*cheese*).
ricxa *n.* rickshaw, pedicab (*drawn by hand or bicycle*).
rie *vt.* laugh. • *n.* laugh, laughter. **rie tra sua dentes** snicker, snigger.
rieta[1] *vt.* & *n.* giggle, titter.
rieta[2] *n.* stream, creek, rivulet, brook, rill.
rif *n.* riff (*music*).
rifa *vt.* raffle. • *n.* raffle, tombola.
Riga *n.* Riga. **Golfo Riga** Gulf of Riga.
rigatoni *n.* rigatoni (*food*).
rigodon *n.* rigaudon, rigadoon (*dance*).
rijida *adj.* stiff, rigid.
rijidi *vi.* & *vt.* stiffen, turn rigid.
rijidia *n.* stiffness, rigidity.
ril *n.* reel (*dance, music*).
rima *vi.*, *vt.* & *n.* rhyme.
rinite *n.* rhinitis, hayfever, coryza.
rino- *pref.* rhino- (*nose*).
rinofarinjite *n.* nasopharyngitis, rhinopharyngitis, common cold.
rinorea *n.* rhinorrhoea, runny nose.
rinosero *n.* rhinoceros, rhino (*Rhinocerotidae*).
rinse *vt.* & *n.* rinse.
rio *n.* river. **rio basa** ford.
rion *n.* guffaw, belly laugh.
ris *n.* rice (*Oryza sativa*). **ris de jasmin** jasmine rice.
risa *adj.* curly, curled. • *n.* curl, ringlet. **risas de lenio** wood shavings, excelsior.
risca *vt.* risk. • *n.* risk, hazard. **risca biolojial** biological hazard, biohazard. **risca de credito** credit risk, credit score. **risca la acaso** take a chance, take pot luck.
riscada *adj.* vulnerable (*species*).
riscosa *adj.* risky; risqué, racy, suggestive, titillating.
risi *vi.* & *vt.* curl.
risole *n.* rissole (*food*).
risoto *n.* risotto (*food*).
ritmal *adj.* prosodic.
ritmo *n.* rhythm, cadence, prosody, rhythmics. **ritmo de tambur** drumbeat. **ritmo e blus** rhythm and blues, R&B.
ritmosa *adj.* rhythmic, rhythmical.
ritual *adj.* ritual, ritualistic, ceremonial, ceremonious, solemn.
rituo *n.* ritual, rite, ceremony, service, observance. **rituo de sposi** wedding, marriage ceremony. **rituo santa** sacred rite, sacrament.
riva *n.* shore, bank, riverbank, waterside. **Riva Ueste** West Bank, Cisjordan.
rival *adj.* riparian (*of riverbanks*).
riviera *n.* riviera.
rizofora *n.* mangrove (*Rhizophora*).
rizoide *adj.* & *n.* rhizoid (*biology*).

rizoma *n.* rhizome (*biology*).
ro *n.* rho (*Greek letter* Ρ, ρ).
roan *adj.* & *n.* roan (*horse*).
roba *n.* dress, robe. **roba de bani** dressing gown, bathrobe, housecoat. **roba de casa** housedress. **roba de coctel** cocktail dress. **roba de note** nightdress, nightgown, nightie. **roba de prete** cassock. **roba de sera** evening gown. **roba de sol** sundress. **roba de sposi** wedding dress, wedding gown. **roba diafana** negligee. **roba gainin** sheath dress. **roba negra peti** little black dress.
robeta *n.* slip (*full-length*). **robeta de note** babydoll (*nightdress*).
robinia *n.* robinia, locust (*tree*: *Robinia*).
robot *n.* robot.
robotal *adj.* robotic (*of robots*).
roboti *vt.* robotize. • *n.* robotization.
robotica *n.* robotics.
robotin *adj.* robotic, robotlike.
roc[1] *adj.* & *n.* rock (*music*). **roc dur** hard rock. **roc e rola** rock and roll. **roc metal** heavy metal. **roc punc** punk rock.
roc[2] *n.* roc (*mythological bird*).
roca[1] *n.* rock, stone. **roca deponeda** sedimentary rock. **roca madral** bedrock. **roca magmal** igneous rock. **roca mutada** metamorphic rock.
roca[2] *vt.* castle (*chess move*). • *n.* castling.
rocefort *n.* roquefort (*cheese*).
roceria *n.* rockery.
roceta *n.* roquet (*croquet*).
roceto *n.* rocket (*missile, engine*).
rocetolojia *n.* rocketology, rocket science.
rocetolojiste *n.* rocketologist, rocket scientist.
rococo *adj.* & *n.* rococo.
rocon *n.* boulder.
rocosa *adj.* rocky. **Montes Rocosa** Rocky Mountains.
rode *vt.* gnaw, nibble.
rodente *adj.* gnawing. • *n.* rodent (*Rodentia*).
rodeo *n.* rodeo (*cattle, contest*).
rodi *n.* roadie (*for touring band*).
rodio *n.* rhodium (*element*).
rododendro *n.* rhododendron (*Rhododendron*).
rodopsina *n.* rhodopsin (*biology*).
rohingia *adj.* & *n.* Rohingya (*person, language*).
roja *adj.* red; red-haired, red-headed, ginger. • *n.* red; redhead. **Mar Roja** Red Sea. **roja calda** red-hot, fervent.
roji *vi.* redden, turn red, blush, flush. • *vt.* redden, turn red, cause to blush. • *n.* blush, flush.
rojin *adj.* reddish. **rojin brun** reddish-brown, auburn, rufous.
rol *n.* role, factor, function, capacity, part (*to play*). **fa la rol de** take the role of, be cast as.
rola *vi.* roll, roll over; taxi (*aircraft*); trundle; tumble; wallow; scroll (*software*). • *vt.* roll, roll over, bowl. • *n.* roll (*action*). **rola de tambur** drumroll.
rolada *n.* roulade, paupiette, braciole (*food*).
rolador *n.* roller.
rolante *adj.* rolling; rollaway (*bed*).
roleta *n.* roulette (*game*).
rolor *n.* roleplayer, actor, player, person with a role to play.
rom *n.* ROM (*read-only memory*).
Roma *n.* Rome.
romaji *n.* rōmaji (*transcription*).
roman *adj.* Roman.
romani *adj.* & *n.* Rom, Romany, Gypsy (*person, language*).
Romania *n.* Romania.
romanian *adj.* & *n.* Romanian.
romanica *adj.* Romanic, Romance; romanesque. • *n.* Romanic, Romance.
romaniol *adj.* & *n.* Romagnol (*person, language*).
romanse *n.* romance.
romansor *n.* romancer.
romantica *adj.* romantic, amatory. • *n.* romantic. **relata romantica** romance, romantic relationship.
romanticisme *n.* romanticism.
romaro *n.* rosemary (*plant*: *Rosmarinus officinalis*).
rombo *adj.* rhomboid. • *n.* rhombus, lozenge.
rombosa *adj.* argyle (*pattern*).
rombozon *n.* rhombozoon (pl. rhombozoa) (*organism*: *Rhombozoa*).
romeo *n.* romeo, lothario, ladies' man.
rompable *adj.* breakable.
rompe *vi.* break, tear, snap; malfunction, go wrong, break down. • *vt.* break, snap, tear up; renege on, go back on, fail to observe (*promise, deal*). • *n.* breakdown, breakage, rupture, tear, failure, malfunction; bust (*economic*). **rompe a du** break in two, snap in two. **rompe de eletrica** power cut, power outage.
rompeda *adj.* broken.
rompegreve *n.* strikebreaker.
rompejelo *n.* icebreaker (*ship*).
rompelingua *n.* tongue twister.
rompente *adj.* breaking. **rompente la timpanes** earsplitting.
rompetesta *n.* puzzle, riddle, brainteaser; mace (*weapon*).
rompor *n.* breaker. **rompor de monopolios** trustbuster.
ronc *interj.* grunt, oink.

ronceta *vt.* & *n.* grunt, oink.
ronci *vt.* growl, snarl, grumble, rumble; snore loudly. • *n.* growl, snarl, grunt, rumble.
roncin *adj.* hoarse.
ronda *adj.* round; pudgy, chubby, tubby, rotund. • *n.* round (*music, drinks, contest*); circle (*of friends*), ring (*of people*), bevy, posse, troop, troupe.
rondi *vi.* & *vt.* round.
rondia *n.* roundness.
rondin *n.* swallow (*bird*: *Hirundinidae*). **Rondin** *n.* Apus (*constellation*).
rondo *n.* rondeau (*poetry*).
ronrona *vt.* & *n.* purr.
rontgen *n.* roentgen (*unit of radiation*).
rontgenio *n.* roentgenium (*element*).
ros *adj.* pink, roseate. • *n.* pink.
rosa *n.* rose (*Rosa*). **rosa spinosa** sweetbrier, sweetbriar, eglantine rose (*Rosa eglanteria, Rosa rubiginosa*).
rosaria *n.* rosary (*prayer, beads*).
rosarieta *n.* chaplet (*beads*).
roseola *n.* roseola, roseola infantum, baby measles.
roseta[1] *n.* rosefinch, purple finch (*Carpodacus*).
roseta[2] *n.* rosette (*botany, decorative ribbon*), cockade.
rosi *vi.* turn pink, blush. • *vt.* turn pink, cause to blush. • *n.* blush.
rosida *n.* rosid (*plant*).
rosin *adj.* pinkish, rosy.
rosinol *n.* nightingale (*Luscinia megarhynchos*).
rosio *n.* dew.
rosiosa *adj.* dewy, bedewed.
rosta *vt.* & *n.* roast.
rostador *n.* roaster. **rostador jirante** rotisserie (*appliance*).
rosteria *n.* rotisserie (*restaurant*).
rostralata *n.* painted snipe (*bird*: *Rostratulidae*).
rota *n.* wheel. **rota de acua** waterwheel. **rota de dentes** gear, cog. **rota de inertia** flywheel. **rota de rola** scroll wheel (*mouse*). **rota idraulical** hydraulic wheel, waterwheel. **rota jigante** Ferris wheel.
roteta *n.* castor.
rotica *adj.* & *n.* rhotic (*sound, dialect*).
rotifero *n.* rotifer (*organism*: *Rotifera*).
rotor *n.* rotor.
rotula *n.* kneecap, patella.
rotunda *n.* rotunda (*building, room*); roundhouse (*for locomotive maintenance*).
roxi *n.* roshi (*monk*).
ru[1] *adj.* rough (*not smooth*), coarse, rugged, nubby.
ru[2] *n.* roux (*food*).
rua *n.* road. **rua sin sorti** dead end, cul-de-sac; stalemate, deadlock, impasse.
Ruanda *n.* Rwanda. **ruanda** *adj.* & *n.* Rwandan.
ruba *vt.* rob, mug, hold up (*steal from by force or threat*). • *n.* robbery, mugging, hold-up, stick-up.
rubarbo *n.* rhubarb (*Rheum*).
rubeola *n.* rubella, German measles.
rubi *n.* ruby (*gem*).
rubia *n.* madder, rubia (*plant, pigment*: *Rubia*); alizarin, crimson.
rubidio *n.* rubidium (*element*).
rublo *n.* ruble, rouble (*currency*).
rubo *n.* bramble (*plant, berry*: *Rubus fruticosus*).
rubor *n.* robber, mugger.
ruca *n.* rocket, roquette, arugula, colewort (*plant*: *Eruca sativa*).
rue *n.* roué, libertine, debauchee.
rueta *n.* lane, path, pathway, alley. **rueta de tira** towpath.
rugbi *n.* rugby (*sport*).
ruia ['ruja] *n.* roughness, coarseness, ruggedness.
ruidador *n.* noisemaker (*device*).
ruidi *vi.* & *vt.* turn noisy, blare.
ruido *n.* noise, cacophony, clamour (US clamor), rumpus, din, racket. **ruido blanca** white noise.
ruidor *n.* noisemaker (*person*).
ruidosa *adj.* noisy, uproarious. **condui ruidosa e enerjiosa** behave boisterously, roughhouse. **ruidosa e enerjiosa** boisterous.
ruina *vt.* ruin, devastate, desolate, ravage. • *n.* ruin, desolation, devastation, doom, havoc, downfall, wreck. **a ruina** (*fall*) to ruins, to pieces, apart. **ruinas** ruins, wreckage.
ruinada *adj.* ruined, ruinous, desolate, devastated, decrepit, derelict, ramshackle. • *n.* (*colloquial*) old fogey, old geezer; jalopy, old banger (*car*). **ruinada par gera** war-torn.
ruji *vt.* & *n.* roar, bellow.
rum *n.* rum (*drink*).
rumans *adj.* Romansh, Romansch (*language*).
rumba *n.* rumba (*dance, music*).
rumor *n.* rumour (US rumor). **rumores** rumours (US rumors), gossip.
rumoror *n.* gossip, rumourmonger (US rumormonger).
runa *n.* rune (*letter*).
runal *adj.* runic.
rupi *n.* rupee (*currency*).
rus *n.* ruse, trick, chicanery, prank, ploy, spoof, wile.
rusce *adj.* & *n.* Russian (*person, language*).
Rusia *n.* Russia.
rusor *n.* trickster, prankster.

rusosa *adj.* crafty, cunning, tricky, devious, artful, wily, sly, shady. **es plu rusosa ca** outwit, outsmart, outthink, outfox.
rusosia *n.* craftiness, cunning, cunningness, deviousness, guile, sleight, trickery.
ruta *vt.* & *n.* burp, belch.
rutenio *n.* ruthenium (*element*).
ruterfordio *n.* rutherfordium (*element*).

S

S[1] [es], **es** *letter* S, s. **con forma de S** S-shaped.
s[2] *abbr.* (*sirca*) c., approx.
-s[3] *suff.* -s (*plural of noun that ends in a vowel*); e.g. *gatos*. See *-es*.
sabatica *adj.* & *n.* sabbatical.
sabe *vt.* know (*fact, details, how to*); e.g. *me no sabe do me ia pone la clave*; *tu sabe elefen*; *el sabe jua xace*. • *n.* knowledge, knowhow. **ci sabe?** who knows? **sabes** items of knowledge, lore. **(tu) sabe** you know (*filler*). See *conose*.
sabetota *n.* know-all, know-it-all, smart aleck, smartarse, smartass, smartypants, wiseguy, wiseacre.
sabor *n.* taste, flavour (US flavor). **con sabor** flavoured (US flavored). **con sabor agu** pungent, sharp-tasting. **con sabor de xasada** gamey. **sabor persistente** aftertaste. **sensa de sabor** sense of taste, gustatory sense. **sin sabor** flavourless (US flavorless), tasteless.
saborea *vt.* savour (US savor), relish, enjoy, love.
saboreor *n.* lover (*of art, music, food, etc.*).
sabori *vi.* taste. • *vt.* flavour (US flavor). **sabori bon** taste good.
saborida *adj.* flavoured (US flavored).
saborinte *n.* flavouring (US flavoring).
saborosa *adj.* tasty, flavourful (US flavorful), strong-tasting, savoury (US savory), palatable.
sabosa *adj.* knowledgeable. • *n.* boffin.
sabota *vt.* & *n.* sabotage.
sabotor *n.* saboteur.
sabre *n.* sabre (US saber). **clica de sabres** sabre (US saber) rattling.
saca *vt.* sack, pillage, maraud, plunder, despoil, ransack.
sacabuta *n.* sackbut (*musical instrument*).
Sacartvelo *n.* Georgia (*Caucasus*). See *cartuli, Jorjia*.
sace *n.* sake (*drink*).
saceta *n.* sachet.
saci[1] *n.* saki monkey (*Pithecia*).
saci[2] *vt.* bag, bag up, put in a bag.
sacin *adj.* sacklike.
saco *n.* bag, sack, sac, tote. **saco de arena** sandbag. **saco de colpa** punching bag, punchbag. **saco de favas** beanbag (*juggling*). **saco de gas** gasbag. **saco de juta** hessian sack, burlap bag, gunnysack. **saco de mone** moneybag. **saco de posta** postbag, mailbag, mailsack. **saco de sela** saddlebag. **saco silindre** duffel bag, duffle bag, kit bag.
sacor *n.* pillager, marauder.
sacral *adj.* sacral.
sacrifia *vt.* & *n.* sacrifice.
sacro *n.* sacrum (*anatomy*).
sacroilial *adj.* sacroiliac.
sacroilio *n.* sacroilium (*anatomy*).
sadisme *n.* sadism.
sadiste *adj.* sadistic. • *n.* sadist.
sadomasocisme *n.* sadomasochism.
sadomasociste *adj.* sadomasochistic.
safari *n.* safari.
safir *n.* sapphire (*gem*).
saga *n.* saga (*story*).
saguaro *n.* saguaro (*cactus: Carnegiea gigantea*).
Sahara *n.* Sahara. **Sahara Ueste** Western Sahara.
saharan *adj.* Saharan.
Sahel *n.* Sahel (*African region*).
saimiri *n.* squirrel monkey (*Saimiri*).
saisi *vt.* seize, grasp, grab, snatch, usurp; abduct, kidnap, ravish, commandeer, requisition. • *n.* abduction, kidnapping. **saisi como ostaje** take (*as*) hostage. **saisi de avion** skyjack. **saisi en viaja** hijack. **saisi se** seize up; freeze, hang (*software*).
saisida *adj.* seized; frozen (*software*).
saisinte *adj.* seizing, grasping. **saisinte la oio** eye-catching, striking.
saison *n.* season.
saisonal *adj.* seasonal; seasonable.
saisor *n.* kidnapper, hijacker. **saisor de avion** skyjacker.
saja *adj.* wise, sage, sagacious, judicious, politic. • *n.* sage, wise person, wise man, wise woman.
sajia *n.* wisdom, sagacity.
sajital *adj.* sagittal.
sal *n.* salt. **sin sal** without salt, unsalted.
sala *n.* room, chamber; ward (*hospital*). **sala de bagaje** cloakroom, luggage room, baggage room. **sala de banio** bathroom. **sala de campana** bell chamber, belfry. **sala de capitan** stateroom. **sala de clase** schoolroom, classroom. **sala de come** dining room. **sala de contas** counting house. **sala de dormi** bedroom, boudoir. **sala de enfantes** nursery, playroom. **sala de entra** antechamber, anteroom, entrance hall. **sala de espeta** waiting room. **sala de fem** boudoir. **sala de femes** ladies' room (*toilet*). **sala de furnis** storeroom, stockroom. **sala de jornalistes** pressroom. **sala de justia** courtroom. **sala de labora** workroom. **sala de lava** washroom. **sala de omes** men's

room (*toilet*). **sala de prete** sacristy. **sala de rede** (*internet*) chatroom. **sala de scalera** stairwell. **sala de sol** sunroom, conservatory. **sala de studia** study (*room*). **sala de te** tearoom. **sala de vesti** dressing room. **sala oscur** darkroom (*photography*). **sala per du** room for two, double room. **sala per un** room for one, single room. **sala prima** first room, homeroom. **sala securida** vault (*bank*).

salada *n.* salad. **salada de col** coleslaw.

salamandra *n.* salamander (four families of *Urodela*, esp. *Salamandridae*).

salami *n.* salami (*food*).

salario *n.* salary, wage, wages, stipend, paycheck, paycheque. **con salario** paid, salaried, non-amateur, professional.

salda *vt.* balance, settle (*account*). • *n.* balance.

saldeta *n.* change.

saleta *n.* closet, compartment. **saleta de comedas** pantry, larder. **saleta de furnis** storage closet, supply closet. **saleta de jacas** cloakroom. **saleta de vestes** clothes closet. **saleta privata** toilet, lavatory, loo, cloakroom, WC.

sali *vt.* salt, salinate. • *n.* salination.

salin *adj.* saline.

saliva *n.* saliva, spittle.

salivi *vt.* salivate, water. • *n.* salivation.

Salix, Mar *n.* Salish Sea.

salmiste *n.* psalmist.

salmo *n.* psalm, canticle, religious poem. **libro de salmos** psalter.

salmon *adj.* salmon (*colour*). • *n.* salmon (*fish*: *Salmo*, *Oncorhynchus*). **salmon fumida** smoked salmon, lox.

salmonela *n.* salmonella.

salmonelose *n.* salmonella (*poisoning*).

salon *n.* living room, drawing room, lounge; great room, hall, chamber. **Salon Alta** Upper House, Senate, House of Lords. **Salon Basa** Lower House, House of Representatives, House of Commons. **salon de balo** ballroom. **salon de bir** beer hall. **salon de conserta** concert hall, auditorium. **salon de dansa** dance hall. **salon de legi** legislative chamber. **salon de presenta** auditorium. **salon de sindicato** guildhall. **salon formal** stateroom.

salopeta *n.* bib overalls, bib-and-brace overalls, dungarees; salopettes, snowsuit.

salosa *adj.* salty, briny, brackish.

salosia *n.* salinity.

salpica *vi.*, *vt.* & *n.* splash, spatter, splatter.

salsa *n.* sauce, dressing; salsa. **salsa de carne** gravy. **salsa de crema** custard. **salsa de poma** apple sauce. **salsa de salada** salad dressing. **salsa de tomate** tomato sauce, spaghetti sauce. **salsa dulse** sweet sauce, dessert topping. **salsa tatar** tartare (US tartar) sauce.

salse *n.* willow (*Salix*).

salsix *n.* sausage. **salsix american** hotdog, frankfurter, frank, wiener. **salsix bolonian** bologna. **salsix de figato** liverwurst.

salsola *n.* tumbleweed, salsola, Russian thistle (*plant*: *Salsola*, *Amaranthus*).

salta *vi.* & *n.* jump, leap, spring, bound, pounce, lunge. **salta a ante** jump forward, jump ahead, flash forward. **salta a sirca** jump around. **salta alta** *v.* perform a high jump. • *n.* high jump. **salta con corda elastica** *v.* bungee-jump. • *n.* bungee jump, bungee jumping. **salta con palo** pole-vault. **salta con paracade** *v.* skydive, parachute. • *n.* skydiving, parachuting. **salta cuantal** quantum leap. **salta de asi a ala** jump around. **salta de la reles** come off the rails, derail. **salta longa** *v.* perform a long jump. • *n.* long jump.

salterio *n.* psaltery (*musical instrument*).

salteta *vi.* start (*with surprise*), jump, flinch, wince. • *vt.* make someone jump.

saltor *n.* jumper, leaper. **saltor alta** high-jumper. **saltor con palo** pole vaulter. **saltor longa** long-jumper.

saluta *vt.* greet, welcome, receive. • *n.* greeting, welcome, salutation. **saluta con mano** wave (*greeting*). **saluta de fusiles** salvo. **saluta inclinada** *v.* & *n.* bow (*respect*). **saluta militar** *v.* & *n.* salute.

salva *vt.* save, rescue; spare; save up; redeem. • *n.* salvation, redemption, salvage.

salvable *adj.* salvageable.

Salvador *n.* El Salvador.

salvadoran *adj.* & *n.* Salvadoran.

salvascermo *n.* screensaver.

salvatempo *n.* timesaver.

salvia *n.* sage, salvia (*plant*: *Salvia*).

salvor *n.* saviour (US savior), rescuer; redeemer.

samara *n.* samara (*botany*).

samarines *adj.* & *n.* Sammarinese. See *San Marino*.

samario *n.* samarium (*element*).

samba *n.* samba (*dance*, *music*).

sambuco *n.* elder, elderberry (*Sambucus*).

Sami *n.* Lapland. **sami** *n.* Sami.

Samoa *n.* Samoa. **Samoa Ueste** Western Samoa.

samoan *adj.* & *n.* Samoan.

samovar *n.* samovar (*urn*).

sampan *n.* sampan (*boat*).

samplador *n.* sampler (*music*).

sample *vt.* sample (*analysis*, *music*). • *n.* sample. **sample tipal** cross-section (*statistics*).

samsara *n.* samsara (*Buddhism*, *Hinduism*).

samurai *n.* samurai.

San[1] *n.* St, Saint (*title*). **Golfo San Jorge** [ˈhorhe] San Jorge Gulf. **Golfo San Laurent** Gulf of Saint Lawrence. **Golfo San Matias** San Matías Gulf. **Rio San Laurent** Saint Lawrence River. **San Kitts e Nevis** Saint Kitts and Nevis. **San Lusia** Saint Lucia. **San Marino** San Marino. **San Nicolas** Saint Nicholas, Santa Claus. **San Tome e Prinsipe** São Tomé and Príncipe. **San Vinsent e la Grenadines** Saint Vincent and the Grenadines. See *citian, nevisian, samarines, sanlusian, santomense, vinsentian.*

san[2] *adj.* & *n.* Bushman, San (*person, language*).

sana[1] *adj.* healthy, hale, salubrious. **mental sana** sane.

Sana[2] *n.* Sana'a.

sanbernardo *n.* Saint Bernard (*dog*).

sandal *n.* sandal.

sandaleta *n.* flip-flop, thong (*simple sandal*).

sandalo *n.* sandalwood (*Santalum album*).

sanduitx *n.* sandwich.

sanga *n.* sangha (*Buddhism*).

sanglota *vt.* & *n.* sob, gasp.

sangria *n.* sangria (*drink*).

sangual *adj.* blood-related.

sangue *n.* blood, gore. **con lias de sangue** consanguine. **de sangue pur** pureblooded, purebred, thoroughbred. **lias de sangue** consanguinity, blood ties. **sangue de vive** lifeblood. **sin sangue** bloodless. **versa de sangue** bloodshed.

sanguefria *n.* sangfroid (*calm*).

sangui *vt.* bleed. • *n.* bleeding, bloodletting. **sangui de nas** nosebleed.

sanguosa *adj.* bloody, gory; bloodshot (*eye*).

sani *vi.* heal, become healthy, get better, recover, recuperate, convalesce. • *vt.* cure, make healthy, make better. **sani spirital** faith healing.

sania *n.* health, wellness, salubriousness. **sania mental** mental health, sanity.

saninte *adj.* wholesome, health-giving, healthful, healthy.

sanitota *n.* cureall, panacea.

sanlusian *adj.* & *n.* Saint Lucian. See *San Lusia.*

sanor *n.* healer. **sanor spirital** faith healer, curandero.

sanscrito *adj.* & *n.* Sanskrit.

santa *adj.* holy, sacred, sacral. • *n.* saint. **santa padronal** patron saint.

santeria *n.* shrine, holy place.

santi *vi.* & *vt.* consecrate, sanctify, hallow; canonize. • *n.* consecration, sanctification; canonization.

santia *n.* holiness, beatitude, sainthood, sanctity.

santida *adj.* hallowed, sacrosanct.

santomense *adj.* & *n.* São Toméan, Santomean. See *San Tome e Prinsipe.*

sanumberto *n.* bloodhound (*dog*).

sapaio *n.* broad-billed sapayoa (*bird*: *Sapayoa aenigma*).

sapateria *n.* shoe shop.

sapato *n.* shoe. **sapato de sporte** athletic shoe, gym shoe, running shoe, trainer, sneaker, plimsoll, pump, sandshoe. **sapato escotada** court shoe, pump (*low-cut*). **sin sapatos** shoeless, barefoot, unshod.

sapator *n.* shoemaker, cobbler.

sapin *adj.* toadlike, toady.

sapo *n.* toad (*Anura*).

sapon *n.* soap.

saponi *vt.* soap.

saponosa *adj.* soapy.

sapota *n.* sapodilla (*tree*: *Manilkara zapota*).

saprofaje *adj.* saprophagous. • *n.* saprophyte.

saprofajia *n.* saprophagy (*biology*).

sarabanda *n.* saraband (*dance, music*).

saraseno *n.* buckwheat (*plant*: *Fagopyrum esculentum*).

sarcasmo *n.* sarcasm, snark.

sarcasmosa *adj.* sarcastic, sardonic, snide.

sarco- *pref.* sarco- (*flesh*).

sarcofago *n.* sarcophagus.

sarcoidose *n.* sarcoidosis (*medical*).

sarcoma *n.* sarcoma (*tumour*). • *n.suff.* -sarcoma.

sarcopenia *n.* sarcopenia (*medical*).

sarda *adj.* & *n.* Sard, Sardinian (*person, language*). **Mar Sarda** Sardinian Sea.

sardas *n.* csardas, czardas (*dance*).

sardina *n.* sardine, pilchard (*Sardina, Sardinops, Sardinella*).

Sardinia *n.* Sardinia.

Sargasso, Mar *n.* Sargasso Sea.

sari *n.* sari (*garment*).

sarin *n.* sarin (*gas*).

sarja *n.* twill, serge (*fabric*).

sarjento *n.* sergeant.

sarong *n.* sarong (*garment*).

sasafras *n.* sassafras (*tree*: *Sassafras albidum*).

sasanan *adj.* Sassanid, Sassanian (*dynasty*).

sasares *adj.* & *n.* Sassarese (*person, language*).

sasia *vt.* satisfy, sate, satiate, gratify, assuage, quench; meet, fulfil (US fulfill) (*requirement*); cover, defray (*cost*). • *n.* satisfaction, satiation, gratification; fulfilment (US fulfillment).

sasiada *adj.* satisfied, content, replete, sated, satiated.

sasiante *adj.* satisfying, satisfactory, rewarding, fulfilling.

Saskatchewan [sasˈkatʃewan] *n.* Saskatchewan (*Canadian province*).

sasofon *n.* saxophone, sax.

sasofoniste *n.* saxophonist.
Sason *n.* Saxony (*German region*). **sason** *adj.* & *n.* Saxon.
satai *n.* satay (*food*).
Satan *n.* Satan.
satanal *adj.* satanic (*of Satan*).
satanin *adj.* satanic (*like Satan*).
satanisme *n.* Satanism.
sataniste *n.* Satanist.
satelite *n.* satellite. **orienta par satelite** satellite navigation, satnav.
sati *n.* sati, suttee (*ritual immolation of widow*).
satin *n.* satin.
satinin *adj.* satiny. • *n.* sateen (*fabric*).
satir *n.* satyr (*mythology*).
satira *adj.* satiric, satirical. • *n.* satire.
satiri *vt.* satirize.
satiriase *n.* satyriasis (*medical*).
satiriste *n.* satirist.
satori *n.* satori (*Buddhism*).
satrap *n.* satrap (*governor*).
satrapia *n.* satrapy.
satura *vt.* saturate, soak through, steep. • *n.* saturation.
saturada *adj.* saturated.
saturdi *n.* Saturday.
Saturno *n.* Saturn (*mythology, planet*).
sauain *n.* samhain (*Celtic festival*).
saudi *adj.* & *n.* Saudi, Saudi Arabian.
sauerbraten *n.* sauerbraten (*food*).
sauna *n.* sauna.
sauternes *n.* sauterne (*wine*).
sava *n.* sap (*of plant*).
savaje *adj.* wild, feral, untamed, savage, brutal, brutish, beastly. • *n.* brute, thug, goon.
savaji *vi.* & *vt.* turn wild, turn savage, brutalize.
savajia *n.* wildness, savagery, brutality.
savana *n.* savanna, grassland, bush.
savoian *adj.* Savoisien, Savoyen.
Savoie *n.* Savoie (*French region*).
Savu *n.* Savu (*island*). **Mar Savu** Savu Sea.
saxifraje *n.* saxifrage (*Saxifraga*).
saximi *n.* sashimi (*food*).
sca *adj.* ska (*music*).
scafal *n.* shelf, ledge, rack, mantel, mantelpiece; scaffold, scaffolding. **scafal de libros** bookshelf. **scafal de ximine** mantelpiece, chimneypiece, chimneyshelf.
scala *n.* ladder; scale (*values, music*). **scala major** major scale (*music*). **scala minor** major scale (*music*). **scala pliable** stepladder.
scalal *adj.* scalar.
scalda *vt.* scald.
scalena *adj.* scalene (*triangle*).
scalera *n.* staircase, stairway, stair, (*flight of*) stairs. **scalera de bancas** bleachers, tiered benches. **scalera de securia** fire escape. **scalera elica** spiral staircase. **scalera rolante** escalator.
scalerin *adj.* stepped, jagged.
scalmo *n.* oarlock, rowlock.
scalpo *n.* scalp.
scama *n.* scale.
scamin *adj.* scale-like.
scamosa *adj.* scaly, squamous.
scanador *n.* scanner.
scandal *n.* scandal, outrage.
scandali *vt.* scandalize, outrage.
scandalinte *adj.* scurrilous.
scandalosa *adj.* scandalous, outrageous.
scande *vt.* scan (*poetry*). • *n.* scansion.
Scandinavia *n.* Scandinavia.
scandinavian *adj.* & *n.* Scandinavian.
scandio *n.* scandium (*element*).
scane *vt.* scan (*with eyes or machine*).
scapula *n.* shoulderblade, scapula.
scarabe *n.* beetle, scarab (*Coleoptera*). **scarabe de maio** cockchafer, May beetle, May bug (*Melolontha*). **scarabe elefantin** weevil (*Curculionoidea*). **scarabe santa** scarab, dung beetle (*Scarabaeus*).
scaramuxa *vi.* skirmish, scrimmage, clash, scuffle; squabble, bicker. • *n.* skirmish, scrimmage, squabble, clash, scuffle, mêlée, fray, affray, fracas.
scarlata *adj.* scarlet, vermilion. • *n.* scarlet.
scarlatina *n.* scarlet fever, scarlatina.
scat *adj.* scat (*music*).
-sce *adj.suff.* & *n.suff.* -ish (*pertaining to a region*); e.g. *rusce*; *norsce*. See *-an*, *-es*, *-i*, *-ica*.
sceletal *adj.* skeletal (*of the skeleton*).
sceletin *adj.* skeletal, skeletonlike.
sceleto *n.* skeleton, framework. **sceleto de sepida** cuttlebone.
scema *n.* scheme, plan (*of action, of payment*); chart, diagram, outline, schema, schematic drawing; timetable. **scema de flue** flowchart. **scema economial** budget. **scema fantasial** pipedream.
scemal *adj.* schematic, scheme-based.
scemi *vt.* outline, plan, mastermind, scheme.
scemor *n.* schemer, planner, mastermind.
scermeta *n.* buckler; gusset.
scermi *vt.* shield, shelter.
scermida *adj.* shielded. **scermida de la venta** sheltered, shielded from the wind.
scermin *adj.* shieldlike, shield-shaped.
scermioio *n.* blinder, blinker.
scermo *n.* screen, shield; monitor. **Scermo** *n.* Scutum (*constellation*). **scermo arjento** silver screen. **scermo de cristal licuida** liquid-crystal display, LCD. **scermo eraldial** coat of arms, blazon. **scermo interatante** touchscreen.
scet *n.* skateboard.
sceti *vt.* skateboard. • *n.* skateboarding.

scetor *n.* skateboarder.
scetx *n.* sketch, skit (*comedy*).
sci *n.* ski; skiing. • *vt.* ski. **sci acual** *vt.* waterski. • *n.* waterski; waterskiing. **sci de distantia longa** *v.* ski long-distance. • *n.* long-distance skiing. **sci savaje** off-piste skiing, backcountry skiing.
scieria *n.* ski slope, piste.
scife *n.* skiff (*boat*).
scifel *n.* skiffle (*music*).
scinco *n.* skink (*lizard: Scincidae*).
scior *n.* skier.
-scise *n.suff.* -schisis (*splitting*).
scizo- *pref.* schizo- (*split*).
scizofrenia *n.* schizophrenia.
scizofrenica *adj.* & *n.* schizophrenic.
scizoide *adj.* schizoid.
scizotipal *adj.* schizotypal.
sclavi *vi.* become enslaved. • *vt.* enslave.
sclavia *n.* slavery, servitude, bondage.
sclavin *adj.* slavish, servile, subservient.
sclavo *n.* slave.
sclavor *n.* slaver, slave master, slave dealer.
sclera *n.* sclera (*anatomy*).
sclero- *pref.* sclero- (*hard*).
scleroderma *n.* scleroderma (*medical*).
sclerose *n.* sclerosis (*medical*). • *n.suff.* -sclerosis.
sclerosica *adj.* sclerotic. • *adj.suff.* -sclerotic.
scola *n.* school, schoolhouse; faculty, department, college (*university*). **scola abitada** boarding school, residential school. **scola de musica** conservatory, conservatoire. **scola de opina** school of thought. **scola prima** primary school, elementary school, grade school.
scolal *adj.* school, scholastic.
scolastica *n.* scholasticism.
scoliose *n.* scoliosis (*medical*).
scoliosica *adj.* scoliotic.
scolor *n.* pupil, schoolchild, schoolboy, schoolgirl.
scolta *n.* scout, boy scout, girl guide, girl scout. **scolta joven** brownie, cub.
scoltisme *n.* scouting, scout movement.
scon *n.* scone (*food*).
scopa *n.* broom, (*large*) brush. **scopa de franjes** mop.
scopi *vt.* sweep, brush.
-scopia *n.suff.* -scopy (*observation*).
scopida *adj.* swept. **scopida par venta** windswept.
scopineva *n.* snowplough (US snowplow).
-scopio *n.suff.* -scope (*observation instrument*).
scopor *n.* sweeper, sweep (*person*). **scopor de ximine** chimneysweep.
scorbuto *n.* scurvy (*medical*).
scoria *n.* scoria, slag (*geology*).
scorpion *n.* scorpion (*Scorpiones*). **Scorpion** *n.* Scorpius, Scorpio (*constellation*).
scotes *adj.* Scottish, Scots. • *n.* Scot (*person*).
Scotia *n.* Scotia. **Mar Scotia** Scotia Sea. **Scotia Nova** Nova Scotia (*Canadian province*).
Scotland *n.* Scotland.
scotoma *n.* scotoma (*medical*).
scrabel *n.* Scrabble (*game*).
scratxa *vt.* & *n.* scratch (*music*).
scrima *vi.* fence. • *n.* fencing, swordplay.
scrimor *n.* fencer.
scrimxa *vt.* scrimshaw (*engrave*).
scrivador *n.* word processor. **scrivador de cd** CD writer, CD burner. **scrivador de disco** CD writer, DVD writer, CD burner, DVD burner. **scrivador de dvd** DVD writer, DVD burner.
scrive *vt.* write; author; burn (*disc*). • *n.* writing (*action, style*). **scrive a sielo** skywrite. **scrive corente** cursive writing. **scrive de mano** handwriting (*style*). **scrive par mano** handwriting, penmanship (*action*). **scrive per un otra** ghostwrite.
scriveda *n.* writing (*content*). **scriveda par mano** handwritten. **scrivedas santa** scriptures, holy texts.
scriveria *n.* escritoire, school desk, small writing desk.
scriveta *vt.* & *n.* scribble, scrawl.
scrivetor *n.* scribbler.
scriviste *n.* scribe, scrivener.
scrivor *n.* writer. **scrivor de colona** columnist. **scrivor ombral** ghostwriter.
scrivoria *n.* authorship.
scrotal *adj.* scrotal.
scroto *n.* scrotum (*anatomy*).
scuadron *n.* squadron; squad (*for team*).
scuax *n.* squash (*sport*).
scuaxor *n.* squash player.
sculta *vt.* sculpt. • *n.* sculpture, statue. **sculta de sira** waxwork, wax figure, wax effigy. **scultas** sculptures, statues, statuary.
sculteta *n.* statuette, figurine.
scultor *n.* sculptor. **Scultor** *n.* Sculptor (*constellation*).
scural *n.* squirrel (*Sciuridae*).
scuter *n.* scooter (*motorcycle*).
se *pron.* himself, herself, itself, oneself, themselves (*reflexive*). **se mesma** himself, herself, itself, oneself, themselves (*emphatically reflexive*).
seanse *n.* seance. **fa un seanse** hold a seance.
sebo *n.* sebum; tallow (*substance*).
seborea *n.* seborrhoea (US seborrhea) (*medical*).
sebosa *adj.* sebaceous. **glande sebosa** sebaceous gland.

sebuano *adj.* & *n.* Cebuano (*person, language*).
seca *adj.* dry, arid.
secador *n.* dryer, drier. **secador de capeles** hairdryer.
secante *n.* secant (*mathematics, geometry*).
seci *vi.* dry, wither, wilt, parch, desiccate. • *vt.* dry, wipe up, wipe away.
secia *n.* dryness, drought. **secia estrema** desiccation.
secida *adj.* dried. **secida par sol** sundried, sunbaked.
secinte *adj.* drying. • *n.* desiccant (*substance*).
seco *n.* caecum (US cecum) (*anatomy*).
secobarbital *n.* seconal (*drug*).
secondo *n.* second (*of time*). **secondo ajuntada** leap second.
secreta *adj.* secret, clandestine, confidential, esoteric, arcane, stealthy, furtive, covert, surreptitious. • *adv.* secretly, in secret, stealthily, in confidence. • *n.* secret, confidence.
secrete *vt.* secrete. • *n.* secretion.
secreteria *n.* secretariat.
secreti *vi.* & *vt.* classify, keep secret.
secretia *n.* secrecy, confidence.
secretor *n.* secretary, clerk.
secretoral *adj.* clerical, secretarial.
secretosa *adj.* secretive, reserved, reticent.
secretosia *n.* secrecy, reticence.
secular *adj.* secular.
seculari *vi.* & *vt.* secularize. • *n.* secularization.
secuoia *n.* sequoia, redwood (*tree: Sequoia sempervirens, Sequoiadendron giganteum*).
secur *adj.* safe, secure. **secur contra acua** waterproof. **secur contra baletas** bulletproof. **secur contra bobos** foolproof, idiotproof. **secur contra bombas** bombproof. **secur contra clima** weatherproof. **secur contra flama** flameproof. **secur contra foco** fireproof. **secur contra frati** shatterproof. **secur contra fura** burglarproof, theftproof. **secur contra lus** lightproof, lightfast. **secur contra malfunsiona** failsafe. **secur contra osidi** rustproof. **secur contra pluve** rainproof. **secur contra tempesta** stormproof. **secur contra umidia** dampproof, moistureproof. **secur per gida** roadworthy. **secur per naviga** seaworthy. **secur per vola** airworthy.
securable *adj.* securable, lockable, lockup.
securador *n.* lock (*door*); safety (*gun*). **securador pendente** padlock.
secureria *n.* safe room, panic room.
securi *vi.* & *vt.* secure, lock; make safe, safeguard; strap up, tether, moor. **securi la polsos** handcuff. **securi la talos** shackle.
securia *n.* safety, security, safekeeping.
securilibro *n.* bookend.
securior *n.* security worker, security officer.
securipolso *n.* handcuff, manacle.
securitalo *n.* fetter, shackle.
secute *vi.* & *vt.* shake, agitate, shake up, judder, wag. • *n.* shaking.
secutesal *n.* salt shaker.
seda *n.* silk. **de seda** (*made of*) silk, silken. **seda de arania** spider silk, gossamer. **Via de Seda** Silk Road.
sede *vt.* cede, concede, yield, surrender, submit, succumb, give up, relinquish, grant, give way, acquiesce, relent, buckle. • *n.* concession, surrender, submission, acquiescence.
sedente *adj.* yielding, submissive, docile.
seder *n.* seder (*Judaism*).
sedilia *n.* cedilla (*diacritic*).
sedin *adj.* silky, silken.
sedo *n.* sedum (*plant: Sedum*).
sedro *n.* cedar (*tree: Cedrus, Thuja*).
sedui *vt.* seduce, entice. • *n.* seduction, enticement.
seduinte *adj.* seducing, seductive.
seduor *n.* seductor, seductress, coquette, minx, tease, tart, tramp, lolita, hussy.
seduosa *adj.* seductive, sultry.
sefalaljia *n.* cephalalgia (*medical*).
sefalica *adj.* cephalic (*of the head*).
sefalo- *pref.* cephalo- (*head*).
sefalopodo *n.* cephalopod (*Cephalopoda*).
sefardi *adj.* Sephardi (*Judaism*). • *n.* Sephardi Jew.
Sefeo *n.* Cepheus (*mythology, constellation*).
segal *n.* rye (*plant: Secale cereale*).
seguador *n.* sequencer (*music*).
segue *vt.* follow, trail, retrace; ensue; honour (US honor), observe, stick to, comply with (*agreement*); succeed (*one's predecessor*); supervene. • *n.* sequence (*order*), run; segue (*transition*). **segue lenta** straggle, dawdle, lag behind. **segue tro prosima** follow too closely, tailgate.
seguensa *vt.* sequence (*biochemistry*).
seguente *adj.* following, next, subsequent, consequent, consequential; consecutive, sequential, successive. • *adv.* next. • *n.* successor; sequel, follow-up; wake, wash (*ship*). • *prep.* following, according to, pursuant to. **seguente de condensa** contrail, vapour (US vapor) trail. **tempo seguente** aftermath, wake.
seguor *n.* follower, acolyte; henchman; successor. **seguores** followers, entourage, retinue.
seja *n.* chair, seat (*including in an elected body*); constituency. **con du sejas** two-seater. **seja baldin** bucket seat. **seja jirante** swivel chair. **seja osilante** rocking chair,

rocker. **seja portada** sedan chair, palanquin, litter. **seja reclinante** recliner, reclining chair, lounger, lazyboy. **seja retro** back seat. **seja rolante** wheelchair. **Seja Santa** Holy See. **seja sumerjinte** ducking stool, cucking stool; dunk tank.

sejeta *n.* small seat, stool. **sejeta de bar** barstool.

sejon *n.* armchair.

sela *n.* saddle. **sela de amazonas** sidesaddle. **sin sela** bareback.

selable *adj.* sealable.

selaco *n.* shark (*Selachimorpha*).

seladon *adj.* celadon (*colour*). • *n.* celadon (*pottery*).

-sele *n.suff.* -coele (US -cele) (*medical*).

selebra *vt.* celebrate, rejoice, exult, revel in. • *n.* celebration, party, gala, bash, prom, fete, festivity. **selebra a lus de candelas** candlelight ceremony. **selebra de casa nova** housewarming. **selebra de coctel** cocktail party. **selebra de sera** soirée. **selebra enebriada** *v.* carouse, binge. • *n.* drunken revelry, bacchanal, bacchanalia. **selebra mascida** masquerade party.

selebrada *adj.* celebrated, renowned. • *n.* celebrity (*person*).

selebrante *adj.* celebrating, jubilant.

selebria *n.* celebrity (*quality*).

selebror *n.* reveller (US reveler); celebrant.

selenio *n.* selenium (*element*).

seleri *n.* celery (*Apium graveolens*).

seleria *n.* saddlery (*place*).

seleucan *adj.* Seleucid (*dynasty*).

selfi *n.* selfie (*photo*).

seli *vt.* seal; stamp.

seliaca *n.* coeliac (US celiac) (*medical*).

selinte *adj.* sealing. • *n.* sealant, caulk. **selinte contra fria** weatherstrip.

selo *n.* seal (*tight closure, wax, etc.*); signet; postage stamp. **selo postal** postage stamp.

selobiosa *n.* cellobiose (*sugar*).

selofan *n.* cellophane.

selor *n.* saddler.

selula *n.* cell (*biology, room*), cubicle. **selula de sangue** blood cell, corpuscle. **selula madrin** stem cell.

selulal *adj.* cellular.

selulite *n.* cellulitis.

seluloide *n.* celluloid (*plastic*).

selulosa *n.* cellulose.

semador *n.* seed drill, seeder.

semafor *n.* semaphore; traffic light, traffic signal.

semafori *vt.* semaphore; lock (*database*).

semana *n.* week. **du semanas** two weeks, fortnight. **en esta semana** this week. **en la semana ante esta** last week. **en la semana pos esta** next week. **en la semana presedente** last week; the previous week. **en la semana seguente** next week; the following week. **en un semana** during one week, in one week, within one week. **pos un semana** in one week, in one week's time. **semana de labora** working week, workweek.

semanal *adj.* weekly.

semantica *n.* semantics.

semantical *adj.* semantic.

sembla *vt.* resemble; e.g. *lo sembla un roca.* • *n.* resemblance.

seme *n.* seed; pip, pit, stone (*fruit*). **seme de pino** pine nut.

sementi *vt.* cement.

semento *n.* cement.

semestre *n.* semester, term.

semetero *n.* cemetery, graveyard, churchyard.

semi[1] *vt.* sow, seed. • *n.* sowing.

semi-[2] *pref.* semi- (*half*). See *emi-, dui-*.

semiacual *adj.* semiaquatic.

semianial *adj.* semiannual, biannual (*twice a year*). • *adv.* semiannually.

semiase *n.* semiaxis (*geometry*). **semiase major** semimajor axis (*astronomy*). **semiase minor** semiminor axis (*astronomy*).

semiconduta *vt.* semiconduct.

semicondutador *n.* semiconductor.

semicondutante *adj.* semiconducting, semiconductive.

semideserto *n.* semidesert.

semidivin *adj.* semidivine.

semidulse *adj.* semisweet.

semifinal *n.* semifinal, semi.

semilicuida *adj.* & *n.* semiliquid.

semimensal *adj.* semimonthly (*twice a month*). • *adv.* twice a month.

semin *n.* semen, sperm.

seminal *adj.* seminal.

seminar *n.* seminar.

seminario *n.* seminary. **seminario iudi** Jewish seminary, yeshiva.

seminariste *n.* seminarian.

semini *vt.* inseminate. • *n.* insemination.

semiotica *n.* semiotics.

semiotical *adj.* semiotic.

semipermeable *adj.* semipermeable.

semiprivata *adj.* semiprivate.

semiprofesal *adj.* semiprofessional.

semiseca *adj.* semiarid.

semisirculo *adj.* semicircular. • *n.* semicircle.

semisolida *adj.* semisolid.

semita *adj.* Semitic. • *n.* Semite.

semitono *n.* semitone.

semitransparente *adj.* semitransparent.

semivaluosa *adj.* semiprecious.

semivocal *adj.* semivocalic. • *n.* semivowel.

semola *n.* semolina (*grains, dessert*).
sempre *adv.* always, forever, ever. **la plu bon de sempre** best ever. **la plu grande de sempre** largest ever. **no sempre** not always, not necessarily. **per sempre** forever. **sempre denova** again and again, time and again, time after time. **sempre min** ever less, less and less, decreasingly. **sempre plu** ever more, more and more, increasingly. **sempre presente** omnipresent, ubiquitous.
sempreverde *adj.* & *n.* evergreen.
sena *n.* scene. **sena miniatur** miniature scene, diorama. **sena retrospetante** flashback. **sena vivante** tableau.
senario *n.* script, screenplay, scenario.
senariste *n.* screenwriter, scriptwriter, scenarist.
senato *n.* senate.
senator *n.* senator.
sene *n.* ash, cinders. **senes** ashes, cinders.
Senegal *n.* Senegal.
senegales *adj.* & *n.* Senegalese.
seneria *n.* crematorium, crematory.
senese *vi.* age, become old, grow old. • *vt.* age. • *n.* old age, senescence, dotage.
senesente *adj.* ageing (US aging), aged, old, elderly, geriatric, senescent. • *n.* old person, elderly person.
senglar *n.* wild boar (*Sus scrofa*).
senglarin *adj.* boarlike, boarish.
seni *vi.* & *vt.* cremate. • *n.* cremation.
senil *adj.* senile.
senilia *n.* senility.
senior *n.* gentleman, lord, master; sir, sire (*form of address*). **Senior** *n.* Mr, Mister; Lord (*religious*). **senioras e seniores** ladies and gentlemen.
seniora *n.* lady; madam, ma'am (*form of address*). **Seniora** *n.* Mrs, Miss, Ms.
senioreta *n.* miss, Miss (*historical form of address for a girl or unmarried woman*).
senioreto *n.* master, Master (*historical form of address for a boy*).
senioria *n.* lordship, ladyship.
seniorisme *n.* manorialism (*feudal*).
seno *n.* breast (*mammary gland*). **a seno** at the breast, suckling. **senos** breasts, bosom, bust.
senotafio *n.* cenotaph.
senozoica *adj.* & *n.* Cenozoic (*geology*).
sensa *vt.* sense (*experience a sensation*). • *n.* sense, sensation, feeling. **sensa comun** common sense. See *senti, sinifia*.
sensador *n.* sensor. **sensador de move** motion sensor.
sensal *adj.* sensory, sensuous, sensate.
sensante *adj.* sentient.
sensorimotor *adj.* sensorimotor (*nerve*).
sensorio *n.* sensorium (*sensory faculties*).
sensosa *adj.* sensitive (*to sensation*).
sensosi *vi.* & *vt.* sensitize.
sensosia *n.* sensitivity, sensibility, sensuality.
sensura *vt.* censor, expurgate, bowdlerize. • *n.* censorship, expurgation, bowdlerization.
sensuror *n.* censor (*person*).
senta *vi.* sit. • *vt.* seat, sit. **senta se** sit down.
sentante *adj.* sitting, seated, sedentary.
sentauro *n.* centaur. **Sentauro** *n.* Centaurus (*constellation*). **Alfa de la Sentauro** Alpha Centauri.
sentenial *adj.* centennial.
sentenio *n.* century.
-sentese *n.suff.* -centesis (*puncturing*).
senti[1] *vt.* feel, be aware of (*emotion, pain*); feel (+ *adjective*), consider oneself to be. • *n.* feeling, sense. **senti ce on es felis** feel happy, consider oneself happy. **senti de bon umor** feel cheerful, consider oneself cheerful. **senti de ja videda** déjà vu. **senti felis** feel happy, consider oneself happy. **senti felisia** feel happiness. See *sensa*.
senti[2] *vi.* & *vt.* split into a hundred parts. • *n.* hundredth (*fraction*). • *pref.* centi- (*a hundredth*).
sentigram *n.* centigram.
sentilitre *n.* centilitre (US centiliter).
sentim *n.* cent, centime, penny, pfennig, pingin (*coin*).
sentimetre *n.* centimetre (US centimeter).
sentina *n.* bilge (*curved hull, compartment*).
sento *det.* (*a*) hundred. • *adj.* hundredth (*ordinal*). **sentos** hundreds.
sentopede *n.* centipede (*Chilopoda*).
sentosa *adj.* sentimental, emotionally sensitive (*having strong or many feelings*).
sentosia *n.* sentimentalism, sensitivity.
Sentrafrica *n.* Central African Republic. See *Republica de Africa Sentral*.
sentrafrican *adj.* & *n.* Central African.
sentral *adj.* central, pivotal.
sentri[1] *vi.* & *vt.* centralize, centre (US center).
sentri-[2] *pref.* centri- (*central*).
sentrifuga *n.* centrifuge.
sentrifugal *adj.* centrifugal.
sentrifugi *vt.* centrifuge.
sentriol *n.* centriole (*biology*).
sentripeta *adj.* centripetal.
sentrisme *n.* centrism.
sentriste *adj.* & *n.* centrist.
sentro *n.* centre (US center); hub. **sentro comersial** shopping centre (US center), shopping mall. **sentro de blanco** bullseye. **sentro de recrea** recreation centre (US center), leisure centre (US center). **sentro de rexerca** research centre (US center), think tank. **sentro de site** downtown, cen-

tre (US center) city, city centre (US center). **sentro de table** centrepiece (US centerpiece). **sentro de telefonia** switchboard, telephone exchange. **sentro eletrical** power station, power plant.

sentror *n.* centre (US center), midfielder (*sport*).

senturion *n.* centurion.

sepal *n.* sepal (*botany*).

separa *vi.* separate, differentiate, discriminate, segregate, break up, secede. • *vt.* separate, differentiate, discriminate, segregate, break up. • *n.* separation, differentiation, discrimination, segregation; breakaway, breakup, secession.

separada *adj.* separate, distinct, discrete, independent, outlying. • *adv.* separately, apart, asunder. • *n.* outlier.

separadisme *n.* separatism, apartheid, segregationism.

separadiste *adj.* separatist, segregationist.

separador *n.* separator.

sepe *n.* hedge, hedgerow.

sepi *vt.* hedge.

sepia *adj.* & *n.* sepia (*colour, pigment*).

sepida *n.* cuttlefish (*Sepiida*).

sepiolita *n.* sepiolite, meerschaum (*substance*).

sepse *n.* sepsis, septicaemia (US septicemia). • *n.suff.* -sepsis (*infection*).

sepsi *vi.* become septic, fester.

sepsica *adj.* septic. • *adj.suff.* -septic.

sera *n.* evening, eve. **a esta sera** this evening, tonight. **a sera** in the evening. **a sera doman** tomorrow evening. **a sera ier** yesterday evening. **a sera oji** this evening, tonight. **la sera ante** the evening before, the eve of. **sera de Res** Epiphany Eve, Twelfth Night.

serafin *n.* seraph (*angel*). **serafines** seraphim.

Seram *n.* Seram (*island*). **Mar Seram** Sea of Seram.

seramica *adj.* ceramic. • *n.* piece of pottery. **arte de seramica** ceramic art, pottery.

seratonina *n.* seratonin.

serbatana *n.* blowgun, blowpipe.

Serbia *n.* Serbia.

serbsce *adj.* Serbian. • *n.* Serbian, Serb.

serca *n.* fence. **serca de palos** palisade. **sercas** fences, fencing.

serci *vt.* fence.

sereal *adj.* & *n.* cereal.

serebral *adj.* cerebral.

serebreta *n.* cerebellum.

serebretal *adj.* cerebellar.

serebri *vt.* rack one's brain, think hard about, puzzle over.

serebro *n.* brain, cerebrum. **serebro fronte** forebrain. **serebro retro** hindbrain.

serebrospinal *adj.* cerebrospinal.

serenada *vt.* & *n.* serenade.

serfia *n.* serfdom.

serfo *n.* serf (*feudal*).

seria *adj.* serious, earnest, solemn, strict, responsible, stringent, weighty. • *n.* seriousness, solemnity, gravity. **sin seria** frivolous.

serial *adj.* serial. • *adv.* in series.

serie *n.* series, spate, succession. **en serie** in series, in sequence, running, consecutive, in a row. **serie de colonas** colonnade. **serie de imajes** series of images, slide show.

serif *n.* serif. **con serif** serif, serifed. **sin serif** sans serif.

serigrafia *n.* serigraphy (*art*).

serigram *n.* serigraph.

serin *n.* serin (*bird: Serinus*).

serio *n.* cerium (*element*).

serisa *n.* cherry (*fruit*).

seriso *n.* cherry (*tree: Cerasus*).

sermon *n.* sermon, homily.

sermonor *n.* preacher.

sero *n.* whey (*milk*); serum (*blood*). **sero de bur** buttermilk.

serolojia *n.* serology.

serolojiste *n.* serologist.

serosa *adj.* serous.

serotonin *n.* serotonin.

serpe *vi.* & *vt.* meander, snake, wind; wriggle, wiggle, writhe, slither. **serpe a via de** wriggle out of, weasel out of.

serpente *adj.* wriggling, wriggly. • *n.* snake, serpent (*Serpentes, Ophidia*). **Serpente** *n.* Serpens (*constellation*). **serpente de mar** sea serpent, sea dragon.

serpentin *adj.* serpentine, meandering, convoluted, sinuous.

serpentor *n.* snake handler, snake charmer; snake eagle (*Circaetinae*). **Serpentor** *n.* Ophiuchus (*constellation*).

serseta *n.* teal (*bird: Anas crecca*).

sersis *n.* redbud, Judas tree (*Cercis*).

serta *adj.* certain, sure, secure, confident, assertive. • *adv.* certainly, surely, definitely, assuredly.

sertable *adj.* checkable, verifiable.

serti *vi.* & *vt.* confirm, check, verify, assure, ensure, make sure, ascertain. • *n.* confirmation, check, assurance. **serti de sona** sound check (*music*).

sertia *n.* certainty; assuredness, confidence.

sertida *adj.* checked, verified.

serumen *n.* earwax, cerumen.

servador *n.* server (*computer, utensil*). **servador ueb** web server.

serval *n.* serval (*wild cat: Leptailurus serval*).

serveta *n.* fawn, baby deer.
servi *vt.* serve (*master, customer, food, drink*); e.g. *servi algun con bir; servi bir a algun.* • *n.* serving, service. **culier de servi** serving spoon. **plato de servi** serving dish, serving plate. **servi publica** service, (*public*) utility. **servi ueb** web service.
servin *adj.* deerlike.
servo[1] *n.* deer (*Cervidae*). **servo fema** doe, hind, female deer. **servo mas** buck, hart, stag, male deer.
servo-[2] *pref.* servo-.
servomacina *n.* servomechanism.
servomotor *n.* servomotor.
servor *n.* server, waiter, waitress, servant. **servor de casa** servant, domestic worker, maid, housemaid, houseboy. **servor de restorante** waiter, waitress. **servor de vesti** valet. **servor xef** headwaiter, maître d'.
servorin *adj.* servantlike, servile.
ses *det.* six. • *adj.* sixth (*ordinal*).
sesa *vi.* & *vt.* cease, stop (*activity, oneself*), quit. • *n.* cessation. **sin sesa** unceasing, incessant, continual, non-stop.
sesal *adj.* sexual, sensual, erotic, venereal.
sesali *vi.* & *vt.* sexualize. • *n.* sexualization.
sesalia *n.* sexuality, sensuality.
sesamo *n.* sesame (*plant, seeds: Sesamum*).
sesar *n.* Caesar (*emperor*).
sesarea *n.* Caesarian (US Cesarian) section.
sesaspara *n.* ceasefire, truce, armistice.
sesdes *det.* sixty. • *adj.* sixtieth (*ordinal*).
sesdesi *n.* sixtieth (*fraction*). • *vi.* & *vt.* split into sixty. • *n.* sixtieth (*fraction*).
sesi *vi.* & *vt.* split into six. • *n.* sixth (*fraction*).
sesia *n.* sexuality (*orientation*).
sesio *n.* caesium (US cesium).
sesion *n.* section, segment; session.
sesional *adj.* sectional.
sesioni *vi.* & *vt.* section, segment, partition, dissect, articulate. • *n.* dissection.
sesionida *adj.* sectioned, segmented, partitioned, dissected, articulated, jointed.
sesisme *n.* sexism.
sesiste *n.* sexist.
sesjemelo *adj.* & *n.* sextuplet.
seso *n.* sex, gender; sexual intercourse, lovemaking. **fa de seso** sex, lovemaking. **fa la seso** have sex, make love. **seso anal** anal sex. **seso bocal** oral sex.
sesosa *adj.* sexy, foxy. • *n.* sexpot, sex bomb.
sespe *n.* turf, sod (*grassy ground*).
sespeta *n.* divot.
sestante *n.* sextant. **Sestante** *n.* Sextans (*constellation*).
sesto *n.* basket. **sesto de dejeta** wastebasket. **sesto de leva** banneton, brotform (*basket for shaping bread*). **sesto de pan** breadbasket. **sesto de pexa** fish basket, creel.
sestodo *n.* cestode, tapeworm (*Cestode*).
sesuple *adj.* sextuple. • *n.* sextet.
set *n.* set (*tennis, etc.*).
seta *n.* sect.
setal *adj.* sectarian.
setaseo *adj.* & *n.* cetacean.
sete *det.* seven. • *adj.* seventh (*ordinal*).
setedes *det.* seventy. • *adj.* seventieth (*ordinal*).
setedesi *n.* seventieth (*fraction*).
setejemelo *n.* & *n.* septuplet.
setembre *n.* September.
seti *vi.* & *vt.* split into seven. • *n.* seventh (*fraction*).
setica *adj.* sceptical (US skeptical). • *n.* sceptic (US skeptic).
seticisme *n.* scepticism (US skepticism).
setisme *n.* sectarianism.
Seto, Mar *n.* Seto Inland Sea.
setor *n.* sector (*geometry*).
setorino *n.* basking shark (*Cetorhinus maximus*).
setro *n.* sceptre (US scepter).
sever *adj.* severe, stern, strict, harsh, acerbic, austere, ascetic, rigorous, draconian, mordant, trenchant, stark, stringent. **sever e subita** fulminating.
severi *vi.* & *vt.* harshen.
severia *n.* severity, strictness, harshness, austerity, rigour (US rigor).
Sexeles *n.pl.* Seychelles. **sexeles** *adj.* & *n.* Seychellois.
sfenoide *n.* sphenoid, sphenoid bone.
sfera *adj.* spherical. • *n.* sphere, orb. **sfera de sielo** celestial sphere.
sferin *adj.* spheroid, spherelike, roundish.
sfigmometre *n.* sphygmomanometer, blood-pressure gauge.
sfinje *n.* sphinx.
sfinter *n.* sphincter (*anatomy*).
si[1] *subord.* if, as long as, provided that.—When *if* means *whether*, the translation is *esce*: *me no sabe esce me pote.* **estra si** except if, unless. **si … no** if … not, unless; e.g. *on no pote aida si on no partisipa.* **si no** if not, otherwise, else. **si sola** if only. **si tal** if so.
si[2] *interj.* yes, indeed, yeah, yay, yea; (*question tag*) is it?, do you?, have they? (*etc., typically implying some uncertainty*). See *no*.
si[3] *n.* si, ti (*musical note*).
sian *adj.* & *n.* cyan, aqua.
siani *vi.* & *vi.* turn cyan.
sianido *n.* cyanide.
sianogram *n.* blueprint.
sianose *n.* cyanosis (*medical*).
siatica *adj.* sciatic (*anatomy*).
siber- *pref.* cyber-.
sibercaferia *n.* cybercafe.

sibercrimin *n.* cybercrime.
sibercriminal *n.* cybercriminal.
sibernetica *n.* cybernetics.
sibernetical *adj.* cybernetic.
siberspasio *n.* cyberspace.
sibila *vt.* & *n.* whistle.
sibileta *n.* whistle, penny whistle.
sibilor *n.* whistler (*bird*: *Pachycephalinae*).
Sibir *n.* Siberia. **Mar Sibir Este** East Siberian Sea.
sibirsce *adj.* & *n.* Siberian.
sibola *n.* scallion (*onion*).
siboleta *n.* chive, chives (*Allium schoenoprasum*).
siborge *n.* cyborg.
siborgio *n.* seaborgium (*element*).
Sibuyan, Mar *n.* Sibuyan Sea.
sic *adj.* & *n.* Sikh.
sicada *n.* cycad (*plant*: *Cycadales*).
sicadela *n.* leafhopper (*insect*: *Cicadella*).
sicala *n.* cicada (*insect*: *Cicadomorpha*).
sicatris *n.* scar, cicatrix.
sicatrisi *vi.* & *vt.* scar, scarify, cicatrize.
sicisme *n.* Sikhism (*religion*).
siclamen *n.* cyclamen (*plant*: *Cyclamen*).
sicle *adj.* cyclic, cyclical, looping. • *n.* cycle, loop; bike. **sicle vil** vicious circle. **sicle virtuosa** virtuous circle.
sicli *vi.* & *vt.* cycle, loop.
siclido *n.* cichlid (*fish*: *Cichlidae*).
siclin *adj.* cyclic.
siclioforo *n.* cycliophor (*organism*: *Cycliophora*).
siclisme *n.* cycling, bicycling (*sport*, *pastime*).
sicliste *n.* cyclist.
siclon *n.* cyclone, typhoon, hurricane.
siclope *n.* cyclops (*mythology*, *crustacean*: *Cyclops*).
siclotron *n.* cyclotron (*particle accelerator*).
siconia *n.* stork (*Ciconiidae*).
side[1] *adj.* thirsty. **side per sangue** bloodthirsty.
-side[2] *n.suff.* -cide (*killing*).
sidi *vi.* thirst, become thirsty. • *vt.* make thirsty.
sidia *n.* thirst.
sido *abbr.* (*sindrom de imunodebilia otenida*) AIDS.
sidra *n.* cider (*alcoholic or not*).
sieca *adj.* blind. **partal sieca** partially blind, purblind. **sieca a blu** tritanopic. **sieca a color** colour-blind (US color-blind), achromatic, monochromatic. **sieca a leteras major** case-blind, case-insensitive. **sieca a roja** protanopic. **sieca a verde** deuteranopic.
sieci *vi.* go blind. • *vt.* blind, dazzle.
siecia *n.* blindness.
sielal *adj.* celestial, heavenly (*of the sky*).
sielin *adj.* heavenly (*like heaven*).
sielo *n.* sky, firmament; heaven. **su sielo** *adj.* open-air, outdoor. • *adv.* outside, outdoors, in the open air, al fresco.
siena *adj.* & *n.* sienna (*colour*). **siena ardeda** burnt sienna. **siena cru** raw sienna.
siensa *n.* science. **siensa de atmosfera** atmospheric science. **siensas umana** human sciences, humanities.
siensal *adj.* scientific.
siensiste *n.* scientist, boffin.
sientolojia *n.* scientology (*religion*).
sientolojiste *n.* scientologist.
siera *n.* saw (*tool*). **siera alternante** jigsaw (*power*), scroll saw, sabresaw, reciprocating saw. **siera arcin** bowsaw. **siera cuadro** whipsaw, pit saw, two-man saw. **siera de banda** band saw. **siera de detalia** jigsaw (*hand*). **siera de junta** mitre (US miter) saw. **siera de mano** handsaw. **siera de table** table saw. **Siera Leon** Sierra Leone. **siera per metal** hacksaw. **siera radial** radial saw. **siera sirculo** circular saw, power saw.
sieraleonian *adj.* & *n.* Sierra Leonean.
siereria *n.* sawmill.
sieri *vt.* saw. • *n.* sawing.
sieribuco *n.* hole saw.
siericurva *n.* coping saw, fretsaw.
sierin *adj.* jagged, serrated, toothlike, sawtooth.
sierini *vi.* & *vt.* serrate.
sieror *n.* sawyer.
sifilis *n.* syphilis (*medical*).
sifilisica *adj.* syphilitic.
sifon *n.* siphon.
sifoni *vt.* siphon.
sifra *n.* code, cipher.
sifri *vt.* encode, encipher, encrypt. • *n.* encryption, encoding.
sigar *n.* cigar.
sigareta *n.* cigarette, fag. **sigareta de canaba** cannabis cigarette, reefer.
sigma *n.* sigma (*Greek letter* Σ, σ, ς).
sigmoide *adj.* sigmoid. • *n.* sigmoid colon (*anatomy*).
sil *n.* lash, eyelash.
silaba *n.* syllable.
silabal *adj.* syllabic.
silabario *n.* syllabary.
silentador *n.* silencer, muffler.
silente *adj.* silent, quiet, mute.
silenti *vi.* fall silent, be quiet, say nothing, shut up. • *vt.* hush.
silentia *n.* silence.
sili *vt.* silo, store in a silo.
silica *n.* silica, silicon dioxide.
silicato *n.* silicate.
silico *n.* silicon (*element*).

silicon *n.* silicone (*substance*).
silicosa *adj.* siliceous.
silida *n.* silage.
silindre *adj.* cylindrical. ● *n.* cylinder; canister.
silio *n.* cilium (pl. cilia) (*biology*).
silo *n.* silo. **silo de misil** missile silo.
silueta *vt.* & *n.* silhouette.
silurian *adj.* & *n.* Silurian (*geology*).
sim- *pref.* sym- (*together*).
simbal *n.* cymbal (*musical instrument*).
simbiose *n.* symbiosis.
simbiosica *adj.* symbiotic. ● *n.* symbiont.
simbol *n.* symbol, sign, token. **simboles** symbols, notation.
simboli *vt.* symbolize. ● *n.* symbolization.
simbolin *adj.* symbolic.
simbolisme *n.* symbolism, imagery.
simbolojia *n.* symbology.
simense *n.* siemens (*unit of conductance*).
simetre *adj.* symmetrical.
simetria *n.* symmetry.
simfito *n.* sawfly (*Symphyta*).
simfonia *n.* symphony.
simfonial *adj.* symphonic.
simfonin *adj.* symphonic.
simia *n.* monkey, small primate (*Simiiformes*, but not *Hominoidea*). **simia afrasian** Old World monkey (*Cercopithecoidea*). **simia american** New World monkey (*Platyrrhini*).
simial *adj.* simian.
simil *adj.* similar, alike, kindred, akin. ● *adv.* similarly, in a similar way. **o simil** or so, or thereabouts, or something like that.
similador *n.* simulator.
simili *vi.* & *vt.* simulate. ● *n.* simulation, simulacrum, likeness.
similia *n.* similarity, similitude.
simitar *n.* scimitar (*sword*).
simonia *n.* simony (*profiting from sacred things*).
simpatia *n.* fellow-feeling, mutual liking, affinity, rapport; being on the same wavelength.
simpatica *adj.* sympathetic (*technical senses*).
simpatiosa *adj.* sympathetic (*feeling rapport, not pity*).
simple *adj.* simple, rudimentary, mere; uncomplicated, plain, straightforward, simplex, simplistic. ● *adv.* simply, merely.
simpli *vi.* & *vt.* simplify; streamline. ● *n.* simplification.
simplia *n.* simplicity.
simultan *adj.* simultaneous, concurrent. ● *adv.* simultaneously, in unison.
simultania *n.* simultaneity, synchronicity, unison.
sin[1] *prep.* without; lacking, devoid of; e.g. *cafe sin lete*; *tu viaja sin bileta*; *leje sin comprende la sinifia*. **sin ce** without; e.g. *la gato entra a la sala sin ce algun vide lo.*
sin-[2] *pref.* syn- (*together*).
Sina *n.* Sinai, Sinai Peninsula.
sinabar *n.* cinnabar (*mineral*).
sinagoga *n.* synagogue.
sinala *adj.* & *n.* Sinhala, Sinhalese (*person, language*).
sinapsal *adj.* synaptic.
sinapse *n.* synapse (*biology*).
sinci *vi.* & *vt.* split into five. ● *n.* fifth (*fraction*).
sincim *n.* twenty-pence piece, twenty-cent piece (*coin*).
sinclo *n.* dipper (*bird*: *Cinclus*).
sinclosoma *n.* whipbird (*Cinclosomatidae*).
sinco *det.* five. ● *adj.* fifth (*ordinal*).
sincodes *det.* fifty. ● *adj.* fiftieth (*ordinal*).
sincodesi *n.* fiftieth (*fraction*).
sincojemelo *adj.* & *n.* quintuplet.
sincopa *vt.* syncopate. ● *n.* syncopation (*music*).
sincrona *adj.* synchronous, synchronic, in sync. ● *n.* synchronism.
sincroni *vi.* synchronize, sync; entrain (*biology*). ● *vt.* synchronize, sync, entrain. ● *n.* synchronization, sync.
sincuple *adj.* quintuple. ● *n.* quintet.
sindi *adj.* & *n.* Sindhi (*person, language*).
sindicati *vi.* & *vt.* syndicate, unionize. ● *n.* syndication.
sindicatisme *n.* unionism, syndicalism.
sindicatiste *n.* unionist, syndicalist.
sindicato *n.* syndicate, labour (US labor) union, trade union, guild.
sindrom *n.* syndrome, disorder. **sindrom de angusa pos trauma** post-traumatic stress disorder. **sindrom de Down** Down syndrome, Down's syndrome. **sindrom de imunodebilia otenida** acquired immune deficiency syndrome, AIDS. **sindrom de osese e compulsa** obsessive-compulsive disorder.
sinema *n.* cinema, movie theatre (US theater). **fan de sinema** moviegoer, film fan, cinema fan. **sinema de casa** home theatre (US theater), home cinema.
sinemafilia *n.* cinemaphilia, love of movies.
sinemafilica *n.* moviegoer, film fan, cinema fan, lover of movies.
sinematografia *n.* cinematography, filmmaking, moviemaking.
sinematografial *adj.* cinematographic.
sinematografiste *n.* cinematographer, filmmaker, moviemaker.
sinemiste *n.* cinematographer, filmmaker, moviemaker.
sinerjia *n.* synergy.
sinerjial *adj.* synergetic, synergistic.
sinestesia *n.* synaesthesia (US synesthesia).

Singapor *n.* Singapore. **singapor** *adj.* & *n.* Singaporean.
singular *adj.* singular. • *n.* singular; single (*music*).
singularia *n.* singularity.
sinia *vt.* signal, signify, denote (*be a sign of*); sign (*use sign language*). • *n.* sign, emblem; character (*typography*); signal. **sinia de "a"** at sign. **sinia de "e"** ampersand. **sinia de ajunta** plus sign. **sinia de daga** dagger, obelus. **sinia de demanda** question mark. **sinia de divide** division sign. **sinia de dolar** dollar sign. **sinia de egalia** equals sign. **sinia de elidi** apostrophe. **sinia de esclama** exclamation mark, exclamation point. **sinia de inferioria** less-than sign. **sinia de inferioria o egalia** less-than-or-equal sign. **sinia de junta** hyphen, dash. **sinia de multipli** multiplication sign. **sinia de numero** number sign. **sinia de omete** caret, omission mark. **sinia de paund** pound sign (*currency*). **sinia de puntua** punctuation mark. **sinia de radis** root sign. **sinia de repete** ditto, ditto mark. **sinia de serti** checkmark, tick. **sinia de sita** quotation mark. **sinia de stela** asterisk. **sinia de superioria** greater-than sign. **sinia de superioria o egalia** greater-than-or-equal sign. **sinia de sutrae** minus sign. **sinia de tabli** tab character. **sinia de tempo** time signature (*music*). **sinia negativa** negative sign, minus sign. **sinia positiva** positive sign, plus sign. **sinia secreta** secret sign, password. **sinia V** V-sign (*victory, insult*). **sinias de tonalia** key signature (*music*). See *bretsel, caracol, ifen.*
sinial *n.* signal (*electric, radio, etc.*); cue. **sinial luminante** flare.
siniali *vt.* signal (*transmit a signal*); cue.
siniante *adj.* denoting, emblematic.
sinica *adj.* cynical. • *n.* cynic.
sinicisme *n.* cynicism.
sinie *n.* swan (*Cygnus*). **Sinie** *n.* Cygnus.
sinieta[1] *n.* cygnet.
sinieta[2] *n.* accent, diacritic, diacritical mark. **sinieta agu** acute accent. **sinieta corta** breve. **sinieta longa** macron. **sinieta nonagu** grave accent.
sinifia *vt.* mean, signify. • *n.* meaning, sense, purport. **sin sinifia** meaningless, senseless.
sinifiosa *adj.* meaningful, significant, momentous.
sinistra *adj.* left (*not right*); port. • *n.* left. **a sinistra** on the left. **a sinistra de** on the left of.
sinistrisme *n.* leftism.
sinistriste *adj.* left-wing, leftist. • *n.* left-winger, leftist.
sinodo *n.* synod (*Christianity*).
sinonim *adj.* synonymous. • *n.* synonym.
sinonimia *n.* synonymy.
sinovia *n.* synovial fluid (*biology*).
sinovial *adj.* synovial. • *n.* synovium, synovial membrane (*biology*).
sinsera *adj.* sincere, genuine, true, committed, whole-hearted, without hypocrisy, without pretence (US pretense).
sinseria *n.* sincerity, commitment.
sinta *n.* ribbon, tape. **sinta aderente** adhesive tape, sticky tape, Sellotape, Scotch tape. **sinta de libro** bookmark.
sintatica *n.* syntax.
sintatical *adj.* syntactic, syntactical.
sintesador *n.* synthesizer, synth. **sintesador de vose** vocoder.
sintesal *adj.* synthetic.
sintese *vt.* synthesize. • *n.* synthesis.
sinteseda *adj.* synthetic, synthesized.
sintil *n.* spark, scintilla.
sintili *vi.* scintillate, spark, sparkle, twinkle, glimmer, shimmer, glisten, glint, glitter, gleam. • *n.* sparkle, twinkle, scintillation, gleam.
sintilinte *adj.* sparkling, sparkly, twinkling, glistening, glittery.
sintom *n.* symptom.
sintomal *adj.* symptomatic.
sintomolojia *n.* symptomatology.
sintur *n.* belt, cincture, sash, strap. **sintur de muni** ammunition belt, ammo belt. **sintur de securia** safety belt. **sintur verde** greenbelt.
sintureta *n.* watchband, watchstrap; armband.
sinturi *vt.* belt, strap.
sinturin *adj.* beltlike, straplike.
sinus *n.* sinus (*anatomy*); sine (*mathematics*).
sinusite *n.* sinusitis (*medical*).
Sion *n.* Zion. **Monte Sion** Mount Zion.
sionisme *n.* Zionism.
sioniste *adj.* & *n.* Zionist.
sipero *n.* sedge, bulrush (*plant: Cyperaceae*).
sipres *n.* cypress (*tree: Cupressaceae*).
sipunculo *n.* sipunculid (*worm: Sipuncula*).
Sir *n.* Sir (*knight's title*).
sira *n.* wax. **sira de abea** beeswax. **sira per brilia** polish.
sirca *prep.* • around, round, surrounding, circling; e.g. *nos ia senta sirca la foco*; *edera crese sirca la tronco*; *me viaja sirca la mundo.* • about, approximately, circa, some; e.g. *a sirca sento anios ante aora*; *la conserta ia comensa sirca la ora dudes.* **a sirca** *prep.* (*moving*) to around. • *adv.* (*positioned or moving*) around; dotted about, here and there.
sircadial *adj.* circadian (*biology*).
sirco[1] *n.* circus.

sirco-[2] *pref.* circum- (*around*).
sircoflexe *n.* circumflex (*diacritic*).
sirconaviga *vt.* circumnavigate. • *n.* circumnavigation.
sircopolal *adj.* circumpolar.
sircoscrive *vt.* circumscribe.
sircoside *vt.* circumcise. • *n.* circumcision.
sircoveni *vt.* bypass, circumvent, work around. • *n.* circumvention.
sircuito *n.* circuit (*electric path*). **con sircuito permanente** hardwired. **sircuito corta** short circuit. **sircuito integrada** integrated circuit. **sircuito primida** printed circuit board. **sircuitos** circuit, circuitry (*components forming an electric path*).
sirculi *vi.* circle, wheel; circulate; mill around. • *vt.* circulate (*air, information*). • *n.* circulation.
sirculo *adj.* circular. • *n.* circle (*including of friends*); circuit (*not electric*). **sirculo de trafica** roundabout, traffic circle.
sirculor *n.* harrier (*bird: Circinae, Polyboroidinae*).
sirena *n.* siren.
sirfido *n.* hoverfly (*Syrphidae*).
sirin *adj.* waxy.
siringa *n.* syringe.
siringi *vt.* syringe.
sirinje *n.* syrinx (*anatomy*).
siripede *n.* barnacle (*crustacean: Cirripedia*).
siro *adj.* & *n.* cirrus (*cloud*).
sirose *n.* cirrhosis (*medical*).
sirsacar *n.* seersucker (*fabric*).
Sirte *n.* Sirte, Surt, Syrte. **Golfo Sirte** Gulf of Sirte, Gulf of Sidra.
sirurjia *n.* surgery. **sirurjia de cor abrida** open-heart surgery. **sirurjia plastica** plastic surgery.
sirurjial *adj.* surgical.
sirurjiste *n.* surgeon. **sirurjiste plastica** plastic surgeon.
sis- *pref.* cis- (*on this side*).
sisa *vt.* & *n.* hiss; whizz, zip, zap.
sisal *n.* sisal (*plant: Agave sisalana*).
sisante *adj.* hissing, sibilant. • *n.* sibilant (*consonant*).
sisel *n.* chisel. **Sisel** *n.* Caelum (*constellation*).
siseli *vt.* chisel, carve. • *n.* carving.
siselor *n.* woodcarver.
Sisilia *n.* Sicily. **Streta Sisilia** Strait of Sicily.
sisilian *adj.* & *n.* Sicilian.
sisjenero *adj.* cisgender.
sismica *adj.* seismic.
sismograf *n.* seismograph.
sismografia *n.* seismography.
sismogram *n.* seismogram.
sismolojia *n.* seismology.
sismolojiste *n.* seismologist.
sisor *n.* scissor, scissors.
sisori *vt.* cut, snip, trim.
sisoron *n.* shears.
sistal *adj.* cystic.
siste *n.* cyst (*biology, medical*).
sistem *n.* system. **sistem de arcivi** filing system (*physical*). **sistem de dijesta** digestive system. **sistem de fix** file system, filing system (*software*). **sistem de maneja contenidas** content management system. **sistem de nervos** nervous system. **sistem de opera** operating system (*software*). **sistem de reprodui** reproductive system. **sistem de scrive** writing system, script. **sistem de sirculi** circulatory system. **sistem de valua local** positional notation, place-value notation (*numerals*). **sistem dinamical** dynamical system. **sistem legal** legal system, jurisprudence. **sistem solal** solar system. **sistem vocal** vowel system, vocalism.
sistemal *adj.* systemic.
sistemosa *adj.* systematic, regular.
sisti *vt.* encyst.
sisticola *n.* cisticola (*bird: Cisticola*).
sistite *n.* cystitis (*medical*).
sisto *n.* cistus, rockrose (*plant: Cistus*).
sistolal *adj.* systolic.
sistole *n.* systole (*biology*).
sistre *n.* cittern (*musical instrument*).
sita[1] *vt.* quote, cite, adduce. • *n.* quotation, citation. **sita jusosa** sound bite.
sita[2] *n.* nuthatch (*bird: Sitta*).
sitadan *n.* citizen, national. **sitadan a stranjer** expatriate, expat. **sitadan comun** ordinary citizen, commoner.
sitadani *vi.* naturalize, become a citizen. • *vt.* naturalize, admit to citizenship. • *n.* naturalization.
sitadania *n.* citizenship.
sitar *n.* sitar (*musical instrument*).
site[1] *n.* city; e.g. *la site Moscva.* **site constituida** chartered city. **site-stato** *n.* city-state. See *urbe.*
-site[2] *n.suff.* -cyte (*cell*).
sitela *n.* sittella (*bird: Daphoenositta*).
siteta *n.* sound bite.
sito- *pref.* cyto- (*cell*).
sitolojia *n.* cytology.
sitolojial *adj.* cytological.
sitolojiste *n.* cytologist.
sitoplasma *n.* cytoplasm (*biology*).
sitosceleto *n.* cytoskeleton (*biology*).
sitra *n.* zither (*musical instrument*).
sitrica *adj.* citric, citrous.
sitron *n.* citron (*tree, fruit: Citrus medica*).
sitronela *n.* citronella (*plant, oil*).

situa *vt.* situate, site, locate. • *n.* situation, site, context, circumstance. **mal situa** bad situation, plight.
situada *adj.* situated, located. **bon situada** convenient, opportune. **es situada** be situated. **mal situada** inconvenient, inopportune.
siverte *n.* sievert (*unit of radiation*).
siveta *n.* civet (*animal*: *Viverridae*).
sivil *adj.* civil, civilized; civilian. • *n.* civilian.
sivili *vi.* & *vt.* civilize. • *n.* civilization (*action*).
sivilia *n.* civilization (*society*, *concept*). **Sivilia de la Vale Indo** Indus Valley Civilization. **Sivilia Minoan** Minoan Civilization.
sivilida *adj.* civilized.
sizijia *n.* syzygy (*astronomy*).
sizijio *n.* clove (*tree*, *spice*: *Syzygium aromaticum*).
Skakerrak *n.* Skakerrak (*strait*).
slalom *n.* slalom (*sport*).
slavica *adj.* Slavic. • *n.* Slav, Slavic.
slip *n.* briefs (*garment*). **slip de fem** knickers, panties. **slip de nada** speedos, swim briefs. **slip de om** Y-fronts, jockey shorts.
slogan *n.* slogan, motto, legend.
sloganor *n.* sloganeer.
Slovenia *n.* Slovenia.
slovenian *adj.* & *n.* Slovenian.
slovensce *adj.* & *n.* Slovak, Slovakian.
Slovensco *n.* Slovakia.
slup *n.* sloop (*boat*).
smegma *n.* smegma (*biology*).
smilax *n.* smilax, sarsaparilla, greenbrier (*plant*: *Smilax*).
smilodon *n.* smilodon, sabretooth (US sabertooth) (*cat*, *tiger*: *Smilodon*).
smorgasbord *n.* smorgasbord (*food*).
snaps *n.* schnapps (*drink*).
soborna *vt.* bribe, suborn. • *n.* bribe, bribery, inducement, kickback, payoff.
sobornable *adj.* bribable, venal.
sobre *adj.* sober.
sobria *n.* sobriety.
sobrin *n.* niece or nephew.
sobrina *n.* niece.
sobrino *n.* nephew.
socratal *adj.* Socratic.
Socrate *n.* Socrates (*philosopher*).
soda *n.* soda, soda water, seltzer.
sodio *n.* sodium.
sodomia *vt.* sodomize, bugger. • *n.* sodomy, buggery.
sodomiste *n.* sodomite.
sofa *n.* sofa, couch, settee. **sofa-leto** *n.* sofa bed, daybed. **sofa sin dorso** divan.
-sofia *n.suff.* -sophy (*wisdom*).
sofisme *n.* sophism, sophistry, casuistry.
sofiste *n.* sophist.
sofistica *vt.* sophisticate. • *n.* sophistication, elegance.
sofisticada *adj.* sophisticated, elegant, chic, classy, debonair, highbrow, rakish, urbane. • *n.* sophisticate.
sofito *n.* ceiling; soffit.
sofla *vi.* blow, waft; chuff (*engine*). • *vt.* blow (*air*), huff. • *n.* blow, waft. **sofla de vitro** glassblowing.
soflada *adj.* blown. **soflada par venta** windblown.
soflador *n.* blower, bellows.
sofleta *vi.* puff, whiffle; chug (*engine*). • *n.* puff.
soflon *n.* gust.
soflor *n.* blower. **soflor de vitro** glassblower.
sofoca *vi.* suffocate, choke. • *vt.* suffocate, choke, smother, stifle. • *n.* suffocation. **sofoca de caldia** swelter.
soia *n.* soya, soybean (*plant*, *seed*: *Glycine max*). **salsa de soia** soy sauce, soya sauce. **seme de soia** soybean, soya bean.
sol[1] *n.* sun.
sol[2] *adj.* & *n.* soul (*music*).
sol[3] *n.* sol, so (*musical note*).
sola *adj.* (*prenominal*) only, sole, single. • *adv.* only, just, solely, exclusively. **sola si** provided that, on condition that.
solal *adj.* solar.
solano *n.* nightshade, horsenettle (*plant*: *Solanum*). **solano negra** black nightshade (*Solanum nigrum*).
solda *vt.* solder, weld.
soldador *n.* soldering iron.
soldato *n.* soldier. **soldato de pede** infantryman, infantry soldier. **soldato montante** cavalryman, trooper. **soldatos** soldiers, troops.
soldi *n.* Sunday. **soldi de pentecoste** Whit Sunday.
soldor *n.* solderer, welder.
soldura *n.* solder.
solea *n.* sole (*fish*: *Soleidae*, *Pleuronetidae*, *Bothidae*). **solea american** American sole (*Achiridae*).
solenoide *n.* solenoid.
soleria *n.* solarium.
solfejo *n.* solfeggio, solfège, sol-fa (*music*).
soli *vt.* sun. **soli se** sun oneself, sunbathe.
solida *adj.* & *n.* solid.
solidi *vi.* & *vt.* solidify; consolidate. • *n.* solidification; consolidation.
solidia *n.* solidity, integrity.
solipsisme *n.* solipsism.
solipsiste *adj.* solipsistic. • *n.* solipsist.
solisita *vt.* ask for, solicit, request, apply for. • *n.* request, requisition, solicitation; petition, application.
solisitor *n.* requester, canvasser.

soliste *n.* soloist. **soliste de gitar** lead guitarist.

solitar *adj.* solitary, alone, lone, lonely, lonesome, isolated, reclusive. • *adv.* in itself, in themselves, by itself, by themselves (*etc.*). • *n.* loner, isolate, recluse.

solitaria *n.* solitude, loneliness, isolation; solitary confinement.

solo[1] *n.* floor, ground. **solo caldinte** heated floor, underfloor heating. **solo de tera** soil, earth. **solo fertil** fertile soil; hotbed.

solo[2] *adj.* solo (*alone*). • *n.* solo (*music*).

Solomon *n.* Solomon. **Isolas Solomon** Solomon Islands. **Mar Solomon** Solomon Sea.

solomones *adj.* & *n.* Solomon Islander.

solosa[1] *adj.* sunny.

solosa[2] *adj.* earthy.

solstisio *n.* solstice. **solstisio de estate** summer solstice. **solstisio de inverno** winter solstice.

solvable *adj.* solvable, soluble, solvent.

solvablia *n.* solvency.

solve *vt.* solve, unravel. • *n.* solution. **solve bela** elegant solution.

solvor *n.* troubleshooter.

soma[1] *vi.* & *vt.* add up (*numbers*). • *n.* sum, total, addition, summation.

soma[2] *n.* soma (*drink*).

somali *adj.* & *n.* Somali, Somalian.

Somalia *n.* Somalia.

somatotropina *n.* somatotropin, human growth hormone.

sombre *adj.* sombre (US somber), bleak, gloomy, dismal, dull, drab, dreary, dingy, dour, grim, lugubrious, downbeat, downcast, saturnine, unsmiling, humourless (US humorless).

sombrero *n.* sombrero (*hat*).

sombria *n.* sombreness (US somberness), bleakness, gloom, gloominess, dreariness.

sona *vi.* sound, ring, chime. • *vt.* sound (*alarm, horn*), ring (*bell*). • *n.* sound. **sin sona** soundless, noiseless. **sona de paso** footstep. **sona de velia** reveille. **sona vocal** vowel sound, vocalism.

sonal *adj.* sound, sonic.

sonambula *vi.* sleepwalk. • *n.* sleepwalking, somnambulism, noctambulation.

sonambulor *n.* sleepwalker, somnambulist, noctambulist.

sonante *adj.* sounding, sonorant. • *n.* sonorant (*phonetics*). **bon sonante** good-sounding, euphonious, mellifluous. **mal sonante** bad-sounding, cacophonous.

sonar *n.* sonar.

sonata *n.* sonata (*music*).

sonda *vt.* & *n.* probe, survey, poll. **sonda a sorti** exit poll. **sonda de opina** opinion poll. **sonda spasial** space probe.

soneto *n.* sonnet (*poetry*).

sonia *vt.* & *n.* dream.

sonin *adj.* dreamlike, phantamagorical. **sonines** phantasmagorica.

sonior *n.* dreamer.

soniosa *adj.* dreamy.

sopa *n.* soup. **sopa clar** clear soup, consommé. **sopa de bivalvo** clam soup. **sopa de col** cabbage soup. **sopa de fava** bean soup. **sopa de filos de ovo** egg drop soup, egg flower soup. **sopa de gal** chicken soup. **sopa de gombo** gumbo. **sopa de lentil** lentil soup. **sopa de onion** onion soup. **sopa de patata** potato soup. **sopa de pavo** turkey soup. **sopa de pex** fish soup. **sopa de poro** leak soup. **sopa de talietas** noodle soup. **sopa de tomate** tomato soup. **sopa de vejetal** vegetable soup, minestrone. **sopa de xampinion** mushroom soup. **sopa ragin** potage.

soprano *adj.* & *n.* soprano.

sorbe *vt.* sip, sup. • *n.* sip. **sorbe ruidosa** *v.* & *n.* slurp.

sorbete *n.* sorbet, sherbet (*dessert*).

sorbo *n.* rowan (*tree: Sorbus*).

sorda *adj.* deaf.

sordador *n.* mute (*musical device*).

sordi *vi.* go deaf. • *vt.* deafen.

sordia *n.* deafness.

sore *n.* sister (*including nun*). **sore par sposi** sister-in-law.

soreria *n.* sisterhood, sorority (*organization*); convent, cloister, nunnery.

soreta *n.* younger sister.

sorgo *n.* sorghum (*plant: Sorghum*).

soria *n.* sisterhood, sisterliness.

sorin *adj.* sisterly.

soron *n.* older sister.

sorsor *n.* witch, wizard, warlock, sorcerer, sorceress. **sorsor fema** sorceress, witch. **sorsor mas** sorcerer, wizard, warlock.

sorsoria *n.* sorcery, witchcraft, wizardry, witchery.

sorti *vi.* go out, get out, exit, leave, evacuate; e.g. *el sorti de la casa.* • *vt.* evacuate (*people from a place*), cause to exit. • *n.* exit, way out, checkout, egress. **sorti de securia** emergency exit.

sosia *n.* society.

sosial *adj.* social, societal; sociable, outgoing, extroverted, gregarious.

sosiali *vi.* & *vt.* socialize.

sosialisme *n.* socialism.

sosialiste *n.* socialist.

sosio- *pref.* socio- (*society*).

sosiobiolojia *n.* sociobiology.

sosiolinguistica *n.* sociolinguistics.
sosiolojia *n.* sociology.
sosiolojial *adj.* sociological.
sosiolojiste *n.* sociologist.
sosiopatia *n.* sociopathy.
sosiopatica *adj.* sociopathic, antisocial.
sote *vt.* sauté (*cookery*). • *n.* sauté.
soto *adj.* Sotho. • *n.* Sotho, Basotho (*person*), Sesotho (*language*).
soviet *adj.* & *n.* soviet.
Soya, Streta *n.* Soya Strait.
spada *n.* sword; spade (*cards*). **spada curva** scimitar.
spadeta *n.* shortsword.
spadin *adj.* swordlike, sword-shaped.
spadon *n.* longsword, broadsword.
spador *n.* swordfighter, swordsman, swordswoman.
spageti *n.* spaghetti.
spala *n.* shoulder.
spaleta *n.* epaulette, epaulet (*shoulder piece*).
spam *n.* spam, junk email.
spami *vt.* spam.
spamor *n.* spammer.
spaniel *n.* spaniel (*dog*).
spara *vt.* shoot, fire (*weapon*). • *n.* shooting, gunfire. **spara antiavional** antiaircraft fire, flak. **spara crusada** crossfire. **spara par aliada** friendly fire.
spartan *adj.* spartan.
sparver *n.* sparrowhawk (*bird*: smaller members of *Accipitrinae*).
spasi *vt.* space, space out. • *n.* spacing.
spasial *adj.* spatial.
spasio *n.* space, room, void. **spasio de gamas** legroom. **spasio de testa** headroom. **spasio sufisinte** elbow room.
spasiosa *adj.* spacious, roomy, capacious, commodious.
spasiotempo *n.* spacetime.
spasma *vi.* & *n.* spasm, twitch. • *n.suff.* -spasm. **spasma de dole** stab of pain, twinge.
spasmica *adj.* spastic. • *adj.suff.* -spastic.
spasmin *adj.* twitchy, jerky.
spatula *n.* spatula; squeegee; putty knife. **spatula de cosini** spatula. **spatula de pex** slotted spatula, fish slice.
spelador *n.* spelling checker, spell checker, spell check.
spelal *adj.* orthographic.
spele *vt.* spell (*word*). • *n.* spelling, orthography.
spende *vt.* spend (*money*, *energy*, *resources*, *time*). • *n.* spending, expense, expenditure, outlay. **spende tro multe** overspend.
sperde *vi.* & *vt.* scatter, disperse, disband; spread, strew, litter; proliferate, perpetuate. • *n.* scattering, dispersal; proliferation. **sperde tra** suffuse. **sperde virusin** spread like a virus, go viral.
sperdeda *adj.* scattered, littered, strewn, diffuse; e.g. *rocas es sperdeda sur la campo*; *un campo con rocas sperdeda*.
sperdeteme *n.* scaremonger, doomsayer, alarmist.
sperdor *n.* spreader. **sperdor de dejetadas** litterbug, litterlout.
sperma *n.* sperm, spermatozoon (pl. spermatozoa).
spermaseti *n.* spermaceti (*substance*).
spermiduto *n.* vas deferens (*anatomy*).
spermiside *n.* spermicide.
speron *n.* spur, goad.
speroni *vt.* spur, goad, urge.
spesa *adj.* thick, stout; stocky, heavyset; bold (*typography*).
spesi *vt.* bolden, embolden (*typography*).
spesia *n.* thickness; boldface.
spesial *adj.* special, especial, exceptional, particular. • *adv.* especially, particularly. **estrema spesial** extremely special, extraordinary.
spesiali *vi.* & *vt.* specialize. • *n.* specialization, speciality, specialty, schtick.
spesialida *adj.* specialized. **tro spesialida** overspecialized.
spesialiste *n.* specialist, expert, consultant, wonk.
spesie *n.* kind, sort, type, species, variation, version, variety. **spesie de comersia** line of business, line of trade.
spesifa *vt.* specify. • *n.* specification.
spesifada *adj.* specified, specific, special, particular, certain. • *n.* feature.
spetaculin *adj.* spectacular, phenomenal.
spetaculo *n.* entertainment, spectacle, show, presentation, production, extravaganza, pageant. **mundo de spetaculo** show business, showbiz.
spetral *adj.* spectral.
spetro *n.* spectrum.
spetroscopi *n.* spectroscopy.
spetroscopial *adj.* spectroscopic.
spetroscopio *n.* spectroscope.
spia *vt.* spy, lurk. • *n.* spying, espionage. **spia par escutador** wiretap.
spicisi *n.* speakeasy (*bar*).
spiga *n.* spike (*flower cluster*); ear (*corn*).
spina *n.* spike, spine, barb, thorn, prickle, spadix; quill (*porcupine*); fishbone; cleat. **spina de jelo** icicle. **spina dorsal** spine, backbone.
spinablanca *n.* hawthorn (*Crataegus*).
spinacer *n.* spinnaker (*sail*).
spinal *adj.* spinal.
spinax *n.* spinach (*plant*, *leaves*: *Spinacia oleracea*).

spineta[1] *n.* American goldfinch, siskin (*Spinus*).
spineta[2] *n.* spicule (*biology*).
spini *vt.* pin.
spinin *adj.* spinelike.
spino *n.* pin; stickpin; prong. **spino de capeles** hairpin. **spino de xapo** hatpin. **spino puiable** thumbtack, drawing pin, pushpin. **spino secur** safety pin.
spinosa *adj.* spiky, spiny, barbed, thorny, prickly, full of spines. • *n.* stickleback (*Gasterosteidae*).
spior *n.* spy, spook.
spiral *adj.* spiral, involute. • *n.* spiral, coil, whorl.
spirali *vi.* & *vt.* spiral, coil, swirl.
spirea *n.* spiraea (US spirea) (*plant*: *Spiraea*).
spirital *adj.* spiritual.
spiritalia *n.* spirituality.
spiritisme *n.* spiritualism.
spiritiste *n.* medium, spiritualist, spiritist, necromancer, channeller (US channeler).
spirito *n.* spirit, soul, atman. **spirito de la eda** zeitgeist.
spiritosa *adj.* numinous, unworldly.
spirobal *n.* tetherball (*game*).
spiroceta *n.* spirochaete (US spirochete) (*bacterium*: *Spirochaetes*).
spise *n.* spice, seasoning, condiment.
spisi *vt.* spice, season.
spisida *adj.* seasoned.
spisosa *adj.* spicy, piquant.
splenectomia *n.* splenectomy (*surgery*).
spleno *n.* spleen (*anatomy*).
spondeal *adj.* spondaic.
spondeo *n.* spondee (*poetry*).
spondilite *n.* spondilitis (*medical*).
sponja *n.* sponge (*cleaning tool*, *organism*: *Porifera*).
sponji *vt.* sponge.
sponjin *adj.* spongy.
sponsor *n.* sponsor.
sponsori *vt.* sponsor.
sponsoria *n.* sponsorship, patronage.
spontan *adj.* spontaneous, candid.
spontania *n.* spontaneity.
spora *n.* spore.
sporan *n.* sporran (*pouch*).
sporocarpo *n.* sporocarp, fruiting body (*botany*).
sporofite *n.* sporophyte.
sporte *n.* sport.
sportor *n.* sportsperson, sportsman, sportswoman.
spos *n.* spouse, husband, wife; mate.
sposa *n.* wife. **de sposa nova** bridal. **sposa de gera** war bride. **sposa futur** bride-to-be. **sposa nova** bride. **sposa pasada** ex-wife. **sposa real** consort (*female*).
sposable *adj.* marriageable.
sposal *adj.* marital, nuptial, conjugal.
sposi *vi.* & *vt.* marry. • *n.* marriage (*action*), wedding. **ante sposi** premarital, prenuptial. **de sposi** bridal. **estra sposi** outside of marriage, illegitimate. **par sposi** in-law, by marriage.
sposia *n.* marriage (*state*), wedlock, matrimony.
sposida *adj.* married. **nova sposida** newlywed.
sposo *n.* husband. **sposo enganada** cuckold. **sposo futur** husband-to-be. **sposo nova** groom, bridegroom. **sposo pasada** ex-husband. **sposo real** consort (*male*).
springboc *n.* springbok (*antelope*: *Antidorcas marsupialis*).
sprinta *vi.* & *n.* sprint.
sprintor *n.* sprinter.
spuma *vi.* foam, froth, lather. • *n.* foam, froth, lather, suds. **spuma de bani** bath foam, bubblebath (*substance*). **spuma de mar** sea foam; meerschaum. **spuma de sapon** soapsuds. **spuma susia** scum.
spumosa *adj.* foamy, frothy, sudsy.
sputa *vt.* spit, expectorate. • *n.* spit, sputum.
sputafoco *n.* fire breather.
sputnic *n.* sputnik.
Sr *abbr.* (*Senior*) Mr.
Sra *abbr.* (*Seniora*) Mrs, Miss, Ms.
sranan *adj.* & *n.* Surinamese (*person*); Sranan Tongo, Taki Taki, Suriname Creole (*language*). See *Suriname*.
sri *n.* gentleman or lady; sir or ma'am (*gender-neutral form of address*). **Sri** *n.* Mr, Ms, Mrs, Miss, Mx. **sris** ladies and gentlemen.
Srilanca *n.* Sri Lanka, Ceylon. **srilanca** *adj.* & *n.* Sri Lankan.
ss *interj.* hiss, psst.
sta *vi.* stand (*be standing*). • *vt.* stand (*cause to stand*). **sta se** stand up. **sta sur manos** *v.* stand on one's hands, do a handstand. • *n.* handstand. **sta sur testa** headstand.
stable *adj.* stable, steady.
stabli *vi.* & *vt.* stabilize. • *n.* stabilization.
stablia *n.* stability.
stablinte *adj.* stabilizing, fixative.
stacato *adj.* staccato.
stadio *n.* stage (*for performance*). **a lado de stadio** ringside, beside the stage. **estra la stadio** offstage.
stadion *n.* stadium, arena. **stadion de bove** bullring.
stadior *n.* stagehand.
stafilococo *n.* staphylococcus (*bacterium*: *Staphylococcus*).
stajia *vi.* intern, apprentice. • *n.* internship, apprenticeship.
stajior *n.* intern, apprentice, trainee, cadet.

stala *n.* stall (*animal, market*), compartment. **stala de dux** shower stall, shower cubicle. **stalas** stable.
stalamita *n.* stalagmite.
stalatita *n.* stalactite.
stali *vt.* stable.
stalor *n.* groom, stable boy.
-stalsia *n.suff.* -stalsis (*contraction*).
stame *n.* stamen (*botany*).
stange *n.* pond.
stangeta *n.* puddle, pool. **stangeta de mar** tidepool, tidal pool, rock pool.
stangi *vi.* & *vt.* puddle, pool.
stania *vi.* stagnate. • *n.* stagnation. **stania con infla** stagflation (*economy*).
staniante *adj.* stagnant, stale, dank, musty, stuffy. • *n.* stagnant water, backwater.
stanio *n.* tin (*element*).
stante *adj.* standing, stationary, stative.
-stase *n.suff.* -stasis.
stasion *n.* station, stop, stopping place. **stasion de autovia** service area, service station, rest area. **stasion de labora** workstation. **stasion final** terminal, terminus. **stasion spasial** space station.
statal *adj.* static (*linguistics*).
state *n.* state (*of affairs*), condition; going; status. **state presente** present state, status quo.
statia *n.* statehood.
statica *n.* statics.
statical *adj.* static.
statina *n.* statin (*drug*).
statiste *n.* statesperson, statesman, stateswoman.
statistica *n.* statistic; statistics (*science*).
statistical *adj.* statistical.
statisticiste *n.* statistician.
stato[1] *n.* state (*political*), government. **stato de polisia** police state. **stato membro** member state. **stato savaje** rogue state. **stato sosial** welfare state. **stato vil** rogue state. **Statos Unida de America** United States. See *SUA, esuan, american.*
-stato[2] *n.suff.* -stat (*measuring tool*).
statoreatador *n.* ramjet (*engine*).
steatita *n.* steatite, soapstone.
steatopijia *n.* steatopygia.
steatopijica *adj.* steatopygous.
steca *n.* steak, beefsteak. **steca T** T-bone steak. **steca tatar** steak tartare.
stegosauro *n.* stegosaur, stegosaurus.
stela *n.* star (*sun, celebrity*); hotshot; asterisk. **stela bela** pin-up. **stela-de-mar** *n.* starfish, sea star (*Asteroidea*). **stela-de-mar plumosa** feather star (*Comatulida*). **stela de matina** morning star (*Venus*). **stela de neutrones** neutron star. **stela de pop** pop star. **stela de roc** rock star. **stela de sera** evening star (*Venus*). **stela joven** starlet. **stela volante** falling star, shooting star.
stelal *adj.* stellar.
steli *vt.* asterisk.
stelin *adj.* starlike, star-shaped.
stelosa *adj.* starry.
stenografia *n.* stenography, shorthand, steno.
stenografiste *n.* stenographer.
stenose *n.* stenosis (*medical*). • *n.suff.* -stenosis.
stensil *n.* stencil; template (*software*).
stensili *vt.* stencil.
stepe *n.* steppe, moor, moorland, heath, heathland. **stepe-foresta** *n.* aspen parkland.
steradian *n.* steradian (*unit of angle*).
sterco *n.* manure.
stercoraro *n.* skua (*bird*: *Stercorarius*).
stereo[1] *adj.* & *n.* stereo (*sound*).
stereo-[2] *pref.* stereo- (*solid*).
stereocimica *n.* stereochemistry.
stereoisomero *n.* stereoisomer.
stereoscopi *n.* stereoscopy.
stereoscopial *adj.* stereoscopic.
stereoscopio *n.* stereoscope.
stereotipal *adj.* stereotypical.
stereotipo *n.* stereotype, cliché.
steril *adj.* sterile, barren, infertile.
sterilador *n.* sterilizer.
sterili *vi.* & *vt.* sterilize. • *n.* sterilization.
sterilia *n.* sterility.
sterna *n.* tern (*bird*: *Sternidae*).
sterno[1] *n.* sternum, breastbone.
sterno[2] *n.* Sterno (*fuel*).
steroide *adj.* steroid, steroidal. • *n.* steroid.
sterol *n.* sterol (*chemistry*).
stetoscopi *vt.* auscultate. • *n.* auscultation, stethoscopy.
stetoscopio *n.* stethoscope.
stigma *n.* stigma.
stilal *adj.* stylistic.
stili *vt.* style, stylize. • *n.* styling, stylization.
stiliste *n.* stylist.
stilo[1] *n.* style. **stilo de capeles** hairdo, hairstyle. **stilo de leteri** lettering style.
stilo[2] *n.* stylus (*writing tool, record player*).
stilton *n.* stilton (*cheese*).
stimula *vt.* stimulate, energize; excite, thrill, pique; arouse, turn on. • *n.* stimulation, stimulus, motive, excitement, excitation, arousal. **stimula tro multe** overexcite.
stimulable *adj.* excitable.
stimulada *adj.* stimulated, excited. **tro stimulada** overexcited.
stimulante *adj.* exciting, thrilling, sensual, arousing, excitatory. • *n.* stimulant.
stiren *n.* styrene (*chemistry*).
Stix *n.* Styx (*mythology*).

stixin *adj.* Stygian.
stoco *n.* rapier (*sword*).
stofa *n.* fabric, material, cloth, textile. **stofa de emeri** emery cloth. **stofa densa** broadcloth. **stofa linosa** oilcloth. **stofa primida** print fabric. See *tela.*
stoferia *n.* cloth factory, cloth store.
stofor *n.* clothmaker, cloth seller.
stoica [sto'ika] *adj.* stoical, stoic. • *n.* stoic.
stoicisme *n.* stoicism.
stolen *n.* stollen (*bread*).
stoma *n.* opening, orifice; stoma (pl. stomata) (*botany, medical*).
stomaco *n.* stomach, tummy; tripe (*food*).
-stomia *n.suff.* -stomy (*surgical opening*).
stona *vt.* amaze, astonish, astound, stun, bedazzle. • *n.* amazement, astonishment. **stona temosa** awe.
stonada *adj.* amazed, astonished, stunned.
stonante *adj.* amazing, wonderful, wondrous, stunning, astonishing, astounding, awesome, stupendous, fantastic.
storno *n.* starling (*Sturnus*). **storno indian** myna, mynah.
stornui *vi.* & *n.* sneeze.
straba *adj.* strabismic, cross-eyed, boss-eyed, wall-eyed. **converjente straba** cross-eyed, esotropic. **diverjente straba** wall-eyed, exotropic.
strabia *n.* strabismus, squint (*strabismic*).
strada *n.* street (*city*), thoroughfare.
stradeta *n.* alley, alleyway, side street (*city*). **stradeta de entra** driveway, drive.
stramonio *n.* jimson weed, jimpson weed (*Datura stramonium*).
strana *adj.* strange, weird, unusual, odd, peculiar, curious, queer, eerie, freaky, uncanny, unworldly, bizarre, eccentric, dotty, kooky, quirky, screwy, wacky. • *n.* weirdo, oddball, dingbat, kook; oddity, peculiarity, eccentricity, kink, quirk, foible.
strangula *vt.* strangle, choke, throttle. • *n.* strangulation.
strangulor *n.* strangler.
strania *n.* strangeness, weirdness, oddness, oddity, peculiarity, eccentricity.
stranjer *adj.* foreign, alien. • *n.* foreigner, outsider, alien, stranger.
stranjeri *vi.* & *vt.* estrange, alienate. • *n.* estrangement, alienation.
stratejia *n.* strategy, stratagem. **stratejia nova** new strategy, initiative.
stratejial *adj.* strategic.
stratejiste *n.* strategist.
strati *vi.* stratify, layer; be coated. • *vt.* coat, layer. • *n.* layering, stratification. **strati interna** line (*something*).
strato *n.* layer, ply; coat (*paint*), coating; stratus (*cloud*); shell (*electron*). **con du stratos** two-layered, two-ply. **strato interna** lining. **stratos** strata. See *fore.*
stratocumulo *adj.* & *n.* stratocumulus (*cloud*).
stratosfera *n.* stratosphere.
stratosferal *adj.* stratospheric.
streptobasilo *n.* streptobacillus (*bacterium: Streptobacillus*).
streptococo *n.* streptococcus (*bacterium: Streptococcus*).
streptomisina *n.* streptomycin (*antibiotic*).
stresa *vt.* & *n.* stress.
stresante *adj.* stressful.
stresor *n.* stressor.
streta *adj.* narrow; tight, taut, snug. • *n.* strait.
streti *vi.* & *vt.* narrow, tighten, constrict. • *n.* narrowing, constriction, stricture.
stretia *n.* narrowness; tightness, tautness, snugness.
streusel *n.* streusel (*cookery*).
stribo *n.* stirrup; stapes (*bone*); abutment (*architecture*).
stricnina *n.* strychnine (*Strychnos nux-vomica*).
striptisa *vi.* & *n.* striptease, strip.
striptisor *n.* stripper, stripteaser.
stroboscopial *adj.* stroboscopic.
stroboscopio *n.* stroboscope, strobe.
strofe *n.* stanza, verse.
stroganov *n.* stroganoff (*food*).
strombo *n.* conch (*mollusc: Strombus*).
strontio *n.* strontium (*element*).
strudel *n.* strudel (*pastry*).
struma *n.* goitre (US goiter) (*medical*).
strumental *adj.* instrumental.
strumentiste *n.* instrumentalist.
strumento *n.* instrument (*musical, medical, scientific, etc.*). **sin strumento** unaccompanied, a cappella. **strumento de cordetas** string instrument. **strumento de percute** percussion instrument. **strumento de teclas** keyboard instrument. **strumento de venta** wind instrument. **strumento lenial de venta** woodwind instrument. **strumento metal de venta** brass instrument.
strutur *n.* structure, frame, framework; phrase (*music*). **strutur de datos** data structure. **strutur de trepa** climbing frame, jungle gym, monkey bars.
strutural *adj.* structural.
struturalisme *n.* structuralism.
struturaliste *n.* structuralist.
struturi *vt.* structure, frame.
struturida *adj.* structured.
stuco *n.* stucco (*plaster*).
studia *vt.* study; pore over. • *n.* study; survey. **studia intensa** study intensively, cram.

studiante *adj.* studying. • *n.* student. **studiante de anio du** second-year student, sophomore. **studiante de anio prima** first-year student, freshman, fresher. **studiante de anio ultima** sixth-former, upperclassman. **studiante nova** freshman, fresher, underclassman. **studiante pasada** ex-student, alumnus, alumna.

studio *n.* studio (*artist's*, *film*, *TV*, *radio*); study (*room*); workshop (*artist's*).

studiosa *adj.* studious.

stufa *n.* stove, cooker, hob. **stufa de alcol** alcohol stove, spirit lamp. **stufa de cerosen** kerosene stove. **stufa portable** portable stove.

stufi *vt.* cook (*on stove*).

stupa *n.* stupa (*Buddhist building*).

stupida *adj.* stupid, dumb, foolish, idiotic, dopey, inane, moronic, simple-minded. • *n.* fool, dummy, idiot, imbecile, moron, dunce, dullard, dimwit, dingbat, featherbrain, numbskull, numpty, ignoramus, bonehead, knucklehead, lamebrain, nitwit, pinhead.

stupidia *n.* stupidity, foolishness, idiocy.

stupor *n.* stupor, trance.

sturion *n.* sturgeon (*fish*: *Acipenseridae*).

sturnela *n.* meadowlark (*bird*: *Sturnella*).

su[1] *prep.* • below, beneath, under, underneath, lower than (*location*, *quantity*, *standard*); e.g. *ombra su la arbores*; *un table su la fenetra*; *un sueter su un jaca*; *labora su esta regulas*; *la temperatur es su zero*. • (*moving*) to below, under; e.g. *pone un cuxin su sua testa*. • *pref.* sub- (*lower in location or hierarchy*); e.g. *sutera*; *sudivide*. **a su** *prep.* (*moving*) to below, under; e.g. *la gato core a su la table*. • *adv.* below, underneath; down, downward, downwards; downstairs. **de su** *prep.* (*moving*) from under. • *adv.* from underneath; from downstairs; up, upward, upwards.

su[2] *adj.* & *n.* Sioux (*person*, *language*).

sua[1] *det.* his, her, its, their. **la sua** his, hers, its, theirs. **sua propre** his own, her own, its own, their own.

SUA[2] *abbr.* (*Statos Unida de America*) USA, US. • *adj.* USA, US, American. See *esuan*.

suacuan *adj.* underwater.

suahili [swa'hili] *adj.* & *n.* Swahili (*person*, *language*).

Suais *n.* Suez. **Canal Suais** Suez Canal. **Golfo Suais** Gulf of Suez.

suami ['swami] *n.* swami (*Hinduism*).

suapare *vi.* show through, be visible through.

suarcivo *n.* subfolder, subdirectory.

suartica *adj.* subarctic.

suasembla *n.* subassembly.

suastica [swa'stika] *n.* swastika.

suatomal *adj.* subatomic.

suave ['swave] *adj.* soft (*hair*, *skin*, *fabric*), smooth; mellow. See *mol*.

suavi ['swavi] *vi.* condition, soften; mellow, smoothe. • *vt.* condition, soften; mellow, smooth.

suavia ['swavia] *n.* softness.

suavinte [swa'vinte] *adj.* softening, emollient. • *n.* conditioner, softener (*substance*).

suazi ['swazi] *adj.* & *n.* Swazi.

Suaziland ['swaziland] *n.* Swaziland.

subasta *vt.* & *n.* auction.

subasteria *n.* auction house.

subastor *n.* auctioneer.

suber *n.* cork (*substance*).

subita *adj.* sudden, abrupt. • *adv.* suddenly, abruptly.

sublima *vi.* & *vt.* sublimate. • *n.* sublimation.

subosce *n.* undergrowth, underbrush, scrub, brushwood (*low-growing vegetation*).

suburban *adj.* suburban. • *n.* suburbanite.

suburbe *n.* suburb. **suburbes** suburbia.

subuteo *n.* hobby.

suca *vt.* suck, suckle. • *n.* suction. **suca a secia** suck dry.

sucamisa *n.* undershirt; singlet, vest (*UK*); camisole.

sucampion *n.* runner-up.

sucampo *n.* subfield (*knowledge*), subdiscipline.

sucapolvo *n.* vacuum cleaner.

sucasangue *n.* leech, bloodsucker (*Hirudinea*).

sucasava *n.* sapsucker (*bird*: *Sphyrapicus*).

sucategoria *n.* subcategory.

suceta *n.* lollipop, lolly; love bite, hickey.

suciaci *n.* sukiyaki (*food*).

suclase *n.* subclass.

sucolie *n.* subset.

sucomite *n.* subcommittee.

sucompania *n.* subsidiary.

suconsensa *adj.* subconscious, subliminal.

suconsensia *n.* subconscious, unconscious (*mind*).

sucontinente *n.* subcontinent.

sucontrata *vt.* subcontract.

sucontrator *n.* subcontractor.

sucorente *n.* undercurrent.

sucotax *n.* succotash (*food*).

sucrosa *n.* sucrose (*sugar*).

sucubo *n.* succubus.

suculente *adj.* succulent.

sucultur *n.* subculture.

sucutanea *adj.* subcutaneous.

suda *vi.* ooze, exude, seep, discharge. • *vt.* ooze, discharge.

Sudafrica *n.* Republic of South Africa. See *Republica de Africa Sude*.

sudafrican *adj.* & *n.* South African.

Sudan *n.* Sudan. **Sudan Sude** South Sudan.
sudani *adj.* & *n.* Sudani.
sude *adj.* south, southern, downstate. • *n.* south. **a sude** southward, southwards. **a sude de** to the south of. **sude-este** *adj.* southeast, southeasterly. • *n.* southeast. **sude-sentral** *adj.* central south. **sude-sude-este** *adj.* & *n.* south-southeast. **sude-sude-ueste** *adj.* & *n.* south-southwest. **sude-ueste** *adj.* southwest, southwesterly. • *n.* southwest.
sudevelopada *adj.* underdeveloped.
sudivide *vi.* & *vt.* subdivide. • *n.* subdivision.
sudocu *n.* sudoku (*puzzle*).
sudui *vi.* subduce. • *n.* subduction (*geology*).
sueba *adj.* & *n.* Suebian. **suebas** Suebians, Suebi (*ancient tribe*).
suentrada *n.* subentry (*in list*).
suesposa *vt.* underexpose. • *n.* underexposure.
suestima *vt.* & *n.* underestimate.
sueter *n.* sweater, pullover, jumper, jersey. **sueter de capeta** hooded sweatshirt, hoodie. **sueter de sporte** sweatshirt. **sueter sin manga** sleeveless sweater, tanktop (*UK*), sweater vest.
sufamilia *n.* subfamily (*biology*).
sufi *adj.* & *n.* Sufi.
sufilo *n.* subphylum.
sufisa *vt.* suffix; e.g. *on sufisa un silaba a un radis*. • *n.* suffix; suffixing, suffixation; extension (*filename*).
sufisi *vi.* suffice, be sufficient, be enough. • *n.* sufficiency, adequacy.
sufisinte *adj.* sufficient, enough, adequate.
sufisme *n.* Sufism (*Islam*).
sufle *n.* soufflé (*food*).
sufrajeta *n.* suffragette.
sufri *vt.* suffer, undergo; e.g. *sufri de depresa*; *sufri un crise mental*. • *n.* suffering, affliction, hardship.
sufror *n.* sufferer.
sugrupo *n.* subgroup.
suhur *n.* suhur, sahur, sehri (*Islam*).
sui *vt.* sweat, perspire. • *n.* perspiration.
suindise *n.* subscript.
suing [swiŋ] *adj.* & *n.* swing, jive, jitterbug, lindy (*dance*, *music*).
suisidal *adj.* suicidal.
suiside *vi.* commit suicide. • *n.* suicide (*action*). **atenta suiside** attempt to commit suicide. **suiside atentada** suicide attempt.
suisidor *n.* suicide (*person*).
suite ['swite] *n.* suite (*furniture*, *rooms*, *music*, *etc.*).
Suiz [swiz] *n.* Switzerland. **suiz** *adj.* & *n.* Swiss.
suje *n.* soot.
sujenero *n.* subgenus.
sujesta *vt.* suggest, evince; remind, call to mind. • *n.* suggestion; connotation.
sujestante *adj.* redolent.
sujestosa *adj.* suggestive.
sujestosia *n.* suggestiveness.
sujetal *adj.* subjective.
sujetalia *n.* subjectivity.
sujeto *n.* subject (*including grammar*), topic.
suji *vt.* soot, blacken with soot.
sujosa *adj.* sooty, black with soot.
sujunta *n.* subordinator, subordinating conjunction.
sujuntiva *adj.* & *n.* subjunctive (*grammar*).
Sulawesi *n.* Sulawesi, Celebes (*island*). **Mar Sulawesi** Celebes Sea.
sulfato *n.* sulphate (US sulfate). **sulfato de magnesio** magnesium sulphate (US sulfate), Epsom salts.
sulfido *n.* sulphide (US sulfide) (*chemistry*).
sulfur *n.* sulphur (US sulfur), brimstone.
sulfurica *adj.* sulphuric (US sulfuric).
sulia *vt.* & *n.* downlink.
sulini *vt.* underline, underscore. • *n.* underlining.
sulinia *n.* underline, underscore (*character*).
sultan *n.* sultan (*governor*).
sultana *n.* sultana (*sultan's wife*).
sultania *n.* sultanate.
Sulu, Mar *n.* Sulu Sea.
sulua *vt.* sublease, sublet.
sulunan *adj.* sublunar (*astronomy*).
sumaco *n.* sumac (*plant*: *Rhus*, *Cotinus*). **sumaco venenosa** poison ivy, poison sumac, poison oak (*Toxicodendron*, *Rhus radicans*, *Rhus vernix*, *Rhus toxicodendron*).
sumarina *n.* submarine, sub.
Sumatra *n.* Sumatra.
Sumba *n.* Sumba (*island*). **Streta Sumba** Sumba Strait.
Sumer *n.* Sumer, Sumeria.
sumerji *vi.* & *vi.* submerge, immerse, submerse, dip, duck, dunk. • *n.* submergence, immersion, dip, dunk.
sumerjor *n.* diver, frogman, aquanaut.
sumina *vt.* undermine.
sumo *n.* sumo (*sport*).
sumor *n.* sumo wrestler.
sumundo *n.* underworld.
suna *n.* Sunnah, Sunna (*Islam*).
sunda *adj.* & *n.* Sunda (*person*, *language*). **Streta Sunda** Sunda Strait.
sunde *n.* sundae (*food*).
suni *adj.* & *n.* Sunni, Sunnite (*Islam*).
sunormal *adj.* subnormal; below par.
suo *n.* sweat, perspiration.

Suomi *n.* Finland. **suomi** *adj.* Finnish. **Golfo Suomi** Gulf of Finland. See *Finland, finsce.*
suorbital *adj.* suborbital.
suordina *vt.* subordinate. • *n.* subordination; suborder (*biology*).
suordinada *adj.* subordinate, secondary, vice-, deputy. • *n.* deputy, commissary.
suosa *adj.* sweaty.
supantala *n.* boxer shorts, boxers.
supasaje *n.* underpass.
superior *adj.* superior, elite; upscale, upmarket. • *n.* superior, higher-up, liege. **Lago Superior** Lake Superior.
superioria *n.* superiority.
superlativa *adj.* & *n.* superlative.
superstisio *n.* superstition.
superstisiosa *adj.* superstitious.
supina *adj.* supine, face up, palm up.
supinador *n.* supinator (*muscle*).
suplica *vt.* implore, entreat, beseech, beg, appeal to, petition, supplicate, importune. • *n.* plea, entreaty, petition, supplication.
supopla *vt.* underpopulate. • *n.* underpopulation.
supoplada *adj.* underpopulated.
suporta *vt.* support, prop up, back up, bolster, underpin, uphold; fund (*financially*); espouse. • *n.* support, backing, aegis, auspices. **suporta finansial** *v.* subsidize. • *n.* financial support, subsidy, grant, funding.
suportable *adj.* supportable.
suportada *adj.* supported, upheld.
suportador *n.* support, supporting device, stand, strut, plinth.
suportor *n.* supporter, sympathizer, proponent, backer; breadwinner; groomsman, usher (*at wedding*).
suportosa *adj.* supportive.
suposa *vt.* suppose, presume, assume, surmise. • *n.* supposition, presumption, assumption, postulate.
suposable *adv.* presumably.
suposada *adj.* supposed, presumptive, putative; so-called (*disparaging*).
supositorimjo *n.* suppository.
supra *prep.* • above, over, higher than (*location, quantity, standard*); e.g. *la teto es supra la sofito*; *un covretota supra tua otra vestes*; *nosa rapidia es supra sento cilometres per ora.* • (*moving*) to above, over; e.g. *el leva la enfante supra sua testa.* • *pref.* super- (*higher in location or hierarchy*); e.g. *suprasil*; *supraumana.* **a supra** *prep.* (*moving*) to above, over. • *adv.* above; up, upward, upwards; upstairs. **de supra** *prep.* (*moving*) from above. • *adv.* from above; from upstairs; down, downward, downwards. **supra tota** above all.
suprabunda *vi.* be overabundant, overflow. • *n.* overabundance, overflow, glut.
suprabundante *adj.* excessive, overabundant.
supracarga *vt.* overload, overburden; supercharge, turbocharge.
supraclase *n.* superclass.
supracomputador *n.* supercomputer.
supracondutador *n.* superconductor.
supradestrui *vt.* & *n.* overkill.
supradosa *vt.* & *n.* overdose.
supradramosa *adj.* overdramatic, overdramatized, sensational, sensationalistic, lurid.
supradramosia *n.* sensationalism.
supraego *n.* superego (*psychology*).
supraengrana *n.* overdrive.
supraeroe *n.* superhero.
supraesposa *vt.* overexpose. • *n.* overexposure.
supraestima *vt.* & *n.* overestimate.
suprafamilia *n.* superfamily (*biology*).
suprafem *n.* superwoman.
suprafilo *n.* superphylum.
supraflue *vi.* overflow. • *n.* overflow, runoff.
suprafluente *adj.* superfluous, excessive.
suprafoli *vt.* overcrowd.
suprafolida *adj.* overcrowded.
supragrupo *n.* supergroup, umbrella group.
supraindise [suprain'dise] *n.* superscript.
supralia *vt.* & *n.* uplink.
supramercato *n.* supermarket.
supramorde *n.* overbite.
supranatural *adj.* supernatural.
supranormal *adj.* supernormal; above par.
supranova *n.* supernova (*star*).
supraom *n.* superman.
supraordina *n.* superorder (*biology*).
supraordinada *adj.* superordinate.
supraorganiza *n.* umbrella organization, umbrella group.
suprapasa *vt.* surpass, exceed, emulate, overshadow, outdo, outclass, outpace, overshoot. • *n.* surplus, excess, profusion, overage. **suprapasa comersial** trade surplus.
suprapasada *adj.* surpassed, overshadowed, dwarfed.
suprapasante *adj.* surpassing, exceeding, excessive, preeminent, profuse, inordinate.
suprapone *vt.* superimpose, overlap, overlay; inlay, composite (*video*); kern (*typography*). • *n.* superimposure, overlap, overlay; lapel. **suprapone par color** chroma key (*video*). **suprapone par scermo blu** blue-screen compositing. **suprapone par scermo verde** green-screen compositing.
suprapopla *vt.* overpopulate. • *n.* overpopulation.

suprapoplada *adj.* overpopulated.
suprapotia *n.* superpower (*of superhero*).
suprapotiosa *adj.* superpowerful. • *n.* superpower (*political*).
supraregala *vt.* overindulge, binge.
suprarenal *adj.* suprarenal.
suprascrive *vt.* overwrite.
suprascriveda *adj.* overwritten. • *n.* palimpsest.
suprasesional *adj.* suprasegmental.
suprasil *n.* eyebrow.
suprasolo *n.* topsoil.
suprasonal *adj.* supersonic.
supraspira *vi.* hyperventilate. • *n.* hyperventilation.
suprasusede *vt.* overachieve.
suprasusedor *n.* overachiever.
supratempo *n.* overtime (*work*).
supratono *n.* overtone.
supraumana *adj.* & *n.* superhuman, Übermensch.
supravalua *vt.* overrate, overvalue.
supraventa *adj.* upwind, windward.
supravide *vt.* supervise, oversee, look over. • *n.* supervision, overseeing, oversight.
supravidor *n.* supervisor, overseer, superintendent, chaperone. **supravidor de carga** cargo supervisor, supercargo.
suprema *adj.* supreme; topmost.
supremia *n.* supremacy.
supresa *vt.* suppress, quash, quell, override. • *n.* suppression.
supresante *n.* suppressant.
suprima *adj.* subprime (*loan*).
suproduida *n.* by-product.
suprogram *n.* subprogram, subroutine.
suproposa *n.* subclause, subordinate clause, dependent clause. **suproposa ajetivin** adjective clause, relative clause. **suproposa averbin** adverb clause. **suproposa nomin** noun clause, content clause.
sur *prep.* • on (*surface, including vertical*), on top of, upon; e.g. *tre libros es sur la table*; *un depinta pende sur la mur*; *un sicatris sur tua dito*; *la vive sur Marte*. • (*moving*) onto; e.g. *la caxa ia cade sur la solo*. • concerning, about, pertaining to (*a topic*); e.g. *me vole parla sur mea vacanse*; *la xica plora sur sua popa perdeda*. **a sur** *prep.* (*moving*) onto, on. • *adv.* on top, on the top, onto the top. **de sur** *prep.* (*moving*) off, off of. • *adv.* off.
sura *n.* calf (*anatomy*).
sureal *adj.* surreal.
surealisme *n.* surrealism.
surealiste *adj.* surrealistic. • *n.* surrealist.
surfa *vt.* surf; browse (*web*). • *n.* surf (*waves*); surfing; browsing. **surfa de vela** windsurfing, sailboarding. **surfa la fola** crowdsurf. **surfa la rede** surf the net.
surfador *n.* web browser.
surfas *n.* surface. **surfas de table** tabletop.
surfasal *adj.* superficial, facile, skindeep, glib, perfunctory. • *adv.* superficially, on the surface.
surfor *n.* surfer.
suri *adj.* & *n.* Syrian.
Suria *n.* Syria.
suricata *n.* meerkat, suricate (*Suricata*).
surie *vt.* & *n.* smile, grin; e.g. *el ia surie sua deleta*. **surie adulante** simper. **surie dentosa** beam. **surie ienin** cheesy grin. **surie vil** *v.* & *n.* smirk.
surimposta *vt.* & *n.* surtax.
Suriname *n.* Suriname, Surinam. See *sranan*.
surion *n.* grin.
surprende *vt.* surprise, startle, astonish, amaze; ambush. • *n.* surprise; ambush.
surprendeda *adj.* surprised, startled, astonished.
surprendente *adj.* surprising. • *adv.* surprisingly.
sursolo *n.* flooring.
survive *vt.* survive. • *n.* survival.
survivente *adj.* surviving, extant.
survivor *n.* survivor, holdover.
suscrive *vt.* sign, autograph, register, underwrite. • *n.* signature, autograph. **suscrive de autor** author's signature; by-line. **suscrive per entra** sign in, check in, register. **suscrive per retira** sign out, check out.
susecretor *n.* undersecretary.
susede *vt.* succeed (*at*), manage to, achieve, accomplish; pass (*test*); e.g. *el ia susede sua esaminas*; *me ia susede abri la botela*. • *n.* success, achievement, accomplishment.
susedor *n.* succeeder, achiever.
susedosa *adj.* successful. • *n.* hit, blockbuster.
susesion *n.* subsection.
susi *vi.* & *vt.* dirty, soil, sully, mess up, besmirch.
susia *adj.* dirty, squalid, sordid, crummy, grimy, grubby, seedy, sleazy; murky (*liquid*). • *n.* dirtiness, dirt, grime, mess.
susida *adj.* dirtied, soiled, sullied.
susiste *vi.* subsist (*stay alive*). • *n.* subsistence.
susolo *n.* subsoil.
susoma *n.* subtotal.
suspende *vt.* suspend, dangle, hang, hang up; adjourn. • *n.* suspense, suspension; cliffhanger; adjournment, abeyance; moratorium.
suspendeda *adj.* suspended, adjourned, in abeyance.
suspendosa *adj.* suspenseful.
suspesie *n.* subtype, subspecies.

suspeta *vt.* suspect. • *n.* suspicion, hunch.
suspetada *adj.* suspected. • *n.* suspect (*person*).
suspetante *adj.* suspicious, askance.
suspetosa *adj.* suspicious (*suspecting, arousing suspicion*).
suspira *vt.* & *n.* sigh. **suspira de lejeri** sigh of relief.
susta *vt.* sustain, support; eke out. • *n.* sustenance.
sustable *adj.* sustainable.
sustantia *n.* substance.
sustantial *adj.* substantial.
sustantivin *adj.* substantival.
sustantivo *n.* substantive, noun.
sustasion *n.* substation.
sustitua *adj.* substitute, replacement, surrogate, sub. • *n.* substitute, replacement, surrogate, stand-in, double, understudy. **sustitua de peril** stunt double, stuntman, stuntwoman. **sustitua jemelin** body double. **sustitua tempora** temporary substitute, replacement, surrogate, stand-in.
sustitui *vi.* & *vt.* substitute, replace; e.g. *la nova sustitui per la vea*. • *n.* substitution. **sustitui per** substitute for, supersede, supplant. **sustitui tempora** replace temporarily, substitute for, stand in for.
sustrato *n.* substrate, lower layer; undercoat. **sustrato de tera** subsoil.
sususede *vt.* underachieve.
sususedor *n.* underachiever.
sutende *vt.* subtend (*botany, geometry*).
suteninte *n.* sublieutenant, second lieutenant, ensign.
sutera *n.* cellar, basement.
suteran *adj.* subterranean, underground.
suteto *n.* attic, loft, garret.
sutil *adj.* subtle, nuanced. • *n.* subtlety, nuance. **sutil nosiva** insidious.
sutilia *n.* subtleness, subtlety.
sutituli *vt.* subtitle.
sutitulo *n.* subtitle (*subheading, transcription*).
sutra *n.* sutra (*aphorism, scripture*).
sutrable *adj.* removable, deletable, delible, deductible. **sutrable de imposta** tax-deductible.
sutrae *vt.* subtract, deduct; remove, take away, delete, expunge; detract. • *n.* subtraction, deduction; removal, deletion.
sutropical *adj.* subtropical.
sutur *n.* suture, surgical stitch. **sutur sajital** sagittal suture.
suturi *vt.* suture. • *n.* suture (*action*).
suumana *adj.* subhuman.
suvacua *adj.* vacuum-sealed.
suvalua *vt.* underappreciate, underrate, undervalue.
suvenir *n.* souvenir, memento, remembrance. **suvenires** souvenirs, memorabilia.
suventa *adj.* downwind, lee, leeward.
suventre *n.* underbelly.
suverti *vt.* subvert, overthrow. • *n.* subversion, overthrow.
suvertinte *adj.* subversive.
suvia [su'via] *n.* underpass.
suxef *n.* deputy head, second-in-command.
suxi *n.* sushi (*food*).
Svalbard *n.* Svalbard, Spitsbergen.
svensce *adj.* Swedish (*person, language*). • *n.* Swedish, Swede.
Sveria *n.* Sweden.

T

T [te], **te** *letter* T, t. **con forma de T** T shaped.
ta *adv.* (*preverbal*) would (*indicating that a finite verb refers to a hypothetical scenario; also used in polite questions*); e.g. *si nos ta ave un mapa, nos no ta es perdeda; tu ta desira plu cafe?*—Unlike *would, ta* does *not* denote a reported future as in *he said he would be here* (*el ia dise ce el va es asi*) and *she would later become an author* (*el ia deveni plu tarda un autor*). **ta ce** would that, may, let (*something happen*); e.g. *ta ce nos vade; ta ce tu deside.* See *ia ta.*
tabaco *n.* tobacco (*plant, leaves: Nicotiana tabacum*).
tabano *n.* horsefly (*Tabanidae*).
tabla *n.* tabla (*musical instrument*).
table *n.* table (*furniture*); board (*game*); table (*of information*), tabulation. **Table** *n.* Mensa (*constellation*). **table basa** low table, coffee table. **table de autopsia** autopsy table, slab. **table de axi** hash table (*software*). **table de contenidas** table of contents. **table de cosina** kitchen table. **table de labora** worktable, workbench, worktop, work surface; desktop (*software*). **table de presa** ironing board. **table de vende** sales counter. **table de xace** chessboard. **table ladal** end table, side table. **table ronda** round table (*including discussion*).
tableta *n.* tablet, slate (*writing*); tablet computer. **tableta de desinia** graphics tablet.
tabli *vi.* tabulate.
tabu [ta'bu] *adj.* taboo, unmentionable. • *n.* taboo.
tabule *n.* tabbouleh (*food*).
taci- *pref.* tachy- (*rapid*).
tacicardia *n.* tachycardia.
tacicardial *adj.* tachycardial.
tacion *n.* tachyon (*particle*).
tacle *vt.* tackle (*sport*). • *n.* tackle.
taco *n.* taco (*food*).
ta-da *interj.* ta-da, hey presto, voilà.
tadjici *adj.* & *n.* Tajik (*person, language*).
Tadjicistan *n.* Tajikistan.
tafel *n.* tafl, tablut, hnefatafl (*game*).
tafeta *n.* taffeta (*fabric*).
tagalog *adj.* & *n.* Tagalog (*person, language*).
tagete *n.* marigold (*Tagetes*).
Tahiti *n.* Tahiti. **tahiti** *adj.* & *n.* Tahitian.
Tai *n.* Thailand, Siam. **tai** *adj.* & *n.* Thai, Siamese (*person, language*). **Golfo Tai** Gulf of Thailand.
taie *n.* waist, waistline.
taiga *n.* taiga, boreal forest.
taitxi *n.* tai-chi, tai-chi chuan.
Taiuan *n.* Taiwan. **taiuan** *adj.* & *n.* Taiwanese.
Taklamakan, Deserto *n.* Taklamakan Desert.
tal *adj.* (*prenominal*) such, this kind of, that kind of. • *adv.* in such a way, in this way, like this, thus, thusly, so, sic. **tal ce** in such a way that. **un tal** such a, of such a kind. See *tan.*
talamo *n.* thalamus (*anatomy*).
talco *n.* talc; talcum powder.
talento *n.* talent, aptitude, gift, flair.
talentosa *adj.* talented, gifted. • *n.* prodigy.
talia *vt.* cut, slice, slash, gash, carve, whittle, incise, hew, sever, butcher. • *n.* cut, slice, slash, gash, incision. **talia de carne** cut of meat. **talia de lardo** rasher. **talia traversal** cross-section, cross-cut.
taliador *n.* cutter, slicer.
taliafilo *n.* wire cutter.
taliagarga *n.* cut-throat, murderer.
taliapaper *n.* paper knife, paper cutter.
talidomida *n.* thalidomide.
talieta *n.* noodle, pasta.
talio *n.* thallium (*element*).
talior *n.* tailor. **talior de petra** stonecutter.
talmud *n.* talmud (*Judaism*).
talmudal *adj.* talmudal.
talo *n.* ankle, talus, astragalus; hock; stem (*plant*), sprig; thallus (*botany*). **talo de fava** beanstalk. **talo vara** clubfoot.
talon *n.* heel. **talon alta** high heel (*shoe*), stiletto.
talpa *n.* mole (*animal: Talpidae*).
talperia *n.* molehill.
tam *n.* tam o'shanter (*hat*).
tamale *n.* tamale (*food*).
tamarin *n.* tamarin (*monkey: Saguinus*).
tamarindo *n.* tamarind (*tree: Tamarindus indica*).
tambur *n.* drum, tambour. **tambur de conga** conga drum. **tambur militar** snare drum. **tambur peti** tabor.
tambureta *n.* tambourine.
tamburi *vt.* drum; signal by drum.
tamia *n.* chipmunk (*Tamias*).
tamil *adj.* & *n.* Tamil (*person, language*).
tamis *n.* sieve, colander, strainer.
tamisi *vt.* sieve, sift, strain.
tampon *n.* swab, wad, pad, padding; paper cartridge (*musket, pistol*). **tampon de fem** tampon.
tan *adv.* to such an extent, so, as; how …! **tan bela** so beautiful, how lovely, how nice. **tan bela ce** so beautiful that. **tan grande como** as big as. **tan multe** so many, so

much. **tan multe ce** so many that, so much that. **tan multe como** as many as, as much as. **tan poca** so little, so few. **tan poca ce** so few that. **un vista tan bela** what a lovely view.

tana *vt.* tan (*leather*). • *n.* tanning (*leather*).

tanatolojia *n.* thanatology.

tancador *n.* tanker. **tancador de petrolio** oil tanker.

tanco *n.* tank, tub, vat, cistern; tank (*military*).

tancini *n.* tankini (*bikini*).

taneria *n.* tannery.

tang *adj.* Tang (*dynasty*).

tanga *n.* thong, G-string (*garment*).

Tanganyika, Lago *n.* Lake Tanganyika.

tangar *n.* tanager (*bird*: *Thraupidae*).

tango *n.* tango (*dance*).

tangram *n.* tangram (*puzzle*).

tanica *adj.* tannic (*chemistry*). **asida tanica** tannic acid.

tanin *n.* tannin.

tanje *vt.* touch lightly, be tangential to, brush against, graze; strum (*guitar*).

tanjente *adj.* tangential, peripheral. • *n.* tangent.

tanjerina *n.* tangerine (*fruit*: *Citrus* × *tangerina*).

tanjerino *n.* tangerine (*tree*).

tanor *n.* tanner.

tantalo *n.* tantalum (*element*).

tantra *n.* tantra (*Buddhism*, *Hinduism*).

tantral *adj.* tantric.

Tanzania *n.* Tanzania.

tanzanian *adj.* & *n.* Tanzanian.

tapaculo *n.* tapaculo (*bird*: *Rhinocryptinae*).

tapador *n.* typewriter.

tape *vi.* tap; patter. • *vt.* tap; type. • *n.* tap, tapping, patter; typing.

tapeti *vt.* upholster. • *n.* upholstery (*action*).

tapeto *n.* carpet, rug, mat; upholstery (*material*). **tapeto de bani** bathmat. **tapeto de porte** doormat. **tapeto imajal** tapestry.

tapetor *n.* upholsterer.

tapi *vt.* plug, seal, cork, cap, stop up.

tapioca *n.* tapioca.

tapir *n.* tapir (*animal*: *Tapirus*).

tapo *n.* plug, seal, cork, bung, spigot, cap, stopper. **tapo de orea** earplug.

tapor *n.* typist.

tarama *n.* taramasalata (*food*).

tarantula *n.* tarantula (*spider*: *Theraphosidae*).

tarda *adj.* late, tardy, overdue, in arrears. • *n.* later part, latter part; latecomer; e.g. *en la tarda de la eda medieval*. **a la plu tarda** at the latest (*no later*). **multe tarda** long overdue. **plu tarda** later.

Tar, Deserto *n.* Great Indian Desert, Thar Desert.

tardi *vi.* grow late. • *vt.* make late, delay.

tardia *n.* lateness.

tardigrado *n.* tardigrade, water bear (*organism*: *Tardigrada*).

tarifa *n.* tariff, duty, rate (*financial*). **tarifa postal** postage (*cost*).

taro *n.* taro (*plant*: *Colocasia esculenta*).

taroci *n.* tarot (*cards*).

tarsal *adj.* tarsal.

tarsio *n.* tarsier (*primate*: *Tarsius*).

tarso *n.* tarsus (*bones*).

tartar *n.* tartar, calculus (*deposit on teeth, in wine*); limescale.

tarte *n.* pie, flan. **tarte de carne** meat pie. **tarte de crema** cream pie, cream flan; custard pie (*missile*). **tarte de fruta** fruit pie. **tarte de ragu** potpie. **tarte merengida de limon** lemon meringue pie.

tartesica *adj.* & *n.* Tartessian.

Tarteso *n.* Tartessos (*ancient city*).

tarteta *n.* tart; patty (*cake*).

tarti *vt.* pie.

tas *n.* cup. **tas de te** teacup; cup of tea.

taseta *n.* demitasse, small cup.

tasi- *pref.* taxi- (*arrangement*).

tasidermia *n.* taxidermy.

tasidermiste *n.* taxidermist.

tasin *adj.* cuplike, cup-shaped.

Tasman, Mar *n.* Tasman Sea.

Tasmania *n.* Tasmania.

taso *n.* rate (*numerical*). **taso de interesa** interest rate. **taso de mori** death rate. **taso de nase** birth rate.

tason[1] *n.* taxon (*biology*).

tason[2] *n.* mug, beaker. **tason de peltre** tankard.

tasonomia *n.* taxonomy.

tasonomial *adj.* taxonomic.

tasonomiste *n.* taxonomist.

tatami *n.* tatami (*mat*).

tatar *adj.* & *n.* Tatar (*person*, *language*).

tatica *n.* tactic, tack. **tatica defendente** countermeasure.

tatical *adj.* tactical.

taticiste *n.* tactician.

tato *n.* tact.

tatosa *adj.* tactful.

tatua *vt.* & *n.* tattoo.

tau *n.* tau (*Greek letter* Τ, τ).

tautolojia *n.* tautology.

taverna *n.* tavern, pub, alehouse, brasserie, roadhouse, saloon. See *bar*, *beveria*.

tavernor *n.* publican.

Taxcent *n.* Tashkent.

taxe *n.* task, chore, job, assignment. **taxes de casa** housework, domestic chores, homemaking. **taxes de scola** schoolwork.

taxi *n.* taxi, cab, taxicab.

taximetre *n.* taximeter.

taxiste *n.* taxi driver, cab driver, cabbie, cabby.
taxo *n.* yew (*tree*: *Taxus*).
taxor *n.* taskmaster.
te *n.* tea (*plant, leaves, drink*: *Camellia sinensis*). **te de bosce** teaberry, checkerberry, boxberry, American wintergreen (*Gaultheria procumbens*).
teatral *adj.* theatrical, theatric. • *n.* play, theatrical performance. **teatral de musica** musical (*play*). **teatral de revista** revue. **teatral mascida** masque, masked play, mummery.
teatro *n.* theatre (US theater) (*place, art*), playhouse, auditorium. **teatro de opera** opera house.
teca *n.* teak (*tree, wood*: *Tectona grandis*).
tecel *n.* dachshund (*dog*).
tecila *n.* tequila (*drink*).
tecla *n.* key. **tecla de entra** enter key, return key. **tecla de spasio** spacebar. **tecla de tabli** tab key. **tecla rapida** shortcut key, accelerator key.
teclador *n.* keyboard.
tecladoreta *n.* keypad. **tecladoreta numeral** numeric keypad.
tecli *vt.* key. • *n.* keypress, keystroke.
tecnesio *n.* technetium (*element*).
tecnica *n.* technique; technics.
tecnical *adj.* technical.
tecniciste *n.* technician.
tecno[1] *adj.* & *n.* techno (*music*).
tecno-[2] *pref.* techno-.
tecnocrata *adj.* technocratic. • *n.* technocrat.
tecnocratia *n.* technocracy.
tecnofilia *n.* technophilia.
tecnofilica *adj.* & *n.* technophile, techie, techy.
tecnofobia *n.* technophobia.
tecnofobica *adj.* technophobic. • *n.* technophobe.
tecnolojia *n.* technology. **tecnolojia alta** high tech. **tecnolojia basa** low tech.
tecnolojial *adj.* technological.
tef *n.* teff (*plant*).
teflon *n.* teflon.
Tehan *n.* South Korea. **tehan** *adj.* & *n.* South Korean. See *Corea Sude*.
teisme [te'isme] *n.* theism.
teiste [te'iste] *adj.* & *n.* theist.
tela *n.* (*piece of*) cloth, towel. **tela de bani** bath towel. **tela de colo** cravat, ascot, neckerchief. **tela de testa** headscarf, kerchief, wimple. **telas de leto** bedclothes, bedding.
tele[1] *n.* (*colloquial*) TV, telly (*television set*).
tele-[2] *pref.* tele- (*remote*).
telecinese *n.* telekinesis, psychokinesis.
telecomanda *vt.* operate by remote control. • *n.* remote control (*action*).
telecomandada *adj.* remote-controlled.
telecomandador *n.* remote control, remote controller.
telecomunica *vt.* telecommunicate. • *n.* telecommunication.
telefon *n.* telephone, phone. **telefon astuta** smartphone. **telefon de porte** doorphone, intercom, talkback.
telefoneta *n.* mobile phone, cellular phone, cellphone, handset.
telefoni *vt.* telephone, phone, call, ring; e.g. *me telefoni a tu; me telefoni la detalias a tu.* • *n.* phone call.
telefonia *n.* telephony, telecommunication.
telefoniste *n.* telephonist, operator.
telefoto *n.* telephoto lens.
telegraf *n.* telegraph.
telegrafi *vt.* telegraph.
telegrafia *n.* telegraphy.
telegram *n.* telegram.
telelabora *vi.* telecommute, telework. • *n.* telecommuting, teleworking.
telelaboror *n.* telecommuter, teleworker.
telemarc *n.* telemark (*skiing*).
telemetre *n.* telemeter; rangefinder.
telemetri *n.* telemetry.
telenovela *n.* soap opera, soap, TV serial, telenovela.
teleolojia *n.* teleology.
teleolojial *adj.* teleological.
telepatia *n.* telepathy.
telepatica *adj.* telepathic. • *n.* telepath.
teleporta *vi.* teleport, teleportation.
teleportador *n.* teleport, teleporter.
telescopial *adj.* telescopic.
telescopio *n.* telescope, spyglass. **Telescopio** *n.* Telescopium (*constellation*).
telesenta *n.* chairlift.
teleta *n.* handkerchief, hanky, napkin. **teleta de bava** (*baby's*) bib. **teleta de bebe** nappy, diaper. **teleta de casola** potholder. **teleta de fem** sanitary napkin, sanitary towel. **teleta de lava** washcloth, washrag, facecloth, flannel; dishcloth, dishrag. **teleta de paper** paper towel, tissue.
teletapador *n.* teleprinter, teletype.
teletape *v.* teleprint, teletype.
televanjelisme *n.* televangelism.
televanjeliste *n.* televangelist.
televide *vt.* view television, watch television.
televidor *n.* television viewer.
televisa *vt.* televise, show on television. • *n.* television (*phenomenon*). **televisa colorosa** colour (US color) television. **televisa de vijila** closed-circuit television, CCTV. **televisa par paia** pay TV.
televisada *adj.* on television, televised.

televisador *n.* television set.
teli *vt.* tile.
telia *n.* tile, shingle.
telica *adj.* telic (*expressing purpose*).
telicia *n.* telicity.
telieta *n.* wafer (*electronics*).
telon *n.* sheet, tablecloth. **telon funeral** funeral cloth, pall.
telonin *adj.* sheetlike.
telugu *adj.* & *n.* Telugu (*person, language*).
telurio *n.* tellurium (*element*).
tema *n.* theme, subject, topic, idea; motif, pattern; thesis. **tema xef** main theme, leitmotif, keynote.
temal *adj.* thematic; on-topic.
teme *vt.* fear, dread. • *n.* fear, dread, angst.
temente *adj.* afraid.
temi *vi.* topicalize (*linguistics*). • *n.* topicalization (*linguistics*).
temosa *adj.* fearful, afraid, alarmed.
tempador *n.* timer (*device*).
tempal[1] *adj.* temporal (*anatomy*). **lobe tempal** temporal lobe. **oso tempal** temporal bone.
tempal[2] *adj.* temporal (*of time*).
tempe *n.* temple (*anatomy*).
tempera[1] *vt.* temper (*emotion, metal, music*). • *n.* temper, temperament.
tempera[2] *n.* tempera (*art*).
temperada *adj.* temperate; mild (*weather*). **bon temperada** well-tempered.
temperatur *n.* temperature. **temperatur ambiente** ambient temperature. **temperatur de sala** room temperature.
tempesta *n.* storm, tempest, squall. **tempesta de arena** sandstorm. **tempesta de foco** firestorm, inferno. **tempesta de venta** windstorm. **tempesta granizosa** hailstorm. **tempesta lamposa** thunderstorm.
tempestosa *adj.* stormy, tempestuous.
templo *n.* temple (*religious*).
tempo *n.* time (*concept, duration, historical period*); tense (*grammar*). **a la mesma tempo** at the same time. **a no tempo** at no time, never. **a tempo** on time, in time, punctually. **a tempo conveninte** at an appropriate time, in due course. **de tempo longa** longstanding. **de tempo partal** part-time. **de tempo plen** full-time. **en tempo real** real-time. **tempo de gera** wartime. **tempo de pausa** time out, rest period. **tempo libre** free time, spare time. See *ves*.
tempora *adj.* temporary, ephemeral, interim, fleeting, transient, makeshift, provisional, transitional. • *adv.* temporarily.
temprana *adj.* early. • *n.* early part; e.g. *en la temprana de 1974*.
temprania *n.* earliness.
tempura *n.* tempura (*food*).
tenable *adj.* holdable, tenable.
tenda *n.* tent, marquee.
tende *vt.* tend, be inclined. • *n.* tendency, propensity, proclivity, inclination, penchant, trend.
tendon *n.* tendon, sinew. **tendon pos la jeno** hamstring.
tendonite *n.* tendonitis, tendinitis.
tendonosa *adj.* sinewy, wiry.
tendor *n.* camper.
tenebrio *n.* meal beetle (*Tenebrio molitor*). **tenebrio larval** mealworm.
tenesino *n.* tennessine (*element*).
teni *vt.* hold, grasp, grip, clutch, cling to, hold on to; detain. • *n.* hold, grasp, grip, clutch. **teni a via** keep away, ward off, deter. **teni como ostaje** hold (*as*) hostage. **teni manos** hold hands.
tenibota *n.* boot jack, boot pull (*for removing boots*).
teniloca *n.* placeholder, surrogate.
teninte *n.* lieutenant.
tenis *n.* tennis. **tenis de table** table tennis, ping-pong.
tenisor *n.* tennis player.
Tennessee [tene'si] *n.* Tennessee (*US state*).
tenor *adj.* & *n.* tenor (*music*).
tenrec *n.* tenrec (*animal: Tenrecidae*).
tensa *vi.* tighten, strain, clench. • *n.* tension, stress, strain. **tensa eletrical** electric tension, electric potential difference, voltage. **tensa sua dentes** grit one's teeth.
tensada *adj.* tense, taut, tight, strained, stressed.
tensal *adj.* tensile.
tensor *n.* tensor.
tenta *vt.* tempt, lure, bait, entice. • *n.* temptation, lure, bait, enticement.
tentable *adj.* temptable, vulnerable (*to temptation*).
tentaculo *n.* tentacle. **tentaculo de oio** eyestalk.
tentaculosa *adj.* tentacled.
tentada *adj.* tempted.
tentante *adj.* tempting. • *n.* lure, bait, decoy.
tentor *n.* tempter, temptress.
teo- *pref.* theo- (*god*).
teocrata *adj.* theocratic. • *n.* theocrat.
teocratia *n.* theocracy.
teodolito *n.* theodolite.
teolojia *n.* theology.
teolojial *adj.* theological.
teolojiste *n.* theologian.
teorem *n.* theorem.
teori *vt.* theorize. • *n.* theorization.
teoria *n.* theory. **teoria cuantal** quantum theory. **teoria de caos** chaos theory. **teoria de categorias** category theory. **teo-**

ria de colies set theory. **teoria de computa** theory of computation. **teoria de computablia** computability theory. **teoria de controla** control theory. **teoria de cordetas** string theory. **teoria de evolui** theory of evolution. **teoria de grafes** graph theory. **teoria de grupos** group theory. **teoria de informa** information theory. **teoria de mesuras** measure theory. **teoria de numeros** number theory. **teoria de ordinas** order theory. **teoria de probablia** probability theory. **teoria legal** jurisprudence.

teorial *adj.* theoretical, theoretic.

teoriste *n.* theorist.

teosofia *n.* theosophy.

teosofiste *n.* theosophist.

tepida *adj.* warm, lukewarm, tepid.

tepidi *vi.* warm (*slightly*).

tepidia *n.* tepidness, tepidity.

tera[1] *n.* land, ground, earth, dirt. • *pref.* terra- (*earth*). **Tera** *n.* Earth (*planet*). **a tera** ashore, on shore. **de tera** earthen. **de tera a aira** surface-to-air, ground-to-air. **de tera a tera** surface-to-surface, ground-to-surface. **tera cultivada** farmland. **tera de nun** no man's land. **tera de trigo** wheatland. **tera nonconoseda** unknown territory, terra incognita. **tera nova** new land, virgin territory. **tera savaje** wilderness, outback. **tera xef** mainland.

tera-[2] *pref.* tera- (*a million million*).

terabait *n.* terabyte.

teracota *n.* terracotta.

teral *adj.* earthly.

teran *adj.* terrestrial, Terran. • *n.* earthling, Terran.

terapia *n.* therapy.

terapiste *n.* therapist.

teraplen *n.* embankment.

teratofobia *n.* teratophobia.

teratofobica *adj.* teratophobic.

teratojen *adj.* teratogenic (*medical*). • *n.* teratogen.

teravada *adj.* Theravada (*Buddhism*).

teraza *n.* terrace, patio, stoop, steps. **teraza de lenio** deck, decking.

terazi *vt.* terrace.

terazida *adj.* terraced, stepped.

terbio *n.* terbium (*element*).

terebentin *n.* turpentine.

teremin *n.* theremin (*musical instrument*).

tereno *n.* terrain. **tereno alta** highland, highlands. **tereno basa** lowland, lowlands. **tereno savaje** badlands.

tereria *n.* terrarium.

teria *n.* teashop, tearoom.

teriaci *n.* teriyaki (*food*).

terier *n.* terrier (*dog*). **terier de Airedale** Airedale terrier.

teritorial *adj.* territorial.

teritorio *n.* territory. **teritorio ultramar** overseas territory. **Teritorios Nordeueste** Northwest Territories.

terma *n.* term, expression. **termas tecnical** technical terms, terminology, jargon.

termal *adj.* thermal.

termina *n.* terminal.

terminolojia *n.* terminology.

terminolojial *adj.* terminological.

terminolojiste *n.* terminologist.

termita *n.* thermite.

termite *n.* termite (*insect: Termitidae* and related families).

termo- *pref.* thermo- (*heat*).

termodinamica *n.* thermodynamics.

termodinamical *adj.* thermodynamic.

termoduple *n.* thermocouple.

termofilia *n.* thermophilia.

termofilica *adj.* thermophilic. • *n.* thermophile.

termometre *n.* thermometer.

termonucleal *adj.* thermonuclear.

termos *n.* thermos, vacuum flask, Dewar flask.

termostato *n.* thermostat.

teror *n.* terror, horror.

terori *vt.* terrify, horrify; terrorize, tyrannize.

terorinte *adj.* terrifying, horrifying, bloodcurdling, spine-chilling.

terorisme *n.* terrorism.

teroriste *n.* terrorist.

terosa *adj.* earthy.

tersiaria *adj.* & *n.* Tertiary (*geology*).

tese *n.* thesis, dissertation, treatise.

tesla *n.* tesla (*unit of magnetic induction*).

tesoreria *n.* treasury, storehouse, exchequer.

tesori *vi.* become treasured, become cherished, become enshrined. • *vt.* treasure, cherish, enshrine.

tesoro *n.* treasure; thesaurus. **tesoro falsa** worthless treasure, goldbrick. **tesoros** treasures, riches, hoard.

tesoror *n.* treasurer.

testa *n.* head, pate, bonce. **con prima sua testa** headlong, head first. **sin testa** headless. **testa de leto** headboard. **testa rasada** shaven head, skinhead.

testal *adj.* textual.

testeta *n.* head (*camera, recording device*).

testi *vt.* head; headbutt. • *n.* header (*soccer*).

testiculal *adj.* testicular.

testiculo *n.* testicle, testis (*anatomy*).

testo *n.* text, document, lyrics. **testo de fonte** source code, source text. **testo ru**

draft, rough draft. **testos** texts, documentation.
testosterona *n.* testosterone.
teta[1] *n.* nipple, teat (*anatomy*).
teta[2] *n.* theta (*Greek letter* Θ, θ).
tetania *n.* tetany (*medical*).
tetano *n.* tetanus, lockjaw (*medical*).
teti *vt.* suckle, breastfeed.
tetin *n.* pacifier, comforter, dummy (*for baby*).
teto *n.* roof, rooftop; deck. **sin teto** roofless, topless. **teto de palia** thatched roof. **teto dur** hardtop (*car*). **teto solal** sunroof.
teton *n.* (*colloquial*) tit, boob, knocker (*breast*).
tetonica *n.* tectonics.
tetonical *adj.* tectonic.
tetor *n.* roofer.
tetra[1] *n.* tetra (*fish*: *Characiformes*). **tetra african** African tetra (*Alestidae*). **tetra american** American tetra (*Characidae*, *Lebiasinidae*).
tetra-[2] *pref.* tetra- (*four*).
tetraedro *adj.* tetrahedral. • *n.* tetrahedron.
tetralojia *n.* tetralogy (*group of four*). **tetralojia de Fallot** tetralogy of Fallot (*medical*).
tetrametre *n.* tetrameter (*poetry*).
tetraplejia *n.* tetraplegia, quadriplegia.
tetraplejica *adj.* & *n.* tetraplegic, quadriplegic.
tetrarca *n.* tetrarch (*governor*).
tetrarcia *n.* tetrarchy.
tetrasiclina *n.* tetracycline (*antibiotic*).
texador *n.* loom. **texador de Jacquard** Jacquard loom. **texador de mano** handloom.
Texas ['teksas] *n.* Texas (*US state*).
texe *vt.* weave; spin. • *n.* weaving. **texe de capeles** hairweaving.
texeda *adj.* woven. • *n.* tissue (*organic*). **texeda a casa** homespun. **texeda scotes** plaid, tartan.
texeta *v.* & *n.* darn.
texon *n.* badger (*Melinae*, *Mellivorinae*, *Taxidiinae*).
texoneria *n.* sett, badger lair, badger burrow.
texor *n.* weaver (*including bird*: *Ploceidae*).
tia *n.* aunt.
tiamina *n.* thiamine (*vitamin*).
Tibet *n.* Tibet. See *Bod.*
tibetan *adj.* & *n.* Tibetan. See *bod.*
tibia *n.* shin, shinbone, tibia.
tic *n.* tic (*spasm*).
tica *n.* tick (*arachnid*: *Ixodoidea*).
ticodroma *n.* wallcreeper (*bird*: *Tichodroma muraria*).
tictac *interj.* tick-tock.
tictaci *vi.* tick (*clock*). • *n.* tick, ticking.
tie *n.* aunt or uncle; (*colloquial*) family member of an older generation.
tifa *n.* cattail, bulrush (*plant*: *Typha*).
tifo *n.* typhus.
tifoide *adj.* & *n.* typhoid.
tigre *n.* tiger (*Panthera tigris*).
tigreta *n.* tiger cub.
Tigris, Rio *n.* Tigris River.
tilde *n.* tilde (*diacritic*).
tilia *adj.* chartreuse, lime. • *n.* linden, lime tree (*Tilia*).
tim *n.* thyme (*plant*: *Thymus*).
timida *adj.* timid, shy, coy, diffident, bashful, faint-hearted, pusillanimous. • *n.* shy person, milquetoast, wallflower.
timidia *n.* timidity, shyness, coyness, diffidence.
timo *n.* thymus (*anatomy*).
timon *n.* rudder, helm. **sin timon** rudderless.
timonor *n.* helmsman.
Timor *n.* Timor. **Mar Timor** Timor Sea. **Timor Este** East Timor.
timoran *adj.* & *n.* Timorese.
timpan *n.* tympanum, eardrum (*anatomy*).
timpano *n.* timpano, timpani, timp, kettle drum.
tin *adj.* avuncular.
tinamo *n.* tinamou (*bird*: *Tinamidae*).
tinca *n.* tench, doctor fish (*Tinca tinca*).
tinea *n.* ringworm, dermatophytosis (*medical*).
tinia *n.* clothes moth (*Tineidae*).
tinito *n.* tinnitus (*medical*).
tinje *vt.* tint, tinge, dye, stain. • *n.* tint, hue, shade; nuance; timbre.
tinjente *adj.* tinting, tinging. • *n.* dye, stain (*substance*).
tinocor *n.* seed-snipe (*bird*: *Thinocoridae*).
tintina *vi.* tinkle, jingle, jangle, clang, clank, clink; ring (*phone*). • *n.* tinkle, jingle, jangle, clang, clank, clink, clangour (US clangor).
tintura *n.* tincture (*medicine*).
tio *n.* uncle. **como tio** avuncular.
tipal *adj.* typical, representative, characteristic. **es tipal de** be typical of, typify.
tipi *n.* tipi, teepee, tepee (*tent*).
tipo *n.* type, sort, kind; type (*printing*). **tipo de dato** data type. **tipo de letera** typeface, font. **tipo movable** movable type.
tipografi *vt.* typeset.
tipografia *n.* typography, typesetting. **tipografia par computador** desktop publishing.
tipografial *adj.* typographic, typographical.
tipografiste *n.* typographer.
tipolojia *n.* typology.
tipolojial *adj.* typological.
tipula *n.* crane fly (*Tipulomorpha*).
tira *vt.* pull, drag, haul, lug, tug, pluck; tow, draw, trail. • *n.* pull, tug, traction. **tira a tera** pull to the ground, pull down, tackle;

shoot down. **tira sua pedes** drag one's feet, shuffle along.
tiracampana *n.* bell pull, bell rope.
tirada *adj.* pulled. **tirada par cavalo** horse-drawn.
tirador *n.* tractor (*with trailer*).
tiramisu [tirami'su] *n.* tiramisu (*dessert*).
tiranal *adj.* tyrannic, tyrannical.
tirania *n.* tyranny, dictatorship, despotism.
tiranin *adj.* tyrannical, tyrantlike.
tiraniosa *adj.* tyrannous.
tirano *n.* tyrant, dictator, despot, strongman; tyrant flycatcher (*bird*: *Tyrannidae*). **es tirano a** tyrannize, boss around, lord it over.
tiranosauro *n.* tyrannosaur, tyrannosaurus (*Tyrannosauridae*).
tiratapo *n.* corkscrew.
tiroide *n.* thyroid (*anatomy*).
tiroidectomia *n.* thyroidectomy (*surgery*).
tisa *vt.* stoke, stir up, incite; tease, tantalize.
tisacafe *n.* coffee stirrer.
tisafoco *n.* poker (*for fire*).
tisanotera *n.* thrips, thunderfly (*Thysanoptera*).
tisante *adj.* teasing. • *n.* trailer, trail (*film, TV*).
-tise *n.suff.* -ptysis (*spitting*).
tisor *n.* troublemaker, provocateur; tease, hussy, tart, tramp, lolita, coquette, minx, jezebel.
titan *n.* Titan.
titanio *n.* titanium.
titi *n.* titi (*monkey*: *Callicebus*).
titila *vt.* tickle; cause to tingle; titillate. • *n.* tickle; titillation.
titilable *adj.* ticklish.
titilosa *adj.* tingly, tingling.
tito *n.* barn owl, bay owl (*Tylonidae*).
titola *vt.* titrate. • *n.* titration, titrimetry.
titulal *adj.* titular.
tituli *vt.* title, entitle, give a title to.
titulo *n.* title, headline, heading; caption (*of image*); rubric, regular column (*magazine*); rank, peerage. **par titulo** *adj.* nominal, in title. • *adv.* nominally, in title. **titulo finansial** security (*tradable asset*). **titulos codal** closing titles, closing credits. **titulos inisial** opening titles, opening credits.
tlingit *adj.* & *n.* Tlingit (*person, language*).
tobagonian *adj.* & *n.* Tobagonian.
tobogan *n.* slide, chute. **tobogan de acua** water slide. **tobogan elica** helter-skelter, spiral slide.
toca *vt.* touch, abut; pluck (*a stringed instrument*). • *n.* touch. • *interj.* touché. **toca con ditos** finger.
tocable *adj.* touchable, tangible.
tocante *adj.* touching. • *n.* tap, flap (*consonant*).
tocata *n.* toccata (*music*).
Tocelau *n.* Tokelau. **tocelau** *adj.* & *n.* Tokelauan.
Tocio *n.* Tokyo.
toco *n.* toque (*cap*).
tofu *n.* tofu, bean curd (*food*).
toga *n.* toga (*garment*).
Togo *n.* Togo.
togoles *adj.* & *n.* Togolese.
tolera *vt.* tolerate, bear, endure, stand, abide, put up with. • *n.* tolerance, endurance, stamina.
tolerable *adj.* bearable, tolerable.
tolerante *adj.* tolerant, easygoing.
tomate *n.* tomato (*Solanum lycopersicum*).
tomba *n.* grave, tomb, crypt, vault, sepulchre (US sepulcher). **tomba coletiva** mass grave.
tombi *vt.* entomb.
tombin *adj.* tomblike, sepulchral.
-tome *n.suff.* -tome (*cutting tool*).
-tomia *n.suff.* -tomy (*cutting*).
-tomica *adj.suff.* -tomic.
tomografia *n.* tomography.
tomtom *n.* tom, tomtom (*drum*).
ton *n.* tonne, metric ton (*1000 kg*).
tona *vi.* & *n.* thunder.
tonal *adj.* tonal.
tonalia *n.* key (*music*).
tong *n.* tong (*secret society*).
Tonga *n.* Tonga.
tongan *adj.* & *n.* Tongan.
tonin *adj.* thunderous.
tono *n.* tone, pitch, musical note; intonation. **tono completa** whole note, semibreve. **tono cuatrida** quarter note, crotchet. **tono des-sesida** sixteenth note, semiquaver. **tono duida** half note, minim. **tono duple** double whole note, breve. **tono muscual** muscle tone. **tono otida** eighth note, quaver. **tono sesdes-cuatrida** sixty-fourth note, hemidemisemiquaver. **tono tredes-duida** thirty-second note, demisemiquaver.
tonsil *n.* tonsil (*anatomy*).
tonsilectomia *n.* tonsillectomy (*surgery*).
tonsilite *n.* tonsillitis (*medical*).
tonsura *n.* tonsure (*shaven head*).
topazio *n.* topaz (*gem*).
tope *adj.* & *n.* taupe (*colour*).
topiaria *n.* topiary.
topo- *pref.* topo-.
topografia *n.* topography.
topografial *adj.* topographic, topographical.
topolojia *n.* topology.
toponim *adj.* toponymic. • *n.* toponym.
tora *n.* Torah (*Judaism*).
torax *n.* thorax.
toraxal *adj.* thoracic.

torba *n.* peat (*soil*).
torca *n.* nut (*for bolt*). **torca papilin** wing nut.
torce *n.* torc (*ornament*).
tore *n.* tower; rook (*chess*). **tore de apartes** apartment block, block of flats. **tore de garda** guard tower, defence (US defense) tower, barbican. **tore de vijila** watchtower, lookout.
toreta *n.* turret.
tori[1] *n.* torii (*gate*).
tori[2] *n.* Tory (*politics*).
tori[3] *vi.* tower (*over*).
torio *n.* thorium (*element*).
tormenta *vt.* torment, bully, scourge, hector; nag, badger, bedevil, beset. • *n.* torment, bullying.
tormentor *n.* tormentor, bully.
torn *n.* (*Latin letter* Þ, þ) thorn.
tornado *n.* tornado.
torneo *n.* tournament, championship; tourney, joust. **torneo de lansias** joust.
torpe *adj.* clumsy, awkward, maladroit, ungainly, ham-fisted, physically inept. • *n.* clumsy person, oaf, clodhopper, lummox.
torpedo *n.* torpedo.
torpi *vi.* fumble, become clumsy. • *vt.* make clumsy.
torpia *n.* clumsiness.
Torres, Streta *n.* Strait of Torres.
torse *vi.* twist, tweak. • *vt.* twist, wring. • *n.* twist, torsion, contorsion, kink. **torse sua colo** crane one's neck, rubberneck.
torsosa *adj.* tortuous, kinky.
torta *n.* cake, pastry, torte. **torta arenin** shortcake (*dessert*). **torta de cafe** coffeecake. **torta de ceso** cheesecake. **torta de Foresta Negra** Black Forest gâteau. **torta de fruta** fruitcake. **torta sponjin** sponge cake.
tortelini *n.* tortellini (*food*).
torteria *n.* pastry shop.
torteta *n.* cupcake. **torteta de xocolada** brownie.
tortilia *n.* tortilla (*food*).
tortor *n.* pastry baker, pastry chef.
tortora *n.* turtledove, collared dove (*Streptopelia*).
tortuga *n.* tortoise, turtle (*Testudines*).
tortura *vt.* & *n.* torture, torment.
torturor *n.* torturer.
torturosa *adj.* torturous, excruciating.
torxa *n.* torch (*flaming*). **torxa per solda** blowtorch.
torxi *vt.* torch (*set fire to*).
torxor *n.* torchbearer.
Toscana *n.* Tuscany (*Italian region*).
tose[1] *vt.* & *n.* cough.
-tose[2] *n.suff.* -ptosis (*sagging*).
-tosia *n.suff.* -tocia (*birth*).
tosta *vt.* toast (*grill*).
tostada *adj.* toasted. • *n.* toast (*bread*).
tostador *n.* toaster.
tota *det.* all (*quantity*), the whole of; e.g. *tota la libros*; *tota la pan*; *tra tota la note*. • *adv.* all. • *pron.* all (*singular or plural*); e.g. *tota de nos*. **a tota veses** on all occasions. **en tota locas** everywhere (*collectively*). **en tota modos** by all means, in every way. **en tota partes** throughout, everywhere (*collectively*). **tota cosas** all things, everything (*collectively*). **tota de mundo** everyone, everybody. **tota no** *det.* none at all, none whatsoever. • *adv.* not at all. **totas** all (*people or things, optional plural pronoun*).
totem *n.* totem.
toxemia *n.* toxaemia (US toxemia).
toxicolojia *n.* toxicology.
toxicolojial *adj.* toxicological.
toxicolojiste *n.* toxicologist.
toxina *n.* toxin. **toxina de botulisme** botulinum toxin.
toxinia *n.* toxicity.
tra *prep.* • through; via; e.g. *acua flue tra la tubos*; *core tra la campos*; *regarda la sielo tra la fenetra*; *de Milano a Roma tra Bologna*. • throughout (*a place or period*); during, for (*an elapsed time or distance actually travelled*); e.g. *la odor es tra la vila*; *leje tra la note*; *on ia esperimenta tra du anios ante trova la solve*. **a tra** *adv.* through. **tra cuando** as long as, so long as. **tra la dia** all day, all the time, continually. **tra la vive** lifelong.
tracea *n.* trachea, windpipe.
traceotomia *n.* tracheotomy.
Tracia *n.* Thrace (*ancient region*).
tradi *vt.* defect, commit treason, betray. • *n.* betrayal, treason, treachery, perfidy; sellout.
tradision *n.* tradition.
tradisional *adj.* traditional, conservative, folksy.
tradisionalisme *n.* traditionalism.
tradisionaliste *n.* traditionalist.
trador *n.* traitor, defector, recreant, quisling.
tradosa *adj.* treasonous, treacherous, perfidious.
traduable *adj.* translatable.
traduador *n.* automatic translator, machine translation system.
tradui *vt.* translate. • *n.* translation. **tradui prestada** loan translation, calque.
traduor *n.* translator.
trae *vt.* bring, deliver, convey. • *n.* delivery.
trafica *vi.* circulate. • *vt.* & *n.* traffic.
traficor *n.* trafficker. **traficor de armas** gunrunner.

tragon *n.* tarragon, estragon (*plant: Artemisia dracunculus*).
tragulo *n.* chevrotain, mouse deer (*Tragulidae*).
trajedia *n.* tragedy.
trajedial *adj.* tragic.
trajicomedia *n.* tragicomedy.
trajicomedial *adj.* tragicomic.
tram *n.* trolley car, tram, streetcar. **tram volante** cable car.
tram-bus *n.* trolleybus.
trama *vt.* texture; shade, shade in, crosshatch; plot (*story*). • *n.* weft, woof, texture; plot (*story*).
trampolin *n.* trampoline, springboard. **trampolin de tufa** diving board.
tramvia *n.* tramway.
trans- *pref.* trans- (*across*).
transatlantica *adj.* transatlantic.
transcontinental *adj.* transcontinental.
transcrive *vt.* transcribe. • *n.* transcription, transcript.
transduador *n.* transducer.
transdui *vt.* transduce. • *n.* transduction.
transe *n.* trance.
transende *vt.* transcend. • *n.* transcendence.
transendentalisme *n.* transcendentalism.
transendente *adj.* transcendent, transcendental.
transesal *adj.* & *n.* transsexual.
transesalia *n.* transsexuality.
transetador *n.* transceiver.
transfemin *adj.* transfeminine.
transfobia *n.* transphobia.
transfobica *adj.* transphobic. • *n.* transphobe.
transfusa *vt.* transfuse. • *n.* transfusion.
Transilvania *n.* Transylvania.
transistor *n.* transistor.
transita *vt.* & *n.* transit.
transitiva *adj.* transitive.
transitivia *n.* transitivity.
transjenero *adj.* transgender. • *n.* transgender person.
transmaral *adj.* transoceanic.
transmasin *adj.* transmasculine.
transmetador *n.* transmitter.
transmete *vt.* transmit (*signal, power, etc.*), broadcast. • *n.* transmission, broadcast.
transmetente *adj.* transmitting.
transparente *adj.* transparent, see-through; open (*government*). • *n.* transparency (*for projection*).
transparentia *n.* transparency.
transpasifica *adj.* transpacific.
transpira *vt.* transpire. • *n.* transpiration.
transplanta *vt.* transplant. • *n.* transplantation.
transpondador *n.* transponder.
transponde *vt.* transpond.
transpone *vt.* transpose. • *n.* transposition.
transporta *vt.* transport, convey; carry, harbour (US harbor) (*disease*). • *n.* transport, transportation. **transporta par avion** transport by air, airlift.
transportador *n.* conveyor, transporter.
transportor *n.* transporter, carrier, courier (*person*). **transportores** carrier, courier (*company*).
transuma *vt.* seasonally move (*livestock*). • *n.* transhumance.
transumante *adj.* transhumant.
transvesti *vt.* cross-dress. • *n.* cross-dressing, transvestism, transvestitism.
transvestida *adj.* cross-dressed, in drag. • *n.* cross-dresser, transvestist, transvestite.
trapa *n.* trap, snare, pitfall; catch, snag (*hidden problem*). **trapa de arena** sand trap, bunker (*golf*).
trapezio *adj.* trapezial, trapezoidal. • *n.* trapezium, trapezoid; trapeze.
trapezior *n.* trapeze artist.
trapezoide *n.* trapezoid.
trapi *vt.* trap, ensnare, snag, corner; strand, maroon; jam, stick (*mechanism*).
trapida *adj.* trapped, ensnared; stranded, marooned; jammed, stuck. **trapida par neva** snowbound.
trapimosca *n.* flypaper, fly ribbon.
trapitota *n.* catchall, ragbag (*miscellaneous category*).
trapo *n.* rag. **trapo de polvo** duster, dustrag.
trapor *n.* trapper.
traposa *adj.* ragged, raggedy, dressed in rags.
trasa *vt.* trace (*outline*); graph. • *n.* tracing; trace, track, trail, spoor, clue. **lasa un trasa** leave a track, leave a trail. **perde trasa de** lose track of. **segue la trasa de** track, follow the track of. **segue un trasa** track, follow a track. **sin un trasa** without a trace. **teni trasa de** keep track of. **trasa de dito** fingerprint.
trasable *adj.* traceable.
trasador *n.* tracer.
traseria *n.* tracery (*architecture*).
traste *n.* fret (*of musical instrument*).
trata *vt.* treat, process; deal with, cover (*a topic*). • *n.* treatment; treaty, pact; deal (*trade*). **trata con medisin** medicate. **trata de uni** act of union. **trata prima** prioritize, put first, make a priority, fast-track.
tratable *adj.* treatable, operable, tractable.
tratablia *n.* tractability.
trateria *n.* processing plant. **trateria de acua** waterworks.

trator *n.* tractor.
trauma *vt.* traumatize. • *n.* trauma.
traumal *adj.* traumatic.
traversa *vt.* cross, go across, traverse, ford; transition; sweep through. • *n.* crossing (*action*), traversal, transition. **traversa nonlegal** cross illegally, jaywalk.
traversal *adj.* cross-, transverse. • *n.* crosspiece; transept.
traversante *adj.* crossing, traversing. • *prep.* crossing, across.
tre *det.* three. • *adj.* third (*ordinal*). • *pref.* great-great-(*grandparent*). **a tre veses** thrice.
trealosa *n.* trehalose (*sugar*).
treava *n.* great-great-grandmother.
treavi *n.* great-great-grandparent.
treavo *n.* great-great-grandfather.
tredes *det.* thirty. • *adj.* thirtieth (*ordinal*). **tredes-alga** *det.* thirty-something. • *adj.* thirty-somethingth (*ordinal*).
tredesi *n.* thirtieth (*fraction*).
trefolia *n.* clover, trefoil (*Trifolium*); cloverleaf; club (*cards*).
trejemelo *adj.* & *n.* triplet.
trelis *n.* truss (*architecture*).
trema *vi.* tremble, shiver, shudder, quiver, quail, quake. • *n.* quake, tremor; tremolo.
tremante *adj.* trembling, quivering, tremulous, tremulent, tremorous, aflutter, aquiver.
tremateria *n.* earthquake.
trematodo *n.* trematode, fluke (*worm*: *Trematoda*).
tremeta *vi.* & *n.* quiver, wobble, jiggle.
tren *n.* train. **tren lenta** slow train, local train. **tren rapida** fast train, express train, express.
treneta[1] *n.* great-great-granddaughter.
treneta[2] *n.* toboggan (*simple sledge*).
trenete *n.* great-great-grandchild.
treneto *n.* great-great-grandson.
treni *vt.* ship (*transport by train*).
treno *n.* sledge, sled, sleigh. **treno de canes** dogsled, dog sleigh. **treno de tre cavalos** three-horse sled, troika.
trensa *vt.* braid, plait, interlace. • *n.* braid, plait. **trensas african** cornrows (*hairstyle*).
trenseta *n.* pigtail (*plaited*).
trepa *vt.* clamber, scramble, climb. • *n.* climbing. **trepa de montanias** mountain climbing, mountaineering.
trepante *adj.* climbing (*including plants*).
trepede *adj.* tripedal, tripodal. • *n.* tripod, trivet.
trepor *n.* climber, mountaineer.
trepunto *n.* ellipsis, dot-dot-dot.
tresobrin *n.* cousin of one's great-grandchildren's generation.
tresobrina *n.* female cousin of one's great-grandchildren's generation.
tresobrino *n.* male cousin of one's great-grandchildren's generation.
tretia [tre'tia] *n.* female cousin of one's great-grandparents' generation.
tretie *n.* cousin of one's great-grandparents' generation.
tretio [tre'tio] *n.* male cousin of one's great-grandparents' generation.
tri[1] *vi.* split into three. • *n.* third (*fraction*).
tri-[2] *pref.* tri- (*three*).
triaje *n.* triage.
trianguli *vt.* triangulate. • *n.* triangulation.
triangulo *adj.* triangular, deltoid. • *n.* triangle. **Triangulo** *n.* Triangulum (*constellation*). **Triangulo Sude** Triangulum Australe (*constellation*).
triasica *adj.* & *n.* Triassic (*geology*).
triatlon *n.* triathlon.
triatlonor *n.* triathlete.
tribal *adj.* tribal.
tribalisme *n.* tribalism.
tribu *n.* tribe. **fem de tribu** tribeswoman. **membro de tribu** tribesperson. **om de tribu** tribesman.
tribui *n.* tribute.
tribuno *n.* tribune (*Roman official, popular leader*).
tricina *n.* trichina (*worm*: *Trichinella*).
tricinose *n.* trichinosis (*medical*).
tricorno *n.* tricorn, tricorne (*hat*).
tricota *vt.* knit.
tricotada *n.* knit (*fabric*), tricot.
tricotero *n.* caddisfly (*Trichoptera*).
tricromata *adj.* trichromatic.
trictrac *n.* backgammon.
trictracor *n.* backgammon player.
tricuspide *n.* tricuspid.
tridente *n.* trident.
tridimensional *adj.* three-dimensional. • *adv.* three-dimensionally, in three dimensions.
trifle *n.* trifle (*dessert*).
triftongo *n.* triphthong (*vowel sound*).
trigliserido *n.* triglyceride (*chemistry*).
trigo *n.* wheat (*Triticum*). **trigo intera** whole wheat.
trigonometria *n.* trigonometry.
trigonometrial *adj.* trigonometric, trigonometrical.
triladal *adj.* trilateral, three-sided.
triler *n.* thriller (*novel, movie*).
trilion *det.* (*a*) trillion, a million million. • *adj.* trillionth (*ordinal*).
trilioni *vi.* split into a trillion parts. • *n.* trillionth (*fraction*).
trilojia *n.* trilogy.
trilojiste *n.* trilogist.
trimestre *n.* trimester, term.
trimetre *n.* trimeter (*poetry*).

tringa *n.* shank, tattler, sandpiper (*bird*: *Tringa*).
trinia *n.* trinity (*Christianity*).
trinial *adj.* triune.
trinialisme *n.* trinitarianism.
trinialiste *adj.* trinitarian.
Trinidad e Tobago *n.* Trinidad and Tobago.
trinidadian *adj.* & *n.* Trinidadian.
trinxa *vt.* & *n.* shred.
trinxador *n.* shredder.
tripanosoma *n.* trypanosome (*organism*).
tripanosomiase *n.* trypanosomiasis, sleeping sickness (*medical*).
tripartisan *adj.* tripartite.
-tripsia *n.suff.* -tripsy (*crushing*).
triptico *n.* triptych (*art*).
triptofan *n.* tryptophan (*amino acid*).
triremo *n.* trireme (*ship*).
-tris *n.suff.* -thrix (*hair*).
trisepe *n.* triceps (*muscle*).
triseratopo *n.* triceratops (*Triceratops*).
trisicle *n.* tricycle, trike.
triste *adj.* sad, unhappy, melancholy, sorry, heavy-hearted. **es triste sin** miss, be sad without. **tan triste** how sad, what a pity, what a shame, such a shame.
tristi *vi.* sadden.
tristia *n.* sadness, sorrow, grief, melancholy, unhappiness.
tristinte *adj.* saddening, poignant.
tristiosa *adj.* full of sadness, sorrowful, woeful, full of grief.
triton *n.* newt (*Pleurodelinae*).
trivia *n.* trivia, guff.
trivial *adj.* trivial, trifling, petty, paltry. • *n.* triviality, trifle (*something trivial*).
trivialia *n.* triviality (*quality*).
tro *adv.* too, too much, excessively. **tro multe** *det.* too many, too much, excessive, inordinate. • *adv.* too much, excessively. **tro poca** *det.* too few, too little, insufficient. • *adv.* too little, insufficiently.
troca *vt.* & *n.* barter, trade.
trocar *n.* trocar (*surgical instrument*).
troceal *adj.* trochaic.
troceo *n.* trochee (*poetry*).
trocor *n.* barterer.
trofeo *n.* trophy.
-trofia *n.suff.* -trophy (*feeding*).
-trofica *adj.suff.* -trophic.
troglodite *n.* troglodyte, caveman, cave dweller; wren (*bird*: *Troglodytidae*).
trogo *n.* trough. **trogo de batiza** baptismal font.
trogon *n.* trogon (*bird*: *Trogonidae*).
Troia *n.* Troy.
troian *adj.* & *n.* Trojan.
trol *n.* troll.
trombo *n.* thrombus, embolism, blood clot.
trombopoiese *n.* thrombopoiesis.
trombose *n.* thrombosis.
trombosite *n.* thrombocyte, platelet.
trompa *n.* horn (*musical instrument*), French horn, trump; trunk (*elephant*). **trompa acual** waterspout. **trompa de Eustacio** Eustachian tube, auditory tube. **trompa de Triton** triton, Triton's trumpet, Triton snail (*Charonia*). **trompa de utero** Fallopian tube.
trompeta *n.* trumpet.
trompetin *adj.* trumpetlike, trumpet-shaped.
trompetiste *n.* trumpeter.
trompetor *n.* trumpeter (*bird*: *Psophia*).
trompi *vt.* trumpet, bray.
trompon *n.* trombone.
tronceta *n.* stem, stalk.
troncetin *adj.* stalklike.
tronco *n.* trunk (*log*, *torso*); fuselage; frustum (*geometry*); stem (*of word*).
troni *vt.* enthrone.
trono *n.* throne.
tropeza *vi.* stumble, trip, trip over, trip up. • *vt.* trip, trip up, cause to stumble. • *n.* stumble, trip. **tropeza de lingua** stumble over one's words, trip over one's tongue.
tropical *adj.* tropical.
tropico *n.* tropic. **Tropico de la Capra** Tropic of Capricorn. **Tropico de la Crabe** Tropic of Cancer.
tropisme *n.* tropism.
troposfera *n.* troposphere.
trota *vi.* & *n.* trot.
troteria *n.* sidewalk, pavement.
trova *vt.* find. • *n.* find, discovery. **trova acaso** accidentally find, come across, stumble upon. **trova se** find oneself; be situated.
trovable *adj.* discoverable, to be found.
truci *vt.* trick.
trucia *n.* trickery.
trucioio *n.* trompe-l'oeil, optical illusion.
truco *n.* trick, ploy; gimmick, schtick; device (*literary*). **truco de majia** magic trick. **truco de mano** legerdemain. **truco perilosa** stunt.
trucor *n.* trickster. **trucor de cartas** cardsharp, cardshark.
trucosa *adj.* tricky.
trufa *n.* truffle (*Tuber* and others).
trumfo *n.* trump (*cards*).
trunca *vi.* truncate. • *n.* truncation; stump.
truncin *adj.* stumpy, squat.
truple *adj.* triple. • *adv.* triply, thrice. • *n.* trio, triad; troika; triumvirate.
truta *n.* trout (*Salmo*, *Oncorhynchus*).
tsar *n.* tsar, czar.
tsaresa *n.* tsarina, czarina.

tsaria *n.* tsardom, czardom.
Tsernagora *n.* Montenegro. See *Montenegro.*
tsernagorsce *adj.* & *n.* Montenegrin.
tsetse *n.* tsetse fly (*Glossina*).
tsuana *adj.* & *n.* Botswanan (*person*), Tswana (*language*). See *Botsuana.*
tsuga *n.* tsuga, hemlock (*tree*: *Tsuga*). **tsuga de Douglas** Douglas fir (*Pseudotsuga*).
tsunami *n.* tsunami.
tu *pron.* you (*singular*).
tua *det.* your (*singular*). **la tua** yours.
tuatara *n.* tuatara (*reptile*: *Sphenodon*).
tuba *n.* tuba (*musical instrument*).
tubal *adj.* tubal.
tuber *n.* tuber (*biology*).
tuberculo *n.* tubercle, apophysis (*biology*).
tuberculose *n.* tuberculosis, TB, consumption.
tuberculosica *adj.* tuberculous, tubercular.
tuberosa *adj.* tuberous.
tubeta *n.* tubule.
tubo *adj.* tubular. • *n.* tube, pipe (*conduit*), channel. **sin tubo** tubeless. **tubo catodal** cathode ray tube. **tubo de acua** water pipe. **tubo de aira** inner tube. **tubo de drena** drainpipe, rainspout, waterspout. **tubo de emetador** exhaust pipe, tailpipe. **tubo de pipa** pipestem. **tubo de proba** test tube. **tubo U** U-bend, U-tube. **tubo vacuida** vacuum tube. **tubos** tubes, pipes, plumbing, pipework.
tubon *n.* large pipe, pipeline.
tucana *n.* toucan (*Ramphastidae*). **Tucana** *n.* Tucana (*constellation*).
tucotuco *n.* tuco-tuco (*rodent*: *Ctenomys*).
tudor *adj.* Tudor.
tufa[1] *vi.* dive, plunge, swoop. • *vt.* dive, plunge, dunk. • *n.* dive, nosedive, swoop, plunge, dunk. **tufa de anjel** swan dive, swallow dive. **tufa libre** *v.* skindive. • *n.* skindiving. **tufa per perlas** *v.* dive for pearls. • *n.* pearl diving.
tufa[2] *n.* tufa, tuff (*rock*).
tufor *n.* diver (*sport*).
tuia ['tuja] *n.* thuja, arborvitae (*tree*: *Thuja*).
tuid [twid] *n.* tweed (*fabric*). **de tuid** tweed.
tuist [twist] *n.* twist (*dance*).
tuita ['twita] *vt.* & *n.* tweet (*Twitter*).
tulio *n.* thulium (*element*).
tulpa *n.* tulip (*Tulipa*).
tumor *n.* tumour (US tumor). **tumor fibrosa** fibroid.
tumorosa *adj.* tumorous.
tumulo *n.* tumulus, barrow, burial mound, kurgan.
tumulta *n.* tumult, riot, uproar, turmoil, mayhem, mêlée, social chaos.
tumultosa *adj.* tumultuous, riotous, chaotic, uproarious.
tun *n.* tuna (*Thunnus*). **tun blanca** albacore, bonito, longfin tuna (*Thunnus alalunga*).
tundra *n.* tundra.
tunel *n.* tunnel, burrow. **tunel carpal** carpal tunnel. **Tunel su la Manga** Channel Tunnel, Chunnel, Eurotunnel.
tuneli *vt.* tunnel, burrow.
tungus *adj.* & *n.* Tungus, Tungusic (*person*, *language*).
Tunis *n.* Tunisia; Tunis (*city*). **Golfo Tunis** Gulf of Tunis.
tunisi *adj.* & *n.* Tunisian.
tupaia *n.* tree shrew (*Scandentia*).
tupelo *n.* tupelo, pepperidge tree (*Nyssa*).
tupi *adj.* & *n.* Tupi (*person*, *language*).
turaco *n.* turaco (*bird*: *Musophagidae*).
turba *vt.* disturb, shake up, stir up, churn up, roil; upset, agitate, distress, cause anxiety to, cause pain to, trouble, harrow. • *n.* trouble, difficulty, unrest; mischief, shenanigans; turbulence. **sin turba** undisturbed. **turba la tera** dig the soil, turn the soil. See *disturba.*
turbable *adj.* disturbable, agitable, capable of getting upset.
turbada *adj.* disturbed, troubled; upset, distraught.
turban *n.* turban.
turbante *adj.* troubling, troublesome, disturbing.
turbina *n.* turbine. **turbina de venta** wind turbine, wind generator, wind power unit, wind energy converter, aerogenerator.
turbosa *adj.* troublesome, naughty, mischievous, impish, rambunctious, rowdy, unruly; turbulent; heavy, rough, choppy (*sea*). • *n.* rascal, scamp, rapscallion, imp, brat, hellion, roughneck, troublemaker.
turbosia *n.* naughtiness, mischief, rambunctiousness.
turces *adj.* & *n.* Turkish.
turcesa *adj.* turquoise (*colour*). • *n.* turquoise (*gem*).
Turcia *n.* Turkey.
turcica *adj.* Turkic (*languages*).
turcmen *adj.* & *n.* Turkmen, Turkmenistani (*person*, *language*).
Turcmenistan *n.* Turkmenistan.
turdo *n.* thrush (*Turdidae*). **turdo roja** American robin (*Turdus migratorius*).
turi *vt.* tour; cruise; go for a ride, take a drive, drive around. • *n.* tour, ride, drive, cruise, excursion, jaunt, junket. **turi a mar** ocean cruise, sea cruise. **turi de bares** pub crawl, bar hop. **turi en caro de fero** hayride. **turi la atraes** tour the attractions, see the sights, sightsee, go sightseeing.
turisme *n.* tourism.
turiste *n.* tourist.

Turkana, Lago *n.* Lake Turkana.
turmalina *n.* tourmaline (*mineral*).
turna *vi.* turn (*to face a new direction*); revolve; e.g. *la parlor turna dramosa.* • *vt.* turn (*something*); careen (*ship*); e.g. *turna un manico; turna se en leto.* • *n.* turn. **turna e returna** toss and turn, turn back and forth. See *jira, verje.*
turnabroca *n.* gimlet.
turnador *n.* lathe.
turnavise *n.* screwdriver. **turnavise crusin** crosshead screwdriver, Phillips-head screwdriver.
turnix *n.* button quail (*bird*: *Turnicidae*).
turno *n.* shift (*work*); turn (*game*). **fa sua turno** do one's shift; take one's turn.
turnor *n.* shiftworker.
turon *n.* turron, torrone (*confectionery*).
tut *n.* & *interj.* toot, hoot, parp.
tuti *vi.* toot, hoot, parp.
tutsi *adj.* & *n.* Tutsi.
Tuvalu *n.* Tuvalu. **tuvalu** *adj.* & *n.* Tuvaluan.
tv *abbr.* (*televisa, televisador*) TV, telly.
txa *interj.* damn, blast, bugger, shit, fuck (*frustration, anger*).
txacra *n.* chakra (*Buddhism, Hinduism*).
Txad *n.* Chad.
txadi *adj.* & *n.* Chadian.
txadica *adj.* Chadic.
txador *n.* chador (*cloak*).
txapareras *n.pl.* chaps (*leggings*).
txapsui *n.* chop suey.
txarango *n.* charango (*guitar*).
txarci *n.* jerky (*food*).
txatni *n.* chutney (*food*).
txatxatxa [tʃatʃaˈtʃa] *n.* cha-cha-cha (*dance, music*).
txau *interj.* (*colloquial*) ciao (*arriving or departing*); hi, yo, goodbye, bye, see you, ta-ta.
txaumen *n.* chow mein, stir-fried noodles.
txedar *n.* cheddar (*cheese*).
txesce *adj.* & *n.* Czech.
Txesco *n.* Czech Republic, Czechia.
txescoslovensce *adj.* & *n.* Czechoslovakian.
Txescoslovensco *n.* Czechoslovakia.
txetxen *adj.* & *n.* Chechen.
Txetxnia *n.* Chechnya.
txi *n.* chi, qi, life energy, life force.
txia *n.* chia (*plant*: *Salvia hispanica*).
txilan *adj.* & *n.* Chilean.
Txile *n.* Chile. **Mar Txile** Chile Sea.
txili *n.* chilli (US chili) pepper, chile, hot pepper (*Capsicum*). **salsa de txili** chilli (US chili) sauce, hot sauce. **txili con carne** chilli (US chili) con carne. **txili polvida** chilli (US chili) powder.
txin *adj.* Qin, Ch'in (*dynasty*).
txing *adj.* Qing, Ch'ing (*dynasty*).
txintxila *n.* chinchilla (*rodent*: *Chinchilla*).
txipotle *n.* chipotle (*pepper*).
txoriso *n.* chorizo (*sausage*).
Txoson *n.* North Korea. **txoson** *adj.* & *n.* North Korean. See *Corea Norde.*
txucot *adj.* & *n.* Chukot, Chukchi (*person, language*).
Txucotca *n.* Chukotka, Chukchi Peninsula. **Mar Txucotca** Chukchi Sea.

U

U[1] [u], **u** *letter* U, u.
u[2] *adj.* & *n.* Wu (*language*).
u[3] *interj.* ooh, wow.
ua *interj.* wah (*baby crying*).
uacari *n.* uakari (*monkey*: *Cacajao*).
uadi *n.* wadi (*valley*).
uafel *n.* waffle (*food*).
ualabi *n.* wallaby (*Macropodidae*).
ualon *adj.* & *n.* Walloon.
Ualonia *n.* Wallonia.
uampum *n.* wampum (*beads*).
uapiti *n.* elk (*US*), wapiti (*Cervus canadensis*).
uarfarin *n.* warfarin (*drug*).
uasabi *n.* wasabi (*plant, sauce*: *Wasabia japonica*).
uau-uau *interj.* woof, bow-wow (*dog*).
uaua *n.* wah-wah (*music*).
Ucraina *n.* Ukraine.
ucrainsce *adj.* & *n.* Ukrainian (*person, language*).
uculele *n.* ukulele (*guitar*).
ueb *adj.* & *n.* web (*internet*).
uergeld *n.* wergeld, weregild (*payment system*).
ueste *adj.* west, western, occidental. • *n.* west, occident. **a ueste** westward, westwards. **a ueste de** to the west of. **ueste-norde-ueste** *adj.* west-northwest. **ueste-sentral** *adj.* central west. **ueste-sude-ueste** *adj.* west-southwest.
uesti *vi.* & *vt.* westernize. • *n.* westernization.
Uganda *n.* Uganda. See *luganda*.
ugandan *adj.* & *n.* Ugandan.
ugonote *n.* Huguenot.
ugrica *adj.* Ugric (*languages*).
ui *interj.* whee, whoopee.
uica *n.* Wicca (*religion*).
uican *adj.* & *n.* Wiccan.
uiguam *n.* wigwam, wickiup, wetu.
uigur [wiˈgur] *adj.* & *n.* Uyghur, Uighur (*person, language*).
uija [ˈwiʒa] *n.* ouija board.
uin *n.* wynn (*Latin letter* Ƿ, ƿ).
uipet *n.* whippet (*dog*).
uisce *n.* whisky, whiskey.
uist *n.* whist (*card game*).
uistiti *n.* marmoset (*monkey*: *Callithrix*).
ulex *n.* gorse, furze (*plant*: *Ulex*).
ulna *n.* ulna (*anatomy*).
ulong *n.* oolong (*tea*).
ulsera *vi.* & *vt.* ulcerate. • *n.* ulcer, sore, ulceration. **ulsera de leto** bedsore. **ulsera jelal** frostbite.
ulserada *adj.* ulcerated, frostbitten.
ulsereta *n.* canker sore, aphthous ulcer.
ultima *adj.* ultimate (*final or most extreme*), last; utmost, prime; eventual. • *adv.* ultimately, eventually, after all. **cuasi ultima** penultimate, second from last, last but one. **du ante la ultima** antepenultimate, third from last, last but two.
ultra *prep.* • beyond, past, across, on the other side of; more than, further than, farther than, exceeding; e.g. *la eglesa es ultra la ponte*; *un taxe ultra mea capasia*; *viaja ultra la rapidia de sona*. • (*moving*) to beyond, to the other side of, across; e.g. *viaja ultra la montes*. • *pref.* ultra-. **a ultra** *prep.* (*moving*) to beyond, to the other side of, across; e.g. *remi un barceta a ultra la lago*. • *adv.* beyond.
ultramar *adj.* overseas.
ultraortodox *adj.* ultraorthodox.
ultrasona *n.* ultrasound.
ultrasonal *adj.* ultrasonic.
ultravioleta *adj.* & *n.* ultraviolet.
ulula *vt.* & *n.* howl, wail.
umaian *adj.* Umayyad, Omayyad (*dynasty*).
umami *n.* umami (*flavour*).
Uman *n.* Oman. **Golfo Uman** Gulf of Oman.
umana *adj.* human. • *n.* human, human being, person. **umanas** humans, humanity, mankind, people.
umani[1] *adj.* & *n.* Omani.
umani[2] *vi.* & *vt.* humanize, anthropomorphize. • *n.* humanization, anthropomorphism.
umania *n.* humanity (*quality*).
umanin *adj.* humanlike, humanoid, anthropoid.
umanisme *n.* humanism.
umaniste *adj.* & *n.* humanitarian, humanist.
umbreta *n.* hammerkop, hammerhead stork, anvilhead (*bird*: *Scopus umbretta*).
Umbria *n.* Umbria (*Italian region*).
umbrian *adj.* & *n.* Umbrian (*person, language*).
umida *adj.* damp, moist, wet; humid (*air*), clammy, close, muggy, sultry.
umidador *n.* humidifier; humidor (*tobacco box*).
umidi *vi.* & *vt.* dampen, moisten, humidify.
umidia *n.* dampness, moisture, wetness, humidity.
umidistato *n.* humidistat.
umil *adj.* humble, modest (*humble*), meek, mild, unassuming, unpretentious, demure.
umili *vi.* & *vt.* humble.
umilia *n.* humility, modesty.
umlaut *n.* umlaut.
umo *n.* humus, mulch (*soil*).

umor *n.* humour (US humor), temper, mood; bodily fluid (*historical*). **bon umor** good mood, good spirits. **de bon umor** in a good mood, cheerful, jovial, light-hearted, sanguine. **de mal umor** in a bad mood, sulking, sulky, sullen, brooding, morose. **de umor variable** moody. **mal umor** bad mood, sulk, snit.
umoriste *n.* humorist.
umorosa *adj.* humorous.
umus *n.* hummus (*food*).
un *det.* a, an, one. • *adj.* first.
Ungaria *n.* Hungary. See *Magiar.*
ungarian *adj.* & *n.* Hungarian.
Ungava, Baia *n.* Ungava Bay.
ungia *n.* nail. **ungia de dito** fingernail. **ungia de pede** toenail.
ungula *n.* hoof.
ungulato *n.* ungulate (*Ungulata*).
uni[1] *vi.* & *vt.* unite, unify. • *n.* union (*action*), unification; union (*result*), coalition, consortium. **Uni de Republicas Sosialistes Soviet** Union of Soviet Socialist Republics. **Uni European** European Union. **Uni Soviet** Soviet Union.
uni-[2] *pref.* uni- (*one*).
unia[1] *n.* unit (*of a larger whole, of measurement*); monad. **unia comersial** commercial unit (*of goods*). **unia de mone** unit of currency.
unia[2] *n.* oneness, solidarity, integrity, unity.
unial *adj.* unitary.
unica *adj.* unique, sole, single, one-off, exclusive, idiosyncratic, inimitable. • *n.* exclusive (*news story*).
unicorno *n.* unicorn. **Unicorno** *n.* Monoceros (*constellation*).
unida *adj.* united, unified. • *adv.* together.
unidimensional *adj.* one-dimensional.
unidiste *adj.* & *n.* unionist.
uniforma *adj.* uniform, unitary, regular. • *n.* uniform (*dress*), livery.
uniformi *vi.* become uniform. • *vt.* make uniform; dress in uniform.
uniformia *n.* uniformity.
uniforminte *adj.* uniforming, procrustean.
uniladal *adj.* unilateral; unrequited.
uniselulal *adj.* unicellular.
unisesal *adj.* unisex.
unitarian *adj.* & *n.* Unitarian.
unitarianisme *n.* Unitarianism (*Christianity*).
univalente *adj.* univalent (*biology*).
universal *adj.* universal; cosmic.
universalisme *n.* universalism (*philosophy, Christianity*).
universaliste *adj.* & *n.* universalist.
universia *n.* university, college, varsity. **universia de diploma** alma mater.
universo *n.* universe, cosmos.
unje *vt.* anoint. • *n.* anointing, unction.
unjente *n.* unguent, ointment, pomade, lotion.
unsial *adj.* uncial (*lettering*).
uoc *n.* wok (*pan*).
uolfram *n.* tungsten, wolfram (*element*).
uolof *adj.* & *n.* Wolof (*person, language*).
uombata *n.* wombat (*Vombatidae*).
uon *n.* won (*currency*).
uonton *n.* wonton (*food*).
upanixad *n.* upanishad (*scripture*).
uple[1] *n.* tuple (*mathematics*); record, struct (*software*).
-uple[2] *adj.suff.* -uple (*numeric multiple*); e.g. *duple, truple, cuatruple.* • *n.suff.* (*group of a specified number of members*).
upsilon *n.* upsilon (*Greek letter* Υ, υ).
ura [uˈra] *interj.* hooray, hurrah, whoopee.
Ural, Montes *n.pl.* Ural Mountains.
uralica *adj.* Uralic (*languages*).
uranio *n.* uranium.
Urano *n.* Uranus (*mythology, planet*).
urato *n.* urate (*chemistry*). **urato de sodio** sodium urate, chalkstone.
urban *adj.* urban, metropolitan. • *n.* city dweller, urbanite.
urbani *vi.* & *vt.* urbanize, citify. • *n.* urbanization.
urbanisme *n.* city planning.
urbaniste *n.* city planner.
urbe *n.* urban area, city area, metropolis. See *site.*
urbolojia *n.* urbanology.
urbolojiste *n.* urbanologist.
urdu *adj.* & *n.* Urdu (*language*).
Urdun *n.* Jordan.
urduni *adj.* & *n.* Jordanian.
urea *n.* urea (*substance*).
uremia *n.* uraemia (US uremia) (*medical*).
uretan *n.* urethane (*substance*).
ureter *n.* ureter (*anatomy*).
uretra *n.* urethra (*anatomy*).
uria[1] *n.* guillemot, murre (*bird: Uria*).
-uria[2] *n.suff.* -uria (*urine*).
urica *adj.* uric (*urine*). • *adj.suff.* -uric.
urieta *n.* murrelet (*bird: Synthliboramphus, Brachyramphus*).
urina *n.* urine.
urinal *adj.* urinary.
urinalise *vt.* urinalyse. • *n.* urinalysis.
urini *vt.* urinate, micturate. • *n.* urination, micturation.
urje *vt.* urge, exhort. • *n.* urge, exhortation.
urjente *adj.* urgent, pressing. • *n.* emergency.
uro *n.* aurochs (*ox: Bos primigenius*).
urolito *n.* urolith, bladder stone.
urolojia *n.* urology.
urolojiste *n.* urologist.
urseta *n.* bear cub.
ursin *adj.* bearlike, ursine.

urso *n.* bear (*Ursidae*). **urso blanca** polar bear. **urso-de-acua** *n.* water bear (*Tardigrada*). **urso de pelux** teddy bear, teddy. **Urso Grande** Ursa Major (*constellation*). **urso gris** grizzly bear. **Urso Peti** Ursa Minor (*constellation*).

URSS *abbr.* (*Uni de Republicas Sosialiste Soviet*) USSR.

urticaria *n.* urticaria, hives (*rash*).

Uruguai *n.* Uruguay.

uruguaia *adj.* & *n.* Uruguayan.

usa *vt.* use, utilize; apply, employ (*force*, *tool*, *method*); wear (*clothes*). • *n.* use, employment, purpose, application; uptake. **comensa usa** start using, take up. **de usa sever** heavy-duty. **usa tro multe** overuse.

usable *adj.* usable.

usada *adj.* used, secondhand. **tro usada** overused, hackneyed, clichéd.

usor *n.* user. **usor de rede** internet user, netizen.

usosa *adj.* useful, utilitarian, purposeful.

usosia *n.* usefulness, utility.

usual *adj.* usual, customary. • *adv.* usually, customarily.

usufruta *n.* usufruct (*right*).

usura *n.* usury.

usuror *n.* usurer, loanshark.

usurosa *adj.* usurous.

usurpa *vt.* usurp.

usurpor *n.* usurper.

Utah ['juta] *n.* Utah (*US state*).

utero *n.* uterus, womb.

utia *n.* hutia (*rodent: Capromyidae*).

util *n.* tool, utensil, implement. **furni utiles nova a** retool. **util de cosini** cooking implement, kitchen utensil. **util de scrive** writing implement. **utiles de arjento** silverware. **utiles de come** cutlery, flatware, eating utensils.

utilitarisme *n.* utilitarianism.

utilitariste *adj.* & *n.* utilitarian.

utopia *n.* utopia.

utopial *adj.* utopian.

utopisme *n.* utopianism.

utopiste *n.* utopian.

u-u *interj.* coo (*pigeon*); twit-twoo, hoo, hoot (*owl*).

uva *n.* grape. **uva seca** raisin, currant.

uvea *adj.* & *n.* Wallisian.

uvo *n.* grape vine (*Vitis*).

uvula *n.* uvula.

uvulal *adj.* uvular. • *n.* uvular (*consonant*).

uzbec *adj.* & *n.* Uzbek, Uzbekistani (*person*, *language*).

Uzbecistan *n.* Uzbekistan.

uzo *n.* ouzo (*drink*).

V

V[1] [ve], **ve** *letter* V, v.
v[2] *abbr.* (*vide*) see.
v[3] *abbr.* (*volum*) vol.
va *adv.* (*preverbal*) (*indicating that a finite verb is in the future tense*) will, shall; e.g. *me va aida tu*; *me ia dise ce me va aida tu*.
vacanse *vi.* vacation, holiday, be on leave, go on leave. • *n.* vacation, holiday, leave, getaway.
vacanseria *n.* vacation spot, resort.
vacansor *n.* vacationer, holidaymaker, holiday traveller (US traveler).
vacua *adj.* empty, hollow, null, void, vacuous. • *n.* vacancy, void; vacuum.
vacui *vi.* empty. • *vt.* empty, evacuate, flush; clear, wipe, erase. • *n.* emptying, evacuation.
vacuia *n.* emptiness, vacuity.
vacuida *adj.* emptied, vacant.
vacuol *n.* vacuole (*biology*).
vada *vi.* wade, paddle.
vade *vi.* go; (*system*) work, function. • *interj.* go, let's go, come on, giddy-up. **como lo vade?** how are you?, how's it going? **vade a** go to, attend (*regularly*). **vade a fa** be just about to do, be just on the point of doing. **vade en dirije a** go towards, head for, make for. **vade par auto** go by car. **vade par pasea** go by foot. **vade per compra** go shopping. **vade per pasea** go for a walk. **vade per vide** go and see, go to see. **vade sur sua via** make one's way. **vade sur un via** take a road, travel a path. **vade tro rapida** speed, commit a speeding offence (US offense).
vaderia *n.* paddling pool, wading pool.
vadi *vt.* ford, cross.
vado *n.* ford, crossing.
vaga *vi.* wander, roam, rove, ramble, traipse, drift, digress, mill around, perambulate; browse (*books*, *goods*). • *n.* wandering, digression. **vaga depresada** mope about. **vaga furtiva** prowl.
vagabon *n.* vagabond, vagrant, hobo, bum, tramp. **vagabon enebriada** wino.
vagabonia *n.* vagrancy.
vagador *n.* rover (*vehicle*).
vagante *adj.* wandering, adrift, errant; itinerant, mobile, peripatetic; stray (*animal*); crooked (*shape*); discursive, rambling.
vagisme *n.* nomadism.
vagiste *n.* nomad.
vago *n.* vagus (*anatomy*).
vagon *n.* wagon, wain; coach, car, carriage (*of train*); trailer (*of truck*). **vagon de bagaje** baggage car. **vagon de carga** freight wagon, boxcar. **vagon de dormi** sleeping car, sleeper. **vagon final** caboose. **vagon restorante** dining car, restaurant car.
vagonor *n.* wagoner, teamster.
vagor *n.* wanderer, drifter, rambler, itinerant.
vajina *n.* vagina.
vajinal *adj.* vaginal.
vajinite *n.* vaginitis (*medical*).
vajraiana *adj.* Vajrayana (*Buddhism*).
valah *adj.* & *n.* Vlach, Wallachian.
Valahia *n.* Wallachia (*Romanian region*).
valciria *n.* Valkyrie (*mythology*).
vale *n.* valley, vale, dale. **a vale** down, downhill, downstream, downward, downwards.
Valensia *n.* Valencia (*Spanish region*).
valente *adj.* valent.
valentia *n.* valence, valency.
valeriana *n.* valerian (*plant*: *Valeriana officinalis*).
valeta *n.* dell, glen.
valga *adj.* & *n.* valgus (*medical*).
Valhala *n.* Valhalla.
valida *adj.* valid, well-founded, cogent; current, in effect.
validi *vi.* & *vt.* validate, ratify, endorse, certify, notarize, probate. • *n.* validation, ratification, endorsement, certification, probate.
validia *n.* validity.
valis *n.* suitcase, valise.
valiseta *n.* carry-on suitcase, handheld luggage.
valison *n.* trunk, portmanteau.
valsa *vi.* & *n.* waltz.
valua *vt.* value, prize. • *n.* value, worth, merit; equity, stock (*financial*). **sin valua** worthless, valueless, pissant.
valuada *adj.* worthy, valued, valuable, meritorious, fine. **es valuada** be worth, be valuable, have value. **la plu valuada** most valuable, inestimable. **valuadas** valuables, riches.
valuosa *adj.* valuable, precious. **valuosas** valuables, riches.
valva *n.* valve; tap, faucet, spigot. **valva de banio** bath tap, bath faucet. **valva de securia** safety valve.
vampir *n.* vampire.
vana *adj.* vain, conceited.
vanadio *n.* vanadium (*element*).
vandal *adj.* Vandalic. • *n.* Vandal (*ancient tribe*); vandal, hooligan.
vandali *vt.* vandalize.
vandalisme *n.* vandalism.

vanelo *n.* lapwing (*bird*: *Vanellinae*).
vanga *n.* vanga (*bird*: *Vangidae*).
vangarda *adj.* avant-garde, vanguard, cutting-edge, latest.
vani *vt.* fan.
vania *n.* vanity.
vanilia *n.* vanilla (*plant*, *flavour*: *Vanilla*).
vanilina *n.* vanillin (*substance*).
vanin *adj.* fanlike, fan-shaped.
vano *n.* fan (*handheld*).
vanta *vt.* & *n.* boast, brag. **vanta a se** gloat, revel.
vantaje *n.* advantage, privilege, benefit, lead.
vantaji *vt.* advantage, privilege, benefit.
vantajosa *adj.* advantageous, opportune.
vantor *n.* boaster, braggart, loudmouth, show-off.
vantosa *adj.* boastful.
Vanuatu *n.* Vanuatu. **vanuatu** *adj.* & *n.* Vanuatuan.
vapor *n.* vapour (US vapor), mist, steam. **vapor nosiva** toxic mist, fumes.
vaporador *n.* vaporizer, nebulizer, evaporator, steamer.
vapori *vi.* evaporate, vaporize; steam (*turn to steam*). • *vt.* evaporate, vaporize; steam (*apply steam to*). • *n.* evaporation.
vaporosa *adj.* steamy, misty, misted.
vara *adj.* & *n.* varus (*medical*).
varano *n.* monitor lizard (*Varanus*).
varia *vi.* & *vt.* vary, range. • *n.* variation, variety, variance, vagary; version, variant; (*in mathematics*) manifold. **varia diferensiable** differentiable manifold. **varia elejeda** cultivar.
variable *adj.* & *n.* variable.
variada *adj.* varied, variegated.
varial *adj.* varietal.
varicosa *adj.* varicose (*medical*).
variola *n.* smallpox.
variosa *adj.* various, several, diverse, sundry. See *diversa*.
varisela *n.* chickenpox.
vasal *n.* vassal, liege (*feudal*).
vasalia *n.* vassalage.
vascular *adj.* vascular.
vasculite *n.* vasculitis (*medical*).
vasectomia *n.* vasectomy (*surgery*).
vasia *n.* pottery.
vasila *vi.* vacillate, hesitate (*between two choices*), waver, falter, equivocate, prevaricate, teeter. • *n.* vacillation, hesitation, indecision.
vasilante *adj.* vacillating, hesitant, indecisive, irresolute, half-hearted.
vasin *n.* vaccine.
vasini *vt.* vaccinate, inoculate. • *n.* vaccination, inoculation.
vasinia *n.* bilberry, blueberry, huckleberry, cranberry (*Vaccinium*). **vasinia blu** blueberry, bilberry, huckleberry (*Vaccinium*). **vasinia de montania** lingonberry (*Vaccinium vitis-idaea*). **vasinia roja** cranberry (*Vaccinium oxycoccos*).
vaso *n.* vase, pot, vessel, urn. **vaso de cafe** coffeepot. **vaso de flores** flower vase. **vaso de losa** earthenware pot, crock. **vaso de note** chamberpot, potty. **vaso de peper** pepperpot. **vaso de pexes** fishbowl. **vaso de sal** salt cellar, saltbox. **vaso de sputa** spittoon. **vaso de te** teapot.
vasoconstrinje *vt.* vasoconstrict.
vasoconstrinjente *n.* vasoconstrictor, vasopressor.
vasodilata *vt.* vasodilate.
vasodilatante *n.* vasodilator.
vason *n.* toilet, toilet bowl, lavatory, loo; commode, potty. **vason urinal** urinal.
vasopresina *n.* vasopressin.
vasor *n.* potter.
vasta *adj.* vast, huge, widespread, large-scale, far-reaching. • *adv.* vastly, widely.
vasti *vi.* become vast, extend hugely, become widespread, spread far and wide. • *vt.* promulgate, spread far and wide.
vastia *n.* vastness.
vasto *n.* lap (*anatomy*).
vate *n.* watt (*unit of power*).
vatia *n.* wattage.
vatican *adj.* Vatican. **Site Vatican** Vatican City.
vea *adj.* old, elderly. • *n.* old person; elder. **deveni tro vea per** outgrow. **la plu vea** oldest, eldest. **plu vea** older, elder.
veber *n.* weber (*unit of magnetic flux*).
vecular *adj.* vehicular.
veculo *n.* vehicle. **veculo acual** watercraft. **veculo de motor** motor vehicle. **veculo funeral** hearse. **veculo madrin** mothership. **veculo spasial** spacecraft.
veda *n.* Veda (*scripture*).
vedal *adj.* Vedic.
vedanta *n.* vedanta (*Hinduism*).
vedantal *adj.* vedantic.
vegan *adj.* & *n.* vegan.
veganisme *n.* veganism.
vei [ˈvei] *vi.* grow old, age. • *vt.* age.
veia [ˈveja] *n.* old age.
vejetal *adj.* vegetable, vegetative. • *n.* vegetable.
vejetali *vi.* vegetate.
vejetalisme *n.* vegetarianism.
vejetaliste *n.* vegetarian.
vela *n.* sail. **vela cuadro** square sail. **vela latina** lateen. **vela xef** mainsail. **Velas** Vela (*constellation*).
velal *adj.* & *n.* velar.

velali *vi.* & *vt.* velarize.
velcro *n.* velcro. **de velcro** (*made of*) velcro.
veleta *n.* vane (*pushed by wind or water*).
veli *vt.* veil, shroud, enshroud.
velia *vi.* waken, awaken, wake up. • *vt.* waken, awaken, wake up, arouse, rouse, roust.
veliada *adj.* awake, wakeful.
veliador *n.* alarm clock.
velida *adj.* veiled.
velin *adj.* sail-like.
velo[1] *n.* veil.
velo[2] *n.* velum, soft palate (*anatomy*).
velosiraptor *n.* velociraptor, raptor (*dinosaur: Velociraptor*).
veluda *n.* velvet, velour. **veluda costelin** corduroy.
veludin *adj.* velvety. • *n.* velveteen.
vena *n.* vein (*anatomy*); lode (*geology*). **estrae la vena de** devein. **vena cava** vena cava. **vena jugulal** jugular vein. **venas** veins; grain (*rock*).
venal *adj.* venous (*of veins*).
vendable *adj.* sellable, saleable, marketable.
vendador *n.* vending machine.
vende *vt.* sell, market, retail, peddle. • *n.* sale; disposal. **per vende** for sale. **vende a mercato** market. **vende major** wholesale. **vende nonlegal** sell illegally, bootleg. **vende per tro poca** undercharge. **vende plu barata ca** undercut. **vende tota** sell out.
venderia *n.* dealership, marketplace.
vendeta *n.* vendetta, feud.
vendor *n.* vendor, seller, clerk, dealer, salesperson, salesman, saleswoman, sales clerk. **vendor de drogas** drug seller, drug dealer, drug pusher. **vendor de libros** bookseller. **vendor de pex** fishmonger. **vendor major** wholesaler. **vendor minor** retailer. **vendor vagante** peddler, pedlar, hawker.
vendoria *n.* salesmanship.
venena *n.* poison, toxin, venom.
veneni *vt.* poison.
venenosa *adj.* poisonous, toxic, venomous.
venerdi *n.* Friday. **venerdi santa** Good Friday.
veneta *n.* venule (*anatomy*).
Veneto *n.* Veneto, Venetia (*Italian region*).
Venezia *n.* Venice.
Venezuela *n.* Venezuela. **Golfo Venezuela** Gulf of Venezuela.
venezuelan *adj.* & *n.* Venezuelan.
veni *vi.* come, arrive. • *vt.* summon, fetch, bring. • *n.* coming, arrival. **me veni de dise** I have just said, I just said (*a moment ago*). **veni de** come from, originate from; (*have*) just. **veni per vide** come and see, come to see.
veninte *adj.* coming, to come, future, next; inbound. **en la semana veninte** next week. **pos la du menses veninte** in two months' time.
venipuntur *n.* venipuncture (*medical*).
venja *vt.* avenge, get even; e.g. *me venja mea ami per la mata par mea enemi*; *me venja la mata de mea ami par mea enemi*; *me venja contra mea enemi*. • *n.* vengeance, revenge, retaliation, retribution, vendetta, payback, reprisal. **venja se** avenge oneself, get revenge, get one's own back, get even, retaliate; e.g. *me venja me per la desonora.*
venjor *n.* avenger.
venjosa *adj.* vengeful, vindictive.
venseo *n.* swift (*bird: Apodidae*).
venta *vi.* blow, be windy. • *n.* wind. **con la venta** downwind, leeward. **contra la venta** upwind, windward. **venta de retro** tailwind. **venta fasante** headwind. **venta norde-este** northeasterly wind, northeaster. **venta sude-ueste** southwesterly wind, southwester.
ventador *n.* fan, ventilator.
venteta *n.* breeze, zephyr.
ventetosa *adj.* breezy, draughty (US drafty).
venti *vt.* ventilate, fan, winnow. • *n.* ventilation.
venton *n.* gale. **venton de neva** blizzard.
ventosa[1] *n.* sucker (*anatomy, rubber cup*).
ventosa[2] *adj.* windy, gusty, blowy.
ventosin *adj.* suckerlike.
ventral *adj.* ventral, of the belly, of the front.
ventre *n.* belly, midriff, front, tummy, gut.
ventriculo *n.* ventricle (*anatomy*).
ventrilocuia *n.* ventriloquy, ventriloquism.
ventrilocuo *n.* ventriloquist.
ventron *n.* paunch, potbelly, beer belly.
venturi *n.* venturi (*tube*).
Venus *n.* Venus (*mythology, planet*).
vera *adj.* true, real, actual, authentic, genuine, veracious, veritable. • *adv.* very, truly, really, actually, indeed, in fact, seriously, sincerely, at all, whatsoever. • *interj.* indeed, true. • *n.* true thing, truth, truism. **en vera no modo** in no way at all, in no way whatsoever. **vera lo ia aveni** it *did* happen (*emphatic*). **vera me desira aida** I *do* want to help (*emphatic*). **vera no** not at all. **vera no cosa** nothing at all, none at all.
veranda *n.* veranda, porch.
verbal *adj.* verbal.
verbena *n.* verbena, vervain (*plant: Verbena*).
verbin *adj.* verbal.
verbo *n.* verb.

verde *adj.* green; verdant. ● *n.* green; greenery, verdure; green (*golf*). **verde de cupre** verdigris.
verdeta *n.* greenfinch (*Chloris*).
verdi *vi.* & *vt.* turn green.
verdin[1] *n.* leafbird (*Chloropsis*).
verdin[2] *adj.* greenish.
verga *n.* yardarm (*for sail*).
vergonia *vi.* be ashamed, feel shame. ● *vt.* shame, humiliate. ● *n.* shame, humiliation. **sin vergonia** shameless, brazen, impenitent, unashamed.
vergoniante *adj.* ashamed.
vergoniosa *adj.* shameful.
veria *n.* truth, trueness, veracity, verity.
verje *vi.* turn, verge, veer, swerve, yaw (*change direction while moving*); e.g. *acel auto no ia indica ce lo va verje a destra.* ● *vt.* & *n.* turn, swerve. **per cada verje** turn by turn (*navigation*). **verje contra la venta** tack. **verje U** U-turn. See *turna*.
verme *n.* worm. **verme de orea** earworm. **verme de tera** earthworm (*Lumbricina*). **verme plata** flatworm, platyhelminth (*Platyhelminthes*). **verme ronda** roundworm, nematode (*Nematoda*).
vermi *vi.* worm (*move like a worm*).
vermiculita *n.* vermiculite.
vermin *adj.* wormlike, vermiform.
vermitxeli *n.* vermicelli (*food*).
Vermont *n.* Vermont (*US state*).
vermute *n.* vermouth (*wine*).
vernis *n.* varnish; glaze. **vernis acuin** shellac.
vernisi *vt.* varnish; glaze.
versa *vi.* & *vt.* pour, tip.
vertebra *n.* vertebra.
vertebral *adj.* vertebral.
vertebrato *adj.* & *n.* vertebrate.
vertical *adj.* vertical, upright; portrait (*orientation*).
vertigo *n.* vertigo, dizziness, lightheadedness.
vertigosa *adj.* dizzy, giddy, light-headed.
veruca *n.* wart, verruca.
verucosa *adj.* warty.
ves *n.* occasion, time, instance; turn (*in a game*), iteration. **a multe veses** frequently, often, oftentimes, usually. **a no ves** on no occasion, at no time. **a poca veses** rarely, seldom, only occasionally. **a un ves** once, one time. **a un ves o un otra** at one time or another, sooner or later. **a un ves pasada** once upon a time. **a veses** at times, sometimes; from time to time, now and then, now and again, on occasion, occasionally. **a veses rara** rarely, seldom, only occasionally. **de ves a ves** from time to time, now and then, now and again, on occasion, occasionally. **du a cada ves** two at a time. **no a esta ves** not this time. See *tempo*.
vesica *n.* bladder (*anatomy*). **vesica bilal** gall bladder.
vesicula *n.* vesicle (*anatomy*).
vespa *n.* wasp, hornet (*Hymenoptera, Apocrita*). **vespa parasital** parasitic wasp.
vespin *adj.* waspish, waspy.
vestal *n.* Vestal, Vestal Virgin.
veste *n.* garment, piece of clothing. **veste alta** top, upper garment. **veste basa** bottom, lower garment. **veste de nada** swimming costume, swimsuit, bathing costume, bathing suit. **veste de sumerjor** wetsuit. **veste de tomba** shroud. **veste desprendeda** castoff. **veste etnical** traditional costume, national dress. **veste spasial** spacesuit. **vestes** clothes, clothing, costume, outfit, dress, apparel, attire, garb, raiment. **vestes de enfantes** childrenswear. **vestes de femes** womenswear. **vestes de nada** swimwear. **vestes de omes** menswear. **vestes fantasin** costume, fancy dress, getup. **vestes pronto** ready-to-wear clothing, pret-à-porter clothing.
vesteria *n.* dressing room, changing room, fitting room; vestry; cloakroom, hatcheck.
vesteta *n.* undergarment. **vestetas** underclothes, undergarments, underwear.
vesti *vt.* clothe, dress (*including wound*); coat (*with paint, etc.*). ● *n.* coat, coating (*paint, etc.*).
vestibulal *adj.* vestibular.
vestida *adj.* clothed, dressed, clad, suited. **nonconveninte vestida** inappropriately dressed, underdressed. **tro calda vestida** dressed too warmly, overdressed. **tro formal vestida** dressed too formally, overdressed. **tro ostentosa vestida** dressed too ostentatiously, overdressed.
vestijial *adj.* vestigial.
vestijio *n.* vestige.
veston *n.* suit, formal attire.
veteran *adj.* & *n.* veteran, vet.
veterinar *adj.* veterinary. **dotor veterinar** veterinarian, vet. **medica veterinar** veterinary medicine.
veti *vt.* veto.
veto *n.* veto.
vetor *n.* vector, one-dimensional array; array (*software*). **vetor de asosia** associative array (*software*).
vetoral *adj.* vector.
vetulicola *n.* vetulicola (*ancient animal: Vetulicola*).
via *n.* way, avenue, route, course, path, approach. **a via** (*go, throw, put*) away, (*saw*) off, (*throw*) out. **a via de** away from. **a via de vias** in the middle of nowhere, in the

back of beyond. **a via de vias comun** off the beaten track. **en via** on the way, en route. **via de rola** taxiway (*airport*). **Via Letin** Milky Way (*astronomy*). **via levada** causeway. **via navigable** waterway. **via ondante** roller coaster. **via periferial** beltway, ringroad, orbital. **via rapida** quick route, shortcut. **via reta** straight, straightaway. **via xef** main road, highway, freeway, throughway, thruway.
viable *adj.* viable.
viablia *n.* viability.
viaduto *n.* viaduct; overpass, flyover.
viaja *vi.* travel. • *n.* journey, trip, voyage, drive. **viaja dial** *v.* & *n.* commute. **viaja per plaser** *v.* & *n.* cruise. **viaja sua via vagante** wend one's way. **viaja tra la mundo** world travel. **viaja tra la ueb** surf the net. **viaja tra tempo** time travel.
viajamania *n.* wanderlust, urge to travel.
viajamanica *adj.* globetrotting, habitually travelling (US traveling). • *n.* globetrotter, habitual traveller (US traveler).
viajor *n.* traveller (US traveler), voyager, passenger, wayfarer. **viajor de mar** seafarer. **viajor dial** commuter. **viajor tra la mundo** world traveller (US traveler), globetrotter. **viajor tra tempo** time traveller (US traveler).
vibra *vi.* vibrate, thrill; flicker (*lights*); trill (*sound*). • *vt.* vibrate, trill, twang. • *n.* vibration, frisson, twang, vibrato, trill.
vibrador *n.* vibrator, buzzer.
vibrafon *n.* vibraphone (*musical instrument*).
vibrante *adj.* vibrating, thrilling; flickering (*lights*); trilled. • *n.* trill (*consonant*).
vibrisa *n.* whisker; barb, barbel (*of fish*).
vibrisin *adj.* whiskerlike.
viburno *n.* viburnum (*plant*: *Viburnum*).
vici *n.* wiki.
vicing *adj.* & *n.* Viking.
Vicipedia *n.* Wikipedia.
Victoria *n.* Victoria. **Lago Victoria** Lake Victoria.
victorian *adj.* Victorian.
vicunia *n.* vicuña (*animal*: *Vicugna vicugna*).
vidable *adj.* visible; macroscopic. **fasil vidable** salient, conspicuous.
vidablia *n.* visibility.
vidador *n.* viewer (*machine*); viewfinder; sight (*gun*).
vidal *adj.* visual.
vide *vt.* see (*including discover*, *understand*), sight, witness; watch (*film*, *sport*). • *n.* sight, vision, eyesight. • *interj.* see, look. **no vide** miss, not see. **(tu) vide** you see (*filler*). **vide tunelin** tunnel vision.
videador *n.* video recorder, video player, VCR, DVD player.
vidente *adj.* seeing, sighted. **partal vidente** partially sighted.
video *adj.* & *n.* video. **video par comanda** video on demand.
videta *vt.* & *n.* glimpse, peek, peep, pry. **videta acaso** *v.* & *n.* glimpse. **videta secreta** *v.* & *n.* peek.
vidua[1] *adj.* widowed. • *n.* widow, widower.
vidua[2] *n.* indigobird, whydah (*Vidua*).
vidui *vi.* become widowed.
viet *adj.* & *n.* Vietnamese (*person*, *language*).
Vietnam *n.* Vietnam.
vijila *vt.* watch, be vigilant, be alert, keep an eye on, monitor. • *n.* watch, vigil, vigilance, surveillance, stakeout. **vijila de tota santas** Halloween, All Hallows' Eve, All Saints' Eve.
vijilante *adj.* vigilant, alert, watchful, hawk-eyed. **es vijilante** be vigilant, watch out, keep a lookout.
vijilor *n.* sentinel, watchman, lookout, proctor. **vijilor estralegal** vigilante.
vil *adj.* vile, loathsome, depraved, ignoble, fiendish. • *n.* villain, scoundrel, crook, con man, miscreant, evildoer, malfeasant, culprit, wrongdoer, reprobate, rogue, scoundrel, fiend.
vila *n.* town. **vila bumante** boomtown. **vila de nase** birthtown, hometown. **vila de universia** campus. **vila provinsal** backwater, boondocks.
vilan *n.* townsman, townswoman, townsperson, townie.
vileta *n.* village. **vileta noncorporada** unincorporated village, hamlet.
viletan *n.* villager.
vilia *n.* vice, villainy, depravity.
vilo *n.* villus (pl. villi) (*anatomy*).
vim *n.* wicker, wattle (*twigs*).
vina *n.* veena (*musical instrument*).
vinagra *n.* vinegar.
vinagreta *n.* vinaigrette.
vinagri *vt.* marinate in vinegar, marinade, pickle.
vinagrida *adj.* pickled.
vinca *n.* vinca, periwinkle (*plant*: *Vinca*).
vineria *n.* winery.
vinieta *n.* vignette, decorative symbol.
vinil *n.* vinyl.
vino *n.* wine. **vendor de vinos** wine merchant, vintner. **vino bolante** sparkling wine. **vino calda** mulled wine, wassail. **vino fortida** fortified wine.
vinofilia *n.* oenophilia (US enophilia) (*love of wine*).
vinofilica *n.* oenophile (US enophile).
vinolojia *n.* oenology (US enology).
vinor *n.* winemaker, vintner.
vinsable *adj.* vincible.

vinsal *adj.* triumphal.
vinse *vt.* beat, defeat, vanquish, surmount, overcome, subdue, trounce; win, be victorious. • *n.* victory, triumph. **vinse inondante** landslide victory. **vinse sin valua** Pyrrhic victory.
vinseda *adj.* & *n.* vanquished, defeated.
vinsente *adj.* victorious, triumphant.
vinsentian *adj.* & *n.* Vincentian, Vincy. See *San Vinsont.*
vinsisme *n.* triumphalism.
vinsor *n.* victor, conqueror, winner.
viola *n.* viola. **viola de rota** hurdy-gurdy, wheel fiddle. **viola vertical** viol, viola de gamba.
viole *vt.* violate, infringe, break (*rule, law*), transgress, defile, desecrate; rape, ravish. • *n.* violation, infringement, infraction, transgression, aggression; rape (*sexual assault*). **viole de patenta** patent infringement.
violente *adj.* violent, harsh, aggressive, militant. • *n.* brute, thug, roughneck.
violentia *n.* violence. **violentia familial** domestic violence, domestic abuse.
violeta *adj.* violet (*colour*). • *n.* violet (*plant: Viola*).
violin *n.* violin, fiddle.
violiniste *n.* violinist, fiddler.
violiste *n.* violist.
violor *n.* violator; rapist.
vipera *n.* viper, adder, asp (*Viperidae*).
vireo *n.* vireo (*bird: Vireonidae*).
Virginia [ver'dʒinja] *n.* Virginia (*US state*). **Virginia Ueste** West Virginia (*US state*).
virgula *n.* comma. **de virgula flotante** floating-point (*number*). **virgula desimal** decimal point.
virjin *adj.* virginal, sexually innocent, chaste. • *n.* virgin, maiden. **Virjin** *n.* Virgo (*constellation*). **Isolas Virjin** Virgin Islands. **Isolas Virjin Brites** British Virgin Islands.
virjinia *n.* virginity, chastity.
virola *n.* virola (*tree: Virola*).
virolojia *n.* virology.
virolojiste *n.* virologist.
virtua *n.* virtue, purity, decency, innocence, righteousness, rectitude.
virtual *adj.* virtual.
virtuosa *adj.* virtuous, pure, decent, innocent, righteous.
virtuosia *n.* decency, righteousness, probity.
virus *n.* virus. **virus de imunodebilia umana** human immunodeficiency virus, HIV.
virusal *adj.* viral (*of viruses*).
vis- *pref.* vice-, deputy (*added to nouns denoting official jobs*); e.g. *visre.*
visa *n.* visa (*for travel*).
visamiral *n.* vice-admiral.
Visayas, Mar *n.* Visayan Sea.
viscio *n.* mistletoe (*Viscum*).
viscomandor *n.* vice-commander, second-in-command.
visconte *n.* viscount.
viscosa *adj.* viscous, thick, sticky, gooey, goopy, gloopy.
viscosia *n.* viscosity, thickness, stickiness, consistency.
vise *n.* screw (*fastener*); bolt (*for nut*). **vise crusin** crosshead screw, Phillips screw. **vise cuadro** square screw, square bolt. **vise de Allen** Allen screw, Allen bolt. **vise esagon** hex-cap screw, hex-cap bolt. **vise nonfininte** wormgear. **vise per lenio** wood screw. **vise per metal** metal screw. **vise ranurida** slot screw.
visera *n.* viscera, guts (*treated as a mass noun*).
viseral *adj.* visceral.
visi *vt.* screw, bolt.
visia *n.* vetch, tare (*plant: Vicia*).
visiera *n.* visor.
visigoto *adj.* Visigothic. • *n.* Visigoth.
visina *adj.* neighbouring (US neighboring), adjoining, adjacent. • *n.* neighbour (US neighbor).
visineria *n.* neighbourhood (US neighborhood). **visineria de lata** shanty town, squatter camp. **visineria misera** slum. **visineria rica** rich neighbourhood (US neighborhood), uptown.
visinia *n.* vicinity.
visita *vt.* visit. • *n.* visit, stopover, call.
visitor *n.* visitor; guest, boarder (*hotel*). **cuantia de visitores** number of visitors, attendance. **visitor invitada** guest.
vismaior *n.* vice-mayor, alderman.
vison *n.* mink (*animal: Mustela vison, Mustela lutreola*).
vispresidente *n.* vice-president.
visre *n.* viceroy.
visrea *n.* vicereine.
visrejente *n.* vice-regent.
vista *n.* view, sight, vista, prospect, landscape, scenery. **con vista bela** scenic. **en vista de** in sight of. **estra vista** out of sight. **ultra vista** out of sight. **vista airal** bird's-eye view. **vista de mar** seascape. **vista de mundo** world view, Weltanschauung. **vista jeneral** overview (*of topic*). **vista ladal** sideview.
vitamina *n.* vitamin. **vitamina C** vitamin C, ascorbic acid.
vite *n.* vine.
vitelo *n.* yolk.
viteria *n.* vineyard.
viteta *n.* tendril.
Viti *n.* Fiji. **viti** *adj.* & *n.* Fijian. See *Fiji.*
vitiligo *n.* vitiligo (*medical*).

vitim *n.* victim, casualty, prey. **sin vitim** victimless.
vitimi *vi.* become a victim, fall prey (*to*), fall foul (*of*). • *vt.* victimize.
vitreta *n.* shotglass; shot (*drink*).
vitri *vi.* vitrify. • *vt.* vitrify; glaze (*window*). • *n.* vitrification.
vitrin *adj.* glassy, glazed, vitreous.
vitriol *n.* vitriol.
vitriolosa *adj.* vitriolic.
vitro *n.* glass (*substance, container*); slide (*microscope*). **en vitro** in vitro. **vitro acrilica** perspex, plexiglass, lucite, polymethyl methacrylate, poly. **vitro colorida** stained glass. **vitro de coniac** brandy glass, snifter. **vitro de fenetra** window pane. **vitro de forno** pyrex. **vitro de vino** wine glass. **vitros** glasses, stemware.
vitror *n.* glazier.
viu *abbr.* (*virus de imunodebilia umana*) HIV.
vive *vi.* live, be alive. • *vt.* cause to live, keep alive. • *n.* life. **de vive intera** lifelong. **en vive** in vivo. **vive intera** lifetime, lifespan. **vive la re** long live the king. **vive plu longa ca** outlive. **vive pos mori** life after death, afterlife, hereafter.
vivente *adj.* alive, live, living. • *n.* creature, organism, lifeform. **viventes savaje** wildlife.
viveria *n.* nursery (*for plants*).
viverna *n.* wyvern (*mythology*).
vivin *adj.* lifelike, vivid.
vivipari *vi.* be viviparous (*give birth to live offspring*).
viviparia *n.* vivipary.
viviparinte *adj.* viviparous.
vivisesioni *vt.* vivisect. • *n.* vivisection.
vivosa *adj.* lively, vivacious, vital, jaunty, spry, spirited, full of life; allegro (*music*). • *n.* lively person, swinger (*socaliser*).
vivosia *n.* liveliness, vitality, esprit, spiritedness.
vixisuaz *n.* vichyssoise (*soup*).
Vixnu *n.* Vishnu (*Hinduism*).
vizir *n.* vizir, vizier (*officer*).
vocabulal *adj.* lexical.
vocabulo *n.* vocabulary, lexicon.
vocal *adj.* vocalic. • *n.* vowel. **vocal abrida** open vowel. **vocal cluida** close vowel. **vocal fronte** front vowel. **vocal media** mid vowel. **vocal media abrida** open-mid vowel. **vocal media cluida** close-mid vowel. **vocal plata** unrounded vowel. **vocal retro** back vowel. **vocal ronda** rounded vowel. **vocal sentral** central vowel.
vocali *vi.* & *vt.* vocalize (*as vowel*).
vocativa *adj.* & *n.* vocative (*grammar*).
vodca *n.* vodka (*drink*).
vodevil *adj.* & *n.* vaudeville, burlesque.
voior *n.* voyeur.
voiorisme *n.* voyeurism.
vola *vi.* & *vt.* fly. • *n.* flight. **vola alta** soar. **vola scemida** scheduled flight. **vola spasial** spaceflight.
volador *n.* aircraft, flying machine.
volante[1] *n.* steering wheel.
volante[2] *n.* shuttlecock.
volatil *adj.* volatile, mercurial.
volatilia *n.* volatility.
volcan *n.* volcano.
volcanal *adj.* volcanic.
volcanolojia *n.* volcanology.
volcanolojiste *n.* volcanologist.
vole *vt.* want, wish, desire, intend, will. • *n.* will, volition, intention; discretion. **a sua vole** at one's discretion. **a vole** at will. **bon voles** best wishes. **ta vole** would like to (*polite*); e.g. *me ta vole du biletas, per favore*; *me ta vole aida, ma me es ja ocupada.* **vole dise** mean, intend to say. **vole ferin** iron will. **vole sabe** wonder, want to know, would like to know.
voleda *adj.* willed, voluntary, deliberate, intended, intentional.
volente *adj.* willing (*actor*); deliberate, intentional. • *adv.* willingly, voluntarily, deliberately, intentionally, on purpose.
voleta *vi.* flutter, go fluttering past.
volibal *n.* volleyball.
volor *n.* flyer; aviator, pilot.
volpal *adj.* vulpine.
volpe *n.* fox (*Vulpes*). **Volpe** *n.* Vulpecula (*constellation*). **volpe fema** vixen.
volpin *adj.* foxlike, vulpine.
volta[1] *vi.* somersault, flip, go head over heels, tumble, topple. • *vt.* flip, send head over heels. • *n.* somersault. **volta ladal** cartwheel. **volta par mano** handspring, cartwheel.
volta[2] *n.* vault (*ceiling*).
voltaica *adj.* voltaic.
volte *n.* volt (*unit of electromotive force*). **cuantia de voltes** voltage.
voltor *n.* tumbler (*acrobat*).
volum *n.* volume (*capacity, loudness, book*).
volumosa *adj.* voluminous.
volunta *n.* will, willpower. **volunta libre** free will.
volvox *n.* volvox (*organism*).
vomita *n.* vomit, sick, puke.
vomiti *vt.* vomit, be sick, throw up, puke, retch, regurgitate, disgorge. • *n.* regurgitation.
vortis *n.* vortex, whirlpool, maelstrom. **vortis de venta** whirlwind.
vortiseta *n.* eddy.
vos *pron.* you (*plural*), you all, ye.

vosa *det.* your (*plural*). **la vosa** yours.
vosal *adj.* vocal (*of the voice*).
vose *n.* voice; articulation. **a vose** aloud, out loud. **vose ativa** active voice. **vose nasal** nasal voice, twang. **vose pasiva** passive voice.
vosi *vt.* voice, utter, vocalize, verbalize, give voice to. • *n.* utterance, vocalism, vocalization.
vota *vi.* vote. • *n.* vote (*individual's, overall process*); ballot, election, poll, voting. **ante vota** pre-election. **caxa de vota** ballot box. **ofisior de vota** returning officer. **paper de vota** ballot paper. **vota direta** plebiscite. **vota jeneral** general election. **vota per** vote for. **vota spesial** special election, by-election. **vota vacua** spoiled vote, spoilt vote, null vote.
voteria *n.* polling place, polling station; voting booth.
votor *n.* voter. **votores** voters, electorate.
vudu *n.* voodoo (*religion*).
vulcani *vt.* vulcanize.
vulgar *adj.* vulgar, indecent, improper, naughty, bawdy, crude, foul-mouthed, rabelaisian, ribald, off-colour (US off-color).
vulgaria *n.* vulgarity.
vultur *n.* vulture (*Aegypiinae, Cathartidae*).
vulva *n.* vulva (*anatomy*).

W

W [wa], **wa** *letter* W, w.
Warszawa [ˈvarʃava] *n.* Warsaw.
Washington [ˈwaʃiŋton] *n.* Washington (*US state, city*).
Wien [vin] *n.* Vienna.
Wisconsin *n.* Wisconsin (*US state*).
Wyoming [wajˈomiŋ] *n.* Wyoming (*US state*).

X

X [eʃ], **ex** *letter* X, x.

xa *n.* shah (*king*).

xabeco *n.* xebec, zebec (*ship*).

xabli *n.* chablis (*wine*).

xacal *n.* jackal (*Canis aureus*, *Canis adustus*, *Canis mesomelas*).

xace *vt.* check (*in chess*). • *n.* chess; check. • *interj.* check.

xacemata *vt.* checkmate. • *n.* checkmate, mate. • *interj.* checkmate.

xacuhatxi *n.* shakuhachi (*flute*).

xal *n.* shawl (*garment*).

xale *n.* chalet (*cottage*).

xama *vi.* & *n.* swarm.

xaman *n.* shaman, sangoma, witch doctor.

xambelan *n.* chamberlain (*officer*).

xamisen *n.* shamisen (*musical instrument*).

xampania *n.* champagne. **xampania multe seca** brut champagne.

xampi *v.* shampoo.

xampinion *n.* mushroom, toadstool (*Agaricomycetes*). **xampinion venenosa** poisonous toadstool.

xampu [ʃamˈpu] *n.* shampoo.

xamroc *n.* shamrock (*Trifolium repens*, *Trifolium dubium*).

xangtxi *n.* xiangqi, Chinese chess.

xantoma *n.* xanthoma (*medical*).

xantopsia *n.* xanthopsia (*medical*).

xapa *n.* veneer.

xaperia *n.* hat shop, millinery.

xapeta *n.* cap, kepi, bonnet. **xapeta academial** mortarboard. **xapeta de bani** bath cap, shower cap.

xapi *vt.* veneer.

xapin *adj.* hatlike.

xapo *n.* hat; header. **xapo de cauboi** cowboy hat. **xapo de jornal** masthead. **xapo de letera** letterhead. **xapo de note** nightcap. **xapo de paje** header. **xapo de palia** straw hat, boater. **xapo de pelo** fur hat; bearskin. **xapo ornosa** headdress. **xapo saturnin** saturn hat, cappello romano. **xapo silindre** top hat.

xapon *n.* akubra, fedora, sombrero, cowboy hat, slouch hat.

xapor *n.* hatter, hatmaker, milliner, haberdasher.

xaria *n.* sharia (*Islam*).

xarif *n.* sharif (*Islam*).

xarlatan *n.* charlatan, mountebank; babbler (*bird*: *Timaliidae*). **xarlatan medical** quack.

xarleston *n.* hi-hat (*cymbals*); charleston (*dance*).

xarnier *n.* hinge.

xarnieri *vt.* hinge.

xarnierida *adj.* hinged.

xarpe *n.* scarf, stole, muffler. **xarpe de muni** bandolier. **xarpe de spada** baldric, sword belt. **xarpe de spala** shoulder belt. **xarpe de taie** cummerbund. **xarpe medical** sling. **xarpe ofisial** sash.

xasa *vt.* chase, hunt, pursue, prey upon. • *n.* chase, hunt, pursuit, predation. **xasa a via** chase away. **xasa de balenas** whaling. **xasa de ereses** auto-da-fé. **xasa de sorsores** witch hunt. **xasa furtiva** prowl. **xasa nonlegal** *vt.* poach. • *n.* poaching. **xasa testas** headhunt.

xasafem *n.* womanizer, philanderer, playboy, gigolo, lothario, romeo, rake, roué, wolf, ladies' man.

xasante *adj.* predatory. **xasante-coliente** *adj.* hunter-gatherer, hunting and gathering.

xasatesta *n.* headhunter.

xasatorpedo *n.* destroyer (*warship*).

xasi *n.* chassis, undercarriage.

xasor *n.* hunter, predator; tracker; hound, hunting dog. **xasor-colior** *n.* hunter-gatherer. **xasor de volpes** foxhound. **xasor nonlegal** poacher.

xcip *adj.* Albanian. • *n.* Albanian (*person, language*). See *albanian*.

Xciperia *n.* Albania. See *Albania*.

xec *n.* sheik, sheikh, shaikh.

xece *n.* cheque (US check) (*money*).

xecel *n.* shekel (*currency*).

xecer *adj.* & *n.* Shaker.

xecerisme *n.* Shakerism (*Christianity*).

xecia *n.* sheikdom, sheikhdom (*post, period, area*).

xef *adj.* chief, main, primary, principal, foremost, premier, prime, key. • *adv.* chiefly, mainly, mostly, primarily, principally, most importantly; e.g. *el bevi xef cafe*; *aira es xef composada de nitrojen*. • *n.* chief, leader, head, headman, chieftain, overlord, sachem. **xef de cosina** chef. **xef de gang** ringleader. **xef de gera** war chief, warlord. **xef de governa** head of government. **xef de orcestra** conductor, orchestra leader. **xef de posteria** postmaster. **xef de securia** head of security, head of intelligence. **xef de sirco** ringmaster. **xef de stasion** station master. **xef de stato** chief of state, head of state. **xef de table** head of the table; croupier. **xef sin potia** figurehead.

xeferia *n.* headquarters, HQ.

xefia *n.* chiefdom, leadership, primacy.

xel *n.* shale (*geology*).
xeliste *n.* cellist, violoncellist.
xelo *n.* cello, violoncello.
xenil *n.* chenille (*yarn*).
xeno- *pref.* xeno- (*foreign*).
xenobiolojia *n.* xenobiology.
xenobiolojiste *n.* xenobiologist.
xenofilia *n.* xenophilia, xenophily.
xenofilica *adj.* xenophilic. • *n.* xenophile.
xenofobia *n.* xenophobia.
xenofobica *adj.* xenophobic. • *n.* xenophobe.
xenon *n.* xenon (*chemistry*).
xenoturbelido *n.* xenoturbellid (*worm*: *Xenoturbellida*).
xerca *vt.* seek, search for, look for, look up, quest after; ask for, solicit. • *n.* search, quest; manhunt. **xerca furtiva** snoop. **xerca per la posto** headhunt (*business*). **xerca rapida** riffle, rifle. **xerca sieca** search blindly, grope. **xerca sua asendentes** trace one's ancestry, search for one's ancestors.
xercada *adj.* sought-after, wanted.
xercador *n.* search engine.
xercaemplea *n.* jobseeker.
xercor *n.* seeker, searcher, prospector.
xeres *n.* sherry (*wine*).
xerif *n.* sheriff (*officer*).
xero- *pref.* xero- (*dry*).
xerofilia *n.* xerophilia.
xerofilica *adj.* xerophilic. • *n.* xerophile, xerophyte.
xeroftalmia *n.* xerophthalmia (*medical*).
xerografia *n.* xerography, electrophotography.
xerografial *adj.* xerographic.
xerostomia *n.* xerostomia (*medical*).
xerpa *adj.* & *n.* Sherpa (*person*, *language*).
xevron *n.* chevron, angle bracket.
xevronosa *adj.* herringbone.
xi *n.* xi (*Greek letter* Ξ, ξ).
xia *adj.* & *n.* Shia, Shiite, Shi'ite (*Islam*).
xiang *adj.* & *n.* Xiang, Hunanese (*language*).
xiatsu *n.* shiatsu (*massage*).
xibolet *n.* shibboleth.
xica *n.* girl; wench; (*colloquial*) gal, chick (*woman*). **xica de cor** girlfriend. **xica de jornales** newsgirl, papergirl. **xica masin** tomboy. **xica minor** jailbait. **xica naive** ingenue. **xica noncortes** impudent girl, minx. **xica ruidosa** boisterous girl, hoyden. **xica vagante** street urchin, guttersnipe, gamine, ragamuffin.
xice *n.* child, kid, kiddie, kiddy, bairn, tyke; (*colloquial*) guy or gal (*person*).
xicle *n.* chicle (*latex*).
xico *n.* boy; (*colloquial*) guy, bloke, chap, fellow, geezer (*man*). **xico de cor** boyfriend. **xico de jornales** newsboy, paperboy. **xico femin** sissy. **xico vagante** street urchin, guttersnipe, gamin.
xicoria *n.* chicory, endive (*plant*: *Cichorium intybus*).
xicungunia *n.* chikungunya (*virus*).
xifon *n.* chiffon (*fabric*).
xilema *n.* xylem (*botany*).
xilia *vt.* & *n.* shriek, scream, screech.
xiliante *adj.* screaming, shrieking; shrill, piercing, harsh, strident, screeching, raucous; garish, loud.
xiling *n.* shilling, schilling (*currency*).
xilo- *pref.* xylo- (*wood*).
xilofaje *adj.* xylophagous. • *n.* xylophage.
xilofon *n.* xylophone.
xilografia *n.* xylography, woodcut printing.
xilografial *adj.* xylographic.
xilogram *n.* xylograph, woodcut.
xilosa *n.* xylose (*sugar*).
ximi *vi.*, *vt.* & *n.* shimmy, wiggle, waggle, jiggle.
ximine *n.* chimney, smokestack; funnel; vent.
ximineria *n.* hearth, hearthside, fireplace, ingle; grate.
ximinte *adj.* waggly, wiggly.
ximpanze *n.* chimpanzee, chimp (*Pan*).
Xina *n.* China. **Mar Xina Este** East China Sea. **Mar Xina Sude** South China Sea. See *Jonguo*.
xines *adj.* Chinese. • *n.* Chinese (*person*, *language*).
xinion *n.* chignon, bun (*hair*).
Xinjiang *n.* Xinjiang, Sinkiang (*Chinese province*).
xinolojia *n.* sinology.
xinolojiste *n.* sinologist.
xinto *n.* shinto (*religion*).
xintoiste *adj.* shintoistic. • *n.* shintoist.
xinxe *n.* bug (*Hemiptera*). **xinxe de acua** waterbug (*Nepomorpha*, *Gerromorpha*). **xinxe de leto** bedbug (*Cimicidae*). **xinxe focosa** firebug (*Pyrrhocoris apterus*). **xinxe scermin** shield bug, stinkbug (*Pentatomomorpha*).
xip *n.* potato crisp (*UK*), potato chip (*US*).
xiroco *n.* sirocco (*wind*).
xirope *n.* syrup. **xirope de asero** maple syrup. **xirope de granada** grenadine.
xiste *n.* schist (*geology*).
xitace *n.* shiitake (*mushroom*: *Lentinula edodes*).
xiva[1] *n.* shiva (*Judaism*).
Xiva[2] *n.* Shiva (*Hinduism*).
xixe *n.* chickpea (*Cicer arietinum*).
xoca *vt.* shock, alarm, appall (US appal), horrify; crash, collide, jolt, jar. • *n.* shock, shocker; jolt, blow of force, brunt; crash, collision. **xoca de colo** whiplash.

xocada *adj.* shocked, aghast, appalled, horrified.
xocante *adj.* shocking, jarring, alarming, appalling, terrible, horrible, horrifying, horrific, horrendous.
xocaoio *n.* eyesore, monstrosity.
xocolada *n.* chocolate.
xocolador *n.* chocolatier.
xogi *n.* shogi, Japanese chess.
xogun *n.* shogun (*tyrant*).
xoji *n.* shoji (*door*).
xova *n.* chough (*bird*: *Pyrrhocorax*). **xova becojala** yellow-billed chough (*Pyrrhocorax graculus*). **xova becoroja** red-billed chough (*Pyrrhocorax pyrrhocorax*).
xucrute *n.* sauerkraut (*food*).
xufelborda *n.* shuffleboard, shovelboard (*game*).
xuta *vt.* shoot, fire (*missile*), launch, fling, hurl, propel, drive; snap, take a photo of, shoot, capture. • *n.* shot, shooting, gunshot. **xuta a platos** clay-pigeon shooting, skeet shooting. **xuta acaso** random shot, potshot.
xutada *n.* shot, bullet, missile.
xutador *n.* wood (*golf club*). **xutador xef** driver (*golf club*).
xutor *n.* shooter, sniper.
xux *interj.* sh.
xuxa *vt.* whisper; prompt; rustle. • *n.* whisper; prompt; rustle, rustling, froufrou.
xuxor *n.* whisperer; prompter.
xva *n.* schwa (*vowel and letter* Ə, ə); shva, shewa' (*Hebrew vowel sign*).
Xvaben *n.* Swabia (*German region*).
xvabes *adj.* Swabian.

Y

Y [ja], **ya** *letter* Y, y.
York Nova *n.* New York State (*US state*).
Yucatan *n.* Yucatán (*Mexican state*). **Penisola Yucatan** Yucatán Peninsula.
Yukon *n.* Yukon (*Canadian province*).

Z

Z [ze], **ze** *letter* Z, z.
zabalion *n.* zabaglione, zabaione (*dessert*).
zada *n.* hoe.
zadi *vt.* hoe.
zafran *n.* saffron (*plant*, *spice*: *Crocus sativus*).
zagaia *n.* assegai (*spear*).
zagruta *vt.* & *n.* zaghrouta, zaghareet (*celebratory ululation*).
Zair *n.* Zaire. See *Republica Democrata de Congo*.
Zambia *n.* Zambia.
zambian *adj.* & *n.* Zambian.
Zanzibar *n.* Zanzibar.
zazen *n.* zazen (*meditation*).
zebra *n.* zebra (*Equus zebra*, *Equus quagga*, *Equus grevyi*).
zebu *n.* zebu, humped cattle (*Bos primigenius indicus*).
Zeland *n.* Zeeland. **Zeland Nova** New Zealand.
zelandes *adj.* New Zealand. • *n.* New Zealander, Kiwi.
zeli *vt.* enthuse.
zelo *n.* zeal, enthusiasm, avidity, alacrity, ardour (US ardor), fervour (US fervor), keenness, brio, gusto, panache, zest.
zelosa *adj.* zealous, enthusiastic, eager, keen, anxious (*for*), passionate, ardent, avid, fanatical, fervent, zestful; hearty, heartfelt, (*emotionally*) warm. **tro zelosa** overenthusiastic, overeager.
zen *n.* Zen.
zeniste *adj.* Zen. • *n.* Zen Buddhist.
zenite *n.* zenith, high point, pinnacle, acme.
zero *det.* zero, no; e.g. *la acua jela a temperatur de zero grados*. • *adj.* zeroth; e.g. *la elemento zero de un vetor*. • *n.* zero, zero point, nought, naught, nil. • *pron.* none, not any, nil; e.g. *zero de la pacetas ia ariva*. See *no*.
zeta *n.* zeta (*Greek letter* Z, ζ).
Zeus *n.* Zeus.
zezea *vt.* & *n.* lisp.
zibelina *n.* sable (*animal*: *Martes zibellina*).
Zica *n.* Zika. **febre de Zica** Zika fever. **virus de Zica** Zika virus.
zigoma *n.* zygoma, cheekbone.
zigoto *n.* zygote (*biology*).
zigurat *n.* ziggurat (*pyramid*).
zigzaga *vi.* & *n.* zigzag.
Zimbabue *n.* Zimbabwe.
zimbabuean *adj.* & *n.* Zimbabwean.
zinci *vt.* zinc, galvanize.
zinco *n.* zinc.
zinia *n.* zinnia (*plant*: *Zinnia*).
zipo *n.* zip, zipper; fly, flies.
zipi *vt.* zip.
zircon *n.* zircon (*mineral*).
zirconio *n.* zirconium (*element*).
zloti *n.* złoty (*currency*).
zo[1] *n.* zoo, menagerie.
zo-[2] *pref.* zoo- (*animal*).
zoco *n.* clog, sabot, wooden shoe.
zocor *n.* clogmaker.
zodiacal *adj.* zodiacal.
zodiaco *n.* zodiac.
zofilia *n.* zoophilia, bestophilia, bestiality.
zofilica *adj.* zoophilic, zoophiliac. • *n.* zoophile, zoophiliac.
zofite *n.* zoophyte.
zojeografia *n.* zoogeography.
zojeografial *adj.* zoogeographical.
zojeografiste *n.* zoogeographer.
zolojia *n.* zoology.
zolojial *adj.* zoological.
zolojiste *n.* zoologist.
zombi *n.* zombie.
zona *n.* zone. **zona de ora** time zone. **zona de presa alta** high-pressure area. **zona de presa basa** low-pressure area.
zonal *adj.* zonal.
Zoroastra *n.* Zoroaster, Zarathustra.
zoroastrisme *n.* Zoroastrianism, Mazdaism (*religion*).
zoroastriste *adj.* & *n.* Zoroastrian.
zuca *n.* pumpkin, squash, gourd, marrow, calabash (*Lagenaria*, *Cucurbita*).
zucar *n.* sugar. **zucar de orzo** barley sugar.
zucari *vt.* sugar, sugarcoat, add sugar to.
zucarosa *adj.* sugary, saccharine, sappy.
zuceta *n.* courgette, zucchini (*Cucurbita pepo*).
zulu *adj.* & *n.* Zulu (*person*, *language*).
zuma *vi.* zoom, zoom in. • *n.* zoom, zooming. **zuma rapida** crash zoom.
zumbador *n.* buzzer.
zumbi *vt.* & *n.* hum, croon; buzz, whir, whirr, drone; whizz, whoosh.
zumbinte *adj.* buzzing, abuzz.

A

a *det.* un.
aardvark *n.* oriteropo.
aardwolf *n.* protele.
abacus *n.* abaco.
abalone *n.* abalon.
abandon *v.* abandona. **with abandon** sin restrinje.
abandonment *n.* abandona.
abase *v.* basi.
abasement *n.* (*action*) basi; (*state*) basia.
abate *v.* calmi.
abattoir *n.* mataderia.
abbacy *n.* (*post, period*) abadia.
abbatial *adj.* abadal.
abbess *n.* abadesa.
abbey *n.* abaderia, monceria.
abbot *n.* abade.
abbreviate *v.* corti.
abbreviation *n.* (*action, result*) corti.
abdicate *v.* renunsia.
abdication *n.* renunsia.
abdicator *n.* renunsior.
abdomen *n.* adomen.
abdominal *adj.* adomenal.
abdominal exercise *n.* eserse adomenal.
abduct *v.* saisi; (*muscle*) dedui.
abduction *n.* saisi; (*muscle*) dedui.
abductor *n.* (*muscle*) deduador.
aberrant *adj.* deviante, nonormal.
aberration *n.* devia, nonormal.
abet *v.* aida.
abeyance *n.* pausa, suspende. **in abeyance** pausada, suspendeda.
abhor *v.* odia.
abhorrence *n.* repulsa.
abhorrent *adj.* repulsante, odiable.
abide *v.* tolera. **abide by** obedi, aseta.
ability *n.* capasia.
abjad *n.* (*writing system*) abjad.
abject *adj.* misera.
abjection *n.* miseria.
abjectness *n.* miseria.
abjuration *n.* rejeta.
abjure *v.* rejeta, renunsia formal.
Abkhaz *adj.* & *n.* (*person, language*) abcaz.
Abkhazia *n.* Abcazia.
Abkhazian *adj.* & *n.* (*person, language*) abcaz.
ablative *adj.* & *n.* (*grammar*) ablativa.
able[1] *adj.* capas, potente. **be able to** pote.
-able[2] *suff.* -able.
able-bodied *adj.* de corpo capas.
ablution *n.* lava.
abnegation *n.* asteni, rejeta, renunsia.
abnormal *adj.* nonormal.
abnormality *n.* (*something abnormal*) nonormal; (*state*) nonormalia.
aboard *prep.* en, sur. • *adv.* a en, a sur. **go aboard** embarca.
abode *n.* abiteria.
abolish *v.* aboli.
abolishment *n.* aboli.
abolition *n.* aboli.
abolitionism *n.* abolisme.
abolitionist *adj.* & *n.* aboliste.
abominable *adj.* odiable, maldisable, maldiseda.
abominate *v.* odia.
abomination *n.* (*feeling*) odia; (*abominable thing*) odiable.
aboriginal *adj.* orijinal.
abort *v.* aborta.
abortion *n.* aborta.
abortionist *adj.* & *n.* abortiste.
abortive *adj.* abortada.
abound *v.* abunda. **abound in** es plen de.
about *prep.* (*concerning*) sur; (*around*) sirca. **be about to do** vade a fa, es a punto de fa.
above *prep.* supra. • *adv.* a supra. **above all** supra tota, ante tota. **above board** sin asconde. **above par** supranormal.
abracadabra *interj.* abracadabra.
abrade *v.* frica, raspa.
abrasion *n.* frica, raspa.
abrasive *adj.* fricosa, raspante.
abreast *adv.* con lado a lado.
abridge *v.* corti.
abroad *adj.* estra la pais.
abrogate *v.* cansela.
abrogation *n.* cansela.
abrupt *adj.* subita.
abscess *n.* aseso.
abscissa *n.* (*coordinate*) axisa.
abscond *v.* fuji furtiva.
abseil *v.* rapela.
absence *n.* asentia.
absent *adj.* asente. **absent without leave** asente sin permete. **become absent** asenti.
absentee *n.* asente.
absent-minded *adj.* distraeda, nonatendente.
absinthe *n.* (*plant, drink*) asinto.
absolute *adj.* asoluta.
absolution *n.* remete.
absolutism *n.* asolutisme.
absolutist *n.* asolutiste.
absolve *v.* remete.
absorb *v.* asorbe; (*cost*) amorti.
absorbent *adj.* asorbente.

absorption *n.* asorbe.
abstain *v.* asteni.
abstainer *n.* astenor.
abstemious *adj.* asteninte.
abstention *n.* asteni. **abstention from voting** asteni de vota.
abstinence *n.* asteni. **abstinence from food** juna.
abstinent *adj.* asteninte.
abstract *adj.* astrata. • *v.* astrati. **abstract out** astrati.
abstraction *n.* (*state*) astratia; (*something abstract*) astrata.
abstractionism *n.* astratisme.
abstractness *n.* astratia.
abstruse *adj.* difisil.
absurd *adj.* asurda.
absurdity *n.* (*quality*) asurdia; (*something absurd*) asurda.
abugida *n.* (*writing system*) abugida.
abundance *n.* abunda.
abundant *adj.* abundante.
abuse *v.* & *n.* maltrata, malusa.
abuser *n.* maltrator.
abusive *adj.* maltratante.
abusiveness *n.* maltrata.
abut *v.* toca.
abutment *n.* (*architecture*) stribo.
abutting *adj.* juntada.
abuzz *adj.* zumbinte.
abysmal *adj.* deplorable.
abyss *n.* presipe, profondon.
Abyssinia *n.* Abisinia.
Abyssinian *adj.* & *n.* abisinian.
AC *n.* corente alternante.
acacia *n.* acasia.
academe *n.* academias.
academia *n.* academias.
academic *adj.* academial, academin. • *n.* profesor.
academician *n.* academiste; profesor.
academy *n.* academia.
academy member *n.* academiste.
Acadia *n.* (*French colony*) Acadia.
Acadian *adj.* & *n.* acadian.
acanthocephalan *n.* (*worm*) acantosefalo.
acanthus *n.* (*plant*) acanto.
a cappella *adj.* sin strumento.
accede *v.* acorda. **accede to** asede.
accelerate *v.* aselera, rapidi.
acceleration *n.* aselera, rapidi.
accelerator *n.* aselerador.
accelerator key *n.* tecla rapida.
accent *n.* (*emphasis*) asentua; (*way of speaking*) pronunsia, dialeto fonetical; (*diacritic*) sinieta.
accentor *n.* (*bird*) asentor.
accentuate *v.* asentua.
accept *v.* aseta.
acceptability *n.* asetablia.
acceptable *adj.* asetable, oce.
acceptance *n.* aseta.
access *v.* & *n.* asede.
accessible *adj.* asedable.
accessory *n.* ajuntable.
accident *n.* (*chance occurrence*) acaso; (*mishap*) asidente, mal fortuna. **by accident** acaso.
accidental *adj.* (*by chance*) acaso; (*by mishap*) asidental. • *n.* (*music*) alterante.
acclaim *v.* aclama.
acclamation *n.* aclama.
acclimate *v.* abitua.
acclimatize *v.* abitua, ajusta.
accolade *n.* premio.
accommodate *v.* (*house*) casi; (*compromise*) compromete; (*change*) ajusta a.
accommodation *n.* abiteria.
accompaniment *n.* acompania.
accompanist *n.* acompaniste.
accompany *v.* acompania.
accomplice *n.* aidor.
accomplish *v.* ateni, reali, susede.
accomplished *adj.* (*skilled*) capas; (*done*) realida.
accomplishment *n.* ateni, reali, susede.
accord *v.* acorda.
accordance *n.* acorda.
according to *prep.* longo, seguente, como diseda par.
accordion *n.* acordion.
accost *v.* avansa parlante a.
account *n.* (*report*) reporta; (*bank, online, etc.*) conta. **account for** justi. **call to account** esije un esplica de. **hold to account** esije un esplica de. **pay on account** paia en partes. **take into account** considera, regarda, atende.
accountable *adj.* encargada, litigable.
accountancy *n.* contablia.
accountant *n.* contor.
accounting *n.* contablia.
account management *n.* maneja de contas.
accoutrement *n.* ajuntable.
accredit *v.* reconose.
accreditation *n.* reconose.
accrete *v.* acrete.
accretion *n.* acrete.
accrual *n.* cumula.
accrue *v.* cumula.
accumulate *v.* cumula, colie.
accumulation *n.* cumula, colie.
accumulator *n.* (*software, cryptography, energy*) cumulador.
accuracy *n.* esatia.
accurate *adj.* esata.
accursed *adj.* maldiseda.
accusation *n.* acusa.

accusative *adj.* & *n.* (*grammar*) acusativa.
accusatory *adj.* acusante.
accuse *v.* acusa. **accuse of wrongdoing** acusa de malcondui.
accused *adj.* & *n.* acusada.
accuser *n.* acusor.
accustom *v.* abitua.
accustomed *adj.* abituada. **become accustomed** abitua.
ace *n.* (*card*) as.
acelomorph (US). See *acoelomorph.*
acerbic *adj.* amarga, asida, sever.
acerbity *n.* amargia.
acetate *n.* asetato.
acetic *adj.* asetica.
acetic acid *n.* asetica.
acetone *n.* asetona.
acetylcholine *n.* asetilcolina.
acetylene *n.* asetilen.
Achaea *n.* (*Greek region*) Acea.
Achaean *adj.* & *n.* acean.
Achaemenid *adj.* & *n.* (*dynasty*) acemenan.
ache *v.* & *n.* dole, doleta.
achene *n.* (*botany*) acenio.
achievable *adj.* atenable, realable.
achieve *v.* ateni, reali, susede.
achievement *n.* ateni, reali, susede.
achiever *n.* susedor.
aching *adj.* doletosa.
achoo *interj.* axu.
achromatic *adj.* acromata, noncromatica; (*colour-blind*) sieca a color.
achy *adj.* doletosa.
acid *adj.* & *n.* asida.
acidic *adj.* asida.
acidification *n.* asidi.
acidify *v.* asidi.
acidity *n.* asidia.
acidophile *n.* asidofilica.
acidophilia *n.* asidofilia.
acidophilic *adj.* asidofilica.
acknowledge *v.* aseta, reconose; atesta.
acknowledgement *n.* reconose.
acme *n.* zenite.
acne *n.* acne.
acoelomorph (US **acelomorph**) *n.* (*organism*) aselomorfo.
acolyte *n.* aidor, seguor.
Aconcagua *n.* Monte Aconcagua.
aconite *n.* aconito.
acorn *n.* cuerca.
acoustic *adj.* acustical.
acoustic guitar *n.* gitar acustical.
acoustician *n.* acusticiste.
acoustics *n.* acustica.
acquaint *v.* informa. **be acquainted with** conose. **become acquainted with** comensa conose.
acquaintance *n.* (*knowledge*) conose; (*person*) conoseda.
acquiesce *v.* sede.
acquiescence *n.* sede.
acquire *v.* oteni.
acquired immune deficiency syndrome *n.* sindrom de imunodebilia otenida, sido.
acquisition *n.* (*action*) oteni; (*thing acquired*) otenida.
acquisitive *adj.* avar, materialiste.
acquit *v.* desculpa, remete.
acquittal *n.* desculpa.
acre *n.* acre.
acrid *adj.* amarga, con odor agu.
acrimonious *adj.* amarga.
acrimony *n.* enemia, malvole, odia.
acrobat *n.* jinasta.
acrobatic *adj.* (*like an acrobat*) jinastin; (*of acrobatics*) jinastial.
acrobatics *n.* jinastia.
acromion *n.* acromion.
acronym *n.* acronim.
acronymic *adj.* acronim.
acronymous *adj.* acronim.
acrophobia *n.* acrofobia.
acropolis *n.* acropoli.
across *prep.* (*crossing*) traversante, a ultra; (*on the other side of*) ultra. **go across** traversa.
acrostic *adj.* & *n.* acrostica.
acroterion *n.* acrotera.
acroterium *n.* acrotera.
acrylic *adj.* & *n.* acrilica.
acrylic acid *n.* asida acrilica.
act *v.* ata; (*pretend*) finje. • *n.* (*thing done, legal document, section of drama*) ata; (*pretence*) finje. **act of kindness** bon ata. **act of union** trata de uni.
actinic *adj.* actinica.
actinide *n.* (*chemistry*) actinido.
actinism *n.* (*chemistry*) actinicia.
actinium *n.* (*element*) actinio.
action *n.* ata.
actionable *adj.* litigable.
activate *v.* ativi.
activation *n.* ativi.
active *adj.* (*including grammar*) ativa.
activeness *n.* ativia.
active voice *n.* vose ativa.
activism *n.* ativisme.
activist *n.* ativiste.
activity *n.* (*state*) ativia; (*something one does*) ata.
actor *n.* ator, rolor.
actress *n.* ator fema.
actual *adj.* real, vera.
actualization *n.* reali.
actualize *v.* reali.
actuarial *adj.* atuarial.
actuary *n.* atuario.

acuity *n.* agia.
acumen *n.* astutia.
acupuncture *n.* agopuntur.
acupuncturist *n.* acupunturiste.
acute *adj.* (*sense*, *angle*) agu; (*medical*) acuta.
acute accent *n.* sinieta agu.
acuteness *n.* agia.
acyclic *adj.* nonsiclin.
ad[1] *n.* anunsia. **small ad** anunsieta.
AD[2] *abbr.* ec (*eda comun*).
adage *n.* proverbo, diseda.
adagio *adj.* adajio.
Adam *n.* Adam.
adamant *adj.* ostinosa.
Adam's apple *n.* poma de Adam.
adapt *v.* ajusta.
adaptability *n.* ajustablia.
adaptable *adj.* ajustable.
adaptation *n.* ajusta.
adaptationism *n.* ajustisme.
adaptationist *n.* ajustiste.
adapter *n.* (*person*) ajustor; (*device*) ajustador.
adaption *n.* ajusta.
adaptive *adj.* ajustal.
add *v.* ajunta. **add up** soma.
addable *adj.* ajuntable.
addendum *n.* ajuntada.
adder *n.* vipera.
addict *v.* abitua. • *n.* dependente, manica.
addicted *adj.* dependente. **addicted to drugs** drogamanica. **grow addicted** abitua.
addiction *n.* abitua, depende, mania.
addictive *adj.* abituante.
add-in *n.* ajuntable.
adding machine *n.* macina de soma.
addition *n.* ajunta, soma. **in addition** ajuntada, en ajunta, plu. **in addition to** en ajunta a. **with the addition of** con ance.
additional *adj.* ajuntada, plu.
addle *v.* putri; (*mind*) confusa.
add-on *n.* ajuntable.
address *v.* & *n.* adirije. **address oneself to** (*audience*, *task*) dirije se a; (*task*) embarca.
addressee *n.* destina.
adduce *v.* sita, alega.
adduct *v.* (*muscle*) adui.
adduction *n.* adui.
adductor *n.* (*muscle*) aduador.
Aden *n.* Aden. **Gulf of Aden** Golfo Aden.
adenoid *n.* adenoide.
adenoidal *adj.* adenoidal.
adept *adj.* capas. • *n.* aderor.
adequacy *n.* sufisi.
adequate *adj.* sufisinte.
adhere *v.* adere.
adherence *n.* adere.
adherent *n.* aderor.
adhesion *n.* adere.
adhesive *adj.* & *n.* aderente.
adhesiveness *n.* adere.
adhesive tape *n.* sinta aderente.
adiabatic *adj.* (*physics*) adiabatica.
adieu *interj.* adio.
adipose *adj.* adipos.
adjacent *adj.* visina, juntada.
adjectival *adj.* ajetival; ajetivin.
adjective *n.* ajetivo.
adjective clause *n.* suproposa ajetivin.
adjective phrase *n.* formula ajetivin.
adjoining *adj.* juntada, visina.
adjourn *v.* pausa, suspende.
adjournment *n.* pausa, suspende.
adjudicate *v.* judi.
adjudicator *n.* judor.
adjunct *n.* ajuntada.
adjure *v.* recomenda forte.
adjust *v.* ajusta.
adjustability *n.* ajustablia.
adjustable *adj.* ajustable.
adjustable wrench *n.* clave ajustable.
adjuster *n.* (*person*) ajustor; (*device*) ajustador.
adjustment *n.* ajusta.
adjutant *n.* aidor militar.
adman *n.* anunsior.
administer *v.* dirije, maneja.
administrate *v.* dirije, maneja.
administration *n.* (*process*) dirije; (*people*) dirijores.
administration charge *n.* paia per maneja.
administrative *adj.* dirijal, manejal.
administrator *n.* dirijor, manejor.
admirable *adj.* amirable.
admiral *n.* amiral. **red admiral** (*butterfly*) atalanta.
admiralship *n.* amiralia.
admiralty *n.* amiralia.
admiration *n.* amira.
admire *v.* amira.
admirer *n.* amiror.
admissible *adj.* asetable.
admission *n.* (*confession*) confesa; (*entrance*) entra.
admit *v.* confesa; aseta; entra, lasa ce on entra, permete entra; (*to citizenship*) sitadani.
admittance *n.* entra. **no admittance** entra proibida.
admixture *n.* misca.
admonish *v.* reproxa.
admonition *n.* reproxa.
ado *n.* ajita, reata.
adobe *n.* adobe.
adolescence *n.* adolese. **pass through adolescence** adolese.
adolescent *adj.* & *n.* adolesente.
adonis *n.* adonis.
adopt *v.* adota, propri.

adoptee *n.* adotada.
adopter *n.* adotor.
adoption *n.* adota.
adoptive *n.* (*child*) adotada.
adorability *n.* adorablia.
adorable *adj.* adorable.
adoration *n.* adora.
adore *v.* adora.
adorer *n.* adoror.
adorn *v.* decora, orna.
adornment *n.* decora, orna.
adposition *n.* (*grammar*) aposada.
adrenal *n.* (*gland*) suprarenal.
adrenaline *n.* epinefrina.
Adriatic *adj.* adriatica.
Adriatic Sea *n.* Mar Adriatica.
adrift *adj.* vagante.
adroit *adj.* capas.
adsorb *v.* adsorbe.
adsorption *n.* adsorbe.
aduki *n.* fava azuci.
adulate *v.* adula.
adulation *n.* adula.
adulator *n.* adulor.
adulatory *adj.* adulante.
adult *adj.* adulte, matur. • *n.* adulte, person matur. **become adult** adulti.
adulter *v.* adultera.
adulterate *v.* adultera.
adulterer *n.* adulteror.
adulterous *adj.* adulterante.
adultery *n.* adultera. **commit adultery** adultera.
adulthood *n.* adultia.
advance *v.* & *n.* avansa, progresa. • *interj.* avansa. • *adj.* fronte.
advanced *adj.* avansada.
advancement *n.* progresa.
advance showing *n.* previde.
advantage *n.* vantaje. • *v.* vantaji. **gain advantage** benefica. **take advantage of** esplota, profita de.
advantageous *adj.* vantajosa.
advent *n.* (*including religious*) ariva.
Adventism *n.* (*Christianity*) adventisme.
Adventist *adj.* & *n.* adventiste.
adventitious *adj.* acaso; nonativa; (*biology*) acaso locada.
adventure *v.* & *n.* aventura.
adventurer *n.* aventuror.
adventurous *adj.* (*activity*) aventurosa; (*person*) aventurante.
adverb *n.* averbo.
adverb clause *n.* suproposa averbin.
adverbial *adj.* averbal; averbin.
adversary *n.* enemi, oposor.
adverse *adj.* enemin, oposante.
adversity *n.* mal fortuna.
advert *n.* anunsia.
advertise *v.* anunsia.
advertisement *n.* anunsia.
advertising *n.* anunsia.
advice *n.* consela; (*notification*) avisa.
advise *v.* consela; (*notify*) avisa.
adviser *n.* conselor.
advisor *n.* conselor.
advocacy *n.* promove.
advocate *v.* defende, promove. • *n.* defendor.
adze *n.* (*tool*) axia.
adzuki *n.* fava azuci.
Aegean *adj.* ejean. • *n.* (*region*) Ejeo.
Aegean Sea *n.* Mar Ejeo.
aegis *n.* proteje, suporta.
-aemia (US **-emia**) *suff.* (*blood*) -emia.
-aemic (US **-emic**) *suff.* -emica.
Aeneid *n.* (*poem*) Eneida.
aeon (US **eon**) *n.* eon.
aerate *v.* airi.
aeration *n.* airi.
aerator *n.* airador.
aerial *adj.* airal. • *n.* antena.
aerial combat *n.* combate airal.
aerial photograph *n.* foto airal.
aerie *n.* nido.
aero- *pref.* airo-.
aerobatics *n.* jinastia de aira.
aerobe *n.* airobio.
aerobic *adj.* airobial.
aerobic exercise *n.* eserse airobial.
aerobics *n.* eserse airobial.
aerodrome *n.* campo de avion.
aerodynamic *adj.* airodinamical.
aerodynamics *n.* airodinamica.
aerofoil *n.* airofolia.
aerogel *n.* airojel.
aerogenerator *n.* turbina de venta.
aerolite *n.* (*meteorite*) airolito.
aerological *adj.* airolojial.
aerology *n.* airolojia.
aeronautical *adj.* aironautical.
aeronautics *n.* aironautica.
aeroplane *n.* avion.
aerosol *n.* airosol.
aerospace *n.* airospasio.
aerostat *n.* (*including balloon*) airostato.
æsc (*letter*). See *ash*[2].
aesthete (US **esthete**) *n.* amor de belia; esteticiste.
aesthetic (US **esthetic**) *adj.* estetical.
aesthetician (US **esthetician**) *n.* esteticiste.
aesthetics (US **esthetics**) *n.* estetica.
aestival (US **estival**) *adj.* estatal.
aetiology (US **etiology**) *n.* etiolojia.
afar *adj.* distante.
affability *n.* amablia.
affable *adj.* amable.

affair *n.* cosa, conserna; (*love*) adultera.
affect *v.* afeta, influe; (*emotionally*) emosia; (*pretend*) finje.
affectation *n.* ostenta.
affected *adj.* egosa, ostentosa, finjosa.
affection *n.* ama, amosia.
affectionate *adj.* amosa.
affidavit *n.* afidavit.
affiliate *v.* parteni. • *n.* membro.
affiliated *adj.* partenente.
affiliation *n.* parteni.
affinity *n.* simpatia.
affirm *v.* afirma.
affirmation *n.* afirma.
affirmative *adj.* afirmante.
affix *v.* & *n.* afisa.
affixation *n.* afisa.
afflict *v.* dole; carga.
affliction *n.* dole; sufri.
affluence *n.* ricia.
affluent *adj.* rica.
afford *v.* (*to buy*) pote compra; (*allow oneself to do*) permete a se.
affordable *adj.* a bon custa.
affray *n.* scaramuxa.
affricate *adj.* & *n.* africante.
affront *n.* ofende.
Afghan *adj.* & *n.* afgani.
Afghan hound *n.* lepror afgani.
Afghani *adj.* & *n.* afgani.
Afghanistan *n.* Afganistan.
Afghanistani *adj.* & *n.* afgani.
aficionado *n.* aderor, fan.
afire *adj.* flaminte.
aflame *adj.* flaminte.
afloat *adj.* flotante.
aflutter *adj.* tremante.
afoot *adj.* comensante, progresante.
aforementioned *adj.* ja notada.
afraid *adj.* temente, temosa.
Afrasian *adj.* afroasian.
afresh *adv.* denova.
Africa *n.* Africa. **South Africa** (*country*) Sudafrica. **Southern Africa** (*region*) Africa sude.
African *adj.* & *n.* african. **South African** sudafrican.
African American *adj.* & *n.* afroamerican.
African tetra *n.* (*fish*) tetra african.
Afrikaans *n.* africans.
Afrikaner *adj.* & *n.* africans.
afro *adj.* & *n.* afro.
Afro-American *adj.* & *n.* afroamerican.
Afro-Asiatic *adj.* afroasian.
Afro-Eurasian *adj.* afroeurasian.
aft *adj.* (*nautical*) popal.
after *prep.* pos. • *subord.* pos cuando. **after all** an con tota, an pos tota, ultima. **one after another** pos lunlotra, la un pos la otra.
afterbirth *n.* plasenta.
afterburner *n.* posardador.
aftereffect *n.* posefeto.
afterglow *n.* (*including emotion*) brasas.
afterimage *n.* posimaje, posimpresa.
afterimpression *n.* posimpresa.
afterlife *n.* vive pos mori.
aftermath *n.* tempo seguente.
afternoon *n.* posmedia.
aftershave *n.* losion de rasa.
aftershock *n.* replica sismica.
aftertaste *n.* sabor persistente.
afterthought *n.* considera tarda.
afterward *adv.* a pos.
afterwards *adv.* a pos.
afterword *n.* epilogo.
again *adv.* denova. **again and again** sempre denova.
against *prep.* contra.
agape[1] *adj.* (*gaping*) baliante.
agape[2] *n.* (*Christian love*) agape.
agar *n.* (*substance*) agar.
agar-agar *n.* (*substance*) agar.
agaric *n.* (*fungus*) agarico.
agate *n.* agata.
agave *n.* (*plant*) agave.
age *n.* (*era, measure of years*) eda. • *v.* vei, senese, gasta. **of the same age** coedal. **old age** eda matur, senese, veia.
aged *adj.* senesente, matur.
ageing (US **aging**) *adj.* senesente.
ageism (US **agism**) *n.* edisme.
ageist (US **agist**) *adj.* ediste.
ageless *adj.* eterna, nonsenesente.
agency *n.* ajenteria, ofisia. **through the agency of** par.
agenda *n.* (*appointments*) ajenda; (*meeting*) ordina de la dia, menu.
agender *adj.* & *n.* ajenero.
agent *n.* ajente.
agglomerate *v.* agrega.
agglomeration *n.* (*action, result*) agrega.
agglutinate *v.* aglutina.
agglutinative *adj.* aglutinante.
aggravate *v.* mali.
aggregate *v.* & *n.* agrega, combina.
aggregation *n.* agrega.
aggress *v.* ataca.
aggression *n.* ataca, viole, combatosia.
aggressive *adj.* atacante, atacosa, coleriosa, combatosa, violente.
aggressor *n.* atacor.
aggrieved *adj.* iritada.
aghast *adj.* xocada.
agile *adj.* ajil.
agility *n.* ajilia.
aging (US). See *ageing*.

agism (US). See *ageism*.
agist (US). See *ageist*.
agitable *adj.* turbable.
agitate *v.* ajita, secute, turba.
agitation *n.* ajita.
agitator *n.* ajitor, provocor.
agitprop *n.* ajitprop.
aglet *n.* gaina de cordeta.
aglow *adj.* ardin, radiante.
agnostic *adj.* & *n.* agnostica.
agnosticism *n.* agnosticisme.
ago *adv.* ante aora, a ante. **a long time ago** a multe tempo ante aora. **two days ago** a du dias ante aora.
agonized *adj.* angusada.
agony *n.* angusa, dolon.
agora *n.* agora.
agoraphobe *n.* agorafobica.
agoraphobia *n.* agorafobia.
agoraphobic *adj.* agorafobica.
agouti *n.* (*rodent*) aguti.
-agra *suff.* (*pain*) -agra.
agrarian *adj.* cultival.
agrarianism *n.* cultivorisme.
agree *v.* (*including grammar*) acorda.
agreeable *adj.* plasente, gustable.
agreeableness *n.* plase.
agreement *n.* acorda. **agreement to coexist** acorda de coesiste. **be in agreement** acorda.
agricultural *adj.* cultival.
agriculturalist *n.* cultivor.
agriculture *n.* cultiva.
agrimony *n.* agrimonia.
agronomic *adj.* agronomial.
agronomical *adj.* agronomial.
agronomist *n.* agronomiste.
agronomy *n.* agronomia.
aground, run *v.* encalia.
ah *interj.* a.
aha *interj.* aha.
ahead *adv.* a ante, a fronte. **ahead of** ante, a fronte de.
ahem *interj.* (*clearing throat*) hm.
ahimsa *n.* (*Buddhism*, *Hinduism*) ahimsa.
ahoy *interj.* he. **ahoy there** alo ala.
aid *v.* & *n.* aida.
aide *n.* aidor.
aide-mémoire *n.* aidamemoria.
AIDS *n.* sido.
aikido *n.* aicido.
ailanthus *n.* (*tree*) ailanto.
aileron *n.* aleta.
ailment *n.* maladia.
aim *v.* punta. • *n.* punta; (*intention*) intende.
aimless *adj.* nondirijeda.
air *n.* aira. • *v.* airi; (*state publicly*) publici. **in the air** en la aira, airal. **in the open air** su sielo. **put on airs** finje superioria.
airbag *n.* cuxin de securia.
air bed *n.* materas inflable.
airborne *adj.* portada par aira.
airbrush *n.* airograf. • *v.* airografi.
air conditioner *n.* frescador.
aircraft *n.* avion, volador.
aircraft carrier *n.* portavion.
aircraft hangar *n.* avioneria.
Airedale terrier *n.* terier de Airedale.
airfare *n.* custa de viaja.
airfield *n.* campo de avion.
airflow *n.* flue de aira.
airfoil (US). See *aerofoil*.
air force *n.* (*military*) forte de aira.
airfreight *v.* & *n.* avioni.
air freshener *n.* desodorinte.
airhead *n.* fol.
air hostess *n.* ospitor de avion.
airless *adj.* sin aira.
airlift *v.* transporta par avion.
airline *n.* airocompania.
airliner *n.* avion comersial.
airlock *n.* clusa de aira.
airmail *v.* & *n.* airoposta, posta airal.
air mattress *n.* materas inflable.
airplane (US). See *aeroplane*.
airport *n.* airoporto.
air purifier *n.* puriaira.
air raid *n.* ataca de aira.
air sac *n.* alveolo.
airship *n.* airostato dirijable.
airsick *adj.* nauseada de vola.
airsickness *n.* maladia de vola.
airspace *n.* airospasio.
air steward *n.* ospitor de avion.
airstream *n.* corente de aira.
airstrip *n.* campo de avion.
airtight *adj.* nonpermeable.
air-to-air *adj.* de aira a aira.
air-to-ground *adj.* de aira a tera.
air-to-surface *adj.* de aira a tera.
air traffic control *n.* controla de trafica airal.
airworthy *adj.* secur per vola.
airy *adj.* airosa.
aisle *n.* coredor.
ajar *adj.* pico abrida.
a.k.a. *abbr.* acc (*ance conoseda como*).
akimbo *adj.* carafin.
akin *adj.* simil.
Akkadian *adj.* & *n.* (*person*, *language*) acad.
Aksum *n.* (*Ethiopian city*) Axum.
akubra *n.* (*hat*) xapon.
akvavit *n.* (*drink*) acuavit.
-al *suff.* (*aldehyde*) -al.
Alabama *n.* (*US state*) Alabama.
alabaster *n.* alabastro. • *adj.* alabastrin.
à la carte *adj.* (*menu*) a la carta.
alack *interj.* ai.

alacrity *n.* zelo.
alarm *v.* alarma, xoca. • *n.* alarma, avertador.
alarm clock *n.* veliador.
alarmed *adj.* alarmada, temosa.
alarmist *n.* sperdeteme.
alas *interj.* ai.
Alaska *n.* (*US state*) Alaska.
Alaskan *adj.* alaskan.
Alaskan Sea *n.* Gulfo Alaska.
alate *adj.* con alas.
Alawi *adj.* & *n.* (*Islam*) alaui.
Alawite *adj.* & *n.* alaui.
alb *n.* camison blanca.
albacore *n.* (*fish*) tun blanca.
Albania *n.* Xciperia, Albania.
Albanian *adj.* & *n.* (*person*, *language*) xcip, albanian.
albatross *n.* albatros; (*golf*) tre su la norma.
albedo *n.* (*astronomy*) albedo.
albeit *subord.* an si.
Albert, Lake *n.* Lago Albert.
Alberta *n.* (*Canadian province*) Alberta.
albinism *n.* albinisme.
albino *adj.* & *n.* albino.
Alboran Sea *n.* Mar Alboran.
album *n.* album.
albumen *n.* albumen.
albumin *n.* (*protein*) albumina.
alburnum *n.* lenio esterna.
alchemical *adj.* alcimical.
alchemist *n.* alcimiciste.
alchemy *n.* alcimica.
alcohol *n.* alcol.
alcoholic *adj.* (*drink*, *content*) alcolosa, de alcol; (*person*) alcolomanica. • *n.* alcolomanica.
alcoholic drink *n.* bevida de alcol.
alcoholism *n.* alcolomania.
alcohol stove *n.* stufa de alcol.
alcove *n.* alcova.
aldehyde *n.* aldehido.
alder *n.* alno.
alderman *n.* vismaior.
aldosterone *n.* (*hormone*) aldosterona.
ale *n.* (*beer*) ale.
alehouse *n.* taverna.
alembic *n.* distilador.
aleph *n.* (*Hebrew letter* א) alef.
alert *adj.* atendente, vijilante. • *v.* & *n.* avisa. **be alert** vijila.
aleurone *n.* (*botany*) aleuron.
Aleut *adj.* & *n.* (*person*, *language*) aleut.
Aleutian *adj.* aleutian.
Aleutian Islands *n.* Isolas Aleutian.
Aleutian Range *n.* Montes Aleutian.
alewife *n.* (*fish*) alosa arengin.
Alexandria *n.* (*Egyptian city*) Alexandria.
Alexandrian *adj.* alexandrian.
alexandrine *adj.* (*poetry*) alexandrin.
alexia *n.* (*medical*) alexia.
alfalfa *n.* alfalfa.
al fresco *adv.* su sielo.
alga *n.* alge. **algae** alges.
algal *adj.* algal.
algebra *n.* aljebra.
algebraic *adj.* aljebral.
algebraist *n.* aljebriste.
Algeria *n.* Jazair.
Algerian *adj.* & *n.* jazairi.
-algia *suff.* (*pain*) -aljia.
-algic *suff.* -aljica.
Algiers *n.* Jazair.
Algonquian *adj.* (*language family*) algoncian.
Algonquin *adj.* & *n.* (*language*) algoncin.
algorithm *n.* algoritmo.
algorithmic *adj.* algoritmal.
alias *n.* alias, nom falsa. • *v.* aliasi.
alibi *n.* alibi.
alidade *n.* (*device*) alidada.
alien *adj.* & *n.* estrateran; stranjer.
alienate *v.* stranjeri; (*emotion*, *law*) aliena.
alienation *n.* stranjeri; (*emotion*, *law*) aliena.
alight *v.* desende.
align *v.* alinia.
alignment *n.* alinia. **get into alignment** alinia se. **in alignment** aliniada.
alike *adj.* simil.
alimentary *adj.* dijestal.
alimentary tract *n.* curso de dijesta.
alimony *n.* pension de divorsa.
alive *adj.* vivente. **be alive** vive.
alizarin *n.* (*pigment*) rubia.
alkali *n.* alcalin.
alkaline *adj.* alcalin.
alkalinity *n.* alcalinia.
alkaliphile *n.* alcalifilica.
alkaliphilia *n.* alcalifilia.
alkaliphilic *adj.* alcalifilica.
alkalization *n.* alcalini.
alkalize *v.* alcalini.
alkaloid *n.* alcaloide.
alkalosis *n.* (*medical*) alcalose.
alkane *n.* alcano.
alkene *n.* (*chemistry*) alcen.
alkyl *n.* (*chemistry*) alcil.
alkyne *n.* (*chemistry*) alcin.
all *det.*, *pron.* & *adv.* tota; (*optional plural pronoun*) totas. **all day** tra la dia. **all over** covrente, a covre de. **all the same** (*however*) an tal. **at all** vera; sin eseta. **not at all** a no grado, tota no, vera no. **on all fours** sur manos e jenos; (*animal*) sur cuatro pedes.
Allah *n.* Dio.
allantois *n.* (*membrane*) alantoide.
allegation *n.* alega, reporta.
allege *v.* alega.
allegiance *n.* fida.
allegorical *adj.* alegorial.

allegory *n.* alegoria.
allegro *adj.* (*music*) vivosa.
allele *n.* (*genetics*) alelo.
alleluia *interj.* aleluia.
allemande *n.* (*dance, music*) alemande.
Allen bolt *n.* vise de Allen.
Allen key *n.* clave exagon.
Allen screw *n.* vise de Allen.
Allen wrench *n.* clave exagon.
allergen *n.* alerjen.
allergenic *adj.* alerjen.
allergic *adj.* alerjica.
allergist *n.* alerjiste.
allergy *n.* alerjia.
alleviate *v.* lejeri.
alley *n.* rueta, stradeta.
alleyway *n.* stradeta.
All Hallows' Eve *n.* vijila de tota santas.
alliance *n.* alia.
alligator *n.* aligator.
all-in-one *adj.* de sola un peso.
alliterate *v.* aletera.
alliteration *n.* aletera.
alliterative *adj.* aleterosa.
allo- *pref.* (*other*) alo-.
allocate *v.* asinia; (*ration*) rasiona.
allocation *n.* asinia; (*ration*) rasiona.
allogamy *n.* estrapoleni.
allopathic *adj.* alopatica.
allopathy *n.* alopatia.
allosaur *n.* alosauro.
allosaurus *n.* alosauro.
allot *v.* asinia.
allotment *n.* asinia; loca asiniada.
allotrope *n.* alotropo.
allotropic *adj.* alotropo.
allotropy *n.* alotropia.
allow *v.* permete, lasa. **allow entry** lasa ce on entra, permete entra. **allow oneself** permete a se.
allowable *adj.* permeteda, asetable.
allowance *n.* contribui, cuota.
alloy *v.* alia. • *n.* aliada.
all right *adj.* & *interj.* oce.
All Saints' Eve *n.* vijila de tota santas.
allspice *n.* pimento.
all-terrain *adj.* multiterenal.
all-terrain vehicle *n.* multiterenal.
allude *v.* refere.
allure *v.* atrae. • *n.* atrae, fasina.
allusion *n.* refere.
alluvial *adj.* aluvial.
alluvium *n.* aluvia.
all-wheel drive *n.* engranada a cuatro rotas.
ally *v.* alia. • *n.* aliada. **ally oneself with** alia se con.
alma mater *n.* universia de diploma.
almanac *n.* almanaco.
almighty *adj.* omnipotente.
almond *n.* (*nut*) amanda; (*tree*) amando.
almondine *adj.* con amandas.
almost *adv.* cuasi. **almost everyone** cuasi cadun.
alms *n.* carita.
almsgiving *n.* carita.
almshouse *n.* povreria.
aloe *n.* (*plant*) aloe.
aloft *adv.* en la aira; a alta.
alone *adj.* solitar.
along *prep.* longo.
alongside *prep.* a lado de.
aloof *adj.* nonamin, nonsosial, distante.
alopecia *n.* calvia.
aloud *adv.* a vose, parlante.
alp *n.* alpe. **Alps** Alpes.
alpaca *n.* (*animal*) alpaca.
Alpenhorn *n.* corno alpan.
alpha *n.* (*Greek letter* A, α) alfa.
alphabet *n.* alfabeta.
alphabetic *adj.* alfabetal.
alphabetical *adj.* alfabetal. **put into alphabetical order** alfabeti.
alphabetize *v.* alfabeti.
Alpha Centauri *n.* Alfa de la Sentauro.
alphanumeric *adj.* alfanumeral.
alphasyllabary *n.* (*writing system*) abugida.
Alphorn *n.* corno alpan.
Alpine *adj.* alpan.
already *adv.* ja. **already mentioned** ja notada.
alright *adj.* & *interj.* oce.
Alsatian *n.* can de pastor deutx.
also *adv.* ance.
Altai *adj.* & *n.* altai.
Altaic *adj.* altaica.
Altai Mountains *n.* Montes Altai.
altar *n.* altar.
altarpiece *n.* arte de altar.
Altay *adj.* & *n.* (*person, language*) altai.
alter *v.* altera.
alterable *adj.* alterable.
alteration *n.* altera.
altercation *n.* luta.
alter ego *n.* otra ego, personalia alternativa.
alternant *n.* alternante.
alternate *v.* alterna. • *adj.* otra posible. • *n.* otra posible.
alternating current *n.* corente alternante.
alternation *n.* alterna.
alternative *adj.* alternativa, elejable, otra posible. • *n.* alternativa, elejable, otra posible. **an alternative idea** un otra idea posible.
alternative personality *n.* personalia alternativa.
alternator *n.* alternador.
althaea *n.* altea.

although *subord.* an si, contra ce, permetente ce.
altimeter *n.* altimetre.
altiplano *n.* plano alta.
altitude *n.* altia.
altitude sickness *n.* maladia de altia.
alto *adj.* & *n.* alto.
altogether *adv.* completa, en junta.
altruism *n.* altruisme.
altruist *n.* altruiste.
altruistic *adj.* altruiste.
alum *n.* (*substance*) alum.
alumina *n.* osido de aluminio.
aluminium (US **aluminum**) *n.* aluminio.
aluminium foil (US **aluminum foil**) *n.* paper de aluminio.
aluminium oxide (US **aluminum oxide**) *n.* osido de aluminio.
alumna *n.* studiante pasada.
alumnus *n.* studiante pasada.
alveolar *adj.* & *n.* alveolal.
alveolitis *n.* alveolite.
alveolus *n.* alveolo.
always *adv.* sempre, a cada ves.
am[1] *v.* (*be*) es.
a.m.[2] *abbr.* am (*ante mediadia*).
amalgam *n.* combina.
amalgamate *v.* combina.
amalgamation *n.* combina.
amandine *adj.* con amandas.
amaranth *n.* amaranto.
amaryllis *n.* (*plant*) amarilis.
amass *v.* asembla.
amateur *n.* amator.
amateurish *adj.* noncapas.
amatory *adj.* romantica.
amaze *v.* stona, mervelia, surprende.
amazement *n.* stona.
Amazon *n.* (*mythology*) amazona; (*region*) Amazonas.
Amazon Rainforest *n.* Foresta Amazonas.
Amazon River *n.* Rio Amazonas.
ambassador *n.* ambasador.
amber *adj.* (*colour*) ambar. • *n.* (*resin*) ambar.
ambergris *n.* (*substance*) ambargris.
ambi- *pref.* ambi-.
ambidextrous *adj.* ambidestrosa.
ambience *n.* ambiente.
ambient *adj.* ambiente.
ambient temperature *n.* temperatur ambiente.
ambiguity *n.* (*quality*) ambiguia; (*something ambiguous*) ambigua.
ambiguous *adj.* ambigua, interpretable.
ambiphile *n.* ambifilica.
ambiphilia *n.* ambifilia.
ambiphilic *adj.* ambifilica.
ambit *n.* limitas.
ambition *n.* aspira.
ambitious *adj.* aspirante.
ambivalence *n.* ambivale.
ambivalent *adj.* ambivalente. **be ambivalent** ambivale.
amble *v.* pasea lenta.
amblyope *n.* ambliopica.
amblyopia *n.* (*medical*) ambliopia.
amblyopic *adj.* ambliopica.
ambrosia *n.* ambrosia.
ambulance *n.* ambulansia.
ambush *v.* & *n.* embosce, surprende.
ameb... (US). See *amoeb...*
ameliorate *v.* boni.
amen *interj.* amen.
amenable *adj.* influable; capas. **amenable to change** fasil cambiable.
amend *v.* cambia. **make amends** compensa.
amendment *n.* cambia.
amenity *n.* desirable.
America *n.* America. **North America** America Norde. **South America** America Sude.
American *adj.* & *n.* american; (*of the US*) esuan, SUA.
American crow *n.* corvo american.
American football *n.* futbal american.
American goldfinch *n.* spineta.
American Indian *adj.* & *n.* american orijinal.
Americanization *n.* americani.
Americanize *v.* americani.
American jay *n.* jai american.
American robin *n.* turdo roja.
American sole *n.* (*fish*) solea american.
American tetra *n.* (*fish*) tetra american.
American wintergreen *n.* te de bosce.
americium *n.* (*element*) amerisio.
Amerindian *adj.* & *n.* american orijinal.
amethyst *n.* ametista.
Amhara *adj.* & *n.* (*person*, *language*) amarina.
Amharic *adj.* & *n.* (*person*, *language*) amarina.
amiable *adj.* amin.
amicable *adj.* amin.
amid *prep.* entre.
amide *n.* (*substance*) amida.
amidst *prep.* entre.
amine *adj.* & *n.* (*chemistry*) amina.
amino acid *n.* aminoasida.
aminobutyric *adj.* aminobutirica.
amir *n.* amir.
Amish *adj.* & *n.* amix.
amiss *adj.* noncoreta.
amity *n.* amia.
ammeter *n.* amperimetre.
ammo *n.* muni.
ammo belt *n.* sintur de muni.
ammonia *n.* amonia.
ammonium *n.* amonio.

ammo vest *n.* jaceta de muni.
ammunition *n.* muni.
ammunition belt *n.* sintur de muni.
amnesia *n.* amnesia.
amnesiac *adj.* & *n.* amnesica.
amnesic *adj.* & *n.* amnesica.
amnesty *v.* & *n.* amnestia.
amnio- *pref.* amnio-.
amniocentesis *n.* amniosentese.
amnion *n.* (*membrane*) amnio.
amniotic *adj.* amnial.
amoeba *n.* ameba.
amoebiside *n.* amebiside.
amoeboid *adj.* amebin.
amok *adj.* amoc. **run amok** furia.
amok syndrome *n.* sindrom amoc.
among *prep.* entre.
amongst *prep.* entre.
amoral *adj.* sin moralia.
amorous *adj.* amosa.
amorousness *n.* amosia.
amorphous *adj.* sin forma.
amortization *n.* amorti.
amortize *v.* amorti.
amount *n.* cuantia.
amp *n.* amper.
ampage *n.* cuantia de amperes.
amperage *n.* cuantia de amperes.
ampere *n.* amper.
ampersand *n.* sinia de "e", bretsel.
amphetamine *n.* amfetamina.
amphi- *pref.* amfi-.
amphibian *n.* amfibio.
amphibious *adj.* amfibin.
amphibrach *n.* amfibraco.
amphitheatre (US **amphitheater**) *n.* amfiteatro.
amphora *n.* amfora.
ample *adj.* bastante. **be ample** basta.
amplification *n.* grandi.
amplifier *n.* fortador.
amplify *v.* grandi.
amplitude *n.* grandia.
amply *adv.* bastante.
ampoule *n.* ampola.
amputate *v.* amputa.
amputated limb *n.* amputada.
amputation *n.* amputa.
amputee *n.* amputada.
amuck *adj.* amoc.
amulet *n.* joala majiosa.
amuse *v.* diverti.
amuse-gueule *n.* deleta.
amusement *n.* diverti.
amusement park *n.* parce de divertis.
amygdala *n.* amigdala.
amyl- *pref.* amil-.
amylase *n.* amilase.
amyloid *n.* amiloide.
amyloidosis *n.* amiloidose.
an *det.* un.
-an *suff.* (*saturated hydrocarbon*) -an.
ana- *pref.* ana-.
Anabaptism *n.* (*Christianity*) anabatisme.
Anabaptist *adj.* & *n.* anabatiste.
anabolic *adj.* anabolal.
anabolism *n.* anaboli.
anabolize *v.* (*biology*) anaboli.
anachronism *n.* anacron.
anachronistic *adj.* anacron.
anacoluthon *n.* nonsegue sintatical.
anaconda *n.* anaconda.
anaemia (US **anemia**) *n.* anemia.
anaemic (US **anemic**) *adj.* anemica.
anaerobe *n.* (*organism*) nonairobio.
anaerobic *adj.* nonairobial.
anaesthesia (US **anesthesia**) *n.* anestesia.
anaesthetic (US **anesthetic**) *n.* anestesente.
anaesthetist (US **anesthetist**) *n.* anestesiste.
anaesthetization (US **anesthetization**) *n.* anestese.
anaesthetize (US **anesthetize**) *v.* anestese.
anagram *n.* anagram.
anagrammatic *adj.* anagramal.
anagrammatize *v.* anagrami.
anal *adj.* anal.
analeptic *adj.* analesica.
analgesic *n.* paradole.
analog (US). See *analogue*.
analogous *adj.* analoja.
analogousness *n.* analojia.
analogue (US **analog**) *adj.* & *n.* analoja.
analogy *n.* (*comparison*) analojia; (*something analogous*) analoja.
anal-retentive *adj.* constrinjeda.
anal sex *n.* seso anal.
analysable (US **analyzable**) *adj.* analisable.
analysand *n.* analiseda.
analyse (US **analyze**) *v.* analise.
analyser (US **analyzer**) *n.* analisador.
analysis *n.* analise.
analyst *n.* analisor.
analytic *adj.* analisal.
analytical *adj.* analisal.
analytic patient *n.* analiseda.
analyz... (US). See *analys...*
anamnesis *n.* (*medical*) anamnese.
anamorphic *adj.* anamorfosal.
anamorphosis *n.* (*optics*, *biology*) anamorfose.
anapaest (US **anapest**) *n.* anapesto.
anapaestic (US **anapestic**) *adj.* anapestal.
anaphor *n.* (*word that refers back*) anafor.
anaphora *n.* anaforia.
anaphoric *adj.* anafor.

anarchic *adj.* anarciosa.
anarchism *n.* anarcisme.
anarchist *n.* anarciste.
anarchy *n.* anarcia.
anastomosis *n.* (*anatomy*) anastomose.
anathema *n.* odiada.
anathematize *v.* odia, maldise.
Anatolia *n.* Anatolia.
Anatolian *adj.* & *n.* anatolian.
anatomical *adj.* anatomial.
anatomist *n.* anatomiste.
anatomy *n.* anatomia.
ancestor *n.* asendente.
ancho *n.* (*chili*) anxo.
anchor *n.* ancor; (*news*) presentor. • *v.* ancori. **drop anchor** cade la ancor. **weigh anchor** leva la ancor.
anchorage *n.* ancoreria.
anchoress *n.* eremita.
anchorite *n.* eremita.
anchorman *n.* presentor de novas.
anchorwoman *n.* presentor de novas.
anchovy *n.* anxoa.
ancient *adj.* antica.
Ancient Egypt *n.* Egipte antica.
ancient times *n.* eda antica.
ancillary *adj.* aidante, ajuntada.
ancylostomiasis *n.* ancilostomiase.
and *conj.* e. **and not** no. **and/or** e/o. **and so** donce. **and so forth** e tal cosas, e tal continuante, etc. **and so on** e tal cosas, e tal continuante, etc. **and then?** (*what happened?*) e a pos? **and whatnot** e tal cosas. **and yet** ma ancora.
Andalusia *n.* (*Spanish region*) Andalusia.
Andaman *n.* Andaman.
Andaman Islands *n.* Isolas Andaman.
Andaman Sea *n.* Mar Andaman.
andante *adj.* (*music*) paseante.
Andes *n.* Andes.
andiron *n.* (*holding logs in a fire*) portatronco.
and/or *conj.* e/o.
Andorra *n.* Andora.
Andorran *adj.* & *n.* andoran.
andro- *pref.* (*male*) andro-.
androecium *n.* (*botany*) androseo.
androgen *n.* androjen.
androgyne *n.* androjine.
androgynous *adj.* androjine.
androgyny *n.* androjinia.
android *adj.* & *n.* androide.
andromeda[1] *n.* (*plant*) andromeda.
Andromeda[2] *n.* (*mythology*, *constellation*) Andromeda.
androphile *n.* androfilica.
androphilia *n.* androfilia.
androphilic *adj.* androfilica.
androphobe *n.* androfobica.
androphobia *n.* androfobia.
androphobic *adj.* androfobica.
-andry *suff.* -andria.
anecdotal *adj.* racontal.
anecdote *n.* raconta.
anemia (US). See *anaemia.*
anemic (US). See *anaemic.*
anemometer *n.* anemometre.
anemone *n.* anemone.
anesth… (US). See *anaesth…*
aneurysm *n.* aneurisme.
anew *adv.* denova.
angel *n.* anjel.
angelfish *n.* pex anjelin.
angelic *adj.* anjelin.
angelica *n.* (*plant*) anjelica.
anger *n.* coleria. • *v.* coleri.
angina *n.* anjina. **angina pectoris** anjina de peto.
angio- *pref.* (*blood vessels*) anjio-.
angioma *n.* anjioma.
angiopathy *n.* anjiopatia.
angioplasty *n.* anjioplastia.
angiosperm *n.* anjiosperma.
angiotensin *n.* anjiotensina.
angle *n.* angulo. • *v.* anguli.
angle bracket *n.* braseta angulo, xevron.
angled joint *n.* junta angulo.
angler *n.* pexor.
Anglican *adj.* & *n.* anglican.
Anglicanism *n.* (*Christianity*) anglicanisme.
anglicism *n.* englesisme.
anglicization *n.* englesi.
anglicize *v.* englesi.
angling *n.* pexa.
Anglo-Saxon *adj.* & *n.* anglosason.
Angola *n.* Angola.
Angolan *adj.* & *n.* angolan.
angora *adj.* (*cat, goat, rabbit*) ancaran.
angostura *n.* angostura.
angry *adj.* coler.
angst *n.* ansia, teme.
angstrom *n.* (*unit of length*) anstrom.
Anguilla *n.* Anguila.
Anguillian *adj.* & *n.* anguilan.
anguish *n.* angusa. **in anguish** angusada.
anguished *adj.* angusada.
angular *adj.* angulo.
angular momentum *n.* momento angulo.
anhydrous *adj.* nonidrosa.
ani *n.* (*bird*) ani.
aniline *n.* (*substance*) anilina.
animal *adj.* & *n.* animal.
animal husbandry *n.* eleva de animales.
animate *v.* anima. • *adj.* animada.
animated character *n.* animada.
animation *n.* (*action, film*) anima.
animator *n.* animor.
anime *n.* (*animation*) anime.
animism *n.* animisme.

animist *adj.* & *n.* animiste.
animosity *n.* odia.
anion *n.* (*chemistry*) anion.
anise *n.* anis.
aniseed *n.* (*plant*) anis; (*seed*) seme de anis.
aniso- *pref.* (*unequal*) aniso-.
ankh *n.* (*cross*) anc.
ankle *n.* talo.
anklebone *n.* oso de talo.
anklet *n.* brasaleta de talo.
ankylosaurus *n.* ancilosauro.
ankylosis *n.* (*medical*) ancilose.
annals *n.* arcivos anial.
anneal *v.* recoce.
annelid *n.* (*worm*) anelido.
annex *v.* ajunta, propri. • *n.* ajuntada.
annexation *n.* ajunta, propri.
annexe *n.* ajuntada.
annihilate *v.* elimina.
annihilation *n.* elimina.
anniversary *n.* aniversario.
anno domini *adv.* de la eda comun.
annona *n.* (*plant*) anona.
annotate *v.* anota.
annotation *n.* anota, nota, glosa.
annotator *n.* anotor.
announce *v.* anunsia, proclama.
announcement *n.* anunsia, proclama.
announcer *n.* anunsior, proclamor.
annoy *v.* irita.
annoyance *n.* irita.
annual *adj.* anial. • *n.* libro anial.
annuity *n.* paia anial.
annul *v.* cansela, nega.
annular *adj.* anelo.
annular eclipse *n.* eclis anelo.
annulment *n.* cansela, nega.
anode *n.* anodo.
anodyne *adj.* blanda. • *n.* paradole.
anoint *v.* unje.
anomalous *adj.* anomal.
anomalousness *n.* anomalia.
anomalure *n.* anomalur.
anomaly *n.* (*quality*) anomalia; (*something anomalous*) anomal.
anomia *n.* (*medical*) anomia.
anon *adv.* pronto.
anonymity *n.* anonimia.
anonymous *adj.* anonim, sin nom.
anorak *n.* (*garment*) anorac.
anorexia *n.* anorexia.
anorexic *adj.* & *n.* anorexica.
another *det.* & *pron.* (*different*) un otra; (*further*) un plu. **another possible idea** un otra idea posible.
anoxia *n.* (*medical*) anosia.
anoxic *adj.* anosica.
answer *v.* responde; (*prayer*) reali. • *n.* responde; (*counterpart*) corespondente; (*to a rival concept*) alternativa. **answer back** replica.
answerable *adj.* (*question*) respondable; (*responsible*) encargada.
answerer *n.* respondor.
answering machine *n.* respondador.
answerphone *n.* respondador.
ant *n.* formica.
antacid *n.* antiasida.
antagonism *n.* oposa.
antagonist *n.* oposor.
antagonistic *adj.* enemin, oposante.
antagonize *v.* oposa.
Antarctic *adj.* antartica. • *n.* Antartica.
Antarctica *n.* Antartica.
Antarctic Ocean *n.* Mar Antartica.
antbird *n.* formicor.
ante- *pref.* ante-.
anteater *n.* formicor.
antecedent *n.* presedente.
antechamber *n.* sala de entra.
antediluvian *adj.* predeluvial.
antelope *n.* antilope.
antenatal *adj.* ante nase, ante pari.
antenna *n.* antena.
antepenultimate *adj.* du ante la ultima.
anterior *adj.* anterior.
anteroom *n.* antesala, sala de entra.
anthelmintic *n.* antielmintal.
anthem *n.* imno.
anther *n.* antera.
anthill *n.* monton de formicas.
anthologist *n.* antolojiste.
anthologization *n.* antoloji.
anthologize *v.* antoloji.
anthology *n.* antolojia.
anthracite *n.* (*substance*) antrasita.
anthrax *n.* antrax.
anthropic *adj.* antroposentral.
anthropic principle *n.* prinsipe antroposentral.
anthropo- *pref.* antropo-.
anthropocentric *adj.* antroposentral.
anthropoid *adj.* umanin.
anthropological *adj.* antropolojial.
anthropologist *n.* antropolojiste.
anthropology *n.* antropolojia.
anthropometric *adj.* antropometrial.
anthropometry *n.* antropometria.
anthropomorphic *adj.* antropomorfe.
anthropomorphism *n.* antropomorfia, umani.
anthropomorphize *v.* umani.
anthropophage *n.* canibal.
anti- *pref.* anti-.
antiabortionist *adj.* & *n.* antiabortiste.
antiageing (US **antiaging**) *adj.* antisenesente.

antiaircraft *adj.* antiavional.
antiaircraft fire *n.* spara antiavional.
anti-alias *v.* desaliasi.
antibacterial *adj.* & *n.* antibaterial.
antibiotic *adj.* & *n.* antibaterial, antimicrobial.
antibody *n.* anticorpo.
anticholinergic *n.* anticolinerjica.
Antichrist *n.* Anticristo.
anticipate *v.* previde, espeta.
anticipation *n.* previde, espeta.
anticlimactic *adj.* deludente.
anticlimax *n.* delude, delude de suspende.
anticlockwise *adj.* contra la orolojo.
anticoagulant *n.* anticoagulante.
anticonvulsant *n.* anticonvulsante.
anticorrosive *adj.* anticorodente.
antics *n.* bufonales, bufonia.
anticyclone *n.* antisiclon.
antidepressant *adj.* & *n.* antidepresante.
antidiabetic *n.* antidiabetica.
antidiarrhoeal (US **antidiarrheal**) *n.* (*drug*) paradiarea.
antidote *n.* contravenena.
antiepileptic *n.* antiepilesica.
antiestablishment *adj.* antisistemal.
antifreeze *n.* parajela.
antifungal *adj.* & *n.* antifungal.
anti-gay *adj.* antige.
antigen *n.* antijen.
antigenic *adj.* antijen.
antigovernment *adj.* antigovernal.
antigravity *n.* antigravita.
Antigua *n.* Antigua. **Antigua and Barbuda** Antigua e Barbuda.
Antiguan *adj.* & *n.* antiguan.
antihelminthic *n.* antielmintal.
antihero *n.* antieroe.
antiheroine *n.* antieroe.
antihistamine *n.* antiistaminal.
anti-inflammatory *adj.* & *n.* antiinflamante.
anti-Jewish *adj.* antiiudiste.
antileprotic *n.* antileprosa.
Antillean *adj.* antilean.
Antilles *n.* Antiles. **Lesser Antilles** Antiles Minor.
antimalarial *n.* antimalarial.
antimatter *n.* antimateria.
antimicrobial *adj.* & *n.* antimicrobial.
antimony *n.* antimonio.
antineutron *n.* antineutron.
antinomy *n.* antinomia.
antioxidant *adj.* & *n.* antiosidinte.
antiparticle *n.* antiparticula.
antipasto *n.* deleta.
antipathetic *adj.* antipatiosa.
antipathy *n.* antipatia, repulsa.
antiperspirant *n.* parasuo.
antiphon *n.* (*music*) antifona.
antiphony *n.* antifonia.
antipodal *adj.* antipoda.
antipode *n.* antipoda.
antipodean *adj.* antipoda.
antipope *n.* antipape.
antiproton *n.* antiproton.
antiprotozoal *n.* antiprotozonal.
antipsychotic *n.* antipsicosica.
antipyretic *n.* antifebral, parafebre.
antiquarian *n.* anticalior.
antiquated *adj.* anticin.
antique *adj.* antica. • *n.* anticalia.
antique seller *n.* anticalior.
antiquity *n.* (*ancient past*) eda antica; (*quality*) anticia.
anti-scratch *adj.* antirascal.
antisemite *n.* antisemita, antiiudiste.
antisemitic *adj.* antisemita, antiiudiste.
antisemitism *n.* antisemitisme, antiiudisme.
antiseptic *adj.* & *n.* antisepsica, antimicrobial.
antishock *adj.* antixocal.
antisocial *adj.* antisosial, sosiopatica.
antispasmodic *n.* antispasmal, paracolico.
antithesis *n.* antitese, oposada.
antithetical *adj.* antitesal, oposante.
antitoxin *n.* antitoxina.
antitrust *adj.* antimonopolial.
antituberculous *n.* (*drug*) antituberculosica.
antitussive *n.* antitosal, paratose.
antivenom *n.* antivenenal.
antiviral *adj.* antivirusal.
antivirus *adj.* antivirusal.
antler *n.* corno, corno de servo.
Antlia *n.* (*constellation*) la Pompa.
antlion *n.* (*insect*) formicaleon.
ant nest *n.* nido de formicas.
antonym *n.* antonim.
antonymous *adj.* antonim.
antonymy *n.* antonimia.
antrum *n.* (*anatomy*) antro.
anura *n.* (*amphibian*) anura.
anus *n.* ano.
anvil *n.* inco.
anvilhead *n.* (*bird*) umbreta.
anxiety *n.* ansia, angusa. **cause anxiety to** turba.
anxiolytic *n.* (*drug*) paransia.
anxious *adj.* ansiosa, angusada; (*eager*) zelosa. **become anxious** ansi.
any *det.* & *pron.* (*doesn't matter which*) cualce, (*optional plural pronoun*) cualces; (*in a question or negative statement*) alga, (*optional plural pronoun*) algas. **any further** plu. **any longer** plu. **any more** plu. **not any** no, zero.
anybody *pron.* (*doesn't matter who*) cualcun; (*in a question or negative statement*) algun.

anyhow *adv.* an tal; (*in any case*) a cualce caso.
anyone *pron.* (*doesn't matter who*) cualcun; (*in a question or negative statement*) algun.
anything *pron.* (*doesn't matter what*) cualce cosa; (*in a question or negative statement*) alga cosa.
anyway *adv.* an tal; (*in any case*) a cualce caso.
anywhere *adv.* (*doesn't matter where*) en cualce loca; (*in a question or negative statement*) en alga loca.
aorist *n.* (*grammar*) aoristo.
aorta *n.* (*anatomy*) aorta.
aortic *adj.* aortal.
aortitis *n.* aortite.
Apache *adj.* & *n.* (*person, language*) apatxe.
apart *adv.* separada, a otra parte; (*fall*) a pesos, a ruina. **apart from** estra.
apartheid *n.* apartait, separadisme.
apartment *n.* aparte.
apartment block *n.* tore de apartes.
apathetic *adj.* apatica.
apathy *n.* apatia, descura.
apatosaurus *n.* apatosauro.
ape *n.* primate.
aperitif *n.* deleta.
aperture *n.* abri, ranur.
aperture priority *n.* (*photography*) primia de abri.
apex *n.* apico.
-aphaeresis (US **-apheresis**) *suff.* -aferese.
aphasia *n.* (*medical*) afasia.
aphasic *adj.* & *n.* afasica.
aphelion *n.* (*astronomy*) afelio.
-apheresis (US). See *-aphaeresis.*
aphid *n.* afido.
aphonia *n.* (*medical*) afonia.
aphonic *adj.* afonica.
aphorism *n.* diseda saja.
aphrodisiac *adj.* & *n.* afrodisica.
aphrodisiacal *adj.* afrodisica.
aphthous ulcer *n.* ulsereta.
apiary *n.* aberia.
apical *adj.* apical.
apiculture *n.* eleva de abeas.
apiece *adv.* per cada.
aplanat *n.* aplanata.
aplanatic *adj.* aplanata.
aplanatic lens *n.* aplanata.
aplasia *n.* (*medical*) aplasia.
aplasic *adj.* aplasica.
aplomb *n.* autofida.
apnea (US). See *apnoea.*
apneic *adj.* apnica.
apnoea (US **apnea**) *n.* (*medical*) apnea.
apo- *pref.* apo-.
apocalypse *n.* apocalise.
apocalyptic *adj.* apocalisal.
apocrypha *n.* apocrifas.
apocryphal *adj.* apocrifa.
apogee *n.* (*astronomy*) apojeo.
apolog (US). See *apologue.*
apologetic *adj.* repentinte.
apologist *n.* defendor.
apologize *v.* demanda per pardona, solisita un pardona, escusa se.
apologue (US **apolog**) *n.* fable moral.
apology *n.* escusa.
aponeurosis *n.* (*anatomy*) aponeurose.
apophysis *n.* (*biology*) tuberculo.
apoplectic *adj.* furiosa.
apoplexy *n.* furia.
apoptosis *n.* apoptose.
apostasy *n.* renunsia.
apostate *n.* renunsior, disentor.
a posteriori *adj.* aposteriori.
apostle *n.* apostol.
apostolic *adj.* apostolal.
apostrophe *n.* sinia de elidi.
apothecary *n.* (*place*) farmasia; (*person*) farmasiste.
apotheosis *n.* divini.
apotheosize *v.* divini.
app *n.* (*software*) ap, programeta.
appal (US). See *appall.*
Appalachia *n.* Apalatxia.
Appalachian *adj.* apalatxian.
Appalachian Mountains *n.* Montes Apalatxian.
appall (US **appal**) *v.* angusa, xoca, ofende.
appalling *adj.* angusante, deplorable, xocante.
apparatus *n.* aparatos. **piece of apparatus** aparato.
apparel *n.* vestes.
apparent *adj.* parente; evidente.
apparition *n.* alusina.
appeal *v.* apela. **appeal to** apela a, suplica.
appear *v.* (*become visible*) apare, (*as an image*) imaji, (*as an outline*) contorni; (*seem*) pare; (*have a certain appearance*) aspeta.
appearance *n.* apare; pare; aspeta. **put in an appearance** apare corta.
appease *v.* pasi.
appeasement *n.* pasi.
appellant *n.* apelor.
appellate court *n.* corte de apela.
append *v.* ajunta.
appendage *n.* apendis, protende.
appendectomy *n.* (*surgery*) apendisectomia.
appendicitis *n.* apendisite.
appendix *n.* (*anatomy, publishing*) apendis; (*addendum*) ajuntada.
appetite *n.* apetito.
appetizer *n.* deleta.
appetizing *adj.* invitante.
applaud *v.* aplaudi.
applauder *n.* aplaudor.
applause *n.* aplaudi.

apple *n.* (*fruit*) poma; (*tree*) pomo.
apple juice *n.* jus de poma.
apple puree *n.* pure de poma.
apple sauce *n.* salsa de poma, pure de poma.
applicable *adj.* aplicable.
applicant *n.* aspiror.
application *n.* (*use*) usa; (*rules*) enforsa; (*request*) solisita; (*software*) ap, program.
applicator *n.* aplicador.
appliqué *n.* (*sewing*) aplica.
apply *v.* (*substance, physical force, oneself*) aplica; (*use*) usa, -i; (*rules*) enforsa; (*be relevant*) pertine. **apply for** solisita.
appoint *v.* (*person*) nomi; (*tasks, resources*) asinia.
appointment *n.* (*meeting*) encontra; (*of tasks*) asinia.
appointment book *n.* ajenda.
appose *v.* aposa.
apposition *n.* aposa.
appraisal *n.* evalua.
appraise *v.* evalua.
appreciate *v.* es grasiosa per; reconose la valua de; (*in value*) aumenta.
appreciative *adj.* grasiosa.
apprehend *v.* catura, aresta.
apprehension *n.* ansia.
apprehensive *adj.* ansiosa.
apprentice *n.* aprendor, stajior. • *v.* stajia.
apprenticeship *n.* stajia.
apprise *v.* informa.
approach *v.* prosimi. • *n.* prosimi; via; (*attitude*) disposa, modo de vive. **approaches** anteurbe.
approachable *adj.* asedable.
appropriate *adj.* aplicable, conveninte, coreta. • *v.* prende, propri. **be appropriate** conveni.
appropriateness *n.* conveni.
appropriation *n.* prende, propri.
approval *n.* aproba.
approve *v.* aproba. **approve of** aproba.
approx. *abbr.* s (*sirca*).
approximant *adj.* & *n.* (*consonant*) aprosiminte.
approximate *adj.* aprosima. • *v.* aprosimi.
approximately *adv.* aprosima, plu o min, sirca.
approximation *n.* aprosimi.
appurtenance *n.* ajuntable, parteninte.
apricot *n.* (*fruit*) abricoca; (*tree*) abricoco.
April *n.* april.
a priori *adj.* apriori.
apron *n.* faldon.
apropos of *adv.* referente a, regardante.
apse *n.* apside.
apsis *n.* apside.
aptitude *n.* talento.
Apus *n.* (*constellation*) la Rondin.
Aqaba *n.* Acaba. **Gulf of Aqaba** Golfo Acaba.
aqua[1] *adj.* & *n.* (*colour*) sian.
aqua-[2] *pref.* acua-.
aquaculture *n.* acuacultur.
aqualung *n.* autorespirador.
aquamarine *adj.* & *n.* acuamarin.
aquanaut *n.* sumerjor.
aquaplane *v.* lisca sur acua.
aquarium *n.* acueria.
Aquarius *n.* (*constellation*) la Acuor.
aquascope *n.* batiscopio.
aquatic *adj.* acual.
aquatint *n.* acuatinje.
aquavit *n.* acuavit.
aqueduct *n.* acuaduto.
aqueous *adj.* acuosa.
aquifer *n.* acuifer.
Aquila *n.* (*constellation*) la Agila.
aquilegia *n.* colombina.
aquiline *adj.* agilin.
Aquitaine *n.* (*French region*) Aciten.
Aquitania *n.* (*French region*) Aciten.
aquiver *adj.* tremante.
Ara *n.* (*constellation*) la Altar.
Arab *adj.* & *n.* arabi.
arabesque *adj.* & *n.* arabesca.
Arabia *n.* Arabia.
Arabian *adj.* & *n.* arabi.
Arabian Peninsula *n.* Penisola Arabi.
Arabian Sea *n.* Mar Arabi.
Arabic *adj.* & *n.* arabi.
Arabic bread *n.* pita.
arable *adj.* cultivable.
arachnid *n.* aracnido.
arachno- *pref.* (*spider*) aracno-.
arachnoid *n.* aracnoide. • *adj.* aranin.
arachnophobe *n.* aracnofobica.
arachnophobia *n.* aracnofobia.
arachnophobic *adj.* aracnofobica.
Arafura Sea *n.* Mar Arafura.
Aragon *n.* (*Spanish region*) Aragon.
Aragonese *adj.* & *n.* aragones.
arak *n.* (*drink*) arac.
Aral Sea *n.* Mar Aral.
Aram *n.* (*biblical region*) Aram.
Aramaean *adj.* & *n.* arami.
Aramaic *adj.* & *n.* arami.
Aramean *adj.* & *n.* arami.
arbalest *n.* (*weapon*) baleston.
arbiter *n.* arbitror.
arbitrage *n.* arbitraje.
arbitrariness *n.* acasia.
arbitrary *adj.* acaso, caprisal.
arbitrary arrest *n.* aresta acaso.
arbitrate *v.* arbitra.
arbitration *n.* arbitra.
arbitrator *n.* arbitror.

arbor (US). See *arbour*.
arboreal *adj.* arboral.
arboretum *n.* arboreria.
arborvitae *n.* (*tree*) tuia.
arbour (US **arbor**) *n.* alcova de jardin, pergola.
arbutus *n.* (*plant*) arbuto.
arc *n.* (*geometry, electrical, narrative*) arco.
arcade *n.* arcada.
arcane *adj.* secreta.
arch[1] *n.* (*architecture*) arco; (*foot*) arco de pede. • *v.* (*back, roof*) arci.
arch-[2] *pref.* (*chief*) arci-.
archaea *n.* (*organism*) arcea.
archaebacterium *n.* (*organism*) arcea.
archaeo- *pref.* arceo-.
archaeological (US **archeological**) *adj.* arceolojial.
archaeologist (US **archeologist**) *n.* arceolojiste.
archaeology (US **archeology**) *n.* arceolojia.
archaeon *n.* arcea.
archaeopteryx *n.* arceopterix.
archaic *adj.* anticin, desusada.
archaism *n.* anticin.
archangel *n.* arcanjel.
archbishop *n.* arcibispo.
archbishopric *n.* arcibispia.
archdiocese *n.* arcibispia.
archduke *n.* arciduxe.
archenemy *n.* arcenemi.
archeo... (US). See *archaeo...*
archer *n.* arcor.
archery *n.* xuta con arco.
archetypal *adj.* arcetipal, model.
archetype *n.* arcetipo, model.
archi- *pref.* arci-.
archimandrite *n.* abade xef.
Archimedes' screw *n.* elicador de Arcimede.
archipelago *n.* arcipelago.
architect *n.* arcitetor.
architectural *adj.* arcitetal.
architecture *n.* arciteta.
architrave *n.* arcitrava.
archival *adj.* arcival.
archive *n.* arciveria. • *v.* arcivi.
archivist *n.* arciviste.
archivolt *n.* arcivolta.
archon *n.* (*Athenian judge*) arconte.
archway *n.* arco.
Arctic *adj.* artica. • *n.* Artica.
Arctic Ocean *n.* Mar Artica.
ardent *adj.* ardente, zelosa.
ardour (US **ardor**) *n.* zelo.
arduous *adj.* fatigante.
are[1] *v.* (*be*) es.
are[2] *n.* (*unit of area*) are.
area *n.* (*measurement*) area; (*region*) rejion. **area code** *n.* prefisa.
areal *adj.* areal.
areca palm *n.* areca.
arena *n.* stadion.
areola *n.* areola.
argentiferous *adj.* arjentifer.
Argentina *n.* Arjentina.
Argentine *adj.* arjentina.
Argentine Sea *n.* Mar Arjentina.
Argentinian *adj.* & *n.* arjentina.
argon *n.* argon.
argot *n.* jergo.
arguable *adj.* disputable.
argue *v.* (*heated*) disputa; (*reasoning*) razona. **argue about** disputa.
argument *n.* (*heated*) disputa; (*reasoning*) razona; (*mathematics, grammar*) partisipante.
argumentative *adj.* disputosa.
argyle *adj.* (*pattern*) rombosa.
arhat *n.* (*saint*) arhat.
aria *n.* aria.
Arianism *n.* (*Christianity*) arianisme.
arid *adj.* seca.
Aries *n.* (*constellation*) la Ovea.
aril *n.* (*botany*) aril.
arillus *n.* (*botany*) aril.
arise *v.* (*stand up*) leva; (*situation*) resulta.
arista *n.* capelon.
aristocracy *n.* (*quality*) aristocratia; (*people*) aristocratas.
aristocrat *n.* aristocrata.
aristocratic *adj.* aristocrata.
aristolochia *n.* (*plant*) aristolocia.
arithmetic *n.* aritmetica. • *adj.* aritmetical.
arithmetical *adj.* aritmetical.
arithmetician *n.* aritmeticiste.
-arium *suff.* (*place*) -eria.
Arizona *n.* (*US state*) Arizona.
ark *n.* arca. **ark of the covenant** arca de la acorda.
Arkansas *n.* (*US state*) Arkansas.
arm[1] *n.* (*anatomy*) braso.
arm[2] *v.* (*with weapons*) arma, furni armas a.
armada *n.* armada, marina.
armadillo *n.* armadilo.
armageddon *n.* apocalise.
armament *n.* (*action*) arma. **armaments** armas.
armature *n.* (*literature, sculpture*) armatur.
armband *n.* sintureta.
armchair *n.* sejon.
armed *adj.* armada, con armas.
armed forces *n.* fortes militar.
Armenia *n.* Haiastan, Armenia.
Armenian *adj.* & *n.* (*person, language*) haiaren, armenian.
armful *n.* plenibraso.
Arminian *adj.* & *n.* arminian.

Arminianism *n.* (*Christianity*) arminianisme.
armistice *n.* sesaspara.
armload *n.* plenibraso.
armlock *n.* clavi de braso.
armoire *n.* armario.
armour (US **armor**) *n.* (*suit*) armur.
armoured (US **armored**) *adj.* blindada.
armoured ship (US **armored ship**) *n.* barcon blindada.
armourer (US **armorer**) *n.* armor.
armour-plate (US **armor-plate**) *v.* blinda.
armour-plated (US **armor-plated**) *adj.* blindada.
armoury (US **armory**) *n.* armeria.
armpit *n.* axila.
armrest *n.* reposabraso.
arms *n.* (*weapons*) armas. **bear arms** porta armas.
army *n.* armada.
arnica *n.* (*plant*) arnica.
aroma *n.* bon odor.
aromantic *adj.* nonromantica.
aromatic *adj.* bonodorinte, bonodorosa.
aromatization *n.* bonodori.
aromatize *v.* bonodori.
around *prep.* sirca. • *adv.* a sirca. **around the clock** a 24 oras de la dia.
arousal *n.* stimula.
arouse *v.* (*from sleep*) velia; (*interest, action*) inspira; (*curiosity*) curiosi; (*excite*) stimula.
arpeggio *n.* arpejio.
arquebus *n.* arcabus.
arrack *n.* arac.
arraign *v.* acusa, litiga.
arraignment *n.* acusa.
arrange *v.* organiza, posa, regula; (*music*) aranja, ordina.
arrangement *n.* organiza, posa; (*music*) aranja, ordina.
arranger *n.* (*music*) aranjor.
array *n.* estende; (*software*) vetor, (*two-dimensional*) matris.
arrears *n.* deta. **in arrears** tarda.
arrest *v.* & *n.* aresta. **under arrest** arestada.
arrhythmia *n.* aritmia.
arrhythmic *adj.* aritmica.
arrival *n.* (*action*) ariva, veni; (*person*) arivor.
arrivals hall *n.* ariveria.
arrive *v.* ariva, veni; (*at port*) atera.
arrogance *n.* egosia.
arrogant *adj.* egosa.
arrow *n.* flexa.
arrowlike *adj.* flexin.
arrowroot *n.* (*plant*) maranta.
arrow-shaped *adj.* flexin.
arroyo *n.* foson.
arse *n.* (*buttocks*) culo.
arsehole *n.* (*anus*) buco de culo; (*insult*) buco de culo, merda.
arselicker *n.* lecaculo.
arsenal *n.* colie de armas; (*place*) armeria.
arsenic *n.* arsenico.
arson *n.* ensende criminal.
arsonist *n.* ensendor criminal.
art *n.* arte.
art deco *adj.* deco. • *n.* arte deco.
arterial *adj.* arterial.
arteriography *n.* arteriografia.
arteriole *n.* arterieta.
arteriosclerosis *n.* arteriosclerose.
arteritis *n.* arterite.
artery *n.* arteria.
artesian *adj.* (*well*) artesian.
artful *adj.* rusosa; artosa.
arthritic *adj.* artritica.
arthritis *n.* (*medical*) artrite.
arthro- *pref.* artro-.
arthropod *n.* artropodo.
arthrosis *n.* artrose.
artichoke *n.* caxofa.
article *n.* (*document, grammar, item*) article. **article of faith** article de crede.
articulate *adj.* bonparlante. • *v.* espresa, pronunsia.
articulated *adj.* sesionida.
articulated lorry *n.* camion sesionida.
articulated truck *n.* camion sesionida.
articulation *n.* (*joint*) junta; (*speech*) pronunsia, vose.
artifact *n.* fabricada, ojeto fabricada.
artifice *n.* artifisia.
artificer *n.* maciniste.
artificial *adj.* artifis.
artificial intelligence *n.* inteleto artifis.
artificiality *n.* artifisia.
artificial language *n.* lingua desiniada.
artillerist *n.* artileriste.
artillery *n.* artileria.
artilleryman *n.* artileriste, canonor.
artisan *n.* artisan.
artist *n.* artiste.
artistic *adj.* (*of art*) artal; (*full of art*) artosa; (*of artist*) artiste.
artistry *n.* capasia.
artless *adj.* (*guileless*) nonenganante; (*writing*) natural.
artsy *adj.* artin.
artwork *n.* obra de arte.
arty *adj.* artin.
Aruba *n.* (*island*) Aruba.
Aruban *adj.* & *n.* aruban.
arugula *n.* (*plant*) ruca.
arum *n.* (*plant*) arum. **bog arum** cala.
Aryan *adj.* & *n.* indoeuropean.
as *adv.* tan. • *subord.* (*like*) como; (*just when*) a cuando; (*while*) en cuando; (*because*) car, con-

siderante ce. **as big as** tan grande como. **as far as** tan distante como; asta. **as for** regardante. **as if** como si. **as it were** on ta dise. **as long as** (*provided*) si; (*while*) tra cuando. **as many as** tan multe como; cuanto. **as many as possible** tan multe como posible. **as much as** tan multe como; cuanto. **as much as possible** tan multe como posible. **as opposed to** contrastada con, en contrasta con. **as regards** en relata con, regardante. **as soon as** direta cuando. **as soon as possible** la plu pronto. **as though** como si. **as well** ance. **as well as** como ance.

asafoetida (US **asafetida**) *n.* (*plant*) asafetida.

asana *n.* (*yoga*) asana.

asbestos *n.* asbesto.

asbestosis *n.* asbestose.

ascarid *n.* (*worm*) ascarido.

ascend *v.* asende.

ascendant *adj.* asendente.

ascender *n.* asendente.

ascension *n.* asende. **right ascension** lonjitude de sielo.

Ascension Day *n.* festa de asende.

ascent *n.* asende.

ascertain *v.* descovre; serti.

ascetic *adj.* asteninte, sever. • *n.* astenor, monce sever.

asceticism *n.* astenisme.

ascorbic acid *n.* vitamina C.

ascot *n.* tela de colo.

ascribe *v.* asinia.

-ase *suff.* (*enzyme*) -ase.

aseptic *adj.* nonsepsica.

asexual *adj.* & *n.* asesal, nonsesal.

asexuality *n.* asesalia.

ash[1] *n.* (*powder*) sene. **ashes** (*of a particular person or thing*) senes.

ash[2] *n.* (*tree*) fresno. (*Latin letter* Æ, æ) ax.

ashamed *adj.* vergoniante. **be ashamed** vergonia.

ashcan *n.* baldon.

ashen *adj.* pal.

A-shirt *n.* camiseta de sporte.

Ashkenazi *adj.* (*Judaism*) axcenazi.

Ashkenazi Jew *n.* axcenazi.

Ashoka *n.* (*Indian emperor*) Axoca.

Ashokan *adj.* axocan.

ashore *n.* a tera.

ashram *n.* (*hermitage*) axram.

ashtray *n.* portasene.

Asia *n.* Asia.

Asia Minor *n.* Anatolia.

Asian *adj.* & *n.* asian.

Asiatic *adj.* & *n.* asian.

aside *adv.* a lado.

-asis *suff.* (*medical*) -ase.

asity *n.* (*bird*) filepita.

ask *v.* demanda. **ask a question** fa un demanda. **ask for** demanda per, solisita, xerca. **ask oneself** demanda a se.

askance *adj.* desaprobante, suspetante.

askew *adj.* apoiada, deslocada.

asleep *adj.* dorminte. **fall asleep** adormi.

asocial *adj.* nonsosial.

asp *n.* vipera.

asparagine *n.* (*amino acid*) asparajina.

asparagus *n.* (*plant, vegetable*) asparago.

aspartame *n.* (*sweetener*) aspartame.

aspartate *n.* (*amino acid*) aspartato.

aspect *n.* (*appearance, feature, grammar*) aspeta; (*feature*) faseta. **continuous aspect** (*grammar*) aspeta continuante.

aspect ratio *n.* proportio de aspeta.

aspen *n.* poplo tremante.

aspen parkland *n.* stepe-foresta.

asperula *n.* (*plant*) asperula.

asphalt *n.* (*concrete*) asfalto; (*viscous pitch*) bitume.

asphodel *n.* (*plant*) asfodelo.

asphyxia *n.* asfixia.

asphyxiate *v.* asfixia.

asphyxiation *n.* asfixia.

aspic *n.* aspica.

aspirate *v.* espira. • *n.* (*consonant*) espirada.

aspiration *n.* aspira; (*phonetics*) espira.

aspire *v.* aspira.

aspirin *n.* aspirina.

ass[1] *n.* (*donkey*) asino.

ass[2] *n.* (*buttocks*) culo.

assail *v.* ataca.

assailable *adj.* atacable.

assailant *n.* atacor.

Assam *n.* (*Indian state*) Asam.

Assamese *adj.* & *n.* asames.

assassin *n.* asasinor.

assassinate *v.* asasina.

assassination *n.* asasina.

assassin bug *n.* reduvido.

assault *v.* & *n.* ataca. **assault rifle** *n.* fusil de ataca. **assault wave** *n.* onda de ataca.

assegai *n.* (*spear*) zagaia.

assemble *v.* asembla.

assembler *n.* (*software*) asemblador.

assembly *n.* reuni; (*political*) asembla. **self-assembly** asemblable.

assembly hall *n.* asembleria.

assembly language *n.* lingua de asembla.

assembly line *n.* cadena de construi.

assemblyman *n.* asemblor.

assembly member *n.* asemblor.

assembly rooms *n.* asembleria.

assemblywoman *n.* asemblor.

assent *v.* acorda. **assent to** aproba.

assert *v.* declara, espresa, reclama, dise forte; (*one's authority*) mostra.

assertion *n.* declara, espresa, reclama, dise forte.
assertive *adj.* serta, autofidante.
assertiveness *n.* autofida.
assess *v.* evalua.
asset *n.* ativa.
asshole *n.* (*anus*) buco de culo; (*insult*) buco de culo, merda.
assiduous *adj.* asidua.
assiduousness *n.* asiduia.
assign *v.* asinia; (*a number to*) numeri.
assignation *n.* encontra.
assignment *n.* asinia, taxe.
assimilate *v.* asorbe.
assimilation *n.* asorbe.
assist *v.* aida.
assistance *n.* aida.
assistant *n.* (*person*) aidor; (*software*) aidador.
asskisser *n.* lecaculo.
associate *v.* asosia, lia, relata. • *n.* asosior. **be associated** pertine, relata.
association *n.* asosia, lia, relata.
associative array *n.* (*software*) vetor de asosia.
assonance *n.* asona.
assonant *adj.* asonante.
assonate *v.* asona.
assorted *adj.* diversa, miscada.
assortment *n.* colie miscada.
assuage *v.* sasia, desintensi.
assume *v.* (*suppose*) suposa; (*responsibility*) oteni; (*pretend*) finje.
assumption *n.* suposa.
assurance *n.* serti.
assure *v.* serti.
assuredness *n.* sertia.
Assyria *n.* (*ancient region*) Asiria.
Assyrian *adj.* & *n.* asirian.
astatic *adj.* astatica.
astatine *n.* (*element*) astato.
aster *n.* (*plant*) aster.
asterid *n.* (*plant*) asterida.
asterisk *n.* stela, sinia de stela. • *v.* steli.
astern *adj.* popal.
asteroid *n.* asteroide, planeteta.
asthenia *n.* (*medical*) astenia. • *suff.* -astenia.
asthenic *adj.* astenica.
asthma *n.* asma.
asthmatic *adj.* & *n.* asmica.
astigmatic *adj.* astigmata.
astigmatism *n.* astigmatia.
astonish *v.* stona, mervelia, surprende. **be astonished** mervelia.
astonishment *n.* stona.
astound *v.* stona.
astragalus *n.* (*plant*) astragalo; (*ankle*) talo.
astrakhan *n.* (*fabric*) caracul.
astral *adj.* astral.
astray *adj.* deviante, perdeda.
astride *adj.* montante.
astringent *adj.* & *n.* astrinjente. **be astringent** astrinje.
astro- *pref.* astro-.
astrobiological *adj.* astrobiolojial.
astrobiologist *n.* astrobiolojiste.
astrobiology *n.* astrobiolojia.
astrolabe *n.* (*device*) astrolabio.
astrologer *n.* astrolojiste.
astrological *adj.* astrolojial.
astrologist *n.* astrolojiste.
astrology *n.* astrolojia.
astronaut *n.* astronauta.
astronomer *n.* astronomiste.
astronomical *adj.* astronomial.
astronomical object *n.* ojeto sielal.
astronomy *n.* astronomia.
astrophysicist *n.* astrofisiciste.
astrophysics *n.* astrofisica.
Asturian *adj.* & *n.* asturian.
Asturias *n.* (*Spanish region*) Asturias.
astute *adj.* astuta.
astuteness *n.* astutia, intelijentia.
asunder *adv.* separada.
asylum *n.* (*state*) refuja; (*place*) refujeria. **give asylum to** refuja.
asymmetrical *adj.* nonsimetre.
asymmetry *n.* nonsimetria.
asymptomatic *adj.* nonsintomal.
asymptote *n.* (*mathematics*) asintota.
asymptotic *adj.* asintotal.
asynchronous *adj.* nonsincrona.
at *prep.* a. **at all** vera; sin eseta. **at first** prima. **at last** final, a fini. **at least** a la min, minima; (*however*) an tal, an con tota. **at most** a la plu, masima. **at once** aora, direta. **at sign** sinia de "a", caracol.
Atacama Desert *n.* Deserto Atacama.
atavism *n.* atavisme, reversa.
atavistic *adj.* ataviste.
ataxia *n.* (*medical*) ataxia.
ataxic *adj.* ataxica.
-ate *suff.* (*chemistry*) -ato.
atheism *n.* ateisme.
atheist *n.* ateiste.
atheistic *adj.* ateiste.
Athens *n.* Atina.
atheroma *n.* (*medical*) ateroma.
atherosclerosis *n.* aterosclerose.
athlete *n.* atleta.
athletic *adj.* atletal.
athletic activity *n.* atletisme.
athletics *n.* atletisme.
athletic shirt *n.* camiseta de sporte.
athletic shoe *n.* sapato de sporte.
atishoo *interj.* axi.
Atlantic *adj.* atlantica.
Atlantic Ocean *n.* Mar Atlantica.
Atlantis *n.* Atlantida.

atlas *n.* libro de mapas.
Atlas Mountains *n.* Montes Atlas.
atlatl *n.* (*spear-throwing device*) lansadardo.
ATM *n.* automata de banco.
atman *n.* spirito.
atmosphere *n.* (*gases*) atmosfera; (*place, event*) ambiente.
atmospheric *adj.* atmosferal.
atmospheric science *n.* siensa de atmosfera.
atoll *n.* atol.
atom *n.* atom.
atomic *adj.* atomal.
atomize *v.* atomi, polvi.
atonal *adj.* nontonal.
atone *v.* espia. **atone for** espia.
atonement *n.* espia.
atonic *adj.* atonica, nonasentuada.
atony *n.* (*medical*) atonia.
atoxic *adj.* nonvenenosa.
-atresia *suff.* (*medical*) -atresia.
atrium *n.* atrio.
atrocious *adj.* asustante, deplorable.
atrocity *n.* odiable.
atrophic *adj.* atrofica.
atrophy *v.* & *n.* atrofia.
atropine *n.* (*substance*) atropina.
at sign *n.* sinia de "a", caracol.
attach *v.* fisa, afisa.
attaché *n.* ajente.
attachment *n.* (*email*) afisa.
attack *v.* & *n.* ataca. **under attack** atacada.
attacker *n.* atacor.
attain *v.* ateni.
attainable *adj.* atenable.
attainment *n.* ateni.
attempt *v.* & *n.* atenta.
attend *v.* (*serve*) atende; (*be at*) es presente a; (*regularly go to*) vade a. **attend to** atende.
attendance *n.* presentia; cuantia de visitores.
attendant *adj.* atendente. • *n.* atendor.
attendee *n.* presente.
attention *n.* atende, interesa. **call attention to** fa ce on persepi. **draw attention** atrae atende. **pay attention to** atende.
attentive *adj.* atendente.
attenuate *v.* debili.
attenuation *n.* debili.
attest *v.* atesta.
attic[1] *n.* suteto.
Attic[2] *adj.* & *n.* (*person, language*) atica.
Attica *n.* (*Greek region*) Atica.
attire *n.* vestes.
attitude *n.* disposa.
attorney *n.* avocato.
attorney general *n.* avocato jeneral.
attract *v.* atrae.
attraction *n.* atrae.
attractive *adj.* atraosa.
attribute *v.* atribui. • *n.* atribuida, cualia, propria.
attribution *n.* atribui.
attrition *n.* erode.
atypical *adj.* nontipal.
aubergine *n.* melonjena.
auburn *adj.* rojin brun. • *n.* brun rojin.
auction *v.* & *n.* subasta.
auctioneer *n.* subastor.
auction house *n.* subasteria.
audacious *adj.* osante.
audacity *n.* osa.
Audh *n.* Auad.
audial *adj.* oreal.
audible *adj.* oiable.
audience *n.* regardores, escutores.
audience size *n.* cuantia de regardores.
audio *adj.* & *n.* audio.
audio cassette *n.* caxeta audio.
audiologist *n.* audiolojiste.
audiology *n.* audiolojia.
audiometer *n.* audiometre.
audiophile *n.* audiomanica.
audio tape *n.* banda audio.
audiovisual *adj.* audiovideo.
audit *v.* & *n.* esamina.
audition *n.* intervisa pratical, mostra.
auditor *n.* esaminor.
auditorium *n.* salon de presenta, salon de conserta, teatro.
auditory *adj.* oreal.
auditory hallucination *n.* alusina oiada.
auditory phonetics *n.* fonetica oreal.
auditory tube *n.* trompa de Eustacio.
auger *n.* elicador.
augment *v.* aumenta, grandi.
augmentation *n.* aumenta, grandi.
augur *n.* augur. • *v.* premostra.
augury *n.* auguria.
august[1] *adj.* (*respected*) respetada.
August[2] *n.* (*month*) agosto.
auk *n.* alco. **little auk** alco.
auklet *n.* (*bird*) alceta.
aulos *n.* (*musical instrument*) aulo.
aunt *n.* tia; (*gender-neutral*) tie.
aura *n.* aura; cualia.
aural *adj.* oreal.
aural speculum *n.* (*medical*) otoscopio.
auricle *n.* orea esterna.
Auriga *n.* (*constellation*) la Caror.
auriscope *n.* otoscopio.
aurochs *n.* (*ox*) uro.
aurora *n.* aurora.
Aurora Australis *n.* aurora sude.
Aurora Borealis *n.* aurora norde.
auscultate *v.* stetoscopi.
auscultation *n.* stetoscopi.
auspices *n.* suporta; (*ancient Rome*) auguria.

auspicious *adj.* fortunosa.
austere *adj.* sever.
austerity *n.* severia.
austerity measures *n.* medias sever.
Australasia *n.* Australasia.
Australasian *adj.* australasian.
Australia *n.* Australia.
Australian *adj.* & *n.* australian.
Australian Aborigine *adj.* & *n.* australian orijinal.
Australian babbler *n.* (*bird*) pomatostomo.
Australian Deserts *n.* Desertos Australian.
Australian wren *n.* maluro.
australopithecus *n.* australopiteco.
Austria *n.* Osteraic.
Austrian *adj.* & *n.* osteraices.
Austronesian *adj.* austronesian.
autarchy *n.* autocratia.
authentic *adj.* autentica, vera.
authenticate *v.* autentici.
authentication *n.* autentici.
authenticity *n.* autenticia.
author *n.* autor. • *v.* scrive.
authoritarian *adj.* & *n.* autoritar, autoritariste.
authoritarianism *n.* autoritarisme.
authoritative *adj.* autoriosa.
authority *n.* (*power*) autoria; (*knowledge*) espertia; (*organization*) autoriosa; (*person*) autoriosa, esperta.
authorization *n.* autori, permete.
authorize *v.* autori, permete.
authorship *n.* autoria, scrivoria.
autism *n.* autisme.
autistic *adj.* autiste.
auto[1] *n.* (*car*) auto.
auto-[2] *pref.* auto-.
autobiographic *adj.* autobiografial.
autobiographical *adj.* autobiografial.
autobiography *n.* autobiografia.
autochthonous *adj.* orijinal.
autoclave *n.* autoclave.
autocracy *n.* autocratia.
autocrat *n.* autocrata.
autocratic *adj.* autocrata.
auto-da-fé *n.* arde de ereses, xasa de ereses.
autodidact *adj.* autoinstruida.
autoerotic *adj.* autoerotica.
autoexposure *n.* autoesposa.
autogamy *n.* autopoleni.
autogiro *n.* autojiro.
autograph *n.* (*signature*) suscrive; (*manuscript*) manoscrito. • *v.* suscrive.
autogyro *n.* autojiro.
autoharp *n.* autoarpa.
autoimmune *adj.* autoimune.
autoimmunity *n.* autoimunia.
automat *n.* automata.
automata *n.* automata.
automate *v.* automati.
automated *adj.* automata.
automatic *adj.* automata; (*response*) reflexe.
automatic translator *n.* traduador.
automation *n.* automati.
automaton *n.* automata.
automobile *n.* auto, automobil.
automobilist *n.* automanica.
automorphic *adj.* automorfe.
automotive *adj.* automobilal.
autonomous *adj.* autonom, nondependente. **become autonomous** autonomi.
autonomy *n.* autonomia.
autopilot *n.* autopilote.
autopsy *n.* autopsia.
autopsy table *n.* table de autopsia.
auto racing *n.* corsa de autos.
autoreplicate *v.* autocopia.
autotroph *n.* autotrof.
autotrophia *n.* autotrofia.
autotrophic *adj.* autotrof.
autumn *n.* autono.
autumnal *adj.* autonal.
autumnal equinox *n.* ecuinote de autono.
auxiliary *adj.* aidante.
auxiliary language *n.* lingua aidante.
avail *v.* (*oneself of*) esplota. **to no avail** futil.
availability *n.* disponablia.
available *adj.* disponable, otenable. **have available** dispone.
avalanche *v.* & *n.* avalanxa.
avant-garde *adj.* vangarda.
avarice *n.* avaria.
avaricious *adj.* avar.
avatar *n.* avatar.
avenge *v.* venja.
avenger *n.* venjor.
avenue *n.* bolevar, via.
aver *v.* afirma.
average *adj.* (*mean*) promedia; (*ordinary*) mediocre. • *n.* promedia. **on average** per promedia.
average Joe *n.* bonom.
averse *adj.* antipatiosa.
aversion *n.* antipatia, repulsa.
avert *v.* (*eyes*) regarda a via, turna sua regarda a via.
avesta *n.* (*scripture*) avesta.
avian *adj.* avial.
aviary *n.* avieria.
aviation *n.* avioni.
aviator *n.* avionor, volor.
aviculture *n.* avicultur.
avid *adj.* zelosa.
avidity *n.* zelo.
avionics *n.* avionica.
avocado *n.* (*fruit, tree*) avocado.
avocation *n.* amato.
avocet *n.* (*bird*) avoseta.

avoid *v.* evita.
avoidable *adj.* evitable.
avoidance *n.* evita.
avoider *n.* evitor.
avow *v.* confesa.
avuncular *adj.* tin, como tio.
Awadh *n.* Auad.
Awadhi *adj.* & *n.* auadi.
await *v.* espeta.
awake *adj.* veliada.
awaken *v.* velia.
award *v.* dona, presenta, premia. • *n.* premio.
awards ceremony *n.* premia.
award-winner *n.* premior.
award-winning *adj.* premiada, campionida.
aware *adj.* consensa. **be aware of** es consensa de; (*emotion, pain*) senti. **become aware** consensi.
awareness *n.* consensia.
awash *adj.* inondada.
away *adv.* de asi, de esta loca; (*go, throw, put*) a via. **away from** a via de. **do away with** aboli.
awe *n.* stona temosa.
awe-inspiring *adj.* merveliosa.
awesome *adj.* merveliosa, stonante.
awful *adj.* asustante, deplorable.
awhile *adv.* per alga tempo.
awhoo *interj.* (*howling*) a-uu.
awkward *adj.* (*clumsy*) torpe; (*difficult*) difisil.
awkwardness *n.* difisilia.
awl *n.* alena.
awn *n.* capelon.
awning *n.* baldacin, fronton; covreveranda.
awol *adj.* asente sin permete.
awry *adj.* deslocada, deviante.
axe (US **ax**) *n.* axa. • *v.* aboli.
axeman (US **axman**) *n.* axor.
axial *adj.* asal.
axillary *adj.* axilal.
axiom *n.* axiom.
axiomatic *adj.* axiomal.
axiomation *n.* axiomi.
axiomatize *v.* axiomi.
axis *n.* ase.
axle *n.* ase.
axman (US). See *axeman*.
axolotl *n.* (*amphibian*) axolote.
axon *n.* (*anatomy*) ason.
ayatollah *n.* aiatola.
aye-aye *n.* (*primate*) aiai.
azalea *n.* (*plant*) azalea.
Azerbaijan *n.* Azerbaidjan.
Azerbaijani *adj.* & *n.* azerbaidjani.
azimuth *n.* (*astronomy*) azimuta.
azoospermia *n.* (*medical*) azospermia.
Azorean *adj.* asoran.
Azores *n.* Asores.
azotemia *n.* (*medical*) azotemia.
Azov, Sea of *n.* Mar Azov.
Aztec *adj.* & *n.* asteca.
azuki bean *n.* fava azuci.
azure *adj.* & *n.* azul.
azure-winged magpie *n.* piga sian.

B

B&B *n.* oteleta.
baa *v.* bala. • *interj.* maa.
babble *v.* babela.
babbler *n.* (*bird*) xarlatan. **Australian babbler** pomatostomo.
babe *n.* bebe.
Bab-el-Mandeb *n.* Streta Mandeb.
babirusa *n.* (*animal*) babirusa.
babka *n.* (*cake*) babca.
baboon *n.* babuin.
baby *adj.* & *n.* bebe.
baby blue *adj.* & *n.* azul.
baby boom *n.* buma de bebes.
baby boomer *n.* bebe de la buma.
baby carriage *n.* caro de bebe.
babycarrier *n.* portabebe.
baby daughter *n.* ficta.
baby deer *n.* serveta.
babydoll *n.* (*nightdress*) robeta de note.
babygro *n.* bodi de bebe.
babyhood *n.* bebia.
Babylonia *n.* Babilonia.
babylonian *adj.* babilonian.
baby measles *n.* roseola.
baby powder *n.* polvo de talco.
baby rabbit *n.* coneta.
babysit *v.* cangari a enfantes.
babysitter *n.* atendor de bebe.
baby sling *n.* portabebe.
baby son *n.* fieta.
baby spider *n.* aranieta.
baccalaureate *n.* laural, diploma laural.
baccarat *n.* (*card game*) bacara.
bacchanal *n.* selebra enebriada.
bacchanalia *n.* selebra enebriada.
bachelor *n.* nonsposida.
bachelorhood *n.* nonsposia.
bachelor's *n.* (*degree*) laural, diploma laural.
bacillus *n.* (*bacterium*) basilo.
back *adj.* (*rear*) retro. • *adv.* (*backwards*) a retro; (*again*) re-. • *n.* (*rear*) retro; (*of body, hand*) dorso; (*of knee*) plia; (*of neck*) nuca. **at the back** a pos. **at the back of** pos, a retro de. **back and forth** de asi a ala. **back up** suporta; (*data*) copia per securia. **get back to** reateni. **get one's own back** venja se. **go back** revade. **go back in** reentra. **go back on** (*promise*) rompe. **in back of** a retro de. **inside the back of** en retro de. **into the back of** en retro de. **on one's back** a dorso. **put one's back to** dorsi. **turn one's back on** dorsi.
backache *n.* dole de dorso.
backbeat *n.* pulsa inversada.
backbend *n.* arci a retro.
backbiting *n.* malacusa.
backboard *n.* (*basketball*) panel de sesto.
backbone *n.* spina dorsal.
backbreaking *adj.* fatigante.
backcountry skiing *n.* sci savaje.
back cover *n.* (*book*) retro.
backdate *v.* predati.
back door *n.* porte retro.
backdrop *n.* fondo.
backer *n.* suportor; (*of horse*) apostor.
backfill *v.* repleni.
backfire *v.* (*engine*) malcombusta, retroflami; (*plan*) contraprodui.
backgammon *n.* trictrac.
backgammon player *n.* trictracor.
background *adj.* fondal. • *n.* fondo.
background documents *n.* documentos fondal.
background information *n.* informa fondal.
background material *n.* documentos fondal.
backing *adj.* fondal. • *n.* suporta.
backing singer *n.* cantor fondal.
backlight *n.* lumina fondal.
backlighting *n.* lumina fondal.
backlog *n.* cumula.
backpack *n.* bolson.
backpacker *n.* bolsonor.
back pain *n.* dole de dorso.
backrest *n.* reposadorso.
backronym *n.* retroacronim.
back seat *n.* seja retro.
backside *n.* posterior, gluteos.
backslash *n.* bara reversada.
backslide *v.* regresa.
backspace *v.* retrospasi.
backstage *n.* (*area*) postadio.
backstory *n.* istoria fondal, nara fondal.
backtrack *v.* resegue sua pasos.
backup *n.* (*data*) copia de securia.
back vowel *n.* vocal retro.
backward *adv.* retrogradal, a pos.
backwards *adv.* a pos, a retro; retro-.
backwater *n.* staniante; vila provinsal.
bacon *n.* lardo.
bacteria *n.* baterias.
bacterial *adj.* baterial.
bactericide *n.* bateriside.
bacteriological *adj.* bateriolojial.
bacteriologist *n.* bateriolojiste.
bacteriology *n.* bateriolojia.
bacteriotherapy *n.* baterioterapia.
bacterium *n.* bateria.
bacterivore *n.* baterivor.

bacterivorous *adj.* baterivor.
Bactria *n.* (*ancient region*) Bactria.
bad *adj.* mal; mal-. **turn bad** mali.
bad breath *n.* alitose.
badge *n.* insinia.
badger *n.* texon. • *v.* tormenta.
badger burrow *n.* texoneria.
badger sett *n.* texoneria.
bad habit *n.* mal abitua.
badinage *n.* conversa replicosa.
badlands *n.* tereno savaje.
bad luck *n.* mal fortuna.
badly adjusted *adj.* malajustada.
badly dressed *adj.* malvestida.
badly positioned *adj.* malposada.
badminton *n.* badminton.
badminton player *n.* badmintonor.
bad mood *n.* mal umor.
badmouth *v.* malacusa, maldise.
bad news *n.* mal novas.
bad omen *n.* mal indica.
bad situation *n.* mal situa.
bad smell *n.* mal odor.
bad-sounding *adj.* mal sonante.
bad-tempered *adj.* disputosa.
Baffin Bay *n.* Baia Baffin.
Baffin Island *n.* Isola Baffin.
baffle *v.* confonde.
bafflegab *n.* babela.
bafflement *n.* confonde.
bag *n.* saco. • *v.* saci. **bag up** saci.
bagatelle *n.* (*trivial thing*) graneta, pico.
bagel *n.* bagel.
bagful *n.* plenisaco.
baggage *n.* bagaje.
baggage car *n.* vagon de bagaje.
baggage room *n.* sala de bagaje.
bagginess *n.* laxia.
baggy *adj.* laxe.
bagpipe *n.* cornamusa.
bagpipes *n.* cornamusa.
baguette *n.* (*bread*) bagete.
bah *interj.* ba.
Baha'i *adj.* bahai. • *n.* (*person*) bahai; (*religion*) bahaisme.
Baha'ism *n.* (*religion*) bahaisme.
Bahamas *n.* Bahamas.
Bahamian *adj.* & *n.* bahaman.
Bahrain *n.* Barain.
Bahraini *adj.* & *n.* baraini.
Baikal, Lake *n.* Lago Baical.
bail[1] *n.* garantia. **out on bail** libre con garantia. **release on bail** libri con garantia.
bail[2] *v.* (*scoop*) copi.
bailiff *n.* enforsor de corte; (*historical*) balio.
bailout *n.* rescate finansial.
bain-marie *n.* baniomaria.
bairn *n.* enfante, xice.
bait *v.* tenta. • *n.* tenta, tentante.
baize *n.* (*fabric*) baieta.
Baja California *n.* California Basa.
Bajan *adj.* & *n.* (*person, language*) barbadian.
bake *v.* forni. • *n.* fornida.
baked beans *n.* gaxa de favas.
baked potato *n.* patata fornida.
bakelite *n.* bacelita.
baker *n.* fornor, panor.
bakery *n.* paneria.
baklava *n.* (*dessert*) baclava.
Balabac Strait *n.* Streta Balabak.
balaclava *n.* balaclava.
balalaika *n.* (*musical instrument*) balalaica.
balance *v.* & *n.* ecuilibra; (*seesaw*) balansi; (*money*) salda. **throw off balance** desecuilibra.
balcony *n.* balcon.
bald *adj.* calva; (*tyre*) gastada. **go bald** calvi.
baldaquin *n.* baldacin.
balderdash *n.* babela.
balding *adj.* calvinte.
baldness *n.* calvia.
baldric *n.* xarpe de spada.
bale *n.* faxo.
Balearic *adj.* balear.
Balearic Islands *n.* Isolas Balear.
Balearic Sea *n.* Mar Balear.
baleen *n.* barba de balena.
Bali *n.* Bali.
balk *v.* esita.
Balkan *adj.* balcan. **Balkans** (*mountains, region*) Balcanes.
ball[1] *n.* (*sphere*) bal; (*testicle*) coion.
ball[2] *n.* (*dance*) balo formal.
ballad *n.* balada.
balladeer *n.* balador.
ballast *n.* balasto. • *v.* balasti.
ballboy *n.* coliebal.
ballerina *n.* baletiste.
ballet *n.* baleto.
ballet dancer *n.* baletiste.
ballgirl *n.* coliebal.
ballistic *adj.* balistical.
ballistics *n.* balistica.
balloon *n.* balon.
balloonist *n.* balonor.
ballot *n.* vota.
ballot box *n.* caxa de vota.
ballot paper *n.* paper de vota.
ballpoint pen *n.* pen de bal.
ballroom *n.* salon de balo.
balm *n.* balsam.
balmy *adj.* estatin.
Baloch *adj.* balotxi.
Balochi *adj.* balotxi.
Balochistan *n.* Balotxistan.
baloney *n.* babela.
balsa *n.* (*tree, wood*) ocroma.

balsam *n.* balsam.
balsamic *adj.* balsamal.
Baltic *adj.* baltica. • *n.* Baltica.
Baltic Sea *n.* Mar Baltica.
Baluch *adj.* balotxi.
Baluchistan *n.* Balotxistan.
baluster *n.* balustre.
balustrade *n.* rel.
bamboo *n.* (*plant*, *stem*) bambu.
ban *v.* & *n.* proibi.
banal *adj.* comun, nonorijinal.
banana *n.* (*plant*, *fruit*) banana.
band[1] *n.* (*strip*) banda.
band[2] *n.* (*people*) bande. **big band** orcestra de jaz.
bandage *n.* banda medical.
band-aid *n.* banda medical aderente.
bandana *n.* bandana.
Banda Sea *n.* Mar Banda.
bandeau *n.* banda de capeles.
bandeau top *n.* portaseno tubo.
banderole *n.* bandera.
bandicoot *n.* bandicute.
bandit *n.* bandito.
banditage *n.* banditia.
bandolier *n.* bandolera, xarpe de muni.
band saw *n.* siera de banda.
bandstand *n.* ciosco de bande.
bandura *n.* (*musical instrument*) bandura.
bandwagon effect *n.* efeto de moda.
bandwidth *n.* largia de banda.
bandylegged *adj.* con gamas arcida.
bane *n.* pesta.
bang *n.* & *interj.* pum. • *v.* pumi.
banger *n.* petardo. **old banger** (*car*) ruinada.
Bangla *adj.* & *n.* (*person*, *language*) bangla.
Bangladesh *n.* Bangladex.
bangle *n.* brasaleta.
bangs *n.* (*hairstyle*) franje.
Bangsamoro *adj.* & *n.* (*Philippine Muslim*) moro.
banish *v.* esclui, espulsa.
banishment *n.* esclui, espulsa.
banister *n.* rel.
banjo *n.* banjo.
banjo player *n.* banjiste.
bank *n.* (*river*) riva; (*mound*) colineta, inclinada; (*money*) banco. • *v.* (*aircraft*) apoia.
bank card *n.* carta de banca.
banker *n.* bancor.
bank holiday *n.* festa nasional.
banking practice *n.* pratica de banco.
banking sector *n.* campo bancal.
banknote *n.* bileta.
bankrupt *adj.* bancarota. • *v.* bancaroti. **go bankrupt** bancaroti.
bankruptcy *n.* bancarotia.
banksia *n.* (*plant*) bancsia.
Ban-Lam *adj.* & *n.* (*person*, *language*) banlam.
banner *n.* bandera.
banneton *n.* (*basket for shaping bread*) sesto de leva.
bannister *n.* rel.
banquet *v.* & *n.* banceta.
banshee *n.* banxi.
banter *v.* & *n.* burleta.
Bantu *adj.* & *n.* (*person*, *language*) bantu.
banyan *n.* figa bangla.
baobab *n.* baobab.
baptism *n.* batiza.
baptismal font *n.* trogo de batiza.
Baptist *adj.* & *n.* batiste.
baptistery *n.* batizeria.
Baptist religion *n.* batisme.
baptistry *n.* batizeria.
baptize *v.* batiza.
bar *n.* (*drinks*) bar; (*rail*) bara; (*ingot*) brice; (*music*) mesura.
barb *n.* spina; (*of fish*) vibrisa.
Barbadian *adj.* & *n.* barbadian.
Barbados *n.* Barbados.
barbarian *adj.* & *n.* barbar.
barbaric *adj.* barbar.
barbarism *n.* barbaria.
barbarous *adj.* barbar.
barbecue *n.* barbecu. • *v.* grili.
barbed *adj.* spinosa.
barbed wire *n.* filo spinosa.
barbel *n.* barbo; (*of fish*) vibrisa.
barbell *n.* bara de pesas.
barbeque *n.* barbecu.
barber *n.* capelor.
barberry *n.* (*plant*) berberis.
barbershop *n.* capeleria.
barbican *n.* tore de garda.
barbie *n.* barbecu.
barbiturate *n.* barbiturica.
barbituric *adj.* barbiturica.
barbituric acid *n.* asida barbiturica.
Barbuda *n.* Barbuda.
Barbudan *adj.* & *n.* barbudan.
barb wire *n.* filo spinosa.
barcarole *n.* canta de gondolor.
bar code *n.* codigo de baras.
bard *n.* barde.
bardic *adj.* bardal.
bare *adj.* nuda. • *v.* nudi.
bareback *adj.* sin sela.
bare-breasted *adj.* con peto nuda.
bare-chested *adj.* con peto nuda.
barefoot *adv.* con pedes nuda, sin sapatos.
barely *adv.* apena, par un capel.
Barents Sea *n.* Mar Barents.
barf *v.* descome.
bargain *v.* negosia. • *n.* barata.
barge *n.* barcasa.
bar hop *n.* turi de bares.

barista *n.* bariste.

baritone *adj.* & *n.* baritono.

barium *n.* (*element*) bario.

bark *v.* abaia. • *n.* (*dog*) abaia; (*tree*) cortex.

barkeep *n.* bariste.

barker *n.* proclamor.

barley *n.* orzo.

barley porridge *n.* gaxa de orzo.

barley sugar *n.* zucar de orzo.

barmaid *n.* bariste.

barman *n.* bariste.

bar mitzvah *n.* barmitsva.

barn *n.* graneria.

barnacle *n.* (*crustacean*) siripede.

barn owl *n.* tito.

barnyard *n.* patio de cultiveria.

barometer *n.* barometre.

baron *n.* baron.

baroness *n.* baronesa.

baronet *n.* baroneta.

barony *n.* baronia.

baroque *adj.* baroca, ornosa.

barracks *n.* caserna.

barracuda *n.* baracuda.

barrage *v.* & *n.* bombarda.

barrel *n.* baril; (*gun*) cano.

barrel factory *n.* barileria.

barrelmaker *n.* barilor.

barrel organ *n.* organo de enrola.

barren *adj.* steril, nonfertil.

barrette *n.* bareta.

barricade *n.* parador.

barrier *n.* ostaculo, parador.

barrister *n.* avocato, avocato de corte.

bar room *n.* bar.

barrow *n.* (*mound*) tumulo, colineta; (*wheeled*) careta.

barstool *n.* sejeta de bar.

bartender *n.* bariste.

barter *v.* & *n.* troca.

barterer *n.* trocor.

barycentre (US **barycenter**) *n.* barisentro.

barycentric *adj.* barisentral.

baryon *n.* (*particle*) barion.

basal *adj.* fundal.

basalt *n.* basalto.

base *adj.* basa. • *n.* funda, pede; (*operations*, *chemistry*, *linguistic*, *numbers*, *baseball*) base; (*chemistry*) alcalin. • *v.* (*something on*) fundi.

baseball *n.* basebal.

baseball player *n.* basebalor.

baseboard *n.* moldur de solo.

base camp *n.* campa de base.

baseless *adj.* sin funda.

basement *n.* sutera.

bash *n.* selebra.

bashful *adj.* timida.

basic *adj.* fundal.

basically *adv.* fundal, a radis.

basic guide *n.* manual prima.

basil *n.* basil.

basilica *n.* basilica.

basilisk *n.* (*lizard*, *mythology*) basilisco.

basin *n.* (*dish*) bol; (*geography*) basin.

basis *n.* funda.

bask *v.* pigri.

basket *n.* sesto.

basketball *n.* (*sport*) bascetbal.

basketball player *n.* bascetbalor.

basking shark *n.* setorino.

basmati rice *n.* basmati.

basophil *n.* basofilica.

basophilia *n.* basofilia.

basophilic *adj.* basofilica.

Basotho *n.* (*person*) soto.

Basque *adj.* & *n.* (*person*, *language*) euscara.

Basque Country *n.* Euscaleria.

bas-relief *n.* releva basa.

bass *adj.* & *n.* (*music*) baso.

bass clef *n.* clave basa.

bass guitar *n.* gitar baso.

bassist *n.* basiste.

bassoon *n.* bason.

bass player *n.* basiste.

Bass Strait *n.* Streta Bass.

bastard *n.* (*illegitimate child*, *insult*) bastardo; (*insult*) puto, puta, fio de puta.

bastardy *n.* bastardia.

baste[1] *v.* (*cookery*) grasi.

baste[2] *v.* (*sewing*) cose laxe.

bastion *n.* bastion.

bat[1] *n.* (*stick*) baston, raceta. • *v.* colpa.

bat[2] *n.* (*animal*) cirotero.

batch *n.* grupo.

batch file *n.* programeta.

bath *n.* (*tub*) banio; (*activity*) bani; (*bathing house*) banieria.

bath cap *n.* xapeta de bani.

bathe *v.* bani.

bather *n.* banior.

bath faucet *n.* valva de banio.

bath foam *n.* spuma de bani.

bath house *n.* banieria.

bathing costume *n.* veste de nada.

bathing suit *n.* veste de nada.

bathmat *n.* tapeto de bani.

bathrobe *n.* roba de bani.

bathroom *n.* sala de banio.

bath tap *n.* valva de banio.

bath towel *n.* tela de bani.

bathtub *n.* banio.

bathwater *n.* acua de banio.

bathyscope *n.* batiscopio.

bathysphere *n.* batisfera.

batik *n.* (*dyeing*) batic.

batiste *n.* (*fabric*) batista.

bat mitzvah *n.* batmitsva.

battalion *n.* batalion.

batten *n.* plance.
batter[1] *v.* (*hit*) bate; (*with stick*) bastoni.
batter[2] *n.* (*mixture*) pasta de frita.
battering ram *n.* ariete.
battery *n.* pila.
battery-powered *adj.* par enerjia de pilas.
battle *v.* & *n.* batalia.
battleaxe (US **battleax**) *n.* axa de gera.
battlecruiser *n.* (*warship*) cruser de batalia.
battlefield *n.* campo de batalia, campo de gera.
battlefront *n.* fronte de batalia.
battleground *n.* campo de batalia.
battlement *n.* merlon.
battleship *n.* barcon blindada, corasida.
bauble *n.* orneta.
Bavaria *n.* Baiern.
Bavarian *adj.* & *n.* baieres.
Bavarian cream *n.* crema baieres.
bavarois *n.* crema baieres.
bawdy *adj.* vulgar.
bawl *v.* & *n.* (*weep*) plora; (*yell*) cria.
bay[1] *n.* (*geography*) baia.
bay[2] *n.* (*recess*) alcova.
bay[3] *n.* (*laurel*) lauro nobil.
bayberry *n.* (*plant*, *berry*) mirica.
Baykal, Lake *n.* Lago Baical.
bay laurel *n.* lauro nobil.
bay leaf *n.* folia de lauro.
bayonet *n.* baioneta.
bayou *n.* pantan.
bay owl *n.* tito.
bay window *n.* fenetra de alcovo.
bazaar *n.* bazar.
bazooka *n.* bazuca.
B-boying *n.* brecdansa.
BBQ *n.* barbecu.
BC *abbr.* aec (*ante la eda comun*).
BCE *abbr.* aec (*ante la eda comun*).
B-cell *n.* limfosite B.
be *v.* es. **be that as it may** an tal.
beach *n.* plaia. • *v.* encalia. **become beached** encalia.
beachfront *n.* fronte de mar.
beacon *n.* faro.
bead *n.* perleta.
beadle *n.* (*officer*) bedel.
beagle *n.* (*dog*) bigel.
beak *n.* beco.
beaker *n.* copa, tason.
beaklike *adj.* becin.
beam *n.* (*light*) raio; (*support*) faxon. • *v.* radia; surie dentosa.
beaming *adj.* radiante.
bean *n.* (*plant*, *seed*) fava. **baked beans** gaxa de favas.
beanbag *n.* (*cushion*) cuxin de favas; (*juggling*) saco de favas.
bean curd *n.* tofu.
beanie *n.* (*cap*) cipa.
beanlike *adj.* favin.
bean porridge *n.* gaxa de favas.
bean-shaped *adj.* favin.
bean soup *n.* sopa de fava.
beanstalk *n.* talo de fava.
bear[1] *v.* tolera; (*carry*) porta; (*give birth*) pari, nase. **bring to bear** punta; enforsa.
bear[2] *n.* (*animal*) urso; (*stock market*) investor pesimiste.
bearable *adj.* tolerable.
bear cub *n.* urseta.
beard *n.* barba.
bearded *adj.* barbida.
bear hug *n.* abrasa ursin.
bearing *n.* (*heading*) dirije; (*machinery*) cosineto.
bearlike *adj.* ursin.
bear market *n.* mercato pesimiste.
Béarnaise *adj.* (*French region*, *sauce*) bearnes.
bearskin *n.* pel de urso; (*hat*) xapo de pelo.
beast *n.* bestia. **beast of burden** bestia de carga.
beastly *adj.* savaje.
beat *v.* (*hit*) bate; (*with stick*) bastoni; (*with whip*) flajeli; (*heart*) bateta; (*music*) pulsa; (*defeat*) vinse. • *n.* (*heart*) bateta; (*music*) pulsa. **beat up** bate.
beaten *adj.* bateda. **off the beaten track** a via de vias comun.
beater *n.* batador, batador eletrical.
beatific *adj.* beatifiante; estasiosa.
beatification *n.* beatifia.
beatify *v.* beatifia.
beatitude *n.* bondise; santia.
beatnik *n.* bitnic.
beau *n.* bela.
Beaufort Sea *n.* Mar Beaufort.
beautician *n.* esteticiste.
beautification *n.* beli.
beautiful *adj.* bela.
beautify *v.* beli.
beauty *n.* belia.
beauty contest *n.* concurso de belia.
beauty parlour (US **parlor**) *n.* beleria.
beauty salon *n.* beleria.
beauty shop *n.* beleria.
beaux arts *n.* artes bela.
beaver *n.* castor.
bebop *n.* (*music*) bebop.
becalm *v.* calmi.
because *subord.* car, par causa ce. **because of** par, par causa de.
bechamel *n.* (*sauce*) bexamel.
beckon *v.* jesti.
become *v.* deveni, -i.
becquerel *n.* (*unit of radioactivity*) becerel.

bed *n.* leto. **air bed** materas inflable. **bed and breakfast** oteleta. **make the bed** ordina la leto.
bedazzle *v.* stona, aturdi.
bedbug *n.* xinxe de leto.
bedclothes *n.* telas de leto.
bedding *n.* telas de leto.
bedevil *v.* tormenta.
bedewed *adj.* rosiosa.
bedfellow *n.* camerada de leto. **be bedfellows** comparti un leto.
bedlam *n.* dementeria.
Bedouin *adj.* & *n.* badaui.
bedpan *n.* bol de leto.
bedpost *n.* colona de leto.
bedraggled *adj.* desordinada.
bedridden *adj.* restrinjeda a leto.
bedrock *n.* roca madral.
bedroom *n.* sala de dormi.
bedside table *n.* comodeta.
bedsore *n.* ulsera de leto.
bedstraw *n.* galia.
bedtime *n.* ora de adormi.
bedwetting *n.* enurese.
bee *n.* abea.
beech *n.* faia.
beechnut *n.* noza de faia.
beef *n.* carne de bove.
beefeater *n.* ioman.
beefsteak *n.* steca.
beefy *adj.* carnosa.
beehive *n.* aberia, nido de abeas.
beekeeper *n.* abeor.
beekeeping *n.* eleva de abeas.
beeline *n.* linia reta. **in a beeline** en linia reta. **make a beeline for** vade en linia reta a.
beep *v.* & *n.* pia.
beeper *n.* piador.
beer *n.* bir.
beer belly *n.* ventron.
beer cellar *n.* cava de bir.
beer hall *n.* salon de bir.
beermat *n.* paragota.
beeswax *n.* sira de abea.
beet *n.* beta.
beetle *n.* scarabe.
beetroot *n.* (*plant*, *vegetable*) beta.
before *prep.* (*space*, *time*) ante. • *subord.* ante cuando. **a long time before** a multe tempo a ante. **before Christ** ante la eda comun. **before now** ante aora. **before the common era** ante la eda comun. **two days before** a du dias a ante.
beforehand *adv.* a ante.
befriend *v.* amini.
befuddle *v.* aturdi.
beg *v.* mendica; (*beseech*) suplica. **beg forgiveness** demanda per pardona.
beget *v.* jenita.
beggar *n.* mendicor.
beggarlike *adj.* mendicorin.
beggarly *adj.* mendicorin.
begin *v.* comensa.
beginner *n.* comensor.
beginning *n.* comensa. • *adj.* comensante. **at the beginning of** a la comensa de.
begonia *n.* begonia.
beguile *v.* encanta.
beguine *n.* (*dance*) bigin.
begun *adj.* comensada.
behalf *n.* benefica. **on behalf of** per.
behave *v.* condui.
behaviour (US **behavior**) *n.* condui.
behaviourism (US **behaviorism**) *n.* conduisme.
behaviourist (US **behaviorist**) *n.* conduiste.
behead *v.* destesti.
behemoth *n.* monstro jigante.
behest *n.* comanda.
behind *prep.* (*space*, *sequence*) pos; (*space*, *motion towards*) a pos, a retro de. • *adv.* a pos. • *n.* posterior, gluteos. **one behind the other** la un pos la otra.
behold *v.* regarda.
beholden *adj.* obligada.
beige *adj.* beje, pal brun.
Beijing *n.* Beijing.
being *adj.* & *n.* esente. **for the time being** per aora, per la presente.
belabour (US **belabor**) *v.* ataca; esplica tro.
Belarus *n.* Bielarus.
Belarusian *adj.* & *n.* bielarusce.
belay *v.* fisa; cansela.
belch *v.* & *n.* ruta.
belfry *n.* sala de campana.
Belgae *n.* (*ancient tribe*) belgas.
Belgian *adj.* & *n.* beljes.
Belgic *adj.* belga.
Belgium *n.* Beljia.
Belgrade *n.* Beograd.
belief *n.* crede.
believable *adj.* credable.
believe *v.* crede.
believer *n.* credor.
belittle *v.* desvalua. **belittle oneself** basi se.
Belize *n.* Beliz.
Belizian *adj.* & *n.* belizan.
bell *n.* campana.
belladonna *n.* (*plant*) beladona.
bell bottle *n.* (*plant*) jasinto de bosce.
bellbottoms *n.* pantalon esvasante.
bellboy *n.* portor.
bell chamber *n.* sala de campana.
belle *n.* bela.
bellflower *n.* campanula.

bellhop *n.* portor.
bellicose *adj.* gerosa.
belligerent *adj.* atacante, enemin.
bell-like *adj.* campanin.
bellman *n.* proclamor.
bellow *v.* & *n.* ruji.
bellows *n.* soflador.
bell pepper *n.* peperon verde.
bell pull *n.* tiracampana, corda de campana.
bell rope *n.* tiracampana, corda de campana.
bell-shaped *adj.* campanin.
bell tower *n.* campaneria.
bellwether *n.* ovea gidante.
belly *n.* ventre.
bellyache *n.* dole de ventre.
belly button *n.* ombilico.
belly dance *n.* dansa de ventre.
belly laugh *n.* rion.
belly shirt *n.* camiseta corta.
belong *v.* parteni.
belonging *adj.* parteninte. **belonging to** de, parteninte a.
belongings *n.* posesedas.
beloved *adj.* & *n.* amada, cara.
below *prep.* su; (*motion towards*) a su. • *adv.* a su. **below par** sunormal.
belt *n.* sintur. • *v.* sinturi. **ammo belt** sintur de muni.
beltane *n.* (*pagan holiday*) beltin.
beltlike *adj.* sinturin.
belt sander *n.* lisador de banda.
beltway *n.* via periferial.
beluga *n.* beluga.
belvedere *n.* belvedere.
bemoan *v.* deplora.
bench *n.* (*seat*) banca.
benchmark test *n.* proba de cualia.
bend *n.* curva, plia. • *v.* curvi, plia; (*limb*) flexe. **bend down** curvi. **the bends** maladia de descompresa.
bendable *adj.* curvable.
bendy *adj.* flexable.
beneath *prep.* su; (*motion towards*) a su. • *adv.* a su.
Benedictine *adj.* & *n.* (*monk*) benedictin.
benediction *n.* bondise.
benefactor *n.* beneficor.
beneficent *adj.* bonvolente.
beneficial *adj.* beneficante.
beneficiary *n.* beneficada.
benefit *v.* benefica, vantaji. • *n.* benefica, vantaje.
benevolence *n.* bonvole.
benevolent *adj.* bonvolente.
Bengal *n.* Bengala. **Bay of Bengal** Golfo Bengala.
Bengali *adj.* & *n.* bangla.
benighted *adj.* nonluminada, nonsabosa.
benign *adj.* nonosiva, noncanserosa.
Benin *n.* Benin.
Beninese *adj.* & *n.* benines.
Beninois *adj.* & *n.* benines.
bent *adj.* (*naturally*) curva; (*out of shape*) curvida.
benzene *n.* benzen.
benzene ring *n.* anelo de benzen.
benzoic *adj.* benzoica.
benzoic acid *n.* asida benzoica.
bequeath *v.* lega.
bequest *n.* lega.
berate *v.* reproxa.
Berber *adj.* & *n.* berber.
berberis *n.* (*plant*) berberis.
bereave *v.* priva.
bereavement *n.* priva.
bereft *adj.* privada.
beret *n.* bereta.
bergamot *n.* bergamota.
bergamot orange *n.* bergamota.
bergamot tree *n.* bergamoto.
Bering *n.* Bering.
Beringia *n.* Beringia.
Bering Sea *n.* Mar Bering.
Bering Strait *n.* Streta Bering.
berkelium *n.* (*element*) bercelio.
Bermuda *n.* Bermuda.
Bermudan *adj.* & *n.* bermudan.
Bermuda shorts *n.* pantala de jenos.
berry *n.* baca.
berrylike *adj.* bacin.
berserk *adj.* furiosa, noncontrolable. **go berserk** furia.
berth *n.* loca asiniada; (*bunk*) leteta.
beryl *n.* (*gem*) beril.
beryllium *n.* (*element*) berilio.
beseech *v.* prea, suplica.
beset *v.* tormenta.
beside *prep.* a lado de.
besides *adv.* plu, en ajunta. • *prep.* en ajunta a.
besiege *v.* aseja, ataca.
besieger *n.* asejor, atacor.
beslipper *v.* pantofli.
besmirch *v.* manxa, susi.
besotted *adj.* oseseda.
bespoke *adj.* par comanda.
besser block *n.* brice de sene.
best *adj.* la plu bon. **do one's best** fa la plu bon cual on pote. **best wishes** *n.* bon voles.
best-case scenario *n.* caso la plu bon.
bestial *adj.* bestin.
bestiality *n.* (*savagery*) bestinia; (*sexual*) zofilia.
bestiary *n.* compendio de bestias.
bestophilia *n.* zofilia.
bestow *v.* dona, presenta.
bestseller *n.* (*book, author*) bonvendeda.

bestselling *adj.* bonvendeda.
bet *v.* & *n.* aposta. **bet against** aposta contra. **bet on** aposta per.
beta *n.* (*Greek letter* Β, β) beta. **in beta** (*being tested*) a beta.
beta blocker *n.* blocinte de resetadores beta.
betail *v.* codi.
beta particle *n.* particula beta.
beta version *n.* varia de beta.
betel *n.* (*plant, stimulant*) betel.
betony *n.* betonica.
betray *v.* tradi.
betrayal *n.* tradi.
betrothed *adj.* prometeda.
better[1] *adj.* plu bon. • *v.* boni. **get better** (*improve*) boni; (*health*) recovre, sani.
better[2] *n.* apostor.
betting game *n.* jua de aposta.
betting parlour (US **parlor**) *n.* aposteria.
betting shop *n.* aposteria.
bettong *n.* (*marsupial*) betong.
bettor *n.* apostor.
between *prep.* entre. **between the two** entre la du. **in between** a entre, entre la du.
bevel *n.* bisel. • *v.* biseli.
bevel gear *n.* pinion cono.
beverage *n.* bevida.
bevy *n.* ronda.
beware *v.* garda se contra.
bewilder *v.* confonde, confusa, aturdi.
bewilderment *n.* confonde, confusa, aturdi.
bewitch *v.* encanta.
beyond *prep.* ultra, plu distante ca; (*motion towards*) a ultra. • *adv.* a ultra. **beyond comprehension** estra comprende. **beyond count** ultra conta. **in the back of beyond** a via de vias.
bezel *n.* montur.
bezique *n.* (*card game*) bezica.
bezoar *n.* (*biology*) bezoar.
Bhojpuri *adj.* & *n.* bodjpuri.
Bhutan *n.* Druciul, Butan.
Bhutanese *adj.* & *n.* drucpa, butan.
Bhutanse *adj.* & *n.* drucpa, butan.
bi- *pref.* bi-.
biannual *adj.* (*twice a year*) semianial.
bias *n.* prejudi; (*fabric*) bies.
biased *adj.* prejudosa.
biathlete *n.* biatlonor.
biathlon *n.* biatlon.
bib *n.* (*baby's*) teleta de bava; (*of overalls*) covrepeto.
bib-and-brace overalls *n.* salopeta.
Bible *n.* Biblia.
biblical *adj.* biblial.
biblio- *pref.* biblio-.
bibliographer *n.* bibliografiste.
bibliographical *adj.* bibliografial.
bibliography *n.* bibliografia.
bibliophile *n.* bibliofilica.
bibliophilia *n.* bibliofilia.
bib overalls *n.* salopeta.
bicameral legislature *n.* legeria con du salones.
bicarbonate *n.* bicarbonato.
bicentenary *n.* aniversario dusento.
bicentennial *n.* aniversario dusento.
biceps *n.* (*muscle*) bisepe.
bicker *v.* scaramuxa.
bicycle *n.* bisicle. • *v.* bisicli.
bicycling *n.* (*sport, pastime*) bisiclisme, siclisme.
bicyclist *n.* bisicliste, sicliste.
bid *v.* & *n.* ofre.
bidder *n.* ofror.
bide one's time *v.* espeta la bon momento.
bidet *n.* bide.
biennial *adj.* duanial.
bier *n.* portacaxon.
bifocal *adj.* bifocal.
bifocals *n.* bifocal.
bifurcate *v.* forci, dui.
bifurcation *n.* forci; (*dualism*) duplisme.
big *adj.* grande.
bigamist *n.* bigamiste.
bigamous *adj.* bigama.
bigamy *n.* bigamia.
big band *n.* orcestra de jaz.
Big Bang *n.* Buma Grande.
bigender *adj.* & *n.* bijenero.
big game *n.* animal xasada.
big-hearted *adj.* jenerosa.
bight *n.* curva; baia. **Great Australian Bight** Baia Australian Grande.
bigmouth *n.* nondiscreta.
bigot *n.* nontoleror.
bigoted *adj.* prejudosa, nontolerante.
bigotry *n.* prejudi, nontolera.
big step *n.* pason.
big toe *n.* diton de pede, halux.
biguine *n.* (*dance*) bigin.
bike *n.* bisicle, sicle.
biker *n.* motosicliste.
bike shorts *n.* pantala de bisicli.
bikini *n.* bicini.
bikini bottom *n.* basa de bicini.
bikini briefs *n.* (*underwear*) minislip; (*of bikini*) basa de bicini.
bikini top *n.* alta de bicini, portaseno de bicini.
bilabial *adj.* & *n.* (*consonant*) bilabial.
bilateral *adj.* biladal. • *n.* (*animal*) bilaterio.
bilberry *n.* vasinia, vasinia blu.
bilby *n.* bilbi.
bile *n.* bile.

bilge *n.* acua de cala; (*curved hull, compartment*) sentina.
bilgewater *n.* acua de cala.
biliary *adj.* bilal.
bilingual *adj.* & *n.* bilingual.
bilingualism *n.* bilingualisme.
bilious *adj.* bilal.
bilk *v.* engana.
bill *n.* (*invoice*) fatura; (*paper money*) bileta; (*legislative*) projeta legal; (*beak*) beco. • *v.* fatura.
billboard *n.* panel de poster.
billet *n.* abiteria. • *v.* casi tempora.
billfold *n.* bolseta, portamone.
billhook *n.* desramador.
billiards *n.* biliardo.
billiards hall *n.* biliarderia.
billiards player *n.* biliardor.
billiards room *n.* biliarderia.
billion *det.* & *pron.* mil milion, bilion.
billionaire *n.* bilionor.
billionth *adj.* (*ordinal*) bilion; (*fraction*) bilioni.
billow *v.* infla.
bimbo *n.* fol.
bimetallic *adj.* bimetal.
bimonthly *adj.* (*once every two months*) dumensal.
bin *n.* baldon. • *v.* baldoni.
binary *adj.* binaria.
bind *v.* lia; (*book*) relia.
binder *n.* folio.
bindery *n.* relieria.
binding *n.* (*cover*) relia.
binge *v.* selebra enebriada; supraregala.
bingo *n.* loto.
binocular *adj.* binoculal.
binoculars *n.* binoculo.
binomial *adj.* binomial. • *n.* binomio.
bio- *pref.* bio-.
biochemical *adj.* biocimical.
biochemistry *n.* biocimica.
biodegradable *adj.* biodegradante.
biodegradation *n.* biodegrada.
biodegrade *v.* biodegrada.
biodiverse *adj.* biodiversa.
biodiversity *n.* biodiversia.
biofuel *n.* biocombustable.
biogenesis *n.* biojenese.
biogeography *n.* biojeografia.
biographer *n.* biografiste.
biographic *adj.* biografial.
biographical *adj.* biografial.
biography *n.* biografia.
biohazard *n.* risca biolojial.
biological *adj.* biolojial.
biological hazard *n.* risca biolojial.
biological warfare *n.* gera biolojial.
biologist *n.* biolojiste.
biology *n.* biolojia.
biomass *n.* biomasa.
biomechanics *n.* biomecanica.
biometric *adj.* biometrial.
biometrical *adj.* biometrial.
biometrics *n.* biometria.
biometry *n.* biometria.
bionic *adj.* bionical.
bionics *n.* bionica.
biophile *n.* biofilica.
biophilia *n.* biofilia.
biophilic *adj.* biofilica.
biophysics *n.* biofisica.
biopsy *n.* biopsia.
biorhythm *n.* bioritmo.
biosphere *n.* biosfera.
biostatistics *n.* biometria.
biosynthesis *n.* biosintese.
biotechnology *n.* biotecnolojia.
bipartite *adj.* (*politics*) bipartisan; (*biology*) bipartida.
biped *n.* bipede.
bipedal *adj.* bipede.
biphasic *adj.* bifasal.
biplane *n.* biplana.
bipolar *adj.* bipolal.
biracial *adj.* birazal.
birch *n.* betul.
bird *n.* avia. **bird of paradise** avia de paradiso. **bird of prey** avia xasante.
bird bath *n.* portacua de avias.
birdcage *n.* caje de avia.
birdcall *n.* clama de avia.
birder *n.* oservor de avias.
bird flu *n.* gripe avial.
birdhouse *n.* casa de avia.
birdie *n.* avieta; (*golf*) un su la norma.
bird's-eye view *n.* vista airal.
birdsong *n.* canta de avias.
birdwatcher *n.* oservor de avias.
biretta *n.* (*cap*) bereta.
biriani *n.* (*food*) biriani.
biro *n.* pen de bal.
birth *n.* nase. **give birth** pari, nase.
birth certificate *n.* documento de nase.
birth control *adj.* & *n.* contraconsepal.
birthday *n.* aniversario.
birthmark *n.* nevo.
birth name *n.* nom orijinal.
birthplace *n.* loca de nase.
birth rate *n.* taso de nase.
birthright *n.* direto natural, erita.
birthstone *n.* petra de zodiaco.
birthtown *n.* vila de nase.
birthwort *n.* (*plant*) aristolocia.
biryani *n.* (*food*) biriani.
Biscay *n.* Biscaia. **Bay of Biscay** Golfo Biscaia.
biscuit *n.* biscoto.
bisect *v.* dui.
bisexual *adj.* bisesal.

bisexuality *n.* bisesalia.
Bishkek *n.* Bixcec.
bishop *n.* (*including chess*) bispo.
bishopric *n.* bispia.
bishopwort *n.* (*plant*) betonica.
Bismarck Sea *n.* Mar Bismarck.
bismuth *n.* bismuto.
bison *n.* bison.
bisque *n.* (*soup*) bisc.
bistro *n.* bistro.
bit[1] *n.* (*tiny piece*) pico. **a bit more of** un plu pico de. **a little bit of** un pico de.
bit[2] *n.* (*bridle*) morso.
bit[3] *n.* (*binary digit*) bitio.
bitch *n.* puta.
bitchy *adj.* odiosa.
bite *v.* morde. **love bite** suceta.
bitmap *n.* imaje matrisin.
bitter *adj.* (*taste*, *emotion*) amarga. **grow bitter** amargi.
bittern *n.* (*bird*) botor.
bitterness *n.* amargia.
bitter orange *n.* orania amarga.
bittersweet *adj.* amarga-dulse.
bitumen *n.* bitume.
bituminous *adj.* bitumosa.
bituminous coal *n.* carbon bitumosa.
bivalve *n.* bivalvo.
bivouac *v.* & *n.* bivaca, campa.
bizarre *adj.* bizara, strana.
blab *v.* esposa.
blabbermouth *n.* esposor.
black *adj.* & *n.* negra; afroamerican; (*sooty*) sujosa. **black and white** blanca-negra, monocromata, acromata.
blackball *v.* rejeta.
black bean *n.* fava negra.
blackberry *n.* (*bush*, *berry*) mora; (*bramble*) rubo.
blackbird *n.* merlo.
blackboard *n.* mureta negra.
blackcurrant *n.* grosela negra.
blacken *v.* negri; (*with soot*) suji.
black eye *n.* oio brunida, ematoma periorbital.
black-eyed bean *n.* fava de oio negra.
Black Forest *n.* Foresta Negra.
Black Forest gâteau *n.* torta de Foresta Negra.
blackhead *n.* punto negra.
black hole *n.* buco negra.
blacklight *n.* lumina ultravioleta.
blacklist *n.* lista negra. • *v.* pone en lista negra.
blackmail *n.* estorse.
black nightshade *n.* solano negra.
blackout *n.* perde de lus; perde de consensia.
black powder *n.* (*gunpowder*) polvo negra.
Black Sea *n.* Mar Negra.
blacksmith *n.* forjor.
black tie *n.* (*suit*) completa de sera.
blacktop *n.* asfalto.
bladder *n.* (*anatomy*) vesica.
bladder stone *n.* urolito.
blade *n.* lama; (*grass*) folia.
blah blah blah *interj.* babela bela.
blame *v.* & *n.* culpa.
blameless *adj.* nonculpable.
blamelessness *n.* nonculpablia.
blameworthy *adj.* culpable.
blanch *v.* blanci; (*cookery*) poxe.
bland *adj.* blanda.
blandness *n.* blandia.
blank *adj.* nondecorada, sin motif; (*deadpan*) sin espresa de fas.
blanket *n.* covreleto.
blare *v.* ruidi.
blasé *adj.* noncurante, nonimpresada.
blaspheme *v.* blasfema, maldise.
blasphemous *adj.* blasfemal.
blasphemy *n.* blasfema, maldise.
blast *v.* & *n.* esplode; colpa. • *interj.* txa. **blast off** enaira, lansa.
blast door *n.* porte contra esplodes.
blasted *adj.* enfernin.
blaster *n.* (*weapon*) colpador.
blast-off *n.* enaira, lansa.
blast wall *n.* mur contra esplodes.
blatant *adj.* clar, evidente; nonfurtiva.
blaze *v.* arde, focon.
blazer *n.* jaca de club; jaca de scola.
blazon *n.* scermo eraldial.
bleach *v.* blanci. • *n.* blancinte.
bleachers *n.* scalera de bancas.
bleak *adj.* sombre. • *n.* (*fish*) alburno.
bleakness *n.* sombria.
bleary *adj.* neblosa.
bleat *v.* bala.
bleed *v.* sangui.
bleep *v.* & *n.* pia.
blemish *v.* & *n.* manxa.
blend *v.* misca, fusa.
blended family *n.* familia fusada.
blender *n.* licuidador, miscador.
blenny *n.* (*fish*) bleni.
bless *v.* bondise.
blessing *n.* bondise.
blight *n.* clorose.
blimp *n.* airostato nonrijida.
blind *adj.* sieca. • *v.* sieci. **go blind** sieci.
blinder *n.* scermioio.
blindfold *n.* banda de oios. • *v.* bandi la oios.
blind man's bluff *n.* jua de sieca.
blind man's buff *n.* jua de sieca.
blindness *n.* siecia.
blini *n.* (*pancake*) blini.
blink *v.* & *n.* palpebri, ginia.
blinker *n.* scermioio.

blintz *n.* (*pancake*) blineta.
bliss *n.* estasia.
blissful *adj.* estasiante.
blister *n.* bula. • *v.* buli.
blithe *adj.* nonconsernada.
blitz *n.* bombarda.
blitzkrieg *n.* gera lampin.
blizzard *n.* venton de neva.
bloat *v.* & *n.* infla.
blob *n.* goton, masa.
bloc *n.* (*alliance*) bloco.
block *n.* (*slab, group of buildings*) bloco; (*of flats*) tore. • *v.* bloci, bari, impedi. **apartment block** tore de apartes. **block and tackle** aparato de puleas.
blockade *n.* impedi.
blockage *n.* bloci.
blockbuster *n.* susedosa.
blocker *n.* blocinte.
blockhouse *n.* fortres.
blog *n.* blog. • *v.* blogi.
blogger *n.* blogor.
blogosphere *n.* blogosfera.
bloke *n.* om, xico.
blond *adj.* & *n.* blonde.
blonde *adj.* & *n.* blonde.
blondness *n.* blondia.
blood *n.* sangue.
bloodbath *n.* masacra, bani de sangue.
blood cell *n.* selula de sangue, emosite.
blood clot *n.* trombo.
bloodcurdling *adj.* terorinte.
bloodhound *n.* (*dog*) sanumberto.
bloodless *adj.* sin sangue.
bloodletting *n.* sangui.
bloodline *n.* linia de sangue, linia de familia.
bloodmobile *n.* bus de dona sangue.
blood money *n.* mone sanguosa.
blood pressure *n.* presa sangual.
blood-pressure gauge *n.* sfigmometre.
blood-related *adj.* (*to do with blood*) sangual.
bloodshed *n.* versa de sangue.
bloodshot *adj.* (*eye*) sanguosa.
bloodsucker *n.* sucasangue.
blood sugar *n.* glucosa.
blood-sugar monitor *n.* monitor de glucosa.
bloodthirsty *adj.* side per sangue.
blood ties *n.* lias de sangue.
blood vessel *n.* duto sangual.
bloody *adj.* sanguosa; (*damned*) enfernin.
bloom *n.* flor. • *v.* flori.
blooper *n.* era comica.
blossom *n.* flor. • *v.* flori.
blot *v.* & *n.* manxa.
blotch *n.* manxa.
blotchy *adj.* manxosa.
blotting paper *n.* paper asorbente.
blouse *n.* blusa.
blow *v.* & *n.* sofla, (*as wind*) venta; (*fuse*) arde; (*hit*) colpa, xoca; (*light blow*) colpeta; (*sex*) suca la pixa de. **blow up** esplode.
blower *n.* (*person*) soflor; (*device*) soflador.
blowfish *n.* fugu.
blowfly *n.* mosca de carne.
blowgun *n.* serbatana.
blowhard *n.* bravator.
blowhole *n.* buco de respira.
blowjob *n.* suca de pixa.
blown *adj.* soflada.
blowout *n.* (*oil*) geser.
blowpipe *n.* serbatana.
blowtorch *n.* torxa per solda.
blowy *adj.* ventosa.
blubber *n.* gras de balena.
bludgeon *v.* bastoni.
blue *adj.* & *n.* (*light*) azul; (*dark*) blu.
bluebell *n.* (*various plants*) campaneta blu; (*genus Mertensia*) mertensia. **common bluebell** jasinto de bosce. **English bluebell** jasinto de bosce. **Scottish bluebell** campanula.
blueberry *n.* vasinia, vasinia blu.
blue-collar worker *n.* laboror par mano.
bluegrass *n.* (*music*) blugras.
blueish *adj.* bluin.
bluejay *n.* jai blu.
blue magpie *n.* piga blu.
blueprint *n.* sianogram.
blues *n.* (*music*) blus.
blue-screen compositing *n.* suprapone par scermo blu.
blue shift *n.* desloca blu.
bluet *n.* (*plant*) blueta.
bluff *v.* & *n.* engana, finje.
bluish *adj.* bluin.
blunder *n.* era grande.
blunt *adj.* nonagu; (*person*) brusca. • *v.* desagi.
bluntness *n.* nonagia.
blur *v.* nebli.
blurb *n.* anunsia.
blurry *adj.* (*image, vision*) neblosa.
blurt *v.* esclama.
blush *v.* & *n.* roji, rosi.
bluster *n.* bravata.
boa *n.* (*snake, scarf*) boa.
board *n.* (*plank*) plance; (*bread, etc.*) planceta; (*game*) table; (*display*) mureta; (*directors*) comite, comite dirijente, dirijores. • *v.* (*go on board*) embarca; (*board up*) planci. **above board** sin asconde. **on board** sur barco; sur avion.
boarder *n.* (*hotel*) visitor.
board game *n.* jua de table.
boarding house *n.* oteleta.
boarding school *n.* scola abitada.
board room *n.* comiteria.
boardshorts *n.* pantala de jenos.

boardwalk *n.* paseria de plances; bolevar a plaia.
boarish *adj.* senglarin.
boast *v.* & *n.* vanta.
boaster *n.* vantor.
boastful *adj.* vantosa.
boat *n.* barco.
boatbill *n.* (*bird*) becobarcin.
boat-billed heron *n.* becobarcin.
boater *n.* xapo de palia.
boatyard *n.* barconeria.
bob *v.* osila; (*gently, curtsy*) osileta; (*for apples*) pexa. • *n.* (*curtsy*) osileta.
bobbin *n.* bobin.
bobbly *adj.* nonplana.
bobby *n.* polisior, polisior engles.
bobcat *n.* lince rojin.
bobolink *n.* (*bird*) bobolince.
bobsled *n.* bob.
bobsledder *n.* bobor.
bobsleigh *n.* bob.
bobwhite *n.* (*bird*) colino.
bocce *n.* (*bowling*) bolo.
bode *v.* premostra.
bodge *v.* & *n.* malfa.
bodger *adj.* malfaor.
bodhisattva *n.* (*Buddhism*) bodisatva.
bodhi tree *n.* pipal.
bodhrán *n.* (*musical instrument*) bodran.
bodice *n.* alta de roba; corseto.
bodiless *adj.* sin corpo.
bodkin *n.* (*needle*) dageta.
body *n.* (*person, animal, vehicle*) corpo; (*garment*) bodi.
body double *n.* sustitua jemelin.
bodyguard *n.* gardacorpo.
body hair *n.* (*one strand*) capeleta; (*collectively*) pelo.
bodylike *adj.* corpin.
body paint *n.* pinta de corpo.
body shape *n.* forma de corpo.
bodystocking *n.* bodi longa.
bodysuit *n.* bodi.
boffin *n.* sabosa; siensiste.
bog *n.* pantan; (*ecology*) pantan torbosa alta. **bogged down** pantanida. **get bogged down** pantani.
bog arum *n.* cala.
bogey *n.* (*bogeyman*) babau; (*mucus*) muco nasal; (*golf*) un supra la norma.
bogeyman *n.* babau, asustor.
boggy *adj.* pantanosa.
bogie *n.* (*wheel system*) bogi.
bogles *n.* babau.
bogus *adj.* falsa.
Bohai Sea *n.* Mar Bohai.
Bohemia *n.* Boemia.
Bohemian *adj.* & *n.* boemian.
Bohol *n.* (*island*) Bohol.
Bohol Sea *n.* Mar Bohol.
bohrium *n.* (*element*) borio.
Boii *n.* (*ancient tribe*) boias.
Boiian *adj.* boia.
boil *v.* boli. • *n.* (*abscess*) aseseta.
boiled egg *n.* ovo bolida.
boiler *n.* caldera.
boilersuit *n.* covretota.
boisterous *adj.* ruidosa e enerjiosa.
boîte *n.* (*nightclub*) cabare.
bok choy *n.* (*cabbage*) boctxoi.
bold *adj.* corajosa, osante; egosa; (*typography*) spesa.
bolden *v.* spesi.
boldface *n.* spesia.
boldness *n.* osa.
bolero *n.* bolero.
bolide *n.* bolide.
Bolivia *n.* Bolivia.
Bolivian *adj.* & *n.* bolivian.
bollocks *n.* (*testicles*) coiones; (*nonsense*) merda de bove. **talk bollocks** parla merda.
bologna *n.* salsix bolonian.
Bolshevik *adj.* & *n.* bolxevic.
bolshy *adj.* disputosa.
bolster *v.* suporta.
bolt[1] *n.* (*for nut*) bulon, vise; (*door, gun*) bareta; (*lightning*) raio. • *v.* buloni, visi.
bolt[2] *v.* (*run away*) fuji.
bolus *n.* (*biology*) bolo.
bomb *n.* bomba. • *v.* bombi.
bombard *v.* bombarda.
bombarde *n.* (*musical instrument*) bombarda.
bombardier *n.* bombor.
bombardment *n.* bombarda.
bombast *n.* bravata.
bombastic *adj.* bravatosa, ostentosa.
bomb detector *n.* detetador de bombas.
bomber *n.* (*person*) bombor; (*aircraft*) bombador.
bombproof *adj.* secur contra bombas.
bombproof structure *n.* parabomba.
bombshell *n.* bomba; (*person*) atraosa.
bomb shelter *n.* refujeria contra esplodes.
Bonaire *n.* (*island*) Bonaire.
bonanza *n.* profita subita.
bonbon *n.* (*confectionery*) bonbon.
bonce *n.* testa.
bond *n.* lia; (*law*) obliga finansial.
bondage *n.* sclavia; (*sexual*) bondaje.
bondsman *n.* garantior.
bone *n.* oso.
bone graft *n.* inserta de oso.
bonehead *n.* stupida.
bone marrow *n.* medula de oso.
boner *n.* (*erection*) pixon.
bonfire *n.* (*celebratory*) foco de festa; (*of rubbish*) foco de jardin.
bong *n.* pipa de acua.

bongo[1] *n.* (*drum*) bongo.
bongo[2] *n.* (*antelope*) bongo.
bonito *n.* (*fish*) tun blanca.
bonk *v.* & *n.* colpa; (*sex*) fode.
bonkers *adj.* bobo.
bon mot *n.* replica.
bonnet *n.* (*cap*) xapeta; (*of vehicle*) capeta, capeta de motor.
bonobo *n.* bonobo.
bonsai *n.* bonsai.
bonus *n.* regala.
bony *adj.* ososa.
boo *v.* desaclama.
boob *n.* (*breast*) mamela, teton; (*mistake*) ereta, lisceta.
booboo *n.* ereta, lisceta.
boob tube *n.* bustier tubo, camiseta gainin.
booby *n.* (*bird*) bobo.
booger *n.* muco nasal.
boogeyman *n.* babau, asustor.
boogie *n.* (*dance, music*) bugi.
boogie-woogie *n.* bugi.
book *n.* libro; (*matches*) libreta. • *v.* (*seat, table*) reserva. **by the book** formal.
bookbinder *n.* relior.
bookbinding *n.* relia.
bookcase *n.* armario de libros.
bookend *n.* securilibro.
book fanatic *adj.* & *n.* libromanica.
bookie *n.* ajente de aposta.
booking *n.* reserva.
bookkeeper *n.* contor.
bookkeeping *n.* contablia.
booklet *n.* libreta.
bookmaker *n.* ajente de aposta.
bookmark *n.* sinta de libro; indicador. • *v.* indica.
bookplate *n.* insinia de libro.
bookseller *n.* vendor de libros.
bookshelf *n.* scafal de libros.
bookshop *n.* libreria.
bookstand *n.* portalibro.
bookworm *adj.* & *n.* libromanica.
Boolean *adj.* lojical.
boom *n.* (*pole*) boma; (*expansion*) buma. • *v.* (*expand*) buma. **baby boom** buma de bebes. **baby boomer** bebe de la buma. **boom and bust** profita e perde.
boomerang *n.* bumerang.
booming *adj.* forte.
boomtown *n.* vila bumante.
boondocks *n.* campania, vila provinsal.
boor *n.* bruta.
boorish *adj.* bruta.
boost *v.* & *n.* aumenta.
booster *n.* (*vaccination*) refortinte.
boot *n.* (*footwear*) bota; (*of vehicle*) portabagaje. • *v.* (*computer*) inisia.
bootblack *n.* limpibota.
Boötes *n.* (*constellation*) la Pastor.
booth *n.* ciosco.
boot jack *n.* (*for removing boots*) tenibota.
bootlace *n.* cordeta.
bootleg *n.* alcol nonlegal. • *v.* emporta nonlegal; vende nonlegal; pirati.
bootlicker *n.* (*sycophant*) lecabota.
boot pull *n.* (*for removing boots*) tenibota.
bootstrap *n.* (*for pulling boot on*) oreta.
bootstrapping *n.* inisia.
booty[1] *n.* benes furada.
booty[2] *n.* (*buttocks*) culo.
booty shorts *n.* minipantala.
booze *n.* alcol, distilada.
bop *n.* balo vivosa.
borage *n.* (*plant*) boraja.
borax *n.* (*substance*) borax.
bordeaux *n.* (*wine*) bordo.
bordello *n.* bordel.
border *n.* (*edge*) borda; (*geography*) frontera. • *v.* (*share an edge with*) borda.
border crossing *n.* pasaje de frontera.
borderland *n.* frontera.
borderless *n.* sin borda.
borderline *n.* frontera. • *adj.* (*just on the edge, personality disorder*) limital.
border tax *n.* imposta de duana, imposta de emporta.
bore[1] *v.* (*be tedious to*) noia. • *n.* (*person*) noior.
bore[2] *v.* (*drill*) fora; (*diameter*) calibre.
bore[3] *n.* (*dance, music*) bure.
boreal forest *n.* taiga.
boredom *n.* noia.
borekale *n.* folia de col.
boring *adj.* noiante, monotonosa.
born *adj.* naseda. **be born** nase.
Borneo *n.* Borneo.
boron *n.* (*element*) boro.
borough *n.* distrito.
borreia *n.* (*dance, music*) bure.
borrow *v.* empresta.
borrower *n.* emprestor.
borry *n.* bure.
borscht *n.* (*soup*) borxt.
borshch *n.* (*soup*) borxt.
Bosnia *n.* Bosnia. **Bosnia and Herzegovina** Bosnia e Hersegovina.
Bosniak *adj.* & *n.* (*person, language*) bosnian.
Bosnian *adj.* & *n.* bosnian.
bosom *n.* peto, senos.
boson *n.* (*particle*) boson.
Bosphorus Strait *n.* Streta Bosporo.
Bosporus Strait *n.* Streta Bosporo.
boss *n.* empleor; padron. **boss someone around** es tirano a algun.
bossa nova *n.* bosanova.
boss-eyed *adj.* straba.
bossy *adj.* autoritar, esijente.
botanical *adj.* botanical.

botanist *n.* botaniciste.
botany *n.* botanica.
botch *v.* & *n.* malfa.
botcher *adj.* malfaor.
both *det.* & *pron.* ambos. **both of us** ambos de nos. **both this and that** e esta e acel; ambos de esta e acel.
bother *v.* disturba, irita.
bothered *adj.* iritada. **be bothered with** disturba se per.
bothersome *adj.* iritante.
Bothnia, Gulf of *n.* Golfo Botnia.
bo tree *n.* pipal.
Botswana *n.* Botsuana.
Botswanan *adj.* & *n.* (*person*) tsuana.
bottle *n.* botela. • *v.* boteli.
bottleneck *n.* colo de botela; (*road*) conjestosa.
bottle opener *n.* abribotela.
bottom *n.* (*lowest part*) basa; (*underside, sea*) fondo; (*anatomy*) posterior, gluteos; (*garment*) veste basa. **at the bottom of** a basa de. **bottom half** basa. **bottoms** (*trousers*) pantalon.
bottom quark *n.* cuarc basa.
botulinum toxin *n.* toxina de botulisme.
botulism *n.* botulisme.
boudoir *n.* sala de fem, sala de dormi.
bouffant *adj.* inflada.
bougainvillea *n.* (*plant*) bugainvilea.
bough *n.* ramon.
bouillabaisse *n.* buliabes.
bouillon *n.* bulion.
boulder *n.* rocon.
boulevard *n.* bolevar.
bounce *v.* bondi. **bounce back** rebondi.
bouncy castle *n.* castel de salta.
bound[1] *v.* & *n.* (*leap*) bondi, salta.
bound[2] *adj.* (*tied*) liada; (*book*) reliada.
bound[3] *adj.* (*travelling*) viajante; (*destined*) destinada.
bound[4] *n.* (*boundary*) frontera, limita. **bounds** limitas.
boundary *n.* frontera, limita.
boundary condition *n.* restrinje limital.
bounded *adj.* limitada, finita.
boundless *adj.* nonlimitada, sin limita, infinita.
bountiful *adj.* abundante, produosa; jenerosa.
bounty *n.* recolie.
bouquet *n.* buce.
bourbon *n.* (*whisky*) borbon.
bourée *n.* (*dance, music*) bure.
bourgeois *adj.* burjes.
bourgeoisie *n.* burjesia.
bourrée *n.* (*dance, music*) bure.
boustrophedon *adj.* & *n.* bustrofedon.
bout *n.* combate, ataca.
boutique *n.* boteca.
boutonnière *n.* flor de boton.
bouzouki *n.* (*musical instrument*) buzuci.
bovine *adj.* boval, bovin. • *n.* bove.
bow[1] *n.* (*weapon, music*) arco; (*knot*) noda papilin.
bow[2] *v.* & *n.* (*bend respectfully*) inclina, saluta inclinada.
bow[3] *n.* (*ship*) proa.
bowdlerization *n.* sensura.
bowdlerize *v.* sensura.
bow drill *n.* forador arcin.
bowel *n.* intestin.
bower *n.* alcova de arbores.
bowerbird *n.* jardinor.
bowl[1] *n.* (*dish*) bol; (*geography*) basin.
bowl[2] *v.* (*ball*) lansa; rola. • *n.* bal de bolo.
bowlegged *adj.* con gamas arcida, con jenos vara.
bowler *n.* (*cricket*) lansor.
bowling *n.* (*sport*) boling.
bowling ball *n.* bal de bolo.
bowls *n.* (*sport*) bolo.
bowsaw *n.* siera arcin.
bow-shaped *adj.* arcin.
bow tie *n.* cravata papilin.
bow window *n.* fenetra de alcovo.
bow-wow *interj.* (*dog*) uau-uau.
box[1] *n.* (*container*) caxa; (*theatre*) lojia. • *v.* caxi.
box[2] *v.* (*fight*) boxe.
box[3] *n.* (*tree*) bux.
boxberry *n.* (*plant*) te de bosce.
boxcar *n.* vagon de carga.
boxer *n.* boxor. **boxers** (*shorts*) supantala.
boxer briefs *n.* minipantala.
boxer shorts *n.* supantala.
boxfish *n.* pex caxin.
boxing glove *n.* ganto de boxe.
boxlike *adj.* caxin.
box office *n.* bileteria.
box set *n.* colie caxida.
box tree *n.* bux.
boxwood *n.* bux.
boxy *adj.* caxin.
boy *n.* xico.
boycott *v.* & *n.* boicota.
boyfriend *n.* ami de cor, xico de cor, amor; (*any male friend*) ami mas.
boyhood *n.* enfantia, jovenia.
boyish *adj.* (*youthful*) joven; (*masculine*) masin.
boy scout *n.* scolta.
boyshorts *n.* minipantala.
bra *n.* portaseno.
bracchial *adj.* brasal.
brace *n.* (*strap*) bretela; (*teeth*) aparato dental; (*of brace and bit*) jirabroca; (*curly bracket*) braseta risa.
bracelet *n.* brasaleta.
brachiopod *n.* braciopodo.

brachiosaur *n.* braciosauro.
brachiosaurus *n.* braciosauro.
brachy- *pref.* (*short*) braci-.
braciole *n.* (*food*) rolada.
bracken *n.* filis aletin.
bracket *n.* braseta. • *v.* braseti. **angle bracket** braseta angulo, xevron. **curly bracket** braseta risa. **in brackets** entre brasetas, brasetida. **round bracket** braseta curva. **square bracket** braseta reta.
brackish *adj.* marin, salosa.
bract *n.* (*botany*) bratea.
bra cup *n.* copa de portaseno.
bradawl *n.* alena.
brady- *pref.* (*slow*) bradi-.
brag *v.* & *n.* vanta.
braggart *n.* vantor, bravator.
Brahma *n.* Brama.
brahman *n.* braman.
Brahmaputra River *n.* Rio Brahmaputra.
brahmin *n.* braman.
braid *v.* & *n.* trensa.
Braille *n.* braille.
brain *n.* serebro.
brainchild *n.* inventada.
brainstorm *n.* brilia de mente.
brainteaser *n.* rompetesta.
brainwash *v.* lava la serebro.
brainwave *n.* brilia de mente.
braise *v.* coce lenta.
brake *n.* freno. • *v.* freni.
brakeman *n.* frenor.
braless *adj.* sin portaseno.
bramble *n.* rubo.
bran *n.* crusca.
branch *n.* ramo. • *v.* rami.
branchlike *adj.* ramin.
brand *n.* (*commercial*) marca.
branding iron *n.* fero de marca.
brandish *v.* brandi.
brandy *n.* coniac.
brandy glass *n.* vitro de coniac.
brash *adj.* egosa.
brass *n.* laton.
brasserie *n.* taverna.
brassiere *n.* portaseno.
brass instrument *n.* strumento metal de venta.
brat *n.* turbosa.
bravado *n.* bravata.
brave *adj.* corajosa. • *v.* fronti corajosa.
bravery *n.* coraje.
bravo *interj.* brava.
brawl *v.* & *n.* combate.
brawn *n.* fortia, musculosia; (*jellied meat*) ceso-de-testa.
brawny *adj.* musculosa.
bray *v.* trompi. • *interj.* i-aa.
brazen *adj.* sin vergonia.
brazier *n.* brasador.
Brazil *n.* Brasil.
Brazilian *adj.* & *n.* brasilera.
Brazil nut *n.* noza de Brazil; (*tree*) nozo de Brazil.
breach *n.* buco, fesur; (*of agreement*) nonsegue. • *v.* penetra.
bread *n.* pan. • *v.* pani. **Arabic bread** pita.
breadbasket *n.* sesto de pan; (*region*) granería.
bread bin *n.* caxa de pan.
bread board *n.* planceta de pan.
breadbox *n.* caxa de pan.
breadcrumb *n.* pico de pan.
breadfruit *n.* fruta de pan; (*tree*) arbor de pan.
bread pan *n.* molda per pan.
bread roll *n.* paneta.
breadwinner *n.* suportor.
break *v.* rompe; (*rule, law*) viole; (*fast*) dejuna. • *n.* (*from activity*) pausa. **break down** (*malfunction*) rompe; (*decompose*) descomposa. **break in** entra par forsa. **break in two** rompe a du. **break out** (*rash*) eruta. **break up** separa. **break wind** flatule.
breakable *adj.* rompable.
breakage *n.* rompe.
breakaway *n.* separa; (*sport*) avansa subita.
breakdance *v.* & *n.* breedansa.
breakdown *n.* (*malfunction*) rompe; (*analysis*) analise.
breaker *n.* (*person*) rompor; (*wave*) onda spumante.
breakfast *n.* come de matina.
breakneck *adj.* lampin.
breakout *n.* evade.
breakpoint *n.* interompe.
breakthrough *n.* avansa grande.
breakup *n.* separa, fini de relata.
breast *n.* (*mammary gland*) seno; (*whole chest*) peto; (*meat*) peto, carne de peto. **at the breast** (*suckling*) a seno.
breastbone *n.* sterno.
breast drill *n.* forador engranada.
breastfeed *v.* dona lete, teti.
breastplate *n.* armur de peto.
breaststroke *n.* ranin.
breath *n.* respira. **bad breath** alitose. **hold one's breath** reteni sua respira. **out of breath** sin aira.
breathalyser (US **breathalyzer**) *n.* alcolometre.
breathe *v.* respira. **breathe in** enspira. **breathe one's last** respira final. **breathe out** espira.
breathing mask *n.* airador.
breathless *adj.* sin aira, sin respira.
breathtaking *adj.* aturdinte, encantante.
breechcloth *n.* covreseso.

breechclout *n.* covreseso.
breeches *n.* pantala.
breech-load *v.* (*gun*) retrocarga.
breechloader *n.* fusil de retrocarga.
breed *v.* reprodui; (*raise animals*) eleva. • *n.* raza.
breeder *n.* (*animals*) elevor.
breeding *adj.* (*kept for breeding*) per reprodui. • *n.* eleva.
breeze *n.* venteta.
breeze block *n.* brice de sene.
breezeway *n.* coredor esterna.
breezy *adj.* ventetosa.
brethren *n.* frates.
Breton *adj.* & *n.* (*person, language*) bresonica.
breve *n.* (*music*) tono duple; (*diacritic*) sinieta corta.
breviary *n.* breviario.
brevity *n.* cortia.
brew *v.* & *n.* (*tea, coffee*) infusa; (*beer*) prepara.
brewer *n.* biror.
brewery *n.* bireria.
briar *n.* erica arborin.
bribable *adj.* sobornable.
bribe *v.* & *n.* soborna.
bribery *n.* soborna.
bric-a-brac *n.* bricabrac.
brick *n.* brice. • *v.* brici. **brick up** brici.
brickie *n.* bricor.
bricklayer *n.* bricor.
bridal *adj.* de sposi, de sposa nova.
bride *n.* sposa nova.
bridegroom *n.* sposo nova.
bridesmaid *n.* dama.
bride-to-be *n.* sposa futur.
bridge[1] *n.* ponte. • *v.* ponti. **bridge the gap** (*metaphor*) ponti la canion.
bridge[2] *n.* (*card game*) brije.
bridle *n.* brida. • *v.* bridi.
brie *n.* (*cheese*) bri.
brief *adj.* corta, consisa. • *v.* instrui; reporta. • *n.* instrui. **briefs** (*garment*) slip.
briefcase *n.* portafolio.
briefing *n.* encontra, instrui, reporta.
brier *n.* erica arborin.
brig *n.* (*ship*) brigantin; (*prison*) prison de barcon.
brigade *n.* brigada.
brigadier *n.* brigador.
brigand *n.* bandito.
brigandage *n.* banditia.
brigantine *n.* brigantin.
bright *adj.* briliante.
brighten *v.* lumina.
brightener *n.* briliante.
brightness *n.* cuantia de brilia.
brilliance *n.* brilia.
brilliant *adj.* briliante.
brim *n.* (*hat, cup*) borda.
brimless *n.* sin borda.
brimstone *n.* sulfur.
brine *n.* marin. • *v.* marini.
bring *v.* (*deliver*) trae; (*summon*) veni. **bring about** reali. **bring back** retrae. **bring nearer** prosimi. **bring out** estrae. **bring to a conclusion** conclui. **bring to bear** enforsa. **bring together** asembla. **bring to life** anima. **bring to the surface** emerji. **bring up** (*child*) eleva; (*topic*) embarca, introdui. **bring up to date** corenti, refresci.
brink *n.* borda.
brinkmanship *n.* politica perilosa.
briny *adj.* marin, salosa.
brio *n.* zelo.
brioche *n.* (*bread*) briox.
briquet *n.* brice de carbon.
briquette *n.* brice de carbon.
brisk *adj.* enerjiosa.
brisket *n.* carne de peto.
bristle *n.* capelon.
Brit *n.* brites.
Britain *n.* Britan. **Great Britain** (*island*) Britan Grande. **New Britain** (*island*) Britan Nova.
Britannia *n.* Britan; (*personification of Britain*) Britania.
britches *n.* pantala.
British *adj.* (*person, language*) brites.
British Columbia *n.* Columbia Brites.
British Virgin Islands *n.* Isolas Virjin Brites.
Briton *n.* brites.
Brittany *n.* Bres.
brittle *adj.* frajil.
broach *v.* (*topic*) embarca, introdui.
broad *adj.* larga; (*daylight*) clar.
broadaxe (US **broadax**) *n.* axon.
broadband *n.* banda larga.
broadband internet *n.* interede de banda larga.
broad bean *n.* fava de visia.
broadbill *n.* (*bird*) eurilaimo.
broad-billed sapayoa *n.* (*bird*) sapaio.
broadcast *v.* & *n.* difusa, radia, transmete.
broadcloth *n.* stofa densa.
broaden *v.* largi.
broadside *n.* bombarda de lado.
broadsword *n.* spadon.
brocade *n.* (*fabric*) brocada.
broccoli *n.* (*plant, vegetable*) brocol.
brochure *n.* libreta.
broil *v.* grili.
broiler *n.* grilia.
broken *adj.* rompeda; (*speech*) nonfluente.
broker *n.* ajente, ajente de intercambia.
brokerage *n.* (*company*) ajenteria de intercambia; (*fee*) paia de intercambia.
bromeliad *n.* (*plant*) bromelia.

bromide *n.* (*chemistry*) bromido.
bromine *n.* bromo.
bronchi *n.* bronco.
bronchial *adj.* broncal.
bronchiole *n.* bronciol.
bronchitis *n.* broncite.
bronchodilator *n.* broncodilatante.
bronchoscope *n.* broncoscopio.
bronchoscopy *n.* broncoscopi.
bronchus *n.* bronco.
brontosaurus *n.* apatosauro.
Bronx cheer *n.* peta de labios.
bronze *n.* bronze. • *adj.* de bronze.
bronze age *n.* eda de bronze.
brooch *n.* brox.
brood *v.* es malumorosa, es preocupada, remastica. • *n.* (*offspring*) projenia. • *adj.* (*kept for breeding*) per reprodui.
brooding *adj.* malumorosa, de mal umor.
brook *n.* rieta.
broom *n.* scopa; (*plant*) jinesta.
broomstick *n.* manico de scopa.
brotform *n.* (*basket for shaping bread*) sesto de leva.
broth *n.* bulion.
brothel *n.* bordel.
brothelkeeper *n.* bordelor.
brother *n.* frate. **older brother** fraton. **younger brother** frateta.
brotherhood *n.* (*quality*) fratia; (*organization*) frateria.
brother-in-law *n.* frate par sposi.
brotherliness *n.* fratia.
brotherly *adj.* fratin.
brouhaha *n.* reata.
brow *n.* fronte.
browbeat *v.* menasa.
brown *adj.* & *n.* brun. • *v.* (*cookery*) bruni. **light brown** pal brun.
brown coal *n.* lignito.
brownie *n.* (*scout*) scolta joven; (*cake*) torteta de xocolada.
brownish *adj.* brunin.
brown lentil *n.* lentil brun.
browse *v.* (*books, goods*) vaga tra; (*web*) surfa.
bruise *v.* & *n.* contusa, bruni.
bruising *n.* contusa, bruni, ematoma.
brunch *n.* come de matina tarda.
Brunei *n.* Brune.
Bruneian *adj.* & *n.* brune.
brunette *adj.* & *n.* brun.
Brunswick, New *n.* (*Canadian province*) Brunswick Nova.
brunt *n.* xoca, colpa xef.
brush[1] *n.* brosa; (*large*) scopa. • *v.* brosi, scopi. **brush against** tanje.
brush[2] *n.* (*scrubland*) bosce de arboretas.
brush finch *n.* aremon.
brushlike *adj.* brosin.
brushoff *n.* rejeta.
brushwood *n.* (*low-growing vegetation*) subosce.
brusque *adj.* brusca.
Brussels *n.* Bruxelles.
Brussels sprout *n.* col de Bruxelles.
brutal *adj.* savaje.
brutality *n.* savajia.
brutalize *v.* savaji.
brut champagne *n.* xampania multe seca.
brute *n.* bruta, savaje, violente.
brutish *adj.* bruta, savaje, violente.
bryozoa *n.* (*organisms*) briozones.
bryozoon *n.* (*organism*) briozon.
bubble *v.* bola. • *n.* bola; (*speech*) balon.
bubble bath *n.* (*substance*) spuma de bani; (*activity*) bani de spuma.
bubble chamber *n.* cambra de bola.
bubblewrap *n.* plastica de bolas.
bubbly *adj.* bolosa.
bubo *n.* bubon.
bubonic *adj.* bubonal.
buccal *adj.* bocal.
buccaneer *n.* pirata.
Bucharest *n.* Bucuresti.
buck *n.* servo mas.
buckaroo *n.* cauboi.
bucket *n.* balde.
bucket seat *n.* seja baldin.
buckle *n.* fibia. • *v.* fibi; (*distort*) desformi; (*give way*) sede.
buckler *n.* (*shield*) scermeta.
buckskin *n.* pel de servo.
bucktooth *n.* dente conein.
buckwheat *n.* (*plant*) saraseno.
bucolic *adj.* campanial.
bud *n.* broto. • *v.* broti.
Buddha *n.* Buda.
Buddhism *n.* budisme.
Buddhist *n.* budiste.
buddleia *n.* (*plant*) budlea.
buddy *n.* ami.
budge *v.* move.
budgerigar *n.* papagaio.
budget *v.* bujeta. • *n.* bujeta, estima, scema economial. **budget for** reserva mone per.
budget-conscious *adj.* frugal.
buffalo *n.* bufalo.
buffer *n.* cuxin; (*software*) pox.
buffet *n.* bufe.
buffet restaurant *n.* buferia.
buffoon *n.* bufon.
buffoonery *n.* farsa, bufonia, bufonales.
bug *n.* (*insect*) xinxe; (*germ*) microbio; (*software*) defeto.
bugaboo *n.* babau.
bugbear *n.* babau.
bug-eyed *adj.* con oios protendente.
bugger *v.* sodomia. • *interj.* txa.
buggery *n.* sodomia.

buggy *n.* caro; careta de bebe.
bugle *n.* corneta natural.
bugler *n.* cornetor.
build *v.* construi. **build badly** malconstrui.
builder *n.* construor.
building *adj.* construinte. • *n.* construida.
building site *n.* construeria.
build-up *n.* (*accumulation*) cumula; (*preparation*) prepara.
built-in *adj.* integrada.
bulb *n.* bulbo; (*light*) ampola.
bulbous *adj.* bulbal, bulbin.
bulbul *n.* (*bird*) bulbul.
Bulgaria *n.* Balgaria.
Bulgarian *adj.* & *n.* (*person, language*) balgarsce.
bulge *n.* bulto, protende. • *v.* bulti, protende. **with bulging eyes** con oios protendente.
bulgur *n.* (*food*) bulgur.
bulimia *n.* bulimia.
bulimic *adj.* & *n.* bulimica.
bulk *adj.* coletiva. • *n.* enormia.
bulkhead *n.* (*ship*) mur; (*retaining wall*) muron.
bulky *adj.* masosa.
bull *n.* bove, bove mas; (*stock market*) investor otimiste.
bulldog *n.* buldog.
bulldozer *n.* buldozer.
bullet *n.* (*missile*) baleta, xutada; (*typography*) punton.
bulletin *n.* avisa; (*newsletter*) revisteta; (*broadcast*) difusa.
bulletin board *n.* mureta de avisas.
bullet point *n.* punton.
bulletproof *adj.* secur contra baletas.
bulletproofing *n.* parabaleta.
bulletproof vest *n.* parabaleta.
bullfight *n.* combate de bove.
bullfighter *n.* combator de bove.
bullfinch *n.* (*bird*) pirula.
bullfrog *n.* rana grande.
bullhorn *n.* megafon.
bull market *n.* mercato otimiste.
bullpen *n.* ensirca de bestias.
bullring *n.* stadion de bove.
bullseye *n.* sentro de blanco; (*confectionery*) confeto de menta peperin.
bullshit *n.* caca de bove, merda de bove. • *v.* parla merda.
bully *v.* tormenta. • *n.* tormentor.
bulrush *n.* (*sedge*) sipero; (*cattail*) tifa.
bulwark *n.* bastion.
bum *n.* (*buttocks*) culo, popa, posterior; (*hobo*) vagabon.
bumble *v.* (*speech*) babela; (*wobble*) bambola; (*bungle*) malfa.
bumblebee *n.* abeon.
bump *v.* (*hit*) colpa. • *n.* colpa; (*lump*) bulto.
bumper *n.* (*of vehicle*) paracolpa.
bumper car *n.* auto de xoca.
bumpkin *n.* campanian.
bumpy *adj.* bultosa.
bun *n.* paneta; (*hairstyle*) xinion; (*buttock*) culeta.
bunch *n.* grupo; (*large quantity*) monton; (*flowers*) buce. **bunches** (*hairstyle*) codetas.
bunco *n.* engana, froda.
bundle *n.* faxo, paco. • *v.* faxi, paci.
bung *n.* tapo.
bungalow *n.* bangalo.
bungee *n.* corda elastica.
bungee jump *v.* & *n.* salta con corda elastica.
bungee rope *n.* corda elastica.
bunghole *n.* buco de baril.
bungle *v.* malfa.
bungler *adj.* malfaor.
bunion *n.* halux valga.
bunk *n.* leteta.
bunk bed *n.* leto castelin.
bunker *n.* (*shelter, container*) buncer; (*golf*) trapa de arena.
bunko *n.* froda.
bunkum *n.* babela.
bunny *n.* coneta.
Bunsen burner *n.* beco de Bunsen.
bunting[1] *n.* (*bird*) emberiza.
bunting[2] *n.* banderetas.
buoy *n.* boia.
buoyant *adj.* flotante.
bur *n.* capsula spinosa.
burble *v.* & *n.* murmura.
burden *v.* & *n.* carga.
burdensome *adj.* cargosa, tro pesosa.
burdock *n.* (*plant*) bardana.
bureau *n.* (*office*) ofisia; (*department*) departe; (*furniture*) buro. **bureau de change** ofisia de intercambia. **bureau of investigation** departe de investiga.
bureaucracy *n.* burocratia.
bureaucrat *n.* burocrata.
bureaucratic *adj.* burocrata.
burgeon *v.* crese rapida.
burger *n.* amburger.
burglar *n.* furor, efrator, furacasa.
burglar alarm *n.* gardador.
burglarize (US). See *burgle*.
burglarproof *adj.* secur contra fura.
burglary *n.* efrata.
burgle (US **burglarize**) *v.* efrata, fura de.
Burgundian *adj.* & *n.* burgunda.
Burgundy *n.* Burgonia. **burgundy** (*colour, wine*) burgonia.
burial *n.* entera.
burial mound *n.* tumulo.
burin *n.* (*tool*) buril.
burka *n.* (*garment*) burca.
Burkinabé *adj.* & *n.* burcinabe.
Burkina Faso *n.* Burcina Faso.
burkini *n.* (*garment*) burcini.

burl *n.* bulto. • *v.* noda.
burlap *n.* juta.
burlap bag *n.* saco de juta.
burlesque *adj.* vodevil. • *n.* vodevil, farsa.
Burma *n.* Miama, Burma.
Burmese *n.* (*person, language*) miama, burman.
burn *v.* arde; (*disc*) scrive. • *n.* (*injury*) ardeda, lesion de arde.
burner *n.* ardador.
burnish *v.* brilia.
burnt cream *n.* crema ardeda.
burnt sienna *n.* siena ardeda.
burp *v.* & *n.* ruta.
burqa *n.* (*garment*) burca.
burqini *n.* (*garment*) burcini.
burr *n.* (*tool*) buril; (*botany*) capsula spinosa.
burrito *n.* burito.
burrow *n.* nido, tunel. • *v.* tuneli.
bursa *n.* (*anatomy*) bursa.
bursar *n.* caxor.
bursitis *n.* (*medical*) bursite.
burst *v.* creve, esplode. • *adj.* creveda. **burst out laughing** esplode con rie.
Burundi *n.* Burundi.
Burundian *adj.* & *n.* burundes.
bury *v.* entera.
bus *n.* bus.
busboy *n.* aidaservor.
bus driver *n.* busor.
busgirl *n.* aidaservor.
bush *n.* arboreta; (*grassland*) savana. **bushes** arboretas, bosceta.
bushbaby *n.* galago.
bush cricket *n.* grilo verde.
bushido *n.* (*samurai code*) buxido.
Bushman *adj.* & *n.* san.
bushtit *n.* (*bird*) ejitalido.
bushy *adj.* (*tail*) brosin.
business *n.* (*activity*) comersia; (*company*) compania; (*concern*) conserna. • *adj.* comersial. **do business** comersia. **that is none of your business** acel no es tua conserna.
business acumen *n.* astutia comersial.
business day *n.* dia de comersia, dia de labora.
businesslike *adj.* comersin.
business lunch *n.* come de negosia.
businessman *n.* comersior.
businessperson *n.* comersior.
business suit *n.* completa de negosia.
businesswoman *n.* comersior.
busser *n.* aidaservor.
bus stop *n.* parabus.
bust[1] *n.* peto, senos; (*sculpture*) busto.
bust[2] *n.* (*economic*) rompe. **go bust** bancaroti.
bustard *n.* (*bird*) otarda.
bustier *n.* (*garment*) bustier.
bustle *n.* ativia.
busy *adj.* ativa, ocupada.
busybody *n.* interferor.
but[1] *conj.* ma. **but still** ma ancora.
but-[2] *pref.* (*chemistry*) but-.
butane *n.* butano.
butch *adj.* masin.
butcher *n.* carnor. • *v.* mata; talia.
butcher's knife *n.* axeta de carnor.
butcher's shop *n.* carneria.
butler *n.* manejor de servores.
butt[1] *v.* (*hit*) colpa.
butt[2] *n.* (*rifle*) posterior; (*buttocks*) culo, popa, posterior.
butt[3] *n.* (*of joke*) blanco.
butt[4] *n.* (*cask*) baril.
butt cheek *n.* (*buttock*) culeta.
butte *n.* colina.
butter *n.* bur. • *v.* buri.
buttercream *n.* crema de bur.
buttercup *n.* ranunculo.
butterfat *n.* gras de bur.
butterfly *n.* papilio, papilio de dia.
butterfly-shaped *adj.* papilin.
buttermilk *n.* sero de bur.
butterscotch *n.* caramel de bur.
buttery *adj.* burin, burosa.
buttock *n.* gluteo.
button *n.* (*fastener, switch*) boton. • *v.* botoni.
buttonhole *n.* buco de boton; flor de boton.
buttonlike *adj.* botonin.
button quail *n.* (*bird*) turnix.
buttress *n.* contraforte.
butyl *n.* (*chemistry*) butil.
butyric *adj.* butirica.
butyric acid *n.* asida butirica.
buxom *adj.* formosa.
buy *v.* compra.
buyer *n.* compror.
buzz *v.* & *n.* zumbi. • *interj.* bzz.
buzzard *n.* buteo.
buzzard-hawk *n.* buteo.
buzzcut *n.* capeles militar.
buzzer *n.* avertador, vibrador, zumbador.
buzzword *n.* parola de moda.
by *prep.* (*made, done, caused, differing*) par; (*by means of*) con, par; (*next to*) a lado de; (*no later than*) ante fini de, a la plu tarda; (*multiplied by*) par; (*divided by*) entre. **by far** clar. **by oneself** (*alone*) solitar; (*unaided*) sin aida. **by the way** en brasetas, en pasa, nota bon.
bye *interj.* asta reuni, asta revide, asta alora, txau.
by-election *n.* vota spesial.
by-law *n.* regula local.
by-line *n.* suscrive de autor.
bypass *v.* evita, sircoveni.
by-product *n.* suproduida.
bystander *n.* oservor.
byte *n.* bait.
Byzantine *adj.* bizantian.

C

c. *abbr.* c (*sirca*).
cab *n.* taxi; (*two-wheeled carriage*) caro lejera.
cabal *n.* cabal.
cabana *n.* cabana.
cabaret *n.* cabare.
cabbage *n.* (*plant, leaves*) col.
cabbage soup *n.* sopa de col.
cabbie *n.* taxiste.
cabby *n.* taxiste.
cab driver *n.* taxiste.
caber *n.* palon.
cabin *n.* (*hut*) cabana; (*ship, aircraft*) cabina.
cabinet *n.* armario; (*politics*) governa; consilio, consilio governante, consilio de ministros.
cabinetmaker *n.* armarior.
cabinetmaking *n.* construi de armarios.
cable *n.* (*bundle of wires*) cable; (*thick rope*) cordon.
cable car *n.* tram volante.
cable tie *n.* fisacable.
caboose *n.* vagon final.
cabriolet *n.* caro lejera.
cacao *n.* cacau.
cacciatore *n.* (*food*) gal de xasor.
cache *n.* (*stash*) reserva; (*memory*) prememoria. • *v.* prememori.
cache-sexe *n.* covreseso.
cachet *n.* prestijia.
cack *n.* (*dung, anything worthless*) caca. • *v.* caci.
cackle *v.* & *n.* cacara.
cacophonous *adj.* mal sonante.
cacophony *n.* ruido.
cactus *n.* cacto.
CAD *n.* desinia aidada par computador.
cadaver *n.* corpo mor.
caddie *n.* (*golf*) portor.
caddisfly *n.* tricotero.
caddy *n.* contenador.
cadence *n.* ritmo.
cadet *n.* stajior.
cadmium *n.* cadmio.
cadre *n.* ecipo.
caduceus *n.* (*herald's wand, medical symbol*) caduseo.
caecum (US **cecum**) *n.* (*anatomy*) seco.
Caelum *n.* (*constellation*) la Sisel.
Caesar *n.* (*emperor*) sesar.
Caesarian section (US **Cesarian section**) *n.* sesarea.
caesium (US **cesium**) *n.* sesio.
café *n.* caferia. **café au lait** cafe con lete calda.
cafeteria *n.* buferia.
caffeinate *v.* cafini.
caffeination *n.* cafini.
caffeine *n.* cafina.
cage *n.* caje. • *v.* caji.
caiman *n.* caiman.
cairn *n.* monumento de rocas.
Cairo *n.* Qahira.
cajole *v.* adula; convinse.
Cajun *adj.* & *n.* cadjen.
cake *n.* torta. • *v.* crosti.
cake batter *n.* gaxa de torta, pasta de torta.
cake mix *n.* gaxa de torta, pasta de torta.
cake pan *n.* molda per tortas.
cakewalk *n.* ateni fasil.
calabash *n.* zuca.
calamity *n.* desastre.
calamus *n.* calamo.
calcaneus *n.* calcaneo.
calcification *n.* calci.
calcify *v.* calci.
calcium *n.* calsio.
calcium carbonate *n.* carbonato de calsio.
calcium-channel blocker *n.* blocinte de canales de calsio.
calcium oxide *n.* osido de calsio.
calculable *adj.* calculable.
calculate *v.* calcula.
calculation *n.* calcula.
calculator *n.* calculador.
calculus *n.* (*mathematics*) calculo; (*deposit on teeth, in wine*) tartar.
caldera *n.* crater volcanal.
Caledonia *n.* Caledonia. **New Caledonia** Caledonia Nova.
Caledonian *adj.* & *n.* caledonian.
calendar *n.* calendario.
calf *n.* boveta; (*anatomy*) sura.
caliber (US). See *calibre*.
calibrate *v.* ajusta.
calibration *n.* ajusta.
calibre (US **caliber**) *n.* calibre.
calico *n.* calico.
California *n.* (*US state*) California. **Baja California** California Basa. **Gulf of California** Golfo California.
californium *n.* (*element*) californio.
caliper (US). See *calliper*.
caliph *n.* califa.
caliphate *n.* califia.
calisthenics *n.* eserse fisical.
call *v.* (*shout*) clama; (*name*) nomi; (*phone*) telefoni; (*attention*) atrae. • *n.* clama; telefoni; visita. **call attention to** fa ce on persepi. **call to account** esije un esplica de. **call to military service** clama a servi militar.

call to mind sujesta, evoca, fa ce on recorda.
calla *n.* (*lily*) cala. **marsh calla** cala.
called *adj.* (*shouted*) clamada; (*named*) nomida. **be called X** es nomida X.
callee *n.* clamada.
calligraphy *n.* caligrafia.
calling *n.* (*vocation*) carera.
calliope *n.* organo de vapor.
calliper (US **caliper**) *n.* calibro.
callous *adj.* calosa.
callousness *n.* calosia.
callow *adj.* nonmatur.
callus *n.* calo.
calm *adj.* calma, cuieta. • *v.* calmi, cuieti. • *n.* calmia, cuietia. **calm down** calmi, cuieti.
calmness *n.* calmia, cuietia.
caloric *adj.* calorial.
calorie *n.* caloria. **large calorie** caloria grande. **small calorie** caloria peti.
calorie-laden *adj.* caloriosa.
calque *n.* tradui prestada.
calumniate *v.* malacusa.
calumniation *n.* malacusa.
calumniator *n.* malacusor.
calumnious *adj.* malacusante.
calumny *n.* malacusa.
Calvary *n.* (*hill*) Calvario.
Calvinism *n.* (*Christianity*) calvinisme.
Calvinist *adj.* & *n.* calviniste.
calypso *adj.* & *n.* calipso.
calyx *n.* calix.
camaraderie *n.* cameradia.
Cambodia *n.* Camputxa.
Cambodian *adj.* & *n.* camputxa.
Cambrian *adj.* & *n.* (*geology*) cambrian.
camel *n.* camel.
camel driver *n.* camelor.
cameleer *n.* camelor.
camellia *n.* (*plant*) camelia.
Camelopardalis *n.* (*constellation*) la Jirafa.
camel rider *n.* camelor.
camembert *n.* (*cheese*) camamber.
cameo *n.* (*jewellery, literature, minor acting role*) cameo.
camera *n.* camera.
cameraman *n.* cameror.
camera operator *n.* cameror.
camerawoman *n.* cameror.
Cameroon *n.* Camerun.
Cameroonian *adj.* & *n.* camerunes.
camisole *n.* sucamisa.
camomile *n.* camomila.
camouflage *v.* & *n.* camofla.
camp *v.* & *n.* campa. **advanced camp** campa avansada.
campaign *v.* & *n.* campania. **campaign for** campania per, batalia per.
campaigner *n.* campanior, batalior.
campanile *n.* campaneria.
Campeche *n.* (*Mexican state*) Campeche. **Bay of Campeche** Baia Campeche.
Campeche Sound *n.* Baia Campeche.
camper *n.* tendor; (*vehicle*) caravan.
campervan *n.* autocaravan.
camphor *n.* camfor.
Campidanese *adj.* & *n.* (*language*) campidanes.
campsite *n.* camperia.
campus *n.* compleso, vila de universia.
can[1] *v.* (*be able to*) pote.
can[2] *n.* (*container*) bote; (*large with spout*) carafon. • *v.* boti, jari.
Canaan *n.* (*biblical region*) Canan.
Canaanite *adj.* & *n.* (*person, language*) cananes.
Canada *n.* Canada.
Canadian *adj.* & *n.* canadian.
canal *n.* canal.
canalboat *n.* barco de canal.
canapé *n.* canape.
canary *n.* canario.
Canary Islands *n.* Isolas Canario.
canasta *n.* (*card game*) canasta.
cancan *n.* (*dance*) cancan.
cancel *v.* cansela, aborta. **be cancelled** aborta.
cancellable (US **cancelable**) *adj.* canselable.
cancellation *n.* cansela.
canceller (US **canceler**) *n.* (*device*) canselador.
cancer[1] *n.* canser.
Cancer[2] *n.* (*constellation*) la Crabe.
cancerous *adj.* canserosa.
candela *n.* candela.
candelabra *n.* candelabro.
candid *adj.* franca; (*photo*) spontan, sin posa.
candidate *n.* aspiror.
candied fruit *n.* fruta confetida.
candle *n.* candela.
candleberry *n.* (*tree*) cucui.
candle extinguisher *n.* estinguador de candela.
candleholder *n.* portacandela.
candlelight ceremony *n.* selebra a lus de candelas.
candlenut *n.* cucui.
candlepower *n.* candela.
candlestick *n.* portacandela.
candour (US **candor**) *n.* onestia.
candy *n.* confetos. • *v.* confeti.
candy bar *n.* bara de confeto.
candy cane *n.* basto de zucar.
candyfloss *n.* coton de zucar.
cane *n.* basto; (*plan*) cana. • *v.* (*punish*) basti; (*prune*) desrami.
cane rat *n.* aulacode.

Canes Venatici *n.* (*constellation*) la Canes de Xasa.
canid *n.* canido.
canine *adj.* canin. • *n.* canido.
canine tooth *n.* dente canin.
Canis Major *n.* (*constellation*) la Can Grande.
Canis Minor *n.* (*constellation*) la Can Peti.
canister *n.* silindre.
canker sore *n.* ulsereta.
cannabinoid *n.* (*drug*) canabinoide.
cannabis *n.* (*plant, drug*) canaba.
cannabis cigarette *n.* sigareta de canaba.
cannabis user *n.* canabor.
cannery *n.* boteria.
cannibal *n.* canibal.
cannibalism *n.* canibalisme.
cannoli *n.* canolos.
cannolo *n.* (*dessert*) canolo.
cannon *n.* (*gun*) canon.
cannonball *n.* bal de canon.
cannoneer *n.* canonor.
cannon fodder *n.* (*soldiers*) carne per canones.
cannonier *n.* canonor.
canoe *n.* canoa. • *v.* vade par canoa.
canoeing *n.* canoisme.
canoeist *n.* canoiste.
canola *n.* (*plant, oil*) colza.
canon[1] *n.* (*literature, music*) canon.
canon[2] *n.* (*priest*) prete regulada.
canonical *adj.* canonal, autoriosa.
canonicalization *n.* normali.
canonicalize *v.* normali.
canonization *n.* santi.
canonize *v.* santi.
can opener *n.* abribote.
canopy *n.* baldacin.
cant *n.* jergo.
cantaloupe *n.* cantalupo.
cantankerous *adj.* disputosa.
cantata *n.* cantada.
canteen *n.* botela de acua; (*restaurant*) caferia, comeria.
canter *v.* & *n.* duigalopa.
canticle *n.* salmo.
cantilever *n.* cantilever. • *v.* cantileveri.
canton *n.* canton. • *v.* casi tempora.
cantor *n.* cantor.
canvas *n.* lona. • *adj.* de lona.
canvass *v.* campania.
canvasser *n.* solisitor.
canyon *n.* canion.
Cao Dai *adj.* & *n.* caodai.
Caodaism *n.* (*religion*) caodai.
Caodaist *adj.* & *n.* caodai.
cap *n.* (*hat*) xapeta; (*upper limit*) limita masima; (*stopper*) tapo. • *v.* tapi; (*price*) limita.
capability *n.* capasia.
capable *adj.* capas, potente. **capable of error** capas de era. **grow capable** capasi.
capacious *adj.* spasiosa.
capacitance *n.* capasia eletrical.
capacitor *n.* condensador.
capacity *n.* capasia; (*role*) rol, posto.
cape *n.* (*headland*) capo; (*cloak*) capa. • *v.* capi.
Cape Breton *n.* Capo Breton.
caper[1] *v.* & *n.* brinca.
caper[2] *n.* (*plant, bud*) capara.
Cape Verde *n.* Capo Verde.
Cape Verdean *adj.* & *n.* capoverdean.
capillary *adj.* & *n.* capilar.
capita, per *adv.* per person.
capital *adj.* & *n.* (*city, economics, architecture*) capital; (*letter*) major.
capitalism *n.* capitalisme.
capitalist *n.* capitaliste.
capitalize *v.* (*finance*) capitali; (*letters*) majori.
capital letter *n.* letera major.
capital punishment *n.* puni de mori.
capitol *n.* (*building*) capitolio.
cappello romano *n.* xapo saturnin.
cappuccino *n.* caputxino.
caprice *n.* capris.
capricious *adj.* caprisosa, caprin.
capriciousness *n.* caprisia.
Capricorn *n.* (*constellation*) la Capra.
Capricornus *n.* (*constellation*) la Capra.
capri pants *n.* pantalon de sura.
capsicum *n.* (*plant, fruit*) peperon.
capsize *v.* inversa.
capstan *n.* enrolador.
capstone *n.* petra ultima.
capsule *n.* capsula.
captain *n.* capitan.
caption *n.* titulo.
captivate *v.* encanta.
captive *adj.* caturada, prisonida, nonlibre.
captivity *n.* nonlibria, prisoni.
captor *n.* caturor.
capture *v.* catura, prende; (*photo*) xuta.
capuchin *n.* (*monkey*) caputxin.
capybara *n.* (*animal*) capibara.
car *n.* auto, automobil; (*train*) vagon. **go by car** vade par auto. **transport by car** automobili.
caracal *n.* (*wild cat*) caracal.
caracara *n.* (*bird*) caracara.
carafe *n.* carafa.
carambola *n.* carambola.
caramel *n.* caramel.
caramel custard *n.* crema de caramel.
caramelize *v.* carameli.
caramel pudding *n.* crema de caramel.
carapace *n.* armur.
carat *n.* (*unit*) carato.
caravan *n.* (*towed vehicle, travellers*) caravan.
caravel *n.* (*ship*) caravela.

caraway *n.* (*plant*) carvi.
carbide *n.* (*chemistry*) carbido.
carbohydrate *n.* carboidrato.
carbon *n.* carbono.
carbonate *n.* carbonato.
carbonated *adj.* gasosa.
carbon dioxide *n.* diosido de carbono.
Carboniferous *adj.* & *n.* (*geology*) carbonifera.
carbonize *v.* carboni.
carbon monoxide *n.* monosido de carbono.
carbon paper *n.* paper de carbono.
carbonyl *n.* (*chemistry*) carbonil.
carboxyl *n.* (*chemistry*) carbosil.
carburate *v.* carbura.
carburation *n.* carbura.
carburetor *n.* carburador.
carburettor *n.* carburador.
carcass *n.* corpo mor.
carcinogen *n.* carsinojen.
carcinogenesis *n.* carsinojenese.
carcinogenic *adj.* carsinojen.
carcinoma *n.* carsinoma.
card *n.* carta.
cardamom *n.* (*plant, spice*) cardamom.
cardboard *n.* carton.
cardboard box *n.* caxa de carton.
card game *n.* jua de cartas.
-cardia *suff.* (*heart*) -cardia.
cardiac *adj.* cardial.
cardigan *n.* cardigan.
cardinal *n.* (*church, bird*) cardinal.
cardio- *pref.* (*heart*) cardio-.
cardiogram *n.* cardiogram.
cardiograph *n.* cardiograf.
cardiography *n.* cardiografia.
cardiological *adj.* cardiolojial.
cardiologist *n.* cardiolojiste.
cardiology *n.* cardiolojia.
cardiomyopathic *adj.* cardiomiopatica.
cardiomyopathy *n.* cardiomiopatia.
cardiopathic *adj.* cardiopatica.
cardiopathy *n.* cardiopatia.
cardiopulmonary *adj.* cardiopulmonal.
cardiopulmonary resuscitation *n.* reanima cardiopulmonal.
cardiotonic *adj.* cardiotonica.
cardiotoxic *adj.* cardionosiva.
cardiovascular *adj.* cardiovascular.
cardlike *adj.* cartin.
card reader *n.* lejecarta.
cardshark *n.* esperta de cartas, trucor de cartas.
cardsharp *n.* esperta de cartas, trucor de cartas.
care *v.* & *n.* (*nurture, means of treatment*) cura. **care for** cura. **I don't care** (*disinterest*) me no cura. **take care of** cura; (*temporarily*) atende.
careen *v.* (*hurtle*) core sin restrinje; (*ship*) turna.
career *n.* carera. • *v.* core sin restrinje.
career man *n.* careror, om de carera.
career-related *adj.* careral.
career woman *n.* careror, fem de carera.
carefree *adj.* sin cura, nonconsernada.
careful *adj.* atendente, curante; (*cautious*) cauta. **be careful** atende.
carefulness *n.* cautia.
care home *n.* ospisio.
careless *adj.* sin atende, nonatendente.
car enthusiast *n.* automanica.
carer *n.* curor.
caress *v.* caresa.
caret *n.* sinia de omete.
caretaker *n.* mantenor; atendor.
cargo *n.* carga.
cargo pants *n.* pantalon de carga.
cargo ship *n.* barcon de carga.
cargo supervisor *n.* supravidor de carga.
Carib *adj.* & *n.* (*language, people*) caribe.
Caribbean *adj.* & *n.* Caribe.
Caribbean Islands *n.* Isolas Caribe.
Caribbean Sea *n.* Mar Caribe.
caribou *n.* reno.
caricature *n.* cartun, imaje esajerada. • *v.* esajera.
carillon *n.* (*music*) carilion.
carina *n.* cilia. **Carina** (*constellation*) la Cilia.
carioca *n.* (*dance*) carioca.
carnage *n.* mori e destrui.
carnal *adj.* erotica.
carnation *n.* cariofilo.
carnelian *n.* (*gem*) cornalina.
carnival *n.* carnaval.
carnival float *n.* caro de carnaval.
carnival worker *n.* carnavalor.
carnivore *n.* carnivor.
carnivorous *adj.* carnivor.
carny *n.* carnavalor.
carob *n.* (*plant*) carobo; (*bean, powder*) caroba.
carol *n.* canta de natal.
Carolina *n.* Carolina. **North Carolina** (*US state*) Carolina Norde. **South Carolina** (*US state*) Carolina Sude.
carom billiards *n.* biliardo franses.
caron *n.* caron.
carotid *adj.* carotide.
carotid artery *n.* arteria carotide.
carouse *v.* selebra enebriada.
carousel *n.* (*entertainment, conveyor belt*) carusel.
carp[1] *n.* (*fish*) carpa.
carp[2] *v.* (*complain*) cexa.
carpal *adj.* (*anatomy*) carpal.
carpal tunnel *n.* tunel carpal.
car park *n.* parce de autos.

carpel *n.* (*botany*) carpel.
Carpentaria, Gulf of *n.* Golfo Carpentaria.
carpenter *n.* carpentor. • *v.* carpenta.
carpenter's square *n.* cuadrador.
carpentry *n.* carpenta.
carpet *n.* tapeto.
carport *n.* garaje partal.
carpus *n.* (*anatomy*) carpo.
car racing *n.* corsa de autos.
carriage *n.* caro; (*luxury*) caron; (*train*) vagon; (*typewriter*) caro. **baby carriage** caro de bebe.
carriage driver *n.* caror.
carriage house *n.* careria.
carriage return *n.* (*character*) reveni de caro.
carriageway *n.* autovia.
carrier *n.* (*person*) transportor; (*company*) transportores. **aircraft carrier** portavion.
carrion *n.* caronia.
carrion crow *n.* corvo comun.
carrot *n.* (*plant*, *root*) carota.
carry *v.* porta, transporta. **carry on** continua. **carry out** esecuta.
carryall *n.* bolson.
carry-on suitcase *n.* valiseta.
carsick *adj.* nauseada de auto.
cart *n.* caro; (*small*) careta.
carte blanche *n.* carta blanca.
cartel *n.* cartel.
Cartesian *adj.* cartesian.
Cartesian coordinate *n.* coordinada cartesian.
Cartesianism *n.* cartesianisme.
Carthage *n.* Cartago.
Carthaginian *adj.* punica.
Carthusian *adj.* & *n.* (*monk*) cartusian.
Carthusian monastery *n.* cartusia.
cartilage *n.* cartilaje.
cartilaginous *adj.* cartilajosa.
cartographer *n.* cartografiste.
cartographic *adj.* cartografial.
cartographical *adj.* cartografial.
cartography *n.* cartografia.
carton *n.* caxa de carton.
cartoon *n.* (*still*) cartun; (*animated*) anima.
cartoon character *n.* animada.
cartoonist *n.* animor; cartuniste.
cartoon strip *n.* banda de cartunes.
cartouche *n.* cartux.
cartridge *n.* cartux.
cartridge pen *n.* pen de cartux.
cartwheel *n.* volta ladal, volta par mano.
caruncle *n.* caruncula.
carve *v.* siseli, talia.
carving *n.* siseli.
carwash *n.* (*machine*) lavador de autos; (*place*) laveria de autos.
caryatid *n.* cariatide.
cascade *v.* & *n.* cascade.
cascading menu *n.* menu cascadente.
cascading stylesheet *n.* folia cascadente de stilo.
case[1] *n.* (*instance*, *law*, *grammar*) caso; (*law*) litiga; (*argument*) razona. **in any case** a cualce caso. **in case** per caso; (*to guard against the possibility that*) per caso ce, per si; (*if it should actually happen that*) en caso ce. **in case of** per caso de; en caso de. **in that case** en acel caso, alora. **it's a case of** lo es un caso de, lo pertine a.
case[2] *n.* (*container*) caxa; (*uppercase*, *lowercase*) leteras major o minor.
case-blind *adj.* sieca a leteras major.
casein *n.* (*protein*) casena.
case-insensitive *adj.* sieca a leteras major.
casement window *n.* fenetra xarnierida.
case-sensitive *adj.* distinguinte leteras major.
caseworker *n.* aidor sosial.
cash *n.* mone, mone fisical. • *v.* (*cheque*) cambia. **cash in** (*cheque*) cambia. **cash in on** esplota, profita de. **in cash** con mone.
cash crop *n.* recolie profitosa.
cashew *n.* (*nut*) anacardia; (*tree*) anacardio.
cashier *n.* caxor.
cash machine *n.* automata de banco.
cashmere *n.* caxmir.
cashpoint *n.* automata de banco.
cash register *n.* caxa rejistrante.
casing *n.* caxa; cartux; (*cable*, *sausage*) gaina.
casino *n.* casino.
cask *n.* baril.
casket *n.* portajoala.
Caspian *adj.* caspian.
Caspian Sea *n.* Caspio, Mar.
cassava *n.* (*tree*, *root*) manioca.
casserole *n.* casolon.
cassette *n.* caxeta. **audio cassette** caxeta audio.
cassia *n.* (*plant*) casia.
Cassiopeia *n.* (*mythology*, *constellation*) Casiopea.
cassock *n.* roba de prete.
cassowary *n.* (*bird*) casuari.
cast[1] *v.* (*throw*) lansa; (*mould*) moldi; (*spell*) encanta. • *n.* (*throw*) lansa; (*container*) molda; (*moulded object*) moldida. **cast a shadow over** ombri. **cast a spell** encanta. **cast out** espulsa.
cast[2] *v.* (*actors*) asinia roles. • *n.* atores. **be cast as** prende la rol de.
castanets *n.* castanieta.
castaway *n.* perdeda a mar.
caste *n.* (*social class*) casta.
Castellano *adj.* & *n.* castelian.
castellate *v.* merloni.
castellation *n.* (*architecture*) merlon.

castigate *v.* reproxa.
Castile *n.* (*Spanish region*) Castelia.
Castilian *adj.* & *n.* (*person, language*) castelian.
casting *n.* moldida.
cast iron *n.* fero moldida.
castle *n.* castel. • *v.* (*chess move*) roca.
castoff *n.* veste desprendeda.
castor *n.* roteta.
castrate *v.* castra.
castration *n.* castra.
castrato *n.* castrada.
casual *adj.* casual; (*speech*) conversal, demotica.
casualness *n.* casualia.
casualty *n.* (*person*) vitim, ferida, mor; (*death*) mori.
casuistry *n.* sofisme.
casus belli *n.* justi de gera.
cat *n.* gato.
cata- *pref.* cata-.
catabolism *n.* cataboli.
catabolize *v.* (*biology*) cataboli.
cataclysm *n.* desastre.
catacomb *n.* catacomba.
Catalan *adj.* & *n.* catalan.
catalepsy *n.* catalesia.
cataleptic *adj.* catalesica.
catalogue (US **catalog**) *n.* catalogo. • *v.* catalogi.
cataloguer (US **cataloger**) *n.* catalogor.
Catalonia *n.* (*Spanish region*) Catalunia.
catalyse (US **catalyze**) *v.* catalise.
catalyst *n.* catalisente.
catalytic *adj.* catalisente.
catalyze (US). See *catalyse*.
catamaran *n.* catamaran.
catamount *n.* puma.
catapult *n.* (*small*) fonda; (*large*) lansapetra. • *v.* lansapetri.
cataract *n.* (*medical*) catarata; (*waterfall*) cascade.
catarrh *n.* cataro.
catastrophe *n.* desastre, apocalise.
catastrophic *adj.* desastrosa.
catatonia *n.* catatonia.
catatonic *adj.* catatonica.
catbird *n.* mimor.
catcall *n.* cria burlante.
catch *v.* catura; (*illness*) reseta, developa; (*bus, etc.*) gania. • *n.* (*latch*) fisador; (*hidden problem*) trapa. **catch cold** developa la gripe. **catch fire** ensende. **catch up** egali. **catch up with** ateni, egali. **play catch-up** atenta egali.
catchall *n.* trapitota; (*wildcard*) bufon.
catcher *n.* caturor, prendor.
catechism *n.* (*Christianity*) catecisme.
categorization *n.* categori.
categorize *v.* categori.
category *n.* categoria.
category theory *n.* teoria de categorias.
cater *v.* furni la come.
caterer *n.* furnor de come.
caterpillar *n.* eruga.
caterpillarlike *adj.* erugin.
caterpillar track *n.* banda erugin.
catfish *n.* pex gatin.
catharsis *n.* purga de emosias.
cathartic *adj.* purgante.
cathedral *n.* catedral.
catheter *n.* cateter.
catheterization *n.* cateteri.
catheterize *v.* cateteri.
cathetus *n.* (*geometry*) cateto.
cathode *n.* catodo.
cathode ray tube *n.* tubo catodal.
cathodic *adj.* catodal.
Catholic *adj.* & *n.* catolica. **catholic** (*eclectic*) ecletica.
Catholicism *n.* catolicisme.
cation *n.* (*chemistry*) cation.
catkin *n.* amento.
catnap *n.* dormeta.
catnip *n.* (*plant*) nepeta.
cattail *n.* (*plant*) tifa.
cattle *n.* boves.
catwalk *n.* paseria, plataforma.
Caucasia *n.* Caucaso.
Caucasian *adj.* (*of the Caucasus*) caucasian; (*white-skinned*) blanca.
Caucasoid *adj.* caucasoide, blanca.
Caucasus *n.* (*region*) Caucaso.
Caucasus Mountains *n.* Montes Caucaso, Caucasos.
caucus *n.* cabal, partito.
caudal *adj.* (*towards the tail*) codal, posterior.
caudate *adj.* codida.
cauldron *n.* calderon.
cauliflower *n.* (*plant, vegetable*) coliflor.
caulk *n.* selinte.
causal *adj.* causal.
causality *n.* causalia.
causation *n.* causa.
cause *v.* causa, resulta, fa ce. • *n.* causa; (*law*) caso; (*target*) ojeto.
causeway *n.* via levada.
caustic *adj.* corodente.
caustic potash *n.* idrosido de potasio.
caustic soda *n.* alcalin corodente, idrosido de sodio.
cauterization *n.* cauteri.
cauterize *v.* cauteri.
cautery *n.* cauterador.
caution *n.* cautia; (*warning*) averti. • *v.* averti.
cautious *adj.* cauta.
cavalcade *n.* parade.
cavalier *n.* cavalor. • *adj.* despetosa.
cavalry *n.* cavalores.

cavalryman *n.* cavalor, soldato montante.
cave *n.* cava.
caveat *n.* avisa.
cave dweller *n.* abitor de cava, troglodite.
caveman *n.* abitor de cava, troglodite.
caver *n.* cavor.
cavern *n.* cavon.
cavewoman *n.* abitor de cava.
caviar *n.* caviar, ovos de pex.
caving *n.* esplora de cavas.
cavity *n.* caveta.
cavort *v.* brinca.
cavy *n.* cavia.
caw *v.* & *n.* abaia. • *interj.* caa.
cayenne *n.* peperon polvida.
cayman *n.* caiman.
Cayman Islands *n.* Isolas Caiman.
CCTV *n.* televisa de vijila.
CCTV camera *n.* camera vijilante.
CD *abbr.* cd.
CD burner *n.* scrivador de cd, scrivador de disco.
CD drive *n.* discador.
CD player *n.* discador.
CD writer *n.* scrivador de cd, scrivador de disco.
CE *abbr.* ec (*eda comun*).
cease *v.* sesa.
ceasefire *n.* sesaspara.
Cebuano *adj.* & *n.* (*person, language*) sebuano.
cecum (US). See *caecum.*
cedar *n.* (*tree*) sedro.
cede *v.* sede.
cedilla *n.* (*diacritic*) sedilia.
ceilidh *n.* (*social event*) celi.
ceiling *n.* sofito; limita masima.
celadon *adj.* (*colour*) seladon. • *n.* (*pottery*) seladon.
-cele (US). See *-coele.*
Celebes *n.* (*island*) Sulawesi.
Celebes Sea *n.* Mar Sulawesi.
celebrant *n.* selebror.
celebrate *v.* selebra, festi.
celebration *n.* selebra.
celebrity *n.* (*person*) selebrada; (*quality*) selebria.
celery *n.* seleri.
celestial *adj.* sielal, de sielo.
celestial mechanics *n.* mecanica de sielo.
celestial object *n.* ojeto sielal.
celestial pole *n.* polo de sielo.
celestial sphere *n.* sfera de sielo.
celiac (US). See *coeliac.*
celibacy *n.* asteni de seso.
celibate *adj.* asteninte.
cell *n.* (*biology, room*) selula.
cellar *n.* sutera.
cellblock *n.* prison.
cellist *n.* xeliste.
cellmate *n.* camerada de selula.
cello *n.* xelo.
cellobiose *n.* (*sugar*) selobiosa.
cellophane *n.* selofan.
cellphone *n.* telefoneta.
cellular *adj.* selulal.
cellular phone *n.* telefoneta.
cellulitis *n.* selulite.
celluloid *n.* (*plastic*) seluloide.
cellulose *n.* selulosa.
Celsius *n.* celsius. **degree Celsius** grado de celsius.
Celt *n.* celta.
Celtiberian *adj.* & *n.* celtiberian.
Celtic *adj.* & *n.* celta.
Celtic Sea *n.* Mar Celta.
cement *n.* semento. • *v.* sementi.
cement block *n.* brice de beton.
cement mixer *n.* miscador de beton.
cemetery *n.* semetero.
cenotaph *n.* senotafio.
Cenozoic *adj.* & *n.* (*geology*) senozoica.
censor *v.* sensura. • *n.* sensuror.
censorship *n.* sensura.
censure *v.* condena.
census *n.* conta de abitores.
cent *n.* sentim. **25-cent piece** cuatrim.
centaur *n.* sentauro.
Centaurus *n.* (*constellation*) la Sentauro.
centenary *n.* aniversario sento.
centennial *adj.* sentenial. • *n.* aniversario sento.
center… (US). See *centre…*
-centesis *suff.* (*puncturing*) -sentese.
centi- *pref.* (*a hundredth*) senti-.
centigrade *n.* celsius. **degree centigrade** grado de celsius.
centigram *n.* sentigram.
centilitre (US (**centiliter**) *n.* sentilitre.
centime *n.* sentim.
centimetre (US **centimeter**) *n.* sentimetre.
centipede *n.* sentopede.
central *adj.* sentral.
Central African *adj.* & *n.* sentrafrican.
Central African Republic *n.* Republica de Africa Sentral, Sentrafrica.
Central America *n.* America Sentral.
centralize *v.* sentri.
central processing unit *n.* computador.
central vowel *n.* vocal sentral.
centre (US **center**) *n.* sentro, media; (*midfielder*) sentror. • *v.* sentri. **off-centre** nonsentral.
centre city (US **center city**) *n.* sentro de site.
centrefold (US **centerfold**) *n.* paje sentral.
centrepiece (US **centerpiece**) *n.* foca, sentro de table.
centri- *pref.* (*central*) sentri-.

centrifugal *adj.* sentrifugal.
centrifuge *n.* sentrifuga. • *v.* sentrifugi.
centriole *n.* (*biology*) sentriol.
centripetal *adj.* sentripeta.
centrism *n.* sentrisme.
centrist *adj.* & *n.* sentriste.
centurion *n.* senturion.
century *n.* sentenio.
cephalalgia *n.* (*medical*) sefalaljia.
cephalic *adj.* (*of the head*) sefalica.
cephalo- *pref.* (*head*) sefalo-.
cephalopod *n.* sefalopodo.
Cepheus *n.* (*mythology*, *constellation*) Sefeo.
ceramic *adj.* seramica.
ceramic art *n.* arte de seramica.
cereal *adj.* & *n.* sereal.
cereal crop *n.* gran.
cereal seed *n.* gran.
cerebellar *adj.* serebretal.
cerebellum *n.* serebreta.
cerebral *adj.* serebral.
cerebral cortex *n.* cortex serebral.
cerebral nerve *n.* nervo serebral.
cerebral palsy *n.* paralise serebral.
cerebrospinal *adj.* serebrospinal.
cerebrum *n.* serebro.
ceremonial *adj.* ritual.
ceremonious *adj.* ritual.
ceremony *n.* rituo.
cerium *n.* (*element*) serio.
certain *adj.* (*undoubted*, *undoubting*) serta; (*specified*) alga, spesifada. **a certain Mrs X** alga Sra X.
certainty *n.* sertia.
certificate *n.* autentici, documento, nota de validi.
certification *n.* autentici, validi.
certified *adj.* (*qualified*) autorida.
certify *v.* autentici, validi.
cerumen *n.* serumen.
cervical *adj.* colal.
cervix *n.* colo de utero.
Cesarian section (US). See *Caesarian section*.
cesium (US). See *caesium*.
cessation *n.* sesa.
cesspit *n.* poso de cloaca.
cesspool *n.* poso de cloaca.
cestode *n.* sestodo.
cetacean *adj.* & *n.* setaseo.
Cetus *n.* (*constellation*) la Balena.
Ceylon *n.* Srilanca.
CGI *n.* (*graphics*) infografia.
chablis *n.* (*wine*) xabli.
cha-cha-cha *n.* (*dance*, *music*) txatxatxa.
Chad *n.* Txad.
Chadian *adj.* & *n.* txadi.
Chadic *adj.* txadica.
chador *n.* (*cloak*) txador.
chadri *n.* (*garment*) burca.
chaetognath (US **chetognath**) *n.* (*worm*) cetognato.
chafe *v.* raspa.
chaff *n.* gluma.
chaffinch *n.* (*bird*) fringilo.
chafing dish *n.* casolon per caldi.
chagrin *n.* embarasa.
chain *n.* (*including shops*, *hotels*) cadena. • *v.* cadeni.
chain mail *n.* malie.
chain reaction *n.* reata en cadena.
chainsaw *n.* motosiera.
chair *n.* seja. • *v.* preside.
chairlift *n.* telesenta.
chairman *n.* presidente.
chairperson *n.* presidente.
chairwoman *n.* presidente.
chakra *n.* (*Buddhism*, *Hinduism*) txacra.
chalaza *n.* (*biology*) calaza.
chalcedony *n.* (*mineral*) calsedonia.
Chalcolithic *adj.* & *n.* calcolitica.
chalet *n.* (*cottage*) xale.
chalice *n.* calix.
chalk *n.* creta. **chalk up** creti.
chalkboard *n.* mureta negra.
chalkstone *n.* urato de sodio.
challenge *v.* & *n.* defia.
challenger *n.* defior.
Chamaeleon *n.* (*constellation*) la Camaleon.
chamber *n.* cambra, sala, salon; (*gun*) cambra. **chamber of commerce** asosia de comersia, ofisia de comersia.
chamberlain *n.* (*officer*) xambelan.
chambermaid *n.* limpor de sala.
chamber music *n.* musica de salon.
chamber orchestra *n.* orcestra de salon.
chamberpot *n.* vaso de note.
chameleon *n.* camaleon.
chamfer *v.* biseli.
chamois *n.* (*animal*) camusa.
chamomile *n.* camomila.
champ *n.* campion.
champagne *n.* xampania.
champion *n.* (*including of a cause*) campion.
championship *n.* torneo.
chamy *n.* (*leather*) camusa.
chance *n.* (*random*) acaso, fortuna; (*opportunity*) bon momento, oportun; probable; (*probability*) probablia. **by chance** acaso. **happy chance** bon acaso. **have the chance to** pote. **take a chance** risca la acaso.
chance encounter *n.* encontra acaso.
chancellery *n.* canseloreria.
chancellor *n.* canselor; (*head of government*) ministro xef.
chancery *n.* canseloreria.
chances *n.* probablia.
chandelier *n.* candelabro.

change *v.* cambia. • *n.* (*including of transport*) cambia; (*money returned*) saldeta.
changeable *adj.* cambiable, mutable.
changeless *adj.* noncambiante.
changing room *n.* vesteria.
channel *n.* canal; tubo. **English Channel** la Manga.
Channel Islands *n.* Isolas de la Manga.
channeller (US **channeler**) *n.* spiritiste.
Channel Tunnel *n.* Tunel su la Manga.
chant *v.* & *n.* canta lenta.
chanty *n.* canta de marinores.
chaos *n.* (*including in mythology*) caos.
chaos theory *n.* teoria de caos.
chaotic *adj.* caososa, tumultosa.
chap *n.* om, xico.
chapel *n.* egleseta.
chaperone *n.* supravidor.
chaplain *n.* eglesor.
chaplet *n.* (*beads*) rosarieta.
chaps *n.* (*leggings*) txapareras.
chapstick *n.* balsam de labio.
chapter *n.* (*book*) capitol; (*society, religious community*) ramo.
char *v.* negri, carboni.
character *n.* (*including in fiction*) carater; (*typography*) sinia.
character code *n.* (*software*) codigo numeral de sinias.
character encoding *n.* (*e.g. UTF-8*) codigo fisical de sinias.
characteristic *adj.* tipal. • *n.* cualia.
characterization *n.* distingui, marca; (*depiction*) representa.
characterize *v.* distingui, marca; (*depict*) representa.
character number *n.* (*software*) numero de sinia.
character repertoire *n.* (*e.g. Unicode*) colie de sinias.
character set *n.* (*e.g. Unicode*) colie de sinias.
charades *n.* jua de mima.
charango *n.* (*guitar*) txarango.
charboil *v.* grili.
charcoal *n.* carbon de lenio.
chard *n.* (*plant*) bleta.
charge *v.* (*accuse*) acusa (formal); (*attack*) ataca; (*entrust*) encarga; (*invoice*) fatura; (*electrically*) carga. • *n.* (*fee*) paia; (*electric*) carga; (*accusation*) acusa. **in charge** encargada, controlante.
charger *n.* cargador.
chariot *n.* caro de gera.
charioteer *n.* caror.
charisma *n.* carisma.
charismatic *adj.* (*religion*) carismal; (*showing charisma*) carismosa.
charitable *adj.* carital; jenerosa.
charitable organization *n.* asosia carital.
charity *n.* carita. • *adj.* carital.
charity shop *n.* bricabraceria.
charlady *n.* limpor.
charlatan *n.* xarlatan.
charleston *n.* (*dance*) xarleston.
charm *v.* encanta. • *n.* encanta; fetix.
charmer *n.* encantor.
charm quark *n.* cuarc encantada.
chart *n.* (*map*) mapa; (*diagram*) scema. • *v.* mapa.
charter *n.* (*of organization*) constitui.
chartered city *n.* site constituida.
charterhouse *n.* cartusia.
chartreuse *adj.* tilia.
charts *n.* (*bestsellers*) parade de susedosas.
charwoman *n.* limpor.
chase *v.* & *n.* xasa. **chase away** xasa a via.
chasm *n.* canion, presipe, profonda, profondon.
chassis *n.* xasi.
chaste *adj.* pur, asteninte, virjin.
chasten *v.* disiplina.
chastise *v.* reproxa.
chastity *n.* virjinia.
chasuble *n.* (*garment*) casula.
chat[1] *v.* & *n.* parleta. **chat up** flirta con.
chat[2] *n.* caturamosca.
chateau *n.* cason de campania.
chatroom *n.* (*internet*) sala de rede.
chat show *n.* program de conversa.
chat-show host *n.* ospitor de conversa.
chattels *n.* posesedas.
chatter *v.* & *n.* parleta; (*teeth*) clica.
chatterbox *n.* parlosa.
chatty *adj.* parlosa.
chauffeur *n.* gidor.
cheap *adj.* barata.
cheapen *v.* redui la custa de; degrada.
cheapness *n.* baratia.
cheapskate *n.* baratamanica.
cheat *v.* froda.
cheater *n.* frodor.
cheatsheet *n.* aidamemoria secreta.
Chechen *adj.* & *n.* txetxen.
Chechnya *n.* Txetxnia.
check[1] *v.* esamina, proba; serti; (*chess*) xace. • *n.* esamina, proba; serti; (*chess*) xace. • *interj.* xace. **check in** suscrive per entra. **check out** suscrive per retira.
check[2] *adj.* & *n.* (*pattern*) cuadro.
check[3] (US). See *cheque*.
checkable *adj.* sertable.
checkbook (US). See *chequebook*.
checked *adj.* sertida; cuadrosa.
checkerberry *n.* (*plant*) te de bosce.
checkered *adj.* cuadrosa.
checkers *n.* (*game*) damas.
check-in *n.* entra.
checklist *n.* lista de sertis.

checkmark *n.* sinia de serti.
checkmate *v.*, *n.* & *interj.* xacemata.
checkout *n.* sorti.
checkpoint *n.* punto de controla.
check-up *n.* esamina, evalua medical.
cheddar *n.* (*cheese*) txedar.
cheek *n.* jena; (*impudence*) noncortesia.
cheekbone *n.* oso de jena, zigoma.
cheekiness *n.* noncortesia.
cheeky *adj.* noncortes.
cheep *v.* (*mouse*, *bird*) pipi. • *interj.* pip.
cheer *v.* & *n.* (*shout*) aclama; (*comfort*) consola. **cheer for** aclama. **cheer up** felisi.
cheerful *adj.* felis, bonumorosa, de bon umor.
cheerfulness *n.* felisia.
cheeriness *n.* felisia.
cheerleader *n.* animor.
cheerless *adj.* nonfelis.
cheerlessness *n.* nonfelisia.
cheers *interj.* joia.
cheery *adj.* felis.
cheese *n.* ceso. **cheese on toast** pan tostada con ceso.
cheese board *n.* planceta de ceso.
cheeseburger *n.* amburger con ceso.
cheesecake *n.* torta de ceso.
cheesecloth *n.* gaza de ceso.
cheesy grin *n.* surie ienin.
cheetah *n.* gepardo.
chef *n.* xef de cosina.
chef's knife *n.* cotel de xef.
chelant *n.* celante.
chelate *v.* (*chemistry*) cela. • *adj.* celada.
chelate complex *n.* celada.
chelating agent *n.* celante.
chelation *n.* cela; celaterapia.
chelation therapy *n.* celaterapia.
chemical *adj.* & *n.* cimical.
chemical warfare *n.* gera cimical.
chemist *n.* cimiciste; (*pharmacist*) farmasiste; (*shop*) farmasia.
chemistry *n.* cimica.
chemosynthesis *v.* cimosintese.
chemosynthetic *adj.* cimosintesal.
chemotherapy *n.* cimoterapia.
chemotroph *n.* (*organism*) cimotrof.
chemotrophia *n.* cimotrofia.
chemotrophic *adj.* cimotrofia.
chenille *n.* (*yarn*) xenil.
cheque *n.* (*money*) xece.
chequebook *n.* libro de xeces.
chereme *n.* (*unit of sign language*) cerem.
cherish *v.* ama, tesori.
cherished *adj.* cara, amada, tesorida.
cherry *n.* (*fruit*) serisa; (*tree*) seriso.
cherub *n.* cerubin.
cherubim *n.* cerubines.
Chesapeake Bay *n.* Baia Chesapeake.
chess *n.* xace.
chessboard *n.* table de xace.
chesspiece *n.* peso de xace.
chest *n.* (*anatomy*) peto; (*container*) caxon. **chest of drawers** comoda.
chestnut *n.* (*tree*, *nut*) castania.
chetognath (US). See *chaetognath.*
chevron *n.* xevron.
chevrotain *n.* tragulo.
chew *v.* mastica.
chew cud *v.* remastica.
chewing gum *n.* goma de mastica.
chewy *adj.* gomin.
chi[1] *n.* (*Greek letter* Χ, χ) ci.
chi[2] *n.* (*life force*) txi.
chia *n.* (*plant*) txia.
chianti *n.* (*wine*) cianti.
chiaroscuro *n.* claroscur.
chiasma *n.* (*genetics*) ciasma.
chic *adj.* modosa, a la moda, de moda, sofisticada.
chicanery *n.* rus.
chick *n.* avieta; (*chicken*) galeta; (*woman*) xica.
chickadee *n.* (*bird*) paro.
chicken *n.* gal; (*young*) galeta; (*meat*) carne de gal.
chicken coop *n.* ensirca de gales.
chickenlike *adj.* galin.
chicken nugget *n.* pepita de gal.
chickenpox *n.* varisela.
chicken soup *n.* sopa de gal.
chickpea *n.* xixe.
chicle *n.* (*latex*) xicle.
chicory *n.* xicoria.
chide *v.* reproxa.
chief *adj.* & *n.* xef. **chief of state** xef de stato.
chiefdom *n.* xefia.
chieftain *n.* xef.
chiffon *n.* (*fabric*) xifon.
chignon *n.* xinion.
Chihuahua *n.* (*Mexican state*) Chihuahua. **chihuahua** (*dog*) chihuahua.
Chihuahuan Desert *n.* Deserto Chihuahua.
chikungunya *n.* (*virus*) xicungunia.
chilblain *n.* eritema cutanea.
child *adj.* enfante. • *n.* enfante, xice; (*son or daughter*) fie.
childbearing *adj.* parinte. • *n.* pari.
childbirth *n.* pari.
childhood *n.* enfantia.
childish *adj.* enfantin.
childlike *adj.* enfantin.
childminder *n.* enfantor.
children's story *n.* fable.
childrenswear *n.* vestes de enfantes.
chile[1] *n.* (*pepper*) txili.
Chile[2] *n.* Txile.

Chilean *adj.* & *n.* txilan.
Chile Sea *n.* Mar Txile.
chili... (US). See *chilli...*
chill *v.* fri.
chilled *adj.* frida.
chilli *n.* (*pepper*) txili. **chilli con carne** txili con carne.
chilli powder *n.* txili polvida.
chilli sauce *n.* salsa de txili.
chilly *adj.* fria.
chime *n.* campana. • *v.* sona.
chimera *n.* (*mythology*) cimera.
chimeric *adj.* imajinal.
chimerical *adj.* imajinal.
chimney *n.* ximine.
chimneypiece *n.* scafal de ximine.
chimneyshelf *n.* scafal de ximine.
chimneysweep *n.* scopor de ximine.
chimp *n.* ximpanze.
chimpanzee *n.* ximpanze.
chin *n.* mento.
Ch'in *adj.* (*dynasty*) txin.
china[1] *n.* porselana.
China[2] *n.* Jonguo, Xina.
chinchilla *n.* (*rodent*) txintxila.
Chinese *adj.* & *n.* (*person, language*) jonguo, xines.
Chinese chess *n.* xangtxi.
Chinese gooseberry *n.* (*plant, fruit*) ciui.
Chinese parsley *n.* coriandro.
Ch'ing *adj.* (*dynasty*) txing.
chink *n.* fesur.
chintz *n.* calico.
chip *n.* (*chipping*) ageta; (*microchip*) microtelia; (*gambling*) fix; (*French fry*) fritada, patata fritada; (*potato crisp*) xip. • *v.* ageti.
chipboard *n.* lenio presada.
chipmunk *n.* tamia.
chipotle *n.* (*pepper*) txipotle.
Chippewa *adj.* & *n.* (*person, language*) odjibua.
chiromancy *n.* ciromansia.
chiropodist *n.* podolojiste.
chiropody *n.* podolojia.
chiropractic *n.* ciropratica.
chiropractor *n.* cipropraticor.
chiropraxis *n.* ciropratica.
chirp *v.* & *n.* pia, grinse.
chisel *n.* sisel. • *v.* siseli.
chit *n.* bileta de deta.
chitin *n.* (*substance*) citina.
chitinous *adj.* citinosa.
chiton *n.* (*garment*) citon.
chitterlings *n.* intestines.
chivalry *n.* cavaloria.
chive *n.* siboleta.
chives *n.* siboleta.
chloranthaceae *n.* clorantasea.
chloride *n.* clorido.
chlorinate *v.* clori.
chlorination *n.* clori.
chlorine *n.* cloro.
chloro- *pref.* (*green*) cloro-.
chlorofluorocarbon *n.* clorofluorocarbono.
chloroform *n.* cloroformo.
chlorophonia *n.* clorofonia.
chlorophyll *n.* clorofila.
chloroplast *n.* cloroplasto.
chlorosis *n.* clorose.
chock *n.* cuneo.
chocolate *n.* xocolada.
chocolate bar *n.* bara de xocolada.
chocolatier *n.* xocolador.
choice *n.* eleje; (*one of several options*) elejable. **of choice** prefereda.
choir *n.* coro.
choke *v.* sofoca, strangula.
cholera *n.* colera.
choleric *adj.* disputosa.
cholesterol *n.* colesterol.
choline *n.* (*substance*) colina.
cholinergic *n.* colinerjica.
choose *v.* eleje.
choosy *adj.* elejente, esijente.
chop *v.* axi. • *n.* (*meat*) costela.
choppy *adj.* (*sea*) turbosa.
chopstick *n.* cuai.
chop suey *n.* txapsui.
choral *adj.* coral.
chorale *n.* coral.
chord[1] *n.* (*music*) acorda.
chord[2] *n.* (*geometry*) corda. **vocal chord** corda vosal, plia vosal.
chordate *n.* (*organism*) cordato.
chore *n.* taxe.
chorea *n.* (*medical*) corea.
choreographer *n.* coreografiste.
choreography *n.* coreografia.
chorion *n.* (*biology*) corion.
chorionic *adj.* corional.
chorister *n.* coriste.
chorizo *n.* (*sausage*) txoriso.
chortle *v.* & *n.* cacareta.
chorus *n.* coro; refren.
chosen *adj.* elejeda. **chosen one** elejeda.
chough *n.* (*bird*) xova.
chow mein *n.* txaumen.
Christ *n.* Cristo.
christen *v.* batiza.
Christendom *n.* mundo cristian.
christening *n.* batiza.
Christian *adj.* & *n.* cristian.
Christianity *n.* cristianisme.
Christianization *n.* cristiani.
Christianize *v.* cristiani.
Christmas *adj.* de natal. • *n.* natal.
Christmas Eve *n.* sera de natal.
Christmas Island *n.* Isola Natal.

Christmas tree *n.* arbor de natal.
chroma key *n.* (*video*) suprapone par color.
chromate *n.* (*chemistry*) cromato.
chromatic *adj.* cromatica.
chrome *n.* cromida.
chrome-plate *v.* cromi.
chromium *n.* cromo.
chromium-plate *v.* cromi.
chromo- *pref.* (*colour*) cromo-.
chromosome *n.* cromosoma.
chronic *adj.* (*medical*) cronica.
chronicle *n.* nara. • *v.* arcivi.
chrono- *pref.* (*time*) crono-.
chronological *adj.* cronolojial.
chronologist *n.* cronolojiste.
chronology *n.* cronolojia.
chronometer *n.* cronometre.
chrysalis *n.* crisalida.
chrysanthemum *n.* crisantemo.
chubby *adj.* ronda.
chuck[1] *v.* lansa; abandona. **chuck out** baldoni.
chuck[2] *n.* (*gripping tool*) portabroca.
chuckle *v.* & *n.* cacareta.
chuff *v.* (*engine*) sofla.
chug *v.* (*engine*) sofleta.
Chukchi *adj.* & *n.* (*person, language*) txucot.
Chukchi Peninsula *n.* Txucotca.
Chukchi Sea *n.* Mar Txucotca.
Chukot *adj.* & *n.* txucot.
Chukotka *n.* Txucotca.
chum *n.* ami.
chumaihuén *n.* (*marsupial*) monito.
chummy *adj.* amin.
chump *n.* fol.
chunder *v.* descome.
chunk *n.* bloco, peson.
Chunnel *n.* Tunel su la Manga.
church *n.* (*building, organization*) eglesa.
churchyard *n.* semetero.
churn *v.* bate. • *n.* batador. **churn up** turba.
chute *n.* tobogan, rampa.
chutney *n.* (*food*) txatni.
chutzpah *n.* ososia.
chyle *n.* (*substance*) cile.
chyme *n.* (*substance*) cimo.
ciao *interj.* (*arriving or departing*) txau.
cicada *n.* (*insect*) sicala.
cicatrix *n.* sicatris.
cicatrize *v.* sicatrisi.
cichlid *n.* (*fish*) siclido.
-cide *suff.* (*killing*) -side.
cider *n.* (*alcoholic or not*) sidra; (*non-alcoholic*) jus de poma.
cigar *n.* sigar.
cigarette *n.* sigareta.
cigarette holder *n.* portasigareta.
cilantro *n.* coriandro.
cilia *n.* (*biology*) silios.
cilice *n.* camisa de juta.
Cilician Sea *n.* Cilicia, Mar.
cilium *n.* (*biology*) silio.
cincture *n.* sintur.
cinder block *n.* brice de sene.
cinders *n.* (*ash*) sene; (*ashes of a particular thing*) senes.
cinema *n.* sinema.
cinema fan *n.* fan de sinema, sinemafilica.
cinemaphilia *n.* sinemafilia.
cinematographer *n.* sinematografiste, sinemiste.
cinematographic *adj.* sinematografial.
cinematography *n.* sinematografia.
cinnabar *n.* (*mineral*) sinabar.
cinnamon *n.* (*plant, spice*) canela.
cipher *n.* sifra.
circa *prep.* sirca.
circadian *adj.* (*biology*) sircadial.
Circinus *n.* (*constellation*) la Compas.
circle *n.* (*including of friends*) sirculo, ronda. • *v.* sirculi.
circling *adj.* sirculinte. • *prep.* sirca.
circuit *n.* (*any path*) curso; (*circular path*) sirculo; (*racetrack*) anelo; (*electric path*) sircuito; (*components forming an electric path*) sircuitos.
circuitous *adj.* nondireta.
circuitry *n.* sircuitos.
circular *adj.* sirculo. • *n.* (*newsletter*) revisteta de grupo.
circular saw *n.* siera sirculo.
circulate *v.* (*air, information*) sirculi; (*vehicles*) trafica.
circulation *n.* sirculi.
circulatory system *n.* sistem de sirculi.
circum- *pref.* (*around*) sirco-.
circumcise *v.* sircoside.
circumcision *n.* sircoside.
circumference *n.* perimetre.
circumflex *n.* (*diacritic*) sircoflexe.
circumnavigate *v.* sirconaviga.
circumnavigation *n.* sirconaviga.
circumpolar *adj.* sircopolal.
circumscribe *v.* sircoscrive.
circumspect *adj.* cauta.
circumstance *n.* situa, caso.
circumvent *v.* sircoveni.
circumvention *n.* sircoveni.
circus *n.* sirco.
cirrhosis *n.* (*medical*) sirose.
cirrus *adj.* & *n.* (*cloud*) siro.
cis- *pref.* (*on this side*) sis-.
cisgender *adj.* sisjenero.
Cisjordan *n.* Riva Ueste.
cistern *n.* tance.
cisticola *n.* (*bird*) sisticola.
cistus *n.* sisto.
citadel *n.* fortres de site.
citation *n.* sita; (*praise*) loda.

cite *v.* sita.
citify *v.* urbani.
citizen *n.* sitadan. **become a citizen** sitadani.
citizenship *n.* sitadania. **admit to citizenship** sitadani.
citric *adj.* sitrica.
citron *n.* (*tree, fruit*) sitron.
citronella *n.* (*plant, oil*) sitronela.
citrous *adj.* sitrica.
citrus fruit *n.* fruta sitrica.
cittern *n.* (*musical instrument*) sistre.
city *n.* site.
city area *n.* urbe.
city centre (US **city center**) *n.* sentro de site.
city dweller *n.* urban.
city hall *n.* ofisia de site.
city planner *n.* urbaniste.
city planning *n.* urbanisme.
city-state *n.* site-stato.
city wall *n.* muron.
civet *n.* (*animal*) siveta.
civic *n.* munisipal.
civil *adj.* (*polite, civilized*) sivil.
civilian *adj.* & *n.* nonmilitar, sivil.
civility *n.* cortesia.
civilization *n.* (*action*) sivili; (*society, concept*) sivilia.
civilize *v.* sivili.
civilized *adj.* sivil, sivilida.
civil servant *n.* ofisior publica.
civil war *n.* gera interna.
clack *v.* & *n.* clace.
clad *adj.* vestida.
clade *n.* (*biology*) clado.
claim *v.* & *n.* (*allege*) alega; (*declare*) declara; (*property, title, to have done*) reclama.
claimant *n.* reclamor.
clairvoyance *n.* clarvide.
clairvoyant *adj.* & *n.* clarvidente. **be clairvoyant** clarvide.
clam *n.* bivalvo.
clamber *v.* trepa.
clammy *adj.* umida.
clamour (US **clamor**) *n.* ruido.
clamp *n.* abrasador.
clamshell *n.* conca de bivalvo.
clam soup *n.* sopa de bivalvo.
clan *n.* clan.
clandestine *adj.* secreta.
clang *v.* & *n.* tintina.
clangour (US **clangor**) *n.* tintina.
clank *v.* & *n.* tintina.
clannish *adj.* escluinte.
clap[1] *v.* aplaudi; (*thump*) pumi.
clap[2] *n.* (*medical*) gonorea.
clapper *n.* (*bell*) batador.
clapperboard *n.* claceta.
claque *n.* aplaudores.
claret *n.* bordo.
clarification *n.* clari.
clarify *v.* clari, espresa clar.
clarinet *n.* clarineta.
clarinettist (US **clarinetist**) *n.* clarinetiste.
clarion *n.* (*trumpet*) claron.
clarity *n.* claria.
clash *v.* & *n.* (*disagree*) desacorda; (*skirmish*) scaramuxa.
clasp *v.* fisa, junta. • *n.* fisador.
class *n.* (*category*) clase, categoria; (*social, school*) clase. **lower class** clase basa. **upper class** clase alta.
class-conscious *adj.* clasiste.
classic *adj.* & *n.* clasica.
classical *adj.* clasica.
classicism *n.* clasicisme.
classification *n.* clasi, categori.
classified advertisement *n.* anunsieta.
classified information *n.* informa secreta.
classify *v.* clasi, categori; (*as secret*) secreti.
classism *n.* clasisme.
classmate *n.* camerada de clase.
classroom *n.* sala de clase.
classy *adj.* sofisticada.
clatter *v.* & *n.* clace.
clause *n.* (*grammar*) proposa; (*law*) restrinje. **adjective clause** suproposa ajetivin. **adverb clause** suproposa averbin. **content clause** suproposa nomin. **coordinate clause** proposa coordinada. **dependent clause** (*grammar*) proposa suordinada, suproposa.
claustrophobe *n.* claustrofobica.
claustrophobia *n.* claustrofobia.
claustrophobic *adj.* claustrofobica.
clavichord *n.* clavicordio.
clavicle *n.* oso de colar, clavicula.
claw *n.* gara. • *v.* gari.
clay *n.* arjila.
clayey *adj.* arjilosa.
clay-pigeon shooting *n.* xuta a platos.
clean *adj.* limpa. • *v.* limpi. **clean up** limpi.
cleaner *n.* (*person*) limpor.
cleanliness *n.* limpia, puria.
cleanser *n.* deterjente; (*makeup*) desmaciante.
clear *adj.* clar. • *v.* vacui. **clear snow** desnevi. **clear up** (*tidy*) reordina.
clear-headed *adj.* con mente clar, atendente.
clearing *n.* (*in forest*) pradeta.
clearing house *n.* ajenteria de compensa.
cleat *n.* spina.
cleavage *n.* (*anatomy*) entreseno; (*neckline*) escota.
cleave *v.* fende.
cleaver *n.* axeta de carnor.
clef *n.* clave de musica.

cleft *adj.* divideda, fendeda. • *n.* fesur.
cleft lip *n.* labio fendeda.
cleft palate *n.* palato fendeda.
clematis *n.* clematis.
clemency *n.* pardona.
clementine *n.* mandarina.
clench *v.* tensa.
clepsydra *n.* orolojo de acua.
cleptocracy *n.* cleptocratia.
cleptocrat *n.* cleptocrata.
clerestory *n.* (*architecture*) clarestorio.
clergy *n.* eglesores. **member of the clergy** eglesor.
clergyman *n.* eglesor mas, prete mas.
clergywoman *n.* eglesor fema, prete fema.
cleric *n.* eglesor.
clerical *adj.* secretoral.
clerk *n.* (*secretary*) secretor; (*sales*) vendor; (*bursar*) caxor.
clever *adj.* astuta, intelijente.
cleverness *n.* astutia.
cliché *n.* clixe, espresa tro usada; stereotipo.
clichéd *adj.* clixe, tro usada.
click *v.* & *n.* (*mouse, link*) clica.
client *n.* cliente.
clientele *n.* clientes.
cliff *n.* falesa, presipe.
cliffhanger *n.* suspende.
cliff railway *n.* funicular.
climactic *adj.* culminante.
climate *n.* clima.
climate change *n.* cambia de clima.
climatic *adj.* climal.
climatology *n.* climatolojia.
climax *v.* & *n.* culmina.
climb *v.* asende; (*clamber, plant*) trepa.
climber *n.* trepor.
climbing frame *n.* strutur de trepa.
clime *n.* clima.
clinch *v.* (*embrace*) abrasa; (*confirm*) confirma. • *n.* abrasa.
clincher *n.* confirma.
cline *n.* (*biology*) clina.
cling *v.* adere. **cling to** teni.
cling film *n.* peleta aderente.
cling wrap *n.* peleta aderente.
clingy *adj.* aderosa.
clinic *n.* clinica.
clinical *adj.* clinical.
clinician *n.* mediciste clinical.
clink *v.* tintina. • *n.* tintina; prison.
clip *n.* (*audio, video, fastener*) clip, estraeda; (*clipping*) frato, estraeda. • *v.* clipi. **clip on** clipi.
clipboard *n.* planceta de clip; (*software*) pox de copia.
clip-on *adj.* de clip.
clippers *n.* (*electric*) cortador.
clipping *n.* frato.
clique *n.* grupo escluinte.
cliquey *adj.* escluinte.
clit *n.* (*clitoris*) clito.
clitic *n.* clitico.
clitoral *adj.* clitorisal.
clitoral hood *n.* prepus.
clitorectomy *n.* clitorectomia.
clitoridectomy *n.* clitorectomia.
clitoris *n.* clitoris.
cloaca *n.* (*anatomy*) cloaca.
cloak *n.* capa. • *v.* capi.
cloakroom *n.* saleta de jacas, vesteria; sala de bagaje; (*toilet*) saleta privata.
clobber *v.* bastoni.
cloche *n.* (*hat*) clox.
clock *n.* orolojo. **alarm clock** veliador. **round the clock** a 24 oras de la dia.
clockmaker *n.* orolojor.
clock rate *n.* frecuentia de orolojo.
clock speed *n.* frecuentia de orolojo.
clockwise *adj.* con la orolojo.
clockwork *adj.* macinal.
clod *n.* masa.
clodhopper *n.* torpe.
clog *n.* (*shoe*) zoco. • *v.* bloci.
clogmaker *n.* zocor.
cloister *n.* (*architecture*) galeria; (*monastery*) monceria, soreria.
clone *v.* & *n.* clone.
close[1] *adj.* (*near, including friend*) prosima; intima; (*humid*) umida. **from close up** de prosima. **have a close shave** evita apena.
close[2] *v.* (*shut*) clui.
closed-circuit television *n.* televisa de vijila.
closed curve *n.* anelo.
closed shop *n.* laboreria sindicatida.
close-fisted *adj.* avar.
close-fitting *adj.* abrasante, corpin.
close-fought *adj.* difisil ganiada.
close-mid vowel *n.* vocal media cluida.
closeness *n.* prosimia.
closet *n.* saleta.
closeup *adj.* macro, prosima. • *n.* macro, foto prosima.
closeup lens *adj.* lente macro.
closeup photography *n.* fotografia prosima.
close vowel *n.* vocal cluida.
closing *adj.* cluinte; codal.
closing credits *n.* titulos codal.
closing quotation mark *n.* cluisita.
closing titles *n.* titulos codal.
closure *n.* clui.
clot *v.* coagula. • *n.* masa, maseta. **clot up** coagula, masi.
cloth *n.* (*material*) stofa; (*piece*) tela.
clothe *v.* vesti.
clothes *n.* vestes.
clothes airer *n.* portaveste.

clothes closet *n.* saleta de vestes.
clothes horse *n.* portaveste.
clothesline *n.* corda de vestes.
clothes moth *n.* tinia, papilio de vestes.
clothespeg *n.* pinse de vestes.
clothespin *n.* pinse de vestes.
clothes pole *n.* portaveste.
clothes rack *n.* portaveste.
clothes rail *n.* portaveste.
clothes rod *n.* portaveste.
cloth factory *n.* stoferia.
clothing *n.* vestes. **piece of clothing** veste.
clothmaker *n.* stofor.
cloth seller *n.* stofor.
cloth store *n.* stoferia.
cloud *n.* (*including software*) nube.
cloudburst *n.* pluvon.
cloudfree *adj.* sin nube.
cloudiness *n.* nubosia.
cloudless *adj.* sin nube.
cloud storage service *n.* ospitafix.
cloudware *n.* programes de nube.
cloudy *adj.* nubosa.
clout *n.* potia.
clove *n.* (*tree, spice*) sizijio.
cloven *adj.* divideda.
clover *n.* trefolia.
cloverleaf *n.* trefolia.
clown *n.* bufon; (*traditional European*) paliaso. • *adj.* bufonal.
clowning *n.* bufonia.
club[1] *n.* (*association*) club, organiza.
club[2] *n.* (*stick*) baston; (*cards*) trefolia. • *v.* bastoni.
clubfoot *n.* talo vara.
clubhouse *n.* casa de club.
club member *n.* clubor.
clubmoss *n.* (*plant*) licopodio.
cluck *interj.* coc-coc-coc.
clue *n.* indica, indiceta, trasa; (*in word game*) defini.
clump *n.* grupo.
clumsiness *n.* torpia.
clumsy *adj.* torpe.
clunk *n.* colpa metalin.
cluster *n.* grupo.
clutch *v.* teni. • *n.* teni; (*mechanism*) embraje. **apply the clutch** embraji.
clutch pencil *n.* portagrafito.
clutter *v.* desordina, foli. • *n.* desordina.
co- *pref.* (*with, together*) co-.
coach *n.* bus; (*carriage*) caro; (*for royalty, weddings, etc.*) caron; (*train*) vagon; (*trainer*) instruor.
coach driver *n.* busor.
coachman *n.* caror.
coagulate *v.* coagula.
coagulation *n.* coagula.
coal *n.* carbon.
coalesce *v.* fusa.
coalition *n.* alia, uni.
coarse *adj.* (*rough*) ru; (*sand*) bruta; (*lewd*) lasiva.
coarseness *n.* ruia.
coast *n.* costa. • *v.* lisca. **off the coast** a lado de costa.
coastal *adj.* costal.
coaster *n.* paragota.
coastguard *n.* gardacosta.
coat *n.* jaca; (*of animal*) pelo; (*of paint, etc.*) covre, strato, vesti. • *v.* covre, strati, vesti. **coat of arms** scermo eraldial. **coat of mail** camison de malie.
coathanger *n.* pendeveste.
coathook *n.* pendejacon.
coating *n.* covre, strato, vesti. • *adj.* covrente. • *prep.* covrente, a covre de.
coauthor *n.* coautor, coscrivor. • *v.* coscrive.
coax *v.* adula.
coaxial *adj.* coasal.
coaxial cable *n.* cable coasal.
cobalt *n.* cobalto.
cobbler *n.* sapator.
cobblestone *n.* petra ronda.
cobble together *v.* improvisa.
cobego *n.* (*flying lemur*) colugo.
cobra *n.* cobra.
cobweb *n.* rede de arania.
coca *n.* (*plant*) coca.
cocaine *n.* cocaina.
coccyx *n.* cosix.
cochlea *n.* coclea.
cochlear *adj.* cocleal.
cock *n.* (*cockerel*) gal mas; (*gun*) martel; (*penis*) pixa.
cockade *n.* roseta.
cock-a-doodle-doo *interj.* cucurucu.
cockatoo *n.* cacatu.
cockchafer *n.* scarabe de maio.
cockerel *n.* gal mas.
cockfight *n.* combate de gales.
cockle *n.* cardio.
cockleshell *n.* conca de cardio.
cockney *adj.* & *n.* cocni.
cockpit *n.* piloteria.
cockroach *n.* cucaraxa.
cockscomb *n.* cresta de gal.
cocktail *n.* coctel.
cocktail dress *n.* roba de coctel.
cocktail party *n.* selebra de coctel.
cocoa *n.* cacau.
co-conspirator *n.* coconspiror.
coconut *n.* (*plant, fruit*) coco.
cocoon *n.* cocon.
cod *n.* (*fish*) gado.
coda *n.* coda, conclui.
coddle *v.* regala.

code *n.* (*laws, software*) codigo; (*secret*) sifra; (*behaviour*) normas. • *v.* codigi. **area code** prefisa. **code of behaviour** normas de condui.

codeine *n.* codeina.

code number *n.* (*software*) numero de sinia.

code point *n.* (*software*) numero de sinia.

code position *n.* (*software*) numero de sinia.

codeword *n.* parola secreta.

codex *n.* manoscrito.

codify *v.* codigi.

codon *n.* (*genetics*) codon.

codpiece *n.* portaseso.

coedit *v.* coedita.

coeditor *n.* coeditor, corevisor.

coeducate *v.* coeduca.

coeducation *n.* coeduca.

coefficient *n.* constante; fator.

-coele *suff.* (*medical*) -sele.

coelenterate *n.* (*organism*) cnidario.

coeliac (US **celiac**) *n.* (*medical*) seliaca.

coerce *v.* forsa.

coercion *n.* forsa.

coexist *v.* coesiste. **agreement to coexist** acorda de coesiste.

coexistence *n.* coesiste.

coffee *n.* (*plant, seed, drink*) cafe.

coffeecake *n.* torta de cafe.

coffeehouse *n.* caferia.

coffeemaker *n.* cafador.

coffeepot *n.* vaso de cafe.

coffee shop *n.* caferia.

coffee stirrer *n.* tisacafe.

coffee table *n.* table basa.

coffer *n.* caxa.

coffin *n.* caxon funeral.

cog *n.* rota de dentes.

cogent *adj.* valida.

cognac *n.* coniac.

cognacy *n.* conasedia.

cognate *adj.* & *n.* conaseda.

cognition *n.* cognisio, pensa.

cognitive *adj.* cognisial.

cognizance *n.* consensia.

cognizant *adj.* consensa.

cognize *v.* conose.

cognomen *n.* conom.

cohabit *v.* coabita.

cohabitant *n.* coabitor.

cohabitation *n.* coabita.

cohabiter *n.* coabitor.

cohere *v.* coere.

coherence *n.* coere.

coherent *adj.* coerente.

cohesion *n.* coere.

cohesive *adj.* coerente.

cohort *n.* grupo.

coil *v.* enrola, spirali. • *n.* enrola, spiral; (*contraceptive*) contraconsepal intrauteral.

coin *n.* moneta.

coincide *v.* coaveni.

coincidence *n.* coaveni. **by coincidence** coaveninte, par coaveni.

coincidental *adj.* coaveninte, par coaveni.

coin collecting *n.* numismatia.

coin collector *n.* numismatiste.

coitus *n.* copula.

coke *n.* (*fuel*) coc.

cola *n.* cola.

colander *n.* tamis.

cold *adj.* fria; (*unfriendly*) nonamin, nonemosiosa, nonsosial. • *n.* fria; (*common cold*) cataro, (*technical*) rinofarinjite. **catch cold** developa la gripe. **have a cold** ave cataro.

cold-hearted *adj.* noncompatiosa.

cold open *n.* (*TV, film*) pretitulo.

cold war *n.* gera fria.

cole *n.* colza.

coleslaw *n.* salada de col.

coleus *n.* (*plant*) coleo.

colewort *n.* (*plant*) ruca.

colic *n.* (*medical*) colico.

coliseum *n.* coloseo.

colitis *n.* (*medical*) colite.

collaborate *v.* colabora.

collaboration *n.* colabora.

collaborative *adj.* colaborante.

collaborator *n.* colaboror.

collagen *n.* colajen.

collapse *v.* & *n.* colasa, cade.

collapsible *adj.* colasable, pliable.

collar *n.* colar.

collarbone *n.* oso de colar, clavicula.

collard greens *n.* folia de col.

collared dove *n.* tortora.

collarless *adj.* sin colar.

collarless shirt *n.* camiseta.

collateral *adj.* coladal; (*damage*) nonintendeda. • *n.* garantia.

colleague *n.* colaboror, asosior.

collect *v.* colie.

collection *n.* colie.

collective *adj.* coletiva. • *n.* (*farm, factory*) coletiva.

collectivism *n.* coletivisme.

collectivist *adj.* & *n.* coletiviste.

collector *n.* colior.

college *n.* universia; (*within a university*) scola.

collegial *adj.* coencargada.

collide *v.* (*several moving objects*) colide; (*one moving object*) xoca.

collider *n.* colidador.

collie *n.* (*dog*) coli, can de pastor scotes.

collision *n.* colide, xoca.

collocate *v.* aposa.

collocation *n.* aposa.

colloid *n.* coloide.

colloidal *adj.* coloide.

colloquial *adj.* conversal, demotica.
colloquium *n.* confere academial.
collude *v.* conspira.
collusion *n.* conspira.
colobus *n.* (*monkey*) colobo.
colocolo *n.* (*wild cat*) colocolo.
colocolo opossum *n.* (*marsupial*) monito.
cologne *n.* parfum.
Colombia *n.* Colombia.
Colombian *adj.* & *n.* colombian.
colon *n.* (*anatomy*) colon; (*punctuation*) dupunto.
colonel *n.* coronel.
colonial *adj.* colonial. • *n.* coloniste.
colonialism *n.* colonialisme.
colonialist *n.* colonialiste.
colonialistic *adj.* colonialiste.
colonic *adj.* colonal.
colonist *n.* coloniste.
colonization *n.* coloni.
colonize *v.* coloni.
colonnade *n.* serie de colonas.
colony *n.* colonia.
colophon *n.* (*publishing*) colofon.
color... (US). See *colour...*
Colorado *n.* (*US state*) Colorado.
Colorado River *n.* Rio Colorado.
colossal *adj.* enorme.
colosseum *n.* coloseo.
colostomy *n.* colostomia.
colostrum *n.* (*biology*) colostro.
colour (US **color**) *n.* color. • *v.* colori. • *adj.* colorida, colorosa.
colour-blind (US **color-blind**) *adj.* sieca a color.
colour blindness (US **color blindness**) *n.* daltonisme.
colour-coded (US **color-coded**) *adj.* codigida par color.
coloured pencil (US **colored pencil**) *n.* lapis colorida.
colourfast (US **colorfast**) *adj.* nonpalinte.
colourful (US **colorful**) *adj.* colorosa.
colouring pencil (US **coloring pencil**) *n.* lapis colorida.
colourless (US **colorless**) *adj.* sin color.
colour television (US **color television**) *n.* televisa colorosa.
colposcope *n.* colposcopio.
colposcopy *n.* colposcopi.
colugo *n.* (*flying lemur*) colugo.
Columba *n.* (*constellation*) la Pijon.
columbine *n.* (*plant*) colombina.
column *n.* (*pillar*, *text*) colona; (*in magazine*) titulo.
columnist *n.* scrivor de colona.
columnlike *adj.* colonin.
colza *n.* (*plant*) colza.
com- *pref.* (*with*, *together*) com-.
coma *n.* coma.
Coma Berenices *n.* (*constellation*) la Capeles de Berenise.
comatose *adj.* comosa.
comb *n.* peten. • *v.* peteni.
combat *v.* & *n.* combate, batalia.
combatant *n.* combator, batalior.
combative *adj.* combatosa.
combination *n.* combina, agrega.
combinatorics *n.* combinatoria.
combine *v.* combina, agrega.
combo *n.* combina; (*musicians*) bande.
combust *v.* combusta.
combustable material *n.* materia combustable.
combustibility *n.* combustablia.
combustible *adj.* & *n.* combustable.
combustion *n.* combusta.
combustion chamber *n.* cambra de combusta.
come *v.* veni; (*orgasm*) ariva. **come across** encontra, trova acaso; (*make an impression*) impresa. **come and see** veni per vide. **come back** reveni. **come back to life** revive. **come from** veni de. **come into** entra a. **come into existence** nase. **come near** prosimi. **come off the rails** salta de la reles. **come on** (*device*) comuta; (*let's go*) vade. **come on to** (*flirt*) fa avansas a. **come together** asembla. **come to life** anima. **come to nothing** aborta. **come up with** (*devise*) inventa, imajina. **to come** veninte, futur.
comeback *n.* reapare, reveni; (*retort*) replica.
comedian *n.* comediste, bromor.
comedic *adj.* comedial.
comedo *n.* (*acne*) punto negra.
comedy *n.* comedia.
comet *n.* (*astronomy*) cometa.
comfort *v.* & *n.* comforta, consola. **take comfort in** es comfortada par.
comfortable *adj.* comfortosa.
comforter *n.* (*for baby*) tetin.
comfy *adj.* comfortosa.
comic *adj.* comedial. • *n.* cartun.
comical *adj.* comica.
comics artist *n.* cartuniste.
comic strip *n.* banda de cartunes.
coming *adj.* veninte. • *n.* veni. **coming out of** veninte de en.
comma *n.* virgula.
command *v.* & *n.* comanda.
commandant *n.* comandor.
commandeer *v.* (*seize control of*) propri, saisi; (*enlist*) envolve.
commander *n.* comandor.
command line *n.* (*software*) linia de comandas.

commandment *n.* regula. **Ten Commandments** decalogo.
commando *n.* comando.
comme ci comme ça *adj.* & *adv.* no bon e no mal.
commemorate *v.* onora.
commemoration *n.* onora.
commemorative *adj.* onoral.
commence *v.* comensa.
commencement *n.* comensa.
commend *v.* loda.
commendable *adj.* lodable.
commendation *n.* loda; premio lodante.
commensurate *adj.* conveninte, proportial.
comment *v.* & *n.* comenta.
commentary *n.* comentas.
commentate *v.* comenta.
commentator *n.* comentor.
commenter *n.* comentor, foromanica.
commerce *n.* comersia.
commercial *adj.* comersial.
commercial aircraft *n.* avion comersial.
commercialization *n.* comersiali.
commercialize *v.* comersiali.
commercial unit *n.* (*goods*) unia comersial; (*shop*) boteca.
commiserate *v.* compatia.
commissar *n.* ofisior.
commissary *n.* delegada, suordinada; ofisior.
commission *v.* encarga; comanda. • *n.* encarga; comanda; (*committee, payment*) comision; (*authorized group*) encargada.
commissionaire *n.* gardaporte.
commissioner *n.* comisionor, comitor.
commit *v.* (*promise*) promete; (*crime*) fa. **commit adultery** adultera. **commit murder** omiside. **commit suicide** suiside. **commit to memory** memori. **commit treason** tradi.
commitment *n.* dedica, obliga, promete; sinseria.
committed *adj.* dedicada; sinsera.
committee *n.* comite.
committee member *n.* comitor.
committee room *n.* comiteria.
commode *n.* (*toilet*) vason; (*furniture*) mobila de vaso de note.
commodious *adj.* spasiosa.
commodity *n.* ben.
commodore *n.* comandor.
common *adj.* (*frequent, shared*) comun; (*shared*) compartida. • *n.* (*land*) campo comun. **have in common** comparti. **in common** comun, compartida.
common agouti *n.* (*rodent*) aguti.
commonality *n.* comunia, compartidia.
common cold *n.* cataro, rinofarinjite.
commoner *n.* sitadan comun.
common era *n.* eda comun. • *adj.* de la eda comun.
commonness *n.* comunia.
common person *n.* person comun.
commonplace *adj.* comun.
common sense *n.* sensa comun.
commonwealth *n.* comunia.
commotion *n.* disturba.
communal *adj.* comunial.
commune *n.* comunia legal.
communicable *adj.* comunicable.
communicate *v.* comunica.
communication *n.* comunica.
communicator *n.* comunicador.
communion *n.* comunia.
communism *n.* comunisme.
communist *n.* comuniste.
community *n.* comunia.
commute *v.* & *n.* viaja dial.
commuter *n.* viajor dial.
comorbid *adj.* (*medical*) comorbosa.
Comorian *adj.* & *n.* comori.
Comoros *n.* Comori.
compact *adj.* compata, consisa; presada. • *v.* compati.
compact camera *n.* camera compata.
compact disc *n.* disco compata.
compactor *n.* compatador.
companion *n.* acompanior, camerada.
companionable *adj.* acompaniable.
companionship *n.* acompania.
company *n.* acompania; (*business*) compania. **in the company of** con, acompaniada par.
company network *n.* rede de compania.
comparable *adj.* comparable.
comparative *adj.* comparada; (*grammar*) comparativa. • *n.* comparativa.
compare *v.* compara.
comparison *n.* compara.
compartment *n.* comparte; saleta; stala.
compartmentalization *n.* comparti.
compartmentalize *v.* comparti.
compass *n.* (*for finding north*) busola; (*for drawing circles*) compas.
compassion *n.* compatia. **feel compassion for** compatia. **worthy of compassion** compatiable.
compassionate *adj.* compatiosa.
compatibility *n.* acorda, conveni.
compatible *adj.* acordable, acordante, armoniosa, conveninte. **be compatible** acorda, conveni.
compatriot *n.* camerada.
compel *v.* (*by law or internal urge*) compulsa; (*physically*) forsa; (*socially*) obliga.
compelling *adj.* nonresistable, fasinante; (*argument*) convinsente.
compendium *n.* compendio.

compensate *v.* compensa; paia.
compensation *n.* compensa; paia.
compete *v.* compete.
competence *n.* capasia.
competent *adj.* capas.
competition *n.* (*action*) compete; (*event*) concurso.
competitive *adj.* competosa.
competitor *n.* competor; concursor.
compile *v.* compila.
compiler *n.* (*person*) compilor; (*software*) compilador.
complacent *adj.* autosasiada.
complain *v.* cexa.
complainer *n.* cexor.
complaint *n.* cexa.
complaisant *adj.* plasente.
complement *v.* completi. • *n.* completinte; (*colour*) oposada.
complementary *adj.* completinte; (*colour*) oposada.
complete *adj.* completa. • *v.* completi.
completeness *n.* completia.
completion *n.* completi.
complex *adj.* complicada. • *n.* (*buildings*, *psychological*) compleso.
complexion *n.* color.
complexity *n.* complica.
compliant *adj.* conformante, obedinte.
complicate *v.* complica.
complication *n.* complica.
complicit *adj.* aidante.
compliment *v.* & *n.* loda. **my compliments** lodas.
comply *v.* obedi; (*with agreement*) segue.
component *adj.* & *n.* composante.
comport *v.* condui.
comportment *n.* condui.
compose *v.* composa. **composed of** composada de.
composer *n.* composor.
composite *adj.* composada. • *v.* (*video*) suprapone.
composition *n.* composa.
compost *n.* descomposada, fertilinte organica.
composure *n.* calmia.
compote *n.* fruta en xirope.
compound *adj.* composada. • *n.* composada; (*buildings*) compleso; (*enclosure*) ensirca.
compound interest *n.* interesa composada.
comprehend *v.* comprende.
comprehensible *adj.* comprendable.
comprehension *n.* comprende.
comprehensive *adj.* completa.
compress *v.* compresa, presa, compati; (*data*) densi.
compression *n.* compresa; densi.
comprise *v.* es composada de.
comprising *adj.* composada de.
compromise *v.* (*make concessions*) compromete; (*endanger*) perili; (*bring into disrepute*) desonora. • *n.* compromete.
compulsion *n.* compulsa.
compulsory *adj.* forsada, obligante.
computability theory *n.* teoria de computablia.
computation *n.* computa.
computational linguistics *n.* linguistica computal.
computational mathematics *n.* matematica computal.
compute *v.* computa.
computer *n.* computador.
computer-aided design *n.* desinia aidada par computador.
computer graphics *n.* infografia.
computer science *n.* informatica.
comrade *n.* camerada.
comradeship *n.* cameradia.
con[1] *n.* (*trick*) froda, engana.
con-[2] *pref.* (*with*, *together*) con-.
con artist *n.* frodor.
concave *adj.* concava.
conceal *v.* asconde.
concede *v.* sede; (*point in an argument*) aseta.
conceit *n.* egosia; (*concept*) conseta.
conceited *adj.* egosa, vana.
conceivable *adj.* consetable, imajinable.
conceive *v.* (*concept*) conseti; (*pregnancy*) consepi.
concentrate *v.* (*attention*, *substance*) consentra.
concentration *n.* consentra; (*relative amount*) proportio.
concentration camp *n.* campa de consentra.
concentration gradient *n.* gradiente de consentra.
concentric *adj.* consentral.
concept *n.* conseta, idea.
conception *n.* (*concept*) conseti; (*pregnancy*) consepi.
conceptual *adj.* consetal.
conceptualize *v.* conseti.
concern *v.* conserna; preocupa. • *n.* conserna; cura. **that is no concern of yours** acel no es tua conserna.
concerning *prep.* sur, consernante.
concert *n.* conserta.
concert hall *n.* salon de conserta.
concertina *n.* consertina.
concerto *n.* conserto.
concession *n.* sede; compromete. **make concessions** compromete.
conch *n.* (*mollusc*) strombo; (*shell*) conca de strombo.
concise *adj.* consisa.
conclave *n.* conclave.

conclude *v.* fini; (*decide*) conclui.
conclusion *n.* fini; (*decision*) conclui.
conclusive *adj.* concluinte.
concoct *v.* (*combine*) combina; (*devise*) inventa.
concoction *n.* combina, prepara.
concomitance *n.* acompania.
concomitant *adj.* acompaniante.
concord *n.* acorda.
concourse *n.* (*foyer*) entra; (*crowd*) fola.
concrete *n.* beton. • *adj.* de beton; (*not abstract*) concreta.
concrete block *n.* brice de beton.
concretion *n.* coagula.
concretize *v.* concreti.
concubine *n.* concubina.
concur *v.* acorda.
concurrent *adj.* simultan, paralel.
concussion *n.* contusa serebral.
condemn *v.* (*disapprove, declare punishment*) condena.
condemnation *n.* condena.
condensate *n.* condensada.
condensation *n.* (*action*) condensa; (*product*) condensada.
condense *v.* (*liquefy*) condensa; (*thicken*) densi.
condensed *adj.* condensada; (*shortened*) consisa.
condensed milk *n.* lete densida.
condenser *n.* condensador.
condescend *v.* finje superioria.
condiment *n.* spise.
condition *n.* (*state*) state; (*medical*) disturba, problem; (*restriction, situation to be met*) restrinje; (*constraint*) constrinje. • *v.* (*fabric*) suavi. **on condition that** sola si, dependente si, con esije ce.
conditional *adj.* dependente.
conditional mood *n.* (*grammar*) moda dependente.
conditioner *n.* suavinte.
condo *n.* condo.
condolence *n.* compatia.
condom *n.* condom.
condominium *n.* condo.
condone *v.* aseta, permete.
condor *n.* condor.
conducive *adj.* beneficante.
conduct *v.* (*carry out*) fa; (*lead*) gida; (*oneself*) condui; (*energy*) conduta. • *n.* (*behaviour*) condui.
conduction *n.* conduta.
conductive *adj.* condutante.
conductor *n.* xef de orcestra; (*bus*) biletor; (*energy*) condutador.
cone *n.* cono.
confabulate *v.* recorda falsa.
confabulation *n.* recorda falsa.
confection *n.* confeto.
confectioner *n.* confetor.
confectionery *n.* confetos.
confectionery bar *n.* bara de confeto.
confederacy *n.* federa.
confederate *v.* federa.
confederation *n.* (*action, result*) federa.
confer *v.* (*discuss*) confere; (*bestow*) dona.
conference *n.* confere.
confess *v.* confesa.
confession *n.* confesa.
confessional *n.* confesoria.
confessor *n.* conselor privata.
confetti *n.* paper trinxada.
confidant *n.* confidada, conselor privata.
confidante *n.* confidada, conselor privata.
confide *v.* confida.
confidence *n.* (*trust*) fida, sertia; (*secret*) privata, secreta; (*secrecy*) privatia, secretia. **in confidence** privata, secreta.
confident *adj.* fidante, serta. **be confident in** fida.
confidential *adj.* privata, secreta, confidada.
confidentiality *n.* privatia.
configurable *adj.* ajustable.
configuration *n.* (*action, result*) ajusta; (*design*) desinia.
configure *v.* ajusta.
confine *v.* restrinje. **confine to bed** restrinje a leto.
confinement *n.* restrinje.
confirm *v.* (*including religious*) confirma; serti; (*action on computer*) aproba.
confirmable *adj.* confirmable.
confirmation *n.* (*including religious*) confirma; serti; (*action on computer*) aproba.
confiscate *v.* confisca, prende.
confiscation *n.* confisca, prende.
conflagration *n.* focon.
conflict *v.* & *n.* desacorda, disputa.
confluence *n.* conflue.
confluent *adj.* confluente.
conform *v.* conforma.
conformist *n.* conformiste.
conformity *n.* conforma.
confound *v.* confonde.
confront *v.* fronti.
confrontation *n.* fronti.
Confucian *n.* confuziste.
Confucianism *n.* confuzisme.
Confucius *n.* (*philosopher*) Kongzi.
confusable *adj.* confusable.
confuse *v.* confusa.
confusion *n.* confusa.
conga *n.* (*dance, music*) conga.
conga drum *n.* conga, tambur de conga.
congeal *v.* conjela.
congenial *adj.* amin.
congenital *adj.* conjenital.
conger *n.* (*eel*) congro.
congest *v.* (*medical, traffic*) conjesta; impedi.

congestion *n.* conjesta; impedi.
congestion charge *n.* paia de conjesta.
conglomerate *v.* & *n.* agrega.
conglomeration *n.* agrega.
Congo *n.* (*region*) Congo. **Democratic Republic of the Congo** Republica Democrata de Congo.
Congolese *adj.* & *n.* congoles.
Congo River *n.* Rio Congo.
congratulate *v.* loda.
congratulation *n.* loda. **congratulations** (*well done*) lodas.
congregate *v.* reuni.
congregation *n.* (*religious*, *administrative*) congrega.
congress *n.* congresa; parlamento. **member of congress** congresor.
congressman *n.* congresor.
congresswoman *n.* congresor.
congruence *n.* acorda.
congruent *adj.* acordante.
congruity *n.* acorda.
congruous *adj.* acordante, armoniosa.
conic *adj.* cono.
conical *adj.* cono.
conifer *n.* conifer.
coniferous *adj.* conifer.
conjecture *v.* divina.
conjoin *v.* junta.
conjugal *adj.* sposal.
conjugate *v.* conjuga.
conjugation *n.* conjuga; (*grammar*) junta. **coordinating conjunction** conjunta. **subordinating conjunction** sujunta.
conjunctiva *n.* (*anatomy*) conjuntiva.
conjunctivitis *n.* conjuntivite.
conjure *v.* apare. **conjure up** evoca.
conjuror *n.* majiste.
conlang *n.* lingua construida.
con man *n.* frodor, vil.
connect *v.* lia, junta; (*electrically*) comuta.
Connecticut *n.* (*US state*) Connecticut.
connecting rod *n.* (*machinery*) biela.
connection *n.* lia, junta; (*electric*) comuta; cambia de bus; cambia de tren.
connective *adj.* liante, juntante.
connivance *n.* conspira.
connive *v.* conspira.
connoisseur *n.* conosor.
connotation *n.* conota, evoca, sujesta.
connote *v.* conota.
conquer *v.* concista.
conqueror *n.* concistor, vinsor.
conquest *n.* concista.
conquistador *n.* concistor.
consanguine *adj.* con lias de sangue.
consanguinity *n.* lias de sangue.
conscience *n.* consiensa.
conscientious *adj.* consiensosa.
conscious *adj.* consensa. **become conscious** consensi.
consciousness *n.* consensia.
conscript *n.* enscriveda.
conscription *n.* enscrive.
consecrate *v.* santi.
consecration *n.* santi.
consecutive *adj.* en serie, seguente.
consensual *adj.* acordada.
consensus *n.* acorda.
consent *v.* & *n.* acorda.
consequence *n.* resulta, efeto.
consequent *adj.* resultante, seguente.
consequential *adj.* resultante, seguente; (*significant*) importante.
consequently *adv.* (*therefore*) donce, alora.
conservation *n.* conserva.
conservationism *n.* conserva de natur.
conservationist *n.* conservor de natur.
conservation site *n.* conserveria.
conservatism *n.* (*political*) conservalisme.
conservative *adj.* tradisional; cauta; (*political*) conservaliste. • *n.* (*political*) conservaliste.
conservatoire *n.* scola de musica.
conservator *n.* conservor.
conservatory *n.* sala de sol; scola de musica.
conserve *v.* conserva.
consider *v.* (*think about*) considera; (*judge to be*) regarda. **considered to be the tallest** regardada como la plu alta. **consider oneself happy** senti felis, senti ce on es felis.
considerable *adj.* notable.
considerate *adj.* compatiosa.
consideration *n.* considera; (*being considerate*) compatia.
considering *adj.* considerante. • *subord.* (*taking into account that*) considerante ce.
consign *v.* consinia.
consignment *n.* consinia.
consignment store *n.* consinieria.
consist *v.* (*of*) es composada; (*in*) ave la inere de.
consistency *n.* (*being consistent*) coere; (*thickness*) densia, viscosia.
consistent *adj.* coerente.
consolation *n.* consola. **find consolation in** es consolada par.
console[1] *v.* (*comfort*) consola.
console[2] *n.* (*control panel*) consol.
consoler *n.* (*person*) consolor.
consolidate *v.* combina; forti, solidi.
consolidation *n.* combina; forti, solidi.
consommé *n.* bulion, sopa clar.
consonant *adj.* & *n.* (*language*, *music*) consonante.
consort *n.* (*female*) sposa real; (*male*) sposo real.
consortium *n.* asosia, uni.

conspicuous *adj.* atraente atende, fasil persepable, fasil vidable.
conspiracy *n.* conspira.
conspiracy theory *n.* teoria de conspira.
conspirator *n.* conspiror.
conspire *v.* conspira.
constable *n.* polisior.
constant *adj.* & *n.* constante.
constellate *v.* constela.
constellation *n.* constela.
consternation *n.* angusa.
constipate *v.* constipa.
constipation *n.* constipa.
constituency *n.* seja.
constituent *adj.* & *n.* composante.
constitute *v.* constitui.
constitution *n.* constitui.
constitutional *adj.* constitual.
constrain *v.* constrinje.
constraint *n.* constrinje.
constrict *v.* (*activity*) constrinje; (*narrow*) magri, streti; (*snake*) presa.
constriction *n.* magri, streti.
construct *v.* construi.
constructed language *n.* lingua construida.
construction *n.* construi. **under construction** en construi.
construction site *n.* construeria.
constructive *adj.* construinte, aidosa.
constructor *n.* construor.
construe *v.* interprete.
consul *n.* consul.
consulate *n.* ambasada, consuleria.
consult *v.* consulta.
consultant *n.* conselor; esperta, spesialiste.
consultation *n.* consulta.
consume *v.* consuma.
consumer *n.* consumor.
consumerism *n.* consumisme.
consumerist *adj.* & *n.* consumiste.
consumer price *n.* custa per la compror.
consummate *adj.* esperta. • *v.* completi.
consumption *n.* consuma; (*illness*) tuberculose.
contact *v.* contata. • *n.* (*touch, person*) contata. **make eye contact with** regarda la oios de.
contact lens *n.* lenteta.
contagious *adj.* infetante, comunicable.
contain *v.* conteni.
container *n.* contenador.
container ship *n.* portacontenador.
contaminant *n.* contaminante.
contaminate *v.* contamina.
contamination *n.* contamina.
contemplate *v.* contempla.
contemplation *n.* contempla.
contemplative *adj.* contemplante.
contemporary *adj.* & *n.* contempora.
contempt *n.* despeta.
contemptible *adj.* despetable.
contemptuous *adj.* despetosa.
contend *v.* luta.
contender *n.* competor.
content[1] *adj.* (*satisfied*) contente, sasiada.
content[2] *n.* (*material included*) contenida, contenidas. **contents** contenidas.
content clause *n.* (*grammar*) suproposa nomin.
contention *n.* (*disagreement*) desacorda, luta; (*assertion*) reclama.
contentious *adj.* controversa.
content management system *n.* sistem de maneja contenidas.
contentment *n.* contentia.
contest *n.* concurso, compete. • *v.* compete, disputa.
contestant *n.* concursor, competor.
context *n.* contesto; situa, ambiente.
contiguity *n.* contata, prosimia.
contiguous *adj.* contatante, continuante.
continent *adj.* (*medical*) conteninte. • *n.* (*geography*) continente.
continental *adj.* continental.
continental shelf *n.* plano continental.
continual *adj.* continuante, nonpausante, nonsesante, sin pausa, sin sesa, tra la dia.
continuance *n.* pospone.
continuation *n.* continua.
continue *v.* continua; (*to exist, linger on*) permane, dura. **to be continued** esta va continua.
continuity *n.* continua.
continuous *adj.* continuante.
continuous aspect *n.* (*grammar*) aspeta continuante.
continuous track *n.* (*on vehicle*) banda erugin.
continuum *n.* continua.
contorsion *n.* torse.
contort *v.* contorse.
contortion *n.* contorse.
contortionist *n.* contorsor.
contour *n.* contorno.
contra- *pref.* contra-.
contraband *n.* contrabanda; benes nonlegal.
contraception *n.* contraconsepi. **emergency contraception** contraconsepi urjente.
contraceptive *adj.* & *n.* contraconsepal. **intrauterine contraceptive device** contraconsepal intrauteral.
contraceptive diaphragm *n.* diaframa contraconsepal.
contract[1] *v.* (*shrink*) contrae, diminui; (*illness*) reseta, developa.

contract[2] *v.* & *n.* (*formal agreement*) contrata, acorda formal.
contraction *n.* contrae.
contractor *n.* contrator.
contractual *adj.* contratal, formal acordada.
contradict *v.* contradise. **contradict oneself** contradise se, autocontradise.
contradiction *n.* contradise.
contradictory *adj.* contradisente.
contrail *n.* seguente de condensa.
contraindicate *v.* contraindica.
contraindication *n.* contraindica.
contralto *adj.* & *n.* (*music*) contralto.
contraption *n.* macineta.
contrapuntal *adj.* contrapuntal.
contrary *adj.* oposante.
contrast *v.* & *n.* contrasta, oposa. **by contrast** par contrasta, a contra. **in contrast to** en contrasta con, contrastada con.
contravene *v.* desacorda con.
contribute *v.* contribui, dona.
contribution *n.* contribui, dona; (*gift*) donada.
contributor *n.* contribuor.
contrite *adj.* repentinte. **feel contrite** repenti.
contrition *n.* repenti.
contrive *v.* inventa.
control *v.* controla. • *n.* controla, restrinje; (*user interface*) aparateta. **air traffic control** controla de trafica airal. **operate by remote control** telecomanda. **out of control** noncontrolable. **take control** prende controla. **under the control of** su controla de.
control freak *adj.* & *n.* controlamanica.
controllable *adj.* controlable.
controller *n.* (*person*) controlor; (*device*) controlador.
control panel *n.* panel de strumentos, consol; (*switches, plugs*) panel de comuta.
control room *n.* controleria.
control theory *n.* teoria de controla.
controversial *adj.* controversa, disputable, disputada.
controversy *n.* (*quality*) controversia; (*something controversial*) controversa.
contusion *n.* contusa.
conundrum *n.* enigma.
convalesce *v.* sani, recovre.
convect *v.* conveta.
convection *n.* conveta.
convective *adj.* convetante.
convene *v.* reuni.
convenience *n.* oportunia.
convenient *adj.* oportun; (*practical*) pratical; (*location*) bon situada.
convent *n.* monceria, soreria.
convention *n.* (*custom*) abitua, pratica; (*meeting*) confere, reuni; (*axiom*) axiom.
conventional *adj.* normal, ortodox.
converge *v.* conflue, converje.
convergence *n.* conflue, converje.
convergent *adj.* converjente.
conversation *n.* conversa.
conversational *adj.* conversal.
converse[1] *v.* (*talk*) conversa.
converse[2] *n.* (*opposite*) reversada.
converser *n.* conversor.
conversion *n.* converti.
convert *v.* converti, cambia. • *n.* convertida. **convert back** reconverti.
convertible *adj.* convertable.
convex *adj.* convesa.
convey *v.* gida, porta, transporta, trae; (*meaning*) espresa.
conveyor *n.* transportador.
conveyor belt *n.* banda transportante.
convict *v.* condena. • *n.* condenada, prisonida.
conviction *n.* (*pronouncement of guilt*) condena; (*belief*) crede.
convince *v.* convinse.
convocation *n.* reuni.
convoke *v.* reuni.
convoluted *adj.* serpentin.
convoy *n.* convoia.
convulse *v.* convulsa.
convulsion *n.* convulsa.
convulsive *adj.* convulsante.
coo *interj.* (*pigeon*) u-u.
cook *v.* coce; (*in oven*) forni; (*on stove*) stufi; (*do cookery*) cosini. • *n.* cosinor.
cookbook *n.* libro de resetas.
cooker *n.* stufa.
cookery *n.* cosini.
cookie *n.* biscoto; (*web*) cuci.
cookie sheet *n.* plata per biscotos.
cooking *n.* (*cookery*) cosini.
cooking implement *n.* util de cosini.
Cook Islands *n.* Isolas Cook.
cookout *n.* coce su sielo.
cookware *n.* benes de coce.
cool *adj.* (*including fashionable*) fresca; a la moda, de moda; (*reception*) nonzelosa. • *v.* fri.
coolant *n.* frinte.
cooled *adj.* frida.
cooper *n.* barilor.
cooperage *n.* barileria.
cooperate *v.* coopera, colabora.
cooperation *n.* coopera, colabora.
cooperative *adj.* cooperante.
co-opt *v.* invita, eleje par comite.
coordinate *v.* coordina. • *n.* coordinada.
coordinate clause *n.* (*grammar*) proposa coordinada.
coordinating conjunction *n.* conjunta.

coordination *n.* coordina.
cop *n.* polisior.
cope *v.* (*with*) maneja.
Copenhagen *n.* Kobenhavn.
copernicium *n.* (*element*) copernisio.
copier *n.* (*person*) copior; (*machine*) copiador.
copilot *n.* copilote.
coping saw *n.* siericurva.
copious *adj.* abundante.
copper *n.* cupre. • *adj.* de cupre. • *v.* cupri.
copper age *adj.* & *n.* calcolitica.
copperplate *n.* (*engraving*) plata de cupre.
coppersmith *n.* cupror.
coprolite *n.* coprolito.
coprolith *n.* coprolito.
copse *n.* bosce.
Copt *n.* copta.
Coptic *adj.* (*Christianity*) copta.
copula *n.* (*grammar*) verbo liante.
copulate *v.* copula.
copulation *n.* copula.
copy *v.* & *n.* copia. **copy and paste** copia e coli.
copybook *n.* libro de modeles.
copy buffer *n.* (*software*) pox de copia.
copyist *n.* copior.
copyreader *n.* coretor.
copyright *n.* direto de autor. • *v.* enscrive su direto de autor.
copywriter *n.* autor de anunsias.
coquette *n.* flirtor, seduor, tisor.
coquettish *adj.* flirtante.
coral *n.* coral.
Coral Sea *n.* Mar Coral.
corbel *n.* (*architecture*) mensula.
Corcovado *n.* Corcovado.
Corcovado Gulf *n.* Golfo Corcovado.
cord *n.* corda. **vocal cord** corda vosal, plia vosal.
cordate *adj.* corin.
corded *adj.* costelin.
cordial *adj.* cortes.
cordite *n.* cordita.
cordless *adj.* sin corda, sin filo.
cordon *v.* & *n.* cordi.
corduroy *n.* veluda costelin.
core *n.* cor. • *v.* descori.
corer *n.* descorador.
corgi *n.* corgi.
coriander *n.* (*plant*, *spice*) coriandro.
cork *n.* (*substance*) suber; (*stopper*) tapo. • *v.* tapi.
cork oak *n.* cuerco de suber.
corkscrew *n.* tiratapo.
corm *n.* (*botany*) cormo.
cormorant *n.* cormoran.
corn[1] *n.* (*maize*) mais; (*any cereal crop*) gran.
corn[2] *n.* (*medical*) calo.
cornea *n.* cornea.
corneal *adj.* corneal.
corner *n.* angulo. • *v.* trapi; (*market*) monopoli.
cornet *n.* (*musical instrument*) corneta.
cornflake *n.* floco de mais.
cornflour *n.* (*starch*) amidon de mais; (*flour*) farina de mais.
cornflower *n.* blueta.
cornice *n.* cornisa, moldur.
Cornish *adj.* (*person*, *language*) cernoica
corn meal *n.* farina de mais.
cornrows *n.* (*hairstyle*) trensas african.
cornstarch *n.* amidon de mais.
cornucopia *n.* corno de abunda.
Cornwall *n.* Cerno.
corny *adj.* bobo.
corolla *n.* (*botany*) corola.
corollary *n.* corolario.
Corona Australis *n.* (*constellation*) la Corona Sude.
Corona Borealis *n.* (*constellation*) la Corona Norde.
coronary *n.* ataca de cor.
coronation *n.* coroni.
coroner *n.* mediciste forense.
coronet *n.* coroneta.
corporal *adj.* corpal. • *n.* (*officer*) caporal.
corporate *n.* (*company*) corpora.
corporate network *n.* rede de compania.
corporate tax *n.* imposta de corpora.
corporation *n.* corpora.
corporeal *adj.* corpal.
corps *n.* (*military*) corpo.
corpse *n.* corpo mor.
corpulent *adj.* obesa.
corpus *n.* (*texts*) corpo.
corpuscle *n.* corpeta, selula de sangue.
corral *n.* ensirca de cavalos; ensirca de bestias.
correct *adj.* coreta. • *v.* coreti. **be correct** dise coreta, razona coreta, razona bon.
correctable *adj.* coretable.
correction *n.* coreti.
correction fluid *n.* licuida de coreti.
corrective glasses *n.* oculo coretinte.
correctness *n.* coretia.
corrector *n.* coretor.
correlate *v.* corelata.
correlation *n.* corelata.
correspond *v.* (*communicate*, *be equivalent*) coresponde; (*match*) acorda.
correspondence *n.* coresponde.
correspondence course *n.* curso par coresponde.
correspondent *n.* (*letter writer*, *reporter*) corespondente; (*reporter*) jornaliste.
corridor *n.* coredor.
corrigible *adj.* coretable.
corroborate *v.* confirma.

corroboration *n.* confirma.
corroboree *n.* balo vivosa.
corrode *v.* corode.
corrosion *n.* corode, osidi.
corrosive *adj.* corodente.
corrugated *adj.* ondante, ondin.
corrugated cardboard *n.* carton ondin.
corrugated iron *n.* fero ondin.
corrupt *v.* mali. • *adj.* frodante, malida.
corruption *n.* mali; froda.
corset *n.* corseto.
corsetiere *n.* corsetor.
Corsica *n.* Corse.
Corsican *adj.* & *n.* (*person*, *language*) corsu.
cortège *n.* prosegue funeral.
cortex *n.* cortex.
Cortez, Sea of *n.* Golfo California.
cortical *adj.* cortexal.
corticosteroid *adj.* & *n.* corticosteroide.
cortisone *n.* (*hormone*) cortisona.
corundum *n.* (*crystal*) corindon.
corvette *n.* (*ship*) corveta.
Corvus *n.* (*constellation*) la Corvo.
coryza *n.* rinite.
cos[1] *n.* (*lettuce*) letuga roman.
cos[2] *subord.* (*because*) car.
cosign *v.* cosuscrive.
cosignatory *n.* cosuscrivor.
cosigner *n.* cosuscrivor.
cosine *n.* cosinus.
cosiness *n.* nidinia.
cosmetic *adj.* & *n.* cosmetica.
cosmetic powder *n.* polvo cosmetica.
cosmetics *n.* macia. **apply cosmetics to** macia.
cosmetologist *n.* cosmetolojiste.
cosmetology *n.* cosmetolojia.
cosmic *adj.* universal.
cosmogony *n.* cosmogonia.
cosmologist *n.* cosmolojiste.
cosmology *n.* cosmolojia.
cosmonaut *n.* astronauta.
cosmopolitan *adj.* de la mundo.
cosmos *n.* universo.
cosponsor *n.* cosponsor. • *v.* cosponsori.
Cossack *adj.* & *n.* cozac.
cosset *v.* regala.
cost *v.* & *n.* custa. **at the cost of** a custa de.
co-star *n.* costela.
Costa Rica *n.* Costa Rica.
Costa Rican *adj.* & *n.* costarican.
cost-conscious *adj.* preocupada de custa.
cost-effective *adj.* nonperosa.
cost-effectiveness *n.* nonperosia.
costly *adj.* custosa, cara.
costume *n.* vestes; (*fancy dress*) vestes fantasin.
cosy (US **cozy**) *adj.* (*place*) nidin; (*person*) nidida.
cot *n.* leteta; leto pliable.
cotangent *n.* cotanjente.
Côte d'Ivoire *n.* Costa de Ivor.
coterie *n.* grupo escluinte.
cotillion *n.* balo de debuantes.
cotinga *n.* (*bird*) cotinga.
cottage *n.* caseta.
cotton *n.* (*plant*, *fibre*) coton. • *adj.* de coton.
cotton candy *n.* coton de zucar.
cotton wool *n.* coton asorbente.
cotyledon *n.* (*botany*) cotiledon.
couch *n.* sofa.
cougar *n.* puma.
cough *v.* & *n.* tose. **cough up** espetora; (*money*, *information*) furni nonvolente.
cough medicine *n.* paratose, antitosal.
cough syrup *n.* calmitose.
could *v.* (*was able*) ia pote; (*would be able*) ta pote.
coulomb *n.* (*unit of charge*) culom.
council *n.* consilio. **local council** comite local.
councillor (US **councilor**) *n.* consilior.
counsel *n.* (*advice*) consela; (*lawyer*) avocato. • *v.* consela.
counselor *n.* conselor.
count[1] *v.* conta. • *n.* (*action*, *amount*) conta. **count down** conta desendente, conta reversada.
count[2] *n.* (*nobleman*) conte.
countable *adj.* contable.
countdown *n.* conta desendente, conta reversada.
countenance *n.* espresa de fas.
counter *n.* (*person*) contor; (*device*) contador; (*game piece*) calculo; (*worktop*) plana. • *v.* oposa. **over the counter** sin prescrive.
counteraccusation *n.* contracusa.
counteract *v.* contramove, oposa.
counterattack *v.* & *n.* contrataca.
counterclaim *n.* contrareclama.
counterclockwise *adj.* contra la orolojo.
countercoup *n.* contracolpa.
countercultural *adj.* contracultural.
counterculture *n.* contracultur. • *adj.* contracultural.
counterespionage *n.* contraspia.
counterfactual *adj.* contrafatal.
counterfeit *adj.* falsa. • *v.* falsi.
counterfeiter *n.* falsor.
counterfeit money *n.* mone falsa.
counterinsurgency *n.* contrarebela.
counterinsurgent *n.* contrarebelor.
counterintuitive *adj.* contra intui.
countermand *v.* nega.
countermeasure *n.* tatica defendente.
counteroffer *n.* ofre respondente.
counterpart *n.* corespondente.
counterpoint *n.* contrapunto.

counterproductive *adj.* contraproduinte. **be counterproductive** contraprodui.
countersink *v.* esvasa.
countertenor *adj.* & *n.* (*music*) alto.
counterterrorism *n.* contraterorisme.
counterterrorist *adj.* & *n.* contrateroriste.
countess *n.* contesa.
counting house *n.* sala de contas.
countless *adj.* ultra conta, sin limita, nonlimitada.
country *n.* pais; (*music*) contri. • *adj.* campanial; (*music*) contri.
country dweller *n.* campanian.
country house *n.* casa campanian; (*large*) cason de campania.
countryman *n.* (*fellow*) paisan.
countryside *n.* campania.
countrywoman *n.* paisan.
county *n.* contia.
coup *n.* colpa, colpa de stato.
coup de grâce *n.* colpa de mori.
coup d'état *n.* colpa de stato.
coupé *n.* (*car*) cupe.
couple *n.* duple. • *v.* onci.
coupler *n.* juntador.
couplet *n.* duple.
coupon *n.* bileta.
courage *n.* coraje.
courageous *adj.* corajosa.
courante *n.* (*dance*, *music*) corente.
courgette *n.* zuceta.
courier *n.* (*person*) mesajor; transportor; (*company*) transportores.
course *n.* (*path*, *study*) curso; (*path*) via; (*of meal*) plato; (*sport*) campo. • *v.* flue, ri. **course of treatment** curso de trata. **first course** plato prima. **go off course** devia. **in due course** a tempo conveninte. **of course** natural, evidente.
courser *n.* (*bird*) cursor.
court *n.* (*law*, *royal*) corte. • *v.* (*courtship*) cortea. **court of appeal** corte de apela. **take to court** litiga.
courteous *adj.* cortes.
courtesan *n.* cortesan.
courtesy *n.* cortesia.
courthouse *n.* corte.
courtier *n.* om de corte, fem de corte.
courting *adj.* corteal.
court martial *n.* corte militar.
courtroom *n.* corte, sala de justia.
courtship *n.* cortea.
courtship display *n.* mostra corteal.
court shoe *n.* sapato escotada.
courtyard *n.* patio.
couscous *n.* (*food*) cuscus.
cousin *n.* cusin; (*of grandchild generation*) dusobrin, dusobrina, dusobrino; (*of great-grandchild generation*) tresobrin, tresobrina, tresobrino; (*of grandparent generation*) dutie, dutia, dutio; (*of great-grandparent generation*) tretie, tretia, tretio.
covalent *adj.* covalente.
cove *n.* baieta.
coven *n.* congrega de sorsores.
covenant *n.* contrata, acorda formal, lia.
cover *v.* covre; (*topic*) trata; (*requirement*) sasia. • *n.* covrente. **cover up** asconde.
coverage *n.* covre.
coverall *n.* covretota.
covering *adj.* & *n.* covrente. • *prep.* covrente, a covre de.
covert *adj.* secreta.
cover-up *n.* asconde.
covet *v.* anela.
cow *n.* bove, bove fema.
coward *n.* coarde.
cowardice *n.* coardia.
cowardly *adj.* coarde, sin coraje.
cowbell *n.* campana de bove.
cowbird *n.* molotro.
cowboy *n.* bovor; (*North American*) cauboi.
cowboy hat *n.* xapo de cauboi, xapon.
cower *v.* acrupi temosa.
cowherd *n.* bovor.
cowl *n.* capeta laxe.
cowlike *adj.* bovin.
co-worker *n.* colaboror.
cowrie *n.* (*shell*, *mollusc*) cauri.
co-write *v.* coscrive.
co-writer *n.* coscrivor.
coy *adj.* timida.
coyness *n.* timidia.
coyote *n.* coiote.
coypu *n.* (*rodent*) coipu.
cozy (US). See *cosy*.
CPR *n.* reanima cardiopulmonal.
CPU *n.* computador.
crab *n.* crabe.
crab apple *n.* poma savaje.
crabby *adj.* iritable, disputosa.
crab plover *n.* (*bird*) droma.
crack *n.* fesur; (*sound*) crac. • *v.* fesuri, frati; (*sound*) craci; (*hack*) pirati. • *interj.* crac.
crack cocaine *n.* crac.
crackdown *n.* colpa forte, colpa sever.
cracker *n.* (*thin and salty*) cracer; (*any biscuit*) biscoto; (*firecracker*) petardo; (*hacker*) pirata de rede.
crackle *v.* & *n.* crepita.
cradle *n.* cuna, leteta.
craft *n.* artisania. • *v.* crea, fabrica.
craftiness *n.* rusosia.
craftsman *n.* artisan.
craftsmanship *n.* artisania.
craftswoman *n.* artisan.
crafty *adj.* rusosa.
crag *n.* presipe.

crake *n.* (*bird*) ral.
cram *v.* pleni; studia intensa.
cramp *n.* (*muscle*) crampo. • *v.* restrinje.
crampon *n.* crampon.
cranberry *n.* vasinia, vasinia roja.
crane *n.* (*bird, machine*) gru. • *v.* (*neck*) torse.
crane fly *n.* tipula.
cranial *adj.* cranial.
cranium *n.* cranio.
crank *n.* manivel. • *v.* maniveli.
crank beater *n.* batador engranada.
crank handle *n.* manivel.
crankshaft *n.* arbor de maniveles.
cranky *adj.* malumorosa.
crap *n.* (*dung, anything worthless*) caca, merda. • *v.* caci.
crappy *adj.* cacin.
crash *v.* (*several moving objects*) colide; (*one moving object*) xoca; (*aircraft*) cade, cade a tera. • *n.* colide; xoca; cade, desastre; (*sound*) pum. • *interj.* pum.
crash course *n.* curso intensa.
crash diet *n.* dieta intensa.
crash zoom *n.* zuma rapida.
crass *adj.* bruta.
crate *n.* caxon.
crater[1] *n.* crater.
Crater[2] *n.* (*constellation*) la Copa.
craton *n.* (*geology*) craton.
cravat *n.* tela de colo.
crave *v.* anela.
crawfish *n.* langosta.
crawl *v.* rampe. **crawl along** move caracolin.
crawler *n.* rampor.
crayfish *n.* crabe de rio.
crayon *n.* pastel de sira.
craze *n.* mania.
crazy *adj.* fol, demente. **go crazy** dementi.
creak *v.* & *n.* (*low-pitched*) cruji; (*high-pitched*) grinse.
creaky *adj.* crujinte; grinsente.
cream *adj.* (*colour*) crema. • *n.* (*substance*) crema. • *v.* (*add cream to*) cremi. **cream of society** crema de sosia.
cream cheese *n.* ceso cremosa.
creamery *n.* cremeria.
cream flan *n.* tarte de crema.
cream pie *n.* tarte de crema.
creamy *adj.* (*creamlike*) cremin; (*full of cream*) cremosa.
crease *v.* & *n.* plia.
create *v.* crea.
creation *n.* (*action*) crea; (*product*) creada.
creative *adj.* creante, creosa, inventosa.
creativity *n.* creosia, inventosia.
creator *n.* creor, autor.
creature *n.* creada, esente, vivente.
credentials *n.* documentos de identia.
credibility *n.* credablia.
credible *adj.* credable.
credit *v.* onora; (*attribute*) atribui. • *n.* (*for achievement*) onora; (*money*) credito. **on credit** par credito.
credit card *n.* carta de credito.
creditor *n.* creditor.
credit risk *n.* risca de credito.
credit score *n.* risca de credito.
credo *n.* crede.
credulity *n.* credosia.
credulous *adj.* credosa.
Cree *adj.* & *n.* (*person, language*) cri.
creed *n.* crede.
creek *n.* rieta.
creel *n.* sesto de pexa.
creep *v.* rampe.
creeper *n.* (*person, plant*) rampor.
creepy *adj.* asustante.
crema catalana *n.* crema catalan.
cremate *v.* seni.
cremation *n.* seni.
crematorium *n.* seneria.
crematory *n.* seneria.
crème anglaise *n.* crema engles.
crème brûlée *n.* crema ardeda.
crème caramel *n.* crema de caramel.
crème de la crème *n.* crema de la crema.
crème de menthe *n.* crema de menta.
crenellate *v.* merloni.
crenellated *adj.* merlonida, merlonin.
crenellation *n.* merlon.
creole *adj.* & *n.* creol.
creosote *n.* creosota.
crêpe *n.* crepe.
crêpe pan *n.* padela de crepes.
crescendo *n.* cresente.
crescent *n.* cresente.
cress *n.* creson.
crest *n.* (*of wave, of bird, heraldic*) cresta; culmina; (*bird*) renoreta. • *v.* culmina; (*wave*) cresti.
Cretaceous *adj.* & *n.* (*geology*) cretasica.
Cretan *adj.* & *n.* critica.
Crete *n.* Criti.
cretin *n.* cretin.
cretinous *adj.* cretin.
crevasse *n.* fesur.
crevice *n.* fesur.
crew *n.* ecipo.
crewcut *n.* capeles militar.
crewel *n.* filo de brode.
crew member *n.* ecipor.
crewneck *n.* colar ronda.
crib *n.* leteta.
cribbage *n.* (*card game*) cribaje.
cricket[1] *n.* (*insect*) grilo.
cricket[2] *n.* (*sport*) criceta.
cricketer *n.* cricetor.
cricket pitch *n.* campo de criceta.

crier *n.* crior, anunsior, proclamor.
crime *n.* crimin.
Crimea *n.* Crim.
Crimean *adj.* & *n.* crimsce.
criminal *adj.* criminal. • *n.* criminor.
criminal attempt *n.* atenta criminal.
criminality *n.* criminalia.
criminalize *v.* criminali.
criminology *n.* criminolojia.
crimp *v.* & *n.* plieta.
crimson *adj.* carmesi. • *n.* carmesi; (*pigment*) rubia.
-crine *suff.* (*secreting*) -crin.
cringe *v.* acrupi temosa.
crinkle *n.* plieta.
crinkled *adj.* plietosa.
crinkly *adj.* plietosa.
crinoid *n.* (*organism*) crinoide.
cripple *v.* descapasi.
crisis *n.* crise.
crisp *adj.* cracosa; (*cloth, paper*) lisa. • *n.* (*potato*) xip.
crispy *adj.* cracosa.
crisscross *adj.* crusante, grilin.
criteria *n.* criterios.
criterion *n.* criterio.
critic *n.* (*opponent*) criticor; (*art*) criticiste, resenior.
critical *adj.* (*opposing*) criticante; (*analysing*) resenial; (*crucial*) esensal; (*crisis*) estrema.
criticism *n.* critica.
criticize *v.* critica.
critique *v.* & *n.* (*opposing*) critica; (*analysing*) resenia.
croak *v.* & *n.* cuaci.
Croatia *n.* Corvatsca.
Croatian *adj.* & *n.* (*person, language*) corvatsce.
crochet *v.* croxe.
crochet hook *n.* ago de croxe.
crochet needle *n.* ago de croxe.
crock *n.* vaso de losa.
crocodile *n.* crocodil.
crocus *n.* croco.
croissant *n.* cresente.
crone *n.* arpia.
crony *n.* ami, camerada.
crook *n.* criminor, vil; (*staff*) basto curva; (*of arm, leg*) plia.
crooked *adj.* (*shape*) apoiada, vagante.
croon *v.* & *n.* canta, zumbi.
crop *n.* cultiva; (*harvest*) recolie. • *v.* (*trim*) corti.
crop rotation *n.* alterna de cultiva.
crop top *n.* camiseta corta.
croquet *n.* (*game, shot*) croceta.
croquette *n.* (*food*) croceta.
crosier *n.* basto curva.
cross *n.* crus. • *adj.* iritada, disputosa; (*transverse*) traversal. • *v.* (*go across*) traversa; (*river*) vadi; (*intersect*) crusa. **cross one's arms** crusa sua brasos. **cross one's legs** crusa sua gamas. **cross out** bari.
crossbar *n.* bara traversante.
crossbeam *n.* faxon traversal.
crossbill *n.* (*bird*) becocrusada.
crossbones *n.* osos crusada.
crossbow *n.* balesta.
crossbred *adj.* ibride.
crossbreed *n.* ibride. • *v.* ibridi.
cross-country running *n.* core tra campania.
cross-country skiing *n.* corsa de sci.
cross-cultural *adj.* intercultural.
cross-culture *adj.* intercultural.
crosscurrent *n.* corente traversal.
cross-cut *n.* talia traversal.
cross-dress *v.* transvesti.
cross-dresser *n.* transvestida.
cross-examination *n.* contrainteroga.
cross-examine *v.* contrainteroga.
cross-eyed *adj.* straba, converjente straba.
cross-faith *adj.* intercredal.
crossfire *n.* spara crusada.
crosshairs *n.* reticulo.
crosshatch *v.* trama.
crosshead screw *n.* vise crusin.
crosshead screwdriver *n.* turnavise crusin.
crossing *adj.* (*going across*) traversante; (*intersecting*) crusante. • *n.* (*going across*) traversa; (*ford*) vado; (*intersection*) crusa. • *prep.* traversante.
crosslike *adj.* crusin.
crossmatching *n.* (*blood types*) conforma de sangue.
crosspiece *n.* traversal.
cross-pollinate *v.* estrapoleni.
cross-pollination *n.* estrapoleni.
cross-reference *v.* & *n.* refere.
crossroads *n.* crus de vias.
cross-section *n.* talia traversal; (*statistics*) sample tipal.
cross-shaped *adj.* crusin.
cross-stitch *n.* punto crusada.
crosstalk *n.* diafonia.
crosswalk *n.* pasaje de traversa.
crossword puzzle *n.* parolas crusada.
crotch *n.* (*anatomy*) entregama, inguin; (*bifurcation*) forci.
crotchet *n.* tono cuatrida.
crouch *v.* acrupi. **crouch down** acrupi se.
croup *n.* (*medical*) crup.
croupier *n.* xef de table.
crouton *n.* cruton.
crow[1] *n.* (*bird*) corvo.
crow[2] *v.* & *n.* (*screech*) abaia. • *interj.* (*caw*) caa; (*cock-a-doodle-doo*) cucurucu. **American**

crow corvo american. **as the crow flies** en linia reta.
crowbar *n.* palanca.
crowd *n.* fola. ● *v.* foli.
crowded *adj.* folida.
crowd-surf *v.* surfa la fola.
crown *n.* corona. ● *v.* coroni; (*as champion*) campioni.
crownlike *adj.* coronin.
crown prince *n.* prinse erital.
crown-shaped *adj.* coronin.
crozier *n.* basto curva.
crucial *adj.* esensal.
crucible *n.* crisol.
crucifix *n.* crus.
crucifixion *n.* crusi.
cruciform *adj.* crusin.
crucify *v.* crusi.
crude *adj.* (*raw*) cru; (*unadjusted*) bruta; (*lewd*) lasiva, vulgar.
cruel *adj.* cruel, calosa, malintendente.
cruelty *n.* cruelia, calosia.
cruise *v.* & *n.* turi, viaja per plaser.
cruise liner *n.* barcon de turi.
cruise missile *n.* misil cruser.
cruiser *n.* (*pleasure boat*) iate; (*warship*) cruser.
cruise ship *n.* barcon de turi.
cruising *adj.* (*travelling at constant speed*) cruser.
crumb *n.* pico de pan. ● *v.* pani.
crumble *v.* desintegra.
crumbly *adj.* desintegrable, granetin.
crummy *adj.* misera, susia.
crumpet *n.* (*cake*) crumpeta.
crumple *v.* plieta, crase.
crumpled *adj.* plietosa.
crunch *n.* & *interj.* crac. ● *v.* craci.
crunchy *adj.* cracinte, cracosa.
crusade *v.* & *n.* crusada.
crusader *n.* crusador.
crush *v.* crase, maxa.
crusher *n.* maxador.
crushing *n.* crase. ● *adj.* (*defeat*) completa.
crust *n.* crosta.
crustacean *n.* crustaseo.
crusty *adj.* crostosa.
crutch *n.* (*support stick*) muleta; (*anatomy*) entregama, inguin.
crux *n.* esense, cor. **Crux** (*constellation*) la Crus.
crwth *n.* (*musical instrument*) crut.
cry *v.* & *n.* (*weep*) plora; (*shout*) cria.
crybaby *n.* plorosa.
cryogenic *adj.* criojen.
cryonic *adj.* criojen.
cryophile *n.* criofilica.
cryophilia *n.* criofilia.
cryophilic *adj.* criofilica.
cryosurgery *n.* criosirurjia.
cryovolcanism *n.* criovolcanisme.
cryovolcano *n.* criovolcan.
crypt *n.* tomba.
crypto- *pref.* cripto-.
cryptographer *n.* criptografiste.
cryptography *n.* criptografia.
cryptologist *n.* criptografiste.
cryptology *n.* criptografia.
crystal *n.* cristal.
crystalline *adj.* cristal.
crystallization *n.* cristali.
crystallize *v.* cristali.
crystallography *n.* cristalografia.
csardas *n.* (*dance*) sardas.
ctenophore *n.* (*organism*) ctenoforo.
cub *n.* (*animal*) joven; (*scout*) scolta joven.
Cuba *n.* Cuba.
Cuban *adj.* & *n.* cuban.
cubbyhole *n.* comparte.
cube *n.* cubo. ● *v.* cubi.
cubemate *n.* camerada de selula.
cube root *n.* radis cubo.
cubic *adj.* cubo.
cubical *adj.* cubo.
cubicle *n.* selula.
cubism *n.* cubisme.
cubist *adj.* & *n.* cubiste.
cubit *n.* codo.
cucking stool *n.* seja sumerjinte.
cuckold *n.* sposo enganada.
cuckoldry *n.* engana sposal.
cuckoo *n.* cucu.
cuckoo shrike *n.* campefaje.
cucumber *n.* concombre.
cuddle *v.* & *n.* abrasa.
cuddly toy *n.* animal de pelux.
cudgel *v.* bastoni.
cue *n.* sinial. ● *v.* siniali.
cuff *n.* polso; (*blood pressure*) manga.
cuirass *n.* corasa.
cuisine *n.* cosini.
cul-de-sac *n.* rua sin sorti.
culinary *adj.* cosinal.
cull *v.* mata la debiles.
culminate *v.* culmina.
culmination *n.* culmina.
culottes *n.* pantala faldin.
culpable *adj.* culpable.
culprit *n.* vil.
cult *n.* culto.
cultist *n.* cultiste.
cultivable *adj.* cultivable.
cultivar *n.* varia elejeda.
cultivatable *adj.* cultivable.
cultivate *v.* cultiva.
cultivation *n.* cultiva.
cultivator *n.* (*person*) cultivor; (*machine*) cultivador.
cultural *adj.* cultural.
culture *n.* cultur; (*medical*) cultiva.

culvert *n.* canal suteran.
Cuman *adj.* & *n.* cuman.
cumbersome *adj.* masosa.
cumbia *n.* (*dance, music*) cumbia.
cumin *n.* (*plant, seed*) cumin.
cummerbund *n.* xarpe de taie.
cumulative *adj.* cumulante.
cumulonimbus *adj.* & *n.* (*cloud*) cumulonimbo.
cumulous *adj.* cumulin, cumulosa.
cumulus *adj.* & *n.* (*cloud*) cumulo.
cuneiform *adj.* & *n.* cuneforma.
cunnilingus *n.* cunilingo.
cunning *adj.* astuta, rusosa. • *n.* astutia, rusosia.
cunningness *n.* rusosia.
cunt *n.* cuno.
cup *n.* tas; (*without handles*) copa. • *v.* (*scoop*) copi; (*in hands, etc.*) ensirca.
cupboard *n.* armario.
cupcake *n.* torteta.
cup holder *n.* portacopa.
Cupid *n.* Cupido.
cuplike *adj.* tasin, copin.
cupola *n.* cupola.
cupped *adj.* copin.
cupric *adj.* cuprica.
cuprite *n.* cuprita.
cuprous *adj.* cuprosa.
cup-shaped *adj.* tasin, copin.
cur *n.* can misera, can coleriosa.
curable *adj.* remediable.
Curaçao *n.* (*island*) Curasau.
curandero *n.* sanor spirital.
curare *n.* (*resin*) curare.
curator *n.* conservor.
curb *n.* borda de troteria.
curd *n.* caliada.
curdle *v.* calia.
curdling agent *n.* caliante.
cure *v.* remedia, sani; (*meat*) prepara.
cureall *n.* sanitota.
cured meat *n.* carne fumida; carne salosa; carne secida.
curettage *n.* cureti.
curette *n.* (*tool*) cureta.
curfew *n.* (*rule*) proibi de sorti; (*time*) ora de retira.
curio *n.* orneta.
curiosity *n.* (*quality*) curiosia; (*novelty item*) noveta. **arouse curiosity** curiosi.
curious *adj.* (*inquisitive*) curiosa; (*strange*) strana.
curium *n.* (*element*) curio.
curl *n.* risa. • *v.* risi. **curl up** enrola.
curled *adj.* risa.
curlew *n.* (*bird*) curlo.
curling *n.* (*sport*) curling.
curly *adj.* risa.
curly bracket *n.* braseta risa.
curly hair *n.* capeles risa.
curmudgeon *n.* disputosa, malumorosa.
curmudgeonly *adj.* malumorosa.
currant *n.* (*plant, fruit*) ribes; (*raisin*) uva seca.
currency *n.* mone.
currency exchange *n.* ofisia de intercambia.
current *adj.* corente, presente; valida. • *n.* (*water, electricity*) corente. **alternating current** corente alternante.
current events *n.* avenis corente, avenis de la ora, avenis nova, novas.
currently *adv.* corente, aora.
curriculum *n.* cursos.
curriculum vitae *n.* resoma de carera.
curry *n.* cari.
curse *v.* & *n.* maldise; (*swear*) blasfema.
cursive writing *n.* scrive corente.
cursor *n.* (*software*) cursor.
cursory *adj.* fretante.
curt *adj.* brusca.
curtail *v.* redui, corti; restrinje.
curtain *n.* cortina.
curtain call *n.* aclama final.
curtsy *v.* plia sua jenos; (*brief*) osileta. • *n.* plia de jenos.
curvaceous *adj.* curvosa, formosa.
curvature *n.* curvia.
curve *n.* curva. • *v.* curvi.
curved *adj.* curva.
curvy *adj.* curvosa.
cushion *n.* cuxin. • *v.* cuxini.
cushion cover *n.* covrecuxin.
cuss *v.* blasfema.
custard *n.* cremeta, salsa de crema; crema de ovos; crema engles.
custard pie *n.* tarte de crema.
custodial *adj.* prisoninte; curante.
custodian *n.* gardor.
custody *n.* aresta; cura. **in custody** arestada.
custom *n.* costum. • *adj.* par comanda.
customary *adj.* costumal, usual.
customer *n.* cliente.
customised *adj.* par comanda.
customizable *adj.* alterable.
customization *n.* altera, personali.
customize *v.* altera, personali.
custom-made *adj.* par comanda.
custom-order *adj.* par comanda.
customs *n.* (*agency*) duana.
customs duty *n.* imposta de duana, imposta de emporta.
customs official *n.* duanor.
cut *v.* talia; (*with knife*) coteli; (*with scissors*) sisori; (*with torch*) ositalia; (*shorten*) corti; (*neckline*) escota; (*deal*) completi, fini. • *n.* (*including of meat*) talia; (*omission*) omete. **cut and paste**

copia e coli. **cut back** redui la spende. **cut down** (*tree*) cade. **cut off** interompe. **cut out** omete.
cutaneous *adj.* cutanea.
cutback *n.* redui.
cute *adj.* adorable, atraosa, beleta, cara, dulse.
cuteness *n.* dulsia.
cuticle *n.* cuticula.
cutie *n.* beleta.
cutlery *n.* utiles de come.
cutlet *n.* costeleta.
cut-off *n.* (*limit*) limita; (*interruption*) interompe.
cut-offs *n.* pantalon cortida.
cutter *n.* (*person*) cortor; (*device*) taliador.
cut-throat *adj.* cruel, sin compatia. • *n.* taliagarga.
cutting board *n.* planceta de talia.
cutting-edge *adj.* vangarda.
cutting torch *n.* ositaliador.
cuttlebone *n.* sceleto de sepida.
cuttlefish *n.* sepida.
CV *n.* resoma de carera.
cyan *adj.* & *n.* sian.
cyanide *n.* sianido.
cyanosis *n.* (*medical*) sianose.
cyber- *pref.* siber-.
cybercafe *n.* sibercaferia.
cybercrime *n.* sibercrimin.
cybercriminal *n.* sibercriminal.
cyberlocker *n.* ospitafix.
cybernetic *adj.* sibernetical.
cybernetics *n.* sibernetica.
cyberspace *n.* siberspasio.
cyborg *n.* siborge.
cycad *n.* (*plant*) sicada.
Cyclades *n.* (*islands*) Ciclades.
cyclamen *n.* (*plant*) siclamen.
cycle *n.* (*loop*, *bike*) sicle. • *v.* (*loop*) sicli; (*bicycle*) bisicli.
cyclic *adj.* sicle, siclin.
cyclical *adj.* sicle.
cycling *n.* (*sport*, *pastime*) bisiclisme, siclisme.
cycling shorts *n.* pantala de bisicli.
cycliophor *n.* (*organism*) sicliotoro.
cyclist *n.* bisicliste, sicliste.
cyclone *n.* siclon.
cyclops *n.* (*mythology*, *crustacean*) siclope.
cyclotron *n.* (*particle accelerator*) siclotron.
cygnet *n.* sinieta.
Cygnus *n.* Sinie.
cylinder *n.* silindre.
cylindrical *adj.* silindre.
cymbal *n.* (*musical instrument*) simbal.
cynic *n.* sinica.
cynical *adj.* sinica.
cynicism *n.* sinicisme.
cypress *n.* (*tree*) sipres.
Cypriot *adj.* & *n.* ciprica.
Cyprus *n.* Cipros.
Cyrillic *adj.* & *n.* cirilica.
cyst *n.* (*biology*, *medical*) siste.
cystic *adj.* sistal.
cystic fibrosis *n.* fibrose sistal.
cystitis *n.* (*medical*) sistite.
-cyte *suff.* (*cell*) -site.
cyto- *pref.* (*cell*) sito-.
cytological *adj.* sitolojial.
cytologist *n.* sitolojiste.
cytology *n.* sitolojia.
cytoplasm *n.* (*biology*) sitoplasma.
cytoskeleton *n.* (*biology*) sitosceleto.
czar *n.* tsar.
czardas *n.* (*dance*) sardas.
czardom *n.* tsaria.
czarina *n.* tsaresa.
Czech *adj.* & *n.* txesce.
Czechia *n.* Txesco.
Czechoslovakia *n.* Txescoslovensco.
Czechoslovakian *adj.* & *n.* txescoslovensce.
Czech Republic *n.* Txesco.

D

dab *v.* colpeta.
dabble *v.* (*in water*) plufi; (*toy with*) jua.
dachshund *n.* (*dog*) tecel.
Dacia *n.* (*ancient region*) Dacia.
dactyl *n.* (*poetry*) datilo.
dactylic *adj.* datilal.
dad *n.* papa.
dadaism *n.* dadaisme.
dadaist *adj.* dadaiste.
daddy *n.* papa.
daddy longlegs *n.* (*arachnid*) gamalonga.
daemon *n.* demon.
daffodil *n.* (*plant*) narsiso.
daft *adj.* fol.
Dagaaba *adj.* & *n.* (*people*) dagara.
Dagare *adj.* & *n.* (*language*) dagara.
dagger *n.* daga; (*typography*) sinia de daga.
daguerreotype *n.* dagereotipo.
dahlia *n.* dalia.
daikon *n.* rabano blanca.
daily *adj.* dial.
dainty *adj.* delicata.
daiquiri *n.* (*drink*) daiciri.
dairy *n.* leteria.
dais *n.* plataforma.
daisy *n.* (*plant*) margarita.
Dakota *adj.* & *n.* (*person, language*) dacota. **North Dakota** (*US state*) Dakota Norde. **South Dakota** (*US state*) Dakota Sude.
dale *n.* vale.
Dalit *adj.* & *n.* (*caste*) dalit.
dally *v.* pigri.
Dalmatia *n.* Dalmasia.
Dalmatian *adj.* dalmasian. • *n.* (*including dog*) dalmasian.
dam *n.* (*river*) parario.
damage *v.* & *n.* dana. **damages** compensa.
Damascus *n.* Dimashq.
damask *n.* (*fabric*) damasco.
dame *n.* dama.
damn *v.* maldise, condena a enferno. • *adj.* enfernin. • *interj.* txa.
damnation *n.* puni eterna.
damned *adj.* enfernin.
damp *adj.* umida.
dampen *v.* umidi; (*deaden*) amorti.
damper *n.* constrinje.
dampness *n.* umidia.
dampproof *adj.* secur contra umidia.
damsel *n.* fem joven.
damselfly *n.* libela.
dance *v.* & *n.* dansa; (*event*) balo. **dance a waltz** dansa un valsa.
dance belt *n.* portaseso.
dance hall *n.* salon de dansa.
dancer *n.* dansor.
dandelion *n.* denteleon.
dander *n.* caspa.
dandruff *n.* caspa.
dandy *n.* dandi.
Dane *n.* danese. **Great Dane** (*dog*) mastin deutx.
danger *n.* peril.
dangerous *adj.* perilosa.
dangle *v.* (*be hanging*) pende; (*cause to hang*) pende, suspende.
Danish *adj.* & *n.* (*person, language*) dansce.
dank *adj.* fria, staniante.
danse macabre *n.* dansa de moria.
Dao *n.* dau.
Daoism *n.* dauisme.
Daoist *n.* dauiste.
daphnia *n.* (*crustacean*) dafnia.
dapper *adj.* bonvestida.
dappled *adj.* manxosa; multicolorosa.
Dardanelles *n.* Streta Dardanelia.
dare *v.* osa.
daredevil *n.* amaperil.
daring *adj.* osante. • *n.* osa.
dark *adj.* & *n.* oscur.
dark blue *adj.* & *n.* blu.
darken *v.* oscuri.
darkness *n.* (*quality*) oscuria; (*gloom*) oscur.
darkroom *n.* (*photography*) sala oscur.
darling *adj.* cara. • *n.* cara, ameta.
darmstadtium *n.* (*element*) darmstatio.
darn *v.* & *n.* texeta, repara.
darnel *n.* (*rye*) lolio.
dart *n.* dardo.
darter *n.* (*bird*) aninga.
Darwinism *n.* darwinisme.
dash *n.* (*punctuation*) sinia de junta, linia orizonal; (*small quantity*) pico. • *v.* (*hopes*) delude.
dashboard *n.* panel de strumentos.
data *n.* datos.
data bank *n.* banco de datos.
database *n.* banco de datos.
data centre (US **center**) *n.* compleso de datos.
data structure *n.* strutur de datos.
data type *n.* tipo de dato.
date[1] *n.* (*calendar*) data; (*appointment*) encontra; (*romantic*) cortea; (*person*) corteor. • *v.* (*determine the date of, write a date on*) dati; (*from*) orijina; (*woo*) cortea. **out of date** desvalidida. **to date** asta aora.
date[2] *n.* (*fruit*) datila; (*tree*) datilo.
dated *adj.* anticin.
dated expression *n.* anticin.
dating *n.* cortea. • *adj.* corteal.

dative *adj.* & *n.* (*grammar*) dativa.
datum *n.* dato.
datura *n.* (*plant*) datura.
daub *v.* colpeta.
daughter *n.* fia; (*gender-neutral*) fie; (*baby*) fieta.
daughter-in-law *n.* fia par sposi.
dauphin *n.* delfin.
Davis Strait *n.* Streta Davis.
dawdle *v.* pigri, segue lenta, avansa min.
dawn *v.* matini. • *n.* lus prima, leva de sol, matini.
dawn chorus *n.* conserta de avias.
day *n.* dia; lus de dia; (*24-hour period*) dia completa. **all day** tra la dia. **one day** a alga dia. **these days** a esta dias.
daybed *n.* sofa-leto.
daybook *n.* jornal de contas.
daybreak *n.* matini, leva de sol.
daydream *v.* & *n.* fantasia.
daydreamer *n.* fantasior.
daylight *n.* lus de dia. **broad daylight** lus clar de dia.
day planner *n.* ajenda.
daytime *n.* dia; lus de dia. • *adj.* diurna.
daze *v.* aturdi.
dazzle *n.* brilion. • *v.* sieci.
DC *n.* corente direta.
D-day *n.* Dia D.
de- *pref.* de-.
deacon *n.* diacon.
deactivate *v.* desativi.
deactivation *n.* desativi.
dead *adj.* mor. **in the dead of night** pos medianote.
deadbeat *n.* pigra.
dead body *n.* corpo mor.
deaden *v.* amorti; mori.
dead end *n.* rua sin sorti.
deadline *n.* limita de tempo.
deadlock *n.* nonprogresa, rua sin sorti.
deadly *adj.* matante.
deadly nightshade *n.* beladona.
deadpan *adj.* nonespresosa, sin espresa de fas.
dead person *n.* mor.
Dead Sea *n.* Mar Mor.
dead skin *n.* pel mor.
deaf *adj.* sorda. **go deaf** sordi.
deafen *v.* sordi.
deafness *n.* sordia.
deal *v.* (*cards*) distribui. • *n.* acorda formal, trata. **deal with** trata.
dealer *n.* vendor.
dealership *n.* venderia.
dealings *n.* ativia.
dean *n.* (*religious, university*) decano.
dear *adj.* cara; (*expensive*) cara, custosa. • *n.* cara, ameta.
dearth *n.* manca, nonsufisi.
death *n.* (*dying*) mori; (*being dead*) moria.
deathbed *n.* leto de mori.
death blow *n.* colpa de mori.
death camp *n.* campa de mata.
death penalty *n.* puni de mori.
death rate *n.* taso de mori.
death row *n.* coredor de mori.
death throes *n.* doles de mori.
death toll *n.* cuantia de mores.
debacle *n.* fiasco.
debase *v.* basi.
debatable *adj.* debatable, discutable.
debate *v.* & *n.* debate, disputa.
debauchee *n.* rue.
debauchery *n.* promiscuia.
debilitate *v.* debili.
debilitation *n.* debili.
debit *n.* deta.
deblur *v.* desnebli.
debonair *adj.* bonvestida, sofisticada.
debride *v.* desbridi.
debridement *n.* desbridi.
debrief *v.* & *n.* intervisa.
debris *n.* detrito.
debt *n.* deta.
debtor *n.* detor.
debug *v.* desdefeti.
debugger *n.* desdefetador.
debunk *v.* desvalidi.
debut *v.* debua. • *n.* debua, apare prima, presenta prima.
debutant *n.* debuante.
debutante *n.* debuante.
deca- *pref.* (*ten*) deca-.
decade *n.* desenio.
decadence *n.* dejenera.
decadent *adj.* dejenerada.
decaffeinate *v.* descafini.
decaffeination *n.* descafini.
decagon *n.* decagon.
decagonal *adj.* decagon.
decagram *n.* decagram.
decahedral *adj.* decaedro.
decahedron *n.* decaedro.
decal *n.* decal.
decalcify *v.* descalci.
decalitre (US **decaliter**) *n.* decalitre.
decalogue (US **decalog**) *n.* decalogo.
decametre (US **decameter**) *n.* decametre.
decant *v.* decanta.
decanter *n.* carafa, decantador.
decapitate *v.* destesti.
decapitation *n.* destesti.
decay *v.* & *n.* dejenera, putri.
decease *n.* mori.
deceased *adj.* & *n.* mor.
deceit *n.* engana.
deceitful *adj.* enganosa.
deceive *v.* engana.

decelerate *v.* lenti.
deceleration *n.* lenti.
December *n.* desembre.
decency *n.* virtua, virtuosia.
decent *adj.* brava, virtuosa.
decent chap *n.* bonom.
decenter (US). See *decentre.*
decentralize *v.* desentri.
decentre (US **decenter**) *v.* desentri.
deception *n.* engana.
deceptive *adj.* enganosa.
dechlorinate *v.* desclori.
deci- *pref.* (*a tenth*) desi-.
decibel *n.* desibel.
decide *v.* deside. **you decide** tu debe deside.
deciduous *adj.* caduca.
decigram *n.* desigram.
decile *n.* (*statistics*) desil.
decilitre (US **deciliter**) *n.* desilitre.
decimal *adj.* desimal.
decimal point *n.* virgula desimal.
decimate *v.* destrui.
decimetre (US **decimeter**) *n.* desimetre.
decipher *v.* desifri.
decipherable *adj.* desifrable.
decision *n.* deside.
decisive *adj.* desidente, nonvasilante.
deck *n.* (*ship*) nivel, (*open upper*) teto; (*terrace*) teraza de lenio; (*cards*) paceta.
deckchair *n.* amaceta.
decking *n.* teraza de lenio.
declaim *v.* proclama.
declaration *n.* declara.
declare *v.* declara.
declassify *v.* desecreti.
declension *n.* (*including grammar*) declina.
declination *n.* declina; (*astronomy*) latitude de sielo.
decline *v.* declina, desende; (*refuse*) refusa.
declutch *v.* desembraji.
deco *adj.* deco. **art deco** arte deco.
decode *v.* desifri.
decolletage *n.* escota profonda.
decompose *v.* descomposa.
decompress *v.* descompresa.
decompression *n.* descompresa.
decompression sickness *n.* maladia de descompresa.
decongest *v.* desconjesta.
decongestant *n.* desconjestante.
decontaminate *v.* descontamina.
decontamination *n.* descontamina.
decor *n.* decora.
decorate *v.* (*including with an honour*) decora; (*ornately*) orna.
decoration *n.* decora; orna.
decorative *adj.* ornal.
decorative symbol *n.* vinieta.
decorator *n.* decoror.
decore *v.* descori.
decorer *n.* descorador.
decorous *adj.* cortes.
decorum *n.* cortesia.
decoupage *n.* (*art*) decupaje.
decouple *v.* dejunta.
decoy *n.* (avia) tentante.
decrease *v.* & *n.* diminui, redui.
decreasingly *adv.* sempre min.
decree *n.* comanda.
decrement *v.* diminui, redui.
decrepit *adj.* ruinada.
decriminalize *v.* descriminali.
decry *v.* denunsia.
decrypt *v.* desifri.
decryption *n.* desifri.
dedicate *v.* dedica.
dedication *n.* dedica.
deduce *v.* dedui.
deducible *adj.* deduable.
deduct *v.* sutrae.
deductible *adj.* sutrable.
deduction *n.* (*deduce*) dedui; (*deduct*) sutrae.
deductive *adj.* deduinte.
deed *n.* ata, fa; (*past*) fada.
deejay *n.* didje.
deem *v.* regarda, reputa.
de-emphasize *v.* desasentua.
de-energize *v.* desenerji.
deep *adj.* profonda; (*tone*) basa. • *n.* profonda.
Deepavali *n.* (*Hindu festival*) divali.
deepen *v.* profondi.
deepness *n.* profondia.
deep snow *n.* nevon.
deer *n.* servo. **baby deer** serveta.
deerlike *adj.* servin.
deer pig *n.* babirusa.
deface *v.* manxa.
de facto *adj.* par fato.
defamation *n.* malacusa.
defame *v.* malacusa.
default *adj.* costumal, inisial, implicada. • *n.* (*value*) implicada, inisial. • *v.* (*on payment*) fali paia. **by default** inisial, par implica.
defeat *v.* vinse. • *n.* defeta.
defeatism *n.* defetisme.
defeatist *n.* defetiste.
defecate *v.* feci.
defecation *n.* feci.
defect[1] *n.* (*flaw*) defeto, nonperfeta; (*glitch*) microbio.
defect[2] *v.* (*change sides*) tradi.
defective *adj.* defetosa, nonperfeta.
defector *n.* trador.
defence (US **defense**) *n.* defende.
defence attorney (US **defense attorney**) *n.* avocato defendente.

defence lawyer (US **defense lawyer**) *n.* avocato defendente.
defenceless (US **defenseless**) *adj.* sin defende.
defence tower (US **defense tower**) *n.* tore de garda.
defend *v.* defende, proteje.
defendant *n.* acusada.
defender *n.* defendor.
defenestrate *v.* lansa de fenetra.
defenestration *n.* lansa de fenetra.
defense... (US). See *defence...*
defensive wall *n.* muron.
defer *v.* pospone.
deference *n.* respeta.
deferential *adj.* adulante.
deferment *n.* pospone.
deferral *n.* pospone.
defiance *n.* defia.
defiant *adj.* defiante.
deficiency *n.* manca, nonsufisi.
deficient *adj.* nonsufisinte.
deficit *n.* manca.
defile *v.* viole.
define *v.* defini.
definite *adj.* definida, serta.
definite article *n.* (*grammar*) article de defini.
definition *n.* defini.
definitive *adj.* defininte.
deflate *v.* defla.
deflation *n.* defla.
deflect *v.* redirije.
deflection *n.* redirije.
deflower *v.* desflori.
defog *v.* desnebli.
defogger *n.* desneblador.
defoliant *n.* desfolinte.
defoliate *v.* desfoli.
deforest *v.* desforesti.
deforestation *n.* desforesti.
deform *v.* desformi, malformi.
deformation *n.* desformi, malformi.
deformity *n.* desformi.
defragment *v.* desfrati.
defragmentation *n.* desfrati.
defraud *v.* froda.
defray *v.* (*pay for*) finansia, sasia.
defrock *v.* despreti.
defrost *v.* dejela.
deft *adj.* destrosa.
defunct *adj.* desusada, descontinuada.
defuse *v.* desativi.
defy *v.* defia.
degenerate *v.* dejenera, mali. • *adj.* dejenerada, malida.
degeneration *n.* dejenera, mali.
degradable *adj.* degradante.
degradation *n.* degrada.
degrade *v.* degrada, basi.
degree *n.* grado; (*academic*) diploma. **to some degree** a alga grado.
degree Celsius *n.* grado de celsius.
degree centigrade *n.* grado de celsius.
degree Fahrenheit *n.* grado de farenhait.
dehumanization *n.* desumani.
dehumanize *v.* desumani.
dehumidifier *n.* desumidador.
dehumidify *v.* desumidi.
dehydrate *v.* desidrata.
dehydration *n.* desidrata.
deidentify *v.* desidentifia.
deification *n.* divini.
deify *v.* divini.
deign *v.* basi se.
deinstall *v.* desinstala.
deism *n.* divinisme.
deist *adj.* & *n.* diviniste.
deistic *adj.* diviniste.
deity *n.* dio, divin.
déjà vu *n.* senti de ja videda.
dejected *adj.* depresada, descorajida.
de jure *adj.* par lege.
Delaware *n.* (*US state*) Delaware.
Delaware Bay *n.* Baia Delaware.
delay *v.* & *n.* pospone, retarda, tardi. **with little delay** pronto. **without delay** sin retarda.
delectable *adj.* deletosa.
delegate *v.* delega. • *n.* delegada.
delegation *n.* delega.
delegitimize *v.* deslegali.
deletable *adj.* sutrable.
delete *v.* sutrae, cansela.
deleterious *adj.* nosiva.
deletion *n.* sutrae.
deli *n.* deleteria.
deliberate *adj.* intendente, intendeda, voleda, volente; (*careful*) curante. • *v.* discute.
deliberation *n.* discute.
delible *adj.* sutrable.
delicacy *n.* deleta, comeda favoreda.
delicate *adj.* delicata, frajil. **delicates** (*garments*) delicatas.
delicatessen *n.* deleteria.
delicious *adj.* deletosa.
delight *v.* & *n.* deleta.
delightful *adj.* deletosa.
delimit *v.* limita.
delimitation *n.* limita.
delineate *v.* defini.
delinquent *adj.* criminal. • *n.* criminor.
delirious *adj.* deliriosa.
delirium *n.* delirio.
deliver *v.* trae.
delivery *n.* trae.
dell *n.* valeta.
delouse *v.* despioli.
delphinium *n.* (*plant*) delfinio.

Delphinus *n.* (*constellation*) la Delfin.
delta *n.* (*Greek letter* Δ, δ) delta; (*river mouth*) delta, estuario.
deltoid *adj.* triangulo. • *n.* (*muscle*) deltoide.
delude *v.* ilude.
deluge *v.* & *n.* deluvia.
delusion *n.* ilude.
deluxe *adj.* lusosa.
demagogue *n.* demagogo.
demagoguery *n.* demagogia.
demagogy *n.* demagogia.
demand *v.* & *n.* esije. **on demand** par comanda.
dematerialization *n.* desmateri.
dematerialize *v.* desmateri.
demean *v.* degrada.
demeanour (US **demeanor**) *n.* condui.
demented *adj.* demente.
dementia *n.* dementia.
demerit *n.* nonvantaje; condena.
demigod *n.* dio minor.
demilitarization *n.* desmilitari.
demilitarize *v.* desmilitari.
deminer *n.* desbombetor.
demise *n.* mori.
demisemiquaver *n.* tono tredes-duida.
demist *v.* desnebli.
demister *n.* desneblador.
demitasse *n.* taseta.
demiurge *n.* demiurgo.
demo[1] *n.* mostra; (*political*) protesta.
demo-[2] *pref.* (*people*) demo-.
demobilization *n.* desmovabli.
demobilize *v.* desmovabli.
democracy *n.* democratia.
democrat *n.* democrata.
democratic *adj.* democrata.
Democratic Republic of the Congo *n.* Republica Democrata de Congo.
democratize *v.* democrati.
demodulate *v.* desmodula.
demographer *n.* demografiste.
demographic *adj.* demografial.
demography *n.* demografia.
demolish *v.* desconstrui, destrui.
demolisher *n.* destruor.
demolition *n.* destrui.
demon *n.* demon.
demonic *adj.* demonal, demonin.
demonization *n.* demoni.
demonize *v.* demoni.
demonology *n.* demonolojia.
demonstrable *adj.* mostrable.
demonstrate *v.* mostra; (*political*) protesta.
demonstration *n.* mostra; (*political*) protesta.
demonstrative *adj.* espresosa; (*grammar*) mostral.
demonym *n.* demonim.
demonymic *adj.* demonim.
demoralize *v.* descoraji.
demo software *n.* programes de proba.
demote *v.* basi, retrosede.
demotic *adj.* demotica.
demotion *n.* basi, retrosede.
demotivate *v.* desmotiva.
demoware *n.* programes de proba.
demur *v.* oposa.
demure *adj.* umil.
demystification *n.* desmisteri.
demystify *v.* desmisteri.
demythologize *v.* desmiti.
den *n.* nido.
Denali, Mount *n.* Monte Denali.
denazification *n.* desnazi.
denazify *v.* desnazi.
dendrite *n.* dendrite.
dendritic *adj.* dendritosa.
dendrochronology *n.* dendrocronolojia.
dendrological *adj.* dendrolojial.
dendrologist *n.* dendrolojiste.
dendrology *n.* dendrolojia.
dengue fever *n.* denge.
deniable *adj.* negable.
denial *n.* (*refusal to admit*) nega; (*refusal to give*) refusa.
denigrate *v.* desvalua.
denim *n.* denim. • *adj.* de denim.
denim shorts *n.* pantala de denim, jina corta.
denizen *n.* abitor.
Denmark *n.* Danmarc.
Denmark Strait *n.* Streta Danmarc.
denoise *v.* desruidi.
denomination *n.* ramo.
denominator *n.* dividente.
denote *v.* indica, sinia.
denouement *n.* conclui.
denounce *v.* denunsia.
denouncement *n.* denunsia.
denouncer *n.* denunsior.
dense *adj.* densa.
density *n.* densia.
dent *v.* & *n.* indente.
dental *adj.* & *n.* dental.
dental floss *n.* filo de dentes.
dental plaque *n.* placa dental.
dental tool *n.* buril.
dentil *n.* (*architecture*) moldur merlonin.
dentin *n.* dentin.
dentine *n.* dentin.
dentist *n.* dentiste.
dentistry *n.* odontia.
dentition *n.* dentes.
dentures *n.* prostese dental.
denude *v.* nudi.
deny *v.* (*refuse to admit*) nega; (*refuse to give*) refusa. **deny oneself** asteni, rejeta, renunsia.

deodorant *n.* desodorinte.
deodorize *v.* desodori.
deodorizer *n.* desodorinte.
deoxyribonucleic *adj.* desosiribonucleal.
deoxyribonucleic acid *n.* asida desosiribonucleal.
depart *v.* parti, asenti.
department *n.* departe; (*of university*) scola.
department store *n.* boteca de departes.
departure *n.* parti.
depend *v.* depende. **depend on** depende de.
dependable *adj.* fidable.
dependant *n.* dependente.
dependence *n.* depende.
dependency *n.* depende.
dependent *adj.* dependente.
dependent clause *n.* (*grammar*) proposa suordinada, suproposa.
depersonalize *v.* despersonali.
depict *v.* imaji, depinta, representa.
depiction *n.* imaje, depinta, representa.
depilate *v.* descapeli.
depilatory *adj.* descapelinte.
deplane *v.* desembarca.
deplete *v.* consuma.
depletion *n.* consuma.
deplorable *adj.* deplorable.
deplore *v.* deplora.
deploy *v.* asinia, ativi, posa.
deployment *n.* asinia, ativi, posa.
depolarization *n.* despolali.
depolarize *v.* despolali.
depopulate *v.* despopla.
depopulation *n.* despopla.
deport *v.* deporta.
deportation *n.* deporta.
deportee *n.* deportada.
depose *v.* despone.
deposit *v.* (*including financial*) depone; presipita.
depositary *n.* fidusior.
deposition *n.* despone.
depository *n.* arciveria.
depot *n.* beneria, reserva.
depraved *adj.* vil.
depravity *n.* vilia.
deprecate *v.* desaproba, desvalua.
deprecation *n.* desaproba, desvalua.
depreciate *v.* desvalua, diminui.
depreciation *n.* desvalua, diminui.
depress *v.* (*push down, sadden*) depresa.
depressant *adj.* depresante.
depression *n.* (*medical, economic, weather*) depresa.
deprivation *n.* priva.
deprive *v.* priva.
deprogramme (US **deprogram**) *v.* desprogrami.
depth *n.* (*quality*) profondia. **depths** (*deep place*) profonda.
deputize *v.* encarga.
deputy *adj.* suordinada. • *n.* suordinada; encargada, representor. • *pref.* vis-.
deputy head *n.* suxef.
derail *v.* desreli, salta de la reles.
derby *n.* (*horse race, sporting event*) derbi.
dereference *v.* (*software*) desrefere.
deregulate *v.* desregula.
deregulation *n.* desregula.
derelict *adj.* descurada, ruinada; (*negligent*) descurante.
deride *v.* burla.
derision *n.* burla.
derisive *adj.* burlante.
derivable *adj.* derivable, deduable.
derivation *n.* deriva, dedui.
derivative *adj.* & *n.* derivada.
derive *v.* deriva, dedui.
dermatitis *n.* dermatite.
dermatology *n.* dermatolojia.
dermatophytosis *n.* (*medical*) tinea.
dermis *n.* (*anatomy*) derma.
derogatory *adj.* degradante.
derriere *n.* posterior.
derring-do *n.* ososia.
dervish *n.* darvix.
desalinate *v.* desali.
desalination *n.* desali.
descale *v.* (*remove scales*) descami; (*remove limescale*) destartari.
descend *v.* desende.
descendant *n.* desendente; projenia.
descendent *adj.* desendente.
descender *n.* desendente.
descent *n.* desende.
describable *adj.* descrivable.
describe *v.* descrive.
describer *n.* descrivor.
description *n.* descrive.
desecrate *v.* viole.
desegregate *v.* desepara.
desegregation *n.* desepara.
deselect *v.* deseleje, desmarca.
desensitize *v.* desensosi.
desert[1] *n.* (*land*) deserto.
desert[2] *v.* (*abandon*) abandona, abandona sua posto. • *n.* (*what one deserves*) merita.
deserted *adj.* abandonada.
deserter *n.* abandonor.
desertification *n.* deserti.
desertion *n.* abandona militar.
deserve *v.* merita.
desiccant *n.* (*substance*) secinte.
desiccate *v.* seci, desumidi.
desiccation *n.* secia estrema.
desiccator *n.* contenador secinte.
design *v.* & *n.* desinia.

designate *v.* identifia.
designation *n.* identifia.
designer *n.* desinior. • *adj.* de moda.
desirable *adj.* desirable, desirada.
desirable feature *n.* desirable.
desire *v.* desira; (*deeply*) anela. • *n.* desira, vole. **if desired** si desirada.
desist *v.* asteni.
desk *n.* buro; (*small writing desk*) scriveria.
desktop *n.* (*software*) table de labora.
desktop computer *n.* computador de table.
desktop PC *n.* pc de table.
desktop publishing *n.* tipografia par computador.
desolate *v.* ruina. • *adj.* ruinada.
desolation *n.* ruina.
despair *v.* & *n.* despera.
desperate *adj.* desperante.
desperation *n.* despera.
despicable *adj.* despetable, despetada.
despise *v.* despeta.
despite *prep.* an con; (*something that has already happened*) an pos. **despite the fact that** an si, contra ce. **despite the lack of** an sin.
despoil *v.* saca.
despondency *n.* descoraji.
despondent *adj.* descorajida.
despot *n.* despota, tirano.
despotate *n.* despotia.
despotic *adj.* despotin.
despotism *n.* tirania.
dessert *n.* (*food*) deser.
dessert topping *n.* salsa dulse.
destabilization *n.* destabli.
destabilize *v.* destabli.
destination *n.* destina.
destine *v.* destina.
destiny *n.* destina, fortuna.
destitute *adj.* povre.
destroy *v.* destrui. **destroy the environment** ecoside.
destroyer *n.* (*person*) destruor; (*warship*) xasatorpedo.
destruction *n.* destrui.
destructive *adj.* destruinte.
desuetude *n.* nonusa.
detach *v.* desfisa.
detachable *adj.* desfisable.
detached *adj.* desfisada; (*person*) nonsosial.
detachment *n.* desfisa.
detail *v.* & *n.* detalia.
detailed *adj.* detaliosa.
detain *v.* teni, deteni.
detect *v.* deteta, persepi.
detection *n.* deteta.
detective *n.* detetor.
detector *n.* detetador.
detente *n.* destensa.
detention *n.* deteni.
detention centre (US **center**) *n.* deteneria.
deter *v.* impedi, preveni, teni a via.
detergent *n.* deterjente.
deteriorate *v.* dejenera, mali.
deterioration *n.* mali.
determination *n.* determina.
determinative *n.* (*grammar*) determinante.
determine *v.* (*decide, discover*) determina.
determined *adj.* determinada, ostinosa. **genetically determined** jenetical determinada.
determiner *n.* (*grammar*) determinante.
determinism *n.* determinisme.
determinist *n.* deterministe.
deterministic *adj.* deterministe, nonacaso.
deterrence *n.* preveni.
deterrent *n.* preveninte.
detest *v.* odia.
detestable *adj.* odiable.
dethrone *v.* destroni.
detonate *v.* detona.
detour *n.* devia.
detox *v.* desveneni.
detoxify *v.* desveneni.
detract *v.* sutrae.
detrimental *adj.* nosiva, ferinte.
detritus *n.* detrito.
detrivore *n.* detrivor.
detrivorous *adj.* detrivor.
detune *v.* desajusta.
deuce *n.* (*cards*) du.
deus ex machina *n.* dio par macina.
deuteranopic *adj.* sieca a verde.
deuterium *n.* (*chemistry*) deuterio.
deuterostome *n.* (*organism*) deuterostomio.
deva *n.* divin.
devaluation *n.* desvalua.
devalue *v.* desvalua.
Devanagari *n.* (*writing system*) devanagari.
devastate *v.* ruina.
devastation *n.* ruina.
devein *v.* estrae la vena de.
develop *v.* developa, crese. **develop immunity** imuni.
developer *n.* developor.
development *n.* developa, crese.
deviant *adj.* deviante.
deviate *v.* devia.
deviation *n.* devia.
device *n.* aparato, macineta; (*literary*) truco.
device driver *n.* (*software*) controlador de aparato.
devil *n.* diablo.
devilish *adj.* diablin, demonin.
devil's tongue *n.* (*plant*) coniac.
devious *adj.* rusosa, enganosa.
deviousness *n.* rusosia.
devise *v.* inventa.

devoid *adj.* (*of*) sin.
devolution *n.* devolui.
devolve *v.* devolui.
Devonian *adj.* & *n.* (*geology*) devonian.
devote *v.* dedica, promete.
devotee *n.* adoror, prometor.
devotion *n.* dedica, promete.
devour *v.* devora.
devout *adj.* relijiosa.
devoutness *n.* relijiosia.
dew *n.* rosio.
Dewar flask *n.* termos.
dewlap *n.* caruncula.
deworm *v.* desvermi, deselminti.
dewormer *n.* antielmintal.
dewy *adj.* rosiosa.
dexterity *n.* destrosia.
dextrose *n.* (*sugar*) destrosa.
dextrous *adj.* destrosa.
dharma *n.* (*religion*) darma.
di- *pref.* (*two*) di-.
dia- *pref.* dia-.
diabetes *n.* diabete.
diabetic *adj.* diabetica.
diabolic *adj.* diablosa.
diabolical *adj.* diablosa.
diachronic *adj.* diacrona.
diacritic *n.* sinieta.
diacritical mark *n.* sinieta.
diadem *n.* coroneta.
diaeresis (US **dieresis**) *n.* (*diacritic*) dierese.
diagnose *v.* diagnose.
diagnosis *n.* diagnose.
diagnostician *n.* diagnosiste.
diagnostics *n.* diagnose.
diagnostic tools *n.* (*software*) programes de diagnose.
diagonal *adj.* diagonal.
diagram *n.* scema.
dial *n.* indicador; (*watch*, *clock*, *compass*) fas; (*telephone*, *radio*, *etc.*) disco. • *v.* (*phone number*) disci.
dialect *n.* dialeto.
dialectic *n.* dialetica.
dialectician *n.* dialeticiste.
dialling code (US **dialing code**) *n.* prefisa.
dialogue (US **dialog**) *n.* conversa, dialogo.
dialogue box (US **dialog box**) *n.* (*software*) dialogo.
dialysis *n.* dialise.
diameter *n.* diametre.
diamond *n.* (*including cards*) diamante.
diamond-shaped *adj.* diamantin.
diaper *n.* teleta de bebe.
diaphanous *adj.* diafana.
diaphragm *n.* diaframa.
diarch *n.* (*governor*) diarca.
diarchy *n.* diarcia.
diarrhoea (US **diarrhea**) *n.* diarea.
diary *n.* (*of experiences*) jornal personal; (*planner*) ajenda. **put in one's diary** ajendi.
diaspora *n.* diaspora.
diastole *n.* (*biology*) diastole.
diastolic *adj.* diastolal.
diatom *n.* (*organism*) diatomea.
diatonic *adj.* diatonica.
diatribe *n.* arenga.
diazepam *n.* diazepam.
dice *n.* dado, dados.
dichotomous *adj.* dicotomial.
dichotomy *n.* dicotomia, duplisme.
dichromatic *adj.* dicromata.
dick *n.* (*penis*) pixa.
dickhead *n.* (*insult*) pixeta.
dicot *n.* (*botany*) dicotiledon.
dicotyledon *n.* dicotiledon.
dictaphone *n.* ditador.
dictate *v.* (*text*) dita; (*decide*) comanda, determina, prescrive.
dictation *n.* dita.
dictator *n.* autocrata, tirano.
dictatorial *adj.* autocrata.
dictatorship *n.* autocratia, tirania.
diction *n.* cualia de parla.
dictionary *n.* disionario.
did *v.* ia fa; (*indicating that a finite verb is in the past tense*) ia. **it *did* happen** (*emphatic*) vera lo ia aveni.
didactic *adj.* instruinte.
didgeridoo *n.* didjeridu.
didjeridu *n.* didjeridu.
die[1] *v.* mori.
die[2] *n.* (*cube*) dado; (*threader*) filetador fema.
dieresis (US). See *diaeresis*.
diesel *n.* gasolio.
diet *v.* & *n.* dieta.
dietary *adj.* dietal.
dieter *n.* dietor.
dietician *n.* dietiste.
differ *v.* difere.
difference *n.* difere.
different *adj.* diferente; nonusual.
differentiable manifold *n.* varia diferensiable.
differential *adj.* & *n.* diferensial.
differential calculus *n.* calculo diferensial.
differential equation *n.* egali diferensial.
differentiate *v.* distingui, separa; (*mathematics*) diferensia.
differentiation *n.* distingui, separa; (*mathematics*) diferensia.
difficult *adj.* difisil, dur. **become difficult** difisili.
difficulty *n.* (*problem*) difisil, problem; turba; (*quality*) difisilia. **with difficulty** difisil; apena.
diffidence *n.* timidia.
diffident *adj.* timida.

diffract *v.* difrata.
diffraction *n.* difrata.
diffuse *v.* difusa; rari. • *adj.* rarida, sperdeda.
diffusion *n.* difusa.
dig *v.* & *n.* escava. **dig the soil** turba la tera. **dig up** desentera; (*plant*) desplanta.
digest *v.* dijesta.
digestible *adj.* dijestable.
digestion *n.* dijesta.
digestive *adj.* dijestal.
digestive system *n.* sistem de dijesta.
digestive tract *n.* curso de dijesta.
digger *n.* escavador.
digit *n.* (*numerical*) dijito; (*finger*, *toe*) dito.
digital *adj.* dijital.
digital audio player *n.* baladador dijital.
digitalis *n.* dijitale.
digitalize *v.* dijitali.
digitize *v.* dijitali.
dignified *adj.* diniosa.
dignify *v.* dini.
dignitary *n.* ofisior alta.
dignity *n.* dinia.
digraph *n.* digram.
digress *v.* vaga.
digression *n.* vaga.
dik-dik *n.* (*antelope*) dicdic.
dike *n.* paramar.
dikkops *n.* (*bird*) burino.
dilapidated *adj.* gastada, nonreparada.
dilapidation *n.* malstate.
dilate *v.* dilata.
dilation *n.* dilata.
dilator *n.* dilatador.
dildo *n.* dildo, consolador.
dilemma *n.* dilema.
dilettante *n.* amator.
diligence *n.* asiduia.
diligent *adj.* asidua.
dill *n.* (*plant*) aneto.
dilute *v.* dilui; rari. • *adj.* diluida; rarida.
diluted *adj.* diluida; rarida.
dilution *n.* dilui.
dim *adj.* oscur. • *v.* oscuri.
dime *n.* (*coin*) desim.
dimension *n.* dimension; (*measurement*) mesura. **in three dimensions** en tre dimensiones, tridimensional.
dimensional *adj.* dimensional.
dimeter *n.* (*poetry*) dimetre.
diminish *v.* diminui.
diminution *n.* diminui.
dimple *n.* indente de jena, indente de surie.
dim sum *n.* (*food*) dimsam.
dimwit *n.* stupida.
din *n.* ruido.
dinar *n.* (*currency*) dinar.
dine[1] *v.* come.
Dine[2] *adj.* & *n.* dine.
diner *n.* comor; (*restaurant*) restorante.
dingbat *n.* strana, bizara; stupida; (*typography*) orna.
dinghy *n.* barceta.
dingo *n.* dingo.
dingy *adj.* sombre.
dining car *n.* vagon restorante.
dining room *n.* sala de come.
dinner *n.* come; come de sera.
dinner jacket *n.* jaca de sera.
dinner theatre *n.* cabare.
dinnertime *n.* ora de come.
dinosaur *n.* dinosauro.
diocese *n.* bispia.
diode *n.* diodo.
Dionysiac *adj.* dionisal.
Dionysian *adj.* dionisal.
Dionysus *n.* Dioniso.
diorama *n.* sena miniatur.
dioxide *n.* diosido.
dioxin *n.* (*substance*) diosina.
dip *v.* & *n.* sumerji.
diphtheria *n.* difteria.
diphthong *n.* (*vowel sound*) diftongo.
diplo- *pref.* (*double*) diplo-.
diploid *adj.* & *n.* diploide.
diploma *n.* diploma.
diplomacy *n.* diplomatia.
diplomat *n.* diplomata.
diplomatic *adj.* diplomata.
diplopia *n.* diplopia.
dipper *n.* (*bird*) sinclo.
dipstick *n.* basto de olio.
dire *adj.* grave.
direct *adj.* direta; (*outspoken*) franca. • *v.* dirije.
direct current *n.* corente direta.
direction *n.* dirije. **in the direction of** a, en dirije a.
directive *n.* comanda.
direct line *n.* linia direta.
directness *n.* francia.
director *n.* dirijor.
directory *n.* (*index*) catalogo; (*software*) arcivo.
dirge *n.* lamenta.
dirigible *n.* airostato dirijable.
dirk *n.* daga.
dirndl *n.* (*costume*) dirndl.
dirt *n.* susia; (*earth*) tera.
dirtiness *n.* susia.
dirty *adj.* susia; (*lewd*) lasiva. • *v.* susi.
dis- *pref.* des-.
disability *n.* descapasia.
disable *v.* descapasi; (*software*) descomuta.
disabled person *n.* descapasida.
disabuse *v.* convinse.
disaccharide *n.* disacarido.
disadvantage *n.* nonvantaje.
disadvantaged *adj.* con nonvantaje.
disagree *v.* desacorda.

disagreeable *adj.* desplasente, nonplasente, iritante.
disagreement *n.* desacorda.
disallow *v.* proibi.
disallowed *adj.* nonpermeteda, proibida.
disambiguate *v.* desambigui.
disambiguation *n.* desambigui.
disappear *v.* desapare.
disappoint *v.* delude.
disappointment *n.* delude.
disapproval *n.* desaproba.
disapprove *v.* desaproba.
disarm *v.* desarma.
disarmament *n.* desarma.
disarray *n.* desordina.
disassemble *v.* desasembla.
disassociate *v.* desasosia.
disassociation *n.* desasosia.
disaster *n.* desastre.
disastrous *adj.* desastrosa.
disavow *v.* nega.
disavowal *n.* nega.
disband *v.* desbandi, desgrupi, sperde.
disbar *v.* esclui.
disbelief *n.* noncrede.
disbelieve *v.* no crede.
disbelieving *adj.* noncredente.
disc *n.* disco.
discard *v.* dejeta, desprende.
discern *v.* deteta, persepi.
discerning *adj.* persepinte.
discharge *v.* descarga; (*liquid, etc.*) suda.
disciple *n.* disiplo.
disciplinarian *n.* disiplinor.
discipline *n.* disiplina, coreti; (*field of study*) campo. • *v.* disiplina.
disc jockey *n.* didje.
disclaim *v.* nega.
disclaimer *n.* renunsia.
disclike *adj.* discin.
disclose *v.* revela.
disclosure *n.* revela.
disco *n.* (*place*) discoteca; (*music*) disco.
discography *n.* discografia.
discolour (US **discolor**) *v.* descolori, malcolori.
discomfort *n.* descomforta.
disconcert *v.* disturba.
disconnect *v.* deslia, dejunta; (*electrically*) descomuta.
disconnection *n.* descomuta.
discontent *adj.* noncontente. • *n.* noncontentia.
discontented *adj.* noncontente.
discontiguous *adj.* noncontatante.
discontinue *v.* descontinua.
discord *n.* desacorda.
discordance *n.* desacorda.
discordancy *n.* desacorda.
discordant *adj.* desacordante.
discotheque *n.* discoteca.
discount *v.* & *n.* desconta.
discount store *n.* boteca descontante.
discourage *v.* descoraji.
discouragement *n.* descoraji.
discourse *n.* parla.
discourteous *adj.* noncortes.
discover *v.* descovre.
discoverable *adj.* descovrable, trovable.
discoverer *n.* descovror.
discovery *n.* descovre, trova.
discredit *v.* desonora.
discreet *adj.* discreta.
discrepancy *n.* devia, nonegalia.
discrete *adj.* separada.
discretion *n.* (*guardedness*) cautia; (*freedom to decide*) vole. **at your discretion** a tua vole.
discretionary *adj.* elejable.
discriminate *v.* distingui, separa; es prejudosa.
discriminating *adj.* distinguinte, elejente.
discrimination *n.* distingui, separa.
disc-shaped *adj.* discin.
discursive *adj.* vagante.
discus *n.* disco.
discuss *v.* discute.
discussion *n.* discute. **up for discussion** discutable.
disdain *v.* & *n.* despeta.
disdainful *adj.* despetosa.
disease *n.* maladia.
disembark *v.* desembarca.
disembodied *adj.* descorpida, sin corpo.
disembowel *v.* desventri.
disenamour (US **disenamor**) *v.* desenama.
disenchant *v.* desencanta.
disenchantment *n.* desencanta.
disenfranchise *v.* proibi de vota.
disengage *v.* (*gear, enemy*) desengrana.
disengagement *n.* desengrana.
disentangle *v.* desmarania.
disfigure *v.* malformi; manxa.
disgorge *v.* vomiti.
disgrace *v.* & *n.* desonora.
disgraceful *adj.* desonorosa.
disguise *v.* & *n.* desembla. • *adj.* desemblante. **be in disguise** desembla. **in disguise** desemblante.
disgust *v.* & *n.* repulsa.
disgusting *adj.* repulsante, ofendente.
dish *n.* plato. **dish of the day** plato de la dia.
disharmony *n.* desarmonia.
dishcloth *n.* teleta de lava.
dish cover *n.* covreplato.
dishearten *v.* descoraji.
dishevel *v.* desordina, despeteni.

dishonest *adj.* nononesta.
dishonesty *n.* nononestia.
dishonour (US **dishonor**) *v.* & *n.* desonora.
dishonourable (US **dishonorable**) *adj.* desonorosa.
dishonoured (US **dishonored**) *adj.* desonorada.
dishpan *n.* bol de lava.
dishrag *n.* teleta de lava.
dishwasher *n.* lavaplato.
dishwashing liquid *n.* deterjente de platos.
disillusion *v.* desilude.
disillusionment *n.* desilude.
disincentive *n.* desmotiva.
disinfect *v.* desinfeta.
disinfectant *adj.* & *n.* desinfetante.
disingenuous *adj.* nonsinsera.
disinherit *v.* deserita.
disintegratable *adj.* desintegrable.
disintegrate *v.* desintegra.
disintegration *n.* desintegra.
disinter *v.* desentera.
disinterest *v.* & *n.* desinteresa.
disjointed *adj.* nonliada.
disk *n.* disco.
disk drive *n.* lejedisco.
dislike *v.* no gusta. • *n.* nongusta; repulsa; (*deep*) antipatia.
dislocate *v.* desloca.
dislocation *n.* desloca.
dislodge *v.* desfisa.
disloyal *adj.* nonfidosa.
disloyalty *n.* nonfida.
dismal *adj.* sombre.
dismantle *v.* desasembla.
dismay *n.* angusa.
dismember *v.* desmembri.
dismiss *v.* (*send away*) envia a via; (*from consideration*) refusa; (*from employment*) desemplea.
dismissal *n.* desemplea.
dismissive *adj.* despetosa.
dismount *v.* desmonta.
disobedience *n.* desobedi.
disobedient *adj.* desobedinte.
disobey *v.* desobedi.
disorder *n.* desordina; (*medical*) disturba, sindrom.
disorderly *adj.* desordinada.
disorganization *n.* desorganiza.
disorganize *v.* desorganiza.
disorganized *adj.* desorganizada, nonordinada.
disorient *v.* desorienta.
disorientate *v.* desorienta.
disorientation *n.* desorienta.
disparage *v.* desvalua.
disparate *adj.* diferente.
disparity *n.* nonegalia.
dispassionate *adj.* nonpasionosa.
dispatch *v.* envia.
dispel *v.* desapare.
dispensable *adj.* nonesesada.
dispensary *n.* (*pharmacy*) farmasia; (*clinic*) clinica.
dispensation *n.* esenta.
dispense *v.* distribui, furni. **dispense with** desprende.
dispenser *n.* (*machine*) furnador.
dispersal *n.* sperde.
disperse *v.* sperde.
dispirit *v.* despiriti.
displace *v.* desloca.
displacement *n.* desloca.
display *v.* mostra.
display case *n.* caxa de esibi.
display window *n.* fenetra de esibi.
displease *v.* desplase.
displeasure *n.* desplase.
disposable *adj.* dejetable, desprendable.
disposal *n.* dejeta, desprende; (*sale*) vende. **have at one's disposal** dispone.
dispose *v.* (*someone to*) disposa. **dispose of** dejeta, desprende.
disposition *n.* disposa.
dispossess *v.* priva.
disproof *n.* contrademostra.
disproportionate *adj.* nonproportial.
disprove *v.* contrademostra.
dispute *v.* & *n.* disputa.
disqualification *n.* descuali.
disqualify *v.* descuali, restrinje.
disregard *v.* iniora.
disrepair *n.* malstate. **in disrepair** nonreparada.
disreputable *adj.* malreputada.
disrepute *n.* malreputa.
disrespect *v.* & *n.* desrespeta.
disrespectful *adj.* desrespetosa.
disrobe *v.* desvesti.
disrupt *v.* disturba.
disruption *n.* disturba.
dissatisfaction *n.* nonsasia.
dissatisfy *v.* nonsasia.
dissect *v.* sesioni; analise.
dissection *n.* sesioni; analise.
dissemble *v.* desembla.
disseminate *v.* difusa.
dissemination *n.* difusa.
dissent *v.* disenti.
dissenter *n.* disentor.
dissention *n.* disenti.
dissertation *n.* tese.
dissident *adj.* oposante.
dissimilar *adj.* nonsimil.
dissipate *v.* disipa.
dissipator *n.* disipador.
dissociate *v.* desasosia.
dissociation *n.* desasosia.

dissociative *adj.* desasosiante.
dissolute *adj.* lasiva.
dissolution *n.* disolve.
dissolvable *adj.* disolvable.
dissolve *v.* disolve.
dissonance *n.* desacorda.
dissonant *adj.* desacordante.
dissuade *v.* desconvinse.
distal *adj.* periferial, distante.
distance *n.* distantia. • *v.* distanti. **from a distance** (*remote*) a distantia. **in the distance** distante.
distant *adj.* distante; (*unfriendly*) nonamin, nonsosial. **grow distant** distanti. **in the distant future** en la futur distante. **in the distant past** en la pasada distante.
distasteful *adj.* desplasente, ofendente, repulsante.
distemper *n.* (*disease*) morva.
distend *v.* infla.
distension *n.* infla.
distil (US **distill**) *v.* distila.
distillate *n.* distilada.
distillation *n.* distila.
distillery *n.* distileria.
distinct *adj.* separada, distinguida, distinguable.
distinction *n.* distingui.
distinctive *adj.* distinguida.
distinguish *v.* distingui.
distinguishable *adj.* distinguable.
distinguishing feature *n.* distinguinte.
distort *v.* contorse.
distortion *n.* contorse.
distract *v.* distrae.
distraction *n.* distrae.
distraught *adj.* ajitada, turbada.
distress *v.* & *n.* angusa, turba.
distribute *v.* distribui, comparti.
distribution *n.* distribui.
distributor *n.* (*person*) distribuor; (*device*) distribuador.
district *n.* distrito. • *adj.* distrital. • *v.* distriti.
distrust *v.* desfida.
disturb *v.* (*minor*) disturba; (*major*) turba.
disturbable *adj.* disturbable; turbable.
disturbance *n.* disturba.
disulphide (US **disulfide**) *n.* (*chemistry*) disulfido.
disunion *n.* desuni.
disunite *v.* desuni.
disuse *v.* desusa. • *n.* nonusa.
ditch *n.* foso, canal.
ditransitive *adj.* (*grammar*) ditransitiva.
ditto *interj.* repete.
ditto mark *n.* sinia de repete.
ditty *n.* canteta.
diuresis *n.* (*medical*) diurese.
diuretic *n.* diuresica.
diurnal *adj.* (*daytime*) diurna; (*once a day*) dial.
diva *n.* diva.
divalent *adj.* divalente; (*grammar*) ditransitiva.
divan *n.* sofa sin dorso.
dive *v.* tufa. • *n.* tufa.
diver *n.* (*sport*) tufor; (*frogman*) sumerjor; (*bird*) gavia.
diverge *v.* diverje.
divergence *n.* diverje.
divergent *adj.* diverjente.
diverse *adj.* diversa, variosa.
diversify *v.* diversi.
diversion *n.* diverti.
diversity *n.* diversia.
divert *v.* (*diverge*) diverje; (*entertain*) diverti.
diverticulitis *n.* (*medical*) diverticulite.
diverticulosis *n.* (*medical*) diverticulose.
diverticulum *n.* (*anatomy*, *medical*) diverticulo.
divest *v.* priva.
divide *v.* divide. **divide into pairs** divide a duples.
divided *adj.* divideda. **divided by** entre, divideda entre.
dividend *n.* dividendo.
divination *n.* divina ritual.
divine *adj.* divin, de dio.
diving board *n.* trampolin de tufa.
divisible *adj.* dividable.
division *n.* (*action*, *part*) divide; (*part*) parte.
division sign *n.* sinia de divide.
divisive *adj.* dividente.
divisor *n.* dividente.
divorce *v.* & *n.* divorsa.
divorcee *n.* divorsada.
divot *n.* sespeta.
divulge *v.* revela, esposa.
Diwali *n.* divali.
dixieland *n.* jaz tradisional.
DIY *n.* bricola.
dizziness *n.* vertigo.
dizzy *adj.* mareada, vertigosa. **feel dizzy** marea. **make dizzy** marea.
dizzying *adj.* mareante.
DJ *n.* didje.
djembe *n.* (*drum*) djembe.
Djibouti *adj.* djibuti. • *n.* (*person*) djibuti; (*country*) Djibuti.
Djiboutian *adj.* & *n.* (*person*) djibuti.
djinn *n.* djini.
DNA *abbr.* adn (*asida desosiribonucleal*).
do[1] *v.* fa; reali. **do again** refa. **do away with** aboli. **do badly** malfa. **do good** fa bon. **do not** (*indicating that a verb is negative*) no. **do not run** no core. **do over** refa; (*beat up*) bate. **do well** fa bon. **do without** maneja sin. **do wrong** fa mal. **do you?** (*question tag, typically implying some uncertainty*) si? **I *do* want to help** (*emphatic*) vera me

desira aida. **it's to do with** lo es un caso de, lo pertine a.
do[2] *n.* (*musical note*) do.
doable *adj.* realable.
Doberman (US **Dobermann**) *n.* (*dog*) doberman.
dobro *n.* (*guitar*) dobro.
docent *n.* gidor, instruor.
docile *adj.* pasosa, sedente.
dock *n.* doca; (*in court*) lojia de acusada. • *v.* doci; (*equipment*) onci.
docker *n.* docor.
docket *n.* (*label*) eticeta; (*to-do list*) ajenda.
dock worker *n.* docor.
doctor *n.* (*medical*) mediciste; (*academic*) dotor. **spin doctor** (*gilder of facts*) doror de fatos.
doctoral *adj.* dotoral.
doctorate *n.* dotoral, diploma dotoral.
doctor fish *n.* tinca.
doctrine *n.* crede, prinsipe.
document *n.* documento, testo; (*legal*) contrata. • *v.* documenti.
documentary *n.* filma atestante.
documentation *n.* documentos, testos; (*action*) documenti.
document wallet *n.* arcivo.
dodge *v.* evita.
dodgem *n.* auto de xoca.
dodgy *adj.* nononesta.
dodo *n.* (*bird*) dodo.
doe *n.* servo fema.
doer *n.* faor.
doff *v.* desapone.
dog *n.* can; (*of gun*) martel.
dogberryism *n.* parola erante.
dogfight *n.* combate airal.
dogged *adj.* ostinosa.
doggerel *n.* mal poesia.
doggie *n.* caneta.
doghouse *n.* caneria, casa de can.
doglike *adj.* canin.
dogma *n.* dogma.
dogmatic *adj.* dogmosa.
dogmatism *n.* dogmisme.
dog pound *n.* ensirca de canes.
dog run *n.* ensirca de canes.
dogsled *n.* treno de canes.
dog sleigh *n.* treno de canes.
dogwood *n.* (*plant, wood*) corneo.
doily *n.* paragota de dentela.
do-it-yourself *n.* bricola.
dole *n.* aida sosial.
dolicho- *pref.* (*long*) dolico-.
doline *n.* dolina.
doll *n.* pupa.
dollar *n.* dolar.
dollar sign *n.* sinia de dolar.
dollop *n.* goton.
dolly *n.* plataforma rolante.
dolmen *n.* (*tomb*) dolmen.
dolomite *n.* (*mineral*) dolomita.
dolphin *n.* delfin.
dolphinfish *n.* mahimahi.
domain *n.* domina.
dome *n.* cupola.
domelike *adj.* cupolin.
dome-shaped *adj.* cupolin.
domestic *adj.* domada.
domestic abuse *n.* violentia familial.
domesticate *v.* doma.
domesticated silkworm *n.* bombis de morero.
domestic chores *n.* taxes de casa.
domestic intelligence agency *n.* departe de securia interna.
domestic policy *n.* politica interna.
domestic violence *n.* violentia familial.
domestic worker *n.* servor de casa.
domicile *n.* abiteria.
dominant *adj.* dominante.
dominate *v.* domina.
domination *n.* domina.
dominator *n.* dominor.
dominatrix *n.* dominor.
domineer *v.* domina.
Dominica *n.* Dominica.
Dominican *adj.* & *n.* (*of Dominica, the Dominican Republic, the monastic order*) dominican.
Dominican Republic *n.* Republica Dominican.
dominion *n.* domina, rena.
domino *n.* domino.
domino effect *n.* reata en cadena.
don[1] *n.* (*university teacher*) profesor.
don[2] *v.* (*put on*) apone.
donate *v.* dona.
donation *n.* (*action*) dona; (*gift*) donada.
donator *n.* donor.
done *adj.* fada.
dongle *n.* (*device*) dongle.
donkey *n.* asino.
donkey driver *n.* asinor.
donkey rider *n.* asinor.
donor *n.* donor.
don't *v.* (*indicating that a verb is negative*) no. **don't laugh** no rie. **don't mention it** no problem. **don't you?** (*question tag, typically expecting the answer yes*) no?
donut *n.* donut.
doobry *n.* aparateta.
doodad *n.* aparateta.
doodle *v.* & *n.* desinieta.
doohickey *n.* aparateta.
doom *v.* condena. • *n.* ruina.
doomsayer *n.* sperdeteme.
doomsday *n.* apocalise.
door *n.* porte. **out of doors** estra casa.
doorbell *n.* campaneta.

door handle *n.* manico de porte.
doorkeeper *n.* gardaporte.
doorknob *n.* manico de porte.
door knocker *n.* bateporte.
doormat *n.* tapeto de porte.
doorphone *n.* comunicador de porte, telefon de porte.
doorpost *n.* gama de porte, palo de porte.
doorstep *n.* grado de porte.
doorstop *n.* paraporte.
doorway *n.* arco de porte.
do-over *n.* refa.
dopamine *n.* dopamina.
dope *v.* drogi.
dopey *adj.* aturdida, stupida.
doppelgänger *n.* fantasma jemelin.
Doppler effect *n.* efeto de Doppler.
dorado *n.* (*fish*) dorado. **Dorado** (*constellation*) la Dorado.
dormant *adj.* dorminte, nonativa.
dormer *n.* (*window*) lucarna.
dormitory *n.* (*sleeping quarters*) dormeria; (*hall of residence*) abitada de studiantes.
dormouse *n.* liron.
dorsal *adj.* dorsal.
dorsal area *n.* dorso.
dorsal fin *n.* pina dorsal.
dose *v.* & *n.* dosa.
dossier *n.* folio.
dot *n.* punto.
dotage *n.* senese.
dot-dot-dot *n.* trepunto.
dote *v.* regala.
dotted *adj.* puntosa. **dotted about** asi e ala, a sirca.
dotterel *n.* caradrio.
dotty *adj.* fol, strana.
double *adj.* duple; (*for two people*) per du. • *n.* duple; (*lookalike*) jemelin, sustitua. • *v.* dupli.
double bass *n.* contrabaso.
double bed *n.* leto per du.
double boiler *n.* baniomaria.
double click *v.* & *n.* (*mouse*) clica duple.
double room *n.* sala per du.
double vision *n.* diplopia.
double whole note *n.* tono duple.
doubt *v.* & *n.* duta.
doubtable *adj.* dutable.
doubtful *adj.* (*person*) dutante, dutosa; (*information*) dutada.
doubting *adj.* dutante, dutosa.
doubtless *adv.* sin duta.
dough *n.* pasta.
doughnut *n.* donut.
Douglas fir *n.* tsuga de Douglas.
dour *adj.* sombre.
douroucouli *n.* (*monkey*) aoto.
dove *n.* pijon.
dovecot *n.* pijoneria.
dovecote *n.* pijoneria.
dovekie *n.* (*bird*) alco.
dovetail *v.* entretexe.
dowdy *adj.* nonmodosa.
dowel *n.* cavil.
down[1] *adv.* a basa, a su, a vale, de supra. • *prep.* a basa de, desendente; (*following or in parallel with*) longo. • *adj.* depresada. **down to** (*until*) asta. **down to earth** pratical. **down with X** aboli X, basi X. **go down** desende; (*oral sex*) fa la seso bocal, leca la cuno, suca la pixa.
down[2] *n.* (*fluff*) peluxeta.
downbeat *adj.* sombre, pesimiste. • *n.* (*music*) pulsa asentuada.
downcast *adj.* sombre.
downfall *n.* defeta, ruina.
downgrade *v.* redui la grado de. • *n.* redui de grado.
downhill *adv.* a vale.
downlink *v.* & *n.* sulia.
download *v.* & *n.* descarga.
downplay *v.* minimi.
downpour *n.* pluvon.
down quark *n.* cuarc desendente.
downriver *adv.* con la flue.
downshift *n.* redui de engrana.
downsize *v.* redui empleadas.
downsizing *n.* redui de empleadas.
Down's syndrome *n.* sindrom de Down.
downstairs *adv.* a su. **from downstairs** de su.
downstate *adj.* sude.
downstream *adv.* a vale, con la corente, con la flue.
downstroke *n.* desendente.
Down syndrome *n.* sindrom de Down.
downtown *n.* sentro de site.
downtrodden *adj.* misera.
downturn *n.* declina.
downward *adj.* a basa, a su, a vale, de supra.
downwards *adv.* a basa, a su, a vale, de supra.
downwind *adj.* suventa, con la venta.
downy *adj.* peluxetin.
dowry *n.* dote.
dox *n.* (*exposure of information*) dox. • *v.* doxi.
doxology *n.* formula de loda.
doyen *n.* decano.
doyenne *n.* decano.
doze *v.* & *n.* dormeta.
dozen *n.* desduple. **dozens** desduples; (*loosely*) deses.
Dr *abbr.* Dr.
drab *adj.* sombre.
drachma *n.* (*currency*) dracma.
Draco *n.* (*constellation*) la Dragon.
draconian *adj.* sever.

draft *n.* testo ru; (*military*) clama a servi militar. • *v.* clama. See also *draught.*
draft animal (US). See *draught animal.*
draftee *n.* clamada, enscriveda.
draftsman (US). See *draughtsman.*
drafty (US). See *draughty.*
drag *v.* tira. **drag and drop** (*software*) lisca e pone. **drag one's feet** tira sua pedes. **in drag** transvestida.
dragnet *n.* rede de draga.
dragon *n.* dragon.
dragonfly *n.* libela.
drag race *n.* corsa de dragsteres.
dragster *n.* (*car*) dragster.
drain *v.* drena. • *n.* cloaca.
drainage *n.* drena.
drainpipe *n.* tubo de drena.
drama *n.* drama; presenta teatral.
dramatic *adj.* dramal, dramosa.
dramatical *adj.* dramosa.
dramatist *n.* dramiste.
dramatization *n.* drami.
dramatize *v.* drami.
dramaturgy *n.* dramaturjia.
drape *v.* drape. • *n.* cortina.
drapery *n.* cortinas.
drastic *adj.* estrema, radisal.
draught (US **draft**) *n.* flueta de aira; (*of ship*) profondia.
draught animal (US **draft animal**) *n.* bestia de tira.
draughts *n.* (*game*) damas.
draughtsman *n.* desinior.
draughty *adj.* con aira fluetante, ventetosa.
Dravidian *adj.* dravidian.
draw *v.* desinia; (*pull*) tira; (*attention*) atrae. • *n.* (*match result*) egal. **draw attention to** fa ce on persepi. **draw lots** estrae fortunas. **draw the line** pone un limita.
drawback *n.* problem, nonvantaje.
drawbridge *n.* ponte levable.
drawer *n.* caxeta.
drawing *n.* desinia, imaje.
drawing pin *n.* spino puiable.
drawing room *n.* salon.
drawl *v.* parla pigra.
drawn *adj.* (*match*) egal, sin ganior.
drawstring *n.* cordeta fronsinte.
dread *v.* teme, preteme, ansi. • *n.* teme, preteme, ansia.
dreadful *adj.* asustante.
dreadlocks *n.* capeles rastafari.
dreadnought *n.* (*warship*) corasida.
dream *v.* & *n.* sonia. **dream of** aspira. **dream up** imajina.
dreamer *n.* sonior, fantasior.
dreamlike *adj.* sonin.
dream world *n.* mundo de sonia.
dreamy *adj.* soniosa.
dreariness *n.* sombria.
dreary *adj.* sombre.
dredge *v.* draga.
dredger *n.* dragador.
dregs *n.* restas, restantes.
dreidel *n.* jireta ivri.
drench *v.* (*soak*) empapa; (*deworm*) desvermi, deselminti. • *n.* (*medicine*) dosa; antielmintal.
dress *n.* (*gown*) roba; (*clothing*) vestes. • *v.* (*person*, *wound*) vesti; (*in uniform*) uniformi. **little black dress** roba negra peti.
dressage *n.* doma esibal.
dresser *n.* comoda.
dressing *n.* (*sauce*) salsa.
dressing gown *n.* roba de bani.
dressing room *n.* sala de vesti, vesteria.
dress shirt *n.* camisa de sera.
dressy *adj.* formal, ordinada.
dribble *v.* & *n.* (*drool*) bava; (*trickle*) flueta; (*ball*) dribla.
dried meat *n.* carne secida.
dried plum *n.* pruna seca.
drier *n.* secador.
drift *v.* vaga.
drifter *n.* vagor.
driftwood *n.* lenio flotante.
drill *v.* fora; (*train*) eserse. • *n.* (*tool*) forador; (*training*) eserse.
drill bit *n.* broca, punto de forador.
drill press *n.* forador colonin.
drink *v.* bevi. • *n.* bevida.
drinkable *adj.* bevable.
drinking establishment *n.* beveria.
drinking straw *n.* palieta.
drinks mat *n.* paragota.
drip *v.* & *n.* gota.
drive *v.* (*vehicle*) gida; (*propel*) xuta. • *n.* viaja, turi; (*gear*) engrana de avansa; (*driveway*) stradeta de entra. **drive around** turi. **drive away** forsa a via. **drive mad** dementi. **take a drive** turi.
drivel *n.* asurda, babela.
driver *n.* (*driver*) gidor, motoriste; (*golf club*) xutador xef; (*software*) controlador.
driveway *n.* stradeta de entra.
driving *n.* motorisme.
drizzle *v.* & *n.* pluveta.
dromedary *n.* dromedario.
drone *v.* zumbi. • *n.* zumbi; (*bee*) abea mas; (*aircraft*) avion sin pilote, (*portable*) avioneta. **drone on** parla monotonosa.
drongo *n.* (*bird*) drongo.
drool *v.* & *n.* bava.
droop *v.* pende.
droopy *adj.* pendente.
drop *v.* cade; (*deliberately*) lasa ce un cosa cade. • *n.* (*liquid*) gota. **drop anchor** cade la ancor. **drop out** abandona.
drop-down list *n.* lista cadente.

drop-down menu *n.* menu cadente.
dropkick *v.* (*martial arts*) cade e pedi, pedi cadente.
droplet *n.* goteta.
dropout *n.* abandonor.
drought *n.* secia.
drove *n.* manada.
drover *n.* manador.
drown *v.* afoca, mori par inonda; (*flood*) inonda.
drowning *n.* afoca, mori par inonda.
drowsiness *n.* dormosia.
drowsy *adj.* dormosa.
drudge *n.* laboror nonsesante.
drudgery *n.* labora sin sesa.
drug *n.* droga. • *v.* drogi.
drug abuse *n.* malusa de drogas.
drug addict *n.* drogamanica. **addicted to drugs** drogamanica.
drug addiction *n.* drogamania.
drug dealer *n.* vendor de drogas.
druggist *n.* farmasiste.
drug habit *n.* drogamania.
drug pusher *n.* vendor de drogas.
drug seller *n.* vendor de drogas.
drugstore *n.* farmasia.
druid *n.* druida.
drum *n.* tambur. • *v.* tamburi.
drumbeat *n.* ritmo de tambur.
drum kit *n.* colie de tambures.
drumroll *n.* rola de tambur.
drumstick *n.* basto de tambur.
drunk *adj.* & *n.* enebriada.
drunkard *n.* enebriada.
drunken *adj.* enebriada.
drunkenness *n.* enebria.
drupe *n.* (*botany*) drupa.
Druze *adj.* & *n.* (*Islam*) durzi.
dry *adj.* seca. • *v.* seci.
dryad *n.* nimfa de bosce.
dryer *n.* secador.
dryness *n.* secia.
dry rot *n.* fungo de lenio.
dry transfer *n.* decal.
drywall *n.* plance de jeso.
dual *adj.* duple; (*grammar*) dual.
dual-boot *v.* (*software*) inisia duple.
dual-format *adj.* de forma duple.
dualism *n.* duplisme.
dualist *n.* dupliste.
duality *n.* duplia, dualia, duplisme.
dub *v.* (*audio*) dupli.
dubious *adj.* dutada.
dubitable *adj.* dutable.
Dublin Bay prawn *n.* omareta.
dubnium *n.* (*element*) dubnio.
ducal *adj.* duxal.
ducat *n.* (*coin*) ducat.
duchess *n.* duxesa.
duchy *n.* duxia. **Duchy of Brittany** Bres.
duck[1] *n.* (*bird*) pato.
duck[2] *v.* (*stoop*) acrupi; (*submerge*) sumerji.
ducking stool *n.* seja sumerjinte.
duckling *n.* pateta.
duct *n.* canal; (*anatomy*) duto.
ductile *adj.* formable.
dud *n.* defetosa.
due *adj.* espetada. **be due** (*deserve*) merita. **due to** par causa de. **in due course** a tempo conveninte.
duel *n.* duel.
duet *n.* duple.
duettist *n.* dupliste.
duffel *n.* dufel.
duffel bag *n.* saco silindre.
duffel coat *n.* jacon de dufel.
dugong *n.* (*animal*) dugong.
dugout *n.* (*trench*) buncer; (*canoe*) canoa escavada.
du jour *adj.* de la dia; de la momento.
duke *n.* duxe.
dulcimer *n.* dulsimer.
dull *adj.* (*boring*) noiante, monotonosa; (*dark*) sombre; (*blunt*) nonagu. • *v.* desagi.
dullard *n.* stupida.
dullness *n.* nonagia.
dulset *adj.* dulse.
duly *adv.* conveninte.
dumb *adj.* (*mute*) muda; (*idiotic*) stupida.
dumbbell *n.* halter.
dumbness *n.* mudia.
dumb waiter *n.* asendeplato.
dummy *adj.* pupetin. • *n.* (*for baby*) tetin; (*idiot*) stupida.
dump *v.* dejeta. • *n.* (*for rubbish*) dejeteria; (*wretched place*) loca misera.
dumping *n.* (*economic*) inonda de mercato.
dumping ground *n.* dejeteria.
dumpling *n.* bal de pasta.
dumpster *n.* portadetrito.
dunce *n.* stupida.
dune *n.* duna.
dung *n.* fece.
dungaree *n.* (*fabric*) calico.
dungarees *n.* (*garment*) salopeta.
dung beetle *n.* scarabe santa.
dungeon *n.* prison suteran.
dunghill *n.* monton de fece.
dunk *v.* & *n.* sumerji, tufa.
dunk tank *n.* seja sumerjinte.
duodenum *n.* (*anatomy*) duodeno.
dupe *n.* fol.
duplex *adj.* duple.
duplicate *v.* dupli.
duplication *n.* dupli.
duplicitous *adj.* enganosa.
duplicity *n.* engana.
dura- *pref.* (*hard*) dura-.

durability *n.* dura.
durable *adj.* durante.
dura mater *n.* (*anatomy*) duramadre.
duramen *n.* lenio interna.
duration *n.* longia.
duress *n.* menasa.
during *prep.* en; (*throughout*) tra.
Dushanbe *n.* Duxanbe.
dusk *n.* lus final, noti.
dusky *adj.* oscur.
dust *n.* polvo. • *v.* (*remove dust*) despolvi; (*cover with dust*) covre con polvo.
dustbin *n.* baldon.
duster *n.* trapo de polvo.
dustheap *n.* dejeteria.
dusting *n.* (*of snow*) neveta.
dust jacket *n.* covrelibro.
dustman *n.* dejetor.
dustpan *n.* padela de polvo.
dustrag *n.* trapo de polvo.
dust-up *n.* disputa.
dusty *adj.* polvosa.
Dutch *adj.* & *n.* nederlandes.
Dutch oven *n.* casolon de fero.
dutiful *adj.* consiensosa.
duty *n.* debe, obliga; (*tax*) tarifa, imposta de ben.
duty-free shop *n.* boteca sin imposta.
duty-free store *n.* boteca sin imposta.
duvet *n.* covreleto.
DVD *n.* dvd.
DVD burner *n.* scrivador de dvd, scrivador de disco.
DVD drive *n.* discador.
DVD player *n.* discador, videador.
DVD recorder *n.* discador.
DVD writer *n.* scrivador de dvd, scrivador de disco.
dwarf *adj.* & *n.* (*including in mythology*) nana.
dwarfed *adj.* ombrida, suprapasada.
dwarfism *n.* nanisme.
dwell *v.* abita.
dwelling *n.* (*place*) abiteria; (*state*) abita.
dwindle *v.* diminui.
dyad *n.* duple.
dyarchy *n.* diarcia.
dye *v.* tinje. • *n.* tinjente.
dyke *n.* paramar.
dynamic *n.* dinamica. • *adj.* dinamical.
dynamical *adj.* dinamical.
dynamical system *n.* sistem dinamical.
dynamics *n.* dinamica.
dynamism *n.* dinamicisme.
dynamite *n.* dinamite.
dynamiter *n.* dinamitor.
dynamo *n.* dinamo.
dynamometer *n.* dinamometre.
dynastic *adj.* dinastial.
dynasty *n.* dinastia.
dyne *n.* (*unit of force*) dine.
dys- *pref.* (*bad, abnormal*) dis-.
dyscalculia *n.* discalculia.
dyscalculic *adj.* discalculica.
dysentery *n.* disenteria.
dysfunctional *adj.* malfunsionante.
dyslexia *n.* dislexia.
dyslexic *adj.* dislexica.
dyspepsia *n.* dispepsia.
dyspepsy *n.* dispepsia.
dyspeptic *adj.* dispepsica.
dysphagia *n.* (*medical*) disfajia.
dysphasia *n.* (*medical*) disfasia.
dysphoria *n.* (*medical*) disforia.
dysplasia *n.* (*medical*) displasia.
dyspnoea (US **dyspnea**) *n.* (*medical*) dispnea.
dysprosium *n.* (*medical*) disprosio.
dystonia *n.* (*medical*) distonia.
dystopia *n.* contrautopia.
dystopian *adj.* contrautopial.
dystrophic *adj.* distrofica.
dystrophy *n.* (*medical*) distrofia.
dysuria *n.* (*medical*) disuria.

E

e- *pref.* (*electronic*) e-.
each *det.* & *pron.* cada. **each in turn** la un pos la otra. **each other** la un la otra, lunlotra, mutua. **each time** a cada ves.
eager *adj.* zelosa.
eagle *n.* agila; (*golf*) du su la norma.
eagle-eyed *adj.* agilin.
eaglet *n.* agileta.
ear *n.* orea; (*corn*) spiga.
earache *n.* dole de orea.
earbuds *n.* escutador.
eardrum *n.* (*anatomy*) timpan.
eared seal *n.* otario.
earful *n.* pleniorea.
earl *n.* conte.
earldom *n.* contia.
earlier *adj.* plu temprana, pasada. • *adv.* a ante. **earlier than** ante. **two days earlier** a du dias a ante.
earliness *n.* temprania.
earlobe *n.* lobe de orea.
early *adj.* temprana; prima; primitiva. **early in** a la comensa de. **in early June** en la temprana de junio.
earmark *n.* marca de orea. • *v.* asinia, indica.
earmuffs *n.* covreorea.
earn *v.* gania.
earner *n.* fonte de revenu.
earnest *adj.* seria.
earnings *n.* revenu.
earphone *n.* escutador.
earphones *n.* escutador.
earpiece *n.* escutador.
earplug *n.* tapo de orea.
earring *n.* orealeta.
earshot, within *adv.* en la campo de oia.
earsplitting *adj.* rompente la timpanes.
earth *n.* tera; (*soil*) solo de tera; (*planet*) Tera. • *v.* (*an electrical device*) lia a tera. **down to earth** pratical. **what on earth?** cual de mundo?
earthbound *adj.* restrinjeda a tera.
Earth Day *n.* festa de la Tera.
earthen *adj.* de tera.
earthenware *n.* losa. • *adj.* de losa.
earthling *n.* teran.
earthly *adj.* teral.
earthquake *n.* trematera.
earthwork *n.* muron de tera.
earthworm *n.* verme de tera.
earthy *adj.* solosa, terosa.
earwax *n.* serumen.
earwig *n.* dermatero.
earworm *n.* verme de orea.
ease *n.* fasilia. • *v.* fasili.
easel *n.* cavaleta.
easier *adj.* plu fasil. **become easier** fasili.
easily *adv.* fasil; (*by far*) clar.
easily damaged *adj.* frajil.
easily learned *adj.* fasil aprendable.
easiness *n.* fasilia.
east *adj.* & *n.* este. **to the east of** a este de.
East Asia *n.* Asia este.
East China Sea *n.* Mar Xina Este.
Easter *n.* pascua. • *adj.* pascual.
Easter bread *n.* pan pascual.
Easter Island *n.* Isola Pascua, Rapanui.
eastern *adj.* este.
east-northeast *adj.* este-norde-este.
East Siberian Sea *n.* Mar Sibir Este.
east-southeast *adj.* este-sude-este.
East Timor *n.* Timor Este.
eastward *adj.* a este.
eastwards *adv.* a este.
easy *adj.* fasil. **easy to learn** fasil aprendable. **take it easy** destensa, reposa.
easygoing *adj.* casual; pasiente, tolerante.
eat *v.* come. **eat out** come en un restorante; (*cunnilingus*) leca la cuno de.
eater *n.* comor.
eatery *n.* comeria.
eating utensils *n.* utiles de come.
eaves *n.* estende de teto.
eavesdrop *v.* escuta secreta, oia secreta.
ebb *n.* (*tide*) esflue.
ebonite *n.* (*rubber*) ebonita.
ebony *n.* ebano.
ebullient *adj.* joiosa.
eccentric *adj.* noncomun, strana; (*orbit*) nonsirculo.
eccentricity *n.* (*quality*) noncomunia, strania; (*quirk*) strana.
ecchymosis *n.* (*medical*) ecimose.
ecclesiastic *adj.* eglesal.
ecdysozoa *n.* (*organisms*) ecdisozones.
ecdysozoon *n.* (*organism*) ecdisozon.
ECG *abbr.* ecg.
ECG scan *n.* eletrocardiogram.
ECG scanner *n.* eletrocardiograf.
echelon *n.* grado.
echidna *n.* ecidna.
echinoderm *n.* (*organism*) ecinodermato.
echo *n.* eco, resona. • *v.* fa un eco, resona, repete.
echo chamber *n.* cambra de resona.
echogram *n.* ecogram.
echograph *n.* ecograf. • *v.* ecografi.
echography *n.* ecografia.
echoic *adj.* ecosa.

echolalia *n.* (*medical*) ecolalia.
echolocate *v.* ecoloca.
echolocation *n.* ecoloca.
éclair *n.* (*cake*) ecler.
eclampsia *n.* (*medical*) eclampsia.
eclectic *adj.* ecletica.
eclecticism *n.* ecleticisme.
eclipse *n.* eclis. • *v.* eclisi.
ecliptic *n.* eclisal. • *adj.* eclisal.
eco- *pref.* eco-.
eco-friendly *adj.* ecolojial sana.
ecological *adj.* ecolojial.
ecologist *n.* ecolojiste.
ecology *n.* ecolojia.
e-commerce *n.* ecomersia.
economic *adj.* economial.
economical *adj.* frugal.
economics *n.* economia.
economist *n.* economiste.
economize *v.* es frugal.
economy *n.* economia.
economy class *n.* clase de turiste.
ecoside *n.* ecoside. **commit ecocide** ecoside.
ecosystem *n.* ecosistem.
ecotone *n.* (*biology*) ecotono.
ecotourism *n.* ecoturisme.
ecstasy *n.* estasia.
ecstatic *adj.* estasiante. **be ecstatic** estasia.
ecto- *pref.* (*outside*) eto-.
ectoderm *n.* (*anatomy*) ectoderma.
-ectomy *suff.* (*surgery*) -ectomia.
ectopia *n.* (*medical*) ectopia.
ectopic *adj.* ectopica.
ectoplasm *n.* ectoplasma.
Ecuador *n.* Ecuador.
Ecuadoran *adj.* & *n.* ecuadoran.
Ecuatoginean *adj.* & *n.* ecuatoginean.
Ecuatorial Guinean *adj.* & *n.* ecuatoginean.
ecumenical *adj.* nonramal.
eczema *n.* (*medical*) eczema.
-ed *suff.* (*indicating that a finite verb is in the past tense*) ia; (*passive participle*) -da.
eddy *n.* vortiseta.
edema (US). See *oedema*.
Eden *n.* Eden.
edge *n.* borda.
edgy *adj.* iritable.
edible *adj.* comable.
edible currant *n.* grosela.
edict *n.* proclama.
edification *n.* educa.
edifice *n.* construida.
edify *v.* educa.
edit *v.* & *n.* edita.
edition *n.* publici; edita; (*periodical*) numero.
editor *n.* (*person*) editor; (*of texts for publication*) revisor; (*software*) editador.
editorial *n.* editorial.
educable *adj.* educable.
educate *v.* educa.
educated guess *n.* divina informada.
education *n.* educa.
educational *adj.* educal; (*teaching*) instruinte.
educator *n.* educor.
educe *v.* dedui, developa.
Edward, Lake *n.* Lago Edward.
-ee *suff.* (*person or thing that is -ed*) -da.
ee-ee-ee *interj.* (*monkey*) i-i-i.
eek *interj.* (*frightened squeal*) i.
eel *n.* angila.
eel-like *adj.* angilin.
eerie *adj.* strana.
eeyore *interj.* (*donkey*) i-aa.
efface *v.* asconde.
effect *n.* (*produced*) efeto, resulta; (*personal*) poseseda. • *v.* (*cause to happen*) reali. **have an effect on** afeta. **in effect** en efeto; enforsada; valida.
effective *adj.* produosa.
effectively *adv.* en efeto.
effectiveness *n.* produosia.
effectual *adj.* produosa.
effectuality *n.* produosia.
effeminate *adj.* femin.
effervesce *v.* bola.
effervescent *adj.* bolante.
effete *adj.* finjosa.
efficacious *adj.* produosa.
efficacy *n.* produosia.
efficiency *n.* capasia, nonperosia.
efficient *adj.* capas, nonperosa.
effigy *n.* pupa.
effloresce *v.* cristali, polvi.
effluent *n.* esfluente.
effort *n.* labora; (*strength exerted*) fortia.
effortless *adj.* fasil, sin labora.
effuse *v.* emete; es parlosa.
e.g. *abbr.* pe (*per esemplo*).
egalitarian *adj.* egaliste.
egalitarianism *n.* egalisme.
egg *n.* ovo.
eggbeater *n.* batcovo; (*mechanical*) batador engranada.
eggbeater drill *n.* forador engranada.
eggcup *n.* portaovo.
egg drop soup *n.* sopa de filos de ovo.
egg flower soup *n.* sopa de filos de ovo.
egg-laying *adj.* oviparinte.
egglike *adj.* ovin.
eggnog *n.* pontxe de ovos, lete de gal.
eggplant *n.* melonjena.
egg-shaped *adj.* ovin.
eggshell *n.* casca de ovo.
eggtimer *n.* orolojo de arena.
egg white *n.* blanca de ovo, albumen.
egg yolk *n.* jala de ovo.

eglantine rose *n.* rosa spinosa.
ego *n.* ego.
egocentric *adj.* egosentral.
egoist *n.* egoiste.
egomania *n.* egomania.
egomaniac *adj.* egomanica.
egomaniacal *adj.* egomanica.
egotism *n.* egosia.
egotistical *adj.* egoiste, egosa.
e-government *n.* egoverna.
egress *n.* sorti.
egret *n.* (*bird*) egreta.
Egypt *n.* Misre, Egipte. **Ancient Egypt** Egipte antica.
Egyptian *adj.* & *n.* misri, egipsian.
Egyptian plover *n.* (*bird*) pluvial de Egipte.
Egyptologist *n.* egiptolojiste.
Egyptology *n.* egiptolojia.
eh? *interj.* (*confusion*) como?; (*requesting confirmation*) no?
eider *n.* (*duck*) eder.
eiderdown *n.* ederdon.
eidetic memory *n.* memoria vivin.
eight *det.* & *pron.* oto.
eightball *n.* bal oto.
eighth *adj.* (*ordinal*) oto. • *n.* (*fraction*) oti. • *pref.* oti-.
eighth note *n.* tono otida.
eightieth *adj.* (*ordinal*) otodes. • *n.* (*fraction*) otodesi.
eighty *det.* & *pron.* otodes.
Eilat, Gulf of *n.* Golfo Acaba.
einsteinium *n.* (*element*) ainstainio.
either *pron.* (*either one*) la un o la otra. **either this or that** o esta o acel.
ejaculate *v.* ejacula.
ejaculation *n.* ejacula.
eject *v.* ejeta, espulsa.
ejection *n.* ejeta, espulsa.
ejective *adj.* & *n.* (*consonant*) ejetada.
eke out *v.* susta, dura.
EKG *abbr.* ecg.
EKG scan *n.* eletrocardiogram.
EKG scanner *n.* eletrocardiograf.
elaborate *adj.* detaliosa. • *v.* esplica.
elaboration *n.* esplica.
Elam *n.* (*ancient civilization*) Elam.
Elamite *adj.* & *n.* elaman.
élan vital *n.* fortia de vive.
elapse *v.* pasa.
elastane *n.* elastan. • *adj.* de elastan.
elastic *adj.* & *n.* elastica.
elastic band *n.* banda elastica.
elasticity *n.* elasticia.
elate *v.* estasia.
elated *adj.* estasiante.
elation *n.* estasia.
elbow *n.* codo.
elbow room *n.* spasio sufisinte.
elder[1] *adj.* plu vea. • *n.* vea; (*religious*) decano. **the elder** (*in names*) major.
elder[2] *n.* (*plant*) sambuco.
elderberry *n.* sambuco.
elderly *adj.* vea, senesente.
elderly person *n.* senesente.
eldest *adj.* la plu vea.
elect *v.* eleje. • *adj.* elejeda.
electability *n.* elejablia.
electable *adj.* elejable.
election *n.* eleje, vota.
elective *adj.* elejal.
elector *n.* elejor.
electoral *adj.* elejal.
electorate *n.* votores.
electric *adj.* eletrical; eletricida.
electrical *adj.* eletrical.
electrical outlet *n.* prende.
electric current *n.* corente eletrical.
electric guitar *n.* gitar eletrical.
electrician *n.* eletriciste.
electricity *n.* eletrica.
electric potential difference *n.* tensa eletrical.
electric prod *n.* basto eletrical.
electric tension *n.* tensa eletrical.
electrification *n.* eletrici.
electrify *v.* eletrici.
electrocardiogram *n.* eletrocardiogram.
electrocardiograph *n.* eletrocardiograf.
electrocardiography *n.* eletrocardiografia.
electrocute *v.* eletrocuta.
electrocution *n.* eletrocuta.
electrode *n.* eletrodo.
electrodynamic *adj.* eletrodinamical.
electrodynamics *n.* eletrodinamica.
electroencephalogram *n.* eletroensefalogram.
electroencephalograph *n.* eletroensefalograf.
electroencephalography *n.* eletroensefalografia.
electrolyse (US **electrolyze**) *v.* eletrolise.
electrolysis *n.* eletrolise.
electrolyte *n.* eletrolito.
electrolytic *adj.* eletrolisal.
electrolyze (US). See *electrolyse*.
electromagnet *n.* eletromagnete.
electromagnetic *adj.* eletromagnetal.
electromagnetism *n.* eletromagnetia.
electromechanical *adj.* eletromecanical.
electromechanics *n.* eletromecanica.
electromotive *adj.* eletromotiva.
electron *n.* eletron.
electronegative *adj.* eletronegativa.
electronic *adj.* eletronical.
electronics *n.* (*science*) eletronica; (*components*) eletronicales.
electrophoresis *n.* eletroforese.

electrophotography *n.* xerografia.
electrophysiology *n.* eletrofisiolojia.
electroplate *v.* eletroplaca.
electropositive *adj.* eletropositiva.
electroshock weapon *n.* arma de xoca eletrical.
electrostatic *adj.* eletrostatical.
electrostatics *n.* eletrostatica.
electrosurgery *n.* eletrosirurjia.
Elefen *adj.* & *n.* elefen. **translate into Elefen** elefeni.
Elefenist *n.* elefeniste.
Elefenize *v.* elefeni.
elegance *n.* sofistica.
elegant *adj.* bela, refinada, sofisticada.
elegibility *n.* elejablia.
elegy *n.* lamenta, poesia de lamenta.
element *n.* (*basic part, including chemical*) elemento.
elementary *adj.* fundal.
elementary school *n.* scola prima.
elephant *n.* elefante.
elephantiasis *n.* elefantiase.
elephantine *adj.* elefantin.
elephant seal *n.* elefante-de-mar.
elephant yam *n.* coniac.
elevate *v.* alti.
elevation *n.* altia.
elevator *n.* asendador.
elevator music *n.* musica de asendador.
elf *n.* elfo.
elfin *adj.* elfin.
elfish *adj.* elfin.
elicit *v.* evoca.
elide *v.* elidi.
eligible *adj.* elejable, cualinte. **be eligible** (*qualify*) cuali.
eliminate *v.* elimina.
elimination *n.* elimina.
elimination match *n.* concurso de elimina.
elision *n.* elidi.
elite *adj.* elite, superior.
elitism *n.* elitisme.
elitist *adj.* elitiste.
elixir *n.* prepara.
Elizabethan *adj.* elizabetan.
elk *n.* uapiti; (*moose*) alce.
ellipse *n.* elise, oval.
ellipsis *n.* trepunto.
ellipsoid *adj.* & *n.* elisoide.
ellipsoidal *adj.* elisoide.
elliptic *adj.* elise.
elliptical *adj.* elise, oval.
elm *n.* olmo.
elocution *n.* bonpronunsia.
elongate *v.* longi.
elongation *n.* longi.
elope *v.* fuji per sposi.
eloquence *n.* bonparla.
eloquent *adj.* bonparlante.
El Salvador *n.* Salvador.
else *adv.* si no.
elsewhere *adv.* a otra parte.
elucidate *v.* clari; esplica.
elude *v.* evita.
elusive *adj.* evitante.
emaciate *v.* magri.
emaciation *n.* magri.
email *v.* & *n.* eposta.
email address *n.* adirije de eposta.
emanate *v.* emerji.
emanation *n.* emerji; emete.
emancipate *v.* libri.
emancipation *n.* libri.
emasculate *v.* desmasi.
emasculation *n.* desmasi.
embalm *v.* balsami.
embankment *n.* teraplen.
embargo *n.* embargo.
embark *v.* embarca.
embarrass *v.* embarasa.
embarrassment *n.* embarasa.
embassy *n.* ambasada.
embattlement *n.* merlon.
embed *v.* caxi.
embellish *v.* beli.
ember *n.* brasa.
embezzle *v.* froda.
embezzlement *n.* froda.
embitter *v.* amargi.
embittered *adj.* amarga.
emblazon *v.* ostenta.
emblem *n.* logo, sinia.
emblematic *adj.* siniante.
embodiment *n.* corpi. **be the embodiment of** corpi.
embody *v.* corpi.
embolden *v.* coraji; (*typography*) spesi.
embolism *n.* embolia, trombo.
embolus *n.* (*medical*) embolo.
emboss *v.* impresa.
embouchure *n.* estuario.
embrace *v.* & *n.* abrasa.
embraceable *adj.* abrasable.
embroider *v.* brode.
embroidery *n.* brode.
embroidery thread *n.* filo de brode.
embroil *v.* envolve.
embryo *n.* embrio.
embryological *adj.* embriolojial.
embryologist *n.* embriolojiste.
embryology *n.* embriolojia.
embryonal *adj.* embrial.
embryonic *adj.* embrial.
emcee *n.* mestre de selebras.
emend *v.* boni, coreti.
emerald *adj.* & *n.* esmeralda.
emerge *v.* emerji.

emergence *n.* emerji.
emergency *n.* crise, urjente.
emergency contraception *n.* contraconsepi urjente.
emergency exit *n.* sorti de securia.
emergency lane *n.* banda de crise.
emergent *adj.* emerjinte.
emerita *adj.* jubilada.
emeritus *adj.* jubilada.
emery *n.* emeri.
emery board *n.* lima de emeri.
emery cloth *n.* stofa de emeri.
emery paper *n.* paper de emeri.
-emesis *suff.* (*vomiting*) -emese.
-emia (US). See *-aemia*.
-emic (US). See *-aemic*.
emigrant *n.* migror.
emigrate *v.* migra de.
emigration *n.* migra.
Emilia *n.* (*Italian region*) Emelia.
Emilian *adj.* & *n.* emelian.
eminence *n.* esele.
eminent *adj.* grande, eselente.
emir *n.* amir.
emirate *n.* amiria.
Emirati *adj.* & *n.* amirati.
emissary *n.* enviada, ambasador, diplomata, representor.
emission *n.* emete.
emit *v.* emete, esflue. **emit smoke** fumi.
emitter *n.* emetador.
emoji *n.* emoji.
emollient *adj.* calminte; (*softening*) suavinte.
emote *n.* mostra emosia.
emoticon *n.* emosicon.
emotion *n.* emosia.
emotional *adj.* (*of the emotions*) emosial; (*feeling emotion*) emosiosa; (*sensitive*) sentosa.
emotive *adj.* emosiante.
emotiveness *n.* emosia.
emotivity *n.* emosia.
empanel *v.* enscrive.
empathetic *adj.* empatica.
empathic *adj.* empatica.
empathy *n.* empatia.
emperor *n.* imperor.
emphasis *n.* asentua.
emphasize *v.* asentua.
emphatic *adj.* asentuante, asentuada.
emphysema *n.* (*medical*) emfisema.
empire *n.* impero.
empirical *adj.* empirical.
empiricism *n.* empiricalisme.
empiricist *n.* empiricaliste.
employ *v.* (*person*) emplea; (*use*) usa.
employability *n.* empleablia.
employable *adj.* empleable.
employee *n.* empleada.
employer *n.* empleor.
employment *n.* (*person*) emplea; (*use*) usa.
emporium *n.* mercato.
empower *v.* autori.
empress *n.* imperoresa.
emptiness *n.* vacuia.
empty *adj.* vacua. • *v.* vacui.
Empty Quarter *n.* (*desert*) Cuatri Vacua.
empty string *n.* (*software*) cadena vacua.
emu *n.* (*bird*) emu.
emulate *v.* suprapasa; imita.
emulation *n.* imita.
emulator *n.* (*software*) imitador.
emulsify *v.* emulsioni.
emulsion *n.* emulsion.
emulsion paint *n.* pinta de emulsion.
en- *pref.* en-.
enable *v.* capasi; (*software*) comuta.
enabler *n.* provocor.
enact *v.* reali; (*plan*) esecuta.
enactment *n.* reali.
enamel *n.* esmalte. • *v.* esmalti.
enamour (US **enamor**) *v.* enama.
encage *v.* caji.
encamp *v.* campa.
encapsulate *v.* capsuli, enclui, ensirca; (*summarize*) resoma.
encapsulation *n.* capsuli.
encase *v.* caxi, enclui.
encephalitis *n.* ensefalite.
encephalogram *n.* ensefalogram.
encephalograph *n.* ensefalograf.
encephalography *n.* ensefalografia.
encephalomyelitis *n.* ensefalomielite.
enchain *v.* cadeni.
enchant *v.* encanta.
enchanter *n.* encantor.
enchantment *n.* encanta.
enchantress *n.* encantor.
enchilada *n.* (*food*) entxilada.
encipher *v.* sifri.
encircle *v.* ensirca.
enclave *n.* enclave.
enclose *v.* enclui, ensirca.
enclosure *n.* ensirca.
encode *v.* (*encrypt*) sifri; (*in a system*) codigi.
encoding *n.* (*encryption*) sifri; (*in a system*) codigi; (*system*) codigo.
encomium *n.* loda.
encompass *v.* (*enclose*) ensirca; (*include*) inclui.
encore *n.* regala.
encounter *v.* encontra.
encourage *v.* coraji.
encouragement *n.* coraji.
encroach *v.* intrui.
encroachment *n.* intrui.
encrust *v.* crosti.
encrustation *n.* crosti.
encrypt *v.* sifri.
encryption *n.* sifri.

encumber *v.* carga.
encyclical *adj.* & *n.* ensiclica.
encyclopaedia (US **encyclopedia**) *n.* ensiclopedia.
encyst *v.* sisti.
end *v.* fini, para. • *n.* fini. **at the end of** a fini de. **in the end** final.
endanger *v.* perili.
endear *v.* cari.
endearing *adj.* amablo.
endeavour (US **endeavor**) *v.* atenta.
endemic *adj.* & *n.* endemica.
ending *adj.* fininte. • *n.* fini; (*grammar*) coda.
endive *n.* (*plant*) xicoria.
endless *adj.* sin fini, nonfininte.
endnote *n.* nota codal.
endo- *pref.* (*inside*) endo-.
endocrine *adj.* (*gland*) endocrin.
endocrinological *adj.* endocrinolojial.
endocrinologist *n.* endocrinolojiste.
endocrinology *n.* endocrinolojia.
endogamous *adj.* endogama.
endogamy *n.* endogamia.
endogenous *adj.* endojenesal.
endogeny *n.* endojenese.
endometrial *adj.* endometrial.
endometriosis *n.* endometriose.
endometrium *n.* endometrio.
endonym *n.* (*local place name*) endonim.
endonymous *adj.* endonim.
endoplasma *n.* endoplasma.
endorphin *n.* endorfina.
endorse *v.* validi, aproba.
endorsement *n.* validi.
endoscope *n.* endoscopio.
endoscopic *adj.* endoscopial.
endoscopy *n.* endoscopi.
endostyle *n.* (*anatomy*) endostilo.
endothelium *n.* (*anatomy*) endotelio.
endow *v.* dona.
endowment *n.* dona.
endpoint *n.* punto de fini.
end table *n.* table ladal.
endurance *n.* (*durability*) dura; (*tolerating*) tolera.
endurance running *n.* core de distantia longa.
endure *v.* (*be long-lasting*) dura; (*tolerate*) tolera. **endure for centuries** dura tra sentenios.
-ene *suff.* (*chemistry*) -en.
enema *n.* enema.
enemy *n.* enemi.
energetic *adj.* enerjiosa.
energize *v.* enerji, stimula.
energy *n.* enerjia.
energy-efficient *adj.* nonperosa de enerjia.
enervate *v.* debili, desenerji.
enervation *n.* debili, desenerji.
Enets *adj.* & *n.* enets.
enfeeble *v.* debili.
enforce *v.* (*rule, etc.*) enforsa; (*force to occur*) forsa.
enforceable *adj.* enforsable.
enforcement *n.* enforsa.
enforcer *n.* enforsor.
enfranchise *v.* permete ce on vota.
engage *v.* (*gear, enemy*) engrana; (*involve*) envolve, partisipa.
engaged *adj.* (*gear*) engranada; (*to be married*) prometeda. **engaged in** (*involved with*) envolveda en.
engagement *n.* (*gear, combat*) engrana; (*to be married*) promete.
engaging *adj.* encantante.
engender *v.* provoca.
engine *n.* motor; (*train*) locomotiva.
engine driver *n.* locomotivor.
engineer *n.* injenior. • *v.* injenia.
engineering *n.* injenia.
England *n.* England.
English *adj.* & *n.* (*person, language*) engles.
English Channel *n.* la Manga.
English horn *n.* (*musical instrument*) corneta engles.
Englishman *n.* engles.
English mile *n.* milia engles.
Englishwoman *n.* engles.
engorge *v.* conjesta, pleni.
engrave *v.* grava.
engraver *n.* gravor.
engraving *n.* grava.
engraving machine *n.* gravador.
engraving tool *n.* buril.
engross *v.* fasina, preocupa.
engulf *v.* engoli.
enhance *v.* boni.
enhancement *n.* boni.
enigma *n.* enigma, misterio.
enigmatic *adj.* enigmosa.
enjoy *v.* gusta, joia; (*relish*) saborea. • *interj.* joia. **enjoy oneself** diverti.
enjoyable *adj.* gustable, plaserosa.
enjoyment *n.* gusta, joia, plaser.
enkephalin *n.* (*biology*) encefalina.
enlarge *v.* grandi.
enlargement *n.* grandi.
enlighten *v.* lumina.
enlightenment *n.* (*including intellectual*) lumina. **Jewish Enlightenment** hascala.
enlist *v.* enscrive, envolve.
enlistment *n.* enscrive.
enliven *v.* refresci.
enmity *n.* enemia.
enneagon *n.* nonagon.
enneagonal *adj.* (*nine-sided*) nonagon.
ennoble *v.* nobili.
ennui *n.* noia.
eno... (US). See *oeno...*
enormity *n.* enormia.

enormous *adj.* enorme.
enough *adv.* sufisinte; (*more than enough*) bastante. **be enough** sufisi. **be more than enough** basta.
en passant *adv.* (*chess*) en pasa.
enquire *v.* demanda.
enquiry *n.* (*question*) demanda; (*investigation*) investiga.
enrage *v.* furia, coleri.
enraged *adj.* furiosa, coleriosa. **be enraged** furia.
enrapture *v.* encanta, estasia.
enrich *v.* rici.
enrol (US **enroll**) *v.* enscrive.
enrolment (US **enrollment**) *n.* enscrive.
en route *adv.* en via.
ensconce *v.* instala. **ensconce oneself** nidi, reposa.
ensemble *n.* bande.
enshrine *v.* conserva, tesori.
enshroud *v.* veli.
ensign *n.* suteninte.
enslave *v.* sclavi.
ensnare *v.* trapi.
ensue *v.* segue.
ensure *v.* serti, garantia.
entablature *n.* entablamento.
entail *v.* implica, nesesa.
entangle *v.* marania.
entente *n.* acorda.
enter *v.* (*place*) entra a; (*data*) entra.
enteritis *n.* enterite.
enter key *n.* tecla de entra.
enterobiasis *n.* (*pinworm infection*) osiurose.
enterprise *adj.* comersial. • *n.* (*project*) emprende.
entertain *v.* diverti.
entertainer *n.* divertor.
entertainment *n.* diverti; spetaculo.
enthrone *v.* troni.
enthuse *v.* zeli.
enthusiasm *n.* zelo; -mania.
enthusiast *n.* fan.
enthusiastic *adj.* zelosa; -manica.
entice *v.* atrae, sedui, tenta.
enticement *n.* atrae, sedui, tenta.
entire *adj.* intera.
entirety *n.* intera.
entitle *v.* tituli, dona un titulo a.
entitled *adj.* titulida; meritante. **be entitled** ave la direto; merita.
entitlement *n.* direto; merita.
entity *n.* cosa, esente; organiza.
entomb *v.* tombi.
entomologist *n.* entomolojiste.
entomology *n.* entomolojia.
entoproct *n.* (*organism*) entoprocto.
entourage *n.* atendores, seguores.
entrails *n.* intestines.
entrain *v.* causa; (*incorporate*) asorbe; (*go on board*) embarca; (*biology*) sincroni.
entrance *n.* (*action, place*) entra.
entrance hall *n.* sala de entra.
entreat *v.* prea, suplica.
entreaty *n.* prea, suplica.
entrench *v.* fundi, radisi.
entrepreneur *n.* emprendor.
entropy *n.* entropia.
entrust *v.* (*responsibility*) encarga; (*valuables, secret*) confida.
entry *n.* (*place*) entra; (*in list*) entrada, numero, punto. **no entry** entra proibida.
entry-level *adj.* per comensores.
entryway *n.* entra.
entwine *v.* entretexe.
enumerate *v.* conta.
enunciate *v.* espresa clar, pronunsia clar; clari.
enuresis *n.* (*medical*) enurese.
envelop *v.* envolve, engoli.
envelope *n.* envelopa.
enviable *adj.* inviable.
envious *adj.* inviosa.
environment *n.* ambiente. **destroy the environment** ecoside.
environmental *adj.* ambiental.
environmentalism *n.* ambientisme.
environmentalist *n.* ambientiste.
environmentally friendly *adj.* ecolojial sana.
envoy *n.* enviada, ambasador, diplomata, representor.
envy *v.* invia. • *n.* invia, jelosia.
enzyme *n.* enzima.
enzymology *n.* enzimolojia.
Eocene *adj.* & *n.* (*geology*) eosene.
eon (US). See *aeon.*
eosin *n.* (*dye*) eosin.
eosinophil *n.* eosinofilica.
eosinophilia *n.* (*medical*) eosinofilia.
eosinophilic *adj.* eosinofilica.
epaulette (US **epaulet**) *n.* (*shoulder piece*) spaleta.
épée *n.* (*sword*) epe.
ephedra *n.* (*plant*) efedra.
ephedrine *n.* (*drug*) efedrina.
ephemera *n.* efemeras.
ephemeral *adj.* efemera, tempora.
epi- *pref.* epi-.
epic *adj.* & *n.* epica.
epicanthic fold *n.* epicanto.
epicanthus *n.* epicanto.
epicene *adj.* androjine.
epicentre (US **epicenter**) *n.* episentro.
epicure *n.* gurme.
epicurean *n.* gurme.
epicureanism *n.* epicurisme.
Epicurus *n.* (*philosopher*) Epicuro.

epidemic *adj.* & *n.* epidemica.
epidemic parotitis *n.* (*medical*) parotidite.
epidemiological *adj.* epidemiolojial.
epidemiologist *n.* epidemiolojiste.
epidemiology *n.* epidemiolojia.
epidermal *adj.* epidermal.
epidermis *n.* epiderma.
epididymis *n.* (*anatomy*) epididimo.
epiglottal *adj.* & *n.* (*consonant*) epiglotal.
epiglottis *n.* epiglote.
epigram *n.* epigram.
epigrammatic *adj.* epigramal.
epigrammatist *n.* epigramor.
epigraph *n.* epigraf.
epilepsy *n.* epilesia.
epileptic *adj.* epilesica.
epilogue (US **epilog**) *n.* epilogo.
epinephrine *n.* epinefrina.
epiphany *n.* epifania; (*festival*) festa de Res.
Epiphany Eve *n.* sera de Res, sera de epifania.
epiphenomenon *n.* epifenomeno.
episcopal *adj.* bispal.
Episcopalian *adj.* & *n.* episcopalian.
Episcopalianism *n.* (*Christianity*) episcopalianisme.
episode *n.* episodio.
episodic *adj.* episodial.
epistemology *n.* epistemolojia.
epistle *n.* letera.
epitaph *n.* enscrive de tomba.
epithelial *adj.* epitelial.
epithelium *n.* (*anatomy*) epitelio.
epithet *n.* epiteto.
epitome *n.* personi.
epitomize *v.* esempli.
epoch *n.* epoca.
eponym *n.* eponim.
eponymous *adj.* eponim.
epoxide *n.* (*chemistry*) eposido.
epoxy *adj.* eposidal.
epoxy resin *n.* resina eposidal.
epsilon *n.* (*Greek letter* E, ε) epsilon.
Epsom salts *n.* sulfato de magnesio.
equal *adj.* egal. **become equal** egali. **without equal** sin egal.
equality *n.* egalia.
equalize *v.* egali.
equalizer *n.* egalinte; (*filter*) egalador.
equals sign *n.* sinia de egalia.
equate *v.* egali.
equation *n.* egali.
equator *n.* ecuator.
equatorial *adj.* ecuatoral.
Equatorial Guinea *n.* Gine Ecuatoral.
equestrian *n.* cavalor. • *adj.* cavaloral.
equi- *pref.* ecui-.
equidistant *adj.* ecuidistante.
equilateral *adj.* ecuiladal.
equilibrium *n.* ecuilibra.
equine *adj.* cavalal.
equinox *n.* ecuinote. **autumnal equinox** ecuinote de autono. **vernal equinox** ecuinote de primavera.
equip *v.* furni.
equipment *n.* aparatos.
equitable *adj.* justa.
equity *n.* (*fairness*) justia; (*financial*) valua.
equivalence *n.* coresponde, egalia, paralelia.
equivalent *adj.* & *n.* corespondente, egal, paralel.
equivocal *adj.* ambigua, interpretable.
equivocate *v.* vasila.
Equuleus *n.* (*constellation*) la Cavaleta.
er[1] *interj.* (*hesitation*) em.
-er[2] *suff.* (*person*) -or; (*tool, machine*) -ador; (*substance, object*) -nte.
era *n.* eda; (*geology*) era.
eradicate *v.* elimina.
eradication *n.* elimina.
erasable *adj.* canselable.
erase *v.* cansela, vacui.
eraser *n.* goma de cansela.
erasure *n.* cansela.
erbium *n.* (*element*) erbio.
erect *v.* erije. • *adj.* erijeda.
erectile *adj.* erijable.
erection *n.* erije.
ergative *adj.* & *n.* (*grammar*) ergativa.
ergo *adv.* & *conj.* donce.
ergonomic *adj.* ergonomial.
ergonomics *n.* ergonomia.
ergot *n.* (*fungus*) ergote.
ergotism *n.* (*medical*) ergotisme.
Eridanus *n.* (*constellation*) Eridano.
Erie, Lake *n.* Lago Erie.
Eritrea *n.* Ertra.
Eritrean *adj.* & *n.* ertri.
erm *interj.* (*hesitation*) em.
ermine *n.* ermino.
erode *v.* erode.
erogenous *adj.* erojen.
Eros *n.* (*mythology*) Eros.
erosion *n.* erode.
erosive *adj.* erodente.
erotic *adj.* erotica, sesal.
erotica *n.* eroticas.
err *v.* era.
errand *n.* misioneta.
errant *adj.* deviante, vagante.
errata *n.* lista de eras.
erratic *adj.* acaso, noncoerente, nonfidable.
erroneous *adj.* erante.
error *n.* era.
ersatz *adj.* nonautentica.
erudite *adj.* erudita.
erudition *n.* eruditia.

erupt *v.* eruta.
eruption *n.* eruta.
-ery *suff.* -eria.
erythema *n.* (*medical*) eritema.
erythro- *pref.* (*red*) eritro-.
erythroblast *n.* (*blood cell*) eritroblasto.
erythrocyte *n.* eritrosite.
erythromycin *n.* (*antibiotic*) eritromisina.
erythropoiesis *n.* (*biology*) eritropoiese.
escalate *v.* grandi.
escalation *n.* grandi.
escalator *n.* scalera rolante.
escapade *n.* aventura.
escape *v.* & *n.* evade, fuji. **have a narrow escape** evita apena.
escapee *n.* evador.
escapism *n.* fantasia, evade de realia.
escargot *n.* caracol.
escarpment *n.* presipe.
-esce *suff.* -i.
eschar *n.* pel mor.
eschew *v.* asteni.
escort *v.* acompania. • *n.* acompanior.
escritoire *n.* scriveria.
-ese *suff.* -es.
Eskimo *adj.* & *n.* inuit.
eso- *pref.* eso-.
esophagus (US). See *oesophagus*.
esoteric *adj.* mistica, secreta; poca conoseda.
esotropic *adj.* converjente straba.
ESP *n.* persepi estrasensal.
especial *adj.* spesial.
Esperantist *adj.* & *n.* esperantiste.
Esperanto *adj.* & *n.* esperanto.
espionage[1] *n.* spia.
e-spionage[2] *n.* (*online stalking*) espia.
esplanade *n.* bolevar a plaia.
espouse *v.* adota, promove, suporta.
espresso *n.* espreso.
esprit *n.* astutia, vivosia.
-ess *suff.* (*formal female title*) -esa.
essay *n.* esajo. • *v.* atenta.
essayist *n.* esajiste.
essence *n.* esense.
essential *adj.* esensal.
establish *v.* fundi, constitui, institui, comensa.
establishment *n.* (*action*) fundi; (*organization*) funda, instituida.
estate *n.* propria.
estate agent *n.* ajente de imobila.
esteem *v.* respeta.
ester *n.* (*chemistry*) ester.
esth… (US). See *aesth…*
estimate *v.* estima, judi. • *n.* estima.
estimation *n.* estima; (*judgement*) judi.
estival (US). See *aestival*.
Estonia *n.* Esti.
Estonian *adj.* & *n.* (*person, language*) esti.
estragon *n.* (*plant*) tragon.
estrange *v.* stranjeri.
estrangement *n.* stranjeri.
estrogen (US). See *oestrogen*.
estrus (US). See *oestrus*.
estuary *n.* estuario.
Estuary English *n.* engles estuarial.
eta *n.* (*Greek letter* Η, η) eta.
etc. *abbr.* etc.
et cetera *adv.* e tal cosas, e tal continuante.
etch *v.* grava.
etching *n.* grava.
eternal *adj.* eterna.
eternalize *v.* eterni.
eternity *n.* eternia.
eth *n.* (*Latin letter* Ð, ð) ed.
eth- *pref.* (*chemistry*) et-.
ethane *n.* etano.
ethanol *n.* etanol.
ethene *n.* etilen.
ether *n.* eter.
ethereal *adj.* eterin.
etherize *v.* eteri.
ethical *adj.* etical.
ethics *n.* normas moral; (*subject*) etica.
Ethiopia *n.* Itiopia.
Ethiopian *adj.* & *n.* itiopian.
Ethiopian Empire *n.* Abisinia.
ethnic *adj.* etnical.
ethnic cleansing *n.* limpi etnical.
ethnic group *n.* etnico; raza.
ethnicity *n.* etnicia.
ethnogenesis *n.* etnojenese.
ethnographer *n.* etnografiste.
ethnography *n.* etnografia.
ethnological *adj.* etnolojial.
ethnologist *n.* etnolojiste.
ethnology *n.* etnolojia.
ethological *adj.* etolojial.
ethologist *n.* etolojiste.
ethology *n.* etolojia.
ethos *n.* cultur; normas.
ethyl *n.* (*chemistry*) etil.
ethylene *n.* etilen.
etiology (US). See *aetiology*.
etiquette *n.* cortesia.
Etruria *n.* Etruria.
Etruscan *adj.* & *n.* etrusca.
-ette *suff.* (*diminutive*) -eta.
etymological *adj.* etimolojial.
etymology *n.* etimolojia.
eu- *pref.* (*good*) eu-.
eubacterium *n.* bateria.
eucalyptus *n.* eucalipto.
eucaryote *n.* (*organism*) eucariota.
eucaryotic *adj.* eucariotal.
eucharist *n.* eucaristia.
euchre *n.* (*card game*) eucre.
Euclid *n.* Euclide.

Euclidean *adj.* euclidal.
Euclidean geometry *n.* jeometria euclidal.
eudicot *n.* (*botany*) eudicota.
eugenetical *adj.* eujenetical.
eugenics *n.* (*science*) eujenetica; (*belief*) eujeneticisme.
eukaryote *n.* eucariota.
eukaryotic *adj.* eucariotal.
eulogize *v.* loda.
eulogy *n.* loda.
eumetazoa *n.* (*organisms*) eumetazones.
eumetazoon *n.* (*organism*) eumetazon.
eunuch *n.* eunuco.
euphemism *n.* parola evitante.
euphonia *n.* (*bird*) eufonia.
euphonious *adj.* bon sonante.
euphonium *n.* eufonio.
euphony *n.* bonsona.
euphorbia *n.* euforbia.
euphoria *n.* estasia.
euphoric *adj.* estasiante.
Eurasia *n.* Eurasia.
Eurasian *adj.* eurasian.
Eurasian eagle owl *n.* buo real.
Eurasian jay *n.* jai eurasian.
Eurasian magpie *n.* piga comun.
eureka *interj.* eureca.
eurhythmic *adj.* armoniosa.
euro *n.* euro.
euro area *n.* eurozona.
Eurocentric *adj.* eurosentriste.
Eurocentrism *n.* eurosentrisme.
Eurocentrist *adj.* & *n.* eurosentriste.
Europe *n.* Europa.
European *adj.* & *n.* european.
Europeanization *n.* europeani.
Europeanize *v.* europeani.
European robin *n.* (*bird*) petirosa.
European Union *n.* Uni European.
europium *n.* (*element*) europio.
eurosceptic (US **euroskeptic**) *adj.* & *n.* eurosetica.
Eurotunnel *n.* Tunel su la Manga.
eurozone *n.* eurozona.
eury- *pref.* (*broad*) euri-.
Eustachian tube *n.* trompa de Eustacio.
euthanase *v.* eutanasia.
euthanasia *n.* eutanasia.
euthanize *v.* eutanasia.
evacuate *v.* evacua, sorti; (*container*) vacui.
evacuation *n.* evacua; vacui.
evacuee *n.* evacuada.
evade *v.* evita.
evader *n.* evitor.
evaluate *v.* evalua.
evaluation *n.* evalua.
evangelical *adj.* evanjelial.
evangelicalism *n.* evanjelialisme.
evangelism *n.* evanjelisme.
evangelist *n.* evanjeliste.
evangelistic *adj.* evanjeliste.
evaporate *v.* vapori.
evaporation *n.* vapori.
evaporator *n.* vaporador.
evasion *n.* evita.
evasive *adj.* evitante.
eve[1] *n.* sera. **the eve of** la sera ante.
Eve[2] *n.* Eva.
even *adj.* (*level*) plana; (*number*) duable. • *adv.* (*emphasizing what follows*) an. **even if** an si. **even less** an min, ancora min. **even more** an plu, ancora plu. **even so** an tal. **even though** an si. **get even** venja, venja se. **not even** an no. **not even once** an nunca.
even-handed *adj.* justa.
evening *n.* sera. **in the evening** a sera. **this evening** a esta sera, a sera oji. **tomorrow evening** a sera doman.
evening gown *n.* roba de sera.
evening meal *n.* come de sera.
evening primrose *n.* enotera.
evening star *n.* (*Venus*) stela de sera.
evening suit *n.* completa de sera.
event *n.* aveni.
eventful *adj.* avenosa.
event horizon *n.* orizon de avenis.
event planner *n.* dirijor de selebra.
eventual *adj.* ultima, futur.
eventually *adv.* ultima, a fini, en la futur distante.
ever *adv.* (*at any time*) a cualce ves; (*forever*) sempre. **best ever** la plu bon de sempre. **better than ever** plu bon ca pasada. **ever less** min e min, sempre min. **ever more** plu e plu, sempre plu, cresente. **ever since** de cuando. **largest ever** la plu grande de sempre.
Everest, Mount *n.* Monte Everest.
evergreen *adj.* & *n.* sempreverde.
evergreen oak *n.* cuerco sempreverde.
everlasting *adj.* eterna.
eversion *n.* eversa.
evert *v.* eversa.
every *det.* & *pron.* cada. **every few years** en cada pico de anios. **every hour** a cada ora. **every morning** a cada matina. **every time** a cada ves. **every two years** en cada duple de anios, en cada anio du.
everybody *pron.* (*individually*) cadun; (*collectively*) tota de mundo.
everyday *adj.* dial.
everyman *n.* cualcun, person comun.
everyone *pron.* (*individually*) cadun; (*collectively*) tota de mundo.
everything *pron.* (*individually*) cada cosa; (*collectively*) tota cosas.

everywhere *adv.* (*individually*) en cada loca, en cada parte; (*collectively*) en tota locas, en tota partes.
evict *v.* descasi, espulsa.
eviction *n.* espulsa.
evidence *n.* atesta; confirma, fato suportante, indica. **give as evidence** atesta. **in evidence** evidente.
evident *adj.* evidente. **become evident** evidenti.
evidential *adj.* atestante.
evidentiary *adj.* atestante.
evil *adj.* malvolente. • *n.* malia.
evildoer *n.* vil.
evil omen *n.* mal indica.
evince *v.* revela; sujesta.
eviscerate *v.* desventri.
evocation *n.* evoca.
evocative *adj.* evocante.
evoke *v.* evoca.
evolution *n.* evolui.
evolutionary *adj.* evolual.
evolutionism *n.* evoluisme.
evolutionist *n.* evoluiste.
evolve *v.* evolui.
ew *interj.* (*disgust*) iu.
ewe *n.* ovea fema.
ex- *pref.* (*former*) pasada; (*outside*) es-.
exacerbate *v.* mali.
exacerbation *n.* mali.
exact *adj.* esata. • *v.* (*demand*) esije; (*revenge*) aplica.
exactitude *n.* esatia.
exaggerate *v.* esajera.
exaggeration *n.* esajera.
exalt *v.* alti, leva, loda.
exaltation *n.* alti, leva, loda.
exam *n.* esamina.
examination *n.* esamina; interoga.
examine *v.* esamina; interoga.
examinee *n.* esaminada.
examiner *n.* esaminor.
example *n.* (*instance*) esemplo; (*for imitation*) esemplo, model. **for example** per esemplo.
exarch *n.* (*bishop*) esarca.
exarchate *n.* esarcia.
exasperate *v.* frustra.
exasperation *n.* frustra.
excavate *v.* escava.
excavation *n.* escava.
excavator *n.* (*person*) escavor; (*machine*) escavador.
exceed *v.* esede, suprapasa.
exceeding *adj.* esedente, suprapasante. • *prep.* ultra.
excel *v.* esele.
excellence *n.* esele, eselentia. **the architect par excellence** la esense de un arcitetor.
excellency *n.* eselentia. **your excellency** eselentia.
excellent *adj.* eselente, multe bon.
excelsior *n.* risas de lenio.
except *v.* eseta. • *prep.* estra, con eseta de, esetante. **except for** estra, con eseta de, esetante. **except if** estra si. **except when** estra cuando.
excepting *prep.* esetante, estra, con eseta de.
exception *n.* eseta. **without exception** sin eseta. **with the exception of** con eseta de, esetante, estra.
exceptional *adj.* spesial.
excerpt *v.* estrae. • *n.* estraeda.
excess *n.* esede, suprapasa.
excessive *adj.* esedente, suprabundante, suprafluente, suprapasante, plu ca nesesada, tro multe.
excessively *adv.* tro, tro multe.
exchange *v.* intercambia. • *n.* intercambia; (*place*) intercambieria; (*phone*) prefisa. **in exchange for** per, par intercambia per.
exchangeable *adj.* intercambiable.
exchange fee *n.* paia de intercambia.
exchanger *n.* intercambior.
exchequer *n.* tesoreria.
excise *v.* estrae. • *n.* imposta interna.
excision *n.* estrae.
excitable *adj.* stimulable.
excitation *n.* stimula.
excitatory *adj.* stimulante.
excite *v.* stimula, ajita.
excitement *n.* stimula, ajita.
exclaim *v.* esclama.
exclamation *n.* esclama.
exclamation mark *n.* sinia de esclama.
exclamation point *n.* sinia de esclama.
exclamatory *adj.* esclamante.
exclude *v.* esclui.
excluding *adj.* & *prep.* escluinte.
exclusion *n.* esclui.
exclusive *adj.* escluinte. • *n.* (*news story*) unica.
exclusively *adv.* sola.
excommunicate *v.* esclui.
excommunication *n.* esclui.
excoriate *v.* despeli.
excrement *n.* escrete, fece.
excrescence *n.* crese.
excrete *v.* escrete.
excretion *n.* escrete.
excretory *adj.* escretal.
excruciating *adj.* torturosa.
exculpate *v.* desculpa.
excursion *n.* turi, esplora.
excusable *adj.* escusable, pardonable.
excuse *v.* & *n.* escusa. **excuse me** pardona me. **excuse oneself** asenti se.
execrable *adj.* despetable, odiable.

execute *v.* (*kill*) mata; (*kill, enact, run software*) esecuta.
execution *n.* mata; esecuta.
executioner *n.* esecutor; (*hangman*) pendor.
executive *n.* dirijor.
executive power *n.* potia de esecuta.
executive producer *n.* produor dirijal.
executor *n.* esecutor; (*of will*) esecutor de atesta.
executrix *n.* esecutor de atesta.
exemplar *n.* esemplo, model.
exemplary *adj.* model.
exemplary practice *n.* pratica model.
exemplary punishment *n.* puni avertinte.
exemplify *v.* esempli.
exempt *v.* esenta. • *adj.* esentada.
exemption *n.* esenta.
exercise *v.* eserse. • *n.* eserse, pratica.
exercise book *n.* libro de eserse.
exerciser *n.* esersor.
exert *v.* forsa. **exert power over** domina.
exertion *n.* (*effort*) eserse; (*strength exerted*) fortia.
exfoliant *n.* desfolinte.
exfoliate *v.* desfoli.
exfoliation *n.* desfoli.
exhalation *n.* espira.
exhale *v.* espira.
exhaust *v.* (*tire*) fatiga; (*use up*) consuma. • *n.* (*vehicle part*) emetador.
exhaustion *n.* fatiga.
exhaustive *adj.* completa.
exhaust pipe *n.* tubo de emetador.
exhibit *v.* esibi, mostra.
exhibition *n.* esibi, mostra.
exhibition hall *n.* esiberia.
exhibitionism *n.* esibisme.
exhibitionist *n.* esibiste.
exhibitor *n.* esibor.
exhilarate *v.* deleta.
exhilaration *n.* deleta.
exhort *v.* urje, coraji.
exhortation *n.* urje, coraji.
exhortative *adj.* corajinte.
exhortatory *adj.* corajinte.
exhumation *n.* desentera.
exhume *v.* desentera.
ex-husband *n.* sposo pasada.
exigent *adj.* esijente.
exile *v.* esclui. • *n.* escluida.
exist *v.* esiste. **cause to exist** crea.
existence *n.* esiste. **come into existence** nase.
existent *adj.* esistente.
existential *adj.* (*of existence*) esistal; (*of existentialism*) esistentialiste.
existentialism *n.* esistentialisme.
existentialist *adj.* & *n.* esistentialiste.
exit *v.* & *n.* sorti.
exit poll *n.* sonda a sorti.
exlibris *n.* insinia de libro.
exo- *pref.* (*outside*) eso-.
exobiological *adj.* esobiolojial.
exobiologist *n.* esobiolojiste.
exobiology *n.* esobiolojia.
exocrine *adj.* (*gland*) esocrin.
exodus *n.* parti.
exogamous *adj.* esogama.
exogamy *n.* esogamia.
exogenous *adj.* esojenesal.
exogeny *n.* esojenese.
exonerate *v.* desculpa.
exoneration *n.* desculpa.
exonym *n.* (*international place name*) esonim.
exonymous *adj.* esonim.
exoplanet *n.* esoplaneta.
exorbitant *adj.* inflada, estorsin.
exorcise *v.* desinfesta.
exorcism *n.* esorsi.
exorcist *n.* esorsiste.
exorcize *v.* esorsi.
exoskeleton *n.* esosceleto.
exosphere *n.* (*atmosphere*) esosfera.
exotic *adj.* esotica.
exotica *n.* esoticas.
exotropic *adj.* diverjente straba.
expand *v.* crese, estende.
expanded polystyrene *n.* polistiren estruida.
expanse *n.* estende.
expansion *n.* crese; (*of abbreviation*) forma completa.
expansionism *n.* estendisme.
expansionist *n.* estendiste.
expansive *adj.* estendosa.
expat *n.* sitadan a stranjer.
expatriate *n.* sitadan a stranjer.
expect *v.* espeta, previde.
expectancy *n.* espeta.
expectant *adj.* espetante.
expectation *n.* espeta, previde.
expectorant *adj.* & *n.* espetorante.
expectorate *v.* espetora, sputa.
expedient *adj.* pratical, oportun; (*appropriate*) conveninte.
expedite *v.* rapidi, aselera.
expedition *n.* mision.
expel *v.* espulsa, esclui.
expend *v.* consuma.
expendable *adj.* desprendable.
expenditure *n.* spende.
expense *n.* custa; spende. **at the expense of** a custa de.
expensive *adj.* custosa, cara.
experience *v.* & *n.* esperia.
experienced *adj.* (*knowledgeable*) esperiosa.
experiential *adj.* esperial.
experiment *v.* & *n.* esperimenta.

experimental *adj.* esperimental.
experimentalist *n.* esperimentor.
experimentation *n.* esperimenta.
experimenter *n.* esperimentor.
expert *adj.* esperta. • *n.* esperta, spesialiste.
expertise *n.* espertia.
expert witness *n.* esperta legal.
expiate *v.* espia.
expiation *n.* espia.
expiration *n.* desvalidi, fini.
expire *v.* desvalidi, fini.
explain *v.* esplica.
explainable *adj.* esplicable.
explanation *n.* esplica.
expletive *n.* blasfema; (*grammar*) pleninte.
explicable *adj.* esplicable.
explicit *adj.* clar; direta, franca.
explode *v.* esplode.
exploit *v.* esplota.
exploitable *adj.* esplotable.
exploitation *n.* esplota.
exploration *n.* esplora.
exploratory *adj.* esplorante.
explore *v.* esplora.
explorer *n.* esploror.
explosion *n.* esplode.
explosive *adj.* & *n.* esplodente.
exponent *n.* esponente.
exponential *adj.* esponental.
exponentiate *v.* esponenti.
exponentiation *n.* esponenti.
export *v.* esporta.
exportation *n.* esporta.
exporter *n.* esportor.
expose *v.* esposa, evidenti. **expose to gas** gasi.
exposed *adj.* esposada; nuda.
exposer *n.* esposor.
exposition *n.* esplica.
exposure *n.* esposa.
ex-president *n.* presidente pasada.
express[1] *v.* espresa.
express[2] *n.* (*train*) tren rapida.
expression *n.* espresa; terma.
expressionism *n.* espresisme.
expressionist *adj.* & *n.* espresiste.
expressionless *adj.* sin espresa de fas.
expressive *adj.* espresosa.
express train *n.* tren rapida.
expropriate *v.* prende la propria de.
expropriation *n.* prende de propria.
expulsion *n.* espulsa.
expunge *v.* elimina, sutrae, cansela.
expurgate *v.* sensura.
expurgation *n.* sensura.
exquisite *adj.* estrema bela.
ex-student *n.* studiante pasada.
extant *adj.* esistente, survivente.
extemporaneous *adj.* improvisada, nonpreparada.
extemporary *adj.* improvisada, nonpreparada.
extemporization *n.* improvisa.
extemporize *v.* improvisa.
extend *v.* estende; (*protrude*) protende; (*become widespread*) vasti.
extendable *adj.* estendable.
extensible *adj.* estendable.
extension *n.* estende; (*something added*) ajuntada; (*filename*) sufisa.
extension module *n.* modulo estendente, ajuntable.
extensive *adj.* estendosa.
extensor *n.* (*muscle*) estendador.
extent *n.* (*size*) estende; (*scope*) limitas; (*degree*) grado. **to no extent** a no grado. **to some extent** a alga grado. **to such an extent** tan. **to the extent that** tan ce; (*inasmuch as*) cuanto.
exterior *adj.* & *n.* esterna.
exteriorize *v.* esterni.
exterminate *v.* mata, elimina.
extermination *n.* mata, elimina.
external *adj.* esterna.
externalize *v.* esterni.
extinct *adj.* estinguida.
extinction *n.* estingui.
extinguish *v.* estingui.
extirpate *v.* elimina.
extirpation *n.* elimina.
extol *v.* loda.
extort *v.* estorse.
extortion *n.* estorse.
extortionate *adj.* estorsin.
extortionist *n.* estorsor.
extra[1] *adj.* plu, ajuntada, ajuntable.
extra-[2] *pref.* (*outer, additional*) estra-.
extract *v.* estrae. • *n.* estraeda.
extraction *n.* estrae; (*thing extracted*) estraeda.
extractor *n.* estrador.
extracurricular *adj.* estra cursos.
extradite *v.* estradi.
extradition *n.* estradi.
extralarge *adj.* estragrande.
extralegal *adj.* estralegal.
extramarital *adj.* estrasposal.
extramural *adj.* estramural.
extraneous *adj.* nonpertinente; esterna.
extraordinary *adj.* estracomun, estrema spesial.
extrapolate *v.* estrapola.
extrapolation *n.* estrapola.
extrasensory *adj.* estrasensal.
extrasensory perception *n.* persepi estrasensal.
extraterrestrial *adj.* & *n.* estrateran.
extravagance *n.* estravagantia.

extravagant *adj.* estravagante.
extravaganza *n.* estravagante, spetaculo.
extraversion *n.* estroverti.
extravert *adj.* & *n.* estrovertida. **be extrovert** estroverti.
extraverted *adj.* estrovertida, sosial.
extreme *adj.* & *n.* estrema.
extreme pain *n.* dolon.
extremism *n.* estremisme.
extremist *adj.* & *n.* estremiste.
extremity *n.* (*furthest point*) estrema, fini; (*quality*) estremia.
extremophile *n.* estremofilica.
extremophilia *n.* estremofilia.
extremophilic *adj.* estremofilica.
extricate *v.* estrae.
extrinsic *adj.* nonesensal; esterna.
extroversion *n.* estroverti.
extrovert *adj.* & *n.* estrovertida. **be extrovert** estroverti.
extroverted *adj.* estrovertida, sosial.
extrude *v.* estrui.
extruder *n.* estruador.
extrusion *n.* estrui.
exuberant *adj.* joiosa.
exude *v.* suda.
exult *v.* selebra.
exultant *adj.* joiosa.
exurb *n.* (*rich outlying suburb*) esurbe.
exurban *adj.* esurban.
exurbanite *n.* esurban.
exurbia *n.* esurbes.
ex-wife *n.* sposa pasada.
eye *n.* oio; (*fastener*) anelo de onca; (*of needle*) anelo. **keep an eye on** atende, monitori, vijila. **look me in the eye** regarda mea oios. **make eye contact with** regarda la oios de.
eyeball *n.* globo de oio.
eye bank *n.* banco de oios.
eyebrow *n.* suprasil.
eye candy *n.* dulse per la oios.
eye catching *adj.* caicinte la oio.
eye chart *n.* carta otometrial.
eyedropper *n.* contagota, pipeta de oio.
eyeful *n.* plenioio.
eyeglasses *n.* oculo.
eyelash *n.* sil.
eyelet *n.* oieta.
eye level *n.* nivel de oio.
eyelid *n.* palpebra.
eyeliner *n.* linioio.
eye-opener *n.* abrioio.
eyepatch *n.* covreoio.
eyepiece *n.* lente de regarda.
eyeshot, within *adv.* en la campo de vide.
eyesight *n.* vide.
eye socket *n.* orbita.
eyesore *n.* xocaoio.
eyestalk *n.* tentaculo de oio.
eyestrain *n.* fatiga de oios.
eyetooth *n.* dente canin superior.
eyewash *n.* lavaoio.
eyewitness *n.* atestor.
eyrie *n.* nido.

F

fa *n.* (*musical note*) fa.
fable *n.* fable.
fabric *n.* stofa.
fabricate *v.* fabrica.
fabrication *n.* fabrica.
fabricator *n.* fabricor.
fabric store *n.* boteca de cose.
fabulous *adj.* noncredable.
façade *n.* fasada.
face *n.* fas; (*honour*) onora. • *v.* (*in a direction*) fasa; (*confront*) fronti. **even in the face of** an con. **face down** prona. **face to face with** con fas a fas con.
facecloth *n.* teleta de lava.
faceless *adj.* anonim.
face mask *n.* masca; masca medical. **face up** supina.
faceoff *n.* fronti; (*sport*) comensa.
facepaint *n.* pinta de fas.
face powder *n.* polvo cosmetica.
face-saving *adj.* salvante de onora.
facet *n.* faseta.
facetious *adj.* bromosa.
facetiousness *n.* bromosia.
facial *adj.* fasal.
facial appearance *n.* aspeta de fas.
facial expression *n.* espresa de fas.
facial hair *n.* capeletas.
facile *adj.* surfasal.
facilitate *v.* fasili.
facilitation *n.* fasili.
facility *n.* (*ease*) fasilia; (*place*) compleso, laboreria, ofisia; (*resource*) recurso.
facing *prep.* a fas de, fasante; frontinte.
facsimile *n.* fasimil.
fact *n.* fato. **in fact** en fato, en realia, vera. **the fact that** la fato ce.
faction *n.* partito, ramo.
factional *adj.* partital.
factionalism *n.* partitisme.
factor *n.* fator; elemento, rol.
factorial *n.* fatoral.
factorize *v.* fatori.
factory *n.* fabriceria.
factotum *n.* fatota.
factual *adj.* fatal.
facula *n.* (*astronomy*) facula.
faculty *n.* capasia; (*university*) scola, profesores.
faculty member *n.* profesor.
fad *n.* moda.
fade *v.* pali. **fade in** apare lenta. **fade out** desapare lenta.
faecal (US **fecal**) *adj.* fecal.
faeces (US **feces**) *n.* fece.
faerie *n.* fe; pais de fes.
Faeroe Islands *n.* Isolas Faro.
Faeroese *adj.* & *n.* faroisce.
fag *n.* (*cigarette*) sigareta.
faggot (US **fagot**) *n.* (*bundle*) faxo.
Fahrenheit *n.* farenhait. **degree Fahrenheit** grado de farenhait.
faience *n.* faiense.
fail *v.* (*not succeed*) fali; (*humiliatingly*) fa un fiasco. **fail to interest** desinteresa. **fail to observe** (*promise, deal*) rompe. **fail to stop** fali para.
failing *adj.* falinte. • *n.* fali.
failsafe *adj.* secur contra malfunsiona.
failure *n.* fali, rompe.
faint *adj.* cuieta, apena persepable. • *v.* desmaia.
faint-hearted *adj.* timida, noncorajosa.
faintness *n.* (*feeling faint*) desmaia.
faint smell *n.* odoreta.
fair[1] *adj.* justa; (*fair-haired*) blonde.
fair[2] *n.* (*entertainment, trade*) feria.
fairground *n.* feria, parce de divertis.
fair-haired *adj.* blonde.
fairly *adv.* justa; (*somewhat*) alga, a alga grado.
fairness *n.* justia.
fairway *n.* (*golf*) curso.
fairy *n.* fe.
fairy-bluebird *n.* irena.
fairyland *n.* pais de fes.
fairylike *adj.* fein.
fairy tale *n.* fable, nara de fes.
fait accompli *n.* fada realida.
faith *n.* fida. **have faith in** fida.
faithful *adj.* fidosa.
faithfulness *n.* fida.
faith healer *n.* sanor spirital.
faith healing *n.* sani spirital.
fajita *n.* (*food*) fajita.
fake *adj.* falsa, nonautentica; (*pretending*) finjente. • *v.* falsi; (*pretend*) finje. • *n.* (*thing*) falsa; (*person*) finjor.
faker *n.* finjor.
fakir *n.* facir.
falafel *n.* (*food*) falafel; (*bread*) pita de falafel.
falcon *n.* falcon.
falconer *n.* falconor.
falconet *n.* falcon.
falconry *n.* falconoria.
Falkland Islands *n.* Isolas Falkland.
fall *v.* cade. • *n.* cade; (*autumn*) autono; (*waterfall*) cascade. **fall asleep** adormi. **fall down** cade. **fall foul** vitimi. **fall guy** portaculpa. **fall ill** maladi. **fall in love** cade en ama, comensa ama, deveni enamada.

fall open abri. **fall out of love** deveni desenamada. **fall prey** vitimi. **fall short** manca. **fall silent** silenti. **fall to earth** cade a tera. **fall to one's knees** cade a jenos.
fallacious *adj.* falsa, erante.
fallacy *n.* crede falsa.
fallback *n.* (*retreat*) retira; (*plan*) alternativa.
fallible *adj.* capas de era.
falling star *n.* stela volante.
Fallopian tube *n.* trompa de utero.
fallout *n.* radioativia.
fallow *adj.* noncultivada.
fallow field *n.* campo reposante.
false *adj.* falsa, nonautentica.
false diamond *n.* diamante falsa.
falsehood *n.* (*quality*) falsia; (*statement*) declara falsa.
false memory *n.* recorda falsa.
falseness *n.* falsia.
false praise *n.* loda falsa.
false teeth *n.* prostese dental.
falsetto *adj.* & *n.* falseto.
falsification *n.* falsi.
falsify *v.* falsi.
falter *v.* esita, vasila, luta.
faltering *adj.* (*speech*) nonfluente.
fame *n.* fama.
familial *adj.* familial.
familiar *adj.* (*well known*) conoseda; (*of the family*) familial; (*like family*) familin. **be familiar with** conose.
familiarity *n.* conose.
familiarize *v.* dona conose a. **familiarize oneself with** comensa conose.
family *n.* familia. **the Brown family** la familia Braun, la Braunes.
family line *n.* linia de familia.
family member *n.* familian; (*of an older generation*) tie.
family name *n.* nom familial.
famine *n.* famion.
famish *v.* fami.
famous *adj.* famosa.
fan *n.* ventador; (*handheld*) vano; (*enthusiast*) fan. • *v.* venti, vani.
fanatic *n.* fan; (*addict*) manica.
fanatical *adj.* zelosa; manica.
fanaticism *n.* mania.
fanciful *adj.* fantasial, imajinal.
fancy *v.* desira; imajina.
fancy dress *n.* vestes fantasin.
fandango *n.* (*dance*) fandango.
fandom *n.* fanes; (*fannishness*) fania.
fanfare *n.* fanfara. **sound a fanfare** fanfara.
fang *n.* denton.
fanlike *adj.* vanin.
fanny *n.* (*UK: vagina*) cuno; (*US: buttocks*) culo.
fan-shaped *adj.* vanin.
fantasize *v.* fantasia.
fantastic *adj.* fantasin; noncredable, stonante.
fantasy *n.* fantasia.
far *adj.* distante. **as far as** tan distante como; (*until*) asta; (*inasmuch as*) cuanto. **by far** clar. **far and away** clar. **far away** distante. **far out** distante. **take far away** distanti.
farad *n.* (*unit of capacitance*) farade.
farce *n.* farsa.
farcical *adj.* farsin.
fare *n.* custa.
Far East *n.* Asia este.
farewell *n.* & *interj.* adio.
far-fetched *adj.* asurda, nonconvinsente.
farina *n.* farina.
farm *v.* cultiva. • *n.* cultiveria; (*breeding animals*) eleveria.
farmable *adj.* cultivable.
farm bird *n.* avia de cultiveria.
farmer *n.* cultivor.
farmhand *n.* peon cultival.
farmhouse *n.* casa de cultiveria.
farmland *n.* tera cultivada.
farmstead *n.* cultiveria.
farmyard *n.* patio de cultiveria.
faro *n.* (*card game*) faro.
Faroe Islands *n.* Isolas Faro.
Faroese *adj.* & *n.* faroisce.
far-reaching *adj.* vasta, estendosa.
Farsi *adj.* & *n.* farsi.
far-sighted *adj.* iperope.
far-sightedness *n.* iperopia.
fart *v.* & *n.* peta, flatule.
farther *det.* plu. • *adv.* plu; plu distante. **farther than** ultra, plu distante ca.
farthing *n.* (*coin*) cuatrim.
fasces *n.* faxo.
fascia *n.* faxa.
fascinate *v.* fasina.
fascination *n.* fasina.
fascism *n.* faxisme.
fascist *adj.* & *n.* faxiste.
fashion *n.* moda. **in fashion** a la moda, de moda. **out of fashion** de moda pasada.
fashionable *adj.* modosa, a la moda, de moda.
fashion designer *n.* modiste.
fashionista *n.* modiste.
fast[1] *adj.* rapida.
fast[2] *v.* juna. **break one's fast** dejuna.
fasten *v.* fisa.
fastenable *adj.* fisable, cluable.
fastener *n.* fisador.
fast food *n.* comeda rapida.
fast-food restaurant *n.* comeria.
fast-forward *v.* avansa rapida.

fastidious *adj.* atendosa.
fast-track *v.* trata prima.
fast train *n.* tren rapida.
fat *n.* gras. • *adj.* obesa; (*fatty*) grasosa.
fatal *adj.* matante.
fatalism *n.* predeterminisme.
fatalist *n.* predeterministe.
fatalistic *adj.* predeterministe.
fatality *n.* mori.
fate *n.* destina, fortuna.
father *n.* padre.
father figure *n.* padrin.
fatherhood *n.* padria.
father-in-law *n.* padre par sposi.
fatherland *n.* propre pais.
fatherless *adj.* sin padre.
fatherly *adj.* padrin.
Father's Day *n.* festa de padres.
father-to-be *n.* padre futur.
fathom *n.* (*unit of length*) ses pedes.
fatigue *v.* fatiga.
fatness *n.* obesia.
fatty *adj.* grasosa.
fatuous *adj.* fol, futil.
fatwa *n.* fatua.
faucet *n.* valva.
fault *n.* (*failing*) fali; (*geology*) falia.
faultless *adj.* sin fali.
faulty *adj.* defetosa.
faun *n.* (*mythology*) fauno.
fauna *n.* animales.
Faustian *adj.* faustian.
fauvism *n.* fauvisme.
fauvist *adj.* & *n.* fauviste.
faux *adj.* falsa, nonautentica.
faux pas *n.* mal paso, era sosial.
fava bean *n.* fava de visia.
favour (US **favor**) *v.* favore, prefere, benefica. • *n.* favore. **do a favour** fa un favore.
favourable (US **favorable**) *adj.* favorable.
favourite (US **favorite**) *adj.* & *n.* favoreda, prefereda.
favouritism *n.* favorisme.
fawn[1] *n.* (*baby deer*) serveta. • *adj.* (*colour*) pal brun.
fawn[2] *v.* (*flatter*) adula.
fax *n.* fax.
fax machine *n.* faxador.
fealty *n.* fida jurada.
fear *v.* & *n.* teme. **fear in advance** preteme.
fearful *adj.* temosa.
fearless *adj.* nontemosa.
fearsome *adj.* asustante.
feasibility *n.* praticalia.
feasible *adj.* posible, realable, pratical.
feast *v.* & *n.* banceta.
feat *n.* ateni.
feather *n.* pluma. • *v.* plumi.
featherbed *n.* leto de plumas, materas de plumas.
featherbrain *n.* stupida.
feather duster *n.* plumon de despolvi.
featherlike *adj.* plumin.
feather mattress *n.* materas de plumas.
feather star *n.* stela-de-mar plumosa.
featherweight boxing *n.* boxe plumin.
feathery *adj.* (*featherlike*) plumin; (*full of feathers*) plumosa.
feature *n.* cualia, cualia spesial, spesifada.
featureless *adj.* sin cualias.
febrifuge *n.* parafebre.
febrile *adj.* febrosa.
February *n.* febrero.
fecal (US). See *faecal.*
feces (US). See *faeces.*
feckless *adj.* nonfidable, nonusosa.
fecund *adj.* fertil.
fed *adj.* nurida. **fed up with** plenida de.
federal *adj.* federal.
federalism *n.* federalisme.
federalist *adj.* & *n.* federaliste.
federalistic *adj.* federaliste.
federate *v.* federa.
Federated States of Micronesia *n.* Statos Federada de Micronesia.
federation *n.* federa.
fedora *n.* (*hat*) xapon.
fee *n.* paia.
feeble *adj.* debil.
feeble-minded *adj.* de mente debil.
feed *v.* nuri; (*into a machine*) flue. • *n.* (*news, software*) flue. **feed again** renuri. **feed back** renuri.
feedback *n.* comentas; (*audio, video*) renuri.
feel *v.* (*emotion, pain*) senti; (*consider oneself to be*) senti; (*seem to be*) pare; (*touch*) palpa.
feeler *n.* palpador.
feeling *n.* (*emotion, pain*) senti; (*sensation*) sensa. **have mixed feelings** ambivale.
feign *v.* finje.
feijoa *n.* (*tree, fruit*) fejoa.
feint *n.* finje, engana.
feisty *adj.* corajosa.
feldspar *n.* (*mineral*) feldspato.
felid *n.* felido.
feline *n.* felido.
fell *v.* cade, colpa a tera, fa ce lo cade.
fellate *v.* fa felatio.
fellatio *n.* felatio.
fellow *n.* om, xico; (*society*) membro.
fellow-feeling *n.* simpatia.
fellow schemer *n.* coconspiror.
fellowship *n.* amia; (*league*) alia.
fellow student *n.* costudiante.
fellow worker *n.* colaboror.
felon *n.* criminor.
felony *n.* crimin major.

felt *n.* feltro.
feltlike *adj.* feltrin.
female *adj.* & *n.* fema.
femaleness *n.* femia.
feminine *adj.* femin.
femininity *n.* feminia.
feminism *n.* femisme.
feminist *n.* femiste.
feminization *n.* femi.
feminize *v.* femi.
femme *adj.* femin.
femoral *adj.* femoral.
femur *n.* femor.
fen *n.* pantan; (*ecology*) pantan torbosa basa.
fence *n.* (*barrier*) serca. • *v.* serci; (*sport*) scrima.
fencepost *n.* palo de serca.
fencer *n.* scrimor.
fencing *n.* sercas; (*sport*) scrima.
fender *n.* (*fireplace*) gardafoco; (*mudguard*) parafango.
fenland *n.* pantan.
fennel *n.* finoio.
fenobarbital *n.* (*drug*) fenobarbital.
fenobarbitone *n.* (*drug*) fenobarbital.
feral *adj.* savaje.
ferment *v.* fermenta.
fermentation *n.* fermenta.
fermium *n.* (*element*) fermio.
fern *n.* filis.
fernlike *adj.* filisin.
ferocious *adj.* ferose.
ferret *n.* furon.
ferric *adj.* ferica.
Ferris wheel *n.* rota jigante.
ferromagnetic *adj.* feromagnetal.
ferrous *adj.* ferosa.
ferry *n.* naveta. • *v.* naveti.
ferryboat *n.* naveta.
ferryman *n.* navetor.
fertile *adj.* fertil.
fertility *n.* fertilia.
fertility drug *n.* medisin de fertilia.
fertilizable *adj.* fertilable.
fertilize *v.* fertili.
fertilizer *n.* fertilinte.
fervent *adj.* zelosa; (*red-hot*) roja calda.
fervour (US **fervor**) *n.* zelo.
fescue *n.* (*plant*) festuca.
fester *v.* putri, sepsi.
festival *n.* (*religious day*, *series of performances*) festa; (*parade*) carnaval.
festive *adj.* festin.
festivity *n.* selebra.
festoon *n.* garlanda. • *v.* garlandi.
feta *n.* (*cheese*) feta.
fetal (US). See *foetal.*
fetch *v.* retrae; (*person*) veni.
fete *n.* feria, selebra; (*charity market*) bazar.
fetid *adj.* apestante.
fetish *n.* fetix.
fetishism *n.* fetixisme.
fetishist *n.* fetixiste.
fetishization *n.* fetixi.
fetishize *v.* fetixi.
fetlock *n.* noca.
fetter *n.* securitalo.
fettuccine *n.* (*pasta*) fetutxine.
fetus (US). See *foetus.*
feud *n.* vendeta, disputa.
feudal *adj.* feudal.
feudal estate *n.* feudo.
feudalism *n.* feudalisme.
feudal manor *n.* feudo.
fever *n.* febre.
fevered *adj.* febrosa.
feverish *adj.* febrosa.
few *det.* & *pron.* (*not many*) poca; (*optional plural pronoun*) pocas. **a few** (*several*) alga, algas, un pico de, un peseta de. **a few less** alga min. **a few more** alga plu. **as few as possible** tan poca como posible. **few less than** poca min ca. **few more than** poca plu ca.
fewer *det.* min.
fewest *det.* (*the smallest quantity of*) la min de.
fey *adj.* fein.
fez *n.* (*hat*) fez.
fiancé *n.* prometeda.
fiancée *n.* prometeda.
fiasco *n.* fiasco.
fiat *n.* comanda.
fib *n.* menteta.
fibre (US **fiber**) *n.* fibre.
fibreglass (US **fiberglass**) *n.* plastica de vitro; (*textile*) fibre de vitro.
fibre optics (US **fiber optics**) *n.* otica de fibres.
fibroblast *n.* (*biology*) fibroblasto.
fibrocyte *n.* (*biology*) fibrosite.
fibroid *adj.* fibrosa. • *n.* tumor fibrosa.
fibrosis *n.* fibrose.
fibrous *adj.* fibrosa.
fibula *n.* (*anatomy*, *brooch*) fibula.
fiche *n.* fix.
fickle *adj.* nonconstante.
fiction *n.* naras.
fictional *adj.* imajinal, naral.
fiction book *n.* libro de imajina.
fictitious *adj.* imajinal.
fiddle *n.* violin. **fiddle with** jueta con.
fiddler *n.* violiniste.
fidelity *n.* fida.
fidget *v.* move ajitada. **fidget with** jueta con.
fidgety *adj.* ajitada.
fiduciary *adj.* fidusial. • *n.* fidusior.
fief *n.* feudo.
fiefdom *n.* feudo.

field *n.* (*grass, knowledge, activity*) campo. **field of vision** campo de vide.
field hockey *n.* hoci de campo.
fiend *n.* vil.
fiendish *adj.* vil.
fierce *adj.* ferose.
fiery *adj.* focosa.
fiesta *n.* carnaval.
fife *n.* (*flute*) fife.
fifth *adj.* (*ordinal*) sinco. • *n.* (*fraction*) sinci.
fifth column *n.* colona sinco.
fiftieth *adj.* (*ordinal*) sincodes. • *n.* (*fraction*) sincodesi.
fifty *det.* & *pron.* sincodes.
fig *n.* (*fruit*) figa; (*tree*) figo.
fight *v.* & *n.* combate, batalia.
fighter *n.* combator, batalior; (*wrestler*) lutor.
fighter aircraft *n.* avion xasante.
figment *n.* ilude.
figurative *adj.* metafor, nonleteral; (*art*) nonastrata.
figure *n.* figur.
figurehead *n.* (*ship*) figur de proa; (*nominal leader*) xef sin potia.
figure-hugging *adj.* abrasante, corpin.
figurine *n.* sculteta.
Fiji *n.* Viti, Fiji.
Fijian *adj.* & *n.* viti, fijian.
filament *n.* fibre, fileta.
filbert *n.* (*nut*) nozeta; (*tree*) nozeto.
filch *v.* fura.
file[1] *n.* (*papers*) arcivo; (*software*) fix. • *v.* arcivi.
file[2] *n.* (*smoothing tool*) lima. • *v.* limi.
file[3] *n.* (*queue*) filo; (*chess*) colona. • *v.* fili.
file cabinet *n.* arcivador.
file card *n.* fix.
file-hosting service *n.* ospitafix.
file manager *n.* (*software*) fixador.
filename *n.* nom de fix.
filer *n.* (*software*) fixador.
file sharing *n.* (*software*) comparti de fixes.
file system *n.* (*software*) sistem de fix.
filet (US). See *fillet.*
filet mignon *n.* filete de bove.
filial *adj.* fial.
filigree *n.* filigrana.
filing cabinet *n.* arcivador.
filing system *n.* (*software*) sistem de fix; (*physical*) sistem de arcivi.
Filipino *adj.* & *n.* filipino.
fill *v.* pleni. **fill in** (*form*) completi. **fill in the blank** pleni la spasio, completi la testo. **fill out** (*form*) completi.
filled *adj.* plen, plenida.
filler *n.* pleninte.
fillet *v.* & *n.* filete.
filling *adj.* pleninte. • *n.* (*action*) pleni; (*substance*) pleninte.
film *v.* filma. • *n.* filma; (*thin skin*) peleta.
film fan *n.* fan de sinema, sinemafilica.
filmmaker *n.* sinematografiste, sinemiste.
filmmaking *n.* sinematografia.
filmography *n.* filmografia.
filmy *adj.* diafana.
filo pastry *n.* pasta folin.
filozoa *n.* (*organisms*) filozones.
filozoon *n.* (*organism*) filozon.
filter *n.* filtro. • *v.* filtri.
filth *n.* mugre.
filthy *adj.* mugrosa; (*lewd*) lasiva.
filtrate *n.* permeada.
filtration *n.* filtri.
fin *n.* pina.
finagle *v.* froda.
final *adj.* & *n.* final.
finale *n.* final.
finalist *n.* finaliste.
finalize *v.* completi.
finally *adv.* final, a fini.
finance *v.* finansia, paia. • *n.* finansia.
financial *adj.* finansial.
financier *n.* finansior.
finch *n.* (*bird*) pinson.
find *v.* & *n.* trova. **able to be found** trovable. **find again** retrova. **find oneself** (*be situated*) trova se. **find out** descovre.
fine[1] *adj.* (*admirable*) amirable, eselente, valuada; (*narrow*) magra; (*delicate*) delicata.
fine[2] *v.* & *n.* (*penalty*) multa.
fine arts *n.* artes bela.
finely chopped *adj.* axida a picos.
fine-tune *v.* ajusteta.
finger *n.* dito. • *v.* diti, toca con ditos. **index finger** dito indicante. **little finger** dito peti. **middle finger** dito media. **ring finger** dito de anelo.
fingerlike *adj.* ditin.
fingernail *n.* ungia de dito.
fingerprint *n.* trasa de dito, impresa de dito.
fingertip *n.* punto de dito.
finial *n.* orna apical.
finicky *adj.* esijente.
finish *v.* & *n.* fini.
finite *adj.* finita, limitada; (*grammar*) finitiva.
Finland *n.* Suomi, Finland. **Gulf of Finland** Golfo Suomi.
Finn *n.* finsce.
Finnic *adj.* finica.
Finnish *adj.* suomi, finsce.
fiord *n.* fiordo.
fir *n.* abeto.
fire *n.* foco; (*destructive*) focon. • *v.* (*gun*) spara, ensende; (*missile*) xuta; (*pottery*) coce; (*from employment*) desemplea. **catch fire** ensende. **on fire** flaminte. **set fire to** ensende.
firearm *n.* fusil.
fireball *n.* bal de foco.

firebomb *n.* bomba de foco. • *v.* bombarda con foco.
fire breather *n.* sputafoco.
fire brigade *n.* brigada de pompores.
firebug *n.* xinxe focosa.
firecracker *n.* petardo.
fire department *n.* brigada de pompores, pomperia.
fire door *n.* parafoco.
fire eater *n.* comefoco.
fire engine *n.* camion de pompores.
fire escape *n.* scalera de securia.
fire extinguisher *n.* estinguador.
firefighter *n.* pompor.
firefly *n.* lampeta.
fireguard *n.* gardafoco.
fire hydrant *n.* idrante.
fireman *n.* pompor.
fireplace *n.* ximineria.
fire plug *n.* idrante.
firepower *n.* potia de spara.
fireproof *adj.* secur contra foco.
fire screen *n.* parafoco.
firestarter *n.* ensendor.
fire station *n.* pomperia.
firestone *n.* petra focosa.
firestorm *n.* tempesta de foco.
fire truck *n.* camion de pompores.
firewall *n.* (*software*) parafoco.
firewood *n.* lenio de foco.
firework display *n.* pirotecnical.
fireworks *n.* focos artal.
firm[1] *adj.* firma, dur; fisada.
firm[2] *n.* compania.
firmament *n.* sielo.
first *adj.* prima, un. • *n.* prima. **at first** prima.
firstborn *adj.* prima naseda.
first course *n.* plato prima.
first floor *n.* (*above ground level*) nivel prima.
first gear *n.* engrana prima.
firsthand *adj.* direta.
firstly *adv.* prima.
first name *n.* nom individua.
first-year *adj.* de anio prima. • *n.* studiante de anio prima.
firth *n.* estuario.
fiscal *adj.* finansial.
fiscorn *n.* (*musical instrument*) fiscorno.
fish *n.* pex. • *v.* pexa.
fish basket *n.* sesto de pexa.
fishbone *n.* oso de pex, spina.
fishbowl *n.* vaso de pexes.
fish crow *n.* corvo pexante.
fisherman *n.* pexor.
fishery *n.* pexeria.
fisheye *n.* oio de pex.
fisheye lens *n.* oio de pex.
fishhook *n.* onca de pexa.
fishing *n.* pexa.
fishing tackle *n.* aparatos de pexa.
fishmonger *n.* vendor de pex.
fish slice *n.* spatula de pex.
fish soup *n.* sopa de pex.
fissile *adj.* fisionable.
fission *n.* fende; (*technical*) fision. **undergo fission** fisioni.
fissionable *adj.* fisionable.
fissure *n.* fesur.
fist *n.* punio.
fistful *n.* plenipunio.
fistula *n.* (*medical*) fistula.
fit[1] *v.* ajusta; (*be the right size for*) cabe. • *adj.* conveninte; (*physically*) en bon forma. **fit around** casi, caxi. **one size fits all** lo es la mesma per cadun.
fit[2] *n.* (*medical, laughter, etc.*) ataca.
fitful *adj.* ajitada.
fitness *n.* (*physical*) bon forma.
fitter *n.* ajustor.
fitting room *n.* vesteria.
five *det.* & *pron.* sinco.
five-cent piece *n.* dudesim.
five-pence piece *n.* dudesim.
five-year-old *n.* enfante de sinco anios.
fix *v.* (*fasten*) fisa; (*repair*) repara. • *n.* repara.
fixable *adj.* fisable; reparable.
fixate *v.* osese.
fixation *n.* osese.
fixative *adj.* & *n.* fisante, stablinte.
fixer *n.* reparor.
fixture *n.* aparato fisada. **light fixture** portabulbo.
fizzy *adj.* gasosa.
fjord *n.* fiordo.
flab *n.* gras.
flabby *adj.* flasida; obesa.
flaccid *adj.* flasida.
flag *n.* bandera. • *v.* marca.
flagellate *v.* flajeli.
flagellation *n.* flajeli.
flagellum *n.* flajelo.
flagman *n.* banderor.
flagon *n.* carafa.
flagpole *n.* palo de bandera.
flagrant *adj.* evidente, nonfurtiva.
flagship *n.* barcon prima.
flagstone *n.* petra plata.
flail *v.* bambola.
flair *n.* talento.
flak *n.* spara antiavional.
flake *n.* floco.
flaky *adj.* flocosa.
flambé *adj.* flaminte.
flamboyant *adj.* estravagante, ostentosa.
flame *n.* flama. • *v.* flami. **flame up** flami.
flamenco *n.* (*dance, music*) flamenco.
flameproof *adj.* secur contra flama.

flame-retardant *adj.* resistente a foco. • *n.* paraflama.
flamethrower *n.* lansaflama.
flaming *adj.* flaminte, flamosa.
flamingo *n.* flamingo.
flammable *adj.* flamable.
flan *n.* (*pie*) tarte; (*crème caramel*) crema de caramel.
Flanders *n.* Flandre.
flange *n.* flanje.
flank *n.* lado.
flannel *n.* (*material*) flanela; (*facecloth*) teleta de lava.
flap *n.* ala; (*consonant*) tocante. • *v.* bate.
flapjack *n.* (*biscuit*) bara de musli; (*pancake*) crepe.
flare *v.* esvasa. • *n.* sinial luminante, misil luminante.
flared *adj.* esvasante.
flares *n.* pantalon esvasante.
flash *n.* (*of light*) flax; (*camera*) flaxador; flaxi, lampi. **quick as a flash** flax.
flashback *n.* retrospeta, sena retrospetante.
flashbulb *n.* bulbo flax.
flasher *n.* esibiste.
flash flood *n.* deluvia subita.
flash forward *v.* salta a ante.
flashlight *n.* lampa de pox.
flash memory *n.* memoria flax.
flask *n.* botela.
flat[1] *adj.* (*level and thin*) plata; (*not bumpy*) plana; (*music*) bemol. • *n.* bemol.
flat[2] *n.* (*apartment*) aparte.
flatbread *n.* pan plata.
flatfish *n.* pex plata.
flat iron *n.* fero calda.
flatland *n.* plano.
flatmate *n.* camerada de aparte, coabitor.
flat-pack *adj.* & *n.* asemblable.
flatten *v.* plati, plani; (*crush*) crase.
flatter *v.* adula, loda; (*garment*) favore.
flatterer *n.* adulor.
flattering *adj.* (*garment*) favorente.
flattery *n.* adula.
flattish *adj.* platin.
flat-top *n.* (*hairstyle*) capeles brosin.
flatulence *n.* flatule.
flatulent *adj.* flatulente.
flatware *n.* utiles de come.
flatworm *n.* verme plata, platielminto.
flaunt *v.* ostenta.
flautist *n.* flautiste.
flavour (US **flavor**) *n.* sabor. • *v.* sabori.
flavoured (US **flavor**) *adj.* saborida, con sabor.
flavourful (US **flavorful**) *adj.* saborosa.
flavouring (US **flavoring**) *n.* saborinte.
flavourless (US **flavorless**) *n.* sin sabor.
flaw *n.* fali, nonperfeta.
flawless *adj.* perfeta.
flax *n.* lino.
flay *v.* despeli.
flea *n.* pulga.
fleabag *n.* misera.
fleabite *n.* morde de pulga.
flea market *n.* mercato de pulgas.
fleawort *n.* (*plant*) plantago.
fleck *n.* manxa.
flection *n.* flexe.
fledgling *n.* avieta.
flee *v.* fuji, evade.
fleece *n.* lana.
fleecy *adj.* peluxetin.
fleet *n.* (*navy*) marina; (*ships or other vehicles*) flotila. • *adj.* rapida.
fleeting *adj.* tempora.
Fleming *n.* (*person*) flames.
Flemish *adj.* (*person, language*) flames.
flense *v.* despeli.
flerovium *n.* (*element*) flerovio.
flesh *n.* carne; (*fruit*) pulpa. • *v.* descarni. **flesh out** (*elaborate*) carni.
fleshpot *n.* lasiveria.
fleshy *adj.* carnosa; (*fruit*) pulposa.
fletch *v.* plumi.
fletcher *n.* flexor.
flex *v.* (*limb, muscle*) flexe.
flexibility *n.* flexablia.
flexible *adj.* flexable, ajustable.
flexible tube *n.* mangera.
flexion *n.* flexe.
flexor *n.* (*muscle*) flexador.
flick *v.* & *n.* colpeta, colpa con dito; lansa con dito.
flicker *v.* (*flame*) dansa; (*lights*) vibra.
flick knife *n.* cotel ejetable.
flies *n.* (*zip*) zipe; (*flap of garment*) covreta.
flight *n.* vola; (*fleeing*) fuji. **flight of stairs** scalera. **put to flight** fuji.
flighty *adj.* nonconstante.
flimflam *n.* (*nonsense*) asurda; (*con trick*) froda.
flimsy *adj.* frajil.
flinch *v.* salteta.
fling *v.* lansa, xuta.
flint *n.* petra focosa.
flintlock *n.* fusil de sintil.
flinty *adj.* nonsedente.
flip *v.* alterna; (*somersault*) volta.
flip-flop *n.* sandaleta.
flippant *adj.* desrespetosa.
flipper *n.* aleta; (*pinball*) pinbal.
flipperlike *adj.* aletin.
flirt *v.* flirta. • *n.* flirtor.
flirtation *n.* flirta.
flirtatious *adj.* flirtante.
flirty *adj.* flirtante.
flit *v.* & *n.* brinca.
float *v.* & *n.* flota.

floatation *n.* flota.
floating-point *n.* (*number*) de virgula flotante.
floccule *n.* floco.
flock *n.* (*birds*) manada; (*congregation*) congrega. • *v.* manadi.
floe *n.* jelo flotante.
flog *v.* flajeli.
flood *v.* & *n.* inonda; (*major*) deluvia.
flood barrier *n.* paradeluvia.
floodgate *n.* (*of lock*) porton.
floodlight *n.* lampa inondante, projetador.
floodlit *adj.* inondada con lus.
floodplain *n.* plano deluvial.
floor *n.* (*ground*) solo; (*sea*) fondo; (*storey*) nivel.
floorboard *n.* plance de solo.
flooring *n.* sursolo.
floor show *n.* cabare.
flop *v.* & *n.* colasa; fa un fiasco.
floppy disk *n.* disco mol.
flora *n.* plantas.
floral *adj.* (*design*) florosa.
Florentine *adj.* fiorentin.
Flores *n.* (*island*) Flores.
Flores Sea *n.* Mar Flores.
floret *n.* floreta.
florid *adj.* ornosa.
Florida *n.* (*US state*) Florida.
Florida Strait *n.* Streta Florida.
florin *n.* florin.
florist *n.* floriste; (*shop*) floreria.
floss *v.* fili sua dentes.
flotation *n.* flota.
flotilla *n.* marineta.
flotsam *n.* flotante.
flounder *v.* bambola.
flour *n.* farina.
flourish *v.* flori; (*wave*) brandi. • *n.* curva ornosa.
flourlike *adj.* farinin.
floury *adj.* (*flourlike*) farinin; (*full of flour*) farinosa.
flout *v.* iniora.
flow *v.* flue, core, ri. • *n.* flue; (*tide*) enflue. **flow in** enflue. **flow out** esflue.
flowchart *n.* scema de flue.
flower *n.* flor. • *v.* flori.
flowerbed *n.* fondo de flores.
flower cluster *n.* masto florinte.
flowerlike *adj.* florin.
flowerpecker *n.* (*bird*) disi.
flowerpot *n.* portaflor.
flower vase *n.* vaso de flores.
flowery *adj.* florosa.
flu *n.* gripe. **avian flu** gripe avial.
fluctuate *v.* flutua.
flue *n.* duto de caldi; duto de fuma.
fluent *adj.* fluente.
fluff *n.* peluxeta.
fluffy *adj.* peluxetin.
fluid *adj.* & *n.* fluente, licuida.
fluid dynamics *n.* dinamica de fluentes.
fluke *n.* (*whale*) aleta de coda; (*worm*) trematodo.
flume *n.* canal.
flunk *v.* fali.
flunkey *n.* lace.
fluoresce *v.* fluorese.
fluorescence *n.* fluorese.
fluorescent *adj.* fluoresente.
fluoride *n.* fluorido; (*in water or toothpaste*) fluorido de sodio.
fluorinate *v.* fluori.
fluorine *n.* fluor.
fluorite *n.* fluorita.
fluorocarbon *n.* fluorocarbono.
fluoroscope *n.* fluoroscopio.
flurry *v.* & *n.* neveta.
flush[1] *v.* (*redden*) roji; (*empty*) vacui; (*toilet*) descarga. • *n.* roji.
flush[2] *adj.* (*surface*) plana; (*text*) aliniada.
flush left *v.* alinia a sinistra.
flush right *v.* alinia a destra.
fluster *v.* ajita.
flute *n.* flauta.
flutist *n.* flautiste.
flutter *v.* & *n.* (*wings*) bateta; (*fly unsteadily*) voleta; (*flag*) ondeta.
fluvial *adj.* rial.
flux *n.* flue.
fly[1] *v.* vola. • *n.* (*zip*) zipe; (*flap*) ala; (*flap of garment*) covreta.
fly[2] *n.* (*insect*) mosca.
fly agaric *n.* amanita.
fly amanita *n.* amanita.
flyby *n.* (*space probe*) pasa per oserva; (*aircraft*) parade volante.
flycatcher *n.* caturamosca.
flyer *n.* volor; (*leaflet*) folia avisante.
fly high *v.* estasia.
flying buttress *n.* arco apoiante.
flying lemur *n.* colugo.
flying machine *n.* volador.
flying phalanger *n.* (*marsupial*) liscor.
flying possum *n.* (*marsupial*) liscor.
flying squirrel *n.* anomalur.
flyover *n.* viaduto.
flypaper *n.* trapimosca.
flypast *n.* (*aircraft*) parade volante.
fly ribbon *n.* trapimosca.
flyswat *n.* colpamosca.
flyswatter *n.* colpamosca.
flywheel *n.* rota de inertia.
foal *n.* cavaleta.
foam *v.* & *n.* spuma.
foam bath *n.* bani de spuma.
foamy *adj.* spumosa.
fob *n.* cadena de orolojeta.

focaccia *n.* (*bread*) focatxia.
focal *adj.* focal.
focal length *n.* distantia focal.
focus *v. & n.* (*light, energy, attention*) foca, consentra. **in focus** focada. **out of focus** nonfocada.
fodder *n.* comeda de bestias.
foe *n.* enemi.
foetal (US **fetal**) *adj.* fetal.
foetus (US **fetus**) *n.* feto.
fog *n.* nebla. **fog up** nebli.
fogey *n.* anticin.
foggy *adj.* neblosa.
foghorn *n.* alarma de nebla.
foible *n.* debil, strana.
foie gras *n.* figato grasosa.
foil *v.* aborta. **aluminium foil** paper de aluminio.
foist *v.* carga.
fold *v.* plia. • *n.* plia; (*sheepfold*) ensirca de oveas. **fold one's arms** crusa sua brasos.
foldable *adj.* pliable.
folder *n.* (*physical*) portapaper; (*software*) arcivo.
folding *adj.* pliable.
folding bed *n.* leto pliable.
folding knife *n.* cotel de pox.
foldout *adj.* abrable.
foliage *n.* folias.
folio *n.* (*book size*) folio.
folk *n.* persones.
folk dance *n.* dansa de folclor.
folklore *n.* folclor.
folk music *n.* musica de folclor.
folk song *n.* canta de folclor.
folksy *adj.* tradisional; casual.
folktale *n.* fable, nara de folclor.
follicle *n.* foliculo.
follow *v.* segue; (*obey*) obedi. **follow back** (*retrace*) resegue.
follower *n.* seguor. **follower of fashion** modiste.
follow-up *n.* seguente.
folly *n.* folia.
foment *v.* provoca.
fond *adj.* amosa; (*hope*) futil. **be fond of** gusta.
fondant *adj.* glasa fondente.
fondle *v.* caresa.
fondness *n.* amosia.
fondue *n.* fondu.
font *n.* tipo de letera.
fontanelle *n.* (*anatomy*) fontanel.
fontina *n.* (*cheese*) fontina.
food *n.* comeda, comable.
food chain *n.* cadena nural.
foodpipe *n.* esofago.
food rationing *n.* divide de comeda.
foodstuff *n.* comable.
fool *n.* fol, stupida. • *v.* jua.
foolhardy *adj.* noncauta.
foolish *adj.* fol, stupida.
foolishness *n.* folia, stupidia.
foolproof *adj.* secur contra bobos.
fool's errand *n.* mision fol.
fool's gold *n.* (*mineral*) pirita.
fool's mission *n.* mision fol.
foot *n.* pede. **by foot** par pede, par pasea. **on foot** par pede, par pasea.
footage *n.* (*film*) metraje.
football *n.* (*sport*) futbal; (*ball*) bal de futbal. **American football** futbal american.
footballer *n.* futbalor.
football pitch *n.* campo de futbal.
football player *n.* futbalor.
footbridge *n.* ponte de pasea.
footer *n.* pede de paje.
foothill *n.* pede de monte.
footlocker *n.* caxa de leto.
footman *n.* lace.
footnote *n.* nota basa.
footpath *n.* paseria.
footprint *n.* impresa de pede; (*environmental*) efeto; (*software*) consuma; (*reception range*) reseteria.
footrest *n.* reposapede.
foot soldier *n.* peon.
footstep *n.* paso; sona de paso.
footstool *n.* reposapede.
fop *n.* dandi.
foppery *n.* dandia.
for *prep.* (*for an intended reason, beneficiary, distance or duration*) per; (*in exchange for, on behalf of*) per; (*with the intention of*) con intende de; (*for an elapsed time or distance actually travelled*) tra. • *subord.* car. **for every** (*in measurements of speed, etc.*) per. **for example** per esemplo. **for instance** per esemplo. **for now** per aora, per la presente. **for sale** per vende. **for the most part** jeneral, per la plu.
forage *v.* foraje.
foramen *n.* (*anatomy*) forame.
foray *n.* ataca, invade.
forbear *v.* asteni.
forbearance *n.* asteni.
forbid *v.* proibi.
forbidden *adj.* proibida, nonpermeteda.
forbidding *adj.* menasante, nonamin.
force *v.* (*strongly or physically*) forsa; (*socially*) obliga. • *n.* (*strength*) fortia; (*military, physics*) forte. **air force** (*military*) forte de aira. **armed forces** fortes militar. **force back** forsa a via.
forceful *adj.* fortiosa.
forceps *n.* pinse medical.
forcible *adj.* fortiosa.
ford *n.* vado, rio basa. • *v.* vadi, traversa.
fore *adj.* fronte. • *interj.* atende.

forearm *n.* braso basa.
forebear *n.* asendente.
forebode *v.* premostra.
foreboding *n.* preteme. **have a foreboding** preteme.
forebrain *n.* serebro fronte.
forecast *v.* & *n.* predise.
foreclose *v.* reposese.
foreclosure *n.* reposese.
forefather *n.* asendente.
forefoot *n.* pede fronte.
foreground *n.* fronte.
forehead *n.* fronte.
foreign *adj.* stranjer.
foreigner *n.* stranjer.
foreign intelligence agency *n.* departe de securia esterna.
foreign minister *n.* ministro de esternas.
foreign policy *n.* politica esterna.
foreign secretary *n.* ministro de esternas.
foreknowledge *n.* preconose. **have foreknowledge of** preconose.
foremost *adj.* xef.
forensic *adj.* forense; legal.
forensics *n.* forensia.
forepart *n.* anterior.
foreplay *v.* & *n.* precopula.
forequarters *n.* (*animal*) anterior.
forerunner *n.* (*person*) presedor; (*thing*) presedente.
foresee *v.* previde, presensa.
foreseeable *adj.* previdable.
foreshadow *v.* premostra.
foreshortening *n.* corti de perspetiva.
foresight *n.* previde.
foreskin *n.* prepus.
forest *n.* foresta. • *v.* foresti.
forestall *v.* retarda.
forest clearance *n.* desforesti.
forested *adj.* forestosa.
forester *n.* forestor.
forest fire *n.* focon savaje.
forest ranger *n.* gardaforesta.
forestry *n.* cultiva de foresta.
foretell *v.* predise.
forethought *n.* preconsidera.
forever *adv.* sempre, per sempre.
forewarn *v.* preaverti.
foreword *n.* prefasa.
forfeit *n.* multa.
forfeiture *n.* multa.
forfend *v.* preveni.
forge *v.* (*metal*) forja; (*money, document*) falsi. • *n.* forjeria.
forger *n.* falsor.
forgery *n.* falsi.
forget *v.* oblida. **forget it** oblida lo.
forgetful *adj.* oblidante.
forget-me-not *n.* (*plant*) no-oblida-me.
forgettable *adj.* oblidable; mediocre.
forgivable *adj.* pardonable.
forgive *v.* pardona.
forgiveness *n.* pardona. **beg forgiveness** demanda per pardona.
forgo *v.* asteni.
fork *n.* force; (*bifurcation*) forci. • *v.* forci, divide, dui.
forked *adj.* forcin, divideda.
forker *n.* forcor.
forklift truck *n.* levacarga.
forklike *adj.* forcin.
fork-shaped *adj.* forcin.
forlorn *adj.* sin espera, abandonada.
form *n.* forma; (*questionnaire*) formulario. • *v.* formi. • *suff.* -forma.
formable *adj.* formable.
formal *adj.* formal.
formal attire *n.* veston.
formaldehyde *n.* formaldehido.
formalin *n.* (*substance*) formalin.
formality *n.* formalia.
format *n.* forma; (*of book, file, etc.*) formato. • *v.* formati.
formation *n.* (*shape*) forma; (*shaping*) formi.
formative *adj.* forminte.
former *adj.* pasada, presedente. **the former** acel, la prima.
formerly *adv.* a ante, pasada, a otra tempos.
form-fitting *adj.* abrasante, corpin.
formica *n.* (*plastic*) formica.
formidable *adj.* forte, intensa; respetable.
formless *adj.* sin forma.
formula *n.* formula.
formulaic *adj.* formulin.
formulary *n.* lista de medisines.
formulate *v.* formula.
formulation *n.* formula.
Fornax *n.* (*constellation*) la Forno.
fornicate *v.* adultera.
fornication *n.* adultera.
fornicator *n.* adulteror.
forsake *v.* abandona.
forsaken *adj.* abandonada.
forswear *v.* renunsia formal.
forsythia *n.* (*plant*) forsitia.
fort *n.* fortres.
forte *adj.* forte.
forth *adv.* a ante.
forthcoming *adj.* futur.
fortieth *adj.* (*ordinal*) cuatrodes. • *n.* (*fraction*) cuatrodesi.
fortification *n.* fortres.
fortified wine *n.* vino fortida.
fortify *v.* forti.
fortissimo *adj.* multe forte.
fortitude *n.* fortia.
fortnight *n.* du semanas.
fortress *n.* fortres.

fortuitous *adj.* (*by chance*) acaso; (*by good luck*) fortunosa.
fortunate *adj.* fortunosa.
fortune *n.* (*destiny*) fortuna; (*wealth*) un monton de mone, un monton de ricia.
fortuneteller *n.* clarvidente.
forty *det.* & *pron.* cuatrodes.
forum *n.* foro.
forumite *adj.* & *n.* foromanica.
forward *adj.* fronte. • *adv.* a fronte; (*moving*) a ante. • *n.* (*sport*) atacor. • *v.* (*document*) avansa. • *interj.* avansa. **go forward** avansa.
forward gear *n.* engrana de avansa.
forward planning *n.* preconsidera.
forwards *adv.* a ante. • *interj.* avansa.
forward slash *n.* bara inclinada.
fossa *n.* (*anatomy*) foso.
fossil *n.* fosil.
fossil fuel *n.* combustable de fosil.
fossilization *n.* fosili.
fossilize *v.* fosili.
foster *v.* coraji.
foster child *n.* enfante tempora adotada.
foster mother *n.* madre tempora adotante.
foster parents *n.* jenitores tempora adotante.
foul *adj.* repulsante. **fall foul** vitimi.
foul-mouthed *adj.* blasfemante, vulgar.
foul-smelling *adj.* malodorosa.
foul-tasting *adj.* malsaborosa.
found *v.* fundi.
foundation *n.* (*base*) funda; (*action*) fundi.
founder *n.* fundor.
foundling *n.* orfan.
foundry *n.* fonderia.
fount *n.* fonte; orijina.
fountain *n.* fonte.
fountainhead *n.* fonte; orijina.
fountain pen *n.* pen de fonte.
four *det.* & *pron.* cuatro. **on all fours** sur manos e jenos; (*animal*) sur cuatro pedes.
four-by-four *n.* multiterenal, engranada a cuatro rotas.
foursome *n.* cuatruple.
fourth *adj.* (*ordinal*) cuatro; (*fraction*) cuatri.
fourth finger *n.* dito de anelo.
fourth root *n.* radis cuatro.
four-wheel drive *n.* multiterenal, engranada a cuatro rotas.
fovea *n.* (*anatomy*) fovea.
fowl *n.* avia de cultiveria; (*meat*) carne de avia.
fox *n.* volpe.
Foxe *n.* Foxe.
Foxe Basin *n.* Baia Foxe.
Foxe Channel *n.* Streta Foxe.
foxglove *n.* dijitale.
foxhole *n.* buco de refuja.
foxhound *n.* xasor de volpes.
foxlike *adj.* volpin.
foxtrot *n.* (*dance, music*) fostrot.
foxy *adj.* sesosa.
foyer *n.* atrio.
fracas *n.* scaramuxa, disputa.
fractal *adj.* fratal.
fraction *n.* frato.
fractional *adj.* fratal.
fractious *adj.* disputosa.
fracture *v.* & *n.* frati.
fragile *adj.* frajil.
fragility *n.* frajilia.
fragment *n.* frato, peso. • *v.* frati.
fragmentation *n.* frati.
fragrance *n.* bon odor.
fragrant *adj.* bonodorinte, bonodorosa.
frail *adj.* frajil.
frailty *n.* debilia.
fraktur *n.* (*lettering*) fractur.
frame *n.* strutur; (*of lens*) montur; (*of picture*) moldur; (*of movie*) imaje; struturi; (*enclose*) ensirca.
framework *n.* strutur, sceleto; (*software*) armatur.
Fram Strait *n.* Streta Fram.
franc *n.* (*currency*) franc.
France *n.* Frans.
franchise *n.* (*commercial*) francisia; (*right to vote*) direto de vota.
Franciscan *adj.* & *n.* fransiscan.
francium *n.* (*element*) fransio.
frangible *adj.* frajil.
frangipani *n.* (*tree*) plumeria.
frank[1] *adj.* (*outspoken*) franca. • *v.* marca como paiada. • *n.* marca de paia; (*hotdog*) salsix american.
Frank[2] *n.* franco.
frankfurter *n.* (*hotdog*) salsix american; (*bun*) paneta de salsix.
frankincense *n.* (*resin*) olibano.
franking mark *n.* marca de paia.
Frankish *adj.* franco.
frankness *n.* francia.
frantic *adj.* manica, panicada.
frappé *adj.* fria.
fraternal *adj.* fratin.
fraternal twin *n.* jemelo nonidentica.
fraternity *n.* (*quality*) fratia; (*organization*) frateria.
fratricide *n.* (*action*) fratiside; (*person*) fratisidor. **commit fratricide** fratiside.
fraud *n.* froda; (*person*) finjor, frodor.
fraudster *n.* frodor.
fraudulent *adj.* frodante.
fraught *adj.* ansiosa. **fraught with** plen de.
fray[1] *v.* (*unravel*) gasta.
fray[2] *n.* scaramuxa; compete.
frayed *adj.* gastada, destexeda.
freaky *adj.* strana.
freckle *n.* punteta.

free *adj.* (*unrestricted*) libre; (*zero-cost*) sin custa. • *v.* libri. **for free** sin custa.
freebie *n.* cosa sin custa.
freedom *n.* libria. **freedom of the press** libria de jornalisme.
freeform *adj.* nonstruturida; improvisada.
freelance *adj.* libre.
freemason *n.* francamason.
freemasonry *n.* francamasonisme.
freephone number *n.* numero sin custa.
free radical *n.* (*chemistry*) radical libre.
freesia *n.* (*plant*) fresia.
free software *n.* (*unrestricted*) programes libre; (*zero-cost*) programes sin custa.
freethinker *n.* pensor libre.
free time *n.* tempo libre.
freeware *n.* programes sin custa.
freeway *n.* via xef.
free will *n.* volunta libre.
freeze *v.* jela; (*software*) saisi se. • *n.* jela.
freezer *n.* jelador.
freight *n.* carga.
freighter *n.* barcon de carga.
freight wagon *n.* vagon de carga.
French *adj.* & *n.* (*person*, *language*) franses.
French door *n.* porte-fenetra.
French fries *n.* fritadas, patatas fritada.
French Guiana *n.* Guian Franses.
French horn *n.* trompa.
French knickers *n.* culote.
French Polynesia *n.* Polinesia Franses.
French window *n.* porte-fenetra.
frenetic *adj.* nonrestrinjeda.
frenzy *n.* panica.
freon *n.* freon.
frequency *n.* frecuentia.
frequency band *n.* banda de frecuentia.
frequent *adj.* frecuente, comun.
frequently *adv.* frecuente, comun, a multe veses.
fresco *n.* (*art*) fresco.
fresh *adj.* fresca; (*water*) dulse; (*flirtatious*) flirtante. **fresh from** resente de.
fresh coat *n.* (*of paint*) revesti.
freshen *v.* fresci. **air freshener** desodorinte.
fresher *n.* studiante nova, studiante de anio prima.
freshly *adv.* nova.
freshman *n.* studiante nova, studiante de anio prima.
freshwater *n.* acua dulse. • *adj.* de acua dulse.
fret[1] *v.* (*worry*) ansi.
fret[2] *n.* (*of musical instrument*) traste.
fretful *adj.* ansiosa.
fretsaw *n.* siericurva.
fretwork *n.* dentela de lenio.
Freudian *adj.* freudiste.
Freudianism *n.* freudisme.
friable *adj.* desintegrable.
friar *n.* frate.
fricassee *n.* (*food*) fricase.
fricative *adj.* & *n.* (*consonant*) fricante.
friction *n.* frica. **cause friction** frica.
Friday *n.* venerdi.
fridge *n.* friador.
fried egg *n.* ovo fritada.
friend *n.* ami. **become friends** amini. **make friends with** amini.
friendliness *n.* aminia.
friendly *adj.* amin, amante.
friendly fire *n.* spara par aliada.
friendship *n.* amia.
friendship tree *n.* crasula.
fries *n.* fritadas, patatas fritada.
Friesland *n.* Frisland.
frieze *n.* friso.
frigate *n.* fregate.
frigatebird *n.* fregate.
fright *n.* asusta.
frighten *v.* asusta, panica.
frightful *adj.* asustante.
frigid *adj.* fria; (*sexually*) sin libido.
frijol *n.* (*bean*) fava roja.
frill *n.* fronsida.
frilly *adj.* fronsosa.
fringe *n.* (*border*, *hairstyle*) franje.
frisbee *n.* frisbi.
Frisia *n.* Frisland.
Frisian *adj.* & *n.* (*person*, *language*) frisce.
frisk *v.* palpa.
frisky *adj.* juosa.
frisson *n.* vibra.
Friulian *adj.* & *n.* (*person*, *language*) furlan.
frivolity *n.* diverti, joia.
frivolous *adj.* nonseria, sin seria.
frizz *v.* crespi.
frizzen *n.* (*of gun*) aser.
frizzy *adj.* crespa.
fro, to and *adv.* de asi a ala.
frock coat *n.* jacon robin.
frog *n.* rana.
froggy *adj.* ranin.
froglike *adj.* ranin.
frogman *n.* sumerjor.
frogspawn *n.* ovipari.
frolic *v.* jua.
from *prep.* de. **from above** de supra. **from ahead** de ante. **from behind** de pos. **from downstairs** de su. **from in front** de ante. **from now on** de aora. **from then on** de alora. **from time to time** de ves a ves, a veses, aora e alora. **from under** de su. **from upstairs** de supra.
frond *n.* folia.
front *adj.* fronte. • *n.* fronte; (*of body*) ventre. **at the front of** a fronte de. **in front** a

ante. **in front of** ante, a fronte de; (*motion towards*) a ante, a fronte de. **inside the front of** en fronte de. **into the front of** en fronte de.
frontal bone *n.* oso fronte.
frontal lobe *n.* lobe fronte.
front door *n.* porte xef.
frontier *n.* frontera, limita.
frontiersman *n.* fronteror.
frontispiece *n.* (*publishing*, *architecture*) frontispis.
front line *n.* frontera.
frontrunner *n.* competor favoreda.
front vowel *n.* vocal fronte.
frost *n.* jelada. • *v.* (*glaze*) glasa.
frostbite *n.* ulsera jelal.
frostbitten *adj.* ulserada.
frosted *adj.* diafana.
frosting *n.* glasa.
frosty *adj.* jelosa.
froth *v.* & *n.* spuma.
frothy *adj.* spumosa.
froufrou *adj.* fronsosa. • *n.* (*rustling*) xuxa.
frown *v.* grima, fronsi sua suprasiles. • *n.* grima.
frozen *adj.* jelada; (*software*) saisida.
frozen fog *n.* nebla jelada.
frozen smoke *n.* airojel.
fructose *n.* (*sugar*) frutosa.
frugal *adj.* frugal.
frugality *n.* frugalia.
frugalness *n.* frugalia.
fruit *n.* fruta, frutas. • *v.* fruti. **bear fruit** fruti.
fruitcake *n.* torta de fruta.
fruiterer *n.* frutor.
fruiterer's *n.* (*shop*) fruteria.
fruitful *adj.* frutosa; fertil.
fruiting body *n.* (*botany*) sporocarpo.
fruition *n.* reali.
fruitless *adj.* futil.
fruitlessness *n.* futilia.
fruit pie *n.* tarte de fruta.
fruity *adj.* frutosa.
frumpy *adj.* nonmodosa, anticin.
frustrate *v.* frustra.
frustration *n.* frustra.
frustum *n.* (*geometry*) tronco.
fry *v.* frita.
fryer *n.* fritador.
frying pan *n.* padela.
fry pan *n.* padela.
fuchsia *adj.* (*colour*) fucsia. • *n.* (*flower*) fucsia.
fuck *v.* (*sex*) fode. • *interj.* (*frustration*, *anger*) txa.
fucking *adj.* (*intensifier*) fodeda.
fudge *n.* caramel mol.
fuel *n.* combustable; (*for engine*) carburante. • *v.* nuri.
fuel cell *n.* pila de combustable.
fufu *n.* (*food*) fufu.
fugal *adj.* fugal.
fugitive *n.* fujor.
fugue *n.* (*music*, *psychology*) fuga.
-ful *suff.* -osa.
fulcrum *n.* fulcro.
fulfil (US **fulfill**) *v.* (*ambition*) reali; (*requirement*) sasia; (*duty*) completi, esecuta.
fulfilling *adj.* (*satisfying*) sasiante, completinte.
fulfilment (US **fulfillment**) *n.* (*of ambition*) reali; (*of requirement*) sasia; (*of duty*) completi.
full[1] *adj.* plen, -osa; (*coverage*) completa. **full of** plen de. **full of life** vivosa. **full of oneself** egosa.
full[2] *v.* (*material*) feltri.
full-board *adj.* (*hotel*) con tre comes.
full-figured *adj.* formosa.
full form *n.* (*of abbreviation*) forma completa.
full moon *n.* luna plen.
fullness *n.* plenia.
full-rigged ship *n.* fregate.
full-scale *adj.* de grandia natural.
full-size *adj.* de grandia natural.
full stop *n.* (*period*) punto.
full-time *adj.* de tempo plen.
fulminate *v.* protesta; esplode.
fulminating *adj.* sever e subita.
fumble *v.* torpi.
fume *n.* fuma.
fumes *n.* gas nosiva, vapor nosiva.
fumigate *v.* fumiga.
fumigation *n.* fumiga.
fumiter *n.* (*plant*) fumaria.
fumitory *n.* fumaria.
fun *n.* diverti, joia. • *adj.* divertinte, joiosa. **have fun** diverti, diverti bon, joia.
funambulist *n.* paseacorda.
function *v.* (*work*) funsiona, vade; (*be operated*) opera. • *n.* (*job*) posto, rol; (*mathematics*, *software*) funsiona.
functional *adj.* funsionante, operante; (*of a function*) funsional.
functionalism *n.* funsionalisme.
functionalist *adj.* & *n.* funsionaliste.
functionalistic *adj.* funsionaliste.
functional programming *n.* programi funsional.
functioning *n.* funsiona, opera. • *adj.* funsionante, operante.
fund *v.* finansia, suporta. • *n.* reserva.
fundamental *adj.* fundal, radisal.
fundamentalism *n.* fundalisme. **Islamic fundamentalism** islamisme.
fundamentalist *adj.* & *n.* fundaliste. **Islamic fundamentalist** islamiste.
fundamentally *adv.* fundal, a radis.
funding *n.* suporta finansial.

fundraiser *n.* (*activity*) recolie de reservas; (*person*) recolior de reservas.
fundraising *n.* recolie de reservas.
Fundy, Bay of *n.* Baia Fundy.
funeral *n.* funera. • *adj.* funeral.
funeral cloth *n.* telon funeral.
funeral march *n.* marxa funeral.
funeral parlour (US **parlor**) *n.* funereria.
funeral procession *n.* prosegue funeral.
funerary *adj.* funeral.
funereal *adj.* funeral.
fungal *adj.* fungal.
fungible *adj.* intercambiable.
fungicide *n.* fungiside.
fungus *n.* fungo.
funicular *adj.* & *n.* funicular.
funk *adj.* & *n.* (*music*) func.
funky *adj.* funcosa.
funnel *n.* (*for pouring*) embuto; (*chimney*) ximine. • *v.* embuti.
funnel-like *adj.* embutin.
funnelweb spider *n.* arania de rede embutin.
funny *adj.* comica.
fur *n.* pelo.
furbelow *n.* fronsida.
furcula *n.* (*wishbone*) furcula.
fur hat *n.* xapo de pelo.
furious *adj.* furiosa. **be furious** furia.
furl *v.* enrola.
Furlan *adj.* & *n.* furlan.
furlike *adj.* pelin.
furlong *n.* (*unit of length*) furlong.
furlough *n.* asentia permeteda.
furnace *n.* fornon.
furnish *v.* (*supply*) furni; (*with furniture*) mobili.
furnishings *n.* mobilas.
furniture *n.* mobilas. **piece of furniture** mobila.
furniture polish *n.* briliamobila.
furore *n.* furia publica; (*craze*) mania.
furrow *n.* (*ploughed*) plia, ranur, ranur de arado; (*wrinkle*) plieta. • *v.* plieta. **furrow one's brow** plieta sua fronte.
furry *adj.* (*furlike*) pelin; (*shaggy*) pelosa.
fur seal *n.* otario.
further *det.* plu. • *adv.* plu; plu distante. **further than** ultra, plu distante ca.
further education *n.* educa ajuntada.
furthermore *adv.* plu, en ajunta.
furthest *adj.* estrema, la plu distante.
furtive *adj.* secreta.
furuncle *n.* (*abscess*) aseseta.
fury *n.* furia.
furze *n.* (*plant*) ulex.
fuse[1] *n.* (*electric*) fondable. • *v.* (*blend*) fusa.
fuse[2] *n.* (*bomb*) mexa.
fuselage *n.* tronco.
fusible *adj.* fusable, fondable.
fusiform *adj.* (*spindle-shaped*) fusin.
fusilier *n.* fusilor.
fusion *n.* fusa.
fuss *n.* reata.
fussy *adj.* esijente, pedante.
fustian *n.* (*fabric*) fustan; (*pompous text*) testo ostentosa.
fusuma *n.* (*screen*) fusuma.
futile *adj.* futil.
futility *n.* futilia.
futon *n.* (*mattress*) futon.
Futunan *adj.* & *n.* futuna.
future *adj.* futur, veninte. • *n.* futur. **in the future** en la futur. **see the future** clarvide.
futurist *n.* futuriste.
futurologist *n.* futurolojiste.
futurology *n.* futurolojia.
fuzz *n.* peluxeta.
fuzzy *adj.* neblosa.

G

gab *v.* babela.
GABA *n.* (*biology*) gaba.
gabardine *n.* (*fabric*) gabardina.
gabble *v.* babela.
gable *n.* fronton.
Gabon *n.* Gabon.
Gabonese *adj.* & *n.* gabones.
gadget *n.* aparato, macineta.
gadolinium *n.* (*element*) gadolinio.
Gaelic *adj.* & *n.* (*person, language*) eres.
gaffe *n.* era sosial.
gag *n.* broma.
gaggle *n.* (*geese*) manada.
Gagulta *n.* (*hill*) Calvario.
gaiety *n.* joia.
gain *v.* gania. • *n.* profita. **gain advantage** benefica. **gain independence** autonomi.
gait *n.* modo de pasea.
gal *n.* xica, joven.
gala *n.* selebra.
galactic *adj.* galasial.
galactose *n.* (*sugar*) galatosa.
galago *n.* (*primate*) galago.
Galápagos Islands *n.* Isolas Galapagos.
galaxy *n.* galasia.
gale *n.* venton.
Galicia *n.* (*Spanish region*) Galisia.
Galician *adj.* & *n.* galego.
galium *n.* (*plant*) galia.
gall *n.* bile.
gallant *adj.* brava.
gall bladder *n.* vesica bilal.
galleon *n.* (*ship*) galeon.
gallery *n.* (*showroom, architecture*) galeria.
galley *n.* (*ship*) galea.
gallium *n.* (*element*) galio.
gallon *n.* galon.
gallop *v.* & *n.* galopa.
gallows *n.* pendador.
gallstone *n.* calculo bilal.
Gallurese *adj.* & *n.* (*person, language*) gadures.
galvanic *adj.* galvanica.
galvanize *v.* zinci.
Gambia *n.* Gambia.
Gambian *adj.* & *n.* gambian.
gambit *n.* comensa riscosa.
gamble *v.* & *n.* aposta.
gambler *n.* juor.
gambling *n.* jua de fortuna.
gambling debt *n.* deta de jua.
gambling game *n.* jua de aposta.
gambol *v.* brinca, jua. • *n.* brinca.
game *n.* jua; (*match*) max; (*animal*) animal xasada; (*meat*) carne xasada. **big game** animal xasada. **game of chance** jua de acaso, jua de fortuna.
gamebird *n.* avia xasada.
gamekeeper *n.* gardaxasa.
gamelan *n.* gamelan.
gamer *n.* juor.
game show *n.* program de concurso.
gamete *n.* gameta.
gametophyte *n.* gametofite.
gamey *adj.* con sabor de xasada.
gamin *n.* xico vagante.
gamine *n.* xica vagante.
gamma *n.* (*Greek letter* Γ, γ) gama.
gamma ray *n.* raio gama.
-gamous *suff.* -gama.
gamut *n.* estende.
-gamy *suff.* (*marriage, mating*) -gamia.
Gan *n.* (*language*) gan.
ganache *n.* (*food*) ganax.
gander *n.* ganso mas.
gang *n.* gang.
Ganges River *n.* Rio Ganga.
ganglion *n.* (*biology*) ganglio.
gangplank *n.* plance de embarca.
gangrene *n.* gangrena.
gangrenous *adj.* gangrenosa.
gangster *n.* gangster.
gangway *n.* plance de embarca.
gannet *n.* (*bird*) bobo.
gantry *n.* cavaleta, gru cavaletin.
gaol *n.* prison.
gaoler *n.* gardor.
gap *n.* buco, fesur; (*to be bridged metaphorically*) canion.
gape *v.* balia.
garage *n.* garaje.
Gara-Gum Desert *n.* Deserto Karakum.
garb *n.* vestes.
garbage *n.* dejetada.
garbage can *n.* baldon.
garbage dump *n.* dejeteria.
garbage heap *n.* monton de dejetadas.
garbage man *n.* dejetor.
garbanzo bean *n.* fava de visia.
garble *v.* malnara.
garden *n.* jardin.
gardener *n.* jardinor.
gardenia *n.* (*plant*) gardenia.
gardening *n.* labora de jardin.
garden sprinkler *n.* duxierba.
gargantuan *adj.* jigante.
gargle *v.* & *n.* gargara.
gargoyle *n.* gargola.
garish *adj.* xiliante.
garland *n.* garlanda. • *v.* garlandi.

garlic *n.* alio.
garlic crusher *n.* presalio.
garlic press *n.* presalio.
garment *n.* veste.
garner *v.* colie.
garnet *n.* (*gem*) granato.
garnish *v.* & *n.* decora.
garotte *n.* garota. • *v.* garoti.
garret *n.* suteto.
garrison *n.* garnison.
garrulous *adj.* parlosa.
garter *n.* (*stocking strap*) lia, bretela de calsa; (*band around leg*) banda de calsa.
garter belt *n.* portalia.
gas *n.* gas. • *v.* gasi.
gasbag *n.* saco de gas; parlosa.
gas can *n.* carafon de gasolina.
gas chamber *n.* cambra de gas.
gaseous *adj.* (*of a gas*) gasal; (*like a gas*) gasin; (*full of gas*) gasosa.
gas giant *n.* jigante de gas, planeton de gas.
gash *v.* & *n.* talia.
gasket *n.* junta selinte.
gaslight *n.* lampa de gas. • *v.* manipula par autoduta.
gasoline *n.* gasolina.
gasoline can *n.* carafon de gasolina.
gasometer *n.* gasometre.
gasp *v.* & *n.* enspireta, enspira subita; (*sob*) sanglota. **last gasp** respira final.
gas pedal *n.* aselerador.
gas station *n.* gasolineria.
gassy *adj.* gasosa.
gastralgia *n.* gastraljia.
gastric *adj.* gastral.
gastritis *n.* gastrite.
gastroenteritis *n.* gastroenterite.
gastroenterologist *n.* gastroenterolojiste.
gastroenterology *n.* gastroenterolojia.
gastrointestinal *adj.* gastrointestinal.
gastronome *n.* gurme.
gastropod *n.* gastropodo.
gastrotrich *n.* (*worm*) gastrotrico.
gas welding *n.* osisolda.
gate *n.* (*field, garden*) porteta; (*castle, town*) porton.
gatehouse *n.* casa de garda.
gatekeeper *n.* gardaporton.
gateway *n.* porteta.
gather *v.* asembla, colie; (*fabric*) fronsi. • *n.* fronsi.
gathering *n.* asembla.
gauche *adj.* nonsofisticada.
gaudy *adj.* ornosa.
Gaul *n.* (*ancient region*) Galia; (*person*) galo.
Gaulish *adj.* (*person, language*) galo.
gaunt *adj.* magra, fatigada.
gauntlet *n.* ganto de armur. **run the gauntlet** core tra bates.
gauss *n.* (*unit of induction*) gaus.
gauze *n.* gaza.
gauzy *adj.* diafana.
gavel *n.* marteleta.
gavotte *n.* (*dance, music*) gavota.
gawk *v.* regarda intensa.
gay *adj.* (*homosexual*) ge; (*cheerful*) bonumorosa. • *n.* ge.
Gaza *n.* Gaza. **Gaza strip** Gaza.
gaze *v.* contempla.
gazebo *n.* belvedere.
gazelle *n.* gazela.
gazette *n.* jornal.
gazpacho *n.* (*soup*) gaspatxo.
GDP *n.* produi interna bruta.
gear *n.* pinion, rota de dentes; (*setting*) engrana.
gearbox *n.* engranador.
gear change *n.* cambia de engrana.
gearshift *n.* lever de engrana.
gearstick *n.* lever de engrana.
gecko *n.* geco.
geek *n.* ganso, manica.
geezer *n.* (*man*) xico; (*old man*) anticin.
gefilte fish *n.* pex plenida.
Geiger counter *n.* contador de Geiger.
geisha *n.* gexa.
gel *n.* jel; (*gelatin*) jelatin. • *v.* jeli.
gelatin *n.* jelatin.
gelatinize *v.* jelatini.
gelatinous *adj.* jelatin.
gelato *n.* (*ice cream*) jelato.
gem *n.* jem.
geminate *v.* jemeli.
gemination *n.* jemeli.
Gemini *n.* (*constellation*) la Jemelos.
-gen *suff.* -jen.
gendarme *n.* polisior, polisior franses.
gender *n.* (*physical*) seso; (*male or female, grammatical*) jenero.
gender-fluid *adj.* de jenero fluente.
gender identity *n.* identia de jenero.
gender-neutral *adj.* ajenero.
gene *n.* jen.
genealogical *adj.* jenealojial.
genealogist *n.* jenealojiste.
genealogy *n.* jenealojia.
general *adj.* jeneral, comun. • *n.* (*officer*) jeneral. **in general** jeneral.
general election *n.* vota jeneral.
generalization *n.* jenerali.
generalize *v.* jenerali.
general-purpose *adj.* multiusal.
general rule *n.* regula jeneral.
generate *v.* jenera.
generation *n.* jenera.
generator *n.* jenerador.
generic *adj.* (*not specific, of a genus*) jeneral.
generosity *n.* jenerosia.

generous *adj.* jenerosa.
genesis *n.* jenese, crea. • *suff.* -jenese.
genetic *adj.* jenetical.
genetically modified *adj.* jenetical alterada.
geneticist *n.* jeneticiste.
genetics *n.* jenetica.
genial *adj.* amin.
-genic *suff.* (*producing*) -jen.
genie *n.* djini.
genital *adj.* jenital. **genitals** jenitales.
genitalia *n.* jenitales.
genitive *adj.* & *n.* (*grammar*) jenitiva.
genius *n.* jenio.
Genoa *n.* (*Italian city*) Genova.
genocide *n.* jenoside.
Genoese *adj.* & *n.* genoves.
genome *n.* jenom.
genotype *n.* jenotipo.
genre *n.* jenero.
genteel *adj.* jentil.
gentile *adj.* & *n.* pagan.
gentle *adj.* jentil, dulse.
gentleman *n.* senior; (*gender-neutral*) sri.
gentleness *n.* jentilia, dulsia.
gentlewoman *n.* dama.
gentrification *n.* burjesi.
gentrify *v.* burjesi.
gentry *n.* clase alta.
genuflect *v.* plia un jeno, ajena se.
genuflection *n.* plia de jeno.
genuflexion *n.* plia de jeno.
genuine *adj.* autentica, vera; (*sincere*) sinsera.
genuineness *n.* autenticia.
genus *n.* jenero.
geo- *pref.* (*Earth*) jeo-.
geocentric *adj.* jeosentral.
geochemistry *n.* jeocimica.
geode *n.* (*geology*) jeodo.
geodesic *adj.* jeodesial.
geodesic dome *n.* cupola jeodesial.
geodesy *n.* jeodesia.
geodetic *adj.* jeodesial.
geographer *n.* jeografiste.
geographical *adj.* jeografial.
geography *n.* jeografia.
geolocate *v.* jeolocali.
geolocation *n.* jeolocali.
geological *adj.* jeolojial.
geologist *n.* jeolojiste.
geology *n.* jeolojia.
geomancy *n.* (*divination*) jeomansia.
geometrical *adj.* jeometrial.
geometrician *n.* jeometriste.
geometrid moth *n.* jeometrido.
geometry *n.* jeometria.
geomorphology *n.* jeomorfolojia.
geophysical *adj.* jeofisical.
geophysics *n.* jeofisica.
geopolitic *adj.* jeopolitical.
geopolitical *adj.* jeopolitical.
geopolitics *n.* jeopolitica.
Georgia *n.* (*Caucasus*) Sacartvelo, Jorjia; (*US state*) Georgia.
Georgian *adj.* & *n.* (*person, language of the Caucasus*) cartuli, jorjian.
geostationary *adj.* jeostable.
geosynchronous *adj.* jeosincrona.
geothermal *adj.* jeotermal.
geranium *n.* jeranio.
gerbil *n.* jerbil.
geriatric *adj.* senesente.
germ *n.* microbio, patojen; (*cereal*) jerme.
German *adj.* & *n.* (*person, language*) deutx.
Germanic *adj.* & *n.* germanica.
germanium *n.* (*element*) germanio.
German measles *n.* rubeola.
German shepherd dog *n.* can de pastor deutx.
Germany *n.* Deutxland.
germfree *adj.* sin microbios.
germicide *adj.* & *n.* antimicrobial.
germinate *v.* jerme.
gerontologist *n.* jerontolojiste.
gerontology *n.* jerontolojia.
gerrymander *v.* manipula distritos elejal.
gerund *n.* jerundio.
gesso *n.* jeso.
gestalt *n.* gestalt.
gestapo *n.* gestapo.
gestate *v.* jesta.
gestation *n.* jesta.
gesticulate *v.* jesti.
gesture *v.* & *n.* jesti.
get *v.* (*obtain*) oteni, prende; (*receive*) reseta; (*become*) deveni. **get back to** reateni. **get better** (*improve*) boni; (*health*) recovre, sani. **get even** venja, venja se. **get off** (*alight*) desende; (*be acquitted*) es desculpada. **get one's own back** venja se. **get out** sorti. **get revenge** venja se. **get rid of** dejeta, desprende; (*abolish*) aboli. **get to know** comensa conose. **get up** leva. **get used to** abitua a.
getaway *n.* (*escape*) evade, fuji; (*vacation*) vacanse.
getaway car *n.* auto de fuji.
get-together *n.* asembla.
getup *n.* vestes fantasin.
gewgaw *n.* orneta.
geyser *n.* geser.
Ghana *n.* Gana.
Ghanaian *adj.* & *n.* ganaian.
ghastly *adj.* macabre.
ghee *n.* (*butter*) gi.
gherkin *n.* concombre vinagrida.
ghetto *n.* geto.
ghillie *n.* aidor de xasa.

ghost *n.* fantasma. **give up the ghost** respira final.
ghostly *adj.* fantasmin.
ghostwrite *v.* scrive per un otra.
ghostwriter *n.* scrivor ombral.
ghoul *n.* (*mythology*) gul.
ghoulish *adj.* macabre.
giant *adj.* jigante, enorme. • *n.* jigante.
giantism *n.* jigantia.
giant planet *n.* planeton.
gibber *v.* babela.
gibberish *n.* babela. • *adj.* babelosa.
gibbet *n.* pendador.
gibbon *n.* gibon.
gibbous *adj.* (*moon*) jibosa.
giblets *n.* organos.
Gibraltar *n.* Jibraltar. **Strait of Gibraltar** Streta Jibraltar.
Gibraltarian *adj.* & *n.* jibraltarian.
giddy *adj.* mareada, vertigosa. **feel giddy** marea.
giddy-up *interj.* vade.
gift *n.* (*present*) donada; (*ability*) talento, capasia.
gifted *adj.* talentosa.
giftwrap *n.* paper de donadas.
gig *n.* gigabait.
giga- *pref.* (*a thousand million*) giga-.
gigabyte *n.* gigabait.
gigantic *adj.* jigante.
gigantism *n.* jigantia.
giggle *v.* & *n.* rieta.
gigolo *n.* jigolo, xasafem, om promiscua.
gigue *n.* (*dance, music*) jiga.
Gila monster *n.* (*lizard*) monstro de Gila.
gild *v.* dora. **gild the lily** dora la lil.
gilder *n.* doror.
gill *n.* (*fish*) brancia; (*mushroom*) lamina.
gillie *n.* aidor de xasa.
gilly *n.* aidor de xasa.
gilt *adj.* dorada.
giltware *n.* benes dorada.
gimbal *n.* cardan.
gimlet *n.* turnabroca.
gimmick *n.* truco.
gimp *n.* coxeor.
gimpy *adj.* coxeante.
gin *n.* jin.
ginger *n.* (*plant, spice*) jinjer. • *adj.* (*hair*) roja, con capeles roja.
gingerbread *n.* pan de jinjer.
ginger nut *n.* biscoto de jinjer.
gingersnap *n.* biscoto de jinjer.
gingham *n.* gingam. • *adj.* de gingam.
gingival *adj.* jenjival.
gingivitis *n.* jenjivite.
ginkgo *n.* (*tree*) ginco.
ginseng *n.* (*plant, root*) jinsen.
giraffe *n.* jirafa.
gird *v.* ensirca.
girder *n.* faxon.
girdle *n.* corseto.
girl *n.* xica.
girlfriend *n.* ami de cor, xica de cor, amor; (*any female friend*) ami fema.
girl guide *n.* scolta.
girlhood *n.* enfantia, jovenia.
girlish *adj.* (*youthful*) joven; (*feminine*) femin.
girl scout *n.* scolta.
girth *n.* perimetre.
gist *n.* esense.
give *v.* dona. **give back** redona. **give birth** pari, nase. **give off** emete. **give the impression** (*of being or doing*) pare. **give up** sede. **give up on** abandona. **give up the ghost** respira final. **give voice to** vosi. **give way** sede.
giveaway *n.* (*freebie*) cosa sin custa; (*indicator*) revelante.
given *adj.* donada; (*taking into account*) considerante.
giver *n.* donor.
gizmo *n.* aparateta.
glacial *adj.* glasial.
glaciate *v.* glasi.
glaciation *n.* glasi.
glacier *n.* glasia.
glaciologist *n.* glasiolojiste.
glaciology *n.* glasiolojia.
glad *adj.* felis, contente.
gladden *v.* felisi.
gladdon *n.* calamo.
glade *n.* (*plant*) pradeta.
gladiator *n.* gladiator.
gladiolus *n.* gladiolo.
glamorize *v.* glamori.
glamorous *adj.* glamorosa.
glamour *n.* glamor.
glance *n.* regardeta, regarda. **glance at** regardeta.
gland *n.* glande.
glans *n.* glande.
glare *v.* (*stare*) grima. • *n.* grima; (*dazzle*) brilion; lus refletada.
glasnost *n.* glasnost.
glass *n.* (*substance, container*) vitro.
glassblower *n.* soflor de vitro.
glassblowing *n.* sofla de vitro.
glasses *n.* (*spectacles*) oculo.
glasses store *n.* oculeria.
glass fibre (US **fiber**) *n.* fibre de vitro.
glasshouse *n.* inverneria.
glass-reinforced plastic *n.* plastica de vitro.
glassware *n.* benes de vitro.
glasswork *n.* fabrica de vitro.
glassy *adj.* vitrin.
glaucoma *n.* glaucoma.

glaze *v.* (*add glass*) vitri; (*add gloss*) glasa; (*varnish*) vernisi. • *n.* glasa; vernis.
glazed *adj.* glasada; (*glassy*) vitrin.
glazier *n.* vitror.
gleam *v.* & *n.* brilia, sintili.
glean *v.* estrae; (*harvest*) colie la resta.
glee *n.* deleta; (*music*) gli.
gleeful *adj.* joiosa.
glen *n.* valeta.
glib *adj.* nonsinsera, surfasal.
glide *v.* & *n.* lisca.
glider *n.* avion liscante; (*marsupial*) liscor.
glimmer *v.* sintili.
glimpse *v.* & *n.* videta, videta acaso.
glint *v.* sintili.
glissando *n.* liscante.
glisten *v.* sintili.
glitch *n.* ereta, lisceta; (*electronic*) defeto, microbio. • *v.* lisceta.
glitter *v.* sintili.
glittery *adj.* sintilinte.
gloat *v.* vanta a se.
glob *n.* goton.
global *adj.* global.
globalism *n.* globalisme.
globalist *n.* globaliste.
globalization *n.* globali.
globalize *v.* globali.
global network *n.* rede global.
global warming *n.* caldi global.
globe *n.* globo.
globetrotter *n.* viajamanica, viajor tra la mundo.
globetrotting *adj.* viajamanica.
globular *adj.* globin.
globule *n.* goton.
globulin *n.* (*protein*) globulina.
glockenspiel *n.* glocenspil.
glomerulus *n.* (*anatomy*) glomerulo.
gloom *n.* oscur; (*mood*) sombria.
gloominess *n.* sombria.
gloomy *adj.* oscur; (*mood*) sombre.
gloop *n.* melma, muco.
gloopy *adj.* melmosa, mucin, viscosa.
glop *n.* melma, muco.
glorify *v.* glori, loda, onora.
glorious *adj.* gloriosa; merveliosa.
glory *n.* gloria, loda, onora. **glory in** es orgulosa de.
gloss *n.* glosa.
glossary *n.* gloseria.
glossy *adj.* glasada, briliante.
glottal *adj.* & *n.* (*consonant*) glotal.
glottis *n.* glote.
glove *n.* ganto.
glovebox *n.* portaganto.
glove compartment *n.* portaganto.
glow *v.* brilieta; (*brightly*) incandese. • *n.* brilieta.
glower *v.* & *n.* grima.
glowing *adj.* ardin.
glow-worm *n.* lampeta.
glucagon *n.* glucagon.
glucose *n.* glucosa.
glucose monitor *n.* monitor de glucosa.
glue *n.* cola. • *v.* coli.
glue gun *n.* pistol de cola.
glug *v.* & *n.* gurgula.
gluon *n.* (*particle*) gluon.
glut *n.* suprabunda.
glutamate *n.* (*chemistry*) glutamato.
glutamic *adj.* glutaminal.
glutamine *n.* (*amino acid*) glutamina.
gluten *n.* gluten.
gluteus *n.* gluteo.
glutton *n.* gloton.
gluttonous *adj.* gloton.
gluttony *n.* glotonia.
glycaemia (US **glycemia**) *n.* glisemia.
glycaemic (US **glycemic**) *n.* glisemial.
glycaemic index (US **glycemic index**) *n.* indise glisemial.
glycerin *n.* gliserol.
glycerine *n.* gliserol.
glycerol *n.* gliserol.
glycogen *n.* (*biology*) glicojen.
glyph *n.* glifo.
GM *adj.* jenetical alterada.
gnarled *adj.* nodosa.
gnarly *adj.* nodosa.
gnash *v.* (*teeth*) mole.
gnat *n.* mosceta, moscito.
gnatcatcher *n.* (*bird*) polioptila.
gnateater *n.* (*bird*) conopofaje.
gnathostomulid *n.* (*organism*) gnatostomulido.
gnaw *v.* rode.
gneiss *n.* (*geology*) gnais.
gnetum *n.* (*plant*) gneto.
gnocchi *n.* bales de pasta.
gnocco *n.* bal de pasta.
gnome *n.* nana.
gnomon *n.* gnomon.
gnostic *adj.* & *n.* gnostica.
gnosticism *n.* gnosticisme.
gnu *n.* gnu.
go[1] *v.* & *interj.* vade; (*depart*) parti. **go and see** vade per vide. **go in** entra. **go out** sorti. **go past** pasa. **go shopping** vade per compra. **go to** (*attend regularly*) vade a. **go viral** sperde virusin.
go[2] *n.* (*game*) go.
goad *n.* speron. • *v.* speroni.
goal *n.* ojeto, (*including sport*) gol.
goalie *n.* golor.
goalkeeper *n.* golor.
goalpost *n.* palo de gol.
goaltender *n.* golor.

goat *n.* capra.
goatee *n.* barbeta.
goatlike *adj.* caprin.
goatskin *n.* pel de capra.
goatsucker *n.* caprimuljo.
gob *n.* (*mouth*) boca; (*lump*) bulto.
gobble *v.* devora. • *interj.* (*turkey*, *peacock*) glu-glu.
gobbledegook *n.* babela.
gobbledygook *n.* babela.
Gobi Desert *n.* Deserto Gobi.
goblet *n.* copa.
goblin *n.* orceta.
gobstopper *n.* confeto dur.
goby *n.* (*fish*) gobio.
god *n.* dio; Dio.
godchild *n.* fie de batiza.
goddaughter *n.* fia de batiza.
goddess *n.* diva.
godfather *n.* padrin, padre de batiza.
godhead *n.* divin.
godless *adj.* sin dio, ateiste.
godlike *adj.* divin.
godmother *n.* madrin, madre de batiza.
godparent *n.* jenitor de batiza.
godsend *n.* donada de Dio.
godson *n.* fio de batiza.
goggles *n.* oculon, oculo protejente.
going *adj.* vadente; partinte. • *n.* state; progresa. **going by** si on considera.
goitre (US **goiter**) *n.* (*medical*) struma.
gold *n.* oro. • *adj.* (*colour*) oro; (*made of gold*) de oro, orosa. **turn to gold** ori.
goldbrick *n.* tesoro falsa.
goldbricker *n.* pigra.
gold bullion *n.* baras de oro.
golden *adj.* (*colour*) oro; (*made of gold*) de oro, orosa.
golden age *n.* eda oro.
golden retriever *n.* (*dog*) retraor oro.
goldenrod *n.* (*plant*) palo de oro.
golden syrup *n.* melasa oro.
gold-filled *adj.* orida.
goldfinch *n.* (*bird*) cardeta. **American goldfinch** spineta.
goldfish *n.* pex oro.
gold medallist (US **medalist**) *n.* medaliste de oro.
gold nugget *n.* pepita de oro.
gold-plate *v.* ori.
goldsmith *n.* oror.
golem *n.* (*mythology*) golem.
golf *n.* (*sport*) golf.
golf buggy *n.* caro de golf.
golf cart *n.* caro de golf.
golf club *n.* baston de golf.
golf course *n.* campo de golf, golferia.
golfer *n.* golfor.
golfing iron *n.* fero de golf.
Golgotha *n.* (*hill*) Calvario.
gonad *n.* gonada.
gondola *n.* gondola.
gondolier *n.* gondolor.
gong *n.* gongo.
gonorrhoea (US **gonorrhea**) *n.* gonorea.
goo *n.* melma, muco.
good *adj.* & *interj.* bon. • *pref.* bon-. **do good** fa bon.
goodbye *interj.* asta reuni, asta revide, adio, txau.
good deed *n.* bon ata.
good enough *adj.* oce.
Good Friday *n.* venerdi santa.
good luck *n.* bon fortuna.
good mood *n.* bon umor.
good-natured person *n.* bonom, bonfem.
goodness *n.* bonia.
good news *n.* bon novas.
good press *n.* bon anunsia.
good publicity *n.* bon anunsia.
good riddance *interj.* bon perde.
goods *n.* benes.
good smell *n.* bon odor.
good-sounding *adj.* bon sonante.
good spirits *n.* bon umor.
goods tax *n.* imposta de ben.
good tidings *n.* bon novas.
good turn *n.* favore.
goodwill *n.* bonvole.
gooey *adj.* melmosa, mucin, viscosa.
goof *v.* & *n.* lisceta.
goofball *n.* bobo.
goofy *adj.* bobo.
google *v.* (*search for*) gugli.
googly *n.* (*cricket*) gugli.
googol *n.* (*number*) gugol.
googolplex *n.* (*number*) gugolplex.
goon *n.* (*fool*) bobo, fol; (*thug*) savaje.
goop *n.* melma, muco.
goopy *adj.* melmosa, mucin, viscosa.
goose *n.* ganso.
gooseberry *n.* grosela spinosa.
goosestep *n.* pasea de ganso.
gopher *n.* (*rodent*) gofer.
gore[1] *n.* (*blood*) sangue.
gore[2] *v.* (*stab*) lansi.
gorge *n.* canion.
gorgeous *adj.* encantante, bela, estrema bela.
gorget *n.* (*throat protector*) covrecolo.
gorgon *n.* arpia.
gorgonzola *n.* gorgonzola.
gorilla *n.* gorila.
gorse *n.* ulex.
gory *adj.* sanguosa.
goshawk *n.* azor.
gosling *n.* ganseta.

gospel *n.* evanjelio; (*music*) gospel. • *adj.* gospel.
gossamer *n.* seda de arania.
gossip *n.* rumores; (*chat*) parleta; (*person*) rumoror.
Goth *n.* goto.
Gothic *adj.* (*person, language*) goto; (*architecture, lettering*) gotica.
Götterdämmerung *n.* ragnaroc.
gouda *n.* (*cheese*) gauda.
goulash *n.* gulax.
gourami *n.* (*fish*) gurami.
gourd *n.* zuca.
gourmand *n.* amor de comeda.
gourmet *n.* gurme.
gout *n.* (*medical*) gota.
govern *v.* governa.
government *n.* governa; stato; consilio governante, consilio de ministros. • *adj.* governal. **head of government** xef de governa.
governor *n.* governor.
governorate *n.* governoria.
grab *v.* saisi.
grace *n.* (*social*) jentilia, refina; (*in movement*) fasilia; (*Christianity*) grasia; (*before meal*) prea de grasias. **your grace** eselentia.
graceful *adj.* jentil, refinada; (*in movement*) fasil.
gracile *adj.* magra.
gracious *adj.* refinada.
grackle *n.* (*bird*) cuiscal.
grade *v.* gradi, ordina.
grade crossing *n.* crusa plana.
grade school *n.* scola prima.
gradient *n.* gradiente.
gradual *adj.* gradal, par grado.
gradualism *n.* gradalisme.
graduate *v.* gradua. • *n.* graduada.
graduation *n.* gradua.
graffiti *n.* grafiti.
graffitied *adj.* grafitosa.
graft *v.* & *n.* (*botany, medical*) inserta.
grain *n.* gran, particula; (*wood*) pelo; (*rock*) venas. **against the grain** contra la pelo.
grainy *adj.* granetin; particulosa.
gram[1] *n.* gram.
-gram[2] *suff.* (*output of device*) -gram.
grammar *n.* gramatica.
grammarian *n.* gramaticiste.
grammatical *adj.* gramatical.
gramme *n.* gram.
gramophone *n.* fonograf.
granary *n.* graneria.
grand *adj.* grandiosa; eselente.
grandchild *n.* nete.
granddaughter *n.* neta; (*gender-neutral*) nete.
grandfather *n.* avo.
grandiloquent *adj.* estravagante, ostentosa.
grandiose *adj.* grandiosa.
grand jury *n.* juria grande.
grandmother *n.* ava.
grandnephew *n.* dusobrino, dusobrin.
grandniece *n.* dusobrina, dusobrin.
grandparent *n.* avi.
grandson *n.* neto; (*gender-neutral*) nete.
granite *n.* granito.
granola *n.* musli.
granola bar *n.* bara de musli.
grant *v.* (*allow*) permete; (*point in an argument*) aseta, sede; (*give*) dona. • *n.* dona, suporta finansial. **grant amnesty to** amnestia.
granted *adj.* permeteda; asetada, sededa; donada. • *subord.* permetente ce, asetante ce, pos aseta ce.
granular *adj.* granetin.
granulate *v.* grani.
granulated *adj.* granin.
granule *n.* graneta.
granulocyte *n.* (*medical*) granulosite.
granulocytopenia *n.* (*medical*) granulositopenia.
granuloma *n.* (*medical*) granuloma.
granulopoiesis *n.* (*medical*) granulopoiese.
grape *n.* uva.
grapefruit *n.* (*fruit, tree*) pomelo.
grape hyacinth *n.* muscari.
grape vine *n.* uvo.
graph[1] *n.* (*diagram*) graf. • *v.* grafi, trasa.
-graph[2] *suff.* (*device*) -graf.
grapheme *n.* grafem.
graphemic *adj.* grafemal.
graphic *adj.* grafica. • *n.* grafica, imaje.
graphical *adj.* grafica.
graphical user interface *n.* interfas grafica de usor.
graphic artist *n.* graficiste.
graphic design *n.* grafica.
graphic designer *n.* graficiste.
graphics program *n.* desiniador, program de desinia.
graphics tablet *n.* tableta de desinia.
graphite *n.* grafito.
graphologist *n.* grafolojiste.
graphology *n.* grafolojia.
graph theory *n.* teoria de grafes.
-graphy *suff.* -grafia.
grapple *v.* luta.
grasp *v.* saisi, teni. • *n.* teni.
grasping *adj.* saisinte; (*greedy*) avar.
grass *n.* erba.
grass fire *n.* focon savaje.
grasshopper *n.* locusta; (*when not swarming*) locusta solitar.
grassland *n.* savana.
grasslike *adj.* erbin.
grassy *adj.* erbosa.

grate[1] *v.* (*cheese*) raspa; (*sound*) grinse. • *n.* grinse.
grate[2] *n.* grilia; ximineria; grilia de ximineria.
grateful *adj.* grasiosa.
grater *n.* raspador.
gratification *n.* sasia.
gratify *v.* sasia.
gratis *adj.* sin custa.
gratitude *n.* grasia.
gratuitous *adj.* sin razona; sin custa.
gratuity *n.* grasieta.
Grau, Mar de *n.* Mar Grau.
grave[1] *n.* tomba.
grave[2] *adj.* (*dire*) grave.
grave accent *n.* sinieta nonagu.
gravedigger *n.* enteror.
gravel *n.* calculos.
graven *adj.* gravada.
gravestone *n.* petra de tomba.
graveyard *n.* semetero.
gravid *adj.* plen; (*pregnant*) ensinta.
gravitate *v.* gravita.
graviton *n.* graviton.
gravity *n.* gravita; (*direness*) gravia; (*seriousness*) seria.
gravity suit *n.* paragravita.
gravy *n.* salsa de carne.
gray[1] (US). See *grey*.
gray[2] *n.* (*unit of radiation*) grai.
grayish (US). See *greyish*.
gray jay (US). See *grey jay*.
graze[1] *v.* (*animals*) come a pasto.
graze[2] *v.* (*scrape skin*) raspa; (*touch lightly*) tanje.
grease *n.* gras. • *v.* grasi.
greasepaint *n.* macia de teatro.
greasy *adj.* grasosa.
great *adj.* major; grande, alta; eselente. • *pref.* (*grandchild*, *grandparent*) du-, tre- (*etc.*). **Alexander the Great** Alexandro la Grande.
Great Australian Bight *n.* Baia Australian Grande.
Great Barrier Reef *n.* Parador Grande de Coral.
Great Basin *n.* Basin Grande.
greatcoat *n.* jacon.
Great Dane *n.* (*dog*) mastin deutx.
Greater Antilles *n.* Antiles Major.
greater jihad *n.* djihad grande.
greater-than-or-equal sign *n.* sinia de superioria o egalia.
greater-than sign *n.* sinia de superioria.
great-grandchild *n.* dunete.
great-granddaughter *n.* duneta.
great-grandfather *n.* duavo.
great-grandmother *n.* duava.
great-grandparent *n.* duavi.
great-grandson *n.* duneto.
great-great-grandchild *n.* trenete.
great-great-granddaughter *n.* treneta.
great-great-grandfather *n.* treavo.
great-great-grandmother *n.* treava.
great-great-grandparent *n.* treavi.
great-great-grandson *n.* treneto.
Great Indian Desert *n.* Deserto Thar.
greatly *adv.* multe, alta.
greatness *n.* eselentia.
great room *n.* salon.
Great Sandy Desert *n.* Cuatri Vacua.
greave *n.* armur de gama.
grebe *n.* (*bird*) grebe.
Grecian *adj.* elinica.
Greece *n.* Elas.
greed *n.* avaria.
greedy *adj.* avar.
Greek *adj.* & *n.* elinica.
green *adj.* verde. • *n.* (*including golf*) verde.
green bean *n.* fava verde.
greenbelt *n.* sintur verde.
greenbrier *n.* (*plant*) smilax.
greenery *n.* plantas, verde.
greenfinch *n.* verdeta.
greengrocer *n.* (*person*) frutor.
greengrocer's *n.* (*shop*) fruteria.
greenhouse *n.* inverneria.
greenhouse effect *n.* efeto invernerial.
greenhouse gas *n.* gas invernerial.
greenish *adj.* verdin.
greenish blue *adj.* verdin azul. • *n.* azul verdin.
Greenland *n.* Calalitnunat, Gronland.
Greenlander *n.* calalit, gronlandes.
Greenlandic *adj.* (*person*, *language*) calalit, gronlandes.
Greenland Sea *n.* Mar Gronland.
green magpie *n.* piga verde.
green pepper *n.* peperon verde.
green room *n.* atrio de presentores.
green-screen compositing *n.* suprapone par scermo verde.
greeny blue *n.* azul verdin.
greeny-blue *adj.* verdin azul.
greet *v.* saluta.
greeting *n.* saluta.
gregarious *adj.* sosial.
Gregorian *adj.* gregorian.
Gregorian chant *n.* canta gregorian.
gremlin *n.* orceta.
Grenada *n.* Grenada.
grenade *n.* granada.
Grenadian *adj.* & *n.* grenadian.
grenadier *n.* (*soldier*) granador.
grenadine *n.* xirope de granada.
Grenadine Islands *n.* Isolas Grenadine.
grey (US **gray**) *adj.* & *n.* gris. • *v.* grisi.
grey area (US **gray area**) *n.* (*of unclear definition*) area neblosa.

greyhound *n.* lepror engles.
greyish (US **gray**) *adj.* grisin.
grey jay (US **gray jay**) *n.* jai gris.
grid *n.* grilia.
grid computing *n.* computa distribuida.
griddle *n.* padela de grili.
gridiron *n.* grilia.
gridiron football *n.* futbal american.
gridlike *adj.* grilin.
gridlock *n.* conjesta sin sorti.
grief *n.* lamenta, tristia.
grievance *n.* cexa.
grieve *v.* lamenta.
grievous *adj.* grave.
griffin *n.* grifon.
griffon *n.* grifon.
grift *v.* froda.
grifter *n.* frodor.
grill *n.* grilia. • *v.* grili.
grillwork *n.* grilia.
grim *adj.* macabre, sombre; (*situation*) grave.
grimace *v.* & *n.* grima.
grime *n.* mugre, susia.
grimy *adj.* mugrosa, susia.
grin *v.* surie; (*skull*) grima. • *n.* surie, surion; (*skull*) grima.
grind *v.* (*to powder*) mole; (*rub*) raspa.
grinder *n.* molador; (*sandwich*) bagete plenida.
grindstone *n.* petra de molin.
griot *n.* (*storyteller*) grio.
grip *v.* teni. • *n.* teni; (*handle*) manico. **lose one's grip on** desteni.
gripe *v.* cexa.
grisly *adj.* macabre, repulsante.
grist *n.* gran; materia usosa.
gristle *n.* cartilaje.
gristly *adj.* cartilajosa.
grit *n.* arena. **grit one's teeth** tensa sua dentes.
gritty *adj.* arenin.
grizzle *v.* grisi.
grizzled *adj.* gris.
grizzly bear *n.* urso gris.
groan *v.* & *n.* jemi; (*creak*) cruji.
grocer *n.* comedor.
grocery *n.* comederia. **groceries** comedas.
grocery store *n.* comederia.
grog *n.* grog, pontxe.
groggy *adj.* mareada.
groin *n.* inguin.
grommet *n.* oieta, anelo fortinte.
groom *n.* (*wedding*) sposo nova; (*horses*) stalor. • *v.* brosi; ordina; prepara.
grooming *n.* cura personal.
groomsman *n.* suportor.
groove *n.* ranur.
groovy *adj.* gustable, modosa.
grope *v.* xerca sieca.
grosbeak *n.* (*bird*) becospesa.
gross *adj.* (*national product, income, profit, tax, tonnage*) bruta; (*raw*) cru; (*disgusting*) repulsante.
gross domestic product *n.* produi interna bruta.
grotesque *adj.* fea, malformida; asustante.
grotto *n.* cava.
grouch *n.* cexor.
grouchy *adj.* cexosa, disputosa.
ground *n.* tera; (*floor*) solo; (*reason*) causa. • *v.* lia a tera.
groundbreaking *adj.* abrinte vias.
ground floor *n.* nivel de tera.
groundhog *n.* monax.
ground jay *n.* jai eurasian.
groundless *adj.* sin funda, sin razona.
ground level *n.* nivel de tera.
ground meat *n.* carne moleda.
groundswell *n.* onda de opina.
ground-to-air *adj.* de tera a aira.
ground-to-surface *adj.* de tera a tera.
groundwater *n.* acua suteran.
groundwork *n.* labora fundal.
group *n.* grupo. • *adj.* grupal. • *v.* grupi. **as a group** grupal, como grupo. **form a group** grupi. **group into pairs** grupi a duples.
grouper *n.* (*fish*) mero, grupor.
groupie *n.* grupi.
group singing *n.* canta grupal.
group theory *n.* teoria de grupos.
grouse *n.* fasian galin.
grout *n.* (*substance*) mortero. • *v.* morteri.
grove *n.* bosce.
grovel *v.* adula.
grow *v.* crese, grandi; (*crops*) cultiva; (*become*) deveni. **grow addicted** abitua. **grow old** senese, vei. **grow up** adulti, maturi.
growable *adj.* cultivable.
grower *n.* cultivor.
growl *v.* & *n.* ronci.
grown-up *adj.* adulte, matur. • *n.* adulte, person matur.
growth *n.* crese, grandi; (*thing that has naturally grown*) crese.
grrr *interj.* (*growling*) grr.
grub *n.* (*insect*) larva; (*food*) comeda.
grubby *adj.* susia; (*greedy*) avar.
grudge *n.* nonpardona.
gruel *n.* gaxa.
gruesome *adj.* macabre, repulsante.
gruff *adj.* bruta, noncortes.
grumble *v.* cexeta; (*rumble*) ronci.
grump *n.* malumorosa.
grumpy *adj.* disputosa.
grunge *adj.* & *n.* (*music*) grunje.
grunt *v.* ronceta. • *n.* ronceta, ronci. • *interj.* ronc.

Grus *n.* (*constellation*) la Gru.
gryphon *n.* grifon.
G-spot *n.* (*anatomy*) punto G.
G-string *n.* (*garment*) tanga.
g-suit *n.* (*gravity suit*) paragravita.
guacamole *n.* (*food*) guacamole.
Guadeloupe *n.* Guadelupe.
Guadeloupean *adj.* guadelupean.
Guam *n.* (*island*) Guam.
Guamanian *adj.* & *n.* guamanian.
Guangdong *n.* Guangdong.
Guang Dong Wa *n.* (*language*) guangdong.
guano *n.* guano.
Guarani *adj.* & *n.* (*person, language*) guarani.
guarantee *v.* & *n.* garantia.
guaranty *n.* garantia.
guard *v.* garda. • *n.* (*action*) garda; (*person*) gardor; (*ticket collector*) biletor; (*device*) gardador.
guardhouse *n.* casa de garda.
guardian *n.* gardor; (*museum, collection*) conservor; (*of child or invalid*) defendor.
guardian angel *n.* anjel gardante.
guardianship *n.* garda.
guardrail *n.* rel gardante.
guard tower *n.* tore de garda.
Guatemala *n.* Guatemala.
Guatemalan *adj.* & *n.* guatemalteca.
guava *n.* (*tree, fruit*) guaiava.
Guayaquil *n.* Guayaquil. **Gulf of Guayaquil** Golfo Guayaquil.
Guernésiais *adj.* & *n.* (*language*) gernsies.
Guernsey *n.* Gernsi.
guerrilla *n.* gerilia.
guerrilla warfare *n.* gera de gerilia.
guess *v.* & *n.* divina.
guesstimate *n.* estima divinante.
guesswork *n.* divina.
guest *n.* invitada, visitor invitada; (*hotel*) visitor.
guest house *n.* oteleta.
guff *n.* trivia.
guffaw *n.* rion. • *v.* claxoni.
GUI *n.* interfas grafica de usor.
Guianan *adj.* & *n.* (*French*) guianes.
guidance *n.* gida.
guide *v.* gida. • *n.* (*person*) gidor; (*scout*) scolta; (*device*) gidador; (*book*) manual.
guidebook *n.* manual.
guideline *n.* regula jeneral.
guidepost *n.* palo de dirije.
guild *n.* corpora; sindicato.
guilder *n.* florin.
guildhall *n.* salon de sindicato.
guile *n.* rusosia.
guileless *adj.* nonenganante.
guillemot *n.* uria.
guillotine *n.* gilotin. • *v.* gilotini.
guilt *n.* culpablia.
guilty *adj.* culpable; (*pleasure*) vergoniosa.
Guinea *n.* Gine. **Gulf of Guinea** Golfo Gine. **New Guinea** Gine Nova.
Guinea-Bissau *n.* Gine-Bisau.
Guinean *adj.* & *n.* ginean.
guinea pig *n.* cavia.
guise *n.* desembla, aspeta.
guitar *n.* gitar. **acoustic guitar** gitar acustical. **bass guitar** gitar baso. **electric guitar** gitar eletrical.
guitarist *n.* gitaristo.
Gujarat *n.* (*Indian state*) Gudjarat.
Gujarati *adj.* & *n.* (*person, language*) gudjarati.
gulag *n.* gulag.
gulf *n.* golfo.
gull *n.* (*bird*) gavota.
gullible *adj.* credosa.
gully *n.* foson.
gulp *v.* engoli.
gulyás *n.* (*soup*) gulax.
gum[1] *n.* (*anatomy*) jenjiva.
gum[2] *n.* goma, resina.
gumbo *n.* (*plant*) gombo; sopa de gombo.
gumboot *n.* bota de cauxo.
gum drop *n.* confeto de jelatin.
gummy *adj.* gomin.
gumshoe *n.* detetor.
gun *n.* fusil.
gunboat *n.* canonera.
gun carriage *n.* caro de canon.
gundi *n.* (*rodent*) gundi.
gunfight *n.* pistoli.
gunfighter *n.* pistolor.
gunfire *n.* spara.
gunge *n.* melma. • *v.* melmi.
gungy *adj.* melmosa.
gunk *n.* melma.
gunman *n.* fusilor, pistolor.
gunnysack *n.* saco de juta. **at gunpoint** su menasa de fusil.
gunpowder *n.* polvo negra.
gunrunner *n.* traficor de armas.
gunshot *n.* xuta.
gunslinger *n.* pistolor.
gunsmith *n.* fabricor de fusiles.
guppy *n.* (*fish*) gupi.
Guptan *adj.* (*dynasty*) guptan.
gurgle *v.* & *n.* gurgula.
gurney *n.* portaferida rolante.
guru *n.* guru.
gush *v.* & *n.* jeta.
gusher *n.* (*oil*) geser.
gusset *n.* scermeta, refortinte.
gust *n.* soflon.
gustatory sense *n.* sensa de sabor.
gusto *n.* zelo.
gusty *adj.* ventosa.
gut *n.* ventre. • *v.* desventri.
gut feeling *n.* senti instintosa.
gutless *adj.* coarde, sin coraje.

guts *n.* intestines, visera.
gutsy *adj.* corajosa.
gutter *n.* (*street, roof*) canaleta.
guttersnipe *n.* enfante misera, xica vagante, xico vagante.
guttural *adj.* gargal, larinjal.
guy *n.* (*man*) xico, om; (*person*) xice, joven.
Guyana *n.* Guiana.
Guyanese *adj.* & *n.* guianan.
guzzle *v.* engoli.
gym *n.* (*gymnasium, fitness club*) jinasio.
gymbag *n.* bolson.
gymnasium *n.* jinasio.
gymnast *n.* jinasta.
gymnastic *adj.* (*of gymnastics*) jinastial; (*like a gymnast*) jinastin.
gymnastics *n.* jinastia.
gymnosperm *n.* (*botany*) gimnosperma.
gym shoe *n.* sapato de sporte.
gymslip *n.* (*dress*) jumper.
gynaeco- (US **gyneco-**) *pref.* (*female*) jineco-.
gynaecological (US **gynecological**) *adj.* jinecolojial.
gynaecologist (US **gynecologist**) *n.* jinecolojiste.
gynaecology (US **gynecology**) *n.* jinecolojia.
gynarch *n.* (*governor*) jinarca.
gynarchy *n.* jinarcia.
gyneco... (US). See *gynaeco...*
gynephile *n.* jinefilica.
gynephilia *n.* jinefilia.
gynephilic *adj.* jinefilica.
gynephobe *n.* jinefobica.
gynephobia *n.* jinefobia.
gynephobic *adj.* jinefobica.
gyno- *pref.* (*female*) jino-.
gynoecium *n.* (*botany*) jineseo.
gyp *n.* dole. • *v.* froda.
gypsum *n.* jeso.
Gypsy *adj.* & *n.* romani.
gyrate *v.* jira.
gyration *n.* jira.
gyre *v.* jira.
gyro *n.* pita elinica.
gyrocopter *n.* autojiro.
gyroplane *n.* autojiro.
gyros *n.* (*bread*) pita elinica.
gyroscope *n.* jiroscopio.
gyrus *n.* (*anatomy*) jiro.

H

ha *interj.* ha.
haberdasher *n.* xapor.
haberdasher's *n.* (*shop*) boteca de cose.
haberdashery *n.* benes de cose.
habit *n.* abitua.
habitability *n.* abitablia.
habitable *adj.* abitable.
habitat *n.* abitada.
habitation *n.* abita.
habit-forming *adj.* abituante.
habitual *adj.* abitual.
habituate *v.* abitua.
habituation *n.* abitua.
haček *n.* (*diacritic*) caron.
hachoir *n.* cotel osilante.
hack *v.* axi; (*software*) pirati.
hackbut *n.* arcabus.
hacker *n.* pirata de rede.
hackneyed *adj.* clixe, tro usada.
hacksaw *n.* siera per metal.
haddock *n.* eglefin.
hadron *n.* (*particle*) adron.
hadrosaur *n.* hadrosauro.
hadrosaurus *n.* hadrosauro.
haem- (US **hem-**) *pref.* (*blood*) em-.
haematemesis *n.* (*medical*) ematemese.
haematite *n.* (*mineral*) ematita.
haemato- *pref.* (*blood*) emato-.
haematology *n.* ematolojia.
haematoma *n.* ematoma.
haematopoiesis *n.* (*biology*) ematopoiese.
haematopoietic *adj.* ematopoiesal.
haematozoa *n.* (*organisms*) ematozones.
haematozoon *n.* (*organism*) ematozon.
haematuria *n.* (*medical*) ematuria.
haemo- *pref.* (*blood*) emo-.
haemocyte *n.* emosite.
haemocytoblast *n.* emositoblasto.
haemodialysis *n.* dialise.
haemoglobin *n.* emoglobina.
haemolytic *adj.* emolitica.
haemopathological *adj.* emopatolojial.
haemopathology *n.* emopatolojia.
haemophilia *n.* emofilia.
haemophiliac *adj.* & *n.* emofilica.
haemopoiesis *n.* (*biology*) ematopoiese.
haemopoietic *adj.* ematopoiesal.
haemorrhage *v.* & *n.* emoraje.
haemorrhagic *adj.* emorajal.
haemorrhoid *n.* emoroide.
haemostasis *n.* (*medical*) emostase.
haemostat *n.* pinse vascular.
haemostatic *adj.* emostasal, parasangual. • *n.* parasangue.
haemotoxin *n.* emotoxina.
hafnium *n.* (*element*) hafnio.
hag *n.* arpia.
hagfish *n.* mixino.
haggard *adj.* fatigada.
haggis *n.* (*food*) hagis.
haggle *v.* negosia.
hagiographer *n.* ajiografiste.
hagiography *n.* ajiografia.
ha ha *interj.* (*laughing*) ha ha.
Haida *adj.* & *n.* (*person*, *language*) haida.
haiku *n.* (*poetry*) haicu.
hail *v.* & *n.* graniza.
hailstone *n.* graniza.
hailstorm *n.* tempesta granizosa.
Hainan *n.* (*island*) Hainan.
hair *n.* (*of the scalp*, *one strand*) capel; (*collectively*) capeles; (*of the face or body*, *or of an animal*) pelo; (*one strand of body hair*) capeleta. **by a hair's breadth** par un capel. **split hairs** es pedante.
hair attachment *n.* peruceta.
hairball *n.* bal de pelo.
hairband *n.* banda de capeles.
hairbrush *n.* brosa de capeles.
haircloth *n.* juta.
haircut *n.* corti de capeles.
hairdo *n.* stilo de capeles.
hairdresser *n.* capelor.
hairdryer *n.* secador de capeles.
hairless *adj.* calva.
hairlike *adj.* capelin.
hairnet *n.* rede de capeles.
hairpiece *n.* peruceta.
hairpin *n.* spino de capeles.
hair salon *n.* capeleria.
hairshirt *n.* camisa de juta.
hairslide *n.* bareta.
hairspray *n.* laca de capeles.
hairstyle *n.* stilo de capeles, moda de capeles.
hairstylist *n.* capelor.
hair tie *n.* portacoda.
hairweaving *n.* texe de capeles.
hairy *adj.* pelosa; (*head*) capelosa.
Haiti *n.* Aiti.
Haitian *adj.* & *n.* aitian.
Haitian Creole *adj.* & *n.* creol aitian.
hajj *n.* (*pilgrimage*) hadj.
hajji *n.* (*pilgrim*) hadji.
haka *n.* (*dance*) haca.
hake *n.* (*fish*) merlusa.
Hakka *adj.* & *n.* (*person*, *language*) haca.
halal *adj.* halal.
halal meat *n.* halal.
halcyon days *n.* eda oro.

hale *adj.* sana.
half *n.* dui. • *adj.* duida, dui-, partal.
half-board *adj.* (*hotel*) con du comes.
half-brother *n.* duifrate.
half-close *v.* (*eyes*) plia.
half full *adj.* duiplen, partal plen.
half-hearted *adj.* vasilante.
half-life *n.* (*of isotope*) duivive.
half light *n.* duilus.
half note *n.* tono duida.
halfpence *n.* duisentim.
halfpenny *n.* duisentim.
half-shirt *n.* camiseta corta.
half-sister *n.* duisore.
half-slip *n.* faldeta.
half-term *n.* (*holiday*) mediatrimestre.
halftime *n.* mediajua.
halftone *n.* mediatinje.
halfway point *n.* media.
halibut *n.* ipogloso.
halitosis *n.* alitose.
hall *n.* (*large room*) salon; (*lobby*) atrio; (*hallway*) coredor. **assembly hall** asembleria. **hall of residence** abitada de studiantes.
hallelujah *interj.* aleluia.
hallmark *n.* marca de cualia, garantia de cualia.
hallow *v.* santi. **All Hallows' Eve** vijila de tota santas.
Halloween *n.* vijila de tota santas.
hallucinate *v.* alusina.
hallucination *n.* alusina.
hallucinatory *adj.* alusinal.
hallucinogen *n.* alusinojen.
hallucinogenic *adj.* alusinojen.
hallux *n.* halux.
hallway *n.* coredor.
halo *n.* areola.
halogen *adj.* & *n.* alojen.
halogen lamp *n.* lampa alojen.
halt *v.* para.
halter *n.* cabestro.
halterneck *n.* camiseta de nuca.
haltertop *n.* camiseta de nuca.
halting *adj.* esitante, nonfluente.
halve *v.* dui.
ham[1] *n.* (*meat*) jamon, carne de porco.
ham[2] *v.* (*theatrically*) ata esajerada. • *n.* ator esajerada.
hamburger *n.* amburger.
ham-fisted *adj.* torpe.
Hamito-Semitic *adj.* afroasian.
hamlet *n.* vileta noncorporada.
hammer *n.* martel. • *v.* marteli.
hammer drill *n.* forador percusente.
hammered dulcimer *n.* dulsimer marteli-da.
hammerhead stork *n.* (*bird*) umbreta.
hammerkop *n.* (*bird*) umbreta.
hammertoe *n.* dito martelin.
hammock *n.* amaca.
hamper *v.* impedi.
Hampshire, New *n.* (*US state*) Hampshire Nova.
hamster *n.* criceto.
hamstring *n.* tendon pos la jeno.
Han *adj.* (*dynasty*) han.
hand *n.* mano; (*clock, compass*) ago, indicador. • *v.* dona. **by hand** par mano. **hand in hand** con mano en mano. **hand out** distri-bui. **hand over** pasa; (*part*) divide. **hand round** distribui. **hands free** con manos libre. **hold hands** teni manos. **made by hand** fabricada par mano. **on one's hands and knees** sur manos e jenos. **on the one hand** a un lado. **on the other hand** a la otra lado.
handbag *n.* bolsa.
handball *n.* (*sport*) handbal.
handbell *n.* campaneta.
handbill *n.* folia avisante.
handbook *n.* manual.
handbrake *n.* freno de mano.
handcar *n.* (*railway maintenance vehicle*) draisin.
handcart *n.* careta.
handclasp *n.* presa de manos.
handcraft *n.* fabrica par mano.
handcuff *n.* securipolso. • *v.* securi la polsos de.
hand drill *n.* forador de mano.
handedness *n.* prefere de mano.
handful *n.* mano, mano plen, plenimano.
hand guard *n.* gardamano.
handgun *n.* pistol, fusil de mano.
handheld computer *n.* computador de mano, aidador personal.
handheld luggage *n.* valiseta.
handhold *n.* manico.
handicap *n.* (*impairment*) descapasia; (*disad-vantage, including golf*) nonvantaje.
handicapped *adj.* descapasida, con nonvan-taje.
handicapped person *n.* descapasida.
handicraft *n.* artisania, fabrica par mano.
handiwork *n.* produida.
handkerchief *n.* teleta.
handle *n.* (*for holding*) manico. • *v.* (*touch with hands*) mani, palpa; (*tool*) maneja.
handlebar *n.* manico.
hand lettering *n.* leteri con mano.
handloom *n.* texador de mano.
handmade *adj.* fabricada par mano.
handmaid *n.* fem servinte.
handmaiden *n.* fem servinte.
handoff *n.* pasa.
handout *n.* (*charity*) carita; (*paper*) folieta.
handover *n.* pasa.
handrail *n.* rel de mano.

handsaw *n.* siera de mano.
handset *n.* telefoneta.
handsewn *adj.* coseda par mano.
handshake *n.* presa de manos.
handsome *adj.* bela.
handspring *n.* volta par mano.
handstand *v.* & *n.* sta sur manos.
handstitched *adj.* coseda par mano.
hand-to-hand combat *n.* combate prosima.
handwork *n.* labora par mano.
handwriting *n.* (*action*) scrive par mano; (*style*) scrive de mano.
handwritten *adj.* scriveda par mano.
handy *adj.* (*convenient*) oportun; (*skilful*) destrosa; (*easy*) fasil.
handyman *n.* fatota.
hang *v.* (*be hanging*) pende; (*cause to hang*) pende, suspende; (*kill by hanging*) pende; (*software*) saisi se. **hang down** pende. **hang up** suspende.
hangar *n.* avioneria.
hanger *n.* pendador.
hangeul *n.* (*writing system*) hangul.
hanging indent *n.* contraindente. **apply a hanging indent to** contraindente.
hangman *n.* pendor.
hangnail *n.* cuticula laserada.
hangover *n.* posenebria.
hangul *n.* hangul.
hangup *n.* neurose.
hank *n.* mexa.
hanker *v.* anela.
hanky *n.* teleta.
hantavirus *n.* (*medical*) hantavirus.
Hanukkah *n.* (*Jewish festival*) hanuca.
ha'penny *n.* duisentim.
haphazard *n.* caos.
hapless *adj.* nonfortunosa.
haplo- *pref.* (*single*) aplo-.
haploid *adj.* & *n.* aploide.
happen *v.* aveni. **happen again** reaveni.
happiness *n.* felisia.
happy *adj.* felis.
happy chance *n.* bon acaso.
hapto- *pref.* (*attachment*) apto-.
harakiri *n.* (*disembowelment*) haraciri.
harangue *v.* arenga.
harass *v.* molesta.
harassment *n.* molesta.
harbinger *n.* indica.
harbour (US **harbor**) *n.* porto. • *v.* refuja; (*disease*) transporta. **outer harbour** anteporto.
hard *adj.* dur; (*difficult*) difisil; (*blow*) forte.
hardback *n.* libro dur.
hardball *n.* basebal.
hardboard *n.* plance compresada.
hard-boil *v.* duri.
hardboiled *adj.* dur bolida.
hard clam *n.* (*mollusc*) mersenaria.
hard-coded *adj.* permanente codigida.
hardcore *adj.* estrema.
hardcover *n.* libro dur.
hard disk *n.* disco dur.
hard drive *n.* disco dur.
harden *v.* duri.
hardened *adj.* calosa.
hard hat *n.* elmo.
hard-headed *adj.* ostinosa.
hard-hearted *adj.* noncompatiosa, nonempatica.
hardly *adv.* apena.
hardness *n.* calosia.
hard-on *n.* (*erection*) pixon.
hard palate *n.* palato dur.
hard rock *n.* roc dur.
hardship *n.* sufri.
hard shoulder *n.* (*of road*) banda de crise, lado de via.
hardtack *n.* biscoto dur.
hardtop *n.* (*car*) teto dur.
hardware *n.* aparatos.
hardware store *n.* boteca de utiles.
hardwired *n.* con sircuito permanente; jenetical determinada.
hard-won *adj.* difisil ganiada.
hardwood *n.* lenio dur.
hard work *n.* asiduia.
hardworking *adj.* asidua.
hardy *adj.* durante.
hare *n.* lepre.
harebell *n.* campanula.
hare-brained *adj.* noncauta, fretante.
Hare Krishna *n.* crixnaisme.
harelip *n.* labio fendeda.
harem *n.* arem.
haricot bean *n.* fava blanca.
hark *v.* escuta.
harken *v.* escuta.
harlequin *n.* arlecin.
harlot *n.* fem promiscua, fem prostituida; (*derogatory*) puta.
harm *v.* feri.
harmful *adj.* nosiva.
harmless *adj.* nonosiva.
harmonic *adj.* & *n.* armonial.
harmonica *n.* armonica.
harmonious *adj.* armoniosa.
harmonium *n.* (*musical instrument*) armonio.
harmonize *v.* armoni.
harmony *n.* armonia.
harness *n.* arnes. • *v.* arnesi.
harp *n.* arpa.
harpist *n.* arpiste.
harpoon *n.* arpon. • *v.* arponi.
harpsichord *n.* clavesimbal.
harpsichordist *n.* clavesimbaliste.

harpy *n.* arpia.
harpy eagle *n.* arpia.
harridan *n.* arpia, fem odiosa.
harrier *n.* (*bird*) circulor.
harrow *n.* raston. • *v.* rasti; (*upset*) angusa, turba.
harry *v.* molesta.
harsh *adj.* sever, dur; violente; (*sound*) xiliante.
harshen *v.* severi.
harshness *n.* severia.
hart *n.* servo mas.
hartebeest *n.* (*antelope*) alselafo.
harvest *v.* & *n.* recolie.
harvester *n.* (*person*) recolior; (*machine*) recoliador; (*arachnid*) gamalonga.
harvestman *n.* falxor; (*arachnid*) gamalonga.
hashish *n.* haxix.
hash sign *n.* (*character*) grilia.
hash table *n.* (*software*) table de axi.
hashtag *n.* (*word*) parola grilida; (*hash sign*) grilia. • *v.* grili.
Hasid *n.* hasidiste.
Hasidic *adj.* hasidiste.
Hasidism *n.* (*Judaism*) hasidisme.
Haskalah *n.* hascala.
hasp *n.* fisador.
hassium *n.* (*element*) hasio.
hassle *v.* irita; molesta. • *n.* peste; (*inconvenience*) nonoportunia.
hassock *n.* cuxin de jenos.
haste *n.* freta.
hasten *v.* freta, rapidi, aselera.
hasty *adj.* fretante.
hat *n.* xapo.
hatband *n.* banda de xapo.
hatbox *n.* portaxapo.
hatch *v.* emerji, sorti de casca. • *n.* porte de asede.
hatchback *adj.* (*car*) con porte retro.
hatcheck *n.* vesteria.
hatchery *n.* incuberia.
hatchet *n.* axeta.
hate *v.* odia.
hate crime *n.* crimin de odia.
hateful *adj.* odiosa.
hate group *n.* grupo de odia.
hate mail *n.* posta de odia.
hatemonger *n.* promovor de odia.
hatlike *adj.* xapin.
hatmaker *n.* xapor.
hatpin *n.* spino de xapo.
hat rack *n.* pendexapo.
hatred *n.* odia.
hat shop *n.* xaperia.
hatstand *n.* pendexapo.
hatter *n.* xapor.
hauberk *n.* camison de malie.
haughty *adj.* egosa.
haul *v.* tira. • *n.* recolie.
haunch *n.* anca e coxa.
haunt *v.* infesta.
haunted *adj.* fantasmosa, infestada.
Hausa *adj.* & *n.* (*person, language*) hausa.
haute couture *n.* moda refinada.
haute cuisine *n.* cosini refinada.
have *v.* ave; (*shower, dream, etc.*) fa; (*indicating that a finite verb is in the past tense*) ia. **have just done** veni de fa, es a fini de fa. **haven't you?** (*question tag, typically expecting the answer yes*) no? **have to** (*social obligation*) debe; (*physical or essential*) nesesa. **have to do with** conserna, pertine a. **have you?** (*question tag, typically implying some uncertainty*) si?
having *adj.* avente. **having found the key** pos trova la clave. **having said that** pos dise acel, an tal.
havoc *n.* ruina.
Hawaii *n.* (*US state*) Hawaii.
Hawaiian *adj.* & *n.* hawaian.
Hawaiian honeycreeper *n.* (*bird*) drepani.
Hawaiian Islands *n.* Isolas Hawaian.
hawk *n.* (*goshawk*) azor; (*buzzard*) buteo; (*kestrel*) falcon.
hawker *n.* vendor vagante.
hawk-eyed *adj.* vijilante.
hawser *n.* cordon.
hawthorn *n.* spinablanca.
hay *n.* feno.
haycart *n.* caro de feno.
hayfever *n.* rinite.
hayloft *n.* feneria.
haymaker *n.* fenor; (*blow*) colpa forte.
hayride *n.* turi en caro de fero.
hayseed *n.* campanian.
haystack *n.* monton de feno.
haywagon *n.* caro de feno.
haywain *n.* caro de feno.
haywire *adj.* acaso, noncoerente, noncontrolable.
hazard *n.* peril, risca.
hazardous *adj.* perilosa.
haze *n.* nebleta.
hazel *n.* nozeto.
hazelnut *n.* nozeta.
hazy *adj.* neblosa.
H-bomb *n.* bomba de idrojen.
he *pron.* (*normally*) el; (*rarely, only for stylistic contrast with* ela) elo. **he himself** (*non-reflexively emphatic*) el mesma. **he who** el ci.
head *n.* testa; (*camera, recording device*) testeta; (*boss*) xef; (*syntax*) nucleo. • *v.* (*hit with head*) testi, colpa con testa; (*lead*) gida. **go head over heels** volta. **head first** con prima sua testa. **head for** vade en dirije a. **head of government** xef de governa. **head of intelligence** xef de securia. **head of security** xef de securia. **head of state** xef

de stato. **head of the table** xef de table. **heads** (*coin*) fas. **per head** per person.
head abbot *n.* abade xef.
headache *n.* dole de testa.
headband *n.* banda de testa.
headboard *n.* testa de leto.
headbutt *v.* & *n.* testi, colpa con testa.
headcheese *n.* (*jellied meat*) ceso-de-testa.
headdress *n.* xapo ornosa.
header *n.* xapo de paje; (*software*) xapo, (*soccer*) testi, colpa con testa.
headgear *n.* covretesta.
headhunt *v.* xasa testas; (*business*) xerca per la posto.
headhunter *n.* xasatesta.
heading *n.* titulo; dirije.
headlamp *n.* faro.
headland *n.* capo, promontania.
headless *adj.* sin testa.
headlight *n.* faro.
headline *n.* titulo.
headlock *n.* clavi de testa.
headlong *adv.* con prima sua testa.
headman *n.* xef.
headmaster *n.* ensenior xef.
headmistress *n.* ensenior xef.
headphones *n.* escutador.
headquarters *n.* xeferia, base.
headrest *n.* reposatesta.
headroom *n.* spasio de testa.
headscarf *n.* tela de testa.
headset *n.* escutador, escutador con microfon.
headstand *n.* sta sur testa.
headstone *n.* petra de tomba.
headstrong *adj.* ostinosa.
headteacher *n.* ensenior xef.
headwaiter *n.* servor xef.
headwater *n.* fonte de rio.
headway *n.* progresa.
headwear *n.* covretesta.
headwind *n.* venta fasante.
headword *n.* (*dictionary*) lema.
heal *v.* remedia, sani.
healer *n.* sanor.
health *n.* sania.
health bar *n.* (*food*) bara natural.
healthcare *n.* aida medical.
healthful *adj.* saninte.
health-giving *adj.* saninte.
healthy *adj.* sana; (*promoting health*) saninte.
heap *v.* pila. • *n.* pila, monton.
hear *v.* oia.
hearing *n.* (*sense of*) oia; (*legal*) escuta.
hearing aid *n.* aidaoia.
hearken *v.* escuta.
hearsay *n.* oiadas.
hearse *n.* veculo funeral.
heart *n.* (*including cards*) cor. **by heart** perfeta.
heartache *n.* (*metaphor*) dole de cor.
heart attack *n.* ataca de cor, infarta miocardial.
heartbeat *n.* bateta de cor.
heartbreak *n.* creve de cor.
heartbreaker *n.* crevecor.
heartbroken *adj.* con cor creveda.
heartburn *n.* iperasidia gastral.
hearten *v.* coraji, felisi.
heartfelt *adj.* zelosa.
hearth *n.* ximineria.
hearthside *n.* ximineria.
heartland *n.* cor de pais.
heartless *adj.* sin cor.
heartlike *adj.* corin.
heart-shaped *adj.* corin.
heartsick *adj.* malada de cor, descorajida.
heartstrings *n.* compatia.
heartthrob *n.* idol, amada.
heartwarming *adj.* felisinte.
heartwood *n.* lenio interna.
hearty *adj.* zelosa.
heat *v.* caldi. • *n.* caldia. **heat up** (*reheat*) recaldi. **in heat** en estro. **on heat** en estro.
heated floor *n.* solo caldinte.
heater *n.* caldador.
heath *n.* (*plant*) erica; (*moor*) stepe.
heathen *adj.* & *n.* pagan.
heather *n.* caluna.
heathland *n.* stepe.
heating *n.* caldi.
heating duct *n.* duto de caldi.
heat sink *n.* disipador de caldia.
heatstroke *n.* ipertermia.
heatwave *n.* onda de caldia.
heave *v.* (*tug*) aranca; (*rise and fall*) onda.
heaven *n.* paradiso, sielo.
heavenly *adj.* (*of the sky*) sielal; (*of heaven*) paradisal, sielal; (*like heaven*) paradisin, sielin.
heavenly body *n.* ojeto sielal.
heaving *adj.* (*rising and falling*) ondosa.
heavy *adj.* pesosa; (*troubling*) turbosa.
heavy-duty *adj.* de usa sever.
heavy-hearted *adj.* triste.
heavy metal *n.* roc metal.
heavyset *adj.* spesa.
heavy snow *n.* nevon.
heavyweight boxing *n.* boxe pesosa.
hebephrenia *n.* (*medical*) ebefrenia.
hebephrenic *adj.* ebefrenica.
Hebraica *n.* ivrisme.
Hebraism *n.* ivrisme.
Hebrew *adj.* & *n.* ivri.
Hebrides *n.* Hebrides. **Inner Hebrides** Hebrides Interna. **Outer Hebrides** Hebrides Esterna.
Hecate Strait *n.* Streta Hecate.

heckle *v.* burla, interompe.
heckler *n.* burlor.
hectare *n.* (*unit of area*) ectare.
hectic *adj.* manica.
hecto- *pref.* (*hundred*) ecto-.
hectogram *n.* ectogram.
hectolitre (US **hectoliter**) *n.* ectolitre.
hectometre (US **hectometer**) *n.* ectometre.
hector *v.* tormenta.
hedge *n.* sepe. • *v.* sepi.
hedgehog *n.* eriso.
hedgerow *n.* sepe.
hedonism *n.* edonisme.
hedonist *n.* edoniste, amor de plaser.
hedonistic *adj.* edoniste.
-hedron *suff.* (*geometric solid*) -edro.
heed *v.* atende.
heedful *adj.* cauta, atendente.
heedfulness *n.* cautia, atende.
heedless *adj.* noncauta, nonatendente, fretosa.
hee haw *interj.* (*donkey*) i-aa.
hee-hee *interj.* (*giggling*) hi hi.
heel *n.* talon. **high heel** (*shoe*) talon alta.
heel bone *n.* calcaneo.
heft *v.* leva.
hefty *adj.* grande, pesosa.
hegemony *n.* ejemonia.
heifer *n.* boveta fema.
height *n.* altia.
heinous *adj.* odiable.
heir *n.* eritor.
heir apparent *n.* eritor legal.
heiress *n.* eritor.
heirloom *n.* eritada de familia.
heist *n.* fura.
hejira *n.* (*Islam*) hidjra.
helical *adj.* elica.
helical gear *n.* pinion elica.
helicoid *adj.* elica.
helicopter *n.* elicotor.
helicopter gunship *n.* elicotor de ataca.
heliocentric *adj.* eliosentral.
heliogravure *n.* fotograva.
heliophile *n.* eliofilica.
heliophilia *n.* (*biology*) eliofilia.
heliophilic *adj.* eliofilica.
heliotrope *adj.* (*colour*) eliotropo. • *n.* (*plant*) eliotropo.
helipad *n.* elisurfas.
heliport *n.* eliporto.
helium *n.* elio.
helix *n.* elica.
hell *n.* enferno. **what the hell?** cual de enferno?
hell-bent *adj.* ostinosa.
Hellene *n.* elinica.
Hellenic *adj.* elinica.
Hellenism *n.* elinisme.
Hellenist *n.* eliniste.
Hellenistic *adj.* eliniste.
hellenization *n.* elinici.
hellenize *v.* elinici.
hellfire *n.* enferno.
hellhole *n.* loca misera.
hellion *n.* turbosa.
hellish *adj.* enfernin.
hello *interj.* alo. **hello there** alo ala.
helm *n.* timon.
helmet *n.* elmo.
helmetlike *adj.* elmin.
helminth *n.* elminto.
helminthiasis *n.* elmintose.
helmintosis *n.* elmintose.
helmsman *n.* timonor.
helot *n.* (*social class*) ilote.
help *v.*, *n.* & *interj.* aida. **help out** aida; (*help to climb out*) aida estrae. **without help** sin aida.
helper *n.* aidor.
helper animal *n.* bestia de servi.
helpful *adj.* aidosa.
helpfulness *n.* aidosia.
helping *adj.* aidante. • *n.* (*food*) comparti.
helpless *adj.* sin defende.
helpmate *n.* aidor.
helter-skelter *n.* tobogan elica.
hem *n.* orlo.
hem- (*US*) See *haem-*.
he-man *n.* musculor.
hemat... (US). See *haemat...*
hemi- *pref.* dui-, emi-.
hemichordate *n.* (*organism*) hemicordato.
hemidemisemiquaver *n.* tono sesdes-cuatrida.
hemiplegia *adj.* emiplejia.
hemiplegic *adj.* emiplejica.
hemisphere *n.* emisfera.
hemline *n.* orlo.
hemlock *n.* (*plant, poison*) conio; (*tree*) tsuga.
hemo... (US). See *haemo...*
hemp *n.* (*plant, material, drug*) canaba.
hemstitch *n.* cose de orlo.
hen *n.* gal fema.
henbane *n.* (*plant*) jusciam.
hence *adv.* de asi.
henceforth *adv.* de aora.
henchman *n.* seguor.
hencoop *n.* ensirca de gales.
henhouse *n.* casa de gales.
henna *n.* (*plant, dye*) hena.
henpeck *v.* critica.
henry *n.* (*unit of inductance*) henri.
hentai *n.* (*manga*) hentai.
heparin *n.* (*medical*) eparina.
hepatic *adj.* epatal. • *n.* (*plant*) epatica.
hepatitis *n.* epatite.

hepta- *pref.* (*seven*) eta-.
heptagon *n.* etagon.
heptagonal *adj.* etagon.
heptameter *n.* (*poetry*) etametre.
heptathlete *n.* etatlonor.
heptathlon *n.* etatlon.
her *pron.* (*normally*) el; (*rarely, only for stylistic contrast with* elo) ela. • *det.* sua. **her highness** sua altia. **her own** sua propre.
herald *n.* eraldo.
heraldic *adj.* eraldial.
heraldry *n.* eraldia.
herb *n.* erba, erba de cosini.
herbaceous *adj.* erbin.
herbal *adj.* erbal.
herbarium *n.* erberia.
herb chopper *n.* cotel osilante.
herbicidal *adj.* erbisidal.
herbicide *n.* erbiside.
herbivore *n.* erbivor.
herbivorous *adj.* erbivor.
herbologist *n.* erbolojiste.
herbology *n.* erbolojia.
Herculean *adj.* herculin.
Hercules *n.* (*mythology, constellation*) Hercule.
herd *n.* manada. • *v.* gida.
herder *n.* pastor.
herding *n.* pastoria.
herdsman *n.* pastor, manador.
herdswoman *n.* pastor.
here *adv.* asi, en esta loca; (*to here*) a esta loca. **here and there** (*dotted about*) asi e ala, a sirca. **here are some ideas** on ave asi alga ideas.
hereafter *n.* vive pos mori.
hereby *adv.* par esta.
hereditary *adj.* erital.
heredity *n.* erita.
herein *adv.* en esta, a en.
heresy *n.* eresia.
heretic *n.* erese.
heretical *adj.* erese.
heritable *adj.* eritable.
heritage *n.* erita.
heritor *n.* eritor.
heritrix *n.* eritor.
hermaphrodite *n.* androjine.
hermaphroditic *adj.* androjine.
hermaphroditism *n.* androjinia.
hermeneutic *adj.* interpretal.
hermetic *adj.* nonpermeable.
hermit *n.* eremita.
hermitage *n.* eremiteria.
hermitic *n.* eremita.
hermitry *n.* eremitia.
hernia *n.* ernia.
herniate *v.* ernia.
herniation *n.* ernia.
hero *n.* eroe; (*sandwich*) bagete plenida.
heroic *adj.* eroin.
heroin *n.* (*drug*) eroina.
heroine *n.* (*hero*) eroe.
heroism *n.* eroisme.
heron *n.* eron.
herpes *n.* erpes.
herpetologist *n.* erpetolojiste.
herpetology *n.* erpetolojia.
herring *n.* arenge.
herringbone *adj.* xevronosa.
hers *pron.* la sua(s).
herself *pron.* (*reflexive*) se; (*emphatically reflexive*) se mesma. **she herself** (*non-reflexively emphatic*) el mesma. **the queen herself** la rea mesma.
hertz *n.* herze.
Herzegovina *n.* Hersegovina.
Herzegovinian *adj.* & *n.* hersegovasce.
hesitant *adj.* esitante; vasilante.
hesitate *v.* esita; (*between two choices*) vasila.
hesitation *n.* esita; vasila.
hessian *n.* juta.
hessian sack *n.* saco de juta.
hetaera *n.* cortesan; (*moth*) etera.
hetero- *pref.* (*different*) etero-.
heterodox *adj.* eterodox.
heterogeneous *adj.* eterojen.
heterosexual *adj.* & *n.* eterosesal.
heterosexuality *n.* eterosesalia.
heterotroph *n.* eterotrof.
heterotrophia *n.* eterotrofia.
heterotrophic *adj.* (*biology*) eterotrof.
heuristic *n.* euristica. • *adj.* euristical.
hew *v.* axi, talia; (*conform*) conforma.
hex- *pref.* (*six*) esa-.
hexadecimal *adj.* exadesimal.
hexagon *n.* exagon.
hexagonal *adj.* exagon.
hexagram *n.* esagram.
hexahedral *adj.* esaedro.
hexahedron *n.* esaedro.
hexameter *n.* exametre.
hex-cap bolt *n.* vise esagon.
hex-cap screw *n.* vise esagon.
hey *interj.* (*hi*) alo; (*attracting attention*) he.
heyday *n.* apico, eda oro.
hey presto *interj.* ta-da.
hi *interj.* alo, txau. **hi there** alo ala.
hiatal hernia *n.* ernia iatal.
hiatus *n.* pausa.
hibachi *n.* (*heater*) hibatxi, brasador.
hibernal *adj.* invernal.
hibernate *v.* inverni.
hibernation *n.* inverni.
hibiscus *n.* (*plant*) ibisco.
hiccough *v.* ica.
hiccup *v.* & *n.* ica.
hick *n.* campanian.

hickey *n.* (*love bite*) suceta; (*thingummy*) aparateta.
hickory *n.* (*tree, nut*) pecan.
hide[1] *v.* asconde. **hide and seek** jua de asconde.
hide[2] *n.* (*skin*) pel.
hideaway *n.* nido.
hideous *adj.* xocante fea.
hideout *n.* asconderia, nido.
hiding *n.* asconde. **be in hiding** asconde.
hiding place *n.* asconderia.
hierarchic *adj.* ierarcial.
hierarchical *adj.* ierarcial.
hierarchy *n.* ierarcia.
hieratic *adj.* (*writing, art*) ieratica.
hieroglyph *n.* ieroglifo.
hieroglyphic *adj.* ieroglifal.
hi-fi *adj.* de fida alta.
high *adj.* alta. **the highs and lows** la altas e la basas.
high-born *adj.* aristocrata, nobil.
highbrow *adj.* sofisticada.
high commissioner *n.* ambasador.
high-end *adj.* estrema lusosa.
higher *adj.* plu alta. **higher than** (*location, quantity, standard*) supra, plu alta ca.
higher education *n.* educa de universia.
higher-up *n.* superior.
highest *adj.* la plu alta. **with the highest praise** con loda masima.
high-fidelity *adj.* de fida alta.
high-handed *adj.* autoritar, egosa.
high heel *n.* (*shoe*) talon alta.
high jump *n.* salta alta.
high-jumper *n.* saltor alta.
highland *adj.* montanial. • *n.* tereno alta, montania.
highlander *n.* montanior.
highlight *v.* & *n.* lumina; (*text*) marca.
highness *n.* altia. **her highness** sua altia. **his highness** sua altia. **your highness** altia.
high plain *n.* plano alta.
high point *n.* zenite.
high-pressure area *n.* antisiclon, zona de presa alta.
high-quality *adj.* de cualia alta.
high-ranking officer *n.* ofisior alta.
high relief *n.* releva alta.
high school *n.* liseo.
high seas *n.* mar alta.
high society *n.* crema de sosia.
high tech *n.* tecnolojia alta.
high tide *n.* marea alta.
highway *n.* via xef; (*motorway*) autovia.
highwayman *n.* bandito.
hi-hat *n.* (*cymbals*) xarleston.
hijab *n.* (*garment*) hidjab.
hijack *v.* saisi en viaja.
hijacker *n.* saisor.
hike *v.* & *n.* pasea longa.
hiker *n.* paseamanica.
hiking *n.* paseamania.
hilarious *adj.* ilario.
hilarity *n.* ilaria.
hill *n.* colina.
hillbilly *n.* montanior.
hillock *n.* colineta.
hilltop *n.* culmina de colina.
hilly *adj.* colinosa.
hilt *n.* (*sword, knife*) manico.
him *pron.* (*normally*) el; (*rarely, only for stylistic contrast with* ela) elo.
Himalaya Mountains *n.* Montes Himalaia.
Himalayan *adj.* himalaian.
Himalayas *n.* (*region*) Himalaia; (*mountains*) Montes Himalaia.
himself *pron.* (*reflexive*) se; (*emphatically reflexive*) se mesma. **he himself** (*non-reflexively emphatic*) el mesma. **the king himself** la re mesma.
hind[1] *adj.* (*rear*) posterior.
hind[2] *n.* (*deer*) servo fema.
hindbrain *n.* serebro retro.
hinder *v.* impedi, interfere.
Hindi *adj.* & *n.* (*language*) hindi.
hindmost *adj.* final.
hindquarters *n.* posterior.
hindrance *n.* impedi.
hindsight *adv.* retrospeta.
Hindu *adj.* & *n.* indu, induiste.
Hinduism *n.* induisme.
Hindustani *adj.* industani.
hinge *n.* xarnier. • *v.* xarnieri.
hint *v.* & *n.* indiceta, aviseta.
hinterland *n.* interna.
hip *n.* anca.
hipbone *n.* oso de anca.
hip-hop *adj.* (*dance, music*) hiphop.
hip-huggers *n.* pantalon de anca.
hippie *n.* hipi.
hippo *n.* ipopotamo.
hippocampus *n.* ipocampo.
Hippocrates *n.* Hipocrate.
Hippocratic oath *n.* jura de Hipocrate.
hippopotamus *n.* ipopotamo.
hippy *n.* hipi.
hipster *n.* dandi. **hipsters** pantalon de anca.
hiragana *n.* (*writing system*) hiragana.
hire *v.* (*rent*) lua; (*employ*) emplea. **hire out** ofre per lua.
hireling *n.* empleada.
hiring *n.* lua.
hirsute *adj.* pelosa.
his *det.* sua. • *pron.* la sua(s). **his highness** sua altia. **his own** sua propre.

Hispanic *adj.* & *n.* latina.
Hispaniola *n.* (*island*) Ispaniola.
hiss *v.* & *n.* sisa. • *interj.* ss.
histamine *n.* istamina.
histogram *n.* istogram.
histologist *n.* istolojiste.
histology *n.* istolojia.
historian *n.* istoriste.
historic *adj.* famosa; (*unprecedented*) sin presedente.
historical *adj.* istorial.
historiographer *n.* istoriografiste.
historiography *n.* istoriografia.
history *n.* istoria.
history-making *adj.* sin presedente.
histrionic *adj.* dramosa.
hit *v.* colpa. • *n.* colpa; (*success*) susedosa. **hit on** imajina; (*flirt*) fa avansas a.
hitchhike *v.* autostopa.
hitchhiker *n.* autostopor.
hither *adv.* asi, a asi, a esta loca.
hit parade *n.* parade de susedosas.
Hittite *adj.* & *n.* (*person*, *language*) hitita.
HIV *abbr.* viu.
hive *n.* (*beehive*) nido, aberia.
hives *n.* (*rash*) urticaria.
hmm *interj.* (*thinking*) hm, mm.
Hmong-Mien *adj.* & *n.* (*person*, *language*) miau-iau.
hnefatafl *n.* (*game*) tafel.
hoagie *n.* (*sandwich*) bagete plenida.
hoagy *n.* (*sandwich*) bagete plenida.
hoard *v.* cumula, reserva. • *n.* reserva; tesoros.
hoarder *n.* cumulor.
hoarding *n.* panel de poster.
hoarfrost *n.* jelada.
hoarse *adj.* roncin.
hoary *adj.* grisin blanca.
hoax *v.* & *n.* engana.
hob *n.* (*stove*) stufa; (*surface beside a fire*) cornisa de foco.
hobbit *n.* hobit.
hobble *v.* coxea; lia la gamas de.
hobby[1] *n.* amato, pasatempo.
hobby[2] *n.* (*bird*) subuteo.
hobbyhorse *n.* basto cavalin; preocupa.
hobbyist *n.* amator.
hobgoblin *n.* elfo.
hobnob *v.* asosia.
hobo *n.* vagabon.
hock[1] *n.* (*joint*) talo.
hock[2] *v.* (*pawn*) impenia.
hockey *n.* hoci.
hockey puck *n.* disco de hoci.
hocus pocus *interj.* abracadabra.
hodgepodge *n.* misca, colie miscada.
Hodgkin's lymphoma *n.* limfoma de Hodgkin.
hoe *n.* zada. • *v.* zadi.
hoedown *n.* balo vivosa.
hog *n.* porco.
hogshead *n.* baril.
hogtie *v.* lia la gamas de, lia la manos e pedes de.
hogwash *n.* asurda.
ho ho ho *interj.* (*deep laughter*) ho ho ho.
hoi polloi *n.* manada.
hoist *v.* leva.
Hokkaido *n.* (*island*) Hokkaido.
Hoklo *adj.* & *n.* (*person*, *language*) holo.
holarctic *adj.* (*ecology*) olartica.
hold *v.* teni; (*event*) ospita, aveni, fa; (*opinion*) opina; (*breath*) reteni. • *n.* (*ship's*) cala. **hold back** freni. **hold hands** teni manos. **hold in** reteni. **hold on to** teni. **hold out** (*hand*) estende; (*endure*) resiste, dura. **hold tight** (*squeeze*) presa. **hold to account** esije un esplica. **hold up** (*raise*) leva; (*delay*) retarda; (*rob*) ruba; (*remain strong*) resiste.
holdable *adj.* tenable.
holdall *n.* bolson.
holder *n.* contenador, portador.
holding company *n.* holding.
holdover *n.* survivor.
hold-up *n.* (*delay*) retarda, pospone; (*robbery*) ruba.
hole *n.* buco; (*piercing*) fora.
hole saw *n.* sieribuco.
holey *adj.* bucosa.
holiday *n.* (*vacation*) vacanse; (*public*, *religious*) festa. • *v.* vacanse.
holidaymaker *n.* vacansor.
holiday traveller (US **traveler**) *n.* vacansor.
holiness *n.* santia.
holism *n.* olisme.
holist *n.* oliste.
holistic *adj.* oliste.
Holland *n.* Nederland.
hollandaise *adj.* olandes.
hollandaise sauce *n.* salsa olandes.
hollow *adj.* vacua, cavetin. • *n.* caveta.
holly *n.* ilex.
hollyhock *n.* (*plant*) alsea.
holmium *n.* (*element*) holmio.
holo- *pref.* (*whole*) olo-.
holocaust *n.* olocausto. **Jewish Holocaust** Olocausto.
Holocene *adj.* & *n.* (*geology*) olosene.
hologram *n.* ologram.
holographic *adj.* olografial.
holography *n.* olografia.
holozoa *n.* (*organisms*) holozones.
holozoon *n.* (*organism*) holozon.
holstein *n.* (*cow*) holstain.
holster *n.* portapistol.
holy *adj.* santa.

Holy Grail *n.* Calix Santa.
holy place *n.* santeria.
Holy See *n.* Seja Santa.
holy texts *n.* scrivedas santa.
homage *n.* onora.
home *n.* casa. • *adv.* a casa. **at home** a casa. **at the home of** a casa de.
homebody *n.* pantoflor.
homebound *adj.* restrinjeda a casa.
home cinema *n.* sinema de casa.
homecoming *n.* reveni a casa.
homegrown *adj.* cultivada a casa.
homeland *n.* propre pais.
homeless *adj.* sin casa.
home loan *n.* presta per casa.
homemade *adj.* fabricada a casa.
homemaker *n.* fem de casa, om de casa.
homemaking *n.* taxes de casa.
homeo... (US). See *homoeo...*
home office *n.* ofisia a casa.
homeowner *n.* proprior de casa.
home page *n.* paje prima.
Homer *n.* Homero.
Homeric *adj.* homeral.
homeroom *n.* sala prima.
home secretary *n.* ministro de internas.
homesick *adj.* anelante sua casa; (*abroad*) anelante sua pais.
homesickness *n.* anela de casa; (*abroad*) anela de pais.
homespun *adj.* texeda a casa.
homestead *n.* imobila.
home theatre (US **theater**) *n.* sinema de casa.
hometown *n.* vila de nase.
homeward *adv.* a casa.
homewards *adv.* a casa.
homework *n.* debe de casa.
homicidal *adj.* omisidal, matante.
homicide *n.* (*action*) omiside; (*person*) omisidor. **commit homicide** omiside.
homily *n.* sermon.
hominid *n.* ominido.
hominy *n.* mais moleda.
homo- *pref.* (*same*) omo-.
homoeo- *pref.* (*same*) omeo-.
homoeopath (US **homeopath**) *n.* omeopatiste.
homoeopathic (US **homeopathic**) *adj.* omeopatica.
homoeopathy (US **homeopathy**) *n.* omeopatia.
homoeostasis (US **homeostasis**) *n.* (*biology*) omeostase.
homoeostatic (US **homeostatic**) *adj.* omeostasal.
homoerotic *adj.* omoerotica.
homogene *adj.* omojen.
homogeneity *n.* omojenia.
homogeneous *adj.* omojen.
homogenize *v.* omojeni.
homolog (US). See *homologue.*
homologous *adj.* omoloja.
homologue (US **homolog**) *n.* omoloja.
homology *n.* (*quality*) omolojia; (*something homologous*) omoloja.
homonym *n.* omonim.
homonymous *adj.* omonim.
homonymy *n.* omonimia.
homophobe *n.* omofobica.
homophobia *n.* omofobia.
homophobic *adj.* & *n.* omofobica.
homophone *n.* omofon.
homophonous *adj.* omofon.
homorganic *adj.* omorganal.
homosexual *adj.* & *n.* omosesal, ge.
homosexuality *n.* omosesalia.
Honduran *adj.* & *n.* onduran.
Honduras *n.* Onduras.
hone *v.* (*sharpen*) agi; (*refine*) developa.
honest *adj.* onesta.
honesty *n.* onestia.
honey *n.* miel; (*sweetheart*) mielin.
honeybee *n.* abea.
honeycomb *n.* favo.
honeydew *n.* (*substance*) mielada.
honeydew melon *n.* melon de inverno.
honeyeater *n.* (*bird*) mielifaje.
honey locust *n.* (*tree*) gleditsia.
honeymoon *n.* luna de miel.
honeysuckle *n.* caprifolia.
Hong Kong *n.* Hongkong.
honk *v.* claxoni.
honor... (US). See *honour...*
honorarium *n.* paia onoral.
honorary *adj.* onoral.
honoree *n.* onorada.
honour (US **honor**) *v.* onora; (*agreement*) reali, segue. • *n.* onora; (*award*) premio lodante. **with honour** onorosa.
honourable (US **honorable**) *adj.* onorable, onorosa.
honourableness (US **honorableness**) *n.* onora.
Honshu *n.* (*island*) Honshu.
hoo *interj.* u-u.
hood[1] *n.* (*garment, of vehicle*) capeta; (*of vehicle*) capeta de motor.
-hood[2] *suff.* -ia.
hooded crow *n.* corvo gris.
hooded sweatshirt *n.* sueter de capeta.
hoodie *n.* (*garment*) sueter de capeta; (*person*) capetor; (*crow*) corvo gris.
hoodlum *n.* criminor.
hoodwink *v.* froda.
hoof *n.* ungula.
hoofbeat *n.* bateta de ungulas.
hoofmark *n.* impresa de ungula.

hoofprint *n.* impresa de ungula.
hook *n.* onca. • *v.* onci. **hook up** onci, junta; (*meet*) encontra.
hookah *n.* pipa de acua.
hook-and-eye closure *n.* oncianelo.
hook-and-eye fastener *n.* oncianelo.
hooked *adj.* oncin.
hooker *n.* fem prostituida.
hookie, play *v.* evita la scola.
hooklike *adj.* oncin.
hookworm *n.* (*worm*) ancilostoma, necator; (*disease*) ancilostomiase, necatoriase.
hooligan *n.* vandal.
hoop *n.* anelo.
hoopla *n.* jua de anelo.
hooray *interj.* ura.
hoot *n.* (*sound*) tut. • *v.* tuti, claxoni. • *interj.* (*owl*) u-u; (*horn*) tut. **hoot with laughter** esplode con rie.
hootenanny *n.* balo vivosa.
hooter *n.* claxon.
hop[1] *v.* brinca. • *n.* brinca; (*event*) balo vivosa.
hop[2] *n.* (*plant*) lupulo.
hope *n.* espera. **hope for** espera.
hopeful *adj.* esperante.
hopefully *adv.* esperable; on espera ce.
hopeless *adj.* sin espera, futil; (*inept*) noncapas.
Hopi *adj.* & *n.* (*person, language*) hopi.
hoplite *n.* (*soldier*) oplita.
hopper *n.* brincor.
hopscotch *n.* brincacuadro.
horde *n.* (*barbarians*) manada.
hordock *n.* (*plant*) bardana.
horizon *n.* orizon.
horizontal *adj.* orizonal.
horizontal band *n.* faxa.
horizontality *n.* orizonalia.
horizontalness *n.* orizonalia.
hormesis *n.* (*biology*) ormese.
hormonal *adj.* ormonal.
hormone *n.* ormon.
hormonelike *adj.* ormonin.
Hormuz *n.* Hormuz. **Strait of Hormuz** Streta Hormuz.
horn *n.* (*animal, music*) corno; (*vehicle*) claxon. **English horn** corneta engles. **French horn** trompa. **horn of plenty** corno de abunda. **sound one's horn** tuti, claxoni.
hornbeam *n.* (*tree*) carpino.
hornbill *n.* (*bird*) calau.
hornet *n.* vespa.
hornlike *adj.* cornin.
hornpipe *n.* (*dance, music*) hornpip; (*musical instrument*) pibgorn.
hornwort *n.* (*plant*) antoserotal.
horny *adj.* (*hornlike*) cornin; (*randy*) libidosa.
Horologium *n.* (*constellation*) la Orolojo.
horology *n.* orolojia.
horoscope *n.* oroscopo.
horrendous *adj.* asustante, xocante, repulsante.
horrible *adj.* asustante, xocante; (*taste*) desplasente, repulsante.
horrid *adj.* asustante; (*taste*) desplasente, repulsante.
horrific *adj.* asustante, xocante.
horrify *v.* asusta, terori, xoca, repulsa.
horror *n.* teror.
horror movie *n.* filma de teror.
hors d'oeuvre *n.* deleta.
horse *n.* cavalo.
horseback *adj.* montante. **on horseback** montante.
horse chestnut *n.* (*tree, nut*) ipocastania.
horse-drawn *adj.* tirada par cavalo.
horsefly *n.* tabano.
horsehair *n.* crinera.
horselike *adj.* cavalin.
horseman *n.* cavalor.
horsemanship *n.* cavaloria.
horsenettle *n.* (*plant*) solano.
horseplay *n.* bufonia.
horsepower *n.* (*measurement*) cavalo.
horse race *n.* corsa de cavalos.
horseracing *n.* corsa de cavalos.
horseradish *n.* rabano forte.
horse rider *n.* cavalor.
horseriding *adj.* cavaloral.
horseshoe *n.* fero de cavalo.
horsetail *n.* (*plant*) ecuisito.
horsewoman *n.* cavalor.
hortative *adj.* corajinte.
horticultural *adj.* orticultural.
horticulture *n.* orticultur.
horticulturist *n.* orticulturiste.
hose *n.* (*tube*) mangera; (*hosiery*) calsas. • *v.* mangeri. **hose down** mangeri.
hosepipe *n.* mangera.
hosiery *n.* calsas.
hospice *n.* ospisio.
hospitable *adj.* bonveninte.
hospital *n.* ospital.
hospital bed *n.* leto rolante.
hospitality *n.* ospitia.
hospitalization *n.* ospitali.
hospitalize *v.* ospitali.
hospital nurse *n.* ospitalor.
hospital worker *n.* ospitalor.
host[1] *v.* ospita. • *n.* (*person*) ospitor; (*computer*) ospitador.
host[2] *n.* (*large number*) multia, monton; (*army*) armada. **a host of** multe.
host[3] *n.* (*Eucharist*) ostia.
hostage *n.* ostaje. **hold hostage** teni como ostaje.
hostelry *n.* otel.

hostess *n.* ospitor. **air hostess** ospitor de avion.
hostile *adj.* enemin; (*environment*) dur.
hostility *n.* (*behaviour*) enemia; (*warfare*) ata de gera.
hot *adj.* calda; (*fashionable*) a la moda, de moda.
hot-air balloon *n.* balon de aira calda.
hotbed *n.* solo fertil.
hotcake *n.* crepe.
hotchpotch *n.* misca, colie miscada.
hotdog *n.* salsix american.
hotdog bun *n.* paneta de salsix.
hotdog roll *n.* paneta de salsix.
hotel *n.* otel.
hotelier *n.* otelor.
hotelkeeper *n.* otelor.
hot flash *n.* ondas de caldia, episodio de caldi.
hot flush *n.* ondas de caldia, episodio de caldi.
hothead *n.* (*angry*) coler, disputosa; (*impetuous*) fretor.
hot-headed *adj.* fretante.
hothouse *n.* inverneria.
hotline *n.* linia direta.
hotpants *n.* minipantala.
hot pepper *n.* txili.
hotrod *n.* bolide.
hot sauce *n.* salsa de txili.
hotshot *n.* stela.
hotspot *n.* punto calda.
hot-swap *v.* cambia calda.
hot-swappable *adj.* calda cambiable.
hot-tempered *adj.* disputosa.
Hottentot *adj.* & *n.* (*person*, *language*) coicoi.
hot tub *n.* banio de vortis.
hound *n.* xasor.
hour *n.* ora. **24 hours a day** a 24 oras de la dia.
hourglass *n.* orolojo de arena.
houri *n.* (*Islam*) huri.
house *n.* casa. • *v.* casi. **House of Commons** Salon Basa. **House of Lords** Salon Alta. **House of Representatives** Salon Basa. **in the house of** a casa de.
houseboat *n.* casa flotante.
houseboy *n.* servor de casa.
housecoat *n.* roba de bani.
housedress *n.* roba de casa.
housefly *n.* mosca de casa.
household *n.* casa, familia.
househusband *n.* om de casa.
housekeeper *n.* manejor de casa.
housekeeping *n.* maneja de casa.
housemaid *n.* servor de casa.
housemate *n.* coabitor.
housesit *v.* garda la casa.
housewarming *n.* selebra de casa nova.
housewife *n.* fem de casa.
housework *n.* taxes de casa.
housing *n.* casas; (*casing*) caxa.
housing estate *n.* compleso de casas.
Houthi *adj.* & *n.* (*Islam*) huti.
hovel *n.* casa misera; cabana bruta.
hover *v.* flota en aira.
hovercraft *n.* liscador.
hoverfly *n.* sirfido.
how *adv.* (*interrogative*) como; (*exclamation*) tan! **how are you?** como lo vade? **how long** como longa, (*intended*) per cuanto tempo, (*elapsed*) tra cuanto tempo. **how lovely!** tan bela! **how sad!** tan triste! **how's it going?** como lo vade?
however *adv.* an tal, ma ancora, contra esta, par contrasta.
howitzer *n.* (*gun*) obus.
howl *v.* & *n.* ulula.
howler monkey *n.* aloata.
how many *det.* & *adv.* cuanto.
how much *det.* & *adv.* cuanto.
howto *n.* instrui.
hoyden *n.* xica ruidosa.
HQ *n.* xeferia, base.
HTML page *n.* paje HTML.
Huang Hai *n.* Mar Huanghai.
Huang He *n.* Rio Huanghe.
hub *n.* sentro; (*computer*) consentrador.
hubcap *n.* covresentro.
hubris *n.* orgulo.
huckleberry *n.* vasinia, vasinia blu.
huckster *n.* frodor.
huddle *v.* foli.
Hudson Bay *n.* Baia Hudson.
Hudson River *n.* Rio Hudson.
Hudson Strait *n.* Streta Hudson.
hue *n.* tinje.
huff *v.* sofla.
huffy *adj.* iritada.
hug *v.* & *n.* abrasa.
huge *adj.* enorme, vasta.
huggable *adj.* abrasable.
Huguenot *n.* ugonote.
huh? *interj.* (*confusion*) como?
hula *n.* (*dance*) hula.
hulk *n.* barcon abandonada.
hull[1] *n.* (*of ship*) casco.
hull[2] *n.* (*of fruit*) casca.
hum *v.* & *n.* zumbi.
human *adj.* & *n.* umana.
human being *n.* umana.
humane *adj.* compatiosa.
human growth hormone *n.* somatotropina.
human immunodeficiency virus *n.* virus de imunodebilia umana, viu.
humanism *n.* umanisme.
humanist *adj.* & *n.* umaniste.

humanitarian *adj.* & *n.* umaniste.
humanities *n.* siensas umana.
humanity *n.* (*humans*) umanas; (*quality*) umania.
humanization *n.* umani.
humanize *v.* umani.
humanlike *adj.* umanin.
humanoid *adj.* umanin.
human sciences *n.* siensas umana.
human trafficking *n.* contrabanda umana.
humble *adj.* umil. • *v.* umili.
humbug *n.* engana; confeto de menta peperin.
humdrum *adj.* noiante.
humerus *n.* (*anatomy*) omero.
humid *adj.* umida.
humidifier *n.* umidador.
humidify *v.* umidi.
humidistat *n.* umidistato.
humidity *n.* umidia.
humidor *n.* (*tobacco box*) umidador.
humiliate *v.* desonora, vergonia.
humiliation *n.* desonora, vergonia.
humility *n.* umilia.
hummingbird *n.* colibri.
hummock *n.* colineta.
hummus *n.* (*food*) umus.
humongous *adj.* jigante.
humor (US). See *humour*.
humorist *n.* umoriste.
humorless (US). See *humourless*.
humorous *adj.* umorosa, comica, comedial.
humour (US **humor**) *n.* (*including bodily fluid*) umor. • *v.* plase.
humourless (US **humorless**) *adj.* sombre.
hump *n.* (*back*) jiba.
humpback whale *n.* megatero.
humped *adj.* jibosa.
humped cattle *n.* zebus.
humus *n.* umo.
Hun *n.* hun.
Hunanese *adj.* & *n.* (*language*) xiang.
hunch *n.* (*hump*) jiba; (*suspicion*) divina. • *v.* (*forward, over*) curvi se a ante.
hunched *adj.* jibosa.
hundred *det.* & *n.* sento. **hundreds** sentos. **one hundred** sento. **two hundred** dusento.
hundredth *adj.* (*ordinal*) sento. • *n.* (*fraction*) senti.
hung *adj.* pendeda, suspendeda. **hung over** malada de posenebria.
Hungarian *adj.* & *n.* magiar, ungarian.
Hungary *n.* Magiar, Ungaria.
hunger *n.* famia. • *v.* fami.
hunger strike *n.* juna political, protesta par juna.
hung parliament *n.* parlamento sin majoria.
hungry *adj.* fame. **go hungry** fami.
hunk *n.* peson.
hunker *v.* acrupi.
Hunnic *adj.* hun.
hunt *v.* & *n.* xasa.
hunter *n.* xasor.
hunter-gatherer *adj.* xasante-coliente. • *n.* xasor-colior.
hunting dog *n.* xasor.
hunting guide *n.* aidor de xasa.
hurdle *n.* ostaculo.
hurdler *n.* corsor de ostaculos.
hurdle race *n.* corsa de ostaculos.
hurdy-gurdy *n.* organo de enrola, viola de rota.
hurl *v.* lansa, xuta.
hurler *n.* lansor.
hurling *n.* hoci eres.
Huron, Lake *n.* Lago Huron.
hurrah *interj.* ura.
hurricane *n.* siclon.
hurrier *n.* fretor.
hurry *v.* freta.
hurt *v.* dole; (*injure*) feri. • *n.* dole. • *adj.* ferida.
hurtful *adj.* angusante, dolente.
hurtle *v.* core sin restrinje.
husband *n.* sposo, spos; (*colloquial*) om.
husbandry *n.* cultiva, eleva. **animal husbandry** eleva de animales.
husband-to-be *n.* sposo futur.
hush *v.* silenti.
husk *n.* gluma.
husky *n.* (*dog*) husci.
hussar *n.* (*soldier*) husar.
Hussite *adj.* & *n.* husiste.
Hussitism *n.* (*Christianity*) husisme.
hussy *n.* seduor, tisor.
hustle *v.* & *n.* freta.
hustler *n.* frodor.
hut *n.* cabana.
hutia *n.* (*rodent*) utia.
Hutterite *adj.* & *n.* (*Christianity*) huterita.
Hutu *adj.* & *n.* (*person, language*) hutu.
hyacinth *n.* jasinto. **grape hyacinth** muscari. **wild hyacinth** jasinto de bosce.
hybrid *adj.* & *n.* ibride.
hybridization *n.* ibridi.
hybridize *v.* ibridi.
hydra *n.* (*organism*) idra; (*mythology, constellation*) Idra.
hydrangea *n.* (*plant*) ortensia.
hydrant *n.* idrante.
hydrate *v.* idrata.
hydration *n.* idrata.
hydrator *n.* idratador.
hydraulic *adj.* idraulical.
hydraulics *n.* idraulica.
hydraulic wheel *adj.* rota idraulical.
hydro- *pref.* (*water*) idro-.

hydrocarbon *adj.* idrocarbonal. • *n.* idrocarbono.
hydrocephalic *adj.* idrosefalica.
hydrocephalus *n.* idrosefalia.
hydrochloric *adj.* idroclorica.
hydrochloric acid *n.* asida idroclorica.
hydrochloride *n.* idroclorido.
hydrodynamic *adj.* idrodinamical.
hydrodynamics *n.* idrodinamica.
hydroelectric *adj.* idroeletrical.
hydroelectricity *n.* idroeletrica.
hydrofoil *n.* idroplana.
hydrogen *n.* idrojen.
hydrogen bomb *n.* bomba de idrojen.
hydrogen peroxide *n.* idrojen perosido.
hydrographer *n.* idrografiste.
hydrographical *adj.* idrografial.
hydrography *n.* idrografia.
hydrologist *n.* idrolojiste.
hydrology *n.* idrolojia.
hydrolyse (US **hydrolyze**) *v.* idrolise.
hydrolysis *n.* idrolise.
hydrolyze (US). See *hydrolyse.*
hydrophile *n.* idrofilica.
hydrophilia *n.* idrofilia.
hydrophilic *adj.* idrofilica.
hydrophobe *n.* idrofobica.
hydrophobia *n.* idrofobia.
hydrophobic *adj.* idrofobica.
hydroplane *n.* avion de mar.
hydroponic *adj.* idroponial.
hydroponics *n.* idroponia.
hydrosphere *n.* idrosfera.
hydrostatic *adj.* idrostatical.
hydrostatic balance *n.* ecuilibra idrostatical.
hydrostatic equilibrium *n.* ecuilibra idrostatical.
hydrostatics *n.* idrostatica.
hydrotherapy *n.* idroterapia.
hydrothermal *adj.* idrotermal.
hydrous *adj.* idrosa.
hydroxide *n.* idrosido.
hydroxyl *adj.* idrosil.
hydrozoa *n.* (*organisms*) idrozones.
hydrozoon *n.* (*organism*) idrozon.
Hydrus *n.* (*constellation*) la Idra Mas.
hyena *n.* iena.
hyena-like *adj.* ienin.
hygiene *n.* ijenia.
hygienic *adj.* ijenial.
hygienist *n.* ijeniste.
hymen *n.* (*anatomy*) imen.
hymn *n.* imno.
hymnal *n.* libro de imnos.
hymnbook *n.* libro de imnos.
hyolith *n.* (*fossil*) hiolito.
hype *n.* anunsia, promove; loda falsa.
hyper- *pref.* iper-.
hyperacidity *n.* iperasidia.
hyperactive *adj.* iperativa.
hyperactivity *n.* iperativia.
hyperbaric *adj.* iperbara.
hyperbola *n.* iperbola.
hyperbole *n.* esajera.
hypercube *n.* ipercubo.
hyperextend *v.* iperestende.
hyperextension *n.* iperestende.
hyperglycaemia (US **hyperglycemia**) *n.* iperglisemia.
hyperglycaemic (US **hyperglycemic**) *adj.* iperglisemica.
hyperhidrosis *n.* (*medical*) iperidrose.
hypericum *n.* iperico.
hyperinflate *v.* iperinfla.
hyperinflation *n.* iperinfla.
hyperkinesia *n.* ipercinesia.
hyperlink *n.* iperlia.
hyperlipidaemia (US **hyperlipidemia**) *n.* (*medical*) iperlipidemia.
hyperostosis *n.* (*medical*) iperostose.
hyperphagia *n.* (*medical*) iperfajia.
hyperplasia *n.* (*medical*) iperplasia.
hyperpyrexia *n.* (*medical*) iperpirexia.
hyperreflexia *n.* (*medical*) ipereflexia.
hypersecrete *v.* (*medical*) ipersecrete.
hypersecretion *n.* ipersecrete.
hypersensitive *adj.* ipersensosa.
hyperstimulate *v.* iperstimula.
hyperstimulation *n.* iperstimula.
hypertension *n.* (*medical*) ipertensa.
hypertensive *adj.* & *n.* ipertensal.
hypertext *n.* ipertesto.
hyperthermia *n.* ipertermia.
hyperthyroidism *n.* (*medical*) ipertiroidia.
hypertonia *n.* (*medical*) ipertonia.
hypertrichosis *n.* (*medical*) ipertricose.
hypertrophy *n.* (*medical*) ipertrofia.
hyperuricaemia (US **hyperuricemia**) *n.* (*medical*) iperurisemia.
hyperventilate *v.* supraspira.
hyperventilation *n.* supraspira.
hyphen *n.* ifen, sinia de junta.
hyphenatable *adj.* ifenable.
hyphenate *v.* ifeni.
hyphenation *n.* ifeni.
hypnagogia *n.* ipnagojia.
hypnagogic *adj.* ipnagojial.
hypno- *pref.* (*sleep*) ipno-.
hypnosis *n.* ipnose.
hypnotherapist *n.* ipnoterapiste.
hypnotherapy *n.* ipnoterapia.
hypnotic *adj.* ipnosal. • *n.* (*sleeping pill*) adorminte.
hypnotism *n.* ipnose.
hypnotist *n.* ipnosiste.
hypnotize *v.* ipnose.
hypnotizer *n.* ipnosiste.

hypo- *pref.* ipo-.
hypochondria *n.* ipocondria.
hypochondriac *adj.* & *n.* ipocondrica.
hypochondriasis *n.* ipocondria.
hypocolius *n.* (*bird*) ipocolio.
hypocrisy *adj.* ipocritia.
hypocrite *n.* ipocrita.
hypocritical *adj.* ipocrita.
hypodermic *adj.* ipodermal.
hypodermis *n.* ipoderma.
hypoglycaemia (US **hypoglycemia**) *n.* ipoglisemia.
hypoglycaemic (US **hypoglycemic**) *adj.* ipoglisemica.
hypogonadism *n.* (*medical*) ipogonadia.
hypokalaemia (US **hypokalemia**) *n.* (*medical*) ipocalemia.
hypomania *n.* (*medical*) ipomania.
hypophysial *adj.* ipofisal.
hypophysis *n.* ipofise.
hypotension *n.* (*medical*) ipotensa.
hypotensive *adj.* & *n.* ipotensal.
hypotenuse *n.* ipotenusa.
hypothalamus *n.* ipotalamo.
hypothermia *n.* ipotermia.
hypothesis *n.* ipotese.
hypothesize *v.* ipotese.
hypothetical *adj.* ipotesal.
hypothyroidism *n.* (*medical*) ipotiroidia.
hypoxaemia (US **hypoxemia**) *n.* iposemia.
hypoxia *n.* (*medical*) iposia.
hyrax *n.* (*animal*) iraco.
hyster- *pref.* (*womb*) ister-.
hysterectomy *n.* (*surgery*) isterectomia.
hysteria *n.* isteria.
hysteric *adj.* isterica.
hysterical *adj.* isterica.

I

I *pron.* me. **I myself** (*emphatic*) me mesma.
-ia *suff.* (*disease*) -ia.
-iac *suff.* (*suffering from a medical condition*) -ica.
iamb *n.* iambo.
iambic *adj.* iambal.
iambus *n.* (*poetry*) iambo.
-ian *suff.* (*pertaining to a region or period*) -an.
-iase *suff.* (*disease*) -iase.
-iatric *suff.* -iatrica.
iatrogenic *adj.* (*caused by doctors*) iatrojen.
-iatry *suff.* -iatria.
I-beam *n.* faxon I.
Iberia *n.* Iberia.
Iberian *adj.* & *n.* iberian.
ibex *n.* (*goat*) ibex.
ibis *n.* (*bird*) ibis.
ibisbill *n.* (*bird*) becoibisin.
-ible *suff.* -able.
-ic[1] *suff.* (*suffering from a medical condition*) -ica.
-ic[2] *suff.* (*chemical valency*) -ica.
ice *n.* jelo. • *v.* (*add icing to*) glasa.
ice age *n.* eda glasial.
iceberg *n.* isberg.
icebound *adj.* maraniada en jelo.
icebox *n.* jelador.
icebreaker *n.* (*ship*) rompejelo.
icecap *n.* glasia.
ice-cold *adj.* jelin, jelin fria.
ice cream *n.* crema jelada.
icefall *n.* cascade jelada.
ice hockey *n.* hoci de jelo.
icehouse *n.* (*storing ice*) jeleria.
Iceland *n.* Island.
Icelander *adj.* & *n.* islansce.
Icelandic *adj.* & *n.* islansce.
icelike *adj.* jelin.
ice rink *n.* patineria.
ichor *n.* (*mythology*, *medical*) icor.
ichthyologist *n.* ictiolojiste.
ichthyology *n.* ictiolojia.
ichthyosaur *n.* ictiosauro.
ichthyosaurus *n.* ictiosauro.
icicle *n.* spina de jelo.
-icide *suff.* (*kill*) -iside.
icing *n.* glasa.
icky *adj.* repulsante.
icon *n.* icon.
iconic *adj.* iconin.
iconoclasm *n.* iconoclasia.
iconoclast *n.* iconoclasiste.
iconoclastic *adj.* iconoclasiste.
icosahedral *adj.* icosaedro.
icosahedron *n.* icosaedro.
ICT *n.* infotecnolojia.
icy *adj.* (*like ice*) jelin; (*covered in ice*) jelosa.
id[1] *n.* (*psychology*) id.
ID[2] *n.* identia.
Idaho *n.* (*US state*) Idaho.
ID card *n.* carta de identia.
-ide *suff.* (*salt*) -ido.
idea *n.* idea.
ideal *adj.* & *n.* ideal.
idealism *n.* idealisme.
idealist *n.* idealiste.
idealistic *adj.* idealiste.
ideality *n.* idealia.
idealization *n.* ideali.
idealize *v.* ideali.
ideate *v.* imajina.
ideation *n.* imajina.
identical *adj.* identica, la mesma.
identical twin *n.* jemelo identica.
identifiable *adj.* identifiable.
identification *n.* identifia.
identifier *n.* marca, identifiante.
identify *v.* identifia.
identity *n.* identia.
identity card *n.* carta de identia.
identity documents *n.* documentos de identia.
identity theft *n.* fura de identia.
ideogram *n.* ideogram.
ideograph *n.* ideogram.
ideological *adj.* ideolojial.
ideologist *n.* ideolojiste.
ideology *n.* ideolojia, filosofia.
idiocy *n.* stupidia.
idiographic *adj.* idiografial.
idiography *n.* idiografia.
idiom *n.* (*expression*) idiom.
idiomatic *adj.* idiomal.
idiopathic *adj.* idiopatica.
idiopathy *n.* idiopatia.
idiosyncrasy *n.* distinguinte, cualia unica.
idiosyncratic *adj.* unica.
idiot *n.* fol, stupida.
idiotic *adj.* fol, stupida.
idiotproof *adj.* secur contra bobos.
idle *adj.* pigra, osiosa; nonusosa. • *v.* pigri; pasa tempo; (*engine*) jira minima.
idleness *n.* pigria.
idler *n.* pigra.
idol *n.* idol.
idolater *n.* idolor.
idolatrous *adj.* idolinte.
idolatry *n.* idoli.
idolize *v.* idoli.
idol worshipper (US **worshiper**) *n.* idolor.
idyll *n.* idilio.

idyllic *adj.* idilin.
i.e. *abbr.* pd (*per dise*).
if *subord.* si, en caso ce; (*whether*) esce. **as if** como si. **if not** si no. **if nothing else** an tal, an con tota. **if only** si sola. **if so** si tal.
-ifer *suff.* (*producing, carrying*) -ifer.
iffy *adj.* nonserta.
iftar *n.* (*meal*) iftar.
-ify *suff.* -i.
igloo *n.* iglu.
igneous *adj.* magmal.
ignite *v.* ensende, inisia.
ignition *n.* ensende, inisia; (*for engine*) inisiador.
ignoble *adj.* vil.
ignominious *adj.* desonorada.
ignominy *n.* desonora.
ignoramus *n.* stupida.
ignorance *n.* nonsabe.
ignorant *adj.* noneducada, nonsabosa.
ignore *v.* iniora.
ignorer *n.* inioror.
iguana *n.* iguana.
iguanodon *n.* iguanodon.
ikebana *n.* (*flower arrangement*) icebana.
ileum *n.* (*anatomy*) ileo.
Iliad *n.* (*poem*) Iliada.
Ilion *n.* (*ancient Troy*) Ilio.
ilium[1] *n.* (*anatomy*) ilio.
Ilium[2] *n.* (*ancient Troy*) Ilio.
ill *adj.* malada. • *pref.* mal-. **fall ill** maladi. **make ill** maladi.
ill-advised *adj.* malconselada.
illegal *adj.* nonlegal.
illegal arrest *n.* aresta nonlegal.
illegal goods *n.* benes nonlegal.
illegality *n.* nonlegalia.
illegalize *v.* deslegali.
illegal occupant *n.* ocupor nonlegal.
illegibility *n.* nonlejablia.
illegible *n.* nonlejable.
illegitimacy *n.* nonlegalia; (*child*) bastardia.
illegitimate *adj.* nonlegal; (*child*) estra sposi.
illeism *n.* (*referring to oneself in the third person*) elisme.
ill-fated *adj.* maldestinada.
ill feeling *n.* odia.
illicit *adj.* nonlegal.
Illinois *n.* (*US state*) Illinois.
illiteracy *n.* nonalfabetisme.
illiterate *adj.* nonalfabetiste.
ill-made *adj.* malcreada.
ill-mannered *adj.* de mal maneras.
illness *n.* maladia.
illogical *adj.* nonlojical.
illogicality *n.* nonlojicalia.
ill-tempered *adj.* disputosa.
illuminate *v.* lumina.
illumination *n.* (*action, result*) lumina.
illusion *n.* ilude; (*optical*) malpersepi; (*hallucination*) alusina.
illusional *adj.* malpersepida.
illusionist *n.* iludiste.
illusive *adj.* iludente; enganosa.
illusory *adj.* iludente, nonreal.
illustrate *v.* desinia, imaji; (*show*) mostra; (*exemplify*) esempli.
illustration *n.* desinia, imaje; mostra.
illustrative *adj.* mostrante.
illustrator *n.* desinior, imajor.
illustrious *adj.* eselente.
ill will *n.* malvole.
ill-willed *adj.* malintendente.
Illyria *n.* Iliria.
Illyrian *adj.* ilirian.
im-[1] (not) *pref.* im-.
im-[2] (in, into) *pref.* im-.
image *n.* imaje. • *v.* imaji.
imagery *n.* imajes; simbolisme.
imaginable *adj.* imajinable.
imaginary *adj.* imajinal.
imaginary beast *n.* bestia imajinal.
imagination *n.* imajina.
imaginative *adj.* imajinosa.
imagine *v.* imajina.
imago *n.* (*biology, psychology*) imago.
imam *n.* (*Islam*) imam.
imbalance *v.* desecuilibra. • *n.* nonecuilibra.
imbecile *n.* fol, stupida.
imbed *v.* caxi.
imbibe *v.* bevi.
IMHO *abbr.* emo (*en mea opina*).
imitate *v.* imita, mima.
imitation *n.* imita, mima.
immaculate *adj.* nonmanxada, perfeta.
immanent *adj.* inerente.
immaterial *adj.* nonmaterial.
immature *adj.* nonmatur.
immaturity *n.* nonmaturia.
immeasurable *adj.* nonmesurable.
immediate *adj.* direta.
immediately *adv.* direta, pronto, la plu pronto, aora, sin retarda.
immense *adj.* enorme.
immensity *n.* enormia.
immerse *v.* sumerji.
immersion *n.* sumerji.
immigrant *n.* migror.
immigrate *v.* migra a.
immigration *n.* migra.
imminent *adj.* prosiminte.
immobile *adj.* nonmovable, nonmovente.
immobilization *n.* desmovabli.
immobilize *v.* desmovabli; freni, restrinje.
immoderate *adj.* nonmoderada.
immodest *adj.* nonmodesta.
immolate *v.* arde sacrifial.
immoral *adj.* nonmoral.

immorality *n.* nonmoralia.

immortal *adj.* nonmortal.

immortality *n.* nonmortalia.

immortalize *v.* nonmortali.

immovable *adj.* nonmovable.

immune *adj.* imune; (*of the immune system*) imunial. **become immune** imuni.

immune deficiency *n.* imunodebilia.

immune system *n.* sistem imunial.

immunity *n.* imunia; (*legal*) esenta.

immunization *n.* imuni.

immunize *v.* imuni.

immunodeficiency *n.* imunodebilia.

immunodeficient *adj.* imunodebil.

immunogen *n.* imunojen.

immunogenic *adj.* imunojen.

immunoglobulin *n.* imunoglobulina.

immunologist *n.* imunolojiste.

immunology *n.* imunolojia.

immunosuppressant *n.* imunosupresante.

immunosuppressive *adj.* imunosupresante.

immunotherapy *n.* imunoterapia.

immutability *n.* nonmutablia.

immutable *adj.* nonmutable.

IMO *abbr.* emo (*en mea opina*).

imp *n.* turbosa.

impact *n.* (*strike*) colpa; (*effect*) efeto. • *v.* colpa.

impair *v.* descapasi.

impairment *n.* descapasia.

impala *n.* (*antelope*) impala.

impale *v.* lansi.

impalpable *adj.* nonpalpable.

impanel *v.* enscrive.

impart *v.* dona, ajunta.

impartial *adj.* nonpartisan.

impasse *n.* rua sin sorti; nonprogresa.

impassion *v.* pasioni.

impassioned *adj.* pasionosa.

impassive *adj.* nonajitable.

impasto *n.* (*painting technique*) impasto.

impatience *n.* nonpasientia.

impatient *adj.* nonpasiente.

impeach *v.* acusa, acusa de malcondui.

impeachment *n.* acusa.

impeccable *adj.* coreta, sin fali.

impede *v.* impedi.

impediment *n.* impedi.

impel *v.* impulsa.

impending *adj.* prosiminte.

impenetrable *adj.* nonpenetrable.

impenitent *adj.* sin regrete, sin vergonia.

imperative *adj.* & *n.* comandante.

imperceptible *adj.* nonpersepable.

imperfect *adj.* nonperfeta.

imperfection *n.* nonperfeta.

imperfective aspect *n.* aspeta nonperfeta.

imperforate *adj.* nonperforada.

imperial *adj.* imperal; (*measurements*) nonmetral.

imperialism *n.* imperalisme.

imperialist *adj.* imperaliste

imperil *v.* perili.

imperishable *adj.* nonputrable; nonmortal.

impermanence *n.* nonpermanentia.

impermanent *adj.* nonpermanente.

impermeable *adj.* nonpermeable.

impersonal *adj.* nonpersonal.

impersonate *v.* imita, finje.

impersonation *n.* imita, finje.

impersonator *n.* imitor, finjor.

impertinence *n.* noncortesia.

impertinent *adj.* noncortes.

imperturbable *adj.* nonajitable.

impervious *adj.* nonpermeable.

impetigo *n.* (*medical*) impetigo.

impetuous *adj.* fretante.

impetus *n.* impulsa.

impinge *v.* intrui. **impinge on** afeta.

impish *adj.* turbosa.

implacable *adj.* nonpasable.

implant *v.* implanta. • *n.* implantada.

implantation *n.* implanta.

implausible *adj.* nonconvinsente.

implement *v.* reali; (*law*) enforsa. • *n.* util.

implementation *n.* reali; enforsa.

implicate *v.* implica.

implication *n.* implica.

implicit *adj.* implicada.

implode *v.* implode.

implore *v.* prea, suplica.

implosion *n.* implode.

implosive *adj.* implodente.

imply *v.* implica.

impolite *adj.* noncortes.

impoliteness *n.* noncortesia.

import *v.* emporta. **have import** importa.

importance *n.* importa.

important *adj.* importante. **be important** importa. **be important to** importa a, conserna. **it's not important** lo no importa. **most important** xef.

important person *n.* person importante.

importation *n.* emporta.

importer *n.* emportor.

imports tax *n.* imposta de emporta, imposta de duana.

importune *v.* suplica.

impose *v.* forsa, pone; (*disturb*) disturba, intrui.

imposition *n.* disturba.

impossibility *adj.* (*quality*) nonposiblia; (*something impossible*) nonposible.

impossible *adj.* nonposible.

imposter *n.* finjor.

impostor *n.* finjor.

impotence *n.* nonpotentia.

impotent *adj.* nonpotente.
impound *v.* confisca.
impoverish *v.* povri.
impoverished *adj.* povre.
impracticable *adj.* nonpratical.
impractical *adj.* nonpratical.
imprecise *adj.* nonesata.
impregnable *adj.* nonpenetrable.
impregnate *v.* ensinti.
impresario *n.* organizor.
impress *v.* impresa.
impression *n.* impresa. **give the impression of** pare.
impressionability *n.* impresablia.
impressionable *adj.* impresable.
Impressionism *n.* (*art*) impresisme.
impressionist *n.* imitor; (*art*) impresiste.
impressive *adj.* impresante.
imprimatur *n.* lisensa de primi; garantia de cualia.
imprint *v.* & *n.* impresa.
imprison *v.* prisoni.
imprisonment *n.* prisoni.
improbability *n.* (*quality*) nonprobablia; (*something improbable*) nonprobable.
improbable *adj.* nonprobable.
impromptu *adj.* improvisada, nonpreparada.
improper *adj.* vulgar.
impropriety *n.* malcondui.
improve *v.* boni; (*situation*) aida.
improvement *n.* boni.
improvisation *n.* improvisa, crea corente.
improvise *v.* improvisa.
imprudent *adj.* nonatendente.
impudence *n.* noncortesia.
impudent *adj.* noncortes.
impugn *v.* disputa.
impulse *n.* impulsa.
impulsion *n.* impulsa.
impulsive *adj.* fretosa, noncauta.
impulsiveness *n.* fretosia, noncautia.
impunity *n.* esenta.
impure *adj.* nonpur.
impurity *n.* nonpuria.
in *prep.* (*space, time*) en; (*point*) a; (*after*) pos; (*language, medium, manner, condition*) en. **in back of** a retro de. **in between** a entre, entre la du. **in exchange for** per, par intercambia per. **in front** a ante. **in front of** ante, a fronte de; (*motion towards*) a ante, a fronte de. **in order that** afin, con intende ce. **in order to** per. **in relation to** en relata con. **in return for** par intercambia per. **in sight of** en vista de. **in spite of** an con; (*something that has already happened*) an pos. **in spite of the fact that** an si, contra ce. **in terms of** en relata con. **in two months' time** pos du menses, pos la du menses veninte.
in-[1] *pref.* (*not*) in-.
in-[2] *pref.* (*in, into*) in-.
inability *n.* noncapasia.
inaccessible *adj.* nonasedable.
inaccuracy *n.* nonesatia.
inaccurate *adj.* nonesata.
inaction *n.* nonativia.
inactive *adj.* nonativa, inerte.
inactivity *n.* nonativia.
inadequacy *n.* nonsufisi.
inadequate *adj.* nonsufisinte.
inadmissible *adj.* nonasetable.
inadvertent *adj.* nonintendeda.
inadvisable *adj.* malconselada.
inalienable *adj.* nonalienable.
inalterable *adj.* nonalterable.
inane *adj.* fol, stupida.
inanimate *adj.* nonanimada.
inapplicable *adj.* nonpertinente.
inappropriate *adj.* nonconveninte, noncoreta.
inappropriately dressed *adj.* nonconveninte vestida.
inarticulate *adj.* malparlante.
inasmuch as *subord.* cuanto.
inattentive *adj.* nonatendente.
inaudible *adj.* nonoiable.
inaugural *adj.* induinte.
inaugurate *v.* indui.
inauguration *n.* indui.
inauspicious *adj.* nonfortunosa.
inboard motor *n.* motor interna.
inborn *adj.* natural, jenetical.
inbound *adj.* veninte.
inbred *adj.* endogama.
inbreed *v.* eleva endogama.
inbreeding *n.* endogamia.
inbuilt *adj.* integrada.
Inca *n.* inca.
incalculable *adj.* noncalculable.
Incan *adj.* inca.
incandesce *v.* incandese.
incandescence *n.* incandese.
incandescent *adj.* incandesente.
incantation *n.* encanta.
incapable *adj.* noncapas, nonpotente.
incapacitate *v.* descapasi.
incarcerate *v.* prisoni.
incarceration *n.* prisoni.
incarnate *v.* incarne.
incarnation *n.* incarne.
incendiary *adj.* ensendente.
incendiary bomb *n.* bomba ensendente.
incense *n.* insenso.
incentive *n.* motiva.
inception *n.* comensa.

incessant *adj.* nonsesante, sin sesa, sin pausa.
incest *n.* insesto.
incestuous *adj.* insestal.
inch *n.* (*unit of length*) diton.
inchoate *adj.* inisial, primitiva.
inchworm *n.* eruga de jeometrido.
incident *n.* aveni.
incidental *adj.* acaso; acompaniante.
incidentally *adv.* en pasa, acaso.
incinerate *v.* arde.
incinerator *n.* ardador.
incipient *adj.* comensante.
incise *v.* talia.
incision *n.* talia.
incisive *adj.* astuta, persepinte.
incisor *n.* dente sisorante.
incite *v.* provoca, tisa.
inclement *adj.* fria; pluvosa.
inclination *n.* tende.
incline *v.* inclina; (*someone to*) disposa. • *n.* inclinada.
inclined *adj.* inclinada; disposada. **be inclined to** es disposada a, tende.
include *v.* inclui.
inclusion *n.* inclui.
inclusive *adj.* incluinte. **inclusive of** incluinte.
incognito *adj.* anonim; desemblante.
incognizant *adj.* nonconsensa.
incoherence *n.* noncoere.
incoherent *adj.* noncoerente.
income *n.* revenu.
income tax *n.* imposta de revenu.
incommensurate *adj.* nonproportial.
incommunicado *n.* sin comunica.
incomparable *adj.* sin compara.
incompatibility *n.* nonacorda, nonarmonia, nonconveni.
incompatible *adj.* nonacordante, nonarmoniosa, nonconveninte.
incompetence *n.* noncapasia.
incompetent *adj.* noncapas.
incomplete *adj.* noncompleta.
incompleteness *n.* noncompletia.
incomprehensibility *n.* noncomprendablia.
incomprehensible *adj.* noncomprendable.
incomprehension *n.* noncomprende.
inconceivable *adj.* nonconsetable, nonimajinable.
inconclusive *adj.* nonconcluinte.
incongruent *adj.* nonacordante.
incongruity *n.* nonacorda.
incongruous *adj.* nonacordante, nonarmoniosa, nonconveninte.
inconsequential *adj.* nonimportante.
inconsiderate *adj.* noncompatiosa.
inconsistency *n.* noncoere.
inconsistent *adj.* noncoerente.
inconsolable *adj.* nonconsolable.
inconspicuous *adj.* nontraente atende, sin atrae atende.
inconstant *adj.* nonconstante.
incontinence *n.* noncontenintia.
incontinent *adj.* noncontenínte.
incontrovertible *adj.* nondisputable.
inconvenience *n.* nonoportunia.
inconvenient *adj.* nonoportun, nonpratical; (*place*) mal situada.
incorporate *v.* asorbe; (*company*) corpora.
incorporation *n.* asorbe; corpora.
incorporeal *adj.* sin corpo.
incorrect *adj.* noncoreta, falsa.
incorrectness *n.* noncoretia.
incorrigible *adj.* noncoretable.
increase *v.* & *n.* crese, grandi; (*increment*) aumenta. **increase by** aumenta con.
increasingly *adv.* sempre plu, cresente.
incredibility *n.* noncredablia.
incredible *adj.* noncredable.
incredulity *n.* noncrede.
incredulous *adj.* noncredente.
increment *v.* & *n.* aumenta.
incremental *adj.* aumental.
incriminate *v.* implica.
incrimination *n.* implica.
incubate *v.* incuba.
incubation *n.* incuba.
incubation period *n.* periodo de incuba.
incubator *n.* incubador.
incubus *n.* incubo.
inculcate *v.* impresa, radisi.
incumbent *adj.* (*necessary*) nesesada; (*in office*) presente.
incur *v.* (*punishment*) incore.
incursion *n.* avansa, invade.
incus *n.* (*anatomy*) inco.
indebted *adj.* debente.
indecent *adj.* vulgar.
indecipherable *adj.* nondesifrable.
indecision *n.* vasila.
indecisive *adj.* vasilante.
indeed *adv.* vera. • *interj.* vera, si.
indefatigable *adj.* nonfatigable.
indefensible *adj.* nondefendable.
indefinite *adj.* nondefinida.
indefinite article *n.* article de nondefini.
indelible *adj.* permanente, nonsutrable, noncanselable.
indelicate *adj.* nontatosa.
indemnity *n.* (*insurance*) asecura; (*compensation*) compensa.
indent *v.* & *n.* indente.
indentation *n.* indente.
independence *n.* autonomia. **gain independence** autonomi.

independent *adj.* (*self-governing*) autonom; (*not connected*) nondependente, separada.
independent clause *n.* proposa autonom.
in-depth *adj.* profonda.
indescribable *adj.* nondescrivable.
indestructible *adj.* nondestruable.
indeterminate *adj.* nondeterminada.
index *n.* (*list*) catalogo; (*serial number*) indise. • *v.* catalogi; indise.
index card *n.* fix.
index finger *n.* dito indicante.
India *n.* Barat, India.
Indian *adj.* & *n.* (*person, language*) barati, indian. **American Indian** american orijinal.
Indiana *n.* (*US state*) Indiana.
Indian Ocean *n.* Mar Indian.
Indic *adj.* indoarian.
indicate *v.* indica.
indication *n.* indica; (*slight*) indiceta.
indicative *n.* (*grammar*) indicante.
indicator *n.* indicador.
indict *v.* acusa.
indictment *n.* condena.
indifference *n.* noncurantia.
indifferent *adj.* (*uninterested*) noncurante, nonimpresada; (*middling*) mediocre.
indigenous *adj.* nativa.
indigent *adj.* povre.
indigestible *adj.* nondijestable.
indigestion *n.* maldijesta.
indignant *adj.* iritada, coler, ofendeda.
indignation *n.* irita, coleria.
indignity *n.* nondinia.
indigo *adj.* indigo.
indigobird *n.* vidua.
indirect *adj.* nondireta.
indiscreet *adj.* nondiscreta.
indiscrete *adj.* nonseparada.
indiscretion *n.* peceta.
indiscriminate *adj.* nondistinguinte, sin distingui.
indispensable *adj.* nesesada.
indisposed *adj.* (*unwell*) malada; (*unwilling*) nonvolente.
indisputable *adj.* nondisputable.
indium *n.* (*element*) indio.
individual *adj.* (*particular*) individua; (*of an individual*) individual. • *n.* individua.
individualism *n.* individualisme.
individualist *adj.* & *n.* individualiste.
individuality *n.* individualia.
indivisible *adj.* nondividable.
Indo-Aryan *adj.* indoarian.
Indochina *n.* Indoxina.
indoctrinate *v.* empapa.
indoctrination *n.* empapa.
Indo-European *adj.* & *n.* indoeuropean.
Indo-Iranian *adj.* & *n.* indoiranian.
indolent *adj.* pigra.
indomitable *adj.* nonconcistable.
Indonesia *n.* Indonesia.
Indonesian *adj.* & *n.* indonesian.
indoor *adj.* en casa.
indoors *adv.* en casa.
indri *n.* (*lemur*) indri.
indubitable *adj.* nondutable.
induce *v.* indui.
inducement *n.* soborna.
induct *v.* indui.
inductance *n.* indui.
induction *n.* indui.
inductive *adj.* induinte.
inductive reasoning *n.* razona induinte.
indulge *v.* favore; regala.
indulgence *n.* favore.
indulgent *adj.* favorente.
Indus *n.* (*constellation*) la Indian.
Indus River *n.* Rio Indo.
industrial *adj.* industrial.
industrialist *n.* industrialiste.
industrialization *n.* industri.
industrialize *v.* industri.
industrious *adj.* asidua.
industry *n.* industria.
Indus Valley Civilization *n.* Sivilia de la Vale Indo.
inebriate *v.* enebria.
inebriation *n.* enebria.
inedible *adj.* noncomable.
ineducable *adj.* noninstruable.
ineffable *adj.* nonespresable.
ineffective *adj.* nonproduosa.
ineffectiveness *n.* nonproduosia.
ineffectual *adj.* nonproduosa.
ineffectuality *n.* nonproduosia.
inefficacious *adj.* nonproduosa.
inefficacy *n.* nonproduosia.
inefficiency *n.* perosia.
inefficient *adj.* perosa.
inelastic *adj.* nonelastica.
inelasticity *n.* nonelasticia.
ineligible *adj.* nonelejable, noncualinte.
inept *adj.* noncapas; (*physically*) torpe.
inequality *n.* nonegalia.
inequity *n.* nonjustia.
inerrant *adj.* nonerante.
inert *adj.* inerte.
inertia *n.* inertia.
inertial *adj.* inertial.
inescapable *adj.* nonevadable.
inestimable *adj.* nonestimable, la plu valuada.
inevitable *adj.* nonevitable.
inexact *adj.* nonesata.
inexcusable *adj.* nonescusable, nonpardonable.
inexhaustible *adj.* nonconsumable.
inexorable *adj.* nonevitable.

inexpensive *adj.* barata.
inexperience *n.* nonesperia.
inexperienced *adj.* sin esperia.
inexpert *adj.* nonesperta.
inexplicable *adj.* nonesplicable.
inextricable *adj.* nonestrable.
infallible *adj.* nonerante, nunca falinte.
infamous *adj.* malfamosa.
infamy *n.* mal fama.
infancy *n.* bebia.
infant *adj.* & *n.* bebe.
infanticide *n.* (*action*) enfantiside; (*person*) enfantisidor. **commit infanticide** enfantiside.
infantile *adj.* enfantin.
infantry *n.* soldatos de pede.
infantryman *n.* soldato de pede.
infantry soldier *n.* soldato de pede.
infarct *v.* (*die through lack of blood*) infarta.
infarction *n.* infarta.
infatuate *v.* enama, osese.
infatuated *adj.* enamada, oseseda.
infatuation *n.* enama, osese.
infeasible *adj.* nonrealable, nonpratical.
infect *v.* infeta.
infection *n.* infeta.
infectious *adj.* infetante, comunicable.
infer *v.* dedui.
inferable *adj.* deduable.
inference *n.* dedui.
inferential *adj.* deduinte.
inferior *adj.* & *n.* inferior.
inferiority *n.* inferioria.
infernal *adj.* enfernal.
inferno *n.* enferno, tempesta de foco.
infertile *adj.* nonfertil, steril.
infertility *n.* nonfertilia.
infest *v.* infesta.
infestation *n.* infesta.
infidel *n.* erese, pagan, noncredor.
infiltrate *v.* infiltra.
infiltration *n.* infiltra.
infinite *adj.* infinita, nonlimitada, sin limita.
infinitesimal *adj.* infinita peti.
infinitive *adj.* & *n.* (*grammar*) infinitiva.
infinity *n.* infinitia.
infirm *adj.* debil.
infirmary *n.* maladeria.
infirmary nurse *n.* maladerior.
infirmity *n.* debilia.
infix *v.* & *n.* infisa.
inflame *v.* inflama; (*provoke*) flami.
inflammable *adj.* flamable.
inflammation *n.* inflama.
inflammatory *adj.* inflamante; (*provocative*) flaminte.
inflatable *adj.* & *n.* inflable.
inflate *v.* infla.
inflation *n.* (*including economic*) infla.
inflect *v.* infleta.
inflection *n.* (*including grammar*) infleta.
inflexible *adj.* nonajustable.
inflict *v.* aplica, forsa.
inflow *n.* enflue.
influence *v.* & *n.* influe, afeta. **have influence over** influe.
influential *adj.* influente.
influenza *n.* gripe.
influx *n.* enflue.
info *n.* informa.
inform *v.* informa. **inform on** informa contra.
informal *adj.* nonformal, casual; (*language*) demotica.
informality *n.* nonformalia.
informant *n.* informor.
information *n.* informa.
information bureau *n.* ofisia de informa.
information office *n.* ofisia de informa.
information overload *n.* inonda de informa.
information science *n.* informatica.
information technology *n.* infotecnolojia.
information theory *n.* teoria de informa.
informative *adj.* informosa.
informer *n.* informor.
infra- *pref.* (*below*) infra-.
infraction *n.* viole, peca. **minor infraction** peceta.
infraorder *n.* infraordina.
infrared *adj.* & *n.* infraroja.
infrastructure *n.* infrastrutur.
infrequent *adj.* nonfrecuente, noncomun, rara; nonperiodal.
infringe *v.* viole.
infringement *n.* viole.
infundibulum *n.* (*anatomy*) embuto.
infuriate *v.* furia.
infuse *v.* infusa.
infusion *n.* infusa.
-ing *suff.* -nte.
ingenious *adj.* injeniosa.
ingenue *n.* xica naive.
ingenuity *n.* injenia.
ingenuous *adj.* naive.
ingenuousness *n.* naivia.
ingest *v.* asorbe, come, consuma.
ingle *n.* ximineria.
ingot *n.* brice.
ingrain *v.* infisa.
ingrate *n.* nongrasiosa.
ingratiate *v.* adula.
ingredient *n.* ingrediente.
ingress *n.* entra.
ingroup *n.* grupo propre.
ingrown *adj.* (*nail*) permeada.
inguinal *adj.* inguinal.
inguinal hernia *n.* ernia inguinal.

Ingush *adj.* & *n.* (*person, language*) ingux.
Ingushetia *n.* Inguxetia.
inhabit *v.* abita.
inhabitability *n.* abitablia.
inhabitable *adj.* abitable.
inhabitant *n.* abitor.
inhalable *adj.* enspirable.
inhalant *n.* medisin enspirable.
inhalation *n.* enspira.
inhale *v.* enspira.
inhaler *n.* enspirador.
inharmonious *adj.* nonarmoniosa.
inhere *v.* inere.
inherent *adj.* inerente, esensal.
inherit *v.* erita.
inheritable *adj.* eritable.
inheritance *n.* erita.
inheritance tax *n.* imposta de erita.
inhibit *v.* constrinje, retarda.
inhibition *n.* retarda.
inhospitable *adj.* nonbonveninte.
inhuman *adj.* nonumana.
inhumane *adj.* noncompatiosa, sin compatia.
inimical *adj.* enemin, impedinte.
inimitable *adj.* nonimitable, unica.
iniquity *n.* nonmoralia.
initial *adj.* inisial, comensal. • *n.* (*letter*) inisial.
initialize *v.* inisia.
initiate *v.* inisia.
initiation *n.* inisia.
initiative *n.* stratejia nova. **showing initiative** automotivada. **take the initiative** inisia.
initiator *n.* inisior.
inject *v.* injeta.
injection *n.* injeta.
injunction *n.* esije judal.
injure *v.* feri.
injurious *adj.* danante, ferinte.
injury *n.* feri.
injustice *n.* nonjustia.
ink *n.* inca. • *v.* inci.
inkblot *n.* manxa de inca.
inkpot *n.* portainca.
inkstand *n.* portainca.
inkwell *n.* fonte de inca.
inland *adj.* interna.
inland tax *n.* imposta interna.
in-law *adj.* par sposi.
inlay *v.* & *n.* (*decoration*) intarsia; (*superimpose*) suprapone.
inlet *n.* baieta.
inmate *n.* prisonida.
inn *n.* otel.
innate *adj.* inata.
innatism *n.* inatisme.
innatist *n.* inatiste.
inner *adj.* interna.
inner ear *n.* orea interna.
Inner Hebrides *n.* Hebrides Interna.
innermost *adj.* la plu interna.
innersole *n.* planta interna.
inner tube *n.* tubo de aira.
innervate *v.* inerva.
innervation *n.* inerva.
innkeeper *n.* otelor.
innocence *n.* (*lack of guilt*) nonculpablia; (*lack of knowledge*) naivia; (*purity*) virtua.
innocent *adj.* (*of crime*) nonculpable; (*naïve*) naive, enfantin, premoral; (*pure*) virtuosa; (*sexually*) virjin; (*not intending harm*) inosente; (*joke*) nonofendente.
innocuous *adj.* nonosiva.
innovate *v.* inova.
innovation *n.* inova.
innovative *adj.* inovosa.
innovator *n.* inovor.
innuendo *n.* insinua.
innumerable *adj.* noncontable, nonumerable, nonlimitada, sin limita, ultra conta.
inoculate *v.* vasini.
inoculation *n.* vasini.
inoffensive *adj.* nonofendente.
inoperable *adj.* nonoperable.
inopportune *adj.* nonoportun; (*place*) mal situada.
inordinate *adj.* suprapasante, tro multe.
inorganic *adj.* nonorganica.
inox steel *n.* aser nonosidinte.
inpatient *n.* pasiente ospitalida.
input *v.* enflue, entra. • *n.* enflue.
inquest *n.* investiga judal.
inquire *v.* demanda.
inquiry *n.* (*question*) demanda; (*investigation*) investiga.
inquisition *n.* incuisisio.
inquisitive *adj.* curiosa.
inroad *n.* avansa, progresa.
insane *adj.* demente. **go insane** dementi.
insane asylum *n.* dementeria.
insanity *n.* dementia.
insatiable *adj.* nonsasiable.
inscribe *v.* enscrive.
inscription *n.* enscrive.
inscrutable *adj.* noncomprendable.
inseam *n.* costur interna.
insect *n.* inseto.
insecticide *n.* insetiside.
insectivore *n.* insetivor.
insectivorous *adj.* insetivor.
insect repellent *n.* repulsante de insetos.
insecure *adj.* (*not safe*) nonsecur; (*unconfident*) nonserta.
insecurity *n.* nonsecuria.
inseminate *v.* semini.
insemination *n.* semini.
insensate *adj.* nonsensante.

insensible *adj.* (*unaware*) nonconsensa; (*imperceptible*) nonsensable.
insensitive *adj.* nonsensosa; (*cruel*) calosa.
insensitivity *n.* nonsensosia; (*cruelty*) calosia.
inseparable *adj.* nonseparable.
insert *v.* introdui; inserta. • *n.* inserta.
insertion *n.* introdui.
inset *v.* & *n.* inserta.
inside *n.* interna. • *prep.* en, a interna de; (*into*) a en. • *adv.* a en, a interna.
inside-out *adj.* eversada. **turn inside-out** eversa.
insider *n.* intima.
insidious *adj.* sutil nosiva.
insight *n.* intui; comprende.
insightful *adj.* intuosa.
insignia *n.* insinia.
insignificant *adj.* nonimportante.
insincere *adj.* nonsinsera.
insincerity *n.* nonsinseria.
insinuate *v.* insinua.
insinuation *n.* insinua.
insipid *adj.* blanda.
insist *v.* insiste.
insistence *n.* insiste.
insistent *adj.* insistente.
insole *n.* planta interna.
insolence *n.* desrespeta; egosia.
insolent *adj.* egosa.
insoluble *adj.* (*substance*) nondisolvable; (*problem*) nonsolvable.
insolvent *adj.* bancarota.
insomnia *n.* insonia.
insomniac *adj.* & *n.* insonica.
inspect *v.* esamina.
inspection *n.* esamina.
inspector *n.* esaminor; (*police*) investigor.
inspiration *n.* inspira.
inspirational *adj.* inspirante.
inspire *v.* inspira.
instability *n.* nonstablia.
install *v.* instala.
installation *n.* instala.
instalment (US **installment**) *n.* episodio, parte; (*payment*) paia partal. **pay by instalments** paia en partes.
instance *n.* caso, ves. **for instance** per esemplo.
instant *n.* momento. • *adj.* pronto, direta.
instantaneous *adj.* direta.
instant camera *n.* camera pronto.
instant coffee *n.* cafe pronto.
instantly *adv.* pronto, direta, la plu pronto.
instant message *n.* mesaje pronto.
instant messaging *n.* mesaji pronto.
instant-on *n.* inisia pronto.
instead *adv.* en loca. **instead of** en loca de.
instep *n.* arco de pede.
instigate *v.* provoca.
instigation *n.* provoca.
instigator *n.* provocor.
instil (US **instill**) *v.* impresa, radisi, fundi.
instinct *n.* instinto.
instinctive *adj.* instintosa.
instinctual *adj.* instintosa.
institute *v.* institui, introdui. • *n.* instituida, organiza.
institution *n.* (*action*) institui; (*organization*) instituida.
institutional *adj.* institual.
institutionalization *n.* normali.
institutionalize *v.* normali.
instruct *v.* instrui.
instruction *n.* instrui.
instructional *adj.* instrual; (*teaching*) instruinte.
instruction book *n.* manual de instrui.
instructive *adj.* instruinte.
instructor *n.* instruor.
instrument *n.* (*musical*, *medical*, *scientific*, *etc.*) strumento.
instrumental *adj.* strumental.
instrumentalist *n.* strumentiste.
instrument bank *n.* consol.
instrument panel *n.* panel de strumentos.
insubordinate *adj.* desobedinte.
insubstantial *adj.* nonmaterial; nonforte.
insufferable *adj.* nontolerable.
insufficiency *n.* nonsufisi, manca.
insufficient *adj.* nonsufisinte, tro poca.
insufflation *n.* ensofla.
insular *adj.* isolal.
insularity *n.* isoli.
insulate *v.* isoli.
insulation *n.* isoli.
insulator *n.* (*device*) isolador.
insulin *n.* insulin.
insult *v.* & *n.* insulta.
insuperable *adj.* nonvinsable.
insurance *n.* asecura.
insurance policy *n.* contrata de asecura.
insurance premium *n.* paia de asecura.
insure *v.* asecura.
insurgence *n.* revolui.
insurgency *n.* rebela.
insurgent *n.* revoluiste.
insurmountable *adj.* nonvinsable.
insurrection *n.* rebela.
insusceptible *adj.* nonafetable.
intact *adj.* intata.
intaglio *n.* (*art technique*) intalio.
intake *n.* enflue.
intangible *adj.* nontocable, nonpalpable, nonmaterial.
intarsia *n.* intarsia.
integer *adj.* & *n.* intero.
integral *adj.* intero; integral. • *n.* (*mathematics*) integral.

integral calculus *n.* calculo integral.
integrate *v.* integra.
integrated circuit *n.* sircuito integrada.
integration *n.* integra.
integrity *n.* solidia; unia.
integument *n.* casca, pel.
intel *n.* (*information*) informa.
intellect *n.* (*faculty*) inteleto; (*smartness*) intelijentia.
intellectual *adj.* (*of the intellect*) inteletal; (*smart*) intelijente. • *n.* (*person*) inteletosa.
intellectualism *n.* inteletalisme.
intellectual property *n.* propria inteletal.
intelligence *n.* intelijentia; (*information*) informa. **artificial intelligence** inteleto artifis.
intelligence quotient *n.* grado de intelijentia.
intelligence test *n.* esamina de intelijentia.
intelligent *adj.* intelijente.
intelligentsia *n.* inteletosas.
intelligible *adj.* comprendable.
intemperate *adj.* nontemperada, nonmoderada.
intend *v.* intende, vole.
intense *adj.* intensa.
intensification *n.* intensi.
intensify *v.* intensi.
intensity *n.* intensia.
intensive *adj.* intensa.
intent *n.* intende.
intention *n.* intende, vole. **with the intention of** con intende de.
intentional *adj.* intendeda, voleda; intendente, volente.
inter[1] *v.* (*bury*) entera.
inter-[2] *pref.* (*between*) inter-, entre-.
interact *v.* interata.
interaction *n.* interata.
interactive *adj.* interatante.
interagency *adj.* interajenterial.
interatomic *adj.* interatomal.
interbreeding *n.* misca de razas.
intercede *v.* interveni.
intercept *v.* intersepi.
interception *n.* intersepi.
intercession *n.* interveni.
interchange *v.* & *n.* intercambia.
interchangeable *adj.* intercambiable.
intercom *n.* comunicador; (*doorphone*) comunicador de porte, telefon de porte.
intercommunicate *v.* intercomunica.
interconnect *v.* interlia.
intercontinental *adj.* intercontinental.
intercontinental missile *n.* misil intercontinental.
intercultural *adj.* intercultural.
interdental *adj.* & *n.* (*consonant*) interdental.
interdepartmental *adj.* interdepartal.
interdepend *v.* interdepende.
interdependent *adj.* interdependente.
interdict *v.* proibi.
interdiction *n.* proibi.
interdisciplinary *adj.* intercampal.
interest *v.* interesa. • *n.* (*including money*) interesa. **be of interest to** interesa, conserna.
interesting *adj.* interesante.
interest rate *n.* taso de interesa.
interface *n.* interfas.
interfaith *adj.* intercredal.
interfere *v.* interfere; disturba.
interference *n.* interfere.
interferon *n.* (*protein*) interferon.
intergalactic *adj.* intergalasial.
intergovernmental *adj.* intergovernal.
interim *adj.* tempora. **in the interim** entretempo.
interior *adj.* & *n.* interna. **in the interior of** a interna de.
interiorize *v.* interni.
interject *v.* interjeta.
interjection *n.* interjeta; (*part of speech*) esclama.
interlace *v.* entretexe; trensa.
interlacing *adj.* entretexeda, entretexable.
interleave *v.* entretexe.
Interlingua *n.* interlingua.
interlinguistics *n.* interlinguistica.
interlink *v.* interlia.
interlock *v.* entretexe.
interlocking *adj.* entretexeda, entretexable.
interlocutor *n.* conversor.
interlope *v.* interfere.
interloper *n.* interferor.
interlude *n.* interval.
intermarriage *n.* intersposi.
intermarry *v.* intersposi.
intermediary *n.* ajente; ajente de intercambia.
intermediate *adj.* media.
interment *n.* restrinje.
interminable *adj.* nonfininte.
intermingle *v.* intermisca.
intermission *n.* interval, pausa.
intermittent *adj.* nonperiodal.
intern *v.* stajia. • *n.* stajior; (*medical graduate*) mediciste comensante.
internal *adj.* interna.
internal combustion engine *n.* motor de combusta interna.
internalize *v.* interni.
international *adj.* internasional.
internationalism *n.* internasionalisme.
internationalist *adj.* internasionaliste.
international language *n.* interlingua.
internecine war *n.* gera interna.
internee *n.* prisonida, restrinjeda.
internet *n.* interede, rede mundal.
internet course *n.* curso enlinia.

internet-savvy *adj.* astuta de rede.
internet user *n.* usor de rede.
internist *n.* (*medical*) interniste.
internment *n.* prisoni.
internship *n.* stajia.
interoffice *adj.* interdepartal.
interpersonal *adj.* interpersonal.
interphase *n.* interfase.
interplanetary *adj.* interplanetal.
interpol *n.* interpol.
interpolate *v.* interpola.
interpolation *n.* interpola.
interpose *v.* interpone.
interpret *v.* interprete.
interpretable *adj.* interpretable.
interpretation *n.* interprete; comprende, persepi.
interpretational *adj.* interpretal.
interpreter *n.* (*person*) interpretor; (*software*) interpretador.
interpretive *adj.* interpreteda.
interrelate *v.* interelata.
interrelation *n.* interelata.
interrelationship *n.* interelata.
interrogate *v.* interoga.
interrogation *n.* interoga.
interrogative adverb *n.* averbo de demanda.
interrogative determiner *n.* determinante de demanda.
interrogative pronoun *n.* pronom de demanda.
interrupt *v.* interompe; (*intrude on*) disturba.
interruption *n.* interompe.
intersect *v.* crusa.
intersection *n.* crusa.
intersex *adj.* intersesal.
intersex person *n.* intersesal.
intersexual *adj.* intersesal.
intersexuality *n.* intersesalia.
intersperse *v.* misca.
interstate *adj.* interstatal.
interstellar *adj.* interstelal.
interstice *n.* interstisio.
interstitial *adj.* interstisial.
intertextual *adj.* intertestal.
intertextuality *n.* intertestalia.
intertwine *v.* entretexe.
interval *n.* (*including musical*) interval.
intervene *v.* interveni.
intervention *n.* interveni.
interview *v.* & *n.* intervisa.
interviewer *n.* intervisor.
interweave *v.* entretexe.
interwoven *adj.* entretexeda.
intestate *adj.* sin atesta.
intestinal *adj.* intestinal.
intestine *n.* intestin. **large intestine** intestin spesa. **small intestine** intestin magra.
intimacy *n.* intimia.
intimate[1] *adj.* (*close*) intima.
intimate[2] *v.* (*state*) declara, insinua.
intimation *n.* declara, insinua.
intimidate *v.* menasa.
intimidation *n.* menasa.
into *prep.* en, a en.
intolerable *adj.* nontolerable.
intolerance *n.* nontolera.
intolerant *adj.* nontolerante.
intonation *n.* tono.
intoxicant *n.* enebriante.
intoxicate *v.* enebria.
intoxication *n.* enebria.
intra- *pref.* (*inner*) intra-.
intractable *adj.* nontratable, noncontrolable.
intramural *adj.* intramural.
intranet *n.* intrarede.
intransigent *adj.* nonacordante, nonconvinsable.
intransitive *adj.* nontransitiva.
intrauterine *adj.* intrauteral.
intrauterine contraceptive device *n.* contraconsepal intrauteral.
intravenous *adj.* intravenal.
intrench *v.* fundi, radisi.
intrepid *adj.* nontemosa.
intricacy *n.* complica.
intricate *adj.* complicada.
intrigue *v.* curiosi, fasina. • *n.* conspira.
intrinsic *adj.* esensal.
intro- *pref.* (*inner*) intro-.
introduce *v.* (*substance, topic, law*) introdui; (*person*) presenta.
introduction *n.* introdui, presenta.
introductory *adj.* introduinte.
introject *v.* (*psychology*) introjeta.
introjection *n.* introjeta.
introspect *v.* introspeta.
introspection *n.* introspeta.
introspective *adj.* introspetante, refletante.
introversion *n.* introverti.
introvert *adj.* & *n.* introvertida.
introverted *adj.* introvertida, nonsosial. **be introverted** introverti.
intrude *v.* intrui. **intrude on** disturba.
intruder *n.* intruor.
intrusion *n.* intrui.
intrusive *adj.* intruosa.
intubate *v.* intuba.
intubation *n.* intuba.
intuit *v.* intui.
intuitable *adj.* intuable.
intuition *n.* intui.
intuitive *adj.* (*person*) intuosa; (*design*) intuable.
Inuit *adj.* & *n.* inuit.
inundate *v.* inonda.
inundation *n.* inonda.

inure *v.* abitua.
inured *adj.* abituada. **become inured** abitua.
invade *v.* invade.
invader *n.* invador.
invalid[1] *adj.* (*not valid*) nonvalida, nonlegal, nonasetable, nonpertinente, mal.
invalid[2] *n.* (*ill or disabled person*) malada, descapasida.
invalidate *v.* desvalidi.
invaluable *adj.* nonestimable.
invariability *n.* nonvariablia.
invariable *adj.* nonvariable.
invariant *adj.* & *n.* constante.
invasion *n.* invade.
invasive *adj.* invadente.
invective *n.* insulta.
inveigle *v.* engana.
invent *v.* inventa.
invention *n.* (*action*) inventa; (*product*) inventada.
inventive *adj.* inventosa.
inventiveness *n.* inventosia.
inventor *n.* inventor.
inventory *n.* lista de benes.
inverse *n.* inversa.
inversion *n.* inversa.
invert *v.* inversa.
invertebrate *adj.* & *n.* nonvertebrato.
invest *v.* investi.
investigate *v.* investiga, esamina.
investigation *n.* investiga.
investigator *n.* investigor, detetor.
investment *n.* investi.
investor *n.* investor.
inviable *adj.* nonrealable.
invigorate *v.* refresci.
invincible *adj.* nonvinsable.
inviolable *adj.* nonviolable.
invisibility *n.* nonvidablia.
invisible *adj.* nonvidable.
invitation *n.* invita.
invite *v.* invita.
in vitro *adj.* en vitro.
in vitro fertilization *n.* fertili en vitro.
in vivo *adj.* en vive.
invocation *n.* clama.
invoice *v.* & *n.* fatura.
invoke *v.* clama.
involute *adj.* complicada; spiral.
involve *v.* envolve.
involved *adj.* envolveda, asosiada.
involvement *n.* envolve.
involving *adj.* envolvente, marcada par.
invulnerable *adj.* nonferable, nonatacable.
iodine *n.* iodo.
ion *n.* (*chemistry*) ion.
Ionia *n.* (*ancient region of Turkey*) Ionia.
Ionian[1] *adj.* (*of Ionia*) ionian.
Ionian[2] *adj.* (*of the Ionian Sea*) ionica.
Ionian Islands *n.* Isolas Ionica.
Ionian Sea *n.* Mar Ionica.
ionic[1] *adj.* (*of ions*) ional.
Ionic[2] *adj.* (*of Ionia*) ionian.
ionization *n.* ioni.
ionize *v.* ioni.
ionosphere *n.* ionosfera.
iora *n.* (*bird*) iora.
iota *n.* (*Greek letter* Ι, ι) iota.
IOU *n.* bileta de deta, promete de paia.
Iowa *n.* (*US state*) Iowa.
IQ *n.* grado de intelijentia.
IQ test *n.* esamina de intelijentia.
Iran *n.* Iran.
Iranian *adj.* & *n.* irani.
Iraq *n.* Irac.
Iraqi *adj.* & *n.* iraci.
irascible *adj.* disputosa.
irate *adj.* coler.
ire *n.* coleria.
Ireland *n.* (*island, country*) Er.
iridescent *adj.* opalin.
iridium *n.* (*element*) iridio.
iris *n.* (*eye, plant*) iris.
Irish *adj.* & *n.* eres.
Irish Sea *n.* Mar Eres.
Irish wolfhound *n.* lepror eres.
irk *v.* irita.
irksome *adj.* iritante.
iron *n.* fero; (*for ironing*) presaveste, fero calda. • *v.* presa.
iron age *n.* eda de fero.
iron-clad *adj.* nonalterable.
iron fist *n.* punio ferin.
ironic *adj.* ironiosa.
ironing board *n.* table de presa.
ironmonger's *n.* (*shop*) boteca de utiles.
iron oxide *n.* osido de fero.
iron pyrite *n.* pirita.
ironware *n.* benes de fero.
iron will *n.* vole ferin.
irony *n.* ironia.
Iroquois *adj.* & *n.* (*person, language*) irocuoi.
irradiate *v.* esposa a radia.
irrational *adj.* nonrazonada, noncoerente; (*person*) nonrazonante.
irreal *adj.* nonreal.
irrealis mood *n.* (*grammar*) moda dependente.
irrecoverable *adj.* nonreganiable; (*illness*) nonremediable.
irredeemable *adj.* nonremetable.
irredentism *n.* (*restoration of territories*) restorisme.
irredentist *n.* restoriste.
irreducible *adj.* nonreduable.
irrefutable *adj.* nonrefutable.

irregular *adj.* caososa, noncoerente, nonsistemosa, nonordinada, nonperiodal, nonregulada, nonormal; (*grammar*) esetosa.
irregularity *n.* noncoere, nonormal; eseta.
irrelevance *n.* nonpertine.
irrelevant *adj.* nonpertinente; academin.
irremediable *adj.* nonremediable.
irremovable *adj.* nonsutrable.
irreparable *adj.* nonreparable.
irreplaceable *adj.* nonrecambiable.
irrepressible *adj.* nonrepresable.
irresistible *adj.* nonresistable.
irresolute *adj.* vasilante.
irrespective *adj.* sin relata. **irrespective of** sin relata con.
irresponsible *adj.* nonfidable.
irretrievable *adj.* nonreprendable.
irreverence *n.* noncortesia.
irreverent *adj.* noncortes.
irreversible *adj.* nonreversable.
irrevocable *adj.* noncanselable.
irrigate *v.* iriga.
irrigation *n.* iriga.
irritability *n.* iritablia.
irritable *adj.* iritable, disputosa.
irritable bowel *n.* colon iritable.
irritant *adj.* iritante.
irritate *v.* irita.
irritation *n.* irita.
is *v.* (*be*) es. **is it?** (*question tag, typically implying some uncertainty*) si.
ischium *n.* (*anatomy*) iscio.
-ish *suff.* (*resembling, somewhat*) -in; (*pertaining to a region*) -es, -ica, -sce.
Isis *n.* (*Egyptian goddess*) Isis.
Islam *n.* islam.
Islamic *adj.* muslim.
Islamism *n.* (*fundamentalism*) islamisme.
Islamist *adj.* & *n.* (*fundamentalist*) islamiste.
island *n.* isola.
isle *n.* isola. **Isle of Man** Isola Man.
islet *n.* isoleta.
-ism *suff.* -isme.
isn't *v.* no es. **isn't it?** (*question tag, typically expecting the answer yes*) no.
iso- *pref.* (*equal*) iso-.
isobar *n.* isobar.
isogloss *n.* isoglosa.
isolate *v.* isoli. • *n.* solitar.
isolated *adj.* isolida, solitar.
isolation *n.* isoli; solitaria.
isolationism *n.* isolisme.
isolationist *adj.* isoliste.
isolator *n.* (*substance*) isolinte.
isomer *n.* (*chemistry*) isomero.
isomeric *adj.* isomeral.
isometric *adj.* isometral.
isomorph *n.* isomorfe.
isomorphic *adj.* isomorfe.
isosceles *adj.* isosele.
isostasy *n.* (*geology*) isostasia.
isotope *n.* isotopo.
isotopic *adj.* isotopo.
isotopy *n.* isotopia.
Israel *n.* Israel.
Israeli *adj.* & *n.* israeli.
Israelite *n.* ivri.
issue *v.* (*provide*) furni; (*publish*) publici; (*statement*) proclama; (*emanate*) emerji. • *n.* problem, difisil; (*topic*) tema, idea; (*publication*) publici; (*periodical*) numero.
-ist *suff.* -iste.
isthmus *n.* istmo.
it[1] *pron.* lo; (*mammal, fish, personified animal*) el. **it could be** lo pote es. **it is hoped that** on espera ce. **it is said that** on dise ce. **it itself** (*non-reflexively emphatic*) lo mesma, el mesma. **it pleases me** lo plase me.
IT[2] *n.* infotecnolojia.
Italian *adj.* & *n.* italian.
Italian sandwich *n.* bagete plenida.
italic *adj.* (*typography*) apoiada, italica.
italicize *v.* apoia, italici.
Italy *n.* Italia.
itch *v.* & *n.* pruri.
itchy *adj.* prurinte.
-ite *suff.* -ito.
item *n.* numero, punto. **item for sale** ben.
itemize *v.* lista, detalia.
iterate *v.* itera.
iteration *n.* itera; ves.
iterative *adj.* iteral.
-itic *suff.* -itica.
itinerant *adj.* vagante, nomada. • *n.* vagor, nomada.
itinerary *n.* curso projetada, ordina de viaja.
-itis *suff.* (*inflammation*) -ite.
its *det.* sua. • *pron.* la sua(s).
itself *pron.* (*reflexive*) se; (*emphatically reflexive*) se mesma. **it itself** (*non-reflexively emphatic*) lo mesma. **this in itself** esta solitar.
-ity *suff.* -ia.
IUD *n.* contraconsepal intrauteral.
Ivorian *adj.* & *n.* ivorian.
-ivorous *suff.* (*eating*) -ivor.
ivory *n.* ivor.
Ivory Coast *n.* Costa de Ivor.
ivy *n.* edera.
-ize *suff.* -i.

J

Jaat *adj.* & *n.* (*person*) jat.
jab *v.* & *n.* colpa, colpa con cotel.
jacana *n.* (*bird*) jacana.
jacaranda *n.* (*tree*) jacaranda.
jack *n.* (*cards*) pajo; (*for lifting*) crico. **jack of all trades** fatota. **jack up** (*lift*) crici.
jackal *n.* xacal.
jackass *n.* asino.
jackboot *n.* bota militar.
jackdaw *n.* monedula.
jacket *n.* (*suit, sports*) jaca.
jacket potato *n.* patata fornida.
jackhammer *n.* martel de aira.
jack-in-the-box *n.* diablo caxida.
jackknife *n.* cotel de pox.
jackpot *n.* premio xef.
Jacquard loom *n.* texador de Jacquard.
jacuzzi *n.* banio de vortis.
jade *adj.* (*colour*) jada. • *n.* (*gem*) jada.
jade plant *n.* crasula.
jagged *adj.* sierin, scalerin.
jaguar *n.* jaguar.
jaguarundi *n.* (*wild cat*) jaguarundi.
jail *n.* prison. • *v.* prisoni.
jailbait *n.* xica minor.
jailbird *n.* prisonida.
jailbreak *n.* evade de prison.
jailer *n.* gardor.
jailhouse *n.* prison.
Jain *adj.* & *n.* jain.
Jain Dharma *n.* (*religion*) jainisme.
Jainism *n.* jainisme.
jalapeño *n.* (*pepper*) jalapenio.
jalopy *n.* ruinada.
jalousie *n.* cortina venezian.
jam[1] *n.* (*fruit preserve*) jalea.
jam[2] *v.* fisa, trapi; (*music*) improvisa.
Jamaica *n.* Jamaica.
Jamaican *adj.* & *n.* jamaican.
Jamaica pepper *n.* (*tree, spice*) pimento.
jamb *n.* gama de porte.
jamboree *n.* asembla.
James Bay *n.* Baia James.
jangle *v.* & *n.* tintina.
janissary *n.* (*soldier*) jeniseri.
janitor *n.* mantenor.
January *n.* janero.
Japan *n.* Nion, Japan. **Sea of Japan** Mar Japan.
Japanese *adj.* & *n.* nion, japanes.
Japanese chess *n.* xogi.
jar *n.* (*container*) jar. • *v.* jari; xoca.
jargon *n.* jergo, parolas tecnical, termas tecnical; (*bafflegab*) babela.
jargon-filled *adj.* jergosa, babelosa.
jarring *adj.* xocante.
jasmine *n.* jasmin.
jasmine rice *n.* ris de jasmin.
Jat *adj.* & *n.* jat.
jaundice *n.* itero.
jaunt *n.* turi.
jaunty *adj.* vivosa.
Java *n.* Djava.
Javanese *adj.* & *n.* (*person, language*) djava.
Java Sea *n.* Mar Djava.
javelin *n.* lansia.
jaw *n.* mandibula.
jawbone *n.* mandibula.
jay *n.* (*bird*) jai. **American jay** jai american.
jaywalk *v.* traversa nonlegal.
jazz *adj.* & *n.* jaz.
jazz orchestra *n.* orcestra de jaz.
jealous *adj.* jelosa.
jealousy *n.* jelosia.
jeans *n.* jina, pantalon de denim.
jean shorts *n.* jina corta, pantala de denim.
jeep *n.* jip.
jeer *v.* burla. • *n.* burla, cria burlante.
jejune *adj.* naive; (*boring*) noiante.
jejunum *n.* (*anatomy*) jejuno.
jell *n.* jel. • *v.* jeli.
jellied alcohol *n.* jelatin de alcol.
jelly *n.* (*fruit preserve*) jalea; (*dessert*) jelatin.
jelly baby *n.* confeto de jelatin.
jelly bean *n.* confeto de jelatin.
jellyfish *n.* medusa.
jeopardize *v.* perili.
jeopardy *n.* peril.
jerboa *n.* (*rodent*) jerboa.
jeremiad *n.* lamenta.
jerk *v.* aranca. • *n.* aranca; (*insult*) culo, pixeta.
jerkin *n.* jaceta.
jerky[1] *adj.* spasmin, convulsante.
jerky[2] *n.* (*food*) txarci, carne secida.
Jèrriais *adj.* & *n.* (*language*) jersies.
jerrycan *n.* carafon de acua; carafon de gasolina.
jersey[1] *n.* sueter.
Jersey[2] *n.* Jersi. **New Jersey** (*US state*) Jersey Nova.
Jerseyman *n.* (*person*) jersies.
Jerusalem *n.* Ieruxalim.
jest *v.* broma.
jester *n.* bromor, bufon.
Jesuit *adj.* & *n.* jesuita.
Jesus *n.* Jesus.
jet[1] *v.* jeta. • *n.* jeta; (*aircraft*) jeto.
jet[2] *n.* (*stone*) jaieta.
jet-black *adj.* jaieta.

jet engine *n.* motor de jeto.
jetlag *n.* desfase de ora.
jet plane *n.* jeto.
jetport *n.* airoporto de jetos.
jet propulsion *n.* propulsa par jeto.
jetsam *n.* dejetadas flotante.
jet stream *n.* corente de jeta.
jettison *v.* dejeta.
jetty *n.* molo.
Jew *n.* iudi.
jewel *n.* (*gem*) jem; (*piece of jewellery*) joala.
jeweller (US **jeweler**) *n.* joalor.
jeweller's shop (US **jeweler's shop**) *n.* joaleria.
jewellery (US **jewelry**) *n.* joalas. **piece of jewellery** joala.
jewellery box *n.* portajoala.
jewellery case *n.* portajoala.
jewellery store *n.* joaleria.
Jewish *adj.* iudi; (*Judaic*) iudiste.
Jewish Enlightenment *n.* hascala.
Jewish Holocaust *n.* Olocausto.
Jewishness *n.* iudia.
Jewry *n.* iudis.
Jews *n.* iudis.
jezebel *n.* tisor.
jiffy *n.* momento. **in a jiffy** pronto.
jig *n.* jiga.
jigger *v.* interfere. • *n.* (*dancer*) jigor; (*alcohol*) dosa.
jiggle *v.* & *n.* ximi, tremeta.
jigsaw *n.* (*puzzle*) puzel; (*hand*) siera de detalia; (*power*) siera alternante.
jigsaw puzzle *n.* puzel.
jihad *n.* djihad.
jihadi *n.* djihadiste.
jihadist *n.* djihadiste.
jilt *v.* abandona.
jimpson weed *n.* stramonio.
jimson weed *n.* stramonio.
Jin *n.* djiniu.
jingle *v.* tintina. • *n.* tintina; (*advertising*) refreneta.
jinni *n.* djini.
jinx *v.* & *n.* encanta, maldise.
Jin-yu *n.* (*language*) djiniu.
jitterbug *adj.* & *n.* (*dance, music*) suing.
jittery *adj.* ansiosa.
jiu-jitsu *n.* (*martial art*) jujutsu.
jive *adj.* & *n.* (*dance, music*) suing.
job *n.* emplea, posto, carera; (*task*) taxe. **do odd jobs** bricola.
jobless *adj.* nonempleada.
jobseeker *n.* xercaemplea.
jockey *n.* joce.
jockey shorts *n.* slip de om.
jockstrap *n.* portaseso.
jocular *adj.* bromosa.
jocularity *n.* bromosia.
jocund *adj.* felis.
jodhpurs *n.* pantalon de cavalor.
Joe, average *n.* bonom.
joey *n.* cangareta.
jog *v.* & *n.* (*run*) core lenta; (*nudge*) puieta.
jogger *n.* coror. **joggers** pantalon de sporte.
jogging bottoms *n.* pantalon de sporte.
join *v.* (*together*) junta; (*become part of*) junta se a. **join with** alia se con.
joiner *n.* (*furniture, doors*) carpentor; (*roofs*) carpentor de teto.
joinery *n.* carpenta.
joint *n.* junta; (*electric*) comuta. **angled joint** junta angulo.
jointed *adj.* sesionida.
joint venture *n.* coemprende.
joist *n.* faxon.
joke *v.* & *n.* broma.
joker *n.* bromor, bufon.
jokester *n.* bromor.
jolly *adj.* felis.
jolt *v.* & *n.* colpa, xoca.
jonquil *n.* (*plant*) joncila.
Jordan *n.* Urdun.
Jordanian *adj.* & *n.* urduni.
jorts *n.* jina corta, pantala de denim.
josh *v.* burleta.
jostle *v.* puxa.
joule *n.* (*unit of energy*) jul.
journal *n.* jornal; (*accounting*) jornal de contas.
journalism *n.* jornalisme.
journalist *n.* jornaliste.
journalistic *adj.* jornaliste.
journalists *n.* jornalistes.
journey *n.* viaja.
journeyman *n.* laboror.
joust *n.* torneo, torneo de lansias.
Jove *n.* Jupiter.
jovial *adj.* bonumorosa, de bon umor.
jowl *n.* caruncula.
joy *n.* joia.
joyful *adj.* joiosa.
joyless *adj.* sin joia.
joyous *adj.* joiosa. **be joyous** joia.
joyride *v.* jira.
joystick *n.* joistic.
jubilant *adj.* selebrante.
jubilee *n.* aniversario.
Judaic *adj.* iudiste.
Judaica *n.* cosas iudi.
Judaism *n.* iudisme.
Judas tree *n.* sersis.
judder *v.* secute.
judge *v.* judi. • *n.* judor.
judgement *n.* judi.
judging *adj.* judinte. • *n.* judi. **judging by** si on considera.
judicial *adj.* judal.

judicial inquiry *n.* investiga judal.
judicial power *n.* potia de judi.
judiciary *n.* juderia.
judicious *adj.* justa, saja.
judo *n.* judo.
jug *n.* carafa; (*large container with spout*) carafon.
juggernaut *n.* camion jigante; forte nonresistable.
juggle *v.* jogla.
juggler *n.* joglor.
juglike *adj.* carafin.
jug-shaped *adj.* carafin.
jugular *adj.* jugulal.
jugular vein *n.* vena jugulal.
juice *n.* jus. **apple juice** jus de poma.
juicer *n.* jusador.
juicy *adj.* jusosa.
juju *n.* encanta, fetix.
ju-jitsu (*also* **jiu-jitsu**, **ju-jutsu**) *n.* jujutsu.
jukebox *n.* automata de discos.
julep *n.* (*drink*) julepo.
julienne *n.* (*food*) juliana.
July *n.* julio.
jumble *v.* misca, acasi. • *n.* misca, acasia.
jumble sale *n.* bazar.
jumbo *adj.* jigante.
jump *v.* salta; (*with surprise*) salteta. • *n.* salta. **jump ahead** salta a ante. **jump around** salta de asi a ala, salta a sirca. **jump forward** salta a ante. **you made me jump** tu ia salteta me.
jumper[1] *n.* (*person or animal that jumps*) saltor.
jumper[2] *n.* sueter; (*dress*) jumper.
jumper dress *n.* jumper.
jumpsuit *n.* covretota.
jumpy *adj.* nervosa.
junco *n.* (*bird*) junco.
junction *n.* junta; (*electric*) comuta.
juncture *n.* momento; (*junction*) junta.
June *n.* junio.
jungle *n.* jungla.
jungle crow *n.* corvo de jungla.
jungle gym *n.* strutur de trepa.
junior *adj.* minor.
juniper *n.* (*plant*) juniper.
junk[1] *n.* bricabrac.
junk[2] *n.* (*boat*) junca.
junk email *n.* spam.
junket *n.* caliada; turi.
junk food *n.* comeda sin nuri.
junkie *n.* drogamanica, manica.
junk shop *n.* bricabraceria.
junkyard *n.* resicleria.
junta *n.* (*government*) junta.
Jupiter *n.* (*mythology*, *planet*) Jupiter.
Jurassic *adj.* & *n.* (*geology*) jurasica.
jurisdiction *n.* autoria.
jurisprudence *n.* filosofia de lege, teoria legal; sistem legal.
jurist *n.* legiste.
juror *n.* jurior.
jury *n.* juria.
jury box *n.* lojia de juria.
just *adj.* (*fair*) justa. • *adv.* (*exactly*) esata; (*only*) sola, mera, no plu ca; en no otra modo ca; (*narrowly*) apena. **be just about to do** vade a fa, es a punto de fa. **have just done** veni de fa, es a fini de fa. **just in case** mera per caso. **just less than** cuasi. **just so** esata tal.
just claim *n.* direto.
justice *n.* justia; (*person*) judor.
justifiable *adj.* justable.
justification *n.* esplica, escusa; (*typography*) alinia plen.
justify *v.* (*explain*) esplica; (*make fair*) justi; (*warrant*) merita; (*typography*) alinia plen.
jut *v.* protende.
jute *n.* (*plant*, *fibre*) juta.
juvenile *n.* joven. • *adj.* jovenal; (*behaviour*) jovenin.
juxtapose *v.* aposa.
juxtaposition *n.* aposa.

K

kabbala *n.* (*Judaism*) cabala.
kabbalah *n.* (*Judaism*) cabala.
kabob *n.* (*kebab*) cebab.
kaboom *interj.* pum.
kabuki *n.* (*drama*) cabuci.
kaftan *n.* (*garment*) caftan.
Kalahari Desert *n.* Deserto Kalahari.
kale *n.* col risa.
kaleidoscope *n.* calidoscopio.
kaleidoscopic *adj.* calidoscopial.
kalimba *n.* (*musical instrument*) calimba.
kangaroo *n.* cangaru.
kanji *n.* (*writing system*) canji.
Kannada *adj.* & *n.* (*person, language*) canada.
Kansas *n.* (*US state*) Kansas.
kappa *n.* (*Greek letter* K, κ) capa.
karakul *n.* (*sheep*) caracul.
Karakum Desert *n.* Deserto Karakum.
karaoke *n.* caraoce.
Kara Sea *n.* Mar Cara.
karat *n.* carato.
karate *n.* carate.
karate expert *n.* carator.
karateka *n.* carator.
Karen *adj.* & *n.* (*person, language*) caren.
Karimata Strait *n.* Streta Karimata.
karma *n.* carma.
kasher *adj.* caxer.
Kashmir *n.* Caxmir.
Kashmiri *adj.* caxmiran.
kata- *pref.* (*down*) cata-.
katakana *n.* (*writing system*) catacana.
katal *n.* (*unit of catalytic activity*) catal.
katana *n.* (*sword*) catana.
Kathmandu *n.* Catmandu.
Kattegat *n.* Kattegat.
katydid *n.* (*bush cricket*) grilo verde.
kava *n.* (*plant*) cava.
kayak *n.* caiac.
kazachok *n.* (*dance*) cozatxoc.
Kazakh *adj.* & *n.* cazac.
Kazakhstan *n.* Cazacstan.
Kazakhstani *adj.* & *n.* (*person, language*) cazac.
kazoo *n.* (*musical instrument*) cazu.
kea *n.* (*bird*) cea.
kebab *n.* cebab.
keel *n.* cilia.
keelhaul *v.* pasa su la cilia.
keen *adj.* (*eager*) zelosa; (*sense*) agu.
keenness *n.* zelo; agia.
keep[1] *v.* (*retain*) reteni; (*in the same state*) manteni; (*remain*) resta; (*doing*) continua, repete; (*from doing*) preveni. **keep alive** vive. **keep a lookout** es vijilante. **keep an eye on** atende; monitori; vijila. **keep away** (*ward off*) teni a via; (*stay away*) resta a via. **keep away from** evita. **keep out** esclui. **keep secret** secreti. **keep track of** teni trasa de.
keep[2] *n.* (*castle*) fortres.
keepsake *n.* recordante.
keffiyeh *n.* (*headdress*) cafia.
keg *n.* barileta.
kelp *n.* fuca.
kelpie *n.* (*mythology, dog*) celpi.
kelvin *n.* (*unit of temperature*) celvin.
kennel *n.* caneria, casa de can.
keno *n.* (*bingo*) loto.
Kentucky *n.* (*US state*) Kentucky.
Kenya *n.* Cenia.
Kenyan *adj.* & *n.* cenian.
kepi *n.* (*hat*) xapeta.
kept woman *n.* concubina.
keratin *n.* ceratin.
keratocyte *n.* ceratinosite.
kerb *n.* borda de troteria.
kerchief *n.* bandana, tela de testa.
Kerguelen Islands *n.* Isolas Kerguelen.
kern *v.* (*typography*) suprapone.
kernel *n.* (*nut*) gran; (*central part*) cor; (*grammar*) nucleo.
kerosene *n.* cerosen.
kerosene stove *n.* stufa de cerosen.
kestrel *n.* falcon.
ketchup *n.* cetxap.
ketone *n.* (*chemistry*) cetona.
kettle *n.* caldera.
kettle drum *n.* timpano.
key *n.* (*lock*) clave; (*keyboard*) tecla; (*music*) tonalia. • *v.* tecli. • *adj.* xef, major.
keyboard *n.* teclador.
keyboard instrument *n.* strumento de teclas.
keychain *n.* cadena de claves, portaclave.
key component *n.* composante major.
key fob *n.* cadena de claves.
keyhole *n.* buco de clave.
keymaker *n.* clavor.
keynote *n.* tema xef.
keypad *n.* tecladoreta.
keypress *n.* tecli.
keyring *n.* portaclave.
key signature *n.* (*music*) armatur, sinias de tonalia.
keystone *n.* clave de arco.
keystroke *n.* tecli.
khagan *n.* (*governor*) han.
khaganate *n.* hania.
khaki *adj.* (*colour*) caci. • *n.* (*fabric*) caci.
khan *n.* han.
khanate *n.* hania.

khat *n.* (*plant, leaves*) cat.
Khmer *adj.* & *n.* (*person, language*) cmer.
Khoi *adj.* & *n.* coicoi.
Khoikhoi *adj.* & *n.* coicoi.
Khoisan *adj.* & *n.* (*person, language*) coisan.
kibbutz *n.* cibuts.
kick *v.* & *n.* pedi, colpa con pede. **kick off** comensa, pedi prima.
kickback *n.* (*recoil*) retira; (*bribe*) soborna.
kickboxer *n.* boxor de pedi.
kickboxing *n.* boxe de pedi.
kicker *n.* pedor.
kickoff *n.* comensa, pedi prima.
kick scooter *n.* patineta.
kickstand *n.* (*bicycle*) cavaleta.
kid *n.* enfante, xice; (*young goat*) capreta.
kiddie *n.* enfante, xice.
kiddy *n.* enfante, xice.
kidnap *v.* saisi, fura. • *n.* fura de enfantes; fura de persones.
kidnapper *n.* saisor, furor.
kidney *n.* ren.
kidney bean *n.* fava roja.
kielbasa *n.* (*sausage*) colbasa.
Kiev *n.* Ciiv.
Kilimanjaro, Mount *n.* Monte Kilimanjaro.
kill *v.* mata.
killdeer *n.* (*bird*) caradrio.
killer *n.* mator.
killer whale *n.* orca.
killing machine *n.* matador.
killing spree *n.* orjia de mata.
killjoy *n.* matajoia.
kiln *n.* fornon.
kilo- *pref.* cilo-.
kilobyte *n.* cilobait.
kilogram *n.* cilogram.
kilolitre (US **kiloliter**) *n.* cilolitre.
kilometre (US **kilometer**) *n.* cilometre.
kilowatt *n.* cilovate.
kilowatt-hour *n.* cilovate-ora.
kilt *n.* cilt, falda scotes.
kilter *n.* ecuilibra.
kimono *n.* cimono.
kin[1] *n.* relatadas.
-kin[2] *suff.* (*diminutive*) -eta.
kinaesthesia (US **kinesthesia**) *n.* cinestesia.
kinaesthetic (US **kinesthetic**) *adj.* cinestesica.
kind[1] *n.* spesie, tipo, jenero.
kind[2] *adj.* compatiosa, jentil, amante, amable.
kindergarten *n.* jardin de enfantes.
kind-hearted *adj.* compatiosa.
kindle *v.* ensende.
kindness *n.* compatia, jentilia, amablia. **act of kindness** bon ata.
kindred *adj.* simil, relatada.
kinesiologist *n.* cinesiolojiste.
kinesiology *n.* cinesiolojia.
kinesth... (US). See *kinaesth...*
kinetic *adj.* cinetica.
kinfolk *n.* relatadas.
king *n.* re.
kingdom *n.* rena.
kingfisher *n.* (*bird*) pexor.
kinglet *n.* renoreta.
kingpin *n.* (*bolt, person*) bulon xef.
king-size *adj.* estragrande.
king-size bed *n.* leto estragrande.
kink *n.* (*twist*) torse; (*flaw*) problem; (*quirk*) strana, bizara.
kinkajou *n.* (*animal*) cincaju.
kinky *adj.* torsosa; bizara.
kinorhynch *n.* (*organism*) cinorinco.
kinship *n.* relata.
kiosk *n.* ciosco.
kipa *n.* (*cap*) cipa.
Kipchak *adj.* & *n.* (*person, language*) ciptxac.
kippah *n.* (*cap*) cipa.
kipper *n.* arenge fumida.
Kiribati *adj.* ciribas. • *n.* (*person*) ciribas; (*country*) Ciribas.
kismet *n.* destina.
kiss *v.* & *n.* besa; (*light kiss*) beseta.
kiss-ass *n.* (*sycophant*) besaculo, besaorea, lecaculo.
kit *n.* (*of equipment*) paco; (*for self-assembly*) asemblable.
kit bag *n.* saco silindre.
kitchen *n.* cosina.
kitchenette *n.* cosineta.
kitchen garden *n.* orteta.
kitchen table *n.* table de cosina.
kitchen utensil *n.* util de cosini.
kitchenware *n.* benes de cosina.
kite *n.* (*toy*) cometa; (*bird*) milan.
kith *n.* relatadas.
kitsch *n.* arte inferior.
kitten *n.* gateta.
Kittian *adj.* & *n.* citian.
kitty *n.* gateta; (*money*) reserva.
Kivu, Lake *n.* Lago Kivu.
kiwi *n.* (*bird, fruit*) ciui; (*New Zealander*) zelandes.
kiwi fruit *n.* ciui.
klaxon *n.* claxon.
kleptocracy *n.* cleptocratia.
kleptocrat *n.* cleptocrata.
kleptomania *n.* cleptomania.
kleptomaniac *adj.* & *n.* cleptomanica.
knack *n.* capasia.
knapsack *n.* bolson.
knave *n.* (*cards*) pajo.
knead *v.* amasa.
kneading machine *n.* amasador.

knee *n.* jeno.
kneecap *n.* rotula.
kneel *v.* ajena. **kneel down** ajena se, cade a jenos.
knee-length shorts *n.* pantala de jenos.
kneeler *n.* cuxin de jenos.
kneepad *n.* covrejeno.
knees *n.* jenos.
knickerbockers *n.* pantala.
knickers *n.* pantaleta, slip de fem. **French knickers** culote.
knickknack *n.* orneta.
knife *n.* cotel.
knight *n.* (*including tarot*) cavalor; (*chess*) cavalo. • *v.* cavalori.
knighthood *n.* titulo de cavalor.
knit *v.* tricota. • *n.* (*fabric*) tricotada.
knitting needle *n.* ago de tricota.
knob *n.* boton; (*penis*) pixa.
knobby *adj.* botonin.
knobhead *n.* (*insult*) pixeta.
knock *v.* & *n.* colpa; (*at door*) bateta. **knock down** cade, colpa a tera, fa ce lo cade; (*building, wall*) desconstrui. **knock out** (*stun*) aturdi; (*from contest*) elimina. **knock over** cade, colpa a tera, fa ce lo cade; desecuilibra.
knockabout comedy *n.* farsa.
knocker *n.* (*door*) batetador; (*breast*) mamela, teton.
knock-kneed *adj.* con jenos valga.
knock-knock *interj.* clac-clac.
knockout *n.* (*contest*) concurso de elimina; (*stun*) aturdi.
knoll *n.* colineta.
knot *v.* & *n.* noda.
knotty *adj.* nodosa.
know *v.* (*by learning: fact, details, how to*) sabe; (*by experience: person, place, etc.*) conose. **know in advance** preconose. **you know** (*filler*) sabe, tu sabe.
know-all *n.* sabetota.
knowhow *n.* sabe.
know-it-all *n.* sabetota.
knowledge *n.* sabe, sabes; (*of person, place, etc.*) conose.
knowledgeable *adj.* sabosa.
known *adj.* conoseda. **known as X** nomida X, conoseda como X.
knuckle *n.* noca.
knucklehead *n.* stupida.
koala *n.* coala.
koan *n.* (*Zen*) coan.
kohl *n.* (*cosmetic*) col.
kohlrabi *n.* (*plant, vegetable*) colirabano.
kola *n.* (*plant, nut, drink*) cola.
Kola Peninsula *n.* Penisola Cola.
kolbassa *n.* (*sausage*) colbasa.
Komodo dragon *n.* (*lizard*) comodo.
Komodo monitor *n.* (*lizard*) comodo.
konjac *n.* (*plant*) coniac.
konjak *n.* (*plant*) coniac.
konnyaku *n.* (*plant*) coniac.
kook *n.* strana, bizara.
kookaburra *n.* cucabura.
kooky *adj.* strana, bizara.
kopek *n.* (*currency*) copec.
Koran *n.* Curan.
Korea *n.* Corea. **North Korea** Txoson, Corea Norde. **South Korea** Tehan, Corea Sude.
Korea Bay *n.* Baia Corea.
Korean *adj.* & *n.* (*person, language*) hangugo, corean. **North Korean** txoson. **South Korean** tehan.
Korean Bay *n.* Baia Corea.
Korea Strait *n.* Streta Corea.
kosher *adj.* caxer.
Kosovan *adj.* & *n.* cosovan.
Kosovo *n.* Cosovo.
koto *n.* (*musical instrument*) coto.
kowtow *v.* (*grovel*) adula; (*kneel*) ajena.
kozachok *n.* (*dance*) cozatxoc.
kraken *n.* cracen.
Kreyol Ayisyen *adj.* & *n.* creol aitian.
krill *n.* (*crustacean*) cril.
kris *n.* (*dagger*) cris.
Krishna *n.* Crixna.
Krishnaism *n.* crixnaisme.
Krishnaist *adj.* & *n.* crixnaiste.
kroužek *n.* (*diacritic*) anelo.
krummhorn *n.* (*musical instrument*) cromorno.
krypton *n.* cripton.
kryptonite *n.* criptonita.
kubasa *n.* (*sausage*) colbasa.
kudos *n.* loda.
kudzu *n.* (*plant*) cudzu.
kufi *n.* (*cap*) cipa.
kufiya *n.* (*headdress*) cafia.
kumquat *n.* cumcuat.
kung fu *n.* cungfu.
Kurd *adj.* & *n.* (*person, language*) curdi.
Kurdish *adj.* & *n.* curdi.
Kurdistan *n.* Curdistan.
kurgan *n.* (*mound*) curgan, tumulo.
Kushan *adj.* (*dynasty*) cuxan.
Kuwait *n.* Cuait.
Kuwaiti *adj.* & *n.* cuaiti.
kvetch *v.* cexa.
kwashiorkor *n.* (*medical*) cuaxiorcor.
kyphosis *n.* (*medical*) cifose.
Kyrgyz *adj.* & *n.* cirgiz.
Kyrgyzstan *n.* Cirgistan.
Kyrgyzstani *adj.* & *n.* (*person, language*) cirgiz.
Kyushu *n.* (*island*) Kyushu.
Kyzylkum *n.* Deserto Kizilkum.

L

la *n.* (*musical note*) la.
lab *n.* laboreria siensal.
labdanum *n.* resina de sisto.
label *n.* eticeta. • *v.* eticeti.
labia *n.* (*anatomy*) labias.
labial *adj.* labial.
labialize *v.* labiali.
labia majora *n.* labias major.
labia minora *n.* labias minor.
labile *adj.* frajil, fasil cambiable; emosiosa.
labiodental *adj.* & *n.* (*consonant*) labiodental.
labium *n.* (*anatomy*) labia.
labor... (US). See *labour...*
laboratory *n.* laboreria, laboreria siensal.
laborious *adj.* laborosa.
labour (US **labor**) *n.* labora; (*giving birth*) pari. **be in labour** pari. **in labour** parinte. **manual labour** labora par mano.
labour camp (US **labor camp**) *n.* campa de labora.
Labour Day (US **Labor Day**) *n.* festa de labora.
laboured (US **labored**) *adj.* (*breathing*) laborosa.
labourer (US **laborer**) *n.* laboror.
labour-saving (US **labor-saving**) *adj.* fasilinte.
labour union (US **labor union**) *n.* sindicato.
Labrador *n.* (*Canadian region*) Labrador; (*dog*) retraor de Labrador.
Labrador retriever *n.* (*dog*) retraor de Labrador.
Labrador Sea *n.* Mar Labrador.
labyrinth *n.* labirinto.
labyrinthine *adj.* labirintin.
Laccadive Sea *n.* Mar Lakshadib.
lace *n.* dentela.
lacerate *v.* lasera.
laceration *n.* lasera.
Lacerta *n.* (*constellation*) la Lezardo.
lacewing *n.* (*insect*) crisopa.
lacework *n.* dentela.
lachrymal *adj.* lacrimal.
lachrymal bone *n.* oso lacrimal.
lachrymatory *adj.* lacrimojen.
lachrymogenic *adj.* lacrimojen.
lack *v.* no ave, nesesa. • *n.* manca, nonsufisi. **lack of knowledge** nonsabe. **the car lacks a wheel** un rota manca de la auto.
lackadaisical *adj.* pigra.
lackey *n.* lace.
lacking *adj.* mancante, nonsufisinte. • *prep.* sin. **be lacking** manca.
lacklustre (US **lackluster**) *adj.* mediocre.
laconic *adj.* consisa.
lacquer *n.* laca.
lacrimal *adj.* lacrimal.
lacrimal bone *n.* oso lacrimal.
lacrosse *n.* (*sport*) lacros.
lactate *v.* leti.
lactation *n.* leti.
lactic *adj.* latica.
lactic acid *n.* asida latica.
lactose *n.* (*sugar*) latosa.
lactulose *n.* (*sugar*) latolosa.
lacuna *n.* buco.
ladanum *n.* resina de sisto.
ladder *n.* scala.
ladies' man *n.* romeo, xasafem.
ladies' room *n.* (*toilet*) sala de femes.
Ladin *adj.* & *n.* (*language*) ladin.
ladle *n.* culieron.
lady *n.* seniora; (*gender-neutral*) sri; (*noble*) dama. **ladies and gentlemen** senioras e seniores, sris.
lady beetle *n.* marieta.
ladybird *n.* marieta.
ladybug *n.* marieta.
ladyfinger *n.* (*biscuit*) biscoto savoian.
ladylike *adj.* damin.
lady's finger *n.* (*biscuit*) biscoto savoian.
ladyship *n.* senioria; damia.
lag *n.* retarda. • *v.* segue lenta, avansa min. **lag behind** segue lenta, avansa min.
lager *n.* bir blonde.
laggard *n.* lenta.
lagniappe *n.* regala.
lagoon *n.* lagon.
lag time *n.* retarda.
laicize *v.* despreti.
lair *n.* nido.
laissez-faire *adj.* libraliste.
laissez-faire economy *n.* economia libraliste.
laity *n.* nonrelijiosas.
lake *n.* lago.
lakeside *n.* fronte de lago.
Lakshadweeb Sea *n.* Mar Lakshadib.
lama *n.* (*Buddhism*) lama.
lamb *n.* oveta; (*meat*) carne de oveta.
lambada *n.* (*dance*) lambada.
lambast *v.* critica.
lambda *n.* (*Greek letter* Λ, λ) lamda.
lame *adj.* (*limping*) coxeante.
lamé *n.* (*fabric*) lame.
lamebrain *n.* stupida.
lamella *n.* lamina.
lament *v.* lamenta.
lamentable *adj.* nonfortunosa.

lamentation *n.* lamenta.
lamina *n.* lamina.
laminate *n.* lamina. • *v.* lamini.
lamination *n.* lamini.
lamp *n.* lampa.
lamplight *n.* lus de lampa.
lamplighter *n.* ensendelampa.
lampoon *v.* burla.
lamppost *n.* palo de lampa.
lamprey *n.* (*animal*) lamprea.
lampshade *n.* paralampa.
lance *n.* lansia. • *v.* lansi.
lancet *n.* bisturi.
land *n.* tera; (*country*) pais. • *v.* atera.
landed *adj.* (*possessing land*) con imobila.
lander *n.* (*space travel*) aterador.
landfall *n.* atera. **make landfall** atera.
landfill *n.* (*site*) dejeteria, entereria.
landing *n.* (*action*) atera; (*staircase*) niveleta.
landing strip *n.* atereria.
landlady *n.* proprior.
landlocked *adj.* sin costa, ensircada par tera.
landlord *n.* proprior.
landlubber *n.* nonmarinor.
landmark *n.* monumento; (*navigation*) punto de refere, loca de orienta. • *adj.* monumental.
landsat *n.* (*satellite network*) landsat.
landscape *n.* vista. • *v.* (*garden*) desinia, projeta. • *adj.* (*orientation*) orizonal.
landscape designer *n.* desinior de jardines.
landscaper *n.* jardinor.
landslide *n.* lisca de tera.
landslide victory *n.* vinse inondante.
landslip *n.* lisca de tera.
lane *n.* (*road*) rueta; (*traffic*) banda.
Langobard *n.* langobarda.
Langobardic *adj.* langobarda.
langoustine *n.* omareta.
language *n.* lingua; (*wording, style*) linguaje. **artificial language** lingua construida, lingua desiniada. **auxiliary language** lingua aidante. **constructed language** lingua construida.
language planning *n.* maneja de linguas.
languid *adj.* pigra.
languish *v.* debili.
languor *n.* letarjia, nonativia.
languorous *adj.* letarjiosa, nonativa.
langur *n.* langur.
lanolin *n.* (*substance*) lanolin.
lantern *n.* lampa.
lanthanide *n.* (*chemistry*) lantanido.
lanthanum *n.* (*element*) lantano.
lanyard *n.* corda.
Lao *adj.* & *n.* lau.
Laos *n.* Lau.
Laotian *adj.* & *n.* (*person, language*) lau.
Lao-Tze *n.* (*philosopher*) Laozi.
Laozi *n.* (*philosopher*) Laozi.
lap[1] *n.* (*anatomy*) vasto, jenos.
lap[2] *n.* (*in a race*) anelo. • *v.* pasa.
lap[3] *v.* (*lick*) leca.
laparoscope *n.* (*medical*) laparoscopio.
laparoscopic *adj.* laparoscopial.
laparoscopy *n.* laparoscopi.
laparotomy *n.* (*medical*) laparotomio.
lapdog *n.* (*dog, person*) can regalada.
lapel *n.* suprapone.
lapidary *adj.* & *n.* (*gem worker*) lapidario.
Lapland *n.* Sami.
lapse *n.* fali.
Laptev Sea *n.* Mar Laptev.
laptop *n.* portable, computador portable.
lapwing *n.* (*bird*) vanelo.
larcenist *n.* furor.
larceny *n.* fura.
larch *n.* (*tree*) larix.
lard *n.* gras, gras de porco.
larder *n.* saleta de comedas.
large *adj.* grande.
large calorie *n.* caloria grande.
large intestine *n.* intestin spesa.
large-scale *adj.* vasta.
largess *n.* (*generosity*) jenerosia; (*gifts*) donadas.
largesse *n.* (*generosity*) jenerosia; (*gifts*) donadas.
lariat *n.* laso.
lark *n.* aloda.
larkspur *n.* (*plant*) consolida; (*delphinium*) delfinio.
larva *n.* larva.
larval *adj.* larval.
laryngeal *adj.* & *n.* larinjal, gargal.
laryngeal prominence *n.* poma de Adam.
laryngitis *n.* larinjite.
laryngopharynx *n.* farinje larinjal.
larynx *n.* larinje.
lasagne *n.* lasanie.
lascivious *adj.* lasiva.
laser *n.* laser. • *v.* laseri.
lash *n.* sil.
lassitude *n.* fatiga.
lasso *n.* laso. • *v.* lasi.
last[1] *adj.* final, ultima; (*latest*) la plu resente. **at last** final, a fini. **last but one** anteultima, cuasi ultima. **last but two** du ante la ultima. **last week** en la semana pasada, en la semana presedente, en la semana ante esta.
last[2] *v.* (*endure*) dura. **last for years** dura tra anios.
lasting *adj.* durante.
latch *n.* fisador. • *v.* fisa.
latchkey child *n.* enfante con clave.
late *adj.* tarda, avansada; (*dead*) lamentada. **grow late** tardi. **in the late 20th century** en la tarda de la sentenio 20.

latecomer *n.* tarda.
lateen *n.* (*sail*) vela latina.
lately *adv.* resente.
lateness *n.* tardia.
late night *n.* note tarda.
latent *adj.* ascondeda.
later *adv.* a pos, plu tarda. **later than** pos. **no later than tomorrow** doman a la plu tarda, ante fini de doman. **two days later** pos du dias.
lateral *adj.* & *n.* (*consonant*) ladal.
lateral approximant *n.* aprosiminte ladal.
lateral fricative *n.* fricante ladal.
lateral thinking *n.* pensa ladal.
lateral thought *n.* pensa ladal.
latest *adj.* la plu nova, vangarda; (*news*) de la ora. **at the latest** a la plu tarda. **latest news** avenis de la ora.
latex *n.* latex.
lath *n.* banda de lenio.
lathe *n.* turnador.
lather *v.* & *n.* spuma.
latifundium *n.* cultiveria grande.
Latin *adj.* & *n.* latina.
Latina *adj.* & *n.* latina.
Latin alphabet *n.* alfabeta roman.
Latin American *adj.* & *n.* latina.
Latino *adj.* & *n.* latina.
latitude *n.* latitude.
latke *n.* (*pancake*) latce.
latrine *n.* latrina.
latter *adj.* tarda. **the latter** esta, la otra.
Latter-day Saints *n.* mormonisme.
lattice *n.* grilia.
latticework *n.* grilia.
Latvia *n.* Latvia.
Latvian *adj.* & *n.* latvisce.
laud *v.* loda.
laudable *adj.* lodable.
laudanum *n.* (*painkiller*) laudano.
laugh *v.* & *n.* rie. **laugh at** burla.
laughable *adj.* riable, burlable.
laughter *n.* rie.
launch *v.* lansa, xuta; (*ship*) envia a mar; (*onto the market*) lansa. • *n.* lansa.
launcher *n.* lansador.
launchpad *n.* lanseria.
launder *v.* lava.
laundered money *n.* mone lavada, mone blancida.
launderer *n.* lavor.
laundromat *n.* laveria.
laundry *n.* laveria.
laureate *adj.* & *n.* laurida, onorada. • *v.* lauri.
laurel *n.* lauro.
lava *n.* (*geology*) lava.
lavage *n.* lava interna.
lavatory *n.* vason; (*room*) saleta privata.
lavender *adj.* (*colour*) lavanda. • *n.* (*plant*) lavanda.
laver *n.* (*seaweed*) nori.
lavish *adj.* lusosa.
law *n.* lege. **by law** par lege.
lawbreaker *n.* criminor, inioror de lege.
lawful *adj.* legal.
lawless *adj.* sin lege.
lawlessness *n.* anarcia.
lawmaker *n.* legor.
lawn *n.* erba, jardin.
lawn bowling *n.* bolo.
lawnmower *n.* cortierba. **unmotorized lawnmower** cortierba puiable.
lawrencium *n.* (*element*) laurensio.
lawsuit *n.* litiga, prosede legal.
lawyer *n.* avocato.
lax *adj.* laxe.
laxative *n.* laxinte, paraconstipa.
lay[1] *v.* pone, reclina; (*eggs*) pone, ovipari, (*internally*) ovovivipari; (*sex*) fode. **lay down** reclina. **lay off** (*employee*) desemplea. **lay out** posa.
lay[2] *adj.* nonrelijiosa.
layaway *n.* reserva. **on layaway** reservada.
layer *n.* strato. • *v.* strati.
layette *n.* dote de bebe.
layman *n.* nonprofesal; nonrelijiosa.
layoff *n.* desemplea.
layout *n.* posa.
layperson *n.* nonprofesal; nonrelijiosa.
laze *v.* pigri.
laziness *n.* pigria.
lazy *adj.* pigra.
lazybones *n.* pigra.
lazyboy *n.* (*chair*) seja reclinante.
lazy eye *n.* ambliopia.
LCD *n.* scermo de cristal licuida.
leach *v.* (*drain*) lixivia.
leachate *n.* lixiviada.
lead[1] *v.* (*guide*) gida. • *n.* vantaje.
lead[2] *n.* (*metal*) plomo; (*pencil*) grafito.
leaden *adj.* plomin.
leader *n.* gidor, xef; capitan; (*authority*) autoriosa; (*economic*) potiosa.
leadership *n.* gida, xefia.
lead guitarist *n.* soliste de gitar.
leading *adj.* gidante; (*initial*) inisial.
leading question *n.* demanda gidante.
lead shot *n.* gran de plomo.
leaf *n.* folia.
leafbird *n.* verdin.
leafhopper *n.* (*insect*) sicadela.
leaflet *n.* folieta.
leaflike *adj.* folin.
leaf monkey *n.* langur.
leafy *adj.* foliosa.
league[1] *n.* (*alliance*) alia.
league[2] *n.* (*unit of length*) lega.

leak *v.* & *n.* gotea; (*information*) esposa.
leakage *n.* gotea.
leak soup *n.* sopa de poro.
leaky *adj.* goteante.
lean[1] *v.* (*tilt*) apoia.
lean[2] *adj.* (*thin*) magra.
leap *v.* & *n.* salta.
leaper *n.* saltor, brincor.
leapfrog *n.* brincadorso.
leap second *n.* secondo ajuntada.
leap year *n.* anio estendeda.
learn *v.* aprende.
learned *adj.* erudita, educada.
learnedness *n.* eruditia.
learner *n.* aprendor.
lease *n.* contrata de lua. • *v.* lua.
leash *n.* corea. • *v.* lia con corea.
least *det.* la min de. • *adv.* la min, minima. • *n.* minima. **at least** a la min, minima; (*however*) an tal, an con tota. **the least helpful person** la person la min aidosa.
leather *n.* cuoro. • *adj.* de cuoro.
leather band *n.* banda de cuoro.
leather-bound book *n.* libro de cuoro.
leathery *adj.* cuorin.
leave[1] *v.* (*in a specified state*) lasa; (*behind*) lasa, abandona; (*depart*) parti de; (*exit*) sorti de; (*school*) fini, gradua. **leave out** omete.
leave[2] *n.* vacanse, asentia permeteda. **be on leave** vacanse. **go on leave** vacanse.
leaven *n.* fermentante.
leavened *adj.* levada.
leavening agent *n.* fermentante.
Lebanese *adj.* & *n.* lubnani.
Lebanon *n.* Lubnan.
lecherous *adj.* lasiva.
lechery *n.* lasivia.
lecithin *n.* (*substance*) lesitina.
lectern *n.* portalibro.
lecture *n.* leson.
lecturer *n.* ensenior, lesonor, presentor.
LED *n.* diodo de lus.
lederhosen *n.* lederhose.
ledge *n.* cornisa; (*shelf*) scafal.
ledger *n.* libro de contas.
lee *adj.* suventa.
leech *n.* sucasangue.
leek *n.* (*plant, vegetable*) poro.
leer *v.* come con sua oios.
leeward *adj.* suventa, con la venta.
leeway *n.* libria.
left[1] *adj.* & *n.* (*not right*) sinistra. **on the left of** a sinistra de.
left[2] *adj.* (*remaining*) restante.
left-align *v.* alinia a sinistra.
left alignment *n.* alinia a sinistra.
left click *v.* & *n.* (*mouse*) clica sinistra.
left-handed *adj.* (*person*) de mano sinistra; (*done*) con mano sinistra.
left-hander *n.* manosinistra.
leftism *n.* sinistrisme.
leftist *adj.* & *n.* sinistriste.
leftover *n.* resta, restante.
left-wing *adj.* sinistriste.
left-winger *n.* sinistriste.
leg *n.* gama.
legacy *n.* (*bequeathed*) lega; (*metaphor*) erita. • *adj.* (*software, hardware*) anticin.
legal *adj.* legal.
legalism *n.* legalisme.
legalist *n.* legaliste.
legalistic *adj.* legaliste.
legality *n.* legalia.
legalization *n.* legali.
legalize *v.* legali.
legend *n.* lejenda, mito, fable; (*motto*) slogan; (*diagram*) esplica.
legendary *adj.* lejendal.
legerdemain *n.* truco de mano.
leggings *n.* (*footless tights*) duicalson; (*protective*) covregamas.
legibility *n.* lejablia.
legible *adj.* lejable.
legion *n.* lejion, armada.
legionnaire *n.* lejionor.
legislate *v.* legi.
legislation *n.* legi.
legislative *adj.* leginte.
legislative branch *n.* (*government*) legeria.
legislative chamber *n.* salon de legi.
legislative power *n.* potia de legi.
legislator *n.* legor.
legislature *n.* legeria.
legist *n.* legiste.
legitimacy *n.* legalia.
legitimate *adj.* legal.
legitimization *n.* legali.
legitimize *v.* legali.
legroom *n.* spasio de gamas.
legume *n.* legum.
lei *n.* (*garland*) le.
leisure *n.* osio. **at leisure** osiosa.
leisure centre (US **center**) *n.* sentro de recrea.
leisurely *adj.* osiosa.
leitmotif *n.* tema xef.
lemma *n.* (*mathematics, philosophy*) lema.
lemming *n.* (*rodent*) leming.
lemon *n.* limon.
lemonade *n.* limonada.
lemonlike *adj.* limonin.
lemon meringue pie *n.* tarte merengida de limon.
lemon squeezer *n.* jusador.
lemony *adj.* (*like lemon*) limonin; (*full of lemon*) limonosa.
lemur *n.* (*primate*) lemur.
lend *v.* presta.

lender *n.* prestor.
length *n.* longia.
lengthen *v.* longi.
lengthways *n.* par longia.
lengthwise *n.* par longia.
lenience *n.* pardona.
leniency *n.* pardona, pardonosia.
lenient *adj.* pardonosa.
lens *n.* lente.
lenslike *adj.* lentin.
lens-shaped *adj.* lentin.
lent *n.* (*Christianity*) cuaresma.
lenten *adj.* cuaresmal.
lenticular *adj.* lentin.
lentil *n.* lentil.
lentil soup *n.* sopa de lentil.
Leo *n.* (*constellation*) la Leon.
Leo Minor *n.* (*constellation*) la Leon Peti.
León *n.* (*Spanish region*) Lion.
Leonese *adj.* & *n.* liones.
leopard *n.* leopardo.
leopard cub *n.* leopardeta.
leotard *n.* bodi de dansa, bodi de sporte.
leper *n.* leprosa.
lepidopteran *n.* papilio.
leprechaun *n.* leprecan.
leprosy *n.* leprosia.
leprous *adj.* leprosa.
-lepsy *suff.* (*medical*) -lesia.
-leptic *suff.* -lesica.
lepton *n.* (*particle*) lepton.
Lepus *n.* (*constellation*) la Lepre.
lesbian *adj.* & *n.* lesbian.
lesbianism *n.* lesbianisme.
lesion *n.* lesion.
Lesothan *adj.* & *n.* lesoto.
Lesotho *n.* Lesoto.
less *det.* & *adv.* min. **less and less** min e min, sempre min. **the less ... the less** min ... min.
lessen *v.* diminui, redui.
Lesser Antilles *n.* Antiles Minor.
lesson *n.* leson.
less-than-or-equal sign *n.* sinia de inferioria o egalia.
less-than sign *n.* sinia de inferioria.
let[1] *v.* permete, lasa; (*lease*) lua; (*wish*) ta ce. **let down** delude. **let go** relasa, desteni. **let it be** amen. **let it snow** (*wish*) ta ce lo neva. **let's go** vade. **to let** (*available to rent*) luable.
-let[2] *suff.* (*diminutive*) -eta.
letdown *n.* delude.
lethal *adj.* matante.
lethargic *adj.* letarjiosa.
lethargy *n.* letarjia.
letter *n.* (*alphabet, postal*) letera. • *v.* leteri.
letterbox *n.* buco de posta.
letterboxed *adj.* (*video*) en ranur orizonal.
letterhead *n.* xapo de letera.
lettering style *n.* stilo de leteri.
Lettish *adj.* & *n.* latvisce.
lettuce *n.* letuga.
letup *n.* pausa.
leuco- *pref.* leuco-.
leucoplast *n.* (*biology*) leucoplasto.
leukaemia (US **leukemia**) *n.* leucemia.
leukocyte *n.* (*blood cell*) leucosite.
lev *n.* (*currency*) lev.
levain *n.* fermentante natural.
Levant *n.* (*Mediterranean region*) Levante.
Levantine Sea *n.* Mar Levante.
levee *n.* paradeluvia, paramar.
level *adj.* plana. • *v.* plani. • *n.* (*tier*) nivel.
level crossing *n.* crusa plana.
level-headed *adj.* calma, pratical.
lever *n.* lever. • *v.* leveri.
leverage *n.* leveri.
leviathan *n.* (*Biblical sea monster*) leviatan.
levitate *v.* leva, flota en aira.
levitation *n.* leva.
levity *n.* bromosia.
levy *v.* forsa.
lewd *adj.* lasiva.
lewdness *n.* lasivia.
lexeme *n.* lexem.
lexical *adj.* vocabulal.
lexical category *n.* categoria sintatical.
lexicographer *n.* lexicografiste.
lexicographical *adj.* lexicografial.
lexicography *n.* lexicografia.
lexicological *adj.* lexicolojial.
lexicologist *n.* lexicolojiste.
lexicology *n.* lexicolojia.
lexicon *n.* vocabulo.
LFN *abbr.* elefen, lfn.
liability *n.* culpablia.
liable *adj.* (*responsible*) culpable; (*disposed*) propensada.
liaise *v.* colabora, coopera, lia.
liaison *n.* lia.
liana *n.* (*plant*) liana.
liar *n.* mentor.
libation *n.* bevida, bevida ofreda.
libel *v.* & *n.* malacusa.
libeller (US **libeler**) *n.* malacusor.
libellous (US **libelous**) *adj.* malacusante.
liberal *adj.* (*political*) libraliste; (*generous*) jenerosa. • *n.* libraliste.
liberal economy *n.* economia libraliste.
liberalism *n.* libralisme.
liberate *v.* libri.
liberation *n.* libri.
liberator *n.* libror.
Liberia *n.* Liberia.
Liberian *adj.* & *n.* liberian.
libertine *adj.* promiscua. • *n.* rue; fem promiscua.
liberty *n.* libria. **at liberty** libre.

libidinal *adj.* libidal.
libidinous *adj.* libidosa.
libido *n.* libido, desira sesal.
Libra *n.* (*constellation*) la Balansa.
librarian *n.* bibliotecor.
library *n.* biblioteca.
libretto *n.* libreta.
Libya *n.* Libia.
Libyan *adj.* & *n.* libi.
licence (US **license**) *n.* lisensa, permete.
licence plate (US **license plate**) *n.* placa de veculo.
license *v.* lisensa.
licentious *adj.* lasiva.
lichen *n.* (*plant*) licen.
lick *v.* & *n.* leca.
licorice *n.* liciris.
lid *n.* covrente.
lie[1] *v.* (*down*) reclina, reposa. **lie back** reclina se. **lie down** reclina se.
lie[2] *v.* & *n.* (*untruth*) menti. **tell a lie** menti.
Liechtenstein *n.* Lictenstain. • *adj.* lictenstaines.
Liechtensteiner *n.* lictenstaines.
lie detector *n.* detetador de mentis.
liege *n.* superior; (*feudal*) vasal.
lien *v.* ipoteca.
lieutenant *n.* teninte.
life *n.* vive. **come back to life** revive. **come to life** anima. **full of life** vivosa. **life after death** vive pos mori.
lifeblood *n.* sangue de vive.
lifeboat *n.* barco de salva.
life energy *n.* txi, fortia de vive.
life expectancy *n.* espeta de vive.
life force *n.* txi, fortia de vive.
lifeform *n.* vivente.
lifeguard *n.* gardor de pisina; gardor de plaia.
life jacket *n.* jaceta inflable.
lifelike *adj.* vivin.
lifeline *n.* corda de salva.
lifelong *adj.* eterna, de vive intera, tra la vive.
life preserver *n.* jaceta inflable.
life signs *n.* indicas de vive.
life-size *adj.* de grandia natural, de grandia vera.
lifespan *n.* vive intera.
lifestyle *n.* cultur, modo de vive.
lifetime *n.* vive intera.
lift *v.* leva, alti. • *n.* (*ride*) pasaje; (*elevator*) asendador. **give a lift to** dona pasaje a. **lift off** enaira.
lift bridge *n.* ponte levable.
lift music *n.* musica de asendador.
lift-off *n.* enaira, lansa.
lift truck *n.* levacarga.
ligament *n.* ligamento.
ligation *n.* lia.
ligature *n.* liante.
light[1] *n.* lus; (*lamp*) lampa. • *v.* (*illuminate*) lumina; (*fire*) ensende. • *adj.* (*colour*) pal. **lights** luses; lampas; aurora.
light[2] *adj.* (*in weight*) lejera.
light blue *adj.* & *n.* azul.
light brown *adj.* pal brun. • *n.* brun pal.
lightbulb *n.* ampola, bulbo de lus.
light-emitting diode *n.* diodo de lus.
lighten *v.* lejeri.
lighter *n.* ensendador, focador.
lightfast *adj.* secur contra lus.
light fixture *n.* portabulbo.
light-headed *adj.* vertigosa.
lightheadedness *n.* vertigo.
light-hearted *adj.* bonumorosa, de bon umor; (*entertaining*) divertinte.
lighthouse *n.* faro.
lighting rail *n.* rel de lampas.
lighting track *n.* rel de lampas.
lightness *n.* lejeria.
lightning *n.* lampo. **like lightning** lampin.
lightning bug *n.* lampeta.
lightning conductor *n.* paralampo.
lightning rod *n.* paralampo.
lightproof *adj.* secur contra lus.
lightshade *n.* paralampa.
lightship *n.* barco de faro.
light socket *n.* portabulbo.
lightvessel *n.* barco de faro.
light weapons *n.* armas lejera.
lightweight *adj.* lejera.
light year *n.* anio de lus.
lignite *n.* lignito.
Liguria *n.* Liguria.
Ligurian *adj.* & *n.* ligurian.
Ligurian Sea *n.* Mar Liguria.
likable (US). See *likeable.*
like[1] *v.* (*be pleased by*) gusta. **I like it** me gusta lo, lo plase me. **I would like** me ta vole. **like it or not** volente o nonvolente.
like[2] *prep.* como. • *subord.* como, como si. • *suff.* -in. **like this** en esta modo, tal.
likeable (US **likable**) *adj.* amable, gustable.
likelihood *n.* probablia.
likely *adj.* probable.
like-minded *adj.* de la mesma mente.
liken *v.* compara.
likeness *n.* simili.
likewise *adv.* ance.
liking *n.* (*mutual*) simpatia.
lilac *adj.* (*colour*) lila; (*plant*) lila.
lilo *n.* materas inflable.
lilt *v.* pronunsia melodiosa.
lily *n.* lil. **calla lily** cala.
lima bean *n.* fava de Lima.
limb *n.* (*arm*, *leg*) membro.
limber *adj.* ajil, flexable.

limbic *adj.* limbica.
limbo[1] *n.* (*religion*) limbo.
limbo[2] *n.* (*dance*) limbo.
Limburg *n.* (*Dutch or Belgian province*) Limburg.
limburger *n.* ceso limburgan.
Limburgian *adj.* limburgan.
Limburgish *adj.* limburgan.
lime[1] *n.* (*substance*) calce.
lime[2] *adj.* (*chartreuse colour*) tilia. • *n.* (*linden tree*) tilia.
lime[3] *n.* (*tree, citrus fruit*) lim.
limelight *n.* (*literal*) lampa de calce.
limerick *n.* limeric.
limescale *n.* tartar.
limestone *n.* calcario.
limit *v.* limita. • *n.* limita, frontera.
limitation *n.* limita.
limitless *adj.* sin limita.
limo *n.* limusin.
limousine *n.* limusin.
limp[1] *v.* & *n.* (*when walking*) coxea.
limp[2] *adj.* (*slack*) flasida.
limper *n.* coxeor.
limpet *n.* lapa.
limpid *adj.* clar.
limpkin *n.* (*bird*) aramo.
linchpin *n.* cavil de rota.
linden *n.* tilia.
lindy *adj.* & *n.* (*dance, music*) suing.
line[1] *n.* linia; (*thread*) filo; (*of people, things*) filo; (*dialogue*) replica. • *v.* (*mark lines on*) lini. **assembly line** cadena de construi. **draw the line** pone un limita. **get in line** pone se en filo. **line of business** spesie de comersia. **line of descent** linia de familia. **line of trade** spesie de comersia. **line up** (*form a line*) fili; (*align*) alinia.
line[2] *v.* (*add layer*) fore, strati interna.
lineage *n.* linia de familia.
lineal *adj.* linial.
linear *adj.* linial.
linear mapping *n.* mapa linial.
linear momentum *n.* momento linial.
linefeed *n.* (*character*) fini de linia.
linen *n.* stofa de lino.
line-up *n.* filo.
-ling *suff.* (*diminutive*) -eta.
linga *n.* (*Hinduism*) linga.
lingam *n.* (*Hinduism*) linga.
linger *v.* persiste, permane.
lingerie *n.* delicatas.
lingering *adj.* persistente; lenta.
lingonberry *n.* vasinia de montania.
Lingua Franca Nova *adj.* elefen. • *n.* lingua franca nova, elefen.
lingual *adj.* lingual.
linguine *n.* (*food*) linguine.
linguist *n.* linguiste.
linguistic *adj.* lingual.
linguistics *n.* linguistica.
liniment *n.* balsam.
lining *n.* fore, strato interna.
link *v.* lia. • *n.* lia; (*of chain*) anelo.
linkage *n.* lia.
linking verb *n.* verbo liante.
linnet *n.* lineta.
lino *n.* linolio.
linoleum *n.* linolio.
linseed *n.* (*plant*) lino; seme de lino. **treated with linseed** linosa.
linseed oil *n.* olio de lino.
lint *n.* peluxeta.
lintel *n.* lintel.
lion *n.* leon.
lion cub *n.* leoneta.
lioness *n.* leon fema.
lionize *v.* leoni.
lip *n.* labio. **with sealed lips** con labios selida.
lip balm *n.* balsam de labio.
lipid *adj.* & *n.* (*chemistry*) lipido.
lipo- *pref.* (*fat*) lipo-.
lipoprotein *n.* lipoprotena.
liposuction *n.* liposuca.
lip-reading *n.* leje de labios.
lip salve *n.* balsam de labio.
lipstick *n.* pintilabio.
lipsync *n.* canta sincrona.
lipsyncher *n.* cantor sincrona.
liquefy *v.* licuidi.
liqueur *n.* licor.
liquid *adj.* & *n.* (*including assets*) licuida.
liquidate *v.* licuidi.
liquidation *n.* licuidi.
liquidator *n.* licuidor.
liquid crystal *n.* cristal licuida.
liquid-crystal display *n.* scermo de cristal licuida.
liquidity *n.* licuidia.
liquidize *v.* licuidi.
liquidizer *n.* licuidador.
liquify *v.* licuidi.
liquor *n.* distilada.
liquorice *n.* liciris.
lira *n.* (*currency*) lira.
Lisbon *n.* Lisboa.
lisp *v.* & *n.* zezea.
list *v.* & *n.* lista.
listen *v.* escuta. **listen back to** (*a recording*) reescuta. **listen to music** escuta musica.
listener *n.* escutor.
listless *adj.* letarjiosa.
listlessness *n.* letarjia.
lit *adj.* luminada.
litany *n.* litania.
liter (US). See *litre*.
literacy *n.* alfabetisme.

literal *adj.* leteral.
literary *adj.* leteratural.
literary work *n.* obra, peso.
literate *adj.* alfabetiste.
literature *n.* leteratur.
-lith *suff.* (*stone*) -lito.
lithe *adj.* ajil.
lithium *n.* litio.
litho- *pref.* (*stone*) lito-.
lithograph *v.* & *n.* litografi.
lithography *n.* litografia.
lithology *n.* litolojia.
lithosphere *n.* litosfera.
lithotroph *n.* litotrof.
lithotrophia *n.* litotrofia.
lithotrophic *adj.* (*biology*) litotrof.
Lithuania *n.* Lietuva.
Lithuanian *adj.* & *n.* lietuvisce.
Lithuanian Jew *n.* litvac.
litigant *n.* litigor.
litigate *v.* litiga.
litigation *n.* litiga.
litigator *n.* litigor.
litigious *adj.* litigosa.
litmus paper *n.* paper de pH.
litotes *n.* (*rhetoric*) litote.
litre (US **liter**) *n.* (*unit of capacity*) litre.
litter *n.* (*rubbish*) dejetada; (*offspring*) bebes, projenia; (*sedan chair*) seja portada. • *v.* sperde.
litter bin *n.* baldon.
litterbug *n.* sperdor de dejetadas.
litterlout *n.* sperdor de dejetadas.
little *adj.* peti. • *det.* & *pron.* (*not much*) poca. **a little** alga, un peseta de; pico. **a little less** alga min. **a little more** alga plu. **as little as possible** tan poca como posible. **little by little** pico e pico. **little less than** poca min ca. **little more than** poca plu ca.
little auk *n.* alco.
little finger *n.* dito peti.
little-known *adj.* poca conoseda, oscur.
little one *n.* peti; (*term of endearment*) fieta.
littoral *adj.* costal.
liturgical *adj.* liturjial.
liturgy *n.* liturjia.
Litvak *adj.* & *n.* litvac.
livability (US). See *liveability*.
livable (US). See *liveable*.
live[1] *v.* (*be alive*) vive; (*dwell*) abita. **live again** revive. **live in** abita.
live[2] *adj.* (*alive*) vivente; (*machine*) comutada; (*broadcast*) direta; (*music*) en conserta. **go live** (*machine*) comuta.
liveability *n.* abitablia.
liveable *adj.* abitable.
lived-in *adj.* abitada.
livelihood *n.* modo de susta.
liveliness *n.* vivosia.
lively *adj.* vivosa.
live oak *n.* cuerco sempreverde.
liver *n.* figato.
liverleaf *n.* epatica.
livermorium *n.* (*element*) livermorio.
liverwort *n.* epatica.
liverwurst *n.* salsix de figato.
livery *n.* uniforma.
livestock *n.* bestias.
livid *adj.* furiosa; (*colour*) purpur.
lividity *n.* purpuria.
living *adj.* vivente. • *n.* modo de susta.
living room *n.* salon.
living will *n.* atesta vival.
lizard *n.* lezardo.
llama *n.* (*animal*) liama.
load *v.* carga. • *n.* carga. **a load of** un monton de, un peson de. **loads of** un monton de, un peson de.
loaf *n.* pan.
loam *n.* (*soil*) lom.
loamy *adj.* lomosa.
loan *v.* & *n.* presta.
loanshark *n.* usuror.
loan translation *n.* tradui prestada.
loathe *v.* odia.
loathsome *adj.* despetable, odiable, vil.
lob *v.* lansa alta.
lobby *n.* (*room*) atrio; (*lobbyists*) promovores. **lobby for** promove.
lobbyist *n.* promovor.
lobe *n.* lobe.
lobed *adj.* lobosa.
lobotomy *n.* lobotomia.
lobster *n.* omaro.
local *adj.* local; (*train*) lenta. **locals** popla local.
locale *n.* ambiente, loca.
localism *n.* localisme.
localization *n.* locali.
localize *v.* locali.
locate *v.* loca, situa.
location *n.* loca.
locative *adj.* & *n.* (*grammar*) locativa.
lock[1] *v.* securi; (*with key*) clavi; (*database*) semafori. • *n.* (*door*) securador; (*waterway*) clusa.
lock[2] *n.* (*hair*) mexa.
lockable *adj.* securable.
locker *n.* caxa secur.
locket *n.* pendente de recorda.
lockjaw *n.* (*medical*) tetano.
locksmith *n.* clavor.
lockup *adj.* securable. • *n.* prison.
locomotion *n.* move.
locomotive *n.* locomotiva.
locomotory *adj.* de move.
locust *n.* locusta, locusta xamante; (*tree*) robinia.

lode *n.* (*geology*) vena.
loden *n.* (*fabric*) loden.
lodge *v.* casi tempora; (*jam*) fisa.
lodger *n.* luor, abitor luante.
loess *n.* (*soil*) loes.
loft *n.* suteto.
lofty *adj.* alta.
log *n.* jornal de viaja; (*software*) jornal de ativia, rejistra; arcivo. • *v.* arcivi; rejistra. **log in** (*software*) entra, autentici, identifia se. **log out** retira, desautentici, desidentifia se.
logarithm *n.* logaritmo.
logarithmic *adj.* logaritmal.
logbook *n.* jornal de viaja.
log cabin *n.* cabana de troncos.
loggia *n.* lojia.
logging *n.* (*industry*) esplota de forestas.
logic *n.* lojica.
logical *adj.* lojical.
logicality *n.* lojicalia.
logistical *adj.* lojistical.
logistics *n.* lojistica.
logjam *n.* conjesta de troncos; (*metaphor*) nonprogresa.
logo[1] *n.* logo.
logo-[2] *pref.* (*words*) logo-.
logophile *n.* logofilica.
logophilia *n.* logofilia.
logophilic *adj.* logofilica.
logorrhoea (US **logorrhea**) *n.* parlamania.
logrunner *n.* (*bird*) ortonis.
Logudorese *adj.* & *n.* (*person*, *language*) logudores.
Logudoro *n.* (*Sardinian region*) Logudoro.
-logy *suff.* (*study*) -lojia.
loin *n.* lombo. **loins** lombo.
loincloth *n.* covreseso.
loiter *v.* espeta furtiva; (*amble*) pigri.
lolita *n.* seduor, tisor.
lollipop *n.* suceta.
lolly *n.* suceta.
Lombard *adj.* & *n.* (*of Lombardy*) lombard; (*Germanic tribe*) langobarda.
Lombardic *adj.* (*person*, *language*) langobarda.
Lombardy *n.* (*Italian region*) Lombardia.
lo mein *n.* (*food*) lomen.
lone *adj.* solitar.
loneliness *n.* solitaria.
lonely *adj.* solitar.
loner *n.* solitar.
lonesome *adj.* solitar.
long[1] *adj.* & *adv.* longa. **as long as** (*provided*) si; (*while*) tra cuando. **for a long time** longa, per tempo longa, tra tempo longa. **for a long way** longa. **long ago** a multe tempo ante aora, a multe tempo a ante, en la pasada distante. **long live the king** vive la re. **no longer** no plu. **two metres long** con du metres de longia.
long[2] *v.* (*for*) anela.
longboat *n.* barco longa, barco vicing.
longbow *n.* arco longa.
long-distance running *n.* core de distantia longa.
long-distance skiing *n.* sci de distantia longa.
longevity *n.* eda grande.
long exposure *n.* (*photography*) esposa lenta.
longfin tuna *n.* tun blanca.
longhouse *n.* casa longa.
longing *n.* anela. **longing for home** anela de casa.
Long Island *n.* Isola Longa.
longitude *n.* lonjitude.
long jump *n.* salta longa.
long-jumper *n.* saltor longa.
long-lasting *adj.* durante.
long overdue *adj.* multe tarda.
longship *n.* barco vicing.
longshoreman *n.* docor.
long shot *n.* foto distante; (*something unlikely*) nonprobable.
long-sighted *adj.* iperope, presbiope.
long-sightedness *n.* iperopia, presbiopia.
longstanding *adj.* de tempo longa.
longsword *n.* spadon.
long-tailed tit *n.* (*bird*) ejitalido.
long-term *adj.* permanente.
long-term memory *n.* memoria de dura longa.
loo *n.* vason; (*room*) saleta privata.
loofah *n.* (*plant*, *sponge*) lufa.
look *v.* regarda; (*seem*) pare; (*have a certain appearance*) aspeta. • *n.* regarda; pare; aspeta. • *interj.* vide. **look after** atende; (*children*) cangari. **look again** reregarda. **look at** regarda. **look away** regarda a via, turna sua regarda a via. **look back** retrospeta. **look down** basi sua regarda, regarda a su. **look down on** despeta, finje superioria. **look down one's nose at** finje superioria. **look for** xerca. **look forward to** espeta zelosa. **look me in the eye** regarda mea oios. **look out** atende. **look over** esamina, supravide. **look up** leva sua regarda, regarda a supra; (*search for*) xerca.
lookalike *adj.* & *n.* jemelin.
looking *adj.* regardante. **looking back** en retrospeta.
lookout *n.* (*person*) vijilor; (*place*) tore de vijila. **keep a lookout** es vijilante.
loom[1] *n.* (*machine*) texador.
loom[2] *v.* (*threaten*) menasa. **loom up** emerji.
loon *n.* gavia.
loony *n.* fol.
loop *n.* (*material*) anelo; (*cycle*) sicle. • *v.* aneli; sicli.
looper *n.* eruga de jeometrido.

loophole *n.* fesur.
looping *adj.* siclinte, sicle.
loopy *adj.* bobo.
loose *adj.* (*not fixed*) nonfisada; (*unsafe*) nonsecur; (*baggy*) laxe.
loosen *v.* laxi.
looseness *n.* laxia.
loot *n.* benes furada.
looter *n.* furor acasiste.
lop *v.* corti.
lope *v.* bondi.
lophophore *n.* (*biology*) lofofora.
lophotrochozoa *n.* (*organisms*) lofotrocozones.
lophotrochozoon *n.* (*organism*) lofotrocozon.
lopper *n.* desramador.
lopsided *adj.* apoiada.
loquacious *adj.* parlosa.
lord *n.* (*noble*) baron; (*gentleman*) senior; (*master*) padron; (*religious*) Senior. **lord it over** es tirano a.
lordship *n.* senioria.
lore *n.* sabes; folclor.
loricifer *n.* (*organism*) lorisifero.
lorikeet *n.* (*bird*) lori.
loris *n.* (*primate*) loris.
lorry *n.* camion. **articulated lorry** camion sesionida.
lorry driver *n.* camionor.
lory *n.* lori.
lose *v.* perde. **lose one's grip on** desteni. **lose track of** perde trasa de.
loser *n.* perdor.
loss *n.* perde. **loss of consciousness** perde de consensia.
lossless *adj.* (*compression*) nonperdente.
lossy *adj.* (*compression*) perdente.
lost *adj.* perdeda. **lost at sea** perdeda a mar.
lot *n.* fortuna; (*plot of land*) peso. **a lot of** un monton de, un peson de. **draw lots** estrae fortunas. **lots of** un monton de, un peson de.
lothario *n.* romeo, xasafem, om promiscua.
lotion *n.* losion, unjente, crema.
lottery *n.* loto.
lotto *n.* loto.
lotus *n.* (*plant*) nelumbo.
loud *adj.* forte; (*garish*) xiliante. **out loud** a vose, parlante.
loudhailer *n.* megafon.
loudmouth *n.* vantor.
loudspeaker *n.* parlador.
Louisiana *n.* (*US state*) Louisiana.
lounge *v.* reposa, pigri. • *n.* salon.
lounger *n.* (*chair*) seja reclinante.
loupe *n.* (*magnifier*) lupa.
louse *n.* (*insect*) piolio.
lousy *adj.* misera.
lout *n.* bruta.
loutish *adj.* bruta.
louvre (US **louver**) *n.* lamina.
lovable (US). See *loveable*.
lovableness (US). See *loveableness*.
love *v.* ama; (*relish*) saborea. • *n.* ama. **fall in love** cade en ama, comensa ama, deveni enamada. **in love** enamada. **love of movies** sinemafilia. **love of words** logofilia. **make love** fa la ama, fa la seso.
loveable *adj.* amable.
loveableness *n.* amablia.
love affair *n.* caso de ama, relata de ama.
love bite *n.* suceta.
loved *adj.* amada. **loved one** amada.
loveliness *n.* belia.
lovelorn *adj.* malada de ama.
lovely *adj.* bela.
lovemaking *n.* fa de ama, fa de seso, seso, copula.
lover *n.* amor, amada; (*of art, music, food, etc.*) saboreor. **lover of movies** sinemafilica. **lover of words** logofilica.
lovesick *adj.* malada de ama.
lovesickness *n.* maladia de ama.
low[1] *adj.* (*position, unkind*) basa. **low in tar** basa de catran.
low[2] *v.* (*moo*) mui.
lowbrow *adj.* nonsofisticada.
low-cut *adj.* escotada.
lowdown *n.* informa.
lower *adj.* basa, plu basa. • *v.* basi. **lower than** (*location, quantity, standard*) su.
lower back *n.* lombo.
lowercase *adj.* minor. • *v.* (*convert to lowercase*) minori.
lowercase letter *n.* letera minor.
lower class *n.* clase basa. • *adj.* de clase basa.
lower course *n.* (*river*) curso basa.
lower garment *n.* veste basa.
Lower House *n.* Salon Basa.
lower layer *n.* sustrato.
lower leg *n.* gama basa.
lower part *n.* basa.
Low German *adj.* & *n.* (*language*) platdeutx.
lowland *n.* tereno basa.
lowlife *n.* bruta.
lowness *n.* basia.
low-pressure area *n.* depresa climal, zona de presa basa.
low relief *n.* releva basa.
Low Saxon *adj.* & *n.* platdeutx.
low table *n.* table basa.
low-tar *adj.* (*cigarette*) basa de catran.
low tech *n.* tecnolojia basa.
low tide *n.* marea basa.
lox *n.* salmon fumida.
loyal *adj.* fidosa.
loyalist *n.* fidiste.

loyalty *n.* fida.
lozenge *n.* (*shape*) rombo; (*pill*) pil rombo.
LSD *n.* (*drug*) lsd.
L-shaped *adj.* con forma de L.
LTM *n.* (*long-term memory*) memoria de dura longa.
luau *n.* (*Hawaiian feast*) luau.
lube *v.* lubrica. ● *n.* lubricante.
lubricant *n.* lubricante.
lubricate *v.* lubrica.
lubrication *n.* lubrica.
lubricious *adj.* lasiva.
lucid *adj.* clar; (*aware*) consensa; (*bright*) briliante, luminosa.
lucidity *n.* claria; consensia; brilia.
Lucifer *n.* diablo.
lucite *n.* vitro acrilica.
luck *n.* fortuna; acaso. **bad luck** mal fortuna. **good luck** bon fortuna.
lucky *adj.* fortunosa.
lucky plant *n.* crasula.
lucrative *adj.* profitosa.
lucre *n.* mone susia.
ludicrous *adj.* asurda, riable, burlable.
ludicrousness *n.* asurdia.
ludo *n.* (*game*) patxisi.
luffa *n.* lufa.
lug *v.* tira.
Luganda *adj.* & *n.* luganda.
luge *n.* (*toboggan*) luje. ● *v.* luji.
luggage *n.* bagaje.
luggage room *n.* sala de bagaje.
lugubrious *adj.* sombre.
lukewarm *adj.* tepida.
lull *v.* calmi.
lullaby *n.* canta de cuna.
lumbago *n.* (*medical*) lumbago.
lumbar *adj.* lombal.
lumbar puncture *n.* perfora lombal.
lumber *n.* lenio.
lumberjack *n.* lenior.
lumen *n.* (*unit of light*) lumen.
luminary *n.* inspiror.
luminous *adj.* luminosa.
lummox *n.* torpe.
lump *n.* (*bulge*) bulto; (*shapeless piece*) masa, maseta. **form lumps** masi.
lumpy *adj.* bultosa.
lunacy *n.* dementia.
lunar *adj.* lunal.
lunatic *n.* demente.
lunatic asylum *n.* dementeria.
lunch *n.* come media.
lunch box *n.* caxa de come.
luncheon *n.* come media.
lunchroom *n.* comeria.
lung *n.* pulmon.
lunge *v.* & *n.* salta.
lungfish *n.* dipno.
lupin *n.* (*plant*) lupin.
lupus[1] *n.* (*medical*) lupus.
Lupus[2] *n.* (*constellation*) la Lupo.
lurch *v.* bambola.
lure *v.* tenta. ● *n.* (*luring*) tenta; (*bait*) tentante.
lurid *adj.* (*shining*) briliante; (*sensational*) supradramosa.
lurk *v.* asconde, spia; espeta furtiva.
lurker *n.* furtiva.
lurking *adj.* ascondeda.
luscious *adj.* deletosa.
lush *adj.* lusosa.
lust *v.* desira sesal. ● *n.* libido, desira sesal.
luster (US). See *lustre.*
lustful *adj.* lasiva, libidosa.
lustre (US **luster**) *n.* brilieta.
lustrous *adj.* briliante.
lusty *adj.* enerjiosa.
lute *n.* luto.
lutefisk *n.* (*food*) lutefisc.
lute player *n.* lutiste.
lutetium *n.* (*element*) lutesio.
Lutheran *adj.* & *n.* luteran.
Lutheranism *n.* (*Christianity*) luteranisme.
lutist *n.* lutiste.
lux *n.* (*unit of light*) lux.
Luxembourg *n.* Luxemburg.
Luxembourgeois *adj.* & *n.* letseburges.
Luxembourger *n.* luxemburges.
Luxembourgish *adj.* luxemburges.
Luxemburgish *adj.* & *n.* letseburges.
luxuriant *adj.* lusosa.
luxurious *adj.* lusosa.
luxury *n.* (*item*) luso; (*state*) lusosia.
Luzon *n.* (*island*) Luzon.
Luzon Strait *n.* Streta Luzon.
lycanthrope *n.* om-lupo.
lycanthropy *n.* om-lupia.
lycee *n.* liseo.
lyceum *n.* liseo.
lychee *n.* (*tree, fruit*) litxi.
lycra *n.* elastan. ● *adj.* de elastan.
Lydia *n.* Lidia.
lye *n.* alcalin corodente, idrosido de potasio, idrosido de sodio.
lymph *n.* limfa.
lymphatic *adj.* limfal.
lymph node *n.* noda limfal; (*swollen*) bubon.
lympho- *pref.* (*lymph*) limfo-.
lymphoblast *n.* (*biology*) limfoblasto.
lymphocyte *n.* limfosite.
lymphocytic *adj.* limfosital.
lymphoid *adj.* limfoide.
lymphoma *n.* limfoma.
lymphopoiesis *n.* (*biology*) limfopoiese.
lynch *v.* linxa.
lynx *n.* lince; (*constellation*) la Lince.
Lyra *n.* (*constellation*) la Lira.
lyre *n.* lira.

lyrebird *n.* menur.
lyric *adj.* lirica.
lyrical *adj.* lirica.
lyricist *n.* parolor.
lyrics *n.* testo.
-lysis *suff.* (*decomposition*) -lise.
lysosome *n.* (*biology*) lisosoma.
-lytic *suff.* -lisica.

M

ma'am *n.* (*form of address*) seniora; (*gender-neutral*) sri.
Maasai *adj.* & *n.* masai.
mac *n.* jacon de pluve.
macabre *adj.* macabre.
macadam *n.* asfalto.
macadamia *n.* (*tree*) macadamia.
Macanese *adj.* & *n.* macau.
Macao *n.* Macau.
macaque *n.* macaca.
macaroni *n.* macaroni.
macaroon *n.* macaron.
Macau *n.* Macau.
macaw *n.* ara.
mace[1] *n.* (*weapon*) rompetesta.
mace[2] *n.* (*spice*) masis.
Macedonia *n.* Macedonia.
Macedonian *adj.* macedonsce.
macerate *v.* empapa.
maceration *n.* empapa.
machete *n.* (*knife*) matxete.
machination *n.* conspira.
machine *n.* macina.
machine gun *n.* mitraliador.
machine gunner *n.* mitralior.
machinery *n.* macinas.
machine translation system *n.* traduador.
machinist *n.* maciniste.
machismo *n.* masia.
macho *adj.* maxo, masiosa.
macintosh *n.* jacon de pluve.
mackerel *n.* macero.
macrame *n.* (*art*) macrame.
macro[1] *n.* (*software*) macro.
macro-[2] *pref.* (*large*) macro-.
macrocephalic *adj.* macrosefalica.
macrocephalous *adj.* macrosefalica.
macrocephaly *n.* (*medical*) macrosefalia.
macrocosm *n.* macrocosmo.
macro lens *adj.* lente macro.
macron *n.* sinieta longa.
macrophage *n.* (*biology*) macrofago.
macro photography *n.* fotografia prosima.
macroscopic *adj.* vidable.
macro zoom lens *n.* lente macro de zuma.
macula *n.* macula.
macula lutea *n.* (*anatomy*) macula.
macular *adj.* macula l.
mad *adj.* (*insane*) demente; (*angry*) coler. **drive mad** dementi. **go mad** dementi.
Madagascar *n.* Madagasicara.
madam *n.* seniora; (*brothelkeeper*) bordelor.
madcap *adj.* bizara, fol.
madden *v.* coleri; dementi.
madder *n.* (*plant, pigment*) rubia.
Madeira *n.* (*island*) Madera.
Madeira Islands *n.* Isolas Madera.
madeleine *n.* (*cake*) madalena.
madhouse *n.* dementeria.
madman *n.* demente.
madness *n.* dementia, folia.
madonna *n.* madona.
madras *n.* (*fabric*) madras.
madrigal *n.* (*music*) madrigal.
madwoman *n.* demente.
maelstrom *n.* vortis.
maestro *n.* mestre.
mafia *n.* mafia.
mafioso *n.* mafior.
magazine *n.* jornal, revista; (*gun*) cargador.
magdalen *n.* prostituida pasada.
mage *n.* majo.
Magellan, Strait of *n.* Streta Magallanes.
Magellanic plover *n.* pluvial de Magalan.
magenta *adj.* & *n.* (*colour*) majenta.
maggot *n.* larva de mosca.
magi *n.* majos.
magic *n.* majia. • *adj.* (*pertaining to magic*) majial; (*full of magic, operating by magic*) majiosa.
magical *adj.* majiosa.
magician *n.* majiste.
magic trick *n.* truco de majia.
magic wand *n.* basto majial.
magistrate *n.* judor local; (*civil law*) judor sivil.
magma *n.* (*geology*) magma.
magmatic *adj.* magmal.
magnanimity *n.* jenerosia.
magnanimous *adj.* jenerosa, bonvolente.
magnate *n.* maniate.
magnesia *n.* osido de magnesio.
magnesium *n.* magnesio.
magnesium oxide *n.* osido de magnesio.
magnesium sulphate (US **sulfate**) *n.* sulfato de magnesio.
magnet *n.* magnete.
magnetic *adj.* magnetal.
magnetic flux density *n.* indui magnetal.
magnetic induction *n.* indui magnetal.
magnetism *n.* magnetia.
magnetization *n.* magneti.
magnetize *v.* magneti.
magnetometer *n.* magnetometre.
magnetometry *n.* magnetometria.
magnification *n.* grandi.
magnificence *n.* gloria.
magnificent *adj.* gloriosa, merveliosa.
magnifier *n.* lupa, lente de grandi.

magnify *v.* grandi.
magnifying glass *n.* lupa, lente de grandi.
magnitude *n.* cuantia; (*astronomy*) cuantia de brilia.
magnolia *n.* magnolia.
magnum opus *n.* obra mestral.
magpie *n.* (*bird*) piga. **azure-winged magpie** piga sian.
magus *n.* majo.
maharajah *n.* (*Indian prince*) maharaja.
maharani *n.* (*Indian princess*) maharani.
maharishi *n.* (*Hinduism*) maharixi.
mahatma *n.* (*holy person*) mahatma.
Mahayana *adj.* (*Buddhism*) mahaiana.
mahi-mahi *n.* mahimahi.
mahjong *n.* (*game*) madjong.
mahogany *n.* (*tree, wood*) mogano. • *adj.* de mogano.
Mahoran *adj.* & *n.* mahores.
Mahore *n.* (*island*) Mahore.
maiasaurus *n.* (*dinosaur*) maiasauro.
maid *n.* servor de casa. **maid of honour** dama de onora.
maiden *n.* fem joven; virjin.
maidenhead *n.* (*anatomy*) imen.
maiden name *n.* nom ante sposi, nom orijinal.
mail[1] *v.* (*letter, parcel*) posta. • *n.* posta. **airmail** posta airal, airoposta.
mail[2] *n.* (*armour*) malie.
mailbag *n.* saco de posta.
mailbox *n.* caxa de posta.
mailman *n.* postor.
mailsack *n.* saco de posta.
mail slot *n.* buco de posta.
maim *v.* feri.
main *adj.* xef. • *n.* mar alta.
main blow *n.* colpa xef.
main clause *n.* proposa major.
Maine *n.* (*US state*) Maine. **Gulf of Maine** Golfo Maine.
mainframe computer *n.* computador sentral.
mainland *n.* continente; tera xef.
mainline *n.* ferovia xef. • *v.* injeta.
mainly *adv.* xef.
mainmast *n.* masto xef.
main road *n.* via xef.
mainsail *n.* vela xef.
mainstream *n.* corente xef, corente dominante. • *adj.* dominante.
maintain *v.* (*preserve*) manteni; (*assert*) declara.
maintenance *n.* manteni.
maintenance man *n.* mantenor.
maintenance woman *n.* mantenor.
main theme *n.* tema xef.
Maithil *adj.* & *n.* (*person, language*) maitili.
Maithili *adj.* & *n.* (*person, language*) maitili.
maître d' *n.* servor xef.
maize *n.* mais.
majestic *adj.* alta, gloriosa, merveliosa.
majesty *n.* altia, gloria. **your majesty** altia.
major *adj.* major; (*officer*) major.
majority *n.* majoria. **the majority of** la plu de.
major scale *n.* (*music*) scala major.
majuscule *n.* letera major.
Makassar Strait *n.* Streta Makasar.
make *v.* crea, fabrica; (*dinner, tea, coffee, beer*) prepara; (*bed*) ordina; (*something happen*) fa ce. **make for** vade en dirije a. **make love** fa la ama, fa la seso. **make one's way** vade sur sua via. **make sure** serti. **make up** (*relationship*) reconsilia; (*cosmetics*) macia. **make war** gera.
maker *n.* fabricor.
makeshift *adj.* tempora.
makeup *n.* composa; (*cosmetics*) macia.
makeup artist *n.* maciste.
makework *n.* labora nonusosa.
Malacca, Strait of *n.* Streta Malaka.
malachite *n.* (*mineral*) malacita.
maladaptation *n.* malajusta.
maladapted *adj.* malajustada.
maladaptive *adj.* malajustada.
maladjusted *adj.* malajustada.
maladjustment *n.* malajusta.
maladroit *adj.* torpe.
malady *n.* maladia.
Malagasy *adj.* & *n.* malagasi.
malaise *n.* descomforta.
malapropism *n.* parola erante.
malaria *n.* malaria.
Malawi *n.* Malaui. **Lake Malawi** Lago Malaui.
Malawian *adj.* & *n.* malaui.
Malay *adj.* & *n.* (*person, language*) melaiu.
Malayalam *adj.* & *n.* (*person, language*) malaialam.
Malaysia *n.* Malaisia.
Malaysian *adj.* & *n.* malaisian.
malcontent *adj.* & *n.* noncontente.
Maldives *n.* Divehi, Maldives.
Maldivian *adj.* & *n.* divehi.
male *adj.* & *n.* mas.
malediction *n.* maldise.
malefactor *n.* criminor.
maleness *n.* masia, omia.
malevolence *n.* malvole.
malevolent *adj.* malvolente.
malfeasant *n.* vil.
malformation *n.* malformi.
malformed *adj.* malformida.
malfunction *v.* malfunsiona, malopera, rompe. • *n.* malfunsiona, malopera, rompe.
Mali *n.* Mali.
Malian *adj.* & *n.* malian.

malice *n.* malvole.
malicious *adj.* malvolente.
maliciousness *n.* malvole.
malign *adj.* malvolente.
malignance *n.* malvole.
malignancy *n.* malvole; canserosia.
malignant *adj.* malvolente; canserosa.
malignity *n.* enemia.
malinger *v.* finje un maladia.
malingerer *n.* finjor de maladia.
mall *n.* bolevar de pasea.
mallard *n.* pato real.
malleable *adj.* martelable.
mallet *n.* martel, martel mol; (*for percussion instrument*) marteleta.
malleus *n.* martel.
mallow *n.* (*plant*) malva.
malnourished *adj.* malnurida.
malnutrition *n.* malnuri.
malodorous *adj.* malodorosa.
malpractice *n.* malpratica.
malt *n.* malta. • *v.* malti.
Malta *n.* Malta.
maltase *n.* (*enzyme*) maltase.
Maltese *adj.* & *n.* malti.
maltose *n.* (*sugar*) maltosa.
Maluku *n.* Maluku.
Maluku Islands *n.* Isolas Maluku.
malware *n.* programes vil.
mama *n.* (*mother*) mama.
mambo *n.* (*dance*) mambo.
mammal *n.* mamal.
mammary *adj.* mamelal.
mammary gland *n.* mamela.
mammillary body *n.* corpo mamelin.
mammogram *n.* mamogram.
mammograph *n.* mamograf. • *v.* mamografi.
mammography *n.* mamografia.
mammon *n.* ricia.
mammoth *n.* mamute.
man *n.* om. **man in the street** person comun, cualcun. **man of the house** om de casa.
manacle *n.* securipolso.
manage *v.* maneja, dirije. **manage to** susede. **manage without** maneja sin.
manageability *n.* manejablia.
manageable *adj.* manejable.
management *n.* dirije; (*directors*) dirijores.
management fee *n.* paia per maneja.
manager *n.* manejor, dirijor.
managerial *adj.* dirijal.
manakin *n.* (*bird*) manacin.
manatee *n.* manati.
mancala *n.* (*game*) mancala.
Manchu *adj.* mandju.
Manchuria *n.* (*Chinese region*) Mandju.
mandala *n.* (*Buddhism*, *Hinduism*) mandala.
mandarin[1] *n.* (*fruit*) mandarina; (*tree*) mandarino.
mandarin[2] *n.* (*official*) mandarin.
Mandarin Chinese *adj.* & *n.* (*language*) putong.
mandarine *n.* (*fruit*) mandarina; (*tree*) mandarino.
mandate *n.* autoria.
mandatory *adj.* obligante.
Mandeb Strait *n.* Streta Mandeb.
mandible *n.* mandibula.
Mandinka *adj.* & *n.* (*person*, *language*) mandinca.
mandola *n.* (*musical instrument*) mandola.
mandolin *n.* (*musical instrument*) mandolin.
mandrake *n.* (*plant*) mandragora.
mandrill *n.* (*monkey*) mandril.
mane *n.* crinera.
maneuver (US). See *manoeuvre*.
manga *n.* (*cartoon*) manga.
manganese *n.* (*element*) manganes.
mange *n.* acariase.
manger *n.* portafeno.
mangey *adj.* acariasica.
mangle *n.* presador. • *v.* mutila.
mango *n.* mango.
mangrove *n.* rizofora.
mangy *adj.* acariasica.
manhandle *v.* (*heavy object*) move laborosa; (*jostle*) puxa.
manhole *n.* buco de cloaca.
manhood *n.* omia.
man-hour *n.* ora de labora.
manhunt *n.* xerca.
Mani *n.* (*prophet*) Mani.
mania *n.* mania. • *suff.* -mania.
maniac *n.* manica.
maniacal *adj.* manica.
manic *adj.* manica. • *suff.* -manica.
manichaean (US **manichean**) *adj.* & *n.* maniste.
manichaeanism (US **manicheanism**) *n.* manisme.
manicure *n.* manicura.
manicurist *n.* manicuror.
manifest *v.* apare, revela. • *adj.* evidente, mostrada. • *n.* (*ship's*) lista de contenidas.
manifestation *n.* mostra, revela.
manifesto *n.* declara.
manifold *n.* (*in mathematics*) varia.
manioc *n.* manioca.
manipulate *v.* manipula.
manipulation *n.* manipula.
manipulator *n.* manipulor.
Manitoba *n.* (*Canadian province*) Manitoba.
manitou *n.* (*life force*) manitu.
mankind *n.* umanas.
manlike *adj.* omin.
manmade *adj.* artifis, fabricada.

manna *n.* (*miracle food*) mana.
Mannar, Gulf of *n.* Golfo Mannar.
manned *adj.* abitada.
mannequin *n.* (*dummy, fashion model*) manicin.
manner *n.* manera, metodo, modo.
mannerism *n.* manera.
manners *n.* cortesia.
mannikin *n.* (*bird*) lonxura.
mannish *adj.* omin.
manoeuvre (US **maneuver**) *v.* & *n.* manobra.
manometer *n.* (*pressure-measuring tool*) manometre.
manorialism *n.* (*feudal*) seniorisme.
manpower *n.* persones disponable.
mansion *n.* cason.
manslaughter *v.* & *n.* mata sin intende.
mantel *n.* scafal.
mantelpiece *n.* scafal, scafal de ximine.
manticore *n.* (*mythology*) manticor.
mantis *n.* (*insect*) mantis.
mantle *n.* (*geology*) litosfera.
mantra *n.* (*meditation*) mantra.
manual *adj.* par mano. • *n.* (*handbook*) manual.
manual exposure *n.* esposa par mano.
manual laborer *n.* laboror par mano.
manual labour *n.* labora par mano.
manual work *n.* labora par mano.
manufacture *v.* & *n.* fabrica.
manufacturer *n.* fabricor.
manufacturing plant *n.* fabriceria.
manumission *n.* libri de sclavia.
manure *n.* sterco.
manuscript *n.* manoscrito.
manwhore *n.* (*insult*) puto.
Manx *adj.* & *n.* manes.
many *det.* & *pron.* multe; (*optional plural pronoun*) multes. **as many as possible** tan multe como posible. **many fewer** multe min. **many more** multe plu. **not many** no multe, poca.
many-sided *adj.* multiladal.
Maoism *n.* (*politics*) maoisme.
Maoist *adj.* maoiste.
Maori *adj.* & *n.* maori.
map *n.* mapa. • *v.* mapa; (*one thing to another*) asosia.
maple *n.* asero.
maple fruit *n.* asera.
maple key *n.* asera.
maple syrup *n.* xirope de asero.
mapmaker *n.* cartografiste.
mapmaking *n.* cartografia.
mapping *n.* mapa; asosia.
mar *v.* manxa.
marabou *n.* (*bird*) marabu.
marabout *n.* (*monk*) marabut.
maraca *n.* (*musical instrument*) maraca.
Maracaibo, Lake *n.* Lago Maracaibo.
Marajó *n.* (*island*) Marajo.
maraschino *n.* (*drink*) marascino.
Marathi *adj.* & *n.* (*person, language*) marati.
marathon *n.* maraton.
marauder *v.* saca. • *n.* sacor.
marble *n.* marmo; (*ball*) bilia. • *adj.* de marmo.
march[1] *v.* marxa. • *n.* marxa.
march[2] *n.* (*land*) marcia.
March[3] *n.* (*month*) marto.
marching band *n.* bande marxante.
marchioness *n.* marcesa.
Mar de Grau *n.* Mar Grau.
mare *n.* cavalo fema.
margarine *n.* margarina.
margarita *n.* (*drink*) margarita.
Margarita Island *n.* Margarita.
marge *n.* margarina.
margin *n.* marjin.
marginal *adj.* marjinal.
marginalization *n.* marjini.
marginalize *v.* marjini.
margrave *n.* marci.
mariachi *n.* (*music*) mariatxi.
Mariana *n.* Mariana.
Marianas *n.* Isolas Mariana.
marigold *n.* calendula; (*genus Tagetes*) tagete.
marihuana *n.* (*plant, drug*) canaba.
marijuana *n.* (*plant, drug*) canaba.
marimba *n.* (*musical instrument*) marimba.
marina *n.* barceria.
marinade *v.* (*in brine*) marini; (*in vinegar*) vinagri.
marinara *n.* (*sauce*) marinara.
marinate *v.* (*in brine*) marini; (*in vinegar*) vinagri.
marine *adj.* maral. • *n.* marinor.
mariner *n.* marinor.
marionette *n.* marioneta.
marionettist *n.* marionetor.
marital *adj.* sposal.
maritime *adj.* maral.
marjoram *n.* (*plant*) majoran.
mark *v.* & *n.* marca.
marker *n.* marcador, indicador.
market *n.* mercato. • *v.* vende, vende a mercato. **go to market** comersiali. **put on the market** comersiali.
marketable *adj.* vendable.
market economy *n.* economia de mercato.
market garden *n.* orto.
marketing *adj.* (*company, expert*) mercatiste.
marketplace *n.* venderia.
market trader *n.* mercator.
marking *n.* marca; (*animals, plants*) manxa.
marksman *n.* fusilor.
marl *n.* (*soil*) marga.

marlin *n.* (*fish*) marlin.
marmalade *n.* marmelada.
Marmara *n.* (*island*) Marmara.
Marmara Sea *n.* Mar Marmara.
marmoset *n.* (*monkey*) uistiti.
marmot *n.* (*rodent*) marmota.
maroon[1] *adj.* (*colour*) bordo.
maroon[2] *v.* encalia, abandona, trapi.
marquee *n.* tenda; (*awning*) baldacin, fronton.
Marquesas Islands *n.* Isolas Marcesas.
marquess *n.* marci.
marquetry *n.* intarsia.
marquis *n.* marci.
marquise *n.* marcesa.
marriage *n.* (*action*) sposi; (*state*) sposia. **by marriage** par sposi.
marriageable *adj.* sposable.
marriage ceremony *n.* rituo de sposi.
marrow *n.* zuca; (*bone*) medula.
marrowbone *n.* oso medulosa.
marry *v.* sposi.
Mars *n.* (*mythology*, *planet*) Marte.
marsh *n.* pantan, pantan arborosa.
marshal *n.* (*officer*) marexal.
Marshallese *adj.* & *n.* majel.
Marshall Islander *n.* majel.
Marshall Islands *n.* Isolas Majel.
marsh calla *n.* cala.
marshland *n.* pantan.
marshmallow *n.* (*plant*) altea; (*confectionery*) nube de zucar.
marshmallow cream *n.* crema de zucar.
marshmallow topping *n.* crema de zucar.
marshy *adj.* pantanosa.
marsupial *adj.* & *n.* marsupial.
marsupium *n.* marsupio.
mart *n.* mercato.
marten *n.* (*animal*) martes.
martial arts *n.* artes militar.
Martian *adj.* & *n.* martan.
martin *n.* (*bird*) martin.
martinet *n.* disiplinor.
martini *n.* (*drink*) martini.
Martiniquan *adj.* & *n.* martinices.
Martinique *n.* (*island*) Martinic.
martyr *n.* martir. • *v.* martiri.
martyrdom *n.* martiria.
marvel *v.* & *n.* mervelia.
marvellous (US **marvelous**) *adj.* merveliosa, eselente.
Marxism *n.* marxisme.
Marxist *n.* marxiste.
Maryland *n.* (*US state*) Maryland.
marzipan *n.* masapan.
Masai *adj.* & *n.* (*person*, *language*) masai.
mascara *n.* negrisil, pintisil.
mascarpone *n.* (*cheese*) mascarpone.
mascot *n.* mascote.
masculine *adj.* masin.
masculinity *n.* masia.
mash *v.* maxa, crase.
mashed peas *n.* gaxa de pisos.
masher *n.* maxador.
mashup *n.* pastix.
mask *n.* masca. • *v.* masci.
masked play *n.* teatral mascida.
masochism *n.* masocisme.
masochist *n.* masociste.
masochistic *adj.* masociste.
mason *n.* petror; (*freemason*) francamason.
masonry *n.* construi de petra; (*freemasonry*) francamasonisme.
masque *n.* teatral mascida.
masquerade party *n.* selebra mascida.
mass[1] *n.* (*lump*, *physics*) masa. **masses** (*populace*) popla. • *adj.* coletiva.
mass[2] *n.* (*religious*) misa.
Massachusetts *n.* (*US state*) Massachusetts.
massacre *v.* & *n.* masacra.
massage *v.* & *n.* masaje.
mass education *n.* educa coletiva.
masseur *n.* masajor.
masseuse *n.* masajor.
mass grave *n.* tomba coletiva.
mass hysteria *n.* isteria coletiva.
massif *n.* (*geology*) masif.
massive *adj.* masosa.
mass media *n.* medias publica.
mass production *n.* produi en serie.
mast *n.* masto.
mast cell *n.* mastosite.
mastectomy *n.* (*surgery*) mastectomia.
master *n.* (*teacher*, *maestro*, *of slaves*) mestre; (*boss*) padron; (*gentleman*) senior; (*historical form of address for a boy*) Senioreto. • *adj.* mestral. • *v.* mestri. **master of ceremonies** mestre de selebras.
masterful *adj.* mestrin.
master key *n.* clave xef.
masterly *adj.* mestrin.
mastermind *n.* (*genius*) jenio; (*of scheme*) scemor. • *v.* scemi.
masterpiece *n.* obra mestral.
master's *n.* (*degree*) mestral, diploma mestral.
masterwork *n.* obra mestral.
mastery *n.* mestria.
masthead *n.* xapo de jornal.
mastic *n.* (*tree*, *resin*) mastica.
masticate *v.* mastica.
mastiff *n.* mastin.
mastocyte *n.* (*biology*) mastosite.
mastodon *n.* mamute.
mastoid *adj.* (*anatomy*) mastoide.
mastoid process *n.* mastoide.
masturbate *v.* masturba.
masturbation *n.* masturba.
mat *n.* tapeto. • *v.* (*tangle*) marania.

matador *n.* mator.
match[1] *v.* (*be equivalent*) coresponde, conforma, egali, acorda; (*sport*) max.
match[2] *n.* (*for lighting fire*) fosfor.
matchbook *n.* libreta de fosfores.
matchbox *n.* caxa de fosfores.
matchless *adj.* sin egal.
matchmaker *n.* ajente de sposi.
matchstick *n.* fosfor.
mate[1] *v.* copula. • *n.* spos; (*pal*) ami.
mate[2] *n.* (*chess*) xacemata.
maté *n.* (*drink*) mate. **yerba maté** erba-de-mate.
material *adj.* material. • *n.* (*matter*) materia; (*supplies*) furnis; (*fabric*) stofa.
materialism *n.* materialisme, consumisme.
materialist *adj.* & *n.* materialiste, consumiste.
materialistic *adj.* materialiste, consumiste.
materialization *n.* materi.
materialize *v.* materi.
material resources *n.* furnis.
material world *n.* mundo consumiste.
maternal *adj.* madral.
maternity *n.* madria. • *adj.* (*leave, dress*) madral.
maternity hospital *n.* ospital de madres.
mathematical *adj.* matematical.
mathematical biology *n.* biolojia matematical.
mathematical chemistry *n.* cimica matematical.
mathematical economy *n.* economia matematical.
mathematical finance *n.* finansia matematical.
mathematical physics *n.* fisica matematical.
mathematician *n.* matematiciste.
mathematics *n.* matematica.
matinee *n.* presenta temprana.
mating *n.* copula.
mating season *n.* periodo corteal.
matriarch *n.* matriarca, madron.
matriarchy *n.* matriarcia.
matricide *n.* (*action*) madriside; (*person*) madrisidor. **commit matricide** madriside.
matriculate *v.* enscrive.
matrilineage *n.* matrilinia.
matrilineal *adj.* matrilinial.
matrimony *n.* sposia.
matrix *n.* (*mathematical*) matris.
matron *n.* dama.
matronym *n.* nom madral.
matryoshka *n.* (*doll*) matrioxca.
matt *adj.* (*dull*) mate.
matte *adj.* (*dull*) mate.
matted *adj.* maraniada.
matter *n.* (*substance*) materia; (*affair*) cosa. • *v.* importa. **it's a matter of** lo es un caso de, lo pertine a. **matter of importance** conserna.
matter-of-fact *adj.* pratical.
mattress *n.* materas. **air mattress** materas inflable.
mature *adj.* matur. • *v.* maturi, adulti.
maturity *n.* maturia.
maudlin *adj.* larmosa.
maul *v.* lasera.
Mauritania *n.* Muritania.
Mauritanian *adj.* & *n.* muritani.
Mauritian *adj.* & *n.* maurisian.
Mauritius *n.* Mauris.
Mauryan *adj.* & *n.* (*dynasty*) maurian.
mausoleum *n.* mausoleo.
mauve *adj.* & *n.* (*colour*) malva.
maven *n.* esperta, conosor.
maverick *n.* nonortodox.
maw *n.* bocon.
maxi- *pref.* masi-.
maxilla *n.* (*bone*) masila.
maxim *n.* diseda.
maximal *adj.* masima.
maximin *n.* (*game theory*) maximin.
maximization *n.* masimi.
maximize *v.* masimi.
maximum *adj.* & *n.* masima. **the maximum** la plu.
may[1] *v.* (*permission, possibility*) pote; (*possibility*) cisa; (*wish*) ta ce.
May[2] *n.* maio.
Mayan *adj.* & *n.* maia.
maybe *adv.* cisa, posible, lo pote es ce.
May beetle *n.* scarabe de maio.
May bug *n.* scarabe de maio.
mayday *interj.* aida.
mayfly *n.* efemera.
mayhem *n.* caos, tumulta.
mayo *n.* maiones.
mayonnaise *n.* maiones.
mayor *n.* maior.
mayoral *adj.* maioral.
maypole *n.* palo de maio.
Mazahua *adj.* & *n.* (*person, language*) mazaua.
Mazdaism *n.* (*religion*) zoroastrisme.
maze *n.* labirinto.
mazurka *n.* (*dance, music*) mazurca.
mbira *n.* (*musical instrument*) calimba.
MC *n.* mestre de selebras.
McKinley, Mount *n.* Monte Denali.
me *pron.* me.
mead *n.* (*drink*) idromel.
meadow *n.* prado.
meadowland *n.* prado.
meadowlark *n.* (*bird*) sturnela.
meagre (US **meager**) *adj.* (*thin*) magra; (*lacking*) mancante, nonsufisinte.

meal *n.* come.
meal beetle *n.* tenebrio.
mealtime *n.* ora de come.
mealworm *n.* tenebrio larval.
mean[1] *v.* sinifia; vole dise, intende.
mean[2] *adj.* (*miserly*) avar; (*unkind*) basa.
mean[3] *adj.* & *n.* (*average*) promedia.
meander *v.* serpe.
meandering *adj.* serpente, serpentin.
meaning *n.* sinifia.
meaningful *adj.* sinifiosa.
meaningless *adj.* sin sinifia.
meanness *n.* (*miserliness*) avaria; (*unkindness*) basia.
means *n.* media, metodo, modo; (*wealth*) ricia. **by all means** en tota modos. **by any means** en cualce modo. **by means of** (*tool*) con; (*method, vehicle*) par. **by no means** en no modo.
mean-spirited *adj.* malvolente.
meant *adj.* intendeda.
meantime *adv.* entretempo. **in the meantime** entretempo.
meanwhile *adv.* entretempo.
measles *n.* morbilio. **baby measles** roseola.
measurable *adj.* mesurable.
measure *v.* mesura; evalua. • *n.* mesura; (*course of action*) media.
measurement *n.* mesura. **measurement of time** mesura de tempo, cronometri.
measure theory *n.* teoria de mesuras.
measuring device *n.* mesurador.
measuring rod *n.* basto de mesura.
measuring stick *n.* basto de mesura.
meat *n.* carne.
meatball *n.* bal de carne.
meat grinder *n.* molin de carne.
meatloaf *n.* pan de carne.
meat pie *n.* tarte de carne.
meatus *n.* (*anatomy*) meato.
meaty *adj.* carnosa.
Mecca *n.* Maca.
mechanic *n.* maciniste.
mechanical *adj.* (*of machinery*) macinal; (*of mechanics*) mecanical.
mechanical pencil *n.* portagrafito.
mechanics *n.* mecanica.
mechanism *n.* macina; (*science, philosophy*) mecanicisme.
mechanist *n.* mecaniciste.
mechanistic *adj.* mecaniciste.
mechanize *v.* macini.
mechanoreceptor *n.* (*neuron*) mecanoresetador.
medal *n.* medalia.
medalist (US). See *medallist.*
medallion *n.* medalion.
medallist (US **medalist**) *n.* medaliste.
meddle *v.* interfere.
meddler *n.* interferor.
meddlesome *adj.* interferente.
media[1] *n.* (*including mass communications*) medias; (*press*) jornalistes.
Media[2] (ancient region) *n.* Media.
median *n.* media.
mediate *v.* arbitra.
mediation *n.* arbitra.
mediator *n.* reconsilior.
medic *n.* mediciste.
medical *adj.* medical.
medical assistance *n.* aida medical.
medical condition *n.* disturba, problem medical.
medical doctor *n.* dotor medical.
medical mask *n.* masca medical.
medical problem *n.* problem medical.
medicate *v.* medisini, trata con medisin.
medication *n.* medisin. **on medication** medisinida.
medicinal *adj.* medisinal.
medicine *n.* (*drugs*) medisin; (*profession*) medica.
medieval *adj.* medieval.
mediocre *adj.* mediocre.
mediocrity *n.* mediocria.
meditate *v.* medita.
meditation *n.* medita.
Mediterranean *adj.* mediteranean. • *n.* (*region, sea*) Mediteraneo.
Mediterranean Basin *n.* Basin Mediteraneo.
Mediterranean Sea *n.* Mar Mediteraneo.
medium *adj.* media. • *n.* (*of communication*) media; (*spiritualist*) spiritiste.
medley *n.* colie, misca.
medulla *n.* medula.
medusa[1] *n.* (*jellyfish*) medusa.
Medusa[2] *n.* (*mythology*) Medusa.
meek *adj.* umil.
meerkat *n.* suricata.
meerschaum *n.* sepiolita, spuma de mar.
meet *v.* encontra; (*reunite*) reuni, asembla; (*formal*) consenta; (*condition*) sasia.
meeting *n.* encontra; reuni, asembla; consenta.
meeting hall *n.* asembleria.
meetinghouse *n.* asembleria.
meg *n.* megabait.
mega- *pref.* (*large, a million*) mega-.
megabyte *n.* megabait.
megalith *n.* megalito.
megalithic *adj.* megalital.
megalo- *pref.* (*large*) megalo-.
megalomania *n.* megalomania.
megalomaniac *n.* megalomanica.
megalomaniacal *adj.* megalomanica.
-megaly *suff.* (*medical*) -megalia.

megaphone *n.* megafon.
meiosis *n.* (*biology*) meiose.
meitnerium *n.* (*element*) maitnerio.
Mekong River *n.* Rio Mecong
melamine *n.* (*plastic*) melamina.
melancholia *n.* melancolia.
melancholiac *adj.* & *n.* melancolica.
melancholic *adj.* melancolica.
melancholy *n.* melancolia, tristia. • *adj.* melancolica, triste, depresada.
Melanesia *n.* Melanesia.
Melanesian *adj.* melanesian.
melange *n.* misca.
melanin *n.* melanin.
melano- *pref.* (*black*) melano-.
melanocarcinoma *n.* (*tumour*) melanoma.
melanocyte *n.* (*biology*) melanosite.
melanoma *n.* melanoma.
melanosis *n.* (*medical*) melanose.
melatonin *n.* (*hormone*) melatonina.
meld *v.* fusa.
mêlée *n.* scaramuxa, tumulta.
mellifluous *adj.* bon sonante.
mellifluousness *n.* bonsona.
mellow *adj.* suave. • *v.* suavi.
melodeon *n.* acordion diatonica.
melodic *adj.* melodiosa.
melodica *n.* (*musical instrument*) melodica.
melodion *n.* acordion diatonica.
melodious *adj.* melodiosa.
melodrama *n.* melodrama.
melodramatic *adj.* melodramosa.
melody *n.* melodia.
melon *n.* melon.
melt *v.* fonde.
meltable *adj.* fondable.
melting pot *n.* crisol.
meltwater *n.* acua dejelada.
member *n.* membro. **member of congress** congresor. **member of parliament** membro de parlamento, parlamentor. **member of the clergy** eglesor.
membership *n.* parteni.
member state *n.* stato membro.
membrane *n.* membrana.
membranelike *adj.* membranin.
membranous *adj.* (*like a membrane*) membranin; (*webbed*) membranosa.
meme *n.* mem.
memento *n.* suvenir, recordante.
memo *n.* nota.
memoir *n.* raconta. **memoirs** autobiografia.
memorabilia *n.* suvenires, recordantes.
memorable *adj.* memorable.
memorandum *n.* nota.
memorial *n.* monumento.
memorialize *v.* eterni.
memorization *n.* memori.
memorize *v.* memori.
memory *n.* (*capacity, including computer*) memoria; (*particular recollection*) recorda. **from memory** (*without notes*) de memoria.
memory aid *n.* aidamemoria.
memory card *n.* carta de memoria.
menace *v.* & *n.* menasa.
menage *n.* casa.
menagerie *n.* zo.
menarche *n.* menstrua prima.
mend *v.* repara, desrompe.
mendable *adj.* reparable.
mendacious *adj.* mentinte.
mendacity *n.* menti.
mendelevium *n.* (*element*) mendelevio.
mendelian *n.* mendeliste.
mendelianism *n.* (*genetics*) mendelisme.
mendelianist *n.* mendeliste.
menhir *n.* (*standing stone*) menir.
menial *adj.* noneducada.
menial worker *n.* peon.
meninge *n.* (*anatomy*) meninje.
meningeal *adj.* meninjal.
meningitis *n.* meninjite.
meniscal *adj.* meniscal.
meniscus *n.* menisco.
Mennonite *adj.* & *n.* menonita.
Mennonitism *n.* (*Christianity*) menonitisme.
menopause *n.* menopausa.
menorah *n.* (*candelabrum*) menora.
menorrhoea (US **menorrhea**) *n.* menorea.
Mensa *n.* (*constellation*) la Table.
men's room *n.* (*toilet*) sala de omes.
menstrual *adj.* menstrual.
menstruate *v.* menstrui.
menstruation *n.* menstrua.
menswear *n.* vestes de omes.
mental *adj.* mental.
mental attitude *n.* disposa mental.
mental breakdown *n.* crise mental.
mental health *n.* sania mental.
mentalism *n.* (*philosophy, psychic*) mentalisme.
mentalist *n.* mentaliste; (*mind reader*) lejemente.
mentalistic *adj.* mentaliste.
mentality *n.* disposa mental.
menthol *n.* mentol.
mention *v.* nota, refere a. • *n.* refere. **already mentioned** ja notada.
mentionable *adj.* notable.
mentor *n.* mestre.
menu *n.* menu.
meow *interj.* miau. • *v.* miaui.
merbromin *n.* (*antiseptic*) merbromina.
mercantile *adj.* comersial.
mercenary *n.* (*soldier*) mersenario.
merchandise *n.* benes.

merchant *n.* mercator.
merciful *adj.* pardonosa.
mercifulness *n.* pardonosia.
merciless *adj.* sin compatia.
mercurial *adj.* volatil.
mercurochrome *n.* (*antiseptic*) merbromina.
mercury[1] *n.* (*element*) mercurio.
Mercury[2] *n.* (*mythology, planet*) Mercurio.
mercy *n.* pardona.
mere *adj.* mera, pur, simple.
merely *adv.* mera, pur, simple; no plu ca, no cosa plu ca.
merengue *n.* (*Dominican dance, music*) merenge.
merge *v.* (*rivers, organizations*) conflue; (*coalesce*) fusa.
merger *n.* conflue; fusa.
meridian *n.* meridiano.
meringue *n.* (*dessert*) merenge.
méringue *n.* (*Haitian dance, music*) merenge aitian.
merit *v.* merita. • *n.* merita, valua.
meritocracy *n.* meritocratia.
meritocrat *n.* meritocrata.
meritocratic *adj.* meritocrata.
meritorious *adj.* valuada.
merlon *n.* (*architecture*) merlon.
mermaid *n.* fe de mar.
merman *n.* fe de mar.
merry *adj.* joiosa.
merry-go-round *n.* carusel.
mesa *n.* colina, plano alta.
mescal *n.* mescal.
mescaline *n.* (*drug*) mescalina.
mesencephalon *n.* (*anatomy*) mesensefalo.
mesentery *n.* (*anatomy*) mesenterio.
mesh *n.* rede.
mesmeric *adj.* ipnosal.
mesmerism *n.* ipnose.
mesmerize *v.* ipnose.
meso- *pref.* (*middle*) meso-.
Mesoamerica *n.* Mesoamerica.
Mesolithic *adj.* & *n.* (*geology*) mesolitica.
mesomycetozoea *n.* (*organisms*) mesomisetozones.
mesomycetozoon *n.* (*organism*) mesomisetozon.
meson *n.* (*particle*) meson.
mesophile *n.* mesofilica.
mesophilia *n.* (*biology*) mesofilia.
mesophilic *adj.* mesofilica.
Mesopotamia *n.* Mesopotamia.
mesothelial *adj.* mesotelial.
mesothelioma *n.* mesotelioma.
mesothelium *n.* (*anatomy*) mesotelio.
mesozoan *n.* (*worm*) mesozon.
Mesozoic *adj.* & *n.* (*geology*) mesozoica.
mesquite *n.* (*plant*) mescite.
mess *n.* desordina; (*tangled*) marania; (*dirt*) mugre, susia. **mess up** desordina; susi; (*hair*) despeteni, marania.
message *n.* mesaje, nota. • *v.* mesaji.
message board *n.* mureta de avisas.
messenger *n.* mesajor.
messiah *n.* maxia.
messianic *adj.* maxial.
messy *adj.* desordinada; (*tangled*) maraniada, despetenida; (*dirty*) mugrosa, susia.
mestiza *adj.* de raza miscada.
mestizo *adj.* de raza miscada.
meta- *pref.* meta-.
metabolic *adj.* metabolal.
metabolism *n.* metaboli.
metabolite *n.* (*biology*) metabolite.
metabolize *v.* metaboli.
metacarpal *adj.* metacarpal.
metacarpus *n.* (*bones*) metacarpo.
metadata *n.* metadatos.
metal *adj.* & *n.* metal.
metal detector *n.* detetador de metales.
metallic *adj.* metal; (*like metal*) metalin.
metallurgical *adj.* metalurjial.
metallurgist *n.* metalurjiste.
metallurgy *n.* metalurjia.
metal screw *n.* vise per metal.
metalwork *n.* arte de metal.
metalworker *n.* metalor.
metalworking *n.* arte de metal.
metamorphic rock *n.* roca mutada.
metamorphism *n.* (*geology*) mutisme.
metamorphosis *n.* muta.
metaphor *n.* metafor.
metaphorical *adj.* metafor.
metaphysical *adj.* metafisical.
metaphysician *n.* metafisiciste.
metaphysics *n.* metafisica.
metastasis *n.* metastase.
metastasize *v.* (*medical*) metastase.
metatarsal *adj.* metatarsal.
metatarsus *n.* (*bones*) metatarso.
metazoa *n.* metazones.
metazoon *n.* (*member of the animal kingdom*) metazon.
meteor *n.* meteor.
meteoric *adj.* meteorin.
meteorite *n.* meteorite.
meteorological *adj.* meteorolojial.
meteorologist *n.* meteorolojiste.
meteorology *n.* meteorolojia.
meter *n.* mesurador.
meter[1] (US). See *metre*.
-meter[2] *suff.* (*measuring tool*) -metre.
meth[1] *n.* metamfetamina.
meth-[2] *pref.* (*chemistry*) met-.
methadone *n.* (*painkiller*) metadon.
methamphetamine *n.* metamfetamina.
methane *n.* metano.

methanol *n.* metanol.
methaqualone *n.* metacualona.
method *n.* metodo.
methodical *adj.* metodosa.
Methodism *n.* (*Christianity*) metodisme.
Methodist *adj.* & *n.* metodiste.
methodology *n.* metodolojia.
methyl *n.* (*chemistry*) metil.
meticulous *adj.* atendosa.
métier *n.* carera.
metonym *adj.* (*substitution of name*) metonim.
metonymy *n.* metonimia.
metre *n.* (*unit of length, poetry*) metre. **two metres long** con du metres de longia.
metric *adj.* metral.
metric ton *n.* (*1000 kg*) ton.
metronome *n.* metronomo.
metropolis *n.* urbe.
metropolitan *adj.* urban.
-metry *suff.* (*measuring*) -metria.
mew *v.* miaui.
Mexican *adj.* & *n.* mexican.
Mexico *n.* Mexico. **Gulf of Mexico** Golfo Mexico. **New Mexico** (*US state*) Mexico Nova.
mezcal *n.* (*drink*) mescal.
mezquite *n.* (*plant*) mescite.
mezuzah *n.* (*parchment*) mezuza.
mezzaluna *n.* cotel osilante.
mezzanine *n.* balcon media.
mezzo-soprano *adj.* & *n.* mediasoprano.
mezzotint *n.* mediatinje.
mi *n.* (*musical note*) mi.
miaow *interj.* miau. • *v.* miaui.
Miao-Yao *adj.* & *n.* miau-iau.
miasma *n.* (*vapour*) miasma.
mic *n.* microfon.
mica *n.* (*mineral*) mica.
Michigan *n.* (*US state*) Michigan. **Michigan** Lago Michigan.
micro- *pref.* (*small, a millionth*) micro-.
microarchitecture *n.* microarciteta.
microbe *n.* microbio.
microbiologist *n.* microbiolojiste.
microbiology *n.* microbiolojia.
microcephalic *adj.* microsefalica.
microcephalous *adj.* microsefalica.
microcephaly *n.* (*medical*) microsefalia.
microchip *n.* microtelia.
microcosm *n.* microcosmo.
microcredit *n.* microcredito.
microfarad *n.* microfarade.
microfilm *n.* microfilma.
microlith *n.* (*geology*) microlito.
micrometer *n.* (*measuring tool*) micrometre.
micrometre (US **micrometer**) *n.* (*unit of length*) micrometre.
micron *n.* (*unit of length*) micron.
Micronesia *n.* Micronesia. **Federated States of Micronesia** Statos Federada de Micronesia.
Micronesian *adj.* & *n.* micronesian.
microphone *n.* microfon.
microplastic *n.* microplastica.
microscope *n.* microscopio.
microscopic *adj.* microscopial.
Microscopium *n.* (*constellation*) la Microscopio.
microsurgery *n.* microsirurjia.
microtome *n.* (*slicing tool*) microtomo.
microtomy *n.* microtomia.
microwave *n.* microonda.
microwave oven *n.* forno de microonda.
micturate *v.* urini.
micturation *n.* urini.
mid- *pref.* media-.
mid-air *adj.* en la aira. **in mid air** en la aira.
midbrain *n.* mesensefalo.
midday *n.* mediadia.
midden *n.* monton de dejetadas; (*dunghill*) monton de fece.
middle *adj.* & *n.* media. **in the middle of** a media de. **in the middle of nowhere** a via de vias. **in the middle of the night** pos medianote.
middle age *n.* (*of life*) eda media.
middle ages *n.* (*history*) eda medieval.
middle class *n.* clase media, burjesia. • *adj.* burjes, de clase media.
middle click *v.* & *n.* (*mouse*) clica media.
Middle East *n.* Asia sude-ueste.
middle finger *n.* dito media.
middleman *n.* ajente media.
middleweight boxing *n.* boxe de pesa media.
middling *adj.* media; (*neither good nor bad*) mediocre.
midfielder *n.* (*sport*) sentror.
midge *n.* mosceta.
midget *adj.* & *n.* nana.
midline *n.* linia media.
midmorning *n.* media de matina.
midnight *n.* medianote.
midperiod *n.* media de periodo.
midpoint *n.* mediapunto.
midriff *n.* ventre, adomen.
midsection *n.* media.
midship *n.* media de barcon.
midst *n.* media.
midstream *n.* media de rio.
midsummer *n.* mediaestate.
midterm *n.* media de periodo.
midtone *n.* mediatinje.
mid vowel *n.* vocal media.
midway *adv.* a media. **midway through** a media de.

midweek *n.* media de semana.
midwife *n.* comadre.
midwifery *n.* comadria.
midwinter *n.* mediainverno.
midyear *n.* media de anio.
might[1] *v.* (*permission, possibility*) pote, ta pote; (*possibility*) cisa.
might[2] *n.* (*power*) potia.
mighty *adj.* potiosa.
migraine *n.* migrania.
migrant *n.* migrante.
migrant worker *n.* laboror migrante.
migrate *v.* migra.
migration *n.* migra.
mike *n.* microfon.
mild *adj.* blanda, nonestrema; (*personality*) umil; (*weather*) temperada.
mildew *n.* mofo.
mile *n.* milia.
mileage *n.* (*distance travelled*) cilometres.
milestone *n.* petra de milia; (*of progress*) monumento.
milieu *n.* ambiente.
militant *adj.* militariste; (*aggressive*) combatosa, violente. • *n.* militariste; ativiste.
militarism *n.* militarisme.
militarist *n.* militariste.
militaristic *adj.* militar.
militarization *n.* militari.
militarize *v.* militari.
military *adj.* militar. • *n.* (*organization*) militar, militares.
military commander *n.* comandor militar.
military court *n.* corte militar.
military haircut *n.* capeles militar.
military officer *n.* ofisior militar.
military service *n.* servi militar.
militia *n.* militia.
militiaman *n.* militior.
militia member *n.* militior.
milk *n.* lete. • *v.* (*animal*) prende lete de.
milkman *n.* letor.
milkshake *n.* lete bateda.
milkvetch *n.* (*plant*) astragalo.
milkweed *n.* (*plant*) asclepia.
milkwort *n.* (*plant*) poligala.
milky *adj.* letin.
Milky Way *n.* (*astronomy*) Via Letin.
mill *n.* molin. • *v.* molini. **mill around** vaga, sirculi.
millefiori *n.* (*art*) milflor.
millefleurs *n.* (*art*) milflor.
millennialism *n.* milenialisme.
millennium *n.* milenio.
miller *n.* molinor.
millet *n.* (*plant*) milio.
milli- *pref.* (*a thousandth*) mili-.
milliard *det.* & *n.* mil milion, bilion.
milligram *n.* miligram.
millilitre (US **milliliter**) *n.* mililitre.
millimetre (US **millimeter**) *n.* milimetre.
milliner *n.* xapor, modiste.
millinery *n.* xaperia.
million *det.* & *n.* milion. **millions** miliones. **one million** milion. **two million people** du milion persones.
millionaire *n.* milionor.
millionth *adj.* (*ordinal*) milion. • *n.* (*fraction*) milioni.
millipede *n.* milipede.
millstone *n.* petra de molin.
milquetoast *n.* timida.
mime *v.* (*perform a mime*) mima. • *n.* mima; (*lip-sync*) canta sincrona; (*person*) mimor.
mimeograph *n.* mimeograf.
mimeography *n.* mimeografia.
mimer *n.* mimor.
mimesis *n.* mima.
mimic *v.* imita. • *n.* (*person*) imitor.
mimicry *n.* imita; mima.
mimosa *n.* (*plant*) mimosa.
minaret *n.* (*mosque tower*) minareta.
mince *v.* axi a picos.
minced meat *n.* carne axida a picos.
mincemeat *n.* fruta axida a picos.
mind *n.* mente, psice; (*opinion*) opina. • *v.* (*pay attention to*) atende; (*be bothered by*) desaproba, es disturbada par. **never mind** oblida lo, lo no importa.
Mindanao *n.* (*island*) Mindanao.
mindful *adj.* consensa.
mindfulness *n.* consensia.
mindless *adj.* sin pensa, sin cura.
Mindoro *n.* Mindoro.
Mindoro Strait *n.* Streta Mindoro.
mind reader *n.* lejemente.
mindset *n.* disposa mental.
mine[1] *pron.* la mea(s).
mine[2] *v.* (*dig*) escava, mina; (*lay mines*) planta bombetas. • *n.* mineria; (*explosive*) bombeta.
mine detector *n.* detetador de bombetas.
minefield *n.* (*physical or metaphorical*) campo de bombetas.
minelayer *n.* bombetador.
miner *n.* escavor.
mineral *adj.* & *n.* mineral.
mineral bath *n.* banieria mineral.
mineralization *n.* minerali.
mineralize *v.* minerali.
mineralogical *adj.* mineralojial.
mineralogist *n.* mineralojiste.
mineralogy *n.* mineralojia.
mineral water *n.* acua mineral.
minestrone *n.* sopa de vejetal.
minesweeper *n.* dragabombeta.
Ming *adj.* (*dynasty*) ming.
mingle *v.* misca.

mini- *pref.* mini-.
miniature *adj.* & *n.* miniatur.
miniature scene *n.* sena miniatur.
miniaturist *n.* miniaturiste.
miniaturization *n.* miniaturi.
miniaturize *v.* miniaturi.
minibike *n.* (*motorcycle*) minimoto.
minibriefs *n.* minislip.
minibus *n.* minibus.
minim *n.* tono duida.
minimal *adj.* minima.
minimalism *n.* minimisme.
minimalist *adj.* & *n.* minimiste.
minimax *n.* (*game theory*) minimax.
minimization *n.* minimi.
minimize *v.* minimi.
minimum *adj.* & *n.* minima. **as a minimum** a la min.
minion *n.* inferior.
miniscule *adj.* pico. • *n.* letera minor.
miniseries *n.* miniserie.
miniskirt *n.* minifalda.
minister *n.* (*government*) ministro; (*clergy*) eglesor. **minister to** cura.
ministerial *adj.* ministral.
ministry *n.* ministreria, ofisia de governa.
minium *n.* (*pigment*) minio.
minivan *n.* (*US*) furgoneta.
mink *n.* (*animal*) vison.
Min Nan *adj.* & *n.* (*person, language*) banlam.
Minnesota *n.* (*US state*) Minnesota.
minnow *n.* (*fish*) pexeta.
Minoan Civilization *n.* Sivilia Minoan.
minor *adj.* & *n.* minor.
minority *n.* minoria. **the minority of** la min de.
minor planet *n.* planeteta.
minor scale *n.* (*music*) scala minor.
minotaur *n.* minotauro.
minstrel *n.* menestrel.
mint[1] *n.* (*plant*) menta; (*confectionery*) confeto de menta.
mint[2] *n.* (*money*) moneria.
minty *adj.* mentin.
minuet *n.* (*dance, music*) minueto.
minus *conj.* (*arithmetic*) min.
minuscule *adj.* pico. • *n.* letera minor.
minus sign *n.* sinia negativa, sinia de sutrae.
minute[1] *n.* (*time*) minuto.
minute[2] *v.* (*take notes*) nota, resoma. **minutes** (*of meeting*) notas, resoma.
minute[3] *adj.* (*tiny*) pico.
minuteman *n.* militior.
minuteness *n.* picia.
minute taker *n.* notor.
minx *n.* seduor, tisor; xica noncortes.
Miocene *adj.* & *n.* (*geology*) miosene.
miracle *n.* miracle, mervelia.
miracleworker *n.* miraclor.
miraculous *adj.* miraclosa.
mirage *n.* miraje.
Mirandes *adj.* & *n.* (*person, language*) mirandes.
mire *n.* pantan, fango.
mired *adj.* pantanida. **become mired** pantani.
mirliton *n.* (*musical instrument*) cazu.
mirror *n.* miror. • *v.* mirori.
mirth *n.* ilaria.
mirthful *adj.* joiosa.
mis- *pref.* mal-.
misadventure *n.* malaventura.
misadvise *v.* malconsela.
misaim *v.* malpunta.
misalign *v.* malalinia.
misalignment *n.* malalinia.
misanthrope *n.* misantrope.
misanthropic *adj.* misantrope.
misanthropist *n.* misantrope.
misanthropy *n.* misantropia.
misapply *v.* malaplica.
misapprehend *v.* malcomprende, malinterprete.
misappropriate *v.* froda.
misappropriation *n.* froda.
misassign *v.* malasinia.
misbehave *v.* malcondui.
misbehaviour (US **misbehavior**) *n.* malcondui.
misbelief *n.* malcrede.
miscalculate *v.* malcalcula.
miscalculation *n.* malcalcula.
miscarriage *n.* aborta natural.
miscarry *v.* aborta, aborta natural.
miscast *v.* malasinia.
miscegenation *n.* misca de razas.
miscellaneous *adj.* diversa, miscada.
miscellany *n.* misca, colie miscada.
mischief *n.* turba, turbosia.
mischievous *adj.* turbosa.
miscible *adj.* miscable.
misclassify *v.* malclasi.
misconceive *v.* malconseti.
misconception *n.* malconseti.
misconduct *n.* malcondui.
misconfigured *adj.* malajustada.
misconstruct *v.* malconstrui.
misconstrue *v.* malinterprete.
miscount *v.* malconta.
miscreant *n.* vil, malcreada.
miscue *v.* & *n.* malsiniali.
misdeal *v.* maldistribui.
misdemeanour (US **misdemeanor**) *n.* crimin minor; peceta. **commit a misdemeanour** peceta.
misdiagnose *v.* maldiagnose.
misdiagnosis *n.* maldiagnose.
misdirect *v.* maldirije.

misdirection *n.* maldirije.
misdistribute *v.* maldistribui.
miser *n.* avar.
miserable *adj.* misera.
miserliness *n.* avaria.
miserly *adj.* avar.
misery *n.* miseria.
misexpress *v.* malespresa.
misfeed *n.* malfa.
misfile *v.* malarcivi.
misfire *v.* (*gun*) malensende.
misfit *n.* malajustada.
misfortune *n.* mal fortuna.
misgovern *v.* malgoverna.
misgovernment *v.* malgoverna.
misguide *v.* malgida.
mishandle *v.* malmaneja.
mishap *n.* mal fortuna.
mishear *v.* maloia.
Mishna *n.* (*Judaism*) mixna.
Mishnah *n.* (*Judaism*) mixna.
misidentify *v.* malidentifia.
misinform *v.* malinforma.
misinterpret *v.* malinterprete.
misjudge *v.* maljudi.
mislay *v.* malpone.
mislead *v.* malgida.
mismanage *v.* malmaneja.
mismatch *v.* & *n.* noncoresponde.
misnamed *adj.* malnomida.
misnomer *n.* malnomida.
miso[1] *n.* (*soup*) miso.
miso-[2] *pref.* (*hate*) miso-.
misogynist *n.* misojine.
misogynistic *adj.* misojine.
misogyny *n.* misojinia.
misperceive *v.* malpersepi.
misperception *n.* malpersepi.
misplace *v.* malpone; (*lose*) perde.
misprint *v.* malprimi. • *n.* malprimida.
mispronounce *v.* malpronunsia.
mispronunciation *n.* malpronunsia.
misquotation *n.* malsita.
misquote *v.* malsita.
misread *v.* maleje.
misrecognize *v.* malreconose.
misreport *v.* malreporta.
misrepresent *v.* malrepresenta, contorse.
misrepresentation *n.* malrepresenta.
misrule *v.* malgoverna.
miss[1] *v.* (*target*) no colpa; (*bus, connection, etc.*) perde; (*fail to see*) no vide; (*fail to hear*) no oia; (*regret the absence of*) es triste sin. • *n.* fali. **have a near miss** evita apena. **the car is missing a wheel** un rota manca de la auto.
Miss[2] *n.* Seniora, Sra; (*gender-neutral*) Sri; (*historical form of address for a girl*) Senioreta.
missal *n.* libro de preas.
misshapen *adj.* malformida.
missile *n.* misil, xutada.
missile launcher *n.* lansamisil.
missile silo *n.* silo de misil.
missing *adj.* mancante, asente. **be missing** manca. **missing in action** perdeda en batalia.
mission *n.* mision; (*station*) misioneria.
missionary *n.* misionor.
Mississippi *n.* (*US state*) Mississippi.
Mississippi River *n.* Rio Mississippi.
missive *n.* letera.
Missouri *n.* (*US state*) Missouri.
Missouri River *n.* Rio Missouri.
misspeak *v.* malespresa.
misspell *v.* malspele.
misstate *v.* maldeclara.
misstep *n.* mal paso. • *v.* fa un mal paso.
mist *n.* (*fog*) nebleta; (*steam*) vapor. **mist up** nebli.
mistakable *adj.* confusable.
mistake *n.* era; (*small*) ereta. • *v.* (*person*) malreconose; (*thing*) malpersepi. **make a mistake** era, fa un mal paso. **make a small mistake** ereta.
mistaken *adj.* erante; (*badly*) erosa.
misted *adj.* vaporosa.
mister[1] *n.* neblador.
Mister[2] *n.* Senior, Sr.
mistletoe *n.* viscio.
mistral *n.* (*wind*) mistral.
mistranslate *v.* maltradui.
mistranslation *n.* maltradui.
mistreat *v.* maltrata.
mistreatment *n.* maltrata.
mistress *n.* mestresa; (*paramour*) concubina.
mistrial *n.* litiga nonconcluinte.
mistrust *v.* desfida.
misty *adj.* vaporosa.
mistype *v.* maltape.
misunderstand *v.* malcomprende.
misuse *v.* malusa; (*waste*) peri.
mite *n.* (*arachnid*) acaro.
miter... (US). See *mitre...*
Mithra *n.* Mitra.
mithraism *n.* mitraisme.
mithraist *adj.* & *n.* mitraiste.
Mithras *n.* Mitra.
mitigate *v.* lejeri, modera, diminui.
mitigation *n.* modera.
mitochondria *n.* (*biology*) mitocondrios.
mitochondrial *adj.* mitocondrial.
mitochondrion *n.* (*biology*) mitocondrio.
mitosis *n.* (*biology*) mitose.
mitral *adj.* (*anatomy*) mitral.
mitre (US **miter**) *n.* (*hat*) mitra; (*joint*) junta angulo.
mitre box (US **miter box**) *n.* caxa de junta.

mitre saw (US **miter saw**) *n.* siera de junta.
mitten *n.* ganteta.
mix *v.* misca; (*shuffle*) acasi.
mixed *adj.* miscada. **have mixed feelings** ambivale.
mixed dish *n.* plato miscada.
mixer *n.* miscador.
mixing machine *n.* miscador.
mixologist *n.* bariste.
mixture *n.* misca.
mix-up *n.* confusa.
mizzenmast *n.* masto posmedial.
mmm *interj.* (*tasty*) mm.
mnemonic *n.* aidamemoria.
moa *n.* (*bird*) moa.
moan *v.* & *n.* jemi.
moat *n.* foso.
mob *n.* (*people, monkeys*) manada; (*crime*) crimin organizada.
mobile *adj.* movable; portable; vagante.
mobile home *n.* casa movable.
mobile phone *n.* telefoneta.
mobility *n.* movablia.
mobilization *n.* movabli.
mobilize *v.* movabli.
mob rule *n.* rena par la manada.
mobster *n.* gangster.
moccasin *n.* (*shoe*) mocasin.
mocha *n.* (*coffee*) moca.
mock *v.* burla. • *adj.* falsa.
mocker *n.* burlor.
mockery *n.* burla.
mockingbird *n.* mimor.
mock trial *n.* litiga falsa.
mock-up *n.* model.
modal *adj.* modal.
mode *n.* (*software, statistics*) moda.
model *adj.* model. • *n.* model, esemplo; (*art, fashion*) model. • *v.* (*make a model of; display clothes*) modeli.
modelling (US **modeling**) *n.* modeli.
modelling clay (US **modeling clay**) *n.* pasta de modeli.
modem *n.* modem.
moderate *v.* modera. • *adj.* moderada, nonestrema.
moderation *n.* modera.
moderator *n.* (*person*) moderor; (*substance*) moderante.
modern *adj.* moderna.
modernism *n.* modernisme.
modernist *n.* moderniste.
modernity *n.* modernia.
modernization *n.* moderni.
modernize *v.* moderni.
modernizer *n.* modernor.
modernness *n.* modernia.
modest *adj.* (*humble*) umil; (*humble, avoiding impropriety*) modesta.
modesty *n.* umilia.
modicum *n.* (*tiny amount*) pico.
modifiable *adj.* alterable.
modification *n.* altera.
modified *adj.* alterada. **genetically modified** jenetical alterada.
modifier *n.* alterante.
modify *v.* altera.
modiste *n.* modiste.
modular *adj.* modulal.
modulate *v.* (*sound, etc.*) modula; (*regulate*) regula.
modulation *n.* modula.
modulator *n.* modulador.
module *n.* modulo.
modulo *prep.* (*mathematics*) modulo.
modulus *n.* modulo.
modus vivendi *n.* acorda de coesiste.
mogul[1] *n.* maniate.
Mogul[2] *adj.* & *n.* (*dynasty*) mugul.
mohair *n.* mohair.
Mohammed *n.* Muhammad.
Mohammedan *adj.* & *n.* muslim.
Mohave Desert *n.* Deserto Mohave.
mohawk *n.* capeles irocuoi.
mohican *n.* capeles irocuoi.
Mohism *n.* (*philosophy*) moisme.
Mohist *adj.* & *n.* moiste.
moiety *n.* dui.
moist *adj.* umida.
moisten *v.* umidi.
moisture *n.* umidia.
moistureproof *adj.* secur contra umidia.
moisturize *v.* idrata.
moisturizer *n.* idratante.
Mojave Desert *n.* Deserto Mohave.
molar *n.* dente molente.
molasses *n.* melasa.
mold... (US). See *mould...*
Moldavia *n.* Moldova.
Moldova *n.* Moldova.
Moldovan *adj.* & *n.* moldovan.
mole[1] *n.* (*animal*) talpa.
mole[2] *n.* (*on skin*) nevo.
mole[3] *n.* (*chemistry*) mol.
molecular *adj.* molecular.
molecule *n.* molecula.
molehill *n.* talperia.
moleskin *n.* camusin.
molest *v.* molesta.
molestation *n.* molesta.
mollify *v.* pasi.
mollusc (US **mollusk**) *n.* molusco.
mollycoddle *v.* regala.
molt (US). See *moult.*
molten *adj.* fondeda.
Molucca *n.* Maluku.

Moluccas *n.* Isolas Maluku.
Molucca Sea *n.* Mar Maluku.
molybdenum *n.* (*element*) molibdeno.
mom *n.* mama.
moment *n.* momento. **for the moment** per aora, per la presente. **of the moment** de la momento. **the right moment** la bon momento.
momentary *adj.* momental.
momentous *adj.* sinifiosa, importante.
momentum *n.* momento. **angular momentum** momento angulo.
mommy *n.* mama.
Monacan *adj.* & *n.* monaces.
Monaco *n.* Monaco.
monad *n.* unia.
monarch *n.* monarca.
monarch butterfly *n.* monarca.
monarchic *adj.* monarcal.
monarchical *adj.* monarcal.
monarchism *n.* monarcisme.
monarchist *adj.* monarciste.
monarchistic *adj.* monarcal.
monarchy *n.* monarcia.
monastery *n.* monceria.
monastic *adj.* moncal.
monasticism *n.* moncisme.
Monday *n.* lundi.
monetary *adj.* monal.
money *n.* mone.
moneybag *n.* saco de mone.
moneychanger *n.* intercambior.
moneylender *n.* prestor.
moneymaker *n.* fonte de revenu.
money tree *n.* crasula.
Mongolia *n.* Mongol.
Mongolian *adj.* & *n.* mongol.
mongoloid *adj.* mongoloide.
mongoose *n.* mangoste.
mongrel *adj.* ibride, de raza miscada. • *n.* ibride.
monicker *n.* nom.
monied *adj.* rica.
moniker *n.* nom.
monism *n.* (*philosophy*) monisme.
monist *n.* moniste.
monito del monte *n.* (*marsupial*) monito.
monitor *n.* monitor; (*screen*) scermo. • *v.* vijila, monitori; manteni.
monitor lizard *n.* varano.
monk *n.* monce, monce mas.
monkey *n.* simia.
monkey bars *n.* strutur de trepa.
monkey wrench *n.* clave engles.
monkish *adj.* moncin.
monkshood *n.* aconito.
mono- *pref.* (*one*) mono-.
monoamine *adj.* & *n.* (*chemistry*) monoamina.
monoblast *n.* (*biology*) monoblasto.
Monoceros *n.* (*constellation*) la Unicorno.
monochromatic *adj.* monocromata; (*colourblind*) sieca a color.
monochrome *adj.* monocromata.
monocle *n.* monoculo.
monocot *n.* monocota.
monocotyledon *n.* (*botany*) monocota.
monocular *adj.* monoculal.
monoculture *n.* monocultiveria.
monocycle *n.* monosicle.
monocyte *n.* (*biology*) monosite.
monocytopoiesis *n.* (*biology*) monositopoiese.
monogamist *n.* monogamiste.
monogamous *adj.* monogama.
monogamy *n.* monogamia.
monogram *n.* inisiales ornal.
monograph *v.* monografi. • *n.* monografia.
monographer *n.* monografiste.
monokini *n.* (*garment*) monocini.
monolingual *adj.* & *n.* monolingual.
monolingual person *n.* monolingual.
monolith *n.* monolito.
monolithic *adj.* monolitin.
monologue (US **monolog**) *n.* monologo.
monomania *n.* monomania.
monomaniac *n.* monomanica.
monomaniacal *adj.* monomanica.
monomer *n.* (*chemistry*) monomer.
monomial *adj.* monomial. • *n.* monomio.
mononucleosis *n.* (*medical*) mononucleose.
monophthong *n.* monoftongo.
monopole *n.* (*particle*) monopolo.
monopolize *v.* monopoli.
monopoly *n.* monopolio.
monopoly money *n.* mone de jua.
monorail *n.* monorel.
monosaccharide *n.* monosacarido.
monosyllabic *adj.* monosilabal.
monosyllable *n.* monosilaba.
monotheism *n.* monoteisme.
monotheist *n.* monoteiste.
monotheistic *adj.* monoteiste.
monotone *n.* monotono.
monotonous *adj.* monotonosa.
monotony *n.* monotonia.
monoxide *n.* monosido.
monsoon *n.* monson.
monster *n.* monstro.
monstrosity *n.* (*eyesore*) xocaoio; (*monstrousness*) monstrinia.
monstrous *adj.* monstrin.
montage *n.* composada, filma composada.
Montana *n.* (*US state*) Montana.
Montenegrin *adj.* & *n.* tsernagorsce, montenegrin.
Montenegro *n.* Tsernagora, Montenegro.
month *n.* mense. **twice a month** a du veses per mense.

monthly *adj.* mensal.
monthly payment *n.* paia mensal.
Montserrat *n.* (*island*) Montserat.
Montserratian *adj.* & *n.* montseratian.
monument *n.* monumento.
monumental *adj.* monumental.
moo *interj.* (*cow*) muu. • *v.* mui.
mood[1] *n.* umor. **bad mood** mal umor. **be in a bad mood** es malumorosa. **in a bad mood** malumorosa, de mal umor. **in a good mood** bonumorosa, de bon umor.
mood[2] *n.* (*grammar*) moda. **conditional mood** (*grammar*) moda dependente.
moody *adj.* de umor variable.
mooli *n.* rabano blanca.
moon *n.* luna.
moonbeam *n.* raio de luna.
moonlight *n.* lus de luna.
moonlit *adj.* luminada par luna.
moonrise *n.* leva de luna.
moonset *n.* reposa de luna.
moonshine *n.* alcol nonlegal.
moonstruck *adj.* enamada.
moonwalk *v.* & *n.* (*dance*) pasea lunal.
moor[1] *n.* (*moorland*) stepe.
moor[2] *v.* (*boat*) lia, securi.
Moor[3] *n.* moro.
Moorish *adj.* moro.
moorland *n.* stepe.
moose *n.* alce.
moo shu *n.* (*food*) muxu.
moot *adj.* discutable, nonserta.
mop *n.* scopa de franjes; (*hair*) crinera. • *v.* limpi.
mope *v.* es malumorosa. **mope about** vaga depresada.
moped *n.* bisicle motorida.
moping *adj.* malumorosa.
moraine *n.* (*geology*) moren.
moral *adj.* moral. • *n.* prinsipe moral, regula moral; (*of story*) leson moral.
moral code *n.* normas moral.
morale *n.* autofida, bonstate.
moralism *n.* moralisme.
moralist *n.* moraliste.
moralistic *adj.* moraliste.
morality *n.* moralia.
moralize *v.* predica.
moralizing *n.* moralisme.
morals *n.* moralia.
morass *n.* pantan.
moratorium *n.* suspende.
moray *n.* morena.
morbid *adj.* morbosa.
morbidity *n.* morbosia.
mordant *adj.* criticante, sever.
more *det.* & *adv.* plu. **more and more** cresente, plu e plu, sempre plu. **more or less** (*approximately*) plu o min. **more than** plu ca, ultra. **more than enough** bastante. **more than ever** plu ca sempre. **more than necessary** plu ca nesesada. **no more** no plu. **the more** [illegible] **the more** plu [illegible] plu.
moreish *adj.* abituante.
moreover *adv.* plu, en ajunta.
morgue *n.* moreria.
moribund *adj.* morinte.
Mormon *adj.* & *n.* mormon.
Mormonism *n.* mormonisme.
morn *n.* matina.
morning *n.* matina. **become morning** matini. **in the morning** a matina. **this morning** a esta matina, a matina oji. **tomorrow morning** a matina doman.
morning-after pill *n.* pil de doman.
morning glory *n.* (*plant*) ipomea.
morning sickness *n.* nausea de ensintia.
morning star *n.* (*Venus*) stela de matina.
Moro *adj.* & *n.* moro.
Moroccan *adj.* & *n.* magribi, marocan.
Morocco *n.* Magrib, Maroco.
Moro Gulf *n.* Golfo Moro.
moron *n.* fol, stupida.
moronic *adj.* stupida.
morose *adj.* malumorosa, de mal umor.
-morph *suff.* -morfe.
morpheme *n.* morfem.
morphine *n.* morfina.
morpho- *pref.* morfo-.
morphological *adj.* morfolojial.
morphology *n.* morfolojia.
Morse code *n.* codigo de Morse.
morsel *n.* peseta.
mortal *adj.* (*able to die*) mortal; (*deadly*) matante.
mortality *n.* (*mortalness*) mortalia; (*death*) mori.
mortar *n.* (*substance, gun*) mortero; (*bowl*) bol de mole. • *v.* morteri. **mortar and pestle** bol e piston.
mortarboard *n.* portamortero; (*hat*) xapeta academial.
mortgage *v.* ipoteca.
mortician *n.* funeror.
mortify *v.* embarasa.
mortise *n.* (*of dovetail joint*) mortasa. • *v.* mortasi.
mortuary *n.* moreria.
mosaic *adj.* & *n.* mosaica.
moscovium *n.* (*element*) moscovio.
Moscow *n.* Moscva.
Moses *n.* Moxe.
mosh *v.* (*dance*) moxa.
mosh pit *n.* moxeria.
Moslem *adj.* & *n.* muslim.
mosque *n.* mascita.
mosquito *n.* moscito.
moss *n.* mos.

mosslike *adj.* mosin.
mossy *adj.* mososa.
most *det.* la plu de. • *adv.* la plu, masima. • *n.* masima. **at most** a la plu, masima. **for the most part** jeneral, xef, per la plu. **the most successful film** la filma la plu susedosa.
mostly *adv.* jeneral, xef, per la plu.
mote *n.* particula.
motel *n.* motel.
moth *n.* papilio, papilio de note.
mothball *n.* bal de naftalina.
mother *n.* madre.
motherboard *n.* (*computer*) carta madral.
mother figure *n.* madrin.
motherhood *n.* madria.
mother-in-law *n.* madre par sposi.
motherland *n.* propre pais.
motherless *adj.* sin madre.
motherly *adj.* madrin.
mother-of-pearl *n.* (*substance*) nacre.
Mother's Day *n.* festa de madres.
mothership *n.* veculo madrin.
mother-to-be *adj.* madre futur.
mother tongue *n.* propre lingua.
motif *n.* motif, tema.
motion *n.* move; (*proposal*) proposa. **in slow motion** de move lenta.
motionless *adj.* nonmovente.
motion sensor *n.* sensador de move.
motivate *v.* motiva. **motivate oneself** automotiva.
motivation *n.* motiva. **self-motivation** automotiva.
motivational *adj.* motivante.
motive *n.* motiva, stimula, razona, intende.
motley *adj.* diversa, eterojen; multicolorosa.
motoneuron *n.* motoneuron.
motor *n.* motor. • *pref.* moto-.
motorbike *n.* motosicle.
motorboat *n.* motobarco.
motorcade *n.* convoia de autos.
motorcycle *n.* motosicle.
motorcycle racing *n.* motosiclisme.
motorcycling *n.* motosiclisme.
motorcyclist *n.* motosicliste.
motor home *n.* autocaravan.
motoring *n.* motorisme.
motorist *n.* motoriste.
motorize *v.* motori.
motorized bicycle *n.* bisicle motorida.
motor neuron *n.* motoneuron.
motor racing *n.* corsa de autos; (*motorbikes*) motosiclisme.
motor vehicle *n.* veculo de motor.
motorway *n.* autovia.
mottled *adj.* manxosa, multicolorosa.
motto *n.* slogan.
moue *n.* mua.
mould[1] (US **mold**) *n.* (*container*) molda; (*cast*) moldida. • *v.* moldi.
mould[2] (US **mold**) *n.* (*fungus*) mofo.
moulding (US **molding**) *n.* (*cast*) moldida; (*decorative*) moldur.
mouldy (US **moldy**) *adj.* mofosa.
moult *v.* muta sua pelo; muta sua plumas.
mound *n.* colineta, monton.
mount *v.* (*climb*) asende; (*ride*) monta; (*campaign*) organiza; (*picture*) afisa; (*one thing on another*) monturi. • *n.* (*mountain*) monte; (*frame*) montur.
mountain *n.* monte; (*mountainous area*) montania. • *adj.* montanial.
mountain climbing *n.* trepa de montanias.
mountain dweller *n.* montanior.
mountaineer *n.* trepor.
mountaineering *n.* trepa de montanias.
mountain lion *n.* puma.
mountainous *adj.* montaniosa.
mountainous area *n.* montania.
mountain pass *n.* colo de monte.
mountain ridge *n.* dorso de montania.
mountains *n.* montes; (*region*) montania.
mountainside *n.* lado de monte.
mountaintop *n.* culmina de monte.
mountebank *n.* frodor, xarlatan.
mounted police officer *n.* polisior montante.
mountie *n.* polisior canadian.
mourn *v.* lamenta.
mourner *n.* lamentor.
mournful *adj.* lamentin; lamentosa.
mouse *n.* mus.
mousebird *n.* colio.
mouse deer *n.* tragulo.
mouselike *adj.* musin.
mouse trail *n.* (*software*) curso de mus.
mousetrap *n.* caturamus.
moussaka *n.* (*food*) musaca.
mousse *n.* (*food*) muse.
moustache *n.* mustax.
mousy *adj.* musin.
mouth *n.* (*anatomy, river, cave*) boca. **by word of mouth** par parla.
mouthful *n.* boca plen, pleniboca.
mouth harp *n.* armonica.
mouth organ *n.* armonica.
mouthpiece *n.* (*music*) beco.
mouthwash *n.* desinfetante de boca.
mouthy *adj.* noncortes.
movable type *n.* tipo movable.
move *v.* move; (*house*) move sua casa, reloca se; (*livestock seasonally*) transuma; (*emotionally*) emosia. • *n.* move; reloca. **move away** distanti.
movement *n.* (*including music*) move; (*community with a cause or direction*) promove.
mover *n.* provocor; potiosa.

movie *n.* filma. **love of movies** sinemafilia.
moviegoer *n.* fan de sinema, sinemafilica.
moviemaker *n.* sinematografiste, sinemiste.
moviemaking *n.* sinematografia.
movie theatre (US **theater**) *n.* sinema.
moving walkway *n.* paseria rolante.
mow *v.* (*grass*) corti la erba; (*with a scythe*) falxi.
mower *n.* (*machine*) cortierba; (*person*) cortor.
Mozabite *adj.* & *n.* (*person, language*) mozabita.
Mozambican *adj.* & *n.* mosambican.
Mozambique *n.* Mosambic.
Mozambique Channel *n.* Streta Mosambic.
Mozarab *n.* mosarabi.
Mozarabic *adj.* mosarabi.
mozzarella *n.* (*cheese*) mozarela.
MP *n.* membro de parlamento, parlamentor.
MP3 player *n.* baladador dijital.
MPV *n.* furgoneta.
Mr *abbr.* Sr (*Senior*); (*gender-neutral*) Sri.
Mrs *abbr.* Sra (*Seniora*); (*gender-neutral*) Sri.
Ms *abbr.* Sra (*Seniora*); (*gender-neutral*) Sri.
mu *n.* (*Greek letter* M, μ) mu.
much *det.* & *pron.* multe. **as much as possible** tan multe como posible. **much less than** multe min. **much more than** multe plu. **not much** no multe, poca.
mucilage *n.* mucilajo.
muck *n.* mugre.
mucky *adj.* mugrosa; (*lewd*) lasiva.
mucous *adj.* mucosa.
mucous membrane *n.* membrana mucosa.
mucus *n.* muco.
mud *n.* fango.
muddiness *n.* fangosia.
muddle *v.* & *n.* confusa.
muddy *adj.* fangosa. • *v.* fangi.
mudguard *n.* parafango.
mudslide *n.* flue de fango.
muenster *n.* (*cheese*) munster.
muesli *n.* musli.
muesli bar *n.* bara de musli.
muezzin *n.* (*caller to prayer*) muezin.
muff *n.* ganton.
muffin *n.* mufin.
muffinman *n.* mufinor.
muffin seller *n.* mufinor.
muffle *v.* amorti.
muffler *n.* silentador; (*scarf*) xarpe.
mufti *n.* (*Islamic scholar*) mufti.
mug *n.* tason. • *v.* ruba.
mugger *n.* rubor.
mugging *n.* ruba.
muggy *adj.* umida.
Mughal *adj.* & *n.* mugul.
mugwort *n.* artemisia.
Muhammad *n.* Muhammad.
Muhammed *n.* Muhammad.
muladi *n.* (*Islam*) muladi.
mulatto *n.* mulato.
mulberry *n.* (*berry*) morera; (*tree*) morero.
mulch *n.* (*soil*) umo.
mule *n.* mulo.
muleteer *n.* mulor.
mulish *adj.* mulin.
mull *v.* considera. **mull over** considera.
mullah *n.* (*Islam*) mula.
mulled wine *n.* vino calda.
mullet *n.* (*fish*) mujil.
mulligatawny *n.* (*soup*) malagatani.
mullion *n.* (*architecture*) mainel.
multi- *pref.* multi-.
multiboot *v.* (*software*) inisia multiple.
multicellular *adj.* multiselulal.
multichannel *adj.* multicanalal.
multicolour (US **multicolor**) *adj.* multicolorosa.
multicoloured (US **multicolored**) *adj.* multicolorosa.
multicore *adj.* multicoral.
multicultural *adj.* multicultural.
multidimensional *adj.* multidimensional.
multidirectional *adj.* multidirijal.
multiethnic *adj.* multietnical.
multifaceted *adj.* multifasetal.
multifunctional *adj.* multiusal.
multigender *adj.* & *n.* nonbinaria.
multilateral *adj.* multiladal.
multilayered *adj.* multistratal.
multilevel *adj.* multinivelal.
multilingual *adj.* multilingual.
multilinial *adj.* multilinial.
multimedia *adj.* multimedial. • *n.* multimedialia.
multinational *adj.* & *n.* multinasional.
multipartite *adj.* multipartital.
multiparty *adj.* multipartital.
multiphase *adj.* multifasal.
multiphasic *adj.* multifasal.
multiple *adj.* & *n.* multiple. **become multiple** multipli.
multiple-choice examination *n.* esamina de elejes multiple.
multiple collision *n.* colide multiple.
multiplex *adj.* multiplesal. • *n.* multipleso.
multiplicand *n.* multiplida.
multiplication *n.* multipli.
multiplication sign *n.* sinia de multipli.
multiplier *n.* multiplinte.
multiply[1] *v.* multipli. **multiplied by** par, multiplida par.
multiply[2] *adv.* multiple, en multe modos.
multipolar *adj.* multipolal.
multipurpose *adj.* multiusal.
multipurpose vehicle *n.* furgoneta.
multiracial *adj.* multirazal.
multistage *adj.* multigradal.

multistorey (US **multistory**) *adj.* multinivelal.
multitalented *adj.* multitalentosa.
multitasking *n.* multitaxia. • *adj.* multitaxal.
multitrack *adj.* multibandal.
multitude *n.* multia. **a multitude of** multe.
multiuser *adj.* multiusoral.
multivalent *adj.* multivalente.
multivariant *adj.* multivariante.
multivariate *adj.* multivariante.
multiverse *n.* multiverso.
mum *n.* mama.
mumble *v.* & *n.* murmura; (*slurred*) farfulia.
mummery *n.* teatral mascida.
mummification *n.* momi.
mummify *v.* momi.
mummy[1] *n.* (*mother*) mama.
mummy[2] *n.* (*preserved*) momia.
mumps *n.* parotidite.
munch *v.* mastica.
mundane *adj.* comun.
mung bean *n.* fava mung.
municipal *n.* munisipal.
municipality *n.* munisipa, comunia legal.
munificence *n.* jenerosia.
munificent *adj.* jenerosa.
munition *n.* (*weapons*) armas; (*ammunition*) muni.
munster *n.* (*cheese*) munster.
muon *n.* (*particle*) muon.
mural *n.* depinta mural.
muralist *n.* (*artist*) muraliste.
murder *v.* & *n.* omiside; (*for political or religious reasons*) asasina. **commit murder** omiside.
murderer *n.* omisidor, taliagarga; asasinor.
murderous *adj.* omisidente.
murder victim *n.* omisideda.
murky *adj.* susia.
murmur *v.* & *n.* murmura.
murphy bed *n.* leto ascondeda.
murrain *n.* maladia de bestias.
murre *n.* (*bird*) uria.
murrelet *n.* (*bird*) urieta.
Musca *n.* (*constellation*) la Mosca.
muscat *n.* muscatel.
muscatel *n.* (*grape, wine*) muscatel.
muscle *n.* musculo.
musclebound *adj.* musculosa.
muscleman *n.* musculor.
muscle relaxant *n.* destensante de musculo.
muscle shirt *n.* camiseta de sporte.
muscle tone *n.* tono muscular.
muscular *adj.* (*of the muscles*) muscular; (*muscly*) musculosa.
musculature *n.* musculos.
musculoskeletal *adj.* musculosceletal.
muse *n.* musa.
museum *n.* museo.
museum guide *n.* gidor de museo.
mush *n.* (*food*) gaxa; (*slop*) gaxin, pulpa. • *v.* gaxi.
mushroom *n.* xampinion.
mushroom soup *n.* sopa de xampinion.
mu shu *n.* (*food*) muxu.
mushy *adj.* gaxin.
mushy peas *n.* gaxa de pisos.
music *n.* musica.
musical *adj.* musical. • *n.* (*play*) teatral de musica.
musical note *n.* tono.
musical piece *n.* peso.
musician *n.* musiciste.
musicologist *n.* musicolojiste.
musicology *n.* musicolojia.
musk *n.* musco.
musk deer *n.* musco.
musket *n.* (*gun*) moscete.
musketeer *n.* moscetor.
musketry *n.* mosceti.
muskrat *n.* (*rodent*) ondatra.
musky *adj.* muscosa.
Muslim *adj.* & *n.* muslim.
muslin *n.* (*fabric*) muselina. • *adj.* de muselina.
muss *v.* desordina.
mussel *n.* (*mollusc*) mul.
must *v.* (*physical or essential*) nesesa; (*social*) debe. • *n.* nesesada. **you must be mistaken** sin duta tu era.
mustache *n.* mustax.
mustang *n.* (*horse*) mustang.
mustard *n.* mostarda.
muster *v.* asembla.
must-have *adj.* & *n.* nesesada.
musty *adj.* staniante.
mutability *n.* mutablia.
mutable *adj.* mutable.
mutagen *n.* mutajen.
mutagenic *adj.* (*genetics*) mutajen.
mutant *n.* mutada.
mutate *v.* muta.
mutation *n.* muta.
mute *adj.* (*unable to speak*) muda; (*silent*) silente. • *n.* (*person*) muda; (*musical device*) sordador. • *v.* mudi.
muteness *n.* mudia.
mutilate *v.* mutila.
mutilation *n.* mutila.
mutineer *n.* rebelor.
mutinous *adj.* rebelante.
mutiny *v.* & *n.* rebela.
mutism *n.* mudia.
mutt *n.* can.
mutter *v.* & *n.* babela; (*slurred*) farfulia.
mutton *n.* carne de ovea.
mutual *adj.* mutua.

mutual insurance *n.* asecura mutua.
mutualize *v.* mutui.
mutual liking *n.* simpatia.
muzak *n.* musica de asendador.
muzz *n.* desordina.
muzzle *n.* (*snout*) boca; (*to prevent biting*) paramorde; (*gun*) boca.
muzzle-load *v.* (*gun*) antecarga.
muzzleloader *n.* fusil de antecarga.
Mx *n.* (*gender-neutral*) Sri.
my *det.* mea.
Myanmar *n.* Miama, Burma.
myasthenia *n.* (*medical*) miastenia.
mycelium *n.* (*biology*) miselio.
mycological *adj.* micolojial.
mycologist *n.* micolojiste.
mycology *n.* micolojia.
myelin *n.* (*biology*) mielin.
myelocyte *n.* (*biology*) mielosite.
myeloid *adj.* (*anatomy*) mieloide.
myeloma *n.* (*medical*) mieloma.
myna *n.* (*bird*) storno indian.
mynah *n.* (*bird*) storno indian.
myo- *pref.* (*muscle*) mio-.
myocardial *adj.* miocardial.
myocardial infarction *n.* infarta miocardial.
myocyte *n.* (*biology*) miosite.
myopia *n.* miopia.
myopic *adj.* miope.
myriad *det.* multe.
myriapod *n.* (*arthropod*) miriapodo.
myrrh *n.* (*tree, resin*) mira.
myrtle *n.* (*plant*) mirto.
mysterious *adj.* misteriosa.
mystery *n.* misterio.
mystic *adj.* & *n.* mistica.
mystical *adj.* mistica.
mystical vision *n.* revela.
mysticism *n.* misticisme.
mystify *v.* confonde.
mystique *n.* carisma.
myth *n.* mito.
mythic *adj.* mital.
mythical *adj.* mital.
mythological *adj.* mitolojial.
mythology *n.* mitolojia.

N

n. *abbr.* n (*numero*).
nab *v.* catura.
Nabatean *adj.* & *n.* (*person, language*) nabatea.
nacelle *n.* (*vehicle part*) nasel.
nacre *n.* nacre.
nacreous *adj.* nacrin, opalin.
Na-Dene *adj.* & *n.* (*person, language*) nadene.
nadir *n.* (*astronomy, misfortune*) nadir.
naevus (US **nevus**) *n.* (*birthmark*) nevo.
nag *v.* tormenta.
nagapie *n.* (*primate*) galago.
Nahuatl *adj.* & *n.* (*person, language*) nauatl.
naiad *n.* nimfa de acua.
nail *n.* (*anatomy*) ungia; (*metal*) clo. • *v.* cloi.
nail clipper *n.* cortiungia.
nail file *n.* lima de ungia.
nail gun *n.* cloador.
nail polish *n.* pintiungia.
naïve *adj.* naive; (*unpretentious*) nonfinjosa.
naïveness *n.* naivia.
naïvety (*also* **naïveté**) *n.* naivia.
naked *adj.* nuda.
nakedness *n.* nudia.
name *n.* nom. • *v.* nomi. **name after** nomi per. **name for** nomi per.
named *adj.* nomida. **be named X** es nomida X.
nameless *adj.* sin nom, nonomida.
namely *adv.* per dise.
nameplate *n.* placa de nom.
namesake *n.* omonim.
Namib Desert *n.* Deserto Namib.
Namibia *n.* Namibia.
Namibian *adj.* & *n.* namibian.
nanny *n.* (*carer*) enfantor; (*colloquial*) nana.
nano- *pref.* (*tiny, a thousand-millionth*) nano-.
nanometre (US **nanometer**) *n.* nanometre.
nanosecond *n.* nanosecondo.
nap[1] *v.* & *n.* dormeta.
nap[2] *n.* (*of fabric*) pelo.
napalm *n.* (*liquid*) napalm.
nape *n.* nuca.
naphtha *n.* (*oil*) nafta.
naphthalina *n.* (*substance*) naftalina.
naphthol *n.* (*substance*) naftol.
napkin *n.* teleta.
nappy *n.* teleta de bebe.
narcissism *n.* narsisisme.
narcissist *n.* narsisiste.
narcissistic *adj.* narsisiste.
narcissus *n.* narsiso.
narco- *pref.* (*stupor*) narco-.
narcolepsy *n.* narcolesia.
narcoleptic *adj.* narcolesica.
narcosis *n.* narcose.
narcotic *adj.* & *n.* narcotica.
nares *n.* (*nostrils*) narinas.
naris *n.* (*nostril*) narina.
narrate *v.* nara.
narration *n.* nara.
narrational *adj.* naral.
narrative *adj.* naral.
narrator *n.* naror.
narrow *adj.* streta; (*thin*) magra. • *v.* streti. **have a narrow escape** evita apena.
narrowboat *n.* barco de canal.
narrow-gauge railway *n.* ferovia streta.
narrowly *adv.* (*only just*) apena.
narrow-minded *adj.* prejudosa.
narrowness *n.* stretia.
narwhal *n.* (*whale*) narval.
nasal *adj.* & *n.* nasal.
nasal cavity *n.* caveta nasal.
nasalize *v.* nasali.
nasal voice *n.* vose nasal.
nascent *adj.* nasente.
nasopharyngitis *n.* cataro.
nasopharynx *n.* farinje nasal.
nasturtium *n.* (*plant*) nasturtio.
nasty *adj.* desplasente, repulsante.
natal *adj.* de nase.
natatorium *n.* naderia.
nation *n.* nasion.
national *adj.* nasional. • *n.* sitadan.
national dress *n.* veste etnical.
national holiday *n.* festa nasional.
nationalism *n.* nasionalisme.
nationalist *n.* nasionaliste.
nationalistic *adj.* nasionaliste.
nationality *n.* nasionalia.
nationalization *n.* nasionali.
nationalize *v.* nasionali.
nationwide *adj.* nasional.
native *adj.* (*to a place*) nativa, orijinal; (*where one was born*) de nase; (*language*) propre. • *n.* nativa.
Native American *adj.* & *n.* american orijinal.
native land *n.* pais de nase.
native land right *n.* direto nativa de tera.
native language *n.* propre lingua.
native title *n.* direto nativa de tera.
native tongue *n.* propre lingua.
nativism *n.* nativisme.
nativist *n.* nativiste.
nativity *n.* natal.
natron *n.* (*substance*) natron.
natter *v.* & *n.* parleta.
natural *adj.* natural.

natural cornet *n.* (*musical instrument*) corneta natural.
naturalist *n.* naturiste.
naturalistic *adj.* naturin.
naturalization *n.* sitadani, naturali.
naturalize *v.* sitadani, naturali.
natural killer cell *n.* limfosite NK.
natural number *n.* numero natural.
natural right *n.* direto natural.
natural satellite *n.* luneta.
natural selection *n.* eleje natural.
natural trumpet *n.* corneta natural.
nature *n.* natur.
naturism *n.* nudisme.
naturist *n.* nudiste.
naugahyde *n.* polivinil cuorin.
naught *n.* zero.
naughtiness *n.* turbosia.
naughty *adj.* turbosa; vulgar, lasiva.
Nauru *n.* Nauero.
Nauruan *adj.* & *n.* nauero.
nausea *n.* nausea.
nauseate *v.* nausea.
nauseation *n.* nausea.
nauseous *adj.* nauseosa.
nautical mile *n.* milia maral.
nautilus *n.* (*mollusc*) nautilo.
Navaho *adj.* & *n.* (*person, language*) dine.
Navajo *adj.* & *n.* (*person, language*) dine.
naval *adj.* marinal.
Navarre *n.* (*Spanish region*) Navara.
nave *n.* (*church*) nave.
navel *n.* ombilico.
navigate *v.* naviga.
navigation *n.* naviga.
navigator *n.* navigor.
navy *n.* marina; (*colour*) blu. • *adj.* blu.
navy bean *n.* fava blanca.
nay *n.* (*flute*) ne.
naysayer *n.* diseno.
Nazi *adj.* & *n.* nazi.
Nazism *n.* nazisme.
NB *abbr.* nb (*nota bon*).
né *adv.* orijinal.
Neanderthal *adj.* & *n.* neandertalan.
near *adj.* prosima. • *v.* prosimi. **bring nearer** prosimi. **have a near miss** evita apena.
nearby *adj.* & *adv.* prosima.
Near East *n.* Asia sude-ueste.
nearly *adv.* cuasi.
nearness *n.* prosimia.
near-sighted *adj.* miope.
near-sightedness *n.* miopia.
neat *adj.* ordinada.
neaten *v.* ordina.
Nebraska *n.* (*US state*) Nebraska.
nebula *n.* nebulosa.
nebulizer *n.* neblador, vaporador.
nebulous *adj.* neblosa.
necatoriasis *n.* (*disease*) necatoriase.
necessarily *adv.* nesesada.
necessary *adj.* nesesada.
necessitate *v.* nesesa, obliga, forsa.
necessity *n.* (*quality*) nesesa; (*thing needed*) nesesada.
neck *n.* colo. **back of the neck** nuca. **neck and neck** con lado a lado.
neckerchief *n.* tela de colo.
necklace *n.* colareta.
neckline *n.* escota.
neckscarf *n.* covrecolo.
necktie *n.* cravata.
necro- *pref.* (*death*) necro-.
necrology *n.* anunsia de mori.
necromancer *n.* necromansiste, spiritiste.
necromancy *n.* (*divination*) necromansia.
necrophile *n.* necrofilica.
necrophilia *n.* necrofilia.
necrophiliac *adj.* & *n.* necrofilica.
necrophobe *n.* necrofobica.
necrophobia *n.* necrofobia.
necrophobic *adj.* necrofobica.
necropolis *n.* necropoli.
necrosis *n.* (*medical*) necrose.
necrotic *adj.* necrosica.
nectar *n.* netar.
nectarine *n.* (*peach*) netarina.
née *adv.* orijinal.
need *v.* nesesa. • *n.* (*quality*) nesesa; (*thing needed*) nesesada. **need to** (*social obligation*) debe; (*physical or essential*) nesesa.
needle *n.* ago.
needlelike *adj.* agin.
needlepoint *n.* brode.
needlework *n.* brode, cose.
needy *adj.* povre.
nefarious *adj.* criminal.
negate *v.* nega.
negation *n.* nega.
negative *adj.* & *n.* (*including photographic*) negativa.
negative sign *n.* sinia negativa.
negativism *n.* negativisme.
negativity *n.* negativia.
neglect *v.* descura.
neglectful *adj.* descurante.
negligee *n.* roba diafana.
negligence *n.* descura.
negligent *adj.* nonatendente; descurante.
negligible *adj.* iniorable.
negotiate *v.* negosia.
negotiation *n.* negosia.
negotiator *n.* negosior.
Negro *adj.* & *n.* afroamerican.
negroid *adj.* negroide.
neigh *interj.* iii.
neighbour (US **neighbor**) *n.* visina.

neighbourhood (US **neighborhood**) *n.* visineria.
neighbouring (US **neighboring**) *adj.* visina.
neighbourly *adj.* amin.
neither *pron.* no la un e no la otra. **neither this nor that** no esta e no acel.
nematode *n.* nematodo, verme ronda.
nematomorph *n.* (*organism*) nematomorfo.
nemertean *n.* (*worm*) nemerteo.
nemesis *n.* arcenemi.
neo- *pref.* (*new*) neo-.
neoclassical *adj.* neoclasica.
neoclassicism *n.* neoclasicisme.
neoclassicist *n.* neoclasiciste.
neocolonial *adj.* neocolonial.
neocolonialism *n.* neocolonialisme.
neocolonialist *adj.* & *n.* neocolonialiste.
neodymium *n.* (*element*) neodimio.
Neolithic *adj.* & *n.* neolitica.
neologism *n.* parola nova.
neon *n.* neon.
neonate *n.* bebeta.
neopagan *adj.* neopagan.
neophyte *n.* comensor.
neoplasm *n.* (*medical*) neoplasma.
neoteny *n.* (*biology*) neotenia.
neotropical *adj.* neotropical.
neotropics *n.* neotropico.
Nepal *n.* Nepal.
Nepalese *adj.* & *n.* nepali.
Nepali *adj.* & *n.* nepali.
nephew *n.* sobrino; (*gender-neutral*) sobrin.
nephritic *adj.* nefritica.
nephritis *n.* (*medical*) nefrite.
nephro- *pref.* (*kidney*) nefro-.
nepotism *n.* netisme.
Neptune *n.* (*mythology*, *planet*) Netuno.
neptunium *n.* (*element*) netunio.
nerd *n.* ganso, manica.
nereid *n.* nimfa de mar.
nerve *n.* nervo; (*courage*) coraje; (*impudence*) noncortesia.
nervous *adj.* (*jumpy*) nervosa, ansiosa; (*of the nerves*) nerval, de nervos.
nervous breakdown *n.* crise mental.
nervousness *n.* nervosia, ansia.
nervous system *n.* sistem de nervos.
-nesia *suff.* (*islands*) -nesia.
-ness *suff.* -ia.
nest *n.* nido. • *v.* nidi; (*embed*) caxi. **build a nest** nidi.
nest box *n.* casa de avia.
nestle *v.* nidi se.
nestling *n.* (*bird*) nidor.
net[1] *n.* rede.
net[2] *adj.* & *adv.* (*money*) neta.
netbook *n.* computador portable peti.
Netherlandish *adj.* & *n.* nederlandes.
Netherlands *n.* Nederland.
Netherlands Antilles *n.* Antiles Nederlandes.
netiquette *n.* cortesia de rede.
netizen *n.* usor de rede.
netsuke *n.* (*sculpture*) netsuce.
nett *adj.* & *adv.* (*money*) neta.
netting *n.* rede.
nettle *n.* ortica.
network *n.* rede. • *v.* redi.
networker *n.* redor.
network user *n.* redor.
neural *adj.* neuronal.
neuralgia *n.* neuraljia.
neuralgic *adj.* neuraljica.
neurasthenia *n.* neurastenia.
neurasthenic *adj.* neurastenica.
neuritic *adj.* neuritica.
neuritis *n.* (*medical*) neurite.
neuro- *pref.* (*nerve*) neuro-.
neurobiologist *n.* neurobiolojiste.
neurobiology *n.* neurobiolojia.
neurological *adj.* neurolojial, neuronal.
neurologist *n.* neurolojiste.
neurology *n.* neurolojia.
neuron *n.* neuron.
neuronal *adj.* neuronal.
neuropathic *adj.* neuropatica.
neuropathy *n.* neuropatia.
neuropeptide *n.* neuropeptido.
neuroscience *n.* neurosiensa.
neuroscientist *n.* neurosiensiste.
neurosis *n.* neurose.
neurosurgeon *n.* neurosirurjiste.
neurosurgery *n.* neurosirurjia.
neurosurgical *adj.* neurosirurjial.
neurotic *adj.* & *n.* neurosica.
neurotoxin *n.* neurotoxina.
neurotransmitter *n.* neurotransmetador.
neuter *adj.* neutra. • *v.* neutri.
neutral *adj.* neutra. • *n.* (*gear*) engrana mor.
neutrality *n.* neutria.
neutralize *v.* neutri.
neutrino *n.* neutrino.
neutron *n.* neutron.
neutronic *adj.* neutronal.
neutron star *n.* stela de neutrones.
neutrophile *n.* neutrofilica.
neutrophilia *n.* neutrofilia.
neutrophilic *adj.* neutrofilica.
Nevada *n.* (*US state*) Nevada.
never *adv.* nunca, a no tempo. **never-ageing** nonsenesente. **never at all** an nunca. **never mind** oblida lo, lo no importa.
nevertheless *adv.* an tal, ma ancora; par contrasta, a cualce caso.
Nevis *n.* Nevis.
Nevisian *adj.* & *n.* nevisian.
nevus (US). See *naevus*.

new *adj.* nova; fresca. **make like new** restora.
newbie *n.* comensor.
newborn *n.* beheta.
New Britain *n.* Britan Nova.
New Brunswick *n.* (*Canadian province*) Brunswick Nova.
New Caledonia *n.* Caledonia Nova.
newcomer *n.* arivor; comensor.
newest *adj.* la plu nova.
Newfoundland *n.* Newfoundland. **Newfoundland and Labrador** (*Canadian province*) Newfoundland e Labrador.
New Guinea *n.* Gine Nova.
New Hampshire *n.* (*US state*) Hampshire Nova.
New Jersey *n.* (*US state*) Jersey Nova.
new land *n.* tera nova.
newly rich *adj.* nova rica.
newlywed *adj.* nova sposida.
New Mexico *n.* (*US state*) Mexico Nova.
new moon *n.* luna oscur.
newness *n.* novia.
news *n.* novas, avenis nova.
newsagent *n.* (*shop*) jornaleria.
news anchor *n.* presentor de novas.
newsboy *n.* xico de jornales.
news bulletin *n.* difusa de novas.
newscast *n.* difusa de novas.
newscaster *n.* presentor de novas.
newsgirl *n.* xica de jornales.
news item *n.* article de novas.
newsletter *n.* revisteta de grupo.
newspaper *n.* jornal dial.
newspaperman *n.* jornaliste.
newspaperwoman *n.* jornaliste.
news presenter *n.* presentor de novas.
newsreader *n.* presentor de novas.
newsreel *n.* filma de novas.
newsstand *n.* jornaleria.
newt *n.* triton.
New Testament *n.* Atesta Nova.
newton *n.* (*unit of force*) neuton.
New World monkey *n.* simia american.
New World sparrow *n.* pasaro american.
New World vulture *n.* condor.
New York State *n.* (*US state*) York Nova.
New Zealand *n.* Zeland Nova. • *adj.* zelandes.
New Zealander *n.* zelandes.
New Zealand wren *n.* acantisita.
next *adj.* seguente; veninte. • *adv.* a pos, seguente. **next to** a lado de.
nexus *n.* rede.
NGO *n.* organiza nongovernal.
niacin *n.* niasina.
nib *n.* (*pen*) beco.
nibble *v.* rode.
Nicaragua *n.* Nicaragua.
Nicaraguan *adj.* & *n.* nicaraguan.
nice *adj.* amable, amin, dulse; bon.
nice guy *n.* bonom.
nice lady *n.* bonfem.
niceness *n.* amablia.
niche *n.* (*alcove, ecological*) nix.
nick *n.* indente. • *v.* indente; (*steal*) fura.
nickel *n.* (*metal*) nicel; (*coin*) dudesim.
nickelodeon *n.* automata de discos.
nickel-plate *v.* niceli.
nickel-plated *adj.* nicelida.
nickname *n.* nometa.
nicotine *n.* nicotina.
nicotinic acid *n.* niasina.
nictate *v.* ginia.
niece *n.* sobrina; (*gender-neutral*) sobrin.
niff *v.* apesta.
Niger *n.* Nijer.
Nigeria *n.* Nijeria.
Nigerian *adj.* & *n.* (*of Nigeria*) nijerian.
Nigerien *adj.* & *n.* (*of Niger*) nijerien.
Niger River *n.* Rio Nijer.
night *n.* note. **at night** a note. **become night** noti.
nightcap *n.* xapo de note.
nightclub *n.* loca de note; cabare.
nightdress *n.* roba de note.
nightfall *n.* noti.
nightgown *n.* roba de note.
nighthawk *n.* caprimuljo.
nightie *n.* roba de note.
nightingale *n.* rosinol.
nightjar *n.* caprimuljo.
nightlight *n.* lampa de note.
nightmare *n.* malsonia. **have a nightmare** malsonia.
nightmarish *adj.* malsonin.
night monkey *n.* aoto.
nightshade *n.* solano.
nightshirt *n.* camisa de note.
night spot *n.* loca de note.
nightstand *n.* comodeta.
nihilism *n.* nihilisme.
nihilist *adj.* & *n.* nihiliste.
nihilistic *adj.* nihiliste.
nihonium *n.* (*element*) nihonio.
nil *adj.* & *n.* zero.
Nilotic *adj.* (*languages*) nilotica.
nimble *adj.* ajil.
nimbleness *n.* ajilia.
nimbus *adj.* (*cloud*) nimbo. • *n.* (*cloud*) nimbo; (*halo*) areola.
nincompoop *n.* bobo, fol.
nine *det.* & *pron.* nove.
nine-pin bowling *n.* boling de nove bastones.
ninetieth *adj.* (*ordinal*) novedes. • *n.* (*fraction*) novedesi.
ninety *det.* & *pron.* novedes.

ninja *n.* ninja.
ninjutsu *n.* (*martial art*) ninjutsu.
ninth *adj.* (*ordinal*) nove; (*fraction*) novi.
niobium *n.* (*element*) niobio.
nip *v.* & *n.* pinsi.
nipple *n.* teta.
nipple shield *n.* covreteta.
niqab *n.* (*veil*) nicab.
nirvana *n.* (*Buddhism*) nirvana.
nit *n.* ovo de piolio.
nitpick *v.* es pedante.
nitpicker *n.* pedante.
nitpicking *n.* pedantia.
nitrate *n.* nitrato.
nitric *adj.* nitrica.
nitric acid *n.* asida nitrica.
nitrite *n.* nitrito.
nitro *n.* nitrogliserina.
nitrogen *n.* nitrojen.
nitrogenous *adj.* nitrojenosa.
nitroglycerine *n.* nitrogliserina.
nitrous *adj.* nitrosa.
nitwit *n.* stupida.
Niue *n.* Niue.
Niuean *adj.* & *n.* niue.
nix *v.* cansela.
no[1] *det.* no, zero. • *interj.* no. **no later than** ante fini de. **no longer** no plu. **no more** no plu; (*down with*) aboli, basi. **no smoking** fumi proibida.
no.[2] (also **№**) *abbr.* n (*numero*).
Noah *n.* Noa.
nobelium *n.* (*element*) nobelio.
nobility *n.* (*quality*) nobilia; (*people*) nobiles.
noble *adj.* & *n.* nobil.
nobody *pron.* nun, no person.
nocebo *adj.* & *n.* (*medical*) nosebo.
nock *v.* & *n.* indente.
noctambulation *n.* sonambula.
noctambulist *n.* sonambulor.
nocturnal *adj.* noturna.
nocturne *n.* (*art*, *music*) noturna.
nod *v.* inclina sua testa; (*in agreement*) acorda con testa, confirma con testa.
node *n.* noda.
nodose *adj.* nodosa.
nodular *adj.* nodulal.
nodule *n.* nodulo.
Noel *n.* natal.
noesis *n.* inteleto.
noetic *adj.* inteletal.
noh *n.* (*drama*) no.
-noid *suff.* (*mind*) -noide.
noise *n.* ruido.
noiseless *adj.* sin sona.
noisemaker *n.* (*person*) ruidor; (*device*) ruidador.
noisy *adj.* ruidosa.
nomad *n.* nomada, vagiste.
nomadic *adj.* nomada.
nomadism *n.* nomadisme, vagisme.
no man's land *n.* tera de nun.
nom de guerre *n.* nom de gera.
nom de plume *n.* nom falsa.
nomenclature *n.* nomes.
nominal *adj.* par nom, par titulo; (*cost*) minima.
nominally *adv.* par titulo.
nominate *v.* nomina, proposa.
nomination *n.* nomina, proposa.
nominative *adj.* & *n.* (*grammar*) nominativa.
nominee *n.* nominada, proposada, aspiror.
non- *pref.* non-.
non-abrasive *adj.* nonraspante.
non-absorbent *adj.* nonasorbente.
non-adhesive *adj.* nonaderente.
non-adjustable *adj.* nonajustable.
nonagon *n.* nonagon.
nonagonal *adj.* nonagon.
non-alcoholic *adj.* nonalcolosa, sin alcol.
non-alcoholic drink *n.* bevida sin alcol.
non-amateur *adj.* con salario.
non-attachment *n.* nonteni.
non-believer *n.* noncredor.
non-binary *adj.* nonbinaria.
non-cancerous *adj.* noncanserosa.
non-central *adj.* nonsentral.
nonchalance *n.* casualia.
nonchalant *adj.* casual.
non-circular *adj.* nonsirculo.
non-combatant *n.* noncombator.
non-committal *adj.* nondedicada.
non-conformist *n.* disentor.
non-conformity *n.* nonconforma.
non-consenting *adj.* nonacordante.
non-corrosive *adj.* noncorodente.
non-denominational *adj.* nonramal.
non-determinist *n.* nondeterministe.
non-deterministic *adj.* nondeterministe.
non-disclosure agreement *n.* acorda de nonrevela.
non-drinker *n.* nonbevor.
none *pron.* zero. **none at all** tota no; tota zero; vera no cosa.
non-empathic *adj.* nonempatica.
non-equivalent *adj.* nonegal.
non-essential *adj.* nonesensal.
nonetheless *adv.* an tal, ma ancora, par contrasta, contra esta, a cualce caso.
non-Euclidean *adj.* noneuclidal.
non-Euclidean geometry *n.* jeometria noneuclidal.
non-existence *n.* nonesiste.
non-existent *adj.* nonesistente.
non-extreme *adj.* nonestrema.
non-fatal *adj.* nonmatante.
non-fiction book *n.* libro de fato.
non-finite *adj.* nonfinitiva.

non-flammable *adj.* nonflamable.
non-fluent *adj.* nonfluente.
non-governmental organization *n.* organiza nongovernal.
non-human *adj.* nonumana.
non-industrial *adj.* nonindustrial.
non-kosher *adj.* noncaxer.
non-linear *adj.* nonlinial.
non-literal *adj.* nonleteral.
non-metal *adj.* & *n.* nonmetal.
non-metric *adj.* nonmetral.
non-native *adj.* nonativa.
non-normative *adj.* nonorminte.
no-no *n.* nonpermeteda, nonasetable.
non-observance *n.* nonsegue.
nonpareil *adj.* sin egal.
non-partisan *adj.* nonpartisan.
non-pathogenic *adj.* nonpatojen.
non-perishable *adj.* nonputrable; nonmortal.
non-poisonous *adj.* nonvenenosa.
non-porous *adj.* nonporosa.
non-professional *n.* nonprofesal.
non-profit *adj.* nonprofitante.
non-proliferation *n.* nonsperde.
non-random *adj.* nonacaso.
non-reflective *adj.* nonrefletante.
non-religious *adj.* nonrelijiosa.
non-renewable *adj.* nonrenovable.
non-resident *n.* nonabitor.
non-residential *adj.* (*not residing*) nonabitante; (*not to do with residence*) nonabital.
non-returnable *adj.* nonreenviable.
non-rigid airship *n.* airostato nonrijida.
non-romantic *adj.* nonromantica.
non-sailor *n.* nonmarinor.
nonsense *n.* asurda. • *interj.* asurda, ba. **talk nonsense** babela.
nonsensical *adj.* asurda.
non sequitur *n.* nonsegue.
non-sexual *adj.* & *n.* nonsesal, asesal.
non-slip *adj.* nonliscosa.
non-smoker *n.* nonfumor.
non-steroidal anti-inflammatory drug *n.* antiinflamante nonsteroidal.
non-stick *adj.* nonaderente.
non-stop *adj.* nonpausante, nonsesante, sin pausa, sin sesa.
non-subscriber *n.* nonenscrivor.
non-toxic *adj.* nonvenenosa, nonosiva.
non-traditional *adj.* nontradisional.
non-union *adj.* nonsindicatal.
non-verbal *adj.* (*not spoken*) nonparlada; (*not expressed in words*) nonparolal.
non-violent *adj.* nonviolente.
non-virulent *adj.* nongrave.
non-viscous *adj.* acuin.
non-volatile *adj.* nonvolatil.
noob *n.* comensor.
noodle *n.* talieta.
noodle soup *n.* sopa de talietas.
noodle strap *n.* breteleta.
nook *n.* alcova.
noon *n.* mediadia.
no one *pron.* nun, no person.
noontime *n.* mediadia.
noose *n.* laso.
noradrenaline *n.* (*hormone*) norepinefrina.
norepinephrine *n.* norepinefrina.
nori *n.* (*seaweed*) nori.
norm *n.* norma.
Norma *n.* (*constellation*) la Cuadrador.
normal *adj.* normal.
normalcy *n.* normalia.
normality *n.* normalia.
normalization *n.* normali.
normalize *v.* normali.
Norman *adj.* & *n.* normande.
Normandy *n.* Normandia.
normative *adj.* (*standardized*) normal; (*standardizing*) norminte.
normoblast *n.* (*blood cell*) normoblasto.
Norse *adj.* nordica.
north *adj.* & *n.* norde. **to the north of** a norde de.
North America *n.* America Norde.
North Carolina *n.* (*US state*) Carolina Norde.
North Dakota *n.* (*US state*) Dakota Norde.
northeast *adj.* & *n.* norde-este.
northeaster *n.* venta norde-este.
northeasterly *adj.* norde-este.
northern *adj.* norde.
Northern Africa *n.* Africa norde.
Northern Ireland *n.* Er Norde.
northern lights *n.* aurora norde.
North Korea *n.* Txoson, Corea Norde.
North Korean *adj.* & *n.* txoson.
north-northeast *adj.* & *n.* norde-norde-este.
north-northwest *adj.* & *n.* norde-norde-ueste.
North Pole *n.* Polo Norde.
North Sea *n.* Mar Norde.
northward *adv.* a norde.
northwards *adv.* a norde.
northwest *adj.* & *n.* norde-ueste.
northwesterly *adj.* norde-ueste.
Northwest Territories *n.* Teritorios Norde-ueste.
Norway *n.* Noria.
Norway lobster *n.* omareta.
Norwegian *adj.* norsce.
Norwegian Sea *n.* Mar Norsce.
nose *n.* nas. • *v.* nasi. **look down one's nose at** finje superioria.
nosebleed *n.* sangui de nas.
nosedive *n.* tufa.
nosegay *n.* buceta.

nosey *adj.* curiosa.
nosh *n.* comeda.
nosologist *n.* nosolojiste.
nosology *n.* nosolojia.
nostalgia *n.* nostaljia.
nostalgic *adj.* nostaljial.
nostril *n.* narina.
nostrum *n.* medisin inferior.
nosy *adj.* curiosa.
not *adv.* no. **not at all** a no grado, tota no, vera no. **not even** an no. **not even once** an nunca. **not many** poca. **not much** poca. **not quite** cuasi, nonesata. **not yet** ancora no.
nota bene *interj.* nota bon.
notable *adj.* notable.
notarize *v.* validi.
notary *n.* notario.
notation *n.* representa, simboles.
notch *n.* indente.
note *v.* (*message, music*) nota; (*scrap of paper*) papereta. • *n.* nota; (*money*) bileta. **make a note of** nota.
notebook *n.* libro de notas; (*small*) libro de pox.
noted *adj.* notada; famosa.
notepad *n.* bloco de notas.
notepaper *n.* paper de letera.
noter *n.* notor.
notetaker *n.* notor.
nothing *n.* no cosa. **come to nothing** aborta. **nothing at all** vera no cosa.
nothingness *n.* noncosia.
notice *n.* (*notification*) avisa; (*displayed information*) nota. • *v.* persepi. **give notice** avisa.
noticeable *adj.* notable, persepable.
noticeboard *n.* mureta de avisas.
notification *n.* avisa.
notify *v.* avisa.
notion *n.* idea.
notions *n.* ideas; (*haberdashery*) benes de cose.
notochord *n.* (*anatomy*) notocorda.
notoriety *n.* fama.
notorious *adj.* malfamosa.
notwithstanding *prep.* an con; (*something that has already happened*) an pos.
nougat *n.* (*confectionery*) nuga.
nought *n.* zero.
noumenon *n.* (*philosophy*) numeno.
noun *n.* nom, sustantivo.
nounal *adj.* nomin.
noun clause *n.* suproposa nomin.
noun phrase *n.* formula nomin.
nourish *v.* nuri.
nourishment *n.* nuri.
nouveau riche *adj.* nova rica.
nova *n.* (*star*) nova.
Nova Scotia *n.* (*Canadian province*) Scotia Nova.
novel *adj.* nova. • *n.* novela.
novelist *n.* novelor.
novella *n.* noveleta.
novelty *n.* (*quality*) novia; (*item*) noveta.
November *n.* novembre.
novena *n.* (*prayers*) novena.
novice *n.* comensor.
novitiate *n.* (*state*) comensa; (*person*) comensor.
novocaine *n.* (*anaesthetic*) procaina.
now *adv.* aora. • *interj.* alora. **for now** per aora, per la presente. **from now on** de aora. **now and again** a veses, de ves a ves, aora e alora. **now and then** a veses, de ves a ves, aora e alora. **now then** alora.
nowadays *adv.* a esta dias, corente.
Nowell *n.* natal.
nowhere *adv.* en no loca, en no parte. **in the middle of nowhere** a via de vias. **nowhere else** en no otra loca.
noxious *adj.* nosiva.
nozzle *n.* boceta.
NSAID *n.* antiinflamante nonsteroidal.
nu *n.* (*Greek letter* Ν, ν) nu.
nuance *n.* tinje, sutil.
nuanced *adj.* sutil.
nub *n.* bulto, protende.
nubbin *n.* bulto.
nubby *adj.* ru.
nubile *adj.* sesal matur.
nuclear *adj.* nucleal.
nuclear bomb *n.* bomba nucleal.
nuclear meltdown *n.* fonde nucleal.
nuclear warfare *n.* gera nucleal.
nuclear warhead *n.* ojiva nucleal.
nucleic *adj.* nucleal.
nucleic acid *n.* asida nucleal.
nucleolus *n.* (*biology*) nucleol.
nucleon *n.* (*particle*) nucleon.
nucleotide *n.* nucleotido.
nucleus *n.* nucleo.
nude *adj.* nuda.
nudge *v.* & *n.* puieta.
nudism *n.* nudisme.
nudist *n.* nudiste.
nudity *n.* nudia.
nugget *n.* pepita.
nuisance *n.* irita, peste.
nuke *n.* bomba nucleal. • *v.* bombi nucleal.
null *adj.* vacua.
nullify *v.* nega.
null string *n.* cadena vacua.
null vote *n.* vota vacua.
numb *adj.* nonsensosa.
number *n.* (*in sequence*) numero; (*quantity*) cuantia. • *v.* numeri.
number plate *n.* placa de veculo.
number sign *n.* sinia de numero, grilia.
number theory *n.* teoria de numeros.

numbness *n.* nonsensosia.
numbskull *n.* stupida.
numeracy *n.* numerisme.
numeral *n.* (*grammar*) numero.
numerate *adj.* numeriste.
numerator *n.* divideda.
numeric *adj.* numeral.
numerical analysis *n.* analise numeral.
numeric keypad *n.* tecladoreta numeral.
numerologist *n.* numerolojiste.
numerology *n.* numerolojia.
numerous *adj.* multe, diversa.
numinous *adj.* diosa, relijiosa, spiritosa.
numismatic *adj.* numismatial.
numismatics *n.* numismatia.
numismatist *n.* numismatiste.
numpty *n.* fol, stupida.
nun *n.* monce, monce fema.
Nunavut *n.* (*Canadian province*) Nunavut.
nunchaku *n.* (*weapon*) nuntxacu.
nunchuk *n.* (*weapon*) nuntxacu.
nunnery *n.* soreria, monceria.
nuptial *adj.* sposal.
nuraghe *n.* (*tower*) nurage.
Nuragic *adj.* (*civilization*) nuragal.
nurse *v.* cura; (*breastfeed*) dona lete; prende lete. • *n.* curor; (*nanny*) enfantor.
nursemaid *n.* enfantor.
nursery *n.* sala de enfantes; (*kindergarten*) jardin de enfantes; (*for plants*) viveria.
nurture *v.* & *n.* cura, eleva.
nut *n.* noza; (*for bolt*) torca; (*testicle*) coion.
nutcracker *n.* crasenoza.
nuthatch *n.* (*bird*) sita.
nuthouse *n.* dementeria.
nutlike *adj.* nozin.
nutmeg *n.* muscada.
nutria *n.* (*rodent*) coipu.
nutrient *n.* nurinte.
nutrition *n.* nuri.
nutritional *adj.* nural.
nutritional yeast *n.* fermentante nural.
nutritionist *n.* nuriste.
nutritious *adj.* nurinte.
nutshell *n.* casca de noza.
nutty *adj.* (*nutlike*) nozin; (*full of nuts*) nozosa; (*eccentric*) bobo.
nuzzle *v.* nasi.
Nyasa, Lake *n.* Lago Malaui.
nyctophile *n.* nictofilica.
nyctophilia *n.* nictofilia.
nyctophilic *adj.* nictofilica.
nylon *n.* nilon.
nymph *n.* nimfa.
nympho *n.* nimfomanica.
nymphomania *n.* nimfomania.
nymphomaniac *adj.* & *n.* nimfomanica.
nystagmus *n.* (*medical*) nistagmo.

O

O *interj.* (*vocative*) o.
oaf *n.* torpe.
oak *n.* cuerco. • *adj.* de cuerco.
oaken *adj.* de cuerco.
oar *n.* remo.
oarlock *n.* scalmo.
oarsman *n.* remor.
oasis *n.* oasis.
oat *n.* avena.
oath *n.* jura. **take oath** jura.
oatmeal *n.* gaxa de avena.
oats *n.* avena.
obdurate *adj.* ostinosa.
obedience *n.* obedi.
obedient *adj.* obedinte.
obelisk *n.* obelisce.
obelus *n.* sinia de daga.
obese *adj.* obesa.
obesity *n.* obesia.
obey *v.* obedi.
obeying *adj.* obedinte.
obfuscate *v.* oscuri.
obi *n.* (*sash*) obi.
obituary *n.* anunsia de mori.
object *n.* (*including grammar*) ojeto. • *v.* oposa, protesta. **object of desire** desirada.
objection *n.* oposa, protesta.
objective *adj.* ojetal, empirical. • *n.* ojeto.
objective lens *n.* lente de ojeto.
objectivity *n.* empiricalia.
object lens *n.* lente de ojeto.
object-oriented programming *n.* programi ojetal.
objet d'art *n.* obra de arte.
oblate *adj.* planida a la polos.
oblation *n.* donada a Dio.
obligate *v.* obliga.
obligated *adj.* obligada. **be obligated** es obligada, debe.
obligation *n.* obliga, promete.
obligatory *adj.* obligante.
oblige *v.* obliga.
oblique *adj.* apoiada.
oblique stroke *n.* bara inclinada.
obliterate *v.* elimina.
obliteration *n.* elimina.
oblivion *n.* estingui, nonconsensia.
oblong *adj.* & *n.* retangulo.
obnoxious *adj.* iritante.
oboe *n.* oboe.
oboist *n.* oboiste.
obscene *adj.* ofendente; lasiva.
obscenity *n.* ofende.
obscurantism *n.* oscurisme.
obscurantist *n.* oscuriste.
obscure *adj.* oscur. • *v.* oscuri.
obscurity *n.* oscuria.
obsequious *adj.* adulante.
observable *adj.* oservable.
observance *n.* rituo.
observant *adj.* oservante.
observation *n.* oserva.
observatory *n.* oserveria.
observe *v.* oserva; (*remark*) comenta; (*comply with*) obedi, segue; (*promise*) reali. **fail to observe** (*promise, deal*) rompe.
observer *n.* oservor.
obsess *v.* osese.
obsession *n.* osese.
obsessive *adj.* osesente. • *n.* osesor.
obsessive-compulsive disorder *n.* sindrom de osese e compulsa.
obsidian *n.* (*rock*) osidiana.
obsolescence *n.* desusa.
obsolete *adj.* desusada.
obstacle *n.* ostaculo, bloco, impedi.
obstacle course *n.* curso de ostaculos.
obstetric *adj.* ostetrical.
obstetrical *adj.* ostetrical.
obstetrician *n.* ostetriciste.
obstetrics *n.* ostetrica.
obstinacy *n.* ostina.
obstinate *adj.* ostinosa.
obstruct *v.* bloci, impedi.
obstruction *n.* bloci, impedi.
obstruent *adj.* & *n.* (*consonant*) constrinjente.
obtain *v.* oteni; (*prevail*) domina.
obtainable *adj.* otenable.
obtrusive *adj.* atraente atende.
obtuse *adj.* nonintelijente, nonsensosa; (*angle*) nonagu.
obvious *adj.* evidente.
obviousness *n.* evidentia.
ocarina *n.* (*musical instrument*) ocarina.
occasion *n.* ves; (*noteworthy event*) aveni. **on each occasion** a cada ves. **on occasion** a veses, de ves a ves, aora e alora.
occasional *adj.* nonfrecuente.
occasionally *adv.* a veses, de ves a ves, aora e alora; (*rarely*) a veses rara, a poca veses.
occident *n.* ueste.
occidental *adj.* ueste.
occipital *adj.* osipital.
occipital bone *n.* oso osipital.
occipital lobe *n.* lobe osipital.
Occitan *adj.* & *n.* (*language*) ositan.
occult *adj.* oculta; ocultiste. • *n.* oculta. • *v.* oculti.
occultation *n.* oculti.
occultism *n.* ocultisme.

occultist *adj.* & *n.* ocultiste.
occupancy *n.* ocupa.
occupant *n.* ocupor.
occupation *n.* ocupa; carera.
occupational *adj.* ocupal.
occupier *n.* ocupor.
occupy *v.* ocupa.
occupying force *n.* ocupor.
occur *v.* aveni.
occurrence *n.* aveni.
ocean *n.* mar.
oceanarium *n.* mareria.
ocean bottom *n.* fondo de mar.
ocean cruise *n.* turi a mar.
ocean floor *n.* fondo de mar.
Oceania *n.* Oseania.
oceanic *adj.* maral.
oceanographer *n.* oseanografiste, marolojiste.
oceanographic *adj.* oseanografial.
oceanography *n.* oseanografia, marolojia.
oceanologist *n.* marolojiste.
oceanology *n.* marolojia.
ocelot *n.* (*wild cat*) oselote.
ochre (US **ocher**) *adj.* (*colour*) ocer. • *n.* (*pigment*) ocer.
octagon *n.* otagon.
octagonal *adj.* otagon.
octal *adj.* (*base eight*) otal.
octane *n.* otano.
Octans *n.* (*constellation*) la Otante.
octant *n.* otante.
octave *n.* otava.
octavo *adj.* (*book size*) otida.
octet *n.* otuple.
octo- *pref.* oto-.
October *n.* otobre.
octodont *n.* (*rodent*) otodon.
octopus *n.* polpo.
octuplet *adj.* & *n.* otojemelo.
ocular lens *n.* lente de regarda.
oculist *n.* oculiste, oftalmolojiste, optometriste.
odalisque *n.* (*slave*) odalisce.
odd *adj.* strana, nonormal, nonusual; (*number*) nonduable.
oddball *n.* strana, bizara.
oddity *n.* (*quality*) strania; (*quirk*) strana.
odd jobs *n.* bricola. **do odd jobs** bricola.
oddness *n.* strania.
odds *n.* (*quality*, *statistic*) probablia. **odds and ends** bricabrac.
ode *n.* (*poem*) ode.
odious *adj.* odiable.
odiousness *n.* odiablia.
odium *n.* odia.
odometer *n.* odometre.
odontologist *n.* odontiste.
odontology *n.* odontia.
odorous *adj.* odorosa.
odour (US **odor**) *n.* odor.
odourless (US **odorless**) *adj.* sin odor, nonolable.
-odynia *suff.* (*pain*) -odinia.
odyssey *n.* odisea.
oedema (US **edema**) *n.* edema.
Oedipal *adj.* edipal.
Oedipus *n.* Edipo.
oenology (US **enology**) *n.* vinolojia.
oenophile (US **enophile**) *n.* vinofilica.
oenophilia (US **enophilia**) *n.* (*love of wine*) vinofilia.
oesophagus (US **esophagus**) *n.* esofago.
oestrogen (US **estrogen**) *n.* estrojen.
oestrus (US **estrus**) *n.* estro, periodo corteal.
of *prep.* de. **of course** natural, evidente.
off *prep.* & *adv.* (*moving from on*) de sur; (*away*) a via. • *adj.* (*machine*) descomutada. **get off** (*alight*) desende; (*be acquitted*) es desculpada. **off of** de sur. **off the beaten track** a via de vias comun. **off the coast** a lado de costa.
offal *n.* intestines, organos.
offbeat *adj.* noncomun.
off-centre (US **off-center**) *adj.* nonsentral.
off-colour (US **off-color**) *adj.* vulgar.
offence (US **offense**) *n.* ofende; (*crime*) crimin; (*attack*) ataca.
offend *v.* ofende.
offender *n.* ofendor.
offense (US). See *offence*.
offensive *adj.* ofendente. • *n.* ataca.
offensiveness *n.* ofende.
offer *v.* & *n.* ofre.
offhand *adj.* casual.
office *n.* (*place*, *job*) ofisia; (*job*) posto.
officeholder *n.* ofisior.
officer *n.* ofisior. **military officer** ofisior militar.
official *adj.* ofisial. • *n.* ofisior; arbitror.
officious *adj.* autoritar.
offline *adj.* estralinia; (*switched off*) descomutada.
offload *v.* descarga.
off-piste skiing *n.* sci savaje.
off-road *adj.* multiterenal.
off-road vehicle *n.* multiterenal.
offset *v.* & *n.* desloca.
offshoot *n.* resulta ladal.
offshore *adj.* & *adv.* costal, a mar; (*finance*) estrateritorial.
offside *adj.* (*sport*) malposada.
offsides *adj.* (*sport*) malposada.
offspring *n.* projenia, enfantes, fies.
offstage *adj.* estra la stadio.
off-topic *adj.* nontemal.
often *adv.* comun, frecuente, a multe veses.

oftentimes *adv.* comun, frecuente, a multe veses.
oganesson *n.* (*element*) oganeson.
ogee *n.* (*architecture, mathematics, etc.*) arco sigmoide.
ogham *n.* (*alphabet*) ogam.
ogive *n.* (*architecture, statistics*) ojiva.
ogle *v.* come con sua oios.
ogre *n.* (*mythology*) ogro.
oh *interj.* o. **oh dear** ai. **oh well** (*mild disappointment*) ma bon, ma oce.
Ohio *n.* (*US state*) Ohio.
Ohio River *n.* Rio Ohio.
ohm *n.* (*unit of resistance*) ome.
-oid *suff.* (*shaped*) -oide.
oil *n.* olio; (*crude*) petrolio. • *v.* oli.
oil-based paint *n.* pinta de olio.
oilcloth *n.* stofa linosa.
oil lamp *n.* lampa de olio.
oil-like *adj.* olin.
oil paint *n.* pinta de olio.
oil pan *n.* caxa de olio.
oil platform *n.* plataforma de petrolio.
oil rig *n.* plataforma de petrolio.
oil tanker *n.* tancador de petrolio.
oily *adj.* (*oil-like*) olin; (*covered in oil*) oliosa.
oink *interj.* ronc. • *v.* & *n.* ronceta.
ointment *n.* unjente.
Ojibwa *adj.* & *n.* odjibua.
OK *interj.* oce, bon. • *adj.* (*good enough*) oce.
okapi *n.* (*animal*) ocapi.
okay *interj.* oce, bon. • *adj.* (*good enough*) oce.
Okhotsk, Sea of *n.* Mar Ohotsc.
Oklahoma *n.* (*US state*) Oklahoma.
okra *n.* gombo.
-ol *suff.* (*chemistry*) -ol.
old *adj.* vea; senesente. **grow old** senese, vei.
old age *n.* eda matur, senese, veia.
old banger *n.* (*car*) ruinada.
Old English *adj.* & *n.* anglosason.
older brother *n.* fraton.
older sister *n.* soron.
old-fashioned *adj.* anticin, de moda pasada.
old fogey *n.* anticin.
old geezer *n.* anticin.
old person *n.* senesente, vea.
Old Testament *n.* Atesta Vea.
Old World monkey *n.* simia afrasian.
oleander *n.* (*plant*) oleandro.
oleo *n.* margarina.
olfaction *n.* ole.
olfactory *adj.* olal.
oligarch *n.* oligarca.
oligarchy *n.* oligarcia.
oligo- *pref.* (*few*) oligo-.
Oligocene *adj.* & *n.* (*geology*) oligosene.
oligosaccharide *n.* (*sugar*) oligosacarido.
olive *adj.* (*colour*) oliva. • *n.* (*fruit*) oliva; (*tree*) olivo.
olive green *adj.* oliva.
Olympia *n.* (*in Greece*) Olimpia.
Olympiad *n.* olimpiada.
Olympian *adj.* & *n.* olimpian.
Olympic *adj.* olimpial.
Olympic Games *n.* Juas Olimpial.
Olympics *n.* Juas Olimpial.
Olympus, Mount *n.* Monte Olimpo.
-oma *suff.* (*tumour*) -oma.
Oman *n.* Uman. **Gulf of Oman** Golfo Uman.
Omani *adj.* & *n.* umani.
Omayyad *adj.* (*dynasty*) umaian.
Ombai Strait *n.* Streta Ombai.
ombudsman *n.* defendor de la popla.
omega *n.* (*Greek letter* Ω, ω) omega.
omelette (US **omelet**) *n.* omeleta.
omelette pan (US **omelet pan**) *n.* padela de crepes.
omen *n.* indica.
omentum *n.* (*anatomy*) omento.
omicron *n.* (*Greek letter* Ο, ο) omicron.
ominous *adj.* menasante.
omission *n.* omete.
omission mark *n.* sinia de omete.
omit *v.* omete, cade, lasa ce lo cade.
omni- *pref.* (*all*) omni-.
omnibus *n.* colie.
omnipotence *n.* omnipotentia.
omnipotent *adj.* omnipotente.
omnipresence *n.* omnipresentia.
omnipresent *adj.* omnipresente, sempre presente.
omniscience *n.* omnisientia.
omniscient *adj.* omnisiente.
omnivore *n.* omnivor.
omnivorous *adj.* omnivor.
on[1] *prep.* (*surface, including vertical*) sur; (*a point in space or time*) a. • *adj.* (*machine*) comutada. **on behalf of** per. **on board** sur barco; sur avion. **on the way** en via. **on the whole** jeneral. **on top** a sur. **on top of** sur.
-on[2] *suff.* (*particle*) -on.
onanism *n.* masturba.
once *adv.* (*one time*) a un ves; (*in the past*) pasada. **at once** aora, direta. **not even once** an nunca. **once every few years** a un ves en cada pico de anios. **once every two years** a un ves en cada duple de anios, a un ves en cada anio du. **once upon a time** a un ves pasada. **this once** a esta ves.
oncological *adj.* oncolojial.
oncologist *n.* oncolojiste.
oncology *n.* oncolojia.
one[1] *det.* un. • *pron.* un; (*as to opposed to the other*) la un; (*an arbitrary person or people in general*) on. **one another** la un la otra, lunlotra. **one by one** individua, pos lunlotra. **one day** a alga dia. **one might say** on ta dise. **one**

size fits all lo es la mesma per cadun. **the ones which** los cual. **the ones who** los ci. **the one which** lo cual. **the one who** el ci.
-one[2] *suff.* (*chemistry*) -ona.
one-dimensional *adj.* unidimensional.
one-dimensional array *n.* (*software*) vetor.
oneiromancy *n.* (*divination*) oniromansia.
oneness *n.* unia.
one-off *adj.* unica.
one-piece *adj.* de un peso.
one-piece swimsuit *n.* bodi de nada.
one-player game *n.* jua solitar.
onerous *adj.* tro pesosa.
oneself *pron.* (*reflexive*) se; (*emphatically reflexive*) se mesma. **by oneself** (*alone*) solitar; (*unaided*) sin aida.
onesie *n.* bodi de bebe.
one-stop shop *n.* boteca completa.
one-way *adj.* de un dirije.
one-way ticket *n.* bileta de un dirije.
ongoing *adj.* corente.
onion *n.* (*plant*, *bulb*) onion.
onion dome *n.* cupola onionin.
onion skin *n.* casca de onion; (*tracing paper*) paper diafana.
onion soup *n.* sopa de onion.
online *adj.* enlinia; (*switched on*) comutada.
online course *n.* curso enlinia.
onlooker *n.* oservor.
only *adj.* sola; (*child*) unica. • *adv.* sola, mera.
on/off switch *n.* boton de comuta.
onomatopoeia *n.* onomatopea.
onomatopoeic *adj.* onomatopeal.
onset *n.* comensa.
onslaught *n.* ataca.
Ontario *n.* Ontario. **Lake Ontario** Lago Ontario.
onto[1] *prep.* sur, a sur.
onto-[2] *pref.* (*existence*) onto-.
ontogenetic *adj.* ontojenial.
ontogeny *n.* (*biology*) ontojenia.
ontologic *adj.* ontolojial.
ontological *adj.* ontolojial.
ontology *n.* ontolojia.
on-topic *adj.* temal.
onus *n.* encarga.
onwards *interj.* a ante, avansa.
onychophor *n.* (*organism*) onicoforo.
onyx *n.* (*mineral*) onix.
oocyte *n.* (*biology*) osite.
ooh *interj.* u.
ooid *n.* (*geology*) olito.
ook *interj.* (*monkey*) i-i-i.
oolite *n.* olito.
oolong *n.* (*tea*) ulong.
oops *interj.* op.
ooze *v.* suda.
opacity *n.* opacia.
opal *n.* (*gem*) opal.
opalescence *n.* opalinia.
opalescent *adj.* opalin.
opaline *adj.* opalin.
opaque *adj.* opaca.
open *v.* abri; (*hand*) esvasa. • *adj.* abrida; nonfurtiva; (*government*) transparente; (*sea*) alta. **in the open air** su sielo. **open out** esvasa. **open to attack** atacable. **open to doubt** dutable. **open to interpretation** interpretable. **open up** abri; esvasa. **wide open** baliante.
openable *adj.* abrable.
open-air *adj.* su sielo.
open-heart surgery *n.* sirurjia de cor abrida.
opening *adj.* abrinte; inisial. • *n.* (*action*, *result*) abri; (*orifice*) stoma; (*performance*) mostra prima.
opening credits *n.* titulos inisial.
opening quotation mark *n.* abrisita.
opening titles *n.* titulos inisial.
openly *adv.* sin asconde.
open-mid vowel *n.* vocal media abrida.
openness *n.* abridia.
open-source *adj.* de fonte abrida.
open vowel *n.* vocal abrida.
openwork *n.* orna par perfora.
opera *n.* (*music*) opera.
operable *adj.* operable, tratable.
opera glasses *n.* binoculo de teatro.
opera house *n.* teatro de opera.
operand *n.* operada.
operant *adj.* (*psychology*) operante.
operate *v.* opera, funsiona, dirije, maneja.
operating system *n.* (*software*) sistem de opera.
operation *n.* opera, funsiona.
operator *n.* operor, dirijor, manejor; (*phone*) telefoniste; (*mathematics*, *logic*) operador.
operetta *n.* opereta.
Ophiuchus *n.* (*constellation*) la Serpentor.
ophthalmia *n.* oftalmite.
ophthalmitis *n.* oftalmite.
ophthalmo- *pref.* (*eye*) oftalmo-.
ophthalmologist *n.* oftalmolojiste.
ophthalmology *n.* oftalmolojia.
ophthalmoplegia *n.* oftalmoplejia.
ophthalmoscope *n.* oftalmoscopio.
ophthalmoscopy *n.* oftalmoscopi.
-opia *suff.* (*eye condition*) -opia.
opiate *n.* (*drug*) opiato.
-opic *suff.* (*eye condition*) -opica.
opine *v.* opina, pensa.
opinion *n.* opina. **have an opinion** opina, pensa.
opinionated *adj.* opinosa.
opinion poll *n.* sonda de opina.
opioid *n.* (*drug*) opioide.
opium *n.* (*drug*) opio.

opossum *n.* (*marsupial*) oposum.
opponent *n.* oposor; criticor.
opportune *adj.* oportun; favorable, vantajosa; (*place*) bon situada.
opportunism *n.* oportunisme, acasisme.
opportunist *n.* oportuniste, acasiste.
opportunistic *adj.* oportuniste, acasiste.
opportunity *n.* oportun, acaso oportun, bon momento; (*something possible*) posible; (*quality*) oportunia. **have the opportunity to** pote.
opposable *adj.* (*thumb*) fasante.
oppose *v.* oposa.
opposed *adj.* oposada. **as opposed to** contrastada con, en contrasta con. **opposed to** oposada a, contra.
opposing *adj.* oposante. • *prep.* contra.
opposite *adj.* oposante, oposada; (*word*) antonim; (*facing*) fasante. • *n.* oposada; (*word*) antonim. • *prep.* a fas de.
opposition *n.* oposa.
oppress *v.* opresa.
oppression *n.* opresa.
oppressive *adj.* opresante.
oppressor *n.* opresor.
opprobrium *n.* desonora.
-opsy *suff.* (*medical*) -opsia.
opt *v.* eleje. **opt in** eleje partisipa. **opt out** eleje no partisipa.
opthalmo- *pref.* (*eye*) otalmo-.
optical *adj.* otical.
optical fibre (US **fiber**) *n.* fibre otical.
optical illusion *n.* ilude de vide, trucioio.
optical scientist *n.* oticiste.
optician *n.* oculiste, optometriste.
optician's *n.* (*shop*) oculeria.
optic nerve *n.* nervo otical.
optics *n.* otica.
optimal *adj.* la plu bon.
optimism *n.* otimisme.
optimist *n.* otimiste.
optimistic *adj.* otimiste.
optimization *n.* masimi.
optimize *v.* masimi.
optimum *adj.* la plu bon.
option *n.* elejable; (*software*) prefere.
optional *adj.* elejable, nonobligante, si desirada.
optometrist *n.* optometriste.
optometry *n.* optometria.
opulence *n.* ricia.
opulent *adj.* lusosa.
opus *n.* obra.
or *conj.* o.
oracle *n.* oraculo.
oracular *adj.* oraculal.
oral *adj.* (*of the mouth*) bocal; (*spoken*) parlada, nonscriveda.
oral defence (US **defense**) *n.* defende de tese.
oral examination *n.* esamina parlada.
oral literature *n.* leteratur parlada.
oral sex *n.* seso bocal.
orange *adj.* (*colour*) orania; (*fruit*) orania.
orange juice *n.* jus de orania.
orangery *n.* oranieria.
orange squeezer *n.* jusador.
orange tree *n.* oranio.
orangey *adj.* oranin.
orangutan *n.* orangutan.
oration *n.* parla.
orator *n.* retoriciste, bonparlor.
oratory[1] *n.* (*speaking*) retorica, parla.
oratory[2] *n.* (*chapel*) oratorio.
orb *n.* sfera.
orbit *v.* & *n.* orbita.
orbital *adj.* orbital. • *n.* via periferial.
orc *n.* (*mythology*) orco.
orca *n.* (*whale*) orca.
orchard *n.* bosce, bosce de frutas; (*market garden*) orto.
orchectomy *n.* (*surgery*) orcectomia.
orchestra *n.* orcestra.
orchestral *adj.* orcestral.
orchestra leader *n.* xef de orcestra.
orchestrate *v.* (*music*) orcestri; (*direct*) dirije.
orchestration *n.* orcestri.
orchid *n.* orcidea.
ordain *v.* comanda; (*religious*) ordina.
ordeal *n.* malesperia.
order *v.* (*food, goods*) comanda; encarga; (*put in order*) ordina. • *n.* comanda; encarga; (*including monks*) ordina. **in order** en ordina. **in order that** afin, con intende ce. **in order to** per. **order of the day** ordina de la dia. **out of order** nonordinada.
orderly *adj.* ordinada.
order theory *n.* teoria de ordinas.
ordinal *adj.* ordinal.
ordinance *n.* proclama.
ordinariness *n.* comunia.
ordinary *adj.* comun, normal; mediocre.
ordinary citizen *n.* sitadan comun.
ordination *n.* (*religious*) ordina.
ordnance *n.* armas, artileria.
Ordovician *adj.* & *n.* (*geology*) ordovisian.
ore *n.* mineral.
oregano *n.* (*plant, spice*) oregano.
Oregon *n.* (*US state*) Oregon.
orexin *n.* (*hormone*) orexina.
organ *n.* (*anatomy, music*) organo.
organdy *n.* organdi.
organelle *n.* (*biology*) organeta.
organic *adj.* (*of biological matter*) organica; (*food*) natural; (*of organs*) organal.
organic fertilizer *n.* fertilinte organica.
organism *n.* organisme, vivente.

organist *n.* organiste.
organization *n.* organiza.
organizational *adj.* organizal.
organize *v.* organiza.
organized crime *n.* crimin organizada.
organizer *n.* organizor.
organophosphorus *n.* (*substance*) organofosforosa.
organotroph *n.* organotrof.
organotrophia *n.* organotrofia.
organotrophic *adj.* (*biology*) organotrof.
organza *n.* (*fabric*) organdi.
orgasm *v.* & *n.* orgasma.
orgasmic *adj.* (*of orgasm*) orgasmal; (*orgasming*) orgasmosa.
orgiastic *adj.* orjial.
orgy *n.* orjia.
oriel *n.* fenetra de alcovo.
orient *v.* orienta. • *n.* este.
oriental *adj.* este.
orientalism *n.* asiamania.
orientalist *adj.* & *n.* asiamanica.
orientate *v.* orienta.
orientation *n.* orienta.
orienteering *n.* corsa de orienta.
orifice *n.* stoma, abri.
origami *n.* origami.
origin *n.* orijina.
original *adj.* orijinal, prima; (*work*, *idea*) noncomun, inventosa, fontosa. • *n.* orijinal, prima.
originality *n.* inventosia.
originate *v.* orijina; fonti. **originate from** veni de. **originate in** es orijinal de.
Orinoco River *n.* Rio Orinoco.
oriole *n.* (*bird*) oriol.
Orion *n.* (*mythology*, *constellation*) Orion.
Oriya *adj.* & *n.* (*person*, *language*) oria.
ornament *n.* decora; (*ornate*) orna.
ornamental *adj.* ornal.
ornate *adj.* ornosa.
ornate curve *n.* curva ornosa.
ornery *adj.* ostinosa.
ornitho- *pref.* ornito-.
ornithological *adj.* ornitolojial.
ornithologist *n.* ornitolojiste.
ornithology *n.* ornitolojia.
Oromo *adj.* & *n.* (*person*, *language*) oromo.
oropharynx *n.* farinje bocal.
orphan *adj.* & *n.* orfan. • *v.* orfani, abandona.
orphanage *n.* orfaneria.
orrery *n.* (*solar system model*) planeterieta.
-orrhaphy *suff.* (*medical*) -orafia.
ortho- *pref.* (*straight*) orto-.
orthodontia *n.* ortodontia.
orthodontic *adj.* ortodontial.
orthodontics *n.* ortodontia.
orthodontist *n.* ortodontiste.
orthodox *adj.* ortodox.
orthodoxy *n.* ortodoxia.
orthogonal *adj.* ortogonal.
orthographic *adj.* ortografial, spelal.
orthography *n.* ortografia, spele.
orthonectid *n.* (*organism*) ortonectido.
orthopaedic (US **orthopedic**) *adj.* ortopedial.
orthopaedics (US **orthopedics**) *n.* ortopedia.
orthopaedist (US **orthopedist**) *n.* ortopediste.
orthopaedy (US **orthopedy**) *n.* ortopedia.
Orwellian *adj.* contrautopial.
oryx *n.* (*antelope*) orix.
Oscan *adj.* & *n.* (*person*, *language*) oscan.
oscillate *v.* osila.
oscillation *n.* osila.
oscillator *n.* osilador.
oscilloscope *n.* osiloscopio.
-ose *suff.* (*chemistry*) -osa.
-osis *suff.* (*medical*) -ose.
Osmanian *adj.* & *n.* osmanian.
Osmanli *adj.* & *n.* osmanian.
osmium *n.* (*element*) osmio.
osmosis *n.* osmose.
osmotic *adj.* osmosal.
osprey *n.* (*bird*) pandion.
Ossetia *n.* Osetia.
Ossetian *adj.* & *n.* (*person*, *language*) osetin.
ossification *n.* osi.
ossify *v.* osi.
ossuary *n.* oseria.
ostensible *adj.* parente.
ostensive *adj.* indicante.
ostentation *n.* ostenta.
ostentatious *adj.* ostentosa, egosa.
osteoarthritis *n.* artrose.
osteologist *n.* osteolojiste.
osteology *n.* osteolojia.
osteopath *n.* osteopatiste.
osteopathic *adj.* osteopatial.
osteopathy *n.* osteopatia.
osteoporosis *n.* osteoporose.
ostomy *n.* (*surgical opening*) ostomia.
ostracism *n.* esclui.
ostracize *v.* esclui.
ostrich *n.* astruzo.
Ostrogoth *n.* ostrogoto.
Ostrogothic *adj.* ostrogoto.
other *adj.* otra; (*additional*) plu. **others** otras. **other than** otra ca, estra, esetante, escluinte. **the other day** a la otra dia, resente.
otherwise *adv.* si no; en otra modo; a otra ves.
otherworldly *adj.* nonatural.
otolaryngologist *n.* otolarinjolojiste.
otolaryngology *n.* otolarinjolojia.
otolith *n.* (*anatomy*) otolito.

otologist *n.* otolojiste.
otology *n.* otolojia.
Otomi *adj.* & *n.* (*person, language*) otomi.
otoscope *n.* otoscopio.
otoscopy *n.* otoscopi.
otter *n.* lutra.
ottoman[1] *n.* (*footstool*) reposapede.
Ottoman[2] *adj.* & *n.* (*empire*) osmanian.
oubliette *n.* prison botelin.
ouch *interj.* au.
Oudh *n.* (*Indian region*) Auad.
ought *v.* debe; (*simple conditional, or polite, or commenting without expectation*) ta debe.
ouija board *n.* uija.
ounce *n.* (*unit of weight*) onsa.
our *det.* nosa.
ours *pron.* la nosa(s).
-ous *suff.* -osa.
oust *v.* despone, esclui, espulsa.
ouster *n.* despone, ejeta.
out *adv.* (*away*) a via. **get out** sorti. **out loud** a vose, parlante. **out of** estra, a estra, de en; (*from among*) entre. **out of breath** sin aira. **out of control** noncontrolable. **out of focus** nonfocada. **out of print** no plu primida. **out of sight** estra vista, ultra vista. **out of the way** (*remote*) isolida; (*done*) en la pasada; (*no longer an obstacle*) no plu un problem. **out of tune** desacordante, malajustada. **out of use** nonusada.
outback *n.* tera savaje.
outbid *v.* ofre plu ca.
outboard motor *n.* motor esterna.
outbound *adj.* partinte.
outbreak *n.* aveni; (*illness*) eruta.
outbred *adj.* esogama.
outbreeding *n.* esogamia.
outburst *n.* esplode.
outcast *n.* escluida, paria.
outclass *v.* suprapasa.
outcome *n.* resulta.
outcry *n.* cria, furia publica.
outdated *adj.* de moda pasada.
outdent *v.* desindente.
outdo *v.* suprapasa.
outdoor *adj.* estra casa, su sielo.
outdoors *adv.* estra casa, su sielo.
outer *adj.* esterna.
outer ear *n.* orea esterna.
outer harbour (US **harbor**) *n.* anteporto.
Outer Hebrides *n.* Hebrides Esterna.
outermost *adj.* estrema.
outfit *n.* vestes, completa.
outflow *n.* esflue.
outfox *v.* es plu astuta ca, es plu rusosa ca.
outgas *v.* relasa.
outgoing *adj.* sosial.
outgrow *v.* deveni tro vea per.
outgun *v.* ave plu armas ca.
outhouse *n.* latrina.
outlandish *adj.* bizara.
outlast *v.* dura plu longa ca.
outlaw *n.* bandito. • *v.* deslegali.
outlay *n.* spende.
outlet *n.* asetador.
outlier *n.* separada.
outline *n.* (*physical*) contorno; (*summary*) resoma; (*diagram*) scema. • *v.* contorni; resoma; scemi.
outlive *v.* vive plu longa ca.
outlook *n.* punto de vista.
outlying *adj.* distante, separada.
outlying regions *n.* bordas.
outmanoeuvre (US **outmaneuver**) *v.* manobra plu bon ca.
outmoded *adj.* de moda pasada.
outnumber *v.* es plu multe ca.
outpace *v.* pasa, suprapasa.
outpatient *n.* pasiente esterna.
outpost *n.* campa avansada, campa isolida.
outpouring *n.* jeta; (*emotion*) esplode.
output *v.* & *n.* esflue.
output tray *n.* platon de esflue.
outrage *n.* coleria; (*event*) scandal. • *v.* coleri, scandali.
outrageous *adj.* scandalosa.
outreach *n.* estende.
outrigger *n.* balansador.
outright *adj.* completa, direta, franca.
outside *n.* esterna. • *adv.* a estra, su sielo. • *prep.* estra.
outsider *n.* stranjer.
outskirts *n.* borda, anteurbe.
outsmart *v.* es plu astuta ca, es plu rusosa ca.
outsource *v.* produi a stranjer; emplea a stranjer.
outsourcing *n.* produi a stranjer; emplea a stranjer.
outspoken *adj.* franca.
outspread *adj.* estendeda.
outstanding *adj.* eselente.
outstretched *adj.* estendeda.
outtake *n.* era comica.
outthink *v.* es plu astuta ca, es plu rusosa ca.
outward *adj.* a estra.
outwards *adv.* a estra.
outwit *v.* es plu astuta ca, es plu rusosa ca.
ouzo *n.* (*drink*) uzo.
oval *adj.* & *n.* oval.
ovarian *adj.* ovarial.
ovary *n.* ovario.
ovate *adj.* oval.
ovation *n.* aplaudi.
oven *n.* forno.
ovenbird *n.* fornor.
oven glove *n.* ganto de cosini.
ovenware *n.* platos de forno.

over *prep.* supra; (*motion towards*) a supra. **all over** covrente, a covre de. **over the top** estravagante.
overabundance *n.* suprabunda.
overabundant *adj.* suprabundante. **be overabundant** suprabunda.
overachieve *v.* suprasusede, ateni plu ca espetada.
overachiever *n.* suprasusedor.
overact *v.* ata esajerada.
overage *n.* suprapasa.
overall *adv.* jeneral.
overalls *n.* covretota.
overanalyse (US **overanalyze**) *v.* analise tro detaliosa.
overbalance *v.* desecuilibra.
overbearing *adj.* egosa.
overbite *n.* supramorde.
overboard *adv.* estra barco, en la mar.
overburden *v.* supracarga.
overcast *adj.* nubosa, covreda.
overcharge *v.* fatura tro multe.
overcoat *n.* jacon.
overcome *v.* vinse.
overcompensate *v.* compensa tro multe.
overconfident *adj.* tro fidante.
overcook *v.* coce tro multe.
overcrowd *v.* suprafoli.
overdevelop *v.* developa tro multe.
overdo *v.* esajera; coce tro multe. **overdo it** labora tro multe.
overdose *v.* & *n.* supradosa.
overdraft *n.* noncovreda, retira noncovreda.
overdramatic *adj.* supradramosa.
overdramatized *adj.* supradramosa.
overdraw *v.* retira tro multe.
overdrawn *adj.* debente.
overdressed *adj.* tro calda vestida; tro formal vestida; tro ostentosa vestida.
overdrive *n.* supraengrana.
overdub *v.* (*audio*) dupli.
overdue *adj.* tarda. **long overdue** multe tarda.
overeager *adj.* tro zelosa.
overeat *v.* come tro multe.
overelaborate *v.* esplica tro.
overenthusiastic *adj.* tro zelosa.
overestimate *v.* & *n.* supraestima.
overexcite *v.* stimula tro multe.
overexcited *adj.* tro stimulada.
overexert *v.* (*oneself*) labora tro multe.
overexplain *v.* esplica tro.
overexpose *v.* supraesposa.
overexposure *n.* supraesposa.
overextend *v.* estende tro multe.
overfamiliar *adj.* noncortes, desrespetosa.
overflow *v.* supraflue, suprabunda. • *n.* supraflue, suprabunda; (*outlet*) diverjador.
overgraze *v.* usa tro multe la pasto.
overgrown *adj.* descurada.
overhang *n.* estende.
overhaul *v.* repara completa.
overhead *adj.* (*cable*) airal.
overhear *v.* oia acaso.
overheard *adj.* acaso oiada.
overindulge *v.* supraregala.
overjoyed *adj.* estasiante.
overkill *adj.* plu ca nesesada. • *v.* & *n.* supradestrui.
overlap *v.* suprapone, covre partal; inclui partal; coaveni partal. • *n.* suprapone.
overlay *v.* & *n.* suprapone.
overload *v.* supracarga.
overlook *v.* (*a view*) regarda.
overlord *n.* renor, xef.
overnight *adv.* a note, per la note, tra la note.
overnight stay *n.* reposa per la note.
overpaid *adj.* tro multe paiada.
overpass *n.* viaduto.
overpopulate *v.* suprapopla.
overpopulation *n.* suprapopla.
overpower *v.* inonda.
overqualified *adj.* tro capas.
overrate *v.* supravalua.
overreach *v.* estende tro multe.
overreact *v.* reata tro forte.
override *v.* supresa.
overripe *adj.* tro matur.
overrule *v.* nega.
overrun *v.* invade.
overseas *adj.* ultramar.
overseas territory *n.* teritorio ultramar.
oversee *v.* supravide.
overseer *n.* supravidor.
oversexed *adj.* tro libidosa.
overshadow *v.* ombri; (*exceed*) suprapasa.
overshoot *v.* suprapasa; fali para.
oversight *n.* nonotada; (*overseeing*) supravide.
overskilled *adj.* tro capas.
oversleep *v.* dormi tro longa.
overspecialized *adj.* tro spesialida.
overspend *v.* spende tro multe.
overstaffed *adj.* con tro multe empleadas.
overstate *v.* esajera.
overstay *v.* permane.
overstimulate *v.* iperstimula.
overstimulation *n.* iperstimula.
overt *adj.* nonfurtiva, evidente.
overtake *v.* pasa.
overtax *v.* imposta tro multe.
overthrow *v.* & *n.* suverti.
overtime *n.* (*work*) supratempo.
overtone *n.* supratono.
overture *n.* (*music*) introdui; (*to communication, negotiation*) invita.
overturn *v.* inversa; (*system*) revolui; (*conviction*) descondena.

overuse *v.* usa tro multe.
overused *adj.* tro usada.
overvalue *v.* supravalua.
overview *n.* (*of topic*) vista jeneral.
overweening *adj.* egosa.
overweight *adj.* obesa, tro pesosa.
overwhelm *v.* inonda.
overwhelming *adj.* inondante; nonresistable.
overwork *v.* labora tro multe.
overwrite *v.* suprascrive.
overwritten *adj.* suprascriveda.
ovi- *pref.* (*egg*) ovi-.
oviduct *n.* (*anatomy*) oviduto.
ovine *adj.* oveal.
oviparity *n.* oviparia.
oviparous *adj.* (*egg-laying*) oviparinte. **be oviparous** ovipari.
oviraptor *n.* (*dinosaur*) oviraptor.
ovoid *adj.* ovin.
ovoviviparity *n.* ovoviviparia.
ovoviviparous *adj.* (*laying eggs within oneself*) ovoviviparinte. **be ovoviviparous** ovovivipari.
ovulate *v.* ovuli.
ovulation *n.* ovuli.
ovule *n.* (*biology*) ovulo.
ovum *n.* ovo.
ow *interj.* au.
owe *v.* (*debt*) debe. **be owed** merita.
owing *adj.* debente. **owing to** par causa de.
owl *n.* buo.
owl-like *adj.* buin.
owl monkey *n.* aoto.
own *adj.* propre. • *v.* posese, ave. **on one's own** sin aida. **on one's own terms** par sua propre metodo.
owner *n.* posesor, proprior.
ownership *n.* (*state*) posese.
ox *n.* bove.
oxcart *n.* caro de bove.
oxidation *n.* osidi.
oxide *n.* osido. **aluminium oxide** osido de aluminio.
oxidize *v.* osidi.
oxyacetylene cutting *n.* ositalia.
oxyacetylene torch *n.* osisoldador.
oxyacetylene welding *n.* osisolda.
oxy-fuel cutting *n.* ositalia.
oxy-fuel welding *n.* osisolda.
oxygen *n.* osijen.
oxygenate *v.* osijeni.
oxymoron *n.* osimoro.
oxymoronic *adj.* osimoro.
oxytocin *n.* (*hormone*) ositosina.
oyster *n.* ostra.
oystercatcher *n.* (*bird*) ostror.
ozone *n.* ozon.

P

p. *abbr.* p (*paje*).
pablum *n.* blanda.
pacarana *n.* (*rodent*) pacarana.
pace *n.* (*step*) paso; (*speed*) rapidia. • *v.* fa un paso.
pacemaker *n.* (*in race*) precorsor; (*medical*) pasmacer.
pacesetter *n.* (*in race*) precorsor.
pachinko *n.* (*pinball*) patxinco.
pachisi *n.* patxisi.
pachy- *pref.* (*thick*) paci-.
pachyderm *n.* pacidermo.
Pacific *adj.* pasifica.
pacification *n.* pasi.
Pacific Ocean *n.* Mar Pasifica.
pacifier *n.* (*for baby*) tetin.
pacifism *n.* pasisme.
pacifist *n.* pasiste.
pacify *v.* pasi.
pack *n.* paco; (*cards*) paceta; (*wolves*) manada. • *v.* paci; (*crowd*) foli.
package *n.* paceta. • *v.* paci.
pack animal *n.* bestia de carga.
packed *adj.* pacida; (*crowded*) folida.
packet *n.* paceta.
packing slip *n.* lista de contenidas.
pact *n.* trata.
pad *n.* cuxineta; (*swab*) tampon; (*notepad*) bloco. • *v.* cuxini, materasi; pleni.
padding *n.* pleninte; tampon.
paddle *n.* remo. • *v.* remi; (*wade*) vada.
paddling pool *n.* vaderia.
paddock *n.* ensirca de cavalos.
paddy *n.* campo de ris.
padlock *n.* securador pendente.
paean *n.* imno, canta de loda.
paederast (US **pederast**) *n.* pedofilica omosesal.
paederasty (US **pederasty**) *n.* pedofilia omosesal.
paediatric (US **pediatric**) *adj.* pediatrica.
paediatrician (US **pediatrician**) *n.* pediatriste.
paediatrics (US **pediatrics**) *n.* pediatria.
paedo- (US **pedo-**) *pref.* (*child*) pedo-.
paedophile (US **pedophile**) *n.* pedofilica.
paedophilia (US **pedophilia**) *n.* pedofilia.
paedophilic (US **pedophilic**) *adj.* pedofilica.
paella *n.* paela.
pagan *adj.* & *n.* pagan.
paganism *n.* paganisme.
page[1] *n.* (*paper*) paje.
page[2] *n.* (*person*) pajo.
pageant *n.* spetaculo.
pageboy *n.* pajo.
pageboy bob *n.* capeles de pajo.
pager *n.* piador.
paginate *v.* numeri la pajes de.
pagination *n.* numeri de pajes.
pagliaccio *n.* paliaso.
pagoda *n.* pagoda.
paid *adj.* paiada; con salario.
pail *n.* balde.
pain *v.* & *n.* dole; (*extreme*) dolon. **cause pain to** dole, turba. **feel pain** dole. **pain in the neck** (*nuisance*) peste.
painful *adj.* dolosa.
painkiller *n.* paradole.
painless *adj.* sin dole.
paint *n.* pinta. • *v.* (*apply paint to*) pinti; (*make a painting*) depinta.
paintbrush *n.* brosa.
painted snipe *n.* (*bird*) rostralata.
painter *n.* (*artist*) depintor; (*decorator*) pintor.
painting *n.* (*art form, artwork*) depinta; imaje.
pair *n.* duple. **in pairs** en duples. **pair up** grupi a duples, divide a duples.
paisley *n.* (*pattern*) caxmiran.
pajamas (US). See *pyjamas.*
Pakistan *n.* Pacistan.
Pakistani *adj.* & *n.* pacistani.
pal *n.* ami.
palace *n.* palasio.
palace coup *n.* colpa de palasio.
paladin *n.* (*knight*) campion.
palaeo- (US **paleo-**) *pref.* (*ancient*) paleo-.
Palaeocene (US **Paleocene**) *adj.* & *n.* (*geology*) paleosene.
palaeographer (US **paleographer**) *n.* paleografiste.
palaeography (US **paleography**) *n.* paleografia.
Palaeolithic (US **Paleolithic**) *adj.* & *n.* paleolitica.
palaeontological (US **paleontological**) *adj.* paleontolojial.
palaeontologist (US **paleontologist**) *n.* paleontolojiste.
palaeontology (US **paleontology**) *n.* paleontolojia.
palaeotropics (US **paleotropics**) *n.* paleotropico.
Palaeozoic *adj.* & *n.* (*geology*) paleozoica.
palanquin *n.* seja portada.
palatable *adj.* saborosa.
palatal *adj.* & *n.* palatal.
palatalize *v.* palatali.
palate *n.* palato.
palatial *adj.* palasin.

Palau *n.* Belau.
Palauan *adj.* & *n.* belau.
pale *adj.* pal. • *v.* pali.
paleness *n.* palia.
paleo... (US). See *palaeo...*
Palestine *n.* Filastin.
Palestinian *adj.* & *n.* filastini.
palette *n.* paleta.
Pali *adj.* & *n.* (*language*) pali.
palimpsest *n.* suprascriveda.
palindrome *n.* palindrom.
palisade *n.* serca de palos.
Palk Bay *n.* Baia Palk.
pall *n.* telon funeral; nube oscur.
palladium *n.* (*element*) paladio.
pallbearer *n.* portor.
pallet[1] *n.* (*straw mattress*) materas de palia.
pallet[2] *n.* (*for stacking goods*) paleta.
palliative *n.* medisin lejerinte, paradole.
pallid *adj.* pal.
pallor *n.* palia.
pally *adj.* amin.
palm[1] *n.* (*tree*) palma.
palm[2] *n.* (*hand*) palma. **palm down** prona. **palm up** supina.
palmate *adj.* palmin.
palmistry *n.* ciromansia, leje de palma.
palmlike *adj.* palmin.
palm reading *n.* ciromansia, leje de palma.
palmtop *n.* aidador personal.
palpable *adj.* palpable.
palpate *v.* palpa.
palpitate *v.* palpita.
palpitation *n.* palpita.
paltry *adj.* magra, nonsufisinte; trivial.
paludarium *n.* (*tank*) pantaneria.
pampas *n.* plano.
pamper *v.* regala.
pamphlet *n.* libreta.
pamplemousse *n.* pampelmus.
pan[1] *n.* (*pot*) casola; (*frying*) padela.
pan[2] *v.* (*camera*) panorama.
pan-[3] *pref.* (*all*) pan-.
Pan[4] *n.* (*mythology*) Pan.
panacea *n.* sanitota.
panache *n.* zelo, estravagantia.
Panama *n.* Panama. **Gulf of Panama** Golfo Panama. **Isthmus of Panama** Istmo Panama.
Panama Canal *n.* Canal Panama.
Panamanian *adj.* & *n.* panaman.
pan-American *adj.* panamerican.
pan-Arabian *adj.* panarabi.
pancake *n.* crepe.
pan control *n.* panoramador.
pancreas *n.* (*anatomy*) pancreas.
panda *n.* panda.
pandemic *adj.* & *n.* pandemica.
pander *v.* regala.
Pandora *n.* (*mythology*) Pandora.
Pandora's box *n.* caxa de Pandora.
pane *n.* panel. **window pane** vitro de fenetra.
panegyric *n.* loda.
panel *n.* (*component*) panel; (*experts*) comite, juria.
panelling (US **paneling**) *n.* panel.
pan flute *n.* flauta de Pan.
pang *n.* dole agu.
pangender *adj.* panjenero.
pangender person *n.* panjenero.
pan-Germanism *n.* pangermanisme.
pangolin *n.* (*animal*) pangolin.
panhandle *v.* mendica.
panic *v.* & *n.* panica.
panicky *adj.* panicante.
panic room *n.* secureria.
Panjab *n.* Pandjab.
panna cotta *n.* crema italian.
panoply *n.* colie grande, esibi.
panorama *n.* panorama.
panpipe *n.* flauta de Pan.
panpipes *n.* flauta de Pan.
pan pot *n.* panoramador.
pansexual *adj.* pansesal.
pant *v.* & *n.* respira rapida.
pantheism *n.* panteisme.
pantheist *n.* panteiste.
pantheistic *adj.* panteiste.
pantheon *n.* panteon.
panther *n.* pantera; leopardo; puma.
panties *n.* pantaleta, slip de fem.
panto *n.* pantomima.
pantomime *v.* mima. • *n.* mima; (*musical comedy*) pantomima.
pantry *n.* saleta de comedas.
pants *n.* (*trousers*) pantalon; (*underpants*) pantaleta.
pantsuit *n.* completa con pantalon.
pantyhose *n.* calson.
pap *n.* pulpa, gaxin; (*insipid entertainment*) blanda.
papa *n.* (*father*) papa.
papacy *n.* papia.
papal *adj.* papal.
papal bull *n.* proclama papal.
paparazzi *n.* paparazos.
paparazzo *n.* paparazo.
papaya *n.* (*fruit*) papaia; (*tree*) papaio.
paper *n.* paper. **scrap of paper** papereta.
paperback *n.* libro mol.
paperboy *n.* xico de jornales.
paper cartridge *n.* (*musket, pistol*) tampon.
paper clip *n.* clip.
paper cutter *n.* taliapaper.
papergirl *n.* xica de jornales.
paperhanger *n.* paperor.
paper knife *n.* taliapaper.
paper towel *n.* teleta de paper.

Papiamento *n.* (*language*) papiamentu.
papier mâché *n.* paper maxada.
papilla *n.* (*anatomy*) papila.
papist *n.* papiste.
paprika *n.* (*plant, fruit, spice*) paprica.
Pap smear *n.* proba de Pap.
Pap test *n.* proba de Pap.
Papuan *adj.* & *n.* papuan.
Papua New Guinea *n.* Papua Gine Nova. **Gulf of Papua** Golfo Papua.
papule *n.* papula.
papyrus *n.* (*plant, paper*) papiro.
par *n.* (*golf*) norma. **above par** supranormal. **below par** sunormal.
para- *pref.* (*additional*) para-.
parable *n.* (*story*) parabola.
parabola *n.* (*curve*) parabola.
parachute *n.* paracade. • *v.* salta con paracade.
parachuting *n.* salta con paracade.
parade *v.* & *n.* parade.
parade float *n.* caro de parade.
paradigm *n.* model.
paradise *n.* paradiso.
paradox *n.* paradox.
paradoxical *adj.* paradoxal.
paradoxical sleep *adj.* dormi paradoxal.
paraffin *n.* parafina; alcano.
paragon *n.* culmina, esemplo perfeta.
paragraph *n.* paragraf.
Paraguay *n.* Paraguai.
Paraguayan *adj.* & *n.* paraguaia.
parakeet *n.* papagaio.
paralegal *adj.* paralegal. • *n.* paralegaliste.
parallax *n.* paralax.
parallel *adj.* & *n.* paralel.
parallelepiped *n.* paralelepipedo.
parallelepipedal *adj.* paralelepipedo.
parallelism *n.* paralelisme.
parallelness *n.* paralelia.
parallelogram *n.* paralelogram.
parallelogrammatic *adj.* paralelogram.
paralympic *adj.* paralimpial.
Paralympic Games *n.* Juas Paralimpial.
paralyse (US **paralyze**) *v.* paralise.
paralysis *n.* paralise.
paralytic *n.* paraliseda.
paralyze (US). See *paralyse.*
paramecium *n.* (*organism*) paramesio.
paramedic *n.* paramediciste.
parameter *n.* parametre.
parameterization *n.* parametri.
parameterize *v.* parametri.
paramilitary *adj.* paramilitar.
paramo *n.* plano alta.
paramount *adj.* suprema importante.
paramour *n.* amor, concubina.
Paraná River *n.* Rio Parana.
paranoia *n.* paranoia.
paranoid *adj.* paranoica.
paranormal *adj.* paranormal.
parapet *n.* parapeto.
paraphernalia *n.* aparatos.
paraphilia *n.* parafilia.
paraphiliac *adj.* & *n.* parafilica.
paraphrase *v.* & *n.* parafrase.
paraplegia *n.* paraplejia.
paraplegic *adj.* & *n.* paraplejica.
parapsychologist *n.* parapsicolojiste.
parapsychology *n.* parapsicolojia.
parasite *n.* parasito.
parasitic *adj.* parasital.
parasitic wasp *n.* vespa parasital.
parasitic worm *n.* elminto.
parasol *n.* parasol.
parasympathetic *adj.* (*nerves*) parasimpatica.
parathyroid *adj.* & *n.* paratiroide.
paratrooper *n.* paracador.
parazoa *n.* (*organisms*) parazones.
parazoon *n.* (*organism*) parazon.
parboil *v.* (*cookery*) poxe.
parcel *n.* paceta.
parch *v.* seci.
parcheesi *n.* patxisi.
parchment *n.* pergamin.
pardalote *n.* (*bird*) pardalote.
pardon *v.* pardona. **pardon me** pardona me.
pardonable *adj.* pardonable.
parent *n.* jenitor.
parenthesis *n.* (*punctuation*) braseta, braseta curva; (*bracketed material*) brasetida.
parenthetical *adj.* entre brasetas.
parenthetical phrase *n.* brasetida.
parenthood *n.* jenitoria.
parenticide *n.* jenitoriside; jenitorisidor. **commit parenticide** jenitoriside.
parenting *n.* eleva de enfantes.
parents *n.* madre e padre.
parent-to-be *n.* jenitor futur.
-paresis *suff.* (*medical*) -parese.
parfait *n.* (*dessert*) parfe.
parfumier *n.* parfumor.
Paria *n.* (*Venezuelan region*) Paria. **Gulf of Paria** Golfo Paria.
pariah *n.* paria.
parietal *adj.* (*anatomy*) parietal.
parietal bone *n.* oso parietal.
parietal lobe *n.* lobe parietal.
parish *n.* parocia.
parishioner *n.* parocian.
parish priest *n.* parocior.
parity *n.* egalia.
park *n.* parce. • *v.* (*vehicle*) parci. **amusement park** parce de divertis.
parka *n.* (*coat*) parca.
parking *n.* parci.

parking lot *n.* parce de autos.
parkinsonism *n.* maladia de Parkinson.
Parkinson's disease *n.* maladia de Parkinson.
parkland *n.* parce.
parkour *n.* parcur.
park ranger *n.* gardaforesta.
parkway *n.* autovia verde.
parlance *n.* jergo, modo de parla.
parley *v.* & *n.* confere.
parliament *n.* parlamento. **member of parliament** membro de parlamento, parlamentor.
parliamentarian *n.* membro de parlamento, parlamentor.
parliamentary *adj.* parlamental.
parmesan *n.* (*cheese*) parmesan.
parochial *adj.* parocial.
parochialism *n.* parocialisme, localisme.
parody *v.* & *n.* parodia.
parole *n.* libria limitada.
parolee *n.* prisonida con libria limitada.
parotid *n.* (*gland*) parotida.
paroxysm *n.* ataca.
parp *n.* & *interj.* tut. • *v.* tuti.
parquet *n.* parceta.
parquetry *n.* (*floor*) parceta.
parricide *n.* (*action*) jenitoriside; (*person*) jenitorisidor. **commit parricide** jenitoriside.
parrot *n.* papagaio.
parry *v.* contramove, oposa.
parse *v.* analise.
parsec *n.* (*unit of length*) parsec.
parser *n.* analisador sintatical.
parsimonious *adj.* frugal.
parsimony *n.* frugalia.
parsley *n.* (*plant*) persil.
parsnip *n.* pastinaca.
parson *n.* eglesor.
parsonage *n.* casa de eglesor.
part *n.* parte; (*to play*) rol. • *v.* divide. **be part of** es un parte de, parteni a, partisipa en. **part of speech** categoria sintatical. **take part** partisipa.
partake *v.* partisipa.
parthenogenesis *n.* (*biology*) partenojenese.
Parthia *n.* (*ancient region*) Partia.
Parthian *adj.* & *n.* partian.
partial *adj.* partal; (*biased*) partisan; (*liking*) favorente.
partiality *n.* favore.
partially sighted *adj.* partal vidente.
participant *n.* partisipor.
participate *v.* partisipa, junta se a.
participation *n.* partisipa.
participle *n.* partisipio.
particle *n.* particula, gran; (*grammar*) paroleta.
particle accelerator *n.* aselerador de particulas.
particleboard *n.* lenio presada.
particular *adj.* individua, spesifada; spesial; esata.
particularly *adv.* spesial.
particulate *adj.* particulin.
parting *n.* (*departure*) parti; (*splitting*) divide.
partisan *adj.* & *n.* partisan.
partition *n.* parte; (*wall*) mureta. • *v.* divide, sesioni.
partitive article *n.* (*grammar*) article de cuantia.
partly *adv.* partal.
partner *n.* (*social*) acompanior; (*business*) asosior. • *v.* asosia.
partnership *n.* asosia.
part payment *n.* paia partal.
partridge *n.* perdis.
part-time *adj.* de tempo partal.
parturition *n.* pari.
party *n.* selebra; (*political*) partito. **be party to** es envolveda en.
pascal *n.* (*unit of pressure*) pascal.
Pashto *adj.* & *n.* (*language*) paxtu.
Pashtun *adj.* & *n.* (*person*) paxtu.
pasigraphy *n.* (*writing system*) pasigrafia.
paska *n.* pan pascual.
pass *v.* (*place, time*) pasa; (*hand over*) pasa, dona; (*law*) aseta; (*test*) susede. **in passing** en pasa. **make a pass at** fa avansas a. **pass away** mori. **pass on** (*illness*) comunica. **pass time** pasa tempo.
passable *adj.* asetable.
passage *n.* (*travel, text, music*) pasaje.
passageway *n.* coredor, pasaje.
passenger *n.* pasajor, viajor.
passepied *n.* (*dance*) paspie.
passer-by *n.* pasor.
passerine *n.* pasarin.
passion *n.* pasion, foco.
passionate *adj.* pasionosa, focosa, zelosa, ardente.
passion flower *n.* pasiflora.
passionless *adj.* nonpasionosa.
passive *adj.* & *n.* (*including grammar*) pasiva.
passive voice *n.* vose pasiva.
passivity *n.* pasivia.
passkey *n.* clave xef, clave restrinjeda.
Passover *n.* (*Judaism*) pesah.
passport *n.* pasaporto.
password *n.* parola secreta, sinia secreta, clave.
past *adj.* & *n.* (*time, tense*) pasada. • *prep.* ultra. **go past** pasa. **in the past** en la pasada.
pasta *n.* pasta, talietas.
paste *n.* pasta; (*spread*) pasta aplicable; (*glue*) cola. • *v.* coli. **copy and paste** copia e coli.
pastel *adj.* & *n.* pastel.

pasteurization *n.* pasteuri.
pasteurize *v.* pasteuri.
pasticcio *n.* pastix.
pastiche *n.* pastix.
pastie *n.* covreteta.
pastime *n.* pasatempo, amato.
pastor *n.* pastor, eglesor, prete, prete mas.
pastoral *adj.* & *n.* (*including art*) pastoral.
pastoralism *n.* pastoria.
past perfect *n.* (*grammar*) pasada perfeta.
pastrami *n.* (*food*) pastrami.
pastry *n.* pasta dulse, torta.
pastry baker *n.* tortor.
pastry chef *n.* tortor.
pastry shop *n.* torteria.
pasturage *n.* pasto.
pasture *n.* pasto.
pat *v.* & *n.* colpeta.
Patagonia *n.* Patagonia.
patch *v.* repara con pesos, desrompe. • *n.* (*repair*) peso.
patchwork *adj.* de pesos.
patchy *adj.* partal.
pate *n.* testa.
pâté *n.* pate, pasta aplicable.
patella *n.* rotula.
patent *v.* & *n.* patenta.
patent infringement *n.* viole de patenta.
patent leather *n.* cuoro vernisida.
paternal *adj.* padral.
paternalism *n.* (*philosophy*) paternalisme.
paternity *n.* padria. • *adj.* (*leave*) padral.
path *n.* curso; via, rueta; (*computer file*) adirije.
pathetic *adj.* misera, povre. • *suff.* -patica.
pathfinder *n.* abrivia.
-pathic *suff.* -patica.
pathname *n.* adirije.
patho- *pref.* (*illness*) pato-.
pathogen *n.* patojen.
pathogenesis *n.* patojenese.
pathogenetic *adj.* patojenesal.
pathogenic *adj.* patojen.
pathological *adj.* patolojial.
pathologist *n.* patolojiste.
pathology *n.* patolojia.
pathos *n.* compatia.
pathway *n.* rueta.
-pathy *suff.* (*illness*) -patia.
patience *n.* pasientia.
patient *adj.* & *n.* (*including medical*) pasiente. **analytic patient** analiseda.
patina *n.* (*sheen*) patina.
patio *n.* teraza.
patois *n.* dialeto.
patriarch *n.* patriarca, padron.
patriarchy *n.* patriarcia.
patricide *n.* (*action*) padriside; (*person*) padrisidor. **commit patricide** padriside.
patrilineage *n.* patrilinia.
patrilineal *adj.* patrilinial.
patrimony *n.* erita.
patriot *n.* patriota.
patriotic *adj.* patriota.
patriotism *n.* patriotisme.
patrol *v.* & *n.* patrulia.
patroller *n.* patrulior.
patrolman *n.* patrulior.
patronage *n.* sponsoria.
patronize *v.* finje superioria.
patron saint *n.* santa padronal.
patronym *n.* nom padral.
patsy *n.* portaculpa.
patter[1] *v.* & *n.* (*tap*) tape.
patter[2] *n.* (*rapid talk*) babela.
pattern *n.* (*repeating*) motif; (*for imitation*) model; (*theme*) tema.
patty *n.* (*cake*) tarteta.
paunch *n.* ventron.
pauper *n.* povre.
paupiette *n.* (*food*) rolada.
pause *v.* & *n.* pausa, reposa. **without pause** sin pausa.
pavane *n.* (*dance, music*) pavana.
pave *v.* pave.
pavement *n.* troteria.
paver *n.* petra plata.
pavilion *n.* pavilion.
paving *n.* (*slabs, asphalt, cobbles*) pave.
paving block *n.* petra de pave, petra cubo.
paving stone *n.* petra de pave, petra plata.
pavlova *n.* (*dessert*) pavlova.
Pavo *n.* (*constellation*) la Pavon.
paw *n.* pedeta.
pawn[1] *n.* (*chess*) peon.
pawn[2] *v.* impenia.
pawnbroker *n.* impenior.
pawnshop *n.* impenieria.
pawpaw *n.* (*tree, fruit*) asimina.
pay *v.* paia. **crime does not pay** crimin no profita. **pay attention to** atende. **pay back** repaia. **pay by instalments** (US **installments**) paia en partes. **pay for** paia per. **pay in advance** prepaia. **pay on account** paia en partes. **pay raise** aumenta de salario. **pay rate per hour** paia per ora. **pay rise** aumenta de salario. **pay TV** televisa par paia.
payable *adj.* paiable; espetada.
pay-as-you-go *adj.* (*phone*) prepaiada.
payback *n.* recompensa; (*revenge*) venja.
paycheck *n.* salario.
paycheque *n.* salario.
payday *n.* dia de paia.
payer *n.* paior.
payload *n.* carga profitosa.
payment *n.* paia.
payment schedule *n.* contrata de paia.

payoff *n.* (*bribe*) soborna; (*investment*) interesa, recompensa.
payroll *n.* lista de salarios.
PC *abbr.* pc (*computador personal*).
PDA *n.* aidador personal.
PDF file *n.* fix PDF.
pea *n.* (*plant, seed*) piso.
peace *n.* pas. **at peace** pasosa.
peaceful *adj.* pasosa.
peacemaker *n.* reconsilior.
peacetime *n.* pas.
peach *adj.* (*colour*) pesca; (*fruit*) pesca; (*tree*) pesco.
peacock *n.* pavon.
peafowl *n.* pavon.
peahen *n.* pavon.
peak *n.* apico, culmina; (*cap*) borda fronte. • *v.* culmina.
peak hour *n.* ora de presa.
peanut *n.* aracide.
peanut butter *n.* bur de aracide.
pear *n.* (*fruit*) pera; (*tree*) pero.
pearl *n.* perla.
pearl diving *n.* tufa per perlas.
pearlike *adj.* perin.
pearly *adj.* perlin.
pear-shaped *adj.* perin.
peasant *n.* campanian, laboror.
peasantry *n.* campanianes.
peat *n.* (*soil*) torba.
peat bog *n.* pantan torbosa.
peatland *n.* pantan torbosa.
pebble *n.* calculo.
pecan *n.* (*tree, nut*) pecan.
peccadillo *n.* peceta.
peccary *n.* (*animal*) pecari.
peck *v.* & *n.* pica; (*kiss*) beseta.
pectin *n.* (*substance*) pectina.
pectoral *adj.* petal.
pectoral fin *n.* pina ladal.
peculiar *adj.* strana.
peculiarity *n.* (*quality*) strania; (*quirk*) strana.
pedagog (US). See *pedagogue*.
pedagogic *adj.* pedagojial.
pedagogical *adj.* pedagojial.
pedagogue (US **pedagog**) *n.* ensenior.
pedagogy *n.* pedagojia.
pedal *n.* pedal. • *v.* pedali.
pedant *n.* pedante.
pedantic *adj.* pedante.
pedantry *n.* pedantia.
peddle *v.* vende.
peddler *n.* vendor vagante.
pede... (US). See *paede...*
pedestal *n.* pedestal.
pedestrian *n.* paseor. • *adj.* mediocre.
pedestrian crossing *n.* pasaje de traversa.
pedi... (US). See *paedi...*
pedicab *n.* (*drawn by hand or bicycle*) ricxa.
pedicure *n.* pedicura.
pedigree *n.* linia de familia, linia de sangue.
pediment *n.* fronton.
pedlar *n.* vendor vagante.
pedo... (US). See *paedo...*
pedometer *n.* podometre.
pee *n.* (*urine*) pisa. • *v.* pisi.
peek *v.* & *n.* videta, videta secreta.
peek-a-boo *n.* jua de cucu.
peel *n.* (*fruit*) casca. • *v.* (*fruit, egg*) descasci. **peel off** descoli.
peeler *n.* descascador.
peep[1] *v.* & *n.* videta.
peep[2] *v.* (*squeak*) pipi. • *interj.* pip.
peephole *n.* buco de spia.
peepul *n.* pipal.
peer[1] *v.* regarda miope.
peer[2] *adj.* & *n.* coedal; nobil.
peerage *n.* titulo; aristocratas.
peerless *adj.* sin egal.
peer pressure *n.* presa de grupo.
peeve *v.* irita.
peevish *adj.* disputosa, iritable.
peg *n.* cavil.
Pegasus *n.* (*mythology, constellation*) Pegaso.
pegboard *n.* panel de caviles.
pejorative *adj.* despetante.
Peking *n.* Beijing.
pekoe *n.* (*tea*) peco.
pelican *n.* pelican.
pelicanlike *adj.* pelicanin.
pellagra *n.* (*medical*) pelagra.
pellet *n.* (*salt, sand, etc.*) gran.
pellucid *adj.* clar.
pelt[1] *v.* (*bombard*) bombarda, colpa.
pelt[2] *n.* (*skin*) pel.
pelvic *adj.* pelvisal.
pelvis *n.* pelvis.
pemphigus *n.* (*medical*) pemfigo.
pen[1] *n.* (*for writing*) pen.
pen[2] *n.* (*enclosure*) ensirca de bestias.
penal *adj.* (*punishment*) penal.
penalize *v.* puni, multa.
penalty *n.* puni, multa; (*football*) puni.
penance *n.* espia, repenti. **do penance** espia.
Penas, Gulf of *n.* Golfo Penas.
penchant *n.* tende.
pencil *n.* lapis.
pencil sharpener *n.* puntilapis.
pendant *n.* pendente.
penduline tit *n.* (*bird*) remize.
pendulous *adj.* pendente.
pendulum *n.* pendulo.
penetrate *v.* penetra.
penetration *n.* penetra.
penguin *n.* pinguin.
pen holder *n.* portapen.
-penia *suff.* (*lack*) -penia.

penicillin *n.* penisilina.
penile *adj.* penisal.
peninsula *n.* penisola.
peninsular *adj.* penisolal.
penis *n.* penis.
penitence *n.* repenti.
penitent *adj.* repentinte. • *n.* repentor. **be penitent** repenti.
penitentiary *n.* prison.
penknife *n.* cotel de pox.
penmanship *n.* (*action*) scrive par mano.
pen name *n.* nom falsa.
pennant *n.* bandereta.
Pennsylvania *n.* (*US state*) Pennsylvania.
penny *n.* sentim.
penny whistle *n.* sibileta.
pension *n.* pension.
pensioner *n.* jubilor.
pensive *adj.* pensosa.
penta- *pref.* (*five*) penta-.
pentacle *n.* (*star*) pentagram.
pentadactyl *adj.* (*biology*) pentadatilo.
pentagon *n.* pentagon.
pentagonal *adj.* pentagon.
pentagram *n.* pentagram.
pentameter *n.* (*poetry*) pentametre.
pentathlete *n.* pentatlonor.
pentathlon *n.* pentatlon.
pentecost *n.* pentecoste.
Pentecostal *adj.* pentecostal.
Pentecostalism *n.* (*Christianity*) pentecostalisme.
penthouse *n.* aparte apical.
pentobarbital *n.* pentobarbital.
pentobarbitone *n.* (*drug*) pentobarbital.
penultimate *adj.* anteultima, cuasi ultima.
penumbra *n.* (*shadow*) penombra.
penurious *adj.* povre.
penury *n.* povria.
peon *n.* peon.
peony *n.* (*plant*) peonia.
people *n.* (*individuals*) persones, umanas; (*a particular community*) popla.
people carrier *n.* furgoneta.
pep *n.* enerjia.
peperomia *n.* (*plant*) peperomia.
pepper *n.* (*hot, sweet, bell*) peperon; (*black, white*) peper. • *v.* peperi.
peppercorn *n.* baca de peper.
pepper grinder *n.* molin de peper.
pepperidge tree *n.* tupelo.
pepper mill *n.* molin de peper.
peppermint *n.* menta peperin.
pepperoni *n.* (*sausage*) salsix de peperon.
pepperpot *n.* vaso de peper.
peppery *adj.* (*like pepper*) peperin; (*full of pepper*) peperosa.
-pepsia *suff.* (*digestion*) -pepsia.
pepsin *n.* (*enzyme*) pepsin.
-peptic *suff.* -pepsica.
peptide *n.* (*chemistry*) peptido.
per[1] *prep.* (*in measurements of speed, etc.*) per; (*shared between*) entre. **per capita** per person. **per head** per person. **per month** per mense. **per person** per person.
per-[2] *pref.* (*thoroughly*) per-.
perahu *n.* (*sailboat*) proa.
perambulate *v.* vaga.
percale *n.* (*fabric*) percal.
perceive *v.* persepi.
percent *n.* persento. **fifty percent** sincodes persentos.
percentage *n.* cuantia persental.
percentage point *n.* persento.
percentile *n.* persentil.
percept *n.* persepida.
perceptible *adj.* persepable.
perception *n.* persepi.
perceptive *adj.* persepinte.
perceptual *adj.* persepal.
perch[1] *n.* (*support*) perxa. • *v.* perxi.
perch[2] *n.* (*fish*) perca.
perching bird *n.* pasarin.
percolate *v.* filtri, permea.
percolator *n.* cafador de filtro.
percuss *v.* percute.
percussion *n.* percute.
percussion cap *n.* capsula de percute.
percussion instrument *n.* strumento de percute.
percussionist *n.* percutiste.
perdition *n.* enferno, puni eterna.
peregrinate *v.* peregrina.
peregrination *n.* peregrina.
peregrine falcon *n.* peregrinor.
peremptory *adj.* brusca, comandante.
perennial *adj.* & *n.* perene.
perfect *adj.* perfeta. • *v.* perfeti, refina.
perfection *n.* perfetia.
perfectionism *n.* perfetisme.
perfectionist *adj.* & *n.* perfetiste.
perfective aspect *n.* (*grammar*) aspeta perfeta.
perfect pitch *n.* orea asoluta.
perfidious *adj.* tradosa.
perfidy *n.* tradi.
perforate *v.* perfora.
perforation *n.* perfora.
perforator *n.* perforador.
perform *v.* fa; (*feat, role, script*) presenta; (*surgery*) opera.
performance *n.* presenta; (*capability*) capasia; (*efficiency*) nonperosia.
performer *n.* presentor, ator.
performing arts *n.* artes de presenta.
perfume *n.* parfum. • *v.* parfumi.
perfumer *n.* parfumor.
perfumery *n.* parfumeria.

perfunctory *adj.* surfasal.
perfusion *n.* permea.
pergola *n.* pergola.
perhaps *adv.* cisa, posible, lo pote es ce.
peri- *pref.* (*around*) peri-.
pericarditis *n.* (*medical*) pericardite.
pericardium *n.* (*anatomy*) pericardio.
perigee *n.* (*astronomy*) perijeo.
perihelion *n.* (*astronomy*) perielio.
peril *n.* peril.
perilla *n.* (*plant*) perila.
perilous *adj.* perilosa.
perimeter *n.* perimetre.
perinatal *adj.* ostetrical.
perineum *n.* (*anatomy*) perineo.
period *n.* periodo; (*punctuation*) punto; (*menstrual*) menstrua.
periodic *adj.* periodal.
periodical *n.* revista.
periodontics *n.* periodontia.
periodontist *n.* periodontiste.
periodontology *n.* periodontia.
periorbita *n.* (*anatomy*) periorbita.
periorbital haematoma (US **hematoma**) *n.* ematoma periorbital.
peripatetic *adj.* vagante, paseante.
peripheral *adj.* periferial, ensircante, tanjente.
periphery *n.* periferia.
periscope *n.* periscopio.
periscopic *adj.* periscopial.
perish *v.* mori.
perishable *adj.* putrable; mortal.
peristalsis *n.* (*biology*) peristalsia.
peristaltic *adj.* peristalsica.
peritoneum *n.* (*anatomy*) peritoneo.
periwinkle[1] *n.* (*plant*) vinca.
periwinkle[2] *n.* (*mollusc*) litorina.
perjure *v.* perjura, atesta falsa.
perjurer *n.* perjuror.
perjury *n.* perjura, atesta falsa. **commit perjury** atesta falsa.
perk[1] *v.* (*up*) felisi.
perk[2] *n.* (*benefit*) benefica.
perky *adj.* restorada.
perm *v.* & *n.* (*hair*) perma.
permafrost *n.* permajelada.
permanence *n.* permane, permanentia.
permanent *adj.* permanente, constante. **be permanent** permane.
permanent wave *n.* (*hair*) perma.
permeable *adj.* permeable.
permeate *v.* permea, estende tra.
permeation *n.* permea.
Permian *adj.* & *n.* (*geology*) permian.
permissible *adj.* permeteda.
permission *n.* permete.
permissive *adj.* regalante.
permit *v.* permete. • *n.* lisensa.
permutate *v.* permuta.
permutation *n.* permuta.
pernicious *adj.* nosiva.
pernickety *adj.* esijente.
perogi *n.* (*dumplings*) pirogi.
peroxide *n.* perosido.
peroxisome *n.* (*biology*) perosisoma.
perpendicular *adj.* & *n.* perpendicular.
perpetrate *v.* esecuta.
perpetrator *n.* esecutor.
perpetual *adj.* eterna.
perpetuate *v.* continua, sperde.
perpetuity *n.* eternia.
perplex *v.* confonde.
perplexity *n.* confonde.
perruquier *n.* perucor.
persecute *v.* persegue.
persecution *n.* persegue.
persecutor *n.* perseguor.
Perseus *n.* (*mythology*, *constellation*) Perseo.
perseverance *n.* persiste, ostina.
persevere *v.* persiste, ostina.
Persia *n.* (*ancient region*) Persia.
Persian *adj.* & *n.* (*person*, *language*) farsi; (*ancient*) persian.
Persian Gulf *n.* Golfo Persian.
persiflage *n.* burleta.
persimmon *n.* (*tree*, *fruit*) caci.
persist *v.* persiste, ostina.
persistence *n.* persiste, ostina.
persistent *adj.* persistente, ostinosa.
persnickety *adj.* esijente.
person *n.* person, umana.
personable *adj.* amin.
personage *n.* person importante.
personal *adj.* personal.
personal computer *n.* computador personal.
personal digital assistant *n.* aidador personal.
personal hygiene *n.* cura personal.
personality *n.* personalia, carater.
personality cult *n.* culto de personalia.
personalization *n.* personali.
personalize *v.* personali.
personal stereo *n.* baladador.
persona non grata *n.* person nondesirada.
personification *n.* personi.
personify *v.* personi.
personlike *adj.* personin.
personnel *n.* empleadas.
perspective *n.* perspetiva; (*attitude*) punto de vista.
perspex *n.* vitro acrilica.
perspicuity *n.* claria.
perspicuous *adj.* clar, clar espresada.
perspiration *n.* (*sweat*) suo; (*sweating*) sui.
perspire *v.* sui.
persuade *v.* convinse.

persuasion *n.* convinse.
persuasive *adj.* convinsente.
pert *adj.* beleta.
pertain *v.* pertine. **pertaining to** pertinente a; (*on the topic of*) sur.
pertinence *n.* pertine.
pertinent *adj.* pertinente.
perturb *v.* disturba, ajita.
perturbation *n.* disturba.
pertussis *n.* pertuse.
Peru *n.* Peru.
peruse *v.* leje, esamina.
Peruvian *adj.* & *n.* peruan.
pervade *v.* permea.
pervasive *adj.* permeante.
perverse *adj.* pervertida.
perversion *n.* perverti.
perversive *adj.* pervertinte.
pervert *v.* perverti.
Pesach *n.* pesah.
pesky *adj.* iritante.
peso *n.* (*currency*) peso.
pessimism *n.* pesimisme.
pessimist *n.* pesimiste.
pessimistic *adj.* pesimiste.
pest *n.* (*creature, nuisance*) peste.
pester *v.* irita.
pesticide *n.* pestiside.
pestilence *n.* pesta.
pestle *n.* piston de mole.
pesto *n.* (*sauce*) pesto.
pet *n.* animal amada, animal de casa. • *v.* caresa.
petal *n.* petal.
petalled (US **petaled**) *adj.* petalosa.
pétanque *n.* bolo.
petard *n.* petardo.
petechia *n.* (*medical*) petecia.
petition *n.* solisita, suplica. • *v.* suplica, apela a.
petrel *n.* (*bird*) petrel.
Petri dish *n.* plato de Petri.
petrification *n.* petri.
petrify *v.* petri.
petro- *pref.* (*stone*) petro-.
petrochemical *adj.* & *n.* petrocimical.
petrodollar *n.* petrodolar.
petrol *n.* gasolina.
petroleum *n.* petrolio.
petrology *n.* petrolojia.
petrol station *n.* gasolineria.
petronia *n.* (*bird*) petronia.
petticoat *n.* faldeta.
pettifogging *n.* pedantia.
petty *adj.* trivial.
petty king *n.* renoreta.
petty kingdom *n.* reneta.
petulant *adj.* malumorosa.
petunia *n.* (*plant*) petunia.
pew *n.* banca.
pewter *n.* (*metal*) peltre.
-pexy *suff.* (*fastening*) -pexia.
peyote *n.* (*plant, drug*) peote.
pfennig *n.* sentim.
pH *n.* pH.
-phage *suff.* (*eater*) -faje.
-phagia *suff.* -fajia.
phago- *pref.* (*eating*) fago-.
phagocyte *n.* fagosite.
phagocytic *adj.* fagosital.
phagocytosis *n.* fagositose.
phalange *n.* (*anatomy*) falanje.
phalanx *n.* (*crowd*) falanje.
phalarope *n.* (*bird*) falaropo.
phallic *adj.* falin.
phallus *n.* falo.
phantamagorical *adj.* sonin.
phantasm *n.* fantasma.
phantasmagorica *n.* sonines.
phantom *n.* fantasma.
pharaoh *n.* faraon.
pharisee *n.* fariseo.
pharmaceutical *adj.* farmasial.
pharmacist *n.* farmasiste.
pharmacological *adj.* farmacolojial.
pharmacologist *n.* farmacolojiste.
pharmacology *n.* farmacolojia.
pharmacy *n.* farmasia.
pharyngeal *adj.* & *n.* (*consonant*) farinjal.
pharyngealize *v.* farinjali.
pharyngeal tonsil *n.* adenoide.
pharyngitis *n.* farinjite.
pharynx *n.* farinje.
phase *v.* & *n.* fase. **be out of phase** desfase. **out of phase** desfaseda. **phase in** introdui gradal. **phase out** retira gradal; descontinua.
phaser *n.* fasador.
pheasant *n.* fasian.
phenol *n.* (*substance*) fenol.
phenolphthalein *n.* (*substance*) fenolftalein.
phenomenal *adj.* spetaculin.
phenomenology *n.* fenomenolojia.
phenomenon *n.* fenomeno.
phenotype *n.* fenotipo.
phenylalanine *n.* (*amino acid*) fenilalanina.
phenylketonuria *n.* (*medical*) fenilcetonuria.
pheromone *n.* feromon.
phew *interj.* fu.
phi *n.* (*Greek letter* Φ, φ) fi.
phial *n.* boteleta.
philander *v.* adultera.
philanderer *n.* xasafem.
philanthropic *adj.* filantrope.
philanthropist *n.* filantropiste.
philanthropy *n.* filantropia.
philatelist *n.* filateliste.
philately *n.* filatelia.

-phile *suff.* -filica.
philharmonic *adj.* filarmonial.
-philia *suff.* (*love*) -filia.
-philiac *suff.* -filica.
-philic *suff.* -filica.
Philippine *adj.* & *n.* pilipina.
Philippines *n.* Pilipinas.
Philippine Sea *n.* Mar Pilipina.
Phillips-head screwdriver *n.* turnavise crusin.
Phillips screw *n.* vise crusin.
philo- *pref.* (*love*) filo-.
philologist *n.* filolojiste.
philology *n.* filolojia.
philosopher *n.* filosofiste.
philosophical *adj.* filosofial.
philosophize *v.* filosofi.
philosophy *n.* filosofia.
philtre (US **philter**) *n.* prepara afrodisica.
phisher *n.* pexor ueb.
phishing *n.* pexa ueb.
phlebitic *adj.* flebitica.
phlebitis *n.* (*medical*) flebite.
phlebotomist *n.* flebotomiste.
phlebotomy *n.* flebotomia.
phlegm *n.* muco.
phlegmatic *adj.* nonajitable.
phloem *n.* (*botany*) floema.
phlox *n.* (*plant*) flox.
pho *n.* (*soup*) fo.
-phobe *suff.* -fobica.
phobia *n.* fobia. • *suff.* -fobia.
phobic *adj.* fobica. • *suff.* -fobica.
Phoenicia *n.* Fenisia.
Phoenician *adj.* & *n.* fenisia.
phoenix *n.* fenix; (*constellation*) la Fenix.
phone[1] *n.* telefon. • *v.* telefoni.
-phone[2] *suff.* (*sound*) -fon.
phone box *n.* ciosco de telefon.
phone call *n.* telefoni.
phone card *n.* carta de telefon.
phoneme *n.* fonem.
phonemic *adj.* fonemal.
phonetic *adj.* fonetical.
phonetics *n.* fonetica.
phoney *adj.* finjente. • *n.* finjor, frodor.
phono- *pref.* fono-.
phonograph *n.* fonograf.
phonological *adj.* fonolojial.
phonology *n.* fonolojia.
phonotactics *n.* fonotatica.
-phony *suff.* (*sound*) -fonia.
-phoria *suff.* (*feeling*) -foria.
-phoric *suff.* -forica.
phoronid *n.* (*organism*) foronido.
phosphate *n.* (*chemistry*) fosfato.
phospholipid *adj.* (*chemistry*) fosfolipido.
phosphoresce *v.* fosforese.
phosphorescent *adj.* fosforesente.
phosphoric acid *n.* asida fosforica.
phosphorus *n.* (*element*) fosfor.
photo[1] *n.* foto, imaje. **take a photo of** fa un foto de, xuta.
photo-[2] *pref.* (*light, photography*) foto-.
photocell *n.* fotoselula.
photochemical *adj.* fotocimical.
photocopy *v.* & *n.* fotocopia.
photoelectric cell *n.* fotoselula.
photogenic *adj.* fotojen.
photograph *n.* foto. • *v.* fotografi.
photographer *n.* fotografiste.
photographic *adj.* fotografial.
photography *n.* fotografia.
photography enthusiast *adj.* & *n.* fotomanica.
photogravure *n.* fotograva.
photojournalism *n.* fotojornalisme, jornalisme fotografial.
photojournalist *n.* fotojornaliste.
photojournalistic *adj.* fotojornaliste.
photon *n.* foton.
photonegative *adj.* evitante lus.
photorealism *n.* fotorealisme.
photorealist *n.* fotorealiste.
photorealistic *adj.* fotorealiste.
photoreceptor *n.* fotoresetador.
photosensitive *adj.* fotosensante.
photosynthesis *n.* fotosintese.
photosynthesize *v.* fotosintese.
phototroph *n.* fototrof.
phototrophia *n.* fototrofia.
phototrophic *adj.* (*biology*) fototrof.
phototropic *adj.* (*botany*) fototropo.
phototropism *n.* fototropia.
photovoltaic *adj.* fotovoltaica.
photovoltaic cell *n.* selula fotovoltaica.
photovoltaic effect *n.* efeto fotovoltaica.
photovoltaics *n.* enerjia solal fotovoltaica.
phrase *n.* (*grammar*) formula; (*music*) frase, strutur. **adjective phrase** formula ajetivin.
phraseology *n.* fraseolojia.
phrenologist *n.* frenolojiste.
phrenology *n.* frenolojia.
Phrygia *n.* Frigia.
Phrygian *adj.* frigian.
phyllo *n.* folin.
phylogenesis *n.* filojenese.
phylogenetic *adj.* filojenetical.
phylogenetics *n.* filojenetica.
phylogeny *n.* (*evolution*) filojenese; (*science*) filojenetica.
phylum *n.* filo.
physical *adj.* fisical.
physical comedy *n.* farsa.
physical currency *n.* mone fisical.
physical exercise *n.* eserse fisical.
physician *n.* dotor medical, mediciste.

physicist *n.* fisiciste.
physics *n.* fisica.
physiognomy *n.* fas; aspeta de fas.
physiological *adj.* fisiolojial.
physiologist *n.* fisiolojiste.
physiology *n.* fisiolojia.
physique *n.* forma de corpo.
-physis *suff.* (*growth*) -fise.
phytochemistry *n.* fitocimica.
pi *n.* (*Greek letter* Π, π) pi.
pia mater *n.* (*anatomy*) piamadre.
pianissimo *adv.* cuieta.
pianist *n.* pianiste.
piano *n.* piano.
pianoforte *n.* piano.
pianola *n.* piano automata, piano de enrola.
piano roll *n.* enrola de piano.
piapiac *n.* jai african.
piastre (US **piaster**) *n.* (*currency*) piastre.
pibgorn *n.* (*musical instrument*) pibgorn.
pica *n.* (*food craving*) pica.
picador *n.* (*bullfighter*) picor.
piccalilli *n.* (*sauce*) picalili.
piccolo *n.* (*flute*) picolo.
pick[1] *v.* (*flower*) prende, colie; (*choose*) eleje. **pick clean** descarni. **pick up** prende, reprende, recolie.
pick[2] *n.* (*pickaxe*) picon.
pickaxe (US **pickax**) *n.* picon.
picket *n.* asembla de grevores; (*stake*) palo. • *v.* protesta.
picketer *n.* grevor, protestor.
pickle *n.* concombre vinagrida. • *v.* vinagri, marini.
pickpocket *n.* furabolsa.
pickup *n.* camioneta.
picky *adj.* esijente.
picnic *v.* & *n.* picnica.
pico- *pref.* (*a million-millionth*) pico-.
picosecond *n.* picosecondo.
picot *n.* aneleta.
pictogram *n.* glifo.
pictograph *n.* glifo.
Pictor *n.* (*constellation*) la Depintor.
pictorial *adj.* imajin.
picture *n.* imaje. • *v.* imaji.
picturesque *adj.* depintin, poesin.
pidgin *n.* (*language*) pijin.
pie *n.* tarte. • *v.* tarti.
piebald *adj.* ducolorida.
piece *n.* peso. **piece of apparatus** aparato. **piece of cake** peso de torta; (*metaphor*) ateni fasil. **piece of clothing** veste. **piece of furniture** mobila. **piece of good luck** bon acaso. **piece of jewellery** joala. **piece of pottery** seramica. **piece of real estate** imobila. **piece together** reconstrui. **to pieces** a pesos, a ruina.
piecemeal *adv.* par partes.
piecework *adj.* paiada par taxe.
pied *adj.* multicolorosa.
pied crow *n.* corvo blanca-negra.
Piedmont *n.* (*Italian region*) Piemonte.
Piedmontese *adj.* & *n.* (*person*, *language*) piemontese.
pie pan *n.* molda per tartes.
pier *n.* molo.
pierce *v.* perfora.
piercing *adj.* (*sound*) xiliante. • *n.* joala perforante.
pieris *n.* (*plant*) andromeda.
pierogi *n.* (*dumplings*) pirogi.
pierrot *n.* paliaso.
pie tin *n.* molda per tartes.
piety *n.* relijiosia.
piffle *n.* babela.
pig *n.* porco.
pig deer *n.* babirusa.
pigeon *n.* pijon.
pigeonhole *n.* comparte.
piggyback *v.* monta la dorso. • *adv.* a dorso.
piggy bank *n.* porceta.
pig-headed *adj.* ostinosa.
piglet *n.* porceta.
piglike *adj.* porcin.
pigment *n.* pigmento.
pigmentation *n.* pigmento.
pigpen *n.* ensirca de porcos, porceria.
pigskin *n.* pel de porco.
pig sty *n.* ensirca de porcos, porceria.
pigtail *n.* (*plaited*) trenseta; (*unplaited*) codetas.
pika *n.* (*animal*) pica.
pike *n.* (*fish*) lusio.
pilaf *n.* (*food*) pilaf.
pilaster *n.* (*column*) pilastro.
pilchard *n.* sardina.
pile[1] *n.* pila, monton. • *v.* pila.
pile[2] *n.* (*of fabric*) pelo.
pile dwelling *n.* casa sur palos.
pile-up *n.* colide multiple; (*accumulation*) cumula.
pilfer *v.* fura, fureta.
pilferage *n.* fureta.
pilgrim *n.* peregrinor.
pilgrimage *n.* peregrina. **make a pilgrimage** peregrina.
pill *n.* pil.
pillage *v.* saca.
pillager *n.* sacor.
pillar *n.* colona.
pillarboxed *adj.* (*video*) en ranur vertical.
pillbox *n.* portapil.
pill bug *n.* (*woodlouse*) onisco.
pillock *n.* bobo.
pillory *v.* & *n.* pilori.
pillow *n.* cuxin, cuxin de testa.
pillowcase *n.* covrecuxin.
pillow talk *n.* conversa intima.

pilot *n.* pilote, volor.
pils *n.* pilsen.
pilsner *n.* (*beer*) pilsen.
pimento *n.* pimento.
pimiento *n.* pimento.
pimp *n.* otenor.
pimpernel *n.* pimpinela.
pimple *n.* papula, pustula.
pin *n.* spino; (*bowling*) baston. • *v.* spini. **feeling pins and needles** formicosa.
piña colada *n.* (*drink*) piniacolada.
pinafore dress *n.* jumper.
piñata *n.* (*container of treats*) piniata.
pinball *n.* pinbal.
pincers *n.* pinse.
pinch *v.* pinsi. • *n.* pinsi; (*of salt*) pico.
pinchpenny *n.* baratamanica.
pincushion *n.* portaspino.
pine[1] *n.* (*tree*) pino.
pine[2] *v.* (*for*) anela.
pineal *adj.* (*anatomy*) pineal.
pineal gland *n.* glande pineal.
pineapple *n.* (*plant, fruit*) ananas.
pinecone *n.* cono de pino.
pine needle *n.* ago de pino.
pine nut *n.* seme de pino.
pinfeather *n.* pluma nonmatur.
pingin *n.* (*coin*) sentim.
ping-pong *n.* tenis de table.
pinhead *n.* stupida.
pinion *n.* pinion.
pink[1] *adj.* & *n.* (*colour*) ros.
pink[2] *n.* (*plant*) dianto.
pinkeye *n.* conjuntivite.
pinkie *n.* dito peti.
pinkish *adj.* rosin.
pinky *n.* dito peti.
pinna *n.* orea esterna.
pinnacle *n.* pinaculo, zenite.
pinochle *n.* (*card game*) pinocle.
pinpoint *v.* locali, detalia.
pinprick *n.* pica de spino.
pinstripes *n.* raios diplomata.
pint *n.* (*unit of capacity*) otigalon.
pinto bean *n.* fava pintida.
pin-up *n.* poster; (*person*) stela bela.
pinwheel *n.* molineta.
pinworm *n.* osiuro.
pinworm infection *n.* osiurose.
Pinyin *n.* (*transcription*) piniin.
pioneer *n.* abrivia; coloniste prima. • *v.* abri la via de.
pioneering *adj.* abrinte vias.
piopio *n.* (*bird*) piopio.
pious *adj.* relijiosa.
pip *n.* seme.
pipal *n.* pipal.
pipe *n.* (*conduit*) tubo; (*large*) tubon; (*smoking*) pipa; (*music*) flauta; (*symbol*) bara vertical.
pipedream *n.* scema fantasial.
pipefish *n.* pex pipin.
pipelike *adj.* pipin.
pipeline *n.* tubon; (*software*) cadena.
piper *n.* flautiste; (*bagpipes*) cornamusor.
pipe-shaped *adj.* pipin.
pipestem *n.* tubo de pipa.
pipe threader *n.* filetador.
pipette *n.* pipeta.
pipevine *n.* (*plant*) aristolocia.
pipework *n.* tubos.
pipsqueak *n.* debil.
piquant *adj.* picante, spisosa.
pique *n.* irita. • *v.* stimula.
piracy *n.* piratia.
piranha *n.* pirania.
pirate *n.* pirata. • *v.* pirati. **make a pirate copy of** pirati.
pirouette *v.* & *n.* pirueta.
Pisces *n.* (*constellation*) la Pexes.
Piscis Austrinus *n.* (*constellation*) la Pex Sude.
piss *n.* (*urine*) pisa. • *v.* pisi.
pissant *adj.* despetable, sin valua.
pistachio *n.* (*tree, nut*) pistaxio.
piste *n.* scieria.
pistil *n.* (*botany*) pistil.
pistol *n.* pistol; fusil de mano. **fight with pistols** pistoli.
pistol fight *n.* pistoli.
piston *n.* piston.
pit[1] *n.* caveta.
pit[2] *n.* (*of fruit*) seme. • *v.* desemi.
pita *n.* pita.
pitch[1] *n.* (*sport*) campo; (*sound*) tono, altia de tono. • *v.* osila.
pitch[2] *n.* (*substance*) bitume.
pitch bend *n.* (*music*) portamento.
pitcher[1] *n.* (*jug*) carafa.
pitcher[2] *n.* (*baseball*) lansor.
pitcher plant *n.* nepentes.
pitchfork *n.* forcon.
piteous *adj.* misera, povre.
pitfall *n.* trapa.
pith *n.* medula.
pithy *adj.* medulosa; (*terse*) consisa.
pitiable *adj.* compatiable, povre.
pitiful *adj.* misera, povre.
pitiless *adj.* sin compatia.
pitohui *n.* (*bird*) pitui.
pit saw *n.* siera cuadro.
pitta[1] *n.* (*bird*) pita.
pitta[2] *n.* (*bread*) pita.
pittance *n.* paia pico.
pituitary *adj.* ipofisal.
pituitary gland *n.* ipofise.
pity *v.* & *n.* compatia. **what a pity** tan triste.
pivot *n.* fulcro. • *v.* pivote, jira.
pivotal *adj.* esensal, sentral.

pixel *n.* pixel.
pixellate *v.* pixeli.
pixellation *n.* pixeli.
pixie *n.* elfo.
pixieish *adj.* elfin.
pixy *n.* elfo.
pizza *n.* piza.
pizzazz *n.* glamor.
pizzeria *n.* pizeria.
pizzicato *n.* pizicato.
placard *n.* carton.
placate *v.* pasi.
placation *n.* pasi.
place *n.* loca. • *v.* loca, pone. **in place of** en loca de. **in the first place** prima. **take place** aveni.
placebo *adj.* & *n.* (*medical*) plasebo.
placeholder *n.* teniloca.
placement *n.* pone.
placenta *n.* plasenta.
placental *adj.* plasental.
place-value notation *n.* (*numerals*) sistem de valua local.
placid *adj.* nonajitable; (*peaceful*) pasosa.
placket *n.* covreta.
placozoa *n.* (*organisms*) placozones.
placozoon *n.* (*organism*) placozon.
plagiarism *n.* plajia.
plagiarist *n.* plajior.
plagiarize *v.* plajia.
plague *v.* & *n.* pesta.
plaid *n.* texeda scotes.
plain *adj.* simple, blanda, comun; nondecorada, sin motif; (*clear*) clar; (*text file*) plata. • *n.* (*land*) plano.
plainchant *n.* canta gregorian.
plainclothesman *n.* polisior desemblante.
plainclothes officer *n.* polisior desemblante.
plainness *n.* blandia.
plainsong *n.* canta gregorian.
plainspoken *adj.* franca.
plains-wanderer *n.* (*bird*) pedionom.
plaintiff *n.* acusor.
plaintive *adj.* lamentin.
plait *v.* & *n.* trensa.
plan *n.* intende, projeta; (*creative*) desinia; (*of action*, *of payment*) scema. • *v.* intende; projeta; desinia; scemi.
planar *adj.* plana.
planarian *n.* (*worm*) planaria.
plane *adj.* plana. • *v.* plani. • *n.* (*surface*) plana; (*tool*) planador.
planer *n.* planador.
planet *n.* planeta. **minor planet** planeteta.
planetarium *n.* planeteria.
planetary *adj.* planetal.
planetesimal *n.* planetesimo.
planetologist *n.* planetolojiste.
planetology *n.* planetolojia.
plangent *adj.* lamentin, resonante.
plank *n.* plance.
planking *n.* faxa.
plankton *n.* plancton.
planned language *n.* lingua desiniada.
planner *n.* scemor.
plant *n.* planta; (*complex*) compleso. • *v.* planta.
plantain[1] *n.* (*weed*) plantago.
plantain[2] *n.* (*plant*, *banana*) plantano.
plantar *adj.* (*of the sole*) plantal.
plantation *n.* cultiveria, cultiveria grande, monocultiveria; (*colony*) colonia.
planter *n.* portaplanta.
planthopper *n.* (*insect*) fulgoro.
plantigrade *adj.* (*biology*) plantigrada.
plant-related *adj.* plantal.
plaque *n.* (*tablet*) placa.
-plasia *suff.* (*growth*) -plasia.
-plasm *suff.* (*growth*) -plasma.
plasma *n.* (*medical*, *gas*) plasma.
plasmacyte *n.* (*biology*) plasmasite.
-plasmic *suff.* -plasmica.
plasmodium *n.* (*organism*) plasmodio.
plaster *n.* (*material*) jeso; (*bandage*) banda medical aderente. • *v.* jesi.
plasterboard *n.* plance de jeso.
plaster cast *n.* molda de jeso.
plastic *adj.* & *n.* plastica. • *suff.* -plastica.
plasticine *n.* pasta de modeli.
plastic surgeon *n.* sirurjiste plastica.
plastic surgery *n.* sirurjia plastica.
plastid *n.* (*biology*) plasto.
-plasty *suff.* (*surgery*) -plastia.
plate *n.* (*dish*) plato; (*layer*) lamina; (*sheet*) plata; (*photographic*, *mechanical*) placa. • *v.* placa.
plateau *n.* plano alta.
platelet *n.* trombosite.
platen *n.* plata.
plate warmer *n.* caldiplato.
platform *n.* plataforma.
plating *n.* placa; faxa.
platinum *n.* platino.
platinum blonde *adj.* & *n.* blanca blonde.
platitude *n.* clixe.
Plato *n.* (*philosopher*) Platon.
platonic *adj.* platonica.
Platonism *n.* platonisme.
platoon *n.* ploton.
Plattdeutsch *adj.* & *n.* platdeutx.
platter *n.* platon.
platyhelminth *n.* platielminto, verme plata.
platypus *n.* ornitorinco.
platyzoa *n.* (*organisms*) platizones.
platyzoon *n.* (*organism*) platizon.
plausible *adj.* credable, convinsente.
play *v.* (*game*, *sport*, *music*, *instrument*, *role*) jua, fa; (*video*) mostra. • *n.* (*theatrical*) teatral, pre-

senta teatral, peso. **play on words** broma de parolas. **play truant** evita la scola.
play area *n.* jueria, patio de enfantes.
playback singer *n.* cantor sincrona.
playbill *n.* poster teatral.
playbook *n.* libro de stratejia.
playboy *n.* xasafem, om promiscua.
player *n.* juor; (*actor*) ator, rolor.
player piano *n.* piano automata, piano de enrola.
playful *adj.* juosa.
playground *n.* (*school*) campo de scola; (*play area*) jueria, patio de enfantes.
playhouse *n.* teatro; (*Wendy house*) casa de jua.
playing card *n.* carta de jua.
playing field *n.* campo de jua.
playmate *n.* ami de jua.
play money *n.* mone de jua.
play-off *n.* desidente, max desidente.
playpen *n.* ensirca de bebe.
playroom *n.* sala de enfantes.
plaything *n.* jueta.
playtime *n.* recrea.
playwright *n.* autor teatral.
plaza *n.* plaza.
plea *n.* suplica.
plead *v.* (*beseech*) prea; (*in court*) declara. **plead ignorance** declara nonsabe.
pleasant *adj.* plasente, amable, comfortante, gustable.
pleasantness *n.* plase.
pleasantry *n.* espresa cortes; (*joke*) broma.
please *v.* plase. • *interj.* per favore. **it pleases me** lo plase me.
pleased *adj.* plaseda. **pleased to meet you** encantada.
pleasing *adj.* plasente. **pleasing on the eye** dulse per la oios.
pleasingness *n.* plase.
pleasurable *adj.* plaserosa.
pleasure *n.* plaser.
pleat *v.* & *n.* (*stitched fold*) plisa.
plebe *n.* comensor.
plebeian *adj.* de clase basa; de la popla comun.
plebiscite *n.* referendo, vota direta.
plectrum *n.* plectro.
pledge *v.* & *n.* promete.
-plegia *suff.* (*paralysis*) -plejia.
-plegic *suff.* -plejica.
Pleiades *n.* (*mythology*, *stars*) Pliades.
Pleistocene *adj.* & *n.* (*geology*) plestosene.
plenary *adj.* completa.
plenipotentiary *adj.* autoriosa.
plenitude *n.* abunda.
plentiful *adj.* abundante.
plenty *n.* abunda. **horn of plenty** corno de abunda.
plenum *n.* (*filled space*) plenida.
pleo- *pref.* (*more*) pleo-.
plesiosaur *n.* plesiosauro.
pleura *n.* (*anatomy*) pleura.
pleural *adj.* pleural.
pleurisy *n.* (*medical*) pleurite.
pleuritis *n.* pleurite.
plexiglass *n.* vitro acrilica.
plexus *n.* (*anatomy*) pleso.
pliable *adj.* pliable, flexable.
pliant *adj.* pliable, flexable.
pliers *n.* pinse.
plight *n.* mal situa.
plimsoll *n.* sapato de sporte.
plinth *n.* suportador.
Pliocene *adj.* & *n.* (*anatomy*) pliosene.
plissé *adj.* plietosa.
plod *v.* & *n.* pasea laborosa.
plop *n.* & *interj.* pluf. • *v.* plufi.
plosive *adj.* & *n.* (*consonant*) esplodente.
plot *v.* conspira; (*story*) trama. • *n.* conspira; (*land*) peso; (*story*) trama.
plotter *n.* conspiror.
plough (US **plow**) *n.* arado. • *v.* aradi.
ploughshare (US **plowshare**) *n.* lama de arado.
plover *n.* (*bird*) pluvial; (*dotterel*) caradrio.
plow (US). See *plough*.
plowshare (US). See *ploughshare*.
ploy *n.* rus, truco.
pluck *v.* tira; (*feathers*) desplumi; (*a stringed instrument*) toca. **pluck out** estrae.
plucky *adj.* corajosa.
plug *n.* (*stopper*) tapo; (*electric*) liador. • *v.* tapi. **plug in** lia.
plugboard *n.* panel de comuta.
plug-in *n.* ajuntable.
plum *adj.* (*colour*) pruna; (*fruit*) pruna; (*tree*) pruno.
plumage *n.* plumas.
plumbago *n.* (*plant*) plumbago.
plumber *n.* plomor.
plumbing *n.* tubos.
plumb line *n.* filo de plomo.
plume *n.* (*feathers*, *smoke*) plumon.
plumeria *n.* plumeria.
plump *adj.* obesa.
plunder *v.* saca.
plunge *v.* & *n.* tufa.
plunging *adj.* tufante; (*neckline*) escotada.
pluperfect *n.* pasada perfeta.
plural *adj.* & *n.* plural.
pluralism *n.* pluralisme.
pluralist *n.* pluraliste.
plurality *n.* pluralia.
pluralize *v.* plurali.
plus *conj.* con ance, como ance; (*arithmetic*) plu.
plush *n.* (*fabric*) pelux.

plush toy *n.* animal de pelux.
plus sign *n.* sinia positiva, sinia de ajunta.
Pluto *n.* (*mythology*, *planet*) Pluto.
plutocracy *n.* plutocratia.
plutocrat *n.* plutocrata.
plutonium *n.* plutonio.
ply *n.* strato.
plywood *n.* lenio stratida.
p.m. *abbr.* pm (*pos mediadia*).
-pnea *suff.* (*breathing*) -pnea.
pneumatic drill *n.* martel de aira.
pneumato- *pref.* (*air*) pneumato-.
pneumo- *pref.* (*air*) pneumo-.
pneumonia *n.* pneumonia.
poach[1] *v.* (*egg*) poxe.
poach[2] *v.* (*hunt*) xasa nonlegal.
poacher *n.* xasor nonlegal.
pocket *n.* pox. • *v.* poxi.
pocketbook *n.* libro de pox; (*wallet*, *bag*) bolsa.
pocket knife *n.* cotel de pox.
pocketwatch *n.* orolojeta.
pod[1] *n.* (*seed*) casca.
pod[2] *n.* (*whales*) manada.
podcast *v.* & *n.* podcasta.
podiatrist *n.* podolojiste.
podiatry *n.* podolojia.
podium *n.* plataforma.
podlike *adj.* cascin.
pod-shaped *adj.* cascin.
poem *n.* poesia; (*religious*) salmo.
poet *n.* poesiste.
poetic *adj.* (*of poetry*) poesial; (*like poetry*) poesin.
poetic licence (US **license**) *n.* permete poesial.
poetry *n.* poesia.
pogrom *n.* (*massacre*) pogrom.
poi *n.* (*food*) poi.
-poiesis *suff.* (*forming*) -poiese.
poignant *adj.* tristinte.
poinsettia *n.* flor de pascua.
point *n.* (*tip*, *dot*, *item*, *scoring*) punto. • *v.* (*aim*) punta; (*point out*) indica. **on the point of** a punto de. **point and click** indica e clica. **point of reference** punto de refere. **point of view** punto de vista; persepi. **points** puntos; (*railway*) force de ferovia. **to the point** consisa.
point-blank *adv.* de prosima.
pointed *adj.* puntida, agu.
pointer *n.* (*software*) refere.
pointillism *n.* (*art*) puntisme.
pointillist *n.* puntiste.
pointless *adj.* futil, sin razona.
pointsman *n.* forcor de ferovia.
pointy *adj.* puntida, agu.
poise *v.* ecuilibra. • *n.* refina.
poised *adj.* preparada; refinada.
poison *n.* venena. • *v.* veneni.
poison ivy *n.* sumaco venenosa.
poison oak *n.* sumaco venenosa.
poisonous *adj.* venenosa.
poisonous toadstool *n.* xampinion venenosa.
poison sumac *n.* sumaco venenosa.
poke *v.* & *n.* puieta.
poker[1] *n.* (*for fire*) tisafoco.
poker[2] *n.* (*card game*) pocer.
Poland *n.* Polsca.
polar *adj.* polal.
polar bear *n.* urso blanca.
polar icecap *n.* glasia polal.
polarity *n.* (*electric*, *magnetic*) polalia.
polarization *n.* polali.
polarize *v.* polali.
polaroid *n.* plastica polalida.
polder *n.* (*reclaimed land*) polder.
pole[1] *n.* palo.
pole[2] *n.* (*magnetic*, *etc.*) polo. **North Pole** Polo Norde. **South Pole** Polo Sude.
Pole[3] *n.* (*Polish person*) polsce.
poleaxe (US **poleax**) *n.* axa de gera.
polecat *n.* furon.
polemic *n.* polemica.
polemicist *n.* polemiciste.
polenta *n.* (*food*) polenta.
pole-vault *v.* salta con palo.
pole vaulter *n.* saltor con palo.
police *n.* polisia.
police box *n.* ciosco de polisia.
policeman *n.* polisior.
police officer *n.* polisior.
police state *n.* stato de polisia.
police station *n.* ofisia de polisia, polisieria.
policewoman *n.* polisior.
policy *n.* politica; (*pledges*) prometes.
policyholder *n.* asecurada.
polio *n.* poliomielite.
poliomyelitis *n.* poliomielite.
polish[1] *v.* (*to make shiny*) brilia. • *n.* sira per brilia.
Polish[2] *adj.* & *n.* (*person*, *language*) polsce.
politburo *n.* politburo.
polite *adj.* cortes.
politeness *n.* cortesia.
politic *adj.* saja.
political *adj.* political.
politician *n.* politiciste.
politicize *v.* politici.
politics *n.* politica.
polka *n.* (*dance*) polca.
polka dots *n.* motif de puntos.
poll *v.* sonda. • *n.* sonda; vota.
pollen *n.* polen.
pollex *n.* polex.
pollinate *v.* poleni.
pollination *n.* poleni.

polling booth *n.* ciosco de vota.
polling place *n.* voteria.
polling station *n.* voteria.
polliwog *n.* raneta.
pollutant *n.* contaminante.
pollute *v.* contamina.
pollution *n.* contamina.
polo *n.* (*sport*) polo. **water polo** polo de acua.
polonaise *n.* (*dance*) polonesa.
polonium *n.* (*element*) polonio.
polo shirt *n.* camisa de polo.
poltergeist *n.* fantasma turbosa.
poly[1] *n.* vitro acrilica.
poly-[2] *pref.* (*many*) poli-.
polyamorous *adj.* poliamial.
polyamory *n.* poliamia.
polyandrous *adj.* poliandrial.
polyandry *n.* (*marriage*) poliandria.
polychromatic *adj.* multicolorosa.
polydactylic *adj.* polidatilo.
polydactyly *n.* (*biology*) polidatilia.
polyester *n.* poliester. • *adj.* de poliester.
polyethylene *n.* polietilen.
polygamist *n.* poligamiste.
polygamous *adj.* poligama.
polygamy *n.* (*marriage, botany*) poligamia.
polyglot *n.* multilingual.
polygon *n.* poligon.
polygonal *adj.* poligon.
polygynous *adj.* polijinial.
polygyny *n.* (*marriage*) polijinia.
polyhedral *adj.* poliedro.
polyhedron *n.* poliedro.
polymath *n.* erudita.
polymer *n.* polimer.
polymeric *adj.* polimerosa.
polymerism *n.* polimeria.
polymerization *n.* polimeri.
polymerize *v.* polimeri.
polymerous *adj.* polimerosa.
polymethyl methacrylate *n.* vitro acrilica.
polymorphic *adj.* polimorfe.
polymorphism *n.* polimorfia.
Polynesia *n.* Polinesia.
Polynesian *adj.* & *n.* polinesian.
polynomial *adj.* polinomial. • *n.* polinomio.
polyp *n.* polipo.
polypeptide *n.* (*chemistry*) polipeptido.
polyphonic *adj.* polifonial.
polyphony *n.* (*music*) polifonia.
polysaccharide *n.* (*sugar*) polisacarido.
polystyrene *n.* polistiren.
polystyrene foam *n.* polistiren estruida.
polysyllabic *adj.* polisilabal.
polysyllable *n.* polisilaba.
polytarp *n.* lona de polietilen.
polytechnic *n.* politecnical.
polytheism *n.* politeisme.
polytheist *n.* politeiste.
polytheistic *adj.* politeiste.
polythene *n.* polietilen.
polythene tarpaulin *n.* lona de polietilen.
polyurethane *n.* poliuretan.
polyvalent *adj.* polivalente.
polyvinyl chloride *n.* polivinil, clorido de polivinil.
pomade *n.* unjente.
pomander *n.* bal bonodorosa.
pomegranate *n.* granada.
pomelo *n.* pampelmus.
pomeranian *n.* (*dog*) pomoran.
pommel *n.* (*sword, saddle*) pomon.
pomp *n.* ostenta.
pompadour *n.* (*hairstyle*) pompador.
pompom *n.* pompon.
pompous *adj.* ostentosa.
poncho *n.* (*garment*) pontxo.
pond *n.* lageta, stange.
ponder *v.* considera.
ponderous *adj.* pesosa.
pong *v.* apesta.
pontiff *n.* pape.
pontifical *adj.* papal.
pontificate *n.* ofisia de pape. • *v.* parla papin.
pontoon *n.* (*boat*) ponton; (*bridge*) ponte de pontones.
pony *n.* cavalo peti.
ponytail *n.* (*hairstyle*) coda de cavalo.
poo *n.* (*dung, anything worthless*) caca. • *v.* caci.
pooch *n.* can.
poodle *n.* canix.
pooh *interj.* (*disgust*) iu.
pool[1] *n.* (*swimming*) pisina; (*puddle*) stangeta. • *v.* stangi.
pool[2] *n.* (*game*) biliardo, biliardo american.
poolhall *n.* biliarderia.
poolroom *n.* biliarderia.
poop *n.* (*dung, anything worthless*) caca. • *v.* caci.
poor *adj.* povre; nonfortunosa; (*quality*) dejetable.
poorhouse *n.* povreria.
pop[1] *n.* & *interj.* pum. • *v.* pumi.
pop[2] *adj.* & *n.* (*music*) pop.
pop[3] *n.* (*dad*) papa.
popcorn *n.* popcorn.
pope *n.* pape.
popgun *n.* fusil de suber.
popinjay *n.* dandi.
poplar *n.* (*tree*) poplo.
poplin *n.* (*fabric*) popelin.
pop music *n.* musica pop.
popover *n.* mufin cavetin.
popper *n.* boton de presa.
poppy *n.* papavera.
poppycock *n.* asurda.
pop star *n.* stela de pop.
populace *n.* popla.

popular *adj.* popular; (*of or by the populace*) poplal.

popularity *n.* popularia.

popularization *n.* populari.

popularize *v.* populari.

populate *v.* popla.

population *n.* (*action, figure*) popla; abitores; cuantia de abitores.

populism *n.* poplisme.

populist *n.* popliste.

populous *adj.* multe poplada.

popup window *n.* fenetra flotante.

porcelain *n.* porselana.

porch *n.* (*covered entrance*) portico; (*veranda*) veranda.

porcine *adj.* porcin.

porcupine *n.* porcospina.

pore[1] *n.* (*opening*) por.

pore[2] *v.* (*over*) studia.

porifer *n.* (*organism*) porifero.

pork *n.* carne de porco.

pork rib *n.* costela de porco.

porn *adj.* & *n.* porno.

porn film *n.* porno.

porno *n.* porno.

pornographer *n.* pornografiste.

pornographic *adj.* pornografial.

pornography *n.* pornografia.

-porosis *suff.* (*medical*) -porose.

porous *adj.* porosa, forosa.

porphyry *n.* (*rock*) porfir.

porpoise *n.* fosena.

porridge *n.* gaxa, gaxa de avena.

porringer *n.* boleta.

port[1] *n.* (*harbour, computer*) porto. **port of call** porto de visita.

port[2] *adj.* & *n.* (*side of ship*) sinistra.

portable *adj.* portable.

portable computer *n.* portable, computador portable.

portable stove *n.* stufa portable.

portage *n.* porta.

portal *n.* porton.

portamento *n.* portamento.

portend *v.* premostra.

portent *n.* indica.

portentous *adj.* menasante.

porter *n.* portor.

portfolio *n.* (*case*) portafolio; (*of work*) galerieta.

porthole *n.* fenetreta.

portico *n.* portico.

portion *n.* parte; comparti.

portly *adj.* obesa.

portmanteau *n.* valison.

portrait *n.* depinta personal, foto personal. • *adj.* (*orientation*) vertical.

portraiture *n.* depinta de persones.

portray *v.* representa.

portrayal *n.* representa.

Portugal *n.* Portugal.

Portuguese *adj.* & *n.* portuges.

Portuguese man-of-war *n.* (*organism*) fisalia.

portulaca *n.* (*plant*) portulaca.

pose *v.* & *n.* posa; (*problem, question*) leva, crea. **pose as** finje.

poser *n.* finjor.

poseur *n.* dandi.

posh *adj.* lusosa, de clase alta.

position *n.* loca; (*arrangement*) posa; (*job*) posto, ofisia. • *v.* loca; posa.

positional notation *n.* sistem de valua local.

positive *adj.* positiva.

positive sign *n.* sinia positiva.

positivity *n.* positivia.

positron *n.* (*particle*) positron.

posse *n.* grupo, ronda.

possess *v.* posese.

possession *n.* (*ownership*) posese; (*item owned*) poseseda.

possessive *adj.* (*person*) posesente; (*grammar*) posesal.

possessor *n.* posesor.

possibility *n.* (*quality*) posiblia; (*something possible*) posible.

possible *adj.* posible. **as much as possible** tan multe como posible.

possibly *adv.* cisa, posible.

post[1] *n.* (*pole*) palo.

post[2] *v.* (*mail*) posta; (*accounting, internet, etc.*) posta; (*publish, display*) publici; (*bill*) fisa. • *n.* (*mail*) posta. **post no bills** no fisa posteres.

post[3] *n.* (*job*) posto. **be posted in** ave sua posto en.

post-[4] *pref.* pos-.

postage *n.* (*cost*) tarifa postal.

postage stamp *n.* selo, selo postal.

postal *adj.* postal.

postalveolar *adj.* & *n.* (*consonant*) posalveolal.

postanal *adj.* posanal.

postbag *n.* saco de posta.

postbox *n.* caxa de posta.

postcard *n.* carta postal.

postcoital *adj.* poscopulal.

postdate *v.* posdati.

poster *n.* poster.

posterboard *n.* carton.

posterior *adj.* posterior.

posterity *n.* desendentes, futur.

posterization *n.* posteri.

posterize *v.* posteri.

postgraduate *adj.* & *n.* posgraduada.

post-haste *adv.* pronto.

posthole *n.* buco de palo.

posthumous *adj.* pos mori.

posting *n.* posta, publici.

Post-it note *n.* papereta aderente.
postman *n.* postor.
postmark *n.* marca postal.
postmaster *n.* xef de posteria.
postmenopausal *adj.* posmenopausal.
postmortem *n.* autopsia.
postnasal *adj.* posnasal.
postnatal *adj.* pos nase, pos pari.
postnominal *adj.* & *n.* (*grammar*) posnomal.
post office *n.* ofisia de posta, posteria.
postoperative *adj.* posirurjial.
post-paid *adj.* (*letter*, *parcel*) prepaiada.
postpartum *adj.* pos pari.
postpone *v.* pospone, retarda.
postponement *n.* pospone.
postposition *n.* (*grammar*) posposada.
postprandial *adj.* pos come.
postscript *abbr.* ps.
post-traumatic *adj.* postraumal.
post-traumatic stress disorder *n.* sindrom de angusa pos trauma.
postulant *n.* aspiror.
postulate *v.* proposa. • *n.* suposa; axiom.
posture *v.* & *n.* posa.
post-war *adj.* posgeral.
postwoman *n.* postor.
posy *n.* buceta.
pot *n.* vaso; (*cooking*) casola. **take pot luck** risca la acaso.
potable *adj.* bevable.
potage *n.* sopa ragin.
potassium *n.* potasio.
potassium hydroxide *n.* idrosido de potasio.
potassium nitrate *n.* nitrato de potasio.
potato *n.* patata. **baked potato** patata fornida.
potato chip *n.* (*French fry*) fritada, patata fritada; (*potato crisp*) xip.
potato masher *n.* maxador de patata.
potato peeler *n.* descascador.
potato soup *n.* sopa de patata.
potbelly *n.* ventron.
potboiler *n.* obra mediocre.
poteen *n.* (*drink*) poitin.
potency *n.* potia.
potent *adj.* potiosa.
potentate *n.* renor.
potential *adj.* posible, potensial. • *n.* (*for future development*, *physics*) potensia.
potentiate *v.* forti.
pothead *n.* canabor.
potheen *n.* (*drink*) poitin.
potholder *n.* teleta de casola.
pothole *n.* dolineta, buco de strada.
potholer *n.* cavor.
pothook *n.* onca de casola.
potion *n.* prepara.
potlatch *n.* (*feast*) patlatx.
potluck *n.* (*meal*) bufe.
potpie *n.* tarte de ragu.
potpourri *n.* bol bonodorosa; misca.
potsherd *n.* frato seramica.
potshot *n.* xuta acaso.
potter[1] *n.* (*pottery maker*) vasor.
potter[2] *v.* (*about*) bricoleta.
pottery *n.* arte de seramica, vasia. **piece of pottery** seramica.
potto *n.* (*primate*) poto.
potty *n.* (*chamberpot*) vaso de note; (*toilet*) vason.
pouch *n.* (*bag*) bolsa; (*anatomy*) pox, marsupio.
poulterer *n.* carnor de avia.
poultice *n.* cataplasma.
poultry *n.* avias de cultiveria; (*meat*) carne de avia.
pounce *v.* & *n.* salta.
pound[1] *n.* (*weight*) libra; (*currency*) paund.
pound[2] *v.* (*strike*) bate; (*grind*) mole.
pound[3] *n.* (*for dogs*) ensirca de canes.
pound sign *n.* (*UK: sterling*) sinia de paund; (*US: weight*) grilia.
pour *v.* versa.
pourboire *n.* donada.
pout *v.* & *n.* mua.
poverty *n.* povria.
POW *n.* prisonida de gera.
powder *n.* polvo. • *v.* polvi; covre con polvo.
powder blue *adj.* & *n.* azul.
powdery *adj.* polvin.
power *n.* (*electric*, *mathematics*) potia; enerjia; capasia; (*person*, *nation*, *etc.*) potiosa. • *v.* propulsa. **exert power over** domina.
powerboat *n.* motobarco.
powerbroker *n.* ajente de potia.
power button *n.* boton de comuta.
power cable *n.* cable eletrical.
power cut *n.* rompe de eletrica.
powerful *adj.* potiosa.
powerhouse *n.* potiosa.
powerless *adj.* noncapas.
power outage *n.* rompe de eletrica.
power plant *n.* sentro eletrical.
power saw *n.* siera sirculo.
power source *n.* fonte de potia.
power station *n.* sentro eletrical.
power supply *n.* fonte de potia.
power switch *n.* boton de comuta.
powwow *n.* confere.
pox *v.* pesta.
pp. *abbr.* p (*pajes*).
practical *adj.* pratical.
practicality *n.* praticalia.
practically *adv.* pratical; (*nearly*) cuasi.
practice *n.* pratica; (*medical*, *legal*) ofisia. • *v.* (US for **practise**) pratica.
practice book *n.* libro de eserse.
practice target *n.* blanco de eserse.

practise (US **practice**) *v.* pratica.
practitioner *n.* praticor.
pragmatic *adj.* pratical.
pragmatics *n.* (*linguistics*) pragmatica.
pragmatism *n.* praticalisme.
pragmatist *n.* praticaliste.
Prague *n.* Praha.
prairie *n.* prado.
prairie dog *n.* (*rodent*) can-de-prado.
praise *v.* & *n.* loda.
praiseworthy *adj.* lodable.
praline *n.* (*food*) pralin.
pram *n.* caro de bebe.
prance *v.* dansa.
prandial *adj.* de come.
prank *n.* rus.
prankster *n.* rusor.
praseodymium *n.* (*element*) praseodimio.
prat *n.* culo; (*insult*) bobo, pixeta.
prate *v.* babela.
pratfall *n.* cade comica.
pratincole *n.* (*bird*) glareola.
prattle *v.* babela.
prawn *n.* gamba.
-praxia *suff.* (*medical*) -praxia.
praxis *n.* pratica.
pray *v.* prea.
prayer *n.* prea.
prayerbook *n.* libro de preas.
pre- *pref.* pre-.
preach *v.* predica.
preacher *n.* sermonor.
preachy *adj.* predicosa.
preadapt *v.* preajusta.
preadjust *v.* preajusta.
preadolescent *adj.* & *n.* preadolesente.
preaffirm *v.* preafirma.
preamble *n.* preambul.
preamp *n.* prefortador.
preamplifier *n.* prefortador.
prearrange *v.* preordina.
Precambrian *adj.* & *n.* (*geology*) precambrian.
precancerous *adj.* precanserosa.
precarious *adj.* perilosa.
precaution *n.* proteje.
precede *v.* presede.
precedence *n.* presede.
precedent *n.* presedente.
precept *n.* prinsipe.
precession *n.* (*astronomy*) presede.
precheck *v.* preesamina.
precinct *n.* distrito.
precious *adj.* valuosa.
precipice *n.* presipe.
precipitate *v.* (*rain*) presipita; (*trigger*) ativi. • *n.* presipitada.
precipitation *n.* presipita.
precipitous *adj.* presipe.
precis *n.* resoma.
precise *adj.* esata.
precision *n.* esatia.
precivilization *n.* presivilia.
preclude *v.* impedi.
precocious *adj.* temprana matur.
precognisant *adj.* preconosente.
precognition *n.* preconose.
precoital *adj.* precopulal.
preconceive *v.* prejudi.
preconception *n.* prejudi.
precondition *n.* restrinje.
pre-credit *n.* pretitulo.
precursor *n.* (*person*) presedor; (*thing*) presedente.
precursory *adj.* presedente, inisial.
pre-cut *adj.* pretaliada.
predate *v.* presede.
predation *n.* xasa.
predator *n.* predor, xasor.
predatory *adj.* xasante.
predawn *adj.* ante leva de sol.
predecessor *n.* (*person*) presedor; (*thing*) presedente.
predefine *v.* predefini.
predestination *n.* predestina.
predestine *v.* predestina.
predetermination *n.* predetermina.
predetermine *v.* predetermina.
predeterminism *n.* predeterminisme.
predeterminist *n.* predeterministe.
predeterministic *adj.* predeterministe.
predicate *v.* & *n.* (*grammar, logic*) predica.
predicative *adj.* & *n.* predicativa.
predict *v.* predise.
predictable *adj.* predisable.
prediction *n.* predise.
predilection *n.* prefere.
predispose *v.* disposa, propensa.
predisposition *n.* disposa, propensa.
predominant *adj.* dominante.
predominate *v.* domina.
predomination *n.* domina.
pre-eclampsia *n.* (*medical*) preeclampsia.
pre-election *adj.* ante vota, preelejal.
preemie *n.* prematur.
preeminent *adj.* suprapasante.
pre-empt *v.* preveni.
pre-emptive *adj.* preveninte.
preen *v.* ordina se, ordina sua plumas.
pre-examine *v.* preesamina.
pre-exist *v.* preesiste.
prefab *n.* prefabrica. • *adj.* prefabricada.
prefabricate *v.* prefabrica.
prefabrication *n.* prefabrica.
preface *v.* & *n.* prefasa.
prefect *n.* prefeto.
prefecture *n.* prefetia, provinse.
prefer *v.* prefere.

preferable *adj.* preferable, plu bon.
preference *n.* prefere; (*item preferred*) preferеda.
preferential *adj.* preferal, favorente.
prefix *v.* & *n.* prefisa.
prefixation *n.* prefisa.
pregame *adj.* prejual.
pregnancy *n.* ensintia.
pregnant *adj.* ensinta. **become pregnant** ensinti.
preheat *v.* precaldi.
prehensile *adj.* prensil.
prehistoric *adj.* preistorial.
prehistorical *adj.* preistorial.
prehistory *n.* preistoria.
prejudge *v.* prejudi.
prejudice *n.* prejudi.
prejudiced *adj.* prejudosa.
prejudicial *adj.* nosiva.
prelate *n.* eglesor alta.
prelim *n.* inisial.
preliminary *adj.* inisial, de comensa. • *n.* (*attempt, round of competition*) inisial, comensa.
preliterate *adj.* nonalfabetiste.
prelude *n.* introdui.
premarital *adj.* ante sposi.
prematch *adj.* prejual.
premature *adj.* prematur.
premature baby *n.* prematur.
premed *adj.* premedical.
premedical *adj.* premedical.
premeditate *v.* preconsidera.
premeditation *n.* preconsidera.
premenstrual *adj.* premenstrual.
premier *adj.* prima, xef.
premiere *v.* debua. • *n.* debua, mostra prima.
premise *n.* (*principle*) premisa. **premises** imobila.
premium *n.* paia ajuntada.
premix *v.* premisca.
premonition *n.* presensa. **have a premonition** presensa.
premoral *adj.* premoral.
prenatal *adj.* ante nase, ante pari, ensintial.
prenominal *adj.* & *n.* (*grammar*) prenomal.
prenuptial *adj.* ante sposi.
preoccupation *n.* preocupa.
preoccupy *v.* preocupa.
preoperative *adj.* presirurjial.
preordain *v.* preordina, predetermina.
preorder *v.* & *n.* precomanda, comanda temprana.
prep *n.* prepara.
prepackage *v.* prepaci.
prepaid *adj.* prepaiada.
preparation *n.* prepara. **preparations** prepara.
prepare *v.* prepara.
prepay *v.* prepaia.
prepayment *n.* prepaia.
preponderance *n.* domina; majoria.
preposition *n.* (*grammar*) preposada.
preposition phrase *n.* (*grammar*) formula de preposada.
preposterous *adj.* asurda.
preposterousness *n.* asurdia.
prepubescent *adj.* preadolesente.
prepuce *n.* (*anatomy*) prepus.
prequel *n.* presedente.
pre-record *v.* prerejistra.
pre-register *v.* preenscrive.
prerequisite *n.* nesesada.
prerogative *n.* direto.
presage *v.* premostra.
presbyopia *n.* presbiopia.
presbyopic *adj.* presbiope.
Presbyterian *adj.* & *n.* presbiterian.
Presbyterianism *n.* (*Christianity*) presbiterianisme.
presbytery *n.* (*priest's house*) preteria.
preschool *adj.* prescolal.
prescient *adj.* clarvidente.
prescribe *v.* prescrive.
prescription *n.* prescrive.
preselect *v.* preeleje.
presence *n.* presentia.
present[1] *adj.* (*time, not absent*) presente; (*time*) corente. • *n.* presente. **at present** a presente, aora. **for the present** per la presente.
present[2] *v.* (*give, introduce*) presenta.
present[3] *n.* (*gift*) donada.
presentable *adj.* presentable.
presentation *n.* presenta; spetaculo.
presenter *n.* presentor.
presentiment *n.* presensa.
presently *adv.* pronto.
preservation *n.* conserva, manteni.
preservative *n.* conservante.
preserve *v.* conserva, manteni; (*with smoke*) fumi. • *n.* (*marmalade*) conserva de fruta.
preset *v.* preajusta.
pre-shrunk *adj.* prelavada.
preside *v.* preside.
presidency *n.* presidentia.
president *n.* presidente.
presidential *adj.* presidental.
press *v.* presa. • *n.* presador; jornalistes; (*publishing house*) casa de publici.
press conference *n.* confere jornaliste.
pressing *adj.* presante; urjente.
pressroom *n.* sala de jornalistes.
press stud *n.* boton de presa.
pressure *v.* & *n.* presa.
pressure cooker *n.* casola de presa.
pressure gradient *n.* gradiente de presa.
pressurization *n.* compresa.

pressurize *v.* compresa; (*someone to do something*) presa.
prestidigitation *n.* majia de mano.
prestige *n.* prestijia.
prestigious *adj.* prestijiosa.
presumably *adv.* suposable.
presume *v.* suposa.
presumption *n.* suposa.
presumptive *adj.* suposada.
presumptuous *adj.* noncortes.
presuppose *v.* presuposa.
presupposition *n.* presuposa.
presurgical *adj.* presirurjial.
presynaptic *adj.* (*biology*) presinapsal.
pret-à-porter clothing *n.* vestes pronto.
pre-teen *n.* preadolesente.
pretence (US **pretense**) *n.* finje.
pretend *v.* finje.
pretender *n.* finjor; (*claimant*) reclamor.
pretense (US). See *pretence*.
pretentious *adj.* ostentosa, finjosa, egosa.
preterite *n.* (*grammar*) pasada.
preternatural *adj.* nonatural.
pre-test *v.* preesamina.
pretext *n.* escusa.
pre-title sequence *n.* pretitulo.
pre-trial *adj.* prelitigal.
prettify *v.* beli.
prettiness *n.* belia.
pretty *adj.* bela, beleta, atraosa.
pretty one *n.* beleta.
pretty thing *n.* beleta.
pre-tune *v.* preajusta.
pretzel *n.* bretsel.
prevail *v.* domina.
prevalence *n.* comunia.
prevalent *adj.* comun.
prevaricate *v.* parla evitante, vasila.
prevarication *n.* parla evitante.
prevent *v.* preveni, impedi.
preventable *adj.* prevenable.
preventative *adj.* preveninte.
prevention *n.* preveni.
preventive *adj.* & *n.* preveninte.
preverbal *adj.* & *n.* (*grammar*) preverbal.
preview *v.* & *n.* previde.
previous *adj.* presedente, pasada.
previously *adv.* a ante, pasada. **a long time previously** a multe tempo a ante.
prevue *n.* previde.
pre-war *adj.* pregeral.
pre-washed *adj.* prelavada.
prey *n.* preda; vitim. **fall prey** vitimi. **prey upon** xasa.
priapism *n.* (*medical*) priapisme.
priapulid *n.* (*worm*) priapulido.
price *n.* custa. • *v.* deside la custa de. **price in the shops** custa per la compror.
priceless *adj.* nonestimable.
pricey *adj.* custosa, cara.
prick *v.* pica. • *n.* pica; (*penis*) pixa. **prick up** erije.
prickle *n.* spina.
prickly *adj.* spinosa; (*tetchy*) disputosa, iritable; (*tingly*) formicosa.
pride *n.* orgulo; (*lions*) manada.
prideful *adj.* orgulosa.
priest *n.* prete, prete mas.
priestess *n.* prete, prete fema.
priesthood *n.* pretia.
priestly *adj.* pretal.
prig *n.* moraliste.
priggery *n.* moralisme.
priggish *adj.* moraliste.
prim *adj.* formal.
primacy *n.* xefia.
primal *adj.* primeval, fundal.
primality *n.* (*of prime number*) primalia.
primary *adj.* prima, xef.
primary care *n.* cura prima.
primary education *n.* educa prima.
primary school *n.* scola prima.
primate *n.* primate; (*small*) simia.
primatologist *n.* primatolojiste.
primatology *n.* primatolojia.
prime[1] *adj.* xef, eselente, ultima; (*number*) primal. • *n.* apico.
prime[2] *v.* prepara.
prime concern *n.* conserna xef.
prime minister *n.* ministro xef.
prime number *n.* numero primal.
primer[1] *n.* (*paint*) pinta prima.
primer[2] *n.* (*textbook*) manual prima.
prime time *n.* ora favoreda.
primeval *adj.* primeval.
primitive *adj.* primitiva; nonsivilida.
primitivism *n.* primitivisme.
primitivist *n.* primitiviste.
primo *adj.* multe bon.
primogeniture *n.* (*state or rights of a firstborn*) primajenita.
primordial *adj.* primeval.
primp *v.* ordina se.
primrose *n.* primula.
primula *n.* (*plant*) primula.
prince *n.* prinse.
princedom *n.* prinsia.
Prince Edward Island *n.* (*Canadian province*) Isola Prinse Edward.
princely state *n.* prinsia.
princess *n.* prinsesa.
principal *adj.* (*main*) xef.
principality *n.* prinsia.
principle *n.* (*rule*) prinsipe. **in principle** de prinsipe.
principled *adj.* prinsiposa.
print *v.* primi. • *n.* primida. **out of print** no plu primida.

printable *adj.* primable.
printed circuit board *n.* sircuito primida.
printed object *n.* primida.
printer *n.* (*person*) primor; (*machine*) primador.
printer driver *n.* controlador de primador.
printer-friendly *adj.* conveninte per primi.
printer-scanner *n.* primador-scanador.
print fabric *n.* stofa primida.
printing house *n.* primeria.
printing press *n.* primador.
printout *n.* (*action*, *result*) primi.
prior *adj.* presedente. **prior to** ante.
prioritize *v.* trata prima; asentua; ordina.
priority *n.* (*quality*) primia; (*main concern*) conserna xef, considera xef. **aperture priority** (*photography*) primia de abri. **make a priority** trata prima.
priory *n.* monceria.
prise *v.* leveri.
prism *n.* prisma.
prismatic *adj.* prismal.
prison *n.* prison.
prison camp *n.* campa de prisoni.
prisoner *n.* prisonida. **prisoner of war** prisonida de gera.
prissy *adj.* esijente.
pristine *adj.* nonmanxada.
privacy *n.* privatia.
private *adj.* privata.
private conversation *n.* conversa privata.
privateer *n.* barcon privata.
private eye *n.* detetor.
private lesson *n.* leson privata.
private sector *n.* campo privata.
private ship *n.* barcon privata.
privet *n.* (*plant*) ligustro.
privilege *n.* vantaje. • *v.* vantaji, favore.
privy *adj.* informada. • *n.* latrina.
prize *n.* premio. • *v.* valua.
prizefight *n.* boxe profesal.
prizefighter *n.* boxor profesal.
prize-winner *n.* premior, campion.
prize-winning *adj.* campionida.
pro *prep.* (*in favour of*) per. • *pref.* (*in favour of*) pro-; (*forward*) pro-.
proa *n.* proa.
probability *n.* (*quality*) probablia; (*something probable*) probable.
probability theory *n.* teoria de probablia.
probable *adj.* probable.
probably *adv.* probable.
probate *v.* & *n.* validi.
probation *n.* libria oservada.
probe *v.* & *n.* sonda; esamina.
probiotic *n.* probiotica.
probity *n.* virtuosia.
problem *n.* problem. **create a problem** fa un problem. **no problem** no problem.
problematic *adj.* problemosa.
proboscis *n.* (*anatomy*) proboside.
pro-business *adj.* procomersial.
procaine *n.* (*anaesthetic*) procaina.
procedure *n.* prosede.
proceed *v.* prosegue. **proceed against** litiga. **proceeds** revenu. **proceed with** comensa.
proceedings *n.* (*society*) jornal de prosegues.
process *v.* prosede, trata; (*move in procession*) prosegue. • *n.* prosede; (*anatomy*) protende.
processing plant *n.* prosederia, trateria.
procession *n.* prosegue.
processor *n.* prosedador.
pro-choice *adj.* proelejal.
proclaim *v.* proclama.
proclamation *n.* proclama.
proclivity *n.* tende.
proconsul *n.* proconsul.
procrastinate *v.* pospone.
procrastination *n.* pospone.
procreate *v.* reprodui.
procreation *n.* reprodui.
procrustean *adj.* uniforminte.
proctologist *n.* proctolojiste.
proctology *n.* proctolojia.
proctor *n.* vijilor.
proctoscope *n.* proctoscopio.
proctoscopy *n.* proctoscopi.
procure *v.* oteni.
procurement *n.* oteni.
procurer *n.* otenor.
prod *v.* & *n.* puieta.
prodigal *adj.* perosa.
prodigious *adj.* enorme.
prodigy *n.* talentosa.
produce *v.* produi; resulta. • *n.* (*fruit and vegetables*) cresedas, produidas.
producer *n.* produor, organizor.
producer-director *n.* produor-dirijor.
product *n.* produida; (*multiplication*) multipli.
production *n.* produi; (*entertainment*) spetaculo.
productive *adj.* produosa.
productiveness *n.* produosia.
productivity *n.* produosia.
prof *n.* profesor.
profanation *n.* blasfema.
profane *adj.* nonsanta, blasfemal.
profanity *n.* maldise.
profess *v.* declara.
profession *n.* profesa, carera.
professional *adj.* profesal; capas; con salario.
professionalism *n.* profesalisme.
professor *n.* profesor. **professors** (*faculty*) profesores.
proffer *v.* estende.
proficiency *n.* capasia.
proficient *adj.* capas.

profile *n.* profil. • *v.* profili.
profiler *n.* profilor.
profit *v.* & *n.* profita. **profit and loss** profita e perde. **profit from** profita de.
profitable *adj.* profitosa.
profiteer *v.* profita nonlegal.
profligate *adj.* perosa.
pro forma *adj.* formal, costumal.
profound *adj.* profonda.
profundity *n.* profondia.
profuse *adj.* suprapasante.
profusion *n.* suprapasa.
progeny *n.* projenia, enfantes.
prognosis *n.* prognose, predise.
prognosticate *v.* predise.
pro-government *adj.* progovernal.
program *n.* (*software*) program. • *v.* programi.
programmatic *adj.* programal.
programme (US **program**) *n.* (*schedule, TV*) program; menu; (*software*) program. • *v.* programi.
programmed cell death *n.* apoptose.
programmer *n.* programor.
programming language *n.* lingua de programi.
progress *v.* & *n.* progresa. **work in progress** labora en curso.
progression *n.* progresa.
progressive *adj.* & *n.* progresiste.
progressivism *n.* progresisme.
prohibit *v.* proibi.
prohibition *n.* proibi.
prohibitionist *n.* proibiste.
prohibitive *adj.* proibinte.
project *v.* (*light, image, voice*) projeta; (*image, voice*) lansa; (*jut out*) protende, estende. • *n.* projeta.
projectile *n.* misil.
projection *n.* projeta; lansa; protende, estende.
projector *n.* projetador.
prokaryote *n.* (*organism*) procariota.
prolapse *n.* (*medical*) prolaso.
prole *n.* proletarial.
prolegomenon *n.* introdui.
proletarian *adj.* & *n.* proletarial.
proletariat *n.* proletaria.
pro-life *adj.* provival.
proliferate *v.* sperde.
proliferation *n.* sperde.
prolific *adj.* produosa, frutosa.
prologue *n.* prefasa.
prolong *v.* longi.
prolongation *n.* longi.
prom *n.* selebra.
promenade *n.* bolevar a plaia, bolevar de pasea.
promethean *adj.* inovosa.
promethium *n.* (*element*) prometio.
prominence *n.* (*protrusion*) protende; (*importance*) importa. **laryngeal prominence** poma de Adam.
prominent *adj.* protendente; importante.
promiscuity *n.* promiscuia.
promiscuous *adj.* promiscua.
promise *v.* & *n.* promete. **full of promise** prometosa.
promising *adj.* prometente, prometosa.
promissory *adj.* prometente.
promontory *n.* promontania, capo.
promote *v.* (*in rank*) alti, leva; (*encourage*) promove.
promoter *n.* promovor.
promotion *n.* alti, leva; promove.
promotional material *n.* presentas de promove.
prompt *v.* & *n.* provoca; puieta; avisa; (*theatre*) xuxa, remente, fa ce on recorda. • *adj.* puntual; rapida.
prompter *n.* xuxor.
promptness *n.* puntualia.
promulgate *v.* promove, vasti.
pronate *v.* proni.
pronation *n.* proni.
pronator *n.* (*muscle*) pronador.
prone *adj.* (*lying flat*) prona; (*susceptible*) propensada.
prong *n.* spino; (*fork*) dente.
pronghorn antelope *n.* antilocapra.
pronominal *adj.* pronomal.
pronoun *n.* pronom.
pronounce *v.* pronunsia.
pronounceable *adj.* pronunsiable.
pronouncement *n.* proclama.
pronunciation *n.* pronunsia.
proof *n.* demostra.
proofing *n.* (*bread*) leva final.
proofread *v.* coreti, releje.
proofreader *n.* coretor.
prop[1] *n.* palo. • *v.* apoia. **prop up** suporta.
prop[2] *n.* (*theatrical*) mobileta.
prop-[3] *pref.* (*chemistry*) prop-.
propaganda *n.* propaganda.
propagandist *n.* propagandiste.
propagandize *v.* propagandi.
propagate *v.* reprodui, estende.
propagation *n.* reprodui, estende.
propane *n.* propano.
propanol *n.* (*chemistry*) propanol.
propel *v.* propulsa, move; (*missile*) xuta.
propellant *n.* propulsante.
propeller *n.* elica.
propelling pencil *n.* portagrafito.
propene *n.* propen.
propensity *n.* propensa, tende.
proper *adj.* coreta, conveninte; (*exclusive*) propre; (*actual*) real.

proper noun *n.* nom propre.
propertied *n.* con imobila.
property *n.* (*premises*) imobila; (*possessions, software*) propria; (*attribute*) cualia.
property tax *n.* imposta de imobila.
prophecy *n.* predise.
prophesy *v.* predise.
prophet *n.* profeta.
prophetic *adj.* predisente.
prophylactic *adj.* preveninte.
prophylaxis *n.* preveni.
propitiate *v.* pasi.
proponent *n.* proposor, defendor, suportor.
proportion *n.* proportio. **in proportion** proportial.
proportional *adj.* proportial.
proportionate *adj.* proportial.
proposal *n.* proposa.
propose *v.* (*including marriage*) proposa.
proposer *n.* proposor.
proposition *n.* proposa.
propound *v.* proposa.
proprietary *adj.* proprial.
proprietor *n.* proprior.
propriety *n.* cortesia.
propriocept *v.* propriosepi.
proprioception *n.* (*sense of one's own movement and orientation*) propriosepi.
propulsion *n.* propulsa.
propylene *n.* (*chemistry*) propen.
pro rata *adv.* proportial.
prorate *v.* distribui proportial.
prosaic *adj.* prosin, mediocre.
proscenium *n.* antestadio.
proscribe *v.* proibi.
prose *n.* prosa.
prosecute *v.* acusa, litiga.
prosecuting attorney *n.* avocato acusante.
prosecution *n.* litiga.
prosecutor *n.* acusor, avocato acusante.
proselytize *v.* promove.
prosodic *adj.* ritmal.
prosody *n.* ritmo.
prospect *n.* vista.
prospective *adj.* futur.
prospector *n.* xercor.
prospectus *n.* anunsia.
prosper *v.* flori; rici.
prosperity *n.* ricia.
prosperous *adj.* rica.
prostaglandin *n.* (*biology*) prostaglandina.
prostate *n.* prostata.
prosthesis *n.* prostese.
prosthetic *adj.* prostesal. • *n.* prostese.
prostitute *v.* prostitui. • *n.* prostituida.
prostitution *n.* prostitui.
prostrate *v.* proni.
protactinium *n.* (*element*) protactinio.
protagonist *n.* eroe.
protanopic *adj.* sieca a roja.
protea *n.* (*plant*) protea.
protean *adj.* flexable, multitalentosa.
protect *v.* proteje.
protection *n.* proteje.
protectionism *n.* protejisme.
protectionist *n.* protejiste.
protective *adj.* protejente.
protector *n.* protejor.
protectorate *n.* (*territory*) protejeda; (*regency*) protejoria.
protégé *n.* disiplo.
protein *n.* protena.
protest *v.* & *n.* protesta.
protestant *adj.* & *n.* protestante.
protestantism *n.* protestantisme.
protestation *n.* protesta.
protester *n.* protestor.
protist *n.* (*organism*) protista.
proto- *pref.* (*first*) proto-.
protocol *n.* (*rules*) protocol.
proton *n.* proton.
proton-pump inhibitor *n.* constrinjente de pompas de protones.
protoplasm *n.* (*biology*) protoplasma.
protostome *n.* (*organism*) protostomio.
prototypal *adj.* prototipal.
prototype *n.* prototipo, model.
prototypical *adj.* prototipal.
protozoa *n.* (*organisms*) protozones.
protozoan *n.* (*organism*) protozon.
protozoic *adj.* protozonal.
protozoon *n.* (*organism*) protozon.
protract *v.* longi.
protractor *n.* angulometre.
protrude *v.* protende.
protrusion *n.* protende.
protuberance *n.* protende, bulto.
proud *adj.* orgulosa. **proud of** orgulosa de.
provability *n.* demostrablia.
provable *adj.* demostrable.
prove *v.* demostra; (*turn out to be*) evidenti.
provenance *n.* orijina.
Provençal *adj.* & *n.* (*person, language*) provensal.
Provence *n.* (*French region*) Provensa.
proverb *n.* proverbo, diseda.
proverbial *adj.* proverbal.
provide *v.* furni.
provided *adj.* furnida. • *subord.* si, sola si, dependente si, con esije ce.
providence *n.* favore divin.
provider *n.* furnor.
province *n.* provinse.
provincial *adj.* provinsal.
provincialism *n.* provinsalisme.
provision *n.* furni; (*law*) restrinje. **provisions** furnis.
provisional *adj.* tempora, per la presente.

proviso *n.* avisa.
provisory *adj.* dependente.
provocateur *n.* provocor, tisor.
provocation *n.* provoca.
provocative *adj.* provocante.
provoke *v.* provoca; resulta.
provolone *n.* (*cheese*) provolone.
provost *n.* diacon; dirijor.
prow *n.* (*of ship*) proa.
pro-war *adj.* progeral.
prowess *n.* capasia.
prowl *v.* vaga furtiva; xasa furtiva.
prowler *n.* furtiva.
proximal *adj.* prosima.
proximity *n.* prosimia.
proxy *n.* representor; (*server*) proxi.
prude *n.* moraliste.
prudence *n.* cautia.
prudent *adj.* cauta.
prudish *adj.* tro modesta.
prune[1] *n.* (*dried plum*) pruna seca.
prune[2] *v.* (*trim*) desrami; corti.
pruning hook *n.* desramador.
prurient *adj.* lasiva.
Prussia *n.* Prusen.
Prussian *adj.* & *n.* prusen.
pry[1] *v.* (*be curious*) curiosi; videta.
pry[2] *v.* (*prise*) leveri.
PS *abbr.* ps (*pos scrive*).
psalm *n.* salmo.
psalmist *n.* salmiste.
psalter *n.* libro de salmos.
psaltery *n.* (*musical instrument*) salterio.
psephological *adj.* psefolojial.
psephologist *n.* psefolojiste.
psephology *n.* psefolojia.
pseudo- *pref.* pseudo-, falsa.
pseudo-national *adj.* falsa nasional.
pseudonym *n.* nom falsa.
pseudonymous *adj.* con nom falsa.
pseudopod *n.* pseudopodo.
pseudopodia *n.* pseudopodos.
pseudopodium *n.* (*anatomy*) pseudopodo.
psi *n.* (*Greek letter* Ψ, ψ) psi.
psilocybin *n.* (*drug*) psilosibina.
psoriasis *n.* (*medical*) psoriase.
psst *interj.* ss.
psyche *n.* psice.
psychedelia *n.* alusinalia.
psychedelic *adj.* alusinal.
psychiatric *adj.* psiciatrica.
psychiatrical *adj.* psiciatrica.
psychiatrist *n.* psiciatriste.
psychiatry *n.* psiciatria.
psychic *adj.* (*of the psyche*) psical; (*paranormal*) psicica.
psycho- *pref.* psico-.
psychoactive *adj.* psicoativa.
psychoanaleptic *adj.* & *n.* psicoanalesica.
psychoanalyse (US **psychoanalyze**) *v.* psicoanalise.
psychoanalysis *n.* psicoanalise.
psychoanalyst *n.* psicoanaliste.
psychoanalytic *adj.* psicoanalisal.
psychoanalytical *adj.* psicoanalisal.
psychoanalyze (US). See *psychoanalyse*.
psychobiology *n.* psicobiolojia.
psychogenic *adj.* (*of psychological origin*) psicojen.
psychokinesis *n.* telecinese.
psycholeptic *adj.* (*medical*) psicolesica.
psychological *adj.* psicolojial.
psychological warfare *n.* gera psicolojial.
psychologism *n.* (*philosophy*) psicolojisme.
psychologist *n.* psicolojiste.
psychology *n.* psicolojia.
psychomotor *adj.* psicomotor.
psychoneurosis *n.* neurose.
psychopath *n.* psicopatica.
psychopathic *adj.* psicopatica.
psychopathology *n.* psicopatolojia.
psychopathy *n.* psicopatia.
psychosexual *adj.* psicosesal.
psychosis *n.* psicose.
psychosocial *adj.* psicososial.
psychosomatic *adj.* psicosomatica.
psychotherapist *n.* psicoterapiste.
psychotherapy *n.* psicoterapia.
psychotic *adj.* psicosica.
psychotropic *adj.* psicotropial.
ptarmigan *n.* perdis blanca.
ptero- *pref.* (*wing*) ptero-.
pterodactyl *n.* pterodatilo.
pterosaur *n.* pterosauro.
Ptolemaic *adj.* ptolemean.
Ptolemean *adj.* ptolemean.
Ptolemy *n.* (*astronomer, dynasty*) Ptolemeo.
-ptosis *suff.* (*sagging*) -tose.
-ptysis *suff.* (*spitting*) -tise.
pub *n.* bar, beveria, taverna.
pub crawl *n.* turi de bares.
puberty *n.* maturi sesal.
pubescent *adj.* sesal maturinte.
pubic *adj.* pubica.
pubic bone *n.* oso pubica.
pubic hair *n.* pelo pubica.
pubis *n.* pubica.
public *adj.* publica. • *n.* popla.
publican *n.* tavernor; (*tax collector*) impostor.
publication *n.* publici.
public domain *n.* domina publica.
public holiday *n.* festa nasional.
publicist *n.* publiciste.
publicity *n.* anunsia, presenta.
publicize *v.* anunsia, presenta.
public official *n.* ofisior publica.
public relations *n.* relatas publica.
public servant *n.* ofisior publica.

public utility *n.* furnor de servi.
publish *v.* publici.
publisher *n.* publicor.
publishing house *n.* casa de publici.
puce *adj.* bordo.
pucker *v.* & *n.* plieta.
puckered *adj.* plietosa.
puckery *adj.* plietosa.
pudding *n.* deser.
puddle *n.* stangeta. • *v.* stangi.
pudenda *n.* jenitales.
pudgy *adj.* ronda, inflada.
pueblo *adj.* & *n.* (*Native American community*) pueblo.
puerile *adj.* enfantin.
Puerto Rican *adj.* & *n.* portorican.
Puerto Rico *n.* Porto Rica.
puff *v.* & *n.* sofleta. **puff up** infla.
puffed-up *adj.* inflada; egosa.
pufferfish *n.* fugu.
puffery *n.* loda falsa.
puffin *n.* papagaio de mar.
puffy *adj.* inflada.
pug *n.* (*dog*) carlino.
pugilism *n.* boxe.
pugilist *n.* boxor.
pugnacious *adj.* disputosa.
puke *v.* vomiti, descome. • *n.* vomita.
pulchritude *n.* belia.
pull *v.* & *n.* tira. **pull a wheelie** capri. **pull back** retira. **pull down** tira a tera.
pullet *n.* gal fema joven.
pulley *n.* pulea.
pullover *n.* sueter.
pulmonary *adj.* pulmonal.
pulp *n.* (*including dental*) pulpa. • *v.* pulpi, maxa.
pulper *n.* maxador.
pulpit *n.* plataforma de predica.
pulpy *adj.* pulposa.
pulsar *n.* (*astronomy*) pulsar.
pulsate *v.* pulsa.
pulsation *n.* pulsa.
pulse *v.* & *n.* pulsa.
pulverize *v.* polvi, mole.
puma *n.* puma.
pumice *n.* (*rock*) pomis.
pummel *v.* bate, bastoni.
pummelo *n.* pampelmus.
pump[1] *n.* pompa. • *v.* pompi.
pump[2] *n.* (*low-cut shoe*) sapato escotada; (*plimsoll*) sapato de sporte.
pumpernickel *n.* pan negra.
pumpkin *n.* zuca.
pun *n.* broma de parolas.
punch[1] *v.* & *n.* (*with fist*) colpa con punio.
punch[2] *v.* (*hole*) perfora. • *n.* perforador.
punch[3] *n.* (*drink*) pontxe.
punchbag *n.* saco de colpa.
punchline *n.* culmina.
punchy *adj.* forte, astuta.
punctilious *adj.* perfetiste.
punctual *adj.* puntual, a tempo; rapida.
punctuality *n.* puntualia.
punctuate *v.* puntua.
punctuation *n.* puntua.
punctuation mark *n.* sinia de puntua.
puncture *v.* & *n.* creve, perfora.
pundit *n.* esperta.
punditry *n.* espertia.
pungent *adj.* con sabor agu; con odor agu.
Punic *adj.* punica.
punish *v.* puni.
punishable *adj.* punable.
punishment *n.* puni.
punitive *adj.* puninte.
Punjab *n.* Pandjab.
Punjabi *adj.* & *n.* pandjabi.
punk *adj.* & *n.* (*music*) punc.
punk rock *n.* roc punc.
punt[1] *n.* (*boat*) barceta de palo.
punt[2] *v.* (*dropkick*) cade e pedi.
puny *adj.* debil, pico.
pup *n.* caneta.
pupa *n.* (*insect*) pupa, crisalida.
pupate *v.* pupi.
pupation *n.* pupi.
pupil[1] *n.* (*student*) aprendor, scolor.
pupil[2] *n.* (*eye*) pupil.
puppet *n.* pupeta.
puppeteer *n.* pupetor.
puppet government *n.* governa pupetin.
puppetlike *adj.* pupetin.
puppet regime *n.* governa pupetin.
puppetry *n.* pupetia.
Puppis *n.* (*constellation*) la Popa.
puppy *n.* caneta.
purblind *adj.* partal sieca.
purchase *v.* compra. • *n.* (*action*) compra; (*object*) comprada.
purchaser *n.* compror.
purdah *n.* (*female seclusion*) purda.
pure *adj.* pur; virtuosa.
pureblooded *adj.* de sangue pur.
purebred *adj.* de sangue pur.
puree *v.* & *n.* (*cookery*) pure. **apple puree** pure de poma.
purely *adv.* pur; mera, en no otra modo ca.
purgative *n.* paraconstipa.
purgatory *n.* purgatorio.
purge *v.* & *n.* purga, elimina.
purification *n.* puri.
purifier *n.* purador. **air purifier** puriaira.
purify *v.* puri.
purism *n.* purisme.
purist *n.* puriste.
puristic *adj.* puriste.
Puritan *adj.* & *n.* puritan.

puritanical *adj.* moraliste.
Puritanism *n.* (*Christianity*) puritanisme.
purity *n.* puria; virtua.
purloin *v.* fura.
purple *adj.* purpur.
purple finch *n.* roseta.
purplish *adj.* purpurin.
purport *v.* finje. • *n.* sinifia.
purpose *n.* intende, razona, usa. **on purpose** intendente, volente.
purposeful *adj.* determinada; usosa.
purpura *n.* (*medical*) purpura.
purr *v.* & *n.* ronrona.
purse *n.* (*handbag*) bolsa; (*for money*) bolseta, portamone. • *v.* (*lips*) plieta.
purser *n.* caxor.
purslane *n.* (*plant*) portulaca.
pursuant to *prep.* seguente.
pursue *v.* xasa.
pursuit *n.* xasa.
purulent *adj.* pusosa.
purvey *v.* furni; (*opinion*) promove.
purveyor *n.* furnor.
pus *n.* (*substance*) pus.
push *v.* (*trolley*, *button*) puia; (*press*) presa; (*slide*) lisca.
pushcart *n.* careta.
pushchair *n.* careta de bebe.
push drill *n.* forador puiable.
push mower *n.* cortierba puiable.
pushover *n.* debil.
pushpin *n.* spino puiable.
push scooter *n.* patineta.
push-up *n.* (*exercise*) pompi.
pushy *adj.* insistente.
pusillanimous *adj.* timida.
puss *n.* gateta.
pussy *n.* gateta; (*vagina*) cuno.
pustule *n.* pustula.
put *v.* pone; (*question*) fa. **put aside** reserva; reservada. **put back** repone. **put back on** (*garment*) reapone. **put down** pone; insulta. **put first** trata prima. **put in an appearance** apare corta. **put on** (*garment*) apone. **put on airs** finje superioria. **put out** (*light*) estingui; (*bother*) disturba. **put to flight** fuji. **put together** junta, asembla. **put to sleep** adormi. **put to work** labora. **put up** erije. **put up with** tolera.
putative *adj.* suposada.
putdown *n.* insulta.
Putonghua *adj.* & *n.* putong.
putrefaction *n.* putri.
putrefy *v.* putri.
putrid *adj.* putrida.
putt *v.* (*golf*) colpeta.
putter[1] *n.* (*golf club*) colpetador.
putter[2] *v.* (*about*) bricoleta.
putty *n.* pasta de lino.
putty knife *n.* spatula.
puzzle *n.* enigma, rompetesta. • *v.* (*perplex*) confonde; (*ponder*) considera, serebri.
puzzlement *n.* confonde.
PVC *n.* polivinil, clorido de polivinil.
pygmy *n.* pigmeo.
pygmy chimpanzee *n.* bonobo.
pyjamas (US **pajamas**) *n.* pajama.
pylon *n.* palon.
pyloric *adj.* piloral.
pylorus *n.* (*anatomy*) piloro.
pyramid *n.* piramide.
pyre *n.* (*bonfire*) pira.
Pyrenean *adj.* pirinean.
Pyrenees *n.* (*region*) Pirineo; (*mountains*) Montes Pirineo.
pyrex *n.* vitro de forno.
pyro- *pref.* (*fire*) piro-.
pyromania *n.* piromania.
pyromaniac *n.* piromanica.
pyromaniacal *adj.* piromanica.
pyrometer *n.* pirometre.
pyrometric *adj.* pirometral.
pyrotechnical *adj.* pirotecnical.
pyrotechnics *n.* pirotecnica.
Pyrrhic victory *n.* vinse sin valua.
Pythagoras *n.* Pitagora.
Pythagorean *adj.* pitagoran.
python *n.* piton.
Pyxis *n.* (*constellation*) la Busola.

Q

qat *n.* (*plant, leaves*) cat.

Qatar *n.* Catar.

Qatari *adj.* & *n.* catari.

qi *n.* (*life force*) txi.

Qin *adj.* (*dynasty*) txin.

Qing *adj.* (*dynasty*) txing.

qua *prep.* como.

quaalude *n.* (*drug*) metacualona.

quack[1] *interj.* (*duck*) cuac. • *v.* & *n.* cuaci.

quack[2] *n.* xarlatan medical.

quadrangle *n.* cuatroangulo, cuatroladal.

quadrangular *adj.* cuatroangulo, cuatroladal.

quadrant *n.* cuadrante.

quadratic *adj.* cuadral.

quadri- *pref.* cuatro-.

quadrilateral *adj.* & *n.* cuatroladal.

quadrille *n.* (*dance, music*) cuadrilia.

quadriplegia *n.* tetraplejia.

quadriplegic *adj.* & *n.* tetraplejica.

quadroon *adj.* & *n.* cuatrinegra.

quadruped *n.* cuatropede.

quadrupedal *adj.* cuatropede.

quadruple *adj.* cuatruple.

quadruplet *adj.* & *n.* cuatrojemelo.

quaff *v.* bevi.

quagga *n.* (*zebra*) cuaga.

quagmire *n.* pantan.

quahog *n.* (*mollusc*) mersenaria.

quail[1] *n.* (*bird*) coturnix.

quail[2] *v.* (*quake*) trema.

quaint *adj.* anticin.

quake *v.* & *n.* trema.

Quaker *adj.* & *n.* cuecer.

Quakerism *n.* (*Christianity*) cuecerisme.

quale *n.* (*philosophy*) cuale.

qualification *n.* cuali.

qualified *adj.* cualida, autorida. **be qualified** ave la capasia, ave la direto.

qualifier *n.* (*grammar*) cualinte.

qualify *v.* (*for something, grammar*) cuali.

qualitative *adj.* cualial.

quality *n.* cualia, atribuida. **quality of life** cualia de vive.

quality test *n.* proba de cualia.

qualm *n.* duta.

quandary *n.* dilema.

quanta *n.* cuantos.

quantification *n.* cuanti.

quantify *v.* cuanti.

quantitative *adj.* cuantial.

quantity *n.* cuantia, conta.

quantum *n.* cuanto.

quantum leap *n.* salta cuantal.

quantum mechanics *n.* mecanica cuantal.

quantum physics *n.* fisica cuantal.

quantum theory *n.* teoria cuantal.

quarantine *v.* & *n.* isoli.

quark *n.* cuarc. **bottom quark** cuarc basa. **charm quark** cuarc encantada. **down quark** cuarc descendente. **strange quark** cuarc strana. **top quark** cuarc alta. **up quark** cuarc asendente.

quarrel *v.* & *n.* disputa. **minor quarrel** disputeta. **quarrel over** disputa.

quarrelsome *adj.* disputosa.

quarry *n.* escaveria.

quart *n.* cuatrigalon.

quarter *n.* cuatri; (*coin*) cuatrim. • *v.* cuatri; (*accommodation*) casi tempora. • *pref.* cuatri-. **quarters** abiteria.

quarter note *n.* tono cuatrida.

quartet *n.* cuatruple.

quarto *adj.* (*book size*) cuatrida.

quartz *n.* cuarzo.

quasar *n.* cuasar.

quash *v.* supresa; (*guilty verdict*) descondena.

quasi- *pref.* cuasi-.

quaternary *adj.* cuatronaria.

quaver *n.* tono otida.

quay *n.* molo.

quayside *n.* molo.

queasy *adj.* nauseada, nauseosa.

Quebec *n.* (*Canadian province*) Quebec.

Quebecois *adj.* & *n.* quebecan.

Quechua *adj.* & *n.* (*person, language*) cetxua.

queen *n.* rea; (*chess, cards*) dama.

queen bee *n.* rea de abeas.

queen-size bed *n.* leto grande.

queer *adj.* strana; (*non-conforming*) cuer; (*gay*) ge. • *n.* cuer, ge.

quell *v.* supresa.

quench *v.* (*fire*) estingui; (*thirst*) sasia.

querulous *adj.* cexosa.

query *n.* demanda.

quesadilla *n.* (*tortilla*) cesadilia.

quest *v.* & *n.* xerca.

question *n.* demanda. • *v.* interoga. **ask a question** fa un demanda. **it's a question of** lo es un caso de, lo pertine a.

questionable *adj.* dutable.

question mark *n.* sinia de demanda.

questionnaire *n.* formulario.

question tag *n.* demanda codal.

quetzal *n.* cetsal.

queue *n.* filo. • *v.* fili. **queue up** fili; pone se en filo.

quibble *v.* es pedante. • *n.* punto pedante.

quiche *n.* cix.

quick *adj.* rapida. **quick as a flash** flax.

quicken *v.* rapidi.
quick route *n.* via rapida.
quicksand *n.* arena movente.
quicksilver *n.* mercurio.
quickstep *n.* (*dance*) cuicstep.
quick-tempered *adj.* disputosa.
quiddity *n.* esense.
quiescence *n.* calmia, inertia, nonativia.
quiescent *adj.* calma, inerte, nonativa.
quiet *adj.* cuieta, silente. • *n.* cuietia.
quieten *v.* cuieti.
quietism *n.* cuietisme.
quietist *n.* cuietiste.
quietness *n.* cuietia.
quill *n.* (*feather*) pluma; (*pen*) pen de pluma; (*porcupine*) spina.
quilt *v.* colxa. • *n.* covreleto.
quince *n.* cidonia.
quinine *n.* cinina.
quinoa *n.* cinua.
quintessence *n.* esense, esemplo perfeta.
quintessential *adj.* perfeta. **the quintessential architect** la esense de un arcitetor.
quintet *n.* sincuple.
quintuple *adj.* sincuple.
quintuplet *adj.* & *n.* sincojemelo.
quip *v.* & *n.* replica.
quipu *n.* (*Inca device*) cipu.
quirk *n.* strana.
quirky *adj.* strana, nonespetada.
quisling *n.* trador.
quit *v.* sesa.
quitclaim *n.* renunsia.
quite *adv.* (*entirely*) intera; (*somewhat*) alga, a alga grado. **not quite** cuasi, nonesata.
quittance *n.* libri.
quiver[1] *v.* & *n.* trema, tremeta.
quiver[2] *n.* (*arrows*) portaflexa.
quixotic *adj.* idealiste.
quiz *n.* cuiz.
quiz show *n.* program de concurso.
quizzical *adj.* confondeda.
quoit *n.* anelo.
quoits *n.* (*game*) jua de anelo.
quoll *n.* (*animal*) cuol.
quorum *n.* cuorum.
quota *n.* cuota.
quotation *n.* sita.
quotation mark *n.* sinia de sita; (*opening*) abrisita; (*closing*) cluisita.
quote *v.* sita.
quotidian *adj.* dial.
quotient *n.* proportio.
Qur'an *n.* Curan.
Qyzylqum *n.* Deserto Kizilkum.

R

R&B *n.* ritmo e blus.
rabbi *n.* rabi.
rabbit *n.* coneo. **baby rabbit** coneta.
rabbit bandicoot *n.* bilbi.
rabbit hutch *n.* caje de coneo.
rabble *n.* manada.
rabelaisian *adj.* vulgar.
rabid *adj.* rabica.
rabies *n.* rabia.
raccoon *n.* prosion.
race[1] *v.* & *n.* (*competition*) corsa.
race[2] *n.* (*racial*) raza.
racecourse *n.* curso de corsa.
racehorse *n.* cavalo de corsa.
racer *n.* corsor.
racetrack *n.* curso de corsa.
raceway *n.* curso de corsa.
rachitis *n.* (*medical*) racite.
racial *adj.* razal.
racing *n.* corsa. **auto racing** corsa de autos.
racism *n.* razisme.
racist *n.* raziste.
rack *n.* scafal; (*for pinion*) bara de dentes. **rack one's brain** serebri.
racket[1] *n.* (*bat*) raceta.
racket[2] *n.* (*din*) ruido; (*criminal*) comersia frodante, crimin organizada.
racketeer *n.* gangster.
racketeering *n.* comersia frodante.
rackett *n.* (*musical instrument*) raceta.
raconteur *n.* racontor, naror.
racquet *n.* raceta.
racquetball *n.* (*sport*) racetabal.
racy *adj.* riscosa.
radar *n.* radar.
radar post *n.* radareria.
radar station *n.* radareria.
radial *adj.* raial, radial.
radial saw *n.* siera radial.
radian *n.* (*unit of angle*) radian.
radiance *n.* radia.
radiant *adj.* radiante.
radiate *v.* radia. • *n.* (*jellyfish*) radiato.
radiation *n.* radia.
radiator *n.* radiador.
radical *adj.* radisal; estrema; estremiste; revoluinte. • *n.* estremiste; revoluiste; (*chemistry*) radical.
radicalism *n.* estremisme.
radicalization *n.* estremi.
radicalize *v.* estremi.
radio *n.* radio. • *v.* radiocomunica. • *pref.* radio-.
radioactive *adj.* radioativa.
radioactivity *n.* radioativia.
radiocommunication *n.* radiocomunica.
radiography *n.* radiografia.
radiological *adj.* radiolojial.
radiologist *n.* radiolojiste.
radiology *n.* radiolojia.
radiophone *n.* radiotelefon.
radiotelephone *n.* radiotelefon.
radiotherapy *n.* radioterapia.
radish *n.* (*plant, root*) rabano.
radium *n.* (*chemistry*) radio.
radius *n.* (*circle*) raio; (*bone*) radio.
radon *n.* (*element*) radon.
raffia *n.* (*plant*) rafia.
raffle *v.* & *n.* rifa.
raft *n.* balsa. • *v.* balsi.
rafter *n.* faxon.
rag *n.* trapo. **dressed in rags** traposa.
raga *adj.* & *n.* (*music*) raga.
ragamuffin *n.* xica vagante.
ragbag *n.* (*miscellaneous category*) trapitota.
rag doll *n.* pupa de trapo.
rage *n.* coleria, furia. • *v.* coleri.
ragged *adj.* traposa, laserada.
ragged left *n.* alinia a destra.
ragged right *n.* alinia a sinistra.
raggedy *adj.* traposa.
raging *adj.* furiosa.
raglan *n.* (*sleeve*) raglan.
ragnarok *n.* ragnaroc.
ragout *n.* ragu.
ragtag *adj.* desorganizada; diversa.
ragtime *adj.* & *n.* (*music*) ragtaim.
raid *v.* & *n.* ataca, invade. **air raid** ataca de aira.
raider *n.* invador.
rail[1] *n.* (*railway, railing*) rel; (*rod*) bara. **come off the rails** salta de la reles.
rail[2] *v.* protesta.
rail[3] *n.* (*bird*) ral.
railing *n.* rel; (*vertical*) balustre.
railroad *n.* ferovia.
railroad track *n.* ferovia, reles.
railroad worker *n.* ferovior.
railway *n.* ferovia.
railwayman *n.* ferovior.
railway worker *n.* ferovior.
raiment *n.* vestes.
rain *v.* & *n.* pluve. **it's raining** lo pluve.
rainbow *n.* arco de sielo.
raincoat *n.* jacon, jacon de pluve.
raindrop *n.* gota de pluve.
rainfall *n.* pluve.
rainforest *n.* foresta pluvosa.
rainproof *adj.* secur contra pluve.
rainspout *n.* tubo de drena.

rainstorm *n.* pluvon.
rainwater *n.* acua de pluve.
rainy *adj.* pluvosa.
raise *v.* alti, leva; (*problem, question*) leva, crea; (*rear*) eleva; (*funds*) recolie. **pay raise** aumenta de salario. **raise again** releva. **raise funds** recolie reservas. **raise one's glass to** brinda.
raisin *n.* uva seca.
raja *n.* (*title*) raja.
rajah *n.* (*title*) raja.
rake[1] *n.* (*tool*) rasto. • *v.* rasti.
rake[2] *n.* (*womanizer*) xasafem.
rakish *adj.* bonvestida, sofisticada.
rally *n.* asembla. • *v.* reenerji.
ram[1] *n.* (*sheep*) ovea mas; (*battering*) ariete. • *v.* puxa.
RAM[2] *n.* (*memory*) ram.
Ramadan *n.* (*Islam*) ramadan.
ramble *v.* vaga.
rambler *n.* vagor.
rambunctious *adj.* turbosa.
rambunctiousness *n.* turbosia.
ramekin *n.* copa de forno.
ramequin *n.* copa de forno.
ramification *n.* rami.
ramjet *n.* (*engine*) statoreatador.
ramp *n.* rampa.
rampage *v.* furia.
rampant *adj.* nonfrenida.
rampart *n.* muron.
ramrod *n.* basto.
ramshackle *adj.* ruinada.
ranch *n.* ranxo.
rancher *n.* ranxor.
ranch house *n.* bangalo.
rancid *adj.* putrida.
rancor (US). See *rancour*.
rancorous *adj.* amarga.
rancour (US **rancor**) *n.* amargia.
rand *n.* (*currency*) rand.
random *adj.* acaso.
randomize *v.* acasi.
randomness *n.* acasia.
random shot *n.* xuta acaso.
randy *adj.* libidosa.
ranee *n.* (*title*) rani.
range *n.* estende; (*mountains*) cadena. • *v.* varia. **a range of** diversa.
rangefinder *n.* telemetre.
rani *n.* (*title*) rani.
rank[1] *n.* grado, titulo; (*chess*) linia. • *v.* gradi, ordina.
rank[2] *adj.* malodorosa.
ranking *n.* gradi.
rankle *v.* irita.
ransack *v.* saca.
ransom *n.* rescate. • *v.* rescati.
ransomware *n.* programes de rescate.
rant *v.* & *n.* arenga, cexa.
rap *v.* bateta; (*music*) rapi. • *n.* bateta; (*music*) rap.
rapacious *adj.* avar.
Rapanui *adj.* rapanui. • *n.* (*person*) rapanui; (*island*) Rapanui, Isola Pascua.
rape[1] *v.* (*assault*) viole.
rape[2] *n.* (*plant*) colza.
rape oil *n.* colza.
rapeseed *n.* colza.
rapeseed oil *n.* colza.
rapid *adj.* rapida.
rapier *n.* (*sword*) stoco.
rapist *n.* violor.
rap music *n.* musica rap.
rappel *v.* rapela.
rapper *n.* (*music*) rapor.
rapport *n.* simpatia.
rapprochement *n.* rearmoni.
rapscallion *n.* turbosa.
rapt *adj.* fasinada.
raptor *n.* predor; (*dinosaur*) velosiraptor.
rapture *n.* estasia.
rare *adj.* rara.
rarefy *v.* rari.
rarely *adv.* rara, a veses rara, a poca veses.
rareness *n.* raria.
rarity *n.* (*quality*) raria; (*rare thing*) rara.
rascal *n.* turbosa.
rash[1] *adj.* (*reckless*) noncauta.
rash[2] *n.* (*medical*) eruta.
rasher *n.* talia de lardo.
rasp *v.* (*sound*) raspa. • *n.* raspador.
raspberry *n.* frambosa; (*sound*) peta de labios.
raspy *adj.* raspante.
rassle *v.* luta.
Rastafari *adj.* & *n.* rastafari.
Rastafarian *adj.* & *n.* rastafari.
raster image *n.* imaje matrisin.
rat *n.* rata. **rat on** informa contra.
ratatouille *n.* (*food*) ratatui.
ratchet *n.* cliceta.
rate *n.* proportio; (*numerical*) taso; (*financial*) tarifa; (*speed*) rapidia. • *v.* gradi.
rather *adv.* alga, a alga grado; (*more precisely*) plu bon, plu esata. **rather than** en loca de.
rathole *n.* rateria.
rathskeller *n.* cava de bir.
ratification *n.* validi.
ratify *v.* validi.
rating *n.* (*measurement*) gradi. **ratings** (*TV*) cuantia de regardores.
ratio *n.* proportio.
ratiocinate *v.* razona.
ration *v.* divide; (*goods*) rasiona. • *n.* parte; rasiona.
rational *adj.* coerente; (*person*) razonante; (*argument*) razonada; (*number*) razonal.

rationale *n.* esplica.
rationalism *n.* razonalisme.
rationalist *adj.* razonaliste.
rationalistic *adj.* razonaliste.
rationalization *n.* esplica, escusa.
rationalize *v.* esplica.
rational thought *n.* razona.
ratlike *adj.* ratin.
rattan *n.* (*fibre*, *plant*) ratan.
rattle *v.* clica; (*worry*) ansi. • *n.* clica; (*toy*, *device*) clicador.
rattled *adj.* (*worried*) ansiosa.
rattler *n.* (*snake*) crotal.
rattlesnake *n.* crotal.
rat trap *n.* rateria.
ratty *adj.* ratin.
raucous *adj.* xiliante.
raunchy *adj.* lasiva.
ravage *v.* ruina.
rave *v.* parla deliriosa; loda zelosa; (*party*) rev.
raven *n.* corvo, corvon.
ravening *adj.* fame, devorante.
ravenous *adj.* fame, devorante.
ravine *n.* canion, foson.
ravioli *n.* (*food*) ravioli.
ravish *v.* encanta; (*kidnap*) saisi, viole.
ravishing *adj.* encantante, estrema bela.
raw *adj.* cru.
rawhide *n.* pel cru.
raw sienna *n.* siena cru.
ray[1] *n.* (*light*, *etc.*) raio.
ray[2] *n.* (*fish*) raia.
rayon *n.* (*fibre*) raion.
raze *v.* destrui.
razor *n.* (*blade*) lama; (*device*) rasador.
razorback *n.* porco savaje.
razorbill *n.* alco.
razor blade *n.* lama.
razor wire *n.* filo lamosa.
razz *n.* peta de labios.
re[1] *n.* (*musical note*) re.
re-[2] *pref.* (*again*, *back*) re-.
reabsorb *v.* reasorbe.
reabsorption *n.* reasorbe.
reaccess *v.* reasede.
reach *v.* ateni, estende a. • *n.* estende. **reach out** estende.
reachable *adj.* atenable.
reacquaint *v.* reinforma. **become reacquainted with** redescovre, recomensa conose.
react *v.* reata.
reactance *n.* reata.
reaction *n.* reata.
reactionary *adj.* reatante. • *n.* reator.
reactivate *v.* reativi.
reactivation *n.* reativi.
reactive *adj.* reatosa.
reactivity *n.* reativia.
reactor *n.* (*person*) reator; (*nuclear*) reatador.
read *v.* leje; (*register*) indica.
readability *n.* lejablia.
readable *adj.* lejable.
readapt *v.* reajusta.
reader *n.* (*person*) lejor; (*machine*) lejador.
readily *adv.* pronto.
readiness *n.* prepara.
reading *n.* (*action*, *interpretation*, *measurement*) leje; indica.
reading device *n.* lejador.
readjust *v.* reajusta.
readmit *v.* reentra.
readmittance *n.* reentra.
read-only *adj.* nonscrivable.
readout *n.* indicador.
ready *v.* prepara. • *adj.* preparada; (*ready-to-wear*, *etc.*) pronto.
reaffirm *v.* reafirma.
reagent *n.* reatante.
real[1] *adj.* real, vera.
real[2] *n.* (*currency*) real.
real estate *n.* imobila.
real estate agent *n.* ajente de imobila.
realign *v.* realinia.
realism *n.* realisme.
realist *n.* realiste.
realistic *adj.* realin.
reality *n.* realia.
reality check *n.* compara con realia.
reality show *n.* program de realia.
realization *n.* reali.
realize *v.* persepi; (*make real*) reali.
reallocate *v.* reasinia; rerasiona.
really *adv.* vera, multe.
realm *n.* rena.
realpolitik *n.* realpolitica.
real-time *adj.* en tempo real.
realtor *n.* ajente de imobila.
realty *n.* imobila.
ream *v.* largi.
reamalgamate *v.* recombina.
reamer *n.* jusador.
reanalyse (US **reanalyze**) *v.* reanalise.
reanimate *v.* reanima.
reap *v.* recolie; (*with a scythe*) falxi.
reaper *n.* falxor.
reappear *v.* reapare.
reappearance *n.* reapare.
reapply *v.* reaplica.
reappoint *v.* reasinia.
reappraise *v.* reevalua.
rear[1] *adj.* (*back*) retro; posterior. • *n.* retro; (*buttocks*) gluteos, posterior, popa. **at the rear** a pos. **rear up** capri.
rear[2] *v.* (*raise*) eleva.
rearm *v.* rearma.
rearmament *n.* rearma.
rearrange *v.* reordina.

rear view *n.* retrovista.
rear-view mirror *n.* miror de retrovista.
reason *v.* razona. • *n.* razona; esplica. **for no reason** sin razona.
reasonable *adj.* razonante, asetable, justa.
reasoning *adj.* razonante. • *n.* razona.
reassemble *v.* reasembla, reconstrui, rejunta.
reassert *v.* redeclara.
reassess *v.* reevalua.
reassign *v.* reasinia.
reassurance *n.* calmi.
reassure *v.* calmi.
reattach *v.* reafisa.
reattain *v.* reateni.
reawaken *v.* revelia.
rebaptize *v.* rebatiza.
rebate *n.* (*business*) desconta.
rebel *v.* rebela. • *n.* rebelor.
rebellion *n.* rebela.
rebellious *adj.* rebelante.
rebirth *n.* renase.
reboot *v.* & *n.* reinisia.
reborn *adj.* renaseda. **be reborn** renase.
rebound *v.* rebondi.
rebroadcast *v.* redifusa.
rebuff *v.* & *n.* rejeta.
rebuild *v.* reconstrui.
rebuilt *adj.* reconstruida.
rebuke *v.* reproxa.
rebus *n.* jua de ieroglifos.
rebut *v.* refuta.
rebuttal *n.* refuta.
recalcitrant *adj.* defiante.
recalculate *v.* recalcula.
recall *v.* recorda; (*withdraw*) retira. • *n.* recorda.
recall election *n.* referendo per retira.
recall referendum *n.* referendo per retira.
recant *v.* retira.
recap *v.* & *n.* resoma.
recapitulate *v.* resoma.
recapture *v.* recatura.
recast *v.* reasinia.
recede *v.* retrosede.
receipt *n.* nota de reseta.
receive *v.* reseta; (*greet*) saluta.
received wisdom *n.* ideas asetada.
receiver *n.* (*device*, *biology*) resetador.
recent *adj.* resente, nova.
receptacle *n.* contenador.
reception *n.* reseta; (*place*) reseteria.
reception area *n.* reseteria.
receptionist *n.* resetiste.
reception range *n.* (*communications*) reseteria.
receptive *adj.* resetante.
recess *n.* alcova.
recession *n.* retrosede.
recessive *adj.* retrosedente.
recharge *v.* recarga.
rechargeable *adj.* recargable.
recheck *v.* reserti.
recidivism *n.* recore.
recidivist *n.* recoror.
recipe *n.* reseta.
recipe book *n.* libro de resetas.
recipient *n.* resetor.
reciprocal *adj.* resiproca, mutua.
reciprocate *v.* resiproci.
reciprocating saw *n.* siera alternante.
reciprocity *n.* resiprocia.
recital *n.* presenta.
recitation *n.* resita.
recite *v.* resita, proclama.
reckless *adj.* fretosa.
recklessness *adj.* fretosia.
reckon *v.* calcula.
reclaim *v.* & *n.* (*property*, *title*) reclama.
reclassify *v.* reclasi.
recline *v.* reclina.
recliner *n.* seja reclinante.
reclining chair *n.* seja reclinante.
reclothe *v.* revesti.
recluse *n.* eremita, solitar.
reclusive *adj.* retirada, solitar.
recoat *v.* & *n.* revesti.
recognition *n.* reconose; (*award*) premio lodante.
recognizable *adj.* reconosable.
recognize *v.* reconose.
recoil *v.* & *n.* retira.
recollect *v.* recorda.
recollection *n.* recorda.
recombinant *adj.* recombinante.
recombine *v.* recombina.
recommence *v.* recomensa.
recommend *v.* recomenda.
recommendation *n.* recomenda.
recommit *v.* refa; reenvia.
recompense *v.* & *n.* recompensa.
recon[1] *n.* (*reconnaissance*) oserva.
recon[2] *n.* (*reconstruction*) reconstrui.
reconcile *v.* reconsilia.
reconciliation *n.* reconsilia.
reconnaissance *n.* oserva, esplora.
reconnect *v.* recomuta, rejunta.
reconnoitre *v.* oserva.
reconsider *v.* reconsidera.
reconstitute *v.* reconstitui.
reconstitution *n.* reconstitui.
reconstruct *v.* reconstrui.
reconstruction *n.* reconstrui.
reconvene *v.* reasembla.
reconvert *v.* reconverti.
recook *v.* recoce.
record *v.* rejistra. • *n.* article, arcivo; (*disc*) disco; (*best performance*) recordo; (*data structure*)

uple. • *adj.* recordo. **in record time** en tempo recordo.
record-breaking *adj.* recordo, sin presedente.
recorder *n.* (*person*) rejistror; (*device*) rejistrador; flauta dulse.
recording *n.* rejistra.
recording device *n.* rejistrador.
record office *n.* arçiveria.
record player *n.* fonograf.
recount *v.* & *n.* reconta.
recoup *v.* regania.
recourse *n.* recurso, alternativa. **have recourse to** nesesa adota.
recover *v.* retrova; (*money*) regania; (*get better*) recovre, sani.
recoverable *adj.* reganiable.
recovery *n.* recovre.
recreant *n.* trador.
recreate *v.* recrea.
recreation *n.* (*repeated creation*) recrea; (*leisure*) jua, pasatempo.
recreational *adj.* recreal.
recreational vehicle *n.* autocaravan.
recreation centre (US **center**) *n.* sentro de recrea.
recriminate *v.* contracusa.
recrimination *n.* contracusa.
recruit *v.* enscrive. • *n.* enscriveda.
rectal *adj.* retal.
rectangle *n.* retangulo.
rectangular *adj.* retangulo.
recti- *pref.* reti-.
rectify *v.* (*in electronics*) reti.
rectilinear *n.* retilinial.
rectitude *n.* virtua.
rector *n.* parocior.
rectory *n.* casa de parocior.
rectum *n.* (*anatomy*) reto.
recumbent bicycle *n.* bisicle orizonal.
recuperate *v.* recovre, sani.
recuperation *n.* recovre.
recur *v.* reaveni, recore, reveni.
recurrence *n.* reaveni, recore.
recurrent *adj.* recorente.
recurse *v.* recorsa.
recursion *n.* recorsa.
recursive *adj.* recorsante.
recuse *v.* asteni.
recyclable *adj.* & *n.* resiclable.
recycle *v.* resicli.
recycle bin *n.* baldon de resicli.
recycling bin *n.* baldon de resicli.
recycling plant *n.* resicleria.
red *adj.* & *n.* roja.
redact *v.* revisa.
red admiral *n.* atalanta.
red-billed chough *n.* xova becoroja.
red blood cell *n.* eritrosite.
redbud *n.* (*tree*) sersis.
Red Cross *n.* Crus Roja.
redcurrant *n.* grosela roja.
redden *v.* roji.
reddish *adj.* rojin.
reddish brown *adj.* rojin brun. • *n.* brun rojin.
redecorate *v.* redecora.
rededicate *v.* rededica.
redeem *v.* remete, salva.
redeemable *adj.* remetable.
redeemer *n.* remetor, salvor.
redefine *v.* redefini.
redemption *n.* remete, salva.
redeploy *v.* reasinia.
redesign *v.* redesinia.
red-haired *adj.* roja, con capeles roja.
redhead *n.* roja.
red-headed *adj.* roja, con capeles roja.
red-hot *adj.* roja calda.
redirect *v.* redirije.
redirection *n.* redirije.
rediscover *v.* redescovre.
rediscuss *v.* rediscute.
redistribute *v.* redistribui.
redistrict *v.* redistriti.
red lead *n.* (*pigment*) minio.
red lentil *n.* lentil roja.
red-light district *n.* lasiveria.
redneck *adj.* coloroja.
redo *v.* refa.
redolent *adj.* recordante, sujestante; odorosa.
redouble *v.* aumenta.
red pepper *n.* peperon roja.
redpoll *n.* (*bird*) gargarosa.
redress *v.* remedia.
Red Sea *n.* Mar Roja.
red shift *n.* desloca roja.
reduce *v.* redui, diminui, desintensi; (*in height*) basi; (*in quantity*) poci; (*in size*) peti; (*to powder*) mole.
reducible *adj.* reduable.
reduction *n.* redui.
reductionism *n.* reduisme.
reductive *adj.* reduinte.
redundancy *n.* dupli.
redundant *adj.* duplinte, plu ca nesesada.
redwing *n.* (*bird*) alaroja.
red-winged blackbird *n.* alaroja american.
redwood *n.* (*tree*) secuoia.
reed *n.* (*plant*) cana; (*of musical instrument*) anxa.
re-educate *v.* reeduca.
reef *n.* resife.
reefer *n.* sigareta de canaba.
reek *v.* apesta, malodori.
reel *n.* (*cylinder*) bobin; (*dance, music*) ril. • *v.* bambola.

re-elect *v.* reeleje.
re-emerge *v.* reemerji.
re-enable *v.* recapasi.
re-enact *v.* rereali.
re-enactment *n.* rereali.
re-energize *v.* reenerji.
re-enforce *v.* reenforsa.
re-engage *v.* reenvolve.
re-enlist *v.* reenscrive.
re-enter *v.* reentra.
re-entry *n.* reentra.
re-establish *v.* reinstitui.
re-evaluate *v.* reevalua.
re-examination *n.* reesamina.
re-examine *v.* reesamina.
re-experience *v.* reesperia.
re-express *v.* reespresa.
refactor *v.* (*software*) refatori.
refamilarize *v.* (*oneself with*) recomensa conose.
refer *v.* refere. **referred to as** conoseda como.
referee *n.* arbitror.
reference *n.* refere, referente. • *v.* refere a.
reference book *n.* libro de consulta, manual.
reference implementation *n.* reali model.
referendum *n.* referendo.
referral *n.* refere.
refill *v.* & *n.* repleni.
refinance *v.* refinansia.
refine *v.* refina.
refinement *n.* refina.
refinery *n.* refineria.
refinish *v.* renovi.
reflect *v.* refleta.
reflection *n.* refleta.
reflective *adj.* refletante.
reflex *n.* reflexe.
reflexive *adj.* reflexe; (*grammar*) refletante.
reflux *n.* (*chemistry*) reflue.
reforest *v.* reforesti.
reform *v.* & *n.* reformi.
reformat *v.* reformati.
reformation *n.* reformi.
reformatory *n.* reformeria.
reformed *adj.* reformida; pasada.
reformism *n.* reformisme.
reformist *adj.* & *n.* reformiste.
reformulate *v.* reformula.
refract *v.* refrata.
refraction *n.* refrata.
refractive *adj.* refratal.
refrain[1] *v.* (*abstain*) asteni.
refrain[2] *n.* (*chorus*) refren.
reframe *v.* restruturi.
refreeze *v.* rejela.
refresh *v.* & *n.* refresci, restora.
refresher *n.* refresci.
refreshment *n.* cometa, restora.
refrigerant *n.* frinte.
refrigerate *v.* fri.
refrigerated *adj.* frida.
refrigeration *n.* fri.
refrigerator *n.* friador.
refry *v.* refrita.
refuel *v.* renuri.
refuge *n.* refuja; (*place*) refujeria. **give refuge to** refuja. **take refuge** refuja se.
refugee *n.* refujada.
refund *v.* & *n.* repaia.
refundable *adj.* repaiable.
refurbish *v.* reconstrui, renovi.
refurbishment *n.* renovi.
refurnish *v.* remobili.
refusal *n.* refusa.
refuse[1] *v.* (*decline*) refusa.
refuse[2] *n.* (*garbage*) dejetada.
refutable *adj.* refutable.
refutation *n.* refuta.
refute *v.* refuta.
regain *v.* regania.
regal *adj.* real.
regale *v.* diverti.
regalia *n.* ornas real.
regard *v.* & *n.* regarda. **as regards** en relata con, consernante, regardante. **with regard to** en relata con, consernante, regardante.
regarding *prep.* en relata con, consernante, regardante.
regardless *prep.* (*of*) an con, sin relata con.
regather *v.* reasembla.
regency *n.* rejentia.
regenerate *v.* rejenera, recrese.
regeneration *n.* rejenera.
regent *adj.* rejente, renante. • *n.* rejente.
regex *n.* (*software*) regex.
reggae *adj.* & *n.* (*music*) rege.
regicide *n.* (*action*) reiside; (*person*) reisidor. **commit regicide** reiside.
regime *n.* governa, rena.
regiment *n.* rejimento.
regimental *adj.* rejimental.
region *n.* rejion.
regional *adj.* rejional, distrital.
regionalism *n.* rejionalisme.
register *v.* (*record*) rejistra; (*for activity*) enscrive, suscrive, suscrive per entra; (*reading*) indica. • *n.* arcivo; (*music, language*) rejistra; (*recorder*) rejistrador.
registered charity *n.* asosia carital.
registrar *n.* rejistror.
registration *n.* enscrive.
registry *n.* arciveria.
regress *v.* regresa.
regression *n.* regresa.
regressive *adj.* regresante.
regressive tax *n.* imposta regresante.

regret *v.* & *n.* regrete, repenti.
regretful *adj.* repentinte.
regrettable *adj.* regretable.
regroup *v.* reuni.
regrow *v.* recrese.
regular *adj.* (*regulated*) regulada; (*consistent*) coerente, normal, sistemosa, uniforma; (*periodic*) periodal.
regular expression *n.* (*software*) regex.
regularity *n.* normalia.
regularize *v.* regula.
regulate *v.* regula.
regulation *n.* regula.
regulator *n.* regulador.
regurgitate *v.* vomiti.
regurgitation *n.* vomiti.
rehabilitate *v.* recapasi.
rehabilitation *n.* recapasi.
reharmonization *n.* rearmoni.
reharmonize *v.* rearmoni.
rehash *v.* rediscute.
rehearsal *n.* pratica.
rehearse *v.* pratica.
reheat *v.* recaldi.
rehouse *v.* recasi.
rehydrate *v.* reidrata.
reify *v.* concreti.
reign *v.* rena.
reignite *v.* reensende.
reimburse *v.* repaia.
reimbursement *n.* repaia.
rein *n.* (*strap*) redin. • *v.* redini.
reincarnate *v.* reincarne.
reincarnation *n.* reincarne.
reindeer *n.* reno.
reinforce *v.* forti, reforti.
reinforced concrete *n.* beton fortida.
reinforcement *n.* (*action*) reforti; (*person, thing*) refortinte.
reinforcement ring *n.* anelo fortinte.
reinsert *v.* reintrodui.
reinspect *v.* reesamina.
reinspection *n.* reesamina.
reinstall *v.* reinstala.
reinstate *v.* repone.
reintegrate *v.* reintegra.
reintegration *n.* reintegra.
reinterpret *v.* reinterprete.
reintroduce *v.* reintrodui.
reinvent *v.* reinventa.
reinvention *n.* reinventa.
reinvestigate *v.* reinvestiga.
reinvigorate *v.* refresci.
reiterate *v.* redise.
reject *v.* rejeta, refusa.
rejection *n.* rejeta, refusa.
rejectionist *adj.* & *n.* rejetiste.
rejoice *v.* joia, selebra.
rejoin *v.* rejunta.
rejoinder *n.* responde.
rejuvenate *v.* rejoveni.
rejuvenation *n.* rejoveni.
relapse *v.* & *n.* recore.
relatable *adj.* relatable.
relate *v.* relata, pertine; conserna; (*story*) raconta, nara.
relation *n.* (*relationship*) relata; (*family member*) relatada. **in relation to** en relata con
relational *adj.* relatal.
relationship *n.* relata; relata de ama.
relative *adj.* relativa; (*family member*) relatada.
relative adverb *n.* (*grammar*) averbo-sujunta.
relative clause *n.* (*grammar*) suproposa ajetivin.
relative pronoun *n.* (*grammar*) pronom-sujunta.
relativistic *adj.* relativial.
relativity *n.* relativia.
relax *v.* destensa, reposa.
relaxant *n.* destensante.
relaxation *n.* destensa, reposa.
relay *n.* (*electric, race*) rele.
relay race *n.* corsa de rele.
relearn *v.* reaprende.
release *v.* relasa, libri; (*publish*) publici, lansa a mercato. • *n.* relasa, libri; publici.
relegate *v.* retrosede.
relegation *n.* retrosede.
relent *v.* moli; sede, retira.
relentless *adj.* nonsedente.
relevance *n.* pertine.
relevant *adj.* pertinente, aplicable. **be relevant** pertine.
reliability *n.* fidablia.
reliable *adj.* fidable.
reliance *n.* depende, fida.
relic *n.* (*object, tradition*) relicia.
relief *n.* (*emotion*) lejeri; (*accentuation*) releva. **throw into relief** releva.
relief agency *n.* ajenteria de aida.
relief map *n.* mapa de releva.
relieve *v.* lejeri.
religion *n.* relijio.
religious *adj.* (*of religion*) relijial; (*displaying religion*) relijiosa.
relinquish *v.* sede, abandona.
reliquary *n.* relicieria.
relish *v.* saborea.
relisten *v.* reescuta.
relive *v.* revive.
reload *v.* recarga.
relocalize *v.* relocali.
relocate *v.* reloca, reloca se.
relocation *n.* reloca.
reluctant *adj.* nonvolente, esitante.
rely *v.* depende, fida.
rem *n.* (*unit of radiation*) rem.

remain *v.* resta, permane. **remains** restas, restantes.
remainder *n.* resta, restante.
remaindered book *n.* libro nonvendeda.
remake *v.* reconstrui, refabrica, recrea.
remark *v.* & *n.* comenta.
remarkable *adj.* notable.
remarry *v.* resposi.
remediable *adj.* remediable.
remedial *adj.* remediante.
remedy *v.* & *n.* remedia.
remember *v.* (*memorize*) memori; (*recall*) recorda.
remembrance *n.* suvenir.
Remembrance Day *n.* Dia de Memoria.
remind *v.* sujesta, evoca, remente, fa ce on recorda.
reminder *n.* remente, recordante; aidamemoria.
reminisce *v.* recorda felis.
remiss *adj.* nonatendente.
remission *n.* remete.
remit *v.* remete.
remittance *n.* paia.
remittent *adj.* flutuante.
remix *v.* remisca.
remnant *n.* resta, restante.
remodel *v.* renovi.
remora *n.* (*fish*) remora.
remorse *n.* regrete, repenti. **feel remorse** repenti.
remorseful *adj.* repentinte.
remortgage *v.* reipoteca.
remote *adj.* distante, a distantia; nonsosial.
remote control *n.* (*action*) telecomanda; (*controller*) telecomandador. **operate by remote control** telecomanda.
remote-controlled *adj.* telecomandada.
remount *v.* remonta.
removable *adj.* desfisable; sutrable.
removal *n.* sutrae; estrae; desfisa.
remove *v.* sutrae; (*extract*) estrae; (*detach*) desfisa; (*garment*) desapone; (*from office*) despone.
REM sleep *adj.* dormi paradoxal.
remunerate *v.* paia.
remuneration *n.* paia.
renaissance *n.* renase. **the Renaissance** la Renase.
renal *adj.* (*of kidneys*) renal.
rename *v.* renomi.
renascence *n.* renase.
renascent *adj.* renasente.
rend *v.* lasera.
render *v.* furni; fa ce, causa ce; (*image, video*) rendere. **render it worthless** fa ce lo es sin valua.
rendezvous *n.* encontra.
rendition *n.* presenta, interprete.
renegade *adj.* & *n.* renegada.
renege *v.* rompe.
renegotiate *v.* renegosia.
renew *v.* renovi.
renewable *adj.* renovable.
renewal *n.* renovi.
renewer *n.* renovor.
renin *n.* (*enzyme*) renin.
rennet *n.* (*substance*) calio.
rennin *n.* (*enzyme*) cimosina.
renounce *v.* renunsia.
renovascular *adj.* (*biology*) renovascular.
renovate *v.* renovi.
renovation *n.* renovi.
renovator *n.* renovor.
renown *n.* fama.
renowned *adj.* selebrada, famosa.
rent *v.* lua. • *n.* custa de lua. **rent out** ofre per lua.
rentable *adj.* luable.
rental *n.* lua. • *adj.* luable.
renter *n.* luor.
renunciation *n.* renunsia.
reoccupation *n.* reocupa.
reoccupy *v.* reocupa.
reoccur *v.* reaveni, recore.
reopen *v.* reabri.
reorder *v.* reordina.
reorganization *n.* reorganiza.
reorganize *v.* reorganiza.
reorient *v.* reorienta.
reorientate *v.* reorienta.
repack *v.* repaci.
repackage *v.* repaci.
repaint *v.* repinti.
repair *v.* repara, desrompe. • *n.* repara.
repairer *n.* reparor.
repairman *n.* reparor.
repair shop *n.* repareria.
repairwoman *n.* reparor.
reparable *adj.* reparable.
reparation *n.* compensa.
repartee *n.* conversa replicosa.
repast *n.* come.
repatriate *v.* renativi.
repatriation *n.* renativi.
repave *v.* repave.
repay *v.* repaia.
repayable *adj.* repaiable.
repayment *n.* repaia.
repeal *v.* cansela.
repeat *v.* repete.
repel *v.* forsa a via; (*disgust*) repulsa.
repellent *adj.* repulsante. • *n.* (*substance*) repulsante.
repent *v.* repenti.
repentance *n.* repenti.
repentant *adj.* repentinte.
repercussion *n.* resulta ladal.

repertoire *n.* colie, colie de presentas, repertorio.
repertory *n.* colie, colie de presentas, repertorio.
repetition *n.* repete.
repetitious *adj.* repetosa.
repetitive *adj.* repetente.
rephrase *v.* redise.
replace *v.* (*old with new*) recambia, cambia; (*new for old*) sustitui; (*place again*) repone.
replaceable *adj.* recambiable.
replacement *adj.* sustitua. • *n.* sustitua, sustitua tempora, recambia.
replay *v.* & *n.* repete, remostra.
replenish *v.* repleni.
replenishment *n.* repleni.
replete *adj.* sasiada.
replica *n.* copia.
replicate *v.* copia, copia esata, reprodui esata.
replication *n.* copia esata, reprodui esata.
replier *n.* respondor.
reply *v.* responde.
repopulate *v.* repopla.
report *v.* & *n.* reporta.
reporter *n.* reportor.
repose *v.* & *n.* reposa.
repository *n.* beneria; arciveria.
repossess *v.* reposese, reprende.
reprehend *v.* reproxa.
reprehensible *adj.* odiable.
represent *v.* representa.
representation *n.* representa.
representative *adj.* representante; tipal. • *n.* representor.
repress *v.* represa.
repressible *adj.* represable.
repression *n.* represa.
repressive *adj.* represante.
reprieve *v.* & *n.* remete.
reprimand *v.* & *n.* reproxa.
reprint *v.* reprimi.
reprisal *n.* venja.
reprise *n.* repete.
reproach *v.* & *n.* reproxa, critica.
reprobate *n.* vil.
reprocess *v.* reprosede.
reproduce *v.* reprodui.
reproduction *n.* reprodui, fasimil.
reproductive system *n.* sistem de reprodui.
repropose *v.* reproposa.
reptile *n.* retil.
reptilian *adj.* retilal.
republic *n.* republica. **Republic of Ireland** Er. **Republic of South Africa** Republica de Africa Sude, Sudafrica. **Republic of the Congo** Republica de Congo.
republican *adj.* & *n.* republiciste.
republicanism *n.* republicisme.
republish *v.* republici.
repudiate *v.* nega.
repudiation *n.* nega.
repugnant *adj.* repulsante.
repulse *v.* repulsa.
repulsive *adj.* repulsante.
reputable *adj.* bonreputada.
reputation *n.* reputa.
repute *v.* reputa. **of good repute** bonreputada. **of ill repute** malreputada.
request *v.* demanda per, solisita. • *n.* solisita.
requester *n.* solisitor.
requiem *n.* misa de moria.
require *v.* nesesa, esije.
requirement *n.* esije, nesesada.
requisite *adj.* nesesada.
requisition *v.* saisi. • *n.* solisita.
re-raise *v.* releva.
re-read *v.* releje.
re-record *v.* rerejistra.
reroute *v.* redirije.
rerun *n.* repete.
resale *n.* revende.
resaler *n.* revendor.
reschedule *v.* reajendi.
rescind *v.* nega.
rescue *v.* salva.
rescuer *n.* salvor.
reseal *v.* reseli.
resealable *adj.* reselable.
research *v.* & *n.* rexerca.
research centre (US **center**) *n.* sentro de rexerca.
research documents *n.* documentos de rexerca.
researcher *n.* rexercor.
research material *n.* documentos de rexerca.
reseat *v.* resenta.
resection *n.* estrae.
resell *v.* revende.
resemblance *n.* sembla.
resemble *v.* sembla.
resent *v.* es ofendeda par; odia.
resentful *adj.* ofendeda; odiosa.
resentment *n.* nonpardona; odia.
reservation *n.* (*seat, table*) reserva; (*doubt*) duta.
reserve *v.* reserva; (*for future use*) reteni. • *n.* reserva; (*wildlife*) conserveria; (*social*) introverti. **in reserve** reservada.
reserved *adj.* reservada; secretosa, introvertida, retirada.
reservist *n.* reserviste.
reservoir *n.* lago de reserva.
reset *v.* & *n.* reinisia.
resettle *v.* relocali.

reside *v.* abita.
residence *n.* abiteria.
residency *n.* abita.
resident *adj.* abitante. • *n.* abitor; (*medical graduate*) mediciste abitante.
residential *adj.* abital; abitante.
residential area *n.* area abital.
residential school *n.* scola abitada.
residual *adj.* restante. • *n.* resta, restante.
residue *n.* resta, restante.
resign *v.* resinia, renunsia.
resignation *n.* resinia, renunsia.
resilient *adj.* durante.
resin *n.* resina.
resinous *adj.* resinosa.
resist *v.* resiste; rebela.
resistance *n.* resiste; rebela; (*movement*) resistente.
resistant *adj.* resistente; (*to pressure*) dur.
resistible *adj.* resistable.
resistor *n.* resistador.
resituate *v.* resitua.
resizable *adj.* de grandia cambiable.
resize *v.* cambia la grandia de.
resole *v.* (*shoe*) recambia la planta de.
resolute *adj.* determinada, nonvasilante.
resolution *n.* (*decision*) deside; (*into parts*) resolve; (*image*) densia.
resolve *v.* (*decide*) deside; (*into parts*) resolve.
resonance *n.* (*reverberation*) resona; (*connotation*) evoca.
resonant *adj.* resonante.
resonate *v.* resona.
resonator *n.* resonador.
resort *n.* vacanseria. **resort to** nesesa adota.
resound *v.* resona.
resource *n.* recurso.
resourceful *adj.* recursosa.
respect *v.* & *n.* respeta.
respectable *adj.* respetable.
respectful *adj.* respetosa.
respective *adj.* propre.
respectively *adv.* en ordina.
respell *v.* respele.
respirator *n.* respirador.
respiratory *adj.* respiral.
respiratory system *n.* sistem de respira.
respiratory tract *n.* curso de respira.
respire *v.* respira.
respite *n.* reposa.
resplendent *adj.* briliante.
respond *v.* responde.
respondent *adj.* respondente. • *n.* respondor.
responder *n.* respondor.
response *n.* responde.
responsibility *n.* encarga, obliga; culpablia. **with shared responsibility** coencargada.
responsible *adj.* encargada, fidable; culpable, litigable; seria.
responsive *adj.* respondente.
rest[1] *v.* & *n.* reposa. **have a rest** reposa.
rest[2] *n.* (*remainder*) resta, restante.
restage *v.* reaveni.
rest area *n.* reposeria; stasion de autovia.
restart *v.* & *n.* reinisia.
restate *v.* reespresa.
restaurant *n.* restorante.
restaurant car *n.* vagon restorante.
restaurateur *n.* restorantor.
restful *adj.* repososa.
restitution *n.* restora; (*recompense*) compensa.
restive *adj.* ajitada.
restless *adj.* ajitada.
restock *v.* repleni.
restoration *n.* restora.
restorationism *n.* restorisme.
restore *v.* restora; (*put back*) repone.
restorer *n.* restoror.
rest period *n.* tempo de pausa.
restrain *v.* restrinje; freni.
restraint *n.* (*device*) freno.
restrict *v.* restrinje.
restricted *adj.* restrinjeda, nonlibre.
restriction *n.* restrinje.
restrictive *adj.* restrinjente.
restructure *v.* restruturi.
rest stop *n.* reposeria.
resubmit *v.* reenvia, reproposa.
resubscribe *v.* reenscrive.
result *v.* & *n.* resulta. **result in** causa, resulta.
resultant *adj.* resultante.
resume[1] *v.* (*continue*) recomensa.
résumé[2] *n.* (*summary*) resoma; (*CV*) resoma de carera.
resupply *v.* refurni.
resurface *v.* reapare.
resurgent *adj.* reanimante.
resurrect *v.* revive.
resurrection *n.* revive.
resuscitate *v.* revive, reanima.
resuscitation *n.* revive.
resuscitator *n.* reanimador.
retail *v.* vende.
retailer *n.* vendor minor.
retain *v.* reteni.
retainer *n.* (*device*) retenador.
retaining wall *n.* muron.
retake *n.* refa.
retaliate *v.* venja se; contrataca.
retaliation *n.* venja; contrataca.
retaliation killings *n.* matas per venja.
retard *v.* retarda.
retch *v.* vomiti.
retell *v.* renara.
retention *n.* reteni.

retest *v.* reesamina.
rethink *v.* repensa.
reticence *n.* secretosia.
reticent *adj.* nonespresosa; secretosa.
reticle *n.* reticulo.
reticular *adj.* reticulal.
reticule *n.* reticulo.
reticulum *n.* (*network, anatomy*) reticulo; (*constellation*) la Rede.
retina *n.* (*anatomy*) retina.
retinal *adj.* retinal.
retinopathic *adj.* retinopatica.
retinopathy *n.* retinopatia.
retinoscope *n.* retinoscopio.
retinoscopy *n.* retinoscopi.
retinue *n.* atendores, seguores.
retire *v.* (*withdraw*) retira; (*from work*) jubila.
retired person *n.* jubilor.
retiree *n.* jubilor.
retirement *n.* jubila.
retirement pension *n.* pension de jubila.
retool *v.* furni utiles nova a.
retort[1] *v.* & *n.* replica.
retort[2] *n.* (*container*) retorta.
retouch *v.* retoca.
retrace *v.* segue, resegue. **retrace one's steps** resegue sua pasos.
retract *v.* retira.
retraction *n.* retira.
retractor *n.* retirador.
retrain *v.* reinstrui.
retreat *v.* retira. • *n.* retira; (*hideaway*) nido.
retrench *v.* redui la spende.
retribution *n.* venja.
retrievable *adj.* reprendable.
retrieval *n.* retrae.
retrieve *v.* retrae; (*pick up*) reprende.
retriever *n.* (*dog*) retraor. **golden retriever** retraor oro.
retro- *pref.* retro-.
retroactive *adj.* retroativa.
retrofit *n.* moderni.
retroflex *adj.* & *n.* (*consonant*) retroflexe.
retrograde *adj.* retrogradal.
retrorocket *n.* retroroceto.
retrospect *adv.* retrospeta. **in retrospect** en retrospeta.
retrospective *n.* retrospeta. • *adj.* retrospetante.
retry *v.* reatenta.
return *v.* (*go back*) revade; (*come back*) reveni; (*give back*) redona; (*send back*) reenvia. • *n.* reveni; revade; redona; (*on investment*) interesa. **in return** par intercambia. **in return for** per, par intercambia per.
returnable *adj.* reenviable.
returning officer *n.* ofisior de vota.
return key *n.* tecla de entra.
return ticket *n.* bileta de vade e reveni.
retype *n.* retape.
reunification *n.* reuni.
reunify *v.* reuni.
reunion *n.* reuni.
reunite *v.* reuni.
reupholster *v.* retapeti.
reusable *adj.* reusable.
reuse *v.* reusa.
revamp *v.* boni, renovi.
reveal *v.* revela, mostra, evidenti.
reveille *n.* sona de velia.
revel *v.* vanta a se. **revel in** selebra.
revelation *n.* revela, abrioio; (*religious*) apocalise.
reveller (US **reveler**) *n.* selebror.
revelry *n.* selebra.
revenge *n.* venja. **get revenge** venja se.
revenue *n.* revenu.
reverberate *v.* resona densa.
reverberation *v.* & *n.* resona; (*merged echoes*) resona densa.
revere *v.* adora.
reverence *n.* adora, onora.
reverend *adj.* (*form of address*) onorable.
reverent *adj.* adorante.
reverie *n.* fantasia.
reverify *v.* reserti.
reversal *n.* reversa.
reverse *v.* reversa. • *n.* (*side*) dorso; (*gear*) engrana de retira. **in reverse** en reversa; reversada.
reverse gear *n.* engrana de retira.
reversible *adj.* reversable.
reversion *n.* reversa.
revert *v.* reversa.
review *v.* resenia. • *n.* resenia; (*periodical*) revista.
reviewer *n.* resenior.
revile *v.* despeta; maltrata.
revise *v.* revisa.
reviser *n.* revisor.
revision *n.* revisa.
revision control system *n.* arcivador de revisas.
revisionist *n.* revisor.
revisit *v.* revisita.
revitalization *n.* revive.
revitalize *v.* revive.
revival *n.* revive.
revive *v.* revive.
revocable *adj.* canselable.
revocation *n.* cansela.
revoke *v.* cansela.
revolt *v.* & *n.* (*local rebellion*) revolta.
revolting *adj.* (*disgusting*) repulsante.
revolution *n.* (*local rebellion*) revolta; (*overthrow of government*) revolui.
revolutionary *adj.* revoluinte. • *n.* revoluiste.

revolutionism *n.* revoluisme.
revolutionist *n.* revoluiste.
revolutionize *v.* revolui.
revolve *v.* jira, turna.
revolver *n.* revolver, fusil de mano.
revolving door *n.* porte caruselin.
revue *n.* teatral de revista.
revulsion *n.* repulsa.
reward *v.* recompensa. • *n.* recompensa, premio.
rewarding *adj.* sasiante.
rewash *v.* relava.
rewind *v.* rebobini.
rewire *v.* refili.
rework *v.* moderni, reconstrui.
rewrap *v.* reenvolve.
rewrite *v.* rescrive.
-rhage *suff.* (*medical*) -raje.
-rhagic *suff.* -rajica.
rhapsody *n.* rapsodia.
rhea1 *n.* (*bird*) rea.
-rhea2 *suff.* (*outflow*) -rea.
rhenium *n.* (*element*) renio.
rheologist *n.* reolojiste.
rheology *n.* reolojia.
rheostat *n.* reostato.
rhesus *adj.* (*medical*) resus.
rhesus macaque *n.* macaca resus.
rhesus monkey *n.* macaca resus.
rhetoric *n.* retorica.
rhetorical *adj.* retorical.
rhetorical question *n.* demanda autorespondente.
rhetorician *n.* retoriciste.
rheum *n.* muco acuin.
rheumatic *adj.* reumatica.
rheumatic disorder *n.* maladia reumatica.
rheumatic fever *n.* febre reumatica.
rheumatism *n.* maladia reumatica.
rheumato- *pref.* reumato-.
rheumatoid *adj.* reumatoide.
rheumatologist *n.* reumatolojiste.
rheumatology *n.* reumatolojia.
-rhexis *suff.* (*rupture*) -rexe.
rhinestone *n.* diamante falsa.
rhinitis *n.* rinite.
rhino1 *n.* rinosero.
rhino-2 *pref.* (*nose*) rino-.
rhinoceros *n.* rinosero.
rhinopharyngitis *n.* rinofarinjite.
rhinorrhoea *n.* (*medical*) rinorea.
rhizoid *adj.* & *n.* (*biology*) rizoide.
rhizome *n.* (*biology*) rizoma.
rho *n.* (*Greek letter* Ρ, ρ) ro.
Rhode Island *n.* (*US state*) Rhode Island.
rhodium *n.* (*element*) rodio.
rhododendron *n.* rododendro.
rhodopsin *n.* (*biology*) rodopsina.
rhomboid *adj.* rombo.
rhombozoa *n.* (*organisms*) rombozones.
rhombozoon *n.* (*organism*) rombozon.
rhombus *n.* rombo.
rhotic *adj.* & *n.* (*sound, dialect*) rotica.
rhubarb *n.* rubarbo.
rhyme *v.* & *n.* rima.
rhythm *n.* ritmo. **rhythm and blues** ritmo e blus.
rhythmic *adj.* ritmosa.
rhythmical *adj.* ritmosa.
rhythmics *n.* ritmo.
Riad *n.* Riad.
rial *n.* rial.
rib *n.* costela; (*fabric*) costelin. • *v.* (*tease*) burleta.
ribald *adj.* vulgar.
ribbed *adj.* costelin.
ribbit *interj.* (*frog*) cuac.
ribbon *n.* sinta.
riboflavin *n.* (*vitamin*) riboflavina.
ribonucleic *adj.* ribonucleal.
ribonucleic acid *n.* asida ribonucleal.
ribonucleotide *n.* ribonucleotido.
ribose *n.* (*sugar*) ribosa.
ribosomal *adj.* ribosomal.
ribosome *n.* (*biology*) ribosoma.
rice *n.* ris.
rice field *n.* campo de ris.
rice milk *n.* lete de ris.
rice porridge *n.* gaxa de ris.
rice pudding *n.* gaxa de ris.
ricer *n.* (*utensil*) estruador.
ricercar *n.* (*music*) rexercar.
rich *adj.* rica; lusosa. **newly rich** nova rica. **rich in iron** rica con fero.
riches *n.* ricia; tesoros, valuadas, valuosas.
rich neighbourhood (US **neighborhood**) *n.* visineria rica.
richness *n.* ricia.
rickets *n.* racite.
rickettsia *n.* (*bacterium*) ricetsia.
rickety *adj.* coxeante.
rickshaw *n.* ricxa.
ricochet *v.* rebondi.
ricotta *n.* (*cheese*) ricota.
rid *v.* libri. **get rid of** dejeta, desprende; (*abolish*) aboli.
riddle1 *n.* (*puzzle*) rompetesta.
riddle2 *v.* (*fill*) permea; (*with holes*) perfora. **riddled with** plen de. **riddled with errors** erosa.
ride *v.* (*horse, cycle*) monta. • *n.* turi. **give a ride to** dona pasaje a. **go for a ride** turi.
ridge *n.* cresta; (*fabric*) costelin.
ridgepole *n.* faxon de cresta.
ridicule *n.* burla.
ridiculous *adj.* asurda, riable, burlable.
ridiculousness *n.* asurdia.
rife *adj.* comun. **be rife with** es plen de.

riff *n.* (*music*) rif.
riffle *v.* xerca rapida.
riffraff *n.* manada.
rifle[1] *n.* (*gun*) fusil, fusil de xasa. **assault rifle** fusil de ataca.
rifle[2] *v.* (*search*) xerca rapida.
rifled *adj.* (*barrel of gun*) raiosa.
rifled bore *n.* cano raiosa.
rifleman *n.* fusilor.
rift *n.* falion.
rift valley *n.* vale de falion.
Riga *n.* Riga. **Gulf of Riga** Golfo Riga.
rigadoon *n.* (*dance*) rigodon.
rigatoni *n.* (*food*) rigatoni.
rigaudon *n.* (*dance*) rigodon.
rigging *n.* aparatos.
right *adj.* (*correct*) coreta; (*not left*) destra. • *n.* destra; (*entitlement*) direto, permete. • *interj.* bon, alora. **be right** razona bon. **by right** par lege. **have the right** ave la direto. **on the right of** a destra de. **right now** aora. **right to vote** direto de vota. **the right moment** la bon momento.
right-align *v.* alinia a destra.
right alignment *n.* alinia a destra.
right angle *n.* angulo reta.
right-angled *adj.* reta.
right ascension *n.* lonjitude de sielo.
right click *v.* & *n.* (*mouse*) clica destra.
righteous *adj.* virtuosa.
righteousness *n.* virtua, virtuosia.
right-handed *adj.* (*person*) de mano destra. • *adv.* (*done*) con mano destra.
right-hander *n.* manodestra.
rightism *n.* destrisme.
rightist *adj.* & *n.* destriste.
right-minded *adj.* bonpensante.
right stuff *n.* cualias nesesada.
right-wing *adj.* destriste.
right-winger *n.* destriste.
rigid *adj.* rijida.
rigid airship *n.* airostato rijida.
rigidity *n.* rijidia.
rigmarole *n.* prosede complicada.
rigor (US). See *rigour*.
rigorous *adj.* sever, atendente.
rigour (US **rigor**) *n.* severia.
rill *n.* rieta.
rim *n.* borda.
rime *n.* nebla jelada.
rimless *n.* sin borda.
rind *n.* (*fruit, cheese*) casca; (*cheese*) crosta.
ring[1] *n.* (*circle*) anelo; (*of people*) ronda. • *v.* aneli.
ring[2] *v.* (*bell*) sona; (*phone*) tintina; (*call by phone*) telefoni.
ring binder *n.* portapaper de anelos.
ring-bound *adj.* reliada con anelos.
ringed *adj.* anelosa.
ringer *n.* finjor, jemelin.
ring finger *n.* dito de anelo.
ringleader *n.* xef de gang.
ringlet *n.* risa.
ringmaster *n.* xef de sirco.
ringroad *n.* via periferial.
ring-shaped *adj.* anelo.
ringside *adj.* a lado de stadio.
ringtail *n.* coda anelida.
ringtoss *n.* jua de anelo.
ringworm *n.* tinea.
rinse *v.* & *n.* rinse.
Rio Grande *n.* Rio Grande.
riot *n.* tumulta.
riotous *adj.* tumultosa.
rip *v.* lasera.
riparian *adj.* (*of riverbanks*) rival.
ripcord *n.* corda de abri.
ripe *adj.* matur.
ripen *v.* maturi.
rip-off *n.* froda.
riposte *n.* replica.
ripple *v.* & *n.* ondeta.
riptide *n.* marea forte.
rise *v.* & *n.* alti, leva, asende. **pay rise** aumenta de salario. **rise again** releva. **rise up** revolta.
risible *adj.* asurda, comica, riable, burlable.
risk *v.* & *n.* risca. **at risk** perilida.
risky *adj.* riscosa.
risotto *n.* (*food*) risoto.
risqué *adj.* riscosa.
rissole *n.* (*food*) risole.
rite *n.* rituo.
ritual *adj.* ritual. • *n.* rituo.
ritualistic *adj.* ritual.
ritzy *adj.* lusosa.
rival *n.* competor, oposor. • *v.* egali.
rivalry *n.* compete.
river *n.* rio.
riverbank *n.* riva.
river bed *n.* fondo de rio.
river bottom *n.* fondo de rio.
River Danube *n.* Rio Danubio.
River Euphrates *n.* Rio Eufrates.
riverine *adj.* (*of rivers*) rial.
river island *n.* isoleta.
River Nile *n.* Rio Nilo.
river rat *n.* coipu.
River Rhine *n.* Rio Reno.
riverside *n.* fronte de rio.
rivet *n.* rebita. • *v.* rebiti.
riveter *n.* rebitor.
riveting *adj.* rebitante; (*interesting*) fasinante.
riviera *n.* riviera.
rivulet *n.* rieta.
Riyad *n.* Riad.
riyal *n.* (*currency*) rial.
RNA *abbr.* arn (*asida ribonucleal*).

roach *n.* cucaraxa.
road *n.* rua.
roadblock *n.* bloci de via.
roadhouse *n.* taverna.
roadie *n.* (*for touring band*) rodi.
roadrunner *n.* (*bird*) jeocucu.
roadside *n.* lado de via. • *adj.* a lado de via.
road sign *n.* avisa de via.
roadworks *n.* labora de via.
roadworthy *adj.* secur per gida.
roam *v.* vaga.
roan *adj.* & *n.* (*horse*) roan.
roar *v.* & *n.* ruji.
roast *v.* & *n.* rosta.
roaster *n.* rostador.
roasting pan *n.* casolon per rosta.
rob *v.* ruba, fura de.
robber *n.* rubor, furor.
robber fly *n.* asilido.
robbery *n.* ruba, fura.
robe *n.* roba.
robin *n.* (*European bird*) petirosa. **American robin** turdo roja.
robinia *n.* robinia.
robot *n.* robot.
robotic *adj.* (*of robots*) robotal; (*robotlike*) robotin.
robotics *n.* robotica.
robotization *n.* roboti.
robotize *v.* roboti.
robotlike *adj.* robotin.
robust *adj.* forte, durante.
roc *n.* (*mythological bird*) roc.
rock[1] *n.* (*substance, boulder*) roca.
rock[2] *v.* (*sway*) osila. • *adj.* & *n.* (*music*) roc. **rock 'n' roll** roc e rola.
rock dove *n.* pijon de rocas.
rocker *n.* seja osilante.
rockery *n.* roceria.
rocket[1] *n.* (*missile, engine*) roceto.
rocket[2] *n.* (*plant*) ruca.
rocket launcher *n.* lansaroceto.
rocketologist *n.* rocetolojiste.
rocketology *n.* rocetolojia.
rocket-propelled *adj.* lansada par roceto.
rocket science *n.* rocetolojia.
rocket scientist *n.* rocetolojiste.
rockfish *n.* pex de rocas.
rockfowl *n.* (*bird*) picatarte.
rocking chair *n.* seja osilante.
rocking horse *n.* cavalo osilante.
rock lobster *n.* langosta.
rock music *n.* musica roc.
rock pigeon *n.* pijon de rocas.
rock pool *n.* stangeta de mar.
rockrose *n.* (*plant*) sisto.
rock sparrow *n.* petronia.
rock star *n.* stela de roc.
rocky *adj.* rocosa.
Rocky Mountains *n.* Montes Rocosa.
rococo *adj.* rococo, ornosa. • *n.* rococo.
rod *n.* bara, basto, palo; (*fishing*) cana.
rodent *n.* rodente.
rodeo *n.* (*cattle, contest*) rodeo.
roe *n.* ovos de pex.
roebuck *n.* capriol mas.
roe deer *n.* capriol.
roentgen *n.* (*unit of radiation*) rontgen.
roentgenium *n.* (*element*) rontgenio.
rogue *n.* vil.
rogue state *n.* stato savaje, stato vil.
Rohingya *adj.* & *n.* (*person, language*) rohingia.
roil *v.* turba.
role *n.* rol. **take the role of** prende la rol de, fa la rol de.
roleplay *n.* jua de roles. • *v.* jua un rol.
roleplayer *n.* rolor.
roll *v.* rola. • *n.* (*action*) rola; (*something rolled up*) enrola. **roll back** reversa, restora. **roll call** clama de nomes. **roll over** rola.
rollaway *adj.* (*bed*) rolante.
rollback *n.* reversa, restora.
roller *n.* rolador.
roller coaster *n.* via ondante.
rollerskate *n.* patin de rotas.
rolling platform *n.* plataforma rolante.
roly-poly *n.* (*woodlouse*) onisco.
Rom[1] *adj.* & *n.* (*person, language*) romani.
ROM[2] *n.* (*memory*) rom.
Romagnol *adj.* & *n.* (*person, language*) romaniol.
romaine lettuce *n.* letuga roman.
rōmaji *n.* (*transcription*) romaji.
Roman *adj.* roman.
Roman alphabet *n.* alfabeta roman.
Roman Catholic *adj.* & *n.* catolica.
Roman Catholicism *n.* catolicisme.
romance[1] *n.* relata romantica; novela rosa; (*medieval*) romanse.
Romance[2] *adj.* & *n.* (*languages*) romanica.
romancer *n.* romansor.
romanesque *adj.* romanica.
Romania *n.* Romania.
Romanian *adj.* & *n.* romanian.
Romanic *adj.* & *n.* romanica.
Roman mile *n.* milia roman antica.
Romansch *adj.* (*language*) rumans.
Romansh *adj.* (*language*) rumans.
romantic *adj.* & *n.* romantica; (*novel*) rosa.
romanticism *n.* romanticisme.
Romany *adj.* & *n.* romani.
Rome *n.* Roma.
romeo *n.* romeo, xasafem.
romp *v.* jua enerjiosa. • *n.* comedia.
romper *n.* bodi de bebe.
rondeau *n.* (*poetry*) rondo.
roof *n.* teto.
roofer *n.* tetor.

roofless *n.* sin teto.
rooftop *n.* teto.
rook[1] *n.* (*bird*) gralia.
rook[2] *n.* (*chess*) tore.
rookery *n.* colonia.
rookie *n.* comensor.
room *n.* sala; (*space*) spasio. **room for one** sala per un. **room for two** sala per du.
roommate *n.* camerada de sala, coabitor.
room temperature *n.* temperatur de sala.
roomy *adj.* spasiosa.
roost *v.* (*birds*) reposa. • *n.* nido, reposeria.
rooster *n.* gal mas.
root *n.* radis. **at root** a radis. **take root** radisi.
root sign *n.* (*mathematics*) sinia de radis.
root vegetable *n.* radis vejetal.
rope *n.* corda; (*thick*) cordon.
rope walker *n.* paseacorda.
roquefort *n.* (*cheese*) rocefort.
roquet *n.* (*croquet*) roceta.
roquette *n.* ruca.
rorqual *n.* (*whale*) balenotera.
rosary *n.* (*prayer, beads*) rosaria.
rose *n.* rosa.
roseate *adj.* (*pink*) ros.
rosebud *n.* broto de rosa.
rosebush *n.* arboreta de rosa.
rosefinch *n.* roseta.
rosemary *n.* (*plant*) romaro.
roseola infantum *n.* (*baby measles*) roseola.
rosette *n.* (*botany, decorative ribbon*) roseta.
rosewater *n.* acua de rosa.
rosewood *n.* (*tree, wood*) palisandro.
roshi *n.* (*monk*) roxi.
rosid *n.* (*plant*) rosida.
rosin *n.* resina.
roster *n.* program de labora.
rostral *adj.* anterior.
rostrum *n.* plataforma.
rosy *adj.* rosin.
rot *v.* & *n.* putri.
rota *n.* program de labora.
rotary *adj.* jirante.
rotate *v.* jira.
rotavator *n.* cultivador.
rote, by *n.* de memoria.
rotifer *n.* (*organism*) rotifero.
rotisserie *n.* (*restaurant*) rosteria; (*appliance*) rostador jirante.
rotor *n.* rotor.
rototiller *n.* cultivador.
rotten *adj.* putrida, descomposada.
rotund *adj.* ronda.
rotunda *n.* (*building, room*) rotunda.
rouble *n.* (*currency*) rublo.
roué *n.* rue, xasafem.
rouge *n.* crema rojinte; polvo rojinte.
rough *adj.* (*not smooth*) ru; (*sea*) turbosa; (*marble, estimate*) bruta; (*approximate*) aprosima. • *n.* (*golf*) bosceta. **diamond in the rough** diamante bruta.
roughage *n.* fibre, comeda fibrosa.
rough draft *n.* testo ru.
rough estimate *n.* estima bruta.
roughhouse *v.* condui ruidosa e enerjiosa.
roughly *adv.* aprosima.
roughneck *n.* turbosa, violente.
roughness *n.* ruia.
roulade *n.* (*food*) rolada.
roulette *n.* (*game*) roleta.
round *adj.* ronda. • *v.* rondi. • *n.* (*music, drinks, contest*) ronda. • *prep.* sirca. **round the clock** a 24 oras de la dia.
roundabout *adj.* nondireta. • *n.* (*merry-go-round*) carusel; (*traffic*) sirculo de trafica.
round bracket *n.* braseta curva.
rounded vowel *n.* vocal ronda.
roundel *n.* disco; medalion ronda.
roundhouse *n.* (*for locomotive maintenance*) rotunda.
roundish *adj.* sferin.
round neck *n.* colar ronda.
roundness *n.* rondia.
round table *n.* (*including discussion*) table ronda.
round-trip ticket *n.* bileta de vade e reveni.
roundup *n.* recolie.
roundworm *n.* verme ronda, nematodo.
rouse *v.* velia.
roust *v.* velia.
roustabout *n.* laboror noninstruida.
rout *v.* fuji.
route *n.* via.
router[1] *n.* (*carpentry tool*) moldurador.
router[2] *n.* (*computer*) dirijador.
routine *n.* costum.
roux *n.* (*food*) ru.
rove *v.* vaga.
rover *n.* (*vehicle*) vagador.
row[1] *n.* (*line*) linia; (*data*) article. **in a row** en serie.
row[2] *v.* (*boat*) remi.
row[3] *v.* & *n.* (*argue*) disputa.
rowan *n.* (*tree*) sorbo.
rowboat *n.* barco de remos.
rowdy *adj.* turbosa.
rower *n.* remor.
rowing boat *n.* barco de remos.
rowlock *n.* (*for oar*) scalmo.
royal *adj.* & *n.* real.
royal family *n.* familia real.
royalism *n.* monarcisme.
royalist *adj.* monarciste.
royalty *n.* familia real. **royalties** diretos de autor.

rub *v.* frota. **rub against** frica. **rub out** cansela.
Rub al Khali *n.* (*desert*) Cuatri Vacua.
rubber *n.* cauxo.
rubber band *n.* banda elastica.
rubber boot *n.* bota de cauxo.
rubberization *n.* cauxi.
rubberize *v.* cauxi.
rubberneck *v.* torse sua colo; fisa con regarda.
rubbish *n.* dejetada. • *adj.* dejetable. • *interj.* asurda, ba.
rubbish bin *n.* baldon.
rubbish heap *n.* dejeteria, monton de dejetadas.
rubble *n.* detrito.
rubdown *n.* frica; (*dry transfer*) decal.
rube *n.* campanian.
rubella *n.* rubeola.
rubenesque *adj.* curvosa, formosa.
rubia *n.* (*plant, pigment*) rubia.
rubidium *n.* (*element*) rubidio.
ruble *n.* rublo.
rubric *n.* titulo.
ruby *n.* (*gem*) rubi.
ruche *n.* fronsida.
rucksack *n.* bolson.
ruckus *n.* disturba.
rudder *n.* timon.
rudderless *adj.* sin timon.
rude *adj.* noncortes.
rudeness *n.* noncortesia.
rudiment *n.* funda.
rudimentary *adj.* fundal; simple.
rue *v.* regrete.
rueful *adj.* regretosa.
ruff *n.* colar fronsosa.
ruffian *n.* bruta.
ruffle *n.* fronsida.
ruffled *adj.* fronsosa.
rufous *adj.* rojin brun.
rug *n.* tapeto.
rugby *n.* (*sport*) rugbi.
rugged *adj.* ru.
ruggedness *n.* ruia.
rugous *n.* brun rojin.
ruin *v.* & *n.* ruina. **ruins** (*wreckage*) ruinas.
ruinous *adj.* destruinte; (*ruined*) ruinada.
rule *v.* rena, governa. • *n.* (*to be followed*) regula; (*reign*) rena, governa. **as a rule** jeneral. **rule of thumb** regula jeneral.
ruler *n.* (*person*) renor; (*tool*) regla.
ruling *n.* judi.
rum *n.* (*drink*) rum.
rumba *n.* (*dance, music*) rumba.
rumble *v.* & *n.* ronci.
rumble strip *n.* (*on road*) banda ru.
ruminant *adj.* remasticante.
ruminate *v.* remastica.
rummage *v.* foraje.
rummy *n.* (*card game*) rami.
rumour (US **rumor**) *n.* rumor. **it is rumoured that** on dise ce.
rumourmonger (US **rumormonger**) *n.* rumoror.
rump *n.* (*rear*) culo; (*hip*) anca.
rumple *v.* desordina.
rumpus *n.* ruido, disturba.
rumrunner *n.* contrabandor.
run *v.* core; (*organization*) dirije, maneja; (*software*) esecuta. • *n.* (*including cricket*) core; (*sequence*) segue; (*for animals*) ensirca. **run aground** encalia. **run amok** furia. **run away** fuji. **run down** dejenera. **run over** (*crush*) crase. **run the gauntlet** core tra bates. **run through** (*pierce*) perfora.
runaway *n.* fujor. • *adj.* noncontrolable.
rundown *adj.* gastada.
rune *n.* (*letter*) runa.
rung *n.* gradeta.
runic *adj.* runal.
runner *n.* coror.
runner-up *n.* sucampion.
running *n.* (*sport*) core. • *adj.* en serie. **endurance running** core de distantia longa.
running shoe *n.* sapato de sporte.
runny *adj.* acuin.
runny nose *n.* rinorea.
run-off *n.* (*water*) supraflue; (*competition*) desidente.
run-of-the-mill *adj.* mediocre.
runt *n.* peti, debil.
runway *n.* atereria.
rupee *n.* (*currency*) rupi.
rupture *n.* rompe; ernia.
rural *adj.* campanial, pastoral.
rural area *n.* campania.
rural person *n.* campanian.
ruse *n.* rus.
rush[1] *v.* & *n.* (*hurry*) freta.
rush[2] *n.* (*plant*) junco.
rush hour *n.* ora de presa.
rusk *n.* biscoto seca.
Russia *n.* Rusia.
Russian *adj.* & *n.* (*person, language*) rusce.
Russian thistle *n.* (*plant*) salsola.
rust *v.* & *n.* osidi.
rustic *adj.* campanial.
rustle *v.* & *n.* (*sound*) xuxa.
rustler *n.* furor de bestias.
rustproof *adj.* noncorodente, nonosidinte, secur contra osidi.
rusty *adj.* osidinte.
rut[1] *n.* (*wheel track*) foseta.
rut[2] *v.* (*deer*) compete corteal. • *n.* compete corteal; periodo corteal.
rutabaga *n.* (*plant, vegetable*) colinabo.

ruthenium *n.* (*element*) rutenio.
rutherfordium *n.* (*element*) ruterfordio.
ruthless *adj.* cruel.
ruthlessness *n.* cruelia.
RV *n.* (*recreational vehicle*) autocaravan.
Rwanda *n.* Ruanda.
Rwandan *adj.* & *n.* ruanda.
rye *n.* (*plant*) segal.
ryegrass *n.* lolio.

S

sabbath *n.* dia santa.
sabbatical *adj.* & *n.* sabatica.
saber... (US). See *sabre...*
sable *n.* (*animal*) zibelina.
sabot *n.* (*shoe*) zoco.
sabotage *v.* & *n.* sabota.
saboteur *n.* sabotor.
sabre (US **saber**) *n.* sabre.
sabre rattling (US **saber rattling**) *n.* clica de sabres.
sabre saw (US **saber saw**) *n.* siera alternante.
sabretooth (US **sabertooth**) *n.* smilodon.
sabretoothed cat (US **sabertoothed cat**) *n.* smilodon.
sabretoothed tiger (US **sabertoothed tiger**) *n.* smilodon.
sac *n.* saco. **air sac** alveolo.
saccharine *adj.* zucarosa.
sacerdotal *adj.* pretal.
sachem *n.* (*leader*) xef.
sachet *n.* saceta.
sack *n.* (*bag*) saco. • *v.* (*employee*) desemplea; (*destroy*) saca.
sackbut *n.* (*musical instrument*) sacabuta.
sackcloth *n.* juta.
sacklike *adj.* sacin.
sacral *adj.* santa; (*of the sacrum*) sacral.
sacrament *n.* rituo santa.
sacred *adj.* santa.
sacred fig *n.* pipal.
sacrifice *v.* & *n.* sacrifia.
sacrificial lamb *n.* portapeca.
sacrilege *n.* blasfema.
sacrilegious *adj.* blasfemal.
sacristy *n.* sala de prete.
sacroiliac *adj.* sacroilial.
sacroilium *n.* (*anatomy*) sacroilio.
sacrosanct *adj.* santida, nonviolable.
sacrum *n.* (*anatomy*) sacro.
sad *adj.* triste.
sadden *v.* tristi.
saddle *n.* sela. • *v.* ensela.
saddlebag *n.* saco de sela.
saddler *n.* selor.
saddlery *n.* (*place*) seleria.
sadism *n.* sadisme.
sadist *n.* sadiste.
sadistic *adj.* sadiste.
sadness *n.* tristia.
sadomasochism *n.* sadomasocisme.
sadomasochistic *adj.* sadomasociste.
safari *n.* safari.
safe *adj.* secur. • *n.* caxa secur. **make safe** securi.
safecracker *n.* furor de caxas secur.
safeguard *v.* securi.
safekeeping *n.* securia.
safe room *n.* secureria.
safety *n.* securia; (*gun*) securador.
safety belt *n.* sintur de securia.
safety cushion *n.* cuxin de securia.
safety pin *n.* spino secur.
safety valve *n.* valva de securia.
safflower *n.* cartamo.
saffron *n.* (*plant*, *spice*) zafran.
sag *v.* pende.
saga *n.* (*story*) saga.
sagacious *adj.* saja.
sagacity *n.* sajia.
sage[1] *adj.* & *n.* (*wise*) saja.
sage[2] *n.* (*plant*) salvia.
sagebrush *n.* (*plant*) artemisia.
saggy *adj.* pendente.
Sagitta *n.* (*constellation*) la Flexa.
sagittal *adj.* sajital.
sagittal crest *n.* cresta sajital.
sagittal plane *n.* plana sajital.
sagittal suture *n.* sutur sajital.
Sagittarius *n.* (*constellation*) la Arcor.
saguaro *n.* (*cactus*) saguaro.
Sahara *n.* Sahara.
Saharan *adj.* saharan.
Sahel *n.* (*African region*) Sahel.
sahur *n.* (*Islam*) suhur.
sail *n.* vela. • *v.* naviga par vela. **go sailing** naviga par vela.
sailboard *n.* plance de vela.
sailboarding *n.* surfa de vela.
sailboat *n.* barco de vela.
sailcloth *n.* lona.
sailfish *n.* pex de vela.
sailing *n.* naviga par vela.
sailing ship *n.* barcon de vela.
sail-like *adj.* velin.
sailor *n.* maror; (*navy*) marinor.
saint *n.* santa; (*title*) San. **All Saints' Eve** vijila de tota santas.
Saint Bernard *n.* (*dog*) sanbernardo.
sainthood *n.* santia.
Saint Kitts and Nevis *n.* San Kitts e Nevis.
Saint Lawrence River *n.* Rio San Laurent. **Gulf of Saint Lawrence** Golfo San Laurent.
Saint Lucia *n.* San Lusia.
Saint Lucian *adj.* & *n.* sanlusian.
Saint Nicholas *n.* San Nicolas.
Saint Vincent and the Grenadines *n.* San Vinsent e la Grenadines.

sake[1] *n.* benefica, interesa. **for its own sake** per sua propre interesa.
sake[2] *n.* (*drink*) sace.
saki monkey *n.* saci.
salacious *adj.* lasiva.
salad *n.* salada.
salad bowl *n.* bol de salada.
salad dressing *n.* salsa de salada.
salamander *n.* salamandra.
salami *n.* (*food*) salami.
salaried *adj.* con salario.
salary *n.* salario.
sale *n.* vende. **for sale** per vende.
saleable *adj.* vendable.
sales clerk *n.* vendor.
sales counter *n.* table de vende.
salesman *n.* vendor.
salesmanship *n.* vendoria.
salesperson *n.* vendor.
sales tax *n.* imposta de vende.
saleswoman *n.* vendor.
salience *n.* importa.
salient *adj.* importante, fasil persepable, fasil vidable.
salinate *v.* sali.
salination *n.* sali.
saline *adj.* salin.
salinity *n.* salosia.
Salish Sea *n.* Mar Salix.
saliva *n.* saliva.
salivary gland *n.* glande salival.
salivate *v.* salivi.
salivation *n.* salivi.
sallow *adj.* jalin.
sally *v.* ataca sortinte.
salmagundi *n.* (*food*) plato miscada.
salmon *adj.* (*colour*) salmon. • *n.* (*fish*) salmon.
salmonella *n.* salmonela; (*poisoning*) salmonelose.
saloon *n.* bar, taverna.
salopettes *n.* salopeta; pantalon de stribos.
salsa *n.* salsa.
salsola *n.* (*plant*) salsola.
salt *n.* sal. • *v.* sali.
saltbox *n.* vaso de sal.
salt cellar *n.* vaso de sal.
salted meat *n.* carne salosa.
saltine *n.* cracer.
saltpetre (US **saltpeter**) *n.* nitrato de potasio.
salt shaker *n.* secutesal.
saltwater *n.* acua salosa. • *adj.* de acua salosa.
salty *adj.* salosa, marin.
salubrious *adj.* sana.
salubriousness *n.* sania.
salutary *adj.* beneficante.
salutation *n.* saluta.
salute *v.* & *n.* saluta militar.
Salvadoran *adj.* & *n.* salvadoran.
salvage *n.* salva.
salvageable *adj.* salvable.
salvation *n.* salva.
salvia *n.* (*plant*) salvia.
salvo *n.* bombarda; saluta de fusiles.
samara *n.* (*botany*) samara, asera.
samaritan *n.* aidosa.
samarium *n.* (*element*) samario.
samba *n.* (*dance, music*) samba.
same *adj.* mesma.
samhain *n.* (*Celtic festival*) sauain.
Sami *n.* sami.
Sammarinese *adj.* & *n.* samarines.
Samoa *n.* Samoa.
Samoan *adj.* & *n.* samoan.
samovar *n.* (*urn*) samovar.
Samoyed *adj.* & *n.* enets.
Samoyedic *adj.* & *n.* (*person, language*) enets.
sampan *n.* (*boat*) sampan.
samphire *n.* finoio de mar.
sample *n.* esemplo; mostra; (*analysis, music*) sample.
sampler *n.* (*music*) samplador.
samsara *n.* (*Buddhism, Hinduism*) samsara.
samurai *n.* samurai.
San *adj.* & *n.* (*person, language*) san.
Sana'a *n.* Sana.
sanatorium *n.* ospitaleta.
sanctification *n.* santi.
sanctify *v.* santi.
sanctimonious *adj.* moraliste.
sanction *n.* puni.
sanctity *n.* santia.
sanctuary *n.* (*state*) refuja; (*place*) refujeria.
sand *n.* arena. • *v.* (*wood*) lisi.
sandal *n.* sandal.
sandalwood *n.* sandalo.
sandbag *n.* saco de arena.
sandbank *n.* banco de arena, parador de arena.
sandbar *n.* parador de arena.
sandblast *v.* areni.
sandbox *n.* caxa de arena.
sand-covered *adj.* arenosa.
sander *n.* lisador.
sandman *n.* arenor.
sandpaper *n.* paper raspante.
sandpiper *n.* (*bird*) calidris, tringa.
sandpit *n.* caxa de arena.
sandshoe *n.* sapato de sporte.
sandstone *n.* arenito.
sandstorm *n.* tempesta de arena.
sand trap *n.* (*golf*) trapa de arena.
sandwich *n.* sanduitx.
sandy *adj.* (*sandlike*) arenin; (*covered in sand*) arenosa.
sane *adj.* mental sana.
sangfroid *n.* (*calm*) sanguefria.

sangha *n.* (*Buddhism*) sanga.
sangoma *n.* (*healer*) xaman.
sangria *n.* (*drink*) sangria.
sanguine *adj.* bonumorosa, de bon umor; otimiste.
sanitary *adj.* ijenial.
sanitary napkin *n.* teleta de fem.
sanitary towel *n.* teleta de fem.
sanitation *n.* ijenia.
sanitation worker *n.* dejetor.
sanitize *v.* ijeni.
sanitizer *n.* ijeninte.
sanitorium *n.* ospitaleta.
sanity *n.* sania mental.
San Jorge Gulf *n.* Golfo San Jorge.
San Marino *n.* San Marino.
San Matías Gulf *n.* Golfo San Matias.
sansa *n.* (*musical instrument*) calimba.
Sanskrit *adj.* & *n.* sanscrito.
sans serif *adj.* sin serif.
Santa Claus *n.* San Nicolas.
Santomean *adj.* & *n.* santomense.
São Toméan *n.* santomense. • *adj.* santomense.
São Tomé and Príncipe *n.* San Tome e Prinsipe.
sap *n.* (*of plant*) sava.
sapient *adj.* razonante.
sapling *n.* arbor joven.
sapodilla *n.* (*tree*) sapota.
sapphic *adj.* lesbian.
sapphire *n.* (*gem*) safir.
sappy *adj.* zucarosa.
saprophagous *adj.* saprofaje.
saprophagy *n.* (*biology*) saprofajia.
saprophyte *n.* saprofaje.
sapsucker *n.* (*bird*) sucasava.
sapwood *n.* lenio esterna.
saraband *n.* (*dance, music*) sarabanda.
Saran wrap *n.* peleta aderente.
sarcasm *n.* sarcasmo.
sarcastic *adj.* sarcasmosa.
sarco- *pref.* (*flesh*) sarco-.
sarcoidosis *n.* (*medical*) sarcoidose.
sarcoma *n.* (*tumour*) sarcoma. • *suff.* -sarcoma.
sarcopenia *n.* (*medical*) sarcopenia.
sarcophagus *n.* sarcofago.
Sard *adj.* & *n.* sarda.
sardine *n.* sardina.
Sardinia *n.* Sardinia.
Sardinian *adj.* & *n.* (*person, language*) sarda.
Sardinian Sea *n.* Mar Sarda.
sardonic *adj.* sarcasmosa.
Sargasso Sea *n.* Mar Sargasso.
sari *n.* (*garment*) sari.
sarin *n.* (*gas*) sarin.
Sarnian *adj.* & *n.* (*person*) gernsies.
sarong *n.* (*garment*) sarong.
sarsaparilla *n.* (*plant*) smilax.
sartorial *adj.* modal.
sash *n.* sintur; xarpe ofisial.
sashay *v.* pasea ostentosa.
sashimi *n.* (*food*) saximi.
Saskatchewan *n.* (*Canadian province*) Saskatchewan.
sass *n.* noncortesia.
sassafras *n.* (*tree*) sasafras.
Sassanian *adj.* (*dynasty*) sasanan.
Sassanid *adj.* sasanan.
Sassarese *adj.* & *n.* (*person, language*) sasares.
sassy *adj.* noncortes.
Satan *n.* Satan, diablo.
satanic *adj.* (*of Satan*) satanal; (*like Satan*) satanin.
Satanism *n.* satanisme.
Satanist *n.* sataniste.
satay *n.* (*food*) satai.
satchel *n.* bolson de spala.
sate *v.* sasia.
sateen *n.* (*fabric*) satinin.
satellite *n.* satelite.
satellite navigation *n.* orienta par satelite.
sati *n.* sati.
satiate *v.* sasia.
satiation *n.* sasia.
satiety *n.* plenia.
satin *n.* satin.
satiny *adj.* satinin.
satire *n.* satira.
satiric *adj.* satira.
satirical *adj.* satira.
satirist *n.* satiriste.
satirize *v.* satiri.
satisfaction *n.* sasia.
satisfactory *adj.* sasiante.
satisfied *adj.* sasiada, contente.
satisfy *v.* sasia.
satnav *n.* orienta par satelite.
satori *n.* (*Buddhism*) satori.
satrap *n.* (*governor*) satrap.
satrapy *n.* satrapia.
saturate *v.* satura.
saturation *n.* satura.
Saturday *n.* saturdi.
Saturn *n.* (*mythology, planet*) Saturno.
saturn hat *n.* xapo saturnin.
saturnine *adj.* sombre.
satyr *n.* (*mythology*) satir.
satyriasis *n.* (*medical*) satiriase.
sauce *n.* salsa. **apple sauce** salsa de poma, pure de poma.
saucepan *n.* casoleta.
saucepan lid *n.* covrecasola.
sauce pot *n.* casoleta.
saucer *n.* plateta.
saucy *adj.* flirtante.
Saudi *adj.* & *n.* saudi.

Saudi Arabia *n.* Arabia Saudi.
Saudi Arabian *adj.* & *n.* saudi.
sauerbraten *n.* (*food*) sauerbraten.
sauerkraut *n.* (*food*) xucrute.
sauna *n.* sauna.
saunter *v.* pasea lenta.
sausage *n.* salsix.
sauté *v.* & *n.* (*cookery*) sote.
sauté pan *n.* padela de sote.
sauterne *n.* (*wine*) sauternes.
savage *adj.* savaje, nonsivilida.
savagery *n.* savajia.
savanna *n.* savana.
savant *n.* erudita.
save *v.* salva; (*money*) salva, reserva, garda; (*data*) fisa. **save face** salva la onora. **save time** gania la tempo. **save up** salva.
savings *n.* reserva.
saviour (US **savior**) *n.* salvor.
Savoie *n.* (*French region*) Savoie.
Savoisien *adj.* savoian.
savour (US **savor**) *v.* saborea.
savoury (US **savory**) *adj.* saborosa.
Savoyen *adj.* savoian.
Savu *n.* (*island*) Savu.
Savu Sea *n.* Mar Savu.
savvy *adj.* astuta. • *n.* astutia.
saw *n.* (*tool*) siera. • *v.* sieri.
sawbuck *n.* cavaleta.
sawdust *n.* polvo de siera.
sawfish *n.* pex de siera.
sawfly *n.* simfito.
sawhorse *n.* cavaleta.
sawmill *n.* siereria.
sawtooth *adj.* sierin.
sawyer *n.* sieror.
sax *n.* sasofon.
saxifrage *n.* saxifraje.
Saxon *adj.* & *n.* sason.
Saxony *n.* (*German region*) Sason.
saxophone *n.* sasofon.
saxophonist *n.* sasofoniste.
say *v.* dise. **say again** redise. **say nothing** silenti. **they say** (*it is rumoured*) on dise.
saying *n.* diseda.
scab *n.* crosta.
scabbard *n.* portaspada.
scaffold *n.* (*scaffolding*) scafal; (*gallows*) ponteta.
scaffolding *n.* ponteta, scafal.
scalar *adj.* scalal.
scald *v.* scalda.
scale[1] *n.* (*values, music*) scala.
scale[2] *n.* scama. **scale back** redui. **scale down** redui. **scale up** grandi.
scale insect *n.* coxinilia.
scale-like *adj.* scamin.
scale model *n.* model proportial.
scalene *adj.* (*triangle*) scalena.
scales *n.* (*for weighing*) balansa, pesador.
scallion *n.* (*onion*) sibola.
scallop *n.* peten.
scalp *n.* scalpo. • *v.* descalpi.
scalpel *n.* bisturi.
scaly *adj.* scamosa.
scam *n.* froda.
scamp *n.* turbosa.
scamper *v.* freta.
scampi *n.* omareta.
scan *v.* (*with eyes or machine*) scane; (*poetry*) scande.
scandal *n.* scandal.
scandalize *v.* scandali.
scandalous *adj.* scandalosa.
Scandinavia *n.* Scandinavia.
Scandinavian *adj.* & *n.* scandinavian.
scandium *n.* (*element*) scandio.
scanner *n.* scanador.
scansion *n.* scande.
scant *adj.* mancante, nonsufisinte.
scanty *adj.* nonsufisinte; revelante.
scapegoat *n.* portaculpa, portapeca.
scapula *n.* scapula, oso de spala.
scar *n.* sicatris. • *v.* sicatrisi.
scarab *n.* scarabe, scarabe santa.
scarce *adj.* rara, mancante.
scarcely *adv.* apena.
scarcity *n.* manca, nonsufisi.
scare *v.* & *n.* asusta, panica.
scarecrow *n.* asustavia.
scaremonger *n.* sperdeteme.
scarf *n.* xarpe.
scarify *v.* sicatrisi.
scarlatina *n.* scarlatina.
scarlet *adj.* & *n.* scarlata.
scarlet fever *n.* scarlatina.
scarlet pimpernel *n.* pimpinela scarlata.
scary *adj.* asustante.
scat *adj.* (*music*) scat.
scatological *adj.* escretemanica.
scatology *n.* escretemania.
scatter *v.* sperde.
scatterbrain *adj.* desorganizada.
scatty *adj.* desorganizada.
scavenge *v.* foraje.
scavenger *n.* forajor.
scenario *n.* caso; (*script*) senario.
scenarist *n.* senariste.
scene *n.* sena.
scenery *n.* vista; (*theatrical*) decora.
scenic *adj.* con vista bela.
scent *n.* odor.
scepter (US). See *sceptre.*
sceptic *n.* setica.
sceptical *adj.* setica, dutante.
scepticism *n.* seticisme.
sceptre (US **scepter**) *n.* setro.
Schadenfreude *n.* plaser odiosa.

schedule *n.* program. • *v.* ajendi.
scheduled *adj.* ajendida; (*flight*) scemida.
schema *n.* scema.
schematic *adj.* scemal.
schematic drawing *n.* scema.
scheme *n.* scema; conspira. • *v.* scemi; conspira.
scheme-based *adj.* scemal.
schemer *n.* scemor, conspiror. **fellow schemer** coconspiror.
schilling *n.* (*currency*) xiling.
-schisis *suff.* (*splitting*) -scise.
schism *n.* fende.
schist *n.* (*geology*) xiste.
schizo- *pref.* (*split*) scizo-.
schizoid *adj.* scizoide.
schizophrenia *n.* scizofrenia.
schizophrenic *adj.* & *n.* scizofrenica.
schizotypal *adj.* scizotipal.
schmooze *n.* parleta.
schmuck *n.* (*insult*) culo, pixeta.
schnapps *n.* (*drink*) snaps.
scholar *n.* erudita.
scholarliness *n.* eruditia.
scholarly *adj.* erudita.
scholarship *n.* (*quality*) eruditia; (*grant*) donada per studia.
scholastic *adj.* scolal.
scholasticism *n.* scolastica.
school[1] *n.* (*place, art, thought*) scola. • *adj.* scolal. • *v.* educa. **high school** liseo. **school of thought** scola de opina.
school[2] *n.* (*fish*) manada.
school age *n.* eda scolal.
schoolbag *n.* bolson de scola.
schoolbook *n.* libro de scola.
schoolboy *n.* scolor mas.
schoolchild *n.* scolor.
school desk *n.* scriveria.
schoolgirl *n.* scolor fema.
schoolhouse *n.* scola.
school leaver *n.* graduante de scola.
schoolmaster *n.* ensenior.
schoolmate *n.* camerada de scola.
schoolmistress *n.* ensenior.
schoolroom *n.* sala de clase.
schoolteacher *n.* ensenior.
schoolwork *n.* taxes de scola.
schoolyard *n.* campo de scola.
schooner *n.* (*ship*) goleta.
schtick *n.* truco, spesiali.
schwa *n.* (*vowel and letter* Ə, ə) xva.
sciatic *adj.* (*anatomy*) siatica.
sciatica *n.* neuraljia siatica.
sciatic nerve *n.* nervo siatica.
sciatic neuralgia *n.* neuraljia siatica.
science *n.* siensa.
science fiction *n.* naras siensal.
scientific *adj.* siensal.
scientist *n.* siensiste.
scientologist *n.* sientolojiste.
scientology *n.* (*religion*) sientolojia.
scimitar *n.* (*sword*) simitar, spada curva.
scintilla *n.* sintil.
scintillate *v.* sintili.
scintillation *n.* sintili.
scion *n.* desendente, critor.
scissor *n.* sisor. **scissors** sisor.
sclera *n.* (*anatomy*) sclera.
sclero- *pref.* (*hard*) sclero-.
scleroderma *n.* (*medical*) scleroderma.
sclerosis *n.* (*medical*) sclerose. • *suff.* -sclerose.
sclerotic *adj.* sclerosica. • *suff.* -sclerosica.
scoff[1] *v.* (*mock*) burla.
scoff[2] *v.* (*devour*) devora, engoli.
scoffer *n.* burlor.
scofflaw *n.* inioror de lege.
scold *v.* reproxa.
scoliosis *n.* (*medical*) scoliose.
scoliotic *adj.* scoliosica.
sconce *n.* portacandela.
scone *n.* (*food*) scon.
scoop *n.* culier. • *v.* copi; escava.
scooter *n.* (*child's*) patineta; (*motorcycle*) scuter.
scope[1] *n.* estende, limitas.
-scope[2] *suff.* (*observation instrument*) -scopio.
-scopy *suff.* (*observation*) -scopia.
scorch *v.* negri.
score *n.* (*points*) puntos; (*music*) partitur. • *v.* ateni, fa; partituri. **score a goal** fa un gol. **score a hole in one** (*golf*) ateni la buco con un colpa.
scoreboard *n.* carta de puntos.
scorecard *n.* carta de puntos.
scorekeeper *n.* rejistror de puntos.
scoria *n.* scoria.
scorn *v.* & *n.* despeta.
scornful *adj.* despetosa.
Scorpio *n.* (*constellation*) la Scorpion.
scorpion *n.* scorpion.
scorpion fly *n.* mecotero.
Scorpius *n.* Scorpion.
Scot *n.* (*person*) scotes.
Scotch tape *n.* sinta aderente.
Scotia *n.* Scotia.
Scotia Sea *n.* Mar Scotia.
Scotland *n.* Scotland.
scotoma *n.* (*medical*) scotoma.
Scots *adj.* scotes.
Scots Gaelic *adj.* & *n.* gailica.
Scottish *adj.* scotes.
Scottish Gaelic *adj.* & *n.* gailica.
scoundrel *n.* vil.
scour *v.* frica.
scourge *v.* tormenta.
scout *n.* (*soldier*) esploror; (*scout movement*) scolta.
scout car *n.* auto esplorante.

scouting *n.* scoltisme.
scout movement *n.* scoltisme.
scowl *v.* grima, fronsi sua suprasiles. • *n.* grima.
scrabble *v.* rasca; (*game*) scrabel. **scrabble at** gari.
scraggly *adj.* ososa.
scram *v.* fuji.
scramble *v.* (*clamber*) trepa; (*mix*) misca, confusa.
scrambled eggs *n.* ovos bateda.
scrambler *n.* confusador.
scrap *v.* aboli. • *n.* peso; metal resiclable. **scrap of paper** papereta.
scrapbook *n.* album.
scrape *v.* raspa.
scraper *n.* raspador.
scrap metal *n.* metal resiclable.
scrappy *adj.* disputosa.
scrapyard *n.* resicleria.
scratch *v.* & *n.* rasca; (*music*) scratxa.
scratchcard *n.* (*instant lottery*) bileta de rasca, bileta de rasca e gania.
scratchpad *n.* bloco de notas.
scratch-resistant *adj.* antirascal.
scrawl *v.* malscrive, scriveta.
scrawny *adj.* ososa.
scream *v.* & *n.* cria, xilia.
screamer *n.* (*bird*) crior.
scree *n.* calculos nonfisada.
screech *v.* & *n.* xilia.
screen *v.* (*conceal*) asconde; (*check*) proba. • *n.* (*partition*, *video panel*) scermo; (*partition*) paravide, (*mesh*) rede.
screen door *n.* porte de rede.
screenplay *n.* senario.
screensaver *n.* salvascermo.
screen window *n.* fenetra de rede.
screenwriter *n.* senariste.
screw *n.* (*fastener*) vise. • *v.* visi; (*sex*) fode. **screw up** malfa.
screwdriver *n.* turnavise.
screwy *adj.* strana.
scribble *v.* & *n.* malscrive, scriveta.
scribbler *n.* scrivetor.
scribe *n.* scriviste.
scrimmage *v.* & *n.* scaramuxa.
scrimp *v.* reserva, es frugal.
scrimshaw *v.* (*engrave*) scrimxa.
script *n.* (*drama*) senario; (*software*) programeta; (*writing system*) sistem de scrive.
scriptures *n.* scrivedas santa.
scriptwriter *n.* senariste.
scrivener *n.* scriviste, notario, caxor.
scroll *n.* libro enrolada; enrola de pergamin. • *v.* (*software*) rola.
scrollbar *n.* bara de rola.
scroll saw *n.* siera alternante.
scroll wheel *n.* (*mouse*) rota de rola.
scrollwork *n.* motif spiral.
scrooge *n.* avar.
scrotal *adj.* scrotal.
scrotum *n.* (*anatomy*) scroto.
scrounge *v.* mendica.
scrub *v.* frota. • *n.* subosce.
scrub-bird *n.* atricorno.
scrubland *n.* bosce de arboretas.
scrubwoman *n.* limpor.
scruff *n.* nuca.
scruffy *adj.* desordinada.
scrum *n.* foleta.
scrumptious *adj.* deletosa.
scrunch *v.* craci.
scrunchie *n.* portacoda.
scruples *n.* dutas, esita moral.
scrutinize *v.* esamina.
scrutiny *n.* esamina.
scuba *n.* autorespirador.
scuff *v.* raspa.
scuffle *v.* & *n.* scaramuxa.
sculpt *v.* sculta.
sculptor *n.* scultor; (*constellation*) la Scultor.
sculpture *n.* sculta.
scum *n.* melma, spuma susia.
scummy *adj.* melmosa.
scurrilous *adj.* scandalinte.
scurry *v.* freta.
scurvy *n.* (*medical*) scorbuto.
scuttle *v.* afonda.
Scutum *n.* (*constellation*) la Scermo.
scythe *n.* falxe. • *v.* falxi.
sea *n.* mar. **at sea** a mar. **under the sea** su mar.
sea anemone *n.* anemone-de-mar.
seabed *n.* fondo de mar.
seabird *n.* avia de mar.
seaborgium *n.* (*element*) siborgio.
sea change *n.* cambion.
seacoast *n.* costa.
sea cow *n.* manati.
sea cruise *n.* turi a mar.
sea cucumber *n.* concombre-de-mar.
sea dragon *n.* serpente de mar.
sea eagle *n.* agila de mar.
sea elephant *n.* elefante-de-mar.
sea embankment *n.* paramar.
seafarer *n.* maror, viajor de mar.
sea floor *n.* fondo de mar.
sea foam *n.* spuma de mar.
seafood *n.* comeda de mar.
seafront *n.* fronte de mar.
seagoing *adj.* maral.
seagrass *n.* erba-de-mar.
seagull *n.* gavota.
seahorse *n.* cavalo-de-mar.
seal[1] *n.* (*tight closure*, *wax*, *etc.*) selo; (*stopper*) tapo. • *v.* seli; tapi.
seal[2] *n.* (*animal*) foca.

sealable *adj.* selable.
sealant *n.* selinte.
sea level *n.* nivel de mar.
sealike *adj.* marin.
sea lily *n.* lil-de-mar.
sea lion *n.* leon-de-mar.
seam *n.* costur.
seaman *n.* marinor.
seamlike *adj.* costurin.
seamster *n.* cosor.
seamstress *n.* cosor.
seance *n.* seanse. **hold a seance** fa un seanse.
seaplane *n.* avion de mar.
seaport *n.* porto.
sear *v.* arde, bruni.
search *n.* xerca. **search for** xerca.
search engine *n.* xercador.
searcher *n.* xercor.
searchlight *n.* projetador.
seascape *n.* vista de mar.
sea serpent *n.* serpente de mar.
seashell *n.* conca.
seashore *n.* costa, plaia.
seasick *adj.* malada de mar, nauseada de mar.
seasickness *n.* maladia de mar.
seaside *n.* borda de mar.
season *n.* saison. • *v.* spisi.
seasonable *adj.* saisonal.
seasonal *adj.* saisonal; (*worker*) migrante.
seasoning *n.* spise.
sea star *n.* stela-de-mar.
seat *n.* (*including in an elected body*) seja. • *v.* senta.
seated *adj.* sentante.
sea urchin *n.* eriso-de-mar.
seawall *n.* muron de mar.
seawater *n.* acua de mar.
seaweed *n.* alges.
seaworthy *adj.* secur per naviga.
sebaceous *adj.* sebosa.
sebaceous gland *n.* glande sebosa.
seborrhoea (US **seborrhea**) *n.* (*medical*) seborea.
sebum *n.* sebo.
secant *n.* (*mathematics, geometry*) secante.
secede *v.* separa.
secession *n.* separa.
seclusion *n.* privatia.
seconal *n.* (*drug*) secobarbital.
second[1] *adj.* (*ordinal*) du. **second from last** anteultima, cuasi ultima. **second to none** min ca nun. **the second highest mountain** la monte du de la plu altas, la monte du la plu alta. **the second one** la numero du.
second[2] *n.* (*of time*) secondo.
secondary *adj.* suordinada.
secondary education *n.* educa de liseo.
secondary infection *n.* infeta ajuntada.
secondary school *n.* liseo.
secondhand *adj.* usada.
second-in-command *n.* suxef, viscomandor.
second lieutenant *n.* suteninte.
second-rate *adj.* inferior.
second-year student *n.* studiante de anio du.
secrecy *n.* secretia, secretosia.
secret *adj.* & *n.* secreta, privata. **in secret** secreta. **keep secret** secreti.
secret agent *n.* ajente secreta.
secretarial *adj.* secretoral.
secretariat *n.* secreteria.
secretary *n.* secretor, notor. **secretary of state** (*for foreign affairs*) ministro de esternas; (*for internal affairs*) ministro de internas.
secrete *v.* secrete.
secretion *n.* secrete.
secretive *adj.* secretosa.
secret service *n.* ajenteria secreta.
secret sign *n.* sinia secreta.
secret society *n.* asosia secreta.
sect *n.* seta.
sectarian *adj.* setal.
sectarianism *n.* setisme.
section *n.* sesion, parte. • *v.* sesioni.
sectional *adj.* sesional.
sector *n.* (*geometry*) setor.
secular *adj.* secular, nonrelijiosa.
secularization *n.* seculari.
secularize *v.* seculari.
securable *adj.* securable.
secure *adj.* (*safe*) secur; (*confident*) serta. • *v.* securi.
security *n.* securia; (*guarantee*) garantia; (*tradable asset*) titulo finansial.
security officer *n.* securior.
security worker *n.* securior.
sedan chair *n.* seja portada.
sedate *adj.* calma. • *v.* calmi.
sedation *n.* calmi.
sedative *adj.* calminte. • *n.* medisin calminte.
sedentary *adj.* sentante; fisada.
seder *n.* (*Judaism*) seder.
sedge *n.* sipero.
sediment *n.* deponeda.
sedimentary *adj.* deponeda.
sedimentary rock *n.* roca deponeda.
sedimentation *n.* depone.
sedition *n.* rebela.
seditious *adj.* rebelante.
seduce *v.* sedui.
seduction *n.* sedui.
seductive *adj.* seduinte, seduosa.
seductor *n.* seduor.
seductress *n.* seduor.

sedum *n.* (*plant*) sedo.
see *v.* (*including discover, understand*) vide. **see again** revide. **see something as** regarda un cosa como. **see the future** clarvide. **see the sights** turi la atraes. **see you** txau, asta reuni, asta revide. **see you later** asta plu tarda. **see you next time** asta alora. **see you tomorrow** asta doman. **you see** (*filler*) vide, tu vide.
seed *n.* seme. • *v.* semi.
seedbed *n.* fondo de semes.
seed drill *n.* semador.
seeder *n.* semador.
seed-snipe *n.* (*bird*) tinocor.
seedy *adj.* susia.
seek *v.* xerca.
seeker *n.* xercor.
seem *v.* (*to do, to be*) pare.
seep *v.* suda, filtri.
seer *n.* previdor.
seersucker *n.* (*fabric*) sirsacar.
seesaw *n.* balansa. • *v.* balansi.
seethe *v.* boli.
see-through *adj.* clar, transparente.
segment *n.* sesion, parte. • *v.* sesioni.
segregate *v.* separa.
segregation *n.* separa.
segregationism *n.* separadisme.
segregationist *adj.* separadiste.
segue *n.* (*transition*) segue.
sehri *n.* (*Islam*) suhur.
seine *v.* (*fish with a dragnet*) pexa con serca.
seismic *adj.* sismica.
seismogram *n.* sismogram.
seismograph *n.* sismograf.
seismography *n.* sismografia.
seismologist *n.* sismolojiste.
seismology *n.* sismolojia.
seize *v.* saisi, prende, aresta. **seize up** (*mechanism*) saisi se.
seizure *n.* prende; (*medical*) ataca.
seldom *adv.* rara, a veses rara, a poca veses.
select *v.* eleje; (*software*) marca.
selection *n.* eleje.
selective *adj.* distinguinte.
selenium *n.* (*element*) selenio.
Seleucid *adj.* (*dynasty*) seleucan.
self *n.* ego. • *pref.* auto-. **I myself** me mesma. **my other selves** la otras de me. **my younger self** la plu joven de me.
self-actualization *n.* autoreali.
self-actualize *v.* autoreali.
self-adhesive *adj.* autoaderente.
self-assembly *adj.* asemblable.
self-assured *adj.* autofidante.
self-confidence *n.* autofida.
self-confident *adj.* autofidante.
self-conscious *adj.* autoconsensa.
self-contradictory *adj.* autocontradisente.
self-control *n.* autorestrinje.
self-controlled *adj.* autorestrinjeda.
self-correct *v.* autocoreti.
self-correcting *adj.* autocoretinte.
self-defence (US **self-defense**) *n.* autodefende.
self-denial *n.* asteni, renunsia.
self-destruct *v.* autodestrui.
self-destructive *adj.* autodestruinte.
self-determination *n.* autodetermina.
self-determine *v.* autodetermina.
self-direct *v.* autodetermina.
self-discipline *n.* autodisiplina.
self-doubt *n.* autoduta.
self-employed *adj.* autoempleada.
self-esteem *n.* autorespeta.
self-evident *adj.* autoevidente.
self-explanatory *adj.* autoesplicante.
self-governing *adj.* autonom.
self-hatred *n.* autoodia.
self-help *n.* autoaida.
self-identity *n.* autoidentia.
selfie *n.* (*photo*) selfi.
self-improvement *n.* autoboni.
selfish *adj.* egoiste.
selfishness *n.* egoisme.
selfless *adj.* compatiosa, sin ego.
self-limit *v.* autoremedia.
self-limited *adj.* (*disease*) autoremediada.
self-loathing *n.* autoodia.
self-made *adj.* autocreada.
self-motivated *adj.* automotivada.
self-motivation *n.* automotiva.
self-pity *n.* autocompatia.
self-pollinate *v.* autopoleni.
self-pollination *n.* autopoleni.
self-portrait *n.* autodepinta.
self-proclaimed *adj.* autonomida.
self-propel *v.* autopropulsa.
self-propulsion *n.* autopropulsa.
self-realization *n.* autoreali.
self-realize *v.* autoreali.
self-regulate *v.* autoregula.
self-replicate *v.* autocopia.
self-replication *n.* autocopia.
self-reproach *n.* autoreproxa.
self-respect *n.* autorespeta.
self-restrained *adj.* autorestrinjeda.
self-restraint *n.* autorestrinje.
self-righteous *adj.* moraliste.
self-rule *n.* autonomia.
self-sacrifice *n.* autosacrifia.
self-satisfied *adj.* autosasiada.
self-service *n.* autoservi.
self-sticking *adj.* autoaderente.
self-styled *adj.* autonomida.
self-sufficient *adj.* autosufisinte, nondependente.
self-taught *adj.* autoinstruida.

sell *v.* vende. **sell out** vende tota.
sellable *adj.* vendable.
seller *n.* vendor.
Sellotape *n.* sinta aderente.
sellout *n.* (*betrayal*) tradi, ipocritia.
seltzer *n.* soda.
selvage *n.* (*edging*) paragasta.
selvedge *n.* (*edging*) paragasta.
semantic *adj.* semantical.
semantics *n.* semantica.
semaphore *n.* semafor.
semblance *n.* pare.
semen *n.* semin.
semester *n.* semestre.
semi *n.* (*match*) semifinal; (*vehicle*) camion sesionida. • *pref.* (*half*) dui-, semi-.
semiannual *adj.* semianial.
semiaquatic *adj.* semiacual.
semiarid *adj.* semiseca.
semiaxis *n.* (*geometry*) semiase.
semibreve *n.* tono completa.
semicircle *n.* semisirculo.
semicircular *adj.* semisirculo.
semicolon *n.* punto-virgula.
semiconduct *v.* semiconduta.
semiconductive *adj.* semicondutante.
semiconductor *n.* semicondutador.
semiconscious *adj.* duiconsensa.
semiconsciousness *n.* duiconsensia.
semidesert *n.* semideserto.
semidivine *adj.* semidivin.
semifinal *n.* semifinal.
semiliquid *adj.* & *n.* semilicuida.
semimajor axis *n.* (*astronomy*) semiase major.
semiminor axis *n.* (*astronomy*) semiase minor.
semimonthly *adj.* (*twice a month*) semimensal.
seminal *adj.* influente; (*of semen*) seminal.
seminar *n.* seminar; confere academial.
seminarian *n.* seminariste.
seminary *n.* seminario.
semiotic *adj.* semiotical.
semiotics *n.* semiotica.
semipermeable *adj.* semipermeable.
semiprecious *adj.* semivaluosa.
semiprivate *adj.* semiprivata.
semiprofessional *adj.* semiprofesal.
semiquaver *n.* tono des-sesida.
semirigid airship *n.* airostato semirijida.
semisolid *adj.* semisolida.
semisweet *adj.* semidulse.
Semite *n.* semita.
Semitic *adj.* semita.
semitone *n.* semitono.
semitrailer truck *n.* camion sesionida.
semitransparent *adj.* semitransparente, diafana.
semivocalic *adj.* semivocal.
semivowel *n.* semivocal.
semolina *n.* (*grains, dessert*) semola.
senate *n.* senato; Salon Alta.
senator *n.* senator.
send *v.* envia; (*as message*) mesaji; (*by raft*) balsi; (*by ship*) barconi. **send away** envia a via. **send back** reenvia. **send head over heels** volta. **send off** envia a via. **send to sleep** adormi.
sender *n.* envior.
send-off *n.* adio.
Senegal *n.* Senegal.
Senegalese *adj.* & *n.* senegales.
senescence *n.* senese.
senescent *adj.* senesente.
seneschal *n.* manejor.
senile *adj.* senil.
senility *n.* senilia.
senior *adj.* major.
seniority *n.* anticia.
sensate *adj.* sensal.
sensation *n.* sensa.
sensational *adj.* supradramosa.
sensationalism *n.* supradramosia.
sensationalistic *adj.* supradramosa.
sense *v.* (*experience a sensation*) sensa. • *n.* sensa; (*emotion*) senti; (*meaning*) sinifia. **make sense** es lojical. **sense of taste** sensa de sabor.
senseless *adj.* sin sinifia.
sensibility *n.* sensosia; (*sensibleness*) praticalia.
sensible *adj.* pratical.
sensitive *adj.* delicata, frajil; (*to sensation*) sensosa; reatosa.
sensitivity *n.* sensosia, sentosia.
sensitize *v.* sensosi.
sensor *n.* sensador.
sensorimotor *adj.* (*nerve*) sensorimotor.
sensorium *n.* (*sensory faculties*) sensorio.
sensory *adj.* sensal.
sensory memory *n.* memoria sensal.
sensory neuron *n.* neuron de sensa.
sensual *adj.* stimulante, sesal, focosa.
sensuality *n.* sesalia, sensosia.
sensuous *adj.* sensal; deletosa, lusosa.
sentence *n.* frase; (*punishment*) condena; (*prison term*) periodo de condena. • *v.* condena.
sentient *adj.* sensante.
sentiment *n.* emosia.
sentimental *adj.* emosiosa, sentosa.
sentimentalism *n.* sentosia.
sentimentality *n.* emosiosia.
sentinel *n.* vijilor.
sentry *n.* gardor.
sepal *n.* (*botany*) sepal.
separate *v.* separa. • *adj.* separada.

separately *adv.* separada; (*elsewhere*) a otra parte.
separation *n.* separa.
separatism *n.* separadisme.
separatist *adj.* separadiste.
separator *n.* separador.
Sephardi *adj.* (*Judaism*) sefardi.
Sephardi Jew *n.* sefardi.
sepia *adj.* (*colour*) sepia. • *n.* (*pigment*) sepia.
sepiolite *n.* sepiolita.
sepoy *n.* polisior barati.
sepsis *n.* sepse. • *suff.* (*infection*) -sepse.
sept *n.* claneta.
September *n.* setembre.
septic *adj.* sepsica. • *suff.* -sepsica. **become septic** sepsi.
septicaemia (US **septicemia**) *n.* sepse.
septum *n.* (*anatomy*) divide.
septuplet *n.* setejemelo.
sepulchral *adj.* tombin.
sepulchre (US **sepulcher**) *n.* tomba.
sequel *n.* seguente.
sequence *n.* ordina, segue, serie. • *v.* ordina; (*biochemistry*) seguensa.
sequencer *n.* (*music*) seguador.
sequential *adj.* seguente.
sequester *v.* isoli; confisca.
sequin *n.* briliante.
sequoia *n.* secuoia.
seraglio *n.* arem; palasio.
Seram *n.* (*island*) Seram. **Sea of Seram** Mar Seram.
serape *n.* (*cloak*) capa.
seraph *n.* (*angel*) serafin.
seraphim *n.* serafines.
seratonin *n.* seratonina.
Serb *n.* serbsce.
Serbia *n.* Serbia.
Serbian *adj.* & *n.* serbsce.
serenade *v.* & *n.* serenada.
serendipity *n.* bon acaso.
serene *adj.* calma, pasosa.
serenity *n.* calmia.
serf *n.* (*feudal*) serfo.
serfdom *n.* serfia.
serge *n.* (*fabric*) sarja.
sergeant *n.* sarjento.
serial *adj.* serial. • *n.* (*TV*) telenovela.
serial killer *n.* mator en serie.
series *n.* serie. **in series** en serie, serial.
serif *n.* serif. • *adj.* con serif.
serifed *adj.* con serif.
serigraph *n.* serigram.
serigraphy *n.* (*art*) serigrafia.
serin *n.* (*bird*) serin.
serious *adj.* seria; (*injury*, *situation*) grave.
seriousness *n.* seria; gravia.
sermon *n.* sermon, predica.
serologist *n.* serolojiste.
serology *n.* serolojia.
serotonin *n.* serotonin.
serous *adj.* serosa.
Serpens *n.* (*constellation*) la Serpente.
serpent *n.* serpente.
serpentine *adj.* serpentin.
serrate *v.* sierini.
serrated *adj.* sierin.
serum *n.* (*blood*) sero.
serval *n.* (*wild cat*) serval.
servant *n.* servor, servor de casa.
servantlike *adj.* servorin.
serve *v.* (*master*, *customer*, *food*, *drink*) servi; (*master*) atende; (*customer*) aida. **serve out** distribui.
server *n.* servor; (*computer*, *utensil*) servador.
service *n.* servi, servi publica; (*religious*) rituo.
service animal *n.* bestia de servi.
service area *n.* stasion de autovia.
service charge *n.* paia per servi.
serviceman *n.* militar.
service provider *n.* furnor de servi.
service station *n.* stasion de autovia.
servicewoman *n.* militar.
servile *adj.* sclavin, servorin.
serving *n.* servi, comparti.
serving dish *n.* plato de servi.
serving plate *n.* plato de servi.
serving spoon *n.* culier de servi.
servitude *n.* sclavia.
servo- *pref.* servo-.
servomechanism *n.* servomacina.
servomotor *n.* servomotor.
sesame *n.* (*plant*, *seeds*) sesamo.
Sesotho *n.* (*language*) soto.
sesquicentennial *n.* aniversario sento sincodes.
sessile *adj.* (*zoology*, *anthropology*) nonmovente, fisada.
session *n.* sesion; (*meeting*) consenta, reuni; (*therapy*, *music*) encontra. **be in session** consenta.
set[1] *v.* prepara; (*sun*, *moon*, *planet*) reposa. • *adj.* preparada. **set fire to** ensende. **set off** (*on journey*) comensa, comensa en via. **set up** institui, comensa.
set[2] *n.* (*collection*) colie; (*tennis*, *etc.*) set.
setback *n.* problem, reversa.
Seto Inland Sea *n.* Mar Seto.
set square *n.* cuadrador.
sett *n.* (*badger's lair*) texoneria; (*paving block*) petra cubo.
settee *n.* sofa.
set theory *n.* teoria de colies.
setting *n.* (*mount*) montur; (*software*) ajusta, prefere.
settle *v.* (*calm*) calmi, reposa; (*colonize*) coloni; (*account*) salda. **settle in** abita.
settlement *n.* (*action*) coloni; (*result*) colonia.

settler *n.* coloniste.
setup *n.* organiza; (*trick*) engana.
seven *det.* & *pron.* sete.
seventh *adj.* (*ordinal*) sete. • *n.* (*fraction*) seti.
seventieth *adj.* (*ordinal*) setedes. • *n.* (*fraction*) setedesi.
seventy *det.* & *pron.* setedes. **be in one's seventies** es en sua desenio oto.
sever *v.* divide, talia.
several *det.* alga, diversa, variosa. • *pron.* alga, algas.
severance pay *n.* paia per desemplea.
severe *adj.* sever.
severity *n.* severia.
sew *v.* cose.
sewage *n.* acua de cloaca.
sewer[1] *n.* (*conduit*) cloaca.
sewer[2] *n.* (*person*) cosor.
sewing *n.* cose.
sewing machine *n.* cosador.
sex *n.* (*category*) seso; (*intercourse*) seso, copula, fa de seso, fa de ama. **anal sex** seso anal. **have sex** copula, fa la seso, fa la ama. **oral sex** seso bocal.
sex bomb *n.* sesosa.
sex drive *n.* libido.
sexism *n.* sesisme.
sexist *n.* sesiste.
sexpot *n.* sesosa, libidosa.
Sextans *n.* (*constellation*) la Sestante.
sextant *n.* sestante.
sextet *n.* sesuple.
sexton *n.* mantenor de eglesa.
sextuple *adj.* sesuple.
sextuplet *adj.* & *n.* sesjemelo.
sexual *adj.* sesal.
sexual identity *n.* identia sesal.
sexual intercourse *n.* seso.
sexuality *n.* (*orientation*) sesia; (*sexualness*) sesalia.
sexualization *n.* sesali.
sexualize *v.* sesali.
sexually transmitted *adj.* sesal comunicada.
sexy *adj.* sesosa.
Seychelles *n.* Sexeles.
Seychellois *adj.* & *n.* sexeles.
sh *interj.* xux.
shabby *adj.* gastada.
shack *n.* cabana bruta.
shackle *n.* securitalo. • *v.* securi la talos de.
shad *n.* (*fish*) alosa.
shaddock *n.* (*fruit, tree*) pampelmus.
shade *n.* (*shadow*) ombra; (*hue*) tinje. • *v.* ombri; (*texture*) trama. **shade in** trama, ombri.
shadow *n.* ombra. • *adj.* ombral. **cast a shadow over** ombri.
shadow box *n.* (*display case*) caxa de esibi.
shadowboxing *n.* boxe solitar.
shadow cabinet *n.* consilio ombral.
shadow government *n.* consilio ombral.
shadowy *adj.* (*shadowlike*) ombrin, (*full of shadows*) ombrosa.
shady *adj.* ombrida; nononesta, rusosa.
shaft *n.* (*axis*) ase; (*tunnel*) duto.
shag *n.* cormoran. • *v.* (*sex*) fode.
shaggy *adj.* pelosa.
shah *n.* (*king*) xa.
shaikh *n.* xec.
shake *v.* secute. **shake hands with** presa manos con. **shake one's head** nega con testa. **shake up** secute; (*upset*) turba.
shakedown *n.* reorganiza; (*extortion*) estorse.
Shaker *adj.* & *n.* xecer.
Shakerism *n.* (*Christianity*) xecerisme.
shakeup *n.* reorganiza.
shakuhachi *n.* (*flute*) xacuhatxi.
shaky *adj.* coxeante.
shale *n.* (*geology*) xel.
shall *adv.* va.
shallow *adj.* basa, nonprofonda; (*breathing*) debil.
sham *n.* finje.
shaman *n.* xaman.
shame *v.* & *n.* vergonia. **feel shame** vergonia. **what a shame** tan triste.
shameful *adj.* vergoniosa.
shameless *adj.* sin vergonia.
shamisen *n.* (*musical instrument*) xamisen.
shammy *n.* camusa.
shampoo *n.* xampu. • *v.* xampi.
shamrock *n.* xamroc.
shank *n.* gama basa; (*bird*) tringa.
shanty *n.* canta de marinores.
shanty town *n.* visineria de lata.
shape *n.* forma. • *v.* formi. **shaped like** con forma de. **with the shape of** con forma de.
shard *n.* frato, frato agu.
share *n.* parte, comparti; (*financial*) asion. • *v.* comparti, intercambia. **share out** comparti, divide. **with shared responsibility** coencargada.
sharecrop *v.* cultiva luante.
sharecropper *n.* cultivor luante.
shared *adj.* compartida, comun.
sharedness *n.* compartidia.
shareholder *n.* asionor.
sharia *n.* (*Islam*) xaria.
sharif *n.* (*Islam*) xarif.
shark *n.* selaco.
sharp *adj.* (*pointed, taste, pain*) agu; (*pointed*) puntida; (*music*) dies. • *n.* dies.
sharpen *v.* agi, punti.
sharpness *n.* agia.
sharpshooter *n.* fusilor.
sharp-tasting *adj.* con sabor agu.

shatter *v.* frati.
shatterproof *adj.* nonrompable, secur contra frati.
shave *v.* rasa; corti la barba. • *n.* rasa; corti de barba. **have a close shave** evita apena.
shaven head *n.* testa rasada.
shaver *n.* rasador.
shaving cream *n.* crema de rasa.
shaving foam *n.* crema de rasa.
shawl *n.* (*garment*) xal.
she *pron.* (*normally*) el; (*rarely, only for stylistic contrast with* elo) ela. **she herself** (*non-reflexively emphatic*) el mesma. **she who** el ci.
sheaf *n.* faxo.
shears *n.* sisoron.
sheath *n.* gaina.
sheathbill *n.* (*bird*) cionis.
sheath dress *n.* roba gainin.
sheathe *v.* gaini.
shed[1] *n.* (*hut*) cabana.
shed[2] *v.* (*tears*) larma; (*skin*) muta, desfoli.
shedload *n.* monton.
sheen *n.* brilieta.
sheep *n.* ovea.
sheepcote *n.* ensirca de oveas.
sheepdog *n.* can de pastor.
sheepfold *n.* ensirca de oveas.
sheepish *adj.* embarasada.
sheep pen *n.* ensirca de oveas.
sheepskin *n.* pel de ovea.
sheer *adj.* diafana.
sheet *n.* telon; (*paper*) folia, paje.
sheetlike *adj.* telonin.
sheet pan *n.* plata de forno.
sheetrock *n.* plance de jeso.
sheet steel *n.* lata.
sheik *n.* xec.
sheikdom *n.* xecia.
sheikh *n.* xec.
sheikhdom *n.* (*post, period, area*) xecia.
shekel *n.* (*currency*) xecel.
shelf *n.* scafal.
shell *n.* (*mollusc, crustacean*) conca; (*egg, animal*) casca; (*animal, plant*) armur; (*ammunition*) cartux; (*electron*) strato. • *v.* (*nut*) descasci.
shellac *n.* laca de goma, vernis acuin.
shellfish *n.* crustaseo, molusco.
shell-like *adj.* concin.
shelter *v.* proteje, scermi, refuja. • *n.* (*state*) refuja; (*place*) refujeria.
shelterbelt *n.* paraventa.
sheltered *adj.* protejeda, scermida de la venta.
shelve *v.* pone sur scafal.
shenanigans *n.* turba.
shepherd *n.* pastor.
shepherdess *n.* pastor.
sherbet *n.* (*dessert*) sorbete.
sheriff *n.* (*officer*) xerif.
Sherpa *adj.* & *n.* (*person, language*) xerpa.
sherry *n.* (*wine*) xeres.
shewa' See *shva*.
Shia *adj.* & *n.* (*Islam*) xia.
shiatsu *n.* (*massage*) xiatsu.
shibboleth *n.* xibolet.
shield *n.* scermo. • *v.* proteje, scermi; (*from view*) asconde.
shield bug *n.* xinxe scermin.
shieldlike *adj.* scermin.
shield-shaped *adj.* scermin.
shift *v.* move, desloca. • *n.* desloca; (*work*) turno. **do one's shift** fa sua turno.
shiftiness *n.* furtivia.
shifting *adj.* nonstable.
shiftworker *n.* turnor.
shifty *adj.* furtiva.
shiitake *n.* (*mushroom*) xitace.
Shi'ite *adj.* & *n.* xia.
shilling *n.* xiling.
shim *n.* cuneo.
shimmer *v.* sintili.
shimmy *v.* & *n.* ximi.
shin *n.* tibia.
shinbone *n.* tibia.
shindig *n.* balo vivosa.
shine *v.* brilia.
shiner *n.* briliante; (*black eye*) oio brunida.
shingle[1] *n.* (*pebbles*) calculos.
shingle[2] *n.* (*tile*) telia.
shinguard *n.* covretibia.
shinobi *n.* (*ninjutsu expert*) ninja.
shinpad *n.* covretibia.
shinto *n.* (*religion*) xinto.
shintoist *n.* xintoiste.
shintoistic *adj.* xintoiste.
shiny *adj.* briliante.
ship[1] *n.* barcon. • *v.* barconi; (*by train*) treni; carga; (*product*) lansa a mercato. **armoured ship** barcon blindada.
-ship[2] *suff.* (*abstract quality*) -ia.
shipmate *n.* camerada de barco.
shipment *n.* carga.
shipshape *adj.* ordinada.
shipwreck *n.* barcon ruinada.
shipwrecked *adj.* perdeda a mar.
shipyard *n.* barconeria.
shire *n.* contia.
shirk *v.* evita.
shirt *n.* camisa; (*simple collarless top*) camiseta. **A-shirt** camiseta de sporte. **T-shirt** camisa T.
shirtsleeve *n.* manga de camisa.
shirttail *n.* coda de camisa.
shish kebab *n.* cebab.
shit *n.* (*dung, anything worthless*) merda. • *v.* merdi. • *interj.* txa.
shiv *n.* cotel.
shiva[1] *n.* (*Judaism*) xiva.

Shiva[2] *n.* (*Hinduism*) Xiva.
shiver *v.* trema.
Shoah *n.* Olocausto.
shoal *n.* parador de arena.
shock *v.* & *n.* xoca, ofende.
shock absorber *n.* amortador, paraxoca.
shocker *n.* xoca.
shockproof *adj.* antixocal.
shockwave *n.* onda sismica; onda de xoca.
shoe *n.* sapato. **athletic shoe** sapato de sporte.
shoebill *n.* (*bird*) becosapatin.
shoehorn *n.* liscasapato.
shoelace *n.* cordeta.
shoeless *adv.* sin sapatos.
shoemaker *n.* sapator.
shoe polish *n.* briliasapato.
shoe shop *n.* sapateria.
shoestring *n.* cordeta.
shogi *n.* xogi.
shogun *n.* (*tyrant*) xogun.
shoji *n.* (*door*) xoji.
shoot *v.* (*missile*) xuta; (*weapon*) spara; (*target*) fusili, mosceti. • *n.* rameta, jerme de radis. **shoot down** tira a tera.
shooter *n.* xutor.
shooting star *n.* stela volante.
shootout *n.* fusili.
shop *n.* boteca. • *v.* compra.
shopkeeper *n.* botecor.
shoplifter *n.* furaboteca.
shopper *n.* compror.
shopping *n.* compra. **go shopping** vade per compra.
shopping cart *n.* careta de compra.
shopping centre (US **center**) *n.* sentro comersial.
shopping mall *n.* sentro comersial.
shopping spree *n.* compra manica.
shopping trolley *n.* careta de compra.
shop steward *n.* portavose de sindicato.
shop window *n.* fenetra de esibi.
shore *n.* costa, plaia; (*river*) riva. **on shore** a tera.
short *adj.* (*length*) corta; (*height*) basa; (*terse*) brusca. • *n.* filmeta. **fall short** manca.
shortage *n.* manca.
shortbread *n.* biscoto arenin.
shortcake *n.* biscoto arenin; (*dessert*) torta arenin.
shortchange *v.* redona tro poca.
short circuit *n.* sircuito corta.
shortcoming *n.* manca.
shortcrust pastry *n.* pasta arenin.
shortcut *n.* via rapida.
shortcut key *n.* (*software*) tecla rapida.
shorten *v.* corti.
shortening *n.* gras.
shortfall *n.* manca.
short film *n.* filmeta.
shorthand *n.* stenografia.
short letter *n.* nota.
shortly *adv.* pronto, pos corta. **shortly after** pronto pos, corta pos.
short pants *n.* pantala.
shorts *n.* pantala; (*underpants*) pantaleta.
short shorts *n.* minipantala.
short-sighted *adj.* miope.
short-sightedness *n.* miopia.
short story *n.* nareta.
shortsword *n.* spadeta.
short-term *adj.* nonpermanente.
short-term memory *n.* memoria de dura corta.
short trousers *n.* pantala.
shortwave *n.* onda corta.
shot *n.* (*action*) xuta; (*bullet*) xutada; (*photo*) foto; (*drink*) vitreta.
shotglass *n.* vitreta.
shotgun *n.* fusil de xasa.
should *v.* debe; (*simple conditional, or polite, or commenting without expectation*) ta debe. **as it should be** como lo debe es.
shoulder *n.* spala.
shoulder belt *n.* xarpe de spala.
shoulderblade *n.* oso de spala, scapula.
shoulder strap *n.* bretela.
shout *v.* & *n.* cria.
shouter *n.* crior.
shove *v.* & *n.* puxa.
shovel *n.* pala. • *v.* (*snow, soil, etc.*) move.
shovelboard *n.* (*game*) xufelborda.
show *v.* mostra; (*on television*) televisa. • *n.* (*entertainment*) gala, spetaculo, estravagante. **show and tell** mostra e dise. **show off** ostenta. **show one's face** apare corta. **show through** suapare. **show up** apare.
showbiz *n.* mundo de spetaculo.
showboat *n.* barco teatral.
show business *n.* mundo de spetaculo.
showcase *n.* caxa de esibi.
showdown *n.* fronti.
shower *n.* (*place, equipment*) dux; (*action*) duxi; (*rain*) pluveta. • *v.* duxi; (*rain*) pluveta. **take a shower** duxi se.
shower cap *n.* xapeta de bani.
shower cubicle *n.* dux, stala de dux.
showerhead *n.* boceta.
shower stall *n.* dux, stala de dux.
showgirl *n.* fem de cabare.
showman *n.* presentor, mestre de selebras.
show-off *n.* vantor.
showroom *n.* galeria.
showy *adj.* ostentosa.
shrapnel *n.* fratos.
shred *v.* & *n.* trinxa.
shredded paper *n.* paper trinxada.
shredder *n.* trinxador.

shrew *n.* (*animal*) musarania; (*harridan*) fem odiosa.
shrewd *adj.* astuta.
shrewdness *n.* astutia.
shriek *v.* & *n.* xilia.
shrike *n.* (*bird*) lanio.
shrill *adj.* xiliante.
shrimp *n.* gamba.
shrine *n.* santeria.
shrink *v.* diminui, peti; (*cower*) acrupi temosa.
shrink wrap *n.* plastica abrasante.
shrivel *v.* plieta.
shrivelled (US **shriveled**) *adj.* plietosa.
shroud *n.* veste de tomba. • *v.* veli.
shrub *n.* arboreta.
shrubbery *n.* arboretas.
shrubby *adj.* arboretin.
shrubland *n.* bosce de arboretas.
shrublike *adj.* arboretin.
shrug *v.* leva sua spalas. • *n.* leva de spalas.
shrunken *adj.* diminuida.
shudder *v.* trema.
shuffle *v.* (*reorder*) misca, acasi; (*drag one's feet*) pantofli, tira sua pedes.
shuffleboard *n.* (*game*) xufelborda.
shun *v.* evita.
shunt *v.* diverje.
shut *v.* clui. • *adj.* cluida. **shut down** (*machine*) descomuta. **shut in** enclui. **shut off** descomuta. **shut up** silenti, clui la boca.
shuteye *n.* dormi.
shutoff *n.* clui; descomuta.
shuttable *adj.* cluable.
shutter *n.* (*window*) covrefenetra; (*camera*) cluador.
shutterbug *n.* fotomanica.
shutter priority *n.* (*photography*) primia de relasador.
shutter release *n.* (*camera*) relasador.
shuttle *n.* naveta. • *v.* naveti.
shuttlecock *n.* volante.
shuttle diplomacy *n.* diplomatia navetal.
shva (also **schwa, shewa'**) *n.* (*Hebrew vowel sign*) xva.
shy *adj.* timida.
shyness *n.* timidia.
shyster *n.* avocato frodante.
si *n.* (*musical note*) si.
Siam *n.* Tai.
Siamese *adj.* & *n.* (*person, language*) tai.
sib *n.* conaseda.
Siberia *n.* Sibir.
Siberian *adj.* & *n.* sibirsce.
sibilant *adj.* & *n.* sisante.
sibling *n.* conaseda.
siblinghood *n.* conasedia.
Sibuyan Sea *n.* Mar Sibuyan.
sic *adv.* tal.
Sicilian *adj.* & *n.* sisilian.
Sicily *n.* Sisilia. **Strait of Sicily** Streta Sisilia.
sick *adj.* malada. • *n.* vomita. **become sick** maladi.
sick bay *n.* maladeria.
sickbed *n.* leto de maladia.
sicken *v.* maladi.
sickle *n.* falxeta.
sickly *adj.* maladiosa.
sickness *n.* maladia. **altitude sickness** maladia de altia.
side *n.* lado. • *adj.* ladal. **at the side** a lado. **on the other side of** ultra. **side by side** a lado de lunlotra, con lado a lado. **take sides** es partisan. **to the other side of** ultra, a ultra.
sidearm *n.* fusil de mano.
sidebar *n.* panel a lado.
sideboard *n.* (*displaying or storing dishes*) comoda de cosina. **sideboards** barba de jenas, pelo de jenas.
sideburns *n.* barba de jenas, pelo de jenas.
sidecar *n.* motocareta.
side effect *n.* resulta ladal.
sidekick *n.* camerada, aidor.
sideloader *n.* levacarga.
sideman *n.* musiciste suportante.
sidesaddle *n.* sela de amazonas.
sideshow *n.* atrae minor.
side street *n.* stradeta.
sideswipe *n.* colpa a lado; critica.
side table *n.* table ladal.
sidetrack *v.* diverje.
sideview *n.* vista ladal.
sidewalk *n.* troteria.
sideways *adv.* a lado, ladal, ladal fasante.
sidle *v.* prosimi furtiva.
Sidra *n.* Sidra. **Gulf of Sidra** Golfo Sirte.
siege *n.* aseja.
siemens *n.* (*unit of conductance*) simense.
sienna *adj.* & *n.* (*colour*) siena.
Sierra Leone *n.* Siera Leon.
Sierra Leonean *adj.* & *n.* sieraleonian.
siesta *n.* dormeta.
sieve *n.* tamis. • *v.* tamisi.
sievert *n.* (*unit of radiation*) siverte.
sift *v.* tamisi.
sigh *v.* & *n.* suspira. • *interj.* ai. **sigh of relief** suspira de lejeri.
sight *n.* (*faculty, thing seen*) vide; (*view*) vista; (*tourist*) monumento, atrae per turistes; (*gun*) vidador. • *v.* vide, oserva. **in sight of** en vista de. **out of sight** estra vista, ultra vista.
sighted *adj.* (*able to see*) vidente.
sighthound *n.* lepror.
sighting *n.* oserva.

sightsee *v.* turi la atraes. **go sightseeing** turi la atraes.
sightseeing boat *n.* barco-bus.
sigma *n.* (*Greek letter* Σ, σ, ς) sigma.
sigmoid *adj.* sigmoide.
sigmoid colon *n.* (*anatomy*) sigmoide.
sign *n.* sinia, simbol, indica. • *v.* (*name*) suscrive; (*use sign language*) sinia. **sign in** suscrive per entra. **sign out** suscrive per retira.
signal *v.* (*signify*) sinia; (*transmit a signal*) siniali; (*by drum*) tamburi. • *n.* sinia; (*electric, radio, etc.*) sinial.
signals corps *n.* corpo de comunica.
signature *n.* suscrive.
signet *n.* selo.
significance *n.* importa. **have significance** importa.
significant *adj.* importante, sinifiosa.
signify *v.* sinifia, sinia.
sign language *n.* lingua de sinia.
signpost *n.* palo de dirije.
Sikh *adj.* & *n.* sic.
Sikhism *n.* (*religion*) sicisme.
silage *n.* silida.
silence *n.* silentia.
silencer *n.* silentador.
silent *adj.* silente.
silhouette *n.* silueta, ombra. • *v.* silueta.
silica *n.* silica, diosido de silico.
silicate *n.* silicato.
siliceous *adj.* silicosa.
silicon *n.* (*element*) silico.
silicon dioxide *n.* diosido de silico, silica.
silicone *n.* (*substance*) silicon.
silk *n.* seda. • *adj.* de seda.
silken *adj.* de seda; (*silky*) sedin.
silkmoth *n.* bombis.
Silk Road *n.* Via de Seda.
silkworm *n.* eruga de seda.
silky *adj.* sedin.
silky-flycatcher *n.* (*bird*) plumasedin.
sill *n.* cornisa.
silliness *n.* bobia, folia.
silly *adj.* bobo, fol.
silo *n.* silo. • *v.* sili.
silt *n.* deponeda.
silty *adj.* particulosa.
Silurian *adj.* & *n.* (*geology*) silurian.
silver *n.* arjento. • *adj.* (*colour*) arjento; (*made of silver*) de arjento. • *v.* arjenti.
silver bullion *n.* baras de arjento.
silverfish *n.* pex arjenta.
silver-plate *v.* arjenti.
silver-plated *adj.* arjentida.
silver screen *n.* scermo arjento.
silversmith *n.* arjentor.
silverware *n.* benes de arjento, utiles de arjento.
silvery *adj.* arjentin.
simian *adj.* simial.
similar *adj.* simil.
similarity *n.* similia.
similarly *adv.* simil. **similarly to** como.
simile *n.* compara.
similitude *n.* similia.
simmer *v.* boli lenta.
simony *n.* (*profiting from sacred things*) simonia.
simper *v.* surie adulante.
simple *adj.* simple.
simple-minded *adj.* de mente simple, stupida.
simple sugar *n.* monosacarido.
simpleton *n.* naive.
simplex *adj.* simple, noncomposada.
simplicity *n.* simplia.
simplification *n.* simpli.
simplify *v.* simpli, fasili.
simplistic *adj.* simple.
simply *adv.* simple, mera, no plu ca, en no modo otra ca.
simulacrum *n.* simili.
simulate *v.* simili.
simulation *n.* simili.
simulator *n.* similador.
simulcast *n.* difusa simultan.
simultaneity *n.* simultania.
simultaneous *adj.* simultan.
sin *v.* & *n.* peca.
Sinai *n.* (*peninsula*) Sina.
since *prep.* de, pos, de pos. • *adv.* a pos. • *subord.* car, considerante ce; de cuando, de pos cuando. **since then** de alora.
sincere *adj.* sinsera, vera.
sincerity *n.* sinseria.
Sindhi *adj.* & *n.* (*person, language*) sindi.
sine *n.* (*mathematics*) sinus.
sinecure *n.* posto fasil.
sinew *n.* tendon, ligamento.
sinewy *adj.* tendonosa.
sinful *adj.* pecosa.
sing *v.* canta.
Singapore *n.* Singapor.
Singaporean *adj.* & *n.* singapor.
singe *v.* negri.
singer *n.* cantor. **backing singer** cantor fondal.
singer-songwriter *n.* cantor-composor.
single *adj.* sola, unica; (*unmarried*) nonsposida; (*for one person*) per un. • *n.* (*music*) singular.
single bed *n.* leto per un.
single click *v.* & *n.* (*mouse*) clica simple.
single father *n.* padre sin sposa.
singlehandedly *adv.* par sola se mesma.
single mother *n.* madre sin sposo.
single room *n.* sala per un.
singlet *n.* sucamisa, camiseta de sporte.
singsong *adj.* cantin, melodiosa.
singular *adj.* & *n.* singular.

singularity *n.* singularia.
Sinhala *adj.* & *n.* sinala.
Sinhalese *adj.* & *n.* (*person, language*) sinala.
sinister *adj.* malvolente.
sink *v.* afonda. • *n.* (*basin*) lavabo.
sinkhole *n.* dolina.
Sinkiang *n.* (*Chinese province*) Xinjiang.
sinking fund *n.* reserva de amorti.
sinner *n.* pecor.
sinologist *n.* xinolojiste.
sinology *n.* xinolojia.
sinuous *adj.* serpentin.
sinus *n.* (*anatomy*) sinus.
sinusitis *n.* (*medical*) sinusite.
Sioux *adj.* & *n.* (*person, language*) su.
sip *v.* & *n.* sorbe.
siphon *n.* sifon. • *v.* sifoni.
sipunculid *n.* (*worm*) sipunculo.
sir *n.* senior; (*gender-neutral*) sri; (*knight's title*) Sir.
sire *n.* (*form of address*) senior.
siren *n.* (*alarm*) alarma, avertador; (*mythology*) sirena.
sirloin *n.* filete.
sirocco *n.* (*wind*) xiroco.
Sirte *n.* Sirte. **Gulf of Sirte** Golfo Sirte.
sisal *n.* (*plant*) sisal.
siskin *n.* spineta.
sissy *n.* xico femin.
sister *n.* (*including nun*) sore. **older sister** soron. **younger sister** soreta.
sisterhood *n.* (*quality*) soria; (*organization*) soreria.
sister-in-law *n.* sore par sposi.
sisterliness *n.* soria.
sisterly *adj.* sorin.
sit *v.* senta. **sit back down** resenta se. **sit down** senta se. **sit on** monta.
sitar *n.* (*musical instrument*) sitar.
sitcom *n.* comedia de situas.
site *v.* & *n.* situa, loca; (*web*) loca ueb, pajeria.
sit-in *n.* protesta par senta.
sittella *n.* (*bird*) sitela.
sitter *n.* atendor.
sitting *adj.* sentante. • *n.* (*meeting*) consenta.
situate *v.* situa.
situated *adj.* situada. **be situated** es situada, trova se.
situation *n.* situa; caso.
situation comedy *n.* comedia de situas.
sit-ups *n.* eserse adomenal.
six *det.* & *pron.* ses.
sixteenth note *n.* tono des-sesida.
sixth *adj.* (*ordinal*) ses. • *n.* (*fraction*) sesi.
sixth-former *n.* studiante de anio ultima.
sixtieth *adj.* (*ordinal*) sesdes. • *n.* (*fraction*) sesdesi.
sixty *det.* & *pron.* sesdes.
sixty-fourth note *n.* tono sesdes-cuatrida.
size *n.* grandia. **one size fits all** lo es la mesma per cadun.
sizeable *adj.* grande.
sizzle *v.* & *n.* crepita.
ska *adj.* (*music*) sca.
Skakerrak *n.* (*strait*) Skakerrak.
skald *n.* barde.
skaldic *adj.* bardal.
skate[1] *n.* (*ice, roller*) patin. • *v.* patini.
skate[2] *n.* (*fish*) raia.
skateboard *n.* scet. • *v.* sceti.
skateboarder *n.* scetor.
skater *n.* patinor.
skedaddle *v.* fuji furtiva.
skeet shooting *n.* xuta a platos.
skein *n.* enrola.
skeletal *adj.* (*of the skeleton*) sceletal; (*skeleton-like*) sceletin.
skeleton *n.* sceleto.
skeletonlike *adj.* sceletin.
skeptic... (US). See *sceptic...*
skerry *n.* isoleta.
sketch *v.* desinia. • *n.* desinia; (*comedy*) scetx.
sketchbook *n.* folio.
sketch pad *n.* bloco de desinias.
skew *adj.* apoiada, nonsimetre. • *v.* apoia, nonsimetri.
skewbald *adj.* ducolorida.
skewer *n.* lansieta. • *v.* lansi.
ski *v.* & *n.* sci.
skid *v.* patini.
skier *n.* scior.
skiff *n.* (*boat*) scife.
skiffle *n.* (*music*) scifel.
skiing *n.* sci. **long-distance skiing** sci de distantia longa.
skilful (US **skillful**) *adj.* capas, destrosa.
skill *n.* capasia.
skilled *adj.* capas.
skillet *n.* padela.
skillful (US). See *skilful.*
skim *v.* (*milk*) descremi; (*read*) leje rapida.
skimmer *n.* (*bird*) becosisorin.
skimp *v.* es frugal.
skimpy *adj.* nonsufisinte; revelante.
skin *n.* pel; (*peel*) casca. • *v.* despeli.
skindeep *adj.* surfasal.
skindiving *n.* tufa libre.
skin graft *n.* inserta de pel.
skinhead *n.* testa rasada.
skink *n.* (*lizard*) scinco.
skinless *adj.* sin pel.
skinny *adj.* magra.
skintight *adj.* abrasante, corpin.
skip[1] *v.* & *n.* brinca; omete.
skip[2] *n.* (*container*) portadetrito.
ski pants *n.* pantalon de stribos.
skipper *n.* brincor.
skipping *n.* brincacorda.

skirmish *v.* & *n.* scaramuxa.
skirt *n.* falda.
skirting board *n.* moldur de solo.
ski slope *n.* scieria.
skit *n.* (*comedy*) scetx.
skittle *n.* baston.
skiver *n.* finjor de maladia.
skort *n.* pantala faldin.
skua *n.* (*bird*) stercoraro.
skulduggery *n.* engana.
skulk *v.* asconde, espeta furtiva.
skull *n.* cranio.
skull cap *n.* cipa.
skunk *n.* mofeta.
sky *n.* sielo.
sky blue *adj.* azul, azul de sielo.
skydive *v.* salta con paracade.
skyjack *n.* saisi de avion.
skyjacker *n.* saisor de avion.
skylark *n.* aloda.
skylight *n.* fenetra de teto.
skyline *n.* orizon.
skyscraper *n.* rascasielo.
skywrite *v.* scrive a sielo.
slab *n.* bloco, peso spesa; table de autopsia.
slack *adj.* laxe.
slackness *n.* laxia.
slacks *n.* pantalon.
slag *n.* (*geology*) scoria.
slag heap *n.* dejeteria.
slake *n.* (*seaweed*) nori.
slalom *n.* (*sport*) slalom.
slam *v.* bate, pumi.
slam dunk *n.* (*basketball*) pum. • *v.* pumi.
slander *v.* & *n.* malacusa.
slanderer *n.* malacusor.
slanderous *adj.* malacusante.
slang *n.* jergo.
slant *v.* apoia.
slanted *adj.* diagonal.
slanting *adj.* apoiada.
slap *v.* & *n.* palmi, colpa con palma.
slapdash *adj.* fretosa, nonatendente.
slapstick *n.* farsa.
slash *v.* talia. • *n.* talia; (*punctuation*) bara. **forward slash** bara inclinada.
slasher *n.* filma de teror.
slat *n.* lamina.
slate *n.* (*rock*) ardosia; (*writing*) tableta.
slaughter *v.* & *n.* masacra, mata.
slaughterhouse *n.* mataderia.
Slav *n.* slavica.
slave *n.* sclavo.
slave dealer *n.* sclavor.
slave master *n.* sclavor.
slaver *n.* sclavor.
slavery *n.* sclavia.
Slavic *adj.* & *n.* slavica.
slavish *adj.* sclavin.
slay *v.* mata.
sleazy *adj.* frodante; susia.
sled *n.* treno.
sledge *n.* treno.
sledgehammer *n.* martelon.
sleek *adj.* lisa, refinada.
sleep *v.* & *n.* dormi. **go to sleep** adormi. **put to sleep** adormi.
sleeper *n.* vagon de dormi.
sleepiness *n.* dormosia.
sleeping car *n.* vagon de dormi.
sleeping pill *n.* adorminte.
sleeping sickness *n.* maladia de dormi, tripanosomiase.
sleepless *adj.* sin dormi.
sleepwalk *v.* sonambula.
sleepwalker *n.* sonambulor.
sleepy *adj.* dormosa.
sleet *v.* & *n.* neva dejelada.
sleeve *n.* manga.
sleeveless *adj.* sin manga.
sleeveless sweater *n.* sueter sin manga.
sleigh *n.* treno.
sleight *n.* rusosia. **sleight of hand** majia de mano.
slender *adj.* magra.
slenderness *n.* magria.
sleuth *n.* detetor.
slice *v.* talia. • *n.* talia; peso.
slicer *n.* taliador.
slick *adj.* liscosa.
slidable *adj.* liscable.
slide *v.* lisca. • *n.* (*chute*) tobogan; (*microscope*) vitro; (*photography*) diapositiva. **water slide** tobogan de acua.
slider *n.* liscador.
slide rule *n.* regla de calcula.
slide show *n.* serie de imajes.
sliding *adj.* liscable.
slight *adj.* minor.
slightly *adv.* pico.
slim *adj.* magra. • *v.* magri.
slime *n.* melma. • *v.* melmi.
slimness *n.* magria.
slimy *adj.* melmosa.
sling *n.* (*harness*) arnes; (*bandage*) xarpe medical; (*catapult*) fonda. • *v.* lansa. **baby sling** portabebe.
slingshot *n.* fondeta.
slink *v.* move furtiva.
slip *v.* lisca; (*mistake*) lisceta, ereta. • *n.* lisca; (*mistake*) lisceta, ereta; (*paper*) fix; (*undergarment*) robeta. **half-slip** faldeta. **slip away** fuji furtiva. **slip of the tongue** ereta de parla. **slip up** lisceta, ereta.
slipcover *n.* covrente desfisable.
slipknot *n.* noda liscante.
slipper *n.* pantofla.
slipperiness *n.* liscosia.

slippery *adj.* liscosa.
slipshod *adj.* nonatendente.
slit *n.* ranur. • *v.* ranuri.
slither *v.* serpe.
sliver *n.* agcta. • *v.* agcti.
slob *n.* porco.
slobber *v.* & *n.* bava.
slog *n.* labora sin sesa.
slogan *n.* slogan.
sloganeer *n.* sloganor.
sloop *n.* (*boat*) slup.
slop *n.* gaxin, pulpa; (*waste water*) acua de cloaca.
slope *v.* inclina. • *n.* inclinada.
sloping *adj.* inclinada.
sloppy *adj.* desordinada, desorganizada; (*baggy*) laxe; (*mushy*) gaxin.
slot *n.* ranur.
sloth *n.* bradipo.
slothful *adj.* pigra.
slot screw *n.* vise ranurida.
slotted spatula *n.* spatula de pex.
slouch hat *n.* xapon.
slough *n.* pel mor.
Slovak *adj.* & *n.* slovensce.
Slovakia *n.* Slovensco.
Slovakian *adj.* & *n.* slovensce.
Slovenia *n.* Slovenia.
Slovenian *adj.* & *n.* slovenian.
slovenly *adj.* desordinada.
slow *adj.* lenta. • *v.* lenti. **in slow motion** de move lenta. **slow down** lenti, retarda.
slowcoach *n.* lenta.
slowdown *n.* lenti.
slow-motion *adj.* de move lenta.
slowpoke *n.* lenta.
slow-release *adj.* con relasa gradal.
slow train *n.* tren lenta.
slub *n.* bulto.
sludge *n.* mugre.
slug *n.* limasa.
sluggard *n.* pigra, lenta.
sluggish *adj.* letarjiosa.
sluggishness *n.* letarjia.
sluice *n.* porton.
sluice gate *n.* porton.
sluiceway *n.* canaleta.
slum *n.* casa misera; visineria misera.
slumber *n.* dormi.
slumlord *n.* proprior esplotante.
slump *v.* & *n.* colasa.
slur *v.* & *n.* farfulia.
slurp *v.* & *n.* sorbe ruidosa.
slurry *n.* fango acuin.
slush *n.* neva dejelada.
slut *n.* puta.
sly *adj.* rusosa.
smack *v.* & *n.* palmi, colpa con palma.
small *adj.* peti; (*letter*) minor.
small ad *n.* anunsieta.
small arms *n.* armas lejera.
small calorie *n.* caloria peti.
small intestine *n.* intestin magra.
smallpox *n.* variola.
smarmy *adj.* adulante.
smart *adj.* (*clever*) astuta, intelijente; (*appearance*) bonvestida, formal, ordinada.
smart aleck *n.* sabetota.
smartarse *n.* sabetota.
smartass *n.* sabetota.
smartphone *n.* telefon astuta.
smartypants *n.* sabetota.
smash *v.* crase.
smear *v.* frota, manxa. • *n.* manxa, manxa frotada.
smegma *n.* (*biology*) smegma.
smell *n.* odor; (*sense*) ole. • *v.* (*produce*) odori; (*detect*) ole. **smell bad** odori mal, malodori. **smell good** odori bon, bonodori.
smellable *adj.* olable.
smelly *adj.* odorosa; (*bad*) malodorinte, malodorosa.
smelt *v.* fonde.
smelter *n.* fondador.
smidgen *n.* pico, goteta.
smilax *n.* (*plant*) smilax.
smile *v.* & *n.* surie.
smilodon *n.* (*sabretooth*) smilodon.
smirk *v.* & *n.* surie vil.
smite *v.* colpa.
smith *n.* forjor.
smithereens *n.* fratos, picos.
smithy *n.* forjeria.
smitten *adj.* enamada.
smock *n.* camison.
smock-frock *n.* camison.
smog *n.* nebla fumosa.
smoke *n.* fuma. • *v.* (*tobacco, food*) fumi.
smoke detector *n.* detetador de fumas.
smoked herring *n.* arenge fumida.
smoked meat *n.* carne fumida.
smoked salmon *n.* salmon fumida.
smokehouse *n.* fumeria.
smokeless *adj.* sin fuma.
smoker *n.* fumor.
smokery *n.* fumeria.
smokestack *n.* ximine.
smoke tree *n.* cotino.
smokey *adj.* fumosa.
smoking *adj.* fuminte. • *n.* fumi. **no smoking** fumi proibida.
smoky *adj.* fumosa.
smolder (US). See *smoulder*.
smooch *v.* besa.
smooth *adj.* lisa, plana; (*person*) suave.
smooth bore *n.* cano lisa.
smoothe *v.* lisi; suavi.
smoother *n.* lisador.

smoothie *n.* pure de fruta.
smoothness *n.* lisia.
smorgasbord *n.* (*food*) smorgasbord.
smother *v.* sofoca.
smoulder (US **smolder**) *v.* ardeta, fumi.
SMS *n.* mesajeta.
smudge *v.* manxa. • *n.* manxa, manxa frotada.
smudgy *adj.* manxosa.
smug *adj.* autosasiada, autofidante.
smuggle *v.* contrabanda.
smuggler *n.* contrabandor.
smut *n.* pornografia.
smutty *adj.* lasiva.
snack *v.* & *n.* cometa.
snafu *n.* caos.
snag *n.* problem, trapa. • *v.* trapi.
snail *n.* caracol. **at a snail's pace** caracolin.
snail mail *n.* posta caracolin.
snake *v.* serpe. • *n.* serpente.
snakebird *n.* aninga.
snakebite *n.* morde de serpente.
snake charmer *n.* serpentor.
snake eagle *n.* serpentor.
snake handler *n.* serpentor.
snap *n.* & *interj.* crac. • *v.* (*sound*) craci; (*break*) rompe; (*photo*) xuta. **snap back** replica. **snap in two** rompe a du.
snap bean *n.* fava verde.
snapdragon *n.* (*plant*) boca de leon.
snap fastener *n.* boton de presa.
snappy *adj.* consisa; (*tetchy*) iritable.
snapshot *n.* foto.
snare *n.* trapa.
snare drum *n.* tambur militar.
snark *n.* sarcasmo.
snarl[1] *v.* & *n.* (*growl*) ronci.
snarl[2] *v.* (*entangle*) marania.
snatch *v.* saisi, aranca.
snazzy *adj.* modosa.
sneak *v.* rampe; informa contra. **sneak away** fuji furtiva. **sneak up** prosimi furtiva.
sneaker *n.* sapato de sporte.
sneakiness *n.* furtivia.
sneaky *adj.* furtiva; enganosa.
sneer *v.* & *n.* grima.
sneeze *v.* & *n.* stornui.
snicker *v.* rie tra sua dentes.
snide *adj.* sarcasmosa.
sniff *v.* & *n.* ensofla.
sniffable *adj.* ensoflable.
snifter *n.* vitro de coniac.
snigger *v.* rie tra sua dentes.
snip *v.* sisori.
snipe *n.* (*bird*) galinago.
sniper *n.* xutor.
snippet *n.* frato.
snippy *adj.* egosa.
snit *n.* mal umor.
snitch *v.* informa contra.
snob *n.* clasiste.
snobbish *adj.* clasiste.
snobby *adj.* clasiste.
snood *n.* rede de capeles.
snooker *n.* biliardo, biliardo engles.
snooker hall *n.* biliarderia.
snoop *v.* xerca furtiva.
snooty *adj.* clasiste.
snooze *v.* & *n.* dormeta.
snore *v.* resona. **snore loudly** ronci.
snorkel *n.* airador.
snort *v.* & *n.* ensofla.
snot *n.* muco nasal.
snotty *adj.* mucosa; (*conceited*) egosa.
snout *n.* beco.
snow *v.* & *n.* neva; (*lightly*) neveta. **snowed in** isolida par neva.
snowball *n.* bal de neva.
snowbank *n.* cresta de neva.
snowboard *n.* plance de neva.
snowbound *adj.* trapida par neva.
snowdrift *n.* duna de neva, monton de neva.
snowdrop *n.* lil de neva.
snow finch *n.* pasaro de neva.
snowflake *n.* floco de neva.
snowline *n.* linia de neva.
snowman *n.* om de neva.
snowmelt *n.* neva fondeda.
snowmobile *n.* mototreno.
snowpack *n.* cumula de neva.
snowplough (US **snowplow**) *n.* scopineva.
snowshoe *n.* raceta de neva.
snow shower *n.* neveta.
snowstorm *n.* nevon.
snowsuit *n.* salopeta.
snowwoman *n.* fem de neva.
snowy *adj.* nevosa.
snowy owl *n.* buo de neva.
snub *v.* iniora.
snuff *n.* ensoflable.
snuffbox *n.* caxa de ensofable.
snuffer *n.* estinguador de candela.
snug *adj.* (*place*) nidin; (*person*) nidida; (*garment*) streta.
snuggle *v.* enrola. **snuggle down** nidi se.
snugness *n.* nidinia; stretia.
so[1] *adv.* (*to such an extent*) tan; (*like this*) tal, en esta modo. • *interj.* alora. • *conj.* (*therefore*) donce, alora. **or so** o simil. **so beautiful** tan bela. **so be it** amen. **so far** (*up to now*) asta aora. **so long as** tra cuando. **so many that** tan multe ce. **so that** (*intention*) afin, con intende ce; (*effect*) tan … ce. **so what?** (*disinterest*) e donce?
so[2] *n.* (*musical note*) sol.

soak *v.* empapa, moia. **soak through** satura. **soak up** asorbe.
soaker *n.* (*rain*) pluvon.
so-and-so *pron.* cualce.
soap *n.* sapon; (*opera*) telenovela. • *v.* saponi.
soapbox *n.* caxon.
soap opera *n.* telenovela.
soapstone *n.* steatita.
soapsuds *n.* spuma de sapon
soapy *adj.* saponosa.
soar *v.* alti, vola alta.
sob *v.* & *n.* sanglota.
sober *adj.* sobre.
sobriety *n.* sobria.
sobriquet *n.* nometa.
so-called *adj.* (*disparaging*) suposada, malnomida. **the so-called X** la X malnomida.
soccer *n.* futbal.
soccer pitch *n.* campo de futbal.
soccer player *n.* futbalor.
sociable *adj.* sosial.
social *adj.* sosial.
social chaos *n.* tumulta.
social convention *n.* abitua sosial, costum.
social gradient *n.* gradiente sosial.
social habit *n.* abitua sosial.
socialism *n.* sosialisme.
socialist *n.* sosialiste.
socialite *n.* om de mundo, fem de mundo, person de mundo.
socialize *v.* sosiali; parleta.
social worker *n.* aidor sosial.
societal *adj.* sosial.
society *n.* sosia, asosia, organiza.
socio- *pref.* (*society*) sosio-.
sociobiology *n.* sosiobiolojia.
sociolinguistics *n.* sosiolinguistica.
sociological *adj.* sosiolojial.
sociologist *n.* sosiolojiste.
sociology *n.* sosiolojia.
sociopath *n.* sosiopatica.
sociopathic *adj.* sosiopatica, antisosial.
sociopathy *n.* sosiopatia.
sock *n.* calseta.
socket *n.* (*joint*) caveta; (*electric*) asetador. **light socket** portabulbo.
Socrates *n.* (*philosopher*) Socrate.
Socratic *adj.* socratal.
sod[1] *n.* (*grassy ground*) sespe.
sod[2] *n.* (*insult*) puto.
soda *n.* soda.
soda ash *n.* carbonato de sodio.
soda water *n.* soda.
sodden *adj.* empapada, acuosa.
sodium *n.* sodio.
sodium bicarbonate *n.* bicarbonato de sodio.
sodium carbonate *n.* carbonato de sodio.
sodium fluoride *n.* fluorido de sodio.
sodium hydroxide *n.* idrosido de sodio.
sodium urate *n.* urato de sodio.
sodomite *n.* sodomiste.
sodomize *v.* sodomia.
sodomy *n.* sodomia.
sofa *n.* sofa.
sofa bed *n.* sofa-leto.
soffit *n.* sofito.
soft *adj.* (*not hard or tough*) mol; (*hair, skin, fabric*) suave; (*sound*) cuieta.
softback *n.* libro mol.
softball *n.* (*sport*) balmol.
soften *v.* moli; suavi.
softener *n.* (*substance*) suavinte.
soft-hearted *adj.* compatiosa.
softness *n.* molia; suavia.
soft palate *n.* (*anatomy*) palato mol, velo.
soft toy *n.* animal de pelux.
software *n.* programes.
softwood *n.* lenio mol.
soggy *adj.* empapada, acuosa.
soil *n.* solo de tera. • *v.* susi.
soirée *n.* selebra de sera.
sojourn *v.* & *n.* reposa.
sol *n.* (*musical note*) sol.
solace *v.* & *n.* consola. **take solace in** es consolada par.
solar *adj.* solal.
solarium *n.* soleria.
solar-powered *adj.* par enerjia solal.
solar system *n.* sistem solal.
solder *v.* solda. • *n.* soldura.
solderer *n.* soldor.
soldering gun *n.* pistol per solda.
soldering iron *n.* fero per solda, soldador.
soldier *n.* soldato.
sole[1] *adj.* (*only*) sola, unica.
sole[2] *n.* (*foot*) planta, fondo de pede; (*shoe*) planta de sapato.
sole[3] *n.* (*fish*) solea. **American sole** solea american.
solecism *n.* era, era sosial.
solely *adv.* sola.
solemn *adj.* formal, ritual, seria.
solemnity *n.* seria.
solenoid *n.* solenoide.
sol-fa *n.* (*music*) solfejo.
solfège *n.* solfejo.
solfeggio *n.* solfejo.
solicit *v.* solisita, xerca.
solicitation *n.* solisita.
solicitor *n.* avocato, avocato personal.
solicitor's clerk *n.* notario.
solicitous *adj.* consernada.
solid *adj.* & *n.* solida.
solidarity *n.* unia.
solidification *n.* solidi.
solidify *v.* solidi.
solidity *n.* solidia.

solid-state drive *n.* memoria de state solida.
solidus *n.* bara inclinada.
soliloquy *n.* monologo.
solipsism *n.* solipsisme.
solipsist *n.* solipsiste.
solipsistic *adj.* solipsiste.
solitaire *n.* jua solitar.
solitary *adj.* solitar.
solitary confinement *n.* solitaria.
solitude *n.* solitaria.
solo *adj.* & *n.* (*music*) solo.
soloist *n.* soliste.
Solomon *n.* Solomon.
Solomon Islander *adj.* & *n.* solomones.
Solomon Islands *n.* Isolas Solomon.
Solomon Sea *n.* Mar Solomon.
solstice *n.* solstisio.
soluble *adj.* (*problem*) solvable; (*substance*) disolvable.
solute *n.* disolveda.
solution *n.* (*problem*) solve; (*liquid mixture*) disolve.
solvable *adj.* solvable.
solve *v.* solve.
solvency *n.* solvablia.
solvent *adj.* solvable. • *n.* disolvente.
soma *n.* (*drink*) soma.
Somali *adj.* & *n.* somali.
Somalia *n.* Somalia.
Somalian *adj.* & *n.* somali.
somatic *adj.* corpal.
somatotropin *n.* somatotropina.
sombre (US **somber**) *adj.* sombre.
sombreness (US **somberness**) *n.* sombria.
sombrero *n.* (*hat*) sombrero, xapon.
some *det.* alga. • *pron.* alga, algas; aprosima, sirca. **some ... or other** alga ... o otra. **some people** alga persones, alga de mundo.
somebody *pron.* algun.
someday *adv.* a alga dia.
somehow *adv.* en alga modo.
someone *pron.* algun.
somersault *v.* & *n.* volta.
something *pron.* alga cosa. **or something like that** o simil.
sometimes *adv.* a veses.
somewhat *adv.* alga, a alga grado.
somewhere *adv.* en alga loca, en alga parte. **somewhere else** en un otra loca.
somnambulism *n.* sonambula.
somnambulist *n.* sonambulor.
somnolence *n.* dormosia.
son *n.* fio; (*gender-neutral*) fie; (*baby*) fieta.
sonar *n.* sonar.
sonata *n.* (*music*) sonata.
song *n.* (*performance*) canta; (*score and lyrics*) cantada.
songbird *n.* avia cantante, cantor.
songbook *n.* libro de cantas.
songfest *n.* canta grupal.
sonic *adj.* sonal.
son-in-law *n.* fio par sposi.
sonnet *n.* (*poetry*) soneto.
sonogram *n.* ecogram.
sonograph *n.* ecograf. • *v.* ecografi.
sonography *n.* ecografia.
sonorant *adj.* & *n.* (*phonetics*) sonante.
sonorous *adj.* resonante, impresante.
soon *adv.* pronto, pos corta. **as soon as** direta cuando. **as soon as possible** la plu pronto. **soon after** pronto pos. **sooner or later** a un ves o un otra.
soonest *adv.* la plu pronto.
soot *n.* suje. • *v.* suji.
soothe *v.* calmi, lejeri, consola.
soothsayer *n.* divinor.
sooty *adj.* sujosa.
sophism *n.* sofisme.
sophist *n.* sofiste.
sophisticate *v.* sofistica. • *n.* sofisticada.
sophistication *n.* sofistica.
sophistry *n.* sofisme.
sophomore *n.* studiante de anio du.
-sophy *suff.* (*wisdom*) -sofia.
soporific *adj.* calminte. • *n.* medisin calminte.
soprano *adj.* & *n.* soprano.
sorbet *n.* sorbete.
sorcerer *n.* sorsor, sorsor mas.
sorceress *n.* sorsor, sorsor fema.
sorcery *n.* sorsoria, majia.
sordid *adj.* susia; desplasente.
sore *adj.* dolosa. • *n.* ulsera.
sorghum *n.* (*plant*) sorgo.
sorority *n.* (*organization*) soreria.
sorrel *n.* (*plant*) osale.
sorrow *n.* tristia.
sorrowful *adj.* tristiosa.
sorry *adj.* triste, repentinte. • *interj.* pardona. **be sorry** repenti, regrete. **feel sorry for** compatia. **I am sorry** pardona me.
sort *n.* spesie, tipo. • *v.* alfabeti, ordina.
sortie *v.* ataca sortinte.
so-so *adj.* no bon e no mal.
Sotho *adj.* & *n.* soto.
soubriquet *n.* nometa.
soufflé *n.* (*food*) sufle.
soul *n.* spirito; (*music*) sol.
soul-destroying *adj.* despiritinte.
soulful *adj.* espresosa.
sound *v.* & *n.* sona. • *adj.* sonal.
sound bite *n.* siteta, sita jusosa.
soundboard *n.* resonador.
sound check *n.* (*music*) serti de sona.

sound engineer *n.* injenior de sona.
sounding board *n.* resonador.
soundless *adj.* sin sona.
soundproof *adj.* acustical isolida. ● *v.* isoli acustical.
soundtrack *n.* banda de sona; (*music*) partitur.
soup *n.* sopa.
soupçon *n.* pico.
soup pot *n.* casola per sopa.
sour *adj.* asida. ● *v.* asidi. **turn sour** asidi.
source *n.* fonte, orijina. ● *adj.* orijinal. **source of income** fonte de revenu.
source code *n.* testo de fonte.
source text *n.* testo de fonte.
sour cream *n.* crema asida.
sourdough *n.* levada natural.
sourness *n.* asidia.
sourpuss *n.* malumorosa.
south *adj.* & *n.* sude. **to the south of** a sude de.
South Africa *n.* Sudafrica.
South African *adj.* & *n.* sudafrican.
South America *n.* America Sude.
South Carolina *n.* (*US state*) Carolina Sude.
South China Sea *n.* Mar Xina Sude.
South Dakota *n.* (*US state*) Dakota Sude.
southeast *adj.* & *n.* sude-este.
southeasterly *adj.* sude-este.
southern *adj.* sude.
Southern Africa *n.* Africa sude.
southern lights *n.* aurora sude.
Southern Ocean *n.* Mar Antartica.
southernwood *n.* (*plant*) abrotano.
South Korea *n.* Tehan, Corea Sude.
South Korean *adj.* & *n.* tehan.
southpaw *n.* manosinistra.
South Pole *n.* Polo Sude.
south-southeast *adj.* & *n.* sude-sude-este.
south-southwest *adj.* & *n.* sude-sude-ueste.
South Sudan *n.* Sudan Sude.
southward *adv.* a sude.
southwards *adv.* a sude.
southwest *adj.* & *n.* sude-ueste.
southwester *n.* venta sude-ueste.
southwesterly *adj.* sude-ueste.
souvenir *n.* suvenir, recordante; (*trinket*) orneta.
sovereign *adj.* autocrata, autonom. ● *n.* monarca.
sovereignty *n.* autocratia, autonomia, domina; monarcia.
soviet *adj.* & *n.* soviet.
Soviet Union *n.* Uni Soviet.
sow *v.* semi.
soya *n.* soia.
soya bean *n.* seme de soia.
soya sauce *n.* salsa de soia.
Soya Strait *n.* Streta Soya.
soybean *n.* (*plant*, *seed*) soia; (*seed*) seme de soia.
soy sauce *n.* salsa de soia.
spa *n.* banieria, banieria mineral, banieria termal; (*hot tub*) banio de vortis.
space *n.* spasio. ● *v.* spasi. **space out** spasi.
spacebar *n.* tecla de spasio.
spacecraft *n.* barcon spasial, veculo spasial.
spaceflight *n.* vola spasial.
spaceman *n.* astronauta.
spaceport *n.* (*science fiction*) porto spasial.
space probe *n.* sonda spasial.
spaceship *n.* barcon spasial.
space shuttle *n.* naveta spasial.
space station *n.* stasion spasial.
spacesuit *n.* veste spasial.
spacetime *n.* spasiotempo.
spacewalk *n.* pasea en spasio.
spacewoman *n.* astronauta.
spacious *adj.* spasiosa.
spade *n.* pala; (*cards*) spada.
spadix *n.* spina.
spaghetti *n.* spageti.
spaghetti hoop *n.* anelo de spageti.
spaghettio *n.* anelo de spageti.
spaghetti ring *n.* anelo de spageti.
spaghetti sauce *n.* salsa de tomate.
spaghetti strap *n.* breteleta.
Spain *n.* Espania.
spam *n.* spam. ● *v.* spami.
spammer *n.* spamor.
span *v.* & *n.* estende.
spandex *n.* elastan. ● *adj.* de elastan.
spangled *adj.* puntosa.
spaniel *n.* (*dog*) spaniel.
Spanish *adj.* & *n.* (*person*, *language*) espaniol.
spank *v.* & *n.* palmi, colpa con palma.
spanner *n.* clave.
spare *v.* salva; eseta. ● *adj.* (*part*) reservada; (*time*) libre.
spare rib *n.* costela de porco.
sparing *adj.* moderada.
spark *n.* sintil. ● *v.* sintili.
sparkle *v.* & *n.* sintili.
sparkling wine *n.* vino bolante.
sparkly *adj.* sintilinte.
spark plug *n.* bujia.
sparrow *n.* pasaro.
sparrowhawk *n.* (*bird*) sparver.
sparrowlike *adj.* pasarin.
sparse *adj.* mancante, nonsufisinte, rarida.
spartan *adj.* spartan.
spasm *v.* & *n.* spasma, contrae, convulsa. ● *suff.* -spasma.
spastic *adj.* spasmica. ● *suff.* -spasmica.
spat *n.* disputeta.
spate *n.* serie.
spathe *n.* (*anatomy*) gaina.
spatial *adj.* spasial.

spatter *v.* salpica.
spatula *n.* spatula, spatula de cosini.
spawn *n.* ovipari.
spay *v.* neutri.
speak *v.* parla.
speakeasy *n.* (*bar*) spicisi.
speaker *n.* parlor; (*orator*) bonparlor; (*legislative*) presidente; (*loudspeaker*) parlador.
spear *v.* lansi. • *n.* lansia.
spearhead *n.* (*attack*) avansada.
spearmint *n.* menta fresca.
spear thrower *n.* lansadardo.
special *adj.* spesial; spesifada.
special effect *n.* efeto spesial.
special election *n.* vota spesial.
special feature *n.* cualia spesial.
specialist *n.* spesialiste, esperta.
speciality *n.* spesiali.
specialization *n.* spesiali.
specialize *v.* spesiali.
special-order *adj.* par comanda.
specialty *n.* spesiali.
species *n.* spesie.
specific *adj.* spesifada.
specification *n.* spesifa.
specify *v.* spesifa.
specimen *n.* esemplo.
specious *adj.* malgidante.
speck *n.* particula, pico.
speckle *n.* manxeta.
speckled *adj.* puntosa.
spectacle *n.* spetaculo, estravagante.
spectacles *n.* (*glasses*) oculo.
spectacular *adj.* spetaculin, dramosa.
spectator *n.* oservor.
specter (US). See *spectre*.
spectral *adj.* spetral, fantasmin.
spectre (US **specter**) *n.* fantasma.
spectroscope *n.* spetroscopio.
spectroscopic *adj.* spetroscopial.
spectroscopy *n.* spetroscopi.
spectrum *n.* spetro.
speculate *v.* divina.
speculation *n.* divina.
speculative *adj.* divinante.
speculator *n.* divinor.
speech *n.* parla; lingua. **part of speech** categoria sintatical.
speech-impaired *adj.* muda.
speechless *adj.* muda.
speed *n.* rapidia. • *v.* vade tro rapida. **speed up** aselera, rapidi.
speedboat *n.* motobarco.
speed bump *n.* jiba lentinte.
speed camera *n.* camera de trafica.
speed hump *n.* jiba lentinte.
speedo *n.* rapidometre.
speedometer *n.* rapidometre.
speedos *n.* (*garment*) slip de nada.
spell[1] *v.* (*letters*) spele.
spell[2] *n.* (*magic*) encanta. **cast a spell** encanta.
spell[3] *n.* (*period*) periodo.
spellbound *adj.* encantada.
spelling *n.* spele.
spelling checker *n.* spelador.
spelunker *n.* cavor.
spelunking *n.* esplora de cavas.
spend *v.* (*money, energy, resources, time*) spende, consuma; (*time*) pasa.
spendthrift *n.* compramanica.
sperm *n.* semin; sperma, spermas.
spermaceti *n.* (*substance*) spermaseti.
spermatozoa *n.* spermas.
spermatozoon *n.* sperma.
spermicide *n.* spermiside.
sperm whale *n.* caxalote.
spew *v.* descome.
sphenoid *n.* sfenoide.
sphenoid bone *n.* sfenoide.
sphere *n.* sfera.
spherelike *adj.* sferin.
spherical *adj.* sfera.
spheroid *adj.* sferin.
sphincter *n.* (*anatomy*) sfinter.
sphinx *n.* sfinje.
sphygmomanometer *n.* sfigmometre.
spice *n.* spise. • *v.* spisi.
spicule *n.* (*biology*) spineta.
spicy *adj.* spisosa.
spider *n.* arania. **baby spider** aranieta.
spider silk *n.* seda de arania.
spider's web *n.* rede de arania.
spidery *adj.* aranin.
spigot *n.* (*stopper*) tapo; (*faucet*) valva.
spike *n.* spina; (*flower cluster*) spiga, masto florinte.
spiked *n.* (*hair*) erisin.
spikenard *n.* (*plant*) nardo.
spiky *adj.* spinosa.
spill *v.* malversa.
spillway *n.* diverjador.
spin *v.* (*whirl*) jira; (*thread*) fili; (*weave*) texe. • *n.* jira; (*political*) dora de fatos, manipula de opina.
spinach *n.* (*plant, leaves*) spinax.
spinal *adj.* spinal.
spinal cord *n.* medula spinal.
spinal tap *n.* perfora lombal.
spindle *n.* fuso.
spindle-shaped *adj.* fusin.
spin doctor *n.* (*gilder of facts*) doror de fatos.
spine *n.* (*barb*) spina; (*backbone*) spina dorsal; (*book*) dorso.
spine-chilling *adj.* terorinte.
spineless *adj.* coarde, sin coraje; (*invertebrate*) nonvertebrato.
spinelike *adj.* spinin.

spinnaker *n.* (*sail*) spinacer.
spinner *n.* filetador fema.
spinning top *n.* jireta.
spinning wheel *n.* macina de fili.
spinoff *n.* derivada, resulta ladal.
spinster *n.* nonsposida.
spinsterhood *n.* nonsposia.
spiny *adj.* spinosa.
spiny anteater *n.* ecidna.
spiny lobster *n.* langosta.
spiraea (US **spirea**) *n.* (*plant*) spirea.
spiral *adj.* & *n.* spiral. ● *v.* spirali.
spiral pattern *n.* motif spiral.
spiral slide *n.* tobogan elica.
spiral staircase *n.* scalera elica.
spire *n.* pinaculo.
spirea (US). See *spiraea*.
spirit *n.* (*soul*) spirito; (*drink*) distilada.
spirited *adj.* vivosa.
spiritedness *n.* vivosia.
spiritist *n.* spiritiste.
spirit lamp *n.* stufa de alcol.
spiritual *adj.* spirital.
spiritualism *n.* spiritisme.
spiritualist *n.* spiritiste.
spirituality *n.* spiritalia.
spirochaete (US **spirochete**) *n.* (*bacterium*) spiroceta.
spit[1] *v.* & *n.* sputa.
spit[2] *n.* palo.
spite *n.* odia. **in spite of** an con; (*something that has already happened*) an pos. **in spite of the fact that** an si, contra ce.
spiteful *adj.* odiosa.
spitfire *n.* coler.
Spitsbergen *n.* Svalbard.
spittle *n.* saliva.
spittoon *n.* vaso de sputa.
splash *n.* (*noise*) pluf; (*splatter*) salpica. ● *v.* plufi; salpica. ● *interj.* pluf.
splashdown *n.* (*of spacecraft*) amar.
splat *n.* & *interj.* pluf. ● *v.* plufi.
splatter *v.* salpica.
splay *v.* estende.
spleen *n.* (*anatomy*) spleno.
splendid *adj.* briliante, merveliosa.
splendour (US **splendor**) *n.* brilia.
splenectomy *n.* (*surgery*) splenectomia.
splenetic *adj.* odiosa.
splice *v.* junta.
splint *n.* (*medical*) ferula.
splinter *n.* ageta. ● *v.* ageti.
splinter bar *n.* bara de molas.
split *v.* & *n.* fende, divide. ● *adj.* fendeda, divideda. **split hairs** es pedante. **split in two** dui.
splitter *n.* (*person*) fendor; (*device*) fendador.
splurge *n.* compramania.
splutter *v.* & *n.* balbuta.
spoil *v.* mali, destrui; (*treat*) regala.
spoiled *adj.* (*food*) malida; (*vote*) vacua.
spoiler *n.* (*plot*) matajoia.
spoilsport *n.* matajoia.
spoke *n.* (*wheel*) raio.
spokesman *n.* portavose, representor.
spokesperson *n.* portavose, representor.
spokeswoman *n.* portavose, representor.
spondaic *adj.* spondeal.
spondee *n.* (*poetry*) spondeo.
spondilitis *n.* (*medical*) spondilite.
sponge *n.* (*cleaning tool, organism*) sponja. ● *v.* sponji.
sponge cake *n.* torta sponjin.
sponge finger *n.* (*biscuit*) biscoto savoian.
spongy *adj.* sponjin.
sponsor *n.* sponsor. ● *v.* sponsori.
sponsorship *n.* sponsoria.
spontaneity *n.* spontania.
spontaneous *adj.* spontan.
spoof *n.* (*parody*) esajera; (*trick*) rus.
spook *n.* fantasma; (*spy*) spior.
spooky *adj.* fantasmosa, asustante.
spool *n.* bobin. ● *v.* bobini.
spoon *n.* culier. ● *v.* (*transfer by spoon*) culieri.
spoonbill *n.* (*bird*) becospatulin.
spoonlike *adj.* culierin.
spoon-shaped *adj.* culierin.
spoor *n.* trasa.
sporadic *adj.* nonperiodal.
spore *n.* spora.
sporocarp *n.* sporocarpo.
sporophyte *n.* sporofite.
sporozoa *n.* (*organisms*) apicomplexas.
sporozoon *n.* (*organism*) apicomplexa.
sporran *n.* (*pouch*) sporan.
sport *n.* sporte.
sportive lemur *n.* lepilemur.
sports *n.* atletisme.
sports bag *n.* bolson.
sportscaster *n.* comentor de sporte.
sports commentator *n.* comentor de sporte.
sports field *n.* campo de sporte.
sportsman *n.* sportor.
sportsperson *n.* sportor.
sportswoman *n.* sportor.
sport utility vehicle *n.* multiterenal.
spot *n.* (*place*) loca; (*dot*) punto; (*stain*) manxa; (*small amount*) pico.
spotlight *n.* lampa de punto.
spotted *adj.* puntosa.
spotty *adj.* puntosa.
spouse *n.* spos.
spout *v.* (*spray*) jeta. ● *n.* jeta; (*jug*) beco.
sprawl *v.* estende.
sprawling *adj.* estendosa.
spray *v.* & *n.* jeta.

spread *v.* (*extend*) estende; (*become widespread*) sperde, difusa, vasti; (*open out*) esvasa; (*butter, etc.*) aplica. • *n.* estende; pasta aplicable.
spreader *n.* sperdor.
spreadsheet *n.* (*software*) program de calcula; (*document*) folio de calcula.
spree *n.* orjia; (*shopping*) compramania.
sprig *n.* talo.
sprightly *adj.* ajil.
spring *n.* (*season*) primavera; (*well*) fonte; (*metal coil*) mola; (*leap*) salta. • *v.* (*leap*) salta; (*originate*) fonti. • *adj.* primaveral.
springboard *n.* trampolin.
springbok *n.* (*antelope*) springboc.
spring-loaded *adj.* cargada par mola.
springtime *n.* primavera.
sprinkle *v.* duxi.
sprinkler *n.* dux.
sprint *v.* & *n.* sprinta.
sprinter *n.* sprintor.
sprite *n.* elfo.
sprocket *n.* dente.
sprout *v.* & *n.* (*young shoot*) jerme.
spruce *n.* (*tree*) pisea.
spry *adj.* vivosa.
spur *n.* speron. • *v.* speroni.
spurge *n.* (*plant*) euforbia.
spurious *adj.* nonvalida.
spurn *v.* rejeta.
spurt *v.* & *n.* jeta.
sputnik *n.* sputnic.
sputter *v.* & *n.* balbuta.
sputum *n.* sputa.
spy *v.* spia. • *n.* spior.
spyglass *n.* telescopio.
spyhole *n.* buco de spia.
squab *n.* (*baby pigeon*) pijoneta.
squabble *v.* & *n.* scaramuxa.
squad *n.* ecipo; (*from which a team is chosen*) scuadron.
squadron *n.* scuadron.
squalid *adj.* misera; susia, mugrosa.
squall *n.* tempesta.
squalour (US **squalor**) *n.* miseria.
squamous *adj.* scamosa.
squander *v.* malspende, peri.
square *adj.* cuadro; (*root*) cuadral. • *n.* (*shape*) cuadro; (*town*) plaza. • *v.* cuadri. **T-square** regla T.
square bolt *n.* vise cuadro.
square bracket *n.* braseta reta.
square dance *n.* dansa cuadro.
square root *n.* radis cuadral, radis du.
square sail *n.* vela cuadro.
square screw *n.* vise cuadro.
squash[1] *v.* crase, maxa. • *n.* (*sport*) scuax.
squash[2] *n.* (*gourd*) zuca.
squash player *n.* scuaxor.
squat *v.* acrupi. • *adj.* truncin. • *n.* casa nonlegal ocupada. **squat down** acrupi se.
squatter *n.* ocupor nonlegal.
squatter camp *n.* visineria de lata.
squawk *v.* & *n.* abaia.
squeak *v.* & *n.* (*creak*) grinse; (*animal, beep*) pia, pipi. • *interj.* pip.
squeaky *adj.* grinsente.
squeal *v.* & *n.* pia longa.
squeegee *n.* spatula.
squeeze *v.* presa; (*lightly*) preseta. **light squeeze** preseta.
squeezer *n.* presador.
squelch *v.* & *n.* gurgula.
squib *n.* petardo.
squid *n.* calamar.
squint *v.* (*to see*) plia sua oios. • *n.* (*medical*) strabia.
squire *n.* atendor.
squirm *v.* contorse.
squirrel *n.* scural.
squirrel monkey *n.* saimiri.
squirt *v.* & *n.* jeta.
squish *v.* maxa.
squishy *adj.* mol.
Sranan Tongo *adj.* & *n.* sranan.
Sri Lanka *n.* Srilanca.
Sri Lankan *adj.* & *n.* srilanca.
S-shaped *adj.* con forma de S.
St *abbr.* San.
stab *v.* & *n.* coteli, colpa con cotel; (*pain*) spasma.
stability *n.* stablia.
stabilization *n.* stabli.
stabilize *v.* stabli.
stable[1] *adj.* stable, constante.
stable[2] *n.* (*horses*) stalas. • *v.* stali.
stable boy *n.* stalor.
staccato *adj.* stacato.
stack *v.* & *n.* pila.
stacker truck *n.* levacarga.
stadium *n.* stadion.
staff *n.* (*of organization*) empleadas, persones; (*stick*) basto curva; (*musical stave*) pentagram.
staffer *n.* empleada.
stag *n.* servo mas.
stage *n.* (*progress*) paso, grado; (*for performance*) stadio. • *v.* aveni.
stagecoach *n.* dilijente.
stagehand *n.* stadior.
stage name *n.* nom teatral.
stagflation *n.* (*economy*) stania con infla.
stagger *v.* bambola; (*events, payments*) gradi.
stagnant *adj.* staniante.
stagnant water *n.* staniante.
stagnate *v.* stania.
stagnation *n.* stania.
staid *adj.* respetable.

stain *v.* manxa; (*dye*) tinje. • *n.* manxa; (*dye*) tinjente.
stained glass *n.* vitro colorida.
stained-glass window *n.* fenetra colorida.
stainless *adj.* sin manxa; nonosidinte.
stainless steel *n.* aser nonosidinte.
stair *n.* grado; (*staircase*) scalera. **stairs** scalera.
staircase *n.* scalera.
stairway *n.* scalera.
stairwell *n.* sala de scalera.
stake[1] *n.* (*pole*) palo.
stake[2] *n.* (*wager*) apostada.
stakeholder *n.* investor.
stakeout *n.* vijila.
stalactite *n.* stalatita.
stalagmite *n.* stalamita.
stale *adj.* nonfresca; staniante.
stalemate *n.* nonprogresa, rua sin sorti.
stalk *n.* tronceta.
stalklike *adj.* troncetin.
stall *n.* ciosco; (*animal, market*) stala; (*delay*) retarda. • *v.* retarda.
stallion *n.* cavalo mas.
-stalsis *suff.* (*contraction*) -stalsia.
stalwart *adj.* fidosa.
stamen *n.* (*botany*) stame.
stamina *n.* dura, tolera.
stammer *v.* & *n.* balbuta.
stamp *v.* (*foot*) piafa; (*mark*) impresa, marca, seli. • *n.* piafa; marca; impresador, marcador.
stamp collector *n.* colior de selos.
stampede *v.* fuji en manada. • *n.* panica.
stance *n.* disposa.
stand *v.* (*be standing, cause to stand*) sta; (*tolerate*) tolera. • *n.* ciosco; (*support*) portador, suportador. **stand for** representa. **stand guard** garda. **stand in** sustitui tempora. **stand on one's hands** sta sur manos. **stand out** es clar; (*jut*) protende. **stand to attention** sta firma. **stand up** sta se. **stand up straight** erije.
standalone *adj.* nondependente.
standard *n.* norma, model. • *adj.* normal.
standardization *n.* normi.
standardize *v.* normi.
standby *n.* pausa.
stand-in *n.* sustitua, sustitua tempora.
standing *adj.* stante. **standing out** clar, fasil persepable.
standoff *n.* nonprogresa.
standoffish *adj.* nonamin.
standstill *n.* para.
stanza *n.* strofe.
stapes *n.* (*bone*) stribo.
staphylococcus *n.* (*bacterium*) stafilococo.
staple[1] *n.* (*fastener*) grapa. • *v.* grapi.
staple[2] *n.* (*food*) comeda major.
staple gun *n.* grapador.
stapler *n.* grapador.
star *n.* (*sun, celebrity*) stela.
starboard *adj.* destra.
starch *n.* amidon. • *v.* amidoni.
starchy *adj.* amidonosa.
stardom *n.* fama.
stare *v.* & *n.* regarda intensa, fisa con regarda.
starfish *n.* stela-de-mar.
starfruit *n.* carambola.
stargaze *n.* contempla la stelas.
stark *adj.* sever.
starlet *n.* stela joven.
starlight *n.* lus de stela.
starlike *adj.* stelin.
starling *n.* storno.
starry *adj.* stelosa.
star-shaped *adj.* stelin.
starship *n.* barcon spasial.
start *v.* & *n.* comensa, inisia; (*with surprise*) salteta.
starter *n.* (*person*) inisior; (*device*) inisiador; (*food*) deleta, plato prima.
starting *adj.* comensante. **starting from** comensante de, partinte de.
starting point *n.* punto de comensa.
startle *v.* surprende.
startup *n.* compania nova. • *adj.* inisial.
startup disk *n.* disco de inisia.
starvation *n.* mori de famia.
starve *v.* mori de famia, fami.
stash *v.* & *n.* asconde, reserva.
-stasis *suff.* -stase.
-stat *suff.* (*measuring tool*) -stato.
state *n.* (*of affairs*) state; (*political*) stato, nasion; (*province*) provinse. • *v.* (*say*) dise, declara, afirma, espresa. **head of state** xef de stato. **state of the art** cresta de la arte, cresta de la tecnolojia.
state attorney *n.* (*civil law*) litigor de stato.
statecraft *n.* arte de governa.
statehood *n.* statia.
statehouse *n.* legeria statal, legeria provinsal.
stateless *adj.* sin nasion.
stately *adj.* diniosa.
statement *n.* declara; (*financial*) fatura.
stateroom *n.* salon formal; sala de capitan.
statesman *n.* statiste.
statesmanship *n.* arte de governa.
statesperson *n.* statiste.
stateswoman *n.* statiste.
static *adj.* statical; (*denoting a state*) statal.
statics *n.* statica.
statin *n.* (*drug*) statina.
station *n.* stasion. **be stationed in** ave sua posto en.
stationary *adj.* nonmovente, stante, firma.

stationer *n.* paperor.
stationer's *n.* (*shop*) papereria.
stationery store *n.* papereria.
station master *n.* xef de staslon.
statistic *n.* statistica.
statistical *adj.* statistical.
statistician *n.* statisticiste.
statistics *n.* (*science*) statistica.
stative *adj.* stante.
statuary *n.* scultas.
statue *n.* sculta.
statuesque *adj.* alta e diniosa.
statuette *n.* sculteta.
stature *n.* grandia.
status *n.* prestijia, state.
status quo *n.* state presente.
statute *n.* lege.
staunch *adj.* dedicada.
stave *n.* (*music*) pentagram.
stay *v.* (*remain*) resta, permane; (*reside temporarily*) reposa. • *n.* reposa; (*of execution*) pospone. **stay away from** evita. **stay for the night** reposa per la note.
stay-at-home *n.* pantoflor.
stay-at-home dad *n.* om de casa.
stay-at-home mom *n.* fem de casa.
staying power *n.* dura.
steadfast *adj.* firma.
steady *adj.* firma, stable; constante.
steak *n.* steca.
steak tartare *n.* steca tatar.
steal *v.* fura; ruba.
stealth *n.* furtivia. **by stealth** furtiva, ascondeda.
stealthiness *n.* furtivia.
stealthy *adj.* furtiva, ascondeda, cuieta, secreta.
steam *n.* vapor. • *v.* (*turn to steam, apply steam to*) vapori. **steam up** nebli.
steamboat *n.* barcon de vapor.
steam engine *n.* macina de vapor.
steamer *n.* vaporador.
steam locomotive *n.* locomotiva de vapor.
steamroller *n.* compatador.
steamship *n.* barcon de vapor.
steamy *adj.* vaporosa.
steatite *n.* steatita.
steatopygia *n.* steatopijia.
steatopygous *adj.* steatopijica.
steed *n.* cavalo.
steel *n.* aser.
steep[1] *adj.* presipe.
steep[2] *v.* satura.
steeple *n.* pinaculo.
steeplechase *n.* corsa de salta.
steeplejack *n.* pinaculor.
steer *v.* dirije, gida.
steering wheel *n.* volante.
stegosaur *n.* stegosauro.
stegosaurus *n.* stegosauro.
stellar *adj.* stelal.
stem *n.* (*plant*) talo, tronceta; (*glass*) gama; (*word*) tronco.
stem cell *n.* selula madrin.
stemware *n.* vitros.
stench *n.* apesta, mal odor.
stencil *n.* stensil. • *v.* stensili.
steno *n.* stenografia.
stenographer *n.* stenografiste.
stenography *n.* stenografia.
stenosis *n.* (*medical*) stenose. • *suff.* (*narrowing*) -stenose.
stentorian *adj.* forte.
step[1] *n.* paso, grado. • *v.* fa un paso. **big step** pason. **steps** (*porch*) teraza. **step by step** par pasos. **take a step** fa un paso.
step-[2] *pref.* (*relation*) estra-.
stepbrother *n.* estrafrate.
stepchild *n.* estraenfante, estrafie.
stepdaughter *n.* estrafia.
stepfamily *n.* familia fusada.
stepfather *n.* estrapadre.
stepladder *n.* scala pliable.
stepmother *n.* estramadre.
stepparent *n.* estrajenitor.
steppe *n.* stepe.
stepped *adj.* scalerin, terazida.
stepping stone *n.* petra de paso.
stepsibling *n.* estraconaseda.
stepsister *n.* estrasore.
stepson *n.* estrafio.
steradian *n.* (*unit of angle*) steradian.
stereo[1] *adj.* & *n.* (*sound*) stereo.
stereo-[2] *pref.* (*solid*) stereo-.
stereochemistry *n.* stereocimica.
stereoisomer *n.* stereoisomero.
stereoscope *n.* stereoscopio.
stereoscopic *adj.* stereoscopial.
stereoscopy *n.* stereoscopi.
stereotype *n.* stereotipo.
stereotypical *adj.* stereotipal.
sterile *adj.* steril, nonfertil.
sterility *n.* sterilia.
sterilization *n.* sterili.
sterilize *v.* sterili.
sterilizer *n.* sterilador.
sterling *n.* paund.
stern[1] *adj.* (*strict*) sever.
stern[2] *n.* (*ship*) popa.
sterno *n.* sterno, jelatin de alcol.
sternum *n.* sterno.
steroid *adj.* & *n.* steroide.
steroidal *adj.* steroide.
sterol *n.* (*chemistry*) sterol.
stethoscope *n.* stetoscopio.
stethoscopy *n.* stetoscopi.
stevedore *n.* docor.
stew *v.* coce lenta. • *n.* ragu.

steward *n.* manejor. **air steward** ospitor de avion. **air stewardess** ospitor de avion.
stick[1] *n.* basto; (*twig*) basteta; (*sport*) raceta.
stick[2] *v.* adere, fisa; (*jam*) trapi; (*put*) pone. **stick no bills** no afisa posteres. **stick out** protende. **stick to** (*follow*) segue. **stick together** coere.
stick bug *n.* fasmido.
sticker *n.* eticeta, aderente.
stickiness *n.* adere; viscosia.
sticking plaster *n.* banda medical aderente.
stick insect *n.* fasmido.
stickleback *n.* spinosa.
stickpin *n.* spino.
stick-up *n.* ruba.
sticky *adj.* aderente, aderosa; viscosa.
sticky label *n.* aderente.
sticky note *n.* papereta aderente.
sticky tape *n.* sinta aderente.
stiff *adj.* rijida.
stiffen *v.* rijidi.
stiffness *n.* rijidia.
stiffy *n.* (*erection*) pixon.
stifle *v.* sofoca.
stigma *n.* stigma.
stigmatize *v.* manxa.
stiletto *n.* (*shoe*) talon alta; (*dagger*) daga magra.
still[1] *adj.* calma; firma. • *adv.* (*ongoing*) ancora; (*nevertheless*) an tal. • *n.* (*photo*) foto. **still be doing** fa ancora, continua fa. **still not** ancora no.
still[2] *n.* (*for distilling*) distilador.
stillbirth *n.* mori fetal.
stillborn *adj.* mor naseda.
still life *n.* natur mor.
stillness *n.* calmia.
stilt *n.* gamon; (*of building*) palo; (*bird*) imantico.
stilton *n.* (*cheese*) stilton.
stimulant *n.* stimulante.
stimulate *v.* stimula.
stimulation *n.* stimula.
stimulus *n.* stimula.
sting *v.* pica. • *n.* pica; (*stinger*) picador.
stinger *n.* picador.
stingray *n.* raia de spina.
stingy *adj.* avar.
stink *v.* apesta, malodori. • *n.* apesta, mal odor.
stinkbug *n.* xinxe scermin.
stinker *n.* malodorosa.
stinking *adj.* apestante, malodorinte, malodorosa.
stinky *adj.* apestosa.
stint *n.* calidris.
stipend *n.* salario, contribui.
stir *v.* jira. **stir up** tisa, provoca; turba.
stir-fried noodles *n.* txaumen.
stir-fry *v.* frita en uoc.
stirrup *n.* stribo.
stirrup pants *n.* pantalon de stribos.
stitch *n.* (*sewing*) punto; (*surgical*) sutur. • *v.* cose, fa un punto.
stitching *n.* cose.
St John's-wort *n.* (*plant*) iperico.
STM *n.* (*short-term memory*) memoria de dura corta.
stoat *n.* ermino.
stock *n.* (*financial*) asion, valua; (*cookery*) bulion; (*supplies*) reservas; (*rifle*) posterior; (*for graft*) portainserta. • *v.* pleni.
stockade *n.* ensirca, ensirca de cavalos.
stockbroker *n.* ajente de cambia.
stock car *n.* auto de serie.
stock exchange *n.* asioneria.
stockholder *n.* asionor.
stocking *n.* calsa.
stock market *n.* asioneria.
stockpile *v.* & *n.* reserva.
stock pot *n.* casola per bulion.
stockroom *n.* sala de furnis.
stocks *n.* pilori.
stocky *adj.* spesa.
stockyard *n.* ensirca de bestias.
stodgy *adj.* monotonosa.
stoic *adj.* & *n.* stoica.
stoical *adj.* stoica.
stoicism *n.* stoicisme.
stoke *v.* tisa.
stole *n.* xarpe.
stolen goods *n.* benes furada.
stolid *adj.* nonajitable.
stollen *n.* (*bread*) stolen.
stoma *n.* (*botany, medical*) stoma.
stomach *n.* stomaco.
stomach ache *n.* dole de stomaco.
stomata *n.* (*botany, medical*) stomas.
stomp *v.* & *n.* (*feet*) piafa.
-stomy *suff.* (*surgical opening*) -stomia.
stone *n.* petra, roca; (*fruit*) seme; (*medical*) calculo. • *v.* bombarda con petras; (*fruit*) desemi.
stone age *n.* eda de petra.
stone-curlew *n.* (*bird*) burino.
stonecutter *n.* talior de petra.
stonelike *adj.* petrin.
stonemason *n.* petror.
stoner *n.* canabor.
stonewall *v.* bloci, retarda.
stonework *n.* construi de petra.
stony *adj.* (*stonelike*) petrin; (*full of stones*) petrosa.
stooge *n.* inferior, lace, burlada.
stool *n.* sejeta.
stoolie *n.* informor.

stool pigeon *n.* informor.
stoop[1] *v.* (*bend down*) curvi.
stoop[2] *n.* (*porch*) teraza.
stop *v.* fini, para, sesa; (*overnight or before resuming*) pausa; (*for passengers*) stasion; (*with stopper*) tapi. • *n.* fini, para, sesa; pausa, loca de pausa. • *interj.* para. **stop up** tapi.
stopgap *n.* covrebuco, pleninte.
stop-off *n.* pausa, loca de pausa.
stopover *n.* pausa; visita.
stopper *n.* tapo.
stopping place *n.* (*along a journey*) loca de pausa; (*for passengers*) stasion.
stopwatch *n.* cronometre.
storage *n.* reserva.
storage closet *n.* saleta de furnis.
store *v.* conserva, reteni. • *n.* reserva; (*shop*) boteca.
storefront *n.* fasada de boteca.
storehouse *n.* beneria, reserva; tesoreria.
storeroom *n.* sala de furnis.
store window *n.* fenetra de esibi.
storey *n.* nivel.
stork *n.* siconia.
storm *n.* tempesta. • *v.* ataca.
stormproof *adj.* secur contra tempesta.
stormy *adj.* tempestosa.
story *n.* nara; (*of building*) nivel.
storybook *n.* libro de fables.
storyteller *n.* naror.
stout *adj.* spesa; (*fat*) obesa. • *n.* bir forte.
stout-hearted *adj.* corajosa.
stove *n.* stufa.
stow *v.* carga.
stowaway *n.* pasajor secreta.
strabismic *adj.* straba.
strabismus *n.* (*squint*) strabia.
straddle *v.* monta.
strafe *v.* mitralia.
straggle *v.* segue lenta, avansa min.
straight *adj.* (*not bent*) reta; (*direct*) direta. • *n.* via reta. **in a straight line** en linia reta. **stand up straight** erije.
straightaway *adv.* direta, pronto, sin retarda. • *n.* via reta.
straightedge *n.* (*tool*) bara reta.
straighten *v.* reti.
straightforward *adj.* fasil, simple; franca.
straight hair *n.* capeles reta.
straightness *n.* retia.
strain *n.* tensa. • *v.* tensa; (*sieve*) tamisi.
strainer *n.* tamis.
strait *n.* streta.
straitjacket *n.* camison de restrinje.
strand[1] *v.* (*leave*) abandona, trapi, encalia.
strand[2] *n.* (*threads or wires*) colie de filos.
strange *adj.* strana, nonormal.
strangeness *n.* strania.
strange quark *n.* cuarc strana.
stranger *n.* nonconoseda, stranjer.
strangle *v.* strangula.
strangler *n.* strangulor.
strangulation *n.* strangula.
strap *n.* banda, sintur, corea; (*shoulder*) bretela, (*thin*) breteleta, cordeta. • *v.* bandi; lia, lia con corea, sinturi. **strap up** securi.
strapless *adj.* sin bretelas.
straplike *adj.* bandin, corein, sinturin.
strap-shaped *adj.* bandin.
strata *n.* stratos.
stratagem *n.* stratejia.
strategic *adj.* stratejial.
strategist *n.* stratejiste.
strategy *n.* stratejia.
stratification *n.* strati.
stratify *v.* strati.
stratocumulus *adj.* & *n.* (*cloud*) stratocumulo.
stratosphere *n.* stratosfera.
stratospheric *adj.* stratosferal.
stratus *n.* (*cloud*) strato.
straw *n.* palia.
strawberry *n.* fresa.
strawberry blonde *adj.* & *n.* roja blonde.
straw hat *n.* xapo de palia.
straw mattress *n.* materas de palia.
stray *v.* devia. • *adj.* deviante; (*animal*) vagante, perdeda.
streak *n.* bandeta.
stream *v.* flue, ri; (*data*) flue. • *n.* rieta.
streamer *n.* banda.
streaming media *n.* medias fluente.
streamline *v.* lisi, simpli.
streamlined *adj.* airodinamical; idrodinamical.
street *n.* (*city*) strada. **man in the street** person comun, cualcun.
streetcar *n.* tram.
street corner *n.* (*general area*) canto.
streetlamp *n.* palo de lampa.
streetlight *n.* palo de lampa.
street price *n.* custa per la compror.
street sign *n.* avisa de via.
street urchin *n.* xice vagante.
streetwalker *n.* fem de strada, fem prostituida.
strength *n.* fortia.
strengthen *v.* forti.
strengthener *n.* refortinte.
strengthening strip *n.* banda fortinte.
strenuous *adj.* esersosa.
streptobacillus *n.* (*bacterium*) streptobasilo.
streptococcus *n.* (*bacterium*) streptococo.
streptomycin *n.* (*antibiotic*) streptomisina.
Stresemann's bushcrow *n.* piga itiopian.
stress *v.* (*tension*) stresa, tensa; (*phonetic*) asentua. • *n.* stresa, angusa; asentua.
stressful *adj.* stresante.

stressor *n.* stresor.
stretch *v.* estende. ● *adj.* elastica.
stretcher *n.* portaferida.
stretchy *adj.* elastica.
streusel *n.* (*cookery*) streusel.
strew *v.* sperde.
strewn *adj.* sperdeda.
striate *adj.* raiosa.
striated *adj.* (*including muscle*) raiosa.
striation *n.* ranur. **glacial striation** rasca glasial.
strict *adj.* sever, seria.
strictly *adj.* sever, seria. **strictly speaking** per dise esata.
strictness *n.* severia.
stricture *n.* restrinje; (*narrowing*) streti.
stride *v.* gami, marxa, pasea grande. ● *n.* pason, gami.
strident *adj.* xiliante.
strife *n.* disputa.
strike *v.* & *n.* colpa; (*protest*) greve. **strike through** (*cross out*) bari.
strikebreaker *n.* rompegreve.
striker *n.* grevor; (*sport*) atacor.
striking *adj.* (*eye-catching*) saisinte la oio.
string *n.* cordeta; (*characters*) cadena.
stringent *adj.* sever, seria.
string instrument *n.* strumento de cordetas.
string literal *n.* (*software*) cadena leteral.
string theory *n.* teoria de cordetas.
stringy *adj.* cordetin.
strip[1] *n.* (*narrow piece*) banda.
strip[2] *v.* (*clothes*) nudi; striptisa.
stripe *n.* (*pattern*) bandeta.
striped *adj.* bandetosa, raiosa.
stripper *n.* striptisor.
striptease *v.* & *n.* striptisa.
stripteaser *n.* striptisor.
stripy *adj.* bandetosa.
strive *v.* compete.
strobe *n.* stroboscopio.
stroboscope *n.* stroboscopio.
stroboscopic *adj.* stroboscopial.
stroganoff *n.* (*food*) stroganov.
stroke *v.* caresa. ● *n.* colpa; (*swimming*) brasi; (*medical*) ataca serebral.
stroll *v.* pasea, pasea lenta.
stroller *n.* careta de bebe.
strong *adj.* forte, durante.
strongbox *n.* caxa secur.
stronghold *n.* fortres.
strongman *n.* musculor; (*leader*) tirano.
strong-smelling *adj.* odorosa.
strong-tasting *adj.* saborosa.
strontium *n.* (*element*) strontio.
struct *n.* (*software*) uple.
structural *adj.* strutural.
structuralism *n.* struturalisme.
structuralist *n.* struturaliste.
structure *n.* strutur. ● *v.* struturi.
structureless *adj.* nonstruturida.
strudel *n.* (*pastry*) strudel.
struggle *v.* & *n.* luta. **struggle for breath** respira laborosa.
strum *v.* (*guitar*) tanje.
strumpet *n.* fem promiscua, fem prostituida, puta.
strut *n.* suportador. ● *v.* pasea grandiosa.
strychnine *n.* stricnina.
stub *n.* (*pencil, cigarette*) peseta; (*entry*) jerme.
stubble *n.* (*straw*) palias basa; (*hair*) capelones.
stubbly *adj.* capelonosa.
stubborn *adj.* ostinosa, mulin.
stubbornness *n.* ostina.
stubby *adj.* corta.
stucco *n.* (*plaster*) stuco.
stuck *adj.* fisada, trapida. **get stuck** deveni fisada, deveni trapida. **stuck in traffic** maraniada en trafica.
stuck-up *adj.* egosa.
stud[1] *n.* (*boot*) crampon.
stud[2] *n.* (*farm*) eleveria. ● *adj.* per reprodui.
studded *adj.* puntosa.
student *n.* studiante. **fellow student** costudiante.
student loan *n.* presta per studia.
student residence *n.* abitada de studiantes.
studio *n.* (*artist's, film, TV, radio*) studio.
studious *adj.* studiosa.
study *v.* studia. ● *n.* studia; (*room*) sala de studia; studio.
stuff *n.* materia. ● *v.* pleni.
stuffed toy *n.* animal de pelux.
stuffing *n.* (*action*) pleni; (*substance*) pleninte.
stuffy *adj.* (*room*) staniante; (*nose*) conjestada.
stuffy nose *n.* conjesta de nas.
stultify *v.* noia.
stumble *v.* tropeza, fa un mal paso; (*over words*) tropeza de lingua. ● *n.* tropeza. **stumble upon** encontra acaso, trova acaso.
stump *n.* trunca.
stumpy *adj.* truncin.
stun *v.* (*daze*) aturdi; (*amaze*) stona.
stun baton *n.* basto eletrical.
stun gun *n.* pistol eletrical.
stunning *adj.* aturdinte; stonante; bela.
stunt *n.* truco perilosa; presenta.
stunt double *n.* sustitua de peril.
stuntman *n.* sustitua de peril.
stuntwoman *n.* sustitua de peril.
stupa *n.* (*Buddhist building*) stupa.
stupefy *v.* aturdi.
stupendous *adj.* stonante.
stupid *adj.* stupida.
stupidity *n.* stupidia.
stupor *n.* stupor.

sturdy *adj.* forte, durante.
sturgeon *n.* (*fish*) sturion.
stutter *v.* & *n.* balbuta.
stye *n.* infeta de palpebra.
Stygian *adj.* stixin.
style *n.* stilo; (*fashion*) moda. • *v.* stili.
stylebook *n.* manual de stilo.
style guide *n.* manual de stilo.
stylesheet *n.* folia de stilo.
stylish *adj.* a la moda, de moda, modosa.
stylist *n.* stiliste.
stylistic *adj.* stilal.
stylization *n.* stili.
stylize *v.* stili.
stylus *n.* (*writing tool, record player*) stilo.
styptic *adj.* parasangual. • *n.* parasangue.
styrene *n.* (*chemistry*) stiren.
styrofoam *n.* polistiren estruida.
Styx *n.* (*mythology*) Stix.
sub[1] *n.* (*submarine*) sumarina; (*sandwich*) bagete plenida; (*substitute*) sustitua; (*subscription*) enscrive.
sub-[2] *pref.* su-.
subarctic *adj.* suartica.
subassembly *n.* suasembla.
subatomic *adj.* suatomal.
subcategory *n.* sucategoria.
subclan *n.* claneta.
subclass *n.* suclase.
subclause *n.* suproposa, proposa suordinada.
subcommittee *n.* sucomite.
subconscious *adj.* suconsensa. • *n.* suconsensia.
subcontinent *n.* sucontinente.
subcontract *v.* sucontrata.
subcontractor *n.* sucontrator.
subculture *n.* sucultur.
subcutaneous *adj.* sucutanea, ipodermal, su pel.
subcutis *n.* ipoderma.
subdirectory *n.* suarcivo.
subdiscipline *n.* sucampo.
subdivide *v.* sudivide.
subdivision *n.* sudivide.
subduce *v.* sudui.
subduction *n.* (*geology*) sudui.
subdue *v.* vinse.
subentry *n.* (*in list*) suentrada.
subfamily *n.* (*biology*) sufamilia.
subfield *n.* (*knowledge*) sucampo.
subfloor *n.* funda de solo.
subfolder *n.* suarcivo.
subgenus *n.* sujenero.
subgroup *n.* sugrupo.
subhuman *adj.* suumana.
subject *n.* (*theme, grammar*) sujeto; (*theme*) tema. • *v.* (*force upon*) carga. **subject to** propensada a; su controla de.
subjective *adj.* sujetal.
subjectivity *n.* sujetalia.
subjugate *v.* concista, domina.
subjunctive *adj.* & *n.* (*grammar*) sujuntiva.
subjunctive mood *n.* moda sujuntiva.
sublease *v.* sulua.
sublet *v.* sulua.
sublieutenant *n.* suteninte.
sublimate *v.* sublima.
sublimation *n.* sublima.
sublime *adj.* merveliosa.
subliminal *adj.* suconsensa.
sublunar *adj.* (*astronomy*) sulunan.
submarine *adj.* su mar. • *n.* sumarina.
submarine sandwich *n.* bagete plenida.
submerge *v.* sumerji.
submergence *n.* sumerji.
submerse *v.* sumerji.
submission *n.* sede.
submissive *adj.* sedente.
submit *v.* (*surrender*) sede; (*information*) presenta, envia, proposa.
subnormal *adj.* sunormal.
suborbital *adj.* suorbital.
suborder *n.* (*biology*) suordina.
subordinate *v.* suordina, inferiori. • *adj.* suordinada.
subordinate clause *n.* proposa suordinada, suproposa.
subordinating adverb *n.* averbo-sujunta.
subordinating conjunction *n.* sujunta.
subordination *n.* suordina, inferiori.
subordinator *n.* (*grammar*) sujunta.
suborn *v.* soborna.
subphylum *n.* sufilo.
subpoena *v.* & *n.* comanda per apare.
subprime *adj.* (*loan*) suprima.
subprime mortgage *n.* ipoteca suprima.
subprogram *n.* suprogram.
subroutine *n.* suprogram.
Subsaharan Africa *n.* Africa susaharan.
subscribe *v.* enscrive; junta se.
subscriber *n.* enscrivor.
subscript *n.* suindise.
subscription *n.* enscrive.
subsection *n.* susesion.
subsequent *adj.* futur, seguente.
subsequently *adv.* a pos, en la futur.
subservient *adj.* sclavin.
subset *n.* sucolie.
subside *v.* calmi.
subsidiary *adj.* ajuntable. • *n.* sucompania.
subsidize *v.* suporta finansial.
subsidy *n.* suporta finansial.
subsist *v.* (*stay alive*) susiste.
subsistence *n.* susiste.
subsoil *n.* susolo, sustrato de tera.
subspecies *n.* suspesie.
substance *n.* sustantia, materia.

substandard *adj.* inferior.
substantial *adj.* sustantial.
substantival *adj.* sustantivin, nomin.
substantive *n.* sustantivo.
substation *n.* sustasion.
substitute *adj.* & *n.* sustitua; nonautentica. • *v.* sustitui.
substitution *n.* sustitui.
substrate *n.* sustrato, funda.
subsume *v.* inclui.
subtend *v.* (*botany*, *geometry*) sutende.
subterfuge *n.* engana.
subterranean *adj.* suteran.
subtitle *n.* (*subheading*, *transcription*) sutitulo. • *v.* sutituli.
subtle *adj.* sutil.
subtleness *n.* sutilia.
subtlety *n.* (*quality*) sutilia; (*something subtle*) sutil.
subtotal *n.* susoma.
subtract *v.* sutrae.
subtraction *n.* sutrae.
subtropical *adj.* sutropical.
subtype *n.* suspesie.
suburb *n.* suburbe.
suburban *adj.* suburban.
suburbanite *n.* suburban.
suburbia *n.* suburbes.
subversion *n.* suverti.
subversive *adj.* suvertinte.
subvert *v.* suverti.
subway *n.* metro.
succeed *v.* susede; (*one's predecessor*) segue.
succeeder *n.* susedor.
success *n.* susede.
successful *adj.* susedosa.
succession *n.* serie; pasa de rena.
successive *adj.* seguente.
successor *n.* (*person*) seguor; (*thing*) seguente.
succinct *adj.* consisa.
succor (US). See *succour*.
succotash *n.* (*food*) sucotax.
succour (US **succor**) *n.* aida.
succubus *n.* sucubo.
succulent *adj.* suculente, jusosa.
succumb *v.* sede.
such *adj.* tal. **in such a way that** tal ce. **such a** un tal. **such and such** alga o otra. **such a shame** tan triste.
suck *v.* suca. **suck dry** suca a secia. **suck off** (*fellatio*) suca la pixa de. **suck up to** adula.
sucker *n.* (*anatomy*, *rubber cup*) ventosa; (*botany*) jerme de radis.
suckerlike *adj.* ventosin.
suckle *v.* suca; (*cause to*) teti.
suckling *adj.* a mamela; a seno.
sucrose *n.* (*sugar*) sucrosa.
suction *n.* suca.
Sudan *n.* Sudan. **South Sudan** Sudan Sude.
Sudani *adj.* & *n.* sudani.
sudden *adj.* subita.
sudoku *n.* (*puzzle*) sudocu.
suds *n.* spuma.
sudsy *adj.* spumosa.
sue *v.* litiga.
Suebi *n.* (*ancient tribe*) suebas.
Suebian *adj.* & *n.* sueba.
Suebians *n.* suebas.
suede *n.* cuoro suave.
suet *n.* gras de ren.
Suez *n.* Suais. **Gulf of Suez** Golfo Suais.
Suez Canal *n.* Canal Suais.
suffer *v.* sufri.
sufferer *n.* sufror.
suffering *n.* sufri, dole.
suffice *v.* sufisi.
sufficiency *n.* sufisi.
sufficient *adj.* sufisinte; (*more than enough*) bastante. **be sufficient** sufisi; basta.
suffix *v.* & *n.* sufisa.
suffixation *n.* sufisa.
suffocate *v.* sofoca.
suffocation *n.* sofoca.
suffrage *n.* direto de vota.
suffragette *n.* sufrajeta.
suffuse *v.* permea, sperde tra.
Sufi *adj.* & *n.* sufi.
Sufism *n.* (*Islam*) sufisme.
sugar *n.* zucar. • *v.* zucari.
sugarbird *n.* promerope.
sugarcane *n.* cana de zucar.
sugarcoat *v.* zucari.
sugarplum *n.* perla de zucar.
sugary *adj.* zucarosa.
suggest *v.* sujesta, proposa.
suggestibility *n.* influablia.
suggestible *adj.* influable.
suggestion *n.* sujesta, proposa.
suggestive *adj.* sujestosa, riscosa.
suggestiveness *n.* sujestosia.
suhur *n.* (*Islam*) suhur.
suicidal *adj.* suisidal.
suicide *n.* (*action*) suiside; (*person*) suisidor. **commit suicide** suiside.
suicide attack *n.* ataca par suiside.
suicide attempt *n.* suiside atentada.
suicide bomber *n.* bomba umana.
suit *v.* conveni. • *n.* (*law*) litiga; (*cards*) familia; (*clothes*) completa, (*formal*) veston.
suitability *n.* conveni.
suitable *adj.* conveninte. **be suitable** conveni.
suitcase *n.* valis.
suite *n.* (*furniture*, *rooms*, *music*, *etc.*) suite.
suited *adj.* conveninte; (*dressed*) vestida.
suitor *n.* corteor.
sukiyaki *n.* (*food*) suciaci.
Sulawesi *n.* Sulawesi.

sulcus *n.* plia.
sulf... (US). See *sulph...*
sulk *v.* mua, es malumorosa. • *n.* mal umor.
sulking *adj.* de mal umor, malumorosa.
sulky *adj.* de mal umor, malumorosa.
sullen *adj.* de mal umor, malumorosa.
sully *v.* susi, manxa.
sulphate (US **sulfate**) *n.* sulfato.
sulphide (US **sulfide**) *n.* sulfido.
sulphur (US **sulfur**) *n.* sulfur.
sulphuric (US **sulfuric**) *adj.* sulfurica.
sulphuric acid (US **sulfuric acid**) *n.* asida sulfurica.
sultan *n.* (*governor*) sultan.
sultana *n.* (*sultan's wife*) sultana.
sultanate *n.* sultania.
sultry *adj.* umida; (*woman*) seduosa.
Sulu Sea *n.* Mar Sulu.
sum *n.* soma.
sumac *n.* (*plant*) sumaco.
Sumatra *n.* Sumatra.
Sumba *n.* (*island*) Sumba.
Sumba Strait *n.* Streta Sumba.
Sumer *n.* Sumer.
Sumeria *n.* Sumer.
summa cum laude *adv.* con loda masima.
summarily *adv.* direta.
summarize *v.* resoma.
summary *n.* resoma.
summary execution *n.* esecuta fretada.
summation *n.* soma.
summer *n.* estate. • *adj.* estatal. • *v.* estati, pasa la estate.
summerhouse *n.* casa de estate.
summer solstice *n.* solstisio de estate.
summertime *n.* estate.
summery *adj.* estatin.
summit *n.* (*peak*) culmina; (*meeting*) confere de xefes.
summon *v.* clama, veni.
summons *v.* & *n.* clama, comanda per apare.
sumo *n.* (*sport*) sumo.
sumo wrestler *n.* sumor.
sump *n.* caxa de olio.
sumptuous *adj.* lusosa.
sun *n.* sol. • *v.* soli. **sun oneself** soli se.
sunbaked *adj.* secida par sol.
sunbathe *v.* bani su sol, soli se.
sunbeam *n.* raio de sol.
sunbed *n.* lecto de sol.
sunbelt *n.* (*sunny region*) banda solosa.
sunbird *n.* netarina.
sunblock *n.* crema solal.
sunburn *n.* arde par sol.
sunburned *adj.* ardeda par sol.
suncream *n.* crema solal.
Sunda *adj.* & *n.* (*person, language*) sunda.
sundae *n.* (*food*) sunde.
Sunda Strait *n.* Streta Sunda.
Sunday *n.* soldi.
sundew *n.* (*plant*) drosera.
sundial *n.* orolojo de sol.
sundown *n.* reposa de sol.
sundress *n.* roba de sol.
sundried *adj.* secida par sol.
sundry *adj.* diversa, variosa.
sunflower *n.* (*plant, bloom*) elianto.
sunglasses *n.* oculo de sol.
sunken *adj.* afondada.
sunlamp *n.* lampa solin, lampa ultravioleta.
sunlight *n.* lus de sol.
sunlit *adj.* luminada par sol.
Sunna *n.* (*Islam*) suna.
Sunnah *n.* (*Islam*) suna.
Sunni *adj.* & *n.* (*Islam*) suni.
Sunnite *adj.* & *n.* (*Islam*) suni.
sunny *adj.* solosa.
sunrise *n.* leva de sol.
sunroof *n.* teto solal.
sunroom *n.* sala de sol, jardin de inverno.
sunset *n.* reposa de sol.
sunshine *n.* brilia de sol.
sunspot *n.* manxa solal.
sunstroke *n.* ipertermia.
suntan *n.* bronze.
sun umbrella *n.* parasol.
sup[1] *v.* (*have dinner*) come.
sup[2] *v.* (*sip*) sorbe.
super- *pref.* supra-.
superannuate *v.* jubila.
superb *adj.* merveliosa.
supercargo *n.* supravidor de carga.
supercharge *v.* supracarga.
supercilious *adj.* egosa.
superclass *n.* supraclase.
supercomputer *n.* supracomputador.
superconductor *n.* supracondutador.
superego *n.* (*psychology*) supraego.
superfamily *n.* (*biology*) suprafamilia.
superficial *adj.* surfasal.
superfluous *adj.* suprafluente, plu ca nesesada.
supergroup *n.* supragrupo.
superhero *n.* supraeroe.
superhighway *n.* autovia.
superhuman *adj.* & *n.* supraumana.
superimpose *v.* suprapone.
superimposure *n.* suprapone.
superintendent *n.* supravidor.
superior *adj.* & *n.* superior. **Lake Superior** Lago Superior.
superiority *n.* superioria.
superlative *adj.* & *n.* superlativa.
superman *n.* supraom.
supermarket *n.* supramercato, comederia.
supernatural *adj.* supranatural.
supernormal *adj.* supranormal.
supernova *n.* (*star*) supranova.

supernumerary *adj.* esedente, plu ca nesesada.
superorder *n.* (*biology*) supraordina.
superordinate *adj.* supraordinada.
superphylum *n.* suprafilo.
superpower *n.* (*of superhero*) suprapotia; (*political*) suprapotiosa.
superpowerful *adj.* suprapotiosa.
superscript *n.* supraindise.
supersede *v.* sustitui per.
supersonic *adj.* suprasonal.
superstition *n.* superstisio.
superstitious *adj.* superstisiosa, credosa.
supervene *v.* interrompe; (*philosophy*) segue.
supervise *v.* supravide.
supervision *n.* supravide.
supervisor *n.* supravidor.
superwoman *n.* suprafem.
supinator *n.* (*muscle*) supinador.
supine *adj.* supina.
supper *n.* come, come de sera.
suppertime *n.* ora de come.
supplant *v.* sustitui per, recambia.
supple *adj.* flexable.
supplement *v.* & *n.* aumenta.
supplemental *adj.* aumental.
supplementary *adj.* aumental, ajuntable, ajuntada, completinte.
supplicate *v.* suplica.
supplication *n.* suplica.
supplier *n.* furnor.
supply *v.* & *n.* furni; (*ammunition*) muni. **supplies** furnis. **supply and demand** ofre e compra.
supply closet *n.* saleta de furnis.
supply convoy *n.* convoia de furnis.
support *v.* suporta, susta; (*advocate*) promove; (*comfort*) consola. • *n.* suporta; consola; (*holder*) portador, suportador.
supportable *adj.* suportable.
support animal *n.* bestia de servi.
supported *adj.* suportada.
supporter *n.* suportor.
supporting device *n.* suportador.
supporting fact *n.* fato suportante.
supporting musician *n.* musiciste suportante.
supportive *adj.* suportosa.
suppose *v.* suposa.
supposition *n.* suposa.
suppository *n.* supositorio.
suppress *v.* supresa.
suppressant *n.* supresante.
suppression *n.* supresa.
suprarenal *adj.* suprarenal.
suprasegmental *adj.* suprasesional.
supremacy *n.* supremia.
supreme *adj.* suprema.
supreme court *n.* corte suprema.
surcharge *n.* paia ajuntada.
surcoat *n.* jacon de cavalor.
sure *adj.* serta. **make sure** serti.
surely *adv.* serta.
surety *n.* garantia; (*person*) garantior.
surf *v.* surfa. • *n.* (*waves*) surfa. **surf the net** surfa la rede, viaja tra la ueb.
surface *n.* surfas. • *v.* apare, emerji. **on the surface** surfasal.
surface-to-air *adj.* de tera a aira.
surface-to-surface *adj.* de tera a tera.
surfboard *n.* plance de surfa.
surfeit *n.* esede.
surfer *n.* surfor.
surge *v.* & *n.* aumenta, avansa; (*emotion*) ondon.
surgeon *n.* sirurjiste.
surgery *n.* sirurjia.
surgical *adj.* sirurjial.
suricate *n.* (*meerkat*) suricata.
Surinam *n.* Suriname.
Suriname *n.* Suriname.
Suriname Creole *adj.* & *n.* (*language*) sranan.
Surinamese *adj.* & *n.* (*person*) sranan.
surly *adj.* bruta, noncortes; disputosa, malumorosa.
surmise *v.* suposa.
surmount *v.* vinse. **be surmounted with** culmina con.
surname *n.* nom familial.
surpass *v.* suprapasa, esede.
surplice *n.* camison blanca.
surplus *n.* suprapasa.
surprise *v.* & *n.* surprende.
surreal *adj.* sureal.
surrealism *n.* surealisme.
surrealist *n.* surealiste.
surrealistic *adj.* surealiste.
surrender *v.* & *n.* sede.
surreptitious *adj.* secreta.
surrey *n.* caro per du.
surrogate *adj.* sustitua. • *n.* sustitua, sustitua tempora, teniloca.
surround *v.* ensirca; (*general environment*) ambie.
surrounding *prep.* sirca.
surroundings *n.* ambiente.
Surt *n.* Sirte.
surtax *v.* & *n.* surimposta.
surveillance *n.* vijila, monitori.
survey *v.* (*investigate*) sonda; (*land*) jeometre. • *n.* sonda; studia.
surveyor *n.* (*land*) jeometror.
survival *n.* survive.
survival kit *n.* paceta de survive.
survive *v.* survive.
survivor *n.* survivor.
susceptibility *n.* propensa.
susceptible *adj.* afetable, propensada.

sushi *n.* (*food*) suxi.
suspect *v.* suspeta. • *n.* (*person*) suspetada.
suspend *v.* (*hang*) pende; (*hang, interrupt*) suspende; (*interrupt*) interompe; (*judgement*) pospone.
suspended animation *n.* anima suspendeda.
suspender *n.* (*shoulder strap*) bretela; (*stocking strap*) lia, bretela de calsa.
suspender belt *n.* portalia.
suspense *n.* suspende.
suspenseful *adj.* suspendosa.
suspension *n.* suspende; interompe.
suspicion *n.* suspeta.
suspicious *adj.* suspetante; (*suspecting, arousing suspicion*) suspetosa.
sustain *v.* susta.
sustainable *adj.* sustable.
sustenance *n.* susta.
sutra *n.* (*aphorism, scripture*) sutra.
suttee *n.* (*ritual immolation of widow*) sati.
suture *n.* sutur; (*action*) suturi. • *v.* suturi.
SUV *n.* (*sport utility vehicle*) multiterenal.
Svalbard *n.* Svalbard.
svelte *adj.* magra.
swab *n.* tampon.
Swabia *n.* (*German region*) Xvaben.
Swabian *adj.* xvabes.
swaddle *v.* envolve.
swag *n.* garlanda; benes furada. • *v.* drape.
swagger *n.* bravata.
swaggering *adj.* bravatosa.
Swahili *adj.* & *n.* (*person, language*) suahili.
swallet *n.* dolina.
swallow[1] *v.* (*eat, engulf*) engoli.
swallow[2] *n.* (*bird*) rondin.
swallow dive *n.* tufa de anjel.
swallowhole *n.* dolina.
swami *n.* (*Hinduism*) suami.
swamp *n.* pantan, pantan erbosa.
swampy *adj.* pantanosa.
swan *n.* sinie.
swan dive *n.* tufa de anjel.
swanky *adj.* lusosa.
swap *v.* & *n.* intercambia.
swappable *adj.* intercambiable.
swarm *v.* xama. • *n.* xama, manada.
swarthy *adj.* brun.
swashbuckler *n.* bravatosa.
swashbuckling *adj.* bravatosa.
swastika *n.* suastica.
swathe *n.* banda.
sway *v.* (*rock*) osila; (*persuade*) convinse, influe.
Swazi *adj.* & *n.* suazi.
Swaziland *n.* Suaziland.
swear *v.* jura; (*curse*) blasfema. **swear in** indui.
swearword *n.* blasfema.
sweat *n.* suo. • *v.* sui.
sweatband *n.* banda de suo.
sweater *n.* sueter.
sweater vest *n.* sueter sin manga.
sweatpants *n.* pantalon de sporte.
sweatshirt *n.* sueter de sporte.
sweatshop *n.* fabriceria misera.
sweaty *adj.* suosa.
swede[1] *n.* (*plant, vegetable*) colinabo.
Swede[2] *n.* (*person*) svensce.
Sweden *n.* Sveria.
Swedish *adj.* & *n.* svensce.
sweep *v.* scopi, limpi; (*thrust*) puxa; (*person*) scopor. **sweep through** traversa.
sweeper *n.* scopor.
sweepstake *n.* aposta coletiva.
sweet *adj.* dulse. • *n.* confeto.
sweet-and-sour *adj.* asida-dulse.
sweetbriar *n.* rosa spinosa.
sweetbrier *n.* rosa spinosa.
sweeten *v.* dulsi.
sweetener *n.* dulsinte.
sweet flag *n.* calamo.
sweetheart *n.* mielin.
sweet lemon *n.* limeta.
sweet lime *n.* limeta.
sweet limetta *n.* limeta.
sweet myrtle *n.* (*plant*) calamo.
sweetness *n.* dulsia.
sweet potato *n.* patata dulse.
sweet sauce *n.* salsa dulse.
swell *v.* infla.
swelter *v.* sofoca de caldia.
swept *adj.* scopida.
swerve *v.* & *n.* verje, devia.
swift *adj.* rapida. • *n.* (*bird*) venseo.
swig *v.* engoli.
swill *v.* engoli; (*swirl*) jira.
swim *v.* & *n.* nada.
swim briefs *n.* slip de nada.
swimmer *n.* nador.
swimming baths *n.* naderia.
swimming complex *n.* naderia.
swimming costume *n.* veste de nada.
swimming pool *n.* pisina.
swimming trunks *n.* pantala de nada.
swim shorts *n.* pantala de nada.
swimsuit *n.* veste de nada; (*one-piece*) bodi de nada.
swimwear *n.* vestes de nada.
swindle *v.* froda.
swindler *n.* frodor.
swine *n.* porco.
swine flu *n.* gripe porcal.
swineherd *n.* porcor.
swing *n.* pendulo; (*dance, music*) suing. • *v.* (*back and forth*) penduli; (*up and down*) balansi; (*club*) brandi. **swing at** atenta colpa, brandi per colpa, lansa un colpa a. **swing round** pivote.

swinger *n.* (*socaliser*) vivosa; (*sex*) intercambior.
swinging *n.* (*sex*) intercambia.
swipe *v.* (*steal*) fura; (*card, finger*) lisca.
swirl *v.* jira, spirali.
Swiss *adj.* & *n.* suiz.
Swiss army knife *n.* cotel composada.
switch *n.* (*electric*) comutador; (*railway*) force de ferovia. **switch back on** recomuta. **switch off** descomuta, clui. **switch on** comuta, abri.
switchblade *n.* cotel ejetable.
switchboard *n.* sentro de telefonia.
switchman *n.* forcor de ferovia.
Switzerland *n.* Suiz.
swivel *v.* jira.
swivel chair *n.* seja jirante.
swollen *adj.* inflada.
swoon *v.* desmaia.
swoop *v.* & *n.* tufa. **in one fell swoop** par sola un colpa.
sword *n.* spada.
sword belt *n.* xarpe de spada.
swordfighter *n.* spador.
swordfish *n.* pex de spada.
swordlike *adj.* spadin.
swordplay *n.* scrima.
sword-shaped *adj.* spadin.
swordsman *n.* spador.
sword swallower *n.* comespada.
swordswoman *n.* spador.
sybarite *n.* edoniste.
sybaritism *n.* edonisme.
sycamore *n.* (*tree*) platan.
sycophancy *n.* adula.
sycophant *n.* adulor.
sycophantic *adj.* adulante.
syllabary *n.* silabario.
syllabic *adj.* silabal.
syllable *n.* silaba.
syllogism *n.* razona deduinte.
sylph *n.* fe de aira.
sylvan *adj.* boscin.
sym- *pref.* (*together*) sim-.
symbiont *n.* simbiosica.
symbiosis *n.* simbiose.
symbiotic *adj.* simbiosica.
symbol *n.* simbol.
symbolic *adj.* simbolin.
symbolism *n.* simbolisme.
symbolization *n.* simboli.
symbolize *v.* simboli.
symbology *n.* simbolojia.
symmetrical *adj.* simetre.
symmetry *n.* simetria.
sympathetic *adj.* (*pity*) compatiosa; (*rapport*) simpatiosa; (*technical senses*) simpatica.
sympathize *v.* compatia.
sympathizer *n.* suportor.
sympathy *n.* compatia.
symphonic *adj.* simfonial, simfonin.
symphony *n.* simfonia.
symposium *n.* confere.
symptom *n.* sintom.
symptomatic *adj.* sintomal.
symptomatology *n.* sintomolojia.
syn- *pref.* (*together*) sin-.
synaesthesia (US **synesthesia**) *n.* sinestesia.
synagogue *n.* sinagoga.
synapse *n.* (*biology*) sinapse.
synaptic *adj.* sinapsal.
sync *v.* & *n.* sincroni. **in sync** sincrona. **out of sync** nonsincrona.
synchronic *adj.* sincrona.
synchronicity *n.* simultania.
synchronism *n.* sincrona.
synchronization *n.* sincroni.
synchronize *v.* sincroni.
synchronous *adj.* sincrona.
syncopate *v.* sincopa.
syncopation *n.* (*music*) sincopa.
syncope *n.* desmaia.
syndicalism *n.* sindicatisme.
syndicalist *n.* sindicatiste.
syndicate *n.* sindicato. • *v.* sindicati.
syndication *n.* sindicati.
syndrome *n.* sindrom.
synergetic *adj.* sinerjial.
synergistic *adj.* sinerjial.
synergy *n.* sinerjia.
synesthesia (US). See *synaesthesia*.
synod *n.* (*Christianity*) sinodo.
synonym *n.* sinonim.
synonym dictionary *n.* disionario de sinonimes.
synonymous *adj.* sinonim.
synonymy *n.* sinonimia.
synopsis *n.* resoma.
synoptic *adj.* resomal.
synovial *adj.* sinovial.
synovial fluid *n.* (*biology*) sinovia.
synovial membrane *n.* (*biology*) sinovial.
synovium *n.* sinovial.
syntactic *adj.* sintatical.
syntactical *adj.* sintatical.
syntactic category *n.* categoria sintatical.
syntax *n.* sintatica.
syntax analyser (US **analyzer**) *n.* analisador sintatical.
synth *n.* sintesador.
synthesis *n.* sintese.
synthesize *v.* sintese.
synthesizer *n.* sintesador.
synthetic *adj.* sintesal, sinteseda, artifis.
syphilis *n.* (*medical*) sifilis.
syphilitic *adj.* sifilisica.
Syria *n.* Suria.

Syrian *adj.* & *n.* suri.
Syrian bread *n.* pita.
syringe *n.* siringa. • *v.* siringi.
syrinx *n.* (*musical instrument*) flauta de Pan; (*anatomy*) sirinje.
Syrte *n.* Sirte.
syrup *n.* xirope.
system *n.* sistem.
systematic *adj.* sistemosa.
systemic *adj.* sistemal.
systole *n.* (*biology*) sistole.
systolic *adj.* sistolal.
syzygy *n.* (*astronomy*) sizijia.

T

tab *n.* (*of page*) oreta; (*bill*) fatura.
tabbed *adj.* con oretas.
tabbouleh *n.* (*food*) tabule.
tabby *adj.* bandetosa.
tab character *n.* sinia de tabli.
tabernacle *n.* baldacin.
tab key *n.* tecla de tabli.
tabla *n.* (*musical instrument*) tabla.
table *n.* (*furniture, of information*) table. **table of contents** table de contenidas.
tableau *n.* sena vivante.
tablecloth *n.* covretable, telon.
table game *n.* jua de table.
tableland *n.* plano alta.
table saw *n.* siera de table.
tablespoon *n.* (*spoon, measurement*) culier de table.
tablet *n.* (*writing*) tableta; (*pill*) pil.
tablet computer *n.* tableta, computador tabletin.
table tennis *n.* tenis de table.
tabletop *n.* surfas de table.
tabloid newspaper *n.* jornal de scandal.
tablut *n.* (*game*) tafel.
taboo *adj.* & *n.* tabu.
tabor *n.* tambur peti.
tabulate *v.* tabli.
tabulation *n.* table.
tachometer *n.* contajira.
tachy- *pref.* (*rapid*) taci-.
tachycardia *n.* tacicardia.
tachycardial *adj.* tacicardial.
tachyon *n.* (*particle*) tacion.
tacit *adj.* implicada.
taciturn *adj.* nonespresosa.
tack *n.* (*nail*) cloeta; (*course of action*) tatica; (*stitch*) punto longa. • *v.* verje contra la venta.
tackle *v.* (*enemy, problem*) fronti, ataca; (*sport*) tacle, tira a tera. • *n.* aparatos; aparatos de vela; (*sport*) tacle.
tacky[1] *adj.* (*sticky*) aderente.
tacky[2] *adj.* (*kitsch*) inferior.
taco *n.* (*food*) taco.
tact *n.* tato.
tactful *adj.* tatosa.
tactic *n.* tatica.
tactical *adj.* tatical.
tactician *n.* taticiste.
tactile *adj.* palpable.
tactless *adj.* nontatosa, noncortes.
tad *n.* pico, goteta.
ta-da *interj.* ta-da.
tadpole *n.* raneta.
taffeta *n.* (*fabric*) tafeta.
taffy *n.* caramel tirada.
tafl *n.* (*game*) tafel.
tag *n.* (*including markup*) eticeta. • *v.* eticeti.
Tagalog *adj.* & *n.* (*person, language*) tagalog.
tag question *n.* demanda codal.
Tahiti *n.* Tahiti.
Tahitian *adj.* & *n.* tahiti.
tai-chi *n.* taitxi.
tai-chi chuan *n.* taitxi.
taiga *n.* taiga.
tail *n.* coda; (*coat*) faldon. **tails** (*coin*) dorso.
tailbone *n.* cosix.
tailed *adj.* (*possessing a tail*) codida.
tailgate *n.* porte retro. • *v.* segue tro prosima.
taillight *n.* lampa retro.
tailor *n.* talior.
tailor-made *adj.* par comanda.
tailpipe *n.* tubo de emetador.
tailwind *n.* venta de retro.
taint *v.* manxa.
Taiwan *n.* Taiuan.
Taiwanese *adj.* & *n.* taiuan.
Taiwanese Hokkien *adj.* & *n.* (*person, language*) holo.
Tajik *adj.* & *n.* (*person, language*) tadjici.
Tajikistan *n.* Tadjicistan.
take *v.* (*including chess*) prende; (*shower, photo, etc.*) fa; (*road*) vade sur. **take a chance** risca la acaso. **take a drive** turi. **take advantage of** esplota, profita de. **take a photo of** fa un foto de, xuta. **take a step** fa un paso. **take a swing at** atenta colpa, brandi per colpa, lansa un colpa a. **take away** sutrae. **take back** reprende, retira. **take by force** saisi par fortia, concista. **take care of** cura; (*temporarily*) atende. **take far away** distanti. **take for a spin** (*a stolen car*) jira. **take hostage** saisi como ostaje. **take in** (*internalize*) interni. **take into account** considera, regarda, atende. **take it easy** destensa, reposa. **take oath** jura. **take off** (*aircraft*) enaira; (*garment*) desapone. **take on** emprende. **take one's time** prende sua tempo. **take one's turn** fa sua turno. **take out** estrae. **take over** emprende, prende controla de. **take part** partisipa. **take place** aveni. **take refuge** refuja se. **take root** radisi. **take sides** es partisan. **take solace in** es consolada par. **take the initiative** inisia. **take turns** alterna. **take up** (*pick up*) prende; (*adopt*) adota, comensa, comensa usa. **take your time** no freta.
takeaway *n.* come retirable.

takeaway restaurant *n.* restorante de comes retirable.
take-off *n.* (*aircraft*) enaira; (*parody*) parodia.
takeout *n.* come retirable.
takeout restaurant *n.* restorante de comes retirable.
taker *n.* prendor.
Taki Taki *adj.* & *n.* sranan.
Taklamakan Desert *n.* Deserto Taklamakan.
talc *n.* talco.
talcum powder *n.* talco, polvo de talco.
tale *n.* nara.
talent *n.* talento, capasia.
talented *adj.* talentosa.
talisman *n.* joala majiosa.
talk *v.* parla. **talk about** parla sur, discute. **talk bollocks** parla merda. **talk bullshit** parla merda. **talk down to** finje superioria. **talk nonsense** babela. **talk of** parla de.
talkative *adj.* parlosa.
talkback *n.* comunicador de porte, telefon de porte.
talk show *n.* program de conversa.
talk-show host *n.* ospitor de conversa.
tall *adj.* alta.
tallow *n.* (*substance*) sebo.
tally *n.* conta. • *v.* acorda.
talmud *n.* (*Judaism*) talmud.
talmudal *adj.* talmudal.
talon *n.* gara.
talus *n.* talo.
tamale *n.* (*food*) tamale.
tamarin *n.* (*monkey*) tamarin.
tamarind *n.* (*tree*) tamarindo.
tambour *n.* tambur.
tambourine *n.* tambureta.
tame *v.* doma. • *adj.* domada.
Tamil *adj.* & *n.* (*person*, *language*) tamil.
tam o'shanter *n.* (*hat*) tam.
tamper *v.* interfere, adultera.
tampon *n.* tampon de fem.
tan *n.* bronze. • *v.* bronzi; (*leather*) tana.
tanager *n.* (*bird*) tangar.
tanbark *n.* cortex de tanin.
tandem *n.* bisicle per du. **in tandem** la un pos la otra.
Tang *adj.* (*dynasty*) tang.
tanga *n.* (*briefs*) minislip.
Tanganyika, Lake *n.* Lago Tanganyika.
tangent *n.* tanjente.
tangential *adj.* tanjente. **be tangential to** tanje.
tangerine *n.* (*fruit*) tanjerina; (*tree*) tanjerino.
tangerine tree *n.* mandarino.
tangible *adj.* tocable, palpable, concreta; real, persepable.
tangle *v.* & *n.* marania.
tangled *adj.* maraniada; (*hair*) despetenida.
tango *n.* (*dance*) tango.
tangram *n.* (*puzzle*) tangram.
tank *n.* (*including military*) tance.
tankard *n.* tason de peltre.
tanker *n.* tancador.
tankini *n.* (*bikini*) tancini.
tank top *n.* (*UK: pullover*) sueter sin manga; (*US: sleeveless shirt*) camiseta de sporte.
tank tread *n.* banda erugin.
tanner *n.* tanor.
tannery *n.* taneria.
tannic *adj.* (*chemistry*) tanica.
tannic acid *n.* asida tanica.
tannin *n.* tanin.
tantalize *v.* tisa.
tantalum *n.* (*element*) tantalo.
tantamount *adj.* egal.
tantra *n.* tantra.
tantric *adj.* tantral.
tantrum *n.* crise coler.
Tanzania *n.* Tanzania.
Tanzanian *adj.* & *n.* tanzanian.
Tao *n.* dau.
Taoism *n.* dauisme.
Taoist *n.* dauiste.
tap[1] *n.* (*faucet*) valva; (*pipe threader*) filetador mas.
tap[2] *v.* (*knock*) tape; (*at door*) bateta; (*medical*) percute. • *n.* tape; bateta; (*consonant*) tocante.
tapaculo *n.* (*bird*) tapaculo.
tap dance *v.* & *n.* clace.
tap dancer *n.* clacor.
tape *n.* banda. • *v.* bandi; rejistra. **audio tape** banda audio. **tape up** bandi. **video tape** banda video.
taper *v.* diminui.
tape recorder *n.* rejistrador de banda.
tapered *adj.* diminuinte.
tapestry *n.* tapeto imajal.
tapeworm *n.* sestodo.
tapioca *n.* tapioca.
tapir *n.* (*animal*) tapir.
tap pants *n.* culote.
taproot *n.* radis major.
tap-tap *interj.* clac-clac.
taqiyah *n.* (*cap*) cipa.
tar *n.* catran; catran de tabaco. • *v.* catrani.
taramasalata *n.* (*food*) tarama.
tarantula *n.* (*spider*) tarantula.
tardigrade *n.* tardigrado.
tardy *adj.* tarda.
tare *n.* (*plant*) visia.
target *n.* ojeto, gol; (*shooting*) blanco.
tariff *n.* tarifa.
tarmac *n.* asfalto.
tarn *n.* lageta.
tarnish *v.* osidi; (*reputation*) manxa. • *n.* osidi.
taro *n.* (*plant*) taro.

tarot *n.* (*cards*) taroci.
tarp *n.* lona catranida.
tarpaper *n.* paper de catran.
tarpaulin *n.* lona catranida.
tarragon *n.* tragon.
tarry *v.* pigri.
tarsal *adj.* tarsal.
tarsier *n.* (*primate*) tarsio.
tarsus *n.* (*bones*) tarso.
tart[1] *adj.* (*taste*) asida.
tart[2] *n.* (*pie*) tarteta.
tart[3] *n.* (*minx*) seduor, tisor.
tartan *n.* texeda scotes.
tartar *n.* tartar.
tartare sauce *n.* salsa tatar.
tartar sauce *n.* salsa tatar.
Tartessian *adj.* & *n.* tartesica.
Tartessos *n.* (*ancient city*) Tarteso.
tartness *n.* asidia.
taser *n.* pistol eletrical.
Tashkent *n.* Taxcent.
task *n.* taxe.
taskmaster *n.* taxor.
Tasmania *n.* Tasmania.
Tasmanian devil *n.* diablo tasmanian.
Tasman Sea *n.* Mar Tasman.
tassel *n.* borla.
taste *v.* (*have flavour*) sabori; (*experience flavour*) proba. • *n.* (*flavour*) sabor; (*experience*) proba; (*liking*) prefere. **taste good** sabori bon.
taste bud *n.* papila de sabor.
tasteful *adj.* plasente.
tasteless *adj.* sin sabor; (*aesthetically*) nonconveninte, repulsante.
tasty *adj.* saborosa.
ta-ta *interj.* txau, asta reuni.
tatami *n.* (*mat*) tatami.
Tatar *adj.* & *n.* (*person, language*) tatar.
tattered *adj.* laserada.
tattle *n.* informa. • *v.* parleta.
tattler *n.* (*bird*) tringa.
tattoo *v.* & *n.* tatua.
tau *n.* (*Greek letter* Τ, τ) tau.
taunt *v.* & *n.* burla.
taupe *adj.* & *n.* (*colour*) tope.
Taurus *n.* (*constellation*) la Bove.
taut *adj.* streta, tensada.
tautness *n.* stretia.
tautology *n.* tautolojia.
tavern *n.* taverna, beveria.
tawdry *adj.* ornosa.
tawny *adj.* oranin brun. • *n.* brun oranin.
tax *v.* & *n.* imposta.
taxable *adj.* impostable.
taxation *n.* imposta.
tax break *n.* pardona de imposta.
tax cut *n.* redui de imposta.
tax-deductible *adj.* sutrable de imposta.
tax dodger *n.* evitor de imposta.
taxfree *adj.* sin imposta.
tax haven *n.* paradiso finansial.
taxi[1] *n.* taxi. • *v.* (*aircraft*) rola. **water taxi** barco-bus.
taxi-[2] *pref.* (*arrangement*) tasi-.
taxicab *n.* taxi.
taxidermist *n.* tasidermiste.
taxidermy *n.* tasidermia.
taxi driver *n.* taxiste.
taximeter *n.* taximetre.
taxiway *n.* (*airport*) via de rola.
taxman *n.* impostor.
taxon *n.* (*biology*) tason.
taxonomic *adj.* tasonomial.
taxonomist *n.* tasonomiste.
taxonomy *n.* tasonomia.
taxpayer *n.* paior de imposta, contribuor.
tax reduction *n.* redui de imposta.
TB *n.* tuberculose.
T-bone steak *n.* steca T.
T-cell *n.* limfosite T.
tchotchke *n.* (*trinket*) orneta.
tea *n.* (*plant, leaves, drink*) te.
teaberry *n.* te de bosce.
teach *v.* (*person*) instrui; (*subject*) ensenia.
teacher *n.* ensenior, mestre.
tea cosy *n.* covrevaso.
teacup *n.* tas de te.
teak *n.* (*tree, wood*) teca.
tea kettle *n.* caldera de te.
teal *n.* (*bird*) serseta.
team *n.* ecipo.
teammate *n.* coecipor.
team member *n.* ecipor.
teamster *n.* camionor, vagonor.
teamwork *n.* coopera.
teapot *n.* vaso de te.
tear[1] *v.* & *n.* (*rip*) lasera, rompe. **tear up** rompe.
tear[2] *v.* & *n.* (*weeping*) larma.
teardrop *n.* larma.
tearful *adj.* larmosa.
tear gas *n.* gas lacrimojen.
tearjerker *n.* crevecor.
tearoom *n.* teria, sala de te.
tearstain *n.* manxa de larmas.
teary *adj.* larmosa.
tease *v.* (*mock*) burla, broma; (*good-naturedly*) burleta; (*tantalize*) tisa. • *n.* burla, broma; (*person*) tisor; (*minx*) seduor.
teasel (*also* **teazel**, **teazle**) *n.* (*plant*) dipsaco.
teaser *n.* burlor.
teashop *n.* teria, boteca de te.
teaspoon *n.* (*spoon, measurement*) culier de te.
teat *n.* (*anatomy*) teta.
teatime *n.* ora de te.
teazel (*also* **teazle**) See *teasel*.
techie *adj.* & *n.* tecnofilica.
technetium *n.* (*element*) tecnesio.

technical *adj.* tecnical.
technical term *n.* terma tecnical.
technician *n.* tecniciste.
technicolor *adj.* colorosa.
technics *n.* tecnica.
technique *n.* tecnica, metodo.
techno *adj.* & *n.* (*music*) tecno. • *pref.* tecno-.
technocracy *n.* tecnocratia.
technocrat *n.* tecnocrata.
technocratic *adj.* tecnocrata.
technological *adj.* tecnolojial.
technology *n.* tecnolojia.
technophile *adj.* & *n.* tecnofilica.
technophilia *n.* tecnofilia.
technophobe *n.* tecnofobica.
technophobia *n.* tecnofobia.
technophobic *adj.* tecnofobica.
tech-savvy *adj.* tecnical astuta.
techy *adj.* & *n.* tecnofilica.
tectonic *adj.* tetonical.
tectonic plate *n.* placa tetonical.
tectonics *n.* tetonica.
teddy *n.* (*bear*) urso de pelux; (*garment*) bodi.
teddy bear *n.* urso de pelux.
tedious *adj.* noiante, monotonosa.
tedium *n.* noia.
tee *n.* (*golf*) portabal; (*T-shirt*) camisa T, camiseta.
tee-hee *interj.* (*giggling*) hi hi.
teem *v.* (*with*) es plen de.
teeming *adj.* plen.
teen *adj.* adolesente.
teenage *adj.* adolesente.
teenager *n.* adolesente. **be a teenager** adolese.
teeny *adj.* pico.
teepee *n.* (*tent*) tipi.
teeter *v.* bambola, osila; (*in choice*) vasila.
teeth *n.* dentes.
teethe *v.* crese dentes.
teething *n.* eruta de dentes.
teetotal *adj.* asteninte.
teetotaller (US **teetotaler**) *n.* astenor de alcol, nonbevor de alcol.
teff *n.* (*plant*) tef.
teflon *n.* teflon.
tele- *pref.* (*remote*) tele-.
telecast *n.* difusa.
telecommunicate *v.* telecomunica.
telecommunication *n.* telecomunica, telefonia.
telecommute *v.* telelabora.
telecommuter *n.* telelaboror.
telegram *n.* telegram.
telegraph *n.* telegraf. • *v.* telegrafi.
telegraphy *n.* telegrafia.
telekinesis *n.* telecinese.
telemark *n.* (*skiing*) telemarc.
telemeter *n.* telemetre.
telemetry *n.* telemetri.
telenovela *n.* telenovela.
teleological *adj.* teleolojial.
teleology *n.* teleolojia.
telepath *n.* telepatica.
telepathic *adj.* telepatica.
telepathy *n.* telepatia.
telephone *n.* telefon. • *v.* telefoni.
telephone booth *n.* ciosco de telefon.
telephone box *n.* ciosco de telefon.
telephone exchange *n.* sentro de telefonia.
telephonist *n.* telefoniste.
telephony *n.* telefonia.
telephoto lens *n.* telefoto.
teleport *v.* teleporta. • *n.* teleportador.
teleportation *v.* teleporta.
teleporter *n.* teleportador.
teleprint *v.* teletape.
teleprinter *n.* teletapador.
telescope *n.* telescopio.
telescopic *adj.* telescopial.
Telescopium *n.* (*constellation*) la Telescopio.
teletype *v.* teletape. • *n.* teletapador.
televangelism *n.* televanjelisme.
televangelist *n.* televanjeliste.
televise *v.* televisa.
television *n.* (*phenomenon*) televisa. **on television** televisada.
television set *n.* televisador.
television viewer *n.* televidor.
telework *v.* telelabora.
teleworker *n.* telelaboror.
telic *adj.* (*expressing purpose*) telica.
telicity *n.* telicia.
tell *v.* dise; informa; (*story*) nara, raconta. **tell a lie** menti. **tell apart** distingui. **tell off** reproxa, critica.
teller *n.* contor.
telltale *adj.* revelante.
tellurium *n.* (*element*) telurio.
telly *n.* (*television set*) tele; (*phenomenon*) tv.
Telugu *adj.* & *n.* (*person, language*) telugu.
temerity *n.* noncautia.
temp *n.* empleada tempora.
temper *n.* tempera, umor. • *v.* (*emotion, metal, music*) tempera; modera.
tempera *n.* (*art*) tempera.
temperament *n.* tempera.
temperate *adj.* temperada.
temperature *n.* temperatur.
temperature gradient *n.* gradiente termal.
temper tantrum *n.* crise coler.
tempest *n.* tempesta.
tempestuous *adj.* tempestosa.
template *n.* model; (*software*) stensil.
temple[1] *n.* (*religious*) templo.
temple[2] *n.* (*anatomy*) tempe.
tempo *n.* rapidia.

temporal[1] *adj.* (*of time*) tempal.
temporal[2] *adj.* (*anatomy*) tempal.
temporal bone *n.* oso tempal.
temporal lobe *n.* lobe tempal.
temporary *adj.* tempora.
temporary shelter *n.* campa.
tempt *v.* tenta.
temptable *adj.* tentable.
temptation *n.* tenta.
tempter *n.* tentor.
temptress *n.* tentor.
tempura *n.* (*food*) tempura.
ten *det.* & *pron.* des. **tens** deses.
tenable *adj.* tenable.
tenacious *adj.* ostinosa, persistente, nonsedente.
tenacity *n.* ostina, persiste.
tenant *n.* luor.
ten-cent piece *n.* desim.
tench *n.* tinca.
Ten Commandments *n.* decalogo.
tend *v.* tende.
tendency *n.* tende.
tendentious *adj.* prejudosa.
tender[1] *adj.* (*food*) mol; (*caring*) compatiosa; (*sensitive*) delicata.
tender[2] *v.* (*offer*) ofre.
tender[3] *n.* (*boat*) barco de embarca.
tenderfoot *n.* comensor.
tenderize *v.* moli.
tenderloin *n.* filete de bove.
tending *adj.* tendente, propensada.
tendinitis *n.* tendonite.
tendon *n.* tendon.
tendonitis *n.* tendonite.
tendril *n.* viteta.
tenement *n.* aparte; aparte misera.
tenet *n.* prinsipe.
Tennessee *n.* (*US state*) Tennessee.
tennessine *n.* (*element*) tenesino.
tennis *n.* tenis.
tennis ball *n.* bal de tenis.
tennis court *n.* campo de tenis.
tennis player *n.* tenisor.
tenon *n.* (*of dovetail joint*) protende.
tenor *adj.* & *n.* (*music*) tenor.
ten-pence piece *n.* desim.
ten-pin bowling *n.* boling de des bastones.
tenrec *n.* (*animal*) tenrec.
tense[1] *adj.* tensada.
tense[2] *n.* (*grammar*) tempo.
tensile *adj.* (*of tension*) tensal; (*stretchable*) estendable.
tension *n.* tensa.
tensor *n.* tensor.
tent *n.* tenda.
tentacle *n.* tentaculo.
tentacled *adj.* tentaculosa.
tentative *adj.* esitosa.
tenth *adj.* (*ordinal*) des. • *n.* (*fraction*) desi.
ten-thousandth *adj.* (*ordinal*) des-mil. • *n.* (*fraction*) desmili.
tenuous *adj.* rarida.
tenure *n.* periodo de ofisia.
tepee *n.* (*tent*) tipi.
tepid *adj.* tepida.
tepidity *n.* tepidia.
tepidness *n.* tepidia.
tequila *n.* (*drink*) tecila.
tera- *pref.* (*a million million*) tera-.
terabyte *n.* terabait.
teratogen *n.* teratojen.
teratogenic *adj.* (*medical*) teratojen.
teratophobia *n.* teratofobia.
teratophobic *adj.* teratofobica.
terbium *n.* (*element*) terbio.
teriyaki *n.* (*food*) teriaci.
term *n.* (*terminology*, *mathematics*) terma; (*office*) periodo; (*course*) trimestre, semestre; (*condition*) restrinje. **in terms of** en relata con. **on one's own terms** par sua propre metodo. **term of office** periodo de ofisia. **terms** (*agreement*) acorda formal.
terminal *n.* (*transport*, *electric*, *computer*) termina; stasion final.
terminate *v.* fini, aborta.
termination *n.* aborta.
terminological *adj.* terminolojial.
terminologist *n.* terminolojiste.
terminology *n.* (*study*) terminolojia; (*vocabulary*) termas tecnical, parolas tecnical.
terminus *n.* fini, stasion final.
termite *n.* termite.
tern *n.* (*bird*) sterna.
terra- *pref.* (*earth*) tera-.
terrace *n.* teraza. • *v.* terazi.
terracotta *n.* teracota.
terragon *n.* (*plant*) estragon.
terrain *n.* tereno.
terra incognita *n.* tera nonconoseda.
Terran *adj.* & *n.* (*earthling*) teran.
terrarium *n.* tereria.
terrestrial *adj.* teran.
terrible *adj.* xocante, asustante.
terrier *n.* (*dog*) terier.
terrific *adj.* enorme; eselente.
terrify *v.* terori, asusta.
territorial *adj.* teritorial.
territory *n.* teritorio.
terror *n.* teror.
terrorism *n.* terorisme.
terrorist *n.* teroriste.
terrorize *v.* terori.
terse *adj.* brusca, consisa.
Tertiary *adj.* & *n.* (*geology*) tersiaria.
tertiary education *n.* educa de universia.
tesla *n.* (*unit of magnetic induction*) tesla.
tesseract *n.* ipercubo.

test *v.* & *n.* (*try out, check*) proba; (*ability*) esamina.
testable *adj.* confirmable.
testament *n.* atesta. **New Testament** Atesta Nova. **Old Testament** Atesta Vea.
testator *n.* atestor.
testicle *n.* testiculo.
testicular *adj.* testiculal.
testify *v.* atesta.
testimonial *n.* atesta.
testimony *n.* atesta.
testis *n.* (*anatomy*) testiculo.
test kit *n.* paceta de proba.
testosterone *n.* testosterona.
test tube *n.* tubo de proba.
tetanus *n.* tetano.
tetany *n.* (*medical*) tetania.
tetchy *adj.* disputosa, iritable.
tête-à-tête *n.* conversa privata.
tether *v.* lia, securi.
tetherball *n.* (*game*) spirobal.
tetra[1] *n.* (*fish*) tetra. **African tetra** tetra african. **American tetra** tetra american.
tetra-[2] *pref.* (*four*) tetra-.
tetracycline *n.* (*antibiotic*) tetrasiclina.
tetrahedral *adj.* tetraedro.
tetrahedron *n.* tetraedro.
tetralogy *n.* (*group of four*) tetralojia. **tetralogy of Fallot** (*medical*) tetralojia de Fallot.
tetrameter *n.* (*poetry*) tetrametre.
tetraplegia *n.* tetraplejia.
tetraplegic *adj.* & *n.* tetraplejica.
tetrarch *n.* (*governor*) tetrarca.
tetrarchy *n.* tetrarcia.
Teutonic *adj.* & *n.* germanica.
Texas *n.* (*US state*) Texas.
text *n.* testo; (*SMS*) mesajeta. • *v.* mesaji.
textbook *n.* libro de aprende.
textile *n.* stofa.
text message *n.* (*SMS*) mesajeta.
textual *adj.* testal.
texture *v.* & *n.* trama.
Thai *adj.* & *n.* tai.
Thailand *n.* Tai. **Gulf of Thailand** Golfo Tai.
thalamus *n.* (*anatomy*) talamo.
thalidomide *n.* talidomida.
thallium *n.* (*element*) talio.
thallus *n.* (*botany*) talo.
than *prep.* & *subord.* ca.
thanatology *n.* tanatolojia.
thank *v.* grasia. **thank God** grasias a Dio. **thank goodness** grasias a Dio. **thank heavens** grasias a la sielo. **thank in advance** pregrasia. **thank you** grasias.
thankful *adj.* grasiosa.
thankless *adj.* (*task*) nongrasiada; (*person*) nongrasiosa.
thanks *n.* & *interj.* grasias. **thanks in advance** pregrasias. **thanks to** con grasias a, par causa de.
Thanksgiving Day *n.* festa de grasia.
Thar Desert *n.* Deserto Tar.
that *det.* acel. • *pron.* acel; (*relative*) cual. • *subord.* ce. **that is to say** per dise, pd. **that kind of** tal. **that one** acel. **that which** lo cual.
thatch *n.* palia. **thatched roof** teto de palia.
thaw *v.* & *n.* dejela.
the *det.* la. **the ones which** los cual. **the ones who** los ci. **the one which** lo cual. **the one who** el ci.
theatre (US **theater**) *n.* (*place, art*) teatro.
theatric *adj.* teatral.
theatrical *adj.* teatral, dramal.
theft *n.* fura; (*by force or threat of force*) ruba.
theftproof *adj.* secur contra fura.
their *det.* sua. **their own** sua propre.
theirs *pron.* la sua(s).
theism *n.* teisme.
theist *adj.* & *n.* teiste.
them *pron.* los.
thematic *adj.* temal.
theme *n.* tema.
themselves *pron.* (*reflexive*) se; (*emphatically reflexive*) se mesma. **they themselves** (*non-reflexively emphatic*) los mesma, (*gender-neutral singular*) el mesma.
then *adv.* (*at that time*) alora; (*next*) a pos; (*therefore*) alora, donce. **from then on** de alora. **the then king** la re alora.
thence *adv.* de ala.
theo- *pref.* (*god*) teo-.
theocracy *n.* teocratia.
theocrat *n.* teocrata.
theocratic *adj.* teocrata.
theodolite *n.* teodolito.
theologian *n.* teolojiste.
theological *adj.* teolojial.
theology *n.* teolojia.
theorem *n.* teorem.
theoretic *adj.* teorial.
theoretical *adj.* teorial.
theorist *n.* teoriste.
theorization *n.* teori.
theorize *v.* teori.
theory *n.* teoria. **theory of computation** teoria de computa. **theory of evolution** teoria de evolui.
theosophist *n.* teosofiste.
theosophy *n.* teosofia.
therapist *n.* terapiste.
therapy *n.* terapia.
Theravada *adj.* (*Buddhism*) teravada.
there *adv.* ala. **there is a problem** on ave un problem. **there were questions** on ia ave demandas.

thereabouts *adv.* prosima. **or thereabouts** o simil.
thereby *adv.* par acel, donce.
therefore *adv.* donce, alora.
theremin *n.* (*musical instrument*) teremin.
thereof *adv.* de esta.
thermal *adj.* termal.
thermal bath *n.* banieria termal.
thermal gradient *n.* gradiente termal.
thermite *n.* termita.
thermo- *pref.* (*heat*) termo-.
thermocouple *n.* termoduple.
thermodynamic *adj.* termodinamical.
thermodynamics *n.* termodinamica.
thermometer *n.* termometre.
thermonuclear *adj.* termonucleal.
thermophile *n.* termofilica.
thermophilia *n.* termofilia.
thermophilic *adj.* termofilica.
thermos *n.* termos.
thermostat *n.* termostato.
thesaurus *n.* tesoro, disionario de sinonimes.
these *det.* esta. • *pron.* estas. **these ones** estas.
thesis *n.* proposa, tema; (*dissertation*) tese.
thespian *n.* ator.
theta *n.* (*Greek letter* Θ, θ) teta.
they *pron.* (*plural*) los; (*gender-neutral singular*) el; (*arbitrary person or people*) on. **they say** (*it is rumoured*) on dise. **they themselves** (*non-reflexively emphatic*) los mesma, (*gender-neutral singular*) el mesma. **they who** los ci; (*gender-neutral singular*) el ci.
thiamine *n.* (*vitamin*) tiamina.
thick *adj.* spesa; (*liquid*) densa, viscosa.
thicken *v.* densi.
thicket *n.* bosceta, marania.
thick-knee *n.* (*bird*) burino.
thickness *n.* spesia; densia, viscosia.
thief *n.* furor.
thigh *n.* coxa.
thighbone *n.* femor.
thimble *n.* dital.
thin *adj.* (*slender*) magra; (*flat*) plata; (*watery*) acuin; (*pastry*) folin. • *v.* magri.
thing *n.* cosa.
thingamabob *n.* aparateta.
thingamajig *n.* aparateta.
thingummy *n.* aparateta.
thingy *n.* aparateta.
think *v.* pensa; (*have opinion*) opina. **think hard** serebri. **think of** (*have in mind*) pensa a, pensa sur; (*think up*) imajina. **think outside the box** pensa ladal. **think up** imajina.
thinker *n.* pensor.
think tank *n.* sentro de rexerca.
thinness *n.* magria.
third *adj.* (*ordinal*) tre. • *n.* (*fraction*) tri. **third from last** du ante la ultima. **to the third power** cubida.
third-party supplier *n.* furnor esterna.
thirst *v.* sidi. • *n.* sidia.
thirsty *adj.* side.
thirtieth *adj.* (*ordinal*) tredes. • *n.* (*fraction*) tredesi.
thirty *det.* & *pron.* tredes.
thirty-second note *n.* tono tredes-duida.
thirty-something *det.* tredes-alga.
thirty-somethingth *adj.* (*ordinal*) tredes-alga.
this *det.* & *pron.* esta. **this kind of** tal. **this once** a esta ves. **this one** esta. **this time** a esta ves.
thistle *n.* cardo.
thither *adv.* ala, a ala.
thong *n.* (*strap*) corea, banda de cuoro; (*briefs*) tanga; (*flip-flop*) sandaleta.
thoracic *adj.* toraxal.
thorax *n.* torax.
thorium *n.* (*element*) torio.
thorn *n.* spina; (*Latin letter* Þ, þ) torn.
thorntree *n.* acasia.
thorny *adj.* spinosa.
thorough *adj.* completa.
thoroughbred *adj.* de sangue pur.
thoroughfare *n.* strada.
thoroughly *adv.* completa.
those *det.* acel. • *pron.* aceles. **those ones** aceles.
though *subord.* an si. **as though** como si.
thought *n.* pensa.
thoughtful *adj.* pensosa.
thoughtless *adj.* sin pensa, sin cura.
thousand *det.* & *n.* mil. **one thousand** mil. **one thousand million** bilion. **thousands** miles.
thousandth *adj.* (*ordinal*) mil. • *n.* (*fraction*) mili.
Thrace *n.* (*ancient region*) Tracia.
thrall *n.* controla.
thrash *v.* bate, bastoni.
thrasher *n.* mimor.
thread *n.* filo, fibre; (*correspondence*) cadena; (*screw, bolt, nut*) fileta. • *v.* (*needle, beads, etc.*) fili.
threadbare *adj.* gastada.
threader *n.* filetador.
threadlike *adj.* filin.
thready *adj.* debil.
threat *n.* menasa.
threaten *v.* menasa.
three *det.* & *pron.* tre.
three-dimensional *adj.* tridimensional, con tre dimensiones, en tre dimensiones.
three-horse sled *n.* treno de tre cavalos.
three-sided *adj.* triladal.

thresh *v.* bate.
thresher *n.* batador.
threshold *n.* entra; (*metaphor*) borda, limita, matini.
thrice *adv.* a tre veses, truple.
thrift *n.* frugalia.
thriftiness *n.* frugalia.
thrifty *adj.* frugal.
thrill *v.* stimula, vibra.
thriller *n.* (*novel, movie*) triler.
thrips *n.* (*insect*) tisanotera.
thrive *v.* flori.
-thrix *suff.* (*hair*) -tris.
throat *n.* garga.
throaty *adj.* gargal.
throb *v.* palpita.
thrombocyte *n.* trombosite.
thrombopoiesis *n.* trombopoiese.
thrombosis *n.* trombose.
thrombus *n.* trombo.
throne *n.* trono.
throng *n.* fola.
throttle *v.* strangula. • *n.* aselerador.
through *prep.* tra. • *adv.* a tra. **through the agency of** par.
throughout *prep.* (*place or period*) tra. • *adv.* en cada parte, en tota partes.
throughway *n.* via xef.
throw *v.* & *n.* lansa. **throw again** relansa. **throw away** baldoni, dejeta, desprende. **throw back** relansa. **throw into relief** releva. **throw off balance** desecuilibra. **throw out** espulsa. **throw up** vomiti, descome.
thrower *n.* lansor.
throw-in *n.* (*football*) lansa de borda.
thrown *adj.* lansada.
thrush *n.* turdo.
thrust *v.* & *n.* puxa.
thruster *n.* puxador.
thruway *n.* via xef.
thud *n.* pum, colpa. • *v.* pumi. • *interj.* pum.
thug *n.* savaje, violente.
thuja *n.* tuia.
thulium *n.* (*element*) tulio.
thumb *n.* diton, polex. **give two thumbs up to** loda duple.
thumbnail *n.* (*image*) imajeta.
thumb piano *n.* (*musical instrument*) calimba.
thumbprint *n.* impresa de diton.
thumbscrew *n.* abrasador de diton.
thumbtack *n.* spino puiable.
thump *v.* & *n.* colpa. • *interj.* pum.
thunder *v.* & *n.* tona.
thunderbird *n.* avia de tona.
thunderbolt *n.* lampo.
thunderclap *n.* colpa de tona.
thunderfly *n.* tisanotera.
thunderous *adj.* tonin.
thundershower *n.* pluveta lamposa.
thunderstorm *n.* tempesta lamposa.
Thursday *n.* jovedi.
thus *adv.* tal, en esta modo; (*therefore*) tal, donce.
thusly *adv.* tal.
thwart *v.* impedi.
thyme *n.* (*plant*) tim.
thymus *n.* (*anatomy*) timo.
thyroid *n.* (*anatomy*) tiroide.
thyroidectomy *n.* (*surgery*) tiroidectomia.
thyroid hormone *n.* ormon tiroidal.
ti *n.* (*musical note*) si.
tiara *n.* coroneta.
Tibet *n.* Bod, Tibet.
Tibetan *adj.* & *n.* (*person, language*) bod, tibetan.
tibia *n.* tibia.
tic *n.* (*spasm*) tic.
tick[1] *v.* (*clock*) tictaci. • *n.* tictaci; (*checkmark*) sinia de serti.
tick[2] *n.* (*arachnid*) tica.
ticket *n.* bileta; (*penalty notice*) multa.
ticket collector *n.* biletor.
ticket office *n.* bileteria.
ticket window *n.* fenetra de bileta.
tickle *v.* & *n.* titila.
ticklish *adj.* titilable.
tick-tock *interj.* tictac.
tidal *adj.* mareal.
tidal mouth *n.* estuario.
tidal pool *n.* stangeta de mar.
tidbit *n.* peseta.
tiddlywink *n.* pulga.
tiddlywinks *n.* jua de pulgas.
tide *n.* marea.
tidepool *n.* stangeta de mar.
tidings *n.* novas.
tidy *v.* ordina. • *adj.* ordinada. **tidy up** reordina.
tie *v.* (*bind*) lia. • *n.* (*garment*) cravata; (*match*) egal.
tiebreak *n.* desidente.
tied *adj.* (*bound*) liada; (*match*) egal, sin ganior.
tier *n.* (*scale, hierarchy*) nivel.
tiered benches *n.* scalera de bancas.
tiger *n.* tigre.
tiger cub *n.* tigreta.
tiger lily *n.* lil tigrin.
tight *adj.* abrasante, streta; (*taut*) tensada. **hold tight** presa. **tights** calson.
tighten *v.* tensa; streti; (*rules*) aumenta.
tight-fisted *adj.* avar.
tight-fitting *adj.* abrasante, corpin.
tight-lipped *adj.* con labios selida.
tightness *n.* stretia.
tightrope *n.* corda tensada.
tightrope walker *n.* paseacorda.
tightwad *n.* baratamanica.

Tigris River *n.* Rio Tigris.
tilde *n.* (*diacritic*) tilde.
tile *n.* telia. • *v.* teli.
till[1] *prep.* (*until*) asta. • *subord.* asta cuando.
till[2] *v.* (*land*) aradi, cultiva.
till[3] *n.* (*for money*) caxa rejistrante.
tiller *n.* cultivador.
tilt *v.* apoia.
timber *n.* lenio.
timberyard *n.* lenieria.
timbre *n.* tinje.
time *n.* (*concept, duration, historical period*) tempo; (*of day*) ora; (*occasion*) ves; (*major historical period*) eda. • *v.* cronometri. **all the time** tra la dia. **ancient times** eda antica. **at no time** a no ves, a no tempo. **at one time or another** a un ves o un otra. **at the same time** a la mesma tempo. **at the same time as** a la mesma tempo como, con ce. **at this time** a esta ora, aora. **at times** a veses. **for a long time** longa. **for some time** (*intended*) per alga tempo, (*elapsed*) tra alga tempo. **for the time being** per aora, per la presente. **from time to time** de ves a ves, a veses, aora e alora. **have a good time** diverti bon. **in time** (*for an event*) a tempo, puntual. **one time** a un ves. **on time** a tempo, puntual. **take your time** no freta. **this time** a esta ves. **time after time** sempre denova. **time and again** sempre denova. **time out** tempo de pausa. **timeout** (*software*) abandona. **two at a time** du a cada ves.
time bomb *n.* bomba-orolojo.
time capsule *n.* capsula de tempo.
timecard *n.* carta de oras.
time-consuming *adj.* consumante de tempo.
time-honoured (US **time-honored**) *adj.* vea onorada.
timekeeper *n.* cronometriste.
timelapse photography *n.* fotografia a intervales.
timeless *adj.* noncambiante; nonsenesente.
time limit *n.* limita de tempo.
time machine *n.* macina de tempo.
timer *n.* (*device*) cronometre, tempador.
time-release *adj.* con relasa gradal.
times *prep.* par, multiplida par.
timesaver *n.* salvatempo.
timescale *n.* calendario.
timesheet *n.* carta de oras.
time signature *n.* (*music*) sinia de tempo.
timestamp *v.* & *n.* indica de ora.
timetable *n.* carta de oras, scema.
time-tested *adj.* longa probada.
time travel *n.* viaja tra tempo.
time traveller (US **traveler**) *n.* viajor tra tempo.
time warp *n.* plia de tempo.
time zone *n.* zona de ora.
timid *adj.* timida, noncorajosa.
timidity *n.* timidia.
timing *n.* judi de tempo; (*measurement*) cronometri.
Timor *n.* Timor.
Timorese *adj.* & *n.* timoran.
Timor Sea *n.* Mar Timor.
timp *n.* timpano.
timpani *n.* (*drum*) timpano.
timpano *n.* (*drum*) timpano.
tin *n.* (*element*) stanio; (*can*) bote. • *v.* boti.
tinamou *n.* (*bird*) tinamo.
tincture *n.* (*medicine*) tintura.
tinder *n.* esca.
tine *n.* dente.
tin foil *n.* paper de aluminio, paper de stanio.
tinge *v.* tinje.
tingle *v.* titila.
tingling *adj.* titilosa, formicosa.
tingly *adj.* titilosa, formicosa.
tininess *n.* picia.
tinker *v.* bricola. • *n.* bricolor.
tinkle *v.* & *n.* tintina.
tinnitus *n.* (*medical*) tinito.
tin opener *n.* abribote.
tinplate *n.* lata.
tinsel *n.* garlanda sintilinte.
tinsmith *n.* lator.
tint *v.* & *n.* tinje.
tiny *adj.* pico.
tiny amount *n.* goteta.
tiny step *n.* paseta.
tip[1] *n.* (*point*) apico, fini, punto.
tip[2] *v.* (*lean*) inclina, versa, apoia. **tip over** cade, desecuilibra, malversa.
tip[3] *n.* (*for service*) grasieta, donada; (*hint*) aviseta. • *v.* grasieta; aviseta.
tipi *n.* (*tent*) tipi.
tipsy *adj.* enebriada, bambolante.
tiptoe *v.* paseta. **on tiptoe** sur ditos de pedes.
tirade *n.* arenga.
tiramisu *n.* (*dessert*) tiramisu.
tire[1] *v.* (*make weary*) fatiga; (*bore*) noia.
tire[2] (US). See *tyre*.
tired *adj.* fatigada.
tiredness *n.* fatiga.
tireless *adj.* nonfatigable.
tiresome *adj.* noiante.
tissue *n.* (*organic*) texeda; (*paper towel*) teleta de paper.
tit[1] *n.* (*bird*) paro.
tit[2] *n.* (*breast*) teton, mamela.
Titan *n.* titan.
titanium *n.* titanio.
titbit *n.* peseta.

tit-for-tat killings *n.* matas per venja.
tithe *n.* desi.
titi *n.* (*monkey*) titi.
titillate *v.* titila.
titillating *adj.* titilante, riscosa.
titillation *n.* titila.
title *n.* titulo. • *v.* tituli. **in title** par titulo.
title bar *n.* (*software*) bara de titulo.
title holder *n.* premior.
titmouse *n.* paro.
titrate *v.* titola.
titration *n.* titola.
titrimetry *n.* titola.
titter *v.* & *n.* rieta.
titular *adj.* titulal.
tizzy *n.* ajita.
T-junction *n.* junta T.
Tlingit *adj.* & *n.* (*person, language*) tlingit.
to *prep.* a; (*in order to*) per. **to and fro** de asi a ala.
toad *n.* sapo.
toadlike *adj.* sapin.
toadstool *n.* xampinion.
toady[1] *v.* (*flatter*) adula. • *n.* adulor.
toady[2] *adj.* (*toadlike*) sapin.
toadyish *adj.* adulante.
toast *v.* (*bread*) tosta; (*raise glass*) brinda. • *n.* tostada, pan tostada; brinda.
toaster *n.* tostador.
toasty *adj.* comfortosa calda.
tobacco *n.* (*plant, leaves*) tabaco.
Tobagonian *adj.* & *n.* tobagonian.
-to-be *suff.* futur.
toboggan *n.* (*simple sledge*) treneta.
toccata *n.* (*music*) tocata.
-tocia *suff.* (*birth*) -tosia.
today *adv.* & *n.* oji.
toddle *v.* bambola.
toddler *n.* paseor nova.
toddy *n.* (*drink*) pontxe.
to-do list *n.* ajenda.
toe *n.* dito de pede, orteo. **big toe** diton de pede, halux.
toenail *n.* ungia de pede.
toffee *n.* caramel dur.
tofu *n.* tofu.
toga *n.* (*garment*) toga.
together *adv.* en junta, juntada, unida; con lunlotra; (*coming together*) a junta.
toggle *v.* (*setting*) alterna. • *n.* comutador.
Togo *n.* Togo.
Togolese *adj.* & *n.* togoles.
toil *v.* & *n.* labora, labora sin sesa.
toilet *n.* (*room*) saleta privata; (*receptacle*) vason.
toilet bowl *n.* vason.
toilet paper *n.* paper de vason.
toiletry *n.* article de lavabo.
toke *v.* enspira.
Tokelau *n.* Tocelau.
Tokelauan *adj.* & *n.* tocelau.
token *n.* simbol; (*counter representing money*) fix.
Tok Pisin *adj.* & *n.* (*language*) pisin.
Tokyo *n.* Tocio.
tolerable *adj.* tolerable.
tolerance *n.* tolera.
tolerant *adj.* tolerante.
tolerate *v.* tolera.
toll *n.* (*payment*) peaje.
tollbooth *n.* ciosco de peaje.
toll-free *adj.* sin custa.
toll-free number *n.* numero sin custa.
tollgate *n.* porteta de peaje.
tom *n.* tomtom.
tomahawk *n.* axeta.
tomato *n.* tomate.
tomato sauce *n.* salsa de tomate.
tomato soup *n.* sopa de tomate.
tomb *n.* tomba.
tomblike *adj.* tombin.
tombola *n.* rifa.
tomboy *n.* xica masin.
tombstone *n.* petra de tomba.
tome[1] *n.* libron.
-tome[2] *suff.* (*cutting tool*) -tome.
tomfoolery *n.* bobia.
-tomic *suff.* -tomica.
tomography *n.* tomografia.
tomorrow *adv.* & *n.* doman. **the day after tomorrow** a la dia pos doman. **tomorrow evening** a sera doman. **tomorrow morning** a matina doman.
tomtom *n.* (*drum*) tomtom.
-tomy *suff.* (*cutting*) -tomia.
ton *n.* (*large quantity*) monton.
tonal *adj.* tonal.
tone *n.* tono.
toner *n.* (*skin conditioner*) astrinjente; (*powder*) polvo xerografial.
tong *n.* (*secret society*) tong.
Tonga *n.* Tonga.
Tongan *adj.* & *n.* tongan.
tongs *n.* pinse; pinse de cosini.
tongue *n.* lingua.
tonguefish *n.* pex linguin.
tongue twister *n.* rompelingua, pleniboca.
tonic *n.* prepara.
tonight *adv.* a esta sera, a sera oji.
tonne *n.* ton.
tonsil *n.* (*anatomy*) tonsil.
tonsillectomy *n.* (*surgery*) tonsilectomia.
tonsillitis *n.* (*medical*) tonsilite.
tonsure *n.* (*shaven head*) tonsura.
too *adv.* (*excessively*) tro; (*also*) ance. **too few** tro poca. **too little** (*amount*) tro poca; (*size*) tro peti. **too many** tro multe. **too much** tro, tro multe.
tool *n.* util.
toolbar *n.* (*software*) bara de utiles.

toolbox *n.* caxa de utiles.
tool shed *n.* cabana de utiles.
tool shop *n.* boteca de utiles.
toot *n.* & *interj.* tut. • *v.* tuti.
tooth *n.* dente.
toothache *n.* dole de dente.
toothbrush *n.* brosa de dentes.
toothed *adj.* dentosa.
tooth extraction *n.* estrae de dente.
toothlike *adj.* sierin.
toothpaste *n.* pasta de dentes.
toothpick *n.* basteta de dentes.
tooth socket *n.* alveolo.
toothy *adj.* dentosa.
top *adj.* alta; (*main*) xef. • *n.* culmina, alta; (*lid*) covrente; (*garment*) camiseta, veste alta. **at the top of** a alta de. **on the top** a sur. **on top of** sur. **over the top** estravagante. **top half** alta. **topped with** culminante con.
topaz *n.* (*gem*) topazio.
topcoat *n.* jacon.
top hat *n.* xapo silindre.
topi *n.* (*cap*) cipa.
topiary *n.* topiaria.
topic *n.* tema, sujeto.
topical *adj.* corente.
topicalization *n.* (*linguistics*) temi.
topicalize *v.* (*linguistics*) temi.
topknot *n.* noda de capeles.
topless *adj.* con peto nuda; (*roofless*) sin teto.
topmost *adj.* la plu alta, suprema.
top-notch *adj.* multe bon, eselente.
topo- *pref.* topo-.
topographic *adj.* topografial.
topographical *adj.* topografial.
topography *n.* topografia.
topology *n.* topolojia.
toponym *n.* toponim.
toponymic *adj.* toponim.
topping *n.* decora.
topple *v.* cade, desecuilibra, volta.
top prize *n.* premio xef.
top quark *n.* cuarc alta.
topsoil *n.* suprasolo.
toque *n.* (*cap*) toco.
Torah *n.* (*Judaism*) tora.
torc *n.* (*ornament*) torce.
torch *n.* (*flaming*) torxa, focador; (*electric*) lampa de pox. • *v.* (*set fire to*) torxi.
torchbearer *n.* torxor, portatorxa.
torii *n.* (*gate*) tori.
torment *v.* & *n.* tormenta, tortura.
tormentor *n.* tormentor.
torn *adj.* laserada.
tornado *n.* tornado.
torpedo *n.* torpedo.
torpidity *n.* letarjia.
torpor *n.* letarjia.
torque *n.* momento de torse.
torrent *n.* deluvia, ondon.
torrential *adj.* deluvial.
Torres, Strait of *n.* Streta Torres.
torrid *adj.* calda e seca; pasionosa.
torrone *n.* (*confectionery*) turon.
torsion *n.* torse.
torte *n.* (*cake*) torta.
tortellini *n.* (*food*) tortelini.
tortilla *n.* (*food*) tortilia.
tortoise *n.* tortuga.
tortuous *adj.* torsosa.
torture *v.* & *n.* tortura.
torturer *n.* torturor.
torturous *adj.* torturosa.
torus *n.* anelo.
Tory *n.* (*politics*) tori.
toss *v.* lansa; (*discard*) baldoni. • *n.* lansa. **toss and turn** turna e returna. **toss out** baldoni.
tosser *n.* (*insult*) pixeta.
toss-up *n.* egal.
tot *n.* bebe.
total *adj.* intera. • *n.* soma.
totalitarian *adj.* autocrata.
totalitarianism *n.* autocratia.
totality *n.* intera.
tote *v.* porta. • *n.* saco.
totem *n.* totem.
totter *v.* bambola.
toucan *n.* tucana.
touch *v.* toca, contata; (*lightly*) tanje; (*feel*) palpa. • *n.* toca, contata; (*sense of*) palpa. **touch oneself** (*masturbate*) diti se. **touch up** retoca.
touchable *adj.* tocable.
touché *interj.* toca.
touchpad *n.* panel de toca.
touchscreen *n.* scermo interatante.
touchy *adj.* iritable.
tough *adj.* dur; durante.
toughen *v.* duri.
toupee *n.* peruca.
tour *v.* & *n.* turi.
tour guide *n.* gidor de turi.
tourism *n.* turisme.
tourist *n.* turiste.
tourist attraction *n.* atrae per turistes.
tourist class *n.* clase de turiste.
tourmaline *n.* (*mineral*) turmalina.
tournament *n.* torneo.
tourney *n.* torneo.
tourniquet *adj.* banda emostasal.
tow *v.* tira.
toward *prep.* a, en dirije a.
towards *prep.* a, en dirije a.
tow bar *n.* bara de tira.
towboat *n.* barco tirante.
towel *n.* tela.
towel rack *n.* portatela.

towel rail *n.* portatela.
tower *n.* tore. • *v.* (*over*) tori.
towhee *n.* (*bird*) pipilo.
tow hitch *n.* bara de tira.
town *n.* vila.
town council *n.* comite de vila.
town hall *n.* ofisia de site.
townhouse *n.* casa de site.
townie *n.* vilan.
township *n.* distrito.
townsman *n.* vilan.
townsperson *n.* vilan.
townswoman *n.* vilan.
towpath *n.* rueta de tira.
toxaemia (US **toxemia**) *n.* toxemia.
toxic *adj.* nosiva, venenosa.
toxicity *n.* toxinia.
toxicological *adj.* toxicolojial.
toxicologist *n.* toxicolojiste.
toxicology *n.* toxicolojia.
toxin *n.* toxina, venena.
toy *n.* jueta. **toy with** jueta con.
toymaker *n.* juetor.
toy windmill *n.* molineta.
trace *v.* (*outline*) trasa; (*pinpoint*) locali. • *n.* trasa, indica; (*tiny amount*) pico. **trace one's ancestry** xerca sua asendentes. **without a trace** sin un trasa.
traceable *adj.* trasable.
tracer *n.* trasador.
tracery *n.* (*architecture*) traseria.
trachea *n.* tracea.
tracheotomy *n.* traceotomia.
tracing *n.* trasa.
tracing paper *n.* paper diafana.
track *n.* (*path*) curso; (*marks left*) trasa; (*mix*) banda; (*music*) peso. • *v.* locali; segue la trasa de. **keep track of** teni trasa de. **leave a track** lasa un trasa. **lose track of** perde trasa de. **off the beaten track** a via de vias comun. **wheel track** foseta.
track-and-field athletics *n.* atletisme lejera.
tracker *n.* xasor.
track lighting *n.* rel de lampas.
track record *n.* istoria.
tracksuit *n.* completa de sporte.
tracksuit bottoms *n.* pantalon de sporte.
tract *n.* curso, duto. **alimentary tract** curso de dijesta. **digestive tract** curso de dijesta. **respiratory tract** curso de respira. **vocal tract** curso de vose.
tractability *n.* tratablia, manejablia.
tractable *adj.* tratable, manejable.
traction *n.* tira.
tractor *n.* trator; (*with trailer*) tirador.
tractor trailer *n.* camion sesionida.
trade *v.* comersia; (*barter*) troca, intercambia. • *n.* comersia; troca, intercambia; (*craft*) artisania.
trade fair *n.* feria.
trademark *n.* marca comersial.
trade-off *n.* compromete.
tradesman *n.* artisan.
trade surplus *n.* suprapasa comersial.
tradeswoman *n.* artisan.
trade union *n.* sindicato.
trade wind *n.* alise.
tradition *n.* tradision.
traditional *adj.* tradisional.
traditional costume *n.* veste etnical.
traditionalism *n.* tradisionalisme.
traditionalist *n.* tradisionaliste.
traffic *v.* & *n.* trafica.
traffic circle *n.* sirculo de trafica.
traffic congestion *n.* conjesta de trafica.
traffic enforcement camera *n.* camera de trafica.
traffic jam *n.* conjesta de trafica.
trafficker *n.* traficor.
traffic light *n.* semafor.
traffic signal *n.* semafor.
tragedy *n.* trajedia.
tragic *adj.* trajedial.
tragicomedy *n.* trajicomedia.
tragicomic *adj.* trajicomedial.
trail *n.* (*path*) curso; (*marks left*) trasa; (*film, TV*) tisante. • *v.* segue; (*vehicle*) tira. **leave a trail** lasa un trasa. **vapour trail** seguente de condensa.
trailblazer *n.* abrivia.
trailer *n.* caravan; (*of truck*) vagon; (*film, TV*) previdet a, tisante.
trailing *adj.* (*positioned last*) codal.
train *v.* (*person, animal*) instrui; (*fitness*) esersE. • *n.* (*vehicle*) tren.
trainee *n.* aprendor, stajior.
train engineer *n.* locomotivor.
trainer *n.* instruor; (*shoe*) sapato de sporte.
training manual *n.* manual de instrui.
traipse *v.* vaga.
trait *n.* cualia.
traitor *n.* trador.
trajectory *n.* curso.
tram *n.* tram.
trammel *n.* restrinje.
trammel net *n.* rede restrinjente.
tramp *n.* vagabon; (*minx*) seduor, tisor.
trample *v.* crase su pede.
trampoline *n.* trampolin.
tramway *n.* tramvia.
trance *n.* transe, stupor.
tranquil *adj.* calma, pasosa.
tranquillize (US **tranquilize**) *v.* calmi.
tranquillizer (US **tranquilizer**) *n.* medisin calminte.

tranquillizing (US **tranquilizing**) *adj.* calminte.
trans- *pref.* (*across*) trans-.
transact *v.* intercambia.
transaction *n.* intercambia.
transatlantic *adj.* transatlantica.
transceiver *n.* transetador.
transcend *v.* transende.
transcendence *n.* transende.
transcendent *adj.* transendente.
transcendental *adj.* transendente.
transcendentalism *n.* transendentalisme.
transcontinental *adj.* transcontinental.
transcribe *v.* transcrive.
transcript *n.* transcrive.
transcription *n.* transcrive.
transduce *v.* transdui.
transducer *n.* transduador.
transduction *n.* transdui.
transept *n.* traversal.
transfeminine *adj.* transfemin.
transfer *v.* & *n.* move, envia, copia, pasa.
transference *n.* pasa.
transfer station *n.* dejeteria.
transfiguration *n.* muta.
transfigure *v.* muta.
transfix *v.* encanta, paralise.
transform *v.* muta, cambia.
transformation *n.* cambia, muta.
transformer *n.* mutador.
transfuse *v.* transfusa.
transfusion *n.* transfusa.
transgender *adj.* & *n.* transjenero.
transgress *v.* viole.
transgression *n.* viole.
transhumance *n.* transuma.
transhumant *adj.* transumante.
transient *adj.* tempora.
transient ischemic attack *n.* ataca serebral.
transistor *n.* transistor.
transit *v.* & *n.* transita.
transition *v.* & *n.* traversa, cambia.
transitional *adj.* tempora.
transitive *adj.* transitiva.
transitivity *n.* transitivia.
translatable *adj.* traduable.
translate *v.* tradui; (*geometry*) reloca.
translation *n.* tradui; (*geometry*) reloca.
translator *n.* traduor.
translucency *n.* diafania.
translucent *adj.* diafana.
transmasculine *adj.* transmasin.
transmigration *n.* reincarne.
transmission *n.* transmete, envia; (*gearbox*) engranador.
transmit *v.* (*signal, power, etc.*) transmete, envia. **sexually transmitted** sesal comunicada.
transmitter *n.* transmetador, enviador.
transmogrify *v.* muta.
transmutation *n.* muta.
transmute *v.* muta.
transoceanic *adj.* transmaral.
transom *n.* lintel.
transpacific *adj.* transpasifica.
transparency *n.* transparentia, claria; (*for projection*) transparente.
transparent *adj.* transparente, clar.
transphobe *n.* transfobica.
transphobia *n.* transfobia.
transphobic *adj.* transfobica.
transpiration *n.* transpira.
transpire *v.* aveni; (*botany*) transpira.
transplant *v.* transplanta.
transplantation *n.* transplanta.
transpond *v.* transponde.
transponder *n.* transpondador.
transport *v.* & *n.* transporta. **transport by car** automobili.
transportation *n.* transporta.
transporter *n.* (*person*) transportor; (*vehicle, etc.*) transportador.
transpose *v.* transpone.
transposition *n.* transpone.
transsexual *adj.* & *n.* transesal.
transsexuality *n.* transesalia.
transverse *adj.* traversal.
transvestism *n.* transvesti.
transvestist *n.* transvestida.
transvestite *n.* transvestida.
transvestitism *n.* transvesti.
Transylvania *n.* Transilvania.
trap *n.* trapa. • *v.* trapi.
trap door *n.* porta de trapa.
trapeze *n.* trapezio.
trapeze artist *n.* trapezior.
trapezial *adj.* trapezio.
trapezium *n.* trapezio.
trapezoid *n.* (*shape*) trapezio; (*bone*) trapezoide.
trapezoidal *adj.* trapezio.
trapper *n.* trapor.
trash *n.* dejetada.
trash can *n.* baldon.
trashy *adj.* dejetable.
trauma *n.* trauma.
traumatic *adj.* traumal.
traumatize *v.* trauma.
travel *v.* viaja. **travel a path** vade sur un via. **urge to travel** viajamania.
travelator *n.* paseria rolante.
travel cost *n.* custa de viaja.
travel guide *n.* libro de viaja.
traveller (US **traveler**) *n.* viajor; nomada. **habitual traveller** viajamanica.
travelogue (US **travelog**) *n.* libro de viaja, filma de viaja.

travel plans *n.* ordina de viaja.
traversal *n.* traversa.
traverse *v.* traversa.
travesty *n.* parodia, malrepresenta.
trawl *v.* draga.
trawler *n.* dragador.
tray *n.* platon.
treacherous *adj.* tradosa.
treachery *n.* tradi.
treacle *n.* melasa.
treacly *adj.* melasin.
tread *n.* paso; (*stair*) grado; (*tyre*) banda de rota. • *v.* fa un paso. **tread on** crase su pede.
treadmill *n.* (*wheel, exercise machine*) paseador.
treason *n.* tradi. **commit treason** tradi.
treasonous *adj.* tradosa.
treasure *n.* tesoro. • *v.* tesori.
treasurer *n.* tesoror.
treasures *n.* tesoros.
treasury *n.* tesoreria.
treat *v.* (*deal with*) trata; (*pamper*) regala. • *n.* regala.
treatable *adj.* tratable.
treatise *n.* tese.
treatment *n.* trata.
treaty *n.* trata.
treble clef *n.* clave alta.
tree *n.* arbor.
tree fort *n.* cabana de arbor.
tree house *n.* cabana de arbor.
treelike *adj.* arborin.
treeline *n.* linia de arbores.
treepie *n.* (*bird*) arboran.
tree shrew *n.* tupaia.
treetop *n.* culmina de arbor.
trefoil *n.* trefolia.
trehalose *n.* (*sugar*) trealosa.
trek *v.* & *n.* pasea longa, pasea laborosa.
trellis *n.* grilia.
trematode *n.* trematodo.
tremble *v.* trema.
tremendous *adj.* enorme, estrema.
tremolo *n.* trema.
tremor *n.* trema.
tremorous *adj.* tremante.
tremulent *adj.* tremante.
tremulous *adj.* tremante.
trench *n.* foso.
trenchant *adj.* persepinte, criticante, sever.
trenchcoat *n.* jacon de foso.
trencher *n.* plato de lenio.
trend *n.* (*tendency*) tende; (*fashion*) moda.
trendy *adj.* a la moda, de moda.
trepidation *n.* ansia.
trespass *v.* invade. **trespass against** ofende.
trespasser *n.* invador.
trestle *n.* cavaleta.
tri- *pref.* (*three*) tri-.
triad *n.* truple.
triage *n.* triaje.
trial *v.* proba. • *n.* (*test*) proba; (*legal*) litiga, prosede legal. **trial and error** atenta e era.
trialware *n.* programes de proba.
triangle *n.* triangulo.
triangular *adj.* triangulo.
triangulate *v.* trianguli.
triangulation *n.* trianguli.
Triangulum *n.* (*constellation*) la Triangulo.
Triangulum Australe *n.* (*constellation*) la Triangulo Sude.
Triassic *adj.* & *n.* (*geology*) triasica.
triathlete *n.* triatlonor.
triathlon *n.* triatlon.
tribal *adj.* tribal.
tribalism *n.* tribalisme.
tribe *n.* tribu.
tribesman *n.* om de tribu.
tribesperson *n.* membro de tribu.
tribeswoman *n.* fem de tribu.
tribunal *n.* judores.
tribune *n.* (*Roman official, popular leader*) tribuno.
tributary *n.* afluente.
tribute *n.* tribui.
triceps *n.* (*muscle*) trisepe.
triceratops *n.* triseratopo.
trichina *n.* (*worm*) tricina.
trichinosis *n.* (*medical*) tricinose.
trichromatic *adj.* tricromata.
trick *n.* (*skill, deception*) truco; (*deception*) rus, froda; (*card games*) prende. • *v.* engana.
trickery *n.* trucia, rusosia.
trickle *v.* & *n.* bava, flueta.
trickster *n.* trucor, rusor.
tricky *adj.* trucosa, rusosa.
tricorn *n.* (*hat*) tricorno.
tricorne *n.* (*hat*) tricorno.
tricot *n.* tricotada.
tricuspid *n.* tricuspide.
tricycle *n.* trisicle.
trident *n.* tridente.
tried *adj.* probada, atentada. **tried and tested** longa probada.
trifle *n.* (*triviality*) trivialia, graneta, pico; (*bauble*) orneta; (*dessert*) trifle. • *v.* jua.
trifling *adj.* trivial.
trigger *n.* gatilio. • *v.* gatili, ativi.
trigger-happy *adj.* gatiliomanica.
triglyceride *n.* (*chemistry*) trigliserido.
trigonometric *adj.* trigonometrial.
trigonometrical *adj.* trigonometrial.
trigonometry *n.* trigonometria.
trike *n.* trisicle.
trilateral *adj.* triladal.
trill *v.* vibra. • *n.* vibra; (*consonant*) vibrante.

trilled *adj.* vibrante.
trillion *det.* & *pron.* milion milion, trilion.
trillionth *adj.* (*ordinal*) trilion. • *n.* (*fraction*) trilioni.
trilogist *n.* trilojiste.
trilogy *n.* trilojia, nara en tre libros.
trim *v.* & *n.* (*shorten*) corti, sisori; (*garnish*) decora. • *adj.* ordinada.
trimester *n.* trimestre.
trimeter *n.* (*poetry*) trimetre.
Trinidad and Tobago *n.* Trinidad e Tobago.
Trinidadian *adj.* & *n.* trinidadian.
trinitarian *adj.* trinialiste.
trinitarianism *n.* trinialisme.
trinity *n.* (*Christianity*) trinia.
Trinity cream *n.* crema ardeda.
trinket *n.* (*bauble*) orneta; (*triviality*) graneta.
trio *n.* truple.
trip *v.* tropeza, fa un mal paso. • *n.* viaja. **trip over one's tongue** tropeza de lingua.
tripartite *adj.* tripartisan.
tripe *n.* (*food*) stomaco.
tripedal *adj.* trepede.
triphthong *n.* (*vowel sound*) triftongo.
triple *adj.* truple.
triple click *v.* & *n.* (*mouse*) clica truple.
triplet *adj.* & *n.* trejemelo.
tripod *n.* trepede.
tripodal *adj.* trepede.
-tripsy *suff.* (*crushing*) -tripsia.
triptych *n.* (*art*) triptico.
trireme *n.* (*ship*) triremo.
tritanopic *adj.* sieca a blu.
trite *adj.* nonorijinal, nonimportante.
triton *n.* trompa de Triton.
Triton snail *n.* trompa de Triton.
Triton's trumpet *n.* trompa de Triton.
triumph *n.* vinse.
triumphal *adj.* vinsal.
triumphalism *n.* vinsisme.
triumphant *adj.* vinsente.
triumvirate *n.* truple.
triune *adj.* trinial.
trivet *n.* trepede.
trivia *n.* trivia.
trivial *adj.* trivial, nonimportante.
triviality *n.* (*quality*) trivialia; (*something trivial*) trivial, graneta.
trivialize *v.* desvalua.
trocar *n.* (*surgical instrument*) trocar.
trochaic *adj.* troceal.
trochee *n.* (*poetry*) troceo.
troglodyte *n.* troglodite.
trogon *n.* (*bird*) trogon.
troika *n.* truple; treno de tre cavalos.
Trojan *adj.* & *n.* troian.
troll *n.* trol.
trolley *n.* careta; (*cart*) caro; (*hospital*) portaferida rolante.
trolleybus *n.* tram-bus.
trolley car *n.* tram.
trollop *n.* fem promiscua, fem prostituida, puta.
trombone *n.* trompon.
trompe-l'oeil *n.* trucioio.
troop *n.* grupo, ronda. **troops** soldatos.
trooper *n.* soldato montante; polisior montante.
troopship *n.* barcon de soldatos.
trope *n.* metafor; motif.
-trophic *suff.* -trofica.
trophy[1] *n.* trofeo.
-trophy[2] *suff.* (*feeding*) -trofia.
tropic *n.* tropico. **Tropic of Cancer** Tropico de la Crabe. **Tropic of Capricorn** Tropico de la Capra.
tropical *adj.* tropical.
tropism *n.* tropisme.
troposphere *n.* troposfera.
trot *v.* & *n.* trota.
troubadour *n.* menestrel.
trouble *v.* & *n.* turba, ajita. **go to the trouble of** disturba se per. **worth the trouble** meritante la labora.
troublemaker *n.* turbosa, tisor.
troubleshoot *v.* diagnose, desrompe.
troubleshooter *n.* solvor.
troublesome *adj.* turbante, turbosa.
trough *n.* trogo; portafeno; (*wave*) depresa.
trounce *v.* vinse.
troupe *n.* ronda, compania.
trouser press *n.* presapantalon.
trousers *n.* pantalon.
trouser suit *n.* completa con pantalon.
trout *n.* truta.
trowel *n.* paleta, desplantador.
Troy *n.* Troia.
truancy *n.* evita de scola.
truant *n.* asente. **play truant** evita la scola.
truce *n.* sesaspara.
truck *n.* camion; (*send by truck*) camioni. **articulated truck** camion sesionida.
truck driver *n.* camionor.
trucker *n.* camionor.
truck farm *n.* orto.
truckload *n.* camion.
truculent *adj.* disputosa.
trudge *v.* & *n.* pasea laborosa.
true *adj.* vera; (*loyal*) fidosa; (*sincere*) sinsera. • *interj.* vera.
true-blue *adj.* fidosa.
true love *n.* (*person*) amada vera.
trueness *n.* veria.
truffle *n.* trufa.
truism *n.* vera.
truly *adv.* vera.

trump *n.* (*cards*) trumfo; (*musical instrument*) trompa.
trumpet *n.* trompeta. • *v.* trompi.
trumpeter *n.* trompetiste; (*bird*) trompetor.
trumpetlike *adj.* trompetin.
trumpet-shaped *adj.* trompetin.
truncate *v.* trunca.
truncation *n.* trunca.
truncheon *n.* baston.
trundle *v.* rola.
trundle bed *n.* leto ascondeda.
trunk *n.* (*log, torso*) tronco; (*box*) valison; (*of vehicle*) portabagaje; (*of elephant*) trompa. **swimming trunks** pantala de nada. **trunks** (*shorts*) pantala.
truss *n.* (*architecture*) trelis.
trust *v.* fida. • *n.* fida; (*legal arrangement*) fidusia.
trustbuster *n.* rompor de monopolios.
trust company *n.* fidusieria.
trustee *n.* dirijor; (*money, property*) fidusior.
trust fund *n.* reserva fidusial.
trusting *adj.* fidante; (*gullible*) credosa, naive.
trustworthy *adj.* fidable.
truth *n.* veria; (*true thing*) vera.
truthful *adj.* onesta.
try *v.* (*attempt*) atenta; (*try out*) proba; (*in court*) litiga. • *n.* atenta; proba. **try on** (*clothes*) proba. **try out** proba.
trypanosome *n.* (*organism*) tripanosoma.
trypanosomiasis *n.* tripanosomiase, maladia de dormi.
tryptophan *n.* (*amino acid*) triptofan.
tryst *n.* encontra romantica.
tsar *n.* tsar.
tsardom *n.* tsaria.
tsarina *n.* tsaresa.
tsetse fly *n.* tsetse.
T-shaped *adj.* con forma de T.
T-shirt *n.* camisa T, camiseta; (*sleeveless*) camiseta de sporte.
T-square *n.* regla T.
tsuga *n.* tsuga.
tsunami *n.* tsunami.
Tswana *adj.* & *n.* (*language*) tsuana.
tuatara *n.* (*reptile*) tuatara.
tub *n.* tance; (*bath*) banio.
tuba *n.* (*musical instrument*) tuba.
tubal *adj.* tubal.
tubal ligation *n.* (*medical*) lia tubal.
tubby *adj.* ronda.
tube *n.* tubo; (*flexible*) mangera.
tubeless *adj.* sin tubo.
tuber *n.* (*biology*) tuber.
tubercle *n.* tuberculo.
tubercular *adj.* tuberculosica.
tuberculosis *n.* tuberculose.
tuberculous *adj.* tuberculosica.
tuberous *adj.* tuberosa.
tube top *n.* bustier tubo, camiseta gainin.
tubular *adj.* tubo.
tubule *n.* tubeta.
Tucana *n.* (*constellation*) la Tucana.
tuck *v.* & *n.* plia. **tuck away** asconde. **tuck into bed** envolve en leto.
tuco-tuco *n.* (*rodent*) tucotuco.
Tudor *adj.* tudor.
Tuesday *n.* martedi.
tufa *n.* (*rock*) tufa.
tuff *n.* (*rock*) tufa.
tuft *n.* mexa.
tufted *adj.* con mexa.
tuftlike *adj.* mexin.
tufty *adj.* mexin.
tug *v.* tira, aranca. • *n.* aranca, tira; (*boat*) barco tirante.
tugboat *n.* barco tirante.
tuition *n.* instrui; custa de instrui.
tuition fee *n.* custa de instrui.
tulip *n.* tulpa.
tulip tree *n.* liriodendro.
tumble *v.* cade; (*acrobat*) volta, rola.
tumbler *n.* (*acrobat*) voltor.
tumbleweed *n.* salsola.
tumescent *adj.* inflada.
tummy *n.* (*belly*) ventre; (*stomach*) stomaco.
tummy button *n.* ombilico.
tumor (US). See *tumour*.
tumorous *adj.* tumorosa.
tumour (US **tumor**) *n.* tumor.
tumult *n.* tumulta, caos.
tumultuous *adj.* tumultosa.
tumulus *n.* tumulo, colineta.
tuna *n.* tun.
tunable *adj.* ajustable.
tundra *n.* tundra.
tune *n.* melodia. • *v.* ajusta. **in tune** bonajustada, acordante. **out of tune** malajustada, desacordante. **tune up** (*music*) ajusta.
tuneful *adj.* melodiosa.
tuner *n.* (*person*) ajustor; (*device*) ajustador.
tune-up *n.* ajusta.
tungsten *n.* uolfram.
Tungus *adj.* & *n.* tungus.
Tungusic *adj.* & *n.* (*person, language*) tungus.
tunic *n.* camison.
tuning fork *n.* force de ajusta.
Tunis *n.* (*city*) Tunis. **Gulf of Tunis** Golfo Tunis.
Tunisia *n.* Tunis.
Tunisian *adj.* & *n.* tunisi.
tunnel *n.* tunel. • *v.* tuneli.
tunnel vision *n.* vide tunelin.
tupelo *n.* tupelo.
Tupi *adj.* & *n.* (*person, language*) tupi.
tuple *n.* (*mathematics*) uple.
turaco *n.* (*bird*) turaco.
turban *n.* turban.

turbid *adj.* fangosa.
turbine *n.* turbina.
turbocharge *v.* supracarga.
turbulence *n.* turba.
turbulent *adj.* turbosa.
turd *n.* fece, merda.
tureen *n.* bol.
turf *n.* sespe.
turgid *adj.* inflada; (*language*) ostentosa.
Turkana, Lake *n.* Lago Turkana.
turkey[1] *n.* pavo.
Turkey[2] *n.* Turcia.
turkey soup *n.* sopa de pavo.
Turkic *adj.* (*languages*) turcica.
Turkish *adj.* & *n.* turces.
Turkmen *adj.* & *n.* turcmen.
Turkmenistan *n.* Turcmenistan.
Turkmenistani *adj.* & *n.* (*person*, *language*) turcmen.
turmeric *n.* (*plant*, *spice*) curcuma.
turmoil *n.* tumulta.
turn *v.* (*to face a new direction*) turna; (*in repeated circles*) jira; (*change direction while moving*) verje, diverje; (*soil*) turba. • *n.* turna; verje; (*game*) turno, ves. **take one's turn** fa sua turno. **take turns** alterna. **turn around** reversa. **turn back and forth** turna e returna. **turn by turn** (*navigation*) per cada verje. **turn down** (*volume*) redui. **turn green** deveni verde, verdi, fa ce lo deveni verde. **turn inside-out** eversa. **turn off** (*machine*) descomuta; (*light*) estingui; (*tap*) clui; (*person*) repulsa. **turn of phrase** espresa. **turn on** (*machine*) comuta; (*light*) ensende; (*tap*) abri; (*person*) stimula, ensende. **turn one's back on** dorsi. **turn out** (*to be*) evidenti. **turn to dust** polvi. **turn up** apare. **turn upside-down** inversa.
turnabout *n.* reversa.
turnagra *n.* (*bird*) piopio.
turncoat *n.* renegada.
turning point *n.* punto de cambia.
turnip *n.* nabo.
turnout *n.* partisipa.
turnpike *n.* autovia.
turnstile *n.* molineta.
turntable *n.* (*record*) plato de disco; (*rail*) plata jirante.
turpentine *n.* terebentin.
turquoise *adj.* (*colour*) turcesa. • *n.* (*gem*) turcesa.
turret *n.* toreta.
turron *n.* turon.
turtle *n.* tortuga.
turtledove *n.* tortora.
turtleneck *n.* colar enrolada.
Tuscany *n.* (*Italian region*) Toscana.
tush *n.* (*buttocks*) culo, popa, posterior.
tusk *n.* denton.
tutelage *n.* garda.
tutor *n.* ensenior privata.
tutorial *n.* leson privata.
Tutsi *adj.* & *n.* tutsi.
Tuvalu *n.* Tuvalu.
Tuvaluan *adj.* & *n.* tuvalu.
tuxedo *n.* jaca de sera.
TV *n.* (*phenomenon*) tv; (*television set*) tele.
TV serial *n.* telenovela.
twaddle *n.* babela.
twang *v.* vibra. • *n.* vibra; (*vocal*) vose nasal.
tweak *v.* & *n.* pinsi, torse; (*minor adjustment*) ajusteta.
tweed *n.* (*fabric*) tuid. • *adj.* de tuid.
tween *n.* preadolesente.
tweet *v.* (*animal*) pia, pipi; (*Twitter*) tuita. • *interj.* pip.
tweeze *v.* & *n.* pinsi.
tweezers *n.* pinseta.
twelfth *adj.* (*ordinal*) des-du. • *n.* (*fraction*) desdui.
Twelfth Night *n.* note des-du, sera de epifania, sera de Res.
twelve *det.* des-du.
twentieth *adj.* (*ordinal*) dudes. • *n.* (*fraction*) dudesi.
twenty *det.* & *pron.* dudes.
twenty-cent piece *n.* (*coin*) sincim. **25-cent piece** cuatrim.
twenty-pence piece *n.* (*coin*) sincim.
twice *adv.* a du veses, duple. **twice a month** semimensal. **twice a year** semianial.
twiddle *v.* jueta con.
twig *n.* basteta.
twilight *n.* duilus, lus prima, lus final. **twilight of the gods** ragnaroc.
twill *n.* sarja.
twin *adj.* & *n.* jemelo.
twin beds *n.* (*two single beds*) letos jemelo.
twine *n.* cordeta.
twinge *n.* spasma de dole.
twinkle *v.* & *n.* sintili.
twirl *v.* jira.
twist *v.* & *n.* torse; (*yank*) aranca; (*dance*) tuist.
twit *n.* fol.
twitch *v.* & *n.* spasma.
twitchy *adj.* spasmin.
twite *n.* (*bird*) lineta.
twitter *v.* & *n.* pia.
twit-twoo *interj.* u-u.
two *det.* & *pron.* du. • *n.* (*cards, etc.*) two. **two at a time** du a cada ves. **two by two** en duples.
two-coloured (US **two-colored**) *adj.* ducolorida.
two-dimensional *adj.* bidimensional.
two-dimensional array *n.* matris.
twofold *adj.* duple.
two-layered *adj.* con du stratos.

two-man saw *n.* siera cuadro.
two-piece *adj.* de du pesos.
two-ply *adj.* con du stratos.
two-seater *adj.* con du sejas.
two-sided *adj.* biladal.
tycoon *n.* maniate.
tyke *n.* enfante, xice.
tympanum *n.* timpan.
type *n.* tipo, spesie, jenero; (*printing*) tipo. • *v.* tape.
typeface *n.* tipo de letera.
typescript *n.* manoscrito.
typeset *v.* tipografi.
typesetting *n.* tipografia.
typewriter *n.* tapador.
typhoid *adj.* & *n.* tifoide.
typhoon *n.* siclon.
typhus *n.* tifo.
typical *adj.* tipal.
typify *v.* marca, es tipal de.
typing mistake *n.* maltape.
typist *n.* tapor.
typo *n.* maltape.
typographer *n.* tipografiste.
typographic *adj.* tipografial.
typographical *adj.* tipografial.
typography *n.* tipografia.
typological *adj.* tipolojial.
typology *n.* tipolojia.
tyrannic *adj.* tiranal.
tyrannical *adj.* tiranal, tiranin.
tyrannize *v.* terori, es tirano a.
tyrannosaur *n.* tiranosauro.
tyrannosaurus *n.* tiranosauro.
tyrannous *adj.* tiraniosa.
tyranny *n.* tirania.
tyrant *n.* tirano.
tyrant flycatcher *n.* (*bird*) tirano.
tyrantlike *adj.* tiranin.
tyre (US **tire**) *n.* numatico.
tzatziki *n.* (*food*) djadjici.

U

uakari *n.* (*monkey*) uacari.
U-bend *n.* tubo U.
Übermensch *adj.* & *n.* supraumana.
ubiquitous *adj.* omnipresente, sempre presente.
ubiquity *n.* omnipresentia.
udder *n.* mamela.
UFO *abbr.* ovn.
Uganda *n.* Uganda.
Ugandan *adj.* & *n.* ugandan.
ugh *interj.* (*disgust*) iu.
uglify *v.* fei.
ugliness *n.* feia.
ugly *adj.* fea. **become ugly** fei.
Ugric *adj.* (*languages*) ugrica.
uh *interj.* (*hesitation*) em.
UHF *n.* frecuentia estrema alta.
uh-oh *interj.* op.
Uighur *adj.* & *n.* (*person*, *language*) uigur.
uilleann pipes *n.* cornamusa eres.
Ukraine *n.* Ucraina.
Ukrainian *adj.* & *n.* (*person*, *language*) ucrainsce.
ukulele *n.* (*guitar*) uculele.
ulcer *n.* ulsera.
ulcerate *v.* ulsera.
ulceration *n.* ulsera.
ulna *n.* (*anatomy*) ulna.
ulterior *n.* (*motive*) ascondeda.
ultimate *adj.* (*final or most extreme*) ultima.
ultimatum *n.* esije ultima.
ultra- *pref.* ultra-.
ultraorthodox *adj.* ultraortodox.
ultrasonic *adj.* ultrasonal.
ultrasonogram *n.* ecogram.
ultrasonograph *n.* ecograf. • *v.* ecografi.
ultrasonography *n.* ecografia.
ultrasound *n.* ultrasona.
ultraviolet *adj.* & *n.* ultravioleta.
ultraviolet lamp *n.* lampa ultravioleta.
um *interj.* (*interjection*) em.
umami *n.* (*flavour*) umami.
Umayyad *adj.* umaian.
umber *adj.* (*colour*) ombra. • *n.* (*pigment*) ombra.
umbilical *adj.* ombilical.
umbilical cord *n.* corda ombilical.
umbilical hernia *n.* ernia ombilical.
umbilicus *n.* ombilico.
umbrage *n.* ofende.
umbrella *n.* parapluve.
umbrella group *n.* supragrupo, supraorganiza.
umbrella organization *n.* supraorganiza.
Umbria *n.* (*Italian region*) Umbria.
Umbrian *adj.* & *n.* (*person*, *language*) umbrian.
umlaut *n.* umlaut.
umpire *n.* arbitror.
umpteenth *adj.* nonumerable.
un- *pref.* (*reverse action*) des-; (*reverse quality*, *absence*) non-.
unabashed *adj.* abrida.
unable *adj.* noncapas, nonpotente.
unacceptable *adj.* nonasetable.
unaccompanied *adj.* nonacompaniada; (*singer*) sin strumento.
unaccustomed *adj.* nonabituada.
unachievable *adj.* nonatenable.
unadaptable *adj.* nonajustable.
unadapted *adj.* nonajustada.
unadjusted *adj.* nonajustada.
unadulterated *adj.* pur.
unaimed *adj.* nondirijeda.
unalike *adj.* nonsimil.
unaltered *adj.* nonalterada.
unambiguous *adj.* nonambigua.
unambitious *adj.* nonaspirante.
unanimity *n.* acorda unida.
unanimous *adj.* en acorda unida.
unanticipated *adj.* nonespetada.
unapologetic *adj.* nonrepentinte.
unappetizing *adj.* noninvitante.
unapproachable *adj.* nonasedable.
unarmed *adj.* sin armas.
unashamed *adj.* sin vergonia.
unassailable *adj.* nonatacable.
unassertive *adj.* nonserta.
unassuming *adj.* umil.
unattainable *adj.* nonatenable.
unattended *adj.* nonatendeda.
unauthorized *adj.* nonpermeteda.
unavailability *n.* nondisponablia.
unavailable *adj.* nondisponable, nonotenable.
unavoidable *adj.* nonevitable.
unaware *adj.* nonconsensa.
unbalance *v.* desecuilibra.
unbar *v.* desbari.
unbearable *adj.* nontolerable.
unbeatable *adj.* nonconcistable.
unbeaten *adj.* nonvinseda.
unbecoming *adj.* nonconveninte.
unbefitting *adj.* nonconveninte.
unbeholden *adj.* nonobligada.
unbeknown to *prep.* nonsabeda par.
unbelievable *adj.* noncredable.
unbelt *v.* desinturi.
unbend *v.* descurvi.
unbiased *adj.* nonprejudosa.
unbind *v.* deslia.

unbleached *adj.* nonblancida.
unblemished *adj.* nonmanxada.
unblock *v.* desbloci, desbari.
unblocked *adj.* desblocida, desbarida, clar.
unbound *adj.* desliada.
unbounded *adj.* nonlimitada, infinita, sin limita.
unbreakable *adj.* nonrompable.
unbridle *v.* desbridi.
unbridling *n.* desbridi.
unbroken *adj.* nonrompeda.
unbuckle *v.* desfibi.
unburden *v.* descarga.
unbutton *v.* desbotoni, abri.
uncanny *adj.* disturbante, misteriosa, strana.
uncap *v.* destapi.
uncaring *adj.* noncurante.
unceasing *adj.* nonsesante, sin sesa.
unceremonious *adj.* nonritual.
uncertain *adj.* nonserta.
unchanging *adj.* noncambiante.
uncharacteristic *adj.* nontipal, nonusual.
uncharted *adj.* nonmapada.
unchecked *adj.* nonsertida.
uncial *adj.* (*lettering*) unsial.
uncivilized *adj.* nonsivilida.
uncle *n.* tio; (*gender-neutral*) tie.
unclean *adj.* nonlimpa, nonpur.
unclear *adj.* nonclar.
unclench *v.* (*fist*) esvasa.
unclip *v.* desclipi.
unclog *v.* desbloci.
uncoil *v.* desenrola.
uncoloured (US **uncolored**) *adj.* noncolorida.
uncombed *adj.* despetenida.
uncomfortable *adj.* noncomfortosa.
uncommon *adj.* noncomun, rara.
uncompleted *adj.* noncompletida.
uncompliant *adj.* nonobedinte.
uncomplicated *adj.* simple.
uncompounded *adj.* noncomposada.
unconcerned *adj.* nonconsernada.
unconditional *adj.* sin restrinje.
unconfident *adj.* nonserta.
unconfigurable *adj.* nonajustable.
unconfined *adj.* nonrestrinjeda.
unconfirmed *adj.* nonconfirmada, nondemostrada, nonsertida.
unconfusable *adj.* nonconfusable.
unconnected *adj.* nonliada.
unconquerable *adj.* nonconcistable.
unconscious *adj.* nonconsensa. • *n.* suconsensia.
unconsciousness *n.* nonconsensia.
unconstitutional *adj.* nonconstitual.
uncontaminated *adj.* noncontaminada, pur.
uncontrollable *adj.* noncontrolable.
uncontrolled *adj.* noncontrolada.
unconventional *adj.* nonortodox, nonusual.
unconvinced *adj.* nonconvinseda.
unconvincing *adj.* nonconvinsente.
uncooked *adj.* cru.
uncork *v.* destapi.
uncorrectable *adj.* noncoretable.
uncorroborated *adj.* nonconfirmada.
uncorrupted *adj.* nonmalida.
uncountable *adj.* noncontable.
uncouth *adj.* bruta, de mal maneras.
uncover *v.* descovre.
uncross *v.* (*arms, legs*) descrusa.
uncrown *v.* descoroni.
unction *n.* unje.
unctuous *adj.* adulante.
uncuff *v.* desecuri la polsos de.
uncultivated *adj.* noncultivada.
uncultured *adj.* noneducada.
uncurable *adj.* nonremediable.
uncurl *v.* desrisi.
uncurtained *adj.* sin cortina.
uncustomary *adj.* noncostumal, nonusual.
uncustomizable *adj.* nonalterable.
uncut *adj.* (*gem*) bruta.
undecided *adj.* nondesideda.
undecorated *adj.* nondecorada.
undedicated *adj.* nondedicada.
undefeated *adj.* nonvinseda, sin defeta.
undefined *adj.* nondefinida.
undemocratic *adj.* nondemocrata.
undemonstrative *adj.* nonespresosa.
undeniable *adj.* nonegable.
undenied *adj.* nonegada.
undependable *adj.* nonfidable.
under *prep.* su; (*motion towards*) a su. • *adv.* a su.
underachieve *v.* sususede, ateni min ca espetada.
underachiever *n.* sususedor.
underappreciate *v.* suvalua.
underarm *n.* axila. • *adj.* axilal.
underbelly *n.* suventre.
underbid *v.* ofre min ca.
underbrush *n.* subosce.
undercarriage *n.* xasi.
undercharge *v.* vende per tro poca.
underclassman *n.* studiante nova.
underclothes *n.* vestetas.
undercoat *n.* sustrato.
undercook *v.* coce tro poca.
undercooked *adj.* tro poca coceda.
undercover *adj.* desemblante.
undercurrent *n.* sucorente.
undercut *v.* vende plu barata ca.
underdeveloped *adj.* sudevelopada.
underdog *n.* nonfavoreda, nonfortunosa.
underdone *adj.* tro poca coceda.
underdressed *adj.* nonconveninte vestida.

underestimate *v.* & *n.* suestima.
underexpose *v.* suesposa.
underexposure *n.* suesposa.
underfloor heating *n.* solo caldinte.
underfoot *adv.* su pede.
undergarment *n.* vesteta.
undergo *v.* sufri, esperia.
undergraduate *adj.* & *n.* pregraduada.
underground *adj.* suteran. • *n.* (*railway*) metro.
underground channel *n.* canal suteran.
underground water *n.* acua suteran.
undergrowth *n.* subosce.
underhanded *adj.* enganosa.
underlie *v.* causa; es la funda de.
underline *v.* sulini. • *n.* (*underlining*) sulini; (*character*) sulinia.
underlying *adj.* fundal.
undermine *v.* sumina.
underneath *prep.* su. • *adv.* a su.
undernourished *adj.* malnurida.
underpaid *adj.* tro poca paiada.
underpants *n.* pantaleta.
underpass *n.* supasaje, suvia.
underpin *v.* suporta.
underpopulate *v.* supopla.
underpopulation *n.* supopla.
underprivileged *adj.* nonfortunosa.
underrate *v.* suvalua.
underscore *v.* sulini. • *n.* (*underscoring*) sulini; (*character*) sulinia.
undersea *adj.* su mar.
undersecretary *n.* susecretor.
undershirt *n.* camiseta, sucamisa.
undershorts *n.* pantaleta; (*boxers*) supantala.
underside *n.* fondo.
undersized *adj.* peti.
underskirt *n.* faldeta.
understaffed *adj.* con tro poca empleadas.
understand *v.* comprende.
understandable *adj.* comprendable.
understate *v.* minimi.
understudy *n.* sustitua.
undertake *v.* emprende, embarca.
undertaker *n.* funeror.
undertaker's *n.* (*funeral parlour*) funereria.
undertaking *n.* emprende, projeta.
undervalue *v.* suvalua.
underwater *adj.* suacuan.
underway *adj.* comensada.
underwear *n.* vestetas.
underweight *adj.* tro lejera.
underworld *n.* sumundo; (*hell*) enferno; (*crime*) criminalia.
underwrite *v.* suscrive.
underwriter *n.* ajente ascurinte, compania ascurinte.
undeserved *adj.* nonmeritada.
undesirable *adj.* nondesirada.
undesired *adj.* nondesirada.
undetected *adj.* nondetetada.
undeterred *adj.* nonimpedida.
undeveloped *adj.* nondevelopada.
undeviating *adj.* nondeviante.
undiagnosed *adj.* nondiagnoseda.
undifferentiated *adj.* nondistinguinte, sin distingui.
undignified *adj.* nondiniosa.
undirected *adj.* nondirijeda.
undirtied *adj.* nonsusida.
undisclosed *adj.* nonrevelada.
undisputed *adj.* nondisputada.
undissolvable *adj.* nondisolvable.
undistinguished *adj.* mediocre.
undisturbed *adj.* nondisturbada, sin turba.
undivided *adj.* nondivideda.
undo *v.* desfa; (*unfasten*) desfisa, abri. **come undone** abri.
undocumented *adj.* nondocumentida, sin documentos.
undoing *n.* desfa.
undoubtable *adj.* nondutable.
undoubted *adj.* nondutada, sin duta.
undress *v.* desvesti.
undue *adj.* nonmeritada, nonesesada.
undulant *adj.* ondante.
undulate *v.* onda.
undulating *adj.* ondante, ondosa.
undulation *n.* onda.
undying *adj.* nonmorinte.
unearth *v.* desentera.
unearthing *n.* desentera.
unearthly *adj.* nonteral.
unease *n.* ansia.
uneasy *adj.* noncuieta.
uneducated *adj.* noneducada.
unelectable *adj.* nonelejable.
unemotional *adj.* nonemosiosa.
unemployed *adj.* nonempleada.
unemployment *n.* nonemplea.
unending *adj.* nonfininte, sin fini.
unenforceable *adj.* nonenforsable.
unenjoyable *adj.* nonplaserosa.
unenlarged *adj.* nongrandida.
unenlightened *adj.* nonluminada.
unenthusiastic *adj.* nonzelosa.
unequal *adj.* nonegal.
unequalled (US **unequaled**) *adj.* sin egal.
unequivocal *adj.* nonambigua, nondutable.
unerasable *adj.* noncanselable.
unerring *adj.* nonerante.
unethical *adj.* nonetical.
uneven *adj.* nonplana.
uneventful *adj.* nonavenosa, calma, pasosa.
unexceptional *adj.* mediocre.
unexciting *adj.* nonstimulante, mediocre.
unexpected *adj.* nonespetada, nonprevideda.

unexplainable *adj.* nonesplicable.
unexploited *adj.* nonesplotada.
unexpressive *adj.* nonespresosa.
unfair *adj.* nonjusta.
unfaithful *adj.* nonfidosa.
unfaithfulness *n.* nonfida.
unfaltering *adj.* nonesitante.
unfamiliar *adj.* nonconoseda.
unfashionable *adj.* nonmodosa.
unfasten *v.* desfisa, abri.
unfathomable *adj.* noncomprendable, nonimajinable.
unfavourable (US **unfavorable**) *adj.* nonfavorable.
unfazed *adj.* nondisturbada.
unfeasible *adj.* nonpratical, nonrealable.
unfeeling *adj.* nonemosiosa, nonsentosa.
unfiltered *adj.* nonfiltrida.
unfinished *adj.* bruta.
unfit *adj.* nonconveninte.
unfixable *adj.* nonreparable.
unfixed *adj.* nonfisada, nonstable.
unflappable *adj.* nonajitable.
unflattering *adj.* nonlodante; (*garment*) nonfavorente.
unflinching *adj.* nonesitante.
unfocused *adj.* nonfocada.
unfold *v.* desplia.
unforeseeable *adj.* nonprevidable.
unforeseen *adj.* nonprevideda.
unforgettable *adj.* nonoblidable.
unforgivable *adj.* nonpardonable.
unfortunate *adj.* nonfortunosa, regretable.
unfortunate occurrence *n.* mal fortuna.
unfounded *adj.* sin funda.
unfree *adj.* nonlibre.
unfree labourer (US **laborer**) *n.* peon.
unfreeze *v.* dejela.
unfriend *v.* desamini.
unfriendly *adj.* nonamin.
unfrock *v.* despreti.
unfrozen *adj.* dejelada.
unfurl *v.* desenrola.
ungainly *adj.* torpe.
Ungava Bay *n.* Baia Ungava.
ungodly *adj.* nonrelijiosa.
ungovernable *adj.* nongovernable.
ungraded *adj.* nongradida.
ungrateful *adj.* nongrasiosa.
ungroup *v.* desgrupi.
unguent *n.* unjente.
ungulate *n.* ungulato.
unhand *v.* desteni.
unhappiness *n.* nonfelisia, tristia.
unhappy *adj.* nonfelis, triste.
unharmed *adj.* nonferida.
unharness *v.* desarnesi.
unhealthy *adj.* nonsana.
unheard *adj.* nonoiada.
unheeded *adj.* iniorada.
unhelpful *adj.* nonaidosa.
unhesitating *adj.* nonesitante.
unhindered *adj.* nonimpedida.
unhinge *v.* dexarnieri; (*mentally*) dementi.
unholy *adj.* nonsanta.
unhook *v.* desonci.
unhorse *v.* colpa de cavalo, cade a tera.
unhurt *adj.* nonferida.
uni- *pref.* (*one*) uni-.
unicameral *n.* con un salon.
unicellular *adj.* uniselulal.
unicorn *n.* unicorno.
unicycle *n.* monosicle.
unification *n.* uni.
unified *adj.* unida.
uniform *adj.* uniforma. • *n.* (*dress*) uniforma. **become uniform** uniformi. **dress in uniform** uniformi.
uniformity *n.* uniformia.
unify *v.* uni.
unilateral *adj.* uniladal.
unilluminated *adj.* nonluminada.
unimaginable *adj.* nonimajinable.
unimpaired *adj.* nondescapasida.
unimpeachable *adj.* nondisputable.
unimpeded *adj.* nonimpedida, nonrestrinjeda.
unimportant *adj.* nonimportante.
unimpressed *adj.* nonimpresada.
unincorporated *n.* noncorporada.
unindent *v.* desindente.
uninformed *adj.* noninformada.
uninhabitable *adj.* nonabitable.
uninhabited *adj.* nonabitada.
uninhibited *adj.* nonrestrinjeda.
uninjured *adj.* nonferida.
uninspired *adj.* mediocre.
uninstall *v.* desinstala.
uninsured *adj.* nonasecurada.
unintelligent *adj.* nonintelijente.
unintelligibility *n.* noncomprendablia.
unintelligible *adj.* noncomprendable.
unintended *adj.* nonintendeda.
uninteresting *adj.* noninteresante.
unintuitable *adj.* nonintuable.
unintuitive *adj.* (*design*) nonintuable; (*person*) nonintuosa.
uninvestigated *adj.* noninvestigada.
uninviting *adj.* noninvitante.
union *n.* (*action, result*) uni. **act of union** trata de uni. **Union of South Africa** Republica de Africa Sude. **Union of Soviet Socialist Republics** Uni de Republicas Sosialistes Soviet.
unionism *n.* sindicatisme.
unionist *adj.* (*policital*) unidiste. • *n.* unidiste; (*trade union*) sindicatiste.
unionize *v.* sindicati.

union steward *n.* portavose de sindicato.
unique *adj.* unica.
unisex *adj.* unisesal; ajenero.
unison *n.* simultania. **in unison** simultan.
unit *n.* (*of a larger whole, of measurement*) unia; (*commercial, residential*) aparte. **unit of currency** unia de mone.
unitard *n.* bodi longa.
Unitarian *adj.* & *n.* unitarian.
Unitarianism *n.* (*Christianity*) unitarianisme.
unitary *adj.* uniforma; (*of units*) unial.
unite *v.* uni.
United Arab Emirates *n.* Amirias Arabi Unida.
United Kingdom *n.* Rena Unida.
United Nations *n.* Nasiones Unida.
United States *n.* Statos Unida de America.
unity *n.* unia.
univalent *adj.* (*biology*) univalente.
universal *adj.* universal.
universalism *n.* (*philosophy, Christianity*) universalisme.
universalist *adj.* & *n.* universaliste.
universal joint *n.* cardan.
universe *n.* universo.
university *n.* universia.
unjoin *v.* dejunta.
unjust *adj.* nonjusta.
unjustifiable *adj.* nonjustable.
unjustified *adj.* nonmeritada; nonrazonada.
unkempt *adj.* desordinada, despetenida.
unkind *adj.* noncompatiosa, basa.
unknowable *adj.* (*person*) nonconosable; (*information*) nonsabable.
unknowing *adj.* nonsabosa.
unknown *adj.* & *n.* (*person*) nonconoseda; (*information*) nonsabeda.
unlabelled (US **unlabeled**) *adj.* noneticetida.
unlatch *v.* desfisa.
unlawful *adj.* nonlegal.
unleaded *adj.* sin plomo.
unlearn *v.* desaprende.
unleash *v.* relasa, libri.
unleavened *adj.* nonfermentada.
unless *subord.* si … no, estra si, estra cuando.
unlicensed *adj.* nonlisensada.
unlikable (US). See *unlikeable.*
unlike *adj.* nonsimil, diferente. • *prep.* no como. **unlike how** no como.
unlikeable (US **unlikable**) *adj.* nonamable.
unlikely *adj.* nonprobable.
unlimited *adj.* nonlimitada, sin limita.
unlisted *adj.* nonlistada.
unliveable (US **unlivable**) *adj.* nonabitable.
unload *v.* descarga.
unlock *v.* desecuri; (*with key*) desclavi; (*database*) desemafori.
unlocked *adj.* nonsecurida.
unlovable *adj.* nonamable.
unloveable *adj.* nonamable.
unlucky *adj.* nonfortunosa.
unmagnified *adj.* nongrandida.
unmanageable *adj.* nonmanejable.
unmanned *adj.* nonabitada.
unmanned aerial vehicle *n.* avion sin pilote.
unmannerly *adj.* noncortes.
unmapped *adj.* nonmapada.
unmark *v.* desmarca.
unmarked *adj.* nonmanxada.
unmarried *adj.* nonsposida.
unmask *v.* desmasci.
unmatched *adj.* sin egal.
unmeasured *adj.* nonmesurada.
unmedicated *adj.* nonmedisinida.
unmentionable *adj.* tabu.
unmerciful *adj.* nonpardonosa.
unmerited *adj.* nonmeritada.
unmistakable *adj.* nonconfusable, evidente.
unmix *v.* desmisca.
unmodifiable *adj.* nonalterable.
unmodified *adj.* nonalterada.
unmotorized lawnmower *n.* cortierba puiable.
unmoved *adj.* nonemosiada.
unmoving *adj.* (*motionless*) nonmovente.
unmuddle *v.* desconfusa.
unnamed *adj.* nonomida.
unnatural *adj.* nonatural.
unnecessary *adj.* nonesesada.
unnerve *v.* descoraji.
unnoted *adj.* nonotada.
unnoticeable *adj.* nonpersepable.
unnoticed *adj.* nonotada.
unobligated *adj.* nonobligada.
unobscured *adj.* nonoscurida.
unobserved *adj.* oservada.
unobstructed *adj.* nonimpedida.
unobtainable *adj.* nonotenable.
unobtrusive *adj.* nontraente atende, sin atrae atende.
unoccupied *adj.* nonocupada.
unofficial *adj.* nonofisial.
unopened *adj.* nonabrida.
unopposed *adj.* nonoposada.
unoriginal *adj.* nonorijinal.
unorthodox *adj.* nonortodox.
unpack *v.* despaci.
unpacking *n.* despaci.
unpaid *adj.* nonpaiada.
unpainted *adj.* nonpintida.
unpalatable *adj.* malsaborosa.
unpasteurized *adj.* nonpasteurida.
unpaved *adj.* nonpaveda.
unperforated *adj.* nonperforada.
unpersuadable *adj.* nonconvinsable.

unpick *v.* destexe.
unpin *v.* despini.
unplanned *adj.* nonespetada, nonintendeda.
unpleasant *adj.* nonplasente, desplasente.
unpleasurable *adj.* nonplaserosa.
unplug *v.* (*electric*) deslia; (*stopper*) destapi.
unpolluted *adj.* noncontaminada.
unpopular *adj.* nonpopular.
unposed *adj.* sin posa.
unpraised *adj.* nonlodada.
unprecedented *adj.* sin presedente.
unpredictable *adj.* nonpredisable.
unprejudiced *adj.* nonprejudosa.
unprepared *adj.* nonpreparada.
unpretentious *adj.* nonfinjosa, modesta, umil.
unpreventable *adj.* nonprevenable.
unprincipled *adj.* nonmoral.
unprintable *adj.* nonprimable.
unproductive *adj.* nonproduosa.
unproductiveness *n.* nonproduosia.
unprofessional *adj.* nonprofesal, noncapas, nonmoral.
unprofitable *adj.* nonprofitosa.
unpronounceable *adj.* nonpronunsiable.
unprotected *adj.* nonprotejeda.
unproven *adj.* nondemostrada.
unpublished *adj.* nonpublicida.
unpunished *adj.* nonpunida.
unqualified *adj.* noncapas, nondutada, nonpreparada.
unquestionable *adj.* nondutable.
unquote *n.* cluisita.
unranked *adj.* nongradida.
unrated *adj.* nongradida.
unravel *v.* destexe, destricota, desmarania, desintegra, gasta; (*mystery*) solve.
unreachable *adj.* nonatenable.
unreadable *n.* nonlejable.
unreadableness *n.* nonlejablia.
unreal *adj.* nonreal.
unreasonable *adj.* nonrazonante.
unreceptive *adj.* nonresetante.
unrecognizable *adj.* nonreconosable.
unrefined *adj.* nonrefinada, (*sugar*) bruta.
unreformed *adj.* nonreformida.
unregarded *adj.* nonregardada, iniorada.
unregretful *adj.* sin regrete.
unregulated *adj.* nonregulada.
unrelated *adj.* nonrelatada.
unrelenting *adj.* nonsedente.
unreliable *adj.* nonfidable.
unremarkable *adj.* mediocre.
unremittent *adj.* nonflutuante.
unremitting *adj.* nonsedente.
unremovable *adj.* nonsutrable.
unrepentant *adj.* nonrepentinte.
unreported *adj.* nonreportada.
unrepresentative *adj.* nonrepresentante.
unrequited *adj.* uniladal.
unreserved *adj.* nonrestrinjeda.
unresponsive *adj.* nonrespondente.
unrest *n.* turba.
unrestrained *adj.* nonrestrinjeda, sin restrinje, nonfrenida.
unrestricted *adj.* nonrestrinjeda, sin restrinje.
unreturnable *adj.* nonreenviable.
unrevealed *adj.* nonrevelada.
unrewarding *adj.* nonsasiante.
unripe *adj.* nonmatur.
unrivalled (US **unrivaled**) *adj.* sin egal.
unroll *v.* desenrola.
unrounded *n.* (*vowel*) plata.
unruffled *adj.* calma.
unruly *adj.* turbosa.
unsaddle *v.* desensela.
unsafe *adj.* nonsecur.
unsaid *adj.* nondiseda.
unsalted *adj.* nonsalida, sin sal.
unsanitary *adj.* nonijenial.
unsatiated *adj.* nonsasiada.
unsatisfactory *adj.* nonsasiante.
unsatisfied *adj.* nonsasiada.
unsatisfying *adj.* nonsasiante.
unsaturated *adj.* nonsaturada.
unscathed *adj.* nonferida.
unscented *adj.* sin odor.
unschooled *adj.* noneducada.
unscientific *adj.* nonsiensal.
unscramble *v.* desconfusa, desmisca.
unscreened *adj.* (*film*) nonmostrada; (*unchecked*) nonprobada, noninvestigada.
unscrew *v.* desvisi.
unscrupulous *adj.* nonmoral.
unseal *v.* deseli, destapi.
unseasonable *adj.* nonsaisonal.
unseasoned *adj.* nonspisida.
unseat *v.* espulsa; colpa de cavalo.
unsecured *adj.* nonsecurida.
unsee *v.* desvide.
unseemly *adj.* nonconveninte.
unseen *adj.* nonvideda.
unselfish *adj.* nonegosa.
unsensing *adj.* nonsensante.
unsentimental *adj.* nonsentosa.
unsettle *v.* disturba.
unshackle *v.* desecuri la talos de.
unshakeable (US **unshakable**) *adj.* ostinosa.
unshaven *adj.* nonrasada.
unshod *n.* (*horse*) sin fero; (*person*) sin sapatos.
unshorn *adj.* nonrasada.
unshown *adj.* nonmostrada.
unsightly *adj.* fea, repulsante.
unskilled *adj.* noneducada, noninstruida.
unsmellable *adj.* nonolable.
unsmiling *adj.* sombre.

unsnarl *v.* desmarania.
unsociable *adj.* nonsosial.
unsocial *adj.* nonsosial.
unsoiled *adj.* nonsusida.
unsold *n.* nonvendeda.
unsolicited *adj.* nonxercada.
unsolvable *adj.* nonsolvable.
unsophisticated *adj.* nonsofisticada, naive, provinsal.
unsorted *adj.* nonordinada.
unspeakable *adj.* nonespresable.
unspecialized *adj.* nonspesialida.
unspoiled *adj.* nonmalida.
unspoken *adj.* nondiseda, nonparlada.
unstable *adj.* nonstable.
unstained *adj.* clar.
unstated *adj.* nondiseda.
unsteady *adj.* bambolante. **be unsteady** bambola.
unsterile *adj.* nonsteril.
unstick *v.* descoli.
unstop *v.* destapi.
unstoppable *adj.* nonparable.
unstrap *v.* desinturi.
unstressed *adj.* nonasentuada.
unstructured *adj.* nonstruturida.
unstylish *adj.* nonmodosa.
unsubscribe *v.* desenscrive, cansela sua enscrive, dejunta se.
unsubstantiated *adj.* nonconfirmada.
unsuccessful *adj.* nonsusedosa.
unsuitability *n.* nonconveni.
unsuitable *adj.* nonconveninte.
unsuited *adj.* nonconveninte.
unsullied *adj.* nonsusida, nonmanxada; nonmalida.
unsung *adj.* nonlodada.
unsupervised *adj.* nonsupravideda.
unsupportable *adj.* nonsuportable.
unsupported *adj.* nonsuportada.
unsure *adj.* nonserta.
unsurpassed *adj.* nonsuprapasada, nonesededa.
unsurprised *adj.* nonsurprendeda.
unsusceptible *adj.* imune.
unsuspected *adj.* nonsuspetada.
unsuspecting *adj.* nonsuspetante.
unsustainable *adj.* nonsustable.
unswayed *adj.* nonconvinseda.
unsweetened *adj.* nondulsida.
unswerving *adj.* nondeviante.
unsympathetic *adj.* noncompatiosa.
unsystematic *adj.* nonsistemosa.
unsystemic *adj.* nonsistemal.
untainted *adj.* nonmanxada.
untamed *adj.* savaje.
untangle *v.* desmarania.
untapped *adj.* nonesplotada.
untaxable *adj.* nonimpostable.
untenable *adj.* nondefendable.
untended *adj.* nonatendeda.
untense *v.* destensa.
untested *adj.* nonprobada.
untether *v.* desecuri.
untethered *adj.* nonsecurida.
unthinkable *adj.* nonpensable.
untidy *adj.* desordinada.
untie *v.* deslia, abri.
untighten *v.* destensa.
until *prep.* asta. • *subord.* asta cuando. **until now** asta aora. **until then** asta alora.
untimely *adj.* nonoportun.
unto *prep.* a.
untold *adj.* nonarada.
untouchable *adj.* nontocable.
untouched *adj.* nontocada.
untraceable *adj.* nontrasable.
untraditional *adj.* nontradisional.
untrainable *adj.* noninstruable.
untrained *adj.* noninstruida.
untranslatable *adj.* nontraduable.
untranslated *adj.* nontraduida.
untransparent *adj.* nontransparente.
untreatable *adj.* nontratable.
untreated *adj.* bruta.
untried *adj.* nonprobada.
untrue *adj.* falsa.
untrueness *n.* falsia, nonveria.
untrustworthy *adj.* nonfidable.
untruth *n.* nonvera; (*untrueness*) nonveria.
untruthful *adj.* mentinte.
untucked *adj.* nonordinada.
untunable *adj.* nonajustable.
untuned *adj.* nonajustada.
unturned *adj.* (*cards*) nonrevelada.
untwist *v.* destorse.
untypical *adj.* nontipal.
unusable *adj.* nonusable.
unused *adj.* (*never used*) nonusada; (*unaccustomed*) nonabituada.
unusual *adj.* nonusual, noncomun, strana.
unusualness *n.* noncomunia.
unvaccinated *adj.* nonvasinida.
unveil *v.* desveli.
unverified *adj.* nonsertida.
unversed *adj.* noncapas.
unviable *adj.* nonrealable.
unvoiced *adj.* nondiseda.
unwanted *adj.* nondesirada.
unwarranted *adj.* nonmeritada.
unweave *v.* destexe.
unwed *adj.* nonsposida.
unwelcome *adj.* nonbonvenida.
unwelcoming *adj.* nonbonveninte.
unwell *adj.* malada.
unwieldy *adj.* masosa.
unwilling *adj.* nonvolente, resistente.
unwillingness *n.* resiste.

unwind *v.* desenrola.
unwise *adj.* nonsaja.
unwitnessed *adj.* nonvideda.
unwitting *adj.* nonespetante.
unworkable *adj.* nonrealable.
unworldly *adj.* nonmundal; nonatural, strana, spiritosa.
unworthy *adj.* nonmeritante.
unwrap *v.* desenvolve.
unwritten *adj.* nonscriveda.
unyielding *adj.* nonsedente.
unzip *v.* dezipi.
up *adv.* a alta, a supra, a monte, de su. • *prep.* a alta de, asendente; (*following or in parallel with*) longo. **bring up to date** corenti, refresci. **get up** leva. **go up** asende. **up for discussion** discutable. **ups and downs** altas e basas, ondas. **up to** asta. **up to date** corente, fresca. **up to now** asta aora.
up-and-coming *adj.* nova emerjinte.
upanishad *n.* (*scripture*) upanixad.
upbeat *adj.* otimiste.
upbraid *v.* reproxa.
upbringing *n.* eleva.
upcoming *adj.* prosiminte.
update *v.* & *n.* corenti, refresci, moderni.
upend *v.* inversa.
upgrade *v.* & *n.* renovi.
upheaval *n.* cambion.
upheld *adj.* suportada.
uphill *adv.* a monte.
uphold *v.* suporta.
upholster *v.* tapeti, materasi.
upholsterer *n.* tapetor.
upholstery *n.* (*material*) tapeto; (*action*) tapeti.
upkeep *n.* manteni.
uplift *n.* leva; felisi.
uplink *v.* & *n.* supralia.
upload *v.* & *n.* carga.
upmarket *adj.* superior.
upon *prep.* sur.
upper *adj.* alta, plu alta.
upper arm *n.* braso alta.
uppercase *adj.* major. • *v.* (*convert to uppercase*) majori.
uppercase letter *n.* letera major.
upper class *n.* clase alta. • *adj.* de clase alta.
upperclassman *n.* studiante de anio ultima.
upper course *n.* (*river*) curso alta.
uppercut *n.* colpa a supra.
upper garment *n.* veste alta.
Upper House *n.* Salon Alta.
upper leg *n.* gama alta.
upper limit *n.* limita masima.
uppermost *adj.* la plu alta.
upper part *n.* alta.
uppity *adj.* egosa.
up quark *n.* cuarc asendente.
upright *adj.* vertical.
uprising *n.* (*local rebellion*) revolta.
upriver *adv.* contra la flue.
uproar *n.* tumulta.
uproarious *adj.* ruidosa, tumultosa; (*hilarious*) ilario.
uproot *v.* desradisi, desplanta.
uprush *n.* (*oil*) geser.
upscale *adj.* superior.
upset *v.* ajita, turba; (*knock over*) malversa. • *adj.* ajitada, turbada.
upshot *n.* resulta.
upside-down *adj.* inversada.
upsilon *n.* (*Greek letter*) upsilon.
upstage *v.* ombri.
upstairs *adv.* a supra. **from upstairs** de supra.
upstanding *adj.* onorosa.
upstart *n.* comensor egosa.
upstate *adj.* norde.
upstream *adj.* a monte, contra la corente, contra la flue.
upstroke *n.* asendente.
upsurge *n.* aumenta.
upswept *adj.* asendente.
upswing *n.* asende.
uptake *n.* usa; asorbe.
uptight *adj.* constrinjeda.
uptown *n.* area abital; visineria rica.
upturn *n.* asende.
upward *adv.* a alta, a supra, a monte, de su.
upwards *adv.* a alta, a supra, a monte, de su.
upwind *adj.* supraventa, contra la venta.
uraemia *n.* (*medical*) uremia.
Uralic *adj.* (*languages*) uralica.
Ural Mountains *n.* Montes Ural.
uranium *n.* uranio.
Uranus *n.* (*mythology*, *planet*) Urano.
urate *n.* (*chemistry*) urato.
urban *adj.* urban.
urban area *n.* urbe.
urbane *adj.* cortes, sofisticada.
urbanite *n.* urban.
urbanization *n.* urbani.
urbanize *v.* urbani.
urbanologist *n.* urbolojiste.
urbanology *n.* urbolojia.
urchin *n.* enfante misera.
Urdu *adj.* & *n.* (*language*) urdu.
urea *n.* (*substance*) urea.
uremia (US). See *uraemia*.
ureter *n.* (*anatomy*) ureter.
urethane *n.* (*substance*) uretan.
urethra *n.* (*anatomy*) uretra.
urge *v.* urje, coraji, speroni; recomenda forte. • *n.* urje. **urge to travel** viajamania.
urgent *adj.* urjente.
-uria *suff.* (*urine*) -uria.
uric *adj.* (*urine*) urica. • *suff.* -urica.

urinal *n.* vason urinal.
urinalyse *v.* urinalise.
urinalysis *n.* urinalise.
urinary *adj.* urinal.
urinate *v.* urini.
urination *n.* urini.
urine *n.* urina.
URL *n.* adirije ueb.
urn *n.* vaso.
urolith *n.* urolito.
urologist *n.* urolojiste.
urology *n.* urolojia.
Ursa Major *n.* (*constellation*) la Urso Grande.
Ursa Minor *n.* (*constellation*) la Urso Peti.
ursine *adj.* ursin.
urticaria *n.* urticaria.
Uruguay *n.* Uruguai.
Uruguayan *adj.* & *n.* uruguaia.
us[1] *pron.* nos. **us both** ambos de nos.
US[2] *abbr.* SUA. • *adj.* esuan, SUA, american.
USA *abbr.* SUA (*Statos Unida de America*).
usable *adj.* usable.
usage *n.* costum.
use *v.* & *n.* usa. **out of use** nonusada. **use up** consuma.
used *adj.* usada; (*accustomed*) abituada. **get used to** abitua a.
useful *adj.* usosa.
useful material *n.* materia usosa.
usefulness *n.* usosia.
useless *adj.* nonusosa, nonusable.
user *n.* usor.
user interface *n.* interfas de usor.
username *n.* nom de usor.
usher *v.* gida. • *n.* gidor; (*at wedding*) suportor.
using *prep.* (*tool*) con; (*method*, *action*) par.
USSR *abbr.* URSS (*Uni de Republicas Sosialiste Soviet*).
usual *adj.* usual, normal.
usufruct *n.* (*right*) usufruta.
usurer *n.* usuror.
usurous *adj.* usurosa.
usurp *v.* usurpa, saisi.
usurper *n.* usurpor, finjor.
usury *n.* usura.
Utah *n.* (*US state*) Utah.
utensil *n.* util.
uterus *n.* utero.
utilitarian *adj.* pratical, usosa; (*philosophy*) utilitariste. • *n.* utilitariste.
utilitarianism *n.* utilitarisme.
utility *n.* (*quality*) usosia; (*public*) servi publica.
utilize *v.* usa.
utmost *adj.* ultima.
utopia *n.* utopia.
utopian *adj.* utopial. • *n.* utopiste.
utopianism *n.* utopisme.
utter[1] *adj.* (*complete*) completa, asoluta.
utter[2] *v.* (*vocally*) dise, vosi.
utterance *n.* dise, vosi.
utterly *adv.* completa, asoluta.
U-tube *n.* tubo U.
U-turn *n.* verje U.
uvula *n.* (*anatomy*) uvula.
uvular *adj.* & *n.* (*consonant*) uvulal.
Uyghur *adj.* & *n.* (*person*, *language*) uigur.
Uzbek *adj.* & *n.* uzbec.
Uzbekistan *n.* Uzbecistan.
Uzbekistani *adj.* & *n.* (*person*, *language*) uzbec.

V

vacancy *n.* vacua.
vacant *adj.* vacuida.
vacate *v.* desocupa.
vacation *v.* & *n.* vacanse.
vacationer *n.* vacansor.
vacation spot *n.* vacanseria.
vaccinate *v.* vasini.
vaccination *n.* vasini.
vaccine *n.* vasin.
vacillate *v.* vasila.
vacillation *n.* vasila.
vacuity *n.* vacuia.
vacuole *n.* (*biology*) vacuol.
vacuous *adj.* vacua.
vacuum *n.* vacua.
vacuum cleaner *n.* sucapolvo.
vacuum flask *n.* termos.
vacuum-sealed *adj.* suvacua.
vacuum tube *n.* tubo vacuida.
vade mecum *n.* (*handbook*) manual.
vagabond *n.* vagabon.
vagary *n.* varia.
vagina *n.* vajina.
vaginal *adj.* vajinal.
vaginal douche *n.* dux vajinal.
vaginitis *n.* (*medical*) vajinite.
vagrancy *n.* vagabonia.
vagrant *n.* vagabon.
vague *adj.* neblosa.
vagus *n.* (*anatomy*) vago.
vain *adj.* (*conceited*) vana; (*futile*) futil. **in vain** futil.
vainglorious *adj.* egosa, vana orgulosa.
vainglory *n.* orgulo vana.
Vajrayana *adj.* (*Buddhism*) vajraiana.
valance *n.* cortina alta; falda de leto.
vale *n.* vale.
valediction *n.* adio.
valedictorian *n.* graduada prima.
valedictory *adj.* adial.
valence *n.* valentia.
Valencia *n.* (*Spanish region*) Valensia.
valency *n.* valentia.
valent *adj.* valente.
valentine *n.* carta de Valentin.
Valentine's Day *n.* festa de Valentin.
valerian *n.* (*plant*) valeriana.
valet *n.* servor de vesti; (*tarot*) pajo.
valgus *adj.* & *n.* (*medical*) valga.
Valhalla *n.* Valhala.
valiant *adj.* corajosa.
valid *adj.* valida, asetable, bon, legal, pertinente.
validate *v.* validi.
validation *n.* validi.
validity *n.* validia.
valise *n.* valis.
valium *n.* diazepam.
Valkyrie *n.* (*mythology*) valciria.
valley *n.* vale.
valor (US). See *valour*.
valorous *adj.* corajosa.
valour (US **valor**) *n.* coraje.
valuable *adj.* valuada, valuosa.
valuables *n.* valuadas, valuosas.
value *v.* & *n.* valua. **have value** ave valua, es valuada.
value-added tax *n.* imposta de valua ajuntada.
valueless *adj.* sin valua.
valve *n.* valva.
vampire *n.* vampir.
van *n.* furgon.
vanadium *n.* (*element*) vanadio.
vandal *n.* (*ancient tribe*, *hooligan*) vandal.
Vandalic *adj.* vandal.
vandalism *n.* vandalisme, dana criminal.
vandalize *v.* vandali.
vane *n.* (*pushed by wind or water*) veleta.
vanga *n.* (*bird*) vanga.
vanguard *n.* vangarda, avansada.
vanilla *n.* (*plant*, *flavour*) vanilia.
vanillin *n.* (*substance*) vanilina.
vanish *v.* desapare.
vanity *n.* vania.
vanquish *v.* vinse.
Vanuatu *n.* Vanuatu.
Vanuatuan *adj.* & *n.* vanuatu.
vapid *adj.* blanda.
vapor (US). See *vapour*.
vaporize *v.* vapori.
vaporizer *n.* vaporador.
vapour *n.* vapor.
vapour trail *n.* seguente de condensa.
varenyky *n.* (*dumplings*) pirogi.
variable *adj.* & *n.* variable.
variance *n.* varia.
variant *n.* varia.
variation *n.* varia; (*kind*) spesie.
varicose *adj.* (*medical*) varicosa.
variegated *adj.* variada, multicolorosa.
varietal *adj.* varial.
variety *n.* varia, diversia; (*kind*) spesie.
various *adj.* variosa, diversa.
varnish *n.* vernis. • *v.* vernisi.
varsity *n.* universia; ecipo prima.
varus *adj.* & *n.* (*medical*) vara.
vary *v.* varia.
vascular *adj.* vascular.
vasculitis *n.* (*medical*) vasculite.

vas deferens *n.* (*anatomy*) spermiduto.
vase *n.* vaso.
vasectomy *n.* (*surgery*) vasectomia.
vasoconstrict *v.* vasoconstrinje.
vasoconstrictor *n.* vasoconstrinjente.
vasodilate *v.* vasodilata.
vasodilator *n.* vasodilatante.
vasopressin *n.* vasopresina.
vasopressor *n.* vasoconstrinjente.
vassal *n.* vasal.
vassalage *n.* vasalia.
vast *adj.* vasta, enorme.
vastness *n.* vastia, enormia.
vat[1] *n.* (*tub*) tance.
VAT[2] *n.* (*tax*) imposta de valua ajuntada.
Vatican *adj.* vatican.
Vatican City *n.* Site Vatican.
vaudeville *adj.* vodevil. • *n.* vodevil; farsa.
vault *n.* tomba; (*bank*) sala securida; (*ceiling*) volta.
VCR *n.* videador.
veal *n.* carne de boveta.
vector *n.* vetor. • *adj.* vetoral.
vector calculus *n.* calculo vetoral.
vector graphic *n.* imaje vetoral.
vector image *n.* imaje vetoral.
Veda *n.* (*scripture*) veda.
vedanta *n.* (*Hinduism*) vedanta.
vedantic *adj.* vedantal.
Vedic *adj.* vedal.
veena *n.* (*musical instrument*) vina.
veer *v.* verje.
vegan *adj.* & *n.* vegan.
veganism *n.* veganisme.
vegetable *adj.* & *n.* vejetal.
vegetable garden *n.* orteta.
vegetable patch *n.* orteta.
vegetable peeler *n.* descascador.
vegetable soup *n.* sopa de vejetal.
vegetarian *n.* vejetaliste.
vegetarianism *n.* vejetalisme.
vegetate *v.* vejetali.
vegetation *n.* plantas.
vegetational *adj.* plantal.
vegetative *adj.* vejetal.
vehement *adj.* forte.
vehicle *n.* veculo.
vehicle registration plate *n.* placa de veculo.
vehicular *adj.* vecular.
veil *n.* velo. • *v.* veli.
vein *n.* (*anatomy*) vena.
Vela *n.* (*constellation*) la Velas.
velar *adj.* & *n.* velal.
velarize *v.* velali.
velcro *n.* velcro. • *adj.* de velcro.
vellum *n.* pergamin de boveta.
velociraptor *n.* velosiraptor.
velocity *n.* rapidia.
velour *n.* veluda.
velum *n.* velo, palato mol.
velvet *n.* veluda.
velveteen *n.* veludin.
velvety *adj.* veludin.
vena cava *n.* vena cava.
venal *adj.* sobornable.
vendetta *n.* vendeta, venja.
vending machine *n.* vendador.
vendor *n.* vendor.
veneer *n.* xapa. • *v.* xapi.
venerable *adj.* onorable, respetada.
venerate *v.* respeta.
venereal *adj.* sesal.
Venetia *n.* (*Italian region*) Veneto.
venetian blind *n.* cortina venezian.
Veneto *n.* Veneto.
Venezuela *n.* Venezuela. **Gulf of Venezuela** Golfo Venezuela.
Venezuelan *adj.* & *n.* venezuelan.
vengeance *n.* venja.
vengeful *adj.* venjosa.
venial *adj.* pardonable.
Venice *n.* Venezia.
venipuncture *n.* (*medical*) venipuntur.
venison *n.* carne de servo.
venom *n.* venena.
venomous *adj.* venenosa.
venous *adj.* (*of veins*) venal.
vent *n.* ximine, boca de venti.
ventilate *v.* venti.
ventilation *n.* venti.
ventilator *n.* ventador.
ventral *adj.* ventral.
ventricle *n.* (*anatomy*) ventriculo.
ventriloquism *n.* ventrilocuia.
ventriloquist *n.* ventrilocuo.
ventriloquy *n.* ventrilocuia.
venture *v.* osa. • *n.* emprende, projeta.
venture capital *n.* capital riscosa.
venturi *n.* (*tube*) venturi.
venue *n.* aveneria.
venule *n.* (*anatomy*) veneta.
Venus *n.* (*mythology*, *planet*) Venus.
Venus flytrap *n.* (*plant*) dionia.
veracious *adj.* vera.
veracity *n.* veria, esatia.
veranda *n.* veranda, lojia.
verb *n.* verbo.
verbal *adj.* verbal; verbin; (*expressed in words*) parolal.
verbal diarrhoea (US **diarrhea**) *n.* parlamania.
verbalize *v.* vosi.
verbatim *adv.* esata.
verb chain *n.* cadena de verbos.
verbena *n.* (*plant*) verbena.
verbiage *n.* parolosia.
verbose *adj.* parolosa.

verbosity *n.* parolosia.
verb phrase *n.* formula verbin.
verdant *adj.* verde, plantosa.
verdict *n.* deside.
verdigris *n.* verde de cupre.
verdure *n.* verde, plantosia.
verge[1] *n.* (*edge*) borda.
verge[2] *v.* (*veer*) verje.
verifiable *adj.* sertable.
verification *n.* autentici.
verify *v.* serti.
verisimilitude *n.* pare de realia.
veritable *adj.* vera.
verity *n.* veria.
vermeil *n.* arjento dorada; bronze dorada.
vermicelli *n.* (*food*) vermitxeli.
vermicide *n.* antielmintal.
vermiculite *n.* vermiculita.
vermiform *adj.* vermin.
vermifuge *n.* antielmintal.
vermilion *adj.* scarlata.
vermin *n.* animales nosiva.
Vermont *n.* (*US state*) Vermont.
vermouth *n.* (*wine*) vermute.
vernacular *adj.* & *n.* demotica.
vernal equinox *n.* ecuinote de primavera.
vernier *n.* balansa fratal.
verruca *n.* veruca.
versatile *adj.* flexable, multiusal.
verse *n.* (*stanza*) strofe; (*poetry*) poesia.
version *n.* (*including of text, product*) revisa; (*kind*) spesie, varia.
version control system *n.* arcivador de revisas.
versus *prep.* contra.
vertebra *n.* vertebra.
vertebral *adj.* vertebral.
vertebrate *adj.* & *n.* vertebrato.
vertex *n.* apico, punto.
vertical *adj.* vertical.
vertical bar *n.* bara vertical.
vertical slash *n.* bara vertical.
vertigo *n.* vertigo.
vervain *n.* (*plant*) verbena.
verve *n.* enerjia.
very *adv.* multe, vera, grande.
very-short-term memory *n.* memoria sensal.
vesicle *n.* (*anatomy*) vesicula.
vesper *n.* prea de sera.
vessel *n.* vaso; (*blood*) duto.
vest *n.* (*undershirt*) sucamisa; (*athletic*) camiseta de sporte; (*US: waistcoat*) jaceta. **ammo vest** jaceta de muni.
Vestal *n.* vestal.
Vestal Virgin *n.* vestal.
vestibular *adj.* vestibulal.
vestibule *n.* atrio.
vestige *n.* vestijio.
vestigial *adj.* vestijial.
vestry *n.* vesteria.
vet[1] *n.* (*medical*) dotor veterinar. • *v.* esamina, autentici.
vet[2] *adj.* & *n.* (*ex-soldier*) veteran.
vetch *n.* visia.
veteran *adj.* & veteran.
Veterans Day *n.* festa de veteranes.
veterinarian *n.* dotor veterinar.
veterinary *adj.* veterinar.
veterinary medicine *n.* medica veterinar.
veto *n.* veto. • *v.* veti, rejeta.
vetulicola *n.* (*ancient animal*) vetulicola.
vex *v.* frustra.
vexation *n.* frustra.
vexatious *adj.* frustrante.
VHF *n.* frecuentia multe alta.
via *prep.* (*place*) tra; (*method, action*) par.
viability *n.* viablia.
viable *adj.* viable, realable, capas de susede.
viaduct *n.* viaduto.
vial *n.* boteleta.
vibrant *adj.* briliante, enerjiosa; pulsante, resonante.
vibraphone *n.* (*musical instrument*) vibrafon.
vibrate *v.* vibra.
vibration *n.* vibra.
vibrato *n.* vibra.
vibrator *n.* vibrador.
viburnum *n.* (*plant*) viburno.
vicar *n.* parocior.
vicarage *n.* casa de parocior.
vicarious *adj.* nondireta.
vice[1] *n.* (*behaviour*) vilia; mal abitua.
vice[2] (US **vise**) *n.* (*tool*) abrasador fisada.
vice-[3] *pref.* vis-, suordinada.
vice-admiral *n.* visamiral.
vice-commander *n.* viscomandor.
vicelike (US **viselike**) *adj.* abrasadorin.
vice-mayor *n.* vismaior.
vice-president *n.* vispresidente.
vice-regent *n.* visrejente.
vicereine *n.* visrea.
viceroy *n.* visre.
vice versa *adv.* en reversa, reversada.
vichyssoise *n.* (*soup*) vixisuaz.
vicinity *n.* visinia. **in the vicinity** prosima.
vicious *adj.* cruel.
vicious circle *n.* sicle vil.
viciousness *n.* cruelia.
vicissitudes *n.* ondas, altas e basas.
victim *n.* vitim. **become a victim** vitimi.
victimize *v.* vitimi.
victimless *adj.* sin vitim.
victor *n.* vinsor.
Victoria *n.* Victoria. **Lake Victoria** Lago Victoria.
Victorian *adj.* victorian.

victorious *adj.* vinsente. **be victorious** vinse.
victory *n.* vinse.
victual *n.* comeda.
vicuña *n.* (*animal*) vicunia.
video *adj.* & *n.* video. **video on demand** video par comanda.
video cassette *n.* caxeta video.
video chat *v.* & *n.* parleta video.
video conference *n.* confere video.
video disc *n.* disco video.
video game *n.* jua video.
video player *n.* videador.
video recorder *n.* videador.
video tape *n.* banda video.
vie *v.* compete.
Vienna *n.* Wien.
Vietnam *n.* Vietnam.
Vietnamese *adj.* & *n.* (*person*, *language*) viet.
view *v.* regarda. • *n.* vista; (*opinion*) opina. **hold a view** opina.
viewer *n.* (*person*) regardor; (*machine*) vidador.
viewfinder *n.* vidador.
viewing figures *n.* cuantia de regardores.
viewpoint *n.* punto de vista.
vigil *n.* vijila.
vigilance *n.* vijila.
vigilant *adj.* vijilante. **be vigilant** vijila.
vigilante *n.* vijilor estralegal, patrulior estralegal.
vigilantism *n.* justia estralegal.
vignette *n.* vinieta.
vigor (US). See *vigour*.
vigorous *adj.* enerjiosa.
vigour (US **vigor**) *n.* enerjia.
Viking *adj.* & *n.* vicing.
Viking boat *n.* barco vicing.
vile *adj.* vil.
vilification *n.* malacusa.
vilify *v.* malacusa, desvalua.
villa *n.* casa campanian.
village *n.* vileta.
villager *n.* viletan.
villain *n.* vil.
villainy *n.* vilia.
villi *n.* (*anatomy*) vilos.
villus *n.* (*anatomy*) vilo.
vinaigrette *n.* vinagreta.
vinca *n.* (*plant*) vinca.
Vincentian *adj.* & *n.* vinsentian.
vincible *adj.* vinsable.
Vincy *adj.* & *n.* vinsentian.
vindicate *v.* desculpa, remete, justi.
vindication *n.* desculpa.
vindictive *adj.* venjosa, odiosa.
vine *n.* vite.
vinegar *n.* vinagra.
vineyard *n.* viteria.
vintage *n.* anio de recolie. • *adj.* de cualia alta.
vintage item *n.* anticalia.
vintner *n.* vinor, vendor de vinos.
vinyl *n.* vinil.
viol *n.* viola vertical.
viola *n.* viola. **viola de gamba** viola vertical.
violate *v.* viole.
violation *n.* viole.
violator *n.* violor.
violence *n.* violentia.
violent *adj.* violente.
violet *adj.* (*colour*) violeta. • *n.* (*plant*) violeta.
violin *n.* violin.
violinist *n.* violiniste.
violist *n.* violiste.
violoncellist *n.* xeliste.
violoncello *n.* xelo.
viper *n.* vipera.
viral *adj.* (*of viruses*) virusal. **go viral** sperde virusin.
vireo *n.* (*bird*) vireo.
virgin *n.* virjin.
virginal *adj.* virjin.
virgin forest *n.* foresta orijinal.
Virginia *n.* (*US state*) Virginia.
Virgin Islands *n.* Isolas Virjin.
virginity *n.* virjinia.
virgin territory *n.* tera nova.
Virgo *n.* (*constellation*) la Virjin.
virile *adj.* masiosa.
virola *n.* (*tree*) virola.
virologist *n.* virolojiste.
virology *n.* virolojia.
virtual *adj.* virtual.
virtually *adv.* cuasi.
virtue *n.* virtua.
virtuoso *n.* mestre.
virtuous *adj.* virtuosa.
virtuous circle *n.* sicle virtuosa.
virulent *adj.* grave, nosiva, infetante; malvolente.
virus *n.* virus, microbio.
visa *n.* (*for travel*) visa.
visage *n.* fas.
Visayan Sea *n.* Mar Visayas.
viscera *n.* visera, intestines.
visceral *adj.* viseral.
viscosity *n.* viscosia.
viscount *n.* visconte.
viscous *adj.* viscosa.
vise (US). See *vice*.
viselike (US). See *vicelike*.
Vishnu *n.* (*Hinduism*) Vixnu.
visibility *n.* vidablia.
visible *adj.* vidable. **become visible** apare. **be visible through** suapare.
Visigoth *n.* visigoto.

Visigothic *adj.* visigoto.
vision *n.* vide; (*hallucination*) alusina; (*mystical*) revela.
visionary *n.* previdor.
visit *v.* & *n.* visita.
visitor *n.* visitor.
visor *n.* visiera.
vista *n.* vista.
visual *adj.* vidal.
visual arts *n.* artes vidable.
visual hallucination *n.* alusina videda.
visual illusion *n.* ilude de vide.
visualize *v.* imajina.
vita *n.* resoma de carera.
vitae *n.* resoma de carera.
vital *adj.* vivosa.
vital force *n.* fortia de vive.
vitality *n.* vivosia.
vitalize *v.* enerji.
vitamin *n.* vitamina.
vitamin C *n.* vitamina C.
vitiate *v.* descapasi.
viticulture *n.* cultiva de uvas.
vitiligo *n.* (*medical*) vitiligo.
vitreous *adj.* vitrin.
vitrification *n.* vitri.
vitrify *v.* vitri.
vitrine *n.* caxa de esibi.
vitriol *n.* vitriol.
vitriolic *adj.* vitriolosa.
vituperate *v.* insulta.
vivacious *adj.* vivosa.
viva voce *n.* defende de tese.
vivid *adj.* vivin.
vivify *v.* anima, refresci.
viviparous *adj.* (*giving birth to life offspring*) viviparinte. **be viviparous** vivipari.
vivipary *n.* viviparia.
vivisect *v.* vivisesioni.
vivisection *n.* vivisesioni.
vixen *n.* volpe fema.
vizier *n.* (*officer*) vizir.
vizir *n.* vizir.
Vlach *adj.* & *n.* valah.
V-neck *n.* escota V. • *adj.* con escota V.
vocabulary *n.* vocabulo.
vocal *adj.* (*of the voice*) vosal; (*outspoken*) franca.
vocal cord *n.* corda vosal, plia vosal.
vocal fold *n.* plia vosal.
vocalic *adj.* vocal.
vocalism *n.* vosi; sona vocal; sistem vocal.
vocalist *n.* cantor.
vocalization *n.* vosi.
vocalize *v.* vosi; (*as vowel*) vocali.
vocal tract *n.* curso de vose.
vocation *n.* carera.
vocative *adj.* & *n.* (*grammar*) vocativa.
vociferous *adj.* forte.
vocoder *n.* sintesador de vose.
vodka *n.* (*drink*) vodca.
vogue *n.* moda.
voice *n.* vose. • *v.* vosi. **active voice** vose ativa. **give voice to** vosi. **passive voice** vose pasiva.
voiced *adj.* vosida, parlada; (*consonant*) con vose.
voiceless consonant *adj.* consonante sin vose.
void *adj.* vacua. • *n.* vacua; spasio.
voilà *interj.* ta-da.
vol. *abbr.* v (*volum*).
Volans *n.* (*constellation*) la Pex Volante.
volatile *adj.* volatil.
volatility *n.* volatilia.
volcanic *adj.* volcanal.
volcanic activity *n.* ativia volcanal.
volcanism *n.* ativia volcanal.
volcano *n.* volcan.
volcanologist *n.* volcanolojiste.
volcanology *n.* volcanolojia.
vole *n.* campaniol.
volition *n.* vole.
volley *n.* bombarda.
volleyball *n.* volibal.
volt *n.* (*unit of electromotive force*) volte.
voltage *n.* tensa eletrical; cuantia de voltes.
voltaic *adj.* voltaica.
voluble *adj.* parlosa.
volume *n.* (*capacity*, *loudness*, *book*) volum.
voluminous *adj.* volumosa.
voluntary *adj.* nonobligante; volente; voleda.
volunteer *n.* bonvolor. • *v.* ofre se; es un bonvolor.
voluptuary *n.* libidosa.
voluptuous *adj.* curvosa, formosa.
volvox *n.* (*organism*) volvox.
vomit *n.* vomita. • *v.* vomiti. **be sick** vomiti.
voodoo *n.* (*religion*) vudu.
voodoo lily *n.* coniac.
voracious *adj.* devorante, nonsasiable.
vortex *n.* vortis.
vote *v.* vota. • *n.* (*individual's*, *overall process*) vota.
voter *n.* votor.
voting booth *n.* voteria, ciosco de vota.
votive offering *n.* ofre prometeda.
vouch *v.* atesta.
voucher *n.* bileta.
vouchsafe *v.* dona; revela.
voussure *n.* (*architecture*) arcivolta.
vow *v.* & *n.* jura.
vowel *n.* vocal.
vowel shift *n.* desloca de vocales.
vowel sound *n.* sona vocal.
vowel system *n.* sistem vocal.
voyage *n.* viaja.
voyager *n.* viajor.

voyeur *n.* voior.
voyeurism *n.* voiorisme.
V-sign *n.* (*victory*, *insult*) sinia V.
VSTM *n.* (*very-short-term memory*) memoria sensal.
vulcanize *v.* vulcani.
vulgar *adj.* (*crude*) vulgar.
vulgarian *n.* bruta.
vulgarity *n.* vulgaria.
Vulgar Latin *n.* latina poplal.
vulgate *n.* demotica.
vulnerable *adj.* ferable; atacable, dolable; (*helpless*) sin defende; (*species*) riscada; (*to temptation*) tentable.
Vulpecula *n.* (*constellation*) la Volpe.
vulpine *adj.* (*of foxes*) volpal; (*like a fox*) volpin.
vulture *n.* vultur.
vulva *n.* (*anatomy*) vulva.

W

wacky *adj.* bizara, strana, comica.
wad *n.* tampon.
waddle *v.* pati.
wade *v.* vada.
wadi *n.* (*valley*) uadi.
wading pool *n.* vaderia.
wafer *n.* (*electronics*) telieta.
waffle[1] *n.* (*food*) uafel.
waffle[2] *v.* (*prattle*) babela.
waft *v.* & *n.* sofla.
wag *v.* secute.
wage *n.* salario. **wage war on** declara un gera contra. **wages** salario.
wager *v.* & *n.* aposta.
wage raise *n.* aumenta de salario.
wage rise *n.* aumenta de salario.
waggle *v.* & *n.* ximi.
waggly *adj.* ximinte.
wagon *n.* caro, vagon.
wagoner *n.* vagonor.
wagtail *n.* (*bird*) motasila.
wah *interj.* (*baby crying*) ua.
wah-wah *n.* (*music*) uaua.
waif *adj.* orfan.
wail *v.* & *n.* ulula.
wain *n.* vagon.
wainscot *n.* panel basa.
wainscotting *n.* panel basa.
wainwright *n.* fabricor de vagones.
waist *n.* taie.
waistband *n.* banda de taie.
waistcoat *n.* jaceta.
waistline *n.* taie.
wait *v.* pausa; (*await*) espeta. • *n.* pausa, pospone, retarda. • *interj.* para.
waiter *n.* servor, servor de restorante.
waiting room *n.* sala de espeta.
waitress *n.* servor, servor de restorante.
waive *v.* desprende.
waiver *n.* renunsia.
wake[1] *v.* velia. **wake up** velia.
wake[2] *n.* (*ship*) seguente; (*aftermath*) tempo seguente.
wakeful *adj.* veliada; atendente.
waken *v.* velia.
wale *n.* (*fabric*) costelin; (*boat*) banda fortinte.
Wales *n.* Cimri.
walk *v.* & *n.* pasea; (*on one's toes*) paseta; (*unsteadily*) bambola. **go for a walk** vade per pasea. **take for a walk** pasea. **walk of life** ocupa.
walker *n.* paseor; (*frame*) aidapasea.
walkie-talkie *n.* radiotelefon.
walking frame *n.* aidapasea.
walking stick *n.* basto de pasea; (*stick insect*) fasmido.
walkman *n.* baladador.
walk-up *n.* aparte sin asendador.
walkway *n.* paseria. **moving walkway** paseria rolante.
wall *n.* mur.
wallaby *n.* ualabi.
Wallachia *n.* (*Romanian region*) Valahia.
Wallachian *adj.* & *n.* valah.
wall bed *n.* leto ascondeda.
wallboard *n.* plance de jeso.
wall cabinet *n.* armario de mur.
wallcreeper *n.* (*bird*) ticodroma.
wallet *n.* bolseta, portamone.
wall-eyed *adj.* straba, diverjente straba.
wallflower *n.* timida.
Wallis and Futuna *n.* Uvea e Futuna.
Wallisian *adj.* & *n.* uvea.
Wallonia *n.* Ualonia.
Walloon *adj.* & *n.* ualon.
wallop *n.* colpa forte.
wallow *v.* rola.
wallpaper *n.* paper de mur.
wallpaperer *n.* paperor.
walnut *n.* noza.
walnut tree *n.* nozo.
walrus *n.* morsa.
waltz *v.* & *n.* valsa.
wampum *n.* (*beads*) uampum.
wan *adj.* pal.
wand *n.* basto majial.
wander *v.* vaga.
wanderer *n.* vagor.
wanderlust *n.* viajamania.
wane *v.* diminui.
wank *v.* (*masturbate*) diti se.
wanker *n.* (*insult*) pixeta.
want *v.* vole. • *n.* nonsufisi.
want ad *n.* anunsieta.
wanted *adj.* xercada; (*criminal*) per catura.
wanting *adj.* mancante, nonsufisinte. **be wanting** manca.
wanton *adj.* promiscua.
wapiti *n.* uapiti.
war *v.* & *n.* gera. **make war** gera.
warble *v.* & *n.* canta melodiosa.
warbler *n.* cantor, avia cantante.
war bride *n.* sposa de gera.
war chief *n.* xef de gera.
war crime *n.* crimin de gera.
ward *n.* (*hospital*) sala; (*person*) dependente; gardada. **ward off** forsa a via, teni a via.
warden *n.* gardor.
warder *n.* gardor.

wardrobe *n.* armario de vestes.
warehouse *n.* beneria.
wares *n.* benes.
warfare *n.* gera.
warfarin *n.* (*drug*) uarfarin.
warhead *n.* ojiva.
warhorse *n.* cavalo de gera.
warlike *adj.* gerosa.
warlock *n.* sorsor, sorsor mas.
warlord *n.* xef de gera, comandor militar.
warm *adj.* alga calda; (*lukewarm*) tepida; (*emotionally*) zelosa. • *v.* caldi; (*slightly*) tepidi.
warm-hearted *adj.* compatiosa.
warmonger *n.* provocor de gera.
warmth *n.* caldia.
warm-up *n.* prepara.
warn *v.* (*of danger*) averti.
warning *n.* averti; avisa.
warning balloon *n.* (*software*) balon de avisa.
warp *v.* contorse. • *n.* (*textiles*) cadena.
warpath, on the *adj.* preparada per batalia.
warrant *n.* comanda. • *v.* merita.
warranty *n.* garantia.
warren *n.* coneria.
warrior *n.* geror.
Warsaw *n.* Warszawa.
warship *n.* barcon de gera.
wart *n.* veruca.
warthog *n.* facocero.
wartime *n.* tempo de gera.
war-torn *adj.* gastada par gera, ruinada par gera.
warty *adj.* verucosa.
wary *adj.* cauta.
wasabi *n.* (*plant*, *sauce*) uasabi.
wash *v.* lava; (*ship*) seguente. **wash up** lava la platos; (*run aground*) encalia.
washbasin *n.* lavabo.
washboard *n.* plance de lava.
washbowl *n.* lavabo.
washcloth *n.* teleta de lava.
washday *n.* dia de lava.
washed *adj.* lavada. **washed out** parada par pluve.
washer *n.* lavor; (*ring*) aneleta.
washerman *n.* lavor, lavaveste.
washerwoman *n.* lavor, lavaveste.
washing machine *n.* (*clothes*) lavaveste; (*clothes*, *dishes*) lavador.
washing out *n.* lava interna.
washing soda *n.* carbonato de sodio.
Washington *n.* (*US state*, *city*) Washington.
washing-up *n.* lava de platos. **do the washing-up** lava la platos.
washing-up bowl *n.* bol de lava.
washing-up liquid *n.* deterjente de platos.
washout *v.* deluvia.
washrag *n.* teleta de lava.
washroom *n.* sala de lava.
washstand *n.* lavabo.
washtub *n.* bol de lava.
washwoman *n.* lavor.
wasp *n.* vespa.
waspish *adj.* vespin.
waspy *adj.* vespin.
wassail *n.* vino calda.
waste *v.* peri; (*money*) malspende. • *n.* peri; (*garbage*) dejetada; (*land*) deserto.
wastebasket *n.* sesto de dejeta.
wasteful *adj.* perosa.
wastefulness *n.* perosia.
wasteland *n.* deserto.
waste water *n.* acua de cloaca.
wastrel *n.* pigra.
watch *v.* oserva, vijila; (*film*, *sport*) regarda, vide. • *n.* vijila; (*timepiece*) orolojeta. **watch again** reregarda. **watch back** (*a recording*) reregarda. **watch out** es vijilante, atende. **watch television** televide.
watchband *n.* sintureta.
watch chain *n.* cadena de orolojeta.
watchdog *n.* (*metaphor*) gardor.
watchful *adj.* vijilante.
watchmaker *n.* orolojor.
watchman *n.* vijilor.
watchstrap *n.* sintureta.
watchtower *n.* tore de vijila.
water *n.* acua. • *v.* acui; (*mouth*) salivi; (*animals*) dona acua a; (*flowers*) duxi. **water down** dilui. **water on the brain** idrosefalia.
water-based paint *n.* pinta de acua.
water bath *n.* (*bain-marie*) baniomaria.
water bear *n.* tardigrado, urso-de-acua.
water bearer *n.* acuor.
waterbed *n.* leto de acua.
waterbird *n.* avia de acua.
water bottle *n.* botela de acua.
water buffalo *n.* bufalo.
waterbug *n.* xinxe de acua.
water bus *n.* barco-bus.
water carrier *n.* acuor.
water chestnut *n.* castania de acua.
water clock *n.* orolojo de acua.
watercolour (US **watercolor**) *n.* acuarela.
watercolour painting (US **watercolor painting**) *n.* depinta de acuarela.
water cooler *n.* friacua.
watercraft *n.* veculo acual.
watercress *n.* creson de acua.
waterfall *n.* cascade.
waterfowl *n.* avia de acua.
waterfront *n.* fronte de acua.
watering can *n.* carafon de acua.
water lily *n.* nimfea.
waterlog *v.* empapa.
waterlogged *adj.* acuosa.

watermark *n.* filigrana.
watermelon *n.* melon acuosa.
water mill *n.* molin de rio.
waterpark *n.* parce acual.
water pipe *n.* tubo de acua; (*smoking*) pipa de acua.
water polo *n.* polo de acua.
waterpower *n.* potia idraulical.
waterproof *adj.* nonpermeable, secur contra acua.
waterproof container *n.* paracua.
water purifier *n.* puriacua.
watershed *n.* basin idrografial; (*turning point*) punto de cambia.
waterside *n.* costa, riva.
waterski *v.* & *n.* sci acual.
waterskiing *n.* sci acual.
water slide *n.* tobogan de acua.
waterspout *n.* (*whirlwind*) trompa acual; (*drainpipe*) tubo de drena.
water taxi *n.* barco-bus.
watertight container *n.* paracua.
water trough *n.* portacua.
waterway *n.* via navigable.
waterwheel *n.* rota de acua, rota idraulical.
waterworks *n.* trateria de acua.
watery *adj.* (*runny*) acuin; (*full of water*) acuosa.
watt *n.* (*unit of power*) vate.
wattage *n.* vatia.
wattle[1] *n.* (*wicker*) vim; (*acacia*) acasia.
wattle[2] *n.* (*dewlap*) caruncula.
wave *n.* (*including of emotion*) onda. • *v.* onda; (*brandish*) brandi; (*greeting*) saluta con mano. **wave of support** onda de opina.
waveband *n.* banda de frecuentia.
waveform *n.* forma de onda.
wave function *n.* funsiona ondal.
wavelength *n.* longia de onda. **being on the same wavelength** simpatia.
wavelet *n.* ondeta.
wavelike *adj.* ondin.
waver *v.* vasila.
wavy *adj.* ondosa.
wax *n.* sira.
waxbill *n.* (*bird*) estrildido.
wax effigy *n.* sculta de sira.
wax figure *n.* sculta de sira.
waxwing *n.* (*bird*) bombisila.
waxwork *n.* sculta de sira.
waxy *adj.* sirin.
way *n.* via; (*of doing*) modo, metodo; (*of behaving*) manera. **be in the way** impedi. **by the way** en brasetas, en pasa, nota bon. **for a long way** longa. **give way** sede. **in any way** en cualce modo. **in every way** en tota modos. **in no way at all** en vera no modo. **in the same way as** en la mesma modo como. **in this way** en esta modo, tal. **make one's way** vade sur sua via. **on the way** en via. **out of the way** (*remote*) isolida; (*done*) en la pasada; (*no longer an obstacle*) no plu un problem. **way of life** modo de vive. **way out** sorti.
wayfarer *n.* viajor.
waylaid *adj.* embosceda.
waylay *v.* embosce.
wayside *n.* lado de via.
wayward *adj.* oposante.
WC *n.* saleta privata.
we *pron.* nos. **we ourselves** (*emphatic*) nos mesma.
weak *adj.* debil; (*food, medicine*) blanda.
weaken *v.* debili.
weakling *n.* debil.
weak-minded *adj.* de mente debil.
weakness *n.* debilia; (*food, medicine*) blandia; (*weak point*) debil.
weal[1] *n.* (*mark*) bulteta, marca de colpa.
weal[2] *n.* (*welfare*) bonstate.
wealth *n.* ricia.
wealthy *adj.* rica.
wean *v.* desteti.
weapon *n.* arma.
weaponry *n.* armas. **light weaponry** armas lejera.
wear *v.* (*clothes*) porta, usa, es vestida en. **wear away** erode. **wear down** erode. **wear out** gasta.
wearable *adj.* portable, aponable.
weariness *n.* fatiga.
weary *adj.* fatigada.
weasel *n.* mustela. **weasel out of** serpe a via de.
weasel-like *adj.* mustelin.
weaselly *adj.* mustelin.
weather *n.* clima; (*colloquial*) aira. • *v.* erode.
weatherbeaten *adj.* gastada par la clima.
weathercock *n.* gal de venta, indicador de venta.
weathered *adj.* gastada par clima.
weather forecaster *n.* presentor de clima.
weather front *n.* fronte meteorolojial.
weatherman *n.* presentor de clima.
weather presenter *n.* presentor de clima.
weatherproof *adj.* secur contra clima.
weatherstrip *n.* selinte contra fria.
weather system *n.* depresa climal.
weathervane *n.* indicador de venta.
weatherwoman *n.* presentor de clima.
weave *v.* texe.
weaver *n.* (*including bird*) texor.
web *n.* membrana; (*internet*) ueb. • *adj.* ueb.
web address *n.* adirije ueb.
web application *n.* program ueb.
webbed *adj.* membranosa.
web browser *n.* surfador.
webcam *n.* camera ueb.
weber *n.* (*unit of magnetic flux*) veber.

webfoot *adj.* pede membranosa.
web log *n.* blog.
web page *n.* paje ueb.
web-savvy *adj.* astuta de ueb.
web server *n.* servador ueb.
web service *n.* servi ueb.
website *n.* loca ueb, pajeria.
wedding *n.* sposi, rituo de sposi.
wedding dress *n.* roba de sposi.
wedding gown *n.* roba de sposi.
wedge *n.* (*including golf club*) cuneo; (*diacritic*) caron.
wedlock *n.* sposia.
Wednesday *n.* mercurdi.
wee[1] *adj.* (*small*) peti.
wee[2] *v.* (*urinate*) pisi.
weed *n.* malerba, planta infestante. • *v.* estrae malerbas de, desmalerbi, desinfesta.
weedkiller *n.* erbiside, desinfestante.
week *n.* semana. **next week** en la semana veninte, en la semana seguente, en la semana pos esta. **the following week** en la semana seguente. **this week** en esta semana.
weekday *n.* dia de semana; dia de labora.
weekend *n.* fini de semana.
weekly *adj.* semanal.
weep *v.* larma, plora.
weepy *adj.* larmosa.
weevil *n.* scarabe elefantin.
weft *n.* trama.
weigh *v.* (*have weight, measure weight*) pesa; (*anchor*) leva.
weighing machine *n.* pesador.
weight *n.* (*measure, object*) pesa.
weightless *adj.* lejera.
weightlessness *n.* lejeria completa.
weightlifter *n.* levor de pesas.
weightlifting *n.* leva de pesas. **weightlifting and wrestling** atletisme pesosa.
weight training *n.* eserse con pesas.
weighty *adj.* seria.
weir *n.* parario.
weird *adj.* strana.
weirdness *n.* strania.
weirdo *n.* strana, bizara.
welcome *v.* & *n.* bonveni, saluta, reseta. • *interj.* bonveni. • *adj.* bonvenida, plasente, gustable. **you're welcome** no problem.
welcomer *n.* resetiste.
weld *v.* solda, osisolda, fusa.
welder *n.* soldor.
welding torch *n.* osisoldador.
welfare *n.* bonstate, cualia de vive; aida sosial.
welfare state *n.* stato sosial.
well[1] *adv.* bon. • *interj.* bon, alora. • *pref.* bon-. **as well** ance. **as well as** como ance.
well[2] *n.* (*shaft*) poso; fonte. • *v.* fonti.
well-adjusted *adj.* bonajustada.
well-being *n.* bonstate, cualia de vive.
well-born *adj.* nobil.
well-dressed *adj.* bonvestida.
well-formed *adj.* bonformida.
well-formedness *n.* bon forma.
well-founded *adj.* valida.
wellington *n.* bota de cauxo.
well-intentioned *adj.* bonintendente.
well-loved *adj.* bon amada.
well-mannered *adj.* de bon maneras.
well-meaning *adj.* bonintendente.
wellness *n.* sania.
well-proportioned *adj.* de bon proportio.
well-spoken *adj.* bonparlante.
well-tempered *adj.* bon temperada.
well-thinking *adj.* bonpensante.
welly *n.* bota de cauxo.
Welsh *adj.* & *n.* (*person, language*) cimrica.
Welsh rabbit *n.* pan tostada con ceso.
Welsh rarebit *n.* pan tostada con ceso.
welt *n.* marca de colpa.
Weltanschauung *n.* vista de mundo.
Weltschmerz *n.* dole de mundo.
wench *n.* fem joven, xica.
wend *v.* (*one's way*) viaja sua via vagante.
Wendy house *n.* casa de jua.
weregild *n.* (*payment system*) uergeld.
werewolf *n.* om-lupo.
wergeld *n.* uergeld.
west *adj.* & *n.* ueste. **to the west of** a ueste de.
West Bank *n.* Riva Ueste.
western *adj.* ueste.
westernization *n.* uesti.
westernize *v.* uesti.
Western Sahara *n.* Sahara Ueste.
Western Samoa *n.* Samoa Ueste.
West Indies *n.* Indias Ueste.
west-northwest *adj.* ueste-norde-ueste.
west-southwest *adj.* ueste-sude-ueste.
West Virginia *n.* (*US state*) Virginia Ueste.
westward *adv.* a ueste.
westwards *adv.* a ueste.
wet *v.* moia. • *adj.* moiada, umida; (*weather*) pluvosa.
wet blanket *n.* matajoia.
wetland *n.* pantan.
wetness *n.* umidia.
wetsuit *n.* paracua, veste de sumerjor.
wetu *n.* (*wigwam*) uiguam.
whack *v.* colpa, colpa forte.
whale *n.* balena.
whale oil *n.* olio de balena.
whaler *n.* balenor.
whaling *n.* xasa de balenas.
wham *n.* colpa forte. • *interj.* pum.
wharf *n.* doca, molo.

what *det.* & *pron.* cual; (*which thing?*) cual cosa?; (*that which*) lo cual. • *interj.* (*confusion*) como? **what a lovely view** un vista tan bela. **what a pity** tan triste. **what a shame** tan triste. **what is the date?** cual es la data? **what is the time?** cual es la ora? **what on earth?** cual de mundo? **what the hell?** cual de enferno?
whatchamacallit *n.* aparateta.
whatever *pron.* cualce cosa. • *subord.* cualce cosa cual. • *interj.* lo no importa.
whatsit *n.* aparateta.
whatsoever *adv.* sin eseta, vera.
wheal *n.* marca de colpa.
wheat *n.* trigo.
wheatland *n.* tera de trigo.
whee *interj.* ui.
wheedle *v.* adula.
wheel *n.* rota. • *v.* sirculi.
wheelbarrow *n.* careta de jardin.
wheelbase *n.* estende de ase.
wheelchair *n.* seja rolante.
wheeled bed *n.* leto rolante.
wheeler-dealer *n.* comersior nononesta.
wheel fiddle *n.* viola de rota.
wheelie *n.* capri. **do a wheelie** capri.
wheel track *n.* foseta.
wheelwright *n.* fabricor de rotas.
wheeze *v.* & *n.* respira ruidosa.
wheezy *adj.* ruidosa respirante.
whelk *n.* busino.
whelp *n.* caneta, om joven.
when *adv.* & *subord.* (*interrogative, relative*) cuando.
whence *adv.* de do.
whenever *adv.* a cualce ora, a cualce ves. • *subord.* sempre cuando.
where *adv.* & *subord.* (*interrogative, relative*) do. **where from** de do. **where to** a do.
whereas *conj.* ma.
wherefore *adv.* perce.
wherever *adv.* a cualce loca. • *subord.* sempre do.
wherewithal *n.* nesesada.
whet *v.* agi.
whether *subord.* esce.
whetstone *n.* petra de agi.
whew *interj.* fu.
whey *n.* (*milk*) sero.
which *det.* & *pron.* (*interrogative, relative*) cual.
whichever *det.* & *pron.* cualce.
whiff *n.* odoreta.
whiffle *v.* sofleta.
while *subord.* (*same time*) en cuando; (*although*) an si, contra ce, ma. **for a while** per alga tempo.
whilst *subord.* (*same time*) en cuando; (*although*) an si, contra ce, ma.
whim *n.* capris.
whimper *v.* & *n.* ploreta, crieta.
whimsical *adj.* caprisosa.
whimsy *n.* (*whim*) capris; (*capriciousness*) caprisia.
whine *v.* cexa.
whiner *n.* cexor.
whiney *adj.* cexosa.
whinge *v.* cexa.
whinger *n.* cexor.
whingey *adj.* cexosa.
whinny *n.* clama dulse. • *interj.* iii.
whiny *adj.* cexosa.
whip *n.* flajelo. • *v.* flajeli; (*into a froth*) bate.
whipbird *n.* sinclosoma.
whiplash *n.* xoca de colo.
whipped cream *n.* crema bateda.
whippet *n.* (*dog*) uipet.
whipping boy *n.* portapeca.
whippoorwill *n.* (*bird*) antrostomo.
whipsaw *n.* siera cuadro.
whir *v.* & *n.* zumbi.
whirl *v.* jira.
whirligig *n.* jirante.
whirlpool *n.* vortis.
whirlpool bath *n.* banio de vortis.
whirlwind *n.* vortis de venta.
whirr *v.* & *n.* zumbi.
whisk *n.* batador.
whisker *n.* vibrisa.
whiskerlike *adj.* vibrisin.
whiskers *n.* barba de jenas.
whiskey *n.* uisce.
whisky *n.* uisce.
whisper *v.* & *n.* xuxa.
whisperer *n.* xuxor.
whist *n.* (*card game*) uist.
whistle *v.* sibila. • *n.* sibila; (*instrument*) sibileta.
whistleblower *n.* denunsior.
whistlepig *n.* (*rodent*) monax.
whistler *n.* (*bird*) sibilor.
white *adj.* & *n.* blanca.
white bean *n.* fava blanca.
white blood cell *n.* limfosite.
whiteboard *n.* mureta blanca.
whitecap *n.* cresta spumosa.
white coffee *n.* cafe con lete.
whitefish *n.* coregon.
whitefly *n.* blanceta.
white heather *n.* erica arborin.
white-hot *adj.* incandesente. **be white-hot** incandese.
white lie *n.* menteta.
whiten *v.* blanci.
whitener *n.* blancinte.
white noise *n.* ruido blanca.
whiteout *n.* (*snowstorm*) nevon; (*correction fluid*) licuida de coreti.
white sauce *n.* bexamel.

White Sea *n.* Mar Blanca.
whitewash *n.* acua de calce. • *v.* pinti con acua de calce.
white whale *n.* beluga.
whither *adv.* do, a do.
whiting *n.* (*fish*) merlan.
whitish *adj.* blancin.
Whit Sunday *n.* soldi de pentecoste.
whittle *v.* talia.
whiz *n.* esperta.
whizz *v.* & *n.* zumbi; (*whoosh*) sisa.
who *pron.* (*interrogative, relative*) ci. **who cares?** (*disinterest*) ba, ci cura? **who knows?** ci sabe?
whoa *interj.* para.
whodunnit *n.* misterio.
whoever *pron.* cualcun. • *subord.* cualcun ci.
whole *adj.* intera. • *n.* intera, completa. **on the whole** jeneral. **the whole of** tota.
whole-hearted *adj.* sinsera.
whole note *n.* tono completa.
whole number *n.* numero natural.
wholesale *n.* vende major.
wholesaler *n.* vendor major.
wholesome *adj.* saninte.
whole wheat *n.* trigo intera.
wholly *adv.* intera.
whom *pron.* (*interrogative, relative*) ci.
whoopee *interj.* ui, ura.
whooping cough *n.* pertuse.
whoops *interj.* op.
whoosh *v.* & *n.* zumbi.
whopper *n.* jigante; (*lie*) menti jigante.
whopping *adj.* jigante.
whore *n.* fem prostituida, puta.
whorehouse *n.* bordel.
whoreson *n.* fio de puta.
whorish *adj.* putin.
whorl *n.* spiral.
whose *det.* (*person*) de ci; (*thing*) de cual.
whosoever *pron.* cualcun.
why *adv.* perce.
whydah *n.* (*bird*) vidua.
Wicca *n.* (*religion*) uica.
Wiccan *adj.* & *n.* uican.
wick *n.* mexa.
wicked *adj.* malvolente.
wicker *n.* (*twigs*) vim. • *adj.* de bastetas.
wicket *n.* (*gate, cricket*) porteta.
wickiup *n.* uiguam.
wide *adj.* larga. **wide open** baliante.
wide-angle lens *n.* lente de angulo larga.
widely *adv.* comun, jeneral, vasta.
widen *v.* largi.
widespread *adj.* vasta. **become widespread** vasti.
widget *n.* aparateta.
widow *n.* vidua.
widowed *adj.* vidua. **become widowed** vidui.
widower *n.* vidua.
width *n.* largia.
wield *v.* brandi.
wiener *n.* salsix american.
wife *n.* sposa, spos; (*colloquial*) fem.
wifebeater *n.* (*shirt*) camiseta de sporte.
wig *n.* peruca.
wiggle *v.* & *n.* ximi, serpe.
wiggly *adj.* ximinte.
wigmaker *n.* perucor.
wigwam *n.* uiguam.
wiki *n.* vici.
Wikipedia *n.* Vicipedia.
wild *adj.* savaje, nonrestrinjeda.
wild boar *n.* senglar.
wildcard *n.* bufon.
wildcat strike *n.* greve nonlegal.
wildebeest *n.* gnu.
wilderness *n.* tera savaje.
wildfire *n.* focon savaje.
wild ginger *n.* asaro.
wild hyacinth *n.* jasinto de bosce.
wildlife *n.* viventes savaje.
wildness *n.* savajia.
wild pig *n.* porco savaje.
wile *n.* engana, rus.
wilful (US **willful**) *adj.* intendeda.
will *n.* vole; (*willpower*) volunta; (*legal document*) atesta final. • *v.* vole; (*indicating that a finite verb is in the future tense*) va. **at will** a vole. **last will and testament** atesta final.
willful (US). See *wilful*.
willing *adj.* volente.
willow *n.* salse.
willowy *adj.* magra.
willpower *n.* volunta.
willy *n.* (*penis*) pixa.
willy-nilly *adv.* volente o nonvolente.
wilt *v.* seci.
wily *adj.* rusosa.
wimp *n.* coarde, debil, blanda.
wimple *n.* tela de testa.
wimpy *adj.* coarde, blanda.
win *v.* (*defeat*) vinse; (*game, battle*) gania.
wince *v.* salteta.
winch *n.* enrolador.
wind[1] *n.* (*weather*) venta; (*flatulence*) flatule. **break wind** flatule.
wind[2] *v.* (*coil*) bobini, enrola, serpe. **wind back** rebobini. **wind up** (*mechanism*) enrola.
windbag *n.* parlosa.
windblown *adj.* soflada par venta.
windbreak *n.* paraventa.
windbreaker *n.* jaca.
windburn *n.* irita par venta.
windcheater *n.* jaca.

windchill *n.* fri par venta.
wind energy converter *n.* turbina de venta.
windfall *n.* profita subita, bon fortuna nonespetada.
wind farm *n.* parce de venta.
wind generator *n.* turbina de venta.
wind instrument *n.* strumento de venta.
windlass *n.* enrolador.
windmill *n.* molin de venta.
window *n.* fenetra.
window blind *n.* cortina enrolante.
window pane *n.* vitro de fenetra.
window shade *n.* cortina enrolante.
windowsill *n.* cornisa de fenetra.
windpipe *n.* tracea.
wind power unit *n.* turbina de venta.
windscreen *n.* paraventa.
windscreen wiper *n.* frotador de paraventa.
windshield *n.* paraventa.
windshield wiper *n.* frotador de paraventa.
windsock *n.* manga de venta.
windstorm *n.* tempesta de venta.
windsurfing *n.* surfa de vela.
windswept *adj.* scopida par venta.
wind tunnel *n.* cambra de venta.
wind turbine *n.* turbina de venta.
windward *adj.* supraventa, contra la venta.
windy *adj.* ventosa. **be windy** venta.
wine *n.* vino.
wine cellar *n.* cava de vino.
wine glass *n.* vitro de vino.
winemaker *n.* vinor.
wine merchant *n.* vendor de vinos.
winepress *n.* presador de vino.
winery *n.* vineria.
wineskin *n.* pel de vino.
wing *n.* ala.
wing collar *n.* colar aletin.
winged *adj.* con alas.
winger *n.* alor.
winglet *n.* aleta.
wingman *n.* alor.
wing nut *n.* torca papilin.
wingspan *n.* estende de alas.
wink *v.* & *n.* ginia.
winkle *n.* (*mollusc*) litorina.
winner *n.* vinsor, ganior, campion.
winnow *v.* venti.
wino *n.* vagabon enebriada.
winsome *adj.* atraosa.
winter *n.* inverno. • *adj.* invernal. • *v.* inverni, pasa la inverno.
winter garden *n.* jardin de inverno.
wintergreen *n.* (*plant*) gaulteria. **American wintergreen** te de bosce.
winterize *v.* prepara per inverno.
winter solstice *n.* solstisio de inverno.
wintry *adj.* invernin, invernosa.
wipe *v.* frota, limpi, vacui. **wipe away** seci. **wipe up** seci.
wipeout *n.* defeta; (*surfing*) cade, fali.
wiper *n.* frotador.
wire *n.* filo, filo metal. • *v.* fili.
wire cutter *n.* taliafilo.
wired connection *n.* lia con filo.
wireless *adj.* sin filo. • *n.* radio.
wireless connection *n.* lia sin filo.
wire stripper *n.* nudifilo.
wiretap *n.* escutador secreta. • *v.* spia par escutador.
wiring *n.* fili.
wiry *adj.* filin; (*person*) tendonosa.
Wisconsin *n.* (*US state*) Wisconsin.
wisdom *n.* sajia. **words of wisdom** disedas saja.
wise *adj.* saja.
wiseacre *n.* sabetota.
wisecrack *n.* broma.
wiseguy *n.* sabetota.
wise person *n.* saja.
wish *v.* & *n.* desira, vole, espera.
wishbone *n.* furcula.
wishful thinking *n.* desira nonpratical.
wish list *n.* lista de desiradas.
wisp *n.* mexa.
wispy *adj.* rarida.
wisteria *n.* (*plant*) glisina.
wistful *adj.* regretosa.
wit *n.* astutia. **to wit** per dise.
witch *n.* sorsor, sorsor fema.
witchcraft *n.* sorsoria.
witch doctor *n.* xaman.
witchery *n.* sorsoria.
witch hazel *n.* amamelia.
witch hunt *n.* xasa de sorsores.
with *prep.* (*having, including, using*) con. **with difficulty** difisil; apena. **with regard to** consernante. **with the addition of** con ance. **with the exception of** con eseta de, esetante, estra. **with the highest praise** con loda masima. **with the intention of** con intende de. **with the shape of** con forma de.
withdraw *v.* retira.
withdrawal *n.* retira.
wither *v.* atrofia, plieta, seci.
withhold *v.* reteni.
within *prep.* en, a interna de; (*a group*) entre. • *adv.* a en, a interna. **from within** de en.
without *prep.* sin. • *subord.* sin ce, evitante ce. **be without** no ave. **without drawing attention** sin atrae atende. **without exception** sin eseta. **without help** sin aida. **without pause** sin pausa.
withstand *v.* resiste, oposa.

witness *n.* atestor. • *v.* esperia, vide.
witness box *n.* lojia de atestor.
witness stand *n.* lojia de atestor.
witter *v.* babela.
witticism *n.* replica, comenta astuta.
wittiness *n.* astutia.
witty *adj.* astuta.
witty conversation *n.* conversa replicosa.
witty reply *n.* replica.
wizard *n.* sorsor, sorsor mas; (*software*) aidador.
wizardry *n.* sorsoria.
wizened *adj.* plietosa.
wobble *v.* & *n.* (*stagger*) bambola; (*shudder*) tremeta.
wobbly *adj.* coxeante; nonplana.
wodge *n.* peson.
woe *n.* mal fortuna.
woeful *adj.* tristiosa.
wok *n.* (*pan*) uoc.
wolf *n.* lupo; (*womanizer*) xasafem.
wolfram *n.* (*element*) uolfram.
wolfsbane *n.* (*plant*) aconito.
Wolof *adj.* & *n.* (*person, language*) uolof.
wolverine *n.* (*animal*) gulo.
woman *n.* fem.
womanhood *n.* femia.
womanish *adj.* femin.
womanizer *n.* xasafem.
womb *n.* utero.
wombat *n.* uombata.
womenswear *n.* vestes de femes.
won *n.* (*currency*) uon.
wonder *n.* (*ask oneself*) demanda a se, vole sabe; (*marvel*) mervelia.
wonderful *adj.* merveliosa, stonante; eselente.
wonderland *n.* pais de mervelias.
wondrous *adj.* stonante.
wonk *n.* asidua, spesialiste.
wonky *adj.* coxeante; apoiada.
wonton *n.* (*food*) uonton.
woo *v.* cortea.
wood *n.* lenio. • *adj.* de lenio, lenial; (*copse*) bosce; (*forest*) foresta; (*golf club*) xutador; (*erection*) pixon.
woodcarver *n.* siselor.
woodchuck *n.* (*rodent*) monax.
woodcock *n.* (*bird*) becasia.
woodcreeper *n.* (*bird*) fornor.
woodcut *n.* xilogram.
woodcut printing *n.* xilografia.
woodcutter *n.* lenior.
wooded *adj.* boscin; forestosa.
wooden *adj.* de lenio, lenial.
wooden shoe *n.* zoco.
woodland *n.* bosce.
woodlouse *n.* onisco.
woodman *n.* boscor.
woodpecker *n.* (*bird*) picor.
wood pigeon *n.* pijon de bosce.
woodpile *n.* pila de lenio.
wood screw *n.* vise per lenio.
wood shavings *n.* risas de lenio.
woodshed *n.* cabana de lenio.
woodsman *n.* boscor.
woodwind instrument *n.* strumento lenial de venta.
woodwork *n.* carpenta.
woodworker *n.* carpentor.
woodworm *n.* larva xilofaje.
woody *adj.* leniosa.
woodyard *n.* lenieria.
wooer *n.* corteor.
woof[1] *interj.* (*dog*) uau-uau.
woof[2] *n.* (*weft*) trama.
woofer *n.* parlador basa.
wool *n.* lana. • *adj.* de lana. **cotton wool** coton asorbente.
wool-covered *adj.* lanosa.
woolgathering *n.* fantasia.
woollen *adj.* de lana.
woolly *adj.* (*made of wool*) de lana; (*covered in wool*) lanosa.
woolly lemur *n.* indri.
woolly mammoth *n.* mamute lanosa.
woomera *n.* lansadardo.
woozy *adj.* mareada. **feel woozy** marea.
word *n.* parola. **by word of mouth** par parla. **in other words** en otra parolas, per dise. **love of words** logofilia. **words of wisdom** disedas saja.
word game *n.* jua de parolas.
wordiness *n.* parolosia.
wording *n.* linguaje.
word-loving *adj.* logofilica.
wordplay *n.* broma de parolas.
word processor *n.* scrivador, program de scrive.
wordsmith *n.* parolor.
word wrap *v.* & *n.* autoflue.
wordy *adj.* parolosa.
work *v.* labora; (*machine, system*) funsiona, opera, vade; (*soil*) cultiva; (*dough*) amasa. • *n.* labora; (*of art, literature, music, etc.*) obra. **in the works** en construi. **manual work** labora par mano. **work around** sircoveni. **work incessantly** labora sin sesa. **work in progress** labora en curso. **work of art** obra de arte. **work out** calcula; (*exercise*) eserse.
workable *adj.* realable.
workaholic *adj.* laboramanica.
workaholism *n.* laboramania.
workbench *n.* table de labora.
workday *n.* dia de labora.
worker *n.* laboror. **fellow worker** colaboror.

worker bee *n.* abea laborante.
workhorse *n.* bestia de carga.
workhouse *n.* laboreria.
working day *n.* dia de labora.
working group *n.* grupo laborante.
working hours *n.* oras de labora.
workingman *n.* laboror.
working masses *n.* popla laborante.
working party *n.* grupo laborante.
working people *n.* popla laborante.
working week *n.* semana de labora.
workload *n.* carga de labora.
workman *n.* laboror.
workmanship *n.* cualia de labora.
workout *n.* eserse.
workplace *n.* laboreria.
workroom *n.* sala de labora.
work schedule *n.* program de labora.
workshop *n.* laboreria, fabriceria, studio.
workstation *n.* stasion de labora.
work surface *n.* table de labora.
worktable *n.* table de labora.
worktop *n.* plana, table de labora.
work-up *n.* prepara; (*medical*) esamina.
workweek *n.* semana de labora.
world *n.* mundo. • *adj.* mundal. **the world's largest** la plu grande de mundo.
worldly *adj.* mundal.
world travel *n.* viaja tra la mundo.
world traveller (US **traveler**) *n.* viajor tra la mundo.
world view *n.* vista de mundo.
world war *n.* gera mundal.
world-weariness *n.* dole de mundo.
worldwide *adj.* global.
worm *n.* verme; (*move like a worm*) vermi; desvermi, deselminti.
wormer *n.* antielmintal.
wormgear *n.* vise nonfininte.
wormhole *n.* buco de verme.
wormlike *adj.* vermin.
worms *n.* elmintose.
wormwood *n.* asinto.
worn *adj.* portada, usada. **worn out** gastada.
worried *adj.* ansiosa.
worrisome *adj.* problemosa.
worry *v.* preocupa, ansi, ajita; es preocupada, remastica. • *n.* preocupa, ansia.
worse *adj.* plu mal.
worsen *v.* mali.
worship *v.* & *n.* adora.
worshiper (US). See *worshipper*.
worshipful *adj.* adorante.
worshipfulness *n.* adora.
worshipper (US **worshiper**) *n.* adoror.
worst-case scenario *n.* caso la plu mal.
worsted *n.* (*yarn, fabric*) lana petenida.
worth *n.* valua, merita. **be worth** es valuada, merita. **worth the effort** meritante la labora.
worthless *adj.* sin valua.
worthless treasure *n.* tesoro falsa.
worthwhile *adj.* meritante la labora.
worthy *adj.* meritante, valuada; (*decent*) brava. **be worthy of** merita. **worthy of compassion** compatiable.
wossname *n.* aparateta.
would *v.* (*indicating that a finite verb refers to a hypothetical scenario, or forming a polite question*) ta. **I would like** me ta vole. **she said she would help** el ia dise ce el va aida. **she would later become an author** el ia deveni plu tarda un autor. **would have** (*past hypothetical*) ia ta. **would that** (*wish*) ta ce.
wound *v.* & *n.* feri.
woven *adj.* texeda.
wow *interj.* u.
wraith *n.* fantasma.
wrangle *v.* gida. • *n.* disputa.
wrangler *n.* bovor.
wrap *v.* envolve. **wrap up** envolve.
wrapped *adj.* envolveda. **be wrapped up in** es envolveda en.
wrapper *n.* paper.
wrapping paper *n.* paper de donadas.
wrath *n.* coleria.
wrathful *adj.* coleriosa.
wreak *v.* causa; forsa.
wreath *n.* garlanda.
wreathe *v.* garlandi.
wreck *n.* ruina; (*ship*) barcon abandonada.
wreckage *n.* ruinas.
wren *n.* (*bird*) troglodite. **Australian wren** maluro.
wrench *v.* aranca. • *n.* clave. **adjustable wrench** clave ajustable.
wrest *v.* aranca.
wrestle *v.* luta.
wrestler *n.* lutor.
wretch *n.* misera.
wretched *adj.* misera.
wretched place *n.* loca misera.
wriggle *v.* serpe. **wriggle out of** serpe a via de.
wriggly *adj.* serpente.
wright *n.* fabricor.
wring *v.* torse; (*extract by wringing*) estorse.
wringer *n.* estorsador.
wrinkle *v.* & *n.* plieta.
wrinkled *adj.* plietosa.
wrist *n.* polso.
wristband *n.* brasaleta.
wristwatch *n.* orolojeta.
writ *n.* comanda.
write *v.* scrive. **write back** rescrive.

write-off *n.* (*cancellation*) cansela; (*wrecked vehicle*) perde completa.
writer *n.* autor, scrivor.
writhe *v.* contorse, serpe.
writing *n.* (*action, style*) scrive; (*content*) scriveda. **artistic writing** caligrafia.
writing desk *n.* scriveria.
writing implement *n.* util de scrive.
writing materials *n.* furnis de scrive.
writing system *n.* sistem de scrive.
written examination *n.* esamina scriveda.
wrong *adj.* noncoreta, falsa, erante, mal. • *v.* & *n.* maltrata. **go wrong** malfunsiona, malopera, rompe.
wrongdoer *n.* vil.
wrongdoing *n.* malcondui, mal fa.
wrong-headed *adj.* malgidada.
wrongness *n.* noncoretia.
wrought iron *n.* fero forjada.
wry *adj.* ironiosa.
Wu *adj.* & *n.* (*language*) u.
wynn[2] *n.* (*Latin letter* Ƿ, ƿ) uin.
Wyoming *n.* (*US state*) Wyoming.
WYSIWYG editor *n.* editador de fasimil.
wyvern *n.* (*mythology*) viverna.

X

xanthoma *n.* (*medical*) xantoma.
xanthopsia *n.* (*medical*) xantopsia.
x-axis *n.* ase x.
x-coordinate *n.* coordinada x.
xebec *n.* xabeco.
xeno- *pref.* (*foreign*) xeno-.
xenobiologist *n.* xenobiolojiste.
xenobiology *n.* xenobiolojia.
xenon *n.* (*chemistry*) xenon.
xenophile *n.* xenofilica.
xenophilia *n.* xenofilia.
xenophilic *adj.* xenofilica.
xenophily *n.* xenofilia.
xenophobe *n.* xenofobica.
xenophobia *n.* xenofobia.
xenophobic *adj.* xenofobica.
xenoturbellid *n.* (*worm*) xenoturbelido.
xero- *pref.* (*dry*) xero-.
xerographic *adj.* xerografial.
xerography *n.* xerografia.
xerophile *n.* xerofilica.
xerophilia *n.* xerofilia.
xerophilic *adj.* xerofilica.
xerophthalmia *n.* (*medical*) xeroftalmia.
xerophyte *n.* xerofilica.
xerostomia *n.* (*medical*) xerostomia.
xerox *v.* fotocopia.
x-height *n.* (*typography*) altia de ex.
Xhosa *adj.* & *n.* (*person, language*) cosa.
xi *n.* (*Greek letter*) xi.
Xiang *adj.* & *n.* xiang.
xiangqi *n.* xangtxi.
Xinjiang *n.* Xinjiang.
X-ray *n.* raio X. • *v.* radiografi.
X-ray image *n.* radiogram.
X-ray machine *n.* radiograf.
xylem *n.* (*botany*) xilema.
xylo- *pref.* (*wood*) xilo-.
xylograph *n.* xilogram.
xylographic *adj.* xilografial.
xylography *n.* xilografia.
xylophage *n.* xilofaje.
xylophagous *adj.* xilofaje.
xylophone *n.* xilofon.
xylose *n.* (*sugar*) xilosa.

Y

-y *suff.* (*pertaining to*) -al; (*similar to*) -in; (*full of*) -osa; (*diminutive*) -eta.
yacht *n.* iate.
yachtsman *n.* iator.
yachtswoman *n.* iator.
yack *v.* & *n.* parleta.
Yahweh *n.* Iaue.
yak[1] *n.* (*mammal*) iac.
yak[2] *v.* & *n.* (*chat*) parleta.
yam *n.* (*plant, tuber*) niama.
yang *n.* (*philosophy*) iang.
yank *v.* & *n.* aranca.
Yankee *adj.* & *n.* (*American*) ianci.
yap *v.* & *n.* abaieta.
yard[1] *n.* (*enclosed*) patio; (*garden*) jardin.
yard[2] *n.* (*unit of length*) iard.
yardarm *n.* (*for sail*) verga.
yardstick *n.* regla.
yarmulke *n.* (*cap*) cipa.
yarn *n.* filo de lana.
yarrow *n.* (*plant*) milfolia.
yaw *v.* verje.
yawn *v.* & *n.* balia.
y-axis *n.* asc y.
yay *interj.* ie, si.
Yazidi *adj.* & *n.* eziditi.
Yazidism *n.* (*religion*) eziditisme.
y-coordinate *n.* coordinada y.
ye *pron.* vos.
yea *interj.* si.
yeah *interj.* ie, si.
year *n.* anio. **five-year-old** enfante de sinco anios. **years gone by** anios pasada.
yearbook *n.* libro anial.
yearly *adj.* anial.
yearn *v.* anela. **yearn for** anela.
yeast *n.* fermento.
yeasty *adj.* fermentosa.
yell *v.* & *n.* cria.
yellow *adj.* & *n.* jala. • *v.* jali.
yellow-billed chough *n.* xova becojala.
yellowish *adj.* jalin.
Yellow River *n.* Rio Huanghe.
Yellow Sea *n.* Mar Huanghai, Mar Jala.
yellowy *adj.* jalin.
yelp *v.* & *n.* cria.
Yemen *n.* Iaman.
Yemeni *adj.* & *n.* iamani.
yen *n.* (*currency*) en.
yeoman *n.* ioman.
yep *interj.* oce.
yerba maté *n.* erba-de-mate.
Yerevan *n.* (*capital*) Ierevan.
yes *interj.* si, oce.
yeshiva *n.* seminario iudi.
yesman *n.* disesi.
yesterday *adv.* & *n.* ier. **the day before yesterday** a la dia ante ier. **yesterday evening** a sera ier. **yesterday morning** a matina ier.
yesteryear *n.* anios pasada.
yet *adv.* (*until now*) asta aora; (*until then*) asta alora. • *conj.* (*however*) an tal. **and yet** ma ancora. **not yet** ancora no.
yeti *n.* ieti.
yew *n.* (*tree*) taxo.
Y-fronts *n.* slip de om.
Yiddish *adj.* & *n.* ides.
yield *v.* furni; (*give up*) sede. • *n.* furni; (*financial*) interesa, recompensa.
yin *n.* (*philosophy*) iin.
yin-yang *n.* iin-iang.
yip *v.* & *n.* abaieta.
-yl *suff.* (*chemistry*) -il.
-yne *suff.* (*chemistry*) -in.
yo *interj.* txau, alo.
yodel *v.* iodle.
yodeller (US **yodeler**) *n.* iodlor.
yodelling (US **yodeling**) *n.* iodle.
yoga *n.* ioga.
yogh *n.* (*Latin letter* Ȝ, ȝ) iog.
yoghurt *n.* iogurte.
yogi *n.* (*yoga expert*) iogi.
yogurt *n.* iogurte.
yoke *n.* iugo.
yokel *n.* campanian.
yolk *n.* vitelo.
yon *det.* acel.
yonder *det.* acel. • *adv.* ala.
yoni *n.* (*Hinduism*) ioni.
yoo-hoo *interj.* (*calling*) alo.
yore *n.* pasada.
Yoruba *adj.* & *n.* (*person, language*) ioruba.
you *pron.* (*singular*) tu; (*plural*) vos; (*arbitrary person or people*) on. **you all** vos. **you could say** on ta dise. **you know** (*filler*) sabe, tu sabe. **you see** (*filler*) vide, tu vide. **you yourself** (*emphatic*) tu mesma. **you yourselves** (*emphatic*) vos mesma.
young *adj.* joven.
younger *adj.* plu joven. **the younger** (*in names*) minor.
younger brother *n.* frateta.
younger sister *n.* soreta.
young person *n.* joven.
youngster *n.* joven.
your *det.* (*singular*) tua; (*plural*) vosa. **your excellency** eselentia. **your grace** eselentia. **your highness** altia. **your majesty** altia.

yours *pron.* (*singular*) la tua(s); (*plural*) la vosa(s).
youth *n.* (*person*) joven; (*youthfulness*) jovenia.
youthful *adj.* joven; (*appearance*) jovenin.
youthfulness *n.* jovenia.
youth hostel *n.* otel de jovenes.
youthlike *adj.* jovenin.
yo-yo *n.* ioio.
ytterbium *n.* (*element*) iterbio.
yttrium *n.* (*element*) itrio.
yuan[1] *n.* (*currency*) iuan.
Yuan[2] *adj.* (*dynasty*) iuan.
Yucatán *n.* (*Mexican state*) Yucatan.
Yucatán Peninsula *n.* Penisola Yucatan.
yucca *n.* (*plant*) iuca.
yuck *interj.* (*disgust*) iu.
Yugoslav *adj.* iugoslavian.
Yugoslavia *n.* Iugoslavia.
Yukon *n.* (*Canadian province*) Yukon.
yule *n.* natal.
yuletide *n.* natal.
yum *interj.* (*tasty*) mm.
yummy *adj.* deletosa.
yuppie *n.* iupi.
yurt *n.* (*tent*) iurt.

Z

zabaglione *n.* (*dessert*) zabalion.
zabaione *n.* (*dessert*) zabalion.
zaftig *adj.* curvosa, formosa.
zaghareet *v.* & *n.* (*celebratory ululation*) zagruta.
zaghrouta *v.* & *n.* (*celebratory ululation*) zagruta.
Zaire *n.* Zair.
Zambia *n.* Zambia.
Zambian *adj.* & *n.* zambian.
zany *adj.* bizara, comica.
Zanzibar *n.* Zanzibar.
zap *v.* colpa; (*whoosh*) sisa.
zap strap *n.* fisacable.
Zarathustra *n.* Zoroastra.
zazen *n.* (*meditation*) zazen.
zeal *n.* zelo.
Zealand, New *n.* Zeland Nova. • *adj.* zelandes.
Zealander, New *n.* zelandes.
zealot *n.* estremiste.
zealotry *n.* estremisme.
zealous *adj.* zelosa.
zebec *n.* (*ship*) xabeco.
zebra *n.* zebra.
zebra finch *n.* (*bird*) mandarin.
zebu *n.* zebu.
Zeeland *n.* Zeland.
zeitgeist *n.* spirito de la eda.
Zen *n.* zen. • *adj.* zeniste.
Zen Buddhist *n.* zeniste.
zenith *n.* zenite; apico.
zephyr *n.* venteta.
zeppelin *n.* airostato rijida.
zero *det.* & *n.* zero.
zero gravity *n.* lejeria completa.
zero point *n.* zero.
zeroth *adj.* zero.
zest *n.* zelo.
zestful *adj.* zelosa.
zesty *adj.* restorada.
zeta *n.* (*Greek letter*) zeta.
Zeus *n.* Zeus.
Zhuang *adj.* & *n.* (*person, language*) djuang.
ziggurat *n.* (*pyramid*) zigurat.
zigzag *v.* & *n.* zigzaga.
Zika *n.* Zica.
Zika fever *n.* febre de Zica.
Zika virus *n.* virus de Zica.
Zimbabwe *n.* Zimbabue.
Zimbabwean *adj.* & *n.* zimbabuean.
zinc *n.* zinco. • *v.* zinci.
zinger *n.* broma.
zinnia *n.* (*plant*) zinia.
Zion *n.* Sion. **Mount Zion** Monte Sion.
Zionism *n.* sionisme.
Zionist *adj.* & *n.* sioniste.
zip *n.* zipe. • *v.* zipi; (*whoosh*) sisa.
zipper *n.* zipe.
zip tie *n.* fisacable.
zircon *n.* (*mineral*) zircon.
zirconium *n.* (*element*) zirconio.
zither *n.* (*musical instrument*) sitra.
złoty *n.* (*currency*) zloti.
zodiac *n.* zodiaco.
zodiacal *adj.* zodiacal.
zombie *n.* zombi.
zonal *adj.* zonal.
zone *n.* zona.
zoo[1] *n.* (*animal park*) zo.
zoo-[2] *pref.* (*animal*) zo-.
zoogeographer *n.* zojeografiste.
zoogeographical *adj.* zojeografial.
zoogeography *n.* zojeografia.
zoological *adj.* zolojial.
zoologist *n.* zolojiste.
zoology *n.* zolojia.
zoom *v.* & *n.* zuma. **zoom in** zuma. **zoom out** dezuma.
zoom lens *n.* lente de zuma.
zoomorphism *n.* animali.
zoomorphize *v.* animali.
zoophile *n.* zofilica.
zoophilia *n.* zofilia.
zoophiliac *adj.* & *n.* zofilica.
zoophilic *adj.* zofilica.
zoophyte *n.* zofite.
Zoroaster *n.* Zoroastra.
Zoroastrian *adj.* & *n.* zoroastriste.
Zoroastrianism *n.* zoroastrisme.
zucchetto *n.* (*cap*) cipa.
zucchini *n.* zuceta.
Zulu *adj.* & *n.* (*person, language*) zulu.
zwieback *n.* biscoto seca.
zygoma *n.* zigoma.
zygote *n.* (*biology*) zigoto.

Elefen per viajores

Parolas simple
Basic words

si	yes
no	no
grasias	thank you
multe grasias	thank you very much
no problem	you're welcome
per favore	please
pardona	sorry, excuse me
alo	hello
adio	goodbye
asta plu tarda	see you later
bon matina	good morning
bon dia	good afternoon
bon sera	good evening
bon note	goodnight
me no comprende	I don't understand
como on dise esta en elefen?	how do you say this in Elefen?
tu parla …?	do you speak …?
engles	English
franses	French
deutx	German
espaniol	Spanish
jonguo; **xines**	Chinese
me	I, me
nos	we, us
tu	you (singular)
vos	you (plural)
el	he, she, him, her
lo	it
los	they, them
cual es tua nom?	what is your name?
encantada!	pleased to meet you!
como lo vade?	how are you?
bon	good
mal	bad
sposa	wife
sposo	husband
fia	daughter
fio	son
madre	mother
padre	father
ami	friend
do es la saleta privata?	where is the toilet, restroom, bathroom?

Dirijes
Directions

a sinistra	left
a destra	right
direta a ante	straight ahead
a supra	above
a su	below
distante	far
prosima	near
longa	long
corta	short
mapa	map
ofisia de informa per turistes	tourist information office

Locas
Places

posteria	post office
museo	museum
banco	bank
ofisia de polisia	police station
ospital	hospital
farmasia	pharmacy, drugstore, chemist
boteca	store, shop
restorante	restaurant
scola	school
eglesa	church
saletas privata	restrooms, toilets
strada	street
rua	road
plaza	plaza, square
monte	mountain
colina	hill
vale	valley
mar	sea, ocean
lago	lake
rio	river
pisina	swimming pool
tore	tower
ponte	bridge

La data
The date

dia	day
semana	week
mense	month
anio	year
lundi	Monday
martedi	Tuesday
mercurdi	Wednesday
jovedi	Thursday
venerdi	Friday
saturdi	Saturday
soldi	Sunday
janero	January
febrero	February
marto	March
april	April
maio	May
junio	June
julio	July
agosto	August
setembre	September
otobre	October
novembre	November
desembre	December
primavera	spring
estate	summer
autono	autumn, fall
inverno	winter
ier	yesterday
oji	today
doman	tomorrow
aniversario	birthday
bon aniversario!	happy birthday!

Numeros
Numbers

zero	0
un	1
du	2
tre	3
cuatro	4
sinco	5
ses	6
sete	7
oto	8
nove	9
des	10
des-un	11
des-du	12
des-tre	13
des-cuatro	14
des-sinco	15
des-ses	16
des-sete	17
des-oto	18
des-nove	19
dudes	20
dudes-un	21
tredes	30
cuatrodes	40
sincodes	50
sesdes	60
setedes	70
otodes	80
novedes	90
sento	100
mil	1000
milion	1 000 000

La ora
The time

cual es la ora?	what time is it?
tre e des-sinco	3:15
tre e un cuatri	3:15
des-sinco e des-sinco	15:15
des-un e tredes	11:30
des-un e un dui	11:30
dudes-tre e tredes	23:30
un e cuatrodes-sinco	1:45
du min un cuatri	1:45
des-tre e cuatrodes-sinco	13:45

Disionario de Lingua Franca Nova

Compras e comes
Shopping and eating

cuanto esta custa?	how much does this cost?
cual es esta?	what is this?
me va compra lo	I will buy it
me vole compra ...	I want to buy ...
tu ave ...?	do you have ...?
tu aseta cartas de credito?	do you accept credit cards?
abrida	open
cluida	closed
carta postal	postcard
selo postal	stamp
poca	few, little
multe	many, much
tota	all
come de matina	breakfast
come media	lunch, dinner
come de sera	supper, dinner
vejetaliste	vegetarian
caxer	kosher
joia!	cheers!
bon sania!	to your health!
la fatura, per favore	the bill (check), please
pan	bread
bevida	drink
cafe	coffee
te	tea
jus	juice
acua	water
bir	beer
vino	wine
sal	salt
peper	pepper
carne	meat
carne de bove	beef
carne de porco	pork
carne de gal	chicken
pex	fish
vejetal	vegetable
fruta	fruit
patata	potato
salada	salad
deser	dessert
crema jelada	ice cream

Viajas
Travel

do es ... ?	where is ...?
cuanto es la custa de un bileta?	how much is a ticket?
un bileta per vade a ..., per favore	one ticket to ..., please
do tu vade?	where are you going?
do tu abita?	where do you live?
tren	train
bus	bus
metro	underground, subway
airoporto	airport
stasion de tren	train station
stasion de bus	bus station
parabus	bus stop
stasion de metro	underground station, subway station
parti	depart, leave
ariva	arrive
lueria de autos	car rental agency
parce de autos	car park, parking lot
otel	hotel
sala	room
reserva	reserve
tu ave un sala vacua per esta note?	do you have a room available for tonight?
no salas vacua	no vacancies
pasaporto	passport

CPSIA information can be obtained
at www.ICGtesting.com
Printed in the USA
BVHW031809180322
631824BV00001B/4

9 781782 012177